THE AFFORDABLE HOUSING READER

The Affordable Housing Reader brings together classic works and contemporary writing on the themes and debates that have invigorated the field of affordable housing policy as well as the challenges arising in achieving the goals of policy on the ground. The reader – aimed at professors, students, and researchers – provides an overview of the literature on housing policy and planning that is both comprehensive and interdisciplinary. It is particularly suited for graduate and undergraduate courses on housing policy offered to students of public policy and city planning.

The volume is structured around the key debates in affordable housing, ranging from the conflicting motivations for housing policy, through analysis of the causes of and solutions to housing problems, to concerns about gentrification and housing and race. Each debate is contextualized in an introductory essay by the editors, and illustrated with a range of texts and articles.

Elizabeth Mueller and Rosie Tighe have brought together in a single volume the best and most influential writings on housing and its importance for planners and policy-makers.

J. Rosie Tighe is an assistant professor in the department of Geography and Planning at Appalachian State University. She is interested in social equity, race and class inequality, and housing affordability issues. Her current research focuses on gentrification, the evolving nature of the American Dream, and community responses to the foreclosure crisis.

Elizabeth J. Mueller is an associate professor of community and regional planning and social work at the University of Texas at Austin. She is interested in the ways that public actions shape the social, economic and political opportunities and experiences of vulnerable communities within cities. Her current work focuses on the tensions between current city planning and housing goals.

The Affordable Housing Reader

Edited by

J. Rosie Tighe

and

Elizabeth J. Mueller

Routledge
Taylor & Francis Group

LONDON AND NEW YORK

First published 2013
by Routledge
2 Park Square, Milton Park, Abingdon, Oxon OX14 4RN

Simultaneously published in the US and Canada
by Routledge
711 Third Avenue, New York, NY 10017

Routledge is an imprint of the Taylor & Francis Group, an informa business

British Library Cataloguing in Publication Data
A catalogue record for this book is available from the British Library

Library of Congress Cataloging in Publication Data
The affordable housing reader / edited by J. Rosie Tighe And Elizabeth J. Mueller.
p. cm.
Includes bibliographical references and index.
1. Low-income housing--United States. 2. Housing policy--United States. 3. Housing--United States--Costs.
I. Tighe, J. Rosie. II. Mueller, Elizabeth J.
HD7287.96.U6A38 2012
363.5'820973--dc23
2012007690

ISBN: 978-0-415-66937-5 (hbk)
ISBN: 978-0-415-66938-2 (pbk)

Typeset in Amasis MT Light and Akzidenz Grotesk
by Saxon Graphics Ltd, Derby

MIX
Paper from
responsible sources
FSC
www.fsc.org   FSC® C004839

Printed and bound in Great Britain by the MPG Books Group

Contents

Plates

Contributors

J. Rosie Tighe is an assistant professor in the department of Geography and Planning at Appalachian State University. She holds a PhD in Community and Regional Planning from the University of Texas at Austin and a Master's Degree in Urban and Environmental Policy and Planning from Tufts University. She is interested social equity, race and class inequality, and housing affordability issues. Her current research focuses on gentrification, the evolving nature of the American Dream, and community responses to the foreclosure crisis.

Elizabeth J. Mueller is an associate professor of community and regional planning and social work at the University of Texas at Austin. She is interested in the ways that public actions shape the social, economic and political opportunities and experiences of vulnerable communities within cities. Her current work focuses on the tensions between current city planning and housing goals. She holds a PhD and MCP from the University of California, Berkeley and was previously an assistant professor of urban policy at the New School for Social Research.

Emily Paradise Achtenberg is a housing policy and development consultant and urban planner who specializes in the preservation of federally-assisted housing. She has assisted community-based nonprofit and governmental organizations in acquiring and preserving more than 3,500 units threatened with expiring use restrictions and subsidy contracts, and she is actively involved in the development of federal, state, and local preservation policies and programs. She is the author of *Stemming the Tide: A Handbook on Preserving Subsidized Multifamily Housing* (2002) and has written about strategies to promote social housing ownership, production, and finance. She was an original member of the Planners Network Steering Committee and is currently a Board member of Citizens' Housing and Planning Association in Boston. She received an MCP from the Massachusetts Institute of Technology.

Philip Ashton is an associate professor at the University of Illinois, Chicago. His primary scholarly focus is the restructuring of U.S. retail finance and its relationship to U.S. central cities. His approach combines the methods of economic geography and industrial organization with theoretical frameworks emphasizing power relations between debtors and creditors. He has used this to produce a series of analyses of the subprime mortgage market that critique conventional interpretations of how minority borrowers and neighborhoods will fare in the "new financial marketplace."

Antonio Bento is an associate professor in Cornell's Charles H. Dyson School of Applied Economics and Management. Bento graduated from the Universidade Nova de Lisboa, Portugal, with a BA in economics in 1996 and earned a PhD in agricultural and resource economics from the University of Maryland in 2000. Prior to joining Cornell, he was a faculty member at the Donald Bren School of Environmental Sciences and Management and the Department of Economics at the University of California-Santa Barbara and, more recently, at the University of Maryland's School of Public Policy. He has also been a consultant to the research division of the World Bank.

Scott Bernstein is the president and co-founder of the Center for Neighborhood Technology (CNT). He studied at Northwestern University, served on the research staff of its Center for Urban Affairs, taught at UCLA and was a founding Board member at the Brookings Institution Metropolitan Center. President Clinton appointed Scott to the President's Council for Sustainable Development, where he co-chaired its task forces on Metropolitan Sustainable Communities and on Cross-Cutting Climate Strategies and to other Federal advisory panels on global warming, development strategy, and science policy. CNT received a 2009 MacArthur Foundation Award for Creative and Effective Institutions.

Chase Billingham is a research associate at the Kitty and Michael Dukakis Center for Urban and Regional Policy and a PhD candidate in the Department of Sociology at Northeastern University.

Barry Bluestone is the Stearns Trustee Professor of Political Economy, the founding director of the Dukakis Center for Urban and Regional Policy and the dean of the School of Public Policy and Urban Affairs at Northeastern University in Boston. He has written hundreds of scholarly articles and is the author/co-author of 11 books, including *Negotiating the Future: A Labor Perspective on American Business* and *Growing Prosperity: The Battle for Growth with Equity in the 21st Century*. He has been a policy adviser for local, state and national officials and representatives. He is a native of Detroit and earned bachelor's, master's and doctoral degrees from the University of Michigan. His areas of specialization include political economy, public policy, labor economics and industrial relations.

Rachel G. Bratt is a professor in the Department of Urban and Environmental Policy and Planning at Tufts University. She is a co-editor of *Critical Perspectives on Housing* (1986) and of *A Right to Housing: Foundation for a New Social Agenda* (2006) and the author of *Rebuilding a Low-Income Housing Policy* (1989). She is also the author or co-author of dozens of academic articles, professional and research reports, and book chapters. In addition to her academic work, she was a professional planner in the City of Worcester, Massachusetts, and has served as a board or advisory committee member for a number of public, private, and nonprofit organizations, including the Consumer Advisory Council of the Federal Reserve Bank, the Citizens' Housing and Planning Association in Boston, and the Wayland, Massachusetts Housing Partnership. She received a PhD from the Massachusetts Institute of Technology's Department of Urban Studies and Planning.

Larry Buron is a Principal Associate in Abt Associates' Housing and Community Revitalization Area. He has 16 years of experience evaluating the impact of government programs on labor market and quality of life outcomes of individuals and communities. He has led studies of HOPE VI, the Section 8/Housing Choice Voucher program, the Low-Income Housing Tax Credit program, and the Neighborhood Stabilization Program.

Arnab Chakraborty is currently an assistant professor of urban and regional planning at the University of Illinois, Urbana-Champaign. He received his PhD in urban planning from the University of Maryland-College Park in 2007. His research interests include land use policy, affordable housing, regional governance, and scenario planning. He has worked with a variety of state and local officials in the US and internationally, particularly in India and China. Among other venues, his research has appeared in Urban Studies, *Journal of the American Planning Association*, *Futures*, and *Cityscape*. He is currently studying the impacts of zoning mix on home foreclosures and developing scenario planning-based approaches to large scale decision-making.

Camille Zubrinsky Charles is Edmund J. and Louise W. Kahn Term Professor in the Social Sciences, Department of Sociology, Graduate School of Education, and the Center for Africana Studies at the University of Pennsylvania. Professor Charles earned her PhD in 1996 from the University of California, Los Angeles, where she was a project manager for the 1992–1994 Multi-City Study of Urban Inequality. Her research interests are in the areas of urban inequality, racial attitudes and intergroup relations, racial residential segregation, racial identity, and minorities in higher education, and she is co-PI of the National Longitudinal Survey of Freshmen. Her work has appeared in *Social Forces, Social Problems, Social Science Research, The DuBois Review*, the *American Journal of Education, the Annual Review of Sociology, the Chronicle of Higher Education*, and *The Root*.

Nestor M. Davidson is an associate professor at the Fordham University School of Law. His scholarship and research concerns property, land use, affordable housing, local government law, and sustainability. His professional legal experience focused on commercial real estate and affordable housing, and he served as Deputy General Counsel at the U.S. Department of Housing and Urban Development. Professor Davidson attended Columbia Law School and clerked for Judge David S. Tatel of the United States Court of Appeals for the District of Columbia Circuit and Justice David H. Souter of the Supreme Court of the United States.

John Emmeus Davis is a partner and co-founder of Burlington Associates in Community Development, LLC, a national consulting cooperative specializing in the design of public programs and private models that support the development of permanently affordable housing and the revitalization of lower-income neighborhoods. He previously worked for the City of Burlington, Vermont, and at the Institute for Community Economics. He has taught at New Hampshire College, the University of Vermont and Massachusetts Institute of Technology. He holds an MS and PhD from Cornell University.

George Galster is the Clarence Hilberry Professor of Urban Affairs at the College of Urban, Labor, and Metropolitan Affairs, Wayne State University. He earned his PhD in Economics from MIT, with undergraduate degrees from Wittenberg and Case Western Reserve Universities. He has published over 100 scholarly articles and book chapters, primarily on the topics of metropolitan housing markets, racial discrimination and segregation, neighborhood dynamics, residential reinvestment, community lending and insurance patterns, and urban poverty. He has been a consultant to the U.S. Department of Housing and Urban Development, numerous municipalities, community organizations, and civil rights groups, and organizations like the National Association of Realtors, American Bankers Association, Fannie Mae, and Chemical Bank Corporation. He served on the Consumer Advisory Council of the Federal Reserve's Board of Governors, and has assumed other leadership positions in community service.

Edward L. Glaeser is the Fred and Eleanor Glimp Professor of Economics at Harvard, where he also serves as Director of the Taubman Center for State and Local Government and the Rappaport Institute for Greater Boston. He studies the economics of cities, and has written scores of urban issues, including the growth of cities, segregation, crime, and housing markets. He has been particularly interested in the role that geographic proximity can play in creating knowledge and innovation. He received his PhD from the University of Chicago in 1992 and has been at Harvard since then.

Erin Godfrey is an Assistant Professor of Applied Psychology at New York University's Steinhardt School of Culture, Education, and Human Development. She earned her PhD in developmental and community psychology from the Graduate School of Arts and Sciences at New York University, with an undergraduate degree from Oberlin College. Her research explores how individuals interact with, understand, and are influenced by the social and political systems in which they are embedded, focusing in particular on policies affecting families and youth from disadvantaged and immigrant backgrounds. Her work has appeared in a variety of peer-reviewed journals, including *Child Development, New Directions in Child and Adolescent Development*, and *Journal of the American Planning Association* as well as edited books such as *Making it Work: Low-wage Employment, Family Life and Child Development*.

Edward G. Goetz is professor of urban and regional planning at the Humphrey School of Public Affairs and director of the Center for Urban and Regional Affairs at the University of Minnesota. He has published articles on housing planning and policy in a range of planning and urban journals. His new book, *New Deal Ruins: Race and Retrenchment in Public Housing*, is published by Cornell University Press.

Joseph Gyourko serves as the Martin Bucksbaum Professor of Real Estate, Finance and Business and Public Policy at The Wharton School of the University of Pennsylvania. He also is Director of the Zell/Lurie Real Estate Center at Wharton and is a Research Associate of the National Bureau of Economic Research.

Chester Hartman is the Director of Research at the Poverty & Race Research Action Council in Washington, D.C. – an organization for which he served as Executive Director and President from its founding in 1990 through 2003. Prior to that, he was a Fellow at the Institute for Policy Studies and founder and chair of the Planners Network, a national organization of progressive urban planners. He has served on the faculty of Harvard, Yale, Cornell, Columbia, University of California-Berkeley, American and the University of North Carolina-Chapel Hill and is an Adjunct Professor of Sociology at George Washington University. Among his recent books are *City for Sale: The Transformation of San Francisco* (2002), *Between Eminence and Notoriety: Four Decades of Radical Urban Planning* (2002), and *Poverty and Race in America: The Emerging Agendas* (2006).

J. David Hulchanski is a professor of housing and community development at the University of Toronto. His scholarship focuses on local and global trends in housing, poverty and social welfare policy; human rights and social justice issues; and social and community development. He holds the University of Toronto's endowed chair in housing, the Dr. Chow Yei Ching Chair in Housing.

Dan Immergluck is Professor of City and Regional Planning at Georgia Tech. Professor Immergluck conducts research on housing and real estate markets, mortgage finance and foreclosures, community reinvestment and fair lending, neighborhood change, and related public policy. He has authored three books, more than 30 articles in scholarly journals and scores of applied research and policy reports. He manages applied research projects at local and national levels. He has testified before Congress and state and local legislative bodies. His work has been cited in a wide variety of government and policy reports.

Mark L. Joseph is an Assistant Professor at the Mandel School of Applied Social Sciences at Case Western Reserve University and a Faculty Associate at the Center on Urban Poverty and Community Development. He received his undergraduate degree from Harvard College and was also a Visiting Scholar at Oxford University. His general research interests are urban poverty and community development. His current research focuses on mixed-income development as a strategy for addressing urban poverty, with particular attention to transforming public housing developments.

Elizabeth K. Julian is a Dallas attorney who has practiced poverty and civil rights law for over 37 years. She is currently the Executive Director of the Inclusive Communities Project, a Dallas-based advocacy organization that works to expand fair and affordable housing opportunities for low income minority families in high opportunity areas of the Dallas Metroplex. Ms. Julian served as Deputy General Counsel for Civil Rights and as Assistant Secretary for Fair Housing and Equal Opportunity at the Department of Housing and Urban Development in the Clinton Administration.

Gerrit-Jan Knaap is executive director of the National Center for Smart Growth Research and Education, is an economist and professor of Urban Studies and Planning in the University of Maryland's School of Architecture, Planning and Preservation. He earned a BS from Willamette University, his MS and PhD from the University of Oregon, and received post-doctoral training at the University of Wisconsin-Madison, all in economics.

Donald A. Krueckeberg was Professor and Associate Dean of the Bloustein School of Planning and Public Policy at Rutgers University. Krueckeberg received a BS from Michigan State University, and both MCP and PhD degrees from the University of Pennsylvania. Dr. Krueckeberg served as President of the Association of Collegiate Schools of Planning and was elected to the College of Fellows of the American Institute of Certified Planners. He received the Distinguished Service Award from the New Jersey Chapter of the American Planning Association in 1984.

Norman Krumholz is a professor at the Maxine Goodman Levin College of Urban Affairs at Cleveland State University. He is a past-president of both the American Planning Association and the American Institute of Certified Planners. Prior to his joining the faculty at CSU, Krumholz served as a planning practitioner in Ithaca, Pittsburg, and Cleveland, where he was planning director for 10 years. Krumholz has written or edited five books on planning and urban neighborhoods, and has published articles in many professional journals. His book, *Making Equity Planning Work: Leadership in the Public Sector* (with Professor John Forester) won the Paul Davidoff award from the Associated Collegiate Schools of Planning for the best progressive book of the year. His equity planning practice in behalf of the poor and working people of Cleveland has become a national model for planners in other large cities who are struggling to retain their industrial and economic base while making their neighborhoods more livable.

Diane K. Levy is a Senior Research Associate in the Metropolitan Housing and Communities Policy Center at the Urban Institute. She has extensive experience studying public housing transformation, neighborhood change, and the impact of both on residents. As part of UI's multi-site HOPE VI Panel Study, Ms. Levy has studied the impact of the program on relocated residents and, for a related project, the redevelopment process and neighborhood impact of HOPE VI in Chicago. She conducted a comparative study of neighborhood revitalization efforts based on mixed-income strategies in the US and the UK and led a study of the purported benefits for families from living in mixed-income communities. Ms. Levy also initiated research into the viability of HOPE VI mixed-income developments. Ms. Levy holds a Masters in both Cultural Anthropology and Regional Planning from the University of North Carolina at Chapel Hill.

Scott Lowe received his PhD from the University of California, Santa Barbara with specialties in environmental economics, applied microeconomics and urban economics. He has a MS in Economics from Oregon State University, and a BA in Economics and Environmental Studies from the University of California, Santa Barbara. Dr. Lowe's primary research interests relate to the influence of regulations on regional and local environmental and socioeconomic conditions. He has published articles and given presentations on the influence of the Clean Air Act on ambient particulate matter and ozone concentrations, on the political economy of the South Coast Air Quality Management District's RECLAIM program, and on the role of inclusionary zoning practices on housing growth in California. His current research addresses historical water use in the western United States.

Peter Marcuse is Professor Emeritus of Urban Planning at Columbia University in New York City. He has a JD from Yale Law School, and a PhD in planning from the University of California at Berkeley. He practiced law in Waterbury, CT, for 20 years, specializing in labor and civil rights law, and was majority leader of its Board of Aldermen, chaired its anti-poverty agency, and was a member of its City Planning commission. He was thereafter Professor of Urban Planning at UCLA, and President of the Los Angeles Planning Commission and member of Community Board 9M in New York City.

George ("Mac") McCarthy has directed the Ford Foundation's Metropolitan Opportunity work since 2008 and has been at the Ford Foundation since 2000. He was previously a senior research associate at the Center for Urban and Regional Studies at the University of North Carolina at Chapel Hill. He has worked as a professor of economics at Bard College; resident scholar at the Jerome Levy Economics Institute; visiting scholar and member of the High Table at King's College of Cambridge University; visiting scholar at the University of Naples, Italy; and research associate at the Centre for Independent Social Research in St. Petersburg, Russia. Mac earned a PhD in economics from the University of North Carolina at Chapel Hill, a master's degree in economics from Duke University and a bachelor's degree in economics and mathematics from the University of Montana.

Kirk McClure is a professor with the Department of Urban Planning at the University of Kansas. His teaching and research address issues of housing, community development and local economic development. McClure generates research on assisted housing for the U.S. Department of Housing and Urban Development. He holds a PhD from the University of California, Berkeley, a master's degree from MIT, as well as degrees from the University of Kansas.

Arthur C. Nelson, FAICP, is Presidential Professor of City and Metropolitan Planning at the University of Utah where he is also Director of the Metropolitan Research Center. For the past 30 years, Dr. Nelson has conducted pioneering research in growth management, urban containment, public facility finance, economic development, and metropolitan development patterns. He has written nearly 20 books and more than 300 other works. Dr. Nelson's current work focuses on how demographic, economics, and housing preference choices will reshape America's metropolitan areas over the next generation.

Kathe Newman is an Associate Professor in the Urban Planning and Policy Development Program at the Edward J. Bloustein School of Planning and Public Policy at Rutgers University and Director of the Ralph W. Voorhees Center for Civic Engagement. Dr. Newman holds a PhD in Political Science from the Graduate School and University Center at the City University of New York. Her research explores how and why cities change and how those changes affect people of color, women, and the poor. She is particularly interested in how capital flows transform urban places. Her research has explored gentrification, foreclosure, urban redevelopment and community participation. Dr. Newman has published articles in *Urban Studies*, *Urban Affairs Review*, *Shelterforce*, *Progress in Human Geography*, *Housing Studies*, *GeoJournal*, and *Environment and Planning A*.

Katherine M. O'Regan is Associate Professor of Public Policy at NYU Wagner Graduate School of Public Service, and faculty director of its Public and Nonprofit MPA program. She teaches and does research on issues at the intersection of poverty and space – the conditions and fortunes of poor neighborhoods and those who live in them. Her current research includes work on a variety of affordable housing topics, from whether the Low Income Tax Credit contributes to increased economic and racial segregation, to whether the presence of housing voucher households contributes to neighborhood crime rates. Among others, she serves on the board of the American Real Estate and Urban Economics Association, the editorial board for the *Journal of Policy Analysis and Management* and the research advisory board for The Reinvestment Fund.

Charles J. Orlebeke is professor emeritus of urban planning and public policy at the University of Illinois, Chicago. He served as Assistant Secretary for Policy Development and Research at the Department of Housing and Urban Development (HUD) during the Nixon Administration and also in the administration of Governor George Romney. His books include *Federal Aid to Chicago* and *New Life at Ground Zero: New York, Home Ownership and the Future of American Cities*.

Rolf Pendall is Director of the Metropolitan Housing and Communities Policy Center at the Urban Institute. His research expertise includes land use planning and regulation; federal, state, and local affordable housing policy and programs; and metropolitan planning and development. Dr. Pendall was previously a tenured professor in the Department of City and Regional Planning at Cornell University. In 2007, Pendall was appointed to a National Academy of Sciences Transportation Research Board panel on links between land use, transportation, energy, and greenhouse gas emissions, helping to produce the report, "Driving and the Built Environment," released in September 2009. Pendall holds a PhD from the University of California at Berkeley, an MS in Community and Regional Planning and an MA in Latin American Studies from the University of Texas at Austin (1989), and a BA in sociology from Kenyon College in Ohio (1984).

Stewart E. Perry has been long active in community economic development (CED) in the U.S. and Canada as both a policy adviser and a designer and manager of CED institutions. As head of the Center for Community Economic Development, he helped create the first finance institution for CED, the Massachusetts Community Development Finance Authority. While at the US Office of Economic Opportunity (1967–69), he helped design and launch the first federal program of support for CDCs. He has headed the Centre for Community Economic Development in Cape Breton, Nova Scotia (1988–93), the Institute for New Enterprise Development (1975–88) and the Center for Community Economic Development (1969–75), both in Cambridge, Mass. His most recent books, as editor, are *Tools and Techniques for Community Renewal and Recovery* (2001) and *The Canadian Social Enterprise Guide* (2nd ed., 2010). He holds a PhD in social relations from Harvard University. Stewart currently lives in Seattle but is a staff associate at the Canadian Center for Community Renewal, specializing in community and development finance.

Stephanie Pollack is Associate Director of the Kitty and Michael Dukakis Center for Urban and Regional Policy at Northeastern University and teaches in the School of Public Policy and Urban Affairs. Her research focuses on transportation policy, transit-oriented development, sustainability and equitable development. Before coming to Northeastern in 2004, Pollack was a senior executive and attorney at the Conservation Law Foundation. From 2004 through 2010 she was also a partner in the strategic environmental consulting firm BlueWave Strategies LLC. She serves on the Massachusetts Department of Transportation's Transportation Advisory Committee, on the steering committee of the Metro Boston Consortium for Sustainable Communities and as co-chair of the Infrastructure Council for the Urban Land Institute's Boston District Council, as well as on the boards of the Boston Society of Architects, Charles River Watershed Association and Health Resources in Action. Pollack holds a BS in Mechanical Engineering, a BS in Public Policy from the Massachusetts Institute of Technology, and a JD from Harvard Law School.

Susan J. Popkin is both Director of The Urban Institute's Program on Neighborhoods and Youth Development and a Senior Fellow in the Metropolitan Housing and Communities Policy Center. A nationally recognized expert on assisted housing and mobility, Dr. Popkin's research has focused on the impact of the radical changes in housing policy over the past decade on the lives of the most vulnerable public and assisted housing families. Prior to joining the Urban Institute, Dr. Popkin was an Associate at Abt Associates, Inc. and an Assistant Professor of Community Health Sciences, School of Public Health, and a Senior Research Specialist at the Prevention Research Center, University of Illinois at Chicago. Dr. Popkin holds a PhD in Human Development and Social Policy from Northwestern University.

john a. powell is an internationally recognized authority in the areas of civil rights and civil liberties and a wide range of issues including race, structural racism, ethnicity, housing, poverty and democracy. He is Director of the Haas Diversity Research Center (HDRC) and The Robert D. Haas Chancellor's Chair in Equity and Inclusion at the University of California-Berkeley. He was formerly Executive Director of the Kirwan Institute for the Study of Race and Ethnicity at The Ohio State University and he holds the Gregory H. Williams Chair in Civil Rights and Civil Liberties at the Moritz College of Law. Previously, he founded and directed the Institute on Race and Poverty at the University of Minnesota. He also served as Director of Legal Services in Miami, Florida and was National Legal Director of the American Civil Liberties Union where he was instrumental in developing educational adequacy theory. He is one of the co-founders of the Poverty and Race Research Action Council and serves on the board of several national organizations. Professor powell has taught at numerous law schools including Harvard and Columbia University. He joined the faculty at The Ohio State University in 2002.

John M. Quigley was the I. Donald Terner Distinguished Professor and Professor of Economics at the University of California-Berkeley. Besides the Department of Economics, he held appointments in the Goldman School of Public Policy and the Haas School of Business. He directed the Berkeley Program on Housing and Urban Policy. His research focussed on the integration of real estate, mortgage, and financial markets; urban labor markets; housing; spatial economics; and local public finance. He was a Fellow of the Regional Science Association and the Homer Hoyt Institute. In 2006, he was elected a Foreign Member of the Royal Swedish Academy of Engineering Sciences. He was the recipient of many scholarly awards including the George Bloom Award for Contributions to Urban Economics.

Jacob Riis was a police reporter whose work appeared in several New York newspapers, documented the living and working conditions of the poor. Through articles, books, photography, and lantern-slide lectures, Riis served as a mediator between working-class, middle-class, and upper-class citizens. He argued for better housing, adequate lighting and sanitation, and the construction of city parks and playgrounds. He portrayed middle-class and upper-class citizens as benefactors and encouraged them to take an active role in defining and shaping their communities. Riis believed that charitable citizens would help the poor when they saw for themselves how "the other half" lived.

William M. Rohe received his PhD from the Pennsylvania State University in 1978. In 2005 he was awarded the Cary C. Boshamer distinguished professorship in city and regional planning for his many important contributions to scholarship. He is co-author of *Planning with Neighborhoods* (University of North Carolina Press), co-editor of *Chasing the American Dream: New Perspectives on Affordable Homeownership* (Cornell University Press) and author of *The Research Triangle: From Tobacco Road to Global Prominence* (University of Pennsylvania Press). He has published over 60 referred articles on the topics of housing and community development policy and practice as well as numerous research reports for federal, state and local government agencies and major foundations. Dr. Rohe has received best article awards from both the *Journal of Planning Education and Research* and the *Journal of the American Planning Association*. His research has been supported by the U.S. Department of Housing and Urban Development, the Ford Foundation, the MacArthur Foundation, and the Fannie Mae Foundation, among others. He currently serves on the editorial boards of the *Journal of Urban Affairs* and *Journal of Planning Literature* and is an associate editor for the journal *Housing Policy Debate*.

Michael H. Schill is Dean of the University of Chicago Law School and a national expert on real estate and housing policy, deregulation, finance, and discrimination. He has written or edited three books and over 40 articles on various aspects of housing, real estate, and property law. He is an active member of a variety of public advisory councils, editorial boards and community organizations. Before joining the faculty of the University of Chicago Law School, he was Dean and Professor of Law at the UCLA School of Law, the Wilf Family Professor in Property Law at New York University School of Law, and professor of urban planning at NYU's Robert F. Wagner Graduate School of Public Service where he also directed the Furman Center for Real Estate and Urban Policy. Prior to that, Schill was a tenured professor of law and real estate at the University of Pennsylvania. He has also been a visiting professor at Harvard Law School.

Anne B. Shlay is Professor of Sociology and Geography and Urban Studies at Temple University. Her work has been funded by the Jesse Ball Dupont Fund, the William Penn Foundation, the Claneil Foundation, other foundations, and local, state and federal government agencies. She was recently Chair of the Community and Urban Sociology Section of the American Sociological Association. She is on the editorial board of *City and Community* and the *Journal of Urban Affairs*. She received the 1999 Temple University Research Award for research productivity. Professor Shlay directed the Center for Public Policy from 1999–2003 and is the former Associate Dean for the College of Liberal Arts at Temple University. In 2006, she was a Fulbright Research Scholar at the School of Public Policy at Hebrew University in Jerusalem. She received her PhD from the University of Massachusetts-Amherst and has held positions at Cornell University and the Johns Hopkins University.

Michael E. Stone, PhD (Princeton University) is a Professor of Community Planning at the University of Massachusetts Boston. For more than 40 years Stone has been involved in teaching, research, policy analysis, program development, technical assistance, and advocacy on housing, living standards, and participatory planning. He works with local community groups, city and state agencies, and national advocacy organizations. He is the author of nearly 50 reports, articles and chapters, and four books. His book *Shelter Poverty: New Ideas on Housing Affordability* has been called "the definitive book on housing and social justice in the United States." His co-authored/co-edited work, *A Right to Housing: Foundation for a New Social Agenda*, published in 2006, has been called "a landmark in progressive housing thought."

Philip Tegeler is the Executive Director at the Policy and Race Research Action Council (PRRAC), a civil rights policy organization based in Washington, D.C. PRRAC's mission is to promote research-based advocacy on structural inequality issues, with a specific focus on the causes and consequences of housing and school segregation. Mr. Tegeler is a civil rights lawyer with experience in fair housing, educational equity, land use law, and institutional reform litigation. Previously, he was with the Connecticut ACLU, where he served as Legal Director from 1997–2003. He also worked with Paul Davidoff as Legal Projects Director at the Metropolitan Action Institute in New York City, and taught in the University of Connecticut School of Law clinical program. He was co-founder and the first board president of the Connecticut Fair Housing Center, served as a member of the Connecticut Housing Coalition Board for nine years, and is an active member of the Housing Justice Network.

Margery Austin Turner is Vice President for Research at the Urban Institute, where she leads efforts to frame and conduct a forward-looking agenda of policy research. A nationally recognized expert on urban policy and neighborhood issues, Ms. Turner has analyzed issues of residential location, racial and ethnic discrimination and its contribution to neighborhood segregation and inequality, and the role of housing policies in promoting residential mobility and location choice. Ms. Turner also served as Deputy Assistant Secretary for Research at the Department of Housing and Urban Development from 1993 through 1996, focusing HUD's research agenda on the problems of racial discrimination, concentrated poverty, and economic opportunity in America's metropolitan areas.

Shannon Van Zandt is Associate Professor and the Coordinator of the Master of Urban Planning program, in the Department of Landscape Architecture and Urban Planning at Texas A & M University. Her research interests are related to low-income housing and sustainable community development. She is particularly interested in understanding the factors which contribute to the spatial distribution of housing and how that distribution affects outcomes for low-income and disadvantaged populations. Her current projects, funded by the National Science Foundation and the Department of Housing and Urban Development, examine housing relocation, social vulnerability to disasters, differences in housing outcomes for owners and renters, and spatial patterns of residential land uses. She teaches courses in housing policy, neighborhood revitalization, land use planning methods, and urban structure. She holds a BED and MUP from Texas A & M University and a PhD from the University of North Carolina.

Alexander von Hoffman is a historian and specialist in housing, community development, and urban affairs. A senior research fellow at the Joint Center for Housing Studies of Harvard University, he is the author of *House by House, Block by Block: The Rebirth of America's Urban Neighborhoods* (2003); *Fuel Lines for the Urban Revival Engine: Neighborhoods, Community Development Corporations, and Financial Intermediaries* (2001); and *Local Attachments: The Making of an American Urban Neighborhood, 1850 to 1920* (1994). His work has also appeared in the *Atlantic Monthly*, the *New York Times*, *Chicago Tribune*, and the *Boston Globe*. Dr. von Hoffman was previously an associate professor of urban planning and design at the Graduate School of Design and a Fellow at the Taubman Center for State and Local Government of the Harvard Kennedy School. He holds a PhD in History from Harvard University.

Susan M. Wachter is Professor of Real Estate and Finance at The Wharton School at the University of Pennsylvania, and Director of the Wharton GIS Lab. She served as Assistant Secretary for Policy Development and Research at the U.S. Department of Housing and Urban Development, from 1998 to 2001 and President of the American Real Estate Urban Economics Association from 1988 to 1989. The author of over 100 publications and ten volumes, Dr. Wachter was Chairperson of the Wharton Real Estate Department from 1996 to 1998. Formerly co-editor of *Real Estate Economics*, she serves on multiple editorial boards and is a Faculty Fellow of The Homer Hoyt Institute for Advanced Real Estate Studies and Academic Fellow at the Urban Land Institute.

Acknowledgements

The editors would like to thank our students and colleagues at Appalachian State University and the University of Texas at Austin for providing feedback on the topics and readings chosen for this volume. It has been our great pleasure to discuss and debate these ideas with them in our courses. We also thank our colleagues Alex Schwartz and Kirk McClure for their kind review of our initial proposal and suggestions for its improvement. The volume is certainly better for their input.

At Routledge, we thank our editor, Alex Hollingsworth, and his wonderful team, especially Louise Fox, Nicole Solano and Fiona Bowler. They were wonderfully patient with our many questions and extremely helpful in guiding us through the intricacies of obtaining permission to use previously published material. In addition, we thank all of the publishers and their staff who gave us permission to reuse materials for this volume, especially Jessica Hanff, managing editor of Housing Policy Debate.

Finally, we thank our families for their support, willingness to pitch in around the house or to walk the dog, or to comply with last minute requests for a "quick read" of an introduction. To Michael, Luke, Andrew and the hounds, our love and gratitude.

Editors' introduction

Housing policy has become headline news in the past few years, for better or worse. It is both an exciting time to teach students about the history of housing policy and a challenging time to discuss what policymakers or practitioners can do to effect positive change. As debate continues to roil around the role of housing in both precipitating and resolving the ongoing financial crisis, we felt it especially important to provide our students with a context for current discussions and a sense of the values and ideological positions underlying debates over solutions. This volume is a step toward those goals.

Several critical themes are woven throughout this book – themes we feel are central to grasping the importance of housing as an area of social policy and to understanding its particular meaning in the U.S. First is the long history of racial exclusion and the role that public policy has played in racializing access to decent housing in the United States. This issue is pervasive and provides a highly charged backdrop to current discussions of where housing opportunities for low-income people ought to be placed. The meaning of neighborhood context for residents cannot be understood absent an awareness of how social norms regarding race have shaped the implementation of housing policies at key points in our history.

A second key theme is the tension between the economic and social goals of housing policy. We see this theme in public discussions of the threat posed by tenement housing at the turn of the twentieth century, in the tensions between urban renewal and public housing embodied in the Housing Act of 1949, in the push to redevelop public housing during the 1990s, and in the current push for mixed-use and transit-oriented development. The political compromises necessary to create policy were shaped by these competing goals and reinforced by our historic aversion to direct production of housing by government. As policy- and decision-making devolves to lower levels of government, these tensions are most apparent and the impediments to progress on social goals more intractable. Local debate is more likely to be framed around the problem of regulation than the need for redistributive justice.

A final theme is the role of housing in the lives of low- and moderate-income residents. A home can serve as a vehicle for economic mobility, as the embodiment of a bundle of benefits linked to social citizenship, and as the embodiment of an individual's right to choose where and how to live. Current discussions regarding the importance of neighborhood setting for residents rely on assumptions about how residents will or should interact with their neighbors, as well as assumptions about the role of more affluent neighbors in establishing social norms or in ensuring that public services are of high quality. Policy gives agency to residents themselves mostly by offering them individual choice. Arguably, legal challenges have stood in as the collective voice of low-income residents.

Many previously held assumptions about the proper focus of housing policy are currently being questioned. To begin with, new ways of defining housing problems, focused on relationships rather than discrete characteristics of housing or people, are emerging. Policy discussions increasingly emphasize that housing is more than shelter, and that its location is central to its value. We see this in debate surrounding "housing first" policies, HOPE VI redevelopment, and the role of Housing Choice Vouchers in providing housing. Housing research focuses not only on the home itself, but also on the demographics of neighbors, the threats or benefits posed by physical aspects of neighborhoods, and by the public services and social relationships present in particular places. Seeing housing as connected to other issues and problems also makes it very context specific and harder to encapsulate in program norms or rules. Yet this broader view also helps us see ways to link housing policy and programs to other policy areas, and to forge new partnerships and coalitions around the needs of low income residents and communities.

The current crisis has also caused us to question the strong policy emphasis on low-income homeownership. Ownership arguably confers several benefits, among them the ability to build wealth and invest in education to foster upward mobility, to offer residents greater security of tenure, and to provide them with the benefits of citizenship that come with property ownership. As the current crisis challenges wealth building as a goal for low-income homeowners, discussion has broadened to encompass new forms of ownership that focus primarily on security of tenure and, to some extent, on the benefits of membership in a community of owners.

Finally, the trajectory of housing policy history reveals a profound shift in how low-income residents fit into existing neighborhoods. Emphasis on mixed income developments and deconcentrating poverty encourages residents to blend in to larger, more affluent groups, rather than to be visible and identifiable as a community or group. Whether such strategies can achieve the scale necessary to change broader social perceptions of the poor is not clear. Whether they can lay the groundwork for reversing broader social patterns of income and racial segregation and exclusion, and what the costs might be for communities, is much debated.

While there are signs of change, important longer term trends continue. Most troubling is the ever-deepening pattern of income inequality in the U.S. The inability of the poor – and increasingly of those further up the income ladder – to afford a decent place to live is driven mostly by lack of income. The gap has widened between the incomes of those at the lower echelons of the labor market and housing costs, yet the federal government has stepped back from providing the deep subsidy necessary to reach the poorest residents. Instead, federal funding agencies have shifted toward providing greater discretion and responsibility to lower levels of government. This pattern is unlikely to change and – at this moment – appears likely to intensify. At the same time, the supply of housing affordable to the population of extremely poor, "hard to house" residents (often elderly, disabled or for other reasons reliant on various forms of public assistance) is declining. Preservation of housing affordable to extremely low-income households is especially important now, due to expiring subsidies and to redevelopment pressures in central cities. The large share of units affordable due simply to age are especially vulnerable to loss. While pressures have been dampened due to the great recession, this a temporary reprieve.

Devolution of discretion and responsibility has arguably led to greater unevenness in responses to housing needs across states and local jurisdictions. The decline in federal funding has emboldened some states and localities to develop their own funding sources and to impose rules requiring inclusion of affordable housing in new residential developments. Yet most jurisdictions do not have such requirements, nor do they have the political will necessary to generate local resources. At the same time, rising emphasis on the need to plan cities for "sustainable" growth presents both opportunities and impediments to the satisfaction of more holistically defined housing needs. Moving forward, it will be increasingly important that housing advocates and policymakers look beyond their traditional agencies and policies to engage new partners in creating appropriate solutions. With census data indicating deepening poverty in suburbia, fear that low-income residents are being pushed out by redevelopment in the name of sustainability is rising among local advocates. Can we learn from past experiences and forge a new path forward?

ORGANIZATION OF THE *READER*

Part 1 puts housing policy in historical context, describing the key ideological and political debates surrounding housing provision. Issues covered include how national policy options and debate are limited by shared understandings of the division between market and government and of the causes of poverty and how poor conditions motivated early housing regulation. Discussion of resulting policies includes the creation of two-tiered systems for offering assistance, thus weakening the prospects for housing targeted at the poor, tensions between addressing the needs of the urban poor and fostering economic development in cities as seen in urban renewal policy, and the extent to which housing is or should be a "right".

Part 2 presents controversies regarding how best to understand housing needs and how measures relate to the proper focus of housing policy. Key issues addressed include how measures relate to assumptions about causes of affordability problems, and how well they do at representing needs across regions and among different types of households. New measures, emphasizing connections between housing and factors thought key to the quality of life or life chances of residents are also discussed. These include the housing and transportation index, and more complex indices of access to opportunity.

Part 3 discusses the provision of homeownership opportunities for low-income households. This section focuses on the rationale and assumptions underlying our policy focus on homeownership, the various strategies undertaken to encourage low-income homeownership and the challenges and risks – both historical and current – to creating low-income homeownership through the financial markets. Specific selections critically discuss the assumptions about the benefits of homeownership for low-income households and the evidence that homeownership yields expected benefits, the formation of the persistent bias against renting, specific policies that have attempted to foster low-income homeownership, and the impact of the ongoing foreclosure crisis on low income neighborhoods. Finally, we include discussion of shared equity forms of ownership.

Part 4 analyzes the federal policy shift away from direct production of affordable housing toward the use of incentives for private production and vouchers for use in private rental housing. Selections in this section consider how well these incentives have worked, as well as ongoing challenges to their effectiveness that have emerged. Key questions tackled in this section include the performance of the federal Low Income Housing Tax Credit as a producer of affordable housing; the challenges to building a stock of affordable housing posed by time-limited incentives; and the pros and cons of Housing Choice Vouchers. Each contribution analyzes both the intent and outcomes of each of these programs, providing insight into their success in terms of economic efficiency, quality of life for residents, and racial and class integration.

Part 5 delves into the "people versus place" debate in urban social policy. For housing policy, this has particular resonance: should we focus on improving conditions in low-income communities (including empowering communities) or facilitate the deconcentration of poverty by encouraging integration of affordable housing into non-poor neighborhoods and communities? This section focuses on policy efforts to transform low-income communities, with emphasis on debates concerning whether policy should focus on transforming poor communities for the benefit of current residents or whether the goal should be to create a greater income mix in these communities (and in the suburbs), and the tensions between these goals. Specific selections cover the motivation for community-based strategies in the 1960s and on how the context for such efforts have changed over time, on the disparate motivations behind dispersal policies in the 1960s and 1980s, the rationale for "mixed income" housing strategies, and on the results of the HOPE VI program for residents. Finally, we consider whether the "people versus place" framing of the discussion is still useful.

Part 6 discusses the role that land use regulations and government subsidies have had in shaping housing policy, affordability and access. It also presents arguments over proposed regulatory solutions to housing shortages. Included are debates regarding the purposes of land use regulation and the proper framing of discussions of over-regulation, how land use regulations shape housing choices and foster a "chain of exclusion" of housing types most often home to racial minorities. Finally, we consider the effects of growth management policies on housing affordability and emerging evidence regarding the impact of transit-oriented development on low-income communities.

Part 7 analyzes how the groundwork for the segregation of U.S. cities and suburbs was established decades ago through numerous mechanisms, including the public housing program and Federal Housing Administration lending policies. This section focuses on the ways that racial exclusion was established and enforced, particularly in suburbs, the fundamental causes and consequences of racial discrimination and segregation, and the challenges to facing building fair housing advocacy coalitions that incorporate the goals of both fair housing and community development proponents. We conclude by presenting the current federal agenda for fair housing.

We hope that this text succeeds in engaging students and scholars of housing policy in discussion of the fundamental challenges to ensuring low income residents have access to safe, decent homes.

J. Rosie Tighe and Elizabeth J. Mueller

PART ONE

Conflicting motivations for housing policy in the U.S.

Plate 1 **Ceru family, 143 Thompson St.** (Lewis Hine, photographer).

INTRODUCTION TO PART ONE

Historically, housing policy in the United States has pursued a variety of policy goals that reach well beyond the bounds of shelter. While housing policy can be viewed as social policy, its primary function was seldom the alleviation of poverty. U.S. housing policy has weathered a particularly disjointed history, throughout which concerns about class and race, as well as opportunity and responsibility, have been constant.

The first efforts to regulate housing focused on housing conditions, relying on the rationale that the poor constituted both threats to public health and to economic development. Public attention to the abysmal conditions in which immigrants lived in the large industrial cities of the late nineteenth and early twentieth centuries were brought to light through investigative reports, pioneering social surveys and public exhibits. Booth's seminal social survey of London, conducted the 1890s and published after the turn of the century, made the connection between working poverty and housing conditions and was influential in subsequent public discussions of housing and planning policy in Britain. In the U.S., the housing exhibit organized by New York's Committee on the Congestion of the Population, following upon the report of the Tenement House Commission in 1894, similarly galvanized public attention and spurred debate.

Arguably the most influential piece to emerge during this period was Jacob Riis' seminal work, *How the Other Half Lives.* The book brought to light the conditions so common in the immigrant centers of America, using striking photographs and strong rhetoric to describe the lives of the poor in America's most prominent cities. However, while conditions in American cities were arguably worse than in Britain, public response favored regulation rather than public provision of adequate housing. As a result, subsequent housing reforms were not focused on aiding the poor and immigrant populations, but to protecting mainstream America from health hazards and threats to property values emanating from the slums. Tensions between serving the needs of poor and creating conditions conducive to private investment remain a central theme in housing policy.

The tensions between the social and economic functions of housing and the constituencies behind each are presented in stark relief in the Urban Renewal policies of the mid-twentieth century. Von Hoffman brings the conflicting roles of housing to life in his description of the adoption of urban renewal policy, highlighting in particular the tensions between social aspects of housing – its role as shelter, the foundation for family life, and for family economic security and neighborhood and community revitalization – and its place in the national economy. He focuses on the influential role of the real estate industry in shaping the federal urban renewal program. For both city planning and housing policy, the fallout from urban renewal would be long-lasting. Urban revitalization programs across the country resulted in wholesale displacement of poor and minority communities, while providing considerable opportunity and incentive for private investment and profit in city centers.

The backlash against Urban Renewal caused profound changes in city planning practice and resulted in a short-lived period during the 1960s of direct federal support for community-based housing development. Activists such as Herbert Gans and Jane Jacobs challenged the notion that "blighted" neighborhoods were the lifeless, economically depressed communities depicted by city planners and developers. In the immediate aftermath of the program, a blue-ribbon committee of business leaders was formed to revisit the issue of housing the nation's poor. The Kaiser Committee's recommendations helped produce a string of innovative programs including Model Cities and others. These programs attempted to respond to the perceived exclusion of residents of "blighted" communities from public discussion of local housing policy priorities while continuing to rely on existing subsidy programs and private participation in the development and management of subsidized housing.

However, the innovation of the 1960s was short-lived. Federally sponsored public housing was aging poorly and took on a reputation for crime, dependence, and corruption. Following the demolition of Pruitt-Igoe in 1972, the Nixon administration placed a moratorium on the production of government-subsidized public housing. An entirely new approach to federal housing policy was instituted, shifting from direct provision to individualized assistance in the form of certificates and vouchers for use in the private housing market. This new approach gave local jurisdictions greater discretion over programs, within the parameters set by federal agencies.

With the passage of the Housing and Community Development Act of 1974, a new approach to funding was adopted. The specific categorical grant programs that comprised 1960s War on Poverty housing and community development programming were eliminated in favor of the more comprehensive Community Development Block Grant program. These changes were followed by an ideological shift in views regarding the size of government and government role in housing production in the 1980s under President Ronald Reagan. Federal housing policy began to evolve into the system of public regulation and financing of primarily private production and lending that exists today.

In this context, those advocating a greater role for government in responding to the housing needs of low-income people face a particular challenge. One response has been largely to understand why past housing policy has gone so terribly wrong. In "Housing Policy and the Myth of the Benevolent State," Peter Marcuse provocatively argues against the idea that federal housing policy has ever acted primarily to provide decent housing for the poor. Indeed, he states that, "an historical analysis of government actions and inactions affecting housing reveals no such housing policy or any common thrust toward one." According to Marcuse, the U.S. government's position on housing has been embodied in a set of policies that were internally contradictory and even self-defeating, lacking in focus, philosophy, clarity of goals, and priorities. As a result, "Any claim to benevolent intervention in the housing situation to bring about more rationally organized and improved housing for the poor is now abandoned altogether."

In the absence of strong, coherent, federal housing policy, the responsibility for financing, producing and managing affordable housing has fallen to the private sector. In his keynote address at the City Futures conference in 2004, former Cleveland planning director Norman Krumholz describes the process through which the private sector has become the dominant force in the housing sector, while the public sector has been relegated to a supporting role – providing incentives, regulations and financing for the production of affordable housing by the private sector. As Krumholz concludes, "None of this should be surprising; affordable housing policy in the U.S. is driven by interest-group politics, popular prejudices and the business considerations that dominate our political system."

Another response has been to focus on reinvigorating the rationale for housing as an area of social policy. Bratt, Hartman, and Stone present a normative vision for a "right to housing" that responds to the stark inequality present in American cities and towns today and to the role of public policy in its creation and perpetuation. Their ambitious goal is to "change the prevailing mind-set and stimulating innovative, aggressive and far-reaching responses to our persistent housing problems."

While subsequent sections in this reader will present particular aspects of housing policy and contemporary debates, the origins of housing policy in conflicting concerns regarding social conditions and economic development, and the failure of key shifts in policy to produce marked improvement in outcomes for those most in need of housing remind us of the importance of forging a clear sense of purpose as a foundation for policy. The original challenge presented by Riis and others at the turn of the twentieth century remains with us: how can we adequately house the poor? The central tension in forging policy responses remains as well: how can we reconcile the social and economic roles of housing? How can we respond without violating tenuous shared values regarding who is deserving of assistance and a role for private producers in the production of affordable housing?

IN THIS PART:

Chapter 1: Riis, Jacob. (1890). *How the Other Half Lives: Studies Among the Tenements of New York*. New York: Charles Scribner's Sons.
Chapter 2: von Hoffman, Alexander. (2008). "The lost history of urban renewal." *Journal of Urbanism: International Research on Placemaking and Urban Sustainability*, 1(3): 281–301.
Chapter 3: President's Committee on Urban Housing. (1968). *A Decent Home*. Committee report. Chair: Edgar Kaiser. Washington, DC: Government Printing Office.
Chapter 4: Marcuse, Peter. (1978). "Housing policy and the myth of the benevolent state." *Social Policy and Administration*, 8(4): 21–26.
Chapter 5: Krumholz, N. (2004). *The Reluctant Hand: Privatization of Public Housing in the US*. Chicago, IL: City Futures.
Chapter 6: Bratt, R. G., M. E. Stone, and C. Hartman. (2009). "Why a right to housing is needed and makes sense: Editors' introduction." *A Right to Housing: Foundation for a New Social Agenda*. Philadelphia, PA: Temple University Press.

REFERENCES AND FURTHER READING

Bauman, J. F., R. Biles and K. M. Szylvian (2000). *From Tenements to the Taylor homes: In Search of an Urban Housing Policy in Twentieth-Century America*. University Park, PA: Pennsylvania State University Press.
Bratt, R. G., C. W. Hartman and A. Meyerson (1986). *Critical Perspectives on Housing*. Philadelphia, PA: Temple University Press.
Burchell, R. and D. Listoken (1995). "Influences on United States housing policy." *Housing Policy Debate*, 6(3): 559–617.
Colton, K. (2003). *Housing in the Twenty-First Century: Achieving Common Ground*. Cambridge, MA: Harvard University Press.
DiPasquale, D. and L. C. Keyes (eds.). (1990). *Building Foundations: Housing and Federal Policy*. Philadelphia, PA: University of Pennsylvania Press.
Friedman, L. M. (1978). *Government and Slum Housing: A Century of Frustration*, Manchester, NH: Ayer Publishing.
Gans, Herbert. (1962). *The Urban Villagers*. New York: The Free Press.
Hayes, Allen R. (1996). *The Federal Government and Urban Housing*. 2nd edition. Albany, NY: State University of New York Press.
Jacobs, J. (1961). *The Death and Life of Great American Cities*. New York: Random House.
Katz, Michael B. (1996). *In the Shadow of the Poorhouse: A Social History of Welfare in America*. New York: Basic Books.
Piven, Frances Fox, and Richard Cloward. (1971). *Regulating the Poor*. 2nd edition. New York: Vintage Books.
Shlay, Anne B. (1995). "Housing in the broader context of the United States." *Housing Policy Debate*, 6(3): 695–720.
Vale, Lawrence. (2000). *From the Puritans to the Projects: Public Housing and Public Neighbors*. Cambridge, MA: Harvard University Press.
von Hoffman, A. (2000). "A study in contradictions: The origins and legacy of the Housing Act of 1949." *Housing Policy Debate*, 11(2): 299–326.

1
From *How the Other Half Lives* (1890)

Jacob Riis

I GENESIS OF THE TENEMENT

THE first tenement New York knew bore the mark of Cain from its birth, though a generation passed before the writing was deciphered. It was the "rear house," infamous ever after in our city's history. There had been tenant-houses before, but they were not built for the purpose. Nothing would probably have shocked their original owners more than the idea of their harboring a promiscuous crowd; for they were the decorous homes of the old Knickerbockers, the proud aristocracy of Manhattan in the early days.

It was the stir and bustle of trade, together with the tremendous immigration that followed upon the war of 1812 that dislodged them. In thirty-five years the city of less than a hundred thousand came to harbor half a million souls, for whom homes had to be found. Within the memory of men not yet in their prime, Washington had moved from his house on Cherry Hill as too far out of town to be easily reached. Now the old residents followed his example; but they moved in a different direction and for a different reason. Their comfortable dwellings in the once fashionable streets along the East River front fell into the hands of real-estate agents and boarding-house keepers; and here, says the report to the Legislature of 1857, when the evils engendered had excited just alarm,

> in its beginning, the tenant-house became a real blessing to that class of industrious poor whose small earnings limited their expenses, and whose employment in workshops, stores, or about the warehouses and thoroughfares, render a near residence of much importance.

Not for long, however.

As business increased, and the city grew with rapid strides, the necessities of the poor became the opportunity of their wealthier neighbors, and the stamp was set upon the old houses, suddenly become valuable, which the best thought and effort of a later age have vainly struggled to efface. Their

> large rooms were partitioned into several smaller ones, without regard to light or ventilation, the rate of rent being lower in proportion to space or height from the street; and they soon became filled from cellar to garret with a class of tenantry living from hand to mouth, loose in morals, improvident in habits, degraded, and squalid as beggary itself.

It was thus the dark bedroom, prolific of untold depravities, came into the world. It was destined to survive the old houses. In their new role, says the old report, eloquent in its indignant denunciation of "evils more destructive than wars,"

> they were not intended to last. Rents were fixed high enough to cover damage and abuse from this class, from whom nothing was expected, and the most was made of them while they lasted. Neatness, order, cleanliness, were never dreamed of in connection with the tenant-house system, as it spread its localities from year to year;

while reckless slovenliness, discontent, privation, and ignorance were left to work out their invariable results, until the entire premises reached the level of tenant-house dilapidation, containing, but sheltering not, the miserable hordes that crowded beneath mouldering, water-rotted roofs or burrowed among the rats of clammy cellars.

Yet so illogical is human greed that, at a later day, when called to account,

the proprietors frequently urged the filthy habits of the tenants as an excuse for the condition of their property, utterly losing sight of the fact that it was the tolerance of those habits which was the real evil, and that for this they themselves were alone responsible.

Still the pressure of the crowds did not abate, and in the old garden where the stolid Dutch burgher grew his tulips or early cabbages a rear house was built, generally of wood, two stories high at first. Presently it was carried up another story, and another. Where two families had lived ten moved in. The front house followed suit, if the brick walls were strong enough. The question was not always asked, judging from complaints made by a contemporary witness, that the old buildings were "often carried up to a great height without regard to the strength of the foundation walls." It was rent the owner was after; nothing was said in the contract about either the safety or the comfort of the tenants. The garden gate no longer swung on its rusty hinges. The shell-paved walk had become an alley; what the rear house had left of the garden, a "court." Plenty such are yet to be found in the Fourth Ward, with here and there one of the original rear tenements.

Worse was to follow. It was

soon perceived by estate owners and agents of property that a greater percentage of profits could be realized by the conversion of houses and blocks into barracks, and dividing their space into smaller proportions capable of containing human life within four walls. ... Blocks were rented of real estate owners, or "purchased on time," or taken in charge at a percentage, and held for under-letting.

With the appearance of the middleman, wholly irresponsible, and utterly reckless and unrestrained, began the era of tenement building which turned out such blocks as Gotham Court, where, in one cholera epidemic that scarcely touched the clean wards, the tenants died at the rate of one hundred and ninety-five to the thousand of population; which forced the general mortality of the city up from 1 in 41.83 in 1815, to 1 in 27.33 in 1855, a year of unusual freedom from epidemic disease, and which wrung from the early organizers of the Health Department this wail: "There are numerous examples of tenement-houses in which are lodged several hundred people that have a *prorata* allotment of ground area scarcely equal to two square yards upon the city lot, court-yards and all included." The tenement-house population had swelled to half a million souls by that time, and on the East Side, in what is still the most densely populated district in all the world, China not excluded, it was packed at the rate of 290,000 to the square mile, a state of affairs wholly unexampled. The utmost cupidity of other lands and other days had never contrived to herd much more than half that number within the same space. The greatest crowding of Old London was at the rate of 175,816. Swine roamed the streets and gutters as their principal scavengers. The death of a child in a tenement was registered at the Bureau of Vital Statistics as "plainly due to suffocation in the foul air of an unventilated apartment," and the Senators, who had come down from Albany to find out what was the matter with New York, reported that "there are annually cut off from the population by disease and death enough human beings to people a city, and enough human labor to sustain it." And yet experts had testified that, as compared with uptown, rents were from twenty-five to thirty per cent, higher in the worst slums of the lower wards, with such accommodations as were enjoyed, for instance, by a "family with boarders" in Cedar Street, who fed hogs in the cellar that contained eight or ten loads of manure; or a one room 12 x 12 with five families living in it, comprising twenty persons of both sexes and all ages, with only two beds, without partition, screen, chair, or table. The rate of rent has been successfully maintained to the present day, though the hog at least has been eliminated.

Lest anybody flatter himself with the notion that these were evils of a day that is happily past and may safely be forgotten, let me mention here three very recent instances of tenement-house life that came under my notice. One was the burning of a rear house in Mott Street, from appearances one of the original tenant-houses that made their owners rich. The fire made homeless ten families, who had paid an average of $5 a month for their mean little cubby-holes. The owner himself told me that it was fully insured for $800, though it brought him in $600 a year rent. He evidently considered himself especially entitled to be pitied for losing such valuable property. Another was the case of a hard-working family of man and wife, young people from the old country, who took poison together in a Crosby Street tenement because they were "tired." There was no other explanation, and none was needed when I stood in the room in which they had lived. It was in the attic with sloping ceiling and a single window so far out on the roof that it seemed not to belong to the place at all. With scarcely room enough to turn around in they had been compelled to pay five dollars and a half a month in advance. There were four such rooms in that attic, and together they brought in as much as many a handsome little cottage in a pleasant part of Brooklyn. The third instance was that of a colored family of husband, wife, and baby in a wretched rear rookery in West Third Street. Their rent was eight dollars and a half for a single room on the top-story, so small that I was unable to get a photograph of it even by placing the camera outside the open door. Three short steps across either way would have measured its full extent.

There was just one excuse for the early tenement-house builders, and their successors may plead it with nearly as good right for what it is worth. "Such," says an official report, "is the lack of houseroom in the city that any kind of tenement can be immediately crowded with lodgers, if there is space offered." Thousands were living in cellars. There were three hundred underground lodging-houses in the city when the Health Department was organized. Some fifteen years before that the old Baptist Church in Mulberry Street, just off Chatham Street, had been sold, and the rear half of the frame structure had been converted into tenements that with their swarming population became the scandal even of that reckless age. The wretched pile harbored no less than forty families, and the annual rate of deaths to the population was officially stated to be 75 in 1,000. These tenements were an extreme type of very many, for the big barracks had by this time spread east

and west and far up the island into the sparsely settled wards. Whether or not the title was clear to the land upon which they were built was of less account than that the rents were collected. If there were damages to pay, the tenant had to foot them. Cases were "very frequent when property was in litigation, and two or three different parties were collecting rents." Of course under such circumstances "no repairs were ever made."

The climax had been reached. The situation was summed up by the Society for the Improvement of the Condition of the Poor in these words: "Crazy old buildings, crowded rear tenements in filthy yards, dark, damp basements, leaking garrets, shops, outhouses, and stables converted into dwellings, though scarcely fit to shelter brutes, are habitations of thousands of our fellow-beings in this wealthy, Christian city." "The city," says its historian, Mrs. Martha Lamb, commenting on the era of aqueduct building between 1835 and 1845, "was a general asylum for vagrants." Young vagabonds, the natural offspring of such "home" conditions, overran the streets. Juvenile crime increased fearfully year by year. The Children's Aid Society and kindred philanthropic organizations were yet unborn, but in the city directory was to be found the address of the "American Society for the Promotion of Education in Africa."

XXV HOW THE CASE STANDS

WHAT, then, are the bald facts with which we have to deal in New York?

I.   That we have a tremendous, ever swelling crowd of wage-earners which it is our business to house decently.

II.   That it is not housed decently.

III.   That it must be so housed here for the present, and for a long time to come, all schemes of suburban relief being as yet utopian, impracticable.

IV.   That it pays high enough rents to entitle it to be so housed, as a right.

V.   That nothing but our own slothfulness is in the way of so housing it, since "the condition of the tenants is in advance of the condition of the houses which they occupy" (Report of Tenement-house Commission).

VI.   That the security of the one no less than of the other half demands, on sanitary, moral, and economic grounds, that it be decently housed.

VII.   That it will pay to do it. As an investment, I mean, and in hard cash. This I shall immediately proceed to prove.

VIII.   That the tenement has come to stay, and must itself be the solution of the problem with which it confronts us.

This is the fact from which we cannot get away, however we may deplore it. Doubtless the best would be to get rid of it altogether; but as we cannot, all argument on that score may at this time be dismissed as idle. The practical question is what to do with the tenement. I watched a Mott Street landlord, the owner of a row of barracks that have made no end of trouble for the health authorities for twenty years, solve that question for himself the other day. His way was to give the wretched pile a coat of paint, and put a gorgeous tin cornice on with the year 1890 in letters a yard long. From where I stood watching the operation, I looked down upon the same dirty crowds camping on the roof, foremost among them an Italian mother with two stark-naked children who had apparently never made the acquaintance of a wash-tub. That was a landlord's way, and will not get us out of the mire.

The "flat" is another way that does not solve the problem. Rather, it extends it. The flat is not a model, though it is a modern, tenement. It gets rid of some of the nuisances of the low tenement, and of the worst of them, the overcrowding – if it gets rid of them at all – at a cost that takes it at once out of the catalogue of "homes for the poor," while imposing some of the evils from which they suffer upon those who ought to escape from them.

There are three effective ways of dealing with the tenements in New York:

I.   By law.

II.   By remodelling and making the most out of the old houses.

III.   By building new, model tenements.

Private enterprise – conscience, to put it in the category of duties, where it belongs – must do the lion's share under these last two heads. Of what the law has effected I have spoken already. The drastic measures adopted in Paris,

in Glasgow, and in London are not practicable here on anything like as large a scale. Still it can, under strong pressure of public opinion, rid us of the worst plague-spots. The Mulberry Street Bend will go the way of the Five Points when all the red tape that binds the hands of municipal effort has been unwound. Prizes were offered in public competition, some years ago, for the best plans of modern tenement-houses. It may be that we shall see the day when the building of model tenements will be encouraged by subsidies in the way of a rebate of taxes. Meanwhile the arrest and summary punishment of landlords, or their agents, who persistently violate law and decency, will have a salutary effect. If a few of the wealthy absentee landlords, who are the worst offenders, could be got within the jurisdiction of the city, and by arrest be compelled to employ proper overseers, it would be a proud day for New York. To remedy the overcrowding, with which the night inspections of the sanitary police cannot keep step, tenements may eventually have to be licensed, as now the lodging-houses, to hold so many tenants, and no more; or the State may have to bring down the rents that cause the crowding, by assuming the right to regulate them as it regulates the fares on the elevated roads. I throw out the suggestion, knowing quite well that it is open to attack. It emanated originally from one of the brightest minds that have had to struggle officially with this tenement-house question in the last ten years. In any event, to succeed, reform by law must aim at making it unprofitable to own a bad tenement. At best, it is apt to travel at a snail's pace, while the enemy it pursues is putting the best foot foremost.

In this matter of profit the law ought to have its strongest ally in the landlord himself, though the reverse is the case. This condition of things I believe to rest on a monstrous error. It cannot be that tenement property that is worth preserving at all can continue to yield larger returns, if allowed to run down, than if properly cared for and kept in good repair. The point must be reached, and soon, where the cost of repairs, necessary with a house full of the lowest, most ignorant tenants, must overbalance the saving of the first few years of neglect; for this class is everywhere the most destructive, as well as the poorest paying. I have the experience of owners, who have found this out to their cost, to back me up in the assertion, even if it were not the statement of a plain business fact that proves itself. I do not include tenement property that is deliberately allowed to fall into decay because at some future time the ground will be valuable for business or other purposes. There is unfortunately enough of that kind in New York, often leasehold property owned by wealthy estates or soulless corporations that oppose all their great influence to the efforts of the law in behalf of their tenants.

There is abundant evidence, on the other hand, that it can be made to pay to improve and make the most of the worst tenement property, even in the most wretched locality. The example set by Miss Ellen Collins in her Water Street houses will always stand as a decisive answer to all doubts on this point. It is quite ten years since she bought three old tenements at the corner of Water and Roosevelt Streets, then as now one of the lowest localities in the city. Since then she has leased three more adjoining her purchase, and so much of Water Street has at all events been purified. Her first effort was to let in the light in the hallways, and with the darkness disappeared, as if by magic, the heaps of refuse that used to be piled up beside the sinks. A few of the most refractory tenants disappeared with them, but a very considerable proportion stayed, conforming readily to the new rules, and are there yet. It should here be stated that Miss Collins's tenants are distinctly of the poorest. Her purpose was to experiment with this class, and her experiment has been more than satisfactory. Her plan was, as she puts it herself, fair play between tenant and landlord. To this end the rents were put as low as consistent with the idea of a business investment that must return a reasonable interest to be successful. The houses were thoroughly refitted with proper plumbing. A competent janitor was put in charge to see that the rules were observed by the tenants, when Miss Collins herself was not there. Of late years she has had to give very little time to personal superintendence, and the care-taker told me only the other day that very little was needed. The houses seemed to run themselves in the groove once laid down. Once the reputed haunt of thieves, they have become the most orderly in the neighborhood. Clothes are left hanging on the lines all night with impunity, and the pretty flower-beds in the yard where the children not only from the six houses, but of the whole block, play, skip, and swing, are undisturbed. The tenants, by the way, provide the flowers themselves in the spring, and take

all the more pride in them because they are their own. The six houses contain forty-five families, and there "has never been any need of putting up a bill." As to the income from the property, Miss Collins said to me last August: "I have had six and even six and three-quarters per cent. on the capital invested; on the whole, you may safely say five and a half per cent. This I regard as entirely satisfactory." It should be added that she has persistently refused to let the corner-store, now occupied by a butcher, as a saloon; or her income from it might have been considerably increased.

Miss Collins's experience is of value chiefly as showing what can be accomplished with the worst possible material, by the sort of personal interest in the poor that alone will meet their real needs. All the charity in the world, scattered with the most lavish hand, will not take its place. "Fair play" between landlord and tenant is the key, too long mislaid, that unlocks the door to success everywhere as it did for Miss Collins. She has not lacked imitators whose experience has been akin to her own. The case of Gotham Court has been already cited. On the other hand, instances are not wanting of landlords who have undertaken the task, but have tired of it or sold their property before it had been fully redeemed, with the result that it relapsed into its former bad condition faster than it had improved, and the tenants with it. I am inclined to think that such houses are liable to fall even below the average level. Backsliding in brick and mortar does not greatly differ from similar performances in flesh and blood.

Backed by a strong and steady sentiment, such as these pioneers have evinced, that would make it the personal business of wealthy owners with time to spare to look after their tenants, the law would be able in a very short time to work a salutary transformation in the worst quarters, to the lasting advantage, I am well persuaded, of the landlord no less than the tenant. Unfortunately, it is in this quality of personal effort that the sentiment of interest in the poor, upon which we have to depend, is too often lacking. People who are willing to give money feel that that ought to be enough. It is not. The money thus given is too apt to be wasted along with the sentiment that prompted the gift.

Even when it comes to the third of the ways I spoke of as effective in dealing with the tenement-house problem, the building of model structures, the personal interest in the matter must form a large share of the capital invested, if it is to yield full returns. Where that is the case, there is even less doubt about its paying, with ordinary business management, than in the case of reclaiming an old building, which is, like putting life into a defunct newspaper, pretty apt to be up-hill work. Model tenement building has not been attempted in New York on anything like as large a scale as in many other great cities, and it is perhaps owing to this, in a measure, that a belief prevails that it cannot succeed here. This is a wrong notion entirely. The various undertakings of that sort that have been made here under intelligent management have, as far as I know, all been successful.

From the managers of the two best-known experiments in model tenement building in the city, the Improved Dwellings Association and the Tenement-house Building Company, I have letters dated last August, declaring their enterprises eminently successful. There is no reason why their experience should not be conclusive. That the Philadelphia plan is not practicable in New York is not a good reason why our own plan, which is precisely the reverse of our neighbor's, should not be. In fact it is an argument for its success. The very reason why we cannot house our working masses in cottages, as has been done in Philadelphia – viz., that they must live on Manhattan Island, where the land is too costly for small houses – is the best guarantee of the success of the model tenement house, properly located and managed. The drift in tenement building, as in everything else, is toward concentration, and helps smooth the way. Four families on the floor, twenty in the house, is the rule of to-day. As the crowds increase, the need of guiding this drift into safe channels becomes more urgent. The larger the scale upon which the model tenement is planned, the more certain the promise of success. The utmost ingenuity cannot build a house for sixteen or twenty families on a lot 25 x 100 feet in the middle of a block like it, that shall give them the amount of air and sunlight to be had by the erection of a dozen or twenty houses on a common plan around a central yard. This was the view of the committee that awarded the prizes for the best plan for the conventional tenement, ten years ago. It coupled its verdict with the emphatic declaration that, in its view, it was "impossible to secure the requirements of physical and moral health within these narrow and arbitrary limits." Houses have been built

since on better plans than any the committee saw, but its judgment stands unimpaired. A point, too, that is not to be overlooked, is the reduced cost of expert superintendence – the first condition of successful management – in the larger buildings.

The Improved Dwellings Association put up its block of thirteen houses in East Seventy-second Street nine years ago. Their cost, estimated at about $240,000 with the land, was increased to $285,000 by troubles with the contractor engaged to build them. Thus the Association's task did not begin under the happiest auspices. Unexpected expenses came to deplete its treasury. The neighborhood was new and not crowded at the start. No expense was spared, and the benefit of all the best and most recent experience in tenement building was given to the tenants. The families were provided with from two to four rooms, all "outer" rooms, of course, at rents ranging from $14 per month for the four on the ground floor, to $6.25 for two rooms on the top floor. Coal lifts, ash-chutes, common laundries in the basement, and free baths, are features of these buildings that were then new enough to be looked upon with suspicion by the doubting Thomases who predicted disaster. There are rooms in the block for 218 families, and when I looked in recently all but nine of the apartments were let. One of the nine was rented while I was in the building. The superintendent told me that he had little trouble with disorderly tenants, though the buildings shelter all sorts of people. Mr. W. Bayard Cutting, the President of the Association, writes to me:

By the terms of subscription to the stock before incorporation, dividends were limited to five per cent. on the stock of the Improved Dwellings Association. These dividends have been paid (two per cent. each six months) ever since the expiration of the first six months of the buildings operation. All surplus has been expended upon the buildings. New and expensive roofs have been put on for the comfort of such tenants as might choose to use them. The buildings have been completely painted inside and out in a manner not contemplated at the outset. An expensive set of fire-escapes has been put on at the command of the Fire Department, and a considerable number of other improvements made. I regard the experiment as eminently successful and satisfactory, particularly when it is considered that the buildings were the first erected in this city upon anything like a large scale, where it was proposed to meet the architectural difficulties that present themselves in the tenement-house problem. I have no doubt that the experiment could be tried to-day with the improved knowledge which has come with time, and a much larger return be shown upon the investment. The results referred to have been attained in spite of the provision which prevents the selling of liquor upon the Association's premises. You are aware, of course, how much larger rent can be obtained for a liquor saloon than for an ordinary store. An investment at five per cent. net upon real estate security worth more than the principal sum, ought to be considered desirable.

The Tenement House Building Company made its "experiment" in a much more difficult neighborhood, Cherry Street, some six years later. Its houses shelter many Russian Jews, and the difficulty of keeping them in order is correspondingly increased, particularly as there are no ash-chutes in the houses. It has been necessary even to shut the children out of the yards upon which the kitchen windows give, lest they be struck by something thrown out by the tenants, and killed. It is the Cherry Street style, not easily got rid of. Nevertheless, the houses are well kept. Of the one hundred and six "apartments," only four were vacant in August. Professor Edwin R. A. Seligman, the secretary of the company, writes to me: "The tenements are now a decided success." In the three years since they were built, they have returned an interest of from five to five and a half per cent. on the capital invested. The original intention of making the tenants profit-sharers on a plan of rent insurance, under which all earnings above four per cent. would be put to the credit of the tenants, has not yet been carried out.

A scheme of dividends to tenants on a somewhat similar plan has been carried out by a Brooklyn builder, Mr. A. T. White, who has devoted a life of beneficent activity to tenement building, and whose experience, though it has been altogether across the East River, I regard as justly applying to New York as well. He so regards it himself. Discussing the cost of building, he says:

There is not the slightest reason to doubt that the financial result of a similar undertaking in any tenement-house district of New York City would be equally good. ... High cost of land is no detriment, provided the value is made by the pressure of people seeking residence there. Rents in New York City bear a higher ratio to Brooklyn rents than would the cost of land and building in the one city to that in the other.

The assertion that Brooklyn furnishes a better class of tenants than the tenement districts in New York would not be worth discussing seriously, even if Mr. White did not meet it himself with the statement that the proportion of day-laborers and sewing-women in his houses is greater than in any of the London model tenements, showing that they reach the humblest classes.

Mr. White has built homes for five hundred poor families since he began his work, and has made it pay well enough to allow good tenants a share in the profits, averaging nearly one month's rent out of the twelve, as a premium upon promptness and order. The plan of his last tenements [...] may be justly regarded as the beau ideal of the model tenement for a great city like New York. It embodies all the good features of Sir Sydney Waterlow's London plan, with improvements suggested by the builder's own experience. Its chief merit is that it gathers three hundred real homes, not simply three hundred families, under one roof. Three tenants, it will be seen, use each entrance hall. Of the rest of the three hundred they may never know, rarely see, one. Each has his private front-door. The common hall, with all that it hands for, has disappeared. The fire-proof stairs are outside the house, a perfect fire-escape. Each tenant has his own scullery and ash-flue. There are no air-shafts, for they are not needed. Every room, under the admirable arrangement of the plan, looks out either upon the street or the yard, that is nothing less than a great park with a play-ground set apart for the children, where they may dig in the sand to their heart's content. Weekly concerts are given in the park by a brass band. The drying of clothes is done on the roof, where racks are fitted up for the purpose. The outside stairways end in turrets that give the buildings a very smart appearance. Mr. White never has any trouble with his tenants, though he gathers in the poorest; nor do his tenements have anything of the "institution character" that occasionally attaches to ventures of this sort, to their damage. They are like a big village of contented people, who live in peace with one another because they have elbow-room even under one big roof.

Enough has been said to show that model tenements can be built successfully and made to pay in New York, if the owner will be content with the five or six per cent. he does not even dream of when investing his funds in "governments" at three or four. It is true that in the latter case he has only to cut off his coupons and cash them. But the extra trouble of looking after his tenement property, that is the condition of highest and lasting success, is the penalty exacted for the sins of our fathers that "shall be visited upon the children, unto the third and fourth generation." We shall indeed be well off, if it stop there. I fear there is too much reason to believe that our own iniquities must be added to transmit the curse still further. And yet, such is the leavening influence of a good deed in that dreary desert of sin and suffering, that the erection of a single good tenement has the power to change, gradually but surely, the character of a whole bad block. It sets up a standard to which the neighborhood must rise, if it cannot succeed in dragging it down to its own low level.

And so this task, too, has come to an end. Whatsoever a man soweth, that shall he also reap. I have aimed to tell the truth as I saw it. If this book shall have borne ever so feeble a hand in garnering a harvest of justice, it has served its purpose. While I was writing these lines I went down to the sea, where thousands from the city were enjoying their summer rest. The ocean slumbered under a cloudless sky. Gentle waves washed lazily over the white sand, where children fled before them with screams of laughter. Standing there and watching their play, I was told that during the fierce storms of winter it happened that this sea, now so calm, rose in rage and beat down, broke over the bluff, sweeping all before it. No barrier built by human hands had power to stay it then. The sea of a mighty population, held in galling fetters, heaves uneasily in the tenements. Once already our city, to which have come the duties and responsibilities of metropolitan greatness before it was able to fairly measure its task, has felt the swell of its resistless flood. If it rise once more, no human power may avail to check it. The gap between the classes in which it surges, unseen, unsuspected by the thoughtless, is widening day by day. No tardy enactment of law, no political expedient, can close it. Against all other dangers our system of government may offer defence and shelter; against this not. I know of but one bridge that will carry us over safe, a bridge founded upon justice and built of human hearts. I believe that the danger of such conditions as are fast growing up around us is greater for the very freedom which they mock. The words of the poet, with whose lines I prefaced this book, are truer to-day, have far deeper meaning to us, than when they were penned forty years ago:

" – Think ye that building shall endure
Which shelters the noble and crushes the poor?"

2
"The lost history of urban renewal"

From *Journal of Urbanism* (2008)

Alexander von Hoffman

Joint Center for Housing Studies, Harvard University, Cambridge, MA, USA

INTRODUCTION

For much of the twentieth century, the people who cared most about the health and form of cities in the USA – including city planners, government officials, and downtown businessmen – considered dilapidated and deteriorating neighborhoods as among the most vexing of problems. The solution they chose was "urban renewal," a term which today is commonly understood to mean the government program for acquiring, demolishing, and replacing buildings deemed slums.

In fact, the original meaning of the term "urban renewal" was quite different. The policy of slum clearance, along with authorizations for public housing intended to replace the demolished homes, was established in the landmark Housing Act of 1949 as "urban redevelopment." Five years later the Housing Act of 1954 instituted the policy of "urban renewal," which was intended to supplant the earlier law with a comprehensive approach to the problem of blighted and slum neighborhoods. In contrast to urban redevelopment, urban renewal stressed not clearance but enforcement of building codes and rehabilitation of substandard buildings. Instead of public housing, it emphasized privately built housing for low-income and displaced families.

This new approach originated in local citizens' movements to use code enforcement and rehabilitation to stabilize and regenerate physically deteriorating neighborhoods. The major trade associations of the housing industry seized on one such effort – the Baltimore Plan – as the basis for a national campaign to spread code enforcement and rehabilitation to rescue blighted neighborhoods. Bitter opponents of public housing, the trade associations wanted to establish the new approach, dubbed "urban renewal," as a national policy. Working out their ideas in round-table conferences hosted by *House and Home* magazine and an advisory committee to President Dwight Eisenhower, representatives of the housing industry virtually wrote code enforcement, rehabilitation, and new private urban housing programs into the Housing Act of 1954.

Yet when it came time to implement the Housing Act of 1954, this attempt to fundamentally shift urban policy failed. Housing codes spread, but enforcement was spotty at best. The new urban housing programs did not catch on with home builders, neighborhood campaigns proved unable to stop the spread of urban blight, and cities continued to pursue the old formula of slum clearance and public housing. As a result, in cities large and small the wrecking ball destroyed hundreds of thousands of homes – many of which were occupied by working class and minority citizens and never replaced. In the popular mind, the distinction between the 1949 and 1954 Laws was lost, and urban renewal became synonymous with demolition. The idea of rehabilitation survived, not as a free-enterprise substitute for public housing, but as a way for grassroots and nonprofit organizations to restore and revive urban communities.

The precise origins of the urban renewal program in the Housing Act of 1954 have been lost even to many historians. Although several scholars have credited the writer Miles Colean with the original idea and noted the influence of private industry through Eisenhower's advisory committee, few, if any, recognized that trade groups formulated much of the 1954 legislation before the advisory committee was formed (Friedman 1968, Scott 1969, Gelfand 1975, Mitchell 1994, Biles 1996, 2000). In his article "The origins and legacy of urban renewal," Weiss (1985) reflects a common misunderstanding by dismissing the 1954 Act as merely changing the name of the 1949 urban redevelopment program. This assertion ignores the housing industry's adamant opposition to the 1949 law and fervent support of the 1954 Act and, conversely, the public housing advocates' enthusiastic support for the 1949 Bill and cool attitude toward the 1954 Law. Most importantly, this interpretation overlooks the different intent and programs of the two laws.

TO CURE THE CITY

During the twentieth century, observers of America's cities became increasingly apprehensive. Since 1920, population growth in most of the nation's great urban centers had slowed from the previous century's breathtaking pace to a crawl, and during the 1930s some cities – notably, Philadelphia, Cleveland, St Louis, and Boston – even lost population. Affluent urban dwellers were defecting to the suburbs, which threatened to undermine the downtown commercial districts and the posh residential areas which depended upon them. Big-city newspaper publishers, department store owners, members of the chambers of commerce, and government officials became alarmed that the loss of tax revenues endangered the economic survival of America's cities.

Urban experts and leaders associated the "decentralization" of people and businesses from the city to the suburbs with the spread of slums and "blight," areas which appeared to be losing economic value and potentially could evolve into slums. To retain middle- and upper-class residents and reverse the spread of blight, the defenders of the American city called for upgrading obsolete building stock, redrawing inadequate street plans, and promoting new downtown development (Teaford 1990, pp. 10–

13, Beauregard 1993, pp. 79–157, Fogelson 2001, Isenberg 2004).

Concerned downtown businessmen, leading real-estate investors, and elected officials focused mostly on downtowns and nearby areas, which often contained grimy factories, train yards, and the homes of industrial workers. The private real-estate industry – particularly the sector that dealt in "respectable," that is, high-end properties – felt that industrial and lower-class areas depressed nearby land values and therefore should be redeveloped either as expensive residences or impressive-looking commercial or office buildings. Obtaining slum real estate was difficult, however, for the paradoxical reason that it was valuable – because demand for homes and businesses was high near the downtown where slums were often located. Consequently, slum landowners – generally small businessmen some of whom themselves rose from or lived in the same benighted neighborhoods – were often reluctant to sell their lucrative properties.

From the 1930s, the housing industry, under the leadership of Herbert U. Nelson, Executive Director of the National Association of Real Estate Boards (NAREB), sought a viable method of urban redevelopment that would allow private entrepreneurs to acquire and rebuild deteriorated sections of the city. To get around the high cost of acquiring inner-city and industrial land, in 1941 Nelson and leading urban realtors called for metropolitan land commissions armed with the power of eminent domain to obtain properties in blighted areas and then sell them to private developers at prices below the current value. The realtors proposed that government provide subsidies or "write-downs" to cover the difference between the purchase cost of inner-city lands and their future value when redeveloped.

In the following years urban redevelopment gained in popularity. Enticed by the notions that planning agencies would coordinate redevelopment and that blighted areas of all sorts could be redeveloped, land-use attorney Alfred Bettman and the city planners came on board, and by 1948 25 state legislatures had adopted urban redevelopment enabling acts. Following the well-publicized example of Pittsburgh's Renaissance coalition of Democratic mayor David Lawrence and Republican financier Richard King Mellon, mayors, businessmen, bankers, and the like in cities across the country formed pro-growth coalitions, which pushed for urban redevelopment projects in the name of civic improvement and local boosterism. The proponents of urban redevelopment, however, said little about the inhabitants of the slums and blighted areas and where they would live after their homes were demolished (Bettman 1943, 1945/1946, Gelfand 1975, Mollenkopf 1983, pp. 112–120, Teaford 1990).

The supporters of urban redevelopment in the main ignored issues of race and class that contributed to the changes in inner-city populations. In the 1920s and 1930s, most perceived that blight and slums were located either in old immigrant quarters – such as New York's Lower East Side and Chicago's Near West Side – or African-American areas, such as Harlem or Chicago's Black Belt. The onset of World War II and the consequent demand for a labor force in the wartime industries triggered large migrations of low-income peoples – blacks and whites from the South, Mexicans, and Puerto Ricans – to America's cities. As working- and lower-class migrants replaced economically better-off residents, some inner-city neighborhoods declined in appearance and value. Moreover, the movement of African Americans – of any income level – into new areas of settlement instigated virulent reactions among whites, who used local institutions and political leaders or even violence to resist the influx of blacks into their neighborhoods. Until the civil rights movement of the 1960s tore off the veil of silence, most white urban leaders rarely spoke of racial conflict in public, preferring instead to pursue policies of racial containment by keeping African Americans in historically African-American neighborhoods, conserving or redeveloping blighted city neighborhoods for whites, and promoting suburban development for whites (Hirsch 1983, Bauman 1987, Sugrue 1996, Freund 2007).

Long before realtors began dreaming of redeveloping the slums into respectable properties for well-to-do whites, reformers of a different sort had laid claim to the problem of the urban slums. As far back as the 1840s, religious, moral, and sanitation reformers exerted themselves to improve or eliminate the congested living quarters of the poor in New York, Boston, Philadelphia, and other large cities. Convinced that these unpleasant physical environments corrupted the health and morals of their inhabitants, housing reformers during the nineteenth and early twentieth centuries campaigned to impose building and sanitary regulations on inner-city properties and demolish the most crowded and unhealthy residences. The reformers worked to replace the slums with parks and model housing projects, but made little progress in breaking up the crowded urban warrens. By the early twentieth century a small band of housing reformers and city planners became impatient with the regulatory approach and began urging Americans to adopt measures similar to the recently enacted government-sponsored housing programs in Europe (Lubove 1962, Culver 1972, Jackson 1976, Rodgers 1998).

In the 1930s the Depression's flood of mortgage foreclosures, collapsing real-estate values, and massive unemployment conferred a sense of urgency on the housing question. Blaming the creation of the slums on private enterprise, a growing number of reformers insisted that only government could provide adequate shelter to the American masses. Urban liberal politicians concurred that the government should help hard-working citizens who through no fault of their own had to live in decrepit and possibly dangerous structures. While the public housers, as the advocates were known, differed on the urgency of demolishing the slums, they knew that arguing the need for slum clearance was a winning strategy for getting low-income public housing. With the political muscle of organized labor and the Catholic Church – and the support of social workers, architects, and planners – the public housers managed to persuade the Roosevelt administration and the Congress to create a long-term public housing program in 1937 to help clear the slums and better house the American people (McDonnell 1957, Radford 1996, von Hoffman 2005).

The private housing industry, however, adamantly objected to public housing. It did not matter that government munificence in the form of the Federal Home Loan Bank System had helped rescue the savings-and-loan associations or that government insurance for private residential mortgages provided by the Federal Housing Administration (FHA) had stabilized the home real-estate business. From the 1930s onwards, private housing financiers, real-estate brokers, and builders denounced the idea of the government directly helping Americans of modest means to obtain homes. It was, they cried, not only a socialistic plot, but also an unjustified give-away to a select undeserving group of people. It soon became evident, if it was not already, that self-interest, as much as ideology, fueled the hatred of the leaders of private industry for public housing.

THE FIGHT OVER URBAN REDEVELOPMENT AND LOW-INCOME HOUSING

During World War II, the soaring demand for homes for defense workers precipitated a political struggle over wartime housing policy. As part of the mobilization of the USA to fight the Axis powers, the government expanded or built from scratch industrial and military sites across the country, overwhelming nearby areas' capacity to house the employees who came streaming in. To organize war production, the federal government curtailed normal residential development and took over the job of issuing housing contracts for the defense workers. Galvanized by the prospect of the government building all defense housing itself, the leaders of the home building industry in 1941 formed the Home Builders Emergency Committee to ensure that private industry would share in the contracts for defense housing. In 1943 the specter of a government-built housing program induced two rival factions of home builders to form the National Association of Home Builders (NAHB), which soon became one of the country's most influential lobbying groups (NAHB 1958, pp. 14–22).

The private industry lobbying appears to have paid off. At first, before the industry fully organized its lobbying efforts, federal government administrators embraced cooperative ownership, public defense housing, regional and local planning, and modernist design, with the thought that these could contribute or serve as prototypes for postwar housing programs. After the reorganization of federal housing departments into the National Housing Agency in 1942, however, the government changed directions and pushed the production of inexpensively constructed temporary dwellings. The representatives of the home builders, realtors, and other industry lobbyists pushed for the new policy, while the housing reform and organized labor interest groups protested that after the war the cheaply

built war workers homes would become slums and bring all public housing into disrepute (Szylvian 2000). This battle set the stage for the long struggle that followed.

As World War II came to an end, the liberal housing reformers and the real-estate and housing industry commenced a bitter political fight over the federal legislation for urban redevelopment and particularly whether it would include public housing. Interest groups, including those representing organized labor, city officials, and social workers, lobbied for public housing and slum clearance as ways to rid the cities of slums and place low-income Americans in decent homes. Answering their call, in 1945 Senators Robert A. Taft, Republican of Ohio, and Allen J. Ellender, Democrat of Louisiana, joined the aging liberal leader Robert Wagner of New York to sponsor legislation that combined urban redevelopment based on slum clearance and "write-down" grants along with a provision to authorize a new round of public housing. On the other side, the real-estate and housing industry groups fought to eliminate public housing, or for that matter, any form of government-provided housing. Seeing that the proposed legislation contained a provision for more public housing, NAREB, the organization that had initiated the idea of urban redevelopment, joined with NAHB and other trade associations to fight the bill (Public Housing 1944, McDonnell 1957, Keith 1973, Hunt 2005b).

The two sides fought inside and outside of Congress for four years until 1949 when the growing popularity of urban redevelopment, a severe postwar shortage, and the Democrats' victories in the 1948 election provided enough political pressure to pass the Taft–Ellender–Wagner bill. Renamed the US Housing Act of 1949, the bill established an urban redevelopment program by funding slum clearance and, as part of the goal of "a decent home and a suitable living environment for every American family," authorized 810,000 new units of public housing over six years. Both Taft and the liberals believed that only the government could provide decent homes for low-income city dwellers and that therefore public housing was needed to replace the homes demolished in urban redevelopment projects. Although the 1949 law did not specifically tie public housing to urban redevelopment projects, it did provide that sites be "predominantly residential" either before or after redevelopment. The clear implication was that clearance projects would involve re-housing slum dwellers either on the site or elsewhere and that only public housing could provide shelter for low-income households (Foard and Fefferman 1960, Davies 1966, Gelfand 1975, Weiss 1985, von Hoffman 2000).

Having lost the battle to prevent the passage of the Housing Act of 1949, the housing industry organizations, especially NAREB and NAHB, launched a ground war against public housing. The trade groups distributed colorfully written and illustrated pamphlets aimed at fanning resentments of programs targeted for low-income people. In the anti-Communist fervor of the time, the enemies of public housing were not above attacking the program as socialist. Armed with anti-housing literature prepared and distributed by the trade associations in Washington, affiliates of the realtors and home builders organized local political campaigns to shut down their public housing authorities, stop projects, and cut off appropriations (NAHB 1949, Realtors' Washington Committee 1949, Journal of Housing 1950a, 1950d, Davies 1966, Freedman 1969). Yet the leaders of the real-estate and building industry knew that to eliminate slum clearance and public housing once and for all, they would need a completely different approach to combat the deterioration of urban neighborhoods.

THE BALTIMORE PLAN

As luck would have it, there emerged during the late 1940s and early 1950s an alternative approach to salvaging slums and preventing neighborhoods from becoming slums. In a score of cities across the United States, local institutions and citizens' groups prodded their governmental officials to stop urban decay by enforcing building codes and rehabilitating residential structures. In Chicago, block clubs and local planning commissions used "conservation" to save neighborhoods from becoming slums. The Philadelphia Redevelopment Authority sponsored Operation Fix-Up in 1949 and incorporated rehabilitation in its redevelopment schemes, an approach which observers likened to the cure of penicillin as opposed to the surgery of clearance. At least 12 cities – including Charlotte, Milwaukee, and St Louis – implemented codes to raise the

health and safety standards of existing buildings, and Boston, Detroit, and Miami were among many urban centers that executed rehabilitation programs to supplement or supplant slum clearance projects. Many of these efforts attempted – usually in vain – to prevent, reverse, or slow down changes in the racial and/or class composition of the population, but, as mentioned above, the public discourse generally ignored this aspect of neighborhood conservation (Journal of Housing 1950b, 1950c, Architectural Forum 1952, Metropolitan Housing and Planning Council 1953, Siegel and Brooks 1953, Bauman 1987, Teaford 1990).

But by far the best known of the citizen neighborhood campaigns occurred in Baltimore, Maryland. The "Baltimore Plan," as it was known, originated in the shocking report of a social worker, Frances Morton, on the atrocious living conditions in the Monument City's poor neighborhoods. A series of vivid newspaper articles published in 1936 spurred the city government to enact tougher sanitation laws and hire an aggressive chief inspector, G. Yates Cook, to enforce them (Millspaugh and Breckenfield 1960).

These actions failed to satisfy Baltimorean reformers, who, led by Morton, in 1941 organized the Citizens' Housing and Planning Association of Baltimore to deal with the city's slums. Criticizing the government for its lax execution of the city's zoning ordinance, the citizens' association urged the creation of an independent city department – free from political influence – to set and enforce minimum housing standards, and, where necessary, demolish delinquent buildings. The reformers further called for a Rehabilitation Commission that would acquire and rebuild substandard structures and then sell or lease the improved buildings (Citizens' Housing and Planning Association of Baltimore 1941). Baltimore officials insisted that the existing agencies could handle the job of cleaning up the slums, and, after some notable accomplishments, the citizens and officials fell to fighting each other over the best way to make "the fix-up idea" work (Seligman 1957, p. 3).

BUSINESSMEN TACKLE THE SLUMS

Despite the conflicts in Baltimore and the reformers' support of public housing and rent control, the housing industry turned the Baltimore Plan into a national symbol of code enforcement and rehabilitation as a way to transform blighted areas into gleaming safe communities. Two leaders in the Baltimore citizens' effort, Guy Hollyday and James Rouse, were prominent members of the Mortgage Bankers Association of America, and Rouse in particular was adept at garnering national attention for the Baltimore Plan. The National Home Builders Association produced a film that cost US$20,000 on the Baltimore Plan as well as magazine articles that pushed enforcement of building codes (NAHB 1948, Report from ACTION 1956, Bloom 2004). NAREB, which had been experimenting with rehabilitation since the 1930s, also jumped on the Baltimore Plan bandwagon (Citizens' Housing and Planning Association of Baltimore 1941, NAREB, Committee on Rehabilitation 1952).

Fortunately for the housing industry, the presidential election of 1952 gave it an opportunity to play a role in shaping policy. As a candidate, Dwight D. Eisenhower had consulted on housing policy with three men affiliated with the Mortgage Bankers of America – its spokesman, James Rouse; its counsel, Samuel Neel; and its consultant, Miles Colean (Colean 1979, Biles 1999). As president, Eisenhower created a business-centered housing agency by filling the top posts at HHFA with industry representatives (Keith 1973).

Turning from their efforts to defeat public housing, NAREB and NAHB both launched coordinated national campaigns to spread the gospel of code enforcement and rehabilitation. In 1952 the successful leader of an anti-public housing campaign in Los Angeles, developer Fritz B. Burns rolled out "Build America Better," a "three-fold attack on urban blight and slums led by the nation's realtors." It consisted of enforcing health, building, and sanitary standards; attracting new construction on cleared or vacant sites through accelerated property tax depreciation; and improving infrastructure such as schools, parks, and streets. The plan kept the federal government out of the picture and said nothing about creating new housing (NAREB 1953, Davies 1958, Keane 2001). From 1952 to 1954, Burns made hundreds of appearances at local chambers of commerce, realtor organizations, and civic groups, while NAREB distributed such publications as A Primer on Rehabilitation

under Local Law Enforcement and Blueprint for Neighborhood Conservation (NAREB, Committee on Rehabilitation 1952, Build America Better Council 1954).

The home builders declared their own campaign, A New Face for America, which closely paralleled that of the realtors. In 1953, the NAHB set up a Department of Housing Rehabilitation and hired G. Yates Cook, a former Baltimore inspector, to direct it. In a hard-hitting pamphlet, A New Face for America – A Program of Action Planned to Stop Slums and Rebuild Our Cities, Cook (1953) laid out a prescription for a slum rehabilitation program that almost matched that of the realtors, except that it included an independent "Blight Commission" like the one the Baltimore reformers had advocated. Not content to exhort, NAHB in late 1953 sponsored a pilot program in New Orleans with the mayor and local businessmen to rehabilitate a block of slums. Cook also organized a code enforcement-and-rehab workshop for city officials and home builders and an NAHB Housing Rehabilitation Committee to convince home builders to emulate the New Orleans slum rehab in their own cities (Brockbank 1953, Cook 1953, Spiegel 1953, Washington Letter of the NAHB 1953, Millspaugh and Breckenfield 1960).

As committed as they were to the code enforcement and rehab plan to save America's cities, the home builders went further. To "halt the march of blight and provide decent, low-cost homes for the great bulk of our people," NAHB leaders called for an effective secondary mortgage market to be organized by Fannie Mae and a host of new mortgage insurance devices to be issued by their favorite agency, the Federal Housing Administration (FHA). The home builders hoped that new legislative tools for the FHA would open the credit gates and allow them to build one million homes a year. Most of these would be in the suburbs, of course, where discrimination in private lending practices and government underwriting would discourage minorities from buying houses. Among the NAHB ideas were the "trade-in house" (in which builders purchase and remodel old houses and resell or rent them); long-term modernization loans on reasonable terms for slum rehab sites, and to further urban redevelopment, easier terms for the FHA program (Section 207) to insure mortgage loans for constructing rental housing.

RENEWAL: A THEORY

Although many invoked the enforcement and fix-up approach as a policy for solving America's urban problems, it was the industry consultant Miles Colean who melded the disparate ideas about blight, code enforcement, and rehabilitation into a coherent theory of urban change. In his 1953 book, *Renewing Our Cities*, Colean made the case for rehabilitation. Colean thought of the problems such as "flight from the central city," "suburban spread," downtown congestion, slums, and blight as an interrelated set of economic problems. Writing from a conservative economist's perspective, Colean worried about raising real-estate values in order to increase urban prosperity (Colean 1953, Gelfand 1975).

For Colean, slums were a part, but only a part, of the illness facing American cities. Rather than simply replacing slums with new housing on a particular site, Colean urged "comprehensive renewal" that would revitalize the city as a whole. In regard to housing, he echoed the realtors call for conservation and rehabilitation over "root-and-branch" clearance. And like the realtors, Colean said little about developing new housing, implying that rehabilitation would leave enough homes to supply the urban population. Yet Colean insisted that cities would have to adopt large-scale planning and improve their schools, traffic, and public works if they were going to revive their economies and beat back blight. In essence, he kicked the neighborhood problems of slums and blight upstairs to metropolitan planners and government administrators, which rendered any real action highly unlikely. Ultimately, comprehensive urban planning would remain out of reach so that Colean's main contributions to national policy were to popularize code enforcement and rehab as an anti-slum strategy and to coin the phrase "urban renewal" to describe it.

THE HOUSING INDUSTRY MAKES POLICY

With plenty of ideas about what to do about housing in America, the housing business interests met to fashion a national policy for the incoming Eisenhower administration. Time, Inc.'s new trade publication, *House and Home*, provided the setting for representatives of the housing industry groups to meet at three conferences – round-table discussions – held between late 1952 and late 1953, from which the editors then wrote up a set of recommendations. The publisher and editors of *House and Home* convened the first two round tables, which were dedicated to housing the low-income family and housing polices for the new Eisenhower administration respectively. The home builders, realtors, and mortgage bankers' trade associations liked the round tables so much, they requested that *House and Home* organize another conference, held in the fall of 1953, to lay out a detailed description and plan for counteracting blight and slums (House and Home 1952, 1953a, 1953b).

The round-table talks served as a precursor to the President's Advisory Committee on Government Housing Policies and Programs, which crafted the main provisions of the Housing Act of 1954. The man credited with suggesting the idea of a housing commission to Eisenhower, Aksel Nielsen, attended the round table held in Rye, New York, in December 1952 as a representative of the Mortgage Bankers Association. He, fellow round-table participant Miles Colean, and HHFA chief Albert Cole selected the members of the advisory committee (Keith 1973, Hunt 2005a). Almost half of committee members they chose had been round-table conferees. More importantly, influential industry figures – such as Richard Hughes and Rodney Lockwood of NAHB and Jim Rouse of the Mortgage Bankers Association – played leading roles in both the round-table conferences and on the Eisenhower committee. Hughes, a vociferous exponent of private enterprise housing programs, and Rouse, a tireless advocate for anti-slum measures, participated in all three round-table conferences. Lockwood and Rouse served as chairmen of the presidential commission's subcommittees where they successfully pressed their points of view on their fellow members House and Home 1952, 1953a, 1953b).

The *House and Home* round-table talks laid out goals and programs, many of which NAHB and other trade associations had proposed earlier and which the President's Advisory Committee would adopt or refine in its report. The round-table participants drew up several targets that were elaborated later in the advisory committee. One was producing a high volume of new homes – at least one million a year – chiefly by guaranteeing the flow of capital. The conferees recommended loosening credit instruments, especially on FHA-insured mortgages, and improving the secondary mortgage market administration by the Federal National Mortgage Association (Fannie Mae).

The industry representatives emphasized the goal of a national housing policy to end slums and provide homes for low-income families. This should be met, they stressed, primarily through code enforcement, rehabilitation, and privately developed low-income housing (House and Home 1953a). The conferees did carry forward elements of the original urban development program by recommending clearance of the worst slums to carry out comprehensive neighborhood and city-wide plans and, remarkably, by allowing as a last resort, municipalities to build some sort of temporary and locally financed public housing (House and Home 1953a).

The industry men did not hold unanimous views on every matter. In the round-table discussions, the issues of federal support for industry and the purpose of federal programs divided the participants. In one camp were hard-core economic conservatives – anti-New Dealers and generally bankers – who dreaded the intervention of the federal government into business activity and even more so if that intervention was aimed at social reform. The conservative bankers called for removing FHA and the Home Loan Bank from the umbrella agency, HHFA, where they had been placed five years earlier, so they would not feel "pressures based on political and welfare state considerations rather than sound economics" (House and Home 1953a, p. 121). On the other side were reformers, such as mortgage bankers Rouse and Ferd Kramer of Chicago and home builders Dick Hughes and Emanuel Spiegel, who believed that government should intervene to overcome both business obstacles and social problems. The activist businessmen called for expanding FHA programs to include mortgage insurance for slum areas and low-income families and proposed that the FHA should assess credit risk in a deteriorated neighborhood "based, not on its present state of decay, but on its condition after the rehabilitation" (House and Home 1953b, p. 107). Both parties agreed that in contrast with programs such as public housing, direct government subsidy should be avoided at all costs.

EISENHOWER'S ADVISORY COMMITTEE GOES TO WORK

The President's Advisory Committee on Government Housing Policies and Programs met in the late fall of 1953 (President's Advisory Committee on Government Housing Policies and Programs 1953). Following the line adopted by the participants in the *House and Home* round tables, the advisory committee urged that the government take action in five major areas: attacking and preventing slums; maintaining existing homes; increasing the volume of new residential construction; assisting low-income families to get homes; and reorganizing the federal housing agency to become more efficient.

Of all its recommendations, the committee declared, those for urban redevelopment were the most important. Borrowing the phrase "urban renewal" and other ideas from Miles Colean's book, Rouse and the subcommittee he chaired – significantly titled the Subcommittee on Urban Redevelopment, Rehabilitation, and Conservation – drew up a new approach to eliminating slums and halting the spread of blight (Subcommittee on Urban Redevelopment, Rehabilitation, and Conservation 1953, Bloom 2004, pp. 72–73). Under the scheme, a new federal Urban Renewal Administration would provide loans, grants, and technical assistance to local communities for planning and renewal projects. The committee insisted that grants for renewal projects go only to cities with a code enforcement program and urged rehabilitation rather than demolition wherever possible. When land was cleared, however, such sites could be used for their logical best use, which was not necessarily housing. Emphasizing planning, the subcommittee recommended that jurisdictions be required to justify their projects by submitting "a workable program" based on analysis of the housing stock and the demand for housing (Subcommittee on Urban Redevelopment, Rehabilitation, and Conservation 1953).

No doubt reflecting Rouse's familiarity with citizens' groups and publicity, the committee also urged the formation of a private national organization to educate and mobilize public opinion for urban renewal based on conservation, enforcement, and rehabilitation. Finally, the urban redevelopment subcommittee also asked for a program for long-term FHA financing in urban renewal areas on terms at least as favorable as those available elsewhere in the city. Reflecting the coordination of thinking on the advisory committee, two other subcommittees – for FHA-VA and low-income families – offered ideas that answered this request for private housing programs.

The FHA-VA subcommittee produced a battery of recommendations that particularly dovetailed with the proposed urban renewal program. Under the chairmanship of home builder Rodney Lockwood, the subcommittee essentially restated several earlier NAHB proposals to promote rehabilitation and reuse of urban housing. These included FHA insurance for repairs of existing single-family homes, loosening the requirements for insurance of existing multifamily dwellings, and bettering the terms on such old NAHB favorites as open-end mortgages (to allow for home repairs and improvements without processing and fees of a new loan), the "trade-in house" program, and FHA insurance for rental housing (such as the Section 207 program) (Subcommittee on FHA and VA Programs and Operations 1953).

In the area of urban housing, Lockwood unveiled proposals for FHA-insurance of urban renewal and low-income housing, which the NAHB had been calling for since the round-table discussions. The subcommittee recommended a new Section 220 of the National Housing Act (of 1934) to allow FHA insurance of loans on liberal terms for the rehabilitation of existing homes and construction of new dwellings in urban renewal sites. To expand private development into the low-income market served by the public housing program, the subcommittee also put forward Section 221, which would offer FHA insurance for 40-year, 100% loans to build homes for sale or rent to families displaced by urban redevelopment (or rehabilitation) or whose income forced them to live in substandard homes (President's Advisory Committee on Government Housing Policies and Programs 1953, Hunt 2005a).

The banker-dominated subcommittee on housing credit facilities also echoed the round-table conferences by calling for an effective body to run the secondary mortgage market and purchase and participate in loans so as to "level peaks and valleys in remote areas of the mortgage market." And as they had in the round-table conferences, the bankers took a narrow approach that shunned any social-welfare functions for the financial system. They called for a new entity – not Fannie Mae – to be entirely privately financed. The subcommittee's conservative recommendations sparked a forceful minority dissent from Richard Hughes, the incoming president of the NAHB. Calling for a "progressive and forward-looking mortgage market," Hughes argued that only a government-financed agency – to wit, Fannie Mae – could pay for the expanding of FHA insurance to cover rehabilitation of the slums and housing for low-income families. Congress, it later turned out, would decide in favor of the NAHB official (Subcommittee on Housing Credit Facilities 1953, pp. 356–366, 360).

The advisory committee offered private industry an ideal opportunity to eliminate finally the public housing program, but – as Bradford Hunt has recounted – it flinched. In an effort to protect public housing, the low-income housing subcommittee recommended two FHA low-income housing programs and continuing public housing until the day that private enterprise actually served very low-income families (Subcommittee on Housing for Low-income Families 1953). Members of the full committee ignored the subcommittee's report, however, and proposed selling off public housing. Ironically, Lockwood, one of the leading foes of public housing, saved the program. Lockwood proposed substitute language calling for his new Section 220 and 221 programs and keeping public housing for the interim until the new private programs took hold. Lockwood's support for continuing the public housing program, Hunt relates, shocked the committee. But after heated and confused discussion, the advisory committee voted to continue this most liberal of New Deal social programs (Hunt 2005a).

THE HOUSING ACT OF 1954

Eisenhower, in his first term and feeling his way to a middle ground between fiscal responsibility and the New Deal government he inherited, embraced the advisory committee's report. The President gave a special address on housing based on the committee's findings. The administration then proposed legislation based on the recommendations, and after some debate, mainly over public housing, the Congress passed the Housing Act of 1954.

The congressional hearings in March of 1954 over what would become the Housing Act of 1954 reflected new political alignments. Not surprisingly, the industry trade associations, led by NAHB and NAREB, generally backed the urban renewal proposals. On the other side, the liberal lobby groups – led by the public housing, labor, and mayors' organizations – supported the new program, albeit grudgingly. The National Housing Conference, for example, endorsed rehabilitation but warned that urban renewal was no substitute for redevelopment and public housing (House and Home 1954).

The new FHA housing programs associated with urban renewal continued to divide the industry representatives between those who accepted government intervention and those who resisted it. Not surprisingly, the activist trade organizations, NAHB and NAREB, endorsed Section 221, the new FHA venture for housing displaced and low-income families, and asked that the legislation raise the ceiling value on loans to cover those – such as to low-income borrowers – that carried greater risk. The various banking associations and the US Chamber of Commerce opposed the new measure as unsound.

In contrast to the mossback banking associations, the pro-public housing groups agreed with NAHB and NAREB and endorsed the new low-cost housing program and concurred that the maximum limit on its loans was too low. The new approach to urban redevelopment housing had created an area of agreement – if not exactly a close coalition – between the left and right.

The political stances at the congressional hearings startled observers. "Strange as it seemed," the trade journal *House and Home* reported, "NAHB took a position closer to that of the CIO and AFL than to any other segment of the private industry (except realtors)." Perhaps more astounding was that "builders, labor, and realtors were in general alignment with public housing in advocating more and more government aid to housing." This might have overstated the matter – a few of the trade groups, notably NAHB and the Mortgage Bankers Association, simply did not comment on the program they had long opposed. Nonetheless it looked at the time like a cease-fire in the public housing wars (House and Home 1954).

Despite the novelty of the urban renewal and FHA programs, public housing as before provoked the greatest struggles in the legislature. Eisenhower had asked for authorization of a relatively modest 35,000 public-housing dwelling-units annually for four years. Liberal organizations asked Congress to raise the number of authorized units to something on the order of 200,000, but arch-conservative Jesse Wolcott led the House of Representatives to remove all public housing from the bill. Nonetheless, the Senate voted to restore the original 35,000 figure, and the conference committee upheld that number.

Other than that, the Congress pretty much transferred the advisory committee's proposals to the Housing Act of 1954. It replaced urban redevelopment with urban renewal, specifying that voluntary repair and rehabilitation could be adopted instead of or along with clearance and rebuilding schemes. To ensure that municipalities adopted the new approach, the law required they submit a "workable program" to receive urban renewal loans or grants. To allow the flexible planning that Colean had called for and weaken the link to public housing, the act reduced the "predominantly residential" provision of the 1949 urban redevelopment program by allowing ten percent of the federal grants to support non-residential projects and enlarging allowable project sites (Gelfand 1975). To promote private development of housing on urban renewal sites and for displaced and low-income families, it contained the new Sections 220 and 221 of the National Housing Act as special mortgage insurance programs, which the NAHB leaders had devised. Also following the home builders' wishes, the 1954 Act liberalized mortgage terms on FHA-loans and allowed FHA to insure open-end mortgages for home repairs. It reorganized Fannie Mae to carry out a secondary-mortgage market operation, and – as NAHB's Hughes had wished – included a provision for "special assistance function" by which it could, if needed, purchase Sections 220 and 221 mortgages. Only the arch-conservative banking lobbyists objected to the social provisions that Colean and they called "barnacles" on the hulls of the FHA and FNMA (Cole 1979, p. 294). For them the status quo policies, in which the FHA served the suburbs and fostered white homeownership sufficed.

THE POLICY FALTERS

The housing industry's first sustained venture into national policy making produced mixed results at best. Armed with the new federal policy they had done so much to create, the activist trade associations continued to pursue their enforcement and rehabilitation campaigns. To encourage its members to develop urban renewal housing projects, NAHB sponsored dozens of local informational meetings and distributed thousands of information kits. NAHB officers urged their members to attend workshops on rehabilitation, develop low-income housing – if for no other reason than to forestall public housing – and even pushed for minority housing. NAREB continued to pursue its Build America Better program, offering consultation services to cities that wished to take up a rehabilitation program. In 1955, James Rouse helped found the American Council to Improve Our Neighborhoods (ACTION), the national citizens' organization that he had proposed in Eisenhower's advisory committee to sponsor research and spread news about neighborhood conservation efforts.

Nonetheless, the implementation of the new urban renewal policy quickly ran into trouble. Despite the NAHB leaders' enthusiasm for urban renewal and the new FHA housing programs, interest among the home builders never materialized. Home builders complained that the construction cost limits and loan terms for Section 221 projects encumbered their efforts, even after Congress liberalized the loan terms. Home builders who tried the Section 220 and 221 programs found it difficult to obtain land from government agencies and to carry out their projects. And, like public housing authorities, the NAHB developers encountered the resistance of middle-class white neighbors who feared that the projects would bring lower-class African Americans. Despite the easing of loan requirements, by 1960 builders had produced just 15,550 dwellings under Section 221 and 1,500 houses under Section 220 (NAHB, Public Housing Committee 1957, NAHB, Urban Renewal Committee 1958, 1959, Fairbanks 1989, pp. 173–174, Mitchell 1994, Hunt 2005a).

A fundamental problem was that the operations and experiences of most home builders were not suited to urban renewal projects, which posed difficulties in land acquisition, took a long time (thereby driving up interim costs), and required both technical knowledge and political skills. The developers who took on urban redevelopment projects were usually large-scale national operators who specialized in complex development projects. Men such as William Zeckendorf and James Scheuer had access to large amounts of capital and could negotiate confidently with pro-growth mayors and their redevelopment authorities. In contrast, most home builders were small-time businessmen who built a small number of houses each year and worked in local areas with which they were familiar. With the exception of a few socially committed home builders such as Leon Weiner of Wilmington, Delaware, home builders found it easier and more profitable to build on vacant lands in the suburbs, where they often received financing from local FHA officials.

Nor were home builders much interested in the rehabilitation program. The business of repair and remodeling old houses and apartment buildings was by its nature idiosyncratic and therefore did not lend itself to efficient replication. Only experienced contractors were willing to tackle this kind of time-consuming and unpredictable work. Stumbling at the gate, NAHB disbanded its Department of Housing Rehabilitation only two years after the passage of the 1954 Housing Act. Since, as one close observer argued, "strict code enforcement will never be possible until a great deal more housing is available to low-and middle-income tenants," the sluggishness of the new programs in combination with anemic appropriations and ugly site battles for public housing did not bode well for economically declining urban neighborhoods (Seligman 1957, p. 129).

As for code enforcement, both local and federal governments honored it more in the breach than in the observance. As had been the case in Baltimore and other cities, local inspection departments proved reluctant to insist that landlords comply with the housing codes. The federal government undermined code enforcement by failing to insist that local governments implement their workable programs. HHFA officials could not bring themselves to deny funds to cities applying for urban renewal funds, and as a result, local governments felt little inducement to enforce housing codes. Starting in 1955, the federal housing agency repeatedly certified workable plans for San Francisco, Cincinnati, and Philadelphia only to discover in 1968 that the vast majority of residences in those cities' code enforcement areas violated local housing codes (National Commission on Urban Problems 1968, Bloom 2004).

By the end of the 1950s, the grassroots movement for neighborhood conservation seemed to falter. No city created the kind of centralized authority over building codes and rehabilitation efforts that the Baltimore leaders concluded was necessary for success. A survey of neighborhood enforcement-and-rehab campaigns found only one that had ever succeeded in truly mobilizing local residents and landlords. Meanwhile, the expansion of low-income minority groups into previously all-white middle-class areas gave a sense that the problem of blight and slums was worsening (Millspaugh and Breckenfield 1960, Horwitt 1992, Santow 2006).

The industry's attempt to stamp out the public housing component of urban redevelopment did not fully succeed either, despite the weak state of the program. Politically, public housing was caught in what one of its creators called "a dreary deadlock" in which it struggled on "not dead but never more than half alive" (Bauer 1957). During the 1950s, the Congress continued to fund the public housing program but at levels far below what it would take to re-house those dislocated by government clearance programs. Furthermore, a combination of federal administrative policies, local bureaucratic inertia, and neighborhood resistance to situating public housing projects in white neighborhoods slowed down the development of even those units that had been authorized. Still, the program survived in urban redevelopment plans – in part because politicians in cities such as Chicago considered it an essential component of racial containment and in part because planners sometimes felt that inner-city ghettos could not attract private investment (Kaplan 1963, Hirsch 1983, Bauman 1987). Hence, some cities continued to demolish old residences and build public housing, most noticeably in the form of tall modernist-style elevator buildings. Funding for public housing actually increased under Democratic administrations during the 1960s, by which time the housing industry no longer considered public housing a threat and stopped trying to kill the program.

A GREAT CONFUSION

Fundamentally, the code enforcement and rehabilitation approach to the slums supplemented but never replaced the earlier notion of urban redevelopment. In fact, the urban renewal concept never really broke from the idea of slum clearance. Private industry anti-slum strategists had always recommended demolishing and replacing those properties that were beyond saving. In 1955, James Rouse himself, along with federal housing official Nathaniel Keith, proposed an urban renewal plan for Washington, D.C., that called for not only "vigorous enforcement of strong housing and building codes and thorough large-scale rehabilitation," but also "spot surgery," and "complete clearance of existing structures" (Bloom 2004, p. 79).

More importantly, pro-development city officials and civic leaders continued to support slum clearance – with or without public housing – during the late 1950s and 1960s. From the beginning, the cities best known for their use of enforcement and rehabilitation – Baltimore, Philadelphia, and Chicago – combined both rehabilitation and clearance for new development often in the same areas (Architectural Forum 1952, 1956). Twelve years after the passage of the 1954 housing law, a government survey found that on average predominantly residential urban renewal projects cleared about a fifth of the projects' land areas (Keyes 1969, p. 5). The watering down of the predominantly residential requirement gave the urban powers-that-be more opportunities for redevelopment schemes. As a result, locales that employed code enforcement and rehabilitation also demolished properties in industrial areas and inner-city ghettos to build highways, civic centers, and commercial developments as well as housing. Despite the hope that the urban renewal approach would preserve existing housing, in the following years the wrecking ball would destroy hundreds of thousands of homes and force their occupants to look for new places to live.

In this context, the public generally never understood "urban renewal" as Colean and real-estate industry leaders had originally envisioned it: a comprehensive approach that stressed code enforcement and rehab first and foremost. Since many of the best-known projects involved demolition of buildings and displacement of their residents, urban renewal became synonymous with a clearance project of any sort. Although in origin and law, urban redevelopment and urban renewal were quite distinct, they became "hopelessly blurred in usage" (Keyes 1969, p. 4). In common parlance, "urban renewal" simply replaced "urban redevelopment."

By whatever name or definition, the policy grew in disfavor. Noting the disproportionate numbers of minority groups who were displaced by redevelopment projects, critics cried out that urban renewal really meant Negro removal. In the early 1960s, frustration with the disruption of city dwellers, destruction of private property, and the seemingly interminable length of time it took to complete renewal projects provoked a political revolt against "urban renewal." Intellectuals of all political stripes soon joined the attack (Jacobs 1961, Worthy 1976, Teaford 1990). By 1974 the urban renewal program had become so unpopular that Congress terminated it and instead instituted wide-ranging block grants that left decisions of whether and how to pursue urban improvements to the discretion of local governments.

ONWARDS WITH ENFORCEMENT AND REHABILITATION

Even as urban renewal lost popularity, code enforcement and building rehabilitation lived on as ways to deal with physical problems in urban housing. Early on the code enforcement and rehabilitation won the support of a key liberal housing group, the National Association of Housing and Redevelopment Officials (NAHRO). In cities across the country, state and city governments established housing courts to deal with landlord-tenant disputes, rent control procedures, and, of course, housing and sanitary code violations. No longer an important weapon in the war against blight, code enforcement devolved to disgruntled tenants who used it as means of redress (Friedman 1968).

In the 1960s, policy makers sought to rescue the increasingly unpopular urban renewal program by increasing the federal funds available for rehabilitating substandard dwellings. In 1964, the federal government bolstered the approach by recognizing a new kind of urban renewal carried out mainly or entirely by code enforcement and extended urban renewal funds to code enforcement activities. The major housing acts of the Lyndon Johnson administration – passed in 1964, 1965, and 1968 – provided financing in various forms for rehabilitation of substandard buildings to assist

them in complying with housing codes. Having entered the urban policy arena with the 1954 Act, NAHB enthusiastically supported Johnson's subsidized low-income housing programs and all but dropped its public opposition to public housing.

Building rehabilitation, with or without code enforcement, eventually found a foothold in urban areas. Long after the housing industry first championed rehabilitation as the solution to slums, nonprofit and low-profit organizations took up the cause of fixing up homes for low-income residents. Soon a rehab element became common in residential renewal proposals (Keyes 1969). In 1978 the Congress established the Neighborhood Reinvestment Corporation (now called NeighborWorks America) to administer a revolving high-risk loan fund to local affiliates to distribute loans to home owners in deteriorated areas to improve their houses. In the 1980s local community development organizations in numerous cities worked to restore inner-city neighborhoods by renovation and remodeling low-income housing. Among the financiers of such projects were two national nonprofit organizations: the Enterprise Foundation, started by James Rouse who at the end of a long career in real-estate development returned to urban revitalization; and the Local Initiative Support Corporation, started by the Ford Foundation. Ironically, the rehab approach to urban renewal, which conservative industry groups originally promoted, now became a centerpiece of a new liberal populist policy for reviving the cities (Whittlesey 1969, von Hoffman 2003).

But during the 1950s and 1960s, federal housing laws, fix-it and code enforcement campaigns, and inducements to home builders were the key weapons in the fight to halt the spread of blight and slums. Such physical improvements, however, could do little to counteract such profound economic and social trends as declining industrial employment, racial discrimination, the shortage of mortgage and business credit in low-income neighborhoods, the ongoing departure of middle-class residents to the suburbs, and the consequent rise in urban poverty (Wilson 1987). Regardless, by the late 1960s it was clear that code enforcement combined with private rehabilitation and development of housing had failed to stop the decline of urban neighborhoods (Gribetz and Grad 1966, Friedman 1968,

National Commission on Urban Problems 1968, President's Committee on Urban Housing 1969). By then the public mind thought of the private industry's great hope for saving the cities simply as slum clearance, which it labeled and denounced as urban renewal.

REFERENCES

Architectural Forum, 1952. The Philadelphia cure: clearing slums with penicillin, not surgery. *Architectural Forum*, 96, 112–119.

Architectural Forum, 1956. Philadelphia's redevelopment. *Architectural Forum*, 105, 128–135.

Bauer, C., 1957. The dreary deadlock of public housing. *Architectural Forum*, 106, 140–142.

Bauman, J.F., 1987. *Public housing, race, and renewal: urban planning in Philadelphia, 1920–1974*. Philadelphia, PA: Temple University Press.

Beauregard, R.A., 1993. *Voices of decline: the postwar fate of US cities*. Cambridge, MA: Blackwell.

Bettman, A., 1943. Requirements of a sound urban redevelopment statute. *American City*, 58, 49–50.

Bettman, A., 1945/1946. Statement to the Honorable Chairman and Members, Sub-Committee on Housing and Urban Redevelopment, Committee on Postwar Planning, U.S. Senate. Postwar economic policy and planning [1945]. Repr. In: A.C. Comey, ed. Alfred Bettman, *City and regional planning papers*. Cambridge, MA: Harvard University Press, 99–107.

Biles, R., 1996. Public housing in the Eisenhower Administration. Paper presented at the Annual Meeting of the Social Science History Association, New Orleans, LA, USA, 16 October.

Biles, R., 1999. Public housing policy in the Eisenhower Administration. *Mid-America*, 81, 5–26.

Biles, R., 2000. Public housing and the postwar urban renaissance, 1949–1973. In: J.F. Bauman, R. Biles and K.M. Szylvian, eds. *From tenements to the Taylor homes: in search of an urban housing policy in twentieth-century America*. University Park, PA: Pennsylvania State University Press, 143–162.

Bloom, N.D., 2004. *Merchant of illusion: James Rouse, America's salesman of the businessman's utopia*. Columbus, OH: Ohio State University Press.

Brockbank, A.E., 1953. Cities must fight blight or face economic bankruptcy. *NAHB Correlator*, 7 (10), 4–6.

Build America Better Council, 1954. *Blueprint for action: to build America better, a check list for real estate boards*. Washington, D.C.: National Association of Real Estate Boards.

Citizens' Housing and Planning Association of Baltimore, 1941. *Blighted areas and the defense program*. Baltimore, MD: Maryland State Planning Commission.

Cole, A.M., 1979. Federal housing program. In: G.S. Fish, ed. *The story of housing*. New York, NY: Macmillan, 278–331.

Colean, M.L., 1953. *Renewing our cities*. New York, NY: Twentieth Century Fund.

Colean, M.L., 1979. A national policy on federal intervention in mortgage finance and community development. In: G.S. Fish, ed. *The story of housing*. New York, NY: Macmillan, 268–276.

Cook, G.Y., 1953. *A new face for America: a program of action planned to stop slums and rebuild our cities*. Washington, D.C.: National Association of Home Builders (NAHB).

Culver, D.M., 1972. Tenement house reform in Boston, 1846–1898. PhD dissertation, Boston University, Boston, MA.

Davies, J.P., 1958. *Real estate in American history*. Washington, D.C.: Public Affairs Press.

Davies, R.O., 1966. *Housing reform during the Truman administration*. Columbia, MO: University of Missouri Press.

Fairbanks, R., 1989. *Making better citizens: housing reform and the community development strategy in Cincinnati, 1890–1960*. Urbana and Chicago, IL: University of Illinois Press.

Foard, A.A. and Fefferman, H., 1960. Federal urban renewal legislation. *Law and Contemporary Problems*, 25, 635–684.

Fogelson, R.M., 2001. *Downtown: its rise and fall, 1880–1950*. New Haven, CT: Yale University Press.

Freedman, L., 1969. *Public housing; the politics of poverty*. New York, NY: Holt, Rinehart & Winston.

Freund, D.M.P., 2007. *Colored property: state policy and white racial politics in suburban America*. Chicago, IL: University of Chicago Press.

Friedman, L.M., 1968. *Government and slum housing, a century of frustration*. Chicago, IL: Rand McNally.

Gelfand, M.I., 1975. *A nation of cities: the federal government and urban America, 1933–1965*. New York, NY: Oxford University Press.

Gribetz, J. and Grad, F.P., 1966. Housing code enforcement sanctions and remedies. *Columbia Law Review*, 66, 1254–1290.

Hirsch, A.R., 1983. *Making the second ghetto, race and housing in Chicago, 1940–1960*. Cambridge: Cambridge University Press.

Horwitt, S., 1992. *Let them call me rebel: Saul Alinsky, his life and legacy*. 2nd ed. New York, NY: Vintage.

House and Home, 1952. Round table report: The low-income family and the too cheap house. *House and Home*, 2, 104–113, 142–146.

House and Home, 1953a. An Eisenhower program for better homes. *House and Home*, 3, 116–125.

House and Home, 1953b. Housing conservation round table: report and recommendations. Leaders of attack on blight agree on recommendations to every city. *House and Home*, 4, 100–113.

House and Home, 1954. Housing Bill hearings. *House and Home*, 5, 33–37.

Housing a Nation, 1966. *Housing a Nation*. Washington, D.C.: Congressional Quarterly Service.

Hunt, D.B., 2005a. How did public housing survive the 1950s? *Journal of Policy History*, 17, 199–200.

Hunt, D.B., 2005b. Was the 1938 United States Housing Act a pyrrhic victory? *Journal of Planning History*, 4, 195–221.

Isenberg, A., 2004. *Downtown America: a history of the place and the people who made it*. Chicago, IL: University of Chicago Press.

Jackson, A., 1976. *A place called home: a history of low-cost housing in Manhattan*. Cambridge, MA: MIT Press.

Jacobs, J., 1961. *The death and life of great American cities*. New York, NY: Random House.

Journal of Housing, 1950a. Grass-roots opposition to public housing has "canned" flavor. *Journal of Housing*, 7, 158–160.

Journal of Housing, 1950b. Stopping slums before they start. *Journal of Housing*, 7, 166–167.

Journal of Housing, 1950c. Housing standards stories from seven cities. *Journal of Housing*, 7, 168–171.

Journal of Housing, 1950d. "Canned" campaign news is bad and good. *Journal of Housing*, 7, 265–268.

Kaplan, H., 1963. *Urban renewal politics; slum clearance in Newark*. New York, NY: Columbia University Press.

Keane, J.T., 2001. *Fritz B. Burns and the development of Los Angeles: the biography of a community developer and philanthropist*. Los Angeles, CA: Historical Society of Southern California.

Keith, N.S., 1973. *Politics and the housing crisis since 1930*. New York, NY: Universe.

Keyes, Jr., L.C., 1969. *The rehabilitation planning game: a study in the diversity of neighborhood*. Cambridge, MA: MIT Press.

Lubove, R., 1962. *The progressives and the slums: tenement house reform in New York City, 1890– 1917*. Pittsburgh, PA: University of Pittsburgh Press.

McDonnell, T.L., 1957. *The Wagner Housing Act – a case study of the legislative process*. Chicago, IL: Loyola University Press.

Metropolitan Housing and Planning Council, 1953. *Conservation: a report to the Conservation Committee of the Metropolitan Housing and Planning Council by its conservation study staff*. Chicago, IL: Metropolitan Housing and Planning Council.

Millspaugh, M. and Breckenfeld, G., 1960. *The human side of renewal: a study of the attitude changes produced by neighborhood rehabilitation*. New York, NY: Ives Washburn.

Mitchell, P.J., 1994. The Housing Act of 1954: impacts on housing. *Planning History Present*, 8, 1–3.

Mollenkopf, J.H., 1983. *The contested city*. Princeton, NJ: Princeton University Press.

National Association of Home Builders (NAHB), 1948. *Slum rehabilitation: the Baltimore story*. Washington, D.C.: NAHB.

National Association of Home Builders (NAHB), 1949. *You've got a stake in this, mister!*. Washington, D.C.: NAHB.

National Association of Home Builders (NAHB), 1958. *History of the National Association of Home Builders of the United States (through 1943)*. Washington, D.C.: NAHB.

National Association of Home Builders (NAHB), Public Housing Committee, 1957. Statement to Chairman Ralph Finitzo, Board of Directors Meeting, San Francisco, September, 1957, Archive Box 03-036. Washington, D.C.: NAHB.

National Association of Home Builders (NAHB), Urban Renewal Committee, 1958. Report of Urban Renewal Committee, Chicago, Illinois, January 17, 1958, Archive Box 03-001. Washington, D.C.: NAHB.

National Association of Home Builders (NAHB), Urban Renewal Committee, 1959. Report of Urban Renewal Committee, Chicago, Illinois,. January 16, 1959. Archive Box 03-001. Washington, D.C.: NAHB.

National Association of Real Estate Boards (NAREB), Committee on Rehabilitation, 1952. *Recommendations on rehabilitation by the Committee on Rehabilitation.* Washington, D.C.: NAREB.

National Association of Real Estate Boards (NAREB), 1953. America can afford to outlaw slums, through realtor's plan, Burns says. *News service release no. 63.* Washington, D.C.: NAREB.

National Commission on Urban Problems, 1968. *Building the American city: report of the National Commission on Urban Problems to the Congress and to the President of the United States.* Washington, D.C.: US Government Printing Office.

President's Advisory Committee on Government Housing Policies and Programs, 1953. *Recommendations on government housing policies and programs, a report.* Washington, D.C.: US Government Printing Office.

President's Committee on Urban Housing, 1969. *A decent home: the report of the President's Committee on Urban Housing.* Washington, D.C.: Government Printing Office.

Public Housing, 1944. Cortright and Nelson receive firm answers. *Public Housing*, 10 (33), 1–2.

Radford, G., 1996. *Modern housing for America: policy struggles in the new era.* Chicago, IL: University of Chicago Press.

Realtors' Washington Committee, 1949. *The world owes me a living.* Washington, D.C.: National Association of Real Estate Boards.

Report from ACTION, 1956. *Report from ACTION*, no. 10, 24–27.

Rodgers, D.T., 1998. *Atlantic crossings: social politics in a progressive age.* Cambridge, MA: Harvard University Press.

Santow, M., 2006. Chicago's "Great Question": Saul Alinsky, Packingtown, and the dilemmas of race in the post-war city. Paper presented at the Boston Immigration and Urban History Seminar, Boston, MA, USA, 26 October 2006.

Scott, M., 1969. *American city planning.* Berkeley, CA: University of California Press.

Seligman, D., 1957. The enduring slums. In: W.H. Whyte, Jr., ed. *The exploding metropolis.* New York, NY: Time, 111–132.

Siegel, J.M. and Brooks, C.W., 1953. *Slum prevention through conservation and rehabilitation.* Washington, D.C.: Subcommittee on Urban Redevelopment, Rehabilitation, and Conservation, Advisory Committee on Government Housing Policies and Programs.

Spiegel, E.M., 1953. NAHB sparks rehabilitation on national front. *NAHB Correlator*, 7 (10), 2–3.

Subcommittee on FHA and VA Programs and Operations, 1953. Appendix 1: Report of the Subcommittee on FHA and VA Programs and Operations. In: *Recommendations on government housing policies and programs, a report.* Washington, D.C.: President's Advisory Committee on Government Housing Policies and Programs/US Government Printing Office.

Subcommittee on Housing Credit Facilities, 1953. Appendix 4: Report of the Subcommittee on Housing Credit Facilities. In: *Recommendations on government housing policies and programs, a report.* Washington, D.C.: President's Advisory Committee on Government Housing Policies and Programs/US Government Printing Office.

Subcommittee on Housing for Low-income Families, 1953. Appendix 3: Report of the Subcommittee on Housing for Low-income Families. In: *Recommendations on government housing policies and programs, a report*. Washington, D.C.: President's Advisory Committee on Government Housing Policies and Programs/US Government Printing Office.

Subcommittee on Urban Redevelopment, Rehabilitation, and Conservation, 1953. Appendix 2: Report of the Subcommittee on Urban Redevelopment, Rehabilitation, and Conservation. In: *Recommendations on government housing policies and programs, a report*. Washington, D.C.: President's Advisory Committee on Government Housing Policies and Programs/US Government Printing Office.

Sugrue, T.J., 1996. *The origins of the urban crisis: race, industrial decline, and housing in Detroit, 1940–1960*. Princeton, NJ: Princeton University Press.

Szylvian, K.M., 2000. The Federal Housing Program during World War II. In: J.F. Bauman, R. Biles and K.M. Szylvian, eds. *From tenements to the Taylor homes: in search of an urban housing policy in twentieth-century America*. University Park, PA: Pennsylvania State University Press, 121–138.

Teaford, J., 1990. *The rough road to renaissance – urban revitalization in America, 1940–1985*. Baltimore, MD: Johns Hopkins University Press.

Von Hoffman, A., 2000. A study in contradictions: the origins and legacy of the Housing Act of 1949. *Housing Policy Debate*, 10, 299–326.

Von Hoffman, A., 2003. *House by house, block by block: the rebirth of America's urban neighborhoods*. New York, NY: Oxford University Press.

Von Hoffman, A., 2005. The end of the dream: the political struggle of America's public houses. *Journal of Planning History*, 4, 222–253.

Washington Letter of the NAHB, 1953. Slum reconstruction pilot demonstration. *Washington Letter of the NAHB*, no. 475 (October), 3.

Weiss, M.A., 1985. The origins and legacy of urban renewal. In: P.J. Mitchell, ed. *Federal housing policy and programs: past and present*. New Brunswick, NJ: Rutgers University, Center for Urban Policy Research.

Whittlesey, R.B., 1969. *The South End row house and its rehabilitation for low-income residents*. Boston, MA: South End Community Development, Inc., Department of Housing and Urban Development.

Wilson, W.J., 1987. *The truly disadvantaged, the inner city, the underclass, and public policy*. Chicago, IL: University of Chicago Press.

Worthy, W., 1976. *The rape of our neighborhoods: and how communities are resisting take-overs by colleges, hospitals, churches, businesses, and public agencies*. New York, NY: Morrow.

3
"Introduction and summary"

From *A Decent Home* (1968)

The President's Committee on Urban Housing, Chairman Edgar F. Kaiser

At the Committee's first meeting on June 2, 1967, the President summarized our charge in these words:

> This Committee's assignment, in short, is to find a way to harness the productive power of America – which has proved it can master space and create unmatched abundance in the market place – to the most pressing unfulfilled need of our society. That need is to provide the basic necessities of a decent home and healthy surroundings for every American family now imprisoned in the squalor of the slums.

In the past 16 months, we have examined all existing Federal housing subsidy programs and every aspect of housing production which we considered relevant to our work. As mentioned in our Chairman's covering letter to the President, we previously submitted a number of recommendations to the White House and to appropriate Departments in the Executive branch. Those earlier recommendations, together with our later suggestions for shaping the Housing and Urban Development Act of 1968 and the contents of this final report, were aimed at two basic goals:

- Rapidly accelerating and increasing the production and rehabilitation of decent housing for the poor.
- Attracting the fullest private participation in developing, sponsoring and managing Federally subsidized housing.

This group of 18 individuals, representing different viewpoints and perspectives, reached early concurrence as a Committee on these principal points underlying our work:

- The need is urgent for speeding up and expanding the Federal programs for housing the urban poor.
- Private enterprise can best provide the muscle, the talent and the major effort – when there are opportunities to earn reasonable profits and to function at maximum efficiency.
- Federal housing assistance is essential for millions of families unable to afford the market price of standard housing.
- Eradication of urban blight, in itself, will not eliminate city slums.

Blocks of overcrowded houses and dilapidated tenements are only the readily seen manifestations of an amalgam of slum-producing problems. Many of them reach deep into the nation's social, political and economic structures.

Within society generally, there remain problems of discrimination – problems of social injustices which cannot be corrected by the necessary legislative action alone, but which require enforcement of civil rights laws and – equally important – constructive and affirmative actions by society itself.

Within urban slums, there are the knotty sociological relations between rundown housing, human behavior, environmental conditions of total neighborhoods, and the disadvantaged life of the poor. Among slum dwellers are the collected and compounded needs for remedial health care and education, skills training for the unemployable, and the interjection of new hope to raise individual motivation for seeking self betterment.

At governmental levels, there are the problems of worsening financial straits for many of the nation's cities and of competing demands and priorities on local and Federal public expenditures.

Better housing alone will not uplift the poor. The Committee emphasizes that stepped up efforts in urban housing must be supported by concentrated and accelerated public and private actions for equipping and enabling the poor to help themselves enter the mainstream of American life.

Furthermore, the most successful programs for bettering housing conditions and economic opportunities cannot, in themselves, produce better environments. Good neighbors are vital for preserving good neighborhoods. Good neighbors are property protective citizens to the fullest extent of their individual capabilities. Antisocial behavior, whether within or outside the slums, impedes and the effort to rebuild America's cities.

As the President said in his message on "The Crisis of the Cities":

The challenge of changing the face of the city and the men who live there summons us all, President and the Congress, Governors and Mayors. The challenge reaches as well into every corporate board room, university, and union headquarters in America. It extends to church and community groups and to the family itself.

It was not this Committee's assignment to seek solutions to all the interwoven problems of what the President called "the squalor of the slums." In view of our specific charge and the work of other National and Presidential commissions, we believed it appropriate for us to consider such problems only insofar as they bear on the provision of housing and specifically, housing for low- and moderate-income families.

Concentrating on housing problems as such, we found no new, simple, and yet practical approach to the challenges of providing decent dwelling places for all the nation's families. The process that delivers housing to the self-supporting consumer and the economic conditions that separate poor families from the market cost of decent housing are more complex than many of us anticipated when embarking on our assignment. Our numerous recommendations in the areas of Federal housing subsidy programs, finance, land, construction manpower, and research and technology in housing are all aimed at reducing these complexities with respect to attainment of the nation's 10-year housing goal, and at attracting maximum private participation in development of housing for low- and moderate-income families.

In some areas of concentration, we found reliable information and data difficult to obtain or conspicuously lacking. As aids in our deliberations, we sought and received opinions and reactions from knowledgeable public and private participants in the housing field. We also commissioned consultants to restudy or probe afresh all major factors in the housing production and delivery processes for both the non-subsidized and subsidized markets: financing and mortgage credit, land availability, efficiency in American housing construction, patterns and practices in the utilization of the homebuilding work force, manpower requirements in the construction trades, and the comparative effectiveness and gaps in Federal housing assistance programs. Other studies, performed for and made available to this Committee, compiled and forecast demographic profiles of the nation's households, so as to project the size of America's challenge in adequately housing the total population and allocating the necessary public and private resources. All studies undertaken for this Committee are published under separate cover in the volumes of Technical Studies.

Based on these consultants' studies and their own independent analyses of factors pertinent to this Committee's assignment, the professional staff produced a series of working papers which in their own judgment reflected the Committee's general thinking and its scope and purpose. This effort was indispensable to us in grasping the dimension and nature of U.S. housing problems and in formulating our proposed solutions. The staff's supportive work often probed deeper into some aspects of the housing field than is reflected in the Committee's recommendations. The staff papers are resented in this volume as an appendix to the Committee's report.

In the literature on public housing policies, private housing production, and American housing needs, this Committee viewed our staff's contribution in the Appendix of this report as a previously unavailable and badly needed reference source. We commend the staff's published work as a guide to any concerned reader seeking fuller understanding of the workings of Federal housing programs: the processes by which dwellings are made available to American consumers, and the sociological, economic and institutional problems that impede these programs and processes from functioning at peak capabilities.

MAJOR CONCLUSIONS

In this report, the Committee has recommended a 10-year goal of 26 million more new and rehabilitated housing units, including at least six million for lower-income families. Attainment of this goal should eliminate the blight of substandard housing from the face of the nation's cities and should provide every American family with an affordable, decent home.

We concluded that new and foreseeable technological breakthroughs in housing production will not by themselves bring decent shelter within economic reach of the millions of house-poor families in the predictable future. To bridge the gap between the marketplace costs for standard housing and the price that lower-income families can afford to pay, appropriations of Federal subsidies are essential and must be substantially increased.

The Housing and Urban Development Act of 1968 sets a goal of 26 million dwellings including six million subsidized units to be built or rehabilitated in the next decade. The Department of Housing and Urban Development has formulated a timetable for attaining the goal of six million subsidized units, which the Committee believes is feasible.

The Committee found that attempts to estimate the total national costs for six million subsidized dwellings and the necessary infrastructures were frustrated by an overwhelming mixture of unpredictable variables. Such estimates were made meaningless by inability to forecast the companion needs for schools, streets, community facilities, public works projects, and governmental and voluntary social services, together with unpredictable interest rates, costs for land and construction, and levels of productivity.

The Committee was able, however, to examine HUD's projections of the Federal subsidy costs for building six million more subsidized dwellings in 10 years, and to compare these projections with our own. Additionally, we assessed the economy's capacity to allocate the necessary resources and were convinced that this goal is attainable in a balanced economy without causing untoward strains. Furthermore, we strongly believe that the goal is necessary and justified for these reasons:

- Decent housing is essential in helping lower-income families help themselves achieve self fulfillment in a free and democratic society.
- Public expenditures for decent housing for the nation's poor, like public expenditures for education and job training, are not so much expenditures as they are essential investments in the future of American society.

The housing needs of the poor, however, cannot be separated from the housing needs for our growing population as a whole. Along with the housing problems of millions of lower-income families, the nation faces a shortage of total housing in the decade ahead. Solutions to the two problems are interdependent and inseparable, both economically and politically.

We believe the American economy can attain the total goal of 26 million additional housing units by 1978. The nation possesses the total resources for its attainment, depending on a determined national commitment to maintain the proper mix of many economic factors. Among the most important factors, in addition to Congressional appropriations of the necessary long-term level of housing subsidies, are responsible fiscal and monetary policies. Without the proper mixture of these two key forces, the realization of a goal of 26 million housing units is doubtful. We recognize that a program of this magnitude could involve difficult choices among alternative applications of resources. In the absence of ideal economic conditions, it could and probably would become necessary to divert resources – labor, material and money – from other activities held at a high priority by many people. Ample mortgage money alone will not create more housing. It is an essential ingredient, but sufficient supplies of manpower, materials and management talent are also keys to the realization of the goal.

A re-making of national priorities, with housing priority upgraded, could become necessary. If any new or major claims were made on our national resources, such re-ranking of priorities would be unavoidable.

The Committee examined the complex subject of mortgage financing. In order to build and rehabilitate millions of dwellings with Federal subsidies and guarantees for low- to middle-income occupants, it is imperative that there be an adequate flow of mortgage funds into this segment of the housing market and that such loans be attractive to a broad group of potential investors. With advice from consultants, staff, and a panel of knowledgeable mortgage specialists, we formulated recommendations aimed making mortgages on low-income housing more competitive with the conventional components of the housing market.

Among our recommendations are:

• All Federally subsidized and Federally insured or guaranteed housing, except public housing, should be financed by bonds insured and guaranteed by the U.S. Government.
• State usury and foreclosure laws applicable to Federally or guaranteed mortgages should be preempted by the Federal Government.
• Permanent statutory ceilings on maximum interest rates for FHA and VA mortgages should be removed

The new Housing Act of 1968 offers the Federal subsidy tools necessary for housing the nation's lower-income families. Private enterprise has demonstrated it can build subsidized housing with speed, efficiency and economies. It must participate fully, along with non-profit sponsors and eligible public agencies, in the development of such housing.

The Committee has reviewed all existing Federal housing programs and has recommended ways to attract more private participation. Among these recommendations are steps to make subsidized housing potentially profitable enough to attract new private participation, including the newly created National Housing Partnership, and others aimed at permitting private developers to respond more freely and efficiently to the needs of the subsidized housing market.

Availability of suitable land for subsidized housing already is a major problem. We have offered a series of recommendations for overcoming some major impediments to land availability. To overcome local impediments to development of subsidized housing, the Federal Government, subject to the Governor's veto, should be empowered to preempt local zoning ordinances which exclude the development of subsidized housing. Additionally, the Federal Government should make Federal land available at realistic costs, and should be empowered to acquire land for lease back to developers of such housing.

Assuming a continuation of current trends, the total building program recommended by this Committee would call for at least a million more man-years in the construction and homebuilding industry by 1975. Already, current local shortages of skilled craftsmen have reached severe levels. The Committee has made recommendations aimed at making job opportunities in construction and homebuilding more attractive and recruiting and training new entrants into the building trades, particularly unemployed minorities who offer a vast but only partially tapped pool of potential recruits.

Building materials generally account for a larger percentage of housing costs than wages for construction workers. The recommended goal of 26 million more dwellings should not be defeated by a critical shortage of building materials, although there may be some temporary strains and upward pressures on building materials' prices.

The Committee is aware that shortages and higher prices of building materials could be minimized by substitutions among materials and by more off-site fabrication. Such steps, which could also produce cost savings, could encounter barriers in restrictive local building codes, labor practices, and work rules. Conditions of widely fluctuating and highly seasonal employment are characteristic of the homebuilding and construction industries. Improved conditions bringing better job security and more full-time, year-round employment should lessen labor's fears which may form the basis for those restrictive work practices which actually do exist.

The Committee has made a number of recommendations aimed at leveling out the seasonal characteristics of employment in homebuilding and construction. We did not conduct any thorough examination of local building codes, inasmuch as the National

Commission on Urban Problems was exploring that issue in depth.

New levels of effort in research and development in the housing industry are essential to achieve attainable cost reductions during the next 10 years. Partly because of its localized and fractionated characteristics, homebuilding has never had the systematic research and concentrated efforts to develop new technologies which characterize most other modern American industries.

We recommend a program for substantially increased Government support to research in the housing field. Our two major recommendations in the area of research and implementation of new technology call for limited Federal preemption of local building codes for subsidized housing, and creation of a national testing institute for building products and systems.

To help put an end to discrimination in the housing market, we recommend strong enforcement of Federal and local open occupancy laws, and effective means for eliminating subtle or unintentional Federal and local impediments to construction of subsidized housing wherever economically feasible.

Two additional challenges within the scope of the recommended housing goals during the next 10 years will be devising ways to replace or rehabilitate nearly nine million dwellings expected to deteriorate into substandard condition and to make better use of existing standard housing for sheltering the nation's lower-income families.

Determining the feasibility of a large scale rehabilitation industry was one of our specific assignments from the President. The Committee reached two major conclusions regarding rehabilitation.

First, we foresee the necessity for a large volume of rehabilitation, contingent on (1) sufficient Federal subsidies to make rehabilitated housing available to the poor, and (2) the support of public policies aimed at encouraging the upgrading of rundown urban neighborhoods. The Committee has made a number of recommendations for facilitating and encouraging rehabilitation of substandard housing: for lower-income families.

Secondly, we do not foresee any substantial change in the individualized and necessarily labor intensive characteristics of the rehabilitation industry, itself. In our judgment,

rehabilitation, although a useful tool, will not lend itself to the massive economies of scale or to the level of industrialization visualized by some observers.

At any current point in time, about 97 to 98 percent of the nation's housing consists of "used" dwellings. In examining the allowable uses of Federal housing subsidies, the Committee found that very few are applicable to existing dwellings unless a substantial amount of rehabilitation is involved. The Committee concluded that subsidies must make greater and more efficient use of existing housing stock and has made a number of recommendations for modifications and additions to Federal housing subsidy programs to accomplish that objective.

FINAL CONCLUSION

The solution to the nation's urban housing problems in providing a decent home for every American family calls for major efforts by the Federal Government, private enterprise, organized labor and state and local governments in creative and affirmative partnerships.

The Committee believes that our nation possesses not only the financial and total resources but also the determination and ingenuity to respond to its housing challenges once the problems are fully understood and the national commitment is clearly made.

The alternative approach to solving the nation's housing problems is clear but, in this Committee's judgment, it is also clearly drastic and as yet unnecessary. Unquestionably, a direct Federal program of land acquisition, public construction, and public ownership and management of subsidized housing would produce the millions of dwellings needed by low-income families within any determined timespan. Such a program, however, would necessitate massive Federal preemption of local private and public prerogatives and decision-making powers.

We believe that the existing approach – reliance on existing subsidy programs and fuller private participation in the development and management of subsidized housing – is sufficient to meet the challenges. If it fails, we would then foresee the necessity for massive Federal intervention with the Federal Government becoming the nation's housing of last resort.

4

"Housing policy and the myth of the benevolent state"

From *Social Policy and Administration* (1978)

Peter Marcuse

Much intellectual analysis of government policies is premised on the myth of the benevolent state. In brief, the myth is that government acts out of a primary concern for the welfare of all its citizens, that its policies represent an effort to find solutions to recognized social problems, and that government efforts fall short of complete success only because of lack of knowledge, countervailing selfish interests, incompetence, or lack of courage.

In the field of housing the view that government policies are addressed to meeting real housing needs or solving housing problems has pervaded the mainstream of the professional literature for the past 30 years. On this basis efforts are made to determine the nature and scope of housing needs, their origins, the mechanisms by which they may be met, the context in which they must be dealt with. Evaluations gauge the results of housing programs against the goal of providing adequate housing for all, and recommendations proposed to better achieve that goal are thought to contribute to improved housing policy.

The analyses informed by this view are not necessarily useless, and some, like Henry Aaron's (1972) are perceptive enough in their criticisms of policy outcomes. But the weakness of most such analyses arises from the assumption that decision makers' mere exposure to the irrationalities in housing policy will be a major factor leading to their improvement. Even those politically sophisticated analyses which attend to interest group pressures, popular prejudices, economic laws, regional conflicts, and the rigidities of bureaucracies still are premised on the belief that, underneath it all, there is a movement toward social amelioration. It is the contention of this paper that the view of the benevolent state in general, and particularly in regard to housing is radically and demonstrably false.

The very phrase "housing policy" is witness to this underlying myth. What is housing policy? It is the set of government actions (and inactions, in the sophisticated view) that is intended to deal with housing problems. Housing policy may indeed be criticized as illogical, incoherent, ineffective; a set of policies, rather than a single policy; a set of policies that is internally contradictory and even self-defeating in particulars; a policy lacking in focus, philosophy, clarity of goals, certainty as to priorities. Yet the underlying existence of a governmental thrust toward the solution of the social problems of housing – of a benevolent state – is implicit in the use of the phrase. The task of analysis is to make clear the goals of housing policy and the means of their achievement, so that the benevolent state may act more rationally to solve housing problems.

Yet an historical analysis of government actions and inactions affecting housing reveals no such housing policy or any common thrust toward one. Housing policy is an ideological artifact – in Manuel Castells's phrase, not a real category. Hypotheses may be formulated as to what state actions one would expect to find if there were, in fact, a housing policy evolving from the efforts of a benevolent state to solve existing problems. These hypotheses may be tested and verified or invalidated. A good starting point may be the benevolent-state account of housing policy as moving from a restrictive approach, i.e., the enactment and enforcement of housing regulations required by mid-nineteenth century health problems, to the more positive contemporary approach of government provision of improved housing facilities.

According to this account substantial government action in the field of housing began in the United States in 1867 with New York's pioneering Tenement House Act. To stem the burgeoning problems of ill housing from which the poor suffered greatly the Tenement House Act prescribed minimum standards for fire safety, ventilation, sanitation, and weather-tightness of roofs for accommodations rented to two or more families.

This marked the beginning of a continuing effort to deal with the problems of ill housing by regulation. Such efforts are thought to be characterized by growing sophistication in definition, scope of coverage, level of standards, and methods of enforcement, culminating in contemporary housing codes and new building standards. State involvement in the actual provision of housing, rather than *mere* regulation, is seen as a different approach directed at the solution of essentially the same problems.

HOUSING REGULATION

Government actions impacted housing in the United States long before 1867, however. While detailed and extensive planning and public construction took place in colonial times in Williamsburg, Savannah, and Philadelphia, these early plans may be considered products of a declining feudal period rather than the responses to a new capitalist urban pattern. But the building regulation adopted by New York in 1766, creating a fire zone in which houses had to be made of stone or brick and roofed with tile or slate, begins a new lineage. It was made in anticipation of growth, in realization of an increasingly complex web of interrelationships within cities, in understanding that mores and social customs could no longer be relied upon to keep individuals from acting in their own private interests in such a way as to impose unnecessary risks on others. The Commissioner's Plan for New York of 1811, laying out a gridiron pattern to facilitate speculation in land, represented a further major involvement of government in the housing field. The mixture of

government action with private enterprise was a continuing and escalating process well before the mid-nineteenth century.

The historic strands that went into the Tenement House Act of 1867, largely unenforceable and wholly unenforced, and the Tenement House Act of 1901, which finally created both meaningful standards and an adequate enforcement mechanism, are not hard to disentangle. First there were health problems, reported officially in New York City as early as 1834, and called attention to beginning in 1843 by the New York Association for Improving the Condition of the Poor, led and financed by wealthy merchants and businessmen (Lubove, 1962, p.4). Smallpox, dysentery, tuberculosis and other diseases were spawned in the slums, but it took the scare of the cholera epidemics in Europe in 1865 to generate real concern. Only by "sanitary reformation … can the inevitable epidemic be mitigated," one observer wrote in 1866, and *Harper's Weekly* prophesied that without health laws, "the City of New York will be left to its own destruction." Lubove summarized (p. 23): "Terror had succeeded where reason, enlightened self-interest and the pleas of humanitarians had failed." But, he noted further,

it was not simply the danger of epidemic stalking out from the downtown ghettoes that panicked the middle class. True, the "stinks of Centre Street [lifted] up their voices," but important also after 1863 was the memory of the terrible July days when the poor streamed out from their gloomy haunts to burn, murder, and pillage. The draft riots, a turbulent protest of the immigrant poor against what they believed was discriminatory conscription, helped prove to New Yorkers that they could not permanently ignore the social and moral condition of the immigrant.

(Lubove, p. 12)

And as the Act of 1867 can be traced in part to the riots of 1863, so can the Act of 1901 be traced in part to the serious social and economic crises of the 1890s.

The political and social integration of the large immigrant population was also seen as directly related to housing standards:

The housing reformer believed that if he could improve the housing of the poor, this would reduce the class and ethnic conflict splitting the urban community into enemy camps. Better housing was needed not only to protect the health of the entire community, but to Americanize the immigrant working-class populations, to impose upon it the middle-class code of manners and morals.

(Lubove, pp. 43, 21)

Both individual antisocial behavior and general economic productivity of labor were linked to the housing codes:

> Unless conditions improved [the Association for the Improvement of the Condition of the Poor] warned [in 1865], the poor would "overrun the city as thieves and beggars endanger public peace and the security of property and life-tax the community for their support, and entail upon it an inheritance of vice and pauperism."

(Lubove, p. 7)

And Lawrence Veiller, the father of the Tenement Act of 1901, sounded the theme of a "stake in society" and home ownership as an incentive "to work industriously, to be economical and thrifty," as part of the case for housing reform (Lubove, p. 132).

It is not necessary to impugn the motives of the leaders of the reform movement, of men like Lawrence Veiller or Jacob Riis, to argue that their actions served the self-interest of the rich. Certainly, liberals, idealists, philanthropists, and other persons of strong charitable inspiration contributed to obtaining passage of laws aimed at preventing the worst of housing conditions in the growing American slums. The point here is rather that the tenement house regulations in the United States, viewed historically, do not mark the beginning of enlightened governmental attitudes toward the slums. Instead, they form an integral part of state actions protecting the existing order from the dangers created by industrialization and urbanization. Regulations governing the use of fireproof construction materials, the provision of streets and highways and public utilities, the granting of franchises for transportation routes and services, and the banning of nuisances were all part of a process beginning well before 1867. Sam Bass Warner (1968, p. 109), referring to Philadelphia, articulated that process as follows:

The popular goal of the private city was a goal to make Philadelphia a moderately safe place for ordinary men and women to go about conducting their own business; the goal was never to help raise the level of living of the poor.

Historically, housing codes were not the beginnings of a benevolent concern for the housing of the poor; they were a continuation of the use of state power to prevent any disturbance – physical, social, or political – of the private conduct of economic affairs. That they also benefited the poor, and that persons of philanthropic motivations supported them, was neither a necessary nor a sufficient cause of their enactment.

In a historical account using real categories, then, the origins of tenement house reform and housing codes would be found in five different chapters: on the economic role and social assimilation of immigrants; on the growth and arrangement of the physical infrastructure of cities, including provisions for handling the external consequences of that infrastructure (this, under the broader category of processes of production); on evolving techniques for the control of deviant individual behavior (following Lubove's emphasis of environmental determinism); and on the devices for insuring domestic tranquility and social/political control of restive groups. Any treatment of the impact on state policy of the benevolent concerns of individuals would be a short one indeed.

PUBLIC PROVISION OF HOUSING

If housing codes were not the beginnings of benevolent policies addressed to remedying housing problems, neither was the public provision of housing for the poor a further manifestation of such concerns. New York City pioneered both in housing regulation and later in housing provision. But the development of the two was discontinuous, contrary to the hypothesis suggested by the myth of the benevolent state.

The New York Tenement House Act of 1901 was the largest single step forward in housing regulation; it created the widespread inner-court layout of apartment buildings in New York and was largely followed in the wave of legislation passed by other states in the two subsequent decades. It was also the basis for the Model Tenement House Act drafted by Lawrence Veiller in 1910 for use by other states.

But Veiller opposed public housing vociferously. He considered governmental assistance to the construction of housing to be socialistic and undesirable class legislation; it would be unfair competition to private capital and would promote the growth of cumbrous and mechanical government systems. Nor was he alone: almost all of the early U.S. reformers agreed that "it was 'bad principle and worse policy' for municipalities 'to spend public money competing with private enterprise in housing the masses.'" (Lubove, 1962, p. 104; see also Jackson, 1976, p. 121). Some outstanding housing reformers (e.g., Edith Elmer Wood) did indeed see housing regulation and public housing as directly interconnected, but it is only with the a priori assumption of a government continuously searching for the best solution to a problem of ongoing and benevolent concern that the linkage between housing codes and public provision of housing becomes direct or substantial.

Nor did private philanthropic sponsorship of housing and the construction of model tenements on a charitable or limited profit basis provide the foundation for subsequent public involvement. In the heyday of the model tenement movement before the turn of the century, a total of 10,000 persons were housed by it; during the same period it is estimated that 750,000 persons were housed in newly built private tenements in New York City (Jackson, 1976, p. 110). No impact of the movement on subsequent public housing legislation can be found.

There is nothing obscure about the motivations for the public provision of housing in the United States. Rather than arising out of a benevolent concern for the poor, housing efforts were more closely related to the manufacture of war supplies to support American efforts in the First World War than with concern to appease the discontent of returning veterans of that war (on the same order although on a much smaller scale than the Homes for Heroes campaign in England and Scotland during the same period), and finally with the provision of employment for the vast army of the unemployed following the Great Depression. A few individuals and organizations did indeed stick with the good fight for public housing throughout all these events; the historic events that shaped decisions, however, were not shaped by those stalwarts.

Indeed, the three major phases in the history of public provision of housing in the United States – the World War I programs, the veterans programs after World War I, and the public housing programs that followed the Great Depression – were themselves largely discontinuous events to be found in different chapters of U.S. history. The U.S. Shipping Board Emergency Fleet Corporation was created under the Shipping Act of 1916 and in 1918 was given the authority to build or requisition housing for "employees and the families of employees of shipyards in which ships are being constructed for the United States." Later in 1918 the United States Housing Corporation was established to help "such industrial workers as are engaged in arsenals and navy yards of the United States and in industries connected with and essential to the national defense, and their families" (Friedman, 1968, p. 95). These actions stem from no earlier involvement of government in housing; they appear right after discussions of tenement house regulations in accounts of housing policy because such accounts are arranged chronologically by artificial theoretical category rather than by organic historical development. The ancestry of these wartime efforts lies rather in the housing built in the factory towns of the late nineteenth century by burgeoning industries: by textiles in Lowell, Massachusetts, and Willimantic, Connecticut, railroad cars in Pullman, Illinois, and rubber tires in Akron, Ohio, coal in the anthracite fields of West Virginia, oil in Bayonne, New Jersey, even piano manufacturing (Steinway) in New York City. The parallels abroad are of course well known; they run from flax mills to candle manufacturers in England (Gauldie, 1974) to the giant coal and iron enterprises of the Ruhr in Germany, which likewise found it necessary to build housing for their workers if they were to harness an adequate and reliable work force. World War I created the same needs in the U.S. cities where war production centered, particularly in the ports, and the state lent its resources to private industry to help meet its needs. If housing units were to be publicly owned when built, their sale to private owners as soon after the war as possible was mandated, and in fact took place. Pullman, not Veiller, was the forebear of the first direct public provision of housing in the United States.

The same historical discontinuity marks what is generally taken as the next stage of supposedly evolving governmental concern with the condition of the poorly housed: the veterans' housing programs adopted by several American states, including Massachusetts and California, in the period following the end of the First World War. Apparently unlike England and Scotland, where the postwar housing activities were directed at the areas of most severe shortage, the American programs assisted returning veterans to purchase single-family homes, regardless of the quality or suitability of their existing housing. Their lineage is as direct to Augustus Caesar and the housing of the returning Roman legions as it is to Lawrence Veiller and the tenement house reformers of New York City.

The Great Depression created the division between the policies of the 1920s and the 1930s. In the case of public housing the division is between policies unrelated to each other in terms of dealing with housing needs. The public housing program finally adopted in 1937 stemmed from concerns about social unrest among unemployed city workers; it hoped to deal with that unrest, not so much through the provision of better housing, but through the provision of jobs. The expansion of the supply of housing was not its goal; indeed, the demolition of an equivalent number of units (of substandard housing) was mandated in the U.S. Housing Act of 1937. As to the relationship to earlier efforts at housing regulation through restrictive codes, Veiller was prepared to testify *against* the Wagner bill in 1936 (McDonnell, 1957, p. 180).

If benevolence was the guiding principle behind state policies affecting housing, one would expect successive major housing acts – after 1937 these would include 1949, 1954, administrative and funding changes in 1964–66, 1968, and 1974 – to show an evolution of sophistication and effectiveness in dealing with the problems of bad housing. History shows no such pattern.

The Housing Act of 1949 did two things: it reinstituted the New Deal public housing program, dormant since World War II, and it laid the groundwork for slum clearance in the United States. The Housing Act of 1937 had coupled the removal of substandard housing with the construction of new public housing, but, as with early English legislation, the slum

clearance effects were hardly visible. The regressive consequences of slum clearance and urban renewal as practiced in the United States after 1949 are by now well known. The program has been criticized, correctly, as destroying more housing than it produced, moving out the poor to make room for the rich, and using public funds to purchase and clear valuable land near central business districts for the private benefit of downtown merchants, property owners, and the business community. Most of such criticism in the United States referred to these events as the "failures of urban renewal" (Bellush and Hausknecht, 1967; Wilson, 1966). The critics speak as if these were perversions of its original intent; as if insufficient foresight, or inadequate understanding of market dynamics, or unanticipated changes in patterns of urban development had led to these consequences. Even radical critiques of the program often saw it as being diverted from its original purpose by local business cliques and real estate interests.

While the preamble to the Housing Act of 1949 calls for "a decent home in a suitable living environment" as the formal goal of national housing policy, the interests supporting Title I, which established the urban redevelopment program, looked to the act as a means of strengthening downtown areas and eliminating blighting uses adjacent to them. Their concern was not with rehousing slum dwellers, but with tearing down slums – at least those casting a blighting influence on major business areas. Nonresidential blight was as obnoxious to them as residential. The very groups who were the strongest opponents of public housing in the United States – the National Association of Real Estate Boards, the United States Savings and Loan League, and, to some extent, the Mortgage Bankers of America – supported the principle of urban redevelopment. The first explicitly saw it as a way to "enable private enterprise to do the job that public housing was supposed to do" (Wilson, 1966, p. 81), in part by forcing slum dwellers out of cheap housing and into the higher priced (and thus theoretically higher quality) market.

The Urban Land Institute, sponsored by land developers and performing research functions for them, and the American Institute of Planners, through its president, Alfred Bettman, one of the early and nationally known proponents of zoning, specifically opposed any statutory requirement that urban redevelopment either clear only residential blighted land or be reused after clearance only for residential purposes. They slowly succeeded: first 10 percent, then 20 percent of projects were exempted from the original requirement that land to be cleared be predominantly residential; the requirement in any event only said predominantly interpreted as meaning 50 percent or more – a formulation which the imaginative drawing of project boundaries could render ineffectual. As one law review commentator lamented, a major reason for these developments, which flew in the face of the benevolent preamble to the original act, was

the position of business interests which normally end to support restrictions on federal expenditures, but are increasingly in favor of reconstructing blighted businesses and industrial properties. Foremost among these are department store owners and mortgage and other lenders concerned about large outstanding investments in downtown retail properties, now suffering competition from suburban shopping centers. (Wilson, 1966, p. 113)

Ten years later, major commercial banking interests, legal and accounting firms, national and international headquarters operations officers, and other specialized interests finding major central-city locations convenient, could easily have been added to the list.

The changes that did occur in the urban renewal program in the 1960s and the passage of the Uniform Relocation Act (1970) giving major assistance to those poor displaced by urban renewal activities came about because the organized resistance of those being displaced was so powerful it could no longer be ignored. Either the process would grind to a halt altogether or the protestors would have to be accommodated. Successive increases in relocation benefits, improvements in administration, and even obligations to construct replacement housing for the displaced were introduced until prorenewal interests felt confident they had made sufficient concessions to enable them to proceed. And the program is proceeding. Current changes, interesting to trace, result not from greater awareness of residential needs but from changing uses of central-city land. The nature of the program was not changed; the political price to be paid

for it had simply been underestimated originally. The provision of relocation assistance was not a result of reawakened benevolence, but of effective protest.

If benevolence was a major factor in the evolution of housing policies, one would expect to find the quantitative levels of production of public housing to be increasing as housing needs increased, and declining as needs declined. Such figures as are available (Aaron, 1972; U.S. Bureau of the Census, 1975; U.S. Dept. of Housing and Urban Development, 1976) indicate a steadily growing need from 1930 through about 1949, and a rather steady decline in absolute numbers needed since 1949. The figures for publicly subsidized units, however, show an altogether different and almost opposite pattern.

The explanation is not hard to find. The U.S. Housing Act of 1937 was adopted to provide jobs, not housing; its construction standards were such that twice as many units might have been provided for the same cost had the provision of housing been its purpose. The private sector saw to it that no such result ensued. After World War II, in a period of major absolute housing shortage, assistance went to private builders and mortgage-lending institutions in the form of financing aids and guarantees, and vast expenditures were made on infrastructure, highways, and related facilities. The suburban boom thus massively encouraged did not aid the poor; it led inexorably to the further decline of central-city housing, neighborhood deterioration, and reductions in public services available to the poor residents left behind by the governmentally encouraged outward movement. Public housing, on the other hand, the only housing program directly providing shelter for the poor, was starved for funds throughout the postwar period.

Accelerated state support of housing construction for families below the level of economically effective demand was not forthcoming until a way was finally found to make it serve private profit. The process is a perfect example of, in Castells's words (1973, p. 12), "the constant tendency ... to make the sectors of public subsidization profitable in order to bring them into line with the criteria of private capital so as to be able to transfer them gradually over to it." The first step was the turnkey construction process, which permitted private builders to do all of the construction on their own land and then sell the completed development to the public authorities. The second step was the perfection of the limited dividend tax benefit approach, which permitted private interests not only to build privately on public land, but to continue to own and manage the resultant publicly subsidized housing. They thus enjoyed the tax benefits of depreciation, with special acceleration provisions, agreeing in return only to limit cash profits. The tax benefits vastly exceeded in value the immediate cash benefit. The final step, being explored today through the Section 8 program of the Housing Act of 1974 and housing allowance experiments will permit private interests to build, own, and manage housing intended for the poor with no limits on profit whatsoever besides those nominally imposed by a requirement that rents be based on an administratively determined competitive level. The state will nevertheless support the payment of rent to the private owner through a subsidy based on the occupant's income. Any claim to benevolent intervention in the housing situation to bring about more rationally organized and improved housing for the poor is now abandoned altogether in favor of a restricted income support to throw into the private market those whose own resources would make their participation in it otherwise profitless. Formal housing policy thus turns parallel to what has always been the largest public program providing housing for the poor: direct welfare payments. The difference between outright welfare and the newer programs is simply its restriction to certain forms of housing and its organization in such a way as to provide more direct benefits to the private providers of the housing.

If the history of state programs directly assisting the positive provision of housing for the poor was to be written according to real categories, it would again be distributed among a number of chapters. The inception of the public housing program would be found in the chapter dealing with the economic and political consequences of the Great Depression. The Housing Act of 1949 and successive legislation dealing with urban renewal would be in the chapter dealing with the evolving economic role of the central city and its consequently changing spatial patterns. A separate chapter on the housing industry would explain much of the postwar evolution of public housing administration and finance. Struggles around

housing would be best treated in a chapter tracing political conflicts since the war, most of them in the section on local politics. Benevolence might serve as a footnote in one or two of such chapters.

Housing policy as a category is not only artificial, it creates a bias from its very use. For housing is a category of a social problem. The policies to be examined are then housing policies, that is, policies addressed to the solution of the housing problem. Thus we find ourselves by the very formulation of the problem granting the basic premise, which a thoroughgoing analysis should begin by questioning: that there is in fact a coherent body of policies addressed to the solution of the housing problem. For if there is, then a benevolent state must be the moving force behind it, and the examination is confined to the forces and patterns which may encourage or interfere with the underlying commitments of such a benevolent state. But it is the very existence of a benevolent state which needs to be questioned, particularly at a time when an apparently liberal shift in federal government administration makes the myth of benevolence particularly seductive.

REFERENCES

Aaron, Henry J. 1972. *Shelter and Subsidies – Who Benefits from Federal Housing Policies?* Washington, D.C.: Brookings Institution.

Bellush, Jewel and Murray Hausknecht, eds. 1967. *Urban Renewal: People, Politics, and Planning.* Garden City: Doubleday.

Castells, Manuel. 1973. *Neo-Capitalism, Collective Consumption and Urban Contradictions: New Sources of Inequality and New Models for Change.* Prepared for the international conference on "Models of Change in Advanced Industrial Societies," held at Monterosso al Mare, November 1973.

Friedman, Lawrence M. 1968. *Government and Slum Housing.* Chicago; Rand McNally & Co.

Gauldie, Enid. 1974. *Cruel Habitation: A History of Working-Class Housing in Britain, 1780–1918.* New York: Harper & Row.

Jackson, A. 1976. *A Place Called Home: A History of Local Housing in Manhattan.* Cambridge, Mass.: MIT Press.

Lubove, R. 1962. *The Progressives and the Slums: Tenement House Reform in New York City, 1890–1917.* University of Pittsburgh Press.

McDonnell, T.L. 1957. *The Wagner Housing Act: A Case Study of a Legislative Process.* Chicago: Loyola University Press.

U.S. Bureau of the Census. 1975. *Historical Statistics of the United States – Colonial Times to 1970.* Washington, D.C.

U.S. Department of Housing and Urban Development. 1976. National Housing Policy Review. *Housing in the Seventies.* Washington, D.C.: GPO.

Warner, Sam Bass, Jr. 1968. *The Private City: Philadelphia in Three Periods of Its Growth.* Philadelphia: University of Pennsylvania Press.

Wilson, James Q., ed. 1966. *Urban Renewal: The Record and the Controversy.* Cambridge, Mass.: MIT Press.

5
From *The Reluctant Hand: Privatization of Public Housing in the U.S.* (2004)

Norman Krumholz

Professor, College of Urban Affairs, Cleveland State University, for the CITY FUTURES Conference, Chicago, July 8–10, 2004

Until the advent of the Great Depression, most American political leaders believed that the private market, with some help from generous philanthropies, could solve the problems of housing the poor. During the era of Progressive Reform, reformers like Mary Kingsbury Simkhovitch, Benjamin Marsh and Lawrence Veiller fought for housing codes and other government regulations to reduce congestion and improve the physical condition of housing. Lawrence Veiller, author of the New York tenement housing legislation of 1901, maintained that housing for the poor would be improved if local government only enforced local building regulations (Scott, 1995). American reformers, unlike their European counterparts, rejected the idea that government should spend public money to build and manage housing for the poor (Lubove, 1962, 104). It soon became clear, however, that without government subsidies housing code enforcement simply raised the cost of housing beyond what the poor and working classes could pay.

Reformers like Mary Simkhovitch, a settlement house worker, and Catherine Bauer, a brilliant journalist/planner and an early hero of social reform, pushed for well-designed, mixed income government subsidized projects including resident-owned cooperatives. They were lonely voices in the wilderness until the economic collapse of the Great Depression when the number of organizations supporting subsidized housing issue expanded widely. Key among the supporters of a public housing bill were liberals, social reformers and unions, anxious to remedy widespread unemployment in the building trades. The reformers were far from a solid block; Veiller, a great supporter of building codes and regulations as a means to end slums, was prepared to testify against subsidized public housing in 1936 (McDonnell, 1957). As the Public Housing Act of 1937 moved through the Congress, the coalition of proponents was outmaneuvered by the real estate industry. Representatives of the politically potent National Association of Real Estate Boards (NAREB) were unremittingly hostile to the idea of public housing. Their representatives warned Congress that the program would destroy the private housing industry, that it would destroy the self-reliance of tenants and that it was "socialistic"; a charge that has had remarkable enduring power. (Congressman Jesse Wolcott, a conservative Republican, charged in 1949 that public housing would "fashion the keys to open the door to socialism in America" (Davies, 1966, 79) and Bob Dole, Republican candidate for the presidency in 1996 told an audience that American public housing is "one of the last bastions of socialism in world"). Instead of providing housing for the poor by having public agencies build and manage such housing, NAREB suggested that the rents of poor tenants be subsidized for use in private apartments through a rent certificate scheme (Orlebeke, 2000, 502). Although NAREB's objections were finally overcome, NAREB successfully managed to limit public housing occupancy to the poor and to give local government power over site selection. The first limitation ended any notions of privately-owned co-op apartments or income mixed communities and the second laid the groundwork for innumerable neighborhood not-in-my-back-yard location conflicts. NAREB also successfully linked public housing to slum clearance by having Congress mandate that one slum house was to be torn down for every public housing unit built. The supply of low-income housing was to be improved but not expanded (Dreier, 2000, 333).

The Housing Act of 1937 produced about 270,000 public housing units by 1939 before the approach of WWII brought production to a virtual halt. Little housing of any kind was built during the war and a major housing shortage emerged after the war and during the birth of the baby-boomer generation. The pent-up demand for housing and worries about the return of pre-war unemployment fueled discussions of new post-war housing legislation which was introduced in 1945 and finally passed four years later as the Wagner-Ellender-Taft Housing Act of 1949. Powerful contenders on both sides failed to reach agreement during this four-year stalemate. On one side were most business leaders, the National Association of Manufacturers, NAREB and its research arm, the Urban Land Institute. Ranged against them were social welfare groups, most unions, most big-city mayors and the Executive Branch. Persistent opposition in the Senate was led by Joseph McCarthy who honed his reactionary skills on public housing before discovering the State Department. In the House, the debate was acrimonious to the point of fisticuffs between two aging democratic members (the contenders were respectively 83 v 69 years old) and featured a crucial roll-call where public housing squeaked through by just five votes (Gelfand, 1975, 151). Truman's come-from-behind victory in the 1948 elections and renewed Democratic control of both Chambers in the 81st Congress provided the housing act with a slim, but working majority and the bill was finally passed by a vote of 227 to 204 (von Hoffman, 2000).

This Act promised "a decent home and a suitable living environment for every American family". This lofty goal raised questions about the meaning of "decent" and seemed to de-emphasize the urgent need for better housing for poor Americans in favor of the general needs of all. As part of the 1949 Housing Act, Congress authorized the construction of 810,000 public housing units to be built over the next six years. However, the opponents of public housing saw to it that Congressional appropriations committees provided the funds for only 25,000 units. Ten years later, fewer than one-quarter of the authorized units had been built (Orlebeke, 2000, 493).

The 1949 Housing Act also included the urban renewal program as Title I of the legislation. Since urban renewal was part of a housing act, and since one of its stated purposes was the removal of slums and blight, it was easy to assume that affordable housing would be the chief focus of the program. However, nothing in Title I mandated the construction of low or moderate income housing. Indeed, the wording of the legislation permitted federal subsidies for projects that destroyed low rent residential slums and replaced them with high rent apartments and commercial structures. Private developers were quick to seize on this language. They also exploited changes in the 1954, 1959 and 1961 Housing Acts that allowed urban renewal projects to contain higher and higher percentages of commercial development and lower percentages of housing. Ultimately, the urban renewal program was rightly criticized from both the left and the right as destroying more low income housing than it built, uprooting minority populations and displacing the poor from their neighborhoods in order to provide for commercial and upper-income housing development (Gans, 1962, Anderson, 1964). Not surprisingly, the very groups who were most strongly opposed to public housing, were the most enthusiastic supporters of Title I. They included NAREB, the U.S. Saving and Loan League and the Mortgage Bankers Association. Ultimately, the political problems created by the widespread use of eminent domain and the wholesale demolitions and relocations under Title I forced the federal government to reconsider the program. First, the program was liberalized to allow for compensation to poor families that were displaced by renewal and finally Title I was terminated and folded into the Community Development Bloc Grant (CDBG) in 1974.

One program that succeeded in providing privately owned, low-income social housing in the U.S. was Section 202 of the Housing Act of 1959. It provided for direct federal loans for up to 50 years at a below-market-interest-rate of 3 percent or less to non-profit housing agencies for the production and management of multifamily rental housing for the elderly and/or the disabled. Housing built under Section 202 could not be privatized during the term of federal financing and regulation. The result was the creation of a group of private and non-profits organizations specializing in low-income social housing (Stone, 2003).

In the 1961 Housing Act Congress began to explore other avenues in which government could subsidize the private sector for a more robust participation in the low-income housing field. One of its most important contributions was Section 221 (d)(3) a rental program for moderate income families, a group that earned too much to be eligible for public housing but too little to afford decent housing in the unassisted private market. Under Section 221 (d)(3) private developers or non-profit sponsors could be eligible for FHA insured three percent loans if they agreed to accept a limited profit and pass along their lower development costs to tenants in the form of lower rents. Production of new housing under 221 (d)(3) turned out to be limited because of a lack of interest on the part of qualified sponsors. As Morton Schussheim (1969, 1) put it, "production of housing for lower income families was a major aim of the (Kennedy and Johnson) Administrations (but) never reached a significant level".

Another effort of the 1961 Housing Act to involve the private market in the production of low income housing was the Section 23 leased housing program. In many older cities with sharply falling populations, whole neighborhoods were being abandoned. Local housing authorities argued that federal law should make it possible for them to acquire, rehabilitate and re-use some of this housing for lower income families. Section 23 was the response: a modest program, but ultimately one with great impact. For the first time, this program allowed local public housing authorities to lease existing privately-owned housing for eligible low-income tenants. Section 23 was the forerunner for much more extensive privatization in the form of housing allowances or rental vouchers to emerge in subsequent housing acts; it was cheaper than conventional public housing and more easily accepted by the community.

In contrast to the disappointing results of the 1949 and 1961 Housing Acts, the 1968 Housing Act, passed in the waning day of The Great Society, produced high volume production results. The 1968 Act called for six million low and moderate income units to be built over the next decade. To accomplish this ambitious goal, the Act offered two new programs: Section 235 which provided home purchasers with mortgages subsidized by the Federal Housing Administration down to one percent, and Section 236 which gave apartment developers insured one percent mortgages enabling them to offer below market rents to low and moderate income families. Congress provided full funding to both programs and subsidized production soared to 197,000 starts in 1969 and 431,000 in 1970 (Orlebeke, 2000, 496). Ironically, the high production in Sections 235 and 236 came under attack from three quarters: first, it was argued that high production in these subsidized programs was overly oriented toward builders and feeding runaway inflation of national housing costs; second it was argued that high housing production, based on the assumption that our cities suffered from a desperate physical housing shortage was incorrect – otherwise why would many city neighborhoods be emptying out and perfectly sound housing being abandoned? The problem seemed to less a shortage of housing than a shortage of income, and all this new housing might be contributing to abandonment. Third, the programs were attacked for their high-cost, shoddy workmanship, and frequent examples of corrupt administration. In the city of Detroit, for example, scandals involving the 235 and 236 programs revealed massive corrupt relationships between bankers, real estate dealers, appraisers and home repair companies.

As time went on, the conventional public housing program began to suffer from a gradual loss in constituency. During the Depression, when President Roosevelt could see "one-third of a nation ill-housed" most American families lived close to the poverty line, about one-third of the labor force was unemployed, and the public housing program was seen by most Americans as desirable and necessary. After WWII, however, American family incomes rose, millions of white families left the cities in favor of the newly-built suburbs, and efforts by housing authorities around the country to integrate new projects into outlying neighborhoods encountered stiff and sometime violent resistance. By the 1960s public housing projects – particularly high-rise projects in big cities – were providing housing for very low income, most African-American families and the projects projected an image of disaster and came to be seen as housing of the last resort. With their constituency falling away, public housing officials were also caught between rising costs of maintenance and falling rents. They began to cut their maintenance and security budgets. Then the well-meaning Booke Amendment to the 1968 Housing Act placed a ceiling on rents of 25 percent of the tenant's income. This further reduced the amount of money available for operating expenses since the original concept assumed that rents would go up parallel to inflation and costs of maintenance. Architects and sociologists who were formerly supporters of public housing began to criticize it. In the late 1960s and early 1970s, architects like Oscar Newman (1972) and sociologists like Lee Rainwater (1970) attacked various projects as inhuman centers of crime and violence. This view of on-going crisis and disaster was reinforced by books like *There Are No Children Here* (Kotlowitz, 1991). The despair that surrounded high- rise public housing projects was powerfully symbolized by the demolition in 1974 of architect Minoru Yamasaki's prize-winning Pruitt-Igoe project in St. Louis after attempts to rehabilitate it had failed. When President Richard Nixon placed a moratorium on all federally-funded housing programs in 1973, many felt his action was long overdue.

Yet, with all the well-publicized failures in large projects and in large cities, overall public housing continued to be a respected part of the housing inventory of many cities. The 40 percent of all public housing which was built for the elderly was overwhelmingly accepted without controversy and smaller public housing agencies in smaller cities reported few difficulties with their buildings. In addition, the public housing program produced millions of jobs. From 1937 to 1970 the public housing program produced 1.3 million units of low-income housing; most of this inventory is still standing and providing decent housing to very low income families. Indeed, the 1991 report by the National Commission on Severely Distressed Public Housing found that 94 percent of the nation's 13,741 projects were providing "decent, safe and sanitary housing at an affordable price" (Stockard, 1998, 241). Only three percent of all public housing agencies were designated as "troubled".

The Nixon Moratorium of 1973 was a watershed in the evolution of low-income housing policy. Up to that time, conventional public housing was mostly a supply-side program in which tangible, "hard" new units were built and maintained by local public housing authorities. The private housing market played only a small role in this program. But around the time of the 1973 Nixon moratorium events began moving toward a shift in policy involving much less reliance on conventional public housing and greater use of the nation's private housing stock through the use of Section 8 housing allowances or vouchers, now called "housing choice vouchers". Vouchers would subsidize rentals by making up the difference between a fixed percentage of a low-income household's income and the fair market rent of a private unit. Vouchers would never cover the full rent of a housing unit and they would never become an entitlement but they offered a choice in perhaps better neighborhoods. The approach was similar to NAREB's rent certificate proposals in 1937.

A test of this proposed program was HUD's 1973 $175 million Experimental Housing Allowance Program (EHAP) in a variety of actual operating conditions. The results of the tests in 12 sites embracing 30,000 households were mixed but generally positive. They suggested that the use of vouchers would not inflate the local market for rental units; that it lowered oppressive rent burdens for participants; and that served as a means of upgrading housing quality, although the upgrades were modest (Winnick, 1995, 107). Congress paid little attention to the EHAP findings, but enacted the Section 8 Housing Assistance Payments Program in 1975 and steadily expanded Section 8 in the Ford and Carter Administrations. The gradual adoption of vouchers since 1975 de-emphasizes the conventional production approach of new units built and maintained by a local housing authority and almost entirely replaces it with demand-side subsidies. Later, production subsidies were made available through tax credits in the Low Income Housing Tax Credit program (LIHTC) which has now become "the primary production vehicle for low income housing in the U.S."(Wallace, 1995, 793). In both the voucher and tax credit programs the private market plays the key role. The Nixon Moratorium and the rising conservative political tide also marked the beginning of the devolution of decision-making in low-income housing production to state and local governments.

The critical forces that pushed the government away from conventional public housing programs toward housing vouchers and tax credits include:

- The waning interest of former advocates in the face of suburban reality and anti-collectivist ideology;
- The horror tales of Cabrini Green and other big-city projects and the graphic destruction of the Pruitt-Igoe project;
- The recognition that the core housing problem in many cities has less to do with shortages and more to do with inadequate income and the need to reduce rent burden;
- The aspect of consumer choice within a given market area, the possibility of desegregation and broader neighborhood acceptance;
- Finally, the rising conservative tide. Most conventional public housing advocates identify themselves as liberal or progressive and support Democratic politics; most supporters of vouchers are interested in privatization and support Republicans. The growth of conservative political power beginning with the 1968 election of Richard Nixon and reinforced by the election of Ronald Reagan, the Congressional coup by Newt Gingrich and the elections of Bush I and II make it likely that the trend toward privatization will continue.

Housing allowances may have carried the day for demand-side subsidy programs, but they are not without problems. For one thing, federal subsidies under Section 8 have been reduced over the past few years; the Reagan Administration required renters to pay 30 percent of their incomes toward rent rather than 25 percent, obviously increasing the rent burden. President George W. Bush is drawing on various HUD programs for his "deficit reduction" strategy. In his FY05 budget proposal to Congress on February 2, 2004, Bush proposed $11.8 billion for the Housing Choice Voucher program (Section 8) which is too little to fully fund all currently authorized vouchers let alone fund any new vouchers. Critics observe that the proposed budget cuts will leave between 113,000 and 137,000 previously authorized

vouchers unfunded. Because of the great demand for vouchers and limited federal appropriations, only a small portion of the needy will be given a subsidy to compete on the open market for a supply of decent vacancies within the rent limit. Landlord resistance in desirable neighborhoods is another problem. NAREB's persistent interest in housing vouchers in 1937 and again in 1949 may reflect the wish of their members to direct a stream of federal subsidies to their least desirable buildings while declining to accept vouchers in their more attractive properties. Racial discrimination may be an added barrier to achieving a reasonable metropolitan distribution of vouchers. Because of the discriminatory workings of the private housing market, reliance on vouchers means that nonwhites will have to deal directly with discrimination as they attempt to use their Section 8 subsidies. HUD rent ceilings as well as discrimination also prevent many minorities from relocating to the suburbs thus concentrating most Section 8 vouchers for use in the central cities. Finally, in this list of problems, is the fact that vouchers never pay all the rent, nor are they an entitlement.

Despite these many real problems, Section 8 tenant-based rental assistance vouchers continue to be very popular. According to HUD report celebrating the 30th anniversary of the creation of housing allowance, vouchers serve 1.4 million families with success rates that are "almost equally high no matter the racial or ethnic group, the age or disability status, or the primary source of income" (HUD, March 2000).

Vouchers are highly flexible and are in demand both as invaluable tools of racial dispersion as exemplified by the Gautreaux program and as tools for neighborhood stabilization as used by community development corporations (CDCs) and other neighborhood advocates.

The Gautreaux program was mandated by a 1976 Supreme Court consent decree which ordered HUD to make available some 5,000 Section 8 vouchers (since increased) in order to relocate mostly African-American tenants in Chicago public housing and waiting lists to white-majority areas within the city or suburbs. Chicago's Metropolitan Leadership Council, a respected open-housing organization was to direct the program with all costs paid by HUD.

By most measures the program has been rated a success. The program administrator scattered about half the participants in white, middle class suburbs and the other half in good, integrated neighborhoods within the central city. The two sets of low-income participants were then compared regarding changes in such indicators as employment, income and education.

In almost all respects, the suburban group scored higher than the group assigned to central city neighborhoods. For the suburban group, employment was higher, school and college attendance and educational scores were higher, and dropout rates were lower (Rosenbaum, 1995).

True, the size of the Gautreaux program was small especially compared with the extensive need and the role of the Metropolitan Leadership Council might have been key to the successful results, but HUD was encouraged by the experiment and determined to expand the effort to a much larger program called Moving to Opportunity (MTO).

MTO, however, quickly ran into difficulties. In 1994, residents of Baltimore County Maryland objected to HUD's plan to move 285 inner-city residents into their neighborhoods under the MTO program. When the request for funding MTO came before Maryland Senator Barbara A. Mikulski's committee, the committee declined to earmark the funds necessary to implement the program.

If Section 8 vouchers offer low-income families (however fraught with difficulties) a way out of the central city, they also offer a way for CDCs to redevelop and stabilize inner city neighborhoods. CDCs are neighborhood-based non-profit housing organizations who have, over the past twenty years, developed most of the new and rehabilitated housing for low and moderate income families in the U.S. For twenty years, they, not the local housing authorities, have been the engines of housing redevelopment in older neighborhoods. (Vidal, 1995).

Typically, CDCs forge alliances with neighborhood residents and businessmen, city officials, various intermediaries and lenders in order to promote reinvestment in their neighborhoods and reverse decline. They target most or all of their benefits toward low and moderate income residents of their neighborhoods and all use Section 8 rent subsidies in their work and would like as many more as they can get.

CDCs also use the Low Income Housing Tax Credit (LIHTC) another program that involves the private market extensively as an essential part of their housing deals. Briefly stated, LIHTC offers profitable corporations an opportunity to invest in low income housing while, at the same time, receiving a reasonable rate of return on their investment. The direct tax write-offs on corporate tax liability made possible by LIHTC now make up about 50–60 percent of the equity capital – that is, invested not borrowed money – in most CDC low income housing developments. In the United States, LIHTC has become the primary and essential subsidy tool for low income housing production. For CDCs, developers, investing corporations, lawyers and accountants participating in (and profiting from) the complicated syndication of tax credits, and limited partners investing in low income housing LIHTC is a way of doing good while doing well, especially since most of the risk is absorbed by the federal government. Not surprisingly, LIHTC is highly popular and Congress permanently renewed the program in 1992.

The uncertainty that surrounds the conventional public housing program in the U.S. is best summarized by the controversy around HOPE VI, HUD's latest attempt to privatize, demolish and otherwise improve "troubled" conventional projects. HOPE VI was created by Congress in 1992. It represents the most serious attempt by the federal government to solve the problems of severely distressed public housing projects and reduce racial segregation and concentrations of poverty. HOPE VI's goals included the following: lowering the concentration of very poor residents and developing mixed-income communities; strengthening surrounding neighborhoods with sustainable development; involving tenants in the planning and implementation of any changes; and leveraging additional resources. Extensively distressed low income housing projects were to be extensively rehabilitated or completely demolished. To bring in capital from new sources, housing authority officials were urged into partnerships with the private or non-profit sectors. No tenant would be left homeless; some of the tenants who would be displaced by HOPE VI demolitions would be given Section 8 vouchers and some were to be included in redeveloped mixed-income properties on and off the original site. These are complicated and in some cases contradictory goals as Quercia and Galster (1997) point out.

Between 1993 and 2001, HUD funded a total of 165 HOPE VI revitalization grants nationally, representing $4.5 billion plus an additional 35 planning grants and another $293 million for demolition (Popkin, *et al.*, 2002,1). In some respects, HOPE VI is similar to welfare reform. Like welfare reform, some tenants are offered the promise of an improvement in their quality of life through a rent voucher or inclusion in a new, mixed-income development, but others who cannot make the transition may suffer because of the loss of their home, no matter how severely distressed.

The difficulties (and the promise) of the HOPE VI program are many; they have been examined elsewhere in a large variety of scholarly studies (Quercia and Galster, 1997; Salama, 1999; Popkin, *et al.*, 2002). To date, only a few major studies of the neighborhood effects of HOPE VI have been completed (Kingsley, *et al.*, 2004). These suggest that there have been some dramatic improvements in many HOPE VI neighborhoods. For example, many HOPE VI neighborhoods report a rise in per capita income of neighborhood residents and in neighborhood lending; and a drop in unemployment rates, concentrated poverty and crime rates (Popkin, *et al.*, 2004, 43).

At the same time, some important questions remain:

1. HUD is using the HOPE VI program to demolish tens of thousands of public housing units and replace them with mixed-income affordable developments on and off the original site. This is the intent of the program and it is working; over 60,000 units of "hard" public housing have already been demolished. Only a small proportion of the new units will be available to very low income tenants, that is, to tenants with 15–20 percent of the area median income. The HOPE VI program, therefore, will significantly and permanently reduce the number of deeply-subsidized hard housing units available for poor families who need housing the most. Does HUD have a back-up strategy to deal with this short-fall?

2. The emphasis on HOPE VI may be accompanied by significant reductions in funding for the conventional public housing program most of which is not severely distressed and is supposed to be extensively rehabilitated under the program. As noted earlier in this paper, 94 percent of all public housing is providing "decent, safe and sanitary housing at affordable prices". If investments in existing public housing are not supported by adequate funds for maintenance, modernization and services they will decline and become eventual candidates for demolition. Will this essential stock be maintained through adequate and routine funding?

3. HUD now seeks to entirely discontinue the HOPE VI program arguing that few projects have been completed over eleven years. In its FY 2004 and FY 2005 budget submissions, the Bush Administration proposed completely eliminating all funding for the program claiming long delays in the completion of various programs. Congress restored funding for the program for FY 2004, but at much lower levels. Yet HOPE VI is now the only source of funding for low income housing and research suggests that it is, on balance, quite successful. Does Congress intend to introduce a new program to fund low income housing?

4. The average cost of new units in HOPE VI on and off-site have never been estimated. It would be important to have accurate figures on the average unit cost in order to determine whether this is a prudent use of scarce federal funds. When does HUD intend to provide such data?

CONCLUSION

This brief overview of the privatization of public housing in the U.S. turns on changes in the United States in the understanding of the "housing problem" and in the political climate. In the Great Depression and the two decades that followed, the problem was understood as a shortage of housing and the remedy was large scale production programs. By the late 1960s, it was clear that in certain cities and certain parts of the country whole neighborhoods were being abandoned, including much housing that was in good condition. In these areas, at least, a physical shortage of housing did not seem to exist and questions about making better use of the existing housing stock began to surface. The President and Congress were also concerned that massive production programs might be feeding inflation in the housing market. The rising tide of conservatism aided the switch from production programs to privatization, reliance on demand-side subsidy programs and tax credits. None of this should be surprising; affordable housing policy in the U.S. is driven by interest-group politics, popular prejudices and the business considerations that dominate our political system.

The present dominance of tenant-based subsidy is part of government's strong and growing thrust toward privatization which now includes: food stamps, Medicare, Medicaid, and even public school vouchers on an extremely limited scale. But housing allowances should not bring an end to production subsidies in low income housing. The thousands of cities in urban America are too diverse, too different to rely on any single subsidy. There are simply too many circumstances where production, not vouchers, is key, and many other circumstances where both should be applied in tandem. In areas of rapid population growth and tight markets, in areas of special-needs housing, and in inner city redevelopment, some mix of tenant-based subsidy and new housing production may be the best answer.

BIBLIOGRAPHY

Anderson, Martin. 1964. *The Federal Bulldozer*. Cambridge, MA: MIT Press.

Davies, Richard. 1966. *Housing Reform During the Truman Administration*. Columbia, MO: University of Missouri Press.

Dreier, Peter. 2000. Labor's Love Lost? Rebuilding Unions' Involvement in Federal Housing Policy. *Housing Policy Debate*. 11 (2): 327–381.

Gans, Herbert J. 1962. *The Urban Villagers: Group and Class in the Life of Italian-Americans*. New York: Free Press.

Gelfand, M.I. 1975. *A Nation of Cities: The Federal Government and Urban America*. New York: Oxford University Press.

HUD. March, 2000. *Section 8 Tenant-Based Housing Assistance: A Look Back After 30 Years*. Washington, D.C.: Dept. of Housing and Urban Development. 1.

Kingsley, G. Thomas, Martin D. Abravanel, Mary Cunningham, Jeremy Gustafson, Arthur J. Naparstek, and Margery Austin Turner. 2004. *Lessons from HOPE VI for the Future of Public Housing*. Washington, D.C.: The Urban Institute.

Kotlowitz, Alex. 1991. *There Are No Children Here: The Story of Two Boys Growing Up In The Other America*. New York: Doubleday.

Lubove, Roy. 1962. *The Progressives and the Slums: Tenement House Reform in New York City, 1890–1917*. Pittsburgh: University of Pittsburgh Press.

McDonnell, Timothy L. 1957. *The Wagner Housing Act: A Case Study of the Legislative Process*. Chicago: Loyola University Press.

Newman, Oscar. 1972. *Defensible Space*. New York: MacMillan.

Orlebeke, Charles, J. 2000. The Evolution of Low Income Housing Policy, 1949 to 1999. *Housing Policy Debate*. 11 (2) 489–517.

Popkin, Susan J. *et al.* 2002. *HOPE VI Panel Study: Baseline Report*. Washington, D.C.: The Urban Institute.

Popkin, Susan J. *et al.* 2004. *A Decade of HOPE VI: Research Findings & Policy Challenges*, Washington, DC: Urban Institute and The Brookings Institution.

Quercia, Roberto and George C. Galster. 1997. The Challenges Facing Public Housing in a Brave New World. *Housing Policy Debate*. 8 (3): 535–69.

Rainwater, Lee. 1970. *Behind Ghetto Walls*. Chicago: Aldine-Atherton.

Rosenbaum, James E. 1995. Changing the Geography of Opportunity by Expanding Residential Choice: Lessons From the Gautreaux Program. *Housing Policy Debate*. 6:1.

Salama, Jerry J. 1999. The Redevelopment of Distressed Public Housing: Early Results from HOPE VI Projects in Atlanta, Chicago and San Antonio. *Housing Policy Debate*. 10 (1): 95–136.

Schussheim, Morton J. 1969. *Toward A New Housing Policy: The Legacy of the 1960s*. New York: Committee for Economic Development.

Scott, Mel. 1995. *American City Planning Since 1890*. Chicago: APA Press.

Stockard, James G. 1998. Public Housing – The Next Sixty Years? In Varady, *et al. New Directions in Urban Public Housing*. Rutgers: Center for Urban Policy Research.

Stone, Michael E. 2003. Shelter Poverty and Social Housing in the UK and US. Paper delivered at the Urban Affairs Association Annual Conference, May, Baltimore, MD.

Vidal, Avis C. 1995. Reintegrating Disadvantaged Communities into the Fabric of Urban Life: The Role of Community Development. *Housing Policy Debate*. 6 (1): 169–229.

von Hoffman, Alexander. 2000. A Study in Contradictions: The Origins and Legacy of the Housing Act of 1949. *Housing Policy Debate*. 11 (2): 299–323.

Wallace, James E. 1995. Financing Affordable Housing in the United States. *Housing Policy Debate*. 6 (4): 785–814.

Winnick, Louis. 1995. The Triumph of Housing Allowance Programs: How a Fundamental Policy Conflict Was Resolved. *Cityscape*. 1 (3): 95–121.

6

"Why a right to housing is needed and makes sense: Editors' introduction"

From *A Right to Housing: Foundation for a New Social Agenda* (2006)

Rachel G. Bratt, Michael E. Stone and Chester Hartman

It is unconscionable that in the 21st century, upwards of a 100 million people in the United States live in housing that is physically inadequate, in unsafe neighborhoods, overcrowded or way beyond what they realistically can afford. Yet it could be quite different. We could and should guarantee high-quality, truly affordable housing in "good" neighborhoods for all and thus finally achieve the National Housing Goal of "a decent home and a suitable living environment for every American family," as articulated by Congress over a half-century ago in the 1949 Housing Act and reaffirmed in subsequent legislative initiatives.[1] [We embrace] the view that a commitment to a Right to Housing should be the foundation not only for housing policy but also for a new social agenda.

The call to adopt and implement a Right to Housing not only has an ethical basis in principles of justice and ideals of a commonwealth. It is also based on a highly pragmatic perspective – the central role that housing plays in people's lives. Given the many ways in which housing is, or can be, the basic building block for a range of related benefits – personal health and safety, employment opportunities, a decent education, security of tenure, economic security – a host of new social relationships and economic opportunities would emerge if a Right to Housing were realized, and the extensive negative impacts of poor housing would largely disappear. A Right to Housing would also go a long way toward countering the

pernicious trend toward our society's extremes of material well-being and opportunity – a trend that is creating larger and larger fissures between the nation's richest and most of the rest of us – but most especially the poorest among us – disparities that have a clear racial dimension as well and that make true democracy impossible.

Just over 60 years ago, in his 1944 State of the Union address to Congress, President Franklin Delano Roosevelt declared that economic security is a necessary ingredient for a democratic society. He further asserted that there was a need for a whole series of economic and social rights, including a Right to Housing. This is part of his message:

> We have come to a clear realization of the fact that true individual freedom cannot exist without economic security and independence. "Necessitous men are not free men." ... These economic truths have become accepted as self-evident. We have accepted, so to speak, a second Bill of Rights under which a new basis of security and prosperity can be established for all – regardless of station, race, or creed. Among these are: the right to a useful and remunerative job ... the right to earn enough to provide adequate food and clothing and recreation ... the right to adequate medical care ... the right to a good education [and along with several other enumerated rights] the right of every family to a decent home. All of these rights spell security. And after

this war is won we must be prepared to move forward in the implementation of these rights, to new goals of human happiness and well-being.

(Roosevelt 1944)[2]

A bold, fresh approach to solving the nation's housing problems is timely because three-fourths of a century of government interventions and a multiplicity of strategies, both public and private, have not been devoted to truly solving the problem. To be sure, gains have been made, and millions of households have been assisted, but the gains and assistance have been partial, piecemeal and transitory at best. Any examination of the array and scale of housing and housing-related problems reveals clearly how painful, pervasive and persistent are these problems. Let us thus finally get past the illusion that merely tinkering with current policies and even appropriating more money will be sufficient to solve our housing problems. Fundamental change is necessary and long overdue.

This is not a new or original insight and call. Back in 1989, the Washington, DC-based Institute for Policy Studies assembled a Working Group on Housing (in which several of *A Right to Housing* contributors – Chester Hartman, Michael Stone, Emily Achtenberg, Peter Dreier, Peter Marcuse and Florence Roisman – participated) that crafted a detailed housing program, put forward in *The Right to Housing: A Blueprint for Housing the Nation.*[3]

That document provided an analysis of the failures of the private market and of government programs similar to what is put forward in *A Right to Housing.* And it included a detailed program for preserving affordable rental housing; promoting affordable homeownership; protecting the stock of government-assisted housing; and producing/financing new affordable housing. First-year program costs – estimated for each element of the program, with administrative costs added – at that time ranged from $29 billion to $88 billion, depending on how rapidly and fully specific program elements were introduced; by way of comparison, at the same time, the highly regressive income tax system for housing provided at least $54 billion in tax breaks for high-income households. The thrust of the various elements was to move substantial portions of the existing housing stock, as well as

new additions, into the nonprofit sector (public as well as private) – "decommodifying housing" was the catchword. Annual costs would steadily decrease as this fundamental shift in the nation's housing stock progressed. Congressman Ron Dellums of California introduced the program in the 101st Congress as H.R. 1122 (A Bill to Provide an Affordable, Secure and Decent Home and Suitable Living Environment for Every American Family). Needless to say, it did not pass. At the end of a hearing on the Bill, Congressman Henry Gonzalez of Texas, then Chair of the Banking, Finance and Urban Affairs Committee and Chair of the Subcommittee on Housing and Community Development, remarked, "What your group has presented is inevitably going to happen.... It is imaginative, it is seminal, it is creative." We agree and hope the arguments herein will hasten its day.

THE PHYSICAL IMPORTANCE OF DECENT HOUSING

Where one lives – particularly if one is poor, and/or a person of color – plays a critical role in fixing a person's place in society and in the local community. Living in substandard housing in a "bad" neighborhood may limit people's ability to secure an adequate education for their children, reduce chances of finding a decent job and deprive them of decent public services and community facilities. The quality of one's housing may also be an outward sign, as well as part of a person's self-image, that in some profound and important ways one has not succeeded.

Housing has always been viewed as one of the necessities of life – a critical element of the "food, clothing and shelter" triumvirate. Stories of homeless people freezing to death each winter provide stark reminders that housing is a fundamental need. In earlier eras, events such as the great Chicago fire of 1871 and the cholera epidemics that swept densely populated urban areas in the early and mid-19th century dramatically made the link between poor housing conditions and health and safety (Friedman 1968). The public response was enactment of tenement house laws, first in New York City and followed by other large cities. The explicit goal was to regulate the "health, safety and morals of tenants" (Wood 1934) as well as to protect the nonpoor who were living in nearby neighborhoods.

Although housing conditions have improved dramatically since the 19th century, poor quality is still a problem facing millions of Americans. Fires due to inadequate wiring or faulty furnaces are still commonplace, and many households are plagued by infestations of vermin and inadequate heating systems. In recent years, there have been compelling demonstrations of the links between health and housing. For example, a project undertaken under the auspices of the Boston Medical Center underscored that poorly maintained housing is closely linked to childhood injuries and lead poisoning, and that damp, moldy interiors are associated with elevated incidences of respiratory disease and asthma. (Sandel *et al.* 1999; see also *Scientific American* 1999, 19–20; Bernstein 1999; Pérez-Peña 2003).

Over the past 30 years, we have learned a great deal about the impact of lead on children's health. Lead poisoning has been called "the most common and devastating environmental disease of young children" (U.S. General Accounting Office 1993, 2). The Centers for Disease Control and Prevention estimates that 434,000 children younger than age six have blood-lead levels above the federal guideline (Avril 2003).[4] Hazards due to lead paint are most serious among poor, nonwhite households, who have a far higher incidence of lead poisoning than their higher-income white counterparts (Leonard *et al.* 1993, 8; National Low Income Housing Coalition 2005). St. Louis, which has the nation's fourth oldest housing stock, has childhood lead poisoning rates about six times the national average. In 1999, the city's lead poisoning prevention program was scheduled to decontaminate about 500 low-income apartments. However, "at that rate, it will finish deleading St. Louis in about 200 years" (Grunwald 1999).

Additional evidence on the connections between poor housing and health comes from a controlled study carried out in England, which revealed that residents living in high-quality public housing in West London were far less likely to become sick than those living in low-quality public housing in East London. Further, researchers concluded that "the costs of failing to provide decent homes in stable environments to families – in the forms of ill health, underachievement, crime and vandalism – will far exceed the investment in adequate maintenance and repair of housing" (cited in Hynes *et al.* 2000, 35–36). Although there may be room for improving our

ability to measure the cost-effectiveness of improved housing, physical problems caused by poor housing should not persist.

THE EMOTIONAL AND SYMBOLIC IMPORTANCE OF HOUSING

In addition to protecting people from the elements and providing (or not providing) physical safety, housing fulfills a variety of critical functions in contemporary society.[5] A landmark study prepared in 1966 for the U.S. Department of Health, Education and Welfare (predecessor to the Department of Health and Human Services) investigated what was known about the relationship between housing and the feelings and behavior of individuals and families. It concluded that "The evidence makes it clear that housing affects perception of one's self, contributes to or relieves stress, and affects health" (Schorr 1966, 3).

A decade later, a study of middle-income people affirmed that an important aspect of the meaning of one's house is

> [T]he sense of permanence and security one could experience. ... In this regard, people spoke of "sinking roots," "nesting," and generally settling down. The house ... seemed to be a powerful symbol of order, continuity, physical safety, and a sense of place or physical belonging.... Closely connected ... was [another] aspect of the house's meaning – the common notion that the house was a refuge from the outside world or even a bastion against that world ...: a desire to escape from other people and from social involvement, the establishment of a place from which others could be excluded, and where, consequently, one could truly be oneself, in control, "more of an individual," capable of loving, and fully human.
>
> (Rakoff 1977, quoted in Stone 1993, 15)

Feminist architectural historian Dolores Hayden has also emphasized the emotional importance of housing: "Whoever speaks of housing must also speak of home; the word means both the physical space and the nurturing that takes place there" (1984, 63). If housing is overcrowded, dilapidated or otherwise inadequate, it is difficult, if not impossible, for family life to function smoothly. Empirical evidence demonstrating the importance of housing for emotional well-being comes from a recent study of the impacts of housing quality on mental health; better-quality housing was related to lower levels of psychological distress (Evans *et al.* 2000, 529).

Jonathan Kozol's poignant account of homeless families in New York City shelters underscores the extent to which grossly inadequate housing conditions contribute to family dysfunction:[6] A lack of privacy creates stress for all family members; the inability to have guests vastly constricts normal social access; children are unable to do homework and adults live in constant fear that their children will be endangered by the harsh social and physical environments (Kozol 1988).

Further, recent research on impacts of homelessness on children has revealed that while "only 5 percent of children entering shelters had a developmental delay requiring specialist evaluation, ... half of the children living in homeless shelters had one or more developmental delays." In addition, although nearly one-half the school-age children in homeless shelters needed special education evaluation, only 22 percent actually received this testing. Children living in shelters also missed far more days of school than did housed children. And, finally, one-half of all children in shelters showed signs of anxiety and depression and demonstrated significantly more behavioral disturbances, such as tantrums and aggressive behavior, than did poor housed children. (Cited in Sandel *et al.* 1999, 39.)

Although it may be difficult to prove that these and other types of problems are *caused* by poor or no housing,[7] it is undeniable that, at the very least, inadequate housing (including long-term residence in shelters) can exacerbate an already problematic situation. A key aspect of family well-being necessarily involves the provision of decent, affordable housing. As a bipartisan task force report declared:

> [A] decent place for a family to live becomes a platform for dignity and self-respect and a base for hope and improvement. A decent home allows people to take advantage of opportunities in education, health and employment – the means to get ahead in our society. A decent home is the important beginning point for growth into the mainstream of American life.
>
> (National Housing Task Force 1988, 3).

More recently, this assertion was echoed by the Congressionally appointed bipartisan Millennial Housing Commission:

> Decent and affordable housing has a demonstrable impact on family stability and the life outcomes of children. Decent housing is an indispensable building block of healthy neighborhoods, and thus shapes the quality of community life.... Better housing can lead to better outcomes for individuals, communities, and American society as a whole.
>
> (2002, 1)[8]

Housing has also been credited as providing a significant boost on the economic ladder due to the opportunity it can present to build assets. Although a key argument [presented here] is that housing need not be viewed as the only or best vehicle for promoting savings and wealth accumulation (see Stone 1993, 195–6, for a discussion of a social alternative to wealth creation through homeownership), and that much more housing can and should be socially and publicly owned, we acknowledge that, at least since the end of World War II, millions of households were able to gain a foothold in the economy through their ability to become homeowners. However, recent research points to several important concerns and risks related to low-income homeownership, including the possibility of financial losses (see Retsinas and Belsky 2002). And of course a central defect of the homeownership push is the enormous racial disparities that exist in homeownership rates and the wealth-generating potential and actuality of home purchase (see Bratt *et al.* 2006, Ch. 4 and Shapiro 2004).[9] Beyond the effects of housing itself, where people live, in terms of neighborhood setting and locational advantage, has a great deal to do with access to both educational opportunities and employment and social networks. (See Bratt *et al.* 2006, Ch. 18.)

IMPORTANCE OF HOUSING IN A NEIGHBORHOOD CONTEXT

Even a cursory overview of this country's community development initiatives reveals that housing has consistently been given a central position. In the urban renewal program, for example, the earliest focus was on "slum" clearance. Later, the emphasis was on housing rehabilitation. As part of the Model Cities program of the mid-1960s, enforcing housing codes, developing "in-fill" housing on vacant land and rehabilitating housing were key components. The Community Development Block Grant (CDBG) program, in existence since 1974, has supported a variety of housing initiatives, with housing responsible for the largest share of CDBG expenditures (The Urban Institute 1995, iv).

During the 1980s and 1990s, nonprofit development organizations proliferated across the country and have become central players in community revitalization efforts. Here, too, there is a significant focus on housing, with the vast majority of these groups involved with housing production or rehabilitation (Vidal 1992, 5). The National Congress for Community Economic Development (NCCED) has estimated that there are more than 3,600 community development corporations (CDCs), which is the dominant type of nonprofit development organization (NCCED 1999). Moreover, housing produced by CDCs "is often a foundation for such activities as business enterprise, economic development, job training, health care and education" (NCCED 1999, 11).

Although many CDCs are acknowledging that their housing initiatives should be viewed in the broader context of comprehensive community revitalization – including the provision of social services, employment training and referrals, health care and substance abuse programs, and enhancing educational opportunities (U.S. General Accounting Office 1995) – the quality of housing is one of the most visible and concrete signs of neighborhood well-being. Housing is, and will continue to be, a central component of virtually any community's rebuilding efforts, and CDCs are likely to continue to play a significant role. (See Bratt et al. 2006, Ch. 16.)

OVERVIEW OF HOUSING NEEDS IN THE UNITED STATES

Despite the universal physical need for shelter, as well as the symbolic and emotional importance of decent housing, housing problems across our nation are serious and widespread. The U.S. Department of Housing and Urban Development (HUD), at the request of Congress, submits occasional reports on "worst case housing needs." These are renter households who have incomes of 50 percent or less of area median income, pay more than 50 percent of their income for rent and utilities and who may also live in severely inadequate quarters,[10] yet do not receive federal assistance. Slightly over 5 million of the nation's approximately 103 million households fall into this category (HUD 2003), with about 15 percent of them living in nonmetropolitan areas (National Low Income Housing Coalition 2001). Yet this figure does not include many of those with serious housing problems, such as the homeless. While estimates of the total number of homeless vary widely – in part a function of the inherent difficulty of counting these people – an often-cited figure is that there are 800,000 homeless people in the United States on any given night. And, over the course of a year, some 3.5 million people may be homeless for varying periods of time (National Low Income Housing Coalition 2005; see Bratt et al. 2006, Ch. 15).

In addition to the literally and virtually homeless are tens of thousands of people who are "pre-homeless" or nearly homeless. In New York City (and doubtless in many other cities with large immigrant populations), there have been numerous illegal conversions of basement space in single-family homes and apartment houses into small (typically, 5' x 8') cubicles, with common kitchens and bathrooms, which present serious fire and health hazards. Officials are reluctant to clamp down on these living arrangements – even if they could systematically find them (estimates range from 10,000 to 50,000 units in New York City alone) – knowing that the consequence of enforcing housing codes would be serious increases in the homelessness population (Wolff 1994). Moreover, illegal units of this sort are not confined to central cities and immigrant populations (Lambert 1996). Among the worst housed of the nearly homeless are migrant farmworkers (Greenhouse 1998).

Owning one's home is of course no guarantee that a family's residence will be problem-free. About 2 million homeowner households lived in housing with moderate or severe problems in 1999,[11] and more than six million homeowner households paid more than 50 percent of their income for housing. About 84 percent of all homeowners facing severe housing problems earned less than 80 percent of area median income (National Low Income Housing Coalition 2001).[12]

Further, in 1999, about 2.6 million households lived in units with more than one person per room (the official measure of overcrowding); about one-half of this group faced overcrowding problems in conjunction with problems of costs and quality (National Low Income Housing Coalition 2001). Finally, and perhaps most depressing of all, the "worst case housing needs" figure does not include the approximately 1.7 million households with severe problems living in subsidized housing (National Low Income Housing Coalition 2001).[13] Included here are public housing units that are waiting to be repaired or substantially rehabilitated as well as thousands of units of privately owned subsidized housing that have a similar backlog of maintenance problems (see National Commission on Severely Distressed Public Housing 1992; England-Joseph 1994; Finkel *et al.* 1999).

Three additional factors are relevant when considering the scope of our housing problems: First, in terms of quality, HUD and Census Bureau criteria for "severely substandard" ignore the stricter, more relevant, legally enforceable local housing code standards. Incorporating such standards into definitions of adequacy would considerably increase the numbers of households living in "inadequate units."[14] Second, a residence that is in decent condition, of the proper size for the household and within their financial means may nonetheless be unacceptably dangerous, isolating and unpleasant – hence substandard – if the surrounding residences and streets fail to meet minimal standards. And third, the affordability criterion embodied in HUD's "worst case" data fails to recognize the severe budgetary problems faced by renter households with incomes above 50 percent of the area median who must spend more than one-half their income for rent. In addition, many other lower-income renter households who pay less than 50 percent of their income for rent may still be paying way too much. This is explored more fully in Stone (2006), which argues that any fixed "proper" rent-to-income ratio standard ignores the realities that household size, income level and the need to pay for nonshelter basics all go into determining whether a given unit is "affordable" for a given household.[15]

What is the best estimate of the bottom line for all of the above housing problems? The National Low Income Housing Coalition (2001) estimates that some 18.5 million homeowner households and 17.2 million renter households are facing either moderate or severe housing problems. Of these 35.7 million households, about 19.5 million earned less than 50 percent of median income,[16] and another 7.5 million earned 50 to 80 percent of median income.[17] The Joint Center for Housing Studies has reached a similar conclusion, presented somewhat differently:

A staggering three in ten US households have housing affordability problems. Fully 14.3 million are severely cost-burdened (spend more than 50 percent of their incomes on housing) and another 17.3 million are moderately cost-burdened (spend 30–50 percent of their incomes on housing). Some 9.3 million households live in overcrowded units or housing classified as physically inadequate. And a disheartening 3.7 million households face more than one of these problems.

(2003, 25)

Using his shelter poverty concept, Michael Stone has found a similarly massive number of households (about 15 million renters and 17 million homeowners in 2001) facing serious housing affordability problems. However, his analysis underscores "a significantly different distribution of the problem: Not all households shelter-poor are paying over 30 percent of their incomes for housing, and not all households paying over 30 percent are shelter-poor."[18] Most strikingly, his approach shows that families with children are more likely to have affordability problems, and that small middle-income households are less likely to have affordability problems, than is suggested by the conventional standard (Bratt *et al.* 2006, Ch. 2).

Another way of looking at housing needs is via estimates of the number of poor households eligible for housing assistance who do not receive it. About two out of three renters with incomes below the poverty line do not receive any housing assistance (Daskal 1998, 35). And, using HUD's higher income limits of eligibility for housing assistance, far more low-income households could receive housing if such funding were available. At the very least, the 5 million households who have "worst case housing needs" would be eligible for a subsidy from HUD.

Housing needs can also be examined by comparing the housing situation of those with the least housing opportunities and resources and those with the most, which are far from evenly distributed. Housing needs among our poorest citizens, discriminated-against racial groups and women heads of household are much more serious than among the population at large. For example, "regardless of income, the incidence of burdens is higher among minorities than whites ..." (Joint Center for Housing Studies 2005, 25). Thus, housing is America's Great Divide. How and where one lives is *the* marker of one's socioeconomic and, to a large extent, racial status in the society and the local community. Moreover, this divide runs through all our major systems: education, health care, employment, criminal justice – in other words, we have developed into a "have/secure" and "have-not/insecure" society.

The extremes of housing consumption are staggering. On the one hand, housing is the most conspicuous form of conspicuous consumption. Mega-mansions are common-place in affluent suburbs, often replacing more modest dwellings that are demolished. And these are not the exclusive domains of the "rich and famous," as large numbers of households rode the wave of economic growth and expansion during the 1990s. A *New York Times* article described this Memphis scene:

> The beige, three-story mansion fills a one-acre lot.... Roof turrets, tall windows, columns that frame the front door at the head of a majestic, sloping driveway all heighten the impression of a palace.... The ranch house next door seems, by comparison, like a shack. "Such houses," observes Kenneth Rosen, who heads the University of California's Fisher Center for Real Estate, "are conspicuous proof that a family has achieved a level of wealth way beyond its physical needs. A mansion, more than luxury cars or anything else, shows everyone in the community that you are rich."
>
> (Uchitelle 1999)

On the other hand, millions of households are facing serious problems securing and paying for decent shelter. The most extreme situation is exemplified by the hundreds of thousands of Americans who, at any given point in time, are without any private domestic space at all – the country's homeless population.

As a society, we seem content to permit such disparities. And the problems can only get worse, as housing costs have been rising faster than incomes for most of the past 30 years. The Joint Center for Housing Studies has noted that: "home prices and rents have continued to outpace general price inflation" (2003, 25).

Moreover, "welfare reform," introduced in 1996, is having a nontrivial impact in the housing area, although its full effects remain to be seen. While a great many TANF recipients (Temporary Assistance for Needy Families, formerly known as AFDC) have entered the workforce, the pay levels for the majority of these jobs still is considerably below what is needed to cover the cost of market rents for apartments. In addition, millions of families who have never been on welfare, and who earn minimum wages or somewhat above, are still unable to afford decent housing (Bratt *et al.* 2006, Ch. 18).

The alarming loss of unsubsidized low-rent units is another important factor contributing to high rental housing costs. Between 1991 and 1997, the number of unsubsidized rental units affordable to extremely low-income households (those with incomes 30 percent or less of area median income) dropped by 370,000 – a 5 percent reduction. At the same time that the low-rent stock has been decreasing, the number of households earning 30 percent or less of median income has been increasing (HUD 2000, 22). According to the Joint Center for Housing Studies,

> In 2001, the 9.9 million renters in the bottom quintile [of income, which was no more than $17,000] outnumbered the supply of these [unsubsidized] units by fully 2 million. Reducing the pool even further, higher-income households occupied 2.7 million of the 7.9 million lowest-cost units.
>
> (2003, 28)

Beyond these important trends, there are deeper causes behind the staggering situation we are observing.

THE ROOTS OF HOUSING PROBLEMS

Housing problems are deeply ingrained in the operation of our economic system and in the ways in which society functions, and they have not emerged in just the past few decades. Rather, this country has a long history of such problems (see, for example, Stone 1993, Chapters 3, 4), the consequence of certain basic institutional arrangements and characteristics of our society. The most important factors include the workings of the private housing market; widening income inequality; persistent and pervasive housing discrimination; overdependence on debt and capital markets to finance housing and public policies that are inadequate to counter these trends and, at worst, exacerbate them.

The illusions of "the Market"

Throughout this nation's history, there has been a struggle between those who believe that we have a collective responsibility, through, but not limited to, government, to "promote the general welfare" and those who assert that the general welfare is and should be best achieved by all pursuing their own self-interest via "the Market," with government doing as little as possible, apart from providing for the common defense. From the Great Depression through the 1970s, the former view predominated, albeit often tempered with ritual apologies for interfering with the alleged virtues of the market. Over the past quarter-century, though, the idealization of the market as the answer to nearly all social and economic problems has emerged as the dominant ideology, with government portrayed not only as outrageously wasteful of "your money," but indeed as the very *cause* of poverty, antisocial behavior, declining educational performance and so forth.

Nowhere has this shift been greater than with regard to housing and housing policy. (A few of the most rabid examples of attacks on government interventions in housing are Salins 1980; Husock 2003.) Public housing has been attacked as an integral part of the culture of welfare dependency as well as the worst of modern urban design. Never mind that most public housing does not fit the stereotypes and that relentless opposition from private real estate interests largely accounts for the failures

of design and siting that do exist. Government assistance for housing the poor, to the extent that it is not opposed entirely, has largely shifted away from housing production to vouchers that ostensibly give recipients the freedom to shop in the "free" housing market. Yet this market tends, in many places, to have little or nothing available, forcing recipients to return their vouchers unused, while in other places, it consists of exploitative landlords who reap windfalls from the vouchers. Rent control has been discredited as allegedly destroying market incentives for landlords and developers to maintain and produce unsubsidized low-rent housing, thus (so the argument goes) causing decay and abandonment of great swaths of urban America. Government is blamed for runaway housing costs and inadequate housing production, through imposition of exclusionary zoning and strict subdivision and permitting regulations. Ironically, to the extent that this latter critique has some legitimacy, the governments responsible are under the control of and acting on behalf of high-income people seeking to protect their wealth from the market.

It is our view that the ideology of the virtuous market is largely a cynical and hypocritical rationalization for selfish individualism and widening inequality. Simplistic theories have been used to divert attention from the underlying causes of housing and other social problems by focusing instead on admittedly flawed, inadequate and often contradictory government responses to those problems. It appears that we have forgotten that markets are social creations, operating on the basis of legal and economic incentives and disincentives established and enforced by governments. The biggest and most profitable businesses get that way by ruthlessly driving out or buying up competitors in order to escape from the strictures of the competitive market whose virtues they proclaim. And they resist mightily government attempts to rein in their monopolistic depredations. But when they fail, to whom do they turn to be bailed out? Why of course, the government via the taxpayers. (See discussion of the savings and loan bailout and the crisis of Fannie Mae and Freddie Mac in Bratt et al. 2006, Ch. 4.)

Furthermore, the efficiency that in theory attaches to competitive "free markets" is at best a one-dimensional efficiency that has no place for distributive justice and neighborhood effects. For example, sharply escalating housing prices in many parts of the country are in fact the response of the free housing market to demand from ever-richer households at the top of the increasingly unequal income distribution. While taxing away some of this speculative wealth would dampen price increases, thereby making housing generally more affordable, and generate some revenue that could be used for low-income housing, such redistribution would ostensibly reduce the efficiency of the housing market. Yet, to add insult to injury, the tax system actually provides incentives for such speculation. Inefficiency on the upside of the market (for instance, windfall profits that the market would not generate without public assistance) does not seem to bother free-market ideologues.

As for so-called neighborhood effects, or externalities, free-market ideology/theory either sees them as beneficial or ignores them. For example, if tearing down smaller, older houses to build mega-mansions results in higher property values and hence higher property taxes and greater economic stress for older homeowners, free-market ideology sees this as a positive externality (the latter are better off because their property values have risen), not as a negative externality because their quality of life has diminished due to increased costs. If the free market produces massive houses on large lots sprawling across the landscape, the costs to natural habitats and watersheds, as well as the costs of increased traffic and air pollution, are largely externalized, for instance, imposed on others in the present and future rather than being part of the calculus of efficiency.

The housing market also treats housing as a commodity – an item that is bought and sold for profit. For the low-income renter or homebuyer, this creates problems at every step of the housing production, development, distribution and financing processes. The final cost of housing is the total of all the many costs involved – including land, building supplies, labor, financing, distribution and conveyance. At each phase of the process, the goal is to maximize profits, which in turn increases costs and reduces affordability.

KEY CAUSAL FACTORS OF HOUSING PROBLEMS – BEYOND THE MARKET

In addition to our view that the private housing market works at cross-purpose with the needs of providing decent, truly affordable housing for all, a number of other factors are at the root of our housing problems. The following offers an overview of these critical themes.

Widening income inequality

Our housing problems are directly and closely connected with the overall structure of our economic system. In contrast with several decades post-World War II, when the gap between the rich and the poor was shrinking, for the past 30 years this trend has changed. We have been mired in a period of sustained and growing income inequality, where the disparity between the upper and lower tiers of the income distribution has become ever wider. Moreover, various subgroups of the population (such as persons of color and single-parent families) are experiencing this disparity with a disproportionate frequency.

Beyond the inequality in income, for most households, the income side of the housing affordability equation is not keeping pace with the escalating costs of housing. Without adequate income, the ability of households to cover the costs of housing is simply impossible. These trends have not "just happened." Instead, they are the outcome of specific policies, goals and initiatives of both government and the corporate sector.

Persistent and pervasive housing discrimination

Not only do people of color have lower incomes than their white counterparts, they are less able to compete in the housing market due to persistent discrimination. Housing discrimination is nothing new (Loewen 2005). While it was a "given" before direct government intervention in housing during the Great Depression, it became codified through the guidelines of the Federal Housing Administration. Indeed, the agency's 1938 underwriting manual advised FHA inspectors who were assessing properties for mortgage insurance to do their job, as follows:

> Areas surrounding a location are investigated to determine whether incompatible racial and social groups are present, for the purpose

of making a prediction regarding the probability of the location being invaded by such groups. If a neighborhood is to retain stability, it is necessary that the properties shall continue to be occupied by the same social and racial classes. A change in social and racial occupancy generally contributes to instability and a decline in values.

(1938, Section 937).

While it took several decades for the FHA to change both its guidelines as well as its mode of operation, the legacy of housing discrimination and, indeed, various ongoing discriminatory practices, is still a grim fact of American life. Much more often than not, neighborhoods are characterized by occupancy by one racial group or another. Moreover, the activities and conscious decisions that have created these patterns are still widely practiced today.

Overdependence on debt and capital markets

Due to the intrinsic nature of housing (bulky, durable, tied to land) and the system of private ownership of almost all housing in this country, the housing sector is extraordinarily dependent on the cost and availability of borrowed money. Mortgage-lending institutions have thus been a dominant force in the housing sector for the past century. Their interests and evolution, including their periodic crises and consequent public policies, have had an enormous impact on the physical landscape of this country and on economic distribution and the stability of the overall economy. On the one hand, the mortgage system has facilitated the construction of vast amounts of housing and the spread of homeownership but has also widened housing inequality, fostered debt entrapment, destroyed neighborhoods and made the nation's economy increasingly unstable and vulnerable to the vagaries of global capital markets.

Flawed and inadequate public policies

Despite and perhaps because of these trends, in recent years, housing equity issues have receded from public and political concern. This has been accompanied by declines in government support for housing programs and subsidies

relative to the growing need for such support. As journalist Jason DeParle concluded in 1996 (and little has changed since), "The Federal Government has essentially conceded defeat in its decades-long drive to make housing affordable to low-income Americans.... Housing has simply evaporated as a political issue." Almost no office holder or candidate for office, at any level of government, gives prominent attention to housing. The Bush Administration's view was expressed in the astounding comment made by HUD Secretary Alphonso Jackson at a May 2004 hearing of the House Committee on Financial Services. In response to a question from one of the committee members, Secretary Jackson "stated that he doesn't talk about housing the poor because 'being poor is a state of mind, not a condition'" (Committee Members Decry HUD Secretary's Comments on the Poor 2004).

But a lack of federal interest in housing was not always the case. Although this interest often grew out of a desire to use housing as a vehicle to attack nonhousing problems (Marcuse 1986), for decades the federal government was a major player in promoting housing for low-income households. What was historically the principal approach – low-rent housing developments built and managed by local housing authorities, with heavy federal subsidies – has been under relentless attack since the 1960s. And the two-decade-long emphasis (from the early 1960s through the early 1980s) in producing subsidized housing through the private sector has also lost favor among federal officials. "Shallower" subsidies provided through the Low Income Housing Tax Credit (LIHTC) and the HOME Investment Partnership program have added some new units but address only a very small fraction of the overall needs for housing affordable to low-income households – they fail to reach far enough down the income distribution, and very few are permanently affordable.

Since its creation in 1986, the LIHTC has contributed to the production of about 1.8 million units but many of these units are not available to those with incomes below 30 percent of median income (National Low Income Housing Coalition 2005).[19] The HOME program has funded the acquisition, construction and rehabilitation of about 800,000 units of housing since its inception in 1990, but again, many of the residents are not the most needy, and most of the units are not permanently affordable (National Low Income Housing Coalition 2005).

Between 1977 and 1994, the number of HUD-assisted households grew by 2.4 million. But this number camouflages a troubling trend: During the period from 1977 to 1983, the annual average increase was 215,000 units; however, between 1984 and 1994, the average annual increase fell to 82,000. From 1995 to 1998, no new funds for assisted housing were provided by Congress. Finally, however, starting in 1999, there was again modest recognition of the need for additional housing assistance, with the appropriation of funds for 50,000 new vouchers in that year, followed by 60,000 and 79,000 in FY2000 and FY2001, respectively (Bratt 2003, based on Dolbeare and Crowley 2002). In FY2002 funding for 26,000 new vouchers was appropriated, but Congress approved no new vouchers in FY2003, FY2004, and FY2005 and HUD requested none for FY2006 (National Low Income Housing Coalition 2005).

It is no surprise that these dismal numbers concerning new households being assisted reflect reductions in the inflated-adjusted level of appropriations for new housing units. Between 1976 and 2004, net new annual federal budget authority for assisted housing dropped from $56.4 billion to $29.25 billion (in constant 2004 dollars)[20] (Dolbeare et al. 2004). In dramatic contrast, the largest form of federal housing aid – the indirect and highly regressive subsidy the tax system provides to homeowners via the homeowner deduction (the ability to deduct from one's taxable income base all property tax and virtually all mortgage interest payments) – was worth over $84 billion in 2004, with the majority of these subsidies going to households in the top two-fifths of the income distribution; nearly 37 percent of housing-related tax subsidies go to those earning over $86,000 (Dolbeare et al. 2004). Including investor deductions, in 2004 housing-related tax expenditures totaled $119.3 billion, four times the budget authority for housing assistance (Dolbeare et al. 2004). In so many ways, the nation's housing system reflects and undergirds the extreme and growing class and race divisions that characterize the society as a whole.

Our flawed public policies are also causing a net loss of subsidized units. Various sources estimate that since the late 1980s, some 200,000

units have been removed from the inventory of assisted housing. This has been due to the loss of over 100,000 units through demolition of some severely deteriorated subsidized housing and as a result of the HOPE VI public housing redevelopment program (National Housing Law Project et al. 2002), as well as the "expiring use" problem: There has been a loss of 60,000 units in some older subsidized housing developments where the owner has prepaid the mortgage and converted the buildings into market-rate dwellings, and a loss of about 40,000 units where owners have opted out of Section 8 contracts (Achtenberg 2002).

The result of all of this is a chronic insufficiency of subsidized low-rent units. A recent estimate of housing needs comes from the Millennial Housing Commission, whose final report stated that

> The addition of 150,000 units annually would make substantial progress toward meeting the housing needs of ELI [extremely low income; at or below 30 percent of area median income] households, but it would take annual production of more than 250,000 units for more than 20 years to close the gap (2002, 18).

One impact of these shortages is long waits for subsidized housing. Based on data collected between 1996 and 1998, HUD estimated that, nationally, the average wait for a public housing unit was 11 months, and for a Section 8 rental assistance voucher, it was 28 months. For the largest public housing authorities (those with over 30,000 units), the wait for a public housing unit was 33 months and 42 months for a Section 8 certificate. In New York City, the wait for either a public housing unit or a Section 8 voucher can be as much as eight years. Between 1998 and 1999, the number of families waiting for assistance increased substantially. The combined waiting list for a Section 8 voucher in 18 cities sampled grew from just under 500,000 to 660,000 households. The 40 waiting lists from those cities examined in the HUD study included about 1 million families. And HUD cautions that these figures may be an underestimate because many housing authorities have closed their waiting lists due to their overwhelming size (HUD 1999, 7–10).

The failings of our housing policies are, in part, due to the government's desire to fulfill a number of economic, social and political goals, beyond the desire to provide housing for the poor. In addition, housing policies are always greatly influenced and shaped by the needs of the private for-profit housing industry – an industry that has a sophisticated and well-financed lobbying component and that has been successful in gaining federal support for their agenda. It is little wonder, therefore, that housing policies have fallen short of the goal of providing decent, affordable housing for those most in need. While [we assert] that our record of federal intervention in housing has been disappointing, regardless of the political party in power, it is acknowledged that somewhat more has been accomplished under Democratic than under Republican Administrations.

ORGANIZING FOR A RIGHT TO HOUSING

Achieving the ambitious vision and goals put forth [here] certainly will require a housing strategy and a movement well beyond what has been seen heretofore in this country. For the most part, housing organizing and activism in the United States have been modest and constrained in time, place and vision. Even in those periods where housing activism has reached a national scale and included aspects of a Right to Housing in its vision, the strategic approach has fallen far short (see Stone 1993, Bratt *et al.* 2006, Ch. 11, 12).

Past social movements have resulted in substantial expansions of basic rights far beyond what has been achieved with regard to housing. Emancipation, women's suffrage, the many gains of the labor movement, and the Civil Rights Movement particularly stand out. The women's movement, the gay and lesbian movement and the disability rights movement are also notable for what they have achieved, however imperfect and incomplete. Indeed, that these are all widely recognized as "movements" and referred to with the definite article "the" attests in some measure to their potency, in striking contrast with housing.

Any viable strategy to achieve a Right to Housing must emerge through a dynamic and participatory process that includes the following principles: understanding and confronting fundamental causes of housing problems; putting forth a vision of truly social housing provision; participating in alliances across issue lines; building organizations committed to leadership development and broadly inclusionary decision-making; generating independent funding for skilled organizers and organizing; and building alliances with trade unions.

***

It is beyond question that as a society we have the resources to provide housing for all that is decent, truly affordable and in supportive communities. What is required is an activist government that has social justice as a prime goal. As well, it requires that housing policy and programs become central concerns and activities beyond the narrow field of housing providers and housing advocates. What is needed is a social movement, in which housing justice becomes linked in an integral way with the many other struggles for justice, opportunity and democratic participation.

Of course, we recognize that in advocating a Right to Housing, there are a host of issues and concerns that need to be addressed and resolved. For example, how much housing, of what quality and in what locations should constitute each person's minimum "right"? Should a Right to Housing include universal design features that would make all units both accessible to people with physical infirmities, as well as to visitors who are physically challenged? What responsibilities should be borne by recipients, and how would those expectations be enforced?

Without diminishing the importance of such questions, we believe that the time is ripe to embark on a serious prior dialogue about the underlying rationale for a Right to Housing. More than 60 years after FDR asserted that the country needs a second Bill of Rights – one that includes a Right to Housing – it is time to make that promise come true.

[We] acknowledge that the realization of a Right to Housing may seem farther away than ever. The U.S. Treasury has been depleted by trillions of dollars in tax cuts and hundreds of billions of dollars for wars on Afghanistan and Iraq. In addition, with further hundreds of billions of dollars being diverted from the already-decimated domestic budget in the aftermath of the 2005 hurricanes in the Gulf Coast region, the expenditure of large sums of money to implement a bold new domestic social policy agenda may be off on a distant horizon.

We believe that the health of a society can be judged by the quality and affordability of its housing for the one-third of a nation least well-off. A society professing deep concern for human needs should not be so profoundly deficient in this area. At the start of a new century, the United States is still facing serious and deeply ingrained housing problems. Housing is so fundamental to human life and well-being that meaningful progress toward achieving a Right to Housing provides an excellent springboard for launching closely related social and economic reforms. The logic is sound. But the call to action has been muffled, and key political actors have, for the most part, been unswayed and missing in action. [We aim to change] the prevailing mind-set and stimulating innovative, aggressive and far-reaching responses to our persistent housing problems.

ACKNOWLEDGEMENT

This is the introduction to *A Right to Housing: Foundation for a New Social Agenda* edited by Rachel G. Bratt, Michael E. Stone and Chester Hartman (2006). All references to *A Right to Housing* in this piece refer to that book or to selections in that book.

Notes

1   The Quality Housing and Work Responsibility Act of 1998 amended the National Housing Goal. It is arguable as to whether the new language constitutes a major or a modest retreat from the original goal, which was to be realized "as soon as feasible." The 1998 Act states

> that the Federal Government cannot through its direct action alone provide for the housing of every American citizen, or even a majority of its citizens, but it is the responsibility of the Government to promote and protect the independent and collective actions of private citizens to develop housing and strengthen their own neighborhoods.

And further, "that the Federal Government should act where there is a serious need that private citizens or groups cannot or are not addressing responsibly" and

> that our Nation should promote the goal of providing decent and affordable housing for all citizens through the efforts and encouragement of Federal, State, and local governments, and by the independent and collective actions of private citizens, organizations, and the private sector.
>
> Title V, Section 505, Sec. 2 (2), (3) and (4), online, available at: www.gpo.gov/fdsys/pkg/ PLAW-105publ276/pdf/ PLAW-105publ276.pdf.

2   While we have never come close to fully implementing FDR's second Bill of Rights, recent proposed legislation suggests that a Right to Housing still has political muscle. The Bringing America Home Act (H.R. 2897), filed in 2003, would provide affordable housing, job training, civil rights protections, vouchers for child care and public transportation, emergency funds for families facing eviction, increased access to health care for all and Congressional support for incomes high enough so that families can support themselves. It would also provide the resources to enable local and state governments to end homelessness. Also introduced in 2003, the National Affordable Housing Trust Fund Act (H.R. 1102) would establish within the Treasury Department a fund to promote the development, rehabilitation and preservation of affordable and safe low-income housing through grants to states and local jurisdictions. The goal is to build and preserve 1.5 million units of rental housing for the lowest-income families over a ten-year period. Initial sources of revenue for the Trust Fund would come from excess Federal Housing Administration insurance reserves and from excess funds generated by the Government National Mortgage Association (Ginnie Mae), a government-sponsored enterprise created in 1968 to support subsidized mortgage lending.

3 The 69-page document, written by Dick Cluster, is available from Community Economics, Inc., jrubenzahl@ communityeconomics.org.

4 A recent study published in the *New England Journal of Medicine* suggests that "lead poisoning might impair children's intelligence at far lower levels than current federal health guidelines ... not only do small amounts of the toxic metal lower a child's intelligence, but each additional unit of lead has a more dramatic effect than at higher levels of exposure" (Avril 2003).

5 According to psychologist Abraham H. Maslow's hierarchy of human needs, the basic, "lowest" need that housing provides is shelter or protection. "Higher" level needs provided by housing include safety or security, a sense of belonging, self-esteem and self-fulfillment. "Lower needs" must be met before "higher needs" (discussed in Meeks 1980, 46–49).

6 Of course, it hardly needs mentioning that even worse than "grossly inadequate housing" is no housing or shelter at all – the most dire form of a housing problem.

7 Even in the case of lead poisoning, where lead-based paint can be found in people's homes, other sources of lead in the environment can pose health risks (such as lead in the soil, gasoline, old school buildings, water contaminated by old lead pipes). Thus, one can never be certain which contaminated source is producing the elevated lead levels that may be observed.

8 Empirical evidence underscores this point. In a longitudinal study of poor and homeless families in New York City, researchers found that

> regardless of social disorders, 80 percent of formerly homeless families who received subsidized housing stayed stably housed, i.e., lived in their own residence for the previous 12 months. In contrast, only 18 percent of the families who did not receive subsidized housing were stable at the end of the study
> (Shinn *et al.* 1998, as cited by National Coalition for the Homeless 1999)

9 There are huge differences in how housing ownership creates unearned wealth. Minority homeowners, who often live in areas with little value appreciation, are sometimes fortunate if they can sell their home for what they paid ten or twenty years earlier (Oliver and Shapiro 1995; Conley 1999; Shapiro 2004). White, middle-class homeowners frequently see their houses rise in value over the years by a factor of five, ten and even more, producing equity that can be drawn upon to provide comfortable retirement and numerous benefits to their offspring: higher education, a substantial inheritance and, most tellingly, financial aid so they can buy they own homes, thus perpetuating, intergenerationally, the widely disparate racial gaps that inhere in homeownership.

10 Defined as units with any one of several serious physical deficiencies, such as plumbing – lacking piped hot water or a flush toilet or lacking both bathtub and shower, for the exclusive use of the residents of the unit; heating, including major systems breakdowns or inadequacies; electrical – either completely lacking or major problems such as exposed wiring and lack of outlets. Other inadequacies that would place a unit in the "severely inadequate" category pertain to serious upkeep problems and significant physical defects in building hallways. A housing unit is termed "moderately inadequate" if it has none of the defects associated with a severely inadequate unit but has significant plumbing breakdowns; unvented heating units; fewer upkeep or hallway problems than in the "severely inadequate" category but still has significant deficits and if it lacks a kitchen sink, range or refrigerator for exclusive use of the residents of the unit (HUD 2000, A28–A29).

11 A moderate housing problem consists of a cost burden between 30 percent and 50 percent of income, occupancy of a unit with moderate physical problems, or overcrowding (more than one person per room); people who are homeless or who have been displaced are viewed as having a severe housing problem. Also included in the latter category are those with cost burdens above 50 percent of income, or occupancy of housing with serious physical problems (National Low Income Housing Coalition 2005).

12 This does not include homeowner households with less serious problems. More than ten million homeowner households earning 80 percent or less of area median income have nontrivial problems with their unit, ranging from open cracks in walls or ceilings, inadequate heat and heating units, and water leaks inside the house (Joint Center for Housing Studies 1998, 68).

13 According to the Joint Center for Housing Studies, adding those households with severe and moderate problems who live in assisted housing, the figure comes to some 3.7 million households (2003, 27).

14 A government report published over 30 years ago still has relevance today:

It is readily apparent that even the most conscientious user of Census data ... would arrive at a total "substandard" housing figure which grossly underestimated the number of dwelling units having serious housing code violations. To use a total thus arrived at as a figure for substandard housing is grossly inadequate and misleading, because it flies in the face of extensive consideration given by health experts, building officials, model code drafting organizations, and the local, state and federal court system to what have become over a period of many years, the socially, politically, and legally accepted minimum standard for housing of human beings in the United States.... Even if public and private efforts eliminate all housing which is substandard under most current federal definitions, there will still be millions of dwelling units below code standard
(Sutermeister 1969, 83, 102)

15 The term "affordable housing" is widely used and generally understood to imply affordable to households with limited income, but, as described more fully in Chapter 2 of Bratt, Hartman and Stone's *A Right to Housing,* we regard affordability not as an inherent characteristic of housing but as a relationship between housing cost and the income of the user household: A multimillion dollar mansion is affordable to a multi-millionaire, a $200 per month

apartment is not affordable to someone with monthly income of $300. Nonetheless, the term "affordable housing" appears throughout many of the book's chapters, given its prevalence in housing studies, popular writings, legislation, program titles and the like.

16 This is calculated as follows from National Low Income Housing Coalition (2001): (1) 87 percent (percent of renter households earning below 50 percent of area median income with severe housing problems) × 7.9 million (number of renter households with severe housing problems)=6.87 million renter households. (2) 46 percent (percent of renter households earning below 50 percent of area median income with moderate housing problems) × 9.3 million (number of renter households with moderate housing problems)=4.28 million renter households. (3) 70 percent (percent of owner households earning below 50 percent of area median income with severe housing problems) × 7.6 million (number of owner households with severe housing problems)=5.32 million owner households with severe housing problems. (4) 28 percent (percent of owner households earning below 50 percent of area median income with moderate housing problems) × 10.9 (number of owner households with moderate housing problems)=3.05 million households with moderate housing problems. Total (1)+(2)+(3)+(4)=19.52 million households earning less than 50 percent of area median income with moderate or severe housing problems.

17 This is calculated as follows from National Low Income Housing Coalition (2001): (1) 7 percent (percent of renter households earning between 50 to 80 percent of area median income with severe housing problems)x 7.9 million (number of renter households with severe housing problems) =0.55 million renter households. (2) 34 percent (percent of renter households earning between 50 to 80 percent of area median income with moderate housing problems) × 9.3 million (number of renter households with moderate housing problems)=3.16 million renter households. (3) 14 percent (percent of owner households earning between 50 to 80 percent of area median income with severe

housing problems) × 7.6 million (number of owner households with severe housing problems) = 1.06 million owner households with severe housing problems. (4) 25 percent (percent of owner households earning between 50 to 80 percent of area median income with moderate housing problems) × 10.9 (number of owner households with moderate housing problems) = 2.73 million households with moderate housing problems. Total (1) + (2) + (3) + (4) = 7.5 million households earning between 50 to 80 percent of area median income with moderate or severe housing problems.

18 Stone (1993) has calculated that, utilizing conservative estimates of costs for nonshelter basics (such as food, clothing, transportation), a staggering 14 million U.S. households (almost three times the number with worst case housing needs) cannot afford to spend a single cent for housing if they are to have enough income to cover these other basic living costs. Among the 45 major metropolitan areas analyzed in a Center on Budget and Policy Priorities study, the percentage of poor renters paying more than 30 percent of their income for housing – HUD's payment standard for families living in subsidized housing – ranged from a low of 65 percent to a high of 92 percent; all but five locales fell in the 70 to 90 percent range; using the 50 percent of income yardstick, the range was from a low of 39 percent to a high of 81 percent; all but 11 locales fell in the 50 to 70 percent range. (Note that in this study the author uses a definition of "poor" pegged to the official poverty line as opposed to HUD's definitions of income, which are in relation to area medians. In 1995, the poverty line for a family of three was $12,158 [Daskal 1998:Table A-1].) By 2003, the poverty line for a family of three had risen to $15,260.

19 The program requires that either 20 percent or more of the units in a given development be occupied by individuals whose income is below 50 percent of the area median income, or at least 40 percent of the units must be occupied by individuals below 60 percent of the area median income (National Low Income Housing Coalition 2005).

20 Another important measure of the level of federal assistance for housing is total dollar outlays. These are payments to maintain and operate the total subsidized housing inventory. This figure has grown significantly since 1976, as the total stock of assisted housing grew during much of this period. However, between 2000 and 2007, assisted housing outlays are projected to drop by nearly $1 billion (Dolbeare *et al.* 2004).

REFERENCES

Achtenberg, Emily P. 2002. *Stemming the Tide: A Handbook on Preserving Subsidized Multifamily Housing.* Washington, D.C.: Local Initiatives Support Corporation.

Avril, Tom. 2003. Study sees increased lead-paint risk. *Boston Sunday Globe*, April 20.

Bernstein, Nina. 1999. Asthma is found in 38% of children in city shelters. *New York Times*, May 5.

Bratt, Rachel G. 2003. Housing for very low-income households: The record of President Clinton, 1993–2000. *Housing Studies*, 18(4): 607–35.

Bratt, Rachel G., Michael E. Stone and Chester Hartman (eds.). 2006. *A Right to Housing: Foundation for a New Social Agenda.* Philadelphia, PA: Temple University Press.

Committee Members Decry HUD Secretary's Comments on the Poor. 2004. Press release from Rep. Barney Frank (Dem. MA), Ranking Democratic Member, May 24.

Conley, Dalton. 1999. *Being Black, Living in the Red: Race, Wealth, and Social Policy in America.* Berkeley/Los Angeles, CA: University of California Press.

Daskal, Jennifer. 1998. *In Search of Shelter: The Growing Shortage of Affordable Rental Housing.* Washington, D.C.: Center on Budget and Policy Priorities.

DeParle, Jason. 1996. Slamming the door. *New York Times Magazine*, October 20.

Dolbeare, Cushing N., and Sheila Crowley. 2002. *Changing Priorities: The Federal Budget and Housing Assistance, 1976–2007.* Washington, D.C.: National Low Income Housing Coalition.

Dolbeare, Cushing N., Irene Basloe Saraf and Sheila Crowley. 2004. *Changing Priorities: The Federal Budget and Housing Assistance, 1976–2005.* Washington, D.C.: National Low Income Housing Coalition.

England-Joseph, Judy A. 1994. Federally assisted housing: Condition of some properties receiving Section 8 project-based assistance is below housing quality standards. Testimony before the Employment, Housing and Aviation Subcommittee, Committee on Government Operations, House of Representatives. Washington, D.C.: U.S. General Accounting Office, GAO/T-RCED-94-273.

Evans, Gary W., Hoi-Yan Erica Chan, Nancy M. Wells and Heidi Saltzman. 2000. Housing quality and mental health. *Journal of Consulting and Clinical Psychology*, 68 (3): 526–30.

Federal Housing Administration. 1938. *Underwriting and Valuation Procedures under Title II of the National Housing Act.* Washington, D.C.: FHA.

Finkel, Meryl, Donna DeMarco, Deborah Morse, Sandra Nolden and Karen Rich. 1999. *Status of HUD-Insured (or -Held) Multifamily Rental Housing in 1995.* Prepared for U.S. Department of Housing and Urban Development by Abt Associates. Contract HC-5964. Washington, D.C.: U.S. Department of Housing and Urban Development.

Friedman, Lawrence M. 1968. *Government and Slum Housing.* Chicago, IL: Rand McNally & Co.

Greenhouse, Steven. 1998. As Economy Booms, Migrant Workers' Housing Worsens. *New York Times,* May 31.

Grunwald, Michael. 1999. Housing crunch worsens for poor. *Washington Post,* October 12.

Hayden, Dolores. 1984. *Redesigning the American Dream: The Future of Housing, Work, and Family Life.* New York: W.W. Norton & Co.

HUD (United States Department of Housing and Urban Development). 1999. *Waiting in Vain: An Update on America's Rental Housing Crisis.* Washington, D.C.: USDHUD.

HUD (United States Department of Housing and Urban Development). 2000. *Rental Housing Assistance – The worsening crisis. A Report to Congress on Worst Case Housing Needs.* Washington, D.C.: USDHUD.

HUD (United States Department of Housing and Urban Development). 2003. *A Report on Worst Case Needs for Housing, 1978–1999: A Report to Congress on Worst Case Housing Needs. Plus Update on Worst Case Housing Needs in 2001.* Washington, D.C.: USDHUD.

Husock, Howard. 2003. *America's Trillion-Dollar Housing Mistake: The Failure of American Housing Policy.* Chicago, IL: Ivan R. Dee.

Hynes, H. Patricia, Doug Brugge, Julie Watts and Jody Lally. 2000. Public health and the physical environment in Boston public housing: A community-based survey and action agenda. *Planning Practice and Research,* 15(1–2): 31–49.

Joint Center for Housing Studies. 1998. *A Decade of Miracles: 1988–1998. Christmas in April Tenth-Year Anniversary Report and 1998 Housing Study.* Cambridge, MA: Harvard University.

Joint Center for Housing Studies. 2003. *The State of the Nation's Housing, 2003.* Cambridge, MA: Harvard University.

Joint Center for Housing Studies. 2005. *The State of the Nation's Housing, 2005.* Cambridge, MA: Harvard University.

Kozol, Jonathan. 1988. *Rachel and Her Children.* New York: Fawcett Columbine.

Lambert, Bruce. 1996. Raid on illegal housing shows the plight of suburbs' working poor. *New York Times,* December 7.

Leonard, Paul A., Cushing N. Dolbeare and Barry Zigas. 1993. *Children and Their Housing Needs.* Washington, D.C.: Center on Budget and Policy Priorities.

Loewen, James W. 2005. *Sundown Towns: A Hidden Dimension of American Racism.* New York: The New Press.

Marcuse, Peter. 1986. Housing policy and the myth of the benevolent state. In *Critical Perspectives on Housing,* eds. Rachel G. Bratt, Chester Hartman and Ann Meyerson. Philadelphia, PA: Temple University Press. pp. 248–258.

Meeks, Carol B. 1980. *Housing.* Englewood Cliffs, NJ: Prentice Hall, Inc.

Millennial Housing Commission. 2002. *Meeting Our Nation's Housing Challenges.* Washington, D.C.: MHC.

National Coalition for the Homeless. 1999. Homeless families with children. *NCH Fact Sheet #7*.

National Commission on Severely Distressed Public Housing. 1992. *The Final Report. A Report to the Congress and the Secretary of Housing and Urban Development*. Washington, D.C.: NCSDPH.

National Housing Law Project, Poverty and Race Research Action Council, Sherwood Research Associates, Everywhere and Now Public Housing Residents Organizing Nationally Together. 2002. *False Hope: A Critical Assessment of the HOPE VI Public Housing Redevelopment Program*. Oakland, CA: The Project.

National Housing Task Force. 1988. *A Decent Place to Live*. Washington, D.C.: NHTF.

National Low Income Housing Coalition. 2001. *Low Income Housing Profile*. Washington, D.C.. NLIHC.

National Low Income Housing Coalition. 2005. *2005 Advocates' Guide to Housing and Community Ddevelopment Policy*. Washington, D.C.: NLIHC.

NCCED (National Congress for Community Economic Development). 1999. *Coming of Age: Trends and Achievements of Community-Based Development Organizations*. Washington, DC.

Oliver, Melvin L., and Thomas M. Shapiro. 1995. *Black Wealth/White Wealth: A New Perspective on Racial Inequality*. New York: Routledge.

Pérez-Peña, Richard. 2003. Study finds asthma in 25% of children in Central Harlem. *New York Times*, April 19.

Rakoff, Robert M. 1977. Ideology in everyday life: The meaning of the house. *Politics and Society*, 7(1):85–104.

Retsinas, Nicolas P., and Eric S. Belsky, eds. 2002. *Low-Income Homeownership: Examining the Unexamined Goal*. Washington, D.C.: The Brookings Institution.

Roosevelt, Franklin Delano. 1944. Unless there is security here at home, there cannot be lasting peace in the world. Message to the Congress on the State of the Union. January 11. In *The Public Papers and Addresses of Franklin D. Roosevelt, 1944–45. Victory and the Threshold of Peace*, ed. Samuel I. Rosenman. 1950. New York: Harper and Brothers.

Salins, Peter. 1980. *The Ecology of Housing Destruction: Economic Effects of Public Intervention in the Housing Market*. New York: Center for Economic Policy Studies.

Sandel, Megan, Joshua Sharfstein and Randy Shaw. 1999. *There's No Place Like Home: How America's Housing Crisis Threatens Our Children*. San Francisco, CA: Housing America and Boston, MA: Doc4Kids Project.

Schorr, Alvin L. 1966. *Slums and Social Insecurity*. Prepared for the U.S. Department of Health, Education and Welfare. Research Report No. 1. Washington, D.C.: U.S. Government Printing Office.

Scientific American. 1999. The invisible epidemic. November, 19–20.

Shapiro, Thomas M. 2004. *The Hidden Cost of Being African American: How Wealth Perpetuates Inequality*. New York: Oxford University Press.

Shinn, Marybeth, Beth C. Weitzman, Daniela Stojanovic, James R. Knickman, Lucila Jimenez, Lisa Duchon, Susan James and David H. Krantz. 1998. Predictors of homelessness among families in New York City: From shelter request to housing stability. *American Journal of Public Health*, 88, 1651–7.

Stone, Michael E. 1993. *Shelter Poverty: New Ideas on Housing Affordability*. Philadelphia, PA: Temple University Press.

Stone, Michael E. 2006. Housing affordability, one third of a nation shelter poor. In *A Right to Housing: Foundation for a New Social Agenda*. Rachel G. Bratt, Michael E. Stone and Chester Hartman (eds.). Philadelphia, PA: Temple University Press.

Sutermeister, Oscar. 1969. Inadequacies and inconsistencies in the definition of substandard housing. In *Housing Code Standards: Three Critical Studies*, Research Report No. 19, Washington, D.C.: National Commission on Urban Problems.

The Urban Institute. 1995. *Federal Funds, Local Choices: An Evaluation of the Community Development Block Grant Program, Vol. 1*. Prepared for the U.S. Department of Housing and Urban Development. Washington, D.C. HUD-PDR-1538(I).

Uchitelle, Louis. 1999. More wealth, more stately mansions. *New York Times*, June 6.

U.S. General Accounting Office. 1993. *Lead-Based Paint Poisoning: Children Not Fully Protected When Federal Agencies Sell Homes to Public*. GAO/RCED-93-38.

U.S. General Accounting Office. 1995. *Welfare Programs: Opportunities To Consolidate and Increase Program Efficiencies*. GAO/HEHS-95-139.

Vidal, Avis C. 1992. *Rebuilding Communities: A National Study of Urban Community Development Corporations*. New York: Community Development Research Center, New School for Social Research.

Wolff, Craig. 1994. Immigrants to life underground: New York illegal roomers live one rung above homeless. *New York Times*, March 13.

Wood, Edith Elmer. 1934. A century of the housing problem. Originally printed as part of a symposium, "Low cost housing and slum clearance," *Law and Contemporary Problems,* Vol. 1. Reprinted in *Urban Housing*, eds. William L.C. Wheaton, Grace Milgram and Margy Ellin Meyerson. 1966. New York: The Free Press, pp. 1–8.

PART TWO

Competing definitions of housing problems

Plate 2 Abandoned house in Detroit, Michigan (photograph by Kevin Bauman –
www.100abandonedhouses.com).

INTRODUCTION TO PART TWO

Over the course of the past century, the motivations for housing policy have swung widely, reflecting tensions between the social and economic roles of housing. Such motivations, along with assumptions about the proper role of government and of the private sector in solving problems are also revealed in the metrics we use to describe problems and make the case for action. Descriptions of "slum conditions," "congestion," and "blight" were used to motivate public regulation and action at various points during the first half of the twentieth century. In the latter part of the century, as housing conditions improved and controversy swirled around place-based strategies, focus has shifted to the affordability of housing.

Affordability problems are most commonly measured by the number or share of households spending above 30 percent of their gross monthly household income on housing costs. Such households are described as "cost burdened." As of 2009, 19.4 million households paid more than half their incomes for housing, of these, 10.1 million were renters. While low-income households are most likely to have such severe burdens, the impact of the current recession is seen in the jump in households earning between $45,000 and $60,000 paying more than 30 percent of their incomes for housing – up 7.9 percentage points since 2001. While the increase was more modest for households earning less than $15,000, close to 80 percent of this group was already housing-cost burdened in 2001 (Joint Center for Housing Studies 2011). A more severe measure of cost burden is the number of households paying more than half of their gross monthly income for housing costs – or having a "severe cost burden." Between 2001 and 2009, the number of such households with "worst case housing needs" has risen by almost 42 percent, representing more than 6 percent of all households in 2009. Such needs are defined as either a severe cost burden or residence in substandard housing. Since only 3 percent of worst case needs were attributable to housing conditions alone, this measure can be largely interpreted to indicate severe affordability problems. Worst case housing needs are heavily concentrated among very low-income renter households: 41 percent of the 17.1 million low income renters had worst case needs in 2009 (Steffen *et al.* 2011).

While affordability has become the dominant frame for describing housing problems, the conceptual and empirical bases for affordability measures as indicators of housing needs are widely challenged. J. David Hulchinski looks to nineteenth century studies of household budgets for the origins of the use of the housing expenditure-to-income ratio. He finds no conceptual basis for using this descriptive ratio to assess ability to pay for housing:

> To define everyone spending more than 30 per cent of income on housing as having a housing problem, for example, takes a descriptive statistical statement (the 30 per cent ratio) and dresses it up as an interpretative measure of housing need (or lack of need).

In fact, HUD's periodic reports on "worst case housing needs" as well as several recent reports on the housing crisis focus instead on those paying more than 50 percent of income (an "extreme cost burden"). Setting the bar higher is more likely to focus attention on the problems of those pushed into crisis by rising housing costs. Wherever the bar is set, however, the cut-off is conceptually arbitrary. Hulchinski argues that we ought avoid completely the use of the term housing affordability since "it does not help bring structure and organisation to our observations."

Others have attempted to create measures that contextualize housing costs and emphasize the meaning of high costs to a family's ability to meet its basic needs. Michael E. Stone's residual income approach takes into account differences in the budgets of households of different size and composition. Large households paying substantial amounts for childcare, for example, cannot pay the same share of monthly income for housing as a household without such needs. Stone's estimates of housing needs in the U.S. since the 1970s reveal a different incidence of "shelter poverty," with a similar share of household income spent on housing yielding higher rates for large households than for small ones. In the 1990s, basic needs budgets were developed by national and local organizations seeking to highlight the amount of income needed to meet basic needs, including housing, taking into account both household size and regional living costs. In addition, the National Low Income Housing Coalition began calculating the hourly "housing wage" needed to rent a home in metropolitan areas around the country.

Despite its flaws, the cost burden measure underlies analysis of gaps in local housing markets between what households at various income levels can afford to pay and the number of units renting for rates affordable to them. Persistent gaps were noted for the lowest income renters in the 1990s, leading to debates over appropriate responses: Were gaps the result of underproduction or were empty units just overpriced? Should households be helped to afford existing units (through vouchers) or should funds be dedicated to production of units? Should the income targeting of programs be changed to better match need? This debate raised a more fundamental question: are affordability problems primarily due to inadequate incomes or to rising housing costs?

While the relationship between declining incomes and housing costs is often noted (see Tilly 2006; Quigley and Raphael 2004), scholars draw different conclusions as to the implications for policy. Glaeser and Gyourko argue that the income side of the affordability gap is properly the domain of anti-poverty policy. They argue that housing policy ought to focus on factors that limit housing production or result in production mismatched to needs. In particular, they emphasize the ways that government regulation of land use and zoning constrain production and that rising housing standards limit lower cost options, consistent with conservative economic arguments about minimizing "interference" in markets. Yet this focus also resonates with fair housing advocates seeking to remove barriers to development of multifamily and rental housing in affluent suburbs. Reducing regulatory barriers to production of affordable housing became a major focus at HUD during the Clinton administration – and continues to this day. (For further discussion of the relationship between land use regulation and housing problems, see Part 6).

New measures attempt to provide more sophisticated assessments of the burden or benefit associated with particular locations. As concern over the environmental impacts of urban development has grown, proposals for more compact and transit-friendly forms of development have come to dominate city planning discussions. Transit advocates, led by the Center for Neighborhood Technology in Chicago and the Center for Transit Oriented Development in California, devised a new measure of affordability that sought to marry housing and transportation costs, much as early planners did in England when devising strategies to decongest London in the late nineteenth century. Their Housing + Transportation index, released in 2010, calculates the joint cost of housing and transportation for households, making clear the high cost of commuting long distances for low income households. Co-location of housing and transit, and joint transportation and housing planning are central themes of the U.S. Department of Housing and Urban Development's new Office of Housing and Sustainable Communities. Yet, as pointed out by Tegeler in his exchange with CNT's Scott Bernstein, this measure may bring its own unintended consequences. In particular, Tegeler fears that it may encourage concentration of affordable housing in low income, minority areas.

In this context, fair housing advocates are proposing new metrics that place current discussions regarding the siting of affordable housing in the context of historic patterns of segregation and exclusion from opportunity. Through a series of lawsuits, advocates have fought for redress of the injuries produced by segregation of public housing through remedies and changes in housing policies that value access to opportunity. In his testimony in Thompson v. HUD, a case brought on behalf of 15,000 families who lived in public housing that was confined to the poorest, most segregated neighborhoods in the Baltimore region, john a. powell argues that legal remedies for segregation must be judged in terms of their ability to provide access to "communities of opportunity." Such places are proximate to various features thought critical to socio-economic mobility including schools, healthy food, parks and open space as well as employment centers. Powell, as director of Ohio University's Kirwan Center, has been a leader in the creation of metrics of access to opportunity. High opportunity areas are identified by mapping the overlap between various spatial measures of opportunity. States and local governments are building in attention to neighborhood context in rules for allocating federal tax credits and through local ordinances.

Current debate around housing goals and metrics seeks to broaden the discussion, shifting away from a focus on cost burdens to more complex measures that capture interrelationships between housing, quality of life and chances for upward mobility experienced by low income residents. These discussions bring us back to underlying motivations for policy: is the purpose of policy to counter the effects of rising income inequality, to address problems in local housing markets, to ensure that the housing rights of minority citizens are upheld, to prevent environmentally damaging sprawl, or some combination of these issues? What problem should we be measuring?

IN THIS PART:

Chapter 7: Hulchanski, J. David. (1995). "The concept of housing affordability: Six contemporary uses of the housing expenditure-to-income ratio." *Housing Studies*, 10(4): 471–491.

Chapter 8: Michael E. Stone. (2006). "What is housing affordability? The case for a residual income approach." *Housing Policy Debate*, 17(1): 151–184.

Chapter 9: Edward L. Glaeser and Joseph Gyuorko. (2008). "How do we know when housing is 'affordable'?" in E.L. Glaeser and J. Gyourko. *Rethinking Federal Housing Policy*. Washington, D.C.: American Enterprise Institute for Public Policy Research.

Chapter 10: Philip Tegeler and Scott Bernstein. (2011). "Counterpoint: The 'housing + transportation' index and fair housing" *Shelterforce (Spring)*.

Chapter 11: john a. powell. (2005). "Remedial phase expert report of john powell in Thompson v. HUD August 19, 2005."

REFERENCES AND FURTHER READING

Burchell, Robert, and David Listokin. (1995). "Influences on US housing policy," *Housing Policy Debate*, 6, 3.

Joint Center for Housing Studies of Harvard University. (2011). *State of the Nation's Housing*. Cambridge, MA: Harvard University.

Lipman, Barbara J. (2006). *A Heavy Load: The Combined Housing and Transportation Burdens of Working Families*. Washington, D.C.: The Center for Housing Policy, October.

McClure, Kirk. (2005). "Deciphering the need in housing markets: A technique to identify appropriate housing policies at the local level." *Journal of Planning Education and Research*, 24(4): 361–378.

Myers, Dowell, and Lonnie Vidaurri. (1996). "Real demographics of housing demand in the United States," *The Lusk Review for Real Estate Development and Urban Transformation* 2, 1: 55–61.

Nelson, Kathryn P. (1994). "Whose shortage of affordable housing? *Housing Policy Debate,* 5, 4: 401–442.

Nelson, Kathryn, and Jill Khadduri. (1992). "To whom should limited housing resources ne directed?" *Housing Policy Debate* 3, 1.

powell, john a. (2002–2003). "Opportunity-based housing." *Journal of Affordable Housing and Community Development Law*, 12, 188.

Quigley, John M., and Steven Raphael. (2004). "Is housing unaffordable? Why isn't it more affordable?" *Journal of Economic Perspectives*, 18(1): 191–214.

Steffen, Barry L., Keith Fudge, Marge Martin, Maria Teresa Souza, David A. Vandenbroucke and Yung G. D. Yao. (2011). *Worst Case Housing Needs 2009: A Report to Congress.* Washington, D.C.: U.S. Department of Housing and Urban Development.

Tilly, Chris. (2006). "The economic environment of housing: Income inequality and insecurity." In Rachel G. Bratt, Michael E. Stone and Chester Hartman, eds. *A Right to Housing: Foundation for a New Social Agenda.* Philadelphia, PA: Temple University Press.

7

"The concept of housing affordability: six contemporary uses of the housing expenditure-to-income ratio"

From *Housing Studies* (1995)

J. David Hulchanski[1]

It must be confessed that the attempt to reduce family needs to a classified budget is a denial of the manifold varieties of human nature ... The idiosyncrasies, vanities, pleasures, and generosities that make life worth living cannot be accounted for in scientific budgets and economic formulae. But even this cold examination of minimum family needs has shown the many variable factors that must enter into household plans; it is clear that simple generalisations and rules-of-thumb for calculating a family's capacity to pay for housing may be quite misleading.

(Humphrey Carver, 1948, p. 86)

In recent years 'housing affordability' has become a common way of summarising the nature of the housing difficulty in many nations. This is in contrast to the 'slum problem', the 'low-rent housing problem', the 'housing shortage' or the 'housing need' definitions of previous decades. A household is said to have a housing affordability problem, in most formulations of the term, when it pays more than a certain percentage of its income to obtain adequate and appropriate housing.

The 'affordability' aspect of this formulation of the housing problem has its roots in 19th century studies of household budgets and in the commonly used turn-of-the-century expression 'one week's pay for one month's rent'. During this century a housing expenditure-to-income ratio began to be used by mortgage lenders and, in recent decades, as part of the selection criteria by private sector landlords in North America (Feins and White, 1977; Gilderbloom, 1985; Lane, 1977). Through the decades the housing expenditure-to-income 'rule of thumb' deemed to be an appropriate indicator of ability to pay gradually shifted upward. In Canada, for example, a 20 per cent rule lasted until the 1950s when somehow a 25 per cent rule came into use, only to be replaced in the 1980s by a 30 per cent 'rule of thumb' (Bacher, 1993; Hulchanski, 1994b). Related to this practical assumption about an 'appropriate' relationship between housing expenditure and income is the work of economists who in the 1950s began to ask questions about the relationship between housing consumption and household income in order to attempt to specify housing demand elasticities for their models (for example, Grebler *et al.*, 1956; Maisel and Winnick, 1966; Reid, 1962; Stigler, 1954; Winnick, 1955; Winger, 1968). During the 1980s the often undefined term 'housing affordability' has come into widespread popular usage in North America and Western Europe with a growing body of literature which, for the most part, finds the term problematic (Bramley, 1994; Hallett, 1993; Hancock, 1993; Kearns, 1992; Linneman and Megbolugbe, 1992; Stone 1990; Whitehead, 1991).

This paper focuses on the following questions. What is the origin of the use of a housing expenditure-to-income ratio? What, if any, are the theoretical and empirical foundations upon which the percentage of income 'rules of thumb' are based? The aim is to determine how valid and reliable the housing expenditure-to-income ratio is as a measure of ability to pay for housing. That is, does such a 'rule' actually measure what its users claim it is measuring?

Based on a review of this history, and on an extensive review of the contemporary housing literature which explicitly uses housing expenditure-to-income ratios, six distinct uses are identified and assessed. The assessment is based on the extent to which each is a valid and reliable measure of what it purports to measure. The six uses are: (1) description; (2) analysis; (3) administration of subsidies; (4) definition of housing need; (5) prediction of the ability to pay; and (6) selection criteria.

The research method used in this paper is historical – the identification of the origins and evolution of the use of housing expenditure 'rules of thumb'. It is also based on content analysis – an examination of how key reports, studies, government documents and the academic housing literature have used and continue to use housing expenditure-to-income ratios. The criteria for assessing the six uses are based on the extent to which they are valid and reliable measures. Validity and reliability are tests of the trustworthiness of the measurement instruments used in research (see for example: Babbie, 1992; Blalock, 1979; Carmines and Zeller, 1979). Validity is a test of the extent to which a measuring instrument adequately and accurately reflects the meaning of the concepts employed. Is the relationship being asserted, for example, what it appears to be – is there an actual direct link between the two things? Or is there error in measurement? Reliability is a test of the consistency of a measure in yielding similar results in repeated trials.

THE SEARCH FOR 'SCIENTIFIC LAWS' OF HOUSEHOLD EXPENDITURE PATTERNS

The intellectual context for the study of household budgets has its roots in the search by the founders of modern social science for 'scientific laws' of social and economic life. The view of the social world as one governed by transcendent religious laws was abandoned for the ideal of an objective knowledge of social and economic phenomena gained through the discovery and study of the 'laws' that regulate human behaviour. The emerging social sciences used the theoretical reasoning and research methods of the natural sciences, on the assumption that the social world could be objectively known in the same way as the natural world could be known. The task was to infer from observation of social activity laws of motion for society similar to those of physics, chemistry and astronomy. It was assumed that if natural scientists could discover the laws of nature so as to control and harness natural phenomena, then social scientists should be able to discover the laws governing social behaviour so as to control and regulate aspects of society. The aim was to develop 'a quantitatively based science that might guide any government in improving the material well-being of its subjects' (Olson, 1993, p. 193). Indeed, the urban social unrest in the early industrialising and urbanising nations of Europe helped give special status to those who sought such laws (Kendall, 1968; Landau and Lazarsfeld, 1968; Lazarsfeld, 1961).

Contemporary housing literature rarely situates itself in this broader historic and intellectual context. The way in which social and economic 'science' evolved affects some fundamental assumptions upon which current housing analysis is based. The source of a number of key assumptions found in contemporary housing theory and practice can be traced to past researchers and their approaches. In the case of the origins of the housing expenditure-to-income 'rules of thumb', the credit is generally attributed to both Ernst Engel and Herman Schwabe, two prominent 19th century German statisticians who formulated the early and widely known 'laws' about the relationship between income and categories of household expenditures (Allen and Bowley, 1935; Feins and Lane, 1981; Feins and White, 1977; Lane, 1977; Reid, 1962; Stigler, 1954; Zimmerman, 1936).

In his study of the use of the housing affordability 'rules of thumb', for example, Lane (1977, pp. 5–6) stated that Ernst Engel 'proposed an 'economic law' which included the proposition that the percentage of income that households spend for lodging and fuel is invariably the same what ever the income'. In contrast Herman Schwabe 'suggested that, as total family income rises, the amount allocated to housing increases at a lower rate'. Lane implied that even though Engel was wrong and

Schwabe was right, the contemporary use of the 25 or 30 per cent 'rule of thumb' defining affordability is closer to Engel's position. To add to the confusion, Margaret Reid, in her 1962 book Housing and Income, a work quoted by many contemporary neo-classical economists who write about the elasticity of housing demand, found 'very substantial evidence' for the 'rejection of the Schwabe law on rent', even though, Reid noted, the Schwabe law 'has long been accepted and many predictions and policies have been formulated with such expectation'. To further add to the confusion over which law was the law, economist George Stigler noted that Engel eventually recognised, based on further empirical evidence, that his earlier formulation of the housing part of his (Engel's) law was indeed wrong (Stigler, 1954, p. 99).

Ernst Engel's 1857 survey of Belgian working-class families was one of the best known statistical analyses of budgets for many decades and the first to draw empirical generalisations from budget data (Allen and Bowley, 1935; Houthakker, 1957; Prais and Houthakker, 1955; Stigler, 1954). On the basis of this study, and the work of Frederic Le Play (1806–82) who published his monumental study of the budgets of working-class families in 1855 (Les ouvriers européens, see Pitts, 1968), Engel proposed his law of consumption: 'The poorer a family, the greater the proportion of total expenditure that must be devoted to the provision of food' (Stigler, 1954). Although his 1857 study was focused on food and the population problem, Engel's law is more general, including all major expenditure categories. The more general law attributed to Engel states that as income increases, the proportions of expenditures on different budget items change and the proportions devoted to the more urgent needs (such as food) decrease while those devoted to luxuries and semi-luxuries increase (Allen and Bowley, 1935, p. 7). In 1868, it was Schwabe who published the first detailed research on the housing part of the household budget, proposing a law related explicitly to housing. In his study of wage and rent data he found that for each income group the percentage of income spent on rent declined as income rose. His law stated: 'The poorer anyone is, the greater the amount relative to his income that he must spend for housing' (Stigler, 1954, p. 100).

After Schwabe published his housing law the subject of housing expenditure patterns became the focus of much debate among analysts of household budgets. The conceptual, theoretical and practical problems were never satisfactorily resolved. What should be included in 'housing' costs: cash rent, some or all utilities, maintenance, furnishings? What is meant by 'income': gross or net, one or all adults' income, children's income if any? What about sharp temporary fluctuations in income and non-cash sources of goods and services which would otherwise have required expenditure of cash income? What about income from roomers, if any? In addition to the primitive nature of the statistical methods, there was little if any standardisation in definitions. As a result, numerous other laws of consumption related to housing flourished from a growing number of academics and government officials based on each of their own particular definitions and analyses of additional sets of budget data. By the mid-1930s Zimmerman was able to identify thirty-six different laws or theories about the relationship of household expenditure and specific budget categories, many related to housing with eight specifically focused on housing (Zimmerman, 1936, pp. 52–53).

The problem with the work of Engel and that of his followers is that the relatively valid relationships identified and the predictions made were peculiar to the food portion of the household budget. In retrospect, we can see that the identification of certain relationships was easy with regard to food, but very difficult in the case of more complex budget categories. Attempts to demonstrate similar laws for other categories of expenditure, especially for housing, therefore, met with much less success. This was due to the inadequacies of the available data and the yet underdeveloped statistical techniques and theoretical assumptions being used. Furthermore housing presented, as it indeed continues to present, numerous conceptual and practical difficulties.

It is fair to conclude, as Stigler did in his 1954 review of this 19th century 'scientific' work, that little of this early research constituted a solid contribution to either theoretical or empirical understanding of consumer behaviour. Rather, this history of attempts to study household consumption is largely a comedy of errors, all kinds of errors – conceptual, theoretical, empirical and methodological. Zimmerman referred to all of this as 'fog which shrouds theories of the relation between rent and the standard of living'. There was, he wrote sarcastically, 'a series of so-called budgetary laws of rent such as the one by Schwabe, the rent law erroneously attributed to Engel, the revised rent law developed by the critics of the spurious law of Engel, and the several other alternative theories ...' (1936, p. 180). By the 1930s the attempt to define 'laws' of housing consumption had run out of steam. Zimmerman's 1936 text on household consumption was one of the last major works to dwell on this approach (Zimmerman, 1936, p. 197).

At the level of day-to-day practice in the housing sector, however, these housing 'laws' and similar sorts of conjectures entered popular usage in yet further distilled and simplified forms. The major practical housing use emerged as the adage 'one week's wage for one month's rent'. By the 1880s a week's wage for a month's rent was a widely used way of describing the housing expenses of many tenants in the US. Kengott's 1912 study of the budgets of workers in Lowell, Massachusetts found, for example, that they usually set aside 20 to 25 per cent for rent, light and fuel (Kengott, 1912, pp. 128–129, 136). Kengott also noted that housing studies in a number of cities in the late 19th century found that the rents consumed 'at least twenty per cent of the earnings of the husband in the family' (Kengott, 1912, p. 57; see also Buder, 1967). This late 19th century adage about 'one week's wage ...' is similar to the late 20th century adage about 25 or 30 per cent of income representing the upper limit of housing affordability. Both are based on not much more than grossly generalised assumptions about the amount that average households tend to or ought to pay for housing (the distinction is rarely made clear) without ever specifying which households are being averaged or how the normative 'ought' statement was derived. What had occurred over the decades was the translation of observations about what some households were spending into assumptions about what they 'ought' to be spending. The summary of all these observations and assumptions then took the easy-to-use format of a ratio of housing expenditure-to-income, which was increasingly referred to in the housing industry as the 'rule of thumb' about the ability of households to pay for housing. As such it also became a 'rule of thumb' about how to minimise risk in renting an apartment or granting a mortgage to a particular household.

SIX CONTEMPORARY USES OF THE HOUSING EXPENDITURE-TO-INCOME 'RULE OF THUMB'

It is far too simple to state that the housing expenditure-to-income ratio is either valid or invalid, useful or not useful, or that it is being used appropriately or inappropriately. Instead, we must ask, in what way is it being used? What is it supposed to be measuring? Does it do so in a valid and reliable manner? In the post-war (mainly North American) housing literature it is possible to find the ratio being used in six distinct ways: (1) description of household expenditures; (2) analysis of trends and comparison of different household types; (3) administration of public housing by defining eligibility criteria and subsidy levels in rent geared-to-income housing; (4) definition of housing need for public policy purposes; (5) prediction of the ability of a household to pay the rent or mortgage; and (6) as part of the selection criteria in the decision to rent or provide a mortgage. Much of the contemporary practical or applied use of the housing expenditure-to-income ratio in the US and Canada relates to defining the ability to pay for housing. This typology helps in the process of distinguishing between valid and invalid, appropriate and inappropriate uses of housing expenditure-to-income ratios. It can also provide an improved vocabulary for those who use the term 'housing affordability'.

The list in Figure 7.1 can be divided into two categories. The first three uses – description, analysis and administration – can be considered quite valid and helpful when used properly by housing researchers and administrators. 'Used properly' means that the research methods and the statistical analysis techniques are properly carried out, i.e. no significant methodological errors are made. This leads to valid and reliable descriptive and analytic statements about the housing expenditures of the different types of households being studied. This type of description and analysis of household expenditure patterns can also be helpful in defining administrative rules about eligibility for means-tested housing programmes.

DESCRIPTION	Describe a typical household's housing expenditure
ANALYSIS	Analyse trends, compare different household types
ADMINISTRATION	Administer rules defining who can access housing subsidies
DEFINITION	Define housing need for public policy purposes
PREDICTION	Predict ability of a household to pay the rent or mortgage
SELECTION	Select households for a rental unit or mortgage

Figure 7.1 The housing expenditure-to-income ratio: six uses of the per cent of income 'rule of thumb'.

The improper and inappropriate use of housing expenditure-to-income ratios, leading to invalid and unreliable results, is due to a variety of theoretical and conceptual errors. Uses four, five and six – definition, prediction, and selection – are all invalid uses for they fail to measure what they claim to be measuring, even if the research methods and the statistical analysis techniques are properly carried out. The ratio is faulty when used to define housing need and to predict the ability of households to pay for housing due in part to a faulty conceptualisation of the income part of the ratio. In addition, it applies a statistical average of a group of households to an individual household, leading to the problem of statistical discrimination (Aigner and Cain, 1977; Galster, 1992; Hulchanski, 1994a; Sunstein, 1991; Thurow, 1975). Each of the six uses is examined below.

(1) Description of household expenditures

Data on housing expenditure-to-income ratios can be useful in describing what different households are spending at selected points in time. Table 7.1, for example, provides 1991 Census data on the percent of income households in Ontario, Canada's largest most urbanised province, pay for housing, making a distinction between home owners without mortgages, home owners with mortgages, and renters. Further details are also provided for different types of renter households. What do these ratios tell us?

There can be no objection to using any ratio of any relationship in an attempt to better describe some aspect of social reality. The problem is the next step, how should this information be interpreted? The subjective part of even the descriptive use of information starts with the very decision about what questions or relationships are to be examined and what data at what level of detail is to be used. Why use ratios? Why not use other types of comparisons? It simply depends on what questions are being asked by the person who compiles certain data in a certain fashion, leaving out other related data. The numbers do not speak for themselves. They are used to demonstrate certain points and contribute to a certain interpretation of what is being examined. What does data about ratios between household income and housing expenditure tell us? Table 7.1, for example, demonstrates that there are different ratios for different household types, something we might have suspected in the first place. Table 7.1 further provides information about the range of differences between the identified household types. This is about it. No claim about 'laws', or 'rules of thumb' or affordability patterns or ability to pay for housing are being made, nor can they be made without adding a great deal more information, analysis and theory, leading to some interpretative statements.

(2) Analysis of trends

Rent-to-income ratios can be used to test hypotheses and to carry out comparative research. In a recent study, for example, Smith (1990) used 'regular housing outlays as a proportion of regular income' to examine the relative position in the housing system of different types of households based on the gender, race and other characteristics of the household head. The concept of 'housing outlays' measures the financial stress incurred

A	B F	C G	D H	E I
Less than 20%	88	38	39	45
	28	35	53	38
20–24.9%	5	18	16	15
	17	16	16	17
25–29.9%	3	14	12	10
	15	13	10	12
30–39.9%	2	14	12	11
	14	13	10	12
40–49.9%	1	6	7	5
	9	7	4	6
50% and over	2	10	15	13
	18	17	8	15
	100	100	100	100
	100	100	100	100
Average income	$58 894	$66 393	$34 971	$39 569
	$21 592	$30 434	$46 535	$39 722
Number of households	1 100 900	1 156 475	1 298 620	626 225
	483 565	958 090	310 850	565 555
30% or more	5%	30%	33%	29%
	40%	37%	22%	33%

Table 7.1 Percentage of household income spent on housing in Ontario. Owners and renters, 1991 Census

Legend for Chart:
A – 1: Percentage of 1990 Household income
B – 2: Owners: Owners without a mortgage %
C – 3: Owners: Owners with mortgages %
D – 4: All renters %
E – 5: Family renter household %

F – 6: Renters: One person renter households %
G – 7: Renters: One income earner in household %
H – 8: Two income earners in households %
I – 9: Renters in Toronto CMA %

Source: Statistics Canada, Housing Costs and Other Characteristics of Canadian Households, Cat 93–330, May 1993.

by individuals in paying rents, rates and mortgage costs (capital and interest components) in order to sustain a position in the housing system. (It is then, a measure of liquidity rather than of assets.) This measure also gives an indication of what portion of people's current disposable income remains for other household expenditures after mandatory housing costs (costs that are inescapable in the short run) have been met (Smith, 1990, p. 77).

Use of housing expenditure-to-income ratios in this fashion does not attempt to identify or make subjective claims about affordability problems. A concept was developed and defined (housing outlays) in order to ask questions about different socio-economic groups. The housing expenditure-to-income ratios were used by Smith to help measure the relative position in the housing system of different groups of households. This adds to our knowledge and understanding about an aspect of current social reality – by isolating certain broad characteristics such as the gender of the head of the household and identifying how these households compared with other households. Smith concluded, for example, that:

In short, as renters, men seem more successful than women in minimising the proportion of income spent on housing, while as home buyers they [men] are more able to allot relatively higher proportions of their income to potentially lucrative housing investments.

(Smith, 1990, p. 85)

This is a comparison among categories of household types, not a sweeping claim about affordability or ability to pay.

This second use of the housing expenditure-to-income ratio takes the descriptive use one step further by using the ratios to help develop concepts and test hypotheses. In Smith's case, the ratio is used as a measure of 'housing outlay' and housing outlay is a measure of the 'financial stress' on groups of households. Data, in the form of housing expenditure-to-income ratios, is gathered to test out hypotheses related to these concepts. There is no simple use of a percentage of income 'rule of thumb'.

Another recent example is the study of US home ownership affordability trends by Gyourko and Linneman (1993). They ask: 'Is a home of a given quality from, say, 15 years ago more affordable or less affordable today to a household similarly situated to the one that occupied the home then?' (Gyourko and Linneman, 1993, p. 40). In this case the price of a specified type of house (holding structural quality and neighbourhood characteristics constant) and the income of specified household types (real household income and occupational wage data) is compared over time to an initial starting date (1960 in this case). There are no sweeping assertions or conclusions about housing affordability in the abstract. There is no mention of a certain ratio of house cost-to-income as being appropriate or affordable. A research question about change over time is asked and answered.

The point here is simply that housing expenditure-to-income ratios can be used in a valid and reliable fashion to test hypotheses and improve our understanding of certain societal trends and dynamics. The ratios, however, do not speak for themselves. The researcher's theoretical and conceptual framework results in certain data being assembled in a certain fashion to identify relationships, interpret them, and draw conclusions.

(3) Administration of public sector housing subsidies

Most countries have some share of the housing stock in the non-market sector. The range in North America and Western Europe is quite broad – from about 5 per cent in the US and Canada to about 40 per cent in the Netherlands (Boelhouwer and van der Heijden, 1992; Dreier and Hulchanski, 1994). These are housing units in projects financed by various government programmes, known generally as public, social or non-profit housing. When housing units are not allocated on a market basis, and when the programme is not universal (that is, not available to everyone equally), regulations define eligibility. The regulations used in many countries include a formula that uses a housing expenditure-to-income ratio.

The income ratio is often but one part of a complex set of administrative regulations assessing eligibility and determining rent levels for subsidised housing. Used in this way the ratio has the effect of keeping out higher income households. It helps serve as a rationing device to target housing subsidy dollars. Administrators in the public sector have to draw a line related to eligibility for programmes which are not universal. Any variety of quantitative and qualitative measures may be employed. The decision as to where to draw the line, that is, what specific definition of eligibility is to be used for a subsidy programme, is a subjective judgement. It cannot be based on an objective scientific determination. Science can inform the debate over the judgement call being made, but it cannot answer normative questions – questions about values and beliefs. What is fair? How do we define 'the poor' or 'the needy'? Science cannot, for example, define the 'poverty line' for a nation. In democratic societies debate over various ways of measuring and defining poverty takes place and then, through elected representatives, a choice is made. 'At some point', as Weale (1983, p. 115) points out, 'the political argument has to stop and the voting begin.' Even then, the debate continues because of the highly subjective value-laden nature of the judgement. Research can help inform this debate and improve our understanding of the issue, as outlined above, by describing and analysing trends.

The administrative use of housing expenditure-to-income ratios in public sector social housing programmes can be confused with the use of the ratios in the private sector (for example uses five and six, prediction of ability to pay and selection of tenants, discussed below). It is, therefore, important to make the distinction between the use of housing expenditure-to-income ratios as maximum income criteria (the public sector usage) and minimum income criteria (the private sector usage). The public sector uses a maximum income measure as a cut-off point to exclude higher income households from non-universal subsidised housing units, while some private sector landlords use a minimum income measure as a cut-off point to exclude lower income households from access to their rental units. The public sector's use is appropriate because the intent is to ration public subsidy dollars by excluding higher income households. The ratio is a valid means of identifying higher income households. The private sector's use is not valid because the intent is to measure (predict) ability to pay rent and then to select tenants based on the assumption that the ratio is a valid part of the criteria used.

In the public and non-profit sectors maximum income criteria are used in the process of defining eligibility for rent geared-to-income housing subsidies, often referred to as 'RGI subsidies'. The aim is to exclude higher income households so as to target lower income households for a particular type of housing subsidy. Even the term, 'rent geared-to-income' makes it clear that income criteria are being applied. They are being used in two ways: to exclude households above a certain income level and to define the amount of subsidy eligible households will receive.

The use of maximum income criteria as part of the process of defining eligibility and subsidy levels for government programmes has a long and relatively undisputed history. Debate takes place over specific cut-off points used in defining eligibility and subsidy levels. For example, in the debate over shifting from the use of 20 to 25 per cent of income in the eligibility and rent setting formula for Canada's public housing, one major federal government sponsored review of public housing programmes argued in favour of using 20 per cent (Dennis and Fish, 1972). It did so on justice and equity considerations, noting that any figure 'will be somewhat arbitrary'.

For purposes of this analysis, the assumption was made that expenditures exceeding 20 per cent of income are excessive for low income households. Any figure chosen will be somewhat arbitrary (Dennis and Fish, 1972, p. 58).

The authors based their equity argument on the fact that the average expenditure on housing for all Canadians in 1969 was 17 per cent, with the top two income quintiles paying 14 per cent.

In the mid-1980s a similar public policy debate took place. The Conservative government, as part of a review of all major government spending programmes, announced that it was shifting the income ratio portion of the eligibility and rent setting formula for housing subsidies from 25 to 30 per cent.

The study team recommends the [introduction of] ... a new federal rent scale graduated from 25 per cent to 30 per cent of total household income, taking into account household size and income level. This scale would be applied to all income-tested households. ... It should be phased in over a three-year period in order to minimise financial hardship on tenants.

(Canada, Task Force on Program Review, 1985, p. 36)

This change was recommended, according to the report, 'in order to reduce subsidies or improve targeting' (Canada, Task Force on Program Review, 1985, p. 36). It was a subjective decision based on certain values and norms about the role of government and about appropriate levels of subsidies. Others with different values objected to the change. One researcher from the Metropolitan Toronto Social Planning Council, for example, said the change in the formula, which reduced subsidies by about $76 million, 'would be putting an additional tax on the poor'. Many others objected to the change, all with similar justice and equity arguments – not with claims that there was something scientific about the 25 per cent ratio (York, 1986).

Debate over which housing expenditure-to-income ratio to use is similar to the public debate over the poverty line. The definition of the dividing line, those included and those excluded, dramatically affects the number of households considered eligible. In 1988, for example, there were 630 000 Canadian households paying between 25 and 30 per cent of their income on housing. If the federal government chose to continue to use the 25 per cent ratio rather than switch to 30 per cent, these 630 000 households would be included resulting in a 50 per cent increase in the number of households considered eligible for social housing assistance (Van Dyk, 1993, p. 36). This demonstrates the arbitrary nature of the public policy choice involved. One choice includes more than half a million households, another choice excludes them. The Canadian federal government, in moving from 25 to 30 per cent, offered no research or scientific justification for the switch in ratios – nor could they offer any.

Maximum income criteria as part of the criteria in means tested programmes, therefore, is a distinctly different use of the housing expenditure-to-income ratio than the other five uses outlined here. There is a long history of using the housing expenditure-to-income ratios in the administrative set of regulations determining eligibility for subsidised housing as well as setting rent levels for the units. There is no claim that the ratio of housing expenditure-to-income used in the formula was selected on the basis of careful scientific study, nor that it is a valid and reliable measure of anything. It is merely used to ration a scarce resource from the point of view of the public interest. This is, however, quite a distinct use from that of defining housing need in general. The administrative use of housing expenditure-to-income ratios should not be confused with the difficult problem of defining housing need.

(4) Definition of housing need

It is common to find the housing expenditure-to-income ratio being used as a 'rule of thumb' for defining housing need for policy and programme purposes, often referred to as 'the housing affordability problem'. This fourth use of the ratio is based on a much too simplistic generalisation about household expenditures and cannot be accepted as valid. To define everyone spending more than 30 per cent of income on housing as having a housing problem, for example, takes a descriptive statistical statement (the 30 per cent ratio) and dresses it up as an interpretative measure of housing need (or lack of need). It does so on the basis of a subjective assertion of what constitutes an 'affordable' housing expenditure for all households. This kind of generalisation is based on an assumption about the cash income required to pay for the other necessities of life.

The selection of a ratio of housing expenditure-to-income has, nonetheless, become a popular and commonly used statement about the nature and scope of the 'housing affordability problem'. Its nature relates to a lack of income, usually assumed to be gross household cash income from employment or transfer payments, and its scope is the number of households paying more than that ratio. For Ontario, as Table 7.1 indicates, 830 000 households, 23 per cent of the 3.56 million households in the province, were paying 30 per cent or more on housing in 1991. Renters and home owners with mortgages comprised most of these households which, some claim, have a 'housing affordability' problem. If they all have a problem, it is a problem of huge proportions: 430 000 renter households, 33 per cent of all renters; 345 000 owner households with mortgages, 30 per cent of all owners with mortgages; and 55 000 owners without mortgages, 5 per cent of this group of owners.

This use of the housing expenditure-to-income ratio is not a valid and reliable method of defining housing need or housing problems. Even without considering the limited definition of income used in the ratio, the sweeping generalisation that spending more than a certain percentage of income on housing means the household has a 'housing problem' is simply not logical. It does not represent the behaviour of real households. Housing researchers recognise that household consumption patterns are extremely diverse and complex. Donnison (1967), for example, referred to the assertion that a certain proportion of income should be devoted to housing as 'a popular but ineptly posed conundrum for which some correspondingly inept solutions have been proposed' and that for individual households 'any reckoning based on the income of the household or its principal earner is likely to be misleading' (Donnison, 1967, pp. 255–256). In his study of housing affordability Marks (1984) identifies and discusses the following weaknesses of the rent-to-income ratio 'as a measure of affordability': it is essentially arbitrary; it does not account for household size, which has a bearing on the choice of an appropriate ratio; it fails to reflect changes in relative prices in all categories of household expenditures; it is not easily adjusted for the amount of housing services being consumed and the substitutions available to the household; and it relies on current rather than permanent income and is subject to seasonal and cyclical sensitivity (Marks, 1984, pp. 25–26). In his research on defining housing measures Stone (1990) notes that the ratio definition of housing need fails to 'grapple in a logically sound way' with the wide variation in what households can actually afford to pay.

Any attempt to reduce affordability of housing to a single percentage of income – no matter how low or high – simply does not correspond to the reality of fundamental and obvious differences among households. Even attempts to establish a few prototypical groups and have somewhat different percentages for each, or set up narrow ranges in order to recognise some differences, fail to grapple in a logically sound way with the range of variation in what households really can afford to pay (Stone, 1990, pp. 50–51).

Households can and do pay a great deal or very little for housing, whatever their income level, as any data on housing expenditure-to-income ratios demonstrate. A definition of housing need based on the ratio is simply not a valid measure. It fails to account for the diversity in household types, stages in the life cycle of the maintainer(s) of each household, the great diversity in household consumption patterns, and the problem of defining income – the focus on only cash income.

(5) Prediction of a household's ability to pay the rent or mortgage

Just as government must define housing need for policy and programme purposes private sector housing and mortgage lending entrepreneurs must minimise risk in the decisions they make. Mortgage lenders and landlords want to do business with households able and willing to pay their monthly rent or mortgage. Willingness is very difficult to assess. Is the use of a housing expenditure-to-income ratio a valid and reliable measure of ability to pay?

The fundamental practical problem with the private sector's use of the housing expenditure-to-income ratio is the definition of 'income' it relies upon. What is household 'income'? What is meant by 'income' in minimum income criteria? The ratio fails to be a valid measure of housing affordability because it relies on the easiest to measure income, money income. It ignores other sources of support, both cash and non-cash, by which households meet their needs. It is the money income, the cash resources which are easiest to measure and, as a result, the easiest to use as a convenient 'rule of thumb' to measure ability to pay. This convenient measure, however, goes much too far in simplifying reality to the point that it does not reflect the reality of most households. The use of the very narrow definition of income as cash income from the formal market economy leads by definition to discrimination against households with limited cash income resources from the formal market economy, such as the unemployed, the underemployed and those in low-paid jobs. It favours those who have a great deal of cash income from this source.

Housing choice is a response to an extremely complex set of economic, social, and psychological impulses. 'Given the variety of circumstances facing different households', Baer writes in his study of housing indicators, 'rules of thumb about the percent of income to be devoted to housing can be extremely misleading in individual cases and therefore in aggregate data as well.' He adds that 'a maximum rent-income ratio for one kind of household may not be appropriate for another, and that imposing the same standard for all households is unrealistic' (Baer, 1976, pp. 383–384). The pattern of household expenditures on housing is far too diverse to be explained by simple principles or averaged statistics about household budgets. There are so many diverse ways in which households meet their basic needs that it is not possible to apply one general rule, or even a set of a couple of related rules, to all households.

Theory and empirical evidence both point to the fact that households meet their basic needs through a variety of methods. As Hulchanski and Michalski (1994) point out, there are five economic spheres by which households can obtain resources (cash and non-cash) for meeting their needs. These are: (1) the domestic economy, internal to the household; (2) the informal economy, the extended family and close acquaintances; (3) the social economy, neighbourhood and community-based groups and agencies; (4) the market economy, the formal marketplace; and (5) the state economy, government. This typology is drawn from the vast body of theory and empirical evidence which indicates that households survive and even thrive in a complex intermingling of different economic spheres with their attendant webs of social relationships. When households find themselves in temporary situations of financial duress, most have other options for substituting certain types of self-provisioning and non-cash exchanges. Indeed, the one general proposition that seems to emerge from the many studies of sources of social and economic support may be stated as follows: households rely upon an extensive network of socio-economic relations to ensure that their basic needs are met, including but not limited to, market earnings (wages, interest, investments, etc.) and government transfer payments (Hulchanski and Michalski, 1994).

In short, the inadequacy in the definition of income used in the housing expenditure-to-income ratio is itself enough to invalidate the use of minimum income criteria as a measure for predicting the ability to pay. The ratio is not a valid and reliable indicator of what it claims to measure. There is no evidence to support its use as a measure of ability to pay for housing. There is a great deal of evidence to the contrary, evidence that many households are paying more than the prescribed ratio. The reality of how households manage to meet their needs, including the need to have the cash to pay their rent, is too complex and diverse to be summarised in one simple measure.

(6) Selection criteria

Minimum income criteria are being used as a key part in the decision for selecting tenants and granting mortgages in North America. This means that many landlords consider the housing expenditure-to-income ratio to be a valid and reliable measure of ability to pay (use no. 5). The use of minimum income criteria in the housing market, unlike the use of maximum income criteria by the public sector, is subject to a great deal of controversy – even to the extent of serious claims that it is a discriminatory practice. In 1992, for example, the Ontario Human Rights Commission estimated that active complaints related to discrimination in

housing represent about 8 per cent of the Commission's total caseload. Many of the housing complaints are connected to the use of minimum income criteria by private sector landlords in evaluating prospective tenants. Many Ontario landlords use household income as part of the criteria in selecting tenants.

When asked 'are there income requirements for your units', nineteen (70 per cent) reported that there are, six reported that there are not any (22 per cent), and two did not respond. Of the nineteen corporations which do have income requirements, fourteen answered the follow-up question: 'What is the rent-to-income ratio that you require?' All but two are between 25 per cent and 33 per cent. The other two are 35 per cent and 40 per cent. Both the mean (the average) and the median rent to income ratio is 31 per cent. (Hulchanski and Weir, 1992, p. 2)

The Ontario Human Rights Commission, in a discussion paper released prior to the establishment of a tribunal to hear the discrimination complaints, stated the following about the use of minimum income criteria:

> To date, landlords have not demonstrated that the use of a minimum income criteria was bona fide or reasonable, and that landlords would suffer undue hardship to refrain from this policy. In order for the continued use of minimum income criteria, it will be necessary for housing providers to demonstrate the rule is bona fide and reasonable ...
> (Ontario Human Rights Commission, 1992, p. 1)

In contrast to this use of housing expenditure-to-income ratios as minimum income criteria, the aim of public sector housing regulations which use maximum income criteria is to assist disadvantaged households by imposing a means-test to determine eligibility. As pointed out above, maximum income cut-offs effectively achieve the exclusion of higher income households. No harm results from excluding these households. In fact, to the extent that their taxes are paying for the means-tested housing subsidies, the aim is to help better target the subsidy dollars. In effect, this helps higher income households by using tax dollars more efficiently. The public sector's eligibility criteria, it should be noted, is based on a variety of discriminatory criteria. Households are separated into eligible and non-eligible groups by many rules and regulations. Income criteria, based on a housing expenditure-to-income ratio, provides but one of the measures.

Where is the evidence to support the use of a housing expenditure-to-income ratio in the selection of tenants so as to decrease the risk of default? After noting that 'there is a relatively low correlation between income and the amount that families spend for shelter' and that 'families at the same income level spend widely varying amounts for housing', Lane (1977) points out that there is 'limited evidence to support this practice' and that even though 'lenders and rental agents use the rule of thumb to identify prospective borrowers and tenants who might not meet their monthly payments', there are many other reasons why people, no matter what their income level, may default on their rent or mortgage payment. 'Defaults and foreclosures', Lane points out, 'are most often associated with unstable incomes or occupations and unexpected family crises such as unemployment, exceptional medical bills or divorce' (Lane, 1977, pp. iv-v).

The use of the rule of thumb is, at present, justified primarily by tradition. What constitutes a 'normal' allocation of income for shelter is not well understood, and even less is known about the maximum housing expenditure a family can make without jeopardising its ability to purchase other necessities (Lane, 1977, p. v).

The conclusion reached by Lane was that 'the rule [of thumb] is both inaccurate and inappropriately used' (Lane, 1977, p. iv). Lane's work was carried out as part of a larger US government sponsored research project related to the use of ability to pay 'rule of thumb' ratios (Burke et al., 1981; Feins and White, 1977; Feins and Lane, 1981; Lane, 1977). There is no reason to challenge these findings. There is no body of research even raising potential problems with the findings of the research by Lane, Feins and White.

The use by entrepreneurs of a minimum income test on potential customers in a marketplace for one of the basic human necessities is quite rightly controversial. It is controversial because it relates to whether it is an acceptable practice for the private use of an arbitrarily selected 'rule of thumb' to be the basis for making distinctions between groups of people. Individual households are not being assessed on the basis of individual characteristics but on their group characteristic – as part of a

very large group with the aggregate characteristic of having a lower than average level of cash income. This is using the category lower than average household income as a negative stereotype. All it effectively achieves is the identification of lower income households. Table 7.2 provides 1992 data on the distribution of housing expenditure-to-income ratios in Ontario on the basis of income quintile. Very few (4.2 per cent) of the middle income quintile pay over 30 per cent of income on rent. No households in the two highest income quintiles pay over 30 per cent. A vast majority of the lowest income quintile (66.4 per cent) and a significant proportion of the second lowest income quintile (21.8 per cent) pay more than 30 per cent of household income on housing. As might be expected, on average, the higher the income, the lower the housing expenditure-to-income ratio. Any statistical measure that is used to deny access to housing which is based on an expenditure-to-income ratio is simply discriminating against households with a lower than average income. By definition these households must pay a higher percentage of income on housing because their incomes are low and there is no such thing as good quality cheap housing. The ratio does not measure the ability to pay rent. It simply identifies lower than average income households who must spend a greater percentage of their income (cash resources) on housing than do above average income households.

All households make choices as to how to allocate not only their cash income but also their total household resources, of which cash from the market is but one important part (Hulchanski and Michalski, 1994). In the case of the application of minimum income criteria in the decision to rent, however, an authority outside the household is imposing its determination of what it considers to be an 'appropriate' budget allocation of the cash income of a particular household. Households with higher than average cash incomes can, of course, easily meet the minimum income criteria (as Tables 7.1 and 7.2 demonstrate for Ontario's households). The 'rule of thumb' measure is not being applied to them. Households with higher than average incomes are, by definition, automatically exempt from that potential constraint on exercising their freedom of choice in the marketplace. These households are also exempt from the potential

A	B / H	C / I	D / J	E / K	F / L	G
Lowest quintile	11.6	12.8	9.3	19.5	14.2	11.0
	5.9	15.8	35.7	66.4	32.7	
2nd quintile	32.1	25.2	29.7	17.4	3.4	0.7
	0.3	25.4	21.8	1.0	–	
Middle quintile	69.2	18.6	8.1	4.2	–	–
	–	–	19.8	4.2	–	
4th quintile	88.4	8.3	3.3	–	–	–
	–	11.8	–	–		
Highest quintile	100.0	–	–	–	–	–
	–	–	7.4	–	–	
Ontario average	43.8	15.6	10.6	12.2	5.9	4.1
	2.2	5.6	100.0	30.0	11.9	

Table 7.2 Housing expenditure-to-income ratios by income quintile. All Ontario households, 1992

Legend for chart:
A – Quintile
B – Under 20%
C – 20 to 24.9%
D – 25 to 29.9%
E – 20 to 39.9%
F – 40 to 49.9%
G – 50 to 59.9%
H – 60 to 69.9%
I – 70% or more
J – Quintile average %
K – % over 30%
L – % over 50%

Source: Statistics Canada, Household Income, Facilities and Equipment Survey, Microdata File, 1992.

constraint on their freedom of choice in deciding for themselves what is an appropriate household budget allocation of their cash resources. Households who fail to meet the minimum income criteria are automatically denied the ability to exercise their freedom of choice in the marketplace and their freedom of choice in allocating the cash portion of their total household resources.

CONCLUSION

Contemporary housing literature rarely situates itself in a broader historic context. The way in which social and economic 'science' evolved affects some of the fundamental assumptions upon which housing analysis today is based. The source of a number of key assumptions found in contemporary housing theory and practice can be traced to past researchers and their approaches. The definition of housing affordability using a 'rule of thumb' ratio of housing expenditure-to-income is one such assumption.

The two parts of this paper cover the 19th century origins and the contemporary implications of the use of the housing expenditure-to-income ratio. The first part answered the questions: What is the origin of the use of a housing expenditure-to-income ratio? What, if any, are the theoretical and empirical foundations upon which the percentage of income 'rules of thumb' are based? The history of attempts to study household consumption demonstrates that it is a history of conceptual, theoretical, empirical and methodological errors.

Yet these housing 'laws' and similar sorts of conjectures entered popular usage in the late 19th and early 20th centuries in even further distilled and simplified forms. What had occurred over the decades was the translation of this casual observation of what some households were spending into assumptions about what they are able to pay and what they ought to be paying. The summary of all these observations and assumptions then took the easy-to-use format of a ratio of housing expenditures-to-income, which was increasingly referred to as the 'rule of thumb' about the ability of households to pay for housing. A 'rule of thumb' is, by definition, not based on science. It is a 'method or procedure derived entirely from practice or experience, without any basis in scientific knowledge' (Oxford English Dictionary, 2nd edn., vol. XIV, p. 232). Since the history of the attempts to define a housing expenditure-to-income ratio as a valid 'law' or 'rule' about household consumption is a history of failure, referring to it as a measure 'without any basis in scientific knowledge' is very appropriate. The 'rule of thumb' does not measure what its users claim it is measuring, whatever the percentage selected.

The ratio can be useful as a valid and reliable quantitative indicator in housing research and analysis (nos. 1 and 2) depending on the nature of the research questions being asked and the methods being used. The housing expenditure-to-income ratio is a misleading and invalid indicator of either housing need or the ability to pay for housing (nos. 4, 5 and 6). Use no. 3, administration of public housing by defining eligibility criteria and subsidy levels in rent geared-to-income housing can make no claim to anything other than being a value-based policy decision – a subjective judgement call made in allocating means-tested subsidies.

Why did the specific ratio used by government and by the private sector shift upward from 20 to 25 per cent and then to 30 per cent over the course of this century (in nos. 3 to 6)? The use of 25 per cent and then 30 per cent in Canada over the past few decades seems to be associated with public sector decisions relating to subsidised housing eligibility and rent levels. Yet this is not a satisfactory, answer because it begs the question of why the public sector shifted the ratio it uses from 25 to 30 per cent. The only possible answer to the question lies in the absolute lack of validity any ratio has as a universal measure or indicator of housing need and ability to pay. No ratio as a generalisable statement about affordability makes any empirical sense. Any ratio used is, therefore, simply arbitrary. All an arbitrary measure requires is for many people to uncritically agree

to use it and not another measure. A scientific measure, however, must pass the tests of validity and reliability and does not depend upon the values or beliefs of individuals (i.e. it is not based on a popularity contest).

There is simply no escaping the fact that household consumption patterns and the means by which households meet their needs are as diverse as the individual humans and their life situations who comprise these households. Since a concept helps 'impose an intellectual organisation upon our observations' and helps 'express our understanding of what is happening' (Harre, 1985, p. 28), housing researchers need to avoid using the term 'housing affordability'. It does not help bring structure and organisation to our observations.

Notes

1   The author wishes to thank Joe Michalski, Melanie Rock and Mari Wilson for research assistance. This paper is based on research carried out for the Ontario Human Rights Commission. An earlier version was presented at the 1994 housing conference sponsored by the European Network for Housing Research.

REFERENCES

Aigner, D.J. and Cain, G.G. (1977) Statistical theories of discrimination in labor markets, Industrial and Labor Relations Review, 30(2), pp. 175–187.

Allen, R.G.D. and Bowley, A.D. (1935) Family Expenditure: A Study of its Variation (London, P.S. King and Son).

Babbie, E. (1992) The Practice of Social Research (Belmont, CA, Wadsworth).

Bacher, J.C. (1993) Keeping to the Marketplace: The Evolution of Canadian Housing Policy (Montreal, McGill-Queen's University Press).

Baer, W.C. (1976) The evolution of housing indicators and housing standards: Some lessons for the future, Public Policy, 24(3), pp. 361–393.

Blalock, H.M., Jr. (1979) Measurement and conceptualization problems: The major obstacle to integrating theory and research,

American Sociological Review, 44, pp. 881–894.

Boelhouwer, P. and van der Heijden, H. (1992) Housing Systems in Europe: Part I, A Comparative Study of Housing Policy (Delft, Delft University Press).

Bramley, G. (1994) An affordability crisis in British housing: dimensions, causes and policy impact, Housing Studies, 9(1), pp. 103–124.

Buder, S. (1967) Pullman: An Experiment in Industrial Order and Community Planning, 1880–1930 (NY, Oxford University Press).

Burke, P., Casey, C. and Doepner, G. (1981) Housing Affordability Problems and Housing Need in Canada and the United States: A Comparative Study (Washington and Ottawa, a joint HUD/CMHC paper).

Canada, Task Force on Program Review (1985) Housing Programs in Search of Balance: A Study Team Report to the Task Force on Program Review (Ottawa, Supply and Services Canada).

Carmines, E.G. and Zeller, R.A. (1979) Reliability and Validity Assessment (Beverly Hills, CA, Sage).

Carver, H. (1948) Houses for Canadians (Toronto, University of Toronto Press).

Dennis, M. and Fish, S. (1972) Programs in Search of a Policy: Low Income Housing in Canada (Toronto, Hakkert).

Donnison, D.V. (1967) The Government of Housing (Penguin Books).

Dreier, P. and Hulchanski, J.D. (1994) The role of non-profit housing in Canada and the United States: some comparisons, Housing Policy Debate, 4(1), pp. 43–80.

Feins, J.D. and Terry S. Lane, T.S. (1981) How Much for Housing? New Perspectives on Affordability and Risk (Cambridge, MA, Abt Books).

Feins, J.D. and C. S. White, Jr. (1977) The Ratio of Shelter Expenditures to Income: Definitional Issues, Typical Patterns and Historical Trends (Cambridge; MA, Abt Associates).

Galster, G.C. (1992) Research on discrimination in housing and mortgage markets: Assessment and future directions, Housing Policy Debate, 3(2), pp. 639–683.

Gilderbloom, J.I. (1985) Social factors affecting landlords in the determination of rent, Urban Life, 14(2), pp. 155–179.

Grebler, L., Blank, D.M. and Winnick, L. (1956) Capital Formation in Residential Real Estate (Princeton).

Gyourko, J. and Linneman, P. (1993) The Affordability of the American dream: an examination of the last 30 years, Journal of Housing Research, 4(1), pp. 39–72.

Hallett, G. (Ed.) (1993) The New Housing Shortage: Housing Affordability in Europe and the USA (London, Routledge).

Hancock, K.E. (1993) 'Can pay? Won't pay?' or economic principles of 'affordability', Urban Studies, 30(1), pp. 127–145.

Harre, R. (1985) The Philosophies of Science (Oxford, Oxford University Press).

Houthakker, H.S. (1957) An international comparison of household expenditure patterns, commemorating the centenary of Engel's law, Econometrica, 25(4), pp. 532–551.

Hulchanski, J.D. (1994a) Discrimination in Ontario's Rental Housing Market: The Role of Minimum Income Criteria (Toronto, Ontario Human Rights Commission).

Hulchanski, J.D. (1994b) The Use of Housing Expenditure-to-Income Ratios: Origins, Evolution and Implications (Toronto, Ontario Human Rights Commission).

Hulchanski, J.D. and Weir, E. (1992) Survey of Corporations Owning or Managing Large Numbers of Rental Apartments in Metro Toronto: Requirement for Last Month's Rent Deposit (Toronto, University of Toronto, Faculty of Social Work, Research Report).

Hulchanski, J.D. and Michalski, J.H. (1994) How Households Obtain Resources to Meet their Needs: The Shifting Mix of Cash and Non-Cash Sources (Toronto, Ontario Human Rights Commission).

Kearns, A. (1992) Affordability for housing association tenants: A key issue for British social housing policy, Journal of Social Policy, 21(4), pp. 525–549.

Kendall, M.G. (1968) The History of Statistical Method, in: International Encyclopedia of the Social Sciences (NY, Macmillan).

Kengott, G.F. (1912) The Record of a City: A Social Survey of Lowell Massachusetts (NY, Macmillan).

Landau, D. and Lazarsfeld, P.F. (1968) Quetelet, Adolphe, International Encyclopedia of the Social Sciences, Vol. 13 (NY, Macmillan).

Lane, T.S. (1977) What Families Spend for Housing – the Origins and Uses of the 'Rules of Thumb' (Cambridge, MA, Abt Associates).

Lazarsfeld, P.F. (1961) Notes on the history of quantification in sociology – sources and problems, in: H. Wolf, (Ed.) Quantification: A History of the Meaning of Measurement in the Natural and Social Sciences (Indianapolis, Bobbs-Merrill).

Linneman, P.D. and I.F. Megbolugbe (1992) Housing affordability: myth or reality? Urban Studies, 29(3/4), pp. 369–392.

Maisel, S.J. and Winnick, L. (1966) Family housing expenditure: elusive laws and intrusive variances, in: W.L.C. Wheaton, G. Milgram and M.E. Meyerson (Eds) Urban Housing (NY, Free Press).

Marks, D. (1984) Housing Affordability and Rent Regulation (Toronto, Ontario Commission of Inquiry into Residential Tenancies, Research Study No. 8).

Olson, R. (1993) The Emergence of the Social Sciences, 1642 –1792 (NY, Twayne Publishers).

Ontario Human Rights Commission (1992) Minimum (Percentage of) Income Requirements in Renter Application (Toronto, The Commission).

Pitts, J.R. (1968) Le Play, Frederic, International Encyclopedia of the Social Sciences, Vol. 9 (NY, Macmillan).

Prais, S.J. and Houthakker, H.S. (1955,1971 2nd printing) The Analysis of Family Budgets (Cambridge, Cambridge University Press).

Reid, M.G. (1962) Housing and Income (Chicago, University of Chicago Press).

Schwabe, H. (1868) Die Verhaltnis von Miethe und Einkommen in Berlin (Berlin).

Smith, S.J. (1990) Income, housing wealth and gender inequality, Urban Studies, 27(1), pp. 67–88.

Stigler, G.J. (1954) The early history of empirical studies of consumer behavior, The Journal of Political Economy, LXII(2), pp. 95–113.

Stone, M.E. (1990) One-Third of a Nation: A New Look at Housing Affordability in America (Washington, DC, Economic Policy Institute).

Sunstein, C.R. (1991) Why markets don't stop discrimination, Social Philosophy and Policy, 8(2), pp. 22–37.

Thurow, L.C. (1975) Generating Inequality: Mechanisms of Distribution in the US Economy (NY, Basic Books).

Van Dyk, N. (1993) A Review of the Core Housing Need Model and the Allocation and Targeting of Federal Housing Assistance (Ottawa, Canadian Housing and Renewal Association).

Weale, A. (1983) Issues of value and principle in social policy, in: M. Loney, D. Boswell and J. Clarke (Eds) Social Policy and Social Welfare (Milton Keynes, Open University Press).

Whitehead, C.M.E. (1991) From need to affordability: An analysis of UK housing objectives, Urban Studies, 28(6), pp. 871–887.

Winger, A.R. (1968) Housing and income, Western Economic Journal, 6(3), pp. 226–232.

Winnick, L. (1955) Housing: has there been a downward shift in consumer preferences? Quarterly Journal of Economics, 69, pp. 85–98.

York, G. (1986) The Nielson Task Force Report, The Globe and Mail [Toronto], 13 March, p. A3.

Zimmerman, C.C. (1936) Consumption and Standards of Living (NY, Van Nostrand).

8

"What is housing affordability? The case for the residual income approach"

From *Housing Policy Debate* (2006)

Michael E. Stone

University of Massachusetts–Boston

INTRODUCTION

What is housing affordability? Most fundamentally, it is an expression of the social and material experiences of people, constituted as households, in relation to their individual housing situations. Affordability expresses the challenge each household faces in balancing the cost of its actual or potential housing, on the one hand, and its nonhousing expenditures, on the other, within the constraints of its income.

However, public policy and the interpretation of individual experiences are mediated through analytical indicators and normative standards of housing affordability that transcend unique individual experiences. Such indicators and standards make it possible to arrive at conclusions – potentially contentious to be sure – about the overall extent of affordability problems and needs, as well as their distribution socially and geographically. They also provide an important foundation for the at least somewhat rational formulation, implementation, and evaluation of policies and practices that deal with affordability.

In the United States, there is widespread acceptance of the ratio of housing cost to income as the appropriate *indicator* of affordability and of the simple "rule of thumb" ratio *standard* (25 percent of income until the early 1980s, 30 percent since then) for assessing housing affordability problems, as well as for determining eligibility and payment levels, explicitly for publicly subsidized rental housing and somewhat more loosely for other rental and ownership programs and financing. The ratio paradigm persists in the United States despite considerable critical discussion in the late 1960s and early 1970s, and some efforts since then, in presenting and applying an alternative residual income approach.

This article begins with an overview of various issues surrounding the meaning of housing affordability, leading to an argument in support of the conceptual soundness of the residual income model. This concept is then briefly set into the historical context of U.S. [...] debates about affordability measures. [...]The following section discusses some of the practical challenges involved in operationalizing a residual income standard: selection of a normative standard for nonhousing items and the treatment of taxes. The article concludes by considering some of the potential implications of the residual income paradigm for the analysis of housing problems and needs [and] for housing subsidy policy.

THE LOGIC OF HOUSING AFFORDABILITY

Semantic and substantive issues relating to affordability

There are several types of tensions in the literature on housing affordability, including but not necessarily limited to the following:

1. Conceptual rigor versus practical policy implications
2. Housing affordability versus "affordable housing"
3. Housing affordability versus housing standards
4. A normative standard of affordability versus empirical analysis of housing costs in relation to incomes

Conceptual rigor versus practical policy implications

Housing subsidy policy is inevitably shaped by factors other than the conceptual clarity of the affordability standard, such as potentially perverse incentives, fiscal constraints, and political interests, among others. This should not, however, diminish intellectual responsibility for rigorous and sound conceptualization, both for purposes of analysis and as an important consideration – if not the sole consideration – in formulating policy.

[…]

Housing affordability versus "affordable housing"

In Britain and the United States, affordability is often expressed in terms of "affordable housing." But affordability is not a characteristic of housing – it is a *relationship* between housing and people. For some people, all housing is affordable, no matter how expensive it is; for others, no housing is affordable unless it is free. "Affordable" housing can have meaning (and utility) only if three essential questions are answered:

1. Affordable to whom?
2. On what standard of affordability?
3. For how long?

Indeed, in light of the discussion in the following section on housing standards, one might also add, meeting what physical standard?

Before the 1980s in the United States, subsidized housing (public and private) was referred to as low-income housing and low- and moderate-income housing, with explicit definitions of "low income" and "moderate income." Although such terms and definitions are still used in determining eligibility under

various housing policies and programs in this country,[1] the term "affordable housing" came into vogue in the 1980s as part of the retreat from public responsibility for the plight of the poor and as affordability challenges moved up the income distribution. Although it still lacks precise and consistent definition, the term has since achieved international stature, and it typically encompasses not only social housing and low-income housing, but also financially assisted housing for middle-income households that find it difficult to purchase houses in the private speculative market.

It thus seems to me that a far more accurate term would be "below-market housing," which properly denotes identifiable segments of the housing stock, without making any unjustifiable general claim of affordability.

Housing affordability versus housing standards

Housing deprivation can take a variety of forms, of which lack of affordability is only one. Households may live in housing that fails to meet physical standards of decency, in overcrowded conditions, with insecure tenure, or in unsafe or inaccessible locations. While each of these other forms of deprivation is logically distinct from lack of affordability, most households that experience one or more of these other forms of deprivation in reality do so because they cannot afford satisfactory housing and residential environments.

If other forms of housing deprivation are largely due to the affordability squeeze, in measuring the extent of affordability problems how should we account for those households that seem *not* to have an affordability problem (as measured by some standard), yet *do* experience one or more other forms of housing deprivation? Simply put, if the cost of obtaining satisfactory dwellings and residential environments within the same housing market area exceeds what such households can afford, then they should reasonably be considered to have an affordability problem even though it is not revealed by applying an economic affordability standard. Only if such a household could afford adequate housing – and if such housing is actually available – might they reasonably be considered to be living in inadequate housing by choice. While housing deprivation is complex and can take various forms, standards for most forms of deprivation are fairly well established, and hence the measurement of deprivation and its relationship to affordability is, in principle, reasonably tractable.

However, can it not be argued that those households that *do* appear to have an affordability problem, yet are "overhoused," might not have an affordability problem if they were not overhoused? This question is the obverse of the one in the previous paragraph and could in principle be answered by a similar analytical technique. The difficulty, of course, arises from the question of what a reasonable, broadly acceptable operational definition of "overhoused" is. Although the relationship between the number of persons in a household and the number of bedrooms (or the total number of rooms) in the dwelling is widely used as an operational definition, this definition in its simplicity tends to be simplistic. For example, a modern garden apartment consisting of two tiny bedrooms, a small living room, and a minuscule kitchen could easily have less than half the usable space of a once luxurious Victorian apartment with one large bedroom, a good-sized living room and dining room, and an eat-in kitchen. Is it reasonable to consider a widow living in the former to be overhoused because the apartment has two bedrooms, but not in the latter because it has one?

A question of greater subtlety that is just as significant for assessing affordability is, should households be considered overhoused if they have rooms for anticipated additional children, for overnight visits from family and friends, for study or hobbies, or for home-based businesses or employment? Thus, the number of households that appear to have an affordability problem, but would not have one if they were not overhoused, is likely to be considerably lower based on some flexible standard rather than a simplistic person/bedroom (or person/room) definition of what it means to be overhoused.

In sum, housing affordability is not really separable from housing standards. An analysis of the extent and distribution of affordability problems that takes into account other forms of housing deprivation would increase the number of households determined to have a true affordability problem, while adjustment for overhousing would decrease it. Because of these offsetting tendencies and definition

difficulties, housing affordability studies should ideally be iterative: applying an economic affordability standard in the first instance, while exploring ways of enhancing the precision of the analysis to account for under- and overhousing.

Lerman and Reeder (1987) and Thalmann (1999, 2003) have developed and applied such quality-based measures, which classify a household as having an affordability problem not on the basis of actual housing cost in relation to income, but on what it would cost to obtain housing of a basic physical standard within a given local housing market. Lerman and Reeder (1987) have developed their model using the ratio standard; Thalmann used a ratio standard in his first article (1999), but a residual income standard in his later one (2003). Both limited their analyses to renters because of the difficulty in consistently defining and measuring homeowner occupancy costs. [...]

A normative standard of affordability versus an empirical analysis of housing costs in relation to incomes

Studies of consumer expenditures have been carried out in Europe and North America since the late 19th century, yielding considerable information about how households have spent their incomes for housing and other items. One way of summarizing the data on housing costs has been to calculate the mean or median ratio of shelter expenditures to income. It has then been assumed that because households on average actually spend this percentage of their incomes for shelter, it is thereby justified as a standard of what it is reasonable to spend.[2] Rapkin rather whimsically noted this confusion when he wrote,

> No discussion of the rent-income ratio can begin without a reference to the familiar belief that one month's rent should approximate one week's salary. It has never been quite clear to me whether this statement purports to be a statistical observation or whether it is a "folkloristic" exhortation to husbandry.
>
> (1957, 8)

Baer (1976) made a useful contribution by explicitly distinguishing between an indicator, which measures empirically the relationship between, say, housing costs and incomes, and a standard, which specifies normatively the appropriate value or values that an indicator should take or not exceed. As he stated with regard to housing affordability:

> Given the variety of circumstances facing different households, rules of thumb about the percent of income to be devoted to housing can be extremely misleading in individual cases and therefore in aggregate data as well. Although generally recognized, the dilemma has largely defied attempts to establish appropriate housing standards.
>
> (Baer 1976, 383)

To illuminate the issue further, Feins and Lane (1981) and Yip (1995), for example, carried out extensive empirical work on the relationship between housing expenditures and incomes in the United States and England, respectively. In both instances, they recognized explicitly the distinction between indicators and standards. Yet they, as well as Baer (1976), ultimately used empirical findings on expenditures as the basis for their normative standards. To be sure, all of these authors rejected the notion of a single normative standard for all types of households. Nonetheless, their proposed standards were derived from actual patterns of expenditures by various subsets of the population.

In reality, what most households actually pay for housing is not what they realistically can "afford": Many pay more, while some pay less, whether measured in money or as a percentage of income. Who pays more and who pays less than they realistically can afford is, of course, not random, but rather is correlated with economic and social circumstances. As a normative concept, an affordability *standard* must have some independent logical or theoretical basis against which households' actual circumstances can be measured. Otherwise, the standard is tautological or arbitrary, and affordability is purely subjective.

Diverse and incompatible definitions of housing affordability

Mathematically, the relationship between housing costs and incomes can be computed either as a ratio or as a difference. These two approaches are the formal foundations of the prevailing affordability paradigm and its principal challenger, respectively.

In practice, however, there appears to be a greater variety of different approaches to defining housing affordability or the lack thereof:

1. Relative – changes in the relationship between summary measures of house prices or costs and household incomes
2. Subjective – whatever individual households are willing to or choose to spend
3. Family budget – monetary standards based on aggregate housing expenditure patterns
4. Ratio – maximum acceptable housing cost/income ratios
5. Residual – normative standards of a minimum income required to meet non-housing needs at a basic level after paying for housing

Relative measures

The relative approach, used widely by the mortgage lending and real estate industries to assess the affordability of the residential sales market, is based on prototypical housing costs, primarily for potential home buyers. The derived indicators enable two or more points in time to be compared as to whether, on average, dwellings for sale have become relatively more or less affordable, typically either in relation to median income or in constant dollars. The technical sophistication of such affordability measures varies, with considerable discussion as to the most appropriate definitions of housing cost and income to use in constructing the measure, as well as the implications of different cost and income definitions (Linneman and Megbolugbe 1992; Pannell and Williams 1994; Weicher 1977).

The most widely cited relative measures in the United States are those of the National Association of Realtors (2005) and the Joint Center for Housing Studies (2004). […] However, in both cases, these measures are really applications of the ratio approach, not a conceptually distinct approach. The relative approaches may thus serve a useful purpose, but provide no independent normative standard for assessing how many and which kinds of households can and cannot afford those properties that are for sale. Nor do they provide any basis for assessing possible affordability stresses of owner-occupiers in their current dwellings, although the Joint Center's renter ratios do provide broad-gauged indicators of renter stress.

Subjective approaches

The second approach rests on the assumption of *homo economicus*. Since households are presumably rational utility-maximizers, every household is by definition paying just what it can afford for housing. Some households may live in undesirable conditions; others may have low incomes that give them few choices; but they all make the choice that is best for them within their constraints. Thus, from this perspective, housing affordability per se has no generalizable meaning; it is neither rationally possible nor socially desirable to establish a normative standard of affordability other than individual choice. As a recent memorandum on affordable housing submitted to a U.K. Parliament Select Committee bluntly stated: "The concept of affordability, of whatever commodity, is essentially subjective" (2002, 2).

More sophisticated versions of this perspective do recognize that the degree of financial flexibility does increase with income (Kempson 1993; Linneman and Megbolugbe 1992). However, while higher-income households for the most part have considerable discretion about how to allocate their resources between housing and other items, and hence for them affordability may be quite subjective, households at the lower end of the income distribution are not simply choosing freely between housing and other needs. Rather, housing costs generally make the first claim on disposable income, so that lower-income households have little discretion in what they can spend for nonhousing items. Thus, the subjectivity of affordability is not only *not* universal, it is not even a continuum that increases with income. Instead, I would contend, there is a threshold or transition zone above which affordability could become increasingly subjective. The important questions then are, What is that threshold or transition zone below which affordability is not subjective, and how can objective affordability below that threshold be defined and measured? These questions are not addressed within this perspective.

Family budget standards approaches

The third approach to conceptualizing housing affordability bases standards on summary measures of what households in the aggregate actually spend. In practice, this has formed the basis for the ratio approach. It has also provided the basis for the budget standards approach of a standardized monetary amount for housing. Since the latter can be understood as a purely income-based standard of affordability, it deserves attention here as a distinct approach.

Although every household has its own unique conditions, historically and socially determined notions of what constitutes a minimum adequate or decent standard of living do exist. They represent norms around which a range of variations can be recognized and about which there certainly could be some philosophical debate. While the experience of poverty is recognized as more than just the inability to secure a socially determined minimum quantity and/or quality of essential goods and services, measurable material deprivation is obviously a central element in poverty. Furthermore, in societies where most basic goods and services are commodities, it is possible, at least in principle, to determine the monetary cost of achieving such a basic material level. This budget standards approach to poverty and income adequacy has a long and honorable history (Bernstein, Brocht, and Spade-Aguilar 2000; Bradshaw 1993; Bradshaw, Mitchell, and Morgan 1987; Citro and Michael 1995; Expert Committee on Family Budget Revisions 1980; Oldfield and Yu 1993; Parker and Nelson 1998; Ruggles 1990).

The budget standards approach involves specification of a market basket of essential items. For housing, food, and most other items, data from consumer expenditure surveys, expert opinions, and, in some cases, opinion surveys and focus groups are used to establish a minimal standard of type, quantity, and quality in a given social context at a given point in time. (The physical standard will of course vary by household type, and this qualifier applies to all of the following.) The physical standard for each item is then priced, and the prices summed to yield a total (after-tax) minimal budget.

If the amounts for housing specified in the standard budgets really do represent the income needed for essentially *any* household of a given type to obtain socially defined minimally adequate housing, then affordability has no independent meaning. In principle, any household whose income is no less than the total budget should be able to meet all of its basic needs, including housing, at the physical quantity and quality represented by the standard.

Due to the inherent nature and variability of housing costs, there are, however, conceptual problems in the treatment of housing costs in the budget standards methodology. While it is well conceptualized and operationalized for other items, *it is flawed with regard to housing.* The issue is revealed by contrasting the budget standards approach and implications for food and housing.

Given the nature of food items – low price variance and high supply elasticity – essentially any household could in principle meet the physical food standard with the amount represented by the specific monetary standard, at least within a particular geographic region.

Housing, by contrast, is highly inhomogeneous. Because it is bulky, durable, and tied to land, it shows high price variance and low supply elasticity – even within a given market area. How then should the minimum standard for housing be priced? If prices are determined for a sample of units meeting the minimum physical standard, the price distribution has a large variance. Which point on the distribution should then be selected for the monetary standard for housing?

If a very low cost is selected (say, the midpoint of the lowest third of the distribution of rents for private market housing, as was the standard in the U.S. Bureau of Labor Statistics [BLS] lower-standard budgets), then most households, despite their best efforts, will not be able to obtain physically adequate housing at the monetary standard unless an extraordinarily large supply of physically adequate housing priced barely above this cost threshold is available. That is, to meet the minimum physical standard, most households would need an income above the total specified by the monetary budget standard. If, however, the monetary standard for housing were set closer to the midpoint of the price distribution, such as the 40th percentile of rents for physically standard units, then some households could spend less than the monetary standard for housing and hence need less income than the total budget, through no virtue of their own.

Others, though not as many as with a lower point on the distribution, would have to spend more. The 40th percentile is the definition of fair market rent (FMR) computed by the U.S. Department of Housing and Urban Development (HUD) and used in recent U.S. budget standards – see Bernstein, Brocht, and Spade-Aguilar (2000).

In sum, housing is unique; the budget standards methodology may be able to specify a reasonably precise *physical* standard for housing, but it cannot establish a precise *monetary* standard. […] Further, in terms of policy, this means that housing affordability problems cannot be explained as just income problems. General and standardized income support alone would be neither efficient nor equitable for solving affordability problems.[3]

The ratio approach

As an indicator for expressing the relationship between housing costs and incomes, the ratio measure has the longest history and widest recognition. Normatively, the ratio approach recognizes that what many households pay for housing in relation to their income is the result of difficult choices among limited and often unsatisfactory alternatives. It asserts that if a household pays more for housing than a certain percentage of its income, then it will not have enough left for other necessities. It usually specifies an explicit ratio of housing cost to income as a standard against which households' actual circumstances can be measured. Yet despite its widespread recognition and acceptance, there is no theoretical or logical foundation for the concept or the particular ratio or ratios that are used.

How can one account for the existence and persistence of the fixed-ratio or percentage-of-income affordability concept? Apart from the mathematical simplicity of the percentage standard, the rationale for the conventional standard – and the rationalization for raising the acceptable level from 25 to 30 percent in the United States in the 1980s – has been built on interpretations of empirical studies of what households actually spend for housing (manifesting the tension discussed earlier). Because ratios are pure numbers, they can be compared across time and space and thus are susceptible to being reified as universal and lawful. Such "laws" then become legitimated as appropriate indicators and as the basis for normative standards.

Even most of those who have rejected the notion of a single ratio *standard* have accepted uncritically the ratio *indicator*. Feins and Lane, for example, after discussing the distinction between indicators and standards, have asserted: "When we apply these terms to the issues of housing affordability, we find that the ratio of shelter expenditures to household income is the appropriate indicator" (1981, 7). (See also Pedone 1988 and Yip 1995; for a critique of such alleged "lawfulness," see Chaplin *et al.* 1994.)

However, there is no logical basis for such an assertion. Once the ratio measure is accepted as the appropriate indicator, ipso facto, the standard must be a ratio or a set of ratios. Yet the notion that a household can adequately meet its nonshelter needs if it has at least a certain percentage of income left after paying for housing implies either that (1) the lower the income of a household, the lower the amount it requires for nonshelter needs, with no minimum whatsoever, or (2) that the normative ratio must diminish with income, all the way to zero below certain incomes. Further, since an affordability standard is intended to measure whether housing costs make an undue claim on household income in relation to other needs, basing such a standard on what people actually pay provides no way of assessing whether they are in fact able to achieve some minimum standard for nonshelter necessities. These logical flaws in the ratio approach lead inexorably to the residual income concept.

The residual income concept of housing affordability

This approach arises from the recognition that because of housing's distinctive physical attributes in comparison with necessities, its cost makes the largest and least flexible claim on after-tax income for most households (in other words, nonhousing expenditures are limited by how much is left after paying for housing). This means that a household has a housing affordability problem if it cannot meet its nonhousing needs at some basic level of adequacy after paying for housing. The appropriate *indicator* of the relationship between housing costs and incomes is thus the difference between them – the residual income left after paying for housing – rather than the ratio.

What are the implications of this logic for an affordability *standard*? If we consider, for example, two households with comparable disposable incomes and suppose that one consists of a single person while the other consists of a couple with three children, obviously the larger household would have to spend substantially more for its nonshelter necessities than the small household to achieve a comparable quality of life. This implies that the larger household can afford to spend less for housing than the small household with the same income. Now if we compare two households of the same size and composition, but with different after-tax incomes, both would need to spend about the same amount to achieve a comparable standard of living for nonshelter items. The higher-income household could thus afford to spend more for housing, both as a percentage of income and in monetary terms.

Generalizing from these examples tells us that since the nonhousing expenses of small households (to achieve a comparable basic standard of living) are, on average, less than those of large households, the former can reasonably devote a higher percentage of income to housing than larger households with the same income. Since low-income and higher-income households of the same size and type require about the same amount of money to meet their nonhousing needs at a comparable basic standard of living, those with lower incomes can afford to devote a smaller percentage of income to housing than otherwise similar higher-income households. In this way, the residual income standard emerges as a sliding scale of housing affordability with the maximum affordable amount and fraction of income varying with household size, type, and income. Indeed, it implies that some households can afford nothing for housing, while others can afford more than any established ratio.

Operationalizing a residual income standard involves using a conservative, socially defined minimum standard of adequacy for nonhousing items. Thus, while the residual income *logic* has broad validity, a particular residual income *standard* is not universal; it is socially grounded in space and time.

Issues involved in selecting such a standard for nonhousing necessities and dealing with personal taxes will be taken up after reviewing the debates about affordability standards in the United States [...]. This literature not only strengthens the argument for the residual income approach, it also helps illuminate some of the practical tasks involved in operation-alizing it.

DEBATES ABOUT AFFORDABILITY STANDARDS

Before the late 1960s in the United States and the late 1980s in Britain, leading housing experts accepted without question the ratio of housing costs to incomes as the appropriate affordability indicator, challenging only the notion of a single ratio as an appropriate normative standard – see Rapkin (1957) and Donnison (1967), respectively.

In the United States, there then followed nearly a decade of considerable intellectual ferment and great progress in reconceptualizing affordability in terms of residual incomes, after which interest diminished until quite recently. [...]

In the 1960s and early 1970s, concern with poverty and urban problems included considerable discussion of housing affordability concepts. A number of U.S. housing analysts looked at affordability in relation to income adequacy and living standards, not merely as a matter of costs, and began questioning the conventional ratio approach to affordability.

The late Cushing Dolbeare appears to have been one of the first to go beyond recognizing the inadequacy of the ratio standard, especially for the poor, and to suggest an alternative. In a pamphlet with a limited circulation, she offered an alternative as part of a proposal for housing grants for the very poor:

> The subsidy might cover the difference between the amount the family could afford for shelter after meeting other basic needs and the cost of shelter – the "residual" approach .... The compelling argument in favor of the residual approach is that it covers, if necessary, the full amount needed for housing, thus assuring that the recipient is able to meet as many ... other basic needs – food, clothing, medical care, etc. – as possible.
>
> (Dolbeare 1966, 12)

The nonshelter standard in this residual income approach was an amount equal to the federal poverty threshold for a household of a given size, minus an estimated typical shelter cost for low-income households of that size.

The issue emerged in the policy arena under the auspices of one of the commissions established in the wake of the urban riots of the mid-1960s. In its 1968 report, the U.S. President's Committee on Urban Housing, asked, "When does a family need a subsidy?" and went on to declare: "Determination of a proper proportion of a family's income for housing requires some difficult value judgments .... The staff concluded that no flat percentage can be equitable for all" (41–42).

Several of the consultants to the committee went a little further in conceptualizing how a variable standard might be developed, but most then retreated to the simpler, conventional ratio standard (G.E. TEMPO 1968; Robert Gladstone and Associates 1968). Another of the consultants did examine the differential effect of household size on housing affordability and in doing so used the concept of a minimum adequate budget that varies with household size. Not surprisingly, he found that smaller households with incomes at the minimum budget level could obtain and afford shelter at higher rent/income ratios than larger households could (von Furstenberg 1968).

Over the next few years, some elements of a consensus on an appropriate approach seemed to be emerging until the issue was submerged by the economic crises of the 1970s. In 1971, a congressional committee published reports on housing affordability standards that it had requested from a number of experts. Three of the reports (Frieden 1971; Lowry 1971; Newman 1971) argued explicitly and strongly for using a residual income approach to analyzing housing needs and subsidy formulas for federal housing programs. Both Newman (1971) and Lowry (1971) suggested that BLS normative family budgets should be used to set the standard for nonhousing expenses.

In the mid-1970s, a big step forward was taken when two research projects – one by Grigsby and Rosenburg (1975) for Baltimore and the other by Stone (1975) for the country as a whole – independently operationalized the residual income approach by using the nonhousing components of the BLS lower budgets and applied this standard to estimate the extent of housing affordability problems. In his study, Stone introduced the term "shelter poverty" to characterize households that, squeezed between income and housing costs, cannot meet their nonshelter needs at the BLS lower-budget standard (1975). Thereafter, Stone continued to update and apply the shelter-poverty standard (1983, 1990, 1993, 1994, 2006), but otherwise there was very little consideration of the residual income approach to housing affordability (at least in the United States) until quite recently. [...]

In recent years, other analysts have expressed tentative recognition of the appropriateness of the residual income approach, as both indicator and standard. For example, Bogdon and Can (1997), in an article on the measurement of local housing affordability problems, compared various approaches, including the ratio measure and the shelter-poverty residual income approach, as well as several others that are actually adaptations of the ratio measure. Ultimately, though, they adopted the ratio measure and its variations for convenience.

Finally, Kutty (2005) has forcefully restated the case for the residual income approach, alluding to the work of Stone (1990, 1993) and others. Most notably, she has operationalized a residual income standard with the nonhousing standard set at two-thirds of the federal poverty threshold and applied it to compute what she calls "housing-induced poverty." As she acknowledges, her choice of a nonshelter standard is lower than the BLS lower-budget standard used by Stone (1990, 1993) and other authors.

[...]

OPERATIONALIZING A RESIDUAL INCOME STANDARD

Two major practical issues have to be dealt with to translate the residual income approach into an operational affordability standard: specifying the monetary level of a minimum standard of adequacy for nonshelter items other than taxes and dealing with personal taxes.

Nonhousing necessities

The residual income literature that has taken up this practical problem mirrors and indeed explicitly rests on the contending approaches to specifying minimum adequate incomes – albeit minus housing. Thus, in this country, one strand has adopted a fraction of the federal poverty threshold as the standard (Budding 1980; Dolbeare 1966; Kutty 2005), while the other has used the nonhousing, nontax items of a family budget standard (Grigsby and Rosenburg 1975; Leonard, Dolbeare, and Lazare 1989; Newman 1971; Stone 1975, 1983, 1990, 1993, 2006).

Dolbeare (1966) proposed using the poverty threshold minus an estimated "typical" shelter cost for low-income households. Budding (1980) proposed using three-quarters of the poverty threshold as the nonhousing standard, while Kutty (2005) has adopted two-thirds of it. This approach has the great virtue of being based on a familiar and widely used monetary standard of adequacy and being computationally simple. However, it reproduces all the problems and limitations of the poverty standard (Bernstein, Brocht, and Spade-Aguilar 2000; Citro and Michael 1995; Expert Committee on Family Budget Revisions 1980; Ruggles 1990) and adds another one of its own: The particular fraction is arbitrary.[4]

The budget standards concepts and methodology have provided a rather less familiar but not necessarily more complex basis for establishing a normative standard for an after-tax basis for residual income. As explained earlier, this approach takes into account the actual cost of a basic market basket of necessities. By explicitly identifying and pricing the various elements, nonhousing items can be extracted so that their total cost is not an arbitrary fraction of the total budget.

The authors who have used the budget standards approach in this country have all relied on the nonshelter, nontax pieces of the BLS lower-standard budgets, updated using corresponding components of the Consumer Price Index (CPI) (Stone 1993). For a while, the BLS itself considered the lower budgets to represent a minimum standard of adequacy, but later retreated from this claim even before the Family Budget program was eliminated in 1981 (Stone 1993). Nonetheless, the composition of goods and services in the BLS budgets was based on consumption patterns in the early 1960s and was not revised to reflect changes in norms and actual consumer buying patterns over time. It is therefore worth asking whether there are more current normative family budgets

Budget Item	BLS Lower Budget[a]		SSS[b] Boston 2003	EPI[c] Boston 2004	U.S. Poverty Threshold[d] 2003
	United States 2003	Boston 2003			
Food	$ 8,701	$ 9,001	$ 6,648	$ 7,044	
Housing furnishings and operations	$ 933	$ 897	nc	nc	
Transportation	$ 2,202	$ 2,390	$ 1,368	$ 3,852	
Clothing	$ 1,176	$ 1,545	nc	nc	
Medical	$ 5,061	$ 6,263	$ 3,204	$ 7,104	
Others goods and services	$ 4,781	$ 5,594	$ 4,200	$ 6,000	
Subtotal	$22,854	$25,690	$15,420	$24,000	$18,660
Child care	nc	nc	$14,712	$15,576	nc
Total	$22,854	$25,690	$30,132	$39,576	$18,660

Table 8.1 Low-cost budget standards, nonhousing items, excluding taxes, for a four-person household (two adults and two children)

[a]Updated from the last BLS lower budget, computed for 1981, using corresponding CPI–U (Consumer Price Index for all Urban Consumers) components.
[b]Pearce (2003).
[c]Economic Policy Institute Basic Family Budgets (Allegretto 2005).
[d]Federal poverty threshold for a four-person family with two children under 18. Unlike the other standards, this includes housing.
nc = not computed.

that might be used to operationalize the residual income approach and how the nonhousing standards of such budgets compare with the updated BLS lower-budget nonhousing standard.

In the United States, the Economic Policy Institute (EPI) has developed a set of basic family budgets (Allegretto 2005; Bernstein, Brocht, and Spade-Aguilar 2000; EPI 2005). Separately, Wider Opportunities for Women (WOW) has developed a so-called "Self-Sufficiency Standard" (SSS), which is also a set of normative basic budgets (Pearce 2003; WOW 2003). Both of these endeavors, unlike the official poverty standard and in response to one of its most widely acknowledged weaknesses, have developed budgets based on the cost of living in local areas, rather than a single national standard. BLS budgets were prepared for local areas as well as for a national standard. While most of the residual income work based on the BLS lower budgets has been national, some has

used updated metropolitan Boston BLS lower budgets (Stone 1989; Stone Werby, and Friedman 2000). Thus a comparison of nonhousing standards has been made using both national and Boston examples. Table 8.1 presents the results for a prototypical four-person household consisting of two adults and two children under 18.

Both the EPI budget and the SSS include child care costs, which, as can be seen, are by far the largest nonshelter cost. With child care costs included, the nonshelter standard implied by these two budgets is far above the updated BLS lower-budget nonhousing standard. Since the BLS budgets did not provide for child care expenses (they assumed a mother at home), comparing the nonhousing standards without child care costs reveals the EPI standard to be quite close to the updated BLS standard, despite substantial differences in composition. The nonhousing, non-child-care SSS, by contrast, is much lower – even lower than the poverty threshold (which includes housing). Nonetheless, the SSS is equal to about five-sixths of the poverty level, somewhat above Kutty's (2005) two-thirds and Budding's (1980) three-quarters. Indeed, if the official poverty threshold were to have any role in setting a uniform national residual income affordability standard, it would at best provide a conservative standard for consumption *excluding* housing and child care.

Personal taxes

The poverty threshold was conceptualized as a standard of inadequate consumption, that is, as a standard for after-tax income. Yet it has routinely been applied to before-tax income, because the decennial census and Current Population Survey (as well as the American Housing Survey and the American Community Survey) obtain only before-tax incomes from respondents. Although Kutty (2005) has recognized this inconsistency, her residual income standard makes no correction for it. Instead, she has adopted two-thirds of the poverty threshold as the total nonhousing standard for consumption and personal taxes. Yet before- and after-tax incomes in general differ substantially, even in prototypical low-income cases. Thus, quite apart from the question of whether a fraction of the poverty threshold is a defensible minimum for nonhousing consumption, failure to take taxes into account generates other distortions. A residual income standard that ignores taxes inevitably leads to considerable misidentification of households with affordability problems.

In contrast to the poverty standard, all of the budget standards models have taken into account personal taxes. However, the computation assumes an after-tax budget, including housing, for each household type. So regardless of whether one uses the budget standards framework or the poverty threshold or some other model for nonhousing consumption, prototypical taxes need to be computed as a function of income as well as household type to fully operationalize a residual income standard – absent data sets that provide after-tax incomes. Stone's shelter-poverty residual income standard (1993) explicitly takes federal and nonfederal income taxes (including credits) and Social Security taxes into account. It is the computation of taxes that makes

operationalization of a residual income standard relatively complex, although algorithms to compute personal taxes for prototypical households are not that difficult to construct.

IMPLICATIONS AND APPLICATIONS

The implications of using a residual income affordability standard differ from the conventional ratio approach in the following areas at least: analysis of housing problems and needs, [and] eligibility and payment standards for housing subsidies. [...]

Analysis of housing problems and needs

Over the decades, on both sides of the Atlantic, several studies have used a residual income approach to measure the incidence of affordability problems for a particular time and place (Grigsby and Rosenburg 1975; Hancock 1993; Kutty 2005; Leonard, Dolbeare, and Lazare 1989; Yip 1995). However, the only works examining affordability trends over time based on a residual income standard and explicitly compared with the ratio approach, are Stone's studies of shelter poverty in the United States (1983, 1990, 1993, 2006).

He has found that since 1970, the incidence of shelter poverty in the aggregate in the United States has been close to the incidence of affordability problems based on the conventional 30 percent of income ratio standard: In 2001, 32.1 million households (15.1 million renters and 17.0 million homeowners) were shelter poor, compared with 34.6 million paying 30 percent or more of their income for rent (Stone 2006). [...] Of course, this is just a coincidence, an artifact of the particular residual income standard and the particular ratio standard. Kutty's much more conservative standard yields a far lower figure for households in what she calls "housing-induced poverty" – 17.2 million (renters and homeowners) in 1999 (2005).

However, Stone's approach reveals a very different distribution of the problem than the one suggested by the ratio approach. This difference points to some of the practical significance of a residual income standard: Small households (of one and two persons) have lower rates of shelter poverty than conventionally measured affordability problems, while larger households have considerably higher rates of shelter poverty than conventionally measured affordability problems (1993, 2006). This difference by household size is to be expected for any residual income standard, simply because any normative standard for nonhousing items will increase monotonically with household size. Essentially, for small households, shelter poverty does not reach as far up the income distribution as conventionally measured affordability problems do, while for larger households, shelter poverty reaches higher than the affordability burdens suggested by the conventional standard do.

Stone has also found that the rate of shelter poverty among small households has declined since 1970 but increased for larger households; this is in contrast to the conventional measure, which has consistently shown small households to be worse off (1993, 2006). His residual income approach thus suggests that affordability problems for families with children are rather more severe than usually thought, with implications for housing production needs as well as for the allocation of subsidies for existing housing.

Eligibility and payment standards for housing subsidies

U.S. rent subsidy formulas have required assisted households to pay a fixed percentage (25 percent until the early 1980s, 30 percent since then) of adjusted income, which is based on certain deductions from gross income (see HUD 2002 for the currently allowed exemptions and deductions). These deductions have recognized, albeit partially and very weakly, the claims of nonhousing items in relation to household size.

Stone has examined some ways in which the residual income approach could be used to reform the formulas for determining assistance levels for U.S. households receiving subsidies (1983, 1993). He has argued that if the logic of residual income affordability is compelling but political support for adoption of the shelter-poverty residual income standard is lacking, subsidy formulas could move closer to the shelter-poverty standard by substantially raising the deductions and simultaneously increasing the percentage of net income recipients pay. [...]

While this approach has the virtue of simplicity, it is problematic in two respects. First, it fails to take into account regional variations in the cost of nonhousing necessities. Second, there are economies of scale in household consumption, so that per capita costs rise monotonically but at a diminishing rate with household size. Equivalency factors used to scale both the poverty level and family budget standards explicitly embody this lack of linearity. Thus, annual determination of standard deductions by locality and household size would result in greater equity in subsidy payments and greater efficiency in their allocation. Development and publication of such standards would be analogous to HUD's annual determination of income limits and FMRs for several hundred geographic areas encompassing the entire country. Income limits are based on an estimate of median family income for each geographic area, which is used as the four-person standard for the area and then scaled up or down to larger and smaller households. FMRs are based on rent distributions in each area for unsubsidized two-bedroom units that recently turned over, scaled up and down for larger and smaller units. Similarly, HUD could determine the residual income deduction standard for a four-person household in each geographic area, to be scaled up and down for larger and smaller households. Once a baseline is established, annual adjustments could be made using the area CPI, excluding housing. As with current policy, additional deductions might be permitted for child care and extraordinary medical expenses.

Stone (1993) has argued that a long-term goal should be to move toward the shelter-poverty standard itself for assisted housing rents, but with some possible adjustments. For one thing, he acknowledges that while a residual income approach suggests that the poorest households can afford nothing for shelter, policy makers and the public have tended to require assisted households to make some minimum out-of-pocket rent payments. Historically, the requirement in public housing was that tenants pay either 25 percent of adjusted income or 5 percent of total income, whichever is higher. Currently, it is 30 percent of adjusted income, 10 percent of total income minus certain income adjustments, or a locally set minimum rent of zero to 50 dollars a month, whichever is the most (HUD 2002).

Of greater significance, Stone has recognized the perverse incentive of using a pure residual income formula for setting rents: Since it would result in housing assistance decreasing by $1 for every $1 increase in disposable income, subsidized households would be unable to increase their resources for nonshelter consumption until they pay the full, unsubsidized cost for their units. Thus, such households would never have an incentive to increase their incomes. He therefore suggests the possibility of reducing "housing assistance by less than one dollar for every dollar of disposable income above the zero threshold" (1983, 271).

[…]

CONCLUSION

This article has examined the foundations of the housing affordability concept, debates about the meaning of affordability, and some of the practical tasks and challenges in operationalizing and applying a residual income affordability indicator and standard. The principal purpose has been to build the case for the residual income concept of housing affordability as sound in its own right and as a compelling alternative to the ratio approach.

Using the conventional ratio concept to define and measure housing affordability has been the prevailing approach because it is simple to understand and apply, because it seems to fit people's commonsense experience, and because it has a long tradition, the imprimatur of venerable historical authority, and the official sanction of most governments.

However, I have argued that the ratio concept is logically unsound and gives a misleading picture of the way households experience the squeeze between housing costs and incomes. A more realistic concept of affordability can be crafted from an understanding of the unique features of housing costs. Such a concept highlights the interaction among incomes, housing costs, and the costs of nonhousing necessities. This residual income approach does not yield a simple rule of thumb ratio. Instead, it leads to a sliding scale, which recognizes that true affordability is sensitive to differences in household composition and income.

Operationalizing a residual income affordability standard is, to be sure, more complex than simply adopting a fixed percentage of income. It is not, however, intractable to do so and does not require econometric analysis or the generation of new data. Over the past few decades, several authors have produced operational residual income standards, although there continues to be some debate about the appropriate nonhousing standard to use (Kutty 2005; Stone 1993, 2006).

Because the residual income model departs in significant ways from the ratio approach, it has a number of implications for policy and practice. First, it offers a more precise and finely honed instrument for assessing housing needs and problems. Second, it points toward revisions in housing subsidy formulas that would result in a more equitable and efficient allocation of subsidies. […]

The residual income approach to housing affordability is neither well known, particularly in this country, nor widely understood, let alone accepted. But it is sound, it is robust, and sooner or later, it will effectively compete with, if not replace, the traditional paradigm of housing affordability.

Notes

1 Moderate income is a term for which there is no longer a precise definition for national policy in the United States, although some state governments do have explicit definitions. But "low income," "very low income" and "extremely low income" are defined by federal statutes and regulations. Each year, the U.S. Department of Housing and Urban Development publishes the income limits for each of these definitions, adjusted for household size, for every geographic area of the United States. See Stone (1994) for a critique.

2 The same confusion could, in principle, arise with residual incomes rather than ratios. It just happens that the ratio indicator has been for the most part unquestioned.

3 For a similar argument, see Thalmann (2003).

4 Indeed, Kutty herself seems to be aware of the limitations (2005).

REFERENCES

Allegretto, Sylvia. 2005. *Basic Family Budgets*. Economic Policy Institute Briefing Paper No. 165. World Wide Web page http://www.epinet.org/briefing papers/165/bp165.pdf (accessed September 1).

Baer, William C. 1976. The Evolution of Housing Indicators and Housing Standards: Some Lessons for the Future. *Public Policy* 24(3):361–93.

Bernstein, Jared, Chauna Brocht, and Maggie Spade-Aguilar. 2000. *How Much Is Enough? Basic Family Budgets for Working Families*. Washington, D.C.: Economic Policy Institute.

Bogdon, Amy S., and Ayse Can. 1997. Indicators of Local Housing Affordability: Comparative and Spatial Approaches. *Real Estate Economics* 25(1):43–80.

Bradshaw, Jonathan, ed. 1993. *Budget Standards for the United Kingdom*. Aldershot, England: Avebury/Ashgate.

Bradshaw, Jonathan, Deborah Mitchell, and Jane Morgan.1987. Evaluating Adequacy: The Potential of Budget Standards. *Journal of Social Policy* 16(2):165–81.

Budding, David W. 1980. *Housing Deprivation among Enrollees in the Housing Allowance Demand Experiment*. Cambridge, MA: Abt Associates, Inc.

Chaplin, Russell, Simon Martin, Jin Hong Yang, and Christine M. E. Whitehead. 1994. *Affordability: Definitions, Measures, and Implications for Lenders*. Cambridge, England: Cambridge University, Department of Land Economy.

Citro, Constance, and Robert Michael, eds. 1995. *Measuring Poverty: A New Approach*. Washington, D.C.: National Academy Press.

Dolbeare, Cushing N. 1966. *Housing Grants for the Very Poor*. Philadelphia: Philadelphia Housing Association.

Donnison, D. V. 1967. *The Government of Housing*. Hammondsworth, England: Penguin.

Economic Policy Institute. 2005. *EPI Issue Guide: Poverty and Family Budgets. Guide to Creating a Basic Family Budget*. World Wide Web page <http://www.epinet.org/content.cfm/issueguides_poverty_instructions> (accessed March 12).

Expert Committee on Family Budget Revisions. 1980. *New American Family Budget Standards*. Washington, D.C.: U.S. Government Printing Office.

Feins, Judith, and Terry Saunders Lane. 1981. *How Much for Housing?* Cambridge, MA: Abt Associates, Inc.

Frieden, Bernard J. 1971. Improving Federal Housing Subsidies: Summary Report. In *Papers Submitted to the Subcommittee on Housing Panels*, U.S. House Committee on Banking and Currency. 92nd Cong., 1st sess., 473–88.

G.E. TEMPO. 1968. United States Housing Needs: 1968–78. In *Technical Studies*, Volume I, U.S. President's Committee on Urban Housing, 1–36. Washington, D.C.: U.S. Government Printing Office.

Grigsby, William G., and Louis Rosenburg. 1975. Urban Housing Policy. New York: APS.

Hancock, Karen E. 1993. Can't Pay? Won't Pay? The Economic Principles of Affordability. *Urban Studies* 30(1):127–45.

Joint Center for Housing Studies. 2004. *State of the Nation's Housing*. Cambridge, MA: Harvard University.

Kempson, Elaine. 1993. *Household Budgets and Housing Costs*. London: Policy Studies Institute.

Kutty, Nandinee K. 2005. A New Measure of Housing Affordability: Estimates and Analytical Results. *Housing Policy Debate* 16(1):113–42.

Leonard, Paul A., Cushing N. Dolbeare, and Edward A. Lazare. 1989. *A Place to Call Home: The Crisis in Housing for the Poor*. Washington, D.C.: Center on Budget and Policy Priorities and Low-Income Housing Information Service.

Lerman, Donald L., and William J. Reeder. 1987. The Affordability of Adequate Housing. *American Real Estate and Urban Economics Association Journal* 15(4):389–404.

Linneman, Peter D., and Isaac F. Megbolugbe. 1992. Housing Affordability: Myth or Reality. *Urban Studies* 28(3/4):369–92.

Lowry, Ira S. 1971. Housing Assistance for Low-Income Urban Families: A Fresh Approach. In *Papers Submitted to the Subcommittee on Housing Panels*, U.S. House Committee on Banking and

Currency. 92nd Cong., 1st sess., 489–523.

National Association of Realtors. 2005. World Wide Web page http://www.realtor.org/ Research.nsf/Pages/Hameth (accessed February 21).

Newman, Dorothy K. 1971. Housing the Poor and the Shelter-to-Income Ratio. In *Papers Submitted to the Subcommittee on Housing Panels*, U.S. House Committee on Banking and Currency. 92nd Cong., 1st sess., 555–78.

Oldfield, Nina, and Autumn C. S. Yu. 1993. *The Cost of a Child: Living Standards for the 1990s*. London: Child Poverty Action Group.

Pannell, Bob, and Peter Williams. 1994. House Prices and Affordability. *Housing Finance* [U.K.] No. 23, August.

Parker, Hermione, and Michael Nelson. 1998. *Low Cost but Acceptable. A Minimum Income Standard for the U.K.: Families with Young Children*. Bristol, England: Policy Press.

Pearce, Diana, with Jennifer Brooks. 2003. *The Self-Sufficiency Standard for Massachusetts*. Prepared for the Women's Educational and Industrial Union. World Wide Web page http://www.weiu.org/pdf_files/MA_Full_Report_Final.pdf (accessed September 5, 2005).

Pedone, Carla. 1988. *Current Housing Problems and Possible Federal Responses*. Washington, DC: Congressional Budget Office.

Rapkin, Chester. 1957. Rent-Income Ratio: Should the Formula for Public Housing Be Changed? *Journal of Housing* 14(1):8–12.

Robert Gladstone and Associates. 1968. The Outlook for United States Housing Needs. In *Technical Studies*, Volume I, U.S. President's Committee on Urban Housing. 37–102. Washington, D.C.: U.S. Government Printing Office.

Ruggles, Patricia. 1990. *Drawing the Line: Alternative Poverty Measures and Their Implications for Public Policy*. Washington, DC: Urban Institute.

Stone, Michael E. 1975. The Housing Crisis, Mortgage Lending, and Class Struggle. *Antipode* 7(2):22–37. Reprinted in *Radical Geography*, ed. Richard Peet, 144–79.

Chicago and London: Maaroufa Press, 1978.

Stone, Michael E. 1983. Housing and the Economic Crisis: An Analysis and Emergency Program. In *America's Housing Crisis: What Is to Be Done?* ed. Chester Hartman, 99–150. Boston and London: Routledge and Kegan Paul.

Stone, Michael E. 1989. Shelter Poverty in Boston: Problem and Program. In *Housing Issues of the 1990s*, ed. Sara Rosenberry and Chester Hartman, 337–78. New York: Praeger.

Stone, Michael E. 1990. *One-Third of a Nation: A New Look at Housing Affordability in America*. Washington, D.C.: Economic Policy Institute.

Stone, Michael E. 1993. *Shelter Poverty: New Ideas on Housing Affordability*. Philadelphia: Temple University Press.

Stone, Michael E. 1994. Comment on Kathryn P. Nelson's "Whose Shortage of Affordable Housing?" *Housing Policy Debate* 5(4):443–58.

Stone, Michael E. 2006. Housing Affordability: One Third of a Nation. In *A Right to Housing: Foundation for a New Social Agenda*, ed. Rachel Bratt, Michael E. Stone, and Chester Hartman, 38–60. Philadelphia: Temple University Press.

Stone, Michael E., Elaine Werby, and Donna Haig Friedman. 2000. *Situation Critical: Meeting the Housing Needs of Lower-Income Massachusetts Residents*. Boston: University of Massachusetts-Boston, Center for Social Policy. World Wide Web page http://www.mccormack. umb.edu/csp/publications/ mccormack%20institute%20report%20 2000.pdf (accessed March 17, 2006).

Thalmann, Phillippe. 1999. Identifying Households Which Need Housing Assistance. *Urban Studies* 36(11):1933–47.

Thalmann, Phillippe. 2003. "House Poor" or Simply "Poor"? *Journal of Housing Economics* 12(4):291–317.

U.K. Parliament, Select Committee on Transport, Local Government, and the Regions. 2002. *Memorandum AFH 20: Affordable Housing in the U.K.* Memoranda Submitted in Testimony. World Wide Web page http://www.publications.parliament. uk/pa/cm200102/cmselect/

cmtlgr/809/809m01.htm   (accessed March 3, 2003).

U.S. Department of Housing and Urban Development, Office of Public and Indian Housing. 2002. *Fact Sheet: How Your Rent Is Determined for Public and Housing Choice Voucher Programs.* Washington, D.C. World Wide Web page http://www.hud.gov/offices/pih/programs/ph/rhiip/rhiip_factsheet.pdf (accessed January 14, 2005).

U.S. President's Committee on Urban Housing. 1968. *A Decent Home: The Report of the Committee.* Washington, D.C.: U.S. Government Printing Office.

von Furstenberg, George. 1968. The Impact of Rent Formulas and Eligibility Standards in Federally Assisted Rental Housing. In *Technical Studies*, Volume I, U.S. President's Committee on Urban Housing. 103–12. Washington, D.C.: U.S. Government Printing Office.

Weicher, John C. 1977. The Affordability of New Homes. *American Real Estate and Urban Economics Association Journal* 5:209–26.

Wider Opportunities for Women. 2003. *Setting the Standard for American Working Families: A Report on the Impact of the Family Economic Self Sufficiency Project Nationwide.* Washington, D.C. World Wide Web pages http://www.wowonline.org and http://www.sixstrategies.org (accessed September 5, 2005).

Yip, Ngai Ming. 1995. Housing Affordability in England. D. Phil. thesis. University of York, Department of Social Policy and Social Work.

9

"How do we know when housing is 'affordable'?"[1]

From *Rethinking Federal Housing Policy* (2008)

Edward L. Glaeser and Joseph Gyourko

A consensus seems to have arisen that housing becomes "unaffordable" when costs rise above 30 percent of household income. This is not only the standard used by the Millennial Housing Commission in its recent report, but also is the basis for a number of U.S. Department of Housing and Urban Development (HUD) policies. Thirty percent is the threshold share of income that voucher recipients are required to contribute toward renting their units. The maximum rent that developers can charge on units financed under the LIHTC program is 30 percent of the income maximum for subsidized renters. We will discuss the details of these programs later. In this chapter, we take issue with both the 30 percent figure and with the idea that housing affordability is best judged by comparing housing costs with income.

Combining income and housing costs in a single affordability metric is a bad idea because it confuses issues of income inequality with problems in the housing market. To better understand why, consider a head of a household earning the $7.25 minimum wage that will apply in the summer of 2009. Working forty hours a week for fifty weeks a year generates a pretax income of $14,500. Homeownership virtually is out of the question because little can be saved for a down payment out of such a low income. Even if that earner pays $600 per month in rent, there will be very little left for consumption of anything other than housing. By any reasonable measure, $600 dollars per month in rent is not unduly expensive; yet it will not be affordable to someone earning the minimum wage. There is no way that producing more housing will change this situation because this is a poverty problem,

not a housing problem. If society wants poor households with this level of income (or less) to consume more housing, it has to transfer resources to them. Low incomes call for a poverty-related response, such as the Earned Income Tax Credit, and perhaps also for in-kind transfers such as health care and housing vouchers.

Housing policy is much better suited to deal with failures specific to the housing market than it is to fight more general social problems. A better approach to affordability is to ask whether housing prices are close to construction costs and whether those construction costs are themselves made artificially high by problems in the housing market. An income standard of affordability makes particularly little sense in cross-city comparisons. As we discuss just below, the most basic model of urban economics predicts significant differences across space in the ratio of income to housing costs, even when the housing market is functioning perfectly.

POVERTY AND HOUSING AFFORDABILITY

It is easy to understand how something like a 30 percent of income standard was established. A poor household earning $15,000 per year cannot afford some of the basic necessities of life such as food, clothing, and transportation if it is spending half its income ($7,500) on shelter. If that family was paying only 30 percent of its income ($4,500) on housing, then its after-housing income would increase by $3,000, and life would get a little bit easier. Basic humanity seems to call out for intervention in the housing market to ease the burden of poor households.

The economist considering this example maintains that the same results can be achieved simply by giving the family an extra $3,000 and leaving the housing market alone. Why get involved with the housing market at all, if the real goal is to give poor people more resources? There is a case for in-kind transfers, which we will discuss later, but those transfers generally are less efficient at reducing income inequality than pure cash transfers.

Fighting inequality via policies to make housing more affordable necessarily interferes with the choices that poor people make. When the government gives the poor housing vouchers, it becomes impossible for them to spend less on housing and more on something else. In addition, if housing affordability policies involve supply-side subsidies that create "affordable" units via tax breaks for developers or inclusionary zoning rules, then the policies target the truly disadvantaged even less effectively. When developers have some input into allocating their below-market-rate units, they may well target them to the richest among those eligible for the apartments. While we can be pretty sure that the benefits associated with a pure income-redistribution program such as the Earned Income Tax Credit are reaped primarily by their poorer recipients, we can also be pretty sure that the Low Income Housing Tax Credit program yields large benefits to the developers who fight for them.[2]

Using an income threshold for housing costs to address income inequality can have unfortunate unintended consequences, including adverse incentive effects. To see this more clearly, we return to our example of a family earning $15,000 per year in a community where free market rents are $7,500 per year. A 30 percent rule implies that this family receives $3,000 in housing aid per year, leaving $10,500 per year in after-housing funds. A family earning $20,000 per year facing the same rule would receive $1,500 per year in housing aid and have $14,000 per year in after-housing income. Note that a $5,000 increase in income is associated with only a $3,500 increase in after-housing earnings. There are many reasons to think that society benefits when poor people face strong incentives to earn more income, yet those incentives are surely weakened by an implicit 30 percent tax on extra earnings.

Larger problems with this housing affordability metric arise when we move away from the very poor and calculate affordability not using rock-bottom housing costs, but those that average people actually face. For example, if we see two middle-income families in the same area, one spending 25 percent of its income on housing, and the other spending 35 percent, does this indicate a housing affordability problem for the second family? Can we say that the affordability problem has increased in severity if more people choose to spend 35 percent of their incomes on housing?

While we certainly can conclude that these households would be better off if housing cost them less, there is no reason to think that 30 percent is some sort of magic threshold. There is also no a priori reason to be troubled if some families decide to spend 35 or 40 percent of their earnings on housing. If these families choose to spend more on their homes, the job of a housing policy should be neither to restrict their choices nor to make their housing artificially inexpensive. The 30 percent threshold sheds little light on the actual functioning of the housing market, and confuses poverty, housing costs, and housing consumption decisions. A better approach is to focus on each outcome separately.

AFFORDABILITY ACROSS SPACE

The 30 percent threshold is particularly problematic for comparisons across markets, especially when discussing the burgeoning middle-class affordability issue. That Americans are highly mobile is one of the reasons. More than 16 percent changed residences between 2005 and 2006, and more than 6 percent moved across counties in the same year (U.S. Census Bureau 2006). The economic approach to cities and regions infers from this mobility that high housing prices are balanced by high income levels or a pleasant quality of life. Moreover, this balance does not imply that people in different places should or will be paying a constant fraction of their income on housing. In fact, giving housing aid to people in high-cost areas to the point where they are spending only 30 percent of their income on housing is likely to be both inequitable and inefficient.

This essential insight can be demonstrated with the following simple example comparing two metropolitan areas with homes of the same quality but with different levels of productivity.[3] In the first market, the average household earns $50,000 per year and homes costs $100,000 each. Further assume that interest, maintenance, and taxes amount to 10 percent of the value of the home. This is the annual user cost of occupying the home for a year, and it amounts to $10,000 (0.1 × $100,000) in this case. Abstracting from any complications associated with changing housing prices or incomes, the household has $40,000 left over to spend on other goods ($50,000 − $10,000 = $40,000).

In the second metropolitan area, productivity is higher so that average households earn $75,000. We assume that all other aspects of these two communities – such as school quality or the weather – are identical. Since people are mobile, they would naturally come to the high-income area unless high housing costs held them back. The standard economic approach to cities implies that incomes net of housing costs need to be equal across space. If they are not, then people will crowd into the high-income area.

This means that the $25,000 difference in household incomes must be offset by a $250,000 difference in housing costs, given the 10 percent user cost of housing we assume. That is, if after-housing incomes are to be equalized across space, then the average house must cost $350,000 in the high-income area. With house prices of $350,000 and annual costs equal to 10 percent of house value (or $35,000), after-housing income is $40,000 ($75,000 − $35,000 = $40,000), which is identical to that in the first market.

In the less productive, low-cost region, households are spending 20 percent of their incomes on housing each year ($10,000 / $50,000 = 0.2). In the high-cost region, households are spending almost 50 percent of their incomes on housing annually ($35,000 / $75,000 = 0.47). An affordability measure based on the ratio of income to house price suggests that the low-cost region is highly affordable, while the high-cost region is unaffordable. But this is clearly not so. People earn the same after-housing incomes in the two areas, as indeed they would have to in order for them to be willing to live in either area. Households are equally well-off in either market. They live in the same quality house and have the same after-housing income to spend

on other goods. Thus, there is no meaningful sense in which housing is less affordable, nor is there an affordability crisis, in the second market. Nobody in that market has any incentive to leave for the cheaper market (presuming they earn the average income in each market, of course).

Our example is not extreme. Average income differences of $25,000 across metropolitan areas are common, and they are generally offset by big differences in housing costs. For example, family income averaged just over $107,000 in the San Francisco primary metropolitan area in 2000, according to the decennial census for that year, compared to about $75,000 in Dallas and Atlanta and only about $66,000 in Phoenix. The gap in housing prices between San Francisco and Atlanta is larger than that implied by differences in their local incomes (assuming a user cost of capital equal to 10 percent), but there is no doubt that a significant fraction of the higher housing prices in the Bay Area is due to the higher incomes earned there.[4]

Policy interventions that try to artificially reduce housing costs in the areas with high income and high housing costs are fundamentally misguided. Imagine a policy that gave housing support to the people in the high-cost area so that their housing costs were only 33 percent of their earnings. In this case, the after-housing income in the high-cost area would be $50,000, while the after-housing income in the low-cost area would remain at $40,000. Before the housing policy, the people in the two regions had the same disposable earnings after paying for housing costs. After the housing policy, the people in the high-income region have become appreciably better off, and inequality has increased.

The disadvantages of such a misguided affordability policy are not limited to increasing inequality across regions. The subsidy would induce people and firms to move to the high-cost region. Assuredly, this would further raise housing prices in the high-cost region, so it would be more of a bonanza to existing homeowners than a relief to renters or home buyers. None of this makes sense from a policy perspective.

In sum, very different price-to-income ratios across housing markets are normal outcomes to be expected when people are free to move across labor and housing markets. One cannot assume that those places where housing prices are a larger multiple of income are less affordable in any economically meaningful sense. Given that basic insight of urban economics, we now turn to what we believe is a more sensible way to define housing affordability.

HOW SHOULD HOUSING AFFORDABILITY BE MEASURED?

Whether government should try to reduce high prices has been debated in many markets, especially for oil in recent years. Of course, just because a good is expensive does not mean the government should intervene to make it cheaper. Economists generally hold that a policy response to high prices is justified only if a market failure, such as that arising from monopoly power, is making prices artificially high. No matter the cause, some reasonable benchmark is necessary if we are going to talk sensibly about affordability, and that benchmark clearly should not be an arbitrary share of an individual's income. Fortunately, in the case of housing, there is a natural measure for considering housing affordability: construction costs.

In a well-functioning housing market with competition among home-builders, supply should be relatively elastic, and price should be determined largely by the cost of construction plus a normal profit for the builder and land assembler.[5] House values above this benchmark level signal that housing is too expensive. Developers have a strong profit incentive to supply new units to the market when prices are well above this level, so if they fail to do so, we can infer that something is standing in their way.

It also is easy to see when there is a gap between house values and construction costs, because we have data on both. Sales prices are publicly recorded, and various consultants to the construction sector provide data on what it costs to build a home in different parts of the country. These cost data surely are imperfect, and they do not include either the cost of land or some of the other soft costs involved in new construction. Yet they serve as a useful benchmark for almost all discussions of housing affordability.

Construction costs literally are the lowest price at which housing can be delivered in a given market. Hence, if prices are close to construction costs, this market is doing a good job of delivering new housing. There can be no market failure that is limiting supply and causing prices to be unduly high.

However, if house prices are significantly greater than construction costs, then we should ask why this gap exists. If the gap simply reflects the high cost of available land because of some natural scarcity, then it will be hard to narrow it without large-scale subsidization or other policies that reduce the value of land. For example, nothing the government could or should do will make land (or housing) costs the same in rural Idaho and midtown Manhattan. Conversely, if this gap reflects a market failure, such as one caused by local government policies that make new construction difficult and render developable land artificially scarce, then effective policies that bring housing costs down are easier to imagine. So, while Manhattan will never be as cheap as Idaho, it is possible to imagine that the price of Manhattan apartments could be much closer to the cost of building them.

Focusing on prices relative to construction costs, moreover, naturally also leads to far more sensible policy outcomes than we can expect from an income-based affordability measure. The long-run market price in an area inevitably reflects the interplay of supply and demand. If we want housing to cost less in an area, the most natural way to achieve that end is to increase supply. Simply put, more houses are the most straightforward way to ensure that housing is not unduly expensive.

Focusing on the gap between prices and construction costs also leads to sensible conclusions about when more housing is needed. If prices are already at or below construction costs, then there will be little room to further reduce costs with new supply unless builders are massively subsidized, and it is hard to see the rationale for that. If prices are above construction costs, then the social cost of new housing well may be lower than its value to consumers, and there can be real gains from new production.

Notes

1   Originally published as Chapter 1 in *Rethinking Federal Housing Policy: How to Make Housing Plentiful and Affordable*, Washington, D.C.: AEI Press, 2008.

Reprinted by permission of the American Enterprise Institute for Public Policy Research, Washington, D.C..

2   Programs such as the LIHTC and Section 8 vouchers cannot avoid introducing some inequality among the poor themselves. Because they are not fully funded mandates, inequality is created simply because some households and not others are lucky enough to receive a voucher or to occupy a subsidized unit.

3   This is a central principle of modern urban economics that was introduced by Sherwin Rosen (1979) and Roback (1982). Unfortunately, it has never influenced the discussion of housing affordability.

4   Our assumption that the annual user costs of living in a home are 10 percent of house value is certainly debatable, but this figure is not extreme, either. The true number varies by income because of mortgage interest deductibility, but 10 percent is well within the range of annual user costs estimated by Poterba (1992), Poterba and Sinai (2008), and other studies of this issue. Reasonable changes in the user cost figure also have no impact on our basic point: using an affordability measure that looks at housing costs relative to income is not useful for cross-metropolitan comparisons.

5   Such a market is characterized by constant returns to scale in economic terms. This does appear to be the case in most markets. See Gyourko and Saiz (2006) for recent evidence supporting the existence of competitive housing construction markets with constant returns to scale.

REFERENCES

Gyourko, Joseph and Albert Saiz. 2006. Construction costs and the supply of housing structure. *Journal of Regional Science* 46, no. 4: 661–80.

Poterba, James. 1992. Taxation and housing: Old questions, new answers. *American Economic Review* 82, no. 2: 237–42.

Poterba, James and Todd Sinai. 2008. Tax expenditures for owner-occupied housing: Deductions for property taxes and mortgage interest and the exclusion of imputed rental income. *American Economic Review*, forthcoming.

Roback, Jennifer. 1982. Wages, rents, and the quality of life. *Journal of Political Economy* 90, no. 6: 1257–78.

Rosen, Sherwin. 1979. Wage-based indexes of urban quality of life. In *Current issues in urban economics*, ed. Peter Mieszkowski and Mahlon Straszheim, 74–104. Baltimore: Johns Hopkins University Press.

U.S. Census Bureau. 2006 American FactFinder. Selected social characteristics in the United States, 2006. http://factfinder.census.gov/servlet/ADPTable?_bm=y&-geo_id=01000US&-qr_name=ACS_2006_EST_G00_DP2&-ds_name=ACS_2006_EST_G00_&-_lang=en&-_sse=on.

10
"Counterpoint: the 'Housing + Transportation Index' and fair housing"

From *Shelterforce* (2011)

Philip Tegeler and Scott Berstein

In 2010, the Center for Neighborhood Technology released its Housing + Transportation Affordability Index, which ranks the affordability of neighborhoods based on a combined housing and transportation cost measure. The index grew out of the recognition that transportation is a growing share of household budgets, and that its cost is directly related to location. Without taking it into account, areas may seem to be "affordable" based on housing cost alone when in fact they impose a high cost burden in terms of transportation. In the following exchange, Philip Tegeler of Poverty and Race Research Action Council and Scott Bernstein of CNT discuss what to do about some of the possible unintended consequences of expanding the definition of affordability that far, but not farther.

PHIL TEGELER: WE NEED A BETTER MEASURE OF OPPORTUNITY[1]

With their comprehensive "Housing + Transportation Affordability Index," the Center for Neighborhood Technology (CNT) has developed a useful tool for estimating the combined cost of housing and transportation – the two largest shares of most family budgets – for homebuyers in 337 metro areas. The index is valuable for moving land use and development decisions away from sprawl, and for informing individual family choices by emphasizing the transportation costs associated with lower priced exurban homes.

However, the index is inappropriate, standing alone, as a tool for siting new low-income family housing. CNT has indicated that it intends the index to be consistent with fair housing goals, but without a strong fair housing overlay, the index has the potential to (once again) steer low-income families into more segregated, higher poverty neighborhoods, because both rental and transportation costs tend to be lower in these neighborhoods.

A recent study by the Urban Institute and the Furman Center found that in Seattle and New York, relative to whites, minorities tend to live in neighborhoods with higher walkability/transit accessibility, but lower opportunity. "The higher density and less auto-dependent neighborhoods that score highly on walkability/transit accessibility measures tend to be more urban and disproportionately populated by racial minorities," it reports. Thus, if housing and transportation costs become the dominant method used by local housing agencies to locate housing for low-income families, it could reinforce separate and unequal development patterns that are the opposite of smart growth.

TRUE COSTS OF HOUSING LOCATION

In order to expand choice and access to opportunity, policymakers should consider not just transportation, but all costs, in particular the direct and indirect costs of living in higher poverty vs. lower poverty communities, in making location decisions.

For example, research has shown that families living in poor neighborhoods pay more for the same groceries than those living in wealthier communities, due to a lack of access to large, chain grocery stores. Small stores lack the range of products or the economies of scale that help drive down prices at chain stores. Groceries constitute a large portion of a household budget for low-income families; one study published by the Kaiser Commission on Medicaid and the Uninsured in 2004 estimates 17 percent. Thus, when calculating the cost of living in a particular neighborhood, ignoring increased food costs could lead to inaccurate assumptions about affordability.

Numerous studies have shown that low-income residents living in disadvantaged neighborhoods also pay more for basic financial services such as check cashing, short-term loans, tax preparation, and money transfers. A low-income family can spend thousands of dollars more in extra costs for these services, depending on the extent to which they use them and the types of services they use, according to a recent Brookings Institution report. High-cost financial service providers such as check cashers are much more densely concentrated in disadvantaged neighborhoods, where banks remain underrepresented.

While the H+T index does account for transportation costs, it does not reflect the possibility that low-income families living in poor communities may pay a higher purchase price for a car than low-income families living in higher-income areas. Families living in poor communities have also been found to pay higher rates for both car insurance and auto loans.

Indirect costs, while difficult to quantify, are also important to consider when evaluating neighborhood costs and benefits. Indirect factors affecting the cost or "value" of a particular neighborhood include: quality of local schools, access to employment, exposure to environmental hazards, exposure to crime, health outcomes, access to different types of social networks, and quality of municipal services.

For example, research indicates that about two-thirds of low-skill job openings are located in predominantly white suburbs, with over half of these jobs accessible by public transportation. Additionally, neighborhood poverty has been shown to negatively affect residents' long-term economic mobility.

When added up, these factors suggest that new low-income family housing should be sited in lower poverty, opportunity-rich communities. They are also a reminder of the need to dramatically improve services and outcomes for low-income families living in neighborhoods where the government has located low-income housing in the past.

DOING BOTH

A recent analysis conducted by the Urban Institute and the NYU Furman Center suggests a better approach to siting affordable housing. The report, *Building Environmentally Sustainable Communities: A Framework for Inclusivity*, combines opportunity metrics with access to transit and walkability to show how low-income families can benefit from smart growth policies without being further marginalized. The UI/Furman report seeks to include fair housing principles in the "sustainability" frame:

There is growing concern from advocates and key stakeholders that communities that are sustainable in the narrower, environmental sense will not necessarily be inclusive, and that efforts to promote environmental sustainability may come at the expense of efforts to improve those households' access to better social and economic opportunities .... But environmental sustainability and inclusion can also be complementary, and an argument can be made that to fully achieve their environmental goals, sustainable communities must be inclusive.

The report goes on to state,

HUD should effectively disqualify tools that increase environmental sustainability without attending to housing affordability or racial/ethnic inclusion. For example, zoning or regulatory changes that focus private sector development around transportation hubs, or restrict development elsewhere without addressing housing affordability, will likely further exclude low- and moderate-income households from desirable, opportunity-rich communities.

The report considers metrics based on three factors, "walkability and transit accessibility," "opportunity" (defined as richness of educational, employment, and quality of life opportunities), and an analysis of where low-income households and people of color already live. Applying these metrics to potential housing locations in New York and Seattle, the report finds a significant number of locations that simultaneously deliver smart growth, opportunity, and social inclusion for low-income families. The report also notes the need to prioritize preservation efforts for existing affordable housing in these neighborhoods.

The report also recommends that low-income families not be *excluded* by siting policies from high-opportunity communities that are not yet fully sustainable, but rather that efforts should be focused on making these communities more sustainable over time, to accommodate a more inclusive population.

State and local housing agencies engaged in siting new affordable housing should weigh these social costs and benefits (as well as their legal obligations under the Fair Housing Act to avoid segregation) rather than relying solely on the "combined costs" of rent and transportation. We also hope that the Center for Neighborhood Technology will consider amending its helpful H+T index to address the special case of low-income housing location.

SCOTT BERNSTEIN: CONSIDER TRANSPORTATION COST TO MAKE FAIR HOUSING PRACTICAL

The Center for Neighborhood Technology's Housing + Transportation (H+T) Affordability Index provides an enhanced understanding of housing affordability by revealing the transportation costs of a given location and adding those costs to location-specific housing expenditures. In addition to helping house and apartment hunters make more informed decisions about where to live, this tool can help policymakers choose where to invest scant public dollars, particularly when siting affordable housing developments.

We agree with Philip Tegeler that using the index in the way he has described could hinder fair housing goals. However, we believe fair housing metrics and the index can be used in tandem to better disclose access to opportunity

and true affordability. Recent analysis by CNT of the Illinois Housing Development Authority's affordable housing sites in the Chicago area and analysis of data directly from the index offer real-world examples that bear out this thinking.

CNT's commitment to creating sustainable, livable cities has always included making housing more affordable. The traditional measure of affordability – inside and outside of housing policy circles – begins and ends with the cost of housing. If a household spends 30 percent or less of its income on a house or apartment, it is considered affordable. Yet, the transportation costs associated with a house or apartment are rarely transparent to families or policymakers and can be significant, equaling or even exceeding outlays for shelter.

Nowhere in current information sources is this hidden cost of location disclosed – not in the U.S. Dept. of Housing and Urban Development's Fair Market Rent measure, not in rental or housing listings such as the Multiple Listing Service, and not in standard housing affordability indices published by HUD. Because relative transportation costs are in large measure a function of specific location, and transportation is overall the second largest household expenditure, this exclusion is a serious omission on both fair housing and consumer protection grounds.

CNT set out to fill this information gap in 2006 by quantifying transportation costs by location in the H+T Index. The index demonstrates how living in a compact, walkable, transit-connected neighborhood can lower a household's expenses and its environmental impact. It also offers a more comprehensive definition of affordability: that combined housing and transportation costs should not exceed 45 percent of household income. Under the traditional affordability definition, 7 in 10 neighborhoods in U.S. metro areas are affordable. Under our new measure, only 4 in 10 neighborhoods are.

These costs and their underlying data have been constructed and disclosed for all 161,000 Census block groups in U.S. metropolitan regions, using 2000 Census data. The index will be updated this year using the new 2005–2009 American Community Survey five-year data and expanded to include areas within micropolitan regions.

CNT has continually tested and refined the index and believes it can be a useful tool for policymakers in deciding where to invest scarce resources, such as those dedicated to the creation of affordable housing. We believe that the transportation costs revealed by the index, used in coordination with traditional fair housing metrics described in Philip Tegeler's article, can ensure that access to opportunity is truly affordable.

A recent analysis by CNT illustrates how the index might be used in a housing policy context. Holding housing costs constant, CNT analyzed how affordable housing financed by the Illinois Housing Development Authority (IHDA) fared between 2001 and 2008 in terms of transportation costs, transit access, and employment access. Holding housing costs constant is appropriate because these developments are all seeking to control housing costs for residents and maintain them at 30 percent or less of household income.

Within the city of Chicago, we found that family housing units located outside of HUD-designated Qualified Census Tracts (QCTs) – in other words, in higher income areas – were more likely to be within a half mile of a train station (86 percent vs. 52 percent) than units located in QCTs. These developments also had markedly better access to regional jobs. Our analysis found that average transportation costs in these neighborhoods were slightly higher

(about $40 per month) than those in low-income areas with IHDA developments.

When our analysis expanded to include suburban developments, however, we found that better access to transit correlated to significantly lower transportation costs (see Figure 10.1). While suburban areas tend to have higher average transportation costs than urban areas, costs vary widely within suburbs, and many suburban locations are both high opportunity and have relatively affordable transportation costs.

Our analysis also revealed that a substantial amount of IHDA-financed affordable housing for seniors had been built in locations with high opportunity and good transit connectivity, but virtually no affordable housing for families had been built in those areas. Neighborhoods with affordable housing developments for seniors had median household incomes about $12,000 higher on average than those with family housing developments and also featured lower average transportation costs.

Chicago suburbs to the west and northwest of the city feature high employment growth, excellent transit infrastructure, and relatively affordable transportation costs, yet these areas contribute far less than their fair share of affordable family housing. Suburban locations generally feature higher average transportation

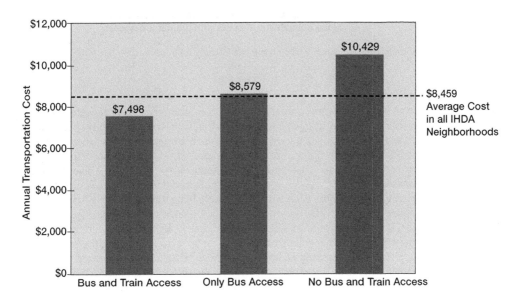

Figure 10.1 Average annual transportation costs in neighborhoods with IHDA developments (80% AMI household).

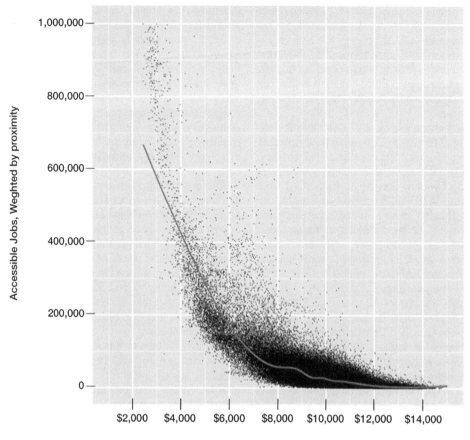

Annual Transportation Expenses for Households Earning AMI

**Locations with low average transportation costs
place households in areas with greater job access**

Figure 10.2 Annual transportation expenses for households earning AMI.

costs than the city, but if policymakers compare apples to apples (weighing developments in urban neighborhoods and suburbs separately), we believe there are significant options for maximizing opportunity while keeping transportation costs low.

Of course every region has different growth patterns, infrastructure systems, and demographic profiles, but CNT's analysis of affordable housing in Chicago demonstrates that enhanced opportunity and affordable transportation are not mutually exclusive. In fact, fair housing metrics and the transportation costs provided by the H+T Index can and should be combined dynamically to produce an optimal distribution

of scarce affordable housing resources. This means that developments featuring the absolute lowest transportation costs should not be promoted if they isolate residents from regional opportunity. But it also means that the impact that transportation costs will have on a household budget must be considered.

A CNT analysis of job access for all 161,000 2000 Census block groups currently covered by the Index also helps illustrate how the tool could be used to improve access to opportunity efforts. We plotted each block group's average transportation costs for the typical regional household and its employment access, which we define as a geographic measure of regional jobs weighted by proximity. Employment access is one of the input variables in the H+T Index. Locations with low transportation costs actually place households in areas with greater overall job access. Access to jobs, in general, is highest where average transportation costs are low. Holding housing costs constant at 30 percent, as they would be with subsidized affordable housing programs, priority should be given to affordable housing developments that are sited in locations where average transportation costs are relatively low, ideally enabling the targeted households to keep these costs at less than 15 to 18 percent of their income.

CNT does not advocate that its index be used to place affordable housing solely where both housing and transportation costs are lowest. We agree with Tegeler that doing so could unduly limit access to opportunity for low-income households. The value of the index is that it can score locations that do well on traditional fair housing criteria based on the transportation cost burden those locations will impose on families. Existing fair housing metrics omit this important piece of information, and the index can fill that gap.

Are there other costs that could or should go into the affordability equation, as Tegeler suggests? Maybe, but that shouldn't stop us from utilizing transportation data, now that we have it. With housing and transportation costs together, we have accounted for the two largest expenditures of low-income households, and the vast majority of those costs are location dependent. Adding transportation costs to the equation makes the process of creating equitable affordable housing a bit more complex; ignoring them exposes families who can least afford it to high transportation costs and volatile gas prices, and runs the risk of undoing the very affordability we are all seeking to create.

Note

1   The author is grateful for the contributions of Hanna Chouest and Caaminee Pandit.

REFERENCES

Kaiser Commission on Medicaid and the Uninsured. (2004). *Challenges and Tradeoffs in Low-Income Family Budgets: Implications for Health Coverage.* Washington, D.C.: The Henry J. Kaiser Family Foundation.

11
"Remedial Phase Report of john powell in Thompson v. HUD August 19, 2005"

john a. powell

INTRODUCTION

To redress the harms created by HUD's failure to desegregate and further fair housing in Baltimore, it is my opinion that a remedy must be implemented that accomplishes two intertwined objectives that lie at the heart of the Fair Housing Act and at the heart of the constitutional obligation to disestablish segregation. The remedy must give African American public housing residents the opportunity to live in racially integrated areas of the Baltimore metropolitan region. It must also ensure that African American public housing residents are able to move to communities that provide the opportunities that have heretofore been denied to them by virtue of the segregated public housing system in Baltimore.

In order to accomplish these twin objectives, I propose a "communities of opportunity" approach to guide the remedy in this matter. This approach is founded upon and informed by decades of research on opportunity and well-being and the determinative role that racial segregation plays in these. It is also informed by the successes and limitations of past public housing policies and programs, and by programs and policies in the housing arena in general. It is a methodology that identifies opportunity-rich areas in the Baltimore region and uses this identification to guide the location of public housing opportunities. As I discuss below, it is also my opinion that this opportunity-oriented targeting of vouchers and housing production should be combined with other remedial features, including supportive services, to ensure that participating public housing residents are

able to successfully access those opportunities afforded by the remedy.

Section I of this report, lays the foundation for the communities of opportunity approach, drawing upon research on the relationship between opportunity and racial segregation in general, and as it specifically relates to past public housing programs (Section IA). I apply this approach to public housing in Baltimore by analyzing the distribution of opportunity in Baltimore and identifying those areas of the region in which housing opportunities should be targeted (Section IB). I also discuss lessons learned from other housing mobility programs that should inform this remedy (Section IC). Furthermore, it is my opinion that the remedy imposed ought to be shaped by several principles and considerations; in Section II of this report I discuss those principles.

[…]

I THE REMEDY SHOULD CONNECT SUBSIDIZED HOUSING RESIDENTS TO COMMUNITIES OF OPPORTUNITY

An effective remedy must connect subsidized housing recipients to areas of opportunity in the Baltimore region. A race-conscious, voluntary remedy that combines vouchers with housing production and other supply-side strategies, and is targeted to integrated communities of opportunity, provides the best mechanism for doing so.

The foundation for this opportunity-based housing model is addressed in Section IA, immediately below. It is based on decades of empirical evidence demonstrating the link between racial segregation and access to opportunity, and has informed a number of housing initiatives throughout the country. In Section IB, of this report, I apply the opportunity-based approach to Baltimore, identifying high and low opportunity areas in the Baltimore region. Not surprisingly, my analysis reveals that African Americans are segregated from high-opportunity communities and that subsidized housing is clustered in segregated low-opportunity areas. The opportunity framework used in this analysis should inform where units are placed and be used to evaluate how the remedial process is progressing. The opportunity maps discussed in this section provide a framework for guiding subsidized housing policy to remedy the segregation facing African American subsidized housing recipients. The high opportunity areas identified in this analysis are locations for further investigation for targeting subsidized housing opportunities. Low opportunity areas should not be designated for remedial housing opportunities. In Section IC, I identify some key lessons learned from other voucher and mobility programs that should inform this remedy.

Opportunity based housing

Whites and people of color have different levels of access to opportunity, and housing segregation is a central cause of this disparity. Ideally, the remedy imposed in this matter should deliberately connect affordable or assisted housing to regional opportunities, such as high performing schools, meaningful employment, viable transportation, quality childcare, responsive health care, and other institutions that facilitate civic and political activity.[1] I refer to such an approach as "opportunity-based housing."

The central premise of opportunity-based housing, borne out of experience, is that residents of a metropolitan area are situated within an interconnected web of opportunities that shape their quality of life.[2] The location of housing is a powerful impediment to or asset for accessing these opportunities and as such housing policies should be oriented towards providing this access wherever it may exist. While policy discussions often focus on the

dichotomy of city and suburb, opportunity is dynamic, as evidenced by the existence of declining inner ring suburbs and redeveloping inner city neighborhoods in many regions today.

The opportunity based housing model in practice

Variants of the opportunity-based housing model can be seen in a number of areas, including fair share and workforce housing strategies. Both models seek to open the region's housing markets to address the exclusionary impact of land use policies.[3] Both aim to connect housing to economic opportunities, implicitly in the case of fair share housing programs such as *Mount Laurel*, and explicitly in the case of work force housing initiatives which seek to create housing opportunities close to regional employment opportunities and affordable at the wages that such opportunities pay.[4] Due to the "win-win" nature of work force housing initiatives (for both housing advocates and employers), work force housing programs are growing across the nation.[5]

The opportunity-based housing framework has been most explicitly accepted in the Chicago region. The region's largest fair housing organization, the Leadership Council for Metropolitan Open Communities (which was charged with administering the Gautreaux program) has embraced the opportunity-based housing framework. As stated by the organization in its 2005 report *The Segregation of Opportunities: The Structure of Advantage and Disadvantage in the Chicago Region,* "The Council has focused its energies on institutional, structural change and recognized housing, where one lives, as a crucial point of access to other economic and life opportunities." The organization has conducted two opportunity mapping exercises in the region to assess if African Americans are separated from opportunity and to frame advocacy efforts to reduce regulatory barriers that bar access to opportunity for African Americans.[6]

Chicago Metropolis 2020 is another regional organization that has embraced the opportunity-based housing framework. The organization was created by business interests but also includes labor, civic, religious and governmental organizations. Metropolis 2020 seeks to guide regional development policy to promote a socially, environmentally and economically healthier region. The organization has embraced the opportunity-based housing framework for future growth of the region. As discussed in the *Metropolitan Housing Index: Housing as Opportunity*, a study analyzing what housing policy reform would improve the region's economy:

> The decision to focus the Index on housing is significant in two respects. First, it underscores our belief that housing is far more than a place to live. A home is also a gateway to opportunity – the most important connection to jobs, schools, transit and community. If we are to provide access to economic opportunity for more Chicago area families, then we must provide a broader range of housing choices throughout the region. Second, the Metropolis Index reinforces our belief that housing, like so many other issues, must be tackled regionally. It is an economic imperative: Workers must have housing choice reasonably close to job centers if our economy is to remain robust.[7]

Metropolis 2020 has moved forward on housing initiatives connecting affordable housing to economic opportunities. The organization also developed a corporate pledge that commits employers to considering public transit access and availability of affordable housing when making expansion of investment decisions. More than 100 business leaders in the Chicago region have signed this pledge.[8]

Principles of opportunity-based housing can also be seen in the framework some states are using for assessing Low Income Housing Tax Credit (LIHTC) applications. Established in 1987, the Low Income Housing Tax Credit program is the largest single source of publicly subsidized affordable housing construction today. The LIHTC program accounts for over $5 billion in federal subsidies annually and the program produced over 800,000 subsidized units in the 1990s (in contrast, HUD's affordable housing production was less than 50,000 units during this time).[9] The Internal Revenue Service administers LIHTC, but individual states have significant flexibility in setting evaluation criteria for the projects. Traditionally, LIHTC has concentrated units in distressed segregated neighborhoods (most notably in the Northeast

and Midwest). Increasingly, however, states are revising their project siting criteria to focus on building in areas of opportunity. LIHTC provides a good example of how affordable housing production can be tied to opportunity. Traditionally, LIHTC evaluation criteria primarily targeted distressed neighborhoods (or Qualified Census Tracts) for investment, but research indicates that preferences for higher poverty neighborhoods declined in state qualified allocation plans in the 1990s.[10] States are now more likely to mandate that the only distressed neighborhoods eligible for credits are those with active revitalization plans and some states have begun to orient LIHTC neighborhood preferences more to economic opportunity.[11] Also, many states integrate other opportunity structures into their site selection evaluation, such as proximity to childcare, access to public transit, and access to nearby services, such as grocery stores and medical facilities.[12]

Several states add incentive scoring "points" in the competitive scoring criteria for Low Income Housing Tax Credit developments in areas of income diversity, population growth or job opportunities.[13] Wisconsin recently modified its scoring criteria to prioritize zip codes with recent job growth for LIHTC investment.[14] LIHTC developers seeking to build affordable housing in these areas are given 5 bonus points when applications for tax credits are reviewed. Minnesota utilizes indices of population growth and job growth to prioritize LIHTC projects.[15] Illinois designed "live near work" criteria (granting 5 bonus points to applicants) to promote LIHTC development in suburban areas with job growth and labor shortages.[16] Although 5 bonus points is not a large component of the total scoring criteria for LIHTC projects, the additional point margin can be critically important due to the high degree of competition between developers for tax credits awards. While these initiatives by individual state are admirable, HUD could and should use its leadership role to have the IRS require all states, including Maryland, to follow suit or at least provide strong incentives for the states to do so.

Elements of the opportunity-based housing concept can also be seen in recently proposed legislation reauthorizing HOPE VI. While it remains to be seen whether the proposed legislation would actually provide access to opportunity, it explicitly acknowledges that housing location is critical "to support excellent outcomes for families; especially children, with emphasis on excellent, high performing neighborhood schools and excellent quality of life amenities, such as first class retail space and green space."[17] In the proposed reauthorization, HOPE VI project evaluation would consider the quality of nearby educational opportunities and continue to focus on siting developments in lower poverty neighborhoods.

A. FOUNDATION OF THE COMMUNITIES OF OPPORTUNITY APPROACH

Beyond the various policies and programs discussed above, the opportunity-based housing model I recommend is based on an extensive body of research identifying the harms of segregation and impact of neighborhood conditions on family well being. Neighborhood conditions have a critical impact on quality of life and access to opportunity. Racial segregation results in segregation from opportunity for African Americans and this isolation inflicts significant harm on African Americans (particularly those in subsidized housing). Mobility programs for subsidized housing recipients prove that accessing higher opportunity communities improves family social, economic and educational well being. Experiences from previous mobility programs also illustrate that the programs must provide support services and counseling for recipients, be fully integrated into regional opportunities, be race-conscious and recognize the constraints of the regional housing market.

The interrelationship of racial segregation and opportunity segregation

The segregation of African Americans results in their isolation from opportunity and clustering of subsidized housing contributes to this isolation. African Americans are primarily segregated into low-opportunity communities, with limited job access, neighborhood instability and poor schools. This opportunity segregation (and the harms associated with it) are present in the Baltimore region and are reinforced by the region's clustering of subsidized housing opportunities.

African Americans remain the most racially segregated population in the nation (in reference to Whites). Despite very modest improvements in recent decades, racial residential segregation remains severe in most metropolitan regions in the United States. Nationally, the average metropolitan region has a dissimilarity index score for African Americans and Whites of .65 in 2000. This means that 65% of the metropolitan African American population would have to relocate in order for them to become fully integrated in our metropolitan regions.[18]

In most metropolitan regions today, few truly integrated communities can be found.[19] In regions with larger African American populations, segregation is even more extreme.[20] Residential segregation (as measured by the dissimilarity index) declined by more than 12 points between 1980 and 2000 in regions that were less than 5% African American, but this decline was only 6 points in regions that were more than 20% African American.[21]

In Baltimore, levels of segregation have decreased slightly over recent decades but the region is still highly segregated. These trends are seen in the dissimilarity index and other segregation indices (including the isolation index, delta index, and absolute centralization index).[22] African Americans primarily live in the City of Baltimore and the western suburbs of Baltimore County. Generally, dissimilarity index scores greater than 0.6 indicate a very high degree of residential segregation. Various analyses of Baltimore indicate dissimilarity index levels greater than 0.71 for the City of Baltimore and greater than 0.67 for the metropolitan area.[23] Others segregation indices also show high levels of residential segregation for the Baltimore region. Analysis by the U.S. Census Bureau using five different measures of segregation finds the Baltimore region to be the 14th most segregated large metropolitan area in the nation as of the 2000 Census.[24]

The segregation of African Americans in metropolitan areas is not just segregation from Whites, but also segregation from opportunities critical to quality of life, stability and social advancement. Bruce Katz and Margery Turner synthesized the impact of this opportunity segregation in the 2003 Brookings Institute research brief *Rethinking Affordable Housing Strategies: An Action Agenda for Local and Regional Leaders.*

Residential segregation denies families of color full and free choice about where to live, while often denying minority neighborhoods the services and resources they need to thrive and grow. As a consequence, minorities' access to quality schools, jobs, and economic opportunity is limited. The most extreme consequences of residential segregation are found in the central cities' large urban areas. Because communities of color experience higher poverty rates than whites, the concentration of minorities in inner city neighborhoods also concentrates poverty and compounds its social costs. As jobs, wealth and economic opportunities have migrated to the suburbs, poor minority communities in the central city have become increasingly isolated and cut off from access to the mainstream of our society and economy. Thus, housing segregation helps sustain economic inequality and contributes to the persistence of urban poverty.[25]

Residential location plays a determinative role in life outcomes and social, physical and mental health.[26] As stated in the findings report of the Congressional bi-partisan Millennial Housing Commission:

> Neighborhood quality plays an important role in positive outcomes for families. Stable housing in an unstable neighborhood does not necessarily allow for positive employment and child education out-comes.[27]

African Americans continue to be concentrated in opportunity-poor inner city neighborhoods. Racial segregation in America results in segregation from opportunities such as employment, high quality education and safe, stable healthy neighborhoods. In the Baltimore region, persistent residential segregation, opportunity segregation, and the concentration of assisted housing in opportunity poor communities is evident. Research suggests that this correlation is apparent to many Whites and that they use the presence or absence of people of color as a proxy for the neighborhood and educational quality of a specific community.[28]

Economic opportunity

Segregation affects the employment opportunities of low-income communities of color by impeding their educational growth and by physically isolating them from job opportunities.[29] As white middle-class populations have moved outward to the fringes of metropolitan areas, businesses and jobs have followed. Policies that restrict the residential choices of public housing residents create a "spatial mismatch" between job opportunities and low-income families that need them.[30] Moreover, gains achieved during the 1990s in closing the gap between African Americans and jobs were generated by increasing the residential mobility of Blacks rather than redistributing employment opportunities.[31] Jobs that remain in central business districts and are geographically accessible from racially and economically segregated neighborhoods are disproportionately unattainable because of a skills mismatch between job seekers and job requirements.[32] Inner cities residents also have more difficulty getting vital information about job openings and support during the application process because of their isolation.[33]

Research by the Brookings Institute in 2005 indicates that the "spatial mismatch" phenomenon persists. Analysis of metropolitan residential patterns and employment in 2000 for the U.S. reveals that 54% of the metropolitan African American population would need to relocate in order to eradicate the mismatch between housing and jobs for African American households. In comparison only 34% of Whites were segregated from employment.[34]

Current transportation policies exacerbate the effects of this spatial mismatch. The lack of viable transit options in most metropolitan areas limits options for those without cars and it prevents central city residents from accessing jobs located in the suburbs.[35] Nationally, people of color tend to rely on public transportation far more than whites, and the distances they must travel to new jobs in regions experiencing spatial mismatch can hurt their employment prospects.[36] In urban areas, African Americans and Latinos together comprise 54% of public transportation users (62% of bus riders, 35% of subway riders, and 29% of commuter rail riders.) Twenty-eight per cent of public transportation users have incomes of $15,000 or less, and 55% have incomes between

$15,000 and $50,000. Only 17 % have incomes above $50,000. Just 7% of white households do not own a car, compared with 24% of African-American households, 17% of Latino households, and 13% of Asian-American households.[37] In addition to the barrier of distance, the employment prospects of transit riders are also diminished by longer commute times relative to car owners and infrequency of service.[38] Spatial isolation contributes to the employment gap between African Americans and Whites, as indicated by a recent survey of spatial mismatch research:

> Our review of recent SMH (spatial mismatch hypothesis) studies clearly suggests that the lack of geographical access to employment is an important factor in explaining labor market outcomes...[39]

Racial segregation is also heavily correlated with concentrated poverty; concentrated poverty is defined as a neighborhood where more than 40% of the population lives in poverty. African Americans and Latinos are the most likely to be segregated into concentrated poverty neighborhoods and 70% of the 7 million people living in concentrated poverty neighborhoods were African American or Latino in 2000.[40] Paul Jargowsky described the detrimental effect of living in concentrated

poverty neighborhoods in his 2002 study of concentrated poverty.

The concentration of poor families and children in high-poverty ghettos, barrios, and slums magnifies the problems faced by the poor. Concentrations of poor people lead to a concentration of the social ills that cause or are caused by poverty. Poor children in these neighborhoods not only lack basic necessities in their own homes, but also they must contend with a hostile environment that holds many temptations and few positive role models. Equally important, school districts and attendance zones are generally organized geographically, so that the residential concentration of the poor frequently results in low-performing schools. The concentration of poverty in central cities also may exacerbate the flight of middle-income and higher-income families to the suburbs, driving a wedge between social needs and the fiscal base required to address them.[41]

On average, African Americans in the Baltimore region live in neighborhoods with higher poverty, higher unemployment and higher vacancy rates than other residents (see Table 11.1). The average African American neighborhood in the Baltimore region has a

Neighborhood Characteristics For the Average Person by Race	Non-Hispanic White		Non-Hispanic Black	
	1990	2000	1990	2000
Indicators of Income				
Median HH Income	$53,985	$57,889	$34,882	$37,549
Per Capita Income	$23,871	$27,008	$15,596	$18,162
% Below Poverty	6.6	6.8	20.8	18.8
Indicators of Human Capital				
% College Educated	25.7	32.3	15.5	20
% Professional	37.9	41.2	27.3	30.9
% Unemployed	3.7	3.7	10	10.1
Indicators of Housing				
% Vacant Housing	5.3	5	8.2	10.7
% Homeowners	69.3	72.7	46.5	52.8

Table 11.1 Neighborhood Characteristics for the average White and African American person in the Baltimore MSA

Source: Table directly adapted from "Separate but Unequal" database from the Mumford Center at: http://mumford.albany.edu/census/SepUneq/PublicSeparateUnequal.htm

Note: Data represents the neighborhood conditions for the average neighborhood by race. Calculations performed by the Mumford Center.

poverty rate that is nearly three times the poverty rate of the average White neighborhood. The vacancy rate in the average African American neighborhood is nearly double the rate for the average White neighborhood. The average African American neighborhood unemployment rate is more than double the rate found in the average White neighborhood.[42]

African Americans are also more likely to be isolated from employment opportunities in the Baltimore region than other residents. Research by the Brookings Institute in 2005 found that nearly 53% of African Americans in the Baltimore region would need to relocate to overcome the mismatch between employment centers and African Americans.[43] This spatial disparity is greatest between African Americans and entry level, low skill employment opportunities and this is particularly problematic for public housing residents who tend to need such jobs. ... [T]he largest clusters of estimated entry level and low skill employment opportunities are found in the suburbs surrounding the City of Baltimore, while African American neighborhoods are found primarily in the central city. Most of the region's recent job growth is oriented toward the suburban fringe of the region, and not well connected to the public transportation network indicating that this mismatch is worsening .... Spatial analysis of projected job growth in the Baltimore region suggests that these trends will worsen in the future. ... [T]he projected fastest growing areas for job growth in the region are primarily outside of both the City of Baltimore and Baltimore County.

Educational opportunity

While the African American labor force is isolated from economic opportunities, African American children remain concentrated in the poorest performing and most economically segregated school districts in the nation. Educational opportunities for most African Americans are segregated by race and class. Almost half of African American students in the U.S. attend a central city school district, compared to 17% of White students.[44] Research measuring dissimilarity for metropolitan school districts in 2000 found that black/white dissimilarity in schools was .65, thus nearly 2 out of 3 children would need to transfer to integrate the nation's

metropolitan school districts. While neighborhood segregation declined slightly during the 1990s, school segregation increased. Racial segregation is accompanied by economic segregation and African American children are much more likely to attend high poverty schools than their white counterparts. The average African American child attends a school with a 65% student poverty rate, compared to 30% for the average White student's school.[45] Segregated high poverty schools are also failing African American students. Three quarters of White students in ninth grade graduate on time while only half of African American students finish high school with a diploma in four years.[46] Researchers feel that this is creating an educational crisis for urban youth, as stated by Gary Orfield at the Harvard Civil Rights Project.

> When an entire racial or ethnic group experiences consistently high dropout rates, these problems can deeply damage the community, its families, its social structure, and its institutions.[47]

Racial and economic segregation harm the quality of education received by children for a number of reasons. Poverty creates numerous challenges for families and their children's learning processes that schools must address. In segregated areas, the scale of these challenges is much greater as the number of kids experiencing them is greater. As one study has found,

> high poverty schools have to devote far more time and resources to family and health crises, security, children who come to school not speaking standard English, seriously disturbed children, children with no educational materials in their homes, and many children with very weak educational preparation.[48]

Low-income students and students of color are also less likely to have qualified teachers, more likely to have teachers who completed an alternative certification program, and more likely to be taught by substitute teachers.[49]

Because of these educational impediments, research has consistently found that both racial and economic segregation negatively affects students. For example, one study finds that there is a "consistent negative effect of high poverty concentrations in school on students' academic achievement."[50] Another study finds that the poverty of a school, far more than the poverty of an individual, determines educational outcomes, and that impoverished students do better if they live in middle-class neighborhoods and/or attend more affluent schools.[51]

Conversely, a wealth of research indicates that students who receive education in integrated environments fare better than their segregated peers. For example, a recent analysis of school desegregation in Louisville, Kentucky found that students of color who attend more integrated schools demonstrate increased academic achievement levels and higher test scores.[52] Intergenerational gains also ensue when students of color attend desegregated schools. One study concludes "improving economic and educational opportunities for one generation of minority individuals raises the socioeconomic status of the next generation, so that those who follow are more apt to begin school at the same starting point as their non-minority classmates."[53] Attending a desegregated school also translates into higher goals for future educational attainment and occupational choices[54] and improved social networks.[55]

The benefits of an integrated education do not just accrue for students of color. Diverse educational settings contribute to all students' ability to participate in a pluralistic society.[56] Blacks and Whites who attend desegregated schools are more likely to attend a desegregated college, live in a desegregated neighborhood, work in a desegregated environment, and possess high career aspirations.[57]

Educational disparity has far reaching implications due to the fact that educational attainment is linked to many life indicators including health, income and employment. There is a strong positive relationship between the education level and health status of an individual; the lower the level of educational attainment the higher incidence of mortality rates and more common the prevalence of specific diseases such as cancer and heart disease.[58] This can be largely attributed to the relationship between educational attainment and earnings. In the United States, each successively higher education level is associated with higher earning power, and data over the last 25 years shows that this gap is only widening.[59] Furthermore, higher levels of educational attainment are associated with greater labor force participation rates and a

lower probability of unemployment. The gap in employment rates between college and high school graduates has been widening steadily as well.[60]

Educational opportunity is segregated by race and class in the Baltimore region. The dissimilarity index for African American and White students in the Baltimore region's schools was .73 in 2000 indicating that nearly 3 of 4 African American students in the region's public schools would need to change schools to desegregate the region's schools.[61] The average African American student in the Baltimore region attends a school with a student poverty rate of 42%, while the average White student attends a school with a 19% student poverty rate.[62]

The majority of African American children in the Baltimore region are concentrated in the Baltimore City school district, the poorest performing district in the region. In 2005, 51% of African American K-12 students in the region attended schools in the Baltimore City district, compared to 23% of the region's total student population.[63] For low-income African American children (those most likely to be living in subsidized housing) this concentration is more extreme. In 2000, 59% of African American children (all persons under 18 years of age) in the Baltimore region were found in the City of Baltimore, while 77% of the region's African American children in poverty (as defined by the Census Bureau in the 2000 Census) were found in the City of Baltimore.[64] Analysis of students who are eligible for free and reduced lunch supports this finding. In 2003, the percentage of economically disadvantaged students (the federal governments definition for free and reduced lunch children) in the Baltimore City School District was 73%, nearly three times the rate of the Baltimore County district (29%), and more than four times the rate of any other district in the region.[65] Test scores in the Baltimore City district are considerably lower than those of its regional counterparts. Only 37% of Baltimore City students who took proficiency exams passed the reading proficiency test and only 26% passed the math proficiency test in 2003. The pass rates for all other districts in the region were approximately double the rates of Baltimore City.[66] The Baltimore City District also contains the lowest percentage of classes taught by highly qualified teachers among all districts in the region. In

2004, almost two-thirds of classes taught in the Baltimore City schools were not taught by highly qualified teachers (65.7%).[67] In comparison, 37.0 % of classes taught in the Baltimore County district were not taught by highly qualified teachers. For other districts in the region this figure was considerably lower: Anne Arundel County (17.8%), Carroll County (13.1%), Harford County (19.9%) and Howard County (18.3%).[68]

[…]Most of the elementary schools in the City of Baltimore perform poorly based on all indicators (with the notable exception of the northern central area within the City of Baltimore). …[T]he highest concentration of schools with large numbers of students eligible for free and reduced lunch (students in poverty) is located in the City of Baltimore. Conversely, low poverty schools are primarily located in the region's suburban counties. Proficiency test scores show similar spatial disparities, with most of the City of Baltimore's elementary schools performing poorly and suburban elementary schools (primarily in Baltimore County and Howard County) performing better. Spatial patterns of teacher qualification also follow these trends; the largest number of schools with large proportions of classes are taught by non-highly qualified teachers located in the City of Baltimore.

Health and environment

Racial and economic segregation also have negative health consequences. A recent study concluded:

> Racial residential segregation is the cornerstone on which black-white disparities in health status have been built in the U.S. Segregation is a fundamental cause of health differences between blacks and whites because it shapes socioeconomic conditions for blacks not only at the individual and household levels but also at the neighborhood and community levels.[69]

Margery Austin Turner and Dolores Acevedo-Garcia, in a review of research on neighborhood effects on health, note that residents of poor, segregated neighborhoods experience poorer health outcomes because of increased exposure to the toxic substances that are dispropor-

tionately sited in their communities, and because of greater barriers to sustaining healthy behaviors such as limited access to adequate grocery stores.[70] Recent research in Maryland finds that Census tracts with higher African American populations and lower socioeconomic status are more likely to be high risk in respect to exposure to cancer-causing air toxins.[71]

A *New York Times* article synthesized research on the negative health effects of living in a racially and economically segregated environment. Among other things, the article noted that research "has shown that people who live in disadvantaged neighborhoods are more likely to have heart attacks than people who live in middle-class neighborhoods, even taking income differences into account."[72] The article also references recent findings from research on the Moving to Opportunity program:

> HUD's most remarkable early findings had to do with health. In Boston, poor children who moved to low-poverty neighborhoods were less likely to experience severe asthma attacks. Adults in New York who moved were less likely to suffer from symptoms of depression and anxiety than those who stayed behind, and adults in Boston were more likely to report that they felt 'calm and peaceful.'[73]

Crime and safety

One of the primary motives for public housing residents' participation in residential mobility programs is the desire to live in a safer neighborhood.[74] This is not surprising given the relationship between segregation, violence, and crime. A number of studies have linked segregation to an increased likelihood of perpetrating and being victimized by violence and crime.[75] The level of stress experienced in high-poverty, isolated neighborhoods contributes substantially to this risk. When parents face a high level of stress, child abuse and neglect, and family breakups are more likely.[76] Children exposed to violence can be more anxious and aggressive when they are in school, and may have trouble concentrating. These and other risk factors have a cumulative effect and this accumulation of risk contributes more significantly than any one factor to the likelihood that young people will be exposed to violence.[77]

Population stability and opportunity

Over the last several decades, many American central cities, including Baltimore, have undergone significant population decline. These population losses have been greatest in cities and neighborhoods that are poor and are racially segregated.[78] This out-migration deepens the levels of racial and economic segregation in these neighborhoods, as those who are able to move are more likely to be affluent and white.

As one would expect, loss of population, particularly upper and middle class population, is accompanied by loss of tax base. This in turn leads to a decline in the quality of municipal services and in the availability of funding for education, resulting in increased tax rates for those who are least able to shoulder them. Also accompanying central city population declines are the out-migration of investment and employment opportunities discussed above.[79] Conversely, more stable neighborhoods tend to have higher property values, higher quality public services, and higher household incomes.[80]

As African Americans and Latinos increasingly move to the suburbs these patterns tend to follow them. They are more likely than whites to move to fiscally stressed suburbs with poor public services. Recent research has found that in major metropolitan areas nearly 80% of African Americans and Latinos who live in the suburbs live in "at-risk suburbs."[81]

Research on Baltimore's inner-ring suburbs, particularly those in Baltimore County and northern Anne Arundel County, illustrates trends similar to the national trends.[82] Although Baltimore's inner-ring suburbs are growing more racially diverse, they are growing more economically isolated and overall population growth has been stagnant. Between 1980 and 2000, Baltimore's inner-ring suburbs experienced a 10% increase in the African American population, while the White population decreased by 15%. The inner-ring suburbs also have a diminishing share of the region's employment, decreasing household income and increasing poverty rates.[83] The Baltimore County suburb of Lochearn illustrates this point; between 1980 and 2000 the African American population increased from 49% of the total population to 78%. During this same time period, its poverty rate nearly doubled while inflation adjusted income and home

values declined. Similar trends were seen in other suburbs like Lansdowne and Woodlawn.[84]

Subsidized housing and opportunity segregation

The clustering of assisted housing reinforces racial and opportunity segregation. Although subsidized housing does not necessarily cause White flight (especially if sited in moderate numbers), the extreme clustering of units in inner city neighborhoods does contribute to racial segregation. As of 2000, three quarters of the nation's traditional assisted housing units were located in central cities while only 37% of the nation's metropolitan population lived in central cities. Low Income Housing Tax Credit projects are also clustered in central city locations: in 2000 58% of all LIHTC units were found in central city locations.[85]

While the average metropolitan neighborhood had a 13% poverty rate in 2000, neighborhoods with traditional assisted housing[86] had a poverty rate of 29%. While only 4% of all metropolitan housing units were in concentrated poverty neighborhoods, more than 11% of assisted housing units were found in concentrated poverty neighborhoods. The average neighborhood with traditional assisted housing had household incomes that were more than 40% lower and home values that were more than 20% lower than the average metropolitan neighborhood.[87] Research in the 50 largest metropolitan regions (where the majority of African Americans live) has identified even greater concentration of assisted housing in high poverty (low-opportunity) areas. Almost 50% of public housing and 27% of project based Section 8 housing is located in a concentrated poverty neighborhood in the 50 largest metropolitan regions.[88] It is my understanding the expert report of Dr. Gerald Webster will illustrate the concentration of subsidized housing in the Baltimore region in segregated lower opportunity communities.

B. IDENTIFYING COMMUNITIES OF OPPORTUNITY IN BALTIMORE

The first step in applying an opportunity-based approach in this remedy is to assess the regional distribution of opportunity.[89] Mapping opportunity in the region requires selecting variables that are indicative of high (or low) opportunity. Once derived, opportunity maps should be used to guide subsidized housing (and affordable housing) policy. For the purpose of this remedy, the identified high opportunity areas should be further considered as potential locations for subsidized housing opportunities. Site-specific impediments may eliminate some locations from consideration and some anomalies may exist, but tracts identified as high opportunity areas provide a geographic framework within which to locate subsidized housing. In the future this analysis should be updated as the remedy progresses. Opportunity is dynamic and additional analysis should be undertaken to identify future potential high opportunity areas not captured in this analysis, in the future the exact measurements and metrics of opportunity may need to be periodically updated.

Measuring opportunity

The opportunity indicators upon which I have focused include measures of economic health, educational opportunity, and neighborhood quality (and/or other quality of life indicators).[90] Economic opportunity is primarily measured by focusing on the availability of jobs and on job growth as a way of determining future areas of job availability.[91] Educational opportunity is primarily measured through student performance measures, teacher qualifications, and student economic status.[92] Neighborhood quality is measured through a wide range of data reflecting neighborhood stability and quality, including housing values, vacancy, poverty rates and crime.[93] For this report, I have gathered data on these opportunity indicators for communities and neighborhoods throughout the Baltimore region.

For present remedial purposes, indicators of opportunity need to be tailored to the unique needs of subsidized housing residents. While opportunity indicators generally focus on standard categories of opportunity (jobs, school quality, and neighborhood quality), for our purposes this should be expanded and framed to address needs that are specific to this population, such as entry-level job access and public transit access. Moreover, the overall guidance provided by opportunity mapping should be employed flexibly so that the individual needs and attributes of public housing residents can be accounted for

in a manner that maximizes desegregation and opportunity access. Indicators of opportunity will be of varying significance for different public housing residents. For example, school quality will be of less importance to elderly residents than to residents in general. Similarly transit access may be less critical for public housing residents that own cars.

Opportunity mapping is a critical step to link subsidized housing to opportunity. Although opportunity mapping provides an understanding of neighborhoods in the region where opportunity is great and where additional in-depth (site-based) analysis should be conducted. Conversely, opportunity mapping identifies where low opportunity areas are located. In the context of this remedy, this opportunity mapping analysis is a critical first step.

Opportunity mapping is grounded in practice

As discussed earlier, principles of opportunity-based housing have informed programs and policies for decades. With advances in research technology and Geographic Information Systems, opportunity mapping has also been increasingly used to guide such policies, as evidenced by several recent housing initiatives. For example, two opportunity-mapping exercises have been conducted in the Chicago region. The most recent assessment by the Leadership Council for Metropolitan Open Communities identifies "communities of opportunity" in the six-county Chicago metropolitan area.[94] The opportunity-mapping project assists in analyzing housing need in the Chicago region as well as assessing the application of housing programs.[95]

The policy of locating subsidized housing based on "impacted" or "non-impacted" areas in the Baltimore consent decree, utilizes some of the principles of opportunity mapping, focusing on an absence of poverty and racial concentration as indicators of opportunity. As seen in Map 13, 2000 Census Tracts that meet the race and poverty impacted areas guidelines (with 2000 African American populations and poverty higher than the regional average) generally coincide with low-opportunity areas in Baltimore. The growth in neighborhood indicator systems in major cities also uses a similar spatial framework to analyze neighborhood distress.[96]

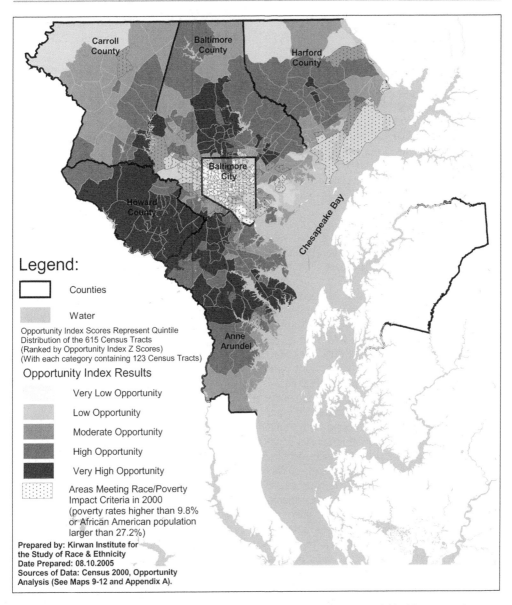

Map 13 Census 2000 tracts meeting race/poverty criteria for impacted areas overlaid with opportunity areas (tracts w/ race of poverty rates higher than 2000 MSA average).

An extensive neighborhood indicator system for the City of Baltimore is already in use. The Baltimore Neighborhood Indicators Alliance (BNIA) utilizes neighborhood indicator analysis to inform housing and development policies. As stated by the BNIA:

The Alliance designed its core functions based on the knowledge that Baltimore needed a common way of understanding how our neighborhoods and overall quality of life are changing over time. Baltimore needed a common threshold from which to have discussions about what is best for changing conditions. Baltimore needed a mechanism to hold itself, and all others who work, live, play, and invest in its neighborhoods, accountable for moving in the right direction.[97]

The private sector utilizes similar models in identifying appropriate locations for residential and commercial investment. Commercial entities make investment decisions based upon market research to quantify a geographic market's relative health by using indicators. The databases used in this type of "cluster analysis" spatially identify locations for new businesses and investments.[98] Similar to opportunity mapping, these indexes provide a first step in site location decisions and are followed by more detailed site-by-site analyses of investment potential.

Indicators and methods

For the purpose of this analysis, opportunity was measured in three primary categories: economic opportunity/mobility, neighborhood health, and educational opportunity. A cumulative map of regional opportunity was created based on all three categories (Map 12). Census Tracts are classified into five groups (very low, low, moderate, high, very high) based on the quintile in which their opportunity index scores fall. Each group contains 123 census tracts. Thus, very low-opportunity areas represent the 123 lowest scoring Census Tracts in the region and very high-opportunity areas represent the 123 highest scoring Census Tracts.

Multiple opportunity indicators were identified and analyzed at the census tract level for each category of opportunity. Data for the opportunity indicators was obtained from multiple sources including the U.S. Census Bureau, state and national school quality databases and the Baltimore Regional Council.[99] […]

Social science research and previous opportunity mapping research guided the selection of indicators chosen for this analysis. Although the precise measurements used to assess indicators are flexible and can be refined, the primary indicators utilized (education, economic opportunity, and neighborhood health) are critical to the opportunity analysis. For example, the manner in which educational quality is measured can be modified, but education as a core indicator of opportunity must be included in the analysis.

Indicators of economic opportunity and mobility

For purposes of the remedy, economic opportunity and mobility must be particularized to the unique employment and mobility needs of African American subsidized housing residents. As indicated by the spatial mismatch literature, proximity to employment is important to accessing employment opportunities. It is apparent from the extensive literature on spatial mismatch that inner city residents do not have access to much of the region's employment opportunities.[100] Jobs are moving further away from the inner city and this disparity is even greater for entry level or low skill jobs.[101]

In addition, lower income central city residents of color are much more dependent on public transportation. In the City of Baltimore, African American auto ownership is very low (an estimated 44% of African American households did not own an automobile in the 2000 Census) and more residents rely on public transit to reach employment. In the 2000 Census, 20% of commuters in the City of Baltimore used public transit to reach work and this figure was even higher for African American commuters (28%).[102]

Given these factors, measures of locally available entry level and low skill jobs, and identification of areas with less competition for entry-level jobs, employment trends, and transit access must be included in an opportunity analysis.[103] Specific economic opportunity indicators data included:

- The number of estimated entry level and low skill employment opportunities within 5 miles of each census tract in 2002.[104] The analysis focuses on entry level and low skill jobs as these are jobs most likely to be attainable for subsidized housing residents.[105]
- The ratio of entry level and low skill employment opportunities per 1,000 residents within 5 miles of each census tract in 2002. This measure helps to determine locations with relatively high demand for entry-level workers. Although low wage jobs may be found in inner-city areas, there are also many low-income workers nearby

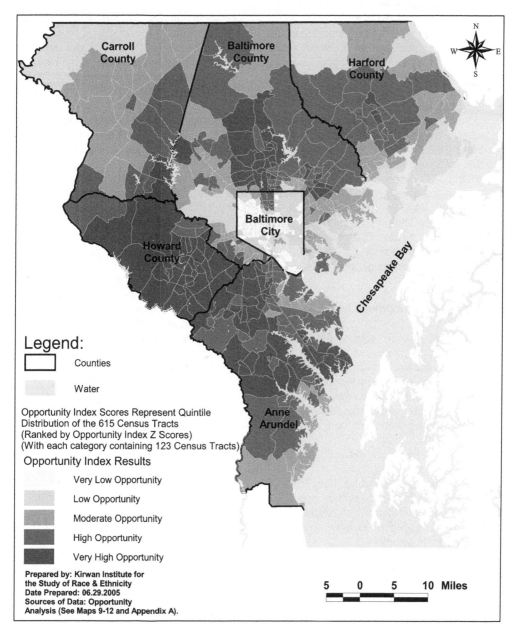

Legend:

☐ Counties

▦ Water

Opportunity Index Scores Represent Quintile
Distribution of the 615 Census Tracts
(Ranked by Opportunity Index Z Scores)
(With each category containing 123 Census Tracts)

Opportunity Index Results

▢ Very Low Opportunity

▢ Low Opportunity

▦ Moderate Opportunity

▩ High Opportunity

■ Very High Opportunity

Prepared by: Kirwan Institute for
the Study of Race & Ethnicity
Date Prepared: 06.29.2005
Sources of Data: Opportunity
Analysis (See Maps 9-12 and Appendix A).

5   0   5   10 Miles

Map 12 Comprehensive Opportunity Index for the Baltimore Region.

• competing for these jobs. Therefore, jobs located near concentrations of low income households may be less accessible to potential employees than jobs outside the urban core. Previous researchers have also utilized a method of "weighting" job accessibility measurements to account for this competition for available jobs.[106]

• The absolute change in employment opportunities within 5 miles of each census tract from 1998 to 2002. This is included to identify areas of increasing employment opportunity.

- The proportion of each census tract within one-half mile of a public transit line. As addressed in the discussion above, public transit is important for low income inner city African Americans. Although transit is highly flexible and can be improved in non transit, high opportunity communities, to best address the direct needs of subsidized housing residents, transit was included as one of the factors in the opportunity analysis.
- The median commute to work time (in minutes). Commute time is a general measure commonly utilized to assess the proximity to regional employment opportunities. The purpose of including this measure was to identify areas that are the most accessible (in respect to travel time) to the region's employment opportunities.

Indicators of neighborhood health

Neighborhood quality affects residents by determining local public and private services; shared norms and social control, peer influences, social networks, crime and violence, and job access.[107] Research shows that living in a severely distressed neighborhood undermines the health and well-being of both adults and children.[108]

Measures of neighborhood health included:

- Rate of population change from 1990 to 2000.[109] As discussed earlier, population declines are associated with neighborhood disinvestment, higher taxation and lower public service quality.[110]
- Estimated crime rates in 2000. Crime and physical deterioration are identified by residents as the most critical elements of neighborhood quality.[111] The crimes include murder, rape, robbery, assault, burglary, theft, and motor vehicle theft. Linking low crime areas to subsidized housing is not unprecedented. A recent article by *The Dallas Morning News* reported that the Dallas Housing Authority will soon stop allowing Section 8 voucher use in areas where crime rates within a ¼ mile of the Section 8 housing development are higher than the city average in the previous six months.[112]
- Poverty rates for the general population in 2000.[113] An extensive body of literature has identified the detrimental impact of concentrated neighborhood poverty on quality of life.[114]
- Vacant property rates in 2000, gathered from the 2000 Census of Population and Housing. As discussed earlier, physical deterioration is a principle indicator of neighborhood quality.[115] Vacant property is also associated with higher crime, higher public service costs, and neighborhood property depreciation and as a threat to public safety.[116]
- Property values for owner occupied homes in 2000, measured as median home value in the 2000 Census.[117] As discussed earlier in this report, more stable neighborhoods tend to have higher property values.[118] Housing prices and neighborhood quality are highly correlated, and housing prices are influenced by many factors, including proximity to jobs and commercial establishments, access to environmental amenities, taxes and public services, and the income level of neighborhood residents.[119]

Indicators of educational opportunity

A comprehensive analysis of educational opportunity should rely on a broad variety of measures. For purposes of this analysis, however, I have focused on a handful of key indicators. These include teacher quality, economic segregation and isolation, and measures of academic proficiency.[120] As discussed in more detail below, measures of educational opportunity include:

- The proportion of elementary and middle school students qualifying for free and reduced lunch in 2004. As stated earlier in this report, school quality and the economic status of its student body have been shown to have significant connections to student performance.[121] Higher poverty schools have been proven to negatively impact student performance, regardless of the individual student's economic status. Also, teachers in higher poverty schools must spend more time to address the additional needs of high poverty students and as a result have less time to focus on teaching course work.
- The proportion of classes not taught by highly qualified teachers in 2004. Teacher

qualifications are important in assessing whether students receive high quality instruction.[122]

- The proportion of elementary and elementary school students proficient in reading in 2004 (as measured by the 3rd and 5th grade Maryland school assessments). Although test scores are not perfect tools to measure student proficiency and may be discriminatory, given the central role that they play in determining advancement and the opportunities available to students, and the importance of scores in the federal No Child Left Behind legislation they must be acknowledged as important measures.
- The proportion of elementary and elementary school students proficient in math in 2004 (as measured by the 3rd and 5th grade Maryland school assessments). See comments above.

Comprehensive opportunity map

I have combined the individual indicators of opportunity to derive a composite map of opportunity for the Baltimore region. The opportunity-based housing framework guides analysis of neighborhoods with respect to a holistic approach to defining opportunity. As Galster and Killen note, the housing, mortgage, criminal, labor, political, social service, educational systems and local social networks are "bound in an immensely complicated nexus of casual interrelationships."[123] While the opportunity-based housing framework empha-sizes housing as the central determinant of opportunity, this is largely because of housing location relative to other opportunity structures, such as jobs and education. Map 12 depicts the overall opportunity index for the Baltimore region. This comprehensive assessment includes all 14-opportunity indicators, measured by averaging standardized scores for the three sub-categories (economic opportunity and mobility, neighborhood health, educational opportunity).

Results

[…][T]he distribution of opportunity has distinct spatial patterns in the region. Economic opportunity and mobility are greatest in three primary areas in the region. North of the City of

Baltimore in Baltimore County, in some areas near downtown Baltimore, and in areas of Howard and Anne Arundel Counties southwest of the City of Baltimore.

[…]Indicators of neighborhood health locate the healthiest neighborhoods almost entirely outside the City of Baltimore. Large clusters of healthy neighborhoods are found in all surrounding counties in the region.

[…][T]he distribution of educational opportunity in the Baltimore region[…] mirror[s] neighborhood health in the region. The distribution of educational opportunity is highly skewed toward the region's suburban counties. All very low educational opportunity census tracts are clustered within the City of Baltimore. The only suburban County with a large concentration of low educational opportunity areas is the portions of Baltimore County west and east of the City of Baltimore.

While the individual opportunity maps provide insight into specific areas for improvement, the comprehensive opportunity map is most critical for informing housing policy as it provides the most complete assessment of opportunity in the region. As seen in Map 12, opportunity-rich areas are distributed throughout the counties in the region but the primary concentration of high-opportunity tracts are found in suburban counties. The largest clusters of very high opportunity tracts are located in central Baltimore County, southern Howard County, northern Anne Arundel County and southern Harford County. The City of Baltimore is the primary location of very low-opportunity tracts in the region, but areas of high opportunity are found on the north central edge of the City of Baltimore.

African Americans are segregated into low opportunity areas

In the Baltimore region, the distribution of opportunity rich and poor communities mirrors patterns of racial segregation. As seen in Map 15, African Americans are segregated away from high-opportunity neighborhoods and into low-opportunity neighborhoods in the Baltimore region. Census tracts identified as very low-opportunity were 81% African American in 2000 and very high-opportunity tracts were only 12% African American in

2000. Conversely, very low-opportunity tracts were 15% White and very high-opportunity tracts were 80% White in 2000. In the six county region, over 72% of African Americans are located in either very low or low-opportunity areas; in contrast only 18% of Whites reside in very low or low-opportunity areas (See Table 11.2).

Racial segregation from opportunity operates independently of income in Baltimore as low-income Whites are considerably less segregated from opportunity than low-income African Americans.[124] Almost 84% of the region's low-income African American households were found in low-opportunity Census Tracts. In comparison, only 33% of the region's low-income White households were found in low-opportunity Census Tracts. More low-income Whites lived in higher opportunity Census Tracts (37%) than lived in low-opportunity Census Tracts (33%). Only 10% of low-income African Americans lived in high-opportunity Census Tracts (See Table 11.3).

Similarly, high-income African Americans do not have the same access to higher opportunity areas as high-income Whites in Baltimore. Sixty seven percent of high-income White households lived in high-opportunity Census Tracts in 2000, while only 30% of high-income African Americans lived in high-opportunity Census Tracts. In 2000, more than half of high-income African American households (56%) lived in low-opportunity Census Tracts, compared to 11% of high-income White households (See Table 11.3).

Affordable housing is deficient in high opportunity areas

Rental housing is primarily clustered in low-opportunity areas but opportunity rich census tracts do contain a significant number of rental housing units. Analysis of price data for these

Number of people by opportunity area 2000	Total population	White population	African American population
Very low opportunity	365,383	56,352	296,633
Low opportunity	460,346	232,819	204,425
Moderate opportunity	508,852	416,234	68,401
High opportunity	594,452	510,440	53,822
Very high opportunity	583,398	467,608	67,957
Percentage of persons by race by opportunity area 2000		White population	African American population
Very low opportunity		15.4%	81.2%
Low opportunity		50.6%	44.4%
Moderate opportunity		81.8%	13.4%
High opportunity		85.9%	9.1%
Very high opportunity		80.2%	11.6%
Percentage region's population by race by opportunity area in 2000	Total population	White population	African American population
Very low opportunity	14.5%	3.4%	42.7%
Low opportunity	18.3%	14.9%	29.7%
Moderate opportunity	20.3%	24.4%	9.4%
High opportunity	23.7%	30.4%	7.5%
Very high opportunity	23.2%	26.9%	10.7%

Table 11.2 Population by race by opportunity area in the Baltimore region in 2000

Source: Opportunity Analysis and Census 2000 STF3 Tract Data.

rental units in high-opportunity areas indicates that it is relatively expensive and thus beyond the means of low-income households. Nearly half of the region's rental housing in 2000 was found in low-opportunity communities (49%). Of the 104,000 rental housing units located in high-opportunity areas, approximately 60% cost more than the HUD fair market rent for a 2 bedroom apartment in the Baltimore region as of 2000 ($643). The region's supply of rental units below fair market rent in 2000 was even more clustered in low-opportunity areas than rental units in general. Only 21% of the 210,000 rental units with rent less than $650 a month were found in high-opportunity communities (See Table 11.4).[125]

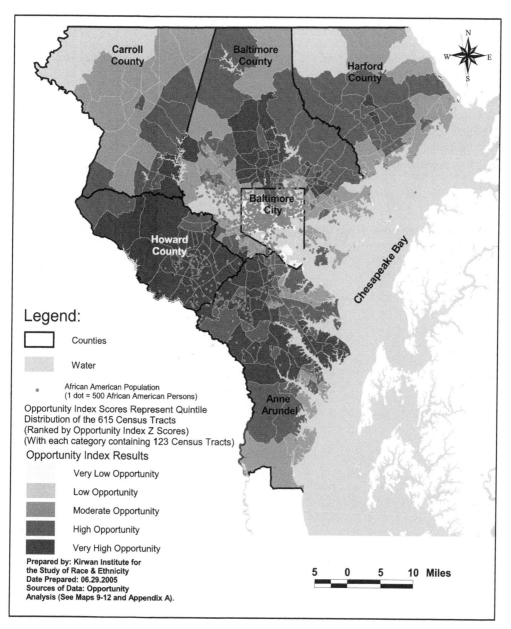

Map 15 Comprehensive opportunity index for the Baltimore region overlaid with African American population in 2000.

Percent of region's households by income and race by opportunity area 2000	Low income Whites	Low income African Am.	Middle income Whites	Middle income African Am.	High income Whites	High income African Am.
Very low opportunity	8.8%	57.5%	3.9%	37.6%	1.7%	24.6%
Low opportunity	23.8%	26.2%	17.0%	34.3%	9.6%	31.0%
Moderate opportunity	26.4%	6.8%	27.2%	10.8%	21.6%	14.2%
High opportunity	24.2%	4.9%	28.4%	7.7%	32.6%	12.7%
Very high opportunity	16.8%	4.6%	23.6%	9.6%	34.6%	17.4%

Percent of region's persons in poverty by race and opportunity area 2000	Region's White pop. in poverty	Region's Af Am. pop. in poverty
Very low opportunity	12.6%	65.8%
Low opportunity	25.8%	20.4%
Moderate opportunity	24.5%	5.8%
High opportunity	21.7%	3.6%
Very high opportunity	15.5%	4.4%

Table 11.3 Population by race and income/poverty by opportunity area in the Baltimore region in 2000

Low Income households earn less than $30K, Middle Income households earn $30K to $60K, High Income households earn more than $60K. This methodology was adopted from the Lewis C. Mumford Center's research on the dynamics residential segregation by race and income, delineating (poor, middle income and affluent households). For more information visit the Mumford Center's website at: http://mumford.albany.edu/census/segregation/home.htm.

Sources of data: Opportunity Analysis and U.S. Census Bureau, 2000 Census Tract Data.

Rental housing characteristics by opportunity area in 2000	Rental units gross rent < $650	Rental units gross rent > $650	% of rental units with rents < $650	% of rental units with rent > $650	% of region's rentals with rents < $650	% of region's rentals with rents > $650
Very low opportunity	71,376	4,025	94.8%	5.3%	34.0%	4.2%
Low opportunity	60,031	14,851	81.4%	20.1%	28.6%	15.6%
Moderate opportunity	35,610	14.587	75.0%	30.7%	17.0%	15.4%
High opportunity	25.924	25,627	46.2%	45.7%	12.3%	27.0%
Very high opportunity	17,076	35,884	32.6%	68.6%	8.1%	37.8%

Table 11.4 Rental housing characteristics by opportunity area in the Baltimore region in 2000

Sources of data: Opportunity Analysis and U.S. Census Bureau, 2000 Census Tract Data.

Subsidized housing is concentrated in low opportunity areas

The region's subsidized housing is primarily clustered in low-opportunity areas. Map 14 illustrates this clustering of subsidized housing sites in 1998 and LIHTC sites in 2001 in low-opportunity areas (primarily in the City of Baltimore) in the region.[126] Nearly two-thirds

of Section 8 voucher households (65%) are located in low-opportunity Census Tracts (Table 11.5). Approximately 20% of all Section 8 households are located in high-opportunity areas, and an even lower percentage of African American Section 8 households are located in high-opportunity areas. Over three-fourths (77%) of all African American Section 8 voucher holders were found in low-opportunity

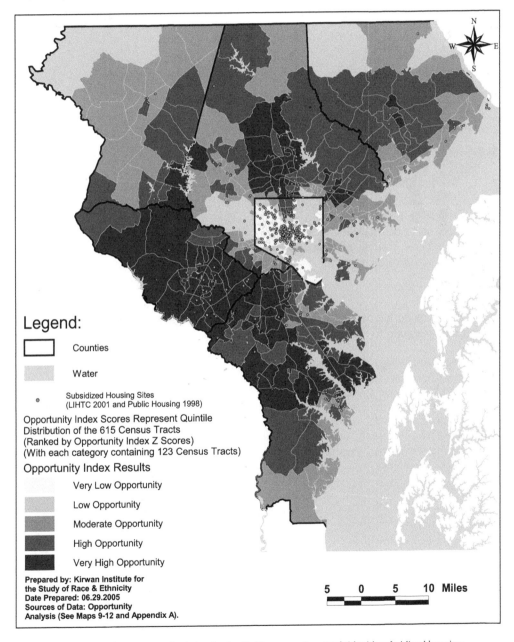

Legend:

☐ Counties

▨ Water

◦ Subsidized Housing Sites
(LIHTC 2001 and Public Housing 1998)

Opportunity Index Scores Represent Quintile
Distribution of the 615 Census Tracts
(Ranked by Opportunity Index Z Scores)
(With each category containing 123 Census Tracts)

Opportunity Index Results

▢ Very Low Opportunity

▢ Low Opportunity

▢ Moderate Opportunity

▢ High Opportunity

▢ Very High Opportunity

Prepared by: Kirwan Institute for
the Study of Race & Ethnicity
Date Prepared: 06.29.2005
Sources of Data: Opportunity
Analysis (See Maps 9-12 and Appendix A).

5　0　5　10　Miles

Map 14 Comprehensive opportunity index for the Baltimore region overlaid with subsidized housing.

Number of units by opportunity area	Section 8 households	White Section 8 households	African American Section 8 households
Very low opportunity	6,701	233	6,436
Low opportunity	5,908	1,138	4,736
Moderate opportunity	2,989	1,737	1,228
High opportunity	2,173	1,193	947
Very high opportunity	1,621	488	1,090
Number of units by opportunity area	Section 8 households	White Section 8 households	African American Section 8 households
Very low opportunity	34.6%	4.9%	44.6%
Low opportunity	30.5%	23.8%	32.8%
Moderate opportunity	15.4%	36.3%	7.8%
High opportunity	11.2%	24.9%	7.3%
Very high opportunity	8.4%	10.2%	7.7%

Table 11.5 Section 8 vouchers by opportunity area

Source: Section 8 Voucher Data from HUD.

Census Tracts, while only 29% of White Section 8 voucher holders were located in these tracts. Conversely, high-opportunity Census Tracts contained 35% of White voucher holders and only 15% of African American Section 8 households (Table 11.5).

Additional considerations when applying opportunity mapping to the remedy

Identifying communities of opportunity is a dynamic process that should adapt to account for the particular needs of subsidized housing recipients and to incorporate new and updated data as it becomes available. The opportunity maps created for this report provide an initial portrait of how opportunity-based housing can be applied to the remedy.

Notes

1 john a. powell, Opportunity-Based Housing, 12-Wtr *J. Affordable Housing and Community Dev. L.* 188.
2 Ibid.
3 Edward Goetz, Fair Share or Status Quo? The Twin Cities Livable Communities Act, 20 *Journal of Planning Education and Research* 39 (2000).
4 Roland Anglin, Searching for Justice: Court-Inspired Housing Policy as a Mechanism for Social and Economic Mobility, 29 *URB. AFF. Q.* 432–53 (1994).
5 Tim Sullivan, Putting the Force in Workforce Housing, 70 *Planning Magazine* 26 (2004).
6 *Communities of Opportunity* (2003) and *Segregation vs. Opportunity* (2005). The Leadership Council for Metropolitan Open Communities: Chicago, IL.
7 Chicago Metropolis 2020. *Metropolitan Housing Index: Housing as Opportunity* (2004) Introduction available online at: http://www.chicagometropolis2020. org/10_20.htm
8 Chicago Metropolis 2020. *The Metropolitan Principles Corporate Pledge FAQ.* Available online at: http://www.chicago metropolis2020.org/10_20faq.htm.
9 Lance Freeman, *Siting Affordable Housing: Location and Neighborhood Trends of Low Income Housing Tax Credit Developments in the 1990s.* Brookings Institute (2004). See also Myron Orfield, Exec. Dir., Institute of Race and Poverty, *Racial Integration and Community Revitalization: Applying the Fair Housing Act to the Low Income Housing Tax Credit*; Draft Working Paper provided by author.

10 Jeremy Gustafasen and J. Christopher Walker, *Analysis of State Qualified Allocation Plans for the Low-Income Housing Tax Credit Program* (2002). Prepared for HUD by the Urban Institute Metropolitan Housing and Communities Policy Center.

11 For an example of a LIHTC program requiring revitalization plans in qualified census tracts please review North Carolina's QAP guidelines at: http://www. nchfa.com/Rental/RD2005qap.aspx

12 Research by Lance Freeman indicates that LIHTC production is still primarily in racially concentrated areas, the program is locating projects in less segregated and lower poverty neighborhoods than other traditional site based subsidized housing programs. See Freeman, op. cit.

13 The State of Minnesota grants bonus LIHTC points for projects built in the top ten and top twenty (job and population growth) counties in the State, for more information visit: http://www.mhfa.state. mn.us/multifamily/HTC2005forms.htm. California grants bonus points for projects in locations with inclusionary housing policies in high income and high job growth areas through its "balanced communities" guidelines. For more information visit: http://www.treasurer. ca.gov/ctcac/programreg/20050608.pdf

14 Source: Low Income Housing Qualified Allocation Plan for the State of Wisconsin. Available online at: http://www.wheda. com/TCA_Appendices/Appdx_T_05.pdf.

15 Tax Credit Allocations: States Reflect in '01, Mull QAP Changes for Next Year, Vol. *Affordable Housing Finance* (September 2001.) Available online at: http://www. housingfinance.com/ahf/articles/ 2001/01SeptQAPchanges/index.html.

16 2005 Qualified Allocation Plan for the Low-income Housing Tax Credit. Illinois Housing Development Authority. "Live near Work" QAP information available online: http://www.ihda.org/ViewPage. aspx?PageID=93.

17 Draft reauthorization bill for the Hope 6 program. Prepared by Senator Barbara Mikulski of Maryland. Introduced on July 27, 2005. For more information visit: http:// mikulski.senate.gov/record.cfm?id =241669. For a summary of the re-

authorization bill visit: http://www.clpha. org/page.cfm?pageID=729.

18 E. Glaeser and J. Vigdor, *Racial Segregation in the 2000 Census* (2001). The Brookings Institution Survey Series. The Brookings Institute, Center on Urban and Metropolitan Policy.

19 Sheryll Cashin, *The Failures of Integration* (2004).

20 Ibid.

21 John Logan, *Ethnic Diversity Grows: Neighborhood Integration Lags Behind* (2001). Lewis Mumford Center for Comparative Urban and Regional Analysis.

22 J. Iceland, D. Weinberg, and E. Steinmetz, *Racial and Ethnic Segregation in the United States: 1980–2000* (2002). U.S. Census Bureau.

23 Logan, op. cit. See also Nancy A. Denton, *American Apartheid: Segregation and the Making of the Underclass* (1993) at 20 ("A simple rule of thumb in interpreting these indices is that values under 30 are low, those between 30 and 60 are moderate, and anything above 60 is high."); Glaeser and Vigdor, op. cit.

24 Iceland, Weinberg, and Steinmetz, op. cit.

25 Bruce Katz and Margery Austin Turner. *Rethinking Affordable Housing Strategies: An Action Agenda for Local and Regional Leaders* (2003). Research Brief, The Brookings Institution, page 7.

26 The Millennial Housing Commission was a bi-partisan federal commission assessing national housing policy and needs. The commission released their final report in 2002. (Hereinafter *Meeting Our Nation's Housing Challenges*).

27 Millennial Housing Commission. *Meeting Our Nation's Housing Challenges* (2002), page 11.

28 Please see race-conscious discussion in Section II.

29 See, e.g., Richard Price and Edwin S. Mills, Race and Residence in Earnings Determination, 17 *J. Urb. Econ.* 1–18 (1985); Mark Alan Hughes, Misspeak Truth to Power: A Geographical Perspective on the 'Underclass' Fallacy, 65 *Econ. Geography* 187 (1989); Harry J. Holtzer, The Spatial Mismatch Hypothesis: What has the Evidence Shown? *Urb. Studies* 105 (1991); and J.F. Kain, The Spatial Mismatch Hypothesis: Three

Decades Later, 3 (2) *Housing Pol'y Deb.* 371 (1992).

30 A 1999 study showed that predominantly white suburbs in the United States contain 69.4% of the low skill jobs, while the central city typically holds 10.2 % of these jobs. Similarly, a recent study found that "metro areas with higher levels of black-white residential segregation exhibit a higher degree of spatial mismatch between blacks and jobs" and that the same applied to other communities of color. See Michael Stoll, Harry Holtzer, and Keith Ihlanfeldt, *Within Cities and Suburbs: Racial Residential Concentration and the Spatial Distribution of Employment Opportunities Across Submetropolitan Areas* (1999).

31 Ibid.

32 These jobs require college degrees more than in any other sub-metropolitan area. Id.

33 See Cong. Office Of Tech. Assessment, *The Technological Reshaping of Metropolitan America* 222 (1995). (Hereinafter *Technological Reshaping*).

34 M. Stoll, *Job Sprawl and the Spatial Mismatch Between Blacks and Jobs* (2005). The Brookings Institute.

35 Robert D. Bullard, Addressing Urban Transportation Equity in the United States, 31 *Fordham Urban Law Journal* 1183 (October 2004).

36 Ibid.

37 Thomas W. Sanchez *et al., Moving to Equity: Addressing Inequitable Effects of Transportation Policies on Minorities,* The Civil Rights Project and Center for Community Change, Harvard University (June 2003).

38 "[T]he time spent traveling per mile for black central city residents is twice that of suburban whites, partly because more whites use their own car to get to work than do blacks (69% for whites versus 43% for blacks) who are more dependent on public transportation." See Congressional Office of Technology Assessment, *Technological Reshaping* 221–22 (1995) (citing Harry Holzer, Keith Ihlanfeldt, and David Sjoquist, Work, Search, and Travel among White and Black Youth, 35 *Journal of Urban Economics* 320–345 (1994).

39 K. Ihlanfeldt, K. and D. Sjoquist, The Spatial Mismatch Hypothesis: A Review of

Recent Studies and Their Implications for Welfare Reform. 9 *Housing Policy Debate* 881 (1998). See also H.J. Holzer, op. cit., page 118 ("The preponderance of evidence from data of the last decade shows that spatial mismatch has a significant effect on black employment").

40 Paul Jargowsky, *Stunning Progress, Hidden Problems: The Dramatic Decline of Concentrated Poverty in the 1990s* (May 2003). The Brookings Institute.

41 Ibid.

42 This data represents the characteristics found in typical neighborhood for the average African American and White resident of the Metropolitan Area. These figures were calculated by the Lewis Mumford Center and can be reviewed online at the "Measuring Neighborhood Inequality," from the "Separate and Unequal" databases on neighborhood characteristics by race. Lewis Mumford Center for Comparative Urban and Regional Analysis.

43 M. Stoll, op. cit.

44 Christopher Swanson, *Who Graduates? Who Doesn't? A Statistical Portrait of Public High School Graduation, Class Of 2001* (February 25, 2004). Education Policy Center, The Urban Institute.

45 John Logan, *Choosing Segregation: Racial Imbalance in American Public Schools, 1990–2000* (March 29, 2002). Lewis Mumford Center for Comparative Urban and Regional Research.

46 G. Orfield, D. Losen,, J. Wald, and C. Swanson. *Losing Our Future: How Minority Youth are Being Left Behind by the Graduation Rate Crisis* (March 2004). A Joint Release By: The Civil Rights Project at Harvard University, The Urban Institute, Advocates for Children of New York and the Civil Society Institute.

47 *Dropouts in America: Confronting the Graduation Rate Crisis.* 2004. Harvard Education Press. Cambridge, MA. Edited by Gary Orfield, page 2.

48 See Gary Orfield and John T. Yun, *Deepening Segregation in American Public Schools* (1997), Harvard Project on School Desegregation. See also, *What Matters Most: Teaching for America's Future, A Report of the National Commission on Teaching America's*

Future (Spring 1996): Summary Report. (Racially segregated schools more often rely upon transitory teachers, have curricula with greater emphasis on remedial courses, higher rates of tardiness and unexcused absence, and lower rates of extracurricular involvement).

49 Linda Darling-Hammond, Recruiting Teachers for the 21st Century: The Foundation for Educational Equity, 68 *Journal of Negro Education* 254, 279 (2000).

50 See William T. Trent, Outcomes of School Desegregation: Findings from Longitudinal Research, 66 *J. Negro Ed.* 255 (1997).

51 Stephen J. Schellenberg, Concentration of Poverty and the Ongoing Need for Title I, in Gary Orfield and Elizabeth H. DeBray eds., *Hard Work for Good Schools: Facts Not Fads in Title I Reform*, 130, 137 (1999). See Michael Kurlaender and John T. Yun, *Is Diversity a Compelling Educational Interest? Evidence From Metropolitan Louisville*, Harvard Civil Rights Project (1999).

52 Ibid.

53 Trent, op. cit.

54 Kurlaender and Yun, op. cit.

55 Amy Stuart Wells, The "Consequences" of School Desegregation: The Mismatch Between the Research and the Rationale, 28 *Hastings Const'l L. Q.* 771, 773 (2001).

56 Kurlaender and Yun, op. cit.

57 Robert Crain and Amy Stuart Wells, Perpetuation Theory and the Long-Term Effects of Schools Desegregation, 531 *Rev. Of Ed'l Research* (Winter 1994); M. Dawkins and J.H. Braddock, The Continuing Significance of Desegregation: School Racial Composition and African American Inclusion in American Society, 53 *J. Negro Ed.* 394 (1994).

58 Center for the Advancement of Health. December 2002. *Life Lessons: Studying Education's Effect on Health*. Vol. 7, No. 12. Healthy People 2010. November 2000. *A Systematic Approach To Health Improvement*.

59 U.S. Census Bureau. Day, J. C. and Newburger, E. C. July 2002. The Big Payoff: Educational Attainment and Synthetic Estimates of Work-Life Earnings.

60 Joint Economic Committee Study. January 2000. *Investment in Education: Private and Public Returns*. United States Congress.

61 School segregation database for Metropolitan Areas by the Lewis Mumford Center for Comparative Urban and Regional Analysis.

62 John Logan. *Choosing Segregation: Racial Imbalance In American Public Schools, 1990–2000* (2002). Lewis Mumford Center for Comparative Urban and Regional Research.

63 Data from Maryland online database for school district indicators and demographics and www.mdreportcard.org.

64 Data from the U.S. Census Bureau, 2000 Decennial Census of Population and Housing. http://www.census.org.

65 Source of data: No Child Left Behind School Partnership Database for Maryland School Districts at: http://www.schoolresults.org.

66 Ibid.

67 Source of data: 2004 Maryland Report Card. Maryland Department of Education at: http://www.msp.msde.state.md.us.

68 Ibid.

69 David R. Williams and Chiquita Collins, Racial Residential Segregation: A Fundamental Cause of Racial Disparities in Health, 116 *Public Health Reports* 404, 405 (Sept.–Oct. 2001). Specific health risks of segregated neighborhoods that the authors reference include: elevated risks of cause-specific and overall adult mortality, infant mortality and tuberculosis; elevated exposure to noxious pollutants and allergens; a lack of recreational facilities; higher cost, poorer quality groceries; and limited access to high quality medical care.

70 Margery Austin Turner and Dolores Acevedo-Garcia, Why Housing Mobility? The Research Evidence Today, 14 *Poverty & Race Research Action Council Newsletter* (January/February 2005).

71 Benjamin J. Apelberg, Timothy J. Buckley and Ronald H. White, Socioeconomic and Racial Disparities in Cancer Risk from Air Toxics in Maryland 113 *Environmental Health Perspectives* (June 2005).

72 Helen Epstein, Enough To Make You Sick?, *The New York Times Magazine* (10/12/03).

73 Ibid.

74 The *Moving To Opportunity Interim Impacts Evaluation* found that "perhaps most notable from the perspective of the families themselves is the fact that they were successful in achieving the goal that loomed largest in their motivation to move out of their old neighborhoods: improvements in safety." Orr, Feins, Jacob, and Beecroft (Abt Associates Inc.) and Sanbonmatsu, Katz, Liebman and Kling (NBER), U.S. Department of Housing and Urban Development Office of Policy Development and Research, Executive Summary of *Moving To Opportunity Interim Impacts Evaluation* (September 2003). Page ix.

75 See, e.g., Robert J. Sampson, Stephen W. Raudenbush, and Felton Earls, Neighborhoods and Violent Crime: A Multi-Level Study of Collective Efficacy, 277 *Science* 918–24 (1997).

76 *Youth and Violence: A Report of The Surgeon General* (January 2001).

77 Ibid.

78 G. Thomas Kingsley and Kathryn L. S. Pettit, Population Growth and Decline in City Neighborhoods, 1 *Urban Institute: Neighborhood Change In Urban America* (December 2002).

79 powell, j. How Government Tax and Housing Policy Have Racially Segregated America in Karen Brown and Mary Louise Fellows, eds., *Taxing America* (1997).

80 See e.g., Chengri Ding and Gerrit-Jan Knaap, Property Values in Inner-City Neighborhoods: The Effects of Homeownership, Housing Investment, and Economic Development, 13 (4) *Housing Policy Debate* 701–727 (2003). It should be noted, however, that stability by itself may not be an unmitigated good. One recent study found that neighborhoods with residential stability and low affluence were associated with poor health outcomes. Christopher R. Browning and Kathleen A. Cagney, Moving Beyond Poverty: Neighborhood Structure, Social Processes and Health, 44 *Journal Of Health And Social Behavior* 552–571 (December 2003).

81 Myron Orfield and Thomas Luce, *Minority Suburbanization and Racial Change: Stable Integration, Neighborhood Transition, and the Need for Regional Approaches*. Report of Institute on Race and Poverty (presentation at the "Race and Regionalism Conference in Minneapolis, MN May 6–7, 2005). "At Risk" suburbs are defined as fiscally stressed suburbs with below average public resources and above average public resource needs.

82 Bernadette Hanlon & Thomas Vicino, *The State of the Inner Suburbs: An Examination of Suburban Baltimore, 1980 to 2000*. Center for Urban Environmental Research and Education, University of Maryland, Baltimore County (2005).

83 Ibid.

84 Ibid.

85 Freeman, op. cit.

86 Note: This figure does not include LIHTC Units. LIHTC units were on average found in neighborhoods with a 19% poverty rate in 2000. Freeman, op. cit.

87 Ibid.

88 Deborah Devine *et al.*, *Housing Choice Voucher Location Patterns: Implications For Participant And Neighborhood Welfare*, U.S. Department of Housing and Urban Development, Office of Policy Development and Research (2003).

89 powell, op. cit.

90 *Communities of Opportunity* (2003) and *Segregation vs. Opportunity* (2005). The Leadership Council for Metropolitan Open Communities, Chicago, IL.

91 Ibid. and *Low Income Housing Qualified Allocation Plan* for the State of Wisconsin.

92 *Communities of Opportunity* (2003) and *Segregation vs. Opportunity* (2005). The Leadership Council for Metropolitan Open Communities, Chicago, IL.

93 Ibid.

94 Ibid.

95 *Segregation vs. Opportunity* (2005). The Leadership Council for Metropolitan Open Communities, Chicago, IL.

96 G. Thomas Kingsley, *Building and Operating Neighborhood Indicator Systems: A Guidebook*, National Neighborhood

Indicators Partnership, The Urban Institute (March 1999).

97 *Baltimore Neighborhood Indicator Alliance.*

98 Cashin, op. cit.

99 For a complete description of all indicator data, see Appendix A in the full report.

100 For more information please review the discussion on spatial mismatch in the "economic opportunity" section of the full report.

101 For more information on spatial mismatch, see Section 1A.

102 U.S. Census Bureau, Census 2000, STF3 data.

103 It is important to note, however, that there is a long history of transportation discrimination and areas with exclusive housing policies are also likely to be areas that resist transit lines. Thus, an opportunity-based housing approach must balance the need to meet the transit needs of residents with the potential for reinforcing the exclusion of public housing residents from opportunity-rich areas that do not participate in the mass transit system. In crafting a remedy, it is important to recognize that the transit system is flexible and, to the greatest extent possible, efforts should be made to overcome transit barriers in otherwise opportunity-rich areas.

104 Five miles is the proximity distance used in previous opportunity mapping analysis. This distance measure could be further refined based on local input and assessment of the potential travel barriers of subsidized housing residents.

105 There are various methodologies to define entry level or low skill employment; this is just one approach utilizing zip code industry business patterns data. It should be noted that this methodology will differ from the methodology used in the expert report of Dr. Basu. From my understanding, Dr. Basu's low wage employment analysis utilized county level occupational employment data, this county level data source is not available at the geographic scale needed for our analysis (zip codes) and therefore was not an applicable methodology for our analysis.

106 Gary Barnes, *Transportation and Regional Growth Study Examines Job Access for Low-Income Households*, Center for Transportation Studies, University of Minnesota (November 2000).

107 Austin Turner and Acevedo-Garcia, op. cit., page 16.

108 Ibid.

109 Although population loss can be more specifically targeted to loss of middle income and higher income residents, in this analysis loss was measured by the total population only. Refinement of this analysis may want to modify this methodology to target these house-holds.

110 Kingsley and Pettit, op. cit.

111 M. R. Greenberg, Improving Neighborhood Quality: A Hierarchy of Needs 10 (3) *Housing Policy Debate* 601–624 (1999).

112 Kim Horner, Rentals in Unsafe Areas Won't Get Vouchers; Dallas Agency's Program Will Make Crime Rates a Factor, *The Dallas Morning News* (08/10/05).

113 Although unemployment is referenced often in the literature in respect to neighborhood conditions, for this analysis poverty was utilized as a better measure of socio-economic status. We had concerns about the accuracy of local unemployment rates and the potential impact of varying degrees of labor force participation distorting the local unemployment rates. Thus, neighborhood unemployment rates may vary significantly based on labor force participation, potentially showing low unemployment if large numbers of the work force have stopped looking for employment.

114 For more information please review discussion on concentrated poverty in the economic opportunity section, earlier in this report.

115 Greenberg, op. cit.

116 For more information on the impacts of vacant and abandoned properties visit the resource page of the National Vacant Property Campaign. Located online at: http://www.vacantproperties.org/facts.html.

117 Much of the research on housing cost and neighborhood quality focuses on homeowner property values and not rents. In this analysis, home values were utilized due to concerns about the statistical validity of data on rental property rents in suburban areas. Some suburban areas have relatively few rental units and only a sample of these units is used to produce Census 2000 gross rent data. Thus, utilizing rents to determine neighborhood quality may be less reliable than utilizing home values.

118 Supre note 80.

119 Ding and Knaap, op. cit.

120 The state of Maryland uses additional indicators of educational quality that were not used in this analysis. These include attendance, absenteeism and graduation rates. For the purpose of this attendance, graduation data was not utilized because of concerns about the validity of this indicator for elementary schools (which were the basis of our analysis).

121 The Century Foundation, *Can Separate Be Equal? The Overlooked Flaw at the Center of No Child Left Behind* (2004).

122 L. Darling-Hammond and B. Berry, Recruiting Teachers for the 21st Century: The Foundation for Educational Equity, 68 (3) *The Journal of Negro Education* 254–279 (1999).

123 George Galster and Sean Killen, The Geography of Metropolitan Opportunity: A Reconnaissance and Conceptual Framework, 6 (1) *Housing Policy Debate* 7–43 (1995).

124 Low Income households earn less than $30K, Middle Income households earn $30K to $60K, and High Income households earn more than $60K. This methodology was adopted from the Lewis C. Mumford Center's research on the dynamics residential segregation by race and income, delineating (poor, middle income and affluent households).

125 Note: gross rent data from Census 2000, the Census gives values in ranges for the number of units within ranges of $ values (e.g. $550 to 699, $600 to 649). Thus $650 was selected as the dividing range to represent units that cost more or less than HUD's 2 bedroom FMR in 2000.

126 Data used in this map was from the HUD 1998 picture of subsidized housing and is not current; LIHTC developments in this data were updated to 2001 but all other data from this map is from 1998. Due to the age of this data, this information will not be consistent with more recent data from the expert report of Gerald Webster. A small number site based data in the HUD 1998 picture of subsidized housing has not geographic information (longitude and latitude coordinates). Due to this missing information these points could not be mapped.

PART THREE

Conflicting views on low income homeownership

WARNING

THIS IS A NOTICE TO VACATE
THE FOLLOWING ADDRESS:

TO ALL OCCUPANTS: A writ of Possession, Cause # _O___ _27___ has been issued
by _Sale of Pos___ Court # _2_ ordering eviction from this property. Your belongings will be
removed if you have not vacated the premises by: _March 10___ _2009_ _10:29AM_
Posted _March 9___ _2009 11:22AM_ Constable, Precinct # _2_
By Deputy _____

ADVERTENCIA

ESTE ES UN AVISO DE EVACUACION DE
DOMICILIO, CASA O APARTAMENTO.

ATENCION TODOS HABITANTES: La Corte a ordenado que se desocupen y dejen los terrenos
que ocupan. Si no cumplen con esta orden para la fecha de: _____ sus
posesiones y efectos seran movidos sin mas advertencia.

Plate 3 Foreclosure notice posted on house in Travis County, Texas, April 2009 (photograph by Meng Qi).

INTRODUCTION TO PART THREE

American poverty policy has a strong history of seeking to reward hard work and encourage self-sufficiency. As such, the vast majority of federal housing initiatives promotes and protects homeownership. American housing policy today reflects its historical roots in trying to distinguish between the worthy and unworthy: encouraging the "submerged middle class" yet discouraging permanent dependency. Policies designed to do so, such as the mortgage interest tax deduction, are not perceived as a "handout," despite the enormous outlay of federal tax dollars involved. Such policies fall in line with the desire to promote stable middle-class communities, yet do little to aid families who are "shelter poor." Such public policies also do little to combat racial and economic segregation and exclusion.

The federal and state emphasis on homeownership resonates with policymakers and voters alike as addressing traditional American values. In contrast, rental housing is often equated with *public housing,* specifically the enormous, cookie-cutter housing projects of the 1950s and 1960s. Popper (1981) affirms that the difference between landowners and the landless is one of the key social divisions in American society. The negative connotations surrounding rental housing and tenants are similar to those surrounding welfare and other federally sponsored programs to aid the poor. For these reasons, programs to support rental-housing development have typically been less politically viable than those fostering homeownership.

As Krueckeberg writes,

> the transformation of the Jeffersonian ideal – the yeoman farmer as the bearer of civic virtue – into the suburban homeowner on what Jackson (1985) has dubbed the "crabgrass frontier" began during the Civil War with the first income tax experiments that provided special tax benefits to homeowners.

Policies emphasizing and encouraging homeownership came to fruition during the Roosevelt Administration. Federal mortgage insurance mitigated risk for banks, allowing them to lend much more freely, and to a new class of Americans – the emerging middle class.

However, as has been pointed out by a number of researchers (Shlay 2006; Rohe *et al.* 2007; Sugrue 2009), homeownership is not necessarily better than renting for many households, and in some cases may actually worsen already shaky finances for low income families, leading to both financial and emotional stress. Shlay (2006) writes,

> Policy should not solely work at getting families into a home-ownership situation without ensuring that it is a viable investment and is in a quality location. Housing policy should not increase risks for families already at risk of a host of problems. It should work at eliminating them or at least minimising their probability of occurring (p. 524).

However, it is important to note that these changes "stabilized the flow of funds to housing during the Depression and set the stage for strong growth in the immediate postwar years" (Lea 1996, 163). FHA insurance, in conjunction with other policies that promoted and enabled suburban homeownership (including the GI Bill and the National Highway Act), increased the homeownership rate increased from 47 percent before the FHA to 62 percent in 1960. By expanding homeownership by the greatest percentage in U.S. history, the FHA also served to expand the tax benefits of the Mortgage Interest Tax Deduction (which had been available to homeowners since 1913).

This system of housing finance existed with few changes through the 1990s, when changes in the mortgage market – including deregulation in the secondary markets – resulted in the creation of a sub-prime mortgage market. The subprime market originated loans to households who did not fit the criteria required by standard mortgage lenders. While these changes resulted in greater access to capital for low-income and minority borrowers, many of the lenders took advantage of their clients by pushing them into mortgages they had little ability to pay back. These "predatory" lenders charged grossly high interest rates to vulnerable populations, particularly poor and minority families. Spurred on by a mortgage system that diluted the risk of lending to marginally qualified applicants, the subprime market grew by 900 percent during the 1990s. By 2008, subprime loans comprised a substantial portion of the housing market, making up nearly 15 percent of all loans in 2008 – increasing from only 7 percent in 1989.

Consequently, between 2006 and 2008, the foreclosure rate increased by 225%, largely as a result from defaults in the subprime sector and a disproportionate number of these foreclosures occur in low income and minority communities. As foreclosures increased and the value of homes fell, the mortgages held by banks and the quasi-public institutions Freddie Mac and Fannie Mae lost tremendous value.

By emphasizing homeownership in the low-income housing policy debate, "ideas about affordable housing policy alternatives ranging from subsidies to co-operatives" have been set aside (Shlay 2006, 527). However, in light of the foreclosure crisis and subsequent economic recession, these alternative approaches have been brought back into the policy spotlight, namely cooperatives. These so-called "shared equity" homeownership approaches apply a cooperative ideal to home and land ownership, providing a more stable and secure form of ownership for low-income households than a traditional mortgage. One of the greatest advantages of Community Land Trusts (CLTs) is that they are organized and controlled by a non-profit organization. Thus, there is considerable support for homeowners after they purchase a home, as the non-profit agency can intervene to prevent default prior to foreclosure (Curtin 2008; Davis 2010). The extremely low foreclosure rate resulting from this model enhances security and stability for both individual owners and the community as a whole.

As banks across the country close and the federal government institutes bailouts, national debate once again centers on housing policy. As the U.S. debt grows higher, it seems appropriate to point out that the total amount lost to subsidies to encourage homeownership is somewhere in the vicinity of $300 billion, or over $3,000 per home-owning household – subsidies that disproportionately favor the wealthy at the expense of the middle and lower classes. The current housing crisis demonstrates not only the importance of housing policy to the overall U.S. economy, but also how minority and low-income households routinely pay the price for poor policymaking.

Provision of homeownership opportunities for low-income households has been a federal policy priority for decades. The strategies undertaken to encourage low-income homeownership and the challenges and risks – both historical and current – to creating low-income homeownership through the financial markets are many and varied. The articles included in this section provide a variety of approaches and perspectives regarding the extent to which government should or should not emphasize or subsidize homeownership, and how potential alternative approaches may or may not improve quality of life for U.S. families.

IN THIS PART:

REFERENCES AND FURTHER READING:

Andrews, Edmund. 2009. *Busted: Life Inside the Great Mortgage Meltdown*. New York: W. W. Norton & Company.
Apgar, William. 2004. *Rethinking Rental Housing: Expanding the Ability of Rental Housing to Serve as a Pathway to Economic and Social Opportunity*. Cambridge, MA: The Joint Center for Housing Policy of Harvard University.
Curtin, Julie Farrell. 2008. "CLTs: A Growing Trend in Affordable Home Ownership." *Journal of Affordable Housing & Community Development Law*, 17(4): 367–394.
Davis, John E. 2010. "More Than Money: What Is *Shared* in Shared Equity Homeownership?" *Journal of Affordable Housing and Community Development Law*. 19 (3/4): 259–277.
Follain, James R. and Lisa Melamed. 1998. "The False Messiah of Tax Policy: What Elimination of the Home Mortgage Interest Deduction Promises and a Careful Look at What It Delivers." *Journal of Housing Research*. Washington, D.C.: Fannie Mae Foundation.
Jackson, Kenneth. 1985. *Crabgrass Frontier*. New York: Oxford University Press.Joint Center for Housing Studies. 2011. *America's Rental Housing: Meeting Challenges, Building On Opportunities*. Cambridge, MA: The Joint Center for Housing Studies of Harvard University.
Joint Center for Housing Studies (2011) *Rental Market Stresses: Impacts of the Great Recession on Affordability and Multifamily Lending*. Cambridge, MA: The Joint Center for Housing Studies of Harvard University
Katz, Allison. 2009. *Our Lot: How Real Estate Came to Own Us*. New York: Bloomsbury.
Lea, Michael J. 1996. "Innovation and the Cost of Mortgage Credit: A Historical Perspective." *Housing Policy Debate* 7(1): 147–174.
Popper, Frank. 1981. *The Politics of Land Use Reform*. Madison, WI: University of Wisconsin Press.
Rohe, W. M. and L. S. Stewart. 1996. "Homeownership and Neighborhood Stability." *Housing Policy Debate*, **7**(1): 37–81.
Rohe, W. M. and H. L. Watson (eds.). 2007. *Chasing the American Dream: New Perspectives on Affordable Homeownership*. Ithaca, NY, Cornell University Press.
Shlay, Anne B. 2006. "Low-Income Homeownership: American Dream or Delusion?" *Urban Studies* 4(3): 511–531.
Sternlieb, G. and J. W. Hughes (1981). *The Future of Rental Housing*. Piscataway, N.J.: Center for Urban Policy Research.
Sugrue, Thomas. 2009. "The New American Dream: Renting." *The Wall Street Journal*, August 14.

Trefzger, J. 1998. "Why Our Federal Income Tax Should Promote Homeownership." *Illinois Real Estate Letter*, 12(3/2): 10.

Watcher, Susan and Michael Smith. 2011. *The American Mortgage System: Crisis and Reform.* Philadelphia, PA: University of Pennsylvania Press.

Wheelock, David C. 2008. "The Federal Response to Home Mortgage Distress: Lessons from the Great Depression." *Federal Reserve Bank of St. Louis Review*, 90(May): 133–148.

Zandi, Mark. 2009. *Financial Shock: Global Panic and Government Bailouts – How We Got Here and What Must Be Done to Fix It.* Upper Saddle River, N.J.: FT Press.

12

"The grapes of rent: A history of renting in a country of owners"

From *Housing Policy Debate* (1999)

Donald A. Krueckeberg

THE BIAS OF OWNERSHIP

In a study of neighborhood development in Minneapolis, suggestively titled "Revenge of the Property Owners," Goetz and Sidney (1994) document the conflict between property owners and lower-income tenants. They found that community organizations were dominated by people who espoused an "ideology of property," a key point of which is that too much rental housing leads to neighborhood decline. Affordable housing policies for renters were to be avoided, according to this dominant faction, because they increase the neighborhood's concentrations of both poverty and transients who have no stake in the neighborhood. Because property owners are less transient and have a stake in the neighborhood's long-term well-being, policy should therefore be crafted to provide benefits for them, halting middle-class flight and attracting investment and stakeholders. This ideology – that owners are better citizens than renters – is a modern manifestation of a bias hardened in stereotypes that has misguided American public policy from colonial times to the present.

Scholars continue to produce evidence to debunk these myths. Rohe and Stegman (1994) studied the impact of homeownership on political and social involvement in Baltimore. They focused on a group of home buyers before and after their purchase of a home, comparing them with a control group of continuing renters. They found that the home buyers were less likely to be neighborly than the continuing renters. Although the home buyers were more likely to participate in neighborhood and block

associations, they did not participate more than renters in other types of community activities. Moreover, those home buyers who bought primarily for investment purposes rather than for shelter and amenity reasons were no more likely to participate in social and political affairs than renters.

Community activism was studied in public housing projects and their stressed inner-city neighborhoods in two New Jersey cities by Greenberg (1998). He found that ownership made no statistically significant difference in discriminating between those who were very active in community affairs and those who were moderately active. However, it did play a role in discriminating between those who were very active and those who were inactive: The inactive people tended to be owners (Greenberg 1998).

Indeed, Kemeny and Marcuse have each put forward the thesis that homeownership fosters values of privatization that inhibit the desire for the public involvement so often deemed characteristic of homeowners (Kemeny 1981; Marcuse 1987). Lundqvist (1998) has performed extensive testing of the impact of tenure form on various kinds of political participation in Sweden, finding no significant substantiation of the thesis except that political party membership is significantly higher among homeowners. However, he finds that the high correlation of education and income with homeownership confounds the analysis and notes that the ideology that property ownership makes good citizens is "deeply engrained in Conservative thinking the world over" (p. 217).

In this article, I argue that from colonial times to the present, a bias in favor of property ownership has been prominent in American public policy. Over time, this bias has manifested itself in several ways: property requirements that denied renters the rights of suffrage in colonial times, land distribution schemes that aggrandized ownership rather than settlement, and finally a variety of regressive federal and state tax policies in which homeowners and the real estate fraternity are enormously subsidized by tenants who are excluded from the largesse they help to supply.

THE COLONIAL HERITAGE: PROPERTY, TAXES, AND SUFFRAGE

A strong historical connection exists among landed property, the property tax, and political representation in the United States. According to our current theory and practice of property tax law, property tax is a tax on the land and improvements on it themselves, not the property owner. This disembodiment of property was not the case when the English first employed the property tax. The concept of apportioning taxes according to ability to pay, or "substance," from which our system derived, "was widely accepted as early as the fourteenth or fifteenth century" in England (Fisher 1996, 12). The concept of taxing possessions rather than people was not generally accepted until perhaps the 17th century because a person of substance without land was virtually inconceivable then.

Property measured a person's substance, and taxes were levied on that basis. Hence, lists of the number and quality of property holdings were kept. As the modern concept of a person with great income but without large landed property holdings became more common, these lists took on a life of their own. The tax came to be regarded as a tax on the properties on the lists rather than on the persons who owned them.

There is an irony in the way we have transformed yet perpetuated this social relationship. If someone were to have stood up in a local town meeting in colonial New England and said, "I am a respected citizen," everyone would have known, by implication, that he or she had property and paid taxes. Today people commonly stand up in local public meetings and declare, "I am a taxpayer!" and everyone is supposed to conclude that these are propertied people deserving of respect. The implication is

that some people do not pay property taxes and therefore have not earned respect. Ownership means privilege over nonownership with reference to the thing owned. That is fundamental to the notion of property rights. If everyone is an owner (of some comparable thing), then there is a basis of equity. But if there is a class of owners and a class of nonowners, then a basis of inequity exists that may not be grounded in any other personal characteristics and behavior other than the act of owning.

In general, in colonial America, "the tax laws overburdened the politically impotent and favored the politically powerful, especially the landed classes" (Becker 1980, 11). Until the American Revolution, class distinctions required that a person have a good deal more than property to qualify to vote. Commonly excluded from the privileges of suffrage were women, Catholics, various non-English Europeans, African Americans, Native Americans, and the poor. Political historian Rogers Smith (1997, 58) tells us:

> The colonists also maintained English class hierarchies in legislating the political rights of even their British members. The "one outstanding and universal requirement" for suffrage was some type of landed property qualification, which disfranchised servants and laborers. Colonial America thus remained in many ways a medieval political world, with power structures defined by titles to estates more than commitments to self-governance.

Only 5 of the 13 colonies relaxed their initial property requirement to include personal property as well as real property. Property, like nationality, race, gender, and religion, was a characteristic of the person, a mark of who the person was. It was evidently less important, however, than racial and gender caste. Ownership of property for most Catholics, all slaves and most ex-slaves, all women, various ethnic groups, and Native Americans did not give them access to full citizenship or the right to vote.

PROPERTY AND TENANCY IN THE CONFEDERATION

In the period of confederation (1776 to 1789), most white males had property and thus could vote. That still represented only about one in six inhabitants. Nonetheless, states increasingly made efforts to replace land requirements with either personal property or taxpaying as the new test for suffrage. Smith (1997, 100) suggests that

[T]he new property tests are better seen as signs of America's eagerness to become a more commercial society. Defenders of the new tests argued that they marked voters as proven contributors to the public weal and sufficiently propertied to act responsibly on financial issues, even if they did not provide republican proofs of economic self-sufficiency. For many Americans excited by liberal visions of commercial prosperity, those warrants sufficed. Indeed, at times Americans described property as "an interest in its own right," rather than a precondition for independent republican citizens.

We see here the development of property as a concept divided between urban and rural interests. Rural interests saw property as the yeoman farmer's source of work and character – personal property that was cared for and valued as a means to produce food and sustain life. Urban interests saw property as something to be bought and sold for a profit, a commodity with a life (market) of its own, "an interest in its own right." The republican virtues of autonomy and independence associated with owning and fruitfully tilling one's own land spoke nobly of the necessity of land for liberty in the Lockean argument against the feudal patterns of landownership by the European aristocracy. But the liberty argument had its dark side as the new American aristocracy belittled its landless in turn.

"Is it not … true," wrote John Adams in 1776, "that men in general, in every society, who are wholly destitute of property, are … too dependent on other men to have a will of their own? … Such is the frailty of the human heart, that very few men who have no property, have any judgment of their own"

(Alexander 1997, 31)

In her history of property and the making of the U.S. Constitution, Nedelsky shows how James Madison and the Federalists defined the problem of good government as a matter of protecting the rights of both people and property. No problem of class conflict is inherent in the goal of protecting people, because rich and poor alike are people and share this need. But when it comes to protecting property, those without it could not be counted on to share in its protection as long as they had none (Nedelsky 1990). The problem, to paraphrase Nedelsky, was, How could we have liberty and justice for all but property only for some? The Madisonian solution was to use property ownership as a boundary or barrier to government infringement on property by ensuring that the majority of citizens, who owned none, would not be eligible for government service, thus keeping the landed minority autonomous from the majority and its potential control of the vote.

The property test for suffrage gradually fell away. By 1828, 14 states still had either taxpaying or property ownership as a test for suffrage. But the language of the debate in New York state in 1821, Heskin (1983) points out, is remarkably similar to the heated debates between landlords and tenants of the 20th century. The opponents of suffrage for tenants characterized landowners as frugal, orderly, moderate, honest, and independent men to whom "we owe all the embellishments and comforts and blessings of life. Who builds our churches? Who erects our hospitals? Who raises our school houses? Those who have property" (Heskin 1983, 6). The landless were excoriated as "ringed and speckled, motley, idle and profligate" (p. 6). Nothing was to be gained by giving them the vote. They had not earned it. They had no property. In 1830, only 6 of the 29 states and territories still had property requirements, although these 6 were important states: Rhode Island, Connecticut, New Jersey, Virginia, Tennessee, and South Carolina. By 1860, only South Carolina retained similar restrictions. Today, property ownership is no longer a requirement for citizenship or the right to vote and participate fully in elections. Of course, the legal barriers built on gender, national origin, poverty, religion, and race are all down as well. But as de facto barriers to political, social, and economic participation, these hurdles remain all too pervasive in our society, and the property bias against renters is among the least recognized and understood.

LAND SALES AND HOMESTEADS: PRIVATIZATION FOR OWNERSHIP

Federal efforts to promote landownership also go back to the colonial era. One form has been the distribution of land to war veterans, a practice that began in colonial times and was repeated after the Revolutionary War and through the Civil War. This benevolence, in part, was a desire to "forestall the evils of a collection of landless, disgruntled ex-soldiers by helping them become landowners" (Mitchell 1985, 40). Once again, the two-sided coin of ownership is evident. On the bright side are liberty, independence, and self-sufficiency; on the other side are the shadow of dependency and the potential for lawlessness for those who have no stake in or pride of ownership.

But land distribution to war veterans was but a drop in the bucket. The federal government found itself the steward of a supply of land constituting 80 percent of the nation's territory while the eastern shore overflowed with crowded populations demanding farms and freedom to expand territorially. Almost all of Illinois, Indiana, Michigan, Ohio, Wisconsin, Alabama, Mississippi, and Tennessee had been ceded to the federal government by 1781. The Louisiana Purchase from France in 1803 more than tripled the inventory of federal lands. The Oregon Compromise of 1846, the Mexican Cession of 1848, and the Alaska Purchase of 1867 piled it on. "There was born," writes Frank Popper, "the largest regional development project in American history, the white settlement of the West" (1984, 120). In 1836, the federal government received 36 percent of its revenue from the sale of public lands. Over time the terms of sale became more and more liberal and instrumental to the accumulation of lands by speculators. "Frontier land was the stock market of the day" (Geisler 1984, 10).

But even then the distribution of the dividends was steeply skewed. Reservations for Native Americans were three times larger in 1873 than they are today. Under the Dawes General Allotment Act of 1887 and the Curtis Act of 1887, many reservations were divided into small family allotments, privatized in a manner similar to that encouraged today in Third World countries by the International Monetary Fund and the World Bank. The land in excess of the individual allotments was then sold to non-Native Americans. On some former reservations, white land owners now outnumbered Native American landowners.

The slogan "40 acres and a mule" fired the imagination of freed slaves after the Civil War. But the concept, to the extent that it was implemented at all, was effective only in the cases of about 40,000 freed slaves on the Sea Islands of South Carolina and Georgia, resulting from a special field order of General William Sherman. The dominant pattern for African Americans was that established by the Bureau of Refugees, Freedmen, and Abandoned Lands, which arranged leases of 40 acres each and established wage and pay scales. However, after Andrew Johnson pardoned many Southerners and restored them to the African-American-occupied lands, the new system looked formidably like the old one:

> The contract labor system and the return of the former slave masters kept the Black man subservient and resulted in the system we know today as sharecropping. Sharecropping was much like slavery; Black people were bound again to land owned by non-Blacks. When the Bureau closed in 1872, it had reestablished and solidified the oppressive land tenure patterns which existed in the antebellum South.
>
> (McDougall 1984, 174)

Even the idea of "40 acres" sounds like something of a fraud when one contrasts it with the Homestead Act of 1862. Lincoln declared, "I am in favor of settling the wild lands into small parcels so that every poor man may have a home" (Robbins 1942, 206). The law originally offered 160 acres essentially for free to a family that would settle on it for 5 years. There were 552,000 original claims over 20 years, but less than half of these managed to fulfill the 5-year requirement. The resulting status of the would-be yeoman was less than the dream had promised. Geisler (1984, 19) sums up the heritage of the period:

> Crop liens and farm debt were intractable, as were the foreclosures and land centralization they hastened. The agricultural census showed that tenancy rose dramatically between 1880 (25 percent of all farms) and 1925 (35 percent) and continued to climb for the next fifteen years. By 1935 some 6.8 million people inhabited America's farmland

in seeming fulfillment of the Jeffersonian ideal. Yet nearly half were tenants. Where the twin faces of tenancy and landlordism appeared, so did socialist ferment.

The condition of tenancy reflected poverty, debt, and socialist – that is, un-American – political sympathies. Tenants were also held responsible for land abuse:

> The *Farm Tenancy Report* of 1937, the 1938 *Yearbook of Agriculture*, and scholarly research of the period viewed tenancy as the source of soil erosion. Such blaming the victim, though later abandoned, may explain why the New Deal land reformers in Washington saw tenants, rather than the prevailing tenure system, as the problem. … The late Depression years saw the demise of the Farm Security Administration through red-baiting and conservative assaults on its budget. Its replacement, the Farmers Home Administration, embodied new federal priorities. Rural landownership as a national concern was supplanted with urban and particularly suburban homeownership expansion – a shift that can be traced to President Hoover's Conference on Home Building and Home Ownership in 1931, foreclosure moratorium laws (such as the 1934 Frazier-Lemke Act), and a revolution in credit fostering the illusion of homeownership and fulfillment of the American dream.
>
> (Geisler 1984, 23–24)

A GRADUAL CHANGE OF STRATEGY: FROM GIVING LAND AWAY TO GIVING INCENTIVES TO BUY

The transformation of the Jeffersonian ideal – the yeoman farmer as the bearer of civic virtue – into the suburban homeowner on what Jackson (1985) has dubbed the "crabgrass frontier" began during the Civil War with the first income tax experiments that provided special tax benefits to homeowners:

> In the Revenue acts of 1864 and 1865 [income] taxpayers were permitted to deduct interest expense and local tax payments. Within these, two categories of expenses related to homeowner-ship: mortgage interest payments and property taxes. The

policy was restated in the first statute implementing the 1913 constitutional amendment establishing the Federal income tax system existing today. The policy has remained virtually unchanged.

> (U.S. Department of Housing and Urban Development 1974)

Carliner (1998), in a recently published article in this journal, argues that these policies should not be considered as evidence of a bias in favor of homeownership because "the deduction of interest expense was not limited to home mortgage interest and the deduction of local and state taxes was not limited to property tax" in these earliest versions of the income tax (p. 301). Indeed, he points out, the distinction between mortgage interest and other consumer interest was not made until the 1986 Tax Reform Act. This argument ignores several important points. First, as Mitchell (1985) points out,

> Every President, from Herbert Hoover [not to mention Lincoln] who started the ball of federal housing policy rolling, to Ronald Reagan who slowed it down, has acknowledged that homeowners are the backbone of the nation and declared his fervent wish that every American household so desiring might join the ranks
>
> (p. 40)

Second, Carliner does not take into account the share of state and local tax collections in the early 20th century taken up by the property tax burden. Today, property taxes are about 30 percent of state and local tax collections, but in 1913 the property tax was 79 percent of state and local tax collections. The income tax exemption of state and local taxes may not have been limited to the property tax, but there was little else to those taxes and hence little incentive to discriminate between them. Third, and similarly, there was less need to distinguish between mortgage debt interest and consumer (nonmortgage) debt interest. In 1912, residential nonfarm mortgage debt was $4.9 billion and consumer debt was $1.6 billion. In 1986, tax expenditures for mortgage interest on owner-occupied homes were $30.4 billion, and tax expenditures for interest on consumer credit were $17.9 billion. We had gone from 33 cents of consumer debt for every dollar of home mortgage to 59 cents of consumer debt tax exemption per dollar of mortgage debt tax exemption, nearly doubling consumer debt's share of the total. It is little wonder that the line was finally drawn between the two to clarify the homeownership policy. The point is that at the time of the establishment of the income tax, there was in fact a near identity between the home mortgage and consumer interest payments and a near identity between the property tax and state and local tax revenues. The property bias was plain to see in these early identities and clarified in subsequent changes.

In 1951 in response to the Korean War and the hardships of mobilization, Congress added a third benefit to homeowners, the deferred capital gains tax provisions. In 1964, to relieve the burden of accumulated capital gains on elderly homeowners, any gains under $20,000 were exempted from the tax. That limit has been raised since, most recently in 1997 to $500,000 for a married couple; the exemption can be claimed every two years and no longer requires sellers to buy an equally or more expensive housing unit before reaching the age threshold for cashing out. The National Multi Housing Council (1997) has estimated that these changes, which no longer require moving up before moving out of homeownership, may in fact increase the demand for rental housing, particularly at the upper end of the market. Although the changes remove a rule that may have prolonged homeownership for a few and certainly will permit earlier downsizing of owned units, the increase in demand for multifamily rental housing, if it materializes, appears to benefit landlords more directly than tenants and high-income tenants far more than low-income tenants.

These tax breaks amount to a great deal of money. In a study that is probably well known to many readers of this journal, Henry Aaron (1972) estimated that in 1966, homeowners paid $7 billion less in taxes "than they would have if they had been governed by the rules applicable to investors in other assets" (p. 55). He attributed $2.9 billion to deductions for property tax and mortgage interest and $4 billion to an imputed net rent exemption (tax on income that would have been taxable if owners had paid themselves rent for their home-as-investment). Federal tax expenditures for 1997 mortgage and property tax deductions were $73.8 billion. We can estimate a tax

expenditure value for the exemption of imputed net rent by assuming that the ratio between the values of the imputed net rent deduction and the mortgage and property tax deduction in Aaron's 1966 estimates holds in 1997. This yields a tax expenditure estimate of $101.8 billion. To these benefits we must add the tax benefits from deferred capital gains ($18.2 billion), capital gains exemptions ($5 billion), and exclusion of interest on owner-occupied mortgage subsidy bonds ($1.7 billion). Thus, the total of these subsidies to homeownership in 1997 was $200.5 billion, or over $3,000 per homeowning household. Aaron's conclusions bear repeating:

> These tax subsidies affect allocation of resources, distribution of income, and the form of legal tenure of housing. Consumption of housing services is greater than it would be in the absence of tax benefits. The increase cannot be gauged precisely, but is about 20 percent in the aggregate. Homeowners in particular reap large benefits – especially those subject to high tax rates, for whom implicit subsidies equal 30 percent or more of the cost of housing services.
>
> (Aaron 1972, 70)

A corollary to Aaron's point is that the benefits of these breaks are not especially large for lower-income homeowners (who tend to itemize deductions less frequently and include the elderly, who are more likely to be mortgage free) and are nonexistent for renters.

Vale (1998) has found that the most recent federal policy initiative to promote homeownership – the sale of public housing to its occupants – may be of limited effectiveness. Although a large majority of occupants of public housing in a Boston study would like to be homeowners, this reverence for the American dream in many cases does not translate into wanting to buy the particular unit occupied in that particular development. Neither does an enhanced desire to own correspond with jobholding and prospects for achieving that end. The policy, Vale implies, has the cart before the horse. What is needed is education and training programs that would develop the economic power of choice.

***

WHO OWNS AMERICA?

In June 1995, a conference titled "Who Owns America?" was held at the University of Wisconsin at Madison, organized by the Land Tenure Center and sponsored by a broad range of interests, including the Ford Foundation and the W. K. Kellogg Foundation. The feeling was that land reform had for too long been seen solely as a Third World concern and it was high time for the issue to be brought home. A second conference, "Who Owns America? II," was held in June 1998, and "Who Owns America? III" is scheduled for the year 2000. What does this question mean?

First of all, the question is open to the interpretation that whoever has title to the land is the sovereign nation. Although much of our history can be interpreted as a battle over control of the nation's resources and destiny, the country is owned by its citizens, past, present, and future. But we do not have the same ownership rights over the nation that we have over other forms of property. No one can legally sell it or destroy it or claim exclusive right to possess it or use it. Why not? Because it is common property. The ground we sit on may not be commonly held, but whatever makes it American ground makes it a shared property. It is not American because of its latitude and longitude but because the space defined by that latitude and longitude is legitimized, protected, and given value by a constitution, a history, and a government that makes that property American. So perhaps a better question is this: Who is at home in America, and what has ownership of property got to do with it?

Second, the question has an empirical ring that suggests it might be easily answered by examining titles to parcels. In one important sense this is true. It is well established, although out of sight and out of mind for most of us, that the federal government still owns nearly a third of the nation's land. Then, in lower orders of magnitude, come huge private holdings: 11 percent of California is owned by 10 private parties; the paper industry owns 37 percent of Maine; in 1968, 39 people owned 44 percent of Hawaii; 8 oil companies own 65 million acres; and so on. Popper (1979) affirms that "the difference between landowners and the landless is one of the key social divisions in contemporary America" (p. 131).

But is homeownership policy designed to break up this massive concentration of power?

No. Indeed, as Geisler (1984) has suggested, the homeownership resulting from federally backed home finance policy is largely an illusion. Most owners have mortgages on their homes. If the mortgaged homeowner doesn't pay the mortgage, he's out. And if the renter doesn't pay the rent, she's out. When the crunch comes, owning and renting are not so different. The number of Americans who own their homes free and clear is only about 25 percent (see table 12.1). A recent survey by the University of Michigan's Survey Research Center for the Federal Reserve Board and the American Financial Services Association shows that the higher one's income and education, the more likely one is to be mortgaged. Aside from the irony conveyed by that statistic, it is even more disturbing to look at the center's findings on the use of second mortgages, whose interest is also tax exempt. Forty-eight percent of those taking out second mortgages do so to consolidate credit card debt, the direct interest on which is not tax deductible, and 20 percent use the money to purchase a car, the direct interest on which is also not tax deductible. Not only are renters suffering from a free-rider problem – homeowners in the income tax commons – but we have also structured the commons so badly that we encourage those free riders to double dip. These dis-benefits come with important racial and spatial maldistributions as well, as shown in Table 12.1.

Third, and most important, the everyday notion of ownership ignores a multitude of claims to the bundle of rights in property by nonowners – claims expressed in taxation and regulation by the public sector and the numerous liabilities of owners for the impacts of their property on the rights and lives of others. Furthermore, laws that recognize that tenants pay property taxes through their rent [...] reinforce an old principle that users of property become invested in that property whether it is theirs in title or not. Oliver Wendell Holmes wrote 100 years ago, "A thing which you have enjoyed and used as your own for a long time ... takes root in your being and cannot be torn away without your resenting the act and trying to defend yourself, however you came by it" (Youngman 1997, 98). John Steinbeck's tenant farmer in *The Grapes of Wrath*, ejected from his land by the owner's men and now facing the tractor about to bulldoze his home, ponders the meaning of the land:

Mortgage-Free Homeownership	(%)	Mortgaged Homeownership (%)	Home Rentership (%)
Total population	25	40	34
African American	16	27	55
Hispanic	15	28	57
Central city	18	32	50
Suburban	24	48	28
Nonmetropolitan	38	36	26

Table 12.1 Homeownership and Rentership in the United States, 1997

Source: The split between owner-occupied and renter-occupied units is based on 1998 data (U.S. Bureau of the Census 1999). The proportion of mortgage-free units is based on *American Housing Survey 1995*. (Rows may not add to 100 due to rounding.)

Funny thing how it is. If a man owns a little property, that property is him, it's part of him, and it's like him. If he owns property only so he can walk on it and handle it and be sad when it isn't doing well, and feel fine when the rain falls on it, that property is him, and some way he's bigger because he owns it. Even if he isn't successful he's big with his property. That is so. ... But let a man get property he doesn't see, or can't take time to get his fingers in, or can't be there to walk on it. ... He can't do what he wants, he can't think what he wants. The property is ... stronger than he is. And he is small, not big. Only his possessions are big – and he's the servant of his property. That is so too.

(Steinbeck 1939, 50–51)

Margaret Jane Radin, legal theorist, put it this way:

A tenancy, no less than a single-family house, is the sort of property interest in which a person becomes self-invested; and after the self-investment has taken place, retention of the interest becomes a priority claim over curtailment of merely fungible interests of others. To pursue the parallel with home ownership, there the owner's interest is personal and the mortgagee's interest is fungible. That is why it seems right to safeguard the owner from losing her home even if it means some curtailment of the mortgagee's interest.

(Radin 1993, 84)

This view represents a doctrinal shift in how legal culture perceives the character of housing, a shift that underlies the revolution that landlord-tenant law underwent in the 1960s. The shift was away from a relationship between landlords and tenants that was subject to minimal legal regulation and toward one of public regulation. At the federal level, the Fair Housing Act of 1968 prohibited discrimination in the private housing market, and at the state level, many statutes created a "warrant of habitability" reversing the traditional rule that held tenants responsible for the care and condition of rental housing. According to Alexander (1997, 360),

The most important aspect of the new "warranty" was that it was nonwaivable: landlords and tenants could not bargain around the new warranty even if they were so inclined. The overall effect of these and other changes was to remove landlord and tenant relations, especially in the residential context, from the realm of private ordering to the domain of public regulation. The new regulatory regime withdrew from landlords many of the traditional prerogatives of property ownership.

Although the traditional relationship between tenant and landlord has tended to put them in opposition to each other, some evidence suggests that they suffer in common the prejudice against tenancy. Richard L. Michaux, past chairman of the National Multi Housing Council, is concerned about the biases in the language we use to discriminate between renters and homeowners. He quotes a local newspaper carrying a typical front-page story

> about the proposed renovation of "…an affordable apartment *complex* of 104 *units* where *tenants* pay …" The article went on to note that "*residents* of nearby *homes* would very much like to see these *units* improved" (Michaux 1996, 26; Michaux's italics).

He calls our attention to the language. Some people live in units in complexes. They're called tenants. Other people live in homes in neighborhoods or communities. They're called residents. Why? According to Michaux, who is also chairman and CEO of Avalon Properties in Alexandria, Virginia:

language

> These words project an image of apartment living as second-class to home ownership, and of apartment dwellers as less fortunate than "residents" of "homes" who live in "communities," an image that is not accurate today.
>
> [D]evelopers are competing with home ownership, which is promoted by no less than federal and state governments. The biases toward home ownership present challenges for the apartment industry to show that we are providing first-class housing for first-class citizens.
>
> (Michaux 1996, 24)

Euclid vs. Ambler Realty

Even the classic defense of zoning by the Supreme Court in *Village of Euclid v. Ambler Realty Co.* (272 U.S. 365 [1926]) displayed an antitenant bias. It noted that "very often the apartment house is a mere parasite, constructed in order to take advantage of the open spaces and attractive surroundings created by the residential character of the district" (Berger and Williams 1997, 813–15). The suggestion of the court is that tenants do not have the character of residents. They have the character of nonresidents. They do not belong.

Not only is the multifamily housing industry trying to change the language to make it less prejudicial, but it is also changing the designs of the buildings and site plans to make apartments look more like traditional single-family housing, putting several apartments in what looks like a large manor house or city row house. As one New Jersey developer put it, " 'It just says home. … I have a home with my own front door. I have

a garage and can use my garage door opener and take my groceries in without walking through a parking lot' " (Shatzman 1998, 83). In racial terms, the apartment renters and their builders are trying to "pass."

These efforts to change the language and the look of apartment living are not so much an attempt to right a centuries-old bias as they are an attempt to respond to market forces, namely the large number of renters-by-choice – renters who can afford to be homeowners but choose not to be. Varady and Lipman (1994), in their study of a National Association of Realtors data set of 2,000 renters, found that three groups of renters, constituting 57 percent of the sample, were not seeking homeownership. They labeled them as lifestyle renters (21 percent), recent college graduates (26 percent), and elderly life-cycle renters (10 percent). The stigma of parasite does not fit. The popular image of renters fails to recognize that one-third of the rental housing in the United States is single-family housing. It is largely invisible.

CONCLUSIONS

American land history amounts to one long struggle to own, not rent. We have seen that property for the elite colonists of America was the guardian of political rights as well as a principal form of wealth. As the property test for suffrage fell away, the privileges of property ownership were distributed through land reform and taxation policies that promoted ownership and accrued to a growing middle class. Property took on a life of its own as a market commodity more than as a custodian of community. The stigma of not owning property and its association with being poor, transient, politically suspect, and different persists in contemporary society, in community politics, in real estate markets, and in our tax structures.

In this article I have argued that we give too much social significance to ownership. Nobody owns the United States the way we own other things in life. We are the inheritors of a nasty and pervasive property bias in our society with roots that run deep, just as other strong biases of gender, race, and nationality still do in spite of our efforts to outlaw them. Our institutions and practices continue to embody and perpetuate the property bias, particularly in the tax system – in the subsidies given to owners but denied to renters and in many of the property tax laws that deny that renters are stakeholders in their communities. The celebration of homeowner-ship in the United States stigmatizes those who don't, can't, or won't buy property. What is needed, it seems, is a civil rights movement for renters. We need federal and state housing policies that seek a balance of tenure choices through incentives that support markets in proportion to the needs and abilities of all consumers. We need a tax system that treats equally all those who call the United States their home and that is hospitable to creating housing security, not just housing debt. Where are the institutions that promote and protect the economic and political interests of renters? Their interests in the United States are as legitimate and permanent as those who buy and sell the illusion of ownership.

REFERENCES

Aaron, Henry J. 1972. *Shelter and Subsidies: Who Benefits from Federal Housing Policies?* Washington, D.C.: Brookings Institution.

Alexander, Gregory S. 1997. *Commodity and Propriety: Competing Visions of Property in American Legal Thought, 1776–1970.* Chicago: University of Chicago Press.

American Housing Survey 1995, H150/95RV Washington, D.C.: U.S. Department of Commerce and U.S. Department of Housing and Urban Development.

Becker, Robert A. 1980. *Revolution, Reform, and the Politics of American Taxation, 1763–1783.* Baton Rouge: Louisiana State University Press.

Berger, Curtis J., and Joan C. Williams. 1997. *Property: Land Ownership and Use.* New York: Aspen.

Carliner, Michael S. 1998. Development of Federal Homeownership "Policy." *Housing Policy Debate* 9(2):299–321.

Fisher, Glenn W. 1996. *The Worst Tax? A History of the Property Tax in America.* Lawrence: University Press of Kansas.

Geisler, Charles C. 1984. A History of Land Reform in the United States: Old Wine, New Bottles. In *Land Reform, American Style,* ed. Charles C. Geisler and Frank J. Popper, 7–31. Totowa, NJ: Rowman and Allanheld.

Goetz, Edward G., and Mara Sidney. 1994. Revenge of the Property Owners: Community Development and the Politics of Property. *Journal of Urban Affairs* 16(4):319–34.

Greenberg, Michael. 1998. Understanding the Civic Activities of the Residents of Inner-City Neighborhoods: Two Case Studies. *Urban Geography* 19(1):68–76.

Heskin, Allan David. 1983. *Tenants and the American Dream: Ideology and the Tenant Movement.* New York: Praeger.

Jackson, Kenneth T. 1985. *The Crabgrass Frontier: The Suburbanization of the United States.* New York: Oxford University Press.

Kemeny, J. 1981. *The Myth of Home Ownership.* London: Routledge & Kegan Paul.

Lundqvist, Lennart J. 1998. Property Owning and Democracy – Do the Twain Ever Meet? *Housing Studies* 13(2):217–31.

Marcuse, Peter. 1987. The Other Side of Housing: Oppression and Liberation. In *Between State and Market: Housing in the Post-Industrial Era,* ed. B. Turner, J. Kemeny, and Lennart J. Lundqvist. Stockholm: Almqvist & Wiksell International.

McDougall, Harold A. 1984. Land Reform and the Struggle for Black Liberation: From Reconstruction to Remote Claims. In *Land Reform, American Style,* ed. Charles C. Geisler and Frank J. Popper, 172–87. Totowa, NJ: Rowman and Allanheld.

Michaux, Richard L. 1996. Reconsidering the Vocabulary of Apartment Living. *National Real Estate Investor* March, pp. 24–26.

Mitchell, J. Paul. 1985. Historical Overview of Federal Policy: Encouraging Homeownership. In *Federal Housing Policy and Programs: Past and Present,* ed. J. Paul Mitchell, 39–46. New Brunswick, NJ: Center for Urban Policy Research.

National Multi Housing Council. 1997. The Rental Housing Market and the Budget Accord. *Research Notes,* August.

Nedelsky, Jennifer. 1990. *Private Property and the Limits of American Constitutionalism: The Madisonian Framework and Its Legacy.* Chicago: University of Chicago Press.

Popper, Frank J. 1979. Ownership: The Hidden Factor in Land Use Regulation. In *Land in America: Commodity or Natural Resource*, ed. Richard N. L. Andrews, 129–35. Lexington, MA: Lexington Books.

Popper, Frank J. 1984. The Ambiguous End of the Sagebrush Rebellion. In *Land Reform, American Style*, ed. Charles C. Geisler and Frank J. Popper, 117–28. Totowa, NJ: Rowman and Allenheld.

Radin, Margaret Jane. 1993. *Reinterpreting Property*. Chicago: University of Chicago Press.

Robbins, Roy M. 1942. *Our Landed Heritage*. Princeton, NJ: Princeton University Press.

Rohe, William M., and Michael A. Stegman. 1994. The Impact of Homeownership on the Social and Political Involvement of Low-Income People. *Urban Affairs Quarterly* 30(1):152–72.

Shatzman, Marci. 1998. Home Sweet Apartment: Single-Family Look Is Still the Trend. *Multifamily Executive* 3(3):82–83.

Smith, Rogers M. 1997. *Civic Ideals: Conflicting Visions of Citizenship in U.S. History*. New Haven, CT: Yale University Press.

Steinbeck, John. 1939. *The Grapes of Wrath*. New York: Viking.

U.S. Bureau of the Census. 1999. *Housing Vacancy Survey Fourth Quarter 1998. Table 6. Homeownership Rates by Area, Fourth Quarter 1998 and 1997*. World Wide Web page www.census.gov/hhes/www/housing/hvs/q498tab6.html (accessed February 26).

U.S. Department of Housing and Urban Development. 1974. *Housing in the Seventies: A Report of the National Housing Policy Review*. Washington, D.C.: U.S. Government Printing Office.

Vale, Lawrence J. 1998. Public Housing and the American Dream: Residents' Views on Buying into "The Projects." *Housing Policy Debate* 9(2):267–98.

Varady, David P., and Barbara J. Lipman. 1994. What Are Renters Really Like? Results from a National Survey. *Housing Policy Debate* 5(4):491–531.

Youngman, Joan M. 1997. Henry George, Property Rights, and Taxation. In *Land Use and Taxation,* ed. H. James Brown, 91–102. Cambridge, MA: Lincoln Institute of Land Policy.

13

"Low-income homeownership: American dream or delusion?"

From *Urban Studies* (2006)

Anne B. Shlay

INTRODUCTION

Since the Great Depression, the hallmark of US housing policy, sine qua non, has been homeownership (Wright, 1983; Hayden, 1985; Jackson, 1985). Historical accounts of the initial motivations behind the push to create a nation of homeowners cite industrialists' interest in homeownership because they feared communism and labour unrest (Hayden, 1981, p. 283) and the belief that stable housing was intrinsically linked to the maintenance of a loyal citizenry (Wright, 1983). But the federal government's push for homeownership, its subsequent intervention in housing markets and its revolutionising of the housing finance industry occurred in the wake of the failed US economy in the late 1920s (Jackson, 1985). Homeownership became a tool to stimulate consumption and increase production while improving Americans' housing conditions (Carliner, 1998). While World War II created a temporary hiatus in the homeownership push, when the troops came home, they were welcomed with federally insured long-term amortisation loans – a central ingredient to the success of a homeownership strategy (Wright, 1983).

It is not clear who pegged homeownership as the American Dream. Homeownership policy, however, has not been about imagining the unattainable but about creating the expectation of owning one's own home. Ideologically, homeownership has been portrayed as a political right seemingly more popular than voting (Shlay, 1985, 1986). Indeed, anthropologist Constance Perin argues that homeownership is symbolically equivalent to citizenship – a status conveyed to the home-buyer through establishing a debt relationship with a bank (Perin, 1977).

Yet homeownership is also valued as the lynch pin for the maintenance and growth of a huge housing infrastructure that includes developers, the financial services industry, the real estate industry, planners, road builders and the like. Homeownership is politically popular, in part, because it has a myriad of constituencies (Buchholz, 2002).

To be sure, homeownership is criticised for escalating suburbanisation, fostering central-city decay, promoting neighbourhood racial change and segregation, and intensifying environmental damage, pollution and waste (Squires, 1994; Wright, 1983; Hayden, 1985; Jackson, 1985; Bradford, 1979). But even its critics fail to come up with good, feasible alternatives given homeownership's enormous popularity. In 2002, 67.9 per cent per cent of US households owned their own homes (US Census, 2002).

Within the US, desires for homeownership have been longstanding. The colonising British, notes historian Kenneth Jackson (1985), quickly organised land into parcels for private consumption. This earliest version of the American dream was not about owning a home *per se* but about owning land. Owning land, however, was not a value indigenous to Americans; Native American Indians did not believe that natural resources such as land could be owned (Jackson, 1985). Detached housing development was enabled by appropriated land from the Indians and fuelled by a strong anti-urban bias imported from England.

The post-World War II growth in homeownership has largely stemmed from housing finance innovations directed at making the purchase of a home possible through a range of guarantees, instruments and incentives as well as increasing the supply of credit through the secondary mortgage market (Lea, 1996; Monroe, 2001). But the beneficiaries of homeownership have historically been working- and middle-class White households, rather than poor households and households of colour (Denton, 2001). In recent years, this has changed. Low-income families represent a new target of homeownership policy. Nationwide, low-income home-ownership is now a policy goal for government at the local, state and federal levels, is claimed as an accomplishment by both the Clinton and Bush presidencies, and is featured in television and radio advertisements.

This paper provides a critical analysis of the recent policy shift to promote low-income homeownership. It examines the ideology and assumptions buttressing this policy, evaluates evidence on the effects of low-income homeownership and assesses the viability of homeownership as a strategy for low-income families.

This paper has several parts. Parts one and two review the rationale for low-income homeownership and the genesis of low-income homeownership policy. Part three examines trends in low-income homeownership and the potential for growth in this market. The fourth part looks at research on the effects of low-income homeownership. The fifth part examines characteristics of metropolitan housing markets that may prevent low-income families from benefiting from homeownership. The final part presents a set of possible policy alternatives to explore for strengthening homeownership and other housing opportunities for low-income families.

THE RATIONALE FOR LOW-INCOME HOMEOWNERSHIP

Within the housing field, there is a longstanding tradition of viewing housing as a source of social problems (Dean, 1949; Hartman, 1975; Wright, 1983). Public interventions in the housing market, including housing codes, zoning, urban renewal and slum clearance, and public housing, were based on a set of beliefs that poor housing caused social, psychological and behavioural problems (Glazer, 1980; Rainwater, 1980; Bellush and Hausknecht, 1967; Gans, 1977; Babcock, 1966). Ideologically, this was rooted, in part, in an anti-urban bias suggested by leaders of the Chicago School of Urban Sociology who worried about the effects of urban size, density and heterogeneity on the breakdown of social norms and community (Bassett and Short, 1980; Fischer, 1982; Baldassare, 1979; Wirth, 1969). To be sure, urbanisation and massive immigration brought with them unhealthy and unsanitary housing conditions. But the rationale for public intervention in housing was linked to the alleged social conditions and social pathologies associated with bad housing. Critics called these unsubstantiated links between housing and behaviour the 'myths of housing reform' (Dean, 1949).

Promoting homeownership, and particularly low-income homeownership, is firmly rooted in this deterministic tradition. Low-income homeownership is expected to bring with it a wide range of social, behavioural, political, economic and neighbourhood changes, many due to behaviours expected with the economic investment that homeownership represents. The goals associated with low-income homeownership are shown in Table 13.1.

The economic goals associated with low-income homeownership are the most intuitive. As with higher-income households, proponents view low-income homeownership as an asset-building strategy for owners to build up equity in their homes (Retsinas and Belsky, 2002b). In addition, low-income homeownership is viewed as a substitute investment for other types, including 401Ks, stocks and mutual funds. It is also viewed as a type of forced savings where making a monthly mortgage payment is similar to putting money in a bank, unlike with making a rental payment. With a fixed-rate mortgage, low-income homeownership is expected to keep housing costs more predictable.

Anticipated social changes are those that affect family well-being because homeownership is believed to give people more control over their housing and, therefore, their lives (Rohe et al., 2002b; Rohe and Stegman, 1994a, 1994b). It is also expected to provide families with more opportunities (Rohe et al., 2002a). For adults, expected social changes include greater life satisfaction, increased participation in voluntary

Family economic	Family social	Political	Neighbourhood
Asset-building	> Social stability	< Criminal activity	> Property values
Substitute investment for 401Ks, stocks, trust funds, etc.	> Family functioning	> Political (voting) participation	> Care of property
Enforced savings	> Satisfaction	> Commitment to employment	> Stability
Created 'fixed' housing costs	> Voluntary/civic participation	> Tax base	< *Graffiti*, litter and other signs of decline
	Children's outcomes (cognitive and behavioural)	> Population growth	
	< Juvenile delinquency		
	> School attendance		
	> Physical and mental health		

Table 13.1 Low-income homeownership rationales/goals

civic organisations and improved physical and psychological health (Dietz and Haurin, 2003). Through homeownership, low-income families are expected to become healthier, happier and more involved in community. For children, homeownership is expected to produce both positive cognitive and behavioural changes resulting in less juvenile delinquency and better school performance (Haurin *et al.*, 2002).

Through a more definitive commitment towards place, low-income homeownership is expected to bring with it changes in political behaviour as well as changes in the local political climate (Gilderbloom and Markham, 1995; Rossi and Weber, 1996; Rohe and Basalo, 1997; Heskin, 1983; Blum and Kingston, 1984; Saunders, 1990). Low-income homeowners are expected to vote more than renters and to be more politically engaged and aware. Low-income homeowner-ship is projected to affect positively the local tax base and to spur local population growth (Rohe *et al.*, 2002a).

At the level of the neighbourhood, low-income homeownership is expected to strengthen local housing markets (Rohe and Stewart, 1996). These homeowners are expected to take better care of their property than renters and therefore create positive

neighbourhood spillovers. Presumably, property values will then rise and abandonment and other forms of blight will decrease (Haurin *et al.*, 2003).

THE GENESIS OF LOW-INCOME HOMEOWNERSHIP POLICY

Homeownership and, in particular, suburbanised homeownership, have deep roots in the activities of the federal government (Jackson, 1985). Yet homeownership has become so entangled with American ideas of social status that it is not entirely evident whether federal policy came to reflect prevailing popular culture or whether desires for homeownership became the ideological manifestation of these political forces. Clearly, public policy and housing preferences have been 'in sync', leading to homeownership's enormous popularity in the US.

The roots of low-income homeownership policy lie in the creation of the Federal Home Administration (FHA) in 1934 and the subsequent establishment of Fannie Mae (Jackson, 1985; van Order, 2000). FHA made homeownership possible for many US households by guaranteeing payment in the event of default. Fannie Mae, Freddie Mac and the evolving Government Sponsored Enterprise (GSE) infrastructure created a secondary market for these loans. These federal interventions in the mortgage market pioneered innovation in mortgage instruments and products, expanded homeownership to the middle class, fuelled suburbanisation and created what economist Michael Lea (1996) calls 'a wonderful life' in mortgage finance where government propelled innovation by sharing risk with the private sector.

But the government also defined risk by developing lending guidelines that made it difficult, if not impossible, to make FHA-insured loans in minority neighbourhoods, racially changing neighbourhoods and older neighbourhoods more generally. By classifying many urban neighbourhoods as poor risks, FHA guidelines effectively redlined cities (Jackson, 1985; Bradford, 1979; Stuart, 2003).

The civil rights movement highlighted FHA's racial and anti-urban bias. Agitation brought about important reforms in the late 1960s. These reforms, largely through the now-infamous 235 programme, increased the availability of FHA finance to minority households. Mortgage brokers heavily marketed FHA loans to inner-city communities using relaxed credit standards for minority home-buyers and massively inflated appraisals (Hays, 1993). Home improvement companies, often in partnership with mortgage companies, bought older homes from the exiting Whites moving to the suburbs and sold them to minorities (a practice known as flipping). Many of these new minority homebuyers could not afford to maintain the homes that they purchased (Bradford, 1979; Squires, 1994). FHA reforms with flawed underwriting, inflated appraisals, scandalous lending practices and massive foreclosures led to wholesale neighbourhood devastation in many city neighbourhoods, particularly in Midwestern and Northeastern cities. The alleged wonderful life in mortgage innovation became a death sentence for many central-city minority neighbourhoods.

With the recognition that lenders were redlining communities, a practice with roots in the neighbourhood underwriting guideline perpetrated by FHA, came the impetus for another innovation in lending – community reinvestment. The logic behind community reinvestment was that mortgage originators, typically savings and loans institutions, had responsibilities to invest in communities that were the source of local deposits (Squires, 1992). Lenders who failed to invest in communities from which they derived deposits were disinvesting from communities by taking their deposits and investing them in someone and somewhere else. An important contribution of the community reinvestment movement was the recognition of the role of private investment decisions in promoting urban decay and inequality (Shlay, 1993).

Sophisticated organising led to the establishment of two federal policies in response to disinvestment, the Home Mortgage Disclosure Act of 1975 (HMDA) and the Community Reinvestment Act of 1977 (CRA). HMDA mandated lenders to report the location of their residential lending, permitting people to document where lenders were making loans. CRA made reinvestment a federal requirement for lenders under federal regulatory oversight (Squires, 1992).

The community reinvestment movement, however, did not advocate for low-income homeownership. But this movement, as it changed form in the last part of the late 20th century, was highly influential in the evolution of low-income homeownership as a desired policy goal.

How did this happen? A variety of forces converged, providing the impetus to move on the low-income homeownership frontier. These included the community reinvestment movement, the collapse of the savings and loan industry, a new political administration in Washington and technological changes in underwriting.

The merger mania and financial restructuring of the 'go-go' 1980s created opportunities for Community Reinvestment Act (CRA) challenges – a regulatory moment when local community groups and others could protest a merger or acquisition based on a lender's lack of compliance with CRA mandates. This led to the negotiation of a host of CRA agreements where lenders committed large amounts of money targeted for urban, minority and low-income lending (National Housing Conference, 2001; Squires, 1992, 2003; Shlay, 1999).

During this same time-period, the collapse of many institutions within the savings and loan industry suggested that prevailing definitions of risk were not firmly grounded in realistic underwriting standards. The understanding that loans to low-income families did not cause savings and loans to fail was accompanied by a growing recognition that low-income loans were profitable and good insurance against loss (Listokin *et al.*, 2002). This perceptual shift fostered a new look at the potential low-income homebuyer.

Lenders were also seeking new markets. Changes in homeownership rates remained flat during the late 1980s and early 1990s, hovering at around 64 per cent (Masnick, 2001). Low-income homebuyers represented a new and untapped market.

Other federal policy initiatives intensified their focus on low-income homeownership. The Federal Housing Enterprises Financial Safety and Soundness Act of 1992 established performance standards for Government Sponsored Enterprises (GSEs Fannie Mae and Freddie Mac) to make homeownership available to a wider variety of households (Case *et al.*, 2002; Fishbein, 2003). The Department of Housing and Urban Development then established target goals for the purchase of loans made to low-and moderate-income homebuyers (less than or equal to the MSA median income) in central cities and to specifically targeted lower households. The GSEs were required to target the 'underserved' markets. Both Fannie Mae and Freddie Mac increased activities around innovating loan products that would help them to meet these goals.

President Clinton also made low-income homeownership part of his housing agenda. He established a policy goal of increasing homeownership to 67.5 per cent (Masnick, 2001; Bratt, 2002). As George Masnick notes, the Clinton administration set this goal and achieved it without either new funding initiatives or momentum from earlier trends. The strategy to accomplish the goal depended heavily on boosting homeownership among groups with low homeownership rates and involved vigorously enforcing fair housing and banking laws already on the books. By partnering with over two dozen public and private organisations that serve as national housing advocates, the Clinton administration developed a far-reaching programme to help minorities and others who have been historically underserved by housing markets (Masnick, 2001, pp. 7–8). In other words, low-income homeownership would be facilitated by eliminating the barriers preventing it, many already against the law but never enforced under previous administrations (Bostic and Surette, 2000). Clinton's home-ownership agenda was not new policy *per se* although it gave increased emphasis to low-income homebuyers.

Technological changes also converged as financial and political institutions began to focus on low-income homeownership. Both the computerisation of the mortgage-lending industry along with automated underwriting cut the time and therefore the cost in underwriting, making home mortgages more accessible to lower-income borrowers (Lea, 1996).

TRENDS AND POTENTIAL IN LOW-INCOME HOMEOWNERSHIP

During the late 1990s, low-income homeownership grew to such an extent that it was labelled a boom (Belsky and Duda, 2002a). From 1993 to 2000, the number of home purchase loans to low-income families grew by 79 per cent (Retsinas and Belsky, 2002a). Home purchases to low-income families and minorities increased more sharply than for other groups (Bostic and Surette, 2000).

The number of low-income minority households increased by more than 800 000, representing 11 per cent of the net increase in homeowners (Belsky and Duda, 2002a). Belsky and Duda (2002a) note that homeownership rates for low-income and minority households grew more rapidly than for other groups. Therefore, a surge in low-income home-ownership, particularly among minority households, constituted a significant proportion of the net growth in homeowner-ship more generally (Retsinas and Belsky, 2002a).

Where have low-income buyers been purchasing homes? Analysis of the spatial patterns associated with these purchases shows that low-income buyers have been moving to neighbourhoods in both suburbs and central cities (Belsky and Duda, 2002a). Some research shows that increases in low-income homeownership have not been accompanied by a reduction in racial and ethnic segregation (Immergluck, 1998). Other research shows that, although Black homeownership increased in neighbourhoods within more racially diverse communities, minority composition in these neighbourhoods was much higher than the national average (Herbert and Kaul, 2005).

What are the prospects for sustaining this growth? This article reports on research that looks at both the demand-and supply-side potential for low-income homeownership.

On the demand side, Eggers and Burke (1996) examined how reducing race- and income-based disparities would affect homeownership rates. Using simulation techniques, they suggested that policy changes to reduce gaps created by race and income could increase low-income and minority homeownership by the year 2000. This research effectively outlined the market's responses to policy changes around fair lending and housing affordability introduced during the Clinton years.

More recent research on the demand side suggests that the market for low-income homeownership has a limit. Looking at mortgage instruments available to serve the low-to-moderate-income market, Listokin *et al.* (2002) examined how many renters could qualify for loans given their income and assets. Using simulation techniques, this research estimated the share of the rental population that could potentially reap the benefits of these mortgage products.

They found that homeownership remained unaffordable for about 80 per cent of renters. This represents 21 million renter families that cannot be served by the low-income mortgage market given the most liberal underwriting standards. Underscoring renters' lack of assets the researchers note that

> With such a trace level of assets, even a 100 per cent LTV (loan to value) mortgage will not facilitate homeownership because of the resources required to meet substantial closing costs
>
> (Listokin *et al.*, 2002, p. 493).

They suggest that additional income and asset supplements are needed to address the renters' financial barriers to homeownership. This includes assistance with housing down-payments (Herbert and Tsen, 2005; Herbert *et al.*, 2005).

Some policy analysts suggest that increasing low-income homeownership solely through credit liberalisation and mortgage lending product innovation may have already reached its limit (Carasso *et al.*, 2005). They speculate that greater emphasis should be placed on low-income homeowners' housing retention and equity accumulation.

Research shows that a large Black-White gap in homeownership remains. This continued gap, argue some researchers, is due not to credit barriers *per se* but to other household characteristics, indicating a limit on how much mortgage finance innovation can increase minority homeownership rates (Gabriel and Rosenthal, 2005). Importantly, some researchers now argue that credit barriers based on discrimination or lack of information may no longer explain gaps in homeownership rates, by income, race and ethnicity (Herbert *et al.*, 2005). Rather, they believe that wealth, income, human capital and employment remain obstacles to homeownership. This does not necessarily absolve discrimination as an explanation in racial and ethnic gaps in homeownership rates. Rather, obstacles to homeownership may be tied more to the legacy of past discrimination that results in racial and ethnic disparities in education, employment and human capital (Masnick, 2004).

At the same time, there are supply-side constraints on homeownership. Research finds that there is a lack of adequate housing units at affordable prices and that affordable homes are being swallowed up by housing price inflation and vacancies (Collins *et al.*, 2002). Few non-mobile housing units are being added to the affordable housing stock. According to Collins *et al.*

> Policymakers need to recognize the failure of filtering as a mechanism to expand the supply of affordable homes
>
> (Collins *et al.*, 2002, p. 198)

With the recognition that filtering may not produce affordable homeownership opportunities for low-income families, research is now examining whether manufacturing housing (modular homes built in factories) is a reasonable homeownership option. It suggests that manufactured housing, under the right conditions, would be a beneficial investment (Boehm and Schlottmann, 2004c).

THE EFFECTS OF LOW-INCOME HOMEOWNERSHIP

What does social science tell us about the impact of low-income homeownership? The literature focuses on three areas of concern:

the social and behavioural effects of homeownership; the economic returns to low-income homeownership; and, the impact of low-income homeownership on children.

Social and behavioural effects of homeownership

Most research on the effects of homeownership, however, is not on low-income homeowners but on middle-and high-income homeowners. The research focus on homeowners at the higher end of the economic spectrum reflects that, by definition, the market for homeownership has been largely the domain of higher-income families (Rohe and Stegman, 1994b).

Research on these largely middle-class homeowners shows positive effects of homeownership. Homeowners, compared with renters, have longer tenure in their housing and comparably less residential mobility. They are more likely to maintain their property and experience greater property value appreciation (Rohe and Stewart, 1996). Homeowners are also more likely than renters to be satisfied and to participate in political and voluntary activities (Rohe et al., 2002b; Blum and Kingston, 1984; DiPasquale and Glaeser, 1999).

Coulson and Fisher (2002) address the relationship between homeownership and mobility directly by examining the impact of homeownership on labour market outcomes. Theorising that homeowners would be constrained in their search for employment because of the costs of relocation, they examined employment differences in renters and owners. If homeowners are constrained, they would be more likely to be unemployed, have longer spells of unemployment and have lower wages than renters. To the contrary, they found just the opposite – that owners experienced less and shorter unemployment and received higher wages compared with renters.

Rossi and Weber (1996) address the effects of homeownership on social characteristics. They examined a wide range of characteristics including household composition, well-being, sociability, marriage and the family, confidence in major American institutions, attitudes towards neighbourhoods, levels of political engagement and views on various public issues. Weak although consistent differences were found between renters and homeowners along

dimensions of life satisfaction, self-esteem and participation in community organisations. Yet for the bulk of their analyses, they found no consistent differences between renters and owners and conclude that "tenure status is not a line of ideological cleavage in American society" (Rossi and Weber, 1996, p. 29).

These effects of homeownership, however, may be confounded by the simultaneous effects of income, education, length of residence and family life cycle (Rossi and Weber, 1996; Rohe and Stegman, 1994b; Blum and Kingston, 1984; DiPasquale and Glaeser, 1999). This is because homeownership may coincide with, or be a product of, being at the stage in the family life cycle when owning one's home is feasible and/or desirable.

Homeowners may become homeowners because they are ready, willing and able to stay in one housing situation for a considerable amount of time. Therefore, these effects of homeownership may be an artifact of a homeowners' self-selection process into this form of housing tenure (Rohe et al., 2002a). Blum and Kingston note in an early study of homeownership that they

> prefer to see homeownership as part of cluster of reinforcing statuses and outlooks that both sustains and creates social attachment.
>
> (Blum and Kingston, 1984, p. 176)

In addition, Rossi and Weber (1996) found that, even when accounting for age and income, there were many family and economic differences between renters and owners. Correlates of homeownership are not necessarily caused by homeownership (DiPasquale and Glaeser, 1999).

Certain behavioural and social characteristics that appear due to homeownership may actually be due to unobserved individual or household characteristics (Dietz and Haurin, 2003). Dietz and Haurin (2003) discuss household planning activities or labour force behaviour associated with the goal of homeownership as being an antecedent, not a consequence of home-ownership.

In addition, it may not be appropriate to generalise findings about middle-income households to behaviours of low-income households. As noted by Rohe and Stegman (1994b, p. 155), 'Social class, ecological conditions, or other factors may result in a very different pattern of involvement among lower-income homeowners'. The effects of homeownership may not be uniform across classes. A report from the National Housing Conference states that

> whether the assumed social benefits of homeownership are really caused by home-ownership or rather are so strongly associated with the types of families that become homeowners, that one cannot truly tease them apart. And this is for all homeowners; arguably, many of the potential benefits of homeownership ought to be lower for very low-income families than for higher-income families.
>
> (National Housing Conference, 2004, p. 4).

An important study that focused directly on the effects of homeownership on low-income families incorporated a quasi-experimental design to compare social, attitudinal and behavioural changes for a sample of recent low-income homebuyers with a sample of low-income Section 8 renters (Rohe and Stegman, 1994a, 1994b; Rohe and Stewart 1996). They interviewed households at three points in time separated by 18-month intervals. Using multivariate techniques that controlled for family, economic, social and housing characteristics, they examined the effects of home-ownership on changes in self-esteem and perceived control, life satisfaction, neighbouring, extent of organisational involvement and the intensity of organisational involvement. They found limited although positive effects of homeownership. Compared with low-income renters, homeowners were more likely to increase their involvement in neighbourhood organisations but not in other types of organisations. Homeowners became more satisfied with their lives compared with renters (Rohe and Stewart, 1996), This may potentially indicate the positive influence of homeownership, but also the problems occurring with living in neighbourhoods of low-income, rental housing.

The economic returns to low-income homeownership

Homeownership is expected to bring economic benefits to low-income families. But, as noted

by Nicolas Retsinas and Eric Belsky (2002a), there is not clear evidence that homeownership delivers economic gains to low-income households. The question is whether homeownership is a good asset-building strategy for low-income families compared with renting. And the answer is, we do not know.

It is difficult to generalise about home-ownership as an investment because the rate of return depends both on the timing and place of purchase (Belsky and Duda, 2002b). The amount of time the property is held and the size of transactions costs are also crucial variables. Whether homeownership brings economic gains to households depends on the timing and location of purchases.

Moreover, the pay-off from homeowner-ship may not result from the sale of one's first home but from re-entering the market and purchasing another house for a significant amount of time (Belsky and Duda, 2002b). As a good investment strategy that pays dividends to homeowners, homeownership may require a long-term, sustained investment in multiple houses. While the potential risk for low-income homeowners rests on timing as to when they enter or exit the housing market, it also rests on whether they can afford to continue to stay in the market for a considerable amount of time. According to Belsky and Duda

> for those who are unable to buy again or whose timing once again triggers a loss, homeownership can turn out to be less than its idealized billing.
>
> (Belsky and Duda, 2002b, p. 219)

When one enters the market is critical (Case and Marynchenko, 2002). Entering the market at the end of a cycle of appreciation may result in buying high, but selling low – obviously not a good situation for any income homebuyer. For low-income home-buyers with fewer assets, the incurred loss may be much more deeply felt than by households with more resources to fall back on.

How long someone owns the house and stays in the market is also a crucial variable. Belsky and Duda (2002b) found that many low-income homeowners sell their homes for less than what they paid for them without experiencing appreciation levels large enough to cover the associated transaction costs.

Once becoming homeowners, low-income households do not stay homeowners like their higher-income counterparts (Boehm and Schlottmann, 2004a). One study found that low-income homebuyers returned to renting at extremely high rates, suggesting that these households need more support after they purchase their homes (Reid, 2004). Incorporating a longitudinal design that followed household housing decisions over time, Boehm and Schlottmann (2004a) found that low-income homeowners, particularly minority ones, were more likely to revert back to renting without ever purchasing a home again. They suggest that for low-income and minority families, homeowner-ship 'may be less beneficial than it otherwise might be' (Boehm and Schlottmann, 2004a, p. 129).

Although many low-income and minority homebuyers transition back from owning to renting, Boehm and Schlottmann (2004b) also find that those who remained homeowners accumulated wealth that their rental counterparts did not. Moreover, the wealth accumulated from homeownership represented the sole net worth of these households who otherwise would be bereft of assets. These low-income and minority homeowners who managed to buck the trend to transition back to renting experienced significant wealth benefits from homeownership.

The strength of the regional economy and low housing market conditions are additional critical variables affecting the profitability of low-income homeownership (Case and Marynchenko, 2002). It may be good to buy in the lower-priced market in Philadelphia in the late 1980s, but not in Los Angeles in the mid 1990s. Where, when and how long represent the big 'ifs' associated with whether low-income homeowners will come out ahead of renting.

In addition, a question is whether homeownership is a good investment compared with others. Goetzmann and Spiegel (2002) argue that homeownership may be a relatively poor asset to invest the bulk of a household's net worth because of its low performance compared with other investments. Of course, the concept of an investment portfolio may seem a bit unrealistic in the context of discussing the financial well-being of low-income households. Given, however, the precarious financial situation of many low-income households and the significance of financial

loss for them, the opportunity costs of their capital should be scrutinised like those of households with more economic resources. Examined along these lines, the conclusions reached by economists Goetzmann and Spiegel in their analysis of housing's economic performance are severe.

Overinvestment in housing by families with modest savings means underinvestment in financial assets that will grow and provide income for retirement. In fact, *encouraging homeownership among low-income families will only increase the wealth gap in the United States* (Goetzmann and Spiegel, 2002, p. 272; emphasis added).

The problem of overrelying on housing as an investment compared with others is compounded by tax issues as well. Mortgage interest deductions are worth more to higher-income people than to low-income households (Collins *et al.*, 1999; Carasso *et al.*, 2005). The economic benefits from mortgage interest deductions to higher-income households mean that lower-income families may be better off renting from higher-income landlords.

The continued high level of racial segregation in most US cities also means that returns to investments may be affected by what has long been regarded as a dual housing market (Denton, 2001). Neighbourhoods of Black homeowners, on average, have been found to be better than those housing Black renters. But the differences between neighbourhoods of White owners and White renters were much larger. Therefore, benefits accrued to White low-income homebuyers may be greater than those accrued to Black low-income homebuyers. Both place, race and neighbourhood are vital parts of the equation when assessing economic benefits to low-income homeownership.

Is homeownership a quality economic investment for low-income families? The answer is complex. The diverse nature of housing markets, the leveraged nature of home purchases, the costs of entering and leaving the homeownership market, the rate of return from housing compared with other investments and differential effects of tax policy on higher-versus lower-income families present questions as to whether low-income homeownership is a uniformly positive economic investment strategy.

The effects of low-income homeownership on children

A significant body of research demonstrates positive benefits of homeownership for children. Children in families of homeowners are more likely to have fewer emotional and behavioural problems (Boyle, 2002), graduate from and perform better in school, have fewer teenage pregnancies (Green and White, 1997) and acquire more education and income (Boehm and Schlottmann, 1999). Moreover, homeowners' children are more likely to become homeowners as adults, therefore continuing this cycle of increased benefits accrued to children who live in homes their parents own (Boehm and Schlottmann, 1999). Boehm and Schlottmann (2002) show that homeowners' children accumulate more wealth because they are more likely to own their homes and acquire greater educational credentials. Regarding children, Green and White (1997) find that homeownership benefits lower-income families more than higher-income families.

Homeownership also has been found to influence the cognitive and behavioural outcomes of young children (Haurin et al., 2002). Children living with homeowning parents tested higher on maths and reading tests. The home environments of homeowners were rated higher in terms of providing cognitive stimulation and emotional support for children.

Finding that homeownership influences child outcomes leads to more questions. How does homeownership affect children? Developmental psychologist Michael Boyle suggests that becoming a homeowner may be as much a process as an outcome with the implication that going through this process may select families more likely to raise children with lower risks of emotional or behavioural problems (Boyle, 2002). Economists Boehm and Schlottmann ask 'which components of owned housing make the biggest difference for children?' (Boehm and Schlottmann, 2002, p. 231). Are homeowning parents more vigilant in watching out for their children because they have an investment in the neighbourhood or do better child outcomes reflect the personal traits of home-buying parents (Green and White, 1997)? Are the skills sets associated with becoming and remaining homeowners similar to those associated with being good parents (Dietz and Haurin, 2003)? Does the effect of home-ownership operate through neighbourhoods, the physical characteristics of housing or what? In other words, are outcomes the direct effects of homeownership or indirect effects that are mediated through other variables? What are the unobserved variables that might explain why homeownership has positive effects on children?

In a major effort to control for some of the previously unobserved variables that may mediate the effects of homeownership, preliminary research has replicated and extended some of the prior research on homeownership and children (Barker and Miller, 2005). It looked at a range of child outcomes including high school drop-out rates, cognitive ability, behavioural problems and ratings of the home environment. Added control variables included residential mobility, wealth, housing type and automobile ownership; the researchers also incorporated some additional methodological techniques. The inclusion of these different measures and methods substantially reduced or eliminated previously found effects of home-ownership, indicating the importance of mediating and unobserved factors that operate coincident with homeownership.

Focusing specifically on low-income homeowners, one study separated the effects of neighbourhood from homeownership *per se* and examined the net effects of tenure and neighbourhood conditions on adult outcomes for children who lived with homeowning low-income parents (Harkness and Newman, 2002). They found that homeownership influenced positive outcomes later in life including less idleness, higher wages and lower levels of welfare receipt.

Neighbourhood conditions affected the magnitude of this effect. Problematic neighbourhood conditions like high rates of poverty and residential instability reduced effects of homeownership and, in some situations, bad neighbourhoods could produce worse outcomes for children with homeowning families. Better neighbourhood conditions increased the positive effects of homeownership. The impact of renting was less affected by neighbourhood conditions. Therefore, this research suggests that homeownership produces positive outcomes but produces the largest effects in combination with being in better neighbourhoods.

Expanding the analysis to compare the effects of homeownership on children living in high-and low-income families, Harkness and Newman (2003) found that homeownership benefits lower-income children more than higher-income children. For higher-income children, positive outcomes were influenced by parent characteristics such as education and income, not homeownership. For lower-income children, homeownership brought with it benefits over and above family characteristics. The difference in homeownership effects for high- versus low-income homeowners stemmed from *a priori* differences between high- and low-income homebuyers. For higher-income homeowners, the alleged effects of homeownership operated through, and are attributed to, parent characteristics.

But it is also not clear how homeownership affects the children within lower-income homeowning families. Harkness and Newman (2003) ask whether the positive effects of homeownership are outcomes of the owned status of housing and its function as an asset or because they increase the residential stability of households?

Research finds consistently positive effects of homeownership on children that operate through adulthood, particularly for low-income children. How homeownership works to deliver these benefits (for example, through family characteristics or residential stability), however, remains undetermined. As noted by Boehm and Schlottmann

If effective housing policies are to be developed, which are also cost-efficient to implement, the intricacies of the process by which children raised in owner-occupied housing benefit from their environment must be better understood
(Boehm and Schlottmann, 2002, p. 424)

METROPOLITAN HOUSING MARKETS AND LOW-INCOME HOMEOWNERSHIP

Within the housing literature, housing is conceptualised as a multidimensional phenomenon that comprises a bundle of characteristics (Shlay, 1995). The housing bundle includes features of the housing unit, neighbourhood composition (family, racial and ethnic and economic), neighbourhood conditions, location, housing type, housing quality and access to schools, services and employment. Housing tenure (renting or owning) is one feature of the overall housing bundle.

But tenure is highly correlated with other housing bundle characteristics (Shlay, 1985, 1986). Owner-occupancy often coincides with better neighbourhood conditions and locations. Are the desired outcomes or alleged effects of homeownership due to ownership *per se* (direct effects of homeownership) or do they stem from other aspects of housing such as location or access to amenities?

A major question is what is being delivered through homeownership? There are no 'pure' tenure effects because of the high correspondence between tenure and other characteristics. In addition, the concept of ownership *per se* is messy in that few households, particularly low-income ones, own their units outright. Ownership is mediated by financial institutions that underwrite the purchase of the home.

Two major housing market characteristics are central variables to homeownership's ability to deliver for low-income families. These include residential location (a home's relationship with space) and financial intermediaries (a household's relationship with sources of housing finance). These two factors can either undermine or support a household's opportunities for success in the low-income housing market.

Location and low-income homeownership

Low-income homeownership is billed as a mechanism for helping neighbourhoods. But what are the risks to low-income families, compared with higher-income families, when buying into this market? Low-income housing is typically more available in neighbourhoods with poor-quality housing (Listokin and Wyly, 2000; Shlay, 1993) although many low-income homebuyers are buying homes outside low-income neighbourhoods (Belsky and Duda, 2002a). Low-income homebuyers face greater risks in terms of costly home repairs, lower rates of appreciation and lower-quality neighbourhood amenities (Retsinas, 1999; Louie *et al.*, 1998). Therefore, low-income homeownership as a policy goal may move already-at-risk households to take on even more risk under conditions of great uncertainty. It is unclear whether policy directed at helping low-income families should encourage people with the least amount of assets to take on more risk.

Low-income homeownership is also promoted as a tool for central-city revitalisation. Like low-income neighbourhoods, central cities, however, may not be good locations for investment, particularly for low-income families. Central cities typically have poorer quality schools and services than suburban locations. Therefore, buying homes in central-city neighbourhoods may not be the best mechanism for providing low-income families with greater access to economic opportunities and upward social mobility (Rohe et al., 2002a). A study of first-time, low-income homebuyers within two heavily subsidised Nehemiah complexes indicated that, although families gained better housing conditions, their new neighbourhoods had poorer schools and higher crime rates than their previous ones (Cummings et al., 2002). It may not be good policy to encourage low-income families to invest in communities with the least resources.

The financial services industry and low-income homeownership

The community reinvestment movement combined with heightened enforcement of the Fair Housing Act has helped to eliminate some credit barriers for prospective low-income homeowners (Squires, 2003) although several significant ones remain (Rosenthal, 2002; Barakova et al., 2003). Low-income homebuyers' recognition by the financial services industry, however, as a potential market for lending has been accompanied by the growth of a new segment of the industry – the subprime lending market. The growth of the subprime lending market represents a major shift in the housing finance industry in the US.

Subprime loans carry higher interest rates and fees to cover the additional risk incurred from making loans to borrowers with problematic credit ratings (Squires, 2004). During the 1990s, the number of subprime loans made in the US grew by 900 per cent (Hurd and Kest, 2003).

A subset of loans made within the subprime lending industry is termed predatory lending (Renuart, 2004). Predatory loans contain excessive terms including points and fees, poor underwriting, high and extended prepayment penalties, flipping and repeated financing, inflated house appraisals and other illegal and deceptive practices (Hurd and Kest, 2003). These loans are considered predatory because lenders use deception, unfairly making these high-priced loans to vulnerable populations (White, 2004). In particular, predatory loans, and subprime loans more generally, are marketed to elderly, low-income and minority families (Stein, 2001). Subprime loans have been disproportionately concentrated in minority communities (Immergluck and Smith, 2004; Calem et al., 2004).

Predatory lending is a process that strips equity from people's homes. While conventional mortgage instruments are used by households to build equity in their property, predatory lending takes equity out of property in the form of excessive fees to lenders – estimated to have reached $2.1 billion annually (Stein, 2001; Renuart, 2004). The estimated total cost of subprime lending is $9.1 billion annually. This does not include the costs of excessive foreclosures (Stein, 2001). Research shows that subprime lending increases the number of foreclosures in communities (Immergluck and Smith, 2004).

Subprime lending in its predatory form has devastating consequences for households and communities, particularly minority, low-income and elderly ones (White, 2004). By increasing the number of low-income and minority homebuyers, policy is increasing the number of households at risk of being preyed upon by predatory lenders. That is, policy designed to promote savings and asset accumulation by low-income families may be serving up potential customers for the subprime lending industry. A reasonable question is whether low-income homeownership places low-income homebuyers at risk of having would-be equity in their homes stripped away by predatory lenders.

HOUSING POLICY ALTERNATIVES FOR LOW-INCOME FAMILIES

Low-income homeownership has been elevated to flagship housing policy status with the goal of providing a myriad of benefits that include asset accumulation, social and behavioural changes for adults and children, increased political involvement, less criminal and deviant behaviour, and neighbourhood improvements that contribute to urban revitalisation. Low-income homeownership is portrayed as a policy that will help to solve complex social and political problems associated with being low-income and as a launching-pad for family socioeconomic mobility.

Yet meeting these goals for low-income families is confounded by many factors including the financial constraints on low-income families that preclude homeownership as an option, low-income families' rapid movement from owning back to renting, risks of overrelying on housing as an investment, negative externalities associated with the location of homes affordable to low-income households and opportunistic and exploitative behaviour by financial intermediaries. Low-income homeownership's ability to deliver is limited precisely by the financially perilous situation of low-income families. With homeownership, potential low-income homebuyers are more at risk because they are low-income.

To address fully the housing needs of low-income families and to provide policy that will enhance their opportunities in way that will permit social and economic advancement, policy needs to account for the multifaceted nature of the housing bundle. Policy should not solely work at getting families into a home-ownership situation without ensuring that it is a viable investment and is in a quality location. Housing policy should not increase risks for families already at risk of a host of problems. It should work at eliminating them or at least minimising their probability of occurring.

With these conditions in mind, this paper offers three general policy directions for low-income housing policy as related to housing tenure: improve access to quality homeownership opportunities through providing households with increased financial supports and incorporating a place-based strategy; increase supports for rental housing; and, initiate support for housing that incorporates alternative tenure forms to conventional renting or owning.

Improve access to quality homeownership opportunities

Solely facilitating low-income families' access to homeownership without altering other aspects of the housing market is unlikely to provide many of the economic, political and social benefits suggested by proponents of low-income homeownership. A successful homeownership strategy will require a more comprehensive approach that works simultaneously at improving local social and physical infrastructure including schools and neighbourhood conditions, protecting families against the exploitation of predatory lenders and breaking down barriers to the inclusion of low-income housing within suburban communities. Delivering on low-income homeownership means delivering on the full set of life-sustaining housing bundle characteristics.

Increasing access to quality homeowner-ship opportunities may mean enlarging direct public subsidy of low-income households (Hockett et al., 2005). Deeper public subsidies of low-income homeownership may mitigate against some of the potential risks of investment in the low-income housing market while increasing opportunities to families who, without subsidy, would not be able to participate (Herbert et al., 2005; Carasso et al., 2005).

Increase supports for rental housing

Tenure relationships exist within the social and political context that defines them. Federal policy supports homeownership and this is part of the reason why homeownership is a desirable housing tenure situation. Policy, in part, makes homeownership a preferred housing option.

The opposite exists for renting. Fewer policies support the production of rental housing or the inclusion of rental units within local communities. To be sure, the Low Income Tax Income Housing Tax Credit (LIHTC) programme and Section 8 subsidies make renting more affordable. But Section 8 funds continue to be cut while complex syndication deals required by the LIHTC do not meet massive unmet needs for affordable units (Orlebeke, 2000) and are inefficient tools for producing low-income housing (Stegman, 1990).

The incentives that exist to encourage landlords to invest in and improve rental housing pale when compared with the array of institutions and supports underlying homeownership. There are no special pools of capital for rental housing. There are few, if any, programmes designed to help renters save for their security deposits or become better consumers except in the context of encouraging them to escape from renting (Sherraden, 1991; Shapiro and Wolff, 2001). Zoning laws often explicitly exclude rental housing from suburbs or relegate it to undesirable locations (Shlay, 1993; Pendall, 2000; Fischel, 2004). While policy helps to make homeownership a positive housing situation, policy helps to make renting a negative housing situation.

Since most low-income families cannot qualify for homeownership without deep subsidies, an important area of exploration is determining how policy can support rental housing as a viable housing option for low-income families. Housing policy has, in part, produced a rental housing market in which the available housing is often undesirable. But rental housing in the abstract is not negative *a priori* but reflects how rental units are packaged as housing bundles.

If housing policy can render rental housing an unattractive housing option, it can also be used to make this type of housing option more desirable. This includes modifying financial incentives for investment and maintenance, enhancing alternative opportunities for household tax benefits and savings, revitalising communities in which rental housing is located, altering the size and physical layout of units, providing tenants with more control over their housing situations and breaking down land use barriers to including rental housing within more well-off communities. We also need to determine how housing subsidies can be delivered to low-income families in a manner that neither stigmatises them nor isolates them within undesirable communities.

Providing attractive and affordable rental housing has been accomplished in small but significant ways within the non-profit sector and community development corporations (Dreier and Hulchanski, 1993; Keyes *et al.*, 1996). Some advocate for supporting the growth of this organisational infrastructure around affordable housing through public-private partnerships and housing trust funds (Walker, 1993; Brooks, 1996; Davis, 1994).

Initiate support for alternative tenure forms

Conceptually, alternative tenure forms do not treat tenure as encapsulating discrete categories (owning or renting) but as a variable that can indicate different forms and degrees of ownership and control (Geisler and Daneker, 2000). Alternative tenure forms tend to socialise ownership so that it is shared among a community. Within typical conventional housing situations, a family unit either owns the property or someone who does not live there owns it. Alternative tenure forms involve ownership among groups of households or residential users. These alternative forms include limited equity co-operatives and land trusts (Miceli *et al.*, 1994; White and Saegert, 1996).

The focus of limited equity co-operatives and land trusts is on collective asset accumulation and social equity. Individual households acquire many of the rights associated with ownership including tax benefits and secure housing. With housing collectively owned, risk is shared and the economic exposure of individual households is held to a minimum.

LOW-INCOME HOMEOWNERSHIP: REASONABLE EXPECTATIONS

Low-income homeownership has been promoted with the expectation that it will engender significant changes for families, neighbourhoods and local housing markets. Yet we lack definitive evidence to substantiate these claims.

It is unclear how many low-income families will be able to become homeowners. Much of the recent increase in low-income and minority homeownership has been the result of increased enforcement within the regulatory environment (for example, CRA, Fair Housing Act) as well as lower interest rates, indicating pent-up demand for homeownership within low-income and minority families. But whether this demand can be sustained is questionable. On the demand side, the vast majority of renters cannot be served by the most lenient available underwriting standards because of economic problems. On the supply side, the affordable housing stock for the low-income homeownership market is not readily available.

Research examining the economic returns from low-income homeownership suggests that a myriad of factors interfere with low-income households' ability to reap material gains from homeownership. Timing, location, finance terms, length of ownership and other factors wreak havoc with whether low-income families will come out ahead or not after becoming homebuyers. Of course, homeownership may have positive outcomes for families even if it is not always a moneymaking venture. But advocating homeownership for families who already have fewer economic resources seems problematic, particularly if homebuyer families' economic circumstances deteriorate more than they would have if they had been renting. This is a crucial area for continued research.

Limited evidence exists on whether low-income homeowners experience social and behavioural changes as a result of their changed housing circumstances. In part, our dearth of knowledge about how homeownership benefits low-income families is for methodological reasons; most research that looks at the effects of homeownership cannot disentangle the impact of family life cycle and class from homeownership on outcomes. It is unclear if homeownership is a cause or consequence of these families' life cycle or economic circumstances.

A growing body of research shows that homeownership has positive educational, social and psychological outcomes for children. Importantly, some studies show higher benefits for lower-income children than for higher-income children. Yet these studies also question how homeownership becomes manifested as a critical variable in children's lives. It is unclear what features of the housing bundle produce positive and therefore also, negative consequence for children. There are many observed variables that may more clearly produce the outcomes attributed to homeownership. Clearly, this is an area where substantially more work is needed.

What homeownership does and why is not well understood because it is difficult to disentangle what homeownership means. Given the multidimensional nature of the housing bundle and the inherent inevitability of predictable housing bundle packaging (by race, class, location, housing type, etc.), what constitutes the homeownership 'treatment' is not clear. Is homeownership secure housing, more space, greater psychological well-being, better neighbourhoods, better communities, the ability to be stable residentially, the accumulation of economic assets or what? Delineating the critical variables associated with homeownership

that produce particular outcomes is another crucial area for research.

But determining how homeownership works on family well-being is also important for developing alternative housing policies that support low-income families. Are there features of homeownership that provide positive benefits that could be configured within a redefined tenure arrangement that approximates renting or some other alternative tenure form to owning? That is, are there features of homeownership that could become a reconstituted tenure form that would eliminate some of the problematic aspects of either renting or owning – for example, by limiting family economic exposure and vulnerability? Can we configure the bundle of housing characteristics with known beneficial consequences for low-income families as a policy tool for supporting these families?

The elevation of low-income homeownership to its current status has deflected political attention away from other policies for affordable housing. As noted over 30 years ago by planner Peter Marcuse

the stance that public policy should take towards homeownership for low-income families lies in the possibilities of institutional changes in existing tenure arrangements, and in the social or political, not the financial characteristics of homeownership.

(Marcuse, 1972, p. 143)

While low-income homeownership has been the predominant focus of housing policy for low-income families, policies supporting public housing, housing vouchers and low-income housing tax credits have been cut, battered and denigrated. By holding centre stage in the low-income housing policy debate, low-income homeownership has crowded out ideas about affordable housing policy alternatives ranging from subsidies to co-operatives.

Many of the policy goals surrounding low-income homeownership are framed by ideological statements about homeownership as the American Dream. But what if these dreams are delusions? Should housing policy be the stuff of dreams or hard-nosed analysis of what works for families, communities and local economies?

REFERENCES

BABCOCK, R. F. (1966) *The Zoning Game.* Madison, WI: University of Wisconsin Press.

BALDASSARE, M. (1979) *Residential Crowding in Urban America.* Berkeley, CA: University of California Press.

BARKER, D. and MILLER, E. (2005) Homeowner-ship and child welfare. Paper presented at Mid Year Meetings of the American Real Estate and Urban Economic Association, May–June. Washington, D.C.

BARAKOVA, I. A., BOSTIC, R. W., CALEM, P. S. and WACHTER, S. M. (2003) Does credit quality matter for homeownership?, *Journal of Housing Economics,* 12(2), pp. 318–336.

BASSETT, K. and SHORT, J. (1980) *Housing and Residential Structure: Alternative Approaches.* New York: Routledge.

BELLUSH, J. and HAUSKNECHT, M. (1967) *Urban Renewal: People, Politics and Planning.* Garden City, NY: Anchor.

BELSKY, E. S. and DUDA, M. (2002a) Anatomy of the low income homeownership boom in the 1990s, in: N. P. RETSINAS and E. S. BELSKY (Eds) *Low-income Homeownership: Examining the Unexamined Goal,* pp. 15–63. Washington, D.C.: The Brookings Institution.

BELSKY, E. S. and DUDA, M. (2002b) Asset appreciation, timing of purchases, and sales, and returns to low-income homeownership, in: N. P. RETSINAS and E. S. BELSKY (Eds) *Low-income Homeownership: Examining the Unexamined Goal,* pp. 208–238. Washington, D.C.: The Brookings Institution.

BLUM, T. C. and KINGSTON, P. W. (1984) Home-ownership and social attachment, *Sociological Perspective,* 27(2), pp. 159–180.

BOEHM, T. and SCHLOTTMAN, A. M. (1999) Does home ownership by parents have an economic impact on their children?, *Journal of Housing Economics,* 8, pp. 217–232.

BOEHM, T. P. and SCHLOTTMAN, A. M. (2002) Housing and wealth accumulation: intergenerational impacts, in: N. P. RETSINAS and E. S. BELSKY (Eds) *Low-income Homeownership: Examining the Unexamined Goal,* pp. 407–426. Washington, D.C.: The Brookings Institution.

BOEHM, T. P. and SCHLOTTMANN, A. M. (2004a) The dynamics of race, income and homeowner-ship, *Journal of Urban Economics,* 55(1), pp. 113–130.

BOEHM, T. P. and SCHLOTTMANN, A. M. (2004b) *Wealth Accumulation and Homeownership: Evidence for Low-income Households.* Washington, D.C.: Office of Policy Development and Research, US Department of Housing and Urban Development.

BOEHM, T. P. and SCHLOTTMANN, A. M. (2004c) *Is Manufacturing Housing a Good Alternative for Low-income Families? Evidence from the American Housing Survey.* Washington, D.C.: Office of Policy Development and Research, US Department of Housing and Urban Development.

BOSTIC, R. W. and SURETTE, B. J. (2000) Have the doors opened wider? Trends in homeownership rates by race and income. Working Paper, April. Board of Governors of the Federal Research System, Washington, D.C.

BOYLE, M. (2002) Home ownership and the emotional and behavioral problems of children and youth, *Child Development,* 73(3), pp. 883–892.

BRADFORD, C. (1979) Financing home ownership: the federal role in neighborhood decline, *Urban Affairs Quarterly,* 14(3), pp. 313–335.

BRATT, R. G. (2002) Housing for very low-income households: the record of President Clinton, 1993–2000. Working Paper W02-8, Joint Center for Housing Studies, Harvard University, Cambridge, MA.

BROOKS, M. E. (1996) Housing trust funds: a new approach to funding affordable housing, in: W. VAN VLIET (Ed.) *Affordable Housing and Urban Redevelopment in the United States: Learning from Failure and Success,* pp. 270–286. Thousand Oaks, CA: Sage.

BUCHHOLZ, T. G. (2002). *Safe at Home: The New Role of Housing in the U.S. Economy.* Washington, D.C.: Home Ownership Alliance.

CALEM, P. S., HERSHAFF, J. E. and WACHTER, S. M. (2004) Neighborhood patterns of subprime lending: evidence from disparate cities, *Housing Policy Debate*, 15(3), pp. 603–622.

CARASSO, A., BELL, E., OLSEN, E. O. and STEUERLE, C. E. (2005) *Improving Home-ownership among Poor and Moderate-income Households*. Washington, D.C.: The Urban Institute (available at http://www.urban.org/url.cfm?ID=311184).

CARLINER, M. (1998) Development of federal homeownership 'policy', *Housing Policy Debate*, 9(2), pp. 299–321.

CASE, B. D., GILLEN, K. and WACHTER, S. M. (2002) Spatial variation in GSE mortgage purchase activity, *Cityscape*, 6(1), pp. 9–35.

CASE, K. and MARYNCHENKO, M. (2002) Home price appreciation in low-and moderate-income markets, in: N. P. RETSINAS and E. S. BELSKY (Eds) *Low-income Homeownership: Examining the Unexamined Goal*, pp. 239–256. Washington, D.C.: The Brookings Institution.

COLLINS, J. M., BELSKY, E. S. and RETSINAS, N. P. (1999) Toward a targeted homeownership tax credit. Working Paper, Brookings Institution Center on Urban and Metropolitan Policy, Washington, D.C.

COLLINS, M., CROWE, D. and CARLINER, M. (2002) Supply-side constraints on low-income home-ownership, in: N. P. RETSINAS and E. S. BELSKY (Eds) *Low-income Homeownership: Examining the Unexamined Goal*, pp. 175–200. Washington, D.C.: The Brookings Institution.

COULSON, N. E. and FISHER, L. M. (2002) Tenure choice and labour market outcomes, *Housing Studies*, 17(1), pp. 35–49.

CUMMINGS, J. L., DIPASQUALE, D. and KAHN, M.E. (2002) Measuring the consequences of promoting inner city homeownership, *Journal of Housing Economics*, 11(3), pp. 330–359.

DAVIS, J. E. (1994) *The Affordable City: Toward a Third Sector Housing Policy*. Philadelphia, PA: Temple University Press.

DEAN, J. P. (1949) The myths of housing reform, *American Sociological Review*, 14(2), pp. 281–288.

DENTON, N. A. (2001) Housing as a means of asset accumulation: a good strategy for the poor?, in: T. M. SHAPIRO and E. N. WOLFF (Eds) *Assets for the Poor: The Benefits of Spreading Asset Ownership*, pp. 232–268. New York: Russell Sage.

DIETZ, R. D. and HAURIN, D. R. (2003) The social and private micro-level consequences of home-ownership, *Journal of Urban Economics*, 54(4), pp. 401–450.

DIPASQUALE, D. and GLAESER, E. L. (1999) Incentives and social capital: are homeowners better citizens?, *Journal of Urban Economics*, 45(2), pp. 354–384.

DREIER, P. and HULCHANSKI, J. D. (1993). The role of nonprofit housing in Canada and the United States: some comparisons, *Housing Policy Debate*, 4(1), pp. 43–80.

EGGERS, F. J. and BURKE, P. E. (1996) Can the national homeownership rate be significantly improved by reaching underserved markets?, *Housing Policy Debate*, 7(1), 83–101.

FISCHEL, W. A. (2004) An economic history of zoning and a cure for its exclusionary effects, *Urban Studies*, 41(2), pp. 317–340.

FISCHER, C. S. (1982) *To Dwell among Friends: Personal Networks in Town and City*. Chicago, IL: University of Chicago Press.

FISHBEIN, A. (2003) Filling the half-empty glass: the role of community advocacy in redefining the public responsibilities of government sponsored housing enterprises, in: G. D. SQUIRES (Ed.) *Organizing Access to Capital: Advocacy and the Democratization of Financial Institutions*, pp. 102–118. Philadelphia, PA: Temple University Press.

GABRIEL, S. A. and ROSENTHAL, S. S. (2005) Homeownership in the 1980s and 1990s: aggregate trends and racial gaps, *Journal of Urban Economics*, 57(1), pp. 101–127.

GANS, H. (1977) Planning for people, not buildings, in: M. STEWART (Ed.) *The City*, pp. 363–386. New York: Penguin.

GEISLER, C. D. and DANEKER, G. (2000) *Property and Values: Alternatives to Public and Private Ownership*. Washington, D.C.: Island Press.

GILDERBLOOM, J. L. and MARKHAM, J. P. (1995) The impact of homeownership on political beliefs, *Social Forces*, 73(4), pp. 1589–1607.

GLAZER, N. (1980) The effects of poor housing, in: J. PYNOOS, R. SCHAFER and C. HARTMAN (Eds) *Housing Urban America*, pp. 164–171. Hawthorne, NY: Aldine.

GOETZMANN, W. N. and SPIEGEL, M. (2002) Policy implications of portfolio choice in under-served mortgage markets, in: N. P. RETSINAS and E. S. BELSKY (Eds) *Low-income Home-ownership: Examining the Unexamined Goal*, pp. 257–274. Washington, D.C.: The Brookings Institution.

GREEN, R. K. and WHITE, M. J. (1997) Measuring the benefits of homeowning: effects on children, *Journal of Urban Economics*, 41, pp. 441–461.

HARKNESS, J. and NEWMAN, S. J. (2002) Home-ownership for the poor in distressed neighborhoods: does this make sense?, *Housing Policy Debate*, 13(3), pp. 597–630.

HARKNESS, J. and NEWMAN, S. J. (2003) Differential effects of homeownership on children from higher-and lower-income families, *Journal of Housing Research*, 14(1), pp. 1–19.

HARTMAN, C. (1975) *Housing and Social Policy*. Englewood, NJ: Prentice-Hall.

HAURIN, D. R., DIETZ, R. D. and WEINBERG, B. A. (2003) The impact of neighborhood home-ownership rates: a review of the theoretical and empirical literature, *Housing Policy Debate*, 13(2), pp. 119–151.

HAURIN, D. R., PARCEL, T. L. and HAURIN, R.J. (2002) Impact of homeownership on child outcomes, in: N. P. RETSINAS and E. S. BELSKY (Eds) *Low-income Homeownership: Examining the Un-examined Goal*, pp. 427–446. Washington, D.C.: The Brookings Institution.

HAYDEN, D. (1981) *The Grand Domestic Revolution: A History of Feminist Designs for American Homes, Neighborhoods and Cities*. Cambridge, MA: MIT Press.

HAYDEN, D. (1985) *Redesigning the American Dream: The Future of Housing, Work, and Family Life*. New York: W.W. Norton.

HAYS, R. A. (1993) *Ownership, Control, and the Future of Housing Policy*. Westport, CN: Greenwood.

HERBERT, C. E. and KAUL, B.(2005) *The Distribution of Homeownership Gains during the 1990s across Neighborhoods*. Washington, D.C.: Office of Policy Development and Research, US Department of Housing and Urban Development.

HERBERT, C. E. and TSEN, W. (2005) *The Potential of Downpayment Assistance for Increasing Homeownership among Minority and Low-income Households*. Washington, D.C.: Office of Policy Development and Research, US Department of Housing and Urban Development.

HERBERT, C. E., HAURIN, D. R., ROSENTHAL, S.S. and DUDA, M. (2005) *Homeownership Gaps among Low-income and Minority Borrowers and Neighborhoods*. Washington, D.C.: Office of Policy Development and Research, US Department of Housing and Urban Development.

HESKIN, A. D. (1983) *Tenants and the American Dream: Ideology and the Tenant Movement*. New York: Praeger.

HOCKETT, D. W. McELWEE, P., PELLETIER, D. and SCHWARTZ, D. (2005) *The Crisis in America's Housing: Confronting Myths and Promoting a Balanced Housing Policy*. Washington, D.C.: National Low Income Housing Coalition.

HURD, M. and KEST, S. (2003) Fighting predatory lending from the ground up: an issue of economic justice, in: G. D. SQUIRES (Ed.) *Organizing Access to Capital: Advocacy and the Democratization of Financial Institutions*, pp. 119–134. Philadelphia, PA: Temple University Press.

IMMERGLUCK, D. (1998) Progress confined: increases in black homebuying and the persistence of racial barriers, *Journal of Urban Affairs*, 20(4), pp. 443–457.

IMMERGLUCK, D. and SMITH, G. (2004) *Risky Business: An Econometric Analysis of the Relationship between Subprime Lending and Neighborhood Foreclosures*. Chicago, IL: Woodstock Institute.

JACKSON, K. T. (1985) *Crabgrass Frontier: The Suburbanization of the United States.* New York: Oxford University Press.

KEYES, L. C., SCHWART, A., VIDA, A. and BRATT, R. G. (1996) Networks and nonprofits: opportunities and challenges in an era of federal devolution, *Housing Policy Debate*, 7(2), 201–229.

LEA, M. J. (1996) Innovation and the cost of mortgage credit: a historical perspective, *Housing Policy Debate*, 7(1), pp. 147–174.

LISTOKIN, D. and WYLY, E. K. (2000) Making new mortgage markets: case studies of institutions, home buyers and communities, *Housing Policy Debate*, 11(3), pp. 575–644.

LISTOKIN, D. D., WYLY, E., SCHMITT, B. and VOICU, I. (2002) *The Potential and Limitation of Mortgage Innovation in Fostering Homeownership in the United States.* Washington, D.C.: The Fannie Mae Foundation.

LOUIE, J., BELSKY, E. S. and MCARDLE, N. (1998) The housing needs of lower-income homeowners. Working Paper W98-9, Joint Center for Housing Studies, Harvard University, Cambridge, MA.

MARCUSE, P. (1972) Homeownership for low income families: financial implications, *Land Economics*, 48(2), pp. 134–143.

MASNICK, G. S. (2001) Home ownership trends and racial inequality in the United States in the 20th century. Working Paper W01-4. Joint Center for Housing Studies, Harvard University, Cambridge, MA.

MASNICK, G. S. (2004) Homeownership and social inequality in the United States, in: K. KURZ and H.-P. BLOSSFELD (Eds) *Homeownership and Social Inequality in Comparative Perspective*, pp. 304–337. Stanford, CA: Stanford University Press.

MICELI, T. J., SAZAMA, G. W. and SIRMANS, C. F. (1994) The role of limited-equity cooperatives in providing affordable housing, *Housing Policy Debate*, 5(4), pp. 469–490.

MONROE, A. (2001) How the Federal Housing Administration affects homeownership. Unpublished paper, Department of Economics, Harvard University.

NATIONAL HOUSING CONFERENCE (2001) Expanding the dream of homeownership, *NHC Affordable Housing Policy Review*, 1(1), pp. 1–51.

NATIONAL HOUSING CONFERENCE (2004) Strengthening the ladder to homeownership for very low-income renters and homeownership retention among very low-income homeowners. Policy paper prepared for the Annie E. Casey Foundation, June.

ORDER, R. van (2000) The U.S. mortgage market: a model of dueling charters, *Journal of Housing Research*, 11(2), pp. 233–255.

ORLEBEKE, C. J. (2000) The evolution of low-income housing policy, 1949–1999, *Housing Policy Debate*, 11(2), pp. 489–520.

PENDALL, R. (2000) Local land use regulation and the chain of exclusion, *Journal of the American Planning Association*, 6(2), pp. 125–142.

PERIN, C. (1977) *Everything in Its Place: Social Order and Land Use in America.* Princeton, NJ: Princeton University Press.

RAINWATER, L. (1980) Fear and the house-as-haven in the lower class, in: J. PYNOOS, R. SCHAFER and C. HARTMAN (Eds) *Housing Urban America*, pp. 187–196. Hawthorne, NY: Aldine.

REID, C. K. (2004) Achieving the American Dream? A longitudinal analysis of the homeownership experiences of low-income households. Working Paper No. 04-04, Center for Studies in Demography and Ecology, University of Washington, Seattle, WA.

RENUART, E. (2004) An overview of the predatory lending process, *Housing Policy Debate*, 15(3), pp. 467–502.

RETSINAS, N. P. (1999) Lower-income homeowners: struggling to keep the dream alive, *Housing Facts and Findings*, 1(3), pp. 1–2.

RETSINAS, N. P. and BELSKY, E. S. (2002a) Examining the unexamined goal, in: N. P. RETSINAS, N. P. and E. S. BELSKY (Eds) *Low-income Home-ownership: Examining the Unexamined Goal*, pp. 1–14. Washington, D.C.: The Brookings Institution.

RETSINAS, N. P. and BELSKY, E. S. (Eds) (2002b) *Low-income Homeownership: Examining the Unexamined Goal.*

Washington, D.C.: The Brookings Institution.

ROHE, W. M. and BASOLO, V. (1997) Long-term effects of homeownership on the self-perceptions and social interactions of low-income persons, *Environment and Behavior*, 29(6), pp. 793–819.

ROHE, W. M. and STEGMAN, M. A. (1994a) The effects of homeownership on the self-esteem, perceived control and satisfaction of low-income people, *Journal of the American Planning Association*, 60(2), pp. 173–184.

ROHE, W. and STEGMAN, M. A. (1994b) The impact of home ownership on the social and political involvement of low-income people, *Urban Affairs Quarterly*, 30(1), pp. 152–172.

ROHE, W. M. and STEWART, L. S. (1996) Home-ownership and neighborhood stability, *Housing Policy Debate*, 7(1), pp. 27–78.

ROHE, W. M., ZANDT, S. VAN and MCCARTHY, G. (2002a) Homeownership and access to opportunity, *Housing Studies*, 17(1), pp. 51–61.

ROHE, W. M., ZANDT, S. VAN and MCCARTHY, G. (2002b) Social benefits and costs of homeowner-ship, in: N. P. RETSINAS and E. S. BELSKY (Eds) *Low-income Homeownership: Examining the Unexamined Goal*, pp. 381–407. Washington, D.C.: The Brookings Institution.

ROSENTHAL, S. S. (2002) Eliminating credit barriers: how far can we go?, in: N. P. RETSINAS and E. S. BELSKY (Eds) *Low-income Homeownership: Examining the Unexamined Goal*, pp. 111–145. Washington, D.C.: The Brookings Institution.

ROSSI, P. H. and WEBER, E. (1996) The social benefits of homeownership: empirical evidence from national surveys, *Housing Policy Debate*, 7(1), pp. 1–35.

SAUNDERS, P. (1990) *A Nation of Homeowners*. London: Unwin Hyman.

SHAPIRO, T. M. and WOLFF, E. N. (2001) *Assets for the Poor: The Benefits of Spreading Asset Ownership*. New York, NY: Russell Sage.

SHERRADEN, M. (1991) *Assets and the Poor: A New American Welfare Policy*. Armonk, NY: M.E. Sharpe, Inc.

SHLAY, A. B. (1985) Castles in the sky: measuring housing and neighborhood ideology, *Environment and Behavior*, 17(5), pp. 593–626.

SHLAY, A. B. (1986) Taking apart the American Dream: the influence of income and family composition on residential preferences, *Urban Studies*, (23)4, pp. 253–270.

SHLAY, A. B. (1993) Shaping place: institutions and metropolitan development patterns, *Journal of Urban Affairs*, 15(5), pp. 387–404.

SHLAY, A. B. (1995) Housing in the broader context in the United States, *Housing Policy Debate*, 6(3), pp. 695–720.

SHLAY, A. B. (1999) Influencing the agents of urban structure: evaluating the effects of community reinvestment organizing on bank lending practices, *Urban Affairs Annual Review*, 35(1), pp. 247–278.

SQUIRES, G. D. (1992) *From Redlining to Reinvestment: Community Responses to Urban Disinvestment*. Philadelphia, PA: Temple University Press.

SQUIRES, G. D. (1994) *Capital and Communities in Black and White: The Intersections of Race, Class and Uneven Development*. Albany, NY: State University of New York Press.

SQUIRES, G. D. (2003) *Organizing Access to Capital: Advocacy and the Democratization of Financial Institutions*. Philadelphia, PA: Temple University Press.

SQUIRES, G. D. (2004) *Why the Poor Pay More: How to Stop Predatory Lending*. Westport, CN: Praeger.

STEGMAN, M. A. (1990) The excessive costs of creative finance: growing inefficiencies in the production of low-income housing, *Housing Policy Debate*, 2(2), pp. 357–372.

STEIN, E. (2001) *Quantifying the Economic Cost of Predatory Lending*. Durham, NC: Coalition for Responsible Lending (http://www.responsible lending.org; accessed 10 May 2004).

STUART, G. (2003) *Discriminating Risk: The U.S. Mortgage Lending Industry in the Twentieth Century*. Ithaca, NY: Cornell University Press.

US CENSUS (2002) *Moving to America: Moving to Homeownership: 1993–2002* (http://www. census.gov/prod/2003pubs/h121-03-1.pdf).

WALKER, C. (1993) Nonprofit housing development: status, trends, and prospects, *Housing Policy Debate*, 4(3), pp. 369–414.

WHITE, A. M. (2004) Risk-based mortgage pricing: present and future research, *Housing Policy Debate*, 15(3), pp. 503–532.

WHITE, A. and SAEGERT, S. (1996) The tenant interim lease program and the development of low-income cooperatives in New York City's most neglected neighborhoods, in: W. van VLIET (Ed.) *Affordable Housing and Urban Redevelopment in the United States: Learning from Failure and Success*, pp. 205–220. Thousand Oaks, CA: Sage.

WIRTH, L. (1969) Urbanism as a way of life, in: R. SENNETT (Ed.) *Classic Essays on the Culture of Cities*, pp. 143–165. New York: Appleton-Century-Crofts.

WRIGHT, G. (1983) *Building the Dream: A Social History of Housing in America*. Cambridge, MA: MIT Press.

14

"More than money: What is *shared* in shared equity homeownership?"

From *Journal of Affordable Housing and Community Development Law* (2010)

John Emmeus Davis

Shared equity homeownership is a sector in flux with new models of resale-restricted, owner-occupied housing, or new permutations of older models, appearing nearly every year. Community land trusts (CLTs), limited equity cooperatives (LECs), and price-restricted houses and condominiums with affordability covenants lasting longer than thirty years remain the signature species within this changing environment, but they are evolving as well. Forced to adapt to the harsh conditions of a fluctuating economy, the shifting requirements of public funding, and the competition for a sustainable niche within a political landscape densely populated with policies and programs favoring tenures very different than themselves, CLTs, LECs, and other forms of shared equity housing have shown remarkable resiliency. They have continually added organizational and operational characteristics that have allowed them not only to survive but to spread to every region of the United States and to other countries as well.

As these models have evolved, so has the conceptual and operational meaning of shared equity homeownership. Previously known as *limited equity housing*, this family of non-governmental, nonmarket tenures is increasingly being called by a different name: *shared equity homeownership*. This name change is not merely cosmetic, a new way of branding an old product. It represents a closer reading of what is actually shared in these unconventional models of owner-occupied housing and a deeper appreciation for what is prudently and practically needed for lower-income renters not only to become homeowners but to sustain homeownership over time.

Shared equity housing, I shall argue here, is more than a mechanism for reallocating the economic value that accrues to residential property so that affordability may be preserved across successive generations of income-eligible homebuyers. It is not only the rewards of homeownership that are shared in CLTs, LECs, and deed-restricted homes but the rights, responsibilities, and risks of homeownership as well. It is not only affordability that is protected by these unconventional models of tenure but housing quality and homeowner security as well. By restructuring the "owner's interest" and introducing a stewardship regime that remains in effect long after a home is sold, shared equity homeownership does what market-rate homeownership often fails to do: it prevents the loss of affordably priced homes, especially when housing markets are very hot or very cold. Shared equity homeownership promises a better outcome for people of modest means: homes that last.

MORE THAN EARNINGS THAT ARE UNILATERALLY LIMITED

In 2004, the National Housing Institute (NHI) commissioned a pioneering study of models of homeownership in which affordability is contractually maintained for many years. As the publisher of *Shelterforce*, a magazine dedicated to presenting timely news about affordable housing and community development, NHI had become aware of a trend that had largely eluded other experts doing research and writing in this field. Many of the articles that NHI was publishing about the proliferation of inclusionary zoning, incentive zoning, housing trust funds, and other municipally sponsored programs for expanding homeownership for families of modest means revealed a growing concern for what happened to these homes *after* they were sold. More and more cities, and a few states as well, were beginning to impose long-term contractual controls over the use and resale of owner-occupied housing being brought within the reach of lower-income homebuyers by the investment of public dollars or the exercise of public powers. Similarly, an increasing number of cities and states were giving priority in distributing their housing largess to CLTs and other nonprofit developers of affordably priced homes that were using ground leases or deed covenants to preserve the affordability of the publicly subsidized, privately owned homes within their portfolios. Despite this rise in governmental support for resale-restricted, owner-occupied housing, most policy research and academic writing about increasing the homeownership rate was still stubbornly focused on mechanisms for removing credit barriers or lowering mortgage payments for the purchase of market-rate homes. Little attention was being paid to nonmarket models of homeownership that restricted the price of publicly assisted homes across multiple resales, maintaining their affordability for many years.

NHI set out to correct this oversight, beginning with a general assessment of what was presently known and not known about the prevalence, variation, and performance of these unconventional forms of tenure. This research was overseen by a national advisory committee of academics, practitioners, and funders recruited by NHI on the basis of each person's prior involvement with at least one of the models under review. None of these models was given priority over another, either in the committee's selection or in the study's design. Rather, NHI took the unprecedented tack of treating these models as a single sector, believing that their similarities matter more than their differences. NHI argued, moreover, that the best way to bring each of these models to scale was to craft policies and programs promoting the sector as a whole.

Halfway through its research process, NHI's advisory committee decided that a new term was needed to describe this sector. Most generic names employed in the past, like *limited equity housing* and *nonspeculative homeownership*, had placed a one-sided emphasis on what homeowners gave up. Their personal earnings, when reselling their ownership interest, were limited. They were forced to relinquish most of the economic gains that accrued to their property. This suggested a burden that was borne unilaterally (and perhaps unfairly) by the individuals who owned and occupied these homes.

Hoping to shed such negative connotations, the search for a more positive and balanced descriptor began. After weighing the pros and cons of dozens of generic names, NHI's advisory committee settled eventually on *shared equity homeownership*. From the beginning, the committee realized that its choice had two significant disadvantages. The term was unfamiliar, requiring considerable explanation, even among practitioners already working with one or more of the models included in this family of tenures. There was also the risk of adding to the confusion that already existed between models of tenure like CLTs and models of finance like shared appreciation mortgages.

These drawbacks notwithstanding, the compelling advantage of shared equity homeownership was its emphasis on what is *shared* between individual homeowners and the larger community, "focusing specifically on how the appreciating value of residential property is regularly created and to whom it rightfully belongs." Only part of a property's unencumbered value is a product of an individual's personal investment in purchasing and improving the property. The rest of it, often the bulk of it, is a product of the community's investment: equity contributed at the time of purchase in the form of a public grant, charitable donation, or municipally mandated concession from a private developer; and equity accruing to the property over time because of public investment in necessary infrastructure (roads, schools, utilities, etc.) and economic growth in the surrounding society.

The latter is what the British call *betterment*. A much older term is *social increment*, coined by John Stuart Mill and popularized by Henry George to describe those gains in land value engendered by the growth and development of society. These gains, according to Mill and George, are "unearned" by private landowners because they had no hand in creating them. They constitute instead "wealth of the community." (Mill 1848) Because society is the cause of this wealth, society is justified in capturing it and using for the common good. The vehicle proposed by Mill and George was to tax it away.

CLTs, LECs, and other forms of resale-restricted, owner-occupied housing employ a different strategy. They lock this socially created value in place, turning residential property into a permanent repository for subsidies invested and gains deposited over time by the larger community. In market-rate homeownership, any unencumbered value that remains in the home after all debts and liens have been discharged belongs to the owner. In shared equity housing, homeowners claim only the equity they created through their own dollars or labors. They also receive a significant return on their investment, usually walking away with more wealth than they had when first buying their homes. Indeed, the asset-building potential of these unconventional models of homeownership can be quite substantial. But departing homeowners do not walk away with all of the value embedded in their homes. Most of this equity, including the entirety of any public subsidies put into the property and a majority of any market gains accruing to the property, remains in the home at resale, reducing its price for the next income-eligible buyer.

Each generation becomes the beneficiary, in effect, of affordability that exists and persists because every dime of the community's wealth has not been removed by the preceding generation of homeowners. To be sure, this intergenerational sharing of wealth results in an absolute cap on the amount of money that sellers might have realized had they been able to purchase and resell conventional, market-priced homes. But this is not really a limitation on *earnings*. The sellers of shared equity homes get

to keep whatever value they have contributed or created themselves. They do not get to pocket what they have not earned, i.e., value that accrues to their land and housing because of the actions of their fellow citizens, near and far.

MORE THAN GAINS THAT ARE FAIRLY ALLOCATED

What is shared in shared equity homeownership, however, goes beyond the back-end distribution of the unencumbered value embedded in residential property. *Equity* is defined more expansively than that, although this broader conceptual and operational reality is often overlooked. When weighing the merits of CLTs, LECs, or deed-restricted homes, too many commentators turn immediately, often exclusively, to the topic of resales. What distinguishes (or damns) these models in their minds is the attempt to regulate the amount of appreciation that departing homeowners may claim as their own. Whatever the model, its resale formula tends to take center stage, provoking an endless debate over whether the gains being pocketed by the housing's sellers are "large enough" to lift them out of poverty or "too much" to preserve the housing's affordability for the next generation of lower-income homebuyers.

Certainly this intergenerational sharing of property-based wealth is a defining feature of CLTs, LECs, deed-restricted homes, and the like, but the equity apportioned by these alternative models of homeownership is more than appreciation. It is more than money. *It is the entirety of the owner's interest*, i.e., the total package of rights, responsibilities, risks, and rewards that accompany the ownership of residential property. In market-rate housing, this package belongs mostly to the homeowner. In shared equity housing, it does not.

The occupants of shared equity housing are also its owners. Individually or collectively, they possess many of the same "sticks" in a property's "bundle of rights" that any other homeowner would customarily hold in the United States, benefits and burdens beyond the reach of most people who rent. In the security and longevity of their tenure; in the control they exercise over their living space; in the responsibilities they assume in financing, maintaining, and improving their homes; in the legacy they leave to their heirs; and in the money they contribute and capture for themselves, those who reside in shared equity housing are homeowners.

At the same time, these unconventional models of housing reshuffle the deck of ownership and control. Many of the rights, responsibilities, risks, and rewards that have traditionally come with owning a home are shared with someone else. Someone other than the homeowner exercises significant control over how the property may be used, financed, improved, priced, and conveyed. Someone other than the homeowner retains a long-term stake in the property, helping the occupants to carry out the responsibilities and to manage the risks of homeownership.

That someone is sometimes a governmental agency, perhaps the same one that provided funding for the housing's development or that required inclusion of affordably priced homes as a condition of the municipality's permission to build. The agency remains vested in the resale-restricted, owner-occupied housing it helped to create. There are also cases of a special purpose, quasi-public entity being set up by multiple municipalities to administer resale controls imposed by smaller municipalities.

More often of late, cities and states have been turning to nonprofit organizations to play this stewardship role on the public's behalf. A community development corporation with a long history of developing rental housing may be asked to monitor and to enforce affordability restrictions on owner-occupied housing that a public agency required. Alternatively, these responsibilities may be assigned to a CLT or an LEC, models in which sharing the owner's interest and preserving affordability are built into the organization's mission and operation at inception.

Different stewards tend to employ different contractual mechanisms for establishing and enforcing this reallocation of the rights, responsibilities, risks, and rewards of ownership. Public agencies tend to favor deed covenants or mortgage instruments. CLTs prefer a ground lease. LECs use a combination of occupancy agreements (sometimes known as a proprietary lease), house rules, corporate bylaws, and share certificates to apportion the owner's interest between the cooperative corporation that owns the property and the cooperative's residents who collectively own and govern the corporation. These preferences are not set in stone. There are public agencies that use ground leasing, for example, and there are CLTs that make frequent use of deed covenants, especially when serving as the long-term steward for affordably priced condominiums that a for-profit developer has been compelled to sprinkle throughout a larger, market-priced project because of inclusionary zoning.

Whoever the steward and whatever the contractual mechanism employed to rearrange the owner's interest, this arrangement must last for a very long time to be considered a form of shared equity homeownership. "Forever" is the gold standard here, with many proponents of shared equity housing willing to countenance nothing less than contractual restrictions on the ownership, use, and resale of owner-occupied homes that never lapse. Others have been willing to settle for longevity rather than permanence, accepting a thirty-year standard as the rule of thumb in deciding which models to count as shared equity homeownership. But in every case, the plan is for the contracts and covenants that reallocate the rights, responsibilities, risks, and rewards of ownership to last more than one generation, spanning multiple resales.

MORE THAN AFFORDABILITY THAT IS DURABLY PRESERVED

The stiffest challenge to any model of shared equity homeownership, and, accordingly, the paramount responsibility of any steward, lies in preserving the affordability of this housing when it is resold. The moment of resale is when there is the most temptation and, in an appreciating real estate market, the greatest financial incentive for sellers and buyers to bypass whatever contractual controls have been placed on the price of the home, the eligibility of the buyer, and the process for transferring the property from one owner to the next. These controls do not take care of themselves. The confidence once vested in self-enforcing covenants has usually proven in practice to be woefully misplaced. Whenever the economic stakes are high enough, there will always be sellers and buyers of resale-restricted housing who find ingenious ways to defeat the equitable allocation of equity and the durable pre-servation of affordability. Painful experience has repeatedly shown that some organizational entity is needed to watch over these homes if the controls contained in a ground lease, deed covenant, share certificate, or mortgage instrument are reliably to do what they were designed to do. As Jim Libby has written, reflecting on his own state's twenty-five-year policy of imposing and enforcing resale restrictions on housing assisted by the Vermont Housing and Conservation Board:

> For resale-restricted, owner-occupied homes in Vermont, ground leases and housing subsidy covenants, both of which limit the homes' resale price, are equally valid and enforceable. Even with clear and enforceable legal documents, however, there is recognition in Vermont that effective and sustainable stewardship is the key to success. An adequately staffed entity must stand behind the housing long after it is first rented or sold, performing the duties of stewardship.
>
> (Libby 2010, 554)

It is the steward's job to see that shared equity homes are continually resold at an affordable price to an eligible buyer. The steward may repurchase the home and, after making any necessary repairs, quickly resell it to another buyer who meets the steward's criteria for eligibility. Alternatively, the steward may oversee a direct seller-to-buyer transfer of the home, monitoring the transaction and intervening, if necessary, to ensure that the price is affordable and the buyer is eligible. Either way, all transfers occur under the steward's watchful gaze and proceed only with the steward's explicit approval.

The preservation of affordability is the purpose and performance for which shared equity homeownership is best known. It is no accident that the greatest expansion in the number of CLTs, LECs, and resale-restricted houses and condominiums has occurred during periods of rapid economic growth and in places where the average price of buying a home has been rising much faster than the average income of local residents. The reliability of these models in maintaining affordability over many years is often touted as the principal reason, even the only reason, for doing shared equity homeownership.

But durable affordability is not the only thing distinguishing these homes from their market-

priced counterparts. Just as the rewards of homeownership are not all that is shared, affordability is not all that is preserved. The long-term survival of shared equity housing and the long-term success of its owners require a steward that is equally attentive to perpetuating the occupancy and quality of these resale-restricted homes and equally protective of the new owners' security of tenure, safeguarding the homeownership opportunities that public funders and their nonprofit partners have made possible.

What is put in place in most models of shared equity housing, therefore, is a multifaceted stewardship regime that does more than merely oversee the transfer of affordably priced homes from one income-eligible buyer to another. The steward is charged with ensuring that shared equity homes continue to be occupied as the principal residence of the same people who own these homes. Absentee ownership is prohibited. Subletting is regulated, if allowed at all. Incentives or penalties are put in place to encourage sound maintenance. LECs, for example, have always established the same sort of reserves for repair and replacement that have long been standard practice in rental housing. In recent years, many CLTs and deed-restricted homeownership programs have followed suit, establishing maintenance escrows or "stewardship funds" to defray the cost of major repairs and system replacements in the residential portfolios under their care.

Stewardship is also focused on managing and minimizing risks that accompany the financing of homeownership, protecting low-income homeowners against the threat of foreclosure. Before a shared equity home is sold, most stewards provide prospective buyers with an intense orientation to their new responsibilities; they impose a screen that prevents their homeowners from entering into predatory or high-cost mortgages; and they carefully match the cost of buying and operating a particular home to the household's ability to carry this added financial burden. After purchase, most stewards regulate the improvement and refinancing of shared equity homes to ensure that homeowners do not assume more debt than they can afford or pledge more equity than they own. Many stewards, CLTs in particular, also insist on being a party to every mortgage, requiring lenders to give the CLT three critical rights in the event of mortgage default: (1) the CLT is notified if the homeowner gets behind in her payments; (2) the CLT gets an opportunity to cure the default on the homeowner's behalf, forestalling foreclosure; and (3) the CLT gets the first shot at buying the property out of foreclosure should the CLT be unsuccessful in helping the homeowner to retain her home. Protections like these are found throughout the sector. They have been demonstratively effective in enhancing the residential security of low-income homeowners, especially when real estate markets cool or collapse. Amid the recent financial crisis, they have been singularly successful in reducing foreclosures among shared equity homes to a fraction of the national foreclosure rate.

A stewardship regime so extensive in the duties it is expected to perform is an indication of just how much the meaning of shared equity homeownership has changed in recent years. The equity that is shared is no longer defined solely by the facility of these models in splitting the proceeds when a home is resold. The models themselves are no longer distinguished solely by their reliability in preserving affordability. What they are and what they do has been recast to ensure the survival and success of the homeownership opportunities they have worked so hard to create.

BETTER THAN HOMES THAT ARE EASILY LOST

Overflowing the conceptual and operational boundaries that once described it, shared equity homeownership must be defined more expansively than before, both in the way the models making up this sector are structured and, equally important, in the way these models perform. The working definition I would propose is the following:

Shared equity homeownership is a generic term for various forms of resale-restricted, owner-occupied housing in which the rights, responsibilities, risks, and rewards of ownership are shared between an income-eligible household who buys the home for a below-market price and an organizational steward who protects the affordability, quality, and security of that home long after it is purchased.

Implicit in this definition is a justification for shared equity homeownership that goes beyond the usual rationale for raising the profile and increasing the scale of this sector. It *is* a vehicle for preventing the community's wealth from being added to the private earnings of individual homeowners. It *is* a means for reallocating the economic gains that accrue to real property. It *is* a mechanism for preserving affordability across successive generations. But shared equity homeownership is more than that. And because it is more, it is better. Better than what? Better than putting precious dollars and precarious people into market-priced homes that are easily lost. Better than homeownership that regularly fails.

Most practitioners of shared equity housing are unaccustomed to making such bold claims for their favorite model. Instead of trumpeting its superiority, they are more likely to be found defending its equivalency, trying modestly to convince a skeptical public or resistant bureaucracy that their nonmarket approach to homeownership is "almost like" conventional homeownership, "almost as good" as market-rate tenures that promise homeowners a rich return on their investment. This is a curious thing. Shared equity homes are less likely to be lost than market-rate homes. Shared equity homeowners are more likely to succeed. Yet the conventional practice of boosting low-income people into market-rate homeownership is rarely subjected to the same scrutiny and skepticism that regularly greets any suggestion that public dollars might be more prudently spent on promoting alternative forms of owner-occupied housing. The notion that these alternative tenures might actually be better than market-rate homeownership is seldom voiced.

Nevertheless, it is becoming harder to ignore the many losses that accumulate year after year among the market-rate homes that low-income households have been helped to purchase through public largess.

Affordable prices are lost when the owners of publicly assisted, market-rate housing are allowed to resell their homes in a rising market for the highest possible price, pocketing 100 percent of the appreciation for themselves. The most egregious of these losses have occurred in cities and counties that have employed inclusionary zoning or some other regulatory incentive or mandate to create thousands of affordably priced homes without long-term controls over their resale. Most of this housing passes into the market within a single decade, earning equity windfalls for the first owners while fetching inflated prices that low- and moderate-income households cannot afford to pay.

Public subsidies are lost when assisted homeowners are allowed to pocket all of the public's investment at resale. Even where a policy of subsidy recapture has replaced a policy of subsidy removal, the value of the public's investment can rapidly erode in a rising market. At the other extreme, in a declining market, this investment can entirely disappear if assisted homes are forced into foreclosure.

Affordable payments are lost when homeowners are boosted into market-priced homes with adjustable-rate mortgages that rise with the market. In a booming economy, moreover, homeowners with adjustable-rate mortgages are not the only ones who see their housing costs climb. A hot market that pushes up real estate values can increase property taxes and insurance costs for all homeowners, many of whom may be unable to bear this added financial burden.

Housing quality is lost when homeowners cannot afford to pay the ongoing cost of repairing their homes or replacing major systems like a roof, foundation, or aging furnace. This tends to happen most often among homeowners with lower incomes who buy homes that are older and in worse condition because that is all they can afford, only later to discover they do not have the means to pay for unexpected repairs.

Homeownership is lost when lifelong renters are unprepared for the new responsibilities of owning a home or, should their circumstances change, the unexpected challenge of meeting financial obligations that can escalate rapidly beyond their means.

Wealth is lost by homeowners and communities alike when home values collapse and foreclosures climb. Communities of color tend to be hit the hardest because subprime mortgages and predatory lending have been heavily concentrated in their neighborhoods. Years of progress helping low-wealth households to gain access to real property and helping low-income communities to reverse the ravages of disinvestment can be wiped out virtually overnight in a wave of foreclosures like the one that began crashing through urban and suburban America after the housing bubble burst in 2006.

Such losses barely registered in our national consciousness until recently. The public was unaware; academics and policy makers were unconcerned. Few expressed much worry about the deadly rate of attrition in this market sector. True, there were a growing number of public officials in hot real estate markets who fretted about the rising per-unit cost of subsidizing homeownership. There were others who lamented the leakage of affordably priced units created through municipal programs like inclusionary zoning. But the desirability of helping low-income households to attain market-rate homes went largely unchallenged, as it does today. Even amid the worst financial meltdown since the Great Depression, most commentators on the causes and remedies for the recent foreclosure crisis have focused on the laxities evident in the way these homes were financed. Almost nothing has been said about the vulnerabilities inherent in the way these homes are owned. The system of financing homeownership has come under close scrutiny. The structure of tenure has not.

Part of the reason is money. Gaining access to an asset that appreciates in value has been extolled and encouraged as one of the surest paths out of poverty. Homeownership provides low-income families with more than a secure place to live. It dangles the golden promise of a low-risk opportunity to accumulate wealth, a gospel of prosperity that has been fervently preached by public officials and private lenders alike.

The hidden flaw in this wealth-building strategy is that many of the homes that low-income households can afford to buy on the open market are located in neighborhoods where real estate appreciation has been chronically low or nonexistent. When low-income households have managed to buy homes in neighborhoods with a stronger record of appreciation, on the other hand, they have often done so using adjustable rate mortgages and other forms of creative financing. Their opportunity for greater wealth has been purchased at the expense of greater risk, exposing these households to financial loss should the market turn against them.

The bigger problem is that first-time homebuyers of modest means tend to fail at an alarming rate, even when using conventional mortgages. Within five years of purchasing a home, nearly half of all low-income home owners fall back into renting. *Failure* is maybe too strong a word for all of this slippage because some people simply come to realize that homeownership is not for them and make a prudent decision to return to tenancy. In many other cases, however, homeownership is wrenched from the hands of low-income households with catastrophic results for both the families who lose their homes and the neighborhoods in which these homes are located. In the prescient words of William Apgar, writing several years before the current foreclosure crisis:

> Unable to properly assess the real risks and responsibilities of homeownership, many low-income and low-wealth families become homeowners even if this choice is a risky and potentially costly mistake. When families take on debt that they are unable to repay, homeownership does not build wealth. Rather, it diverts scarce resources away from meeting other pressing needs.
>
> In the worst case scenario, overextended homeowners may face a financially devastating foreclosure that undermines their ability to gain access to credit and capital for years to come. And, when concentrated in low-income and low-wealth communities, foreclosures can serve to destabilize already distressed communities and undo decades of community revitalization efforts.
>
> (Apgar 2004, 46)

It is not only low-income families that have been "unable to properly assess the risks and responsibilities of homeownership." So have most policy makers. They have been slow to acknowledge the fragility of the homeownership opportunities that governmental resources have made possible. They have been even slower to act in stemming the tide of post-purchase losses that permeate their programs, especially when real estate markets are very hot or very cold. Public dollars, public powers, and creative financing from private lenders continue to be lavished on lifting low-income households across the threshold of ownership with little regard for the long-term fate of hard-earned subsidies, hard-won affordability, and newly minted homeowners on the other side.

Attainability is all. Sustainability is outside the parameters and beyond the horizon of the program's design. Or, in the words of the space age ditty from yesteryear, lampooning the similar myopia of an earlier generation of technocrats: "Once the rockets are up, who cares where they come down? That's not my department, says Wernher von Braun" (Lehrer 1965).

That *is* the "department" of shared equity homeownership. Sustainability is what these nonmarket models do best. For them, it is not enough for low-income families to attain homeownership. They must be able to handle the responsibilities that come with it. They must be able to maintain and retain the homes that are theirs. "Housing policy should not increase risks for families already at risk of a host of problems," warns Anne Shlay. "[I]t should work at eliminating them or at least minimizing their probability of occurring." (Shlay 2006, 524) In short, it should work at helping low-income homeowners to succeed, allowing them to hang onto assets that governmental largess has delivered into their hands.

Attainability sets the bar of public policy much too low. Sustainability aims higher, a lofty aspiration that suffuses every aspect of shared equity housing. Sustainability is woven into the purpose, structure, and operation of shared equity homeownership. It is why the rights, responsibilities, risks, and rewards of ownership are shared. It is why a stewardship regime is put in place: enhancing the chances that affordability, quality, and security will dependably endure; improving the odds that whoever purchases this housing will actually succeed.

Shared equity homeownership is not loss-proof. Regardless of a steward's best efforts, there will be times when a few resale-restricted homes leak out of the system and return to the open market. There will always be home-owners who fail to make necessary repairs or to replace antiquated systems, even with the steward's help. There will always be homeowners who cannot be saved from foreclosure. It is not humanly possible to prevent every failure.

What *can* be done – what shared equity housing is designed to do – is to make failure less frequent, cutting the losses that market-oriented programs calmly accept as a normal cost of doing business when serving people too poor to become homeowners on their own.

When failure does occur, as occasionally but inevitably it must, shared equity housing is also designed to make it less catastrophic.

Engineers would describe such a system as having the capacity for graceful failure. Engineers do not set for themselves the impossible goal of designing a building, an electrical grid, or a computer program that will never fail. They strive, instead, to design systems that are robust and resilient. Such a system fails only in extreme conditions and then fails gracefully. It bends or cracks but does not shatter. It flickers but does not crash. It may even collapse, but with enough warning and backup to protect its most valuable components.

The programmatic design of shared equity homeownership aims for sustainability, but allows for graceful failure. Even when the affordability of shared equity homes is eroded, as sometimes happens at the top of the business cycle if a resale formula has failed to anticipate how fast and wide the gap can grow between housing prices and household incomes, these resale-restricted homes still remain more affordable than their market-rate counterparts. Even when the maintenance of shared equity homes is deferred, as sometimes happens at the bottom of the business cycle when lower wages or lost jobs make it difficult for homeowners to complete costly repairs, a steward is there to restore the quality of these homes before they are conveyed to another buyer. Even when the owners of shared equity homes get behind in their mortgages, as can happen at any time for reasons of health, divorce, or unemployment, the steward is there to arrest the slide toward foreclosure. Should foreclosure occur in spite of the steward's intervention, moreover, there is usually a backup plan for stopping the property's plunge into the market and for returning it to the steward's portfolio of price-restricted housing.

Shared equity homeownership anticipates dangers that rain down the hardest upon the most affordable homes and the most vulnerable homeowners. It then raises a protective umbrella over both, endowing this sector with a resiliency that is missing from the market-priced homes that low-income households usually buy. Shared equity homes are designed to last. They are not as good as homes that are easily lost; they are better.

REFERENCES

Apgar, William. 2004. *Rethinking Rental Housing: Expanding the Ability of Rental Housing to Serve as a Pathway to Economic and Social Opportunity.* Harvard University, MA: Joint Center for Housing Studies, Working Paper Series, W04–11.

Lehrer, Tom. 1965. "Wernher Von Braun."

Libby, James M. 2010. "The Challenge of Perpetuity", in Davis, John E. (Ed.) *The Community Land Trust Reader.* Cambridge, MA: Lincoln Institute of Land Policy.

Mill, John Stuart. 1848. "On the General Principles of Taxation", in *Principles Of Political Economy With Some Of Their Applications To Social Philosophy* William James Ashley ed., New York: Charles C. Little and James Brown.

Shlay, Anne B. 2006. "Low-Income Homeownership: American Dream or Delusion?" *Urban Studies.* 43(3): 511–531.

15

"The social benefits and costs of homeownership: A critical assessment of the research"

From Low Income Homeownership: Examining the Unexamined Goal (2002)

William M. Rohe, Shannon Van Zandt and George McCarthy

I. INTRODUCTION

Homeownership is often thought to be an essential ingredient of the "American Dream." Living in a single-family, owner-occupied dwelling unit is central to the American conception of a secure and successful life. Study after study has found that a large proportion of Americans would rather own than rent a home. In a recent national survey, for example, 86 percent of all respondents felt that people are better off owning than renting a home, and 74 percent believe that people should purchase a home as soon as they can afford it, regardless of their marital status or whether they had children in the household. Of the renters surveyed, 67 percent said they rent because they are unable to afford to own, while 26 percent said it was a matter of choice. Moreover, a full 57 percent of renters said that buying a home is a very important priority in their lives (Fannie Mae 1994).

Recent trends in homeownership

Interest in homeownership among Americans has been encouraged and supported by a variety of federal programs and policies, including the federal tax code, Federal Housing Administration (FHA) programs, and the Clinton Administration's National Homeownership Strategy. The federal commitment to and subsidy of homeownership has often been justified by claims that it has a variety of social and economic benefits both to individuals and to the society as a whole. In this article, we look exclusively at arguments for the social benefits of homeownership.[1] The introduction to the National Homeownership Strategy (1995) includes the following passages:

> Homeownership is a commitment to strengthening families and good citizenship.

> Homeownership enables people to have greater control and exercise more responsibility over their living environment.

> Homeownership is a commitment to community. Homeownership helps stabilize neighborhoods and strengthen communities. It creates important local and individual incentives for maintaining and improving private property and public spaces.

What evidence is there for these claims? Are they based on "conventional wisdom" or sound empirical research? How about the costs of homeownership? Is there a "downside" that is ignored in the rush to support homeownership? In answering these questions, we seek to accomplish several objectives:

- Provide a comprehensive and critical review of the literature on the purported social impacts of homeownership;

- Present a balanced view of both the potential benefits and potential costs of homeownership; and
- Develop an agenda for future research on the benefits and costs of homeownership.

II. INDIVIDUAL SOCIAL IMPACTS

In this section the assertions that homeownership engenders healthier and happier individuals are examined. Personal investment in home and neighborhood are thought to lead to improved levels of social, psychological, emotional and financial health. However, it is not clear that these outcomes are causally related to homeownership. As will be shown, the research literature on many of these topics is sparse and much leaves something to be desired methodologically. Moreover, some research that suggests that, under certain circumstances, homeownership has negative impacts on psychological and physical health.

Homeownership and satisfaction

The theory

Given the social and economic benefits often attributed to it, homeownership might be expected to have a positive impact on a person's life or residential satisfaction. Life satisfaction is defined as a person's level of contentment with all aspects of his or her life (Campbell 1976; Fernandez and Kulik 1981). Residential satisfaction is more narrowly defined satisfaction with both the housing unit and the surrounding neighborhood (Rohe and Stewart 1996).

Homeownership may contribute to life satisfaction in a number of ways. First, buying a home is an important goal for many Americans (Fannie Mae 1998, 1999). In American society, buying a home is a rite-of-passage symbolizing that a person has achieved a certain economic status. Thus, attaining this goal should increase an individual's satisfaction with his or her life.

Second, many homeowners find satisfaction in both maintaining and improving their homes (Saunders 1990). Renters are less inclined to engage in these activities since they will not reap the economic benefits of improvements

upon leaving their units and since they are less attached to their units (Austin and Baba 1990; Galster 1987; Saunders 1990).

Third, compared to renters, homeowners have greater latitude in customizing units to suit their own tastes. Their living environments are likely to better support their styles of life, thus increasing their satisfaction with both the residence and life in general (Galster 1987). Finally, homeowners are more likely to have accumulated additional wealth through a combination of mortgage amortization and home price appreciation. These, in turn, may contribute to their satisfaction with life.

These arguments, however, assume that the homeownership experience is a positive one. If the homeowner is faced with major unexpected problems with the home or the surrounding neighborhood, or the value of the home depreciates, homeownership might be expected to decrease satisfaction.

The evidence

The limited research evidence on the relationship between homeownership and life satisfaction tends to support a positive association. Rossi and Weber (1996) report a positive relationship between homeownership and both self-satisfaction and happiness in an analysis using a National Survey of Families and Households. They found no significant relationship between homeownership and happiness, however, in an analysis of data from the General Social Survey. Control variables used in the study were confined to age and socioeconomic status, so as the authors acknowledge, other unobserved variables could account for this association.

In a longitudinal study, Rohe and his colleagues surveyed both a group of homebuyers and a comparison group of continuing renters in Baltimore. After one and one-half years the homebuyers were found to have experienced a statistically significant increase in their ratings of life satisfaction (Rohe and Stegman 1994a). Moreover, based on a second follow-up survey, homeowners still reported higher ratings of life satisfaction three years after purchasing their homes (Rohe and Basolo 1997). These results were found in spite of the purchased units being in relatively less desirable neighborhoods.

The research done on the determinants of residential satisfaction consistently finds that homeowners are more satisfied with their dwelling units, even after the influences of household, dwelling unit and neighborhood characteristics are controlled for (Danes and Morris 1986; Kinsey and Lane 1983; Lam 1985; Morris, Crull and Winter 1976; and Varady 1983). In one of the stronger studies on this topic, Lam (1985) analyzed survey data from a large national sample of adults. He constructed a housing satisfaction measure based on four survey items that, based on factor analysis, seemed to be measuring the same underlying construct. After controlling for a host of demographic, housing unit and neighborhood characteristics using OLS regression procedures, he found homeowners to be substantially more satisfied with their homes than renters.

In a study of homeowners in Wooster, Ohio, and Minneapolis, Minnesota, however, Galster (1987) finds that the level of residential satisfaction is determined by characteristics of the individual, the housing unit and the surrounding neighborhood. Galster suggests that a number of homeowners "appear to translate similar residential contexts into quite different degrees of residential satisfaction." Homeowners in later stages of the life-cycle, for example, tended to be more satisfied with their living situation regardless of the characteristics of the unit or neighborhood. The adequacy of interior space and plumbing facilities (measured by rooms per person and bathrooms per person) were also highly related to the level of residential satisfaction. Satisfaction levels were also found to be higher among those owning newer units. Finally, measures of the physical and socioeconomic status of the neighborhood proved to be strong predictors of neighborhood satisfaction. Other studies on this topic tend to find similar results (Danes and Morris 1986; Kinsey and Lane 1983; and Lane and Kinsey 1980).

Overall assessment

Future studies might delve deeper into the specific explanations for why homeowners are more satisfied. At this point, the basic relationship is well established but we are still inferring the reasons for this relationship. A comparison of different types of ownership,

such as condominium, cooperative, community land trust and fee simple, may provide additional insights on this issue. Each of those types of ownership confers a different set of benefits and those differences may result in differing levels of satisfaction.

Homeownership and psychological health

This section assesses the claims that homeownership has a variety of positive impacts on psychological health. Not unlike the mechanisms that are thought to lead to residential and life satisfaction, some have argued that the social status and personal freedom associated with homeownership leads to higher levels of self-esteem and perceived control over life. Others have argued that homeownership contributes to both psychological and physical health as homeowners have additional assets that can be used to pay for improved health care. Compared to renters, homeowners also have additional security of tenure, which may result in a less stressful life.

The theory

Coopersmith (1967) defines self-esteem as an individual's personal judgment of his or her own worthiness. Based on Rosenberg's principles of self-esteem, Rohe and Stegman (1994a) suggest three distinct mechanisms by which homeownership can contribute to a person's self-esteem.

First, self-esteem may be influenced by how he or she is viewed by others. If others hold a person in high regard, that person's self-esteem is likely to be higher. Given that homeowners are afforded higher social status in American society (Doling and Stafford 1989; Dreier 1982; Marcuse 1975; Perin 1977), they are likely to internalize this status in the form of higher self-esteem.

Second, self-esteem may be influenced by how individuals see themselves as compared to others. If they see themselves doing better that those around them, they are likely to have higher levels of self-esteem. Homeowners may take their housing tenure as an indication that they are doing better than many, particularly renters. This self-perception may be particularly true for lower-income persons whose acquaintances are more likely to be renters.

Third, self-esteem may be influenced by self-assessments of their own actions and their outcomes. People who are successful in accomplishing their goals see this as evidence of their own competence. Since homeownership is a goal for an overwhelming majority of Americans (Fannie Mae 1998, 1999; Tremblay, et al. 1980), having achieved it may contribute to greater self-esteem.

Self-efficacy, sometime referred to as perceived control, refers to an individual's belief that he or she is largely in command of important life events rather than being subject to fate or to the will of others. In addition to increases in self-efficacy that may result from the successful purchase of a home, compared to renters, homeowners may have more actual control over important aspects of everyday life. Owners are not, for example, dependent on the decisions of landlords concerning rent increases or lease renewals. In addition, homeowners are better able to control who enters their units. Finally, homeowners are free to make modifications to the units to suit their needs and tastes. This enhanced control over their homes, the argument goes, may positively impact the more general sense of perceived control over life events thus leading to greater psychological and physical health.

A counter argument, however, suggests that homeowners, particularly lower-income homeowners, do not have as much actual control as some have claimed. Financial instability puts lower-income households at risk of losing their homes due to mortgage foreclosure. The psychological impact of homeownership could be negative if a person is unable to pay their mortgage and is forced from his or her home. It may also be negative if the house is found to have major problems or if owners do not have sufficient incomes to maintain their homes. Being forced out of one's home is a particularly distressing experience. Given that owners may stand to lose their equity in a foreclosure and that foreclosure can be a psychologically traumatic experience, low-income homeowners may actually feel less in control of their living situations than do low-income renters (Doling and Stafford 1989; Hoffmann and Heistler 1988). Further, homeownership may tie low-income people to declining areas where the number of good jobs is dwindling, eroding their perceived control over life events (Lauria 1976).

The evidence

Although far from conclusive, the weight of the relatively scant empirical evidence supports the idea that homeownership may contribute to a person's self-esteem. Out of the five studies reviewed, four provided a limited amount of evidence for a positive association between homeownership and self-esteem (Rohe and Stegman 1994a; Rohe and Basolo 1997; Balfour and Smith 1996; Rossi and Weber 1996; Clark 1997). While several studies have found that homebuyers report higher levels of self-esteem, one of the strongest studies on this topic found that buying a home had no significant impact on self-esteem, suggesting that such a positive relationship may need to be qualified (Rohe and Stegman 1994a).

Based on focus groups conducted by Balfour and Smith (1996) as part of a case study of a lease purchase program sponsored by the Cleveland Housing Network, the authors conclude that "[t]he opportunity to secure low-cost housing and to work toward homeownership elevate [the individual's] status in society and contributes to personal security and self-esteem." In a second qualitative study based on in-depth interviews with a non-random sample, Rakoff (1977: 93) suggests,

> …people spoke of the self-judging they went through, seeing evidence of their own success or failure in life in the quality or spaciousness of their houses, in their ability or inability to "move up" to better houses periodically, or even in the mere fact of owning … property …."

In analyzing survey data from the National Survey of Families and Households, Rossi and Weber (1996) report that homeowners were more likely to agree to the statement, "I do things as well as anyone," a question meant to assess a person's self-esteem. Yet homeowners are likely to be different from renters in a variety of ways, and these variations may account for the differences found. Homeowners are likely to have higher incomes, education levels and occupational statuses, and are more likely to be older and married with children

(Carliner 1973). Rossi and Weber did not control for many of the variables that they acknowledge could account for the results, including household composition, housing conditions, or marital status. Further, most studies on this topic measure self-esteem with a potentially more reliable index composed of multiple questions.

Another empirical study conducted by Clark (1997) relied on a survey of 1,618 black respondents from the National Survey of Black Americans. A structural equations model was developed from these data that shows a significant but weak positive relationship between homeownership and self-esteem. Potentially confounding influences of housing type, size, and condition were not considered nor were other potentially important social characteristics, such as the presence of children and marital status.

One of the strongest studies on this topic was conducted by Rohe and his colleagues (Rohe and Stegman 1994a; Rohe and Basolo 1997). They employed a panel study of 143 persons who had signed contracts to purchase newly constructed row houses on four sites in central city Baltimore. The panel was interviewed three times – before move-in and then at two eighteen-month intervals. This study also surveyed members of a comparison group of Section 8 renters with comparable wage incomes at the same time intervals. Surveys included a single direct question asking respondents if they thought buying a home had a positive, negative or no impact on their self-esteems, as well as a five-question self-esteem index developed by Hoyle (1987).

The analysis involved a simple frequency count of the homeowners who felt that homeownership had had a positive impact on their self-esteems and the use of multiple regression models to assess the relative change in self-esteem index between the homeowners and continuing renters while controlling for potentially confounding variables. The results indicate that at the time of the second interview, 85 percent of the homebuyers said being a homeowner has made them feel better about themselves. The analysis of the self-esteem index, however, found no statistically significant differences between the self-esteem of the homebuyers and continuing renters. The analysis of the third set of interviews found similar results.

Rohe and his colleagues offered three explanations for the lack of statistically significant relationships between homeownership and the self-esteem index. First, the impact of homeownership on self-esteem may have been too small to detect given the relatively small sample sizes and the relatively crude measure used. Second, buying a home may simply not be enough to alter what some believe to be a very stable self-perception (Rosenberg 1979). Finally, the type of housing units purchased as well as the condition of the neighborhoods surrounding these units may have dampened any impacts that homeownership may have on self-esteem.[2]

Overall assessment

Additional research on the impacts of homeownership on self-esteem and perceived control is clearly needed. The research conducted to date suffers from a variety of methodological problems including small sample sizes, a lack of adequate controls for possible confounding influences, inadequately developed measures and social expectancy bias. Assuming there really is a positive association between homeownership and psychological health, much more information about the process involved and the specific circumstances under which this relationship will hold is needed.

In addition, little, if any, research exists on the impacts of foreclosure on a person's self-esteem or any other psychological constructs. Not everyone is a successful homeowner and, given the current push to increase the homeownership rate, the number of foreclosures is likely to increase. We should have a better understanding of the impacts of these foreclosures on the persons involved.

Homeownership and physical health

How might homeownership impact physical health? One answer is that owner-occupied units, at least in the United States, are typically kept in better condition, so homeowners are less likely to be subject to problems related to inadequate heating and cooling systems and infestations of bugs and rodents. But the critical variable here is housing condition, rather than homeownership per se. One might ask whether homeownership has an independent effect, once housing condition is taken into account.

The theory

One argument is that homeownership provides individuals with additional assets that can be drawn upon in times of need. Page-Adams and Vosler (1997), for example, argue that recent economic restructuring has left many people feeling economically, socially and psychologically vulnerable. Homeowners are in a better position to handle this vulnerability because they have an asset in the form of home equity that can be drawn on to get them through hard times. Rasmussen and his colleagues (1997) also argue that home equity can be used by the elderly to cover the increasing "out of pocket" costs of health care, suggesting that they are able to afford a higher level of care and hence remain healthy longer.

Others argue that homeownership leads to "ontological security" which might be expected to have a positive impact on physical health by promoting a general sense of well-being (Saunders 1990). A counter argument, however, has been put forth by Nettleton and Burrows (1998). They suggest that mortgage indebtedness can lead to insecurity, anxiety and fear, particularly for those who are at risk of losing their homes. Recent trends such as variable interest rates and less secure employment may mean that some homeowners feel insecure about losing their homes.

The evidence

Homeownership is a variable included in many studies of physical health but it is seldom the main emphasis of these studies. Rather, it is often included as a control variable with little attention being paid to its independent impact on health. While these studies tend to show that homeowners are healthier, physically as well as psychologically, they do not control for the potentially confounding influences of both other characteristics of the housing units and the surrounding neighborhoods (Baker 1997; Greene and Ondrich 1990; Kind, et al. 1998; Lewis, et al. 1998). Given that owner-occupied homes, when compared to rental properties,

tend to be larger, detached units in better repair, it is not surprising to find positive associations between homeownership and health.

Several studies have, however, been explicitly designed to assess the impacts of homeownership on health. Macintyre et al. (1998) studied approximately 1,500 persons in Scotland. After controlling for age, sex, income and self-esteem, the authors report that homeowners scored higher on general health questionnaires as well as a number of more specific health indicators. In a study based on two surveys of Americans, Rossi and Weber (1996) analyzed data from the National Study of Family Health and found more positive self-assessments of physical health among homeowners, although the control variables were limited to age and socioeconomic status. Data from the General Social Survey, however, indicated no significant relationship between homeownership and health.

Page-Adams and Vosler (1997) studied 193 factory workers who were being laid off from their jobs. The results of a multivariate analysis indicate that, after controlling for income and education, homeowning workers reported significantly less economic strain, depression, and problematic alcohol use than did renters. These findings suggest that the economic and/or psychological stability engendered by homeownership may dampen stress related to job loss, although one wonders about stress associated with worrying about making mortgage payments. That issue was not addressed in the research.

Robert and House (1996) analyzed data from the American's Changing Lives data set, which contains interview data on 3,617 respondents 25 years or older. After controlling for education and income, they report that homeownership was associated with "functional health" (a measure of physical limitations) but not to the number of chronic conditions or to self-rated health.

Nettleton and Burrows (1998) studied the health impacts of having difficulty making mortgage payments. They analyzed data from more than 3,500 persons from the British Household Panel Survey at two time intervals: 1991 to 1992 and 1994 to 1995. Results indicate that having difficulty making mortgage payments was associated with lower scores on a general well-being scale among both men and women and it increased the likelihood of men visiting their general practitioners. Control variables included in this study were: income changes, physical health problems (a dichotomous measure), employment changes, number of household members employed, age, residential mobility and mortgage problems. These findings suggest that the impact of homeownership on health is contingent on whether the homeowner is able to keep up with his or her payments.

Overall assessment

The weight of the limited evidence on the relationship between homeownership and health suggests that there is a positive association between homeownership and health, as long as the household is current on its mortgage payments. The existing studies, however, do not adequately control for potentially confounding variables including socioeconomic status and housing and neighborhood conditions. Thus, it seems premature to conclude that there is a causal relationship between homeownership and health.

Furthermore, the existing research has not identified the mechanism or mechanisms through which ownership impacts health. Is it simply that homeowners tend to live in higher quality units, thus they are not exposed to health-threatening physical conditions? If so, more aggressive code enforcement or other means of improving the condition of rental properties would address this problem. Or, does homeownership impact health by providing owners with greater psychological security? If that is true, the Nettleton and Burrows study suggests that the impacts of homeownership are contingent on whether a homeowner is having difficulty meeting mortgage payments.

III. SOCIETAL SOCIAL IMPACTS

This section assesses the claims that home-ownership contributes to the overall health of society by fostering social stability, social involvement and socially desirable behaviors among both youth and adults. Homeownership is thought to lead to social stability in that homeowners move less frequently than renters. Longer tenure, along with greater economic investment in their homes, is thought to cause

homeowners to take better care of their properties. Better maintenance may contribute to both the overall attractiveness of the area and local property values (Rohe and Stewart 1996).

Homeownership is also thought to lead to higher levels of participation in local voluntary organizations and political activities as homeowners seek to protect their economic and emotional investments in their communities. Homeownership is also thought to influence behaviors such as school performance and teen parenthood among children as well as substance abuse among adults. As we will see, the research findings tend to confirm an association between homeownership and both neighborhood stability and socially or civically desirable behaviors. It is not clear, however, whether homeownership actually causes greater stability and participation, or whether those who are more likely to stay put are prone to buy homes. Further, as the transaction costs associated with home buying continue to decline, we may see a decline in the stability currently associated with homeownership, along with all its putative benefits.

Homeownership and neighborhood stability

Neighborhood stability refers to the average length of tenure among neighborhood residents. Less turnover equals greater neighborhood stability. Neighborhood stability does not necessarily equal neighborhood health however, nor does it necessarily imply stability in property values, although these benefits may be associated with stability.

The theory

The relationship between homeownership and neighborhood stability can be seen from two perspectives – the housing tenure literature and the housing mobility literature. Thomas Boehm notes, "we have two distinct literatures; the mobility [literature] says that owners are unlikely to move, while the tenure [literature] maintains that movers are unlikely to own" (1981: 375). Empirical evidence from both bodies of literature bears out these relationships (Goodman 1974; Roistacher 1974; Rossi 1955; Speare 1970; Varady 1983).

Rohe and Stewart (1996) suggest that homeownership impacts stability through two mechanisms. The first mechanism involves the human capital accumulated through age, education and income. Homeowners tend to be higher-income, family households with older, more educated household heads. These households anticipate staying in a home for a longer period of time. The second process is related to the additional interests that homeowners have in their homes. While both renters and homeowners have use interests in their homes, homeowners also have exchange interests. "This combination of interests seems to provide powerful incentives for owner-occupants to maintain their properties at a higher standard and to join organizations that protect the collective interests of homeowners in the area" (Rohe and Stewart 1996: 71).

Collectively, homeownership is thought to confer benefits to the neighborhood by stabilizing property values, encouraging maintenance and upkeep of properties and improving social conditions like high school dropout rates or crime rates (Rohe and Stewart 1996). Economically, the individual may benefit from neighborhood stability through stable or increasing property values. Further, individuals are thought to benefit socially by becoming more invested in their communities. Rohe and Stewart suggest that, beyond homeownership, "living in a relatively stable neighborhood will further encourage participation in community organizations, local social interaction and attachment, property maintenance, neighborhood satisfaction, and positive expectations about the future of the neighborhood" (1996: 54-55).

Housing policy-makers interpret these theories to suggest that increasing homeownership rates will result in both economic and social benefits to residents. However, actions taken to promote neighborhood stability through increasing homeownership may be at the cost of individual mobility. The decreased mobility associated with homeownership among individuals and households living in distressed neighborhoods may perpetuate the kinds of social problems associated with these environments (see Wilson 1987; Jargowsky 1997; Ellen and Turner 1997). In recent years, indices of both dissimilarity and isolation have increased, meaning that more poor households are living in areas of concentrated poverty, with less access to people different than themselves (Abramson *et al.* 1995). Segregation and isolation stunt the ability of neighborhood residents to improve neighborhood social characteristics, such as levels of employment and the number of families on public assistance, as well as physical characteristics like the number of dilapidated houses or the median value of homes (Massey and Fong 1990).

The evidence

Homeowners are indeed far less likely to move than renters. While renters maintain their residences for a median duration of 2.1 years, homeowners stay in one residence for a median of 8.2 years. More than 70 percent of renters have lived in their current residence for fewer than four years, while more than 70 percent of owners have lived in their current residence for more than four years (Hansen *et al.* 1998). This decreased residential mobility among homeowners confers benefits to both the neighborhood of residence and the individual household. Yet, it may also have unexpected costs.

The most comprehensive and explicit examination of the relationship between homeownership and neighborhood stability was conducted by Rohe and Stewart (1996). While most empirical studies use tenure as a control variable for examining the number and frequency of household moves, they do not examine the impact on the neighborhood. Rohe and Stewart's examination included an empirical analysis of Census data for 1980 and 1990. They used these data to test the impact of homeownership rates on two measures of neighborhood stability – length of tenure and property values. Beyond the expected finding that homeowners tend to stay longer in one home than do renters, they found that an increase in neighborhood homeownership levels over time leads to an increase in the property values of single-family, owner-occupied units. Rohe and Stewart (1996: 66) predict that "each percentage point increase in the homeownership rate of a tract would yield about a $1,600 increase in the property value of the average single-family home over a ten-year period."

While high homeownership levels have been linked to neighborhood stability, low levels of homeownership within a neighborhood have been empirically correlated with high levels of social problems. Galster *et al.* (2000), in a study of neighborhood threshold effects, found that various social indicators – female headship rate, male labor force nonparticipation, overall nonemployment rate, and poverty rate – are sensitive to homeownership rates in the neighborhood. Their analysis of Census and other statistical data from the nation's 100 largest metropolitan areas indicates that when renter-occupancy reaches a level of 85.5 percent, the census tract experiences a rapid and progressive increase in the aforementioned social indicators. These findings indirectly support the policy view that at least in some neighborhoods, expanding levels of home-ownership may counteract neighborhood decline.

Yet, a growing body of empirical literature suggests that, in some instances, rather than improving the environment for residents of distressed neighborhoods, homeownership acts to trap households in those neighborhoods. In those cases, length of tenure may reflect the greater obstacles to mobility among homeowners rather than a desire to stay put. The literature identifies four groups that may be particularly susceptible to isolation within neighborhoods of poor quality: low-income households, black households, female-headed households, and older homeowners.

South and Deane (1993) use American Housing Survey data to study the relationship between race and residential mobility. After controlling for a variety of relevant variables, their analysis shows that both low-income and black households are more likely to find themselves living in distressed or declining neighborhoods. Further, these households are less likely to translate dissatisfaction into a move. As with the general population, homeownership consistently appears as a deterrent to mobility.

In a series of recent studies, South and Crowder use national longitudinal data from the Panel Study of Income Dynamics (PSID) to examine factors affecting the mobility of nontraditional and minority households. While controlling for a number of demographic, geographic, socioeconomic and life-cycle characteristics, these studies do not take into account housing conditions or residential satisfaction, both important factors when evaluating residential mobility. They do report, however, that low-income households and minority households that start out in poor neighborhoods are unlikely to move to a neighborhood of better quality. Rather, they move into neighborhoods of similar or worse quality, if they move at all (South and Crowder 1997; 1998a).

Female-headed households may also be at a disadvantage. South and Crowder (1998b) found that, among female heads of household, marrying and finding employment facilitated a move from a poor neighborhood to a nonpoor one, while age and homeownership deterred such a move. Black single mothers are less likely than nonblack single mothers to escape distressed neighborhoods, and neither cohabitation nor public aid alleviate this result.

Noting the consistent and strong impact of age as an impediment to mobility, Burkhauser and his colleagues (1995) examined whether older homeowners are trapped in distressed neighborhoods. Using the Panel Study of Income Dynamics data set and Census data, they found that older homeowners are the most likely among all groups to be living in distressed neighborhoods. Further, of those living in distressed neighborhoods, older homeowners are the least likely to move out of them, even among those with some socioeconomic means. These findings suggest that rather than being trapped, elderly homeowners simply choose to remain in spite of the deteriorating conditions. The authors suggest that elderly homeowners stay due to the extensive attachment they have to their neighborhoods, coupled with the relatively high economic and psychological costs of moving.

Overall assessment

Although the relationship between home-ownership and mobility is straightforward and well documented, the impacts of decreased mobility, caused by homeownership or other structural impediments, are not so well established. The tension between individual mobility and group stability remains unresolved within housing policy. While homeownership has been shown to improve neighborhood stability, thus conferring certain benefits to the individual, at the same time it restricts individual mobility, which in certain instances may stunt the individual or household's ability to escape a neighborhood of poor quality and move to better one. Although facilitating homeownership among disadvantaged groups may enable them to escape distressed neighborhoods, it may also lead to the entrapment of such households in declining neighborhoods, thus perpetuating rather than improving the problems associated with such neighborhoods.

While the aforementioned studies clearly indicate that disadvantaged groups are less likely to move out of distressed neighborhoods, and that homeownership is an obstacle to such movement, it is not clear whether recent efforts to make homeownership more widely available to underserved populations are counteracting or exacerbating the effect. Further research is needed to establish the conditions under which these outcomes occur, as well as to propose methods to facilitate the more desirable result.

Homeownership and social involvement

American society values participation in both voluntary associations and political organizations. In our capitalist-oriented democracy, participation in voluntary associations is needed to address some of the social issues and problems that are either beyond the influence of government or beyond our willingness to support government programs to adequately address those problems. At the same time, our democratic form of government is based on the assumption that citizens will actively participate in the governance process. At the very least, citizens are expected to vote in local and national elections, if not become more involved by participating in political campaigns or serving on local advisory committees. Thus, if homeownership encourages participation in either voluntary or political organizations, it is having a positive impact on American society.

The theory

Why should homeowners participate more than renters in both voluntary organizations and political activities? Several arguments have been put forward. First, homeowners may be more likely to participate in local voluntary and political activities because they have an economic investment in their homes and they see participation in voluntary and political organizations as a means of protecting that investment (Baum and Kingston 1984; Rohe and Stewart 1996). The equity homeowners have in their homes is affected by conditions in the surrounding neighborhood, thus homeowners work to influence these conditions through participating in both volunteer organizations and becoming active in local political affairs. Renters, on the other hand, lack this strong economic incentive to get involved.

A second economic argument for why homeowners may be more civically active is that, compared to renters, the transaction costs associated with moving are higher (Cox 1982). Owners often incur significant expenses in both selling their existing homes and buying a new one. If a deterioration in neighborhood conditions forces homeowners to move, it can result in thousands of dollars in costs. Thus, there is greater economic incentive for owners to join neighborhood or community associations that work to maintain physical and social conditions in their neighborhoods.

A third explanation for why homeowners may be more actively involved in voluntary and political activities is that they tend to stay in their homes longer and may come to identify with their homes more strongly. Baum and Kingston (1984: 163), for example, suggest that "such feelings as pride of ownership may induce certain social psychological orientations not related to economic concerns that foster or reinforce particular social attachments." Thus, a greater attachment to place may motivate homeowners to participate in voluntary and political organizations at a higher rate.

A heightened concern about property values, transaction costs and attachments among homeowners may also have social costs, however, in the form of inappropriate discrimination against various social groups including racial and ethnic minorities and renters. Neighborhood and other voluntary groups often engage in efforts to exclude those groups from their neighborhoods, thinking that their inclusion would threaten both their economic and social-psychological investments there. Participation at the municipal government level may also result in policies, such as exclusionary zoning, that greatly restrict the ability of lower-income families to move into communities.

The evidence

The empirical evidence on the relationship between homeownership and participation in both voluntary organizations and local political activity is both extensive and consistent. After controlling for income, education and other socioeconomic characteristics, homeowners are indeed more likely than renters to participate in voluntary organizations and engage in local political activity (Ahlbrandt and Cunningham 1979; Baum and Kingston 1984; Cox 1982; Lyons and Lowery 1989; Guest and Oropesa 1986; Rohe and Stegman 1994b; Rossi and Weber 1996). Yet, limitations in the design of most of the extant research does not fully account for the possibility of a spurious relationship between participation and homeownership. In other words, certain persons may have an underlying propensity for social involvement that leads them to both participate in voluntary and political activities, and to buy a home.

DiPasquale and Glaeser (1999) analyzed data from the General Social Survey. After controlling for age, race, gender, marital status, children, income, education and city size they found that homeownership had a strong correlation with the number of non-professional organizations belonged to, knowledge of local political leaders, voting and involvement in activities designed to solve local problems. Their results indicate that compared to renters, homeowners are

> approximately ten percent more likely to work to solve local problems or know their U.S. representatives by name. They are 13 percent more likely to know the identity of their school board head. Homeowners are 16 percent more likely to vote in local elections. On average, they are members of 0.22 more non-professional organizations than non-owners.
>
> (1999: 3)

Cox (1982), in a study of 400 adults in the Columbus, Ohio metropolitan area, found that compared to renters, homeowners were more likely to attend meetings, send letters and engage in other political activities. Furthermore, to test whether economic incentives motivated homeowners to participate more, he tested to see whether homeowners who said making a

profit was an important reason for purchasing a home were more likely to participate than those who said it was not. His results show no significant differences in the participation of those with strong and weak profit orientations.

Rohe and Stegman (1994b), in a longitudinal study of a group of low-income homebuyers and a comparison group of continuing renters in Baltimore, report that the homebuyers were more likely to participate in neighborhood and block associations but not other types of community organizations. They also report that homebuyers who perceived more neighborhood problems or who emphasized economic reasons for buying were no more likely to participate in social and political affairs.

Finally, Kingston and Fries (1994) analyzed data from the General Social Survey to see if there are differences in the social and political participation of male and female homeowners. They report that, compared to renters, both male and female homeowners were more inclined to vote in local elections, but that only female homeowners were more likely to be working to solve community problems. This is one of the few studies, however, that did not find a positive relationship between homeownership and participation in voluntary organizations.

Overall assessment

The existing research on homeownership and participation in voluntary organizations and political activity supports the idea that homeowners are more actively involved. The reason or reasons behind this higher participation rate, however, are still not clear. None of the studies on this topic have totally ruled out the possibility that the association between homeownership and social and political participation is spurious. Although unlikely, there may be a more fundamental orientation toward social involvement that predisposes people to both participate in voluntary and political activity and to purchase homes.

Moreover, the most compelling theory for why homeowners should participate more is that they seek to protect the economic investment in their homes. Yet, studies that tested to see whether investment orientation influenced participation rates found no support for this proposition (Cox 1982; DiPasquale and

Glaeser 1999; Rohe and Stegman 1994b). DiPasquale and Glaeser (1999) suggest that the lower mobility rates among homeowners may explain the higher rates of involvement among homeowners, but their evidence is far from convincing. Thus, additional research is needed to understand the mechanisms and motivations behind the higher participation rate among homeowners.

Homeownership and socially desirable youth behaviors

Neighborhood stability and social involvement reflect a commitment to producing and maintaining a quality environment. Recently, several writers have suggested that such a commitment can lead to better school performance among youth, lower school dropout rates and lower rates of teen parenthood. Homeownership is thought to be directly or indirectly responsible for these socially desirable behaviors and outcomes among youth.

The theory

Green and White (1997) offer several possible explanations for how homeownership may impact socially desirable behaviors among local youth. First, homeowners may acquire both "do-it-yourself skills" from doing their own home maintenance and financial skills from having to meet the costs of home repairs. These skills may then be transferred to the children in homeowning households. It is hard to imagine, however, that home maintenance skills translate into lower levels of adolescent crime, pregnancy, and drug use and higher levels of educational attainment and employment. Yet, as Boehm and Schlottman (1999) show, children of homeowners are more likely to become homeowners themselves, suggesting that the homeowning ethic may be passed down generationally.

A second argument is that because homeowners have a greater financial stake in their neighborhoods they will be more concerned with any anti-social behaviors of local children, including their own, since they may negatively impact property values. Thus, homeowners may monitor their children's

behavior more closely. Haurin and his colleagues (2000) suggest that greater investment in owned property leads to an improved home environment, one that is supportive of cognitive and emotional development in a child. The increased social capital that results from a stable home environment helps children develop stable and strong relationships with their parents and others, diminishing involvement in undesirable behavior.

Third, homeowners tend to stay longer in a neighborhood, making them more effective monitors of children in the neighborhood. This hypothesis suggests a role for the neighborhood in turning out well-behaved youngsters through, for example, collective socialization or peer influences (Jencks and Mayer 1990; Ellen and Turner 1997). While most researchers acknowledge the greater influence of family and personal characteristics on youth behavior, neighborhood conditions may still play an important role. Because of the high correlation between homeownership and neighborhood quality, however, these impacts may be difficult to disentangle.

The evidence

Four studies that addressed the relationship between homeownership and socially desirable youth behaviors were identified. Essen and his colleagues (1978) used the National Child Development Study to assess the impacts of homeownership on the school performance of 16-year-olds in Britain. After controlling for housing conditions, region, family size, gender, social class, parental education and parental school visits, they found that children of homeowners performed better on both reading and math tests.

Green and White (1997) studied the relationships between homeownership and both staying in school and teenage parenthood. They performed separate analyses on data from the Panel Study of Income Dynamics, the Public Use Microsample from the 1980 Census and the High School and Beyond data set. In each of these analyses, they controlled for a variety of sociodemographic variables including race, family income, parent education, family composition, size and work status. They report that in all three analyses, the children of homeowners were less likely than the children of renters to drop out of high school or to have children as teenagers. Both effects are largest for children of low-income households. To test for selection bias, they used a bivariate probit technique to take account of differences between parents who choose to own versus rent. No support for selection bias was found.

Boehm and Schlottman (1999) examine the impact of homeownership on children's productivity through educational attainment and their housing choices as young adults, using data from the Panel Study of Income Dynamics. After controlling for variables that are thought to influence educational attainment, including personal characteristics, parents' educational background, parents' income and family size, they find that homeownership is a highly significant predictor of educational attainment, even with an additional control for average house value. Based on these results, Boehm and Schlottman conclude that increased educational attainment is the primary channel by which the children of homeowners might benefit. They go on to show that children raised in owned homes translate their greater educational attainment into both increased earnings and homeownership for themselves.

Finally Haurin, Parcel and Haurin (2000) analyze the impact of owning on both cognitive and behavioral child outcomes. They use panel data from the National Longitudinal Survey of Youth. Using a model that helps overcome many of the threats to causal attribution, the authors are able to explicitly credit improvements in child outcomes to an improvement in the quality of the home environment.[3] Even when controlling for a predisposition for homeowners to provide better environments (selection bias), the researchers found that homeowners offer a more stimulating and supportive home environment.

Haurin and colleagues then looked at how this improved environment impacted child outcomes. Outcomes analyzed included cognitive skills – reading recognition and math achievement – and behavioral problems like having a bad temper, being argumentative and feeling worthless, as reported by the child's mother. While these behaviors are not necessarily "socially undesirable," they might be expected to predict delinquent behavior as the child grows into adolescence. For each of the child outcomes, the researchers found that homeowning significantly and substantively

raised cognitive outcomes and reduced behavioral problems. Yet, while Haurin and his colleagues found homeowning improved the home environment by 16 to 22 percent, the improvement in child outcomes ranged from four to seven percent. Such a reduction in the magnitude of the effect suggests that many other factors influence child behavior. These unidentified factors may be expected only to increase in importance as the child matures.

Overall assessment

Although Green and White's (1997) findings of positive associations between homeownership and both staying in school and avoiding teenage parenthood are intriguing, other unobserved variables, such as family assets or neighborhood conditions like peer influences, may be responsible for those results. Haurin, Parcel and Haurin's (2000) findings are indeed compelling, but cannot tell us much about how these children will behave as adolescents. Although further findings from National Longitudinal Study of Youth hold promise, there is simply not enough research on this topic to draw any firm conclusions at this time.

Future research needs to address the impacts of homeownership on a full set of possible youth behaviors including youth employment, educational attainment, sexual behavior, drug use, and crime. In particular, the impact of homeownership on adolescent crime is a fruitful topic for research. While some studies have examined the differences in crime rates among urban and suburban teenagers, few if any have looked at the independent impact of homeownership. Sampson, Raudenbush and Earls (1997), for example, used owner-occupation as a measure of residential stability and found that it did indeed ameliorate the rate of violent crime at the neighborhood level.

IV. CONCLUSION

Evidence exists for a variety of positive social impacts of homeownership for both individuals and to society. This evidence, however, is stronger for certain social impacts and weaker for others. Considerable evidence suggests, for example, that homeowners are more likely to be satisfied with their homes and neighborhoods, more likely to participate in voluntary and political activities and more likely to stay in their homes longer periods of time. Some doubt still exists, however, whether these relationships are causal, since most of the studies do not adequately account for the self-selection of households to owner and renter occupancy.

Evidence of the impacts of homeownership on other social variables is more sparse and, in some instances, less consistent. Some evidence suggests that homeownership leads to increased self-esteem except for those buying in neighborhoods with dilapidated housing, social problems and poor reputations. The limited amount of evidence on the relationship between homeownership and life satisfaction tends to support a positive relationship. Similarly, the limited amount of research on homeownership and health points to a positive association as long as the homeowners are current on their mortgage payments. The mechanism through which homeownership impacts health, however, has not been clearly identified. Finally, the research on the impacts of homeownership on both perceived control and socially desirable youth behaviors is simply too sparse to draw conclusions at this time.

Very little research exists on potential negative social impacts of homeownership. One British study that suggests that those who are behind on mortgage payments suffer negative health consequences (Nettleton and Burrows 1998). Some evidence also suggests that homeowners are less likely to move from high poverty areas, although the consequences of this are not clear. No research on potentially important topics including the impacts of mortgage payment delinquency or default on self-esteem, sense of control, life satisfaction and other social variables was identified.

Policy implications

Public policy that encourages homeownership has often been justified by claims that it has a variety of benefits both to both individuals and to society. Considerable, although not irrefutable, evidence exists for several of those claims. Given these benefits, there is justification for public policies that encourage and support homeownership. Whether the costs of these policies are reasonable given the anticipated

benefits is a separate question beyond the scope of this article.

The research on the impacts of homeownership also suggests that these benefits may not accrue to all homeowners. The possibility of these negative impacts suggests that those involved in promoting homeownership should be careful not to oversell homeownership, particularly among those who are less likely to be successful homeowners. Recent public policy has been focused on making homeownership available to lower-income families. Although this is clearly an important and worthy goal, not everyone is capable of becoming a successful homeowner. Homeownership counseling may help lower-income homebuyers be successful homeowners, but at this point there is very little research evidence on this topic. Caution should be exercised in encouraging homeownership among those with a relatively low probability of success. Encouraging persons to buy homes that they end up losing would do them a great disservice.

Similarly, caution should be exercised in encouraging households to purchase homes in areas that do not have a reasonable probability of stable or increasing property values and healthy social conditions. The designers of many neighborhood revitalization programs adopt homeownership as the central element of their revitalization strategy. However, efforts to increase the homeownership rate in the target area must be accompanied by investments in infrastructure and services. Otherwise the homebuyers may not realize either the economic or social benefits of homeownership. If people buy in areas characterized by depreciating property values and serious social problems, the American Dream could turn into the American Nightmare.

Future research

Our review of the literature on the social impacts of homeownership suggests both general and specific recommendations on future research. These recommendations address methodological issues in how this research is conducted as well as specific topics in need of additional research.

Future research needs to do a better job of addressing self-selection bias. The self-selection of people into homeownership and rental occupancy represents a significant threat to the validity of most of the research done on the impacts of homeownership, making it impossible to determine the causal direction of any relationships found. Although we cannot randomly assign people to homeownership or rental occupancy, there are statistical techniques that can help account for the self-selection problem. In particular, a two-stage modeling technique developed by Heckman (1979) can be used to predict who becomes a homeowner based on known social and economic characteristics. The prediction is then used to develop an independent variable used to capture the effect of selection bias in the primary regression model. Rohe and Stewart (1996) used the technique in their study of homeownership on neighborhood stability.

Another approach to addressing the self-selection problem is through longitudinal research designs. Longitudinal designs allow for the measurement of key variables before and after the subjects become homeowners, allowing for the establishment of temporal sequences that are important in establishing causality.

Future research needs to do a better job controlling for potentially confounding variables. Much of the existing research on the impacts of homeownership fails to adequately control for alternative explanations for the relationships found. Homeownership is strongly correlated with income, education, age, stage in the life cycle, marital status, race, the presence of children, and employment tenure and security. However, many studies fail to control for one or more of these variables. Further, owner-occupied units tend to be larger, better-maintained, single family detached dwelling units located in more desirable neighborhoods. To truly isolate the impacts of owning, these variables must also be controlled.

Future research needs to better identify the mechanisms though which homeownership influences various social variables. Much of the existing research on the impacts of homeownership finds associations between homeownership and the social and economic variables under study and then goes on to infer the process or mechanism through which it is thought to produce those impacts. Future research needs to actually test them. The intermediate variables through which

homeownership is thought to act need to be identified, measured and tested.

Future research needs to better identify the circumstances under which ownership leads to both positive and negative outcomes. Most of the existing research on the impacts of homeownership does not recognize that the homeownership experience may not be the same for all types of home buyers or for those who buy in different neighborhoods or housing markets. This review of the literature suggests a bias, particularly among American researchers, toward testing for evidence of purported positive impacts of homeownership. In particular, we know very little about: the social-psychological or economic impacts of mortgage payment stress or mortgage default; the role of homeownership in potentially trapping persons in neighborhoods that they would rather leave; and the relationship between homeownership and efforts to exclude minorities, renters and others from neighborhoods.

To develop a more balanced view of the impacts of homeownership and to better understand how to avoid the downside of homeownership these questions should be addressed in future research.

Notes

1 For a discussion of economic costs and benefits, see McCarthy, Van Zandt and Rohe, 2001.

2 The units purchased by the sample of homebuyers were all attached row houses with small front and/or back yards. These units do not fit the more traditional image of an owner-occupied home – a detached dwelling with an ample yard. In addition, the surrounding neighborhoods had abandoned properties as well as a relatively high level of crime and other social problems. These factors could have inhibited the impacts that owning a home had on the buyers' self-esteem.

3 The quality of the home environment is measured by the Home Observation for Measurement of the Environment (HOME) scale (Bradley and Caldwell 1984). This scale includes cognitive variables measuring how much the child is cognitively stimulated, social variables like responsiveness and warmth, and physical

variables including the amount of sensory input and organization of the physical environment.

REFERENCES

Abramson, A. J., M. S. Tobin, *et al.* 1995. The Changing Geography of Metropolitan Opportunity: The Segregation of the Poor in U.S. Metropolitan Areas, 1970 to 1990. *Housing Policy Debate* 6(1): 45–72.

Ahlbrandt, R., and J. Cunningham. 1979. *A New Public Policy for Neighborhood Preservation.* New York, Praeger Publications.

Austin, D., and Y. Baba. 1990. Social Determinants of Neighborhood Attachments. *Sociological Spectrum* 10: 59–78.

Baker, D. 1997. Inequality in Health and Health Service Use for Mothers of Young Children in South West England. *Journal of Epidemiology and Community Health* 51(1): 74–9.

Balfour, D. L., and J. L. Smith. 1996. Transforming Lease-Purchase Housing Programs for Low Income Families: Towards Empowerment and Engagement. *Journal of Urban Affairs* 18(2): 173–88.

Baum, T., and P. Kingston. 1984. Homeownership and Social Attachment. *Sociological Perspectives* 27(2): 159–80.

Boehm, T. P. 1981. Tenure Choice and Expected Mobility – A Synthesis. *Journal of Urban Economics* 10(3): 375–89.

Boehm, T. P. and A. Schlottmann. 1999. Does Home Ownership by Parents Have an Economic Impact on Their Children? Paper presented at the American Real Estate and Urban Economics Association Mid Year Meeting, New York, NY.

Bradley, R. H., and B. M. Caldwell. 1984. The HOME Inventory and Family Demographics. *Developmental Psychology* 20: 315–20.

Burkhauser, R. V., B. A. Butrica, *et al.* 1995. Mobility Patterns of Older Homeowners: Are Older Homeowners Trapped in Distressed Neighborhoods? *Research on Aging* 17(4): 363–84.

Campbell, A. 1976. Subjective Measures of Well-Being. *American Psychologist* 31: 117–24.

Carliner, G. 1973. *Determinants of Home Ownership. Institute for Research on Poverty.* Madison, WI: University of Wisconsin.

Clark, H. 1997. A Structural Equation Model of the Effects of Homeownership on Self-Efficacy, Self-Esteem, Political Involvement and Community Involvement in African-Americans. Doctoral Dissertation, School of Social Work, Arlington, TX: University of Texas at Arlington.

Coopersmith, S. 1967. *The Antecedents of Self-Esteem.* San Francisco, CA: W. H. Freeman.

Cox, K. 1982. Housing Tenure and Neighborhood Activism. *Urban Affairs Quarterly* 18(1): 107–29.

Danes, S., and E. Morris 1986. Housing Status, Housing Expenditures and Satisfaction. *Housing and Society* 13: 32–43.

DiPasquale, D., and E. L. Glaeser 1999. Incentives and Social Capital: Are Homeowners Better Citizens? *Journal of Urban Economics* 45(2): 354–84.

Doling, J., and B. Stafford. 1989. *Home Ownership: The Diversity of Experience.* Aldershot, England: Gower.

Dreier, P. 1982. The Status of Renters in the United States. *Social Forces* 30(December): 179–98.

Ellen, I. G., and M. A. Turner. 1997. Does Neighborhood Matter? Assessing Recent Evidence. *Housing Policy Debate* 8(4): 833–66.

Essen, J., K. Fogelman, and J. Head. 1978. Childhood Housing Experiences and School Attainment. *Child Care, Health and Development* 4: 41–58.

Fannie Mae. 1994. *Fannie Mae National Housing Survey 1994.* Washington, D.C.: Fannie Mae.

——1998. *Fannie Mae National Housing Survey 1998.* Washington, D.C.: Fannie Mae.

——1999. *Fannie Mae National Housing Survey 1999.* Washington, D.C.: Fannie Mae.

Fernandez, R. M., and J. C. Kulik. 1981. A Multi-level Model of Life Satisfaction: Effects of Individual Characteristics and Neighborhood Composition. *American Sociological Review* 46(6): 840–50.

Galster, G. C. 1987. *Homeowners and Neighborhood Reinvestment*. Durham, NC: Duke University Press.

Galster, G. C., R. Quercia and A. Cortes. 2000. Identifying Neighborhood Thresholds: An Empirical Investigation. *Housing Policy Debate* 11(3): 701–32.

Goodman, J. 1974. Local Residential Mobility and Family Housing Adjustments. In *Five Thousand American Families – Patterns of Economic Progress*. Edited by J. Morgan. Ann Arbor, MI: Institute for Survey Research, University of Michigan.

Green, R., and M. White. 1997. Measuring the Benefits of Homeowning: Effect on Children. *Journal of Urban Economics* 41: 441–61.

Greene, V. L., and J. I. Ondrich. 1990. Risk Factors for Nursing Home Admissions and Exits: A Discrete Time-Hazard Function-Approach. *Journals of Gerontology* 45(6): S250–S258.

Guest, A. W., and R. S. Oropesa. 1986. Informal Social Ties and Political Activity in the Metropolis. *Urban Affairs Quarterly* 21(4): 550–74.

Hansen, J. L., J. P. Formby and W. J. Smith. 1998. Estimating the Income Elasticity of Demand for Housing: A Comparison of Traditional and Lorenz-Concentration Curve Methodologies. *Journal of Housing Research* 7: 328–42.

Haurin, D. R., T. Parcel and R. J. Haurin. 2000. The Impact of Home Ownership on Child Outcomes. Unpublished manuscript.

Heckman, J. J. 1979. Sample Selection Bias as a Specification Error. *Econometrica* 47: 153–61.

Hoffman, L., and B. Heistler. 1988. Home Finance: Buying and Keeping a House in a Changing Financial Environment. In *Handbook of Housing and the Built Environment in the United States*. Edited by Huttman and van Vleit. New York: Greenwood Press.

Hoyle, R., 1987. *Tapping Substantive Dimensions of Self-Esteem: The Multifaceted Evaluation of Self Inventory*. Chapel Hill, NC: Department of Psychology, University of North Carolina at Chapel Hill.

Jargowsky, P. 1997. *Poverty and Place: Ghettos, Barrios, and the American City*. New York: Russell Sage.

Jencks, C., and S. Mayer. 1990. The Social Consequences of Growing Up in a Poor Neighborhood. In *Inner-City Poverty in the United States*. Edited by L. Lynn Jr. and M. McGeary. Washington, D.C.: National Academy Press.

Kind, P., P. Dolan, *et al.* 1998. Variations in Population Health Status: Results from a United Kingdom National Questionnaire Survey. *British Medical Journal* 316(7133): 736–41.

Kingston, P., and J. Fries. 1994. Having a Stake in the System: The Sociopolitical Ramifications of Business and Home Ownership. *Social Science Quarterly* 75(3): 679–86.

Kinsey, J., and S. Lane. 1983. Race, Housing Attributes, and Satisfaction with Housing. *Housing and Society* 10: 98–116.

Lam, J. 1985. Type of Structure, Satisfaction and Propensity to Move. *Housing and Society* 12: 32–44.

Lane, S., and J. Kinsey. 1980. Housing Tenure Status and Housing Satisfaction. *Journal of Consumer Affairs* 14(Winter): 341–65.

Lauria, D. 1976. Wealth, Capital and Power: The Social Meaning of Home Ownership. *Journal of Interdisciplinary History* 7(2): 261–82.

Lewis, G., P. Bebbington, *et al.* 1998. Socioeconomic Status, Standard of Living, and Neurotic Disorder. *Lancet* 352(9128): 605–09.

Lyons, W., and D. Lowery. 1989. Citizen Reponses to Dissatisfaction in Urban Communities: A Partial Test of a General Model. *Journal of Politics* 15(4): 841–68.

Macintyre, S., A. Ellaway, *et al.* 1998. Do Housing Tenure and Car Access Predict Health Because They are Simply Markers of Income or Self-Esteem? A Scottish Study. *Journal of Epidemiology and Community Health* 52(10): 657–64.

Marcuse, P. 1975. Residential Alienation, Home Ownership and the Limit of Shelter Policy. *Journal of Sociology and Social Welfare* 3(November): 181–203.

Massey, D. S., and E. Fong. 1990. Segregation and Neighborhood Quality. *Social Forces* 69(1): 15–32.

McCarthy, G., S. Van Zandt and W. M. Rohe. 2001. The Economic Costs and Benefits of Homeownership: A Critical Assessment of the Research. Forthcoming Working

Paper. Research Institute for Housing America.

Morris, E., S. Crull, *et al.* 1976. Housing Norms, Housing Satisfaction and the Propensity to Move. *Journal of Marriage and the Family* 38: 309–20.

Nettleton, S., and R. Burrows. 1998. Mortgage Debt, Insecure Home Ownership and Health: An Exploratory Analysis. *Sociology of Health and Illness* 20(5): 731–53.

Page-Adams, D., and N. Vosler. 1997. *Homeownership and Well-Being Among Blue-Collar Workers.* St. Louis, MO, Washington University in St. Louis, George Warren Brown School of Social Work, Center for Social Development.

Perin, C. 1977. *Everything in Its Place.* Princeton, NJ: Princeton University Press.

Rakoff, R. 1977. Ideology in Everyday Life: The Meaning of the House. *Politics and Society* 7: 85–104.

Rasmussen, D. W., I. F. Megbolugbe, *et al.* 1997. The Reverse Mortgage as an Asset Management Tool. *Housing Policy Debate* 8(1): 173–94.

Robert, S., and J. S. House. 1996. SES Differentials in Health by Age and Alternative Indicators of SES. *Journal of Aging and Health* 8(3): 359–88.

Rohe, W. M., and V. Basolo. 1997. Long-Term Effects of Homeownership on the Self-Perceptions and Social Interaction of Low-Income Persons. *Environment and Behavior* 29(6): 793–819.

Rohe, W. M., and M. A. Stegman. 1994a. The Impacts of Home Ownership on the Self-Esteem, Perceived Control and Life Satisfaction of Low-Income People. *Journal of the American Planning Association* 60(1): 173–84.

Rohe, W. M., and M. Stegman. 1994b. The Impact of Home Ownership on the Social and Political Involvement of Low-Income People. *Urban Affairs Quarterly* 30(September): 152–72.

Rohe, W. M., and L. S. Stewart. 1996. Home Ownership and Neighborhood Stability. *Housing Policy Debate* 7(1): 37–81.

Roistacher, E. 1974. Residential Mobility. In *Five Thousand American Families – Patterns of Economic Progress.* Edited by J. Morgan. Ann Arbor, MI: Institute for Survey Research, University of Michigan.

Rosenberg, M. 1979. *Conceiving the Self.* Malabar, FL: Robert E. Krieger Publishing Company.

Rossi, P. 1955. *Why Families Move.* Glencoe, IL: The Free Press.

Rossi, P. H., and E. Weber. 1996. The Social Benefits of Homeownership: Empirical Evidence From National Surveys. *Housing Policy Debate* 7(1): 1–35.

Sampson, R. J., S. W. Raudenbush and F. Earls. 1997. Neighborhoods and Violent Crime: A Multilevel Study of Collective Efficacy. *Science* 277: 918–23.

Saunders, P. 1990. *A Nation of Home Owners.* London: Unwin Hyman.

South, S. J., and K. D. Crowder. 1997. Escaping Distressed Neighborhoods: Individual, Community, and Metropolitan Influences. *American Journal of Sociology* 102(4): 1040–84.

South, S. J., and K. D. Crowder. 1998a. Residential Mobility Between Cities and Suburbs: Race, Suburbanization and Back-to-the-City Moves. *Demography* 34(4): 525–38.

South, S. J., and K. D. Crowder. 1998b. Avenues and Barriers to Residential Mobility among Single Mothers. *Journal of Marriage and the Family* 60(4): 866–77.

South, S. J., and G. D. Deane. 1993. Race and Residential Mobility: Individual Determinants and Structural Constraints. *Social Forces* 72(1): 147–67.

Speare Jr., A. 1970. Home Ownership, Life Cycle Stage, and Residential Mobility. *Demography* 7(4): 449–58.

Tremblay, K. R., D. A. Dillman, *et al.* 1980. An Examination of the Relationship Between Housing Preferences and Community-Size Preferences. *Rural Sociology* 45(3): 509–19.

Varady, D. 1983. Determinants of Residential Mobility Decisions. *Journal of the American Planning Association* 49: 181–99.

Wilson, W. J. 1987. *The Truly Disadvantaged: The Inner-City, the Underclass, and Public Policy.* Chicago: University of Chicago Press.

16
"High-risk lending and public policy, 1995–2008"

From *Foreclosed: High-Risk Lending, Deregulation and the Undermining of America's Mortgage Market* (2009)

Dan Immergluck

Much of the media coverage of the 2007–08 mortgage crisis gave the impression that the problems of high-risk lending had come as a total surprise to policymakers. There was little mention of well-documented problems in the high-risk mortgage market and the decade-long policy battle over regulating subprime loans. Federal regulators were said to be "asleep at the wheel" and somehow missed this major development in credit markets (Levitt 2008.) In fact, major problems in the subprime mortgage market had been recognized as early as the 1990s, and significant policy debates had occurred continually since then. The increase in subprime lending from 2002 to 2007 was not the first boom in subprime lending. Although there were some minor changes in federal regulation in 2001, the financial services industry successfully fought off most calls for increased regulation and even had the assistance of some federal regulators in overriding state attempts to regulate lending more strongly.

***

Among the policy debates that received substantial media attention in 2007 and 2008 were those concerning proposals to assist distressed borrowers in foreclosure or at risk of foreclosure. Although I will address some of these proposals in this chapter, I will focus more on earlier policy debates around increased regulation of the mortgage lending industry. To establish policy proposals for reforming and restructuring mortgage markets going forward, which will be covered in the final chapter, it is

critical to understand the policy debates that have occurred in recent decades.

POLICY DEBATES OVER REGULATING HIGH-RISK MORTGAGE LENDING, 1995–2008

As problems of predatory lending and higher foreclosure rates among subprime loans came to light in the late 1990s, consumer and community groups around the country became increasingly focused on the issue. There were concerns and policy debates over predatory and high-cost lending before the late 1990s, however. In the late 1980s and early 1990s, Washington, D.C.-based consumer advocates such as the National Consumer Law Center and others worked to get the Home Ownership and Equity Protection Act (HOEPA) passed in 1994. HOEPA had been focused on increasing regulation of very high-cost home equity and refinancing loans. It established a threshold of loan pricing, with loans priced over this threshold becoming subject to special disclosures, and it prohibited certain loan practices and terms. Consumer advocates argued for stronger restrictions on high-cost loans, but were successful only in obtaining regulations that relied primarily on increasing disclosures to borrowers.

Although HOEPA may have had some effect on small, "hard-money" lenders that charged interest rates in the high teens and low twenties, it did not restrain subprime lending in any meaningful way and may have, in fact, provided the regulatory context for the growth of the market. Besides relying mostly on additional disclosures as the fundamental way to protect borrowers, HOEPA employed pricing thresholds or "triggers" over which proscriptive regulations would kick in. However, these thresholds were generally much too high to address the vast majority of subprime loans and easily could be avoided by pricing just under the threshold or by shifting pricing from interest rates to up-front or contingent fees that were not included in the pricing calculations. The subprime market actually grew faster after 1995, especially for refinance lending, the primary target of HOEPA. With the explosion of the subprime market came the growth of predatory lending and, soon, an increase in defaults and foreclosures as well.

In 1997, the Federal Reserve Board, which is responsible for adopting regulations under HOEPA, examined early implementation of the law. The following year, the Board, together with the Department of Housing and Urban Development, issued a joint report to Congress that addressed issues such as loan flipping, credit insurance, and related issues of abusive and predatory lending. However, few of the recommendations were implemented.

Some states moved to increase regulation of subprime lending in the mid- to late 1990s (Bostic *et al.* 2008). Some restricted the use of prepayment penalties or balloon payments in mortgages. Other states tightened mortgage broker and banker licensing and regulation. However, these laws were generally not very comprehensive and attacked only small pieces of the abusive and predatory lending problem.

As subprime lending reached a critical mass in the late 1990s, the disproportionate concentration of high-risk loans in urban neighborhoods began to be felt more acutely, especially in the form of foreclosures and abandoned housing. Moreover, subprime and predatory lending became not just a consumer issue but also posed problems for community development. Concentrated foreclosures hurt neighborhoods and cities, adding to the unfairness of the loss of homes to individual families.

North Carolina makes the first move toward comprehensive regulation

Advocates for stronger mortgage regulation found success first at the state and local levels.

In North Carolina, a state with a strong history of community reinvestment activism, a number of organizations became involved in the issue. These included the country's largest community development credit union, the Center for Self-Help, as well as the Community Reinvestment Association of North Carolina and the North Carolina Fair Housing Center. This group formed the hub of the Coalition for Responsible Lending, which was able to gain the support of a major statewide elected official, the attorney general, who played a significant role in the legislative campaign. The legislature's black caucus was also supportive.

Advocates for increased regulation of subprime home loans in North Carolina developed a bill that would go far beyond HOEPA in limiting the practices that could be used in making high-cost loans. In the summer of 1999 the North Carolina legislature passed the first comprehensive antipredatory-lending state legislation in the country. The bill followed the threshold approach of HOEPA but set the triggers significantly lower so that the law would capture a substantial segment of subprime loans while avoiding prime loans. It then prohibited certain lending features that, in the case of high-cost lending, were often viewed as predatory. Surprisingly, especially in the light of the later fierce battles in other states, the bill was supported by both the Mortgage Bankers Association of North Carolina and the North Carolina Association of Mortgage Brokers.

Following passage of the North Carolina law, two states, New York and Massachusetts, issued regulations aimed at the predatory lending problem, although these measures were substantially weaker than the North Carolina legislation. Other states began debating similar measures. On the local level, the City of Chicago and Cook County, Illinois, each proposed local ordinances aimed at the problem in early 2000. Unlike the North Carolina legislation, the Chicago and Cook County ordinances did not call for regulating lenders. Rather, the proposals relied on a significant history of local laws aimed at encouraging banks to be socially responsible by linking government financial business to responsible banking. Chicago, for example, had an ordinance dating back to 1974 that required banks accepting municipal deposits to disclose data on their lending in the city.

The Chicago ordinance and others like it in Oakland, Atlanta, Dayton, Cleveland, and Detroit sought to withdraw municipal business from firms engaged in predatory lending. These laws followed earlier municipal deposit ordinances aimed at encouraging banks to reinvest in urban neighborhoods. They also bore close resemblance to antiapartheid ordinances that many cities passed in the 1980s, in which cities refused to do business with firms that invested in South Africa. The industry responded quickly by appealing to state legislatures, where they had more lobbying experience and relationships, to override the local ordinances. Some of the local predatory lending ordinances – including those in Detroit, Dayton, and Cleveland – were soon overridden by state legislation or court decisions. By preempting these incentive ordinances, state legislatures or courts told local governments that they did not have a right to choose the financial institutions with which they did business.

Stiff opposition: lenders, the GSEs, and the credit rating agencies fight state regulation of high-risk lending

Following the initial actions of a few early states, other states continued to consider more comprehensive antipredatory lending regulations. By 2003, the National Conference of State Legislatures listed more than thirty states as having passed predatory lending statutes, and by the beginning of 2007 only seven states had no sort of "mini-HOEPA" statutes or sets of laws restricting prepayment penalties, balloon payments, or predatory practices or terms (Bostic *et al.* 2008; National Conference of State Legislatures 2003). However, there was great variation in both what sorts of loans these statutes covered and the extent to which the laws proscribed certain practices or products. Many state statutes were not very comprehensive or very strong. Some essentially just re-created HOEPA protections in state law. Many so-called antipredatory lending laws at the state level had been heavily influenced by state banking lobbyists. The result was that the pricing thresholds over which the regulations would kick in were often the same as the very high federal HOEPA thresholds and the restrictions themselves were often very minimal.

When consumer advocates and community organizations made efforts to strengthen lending regulations, they were often thwarted by industry advocates and lobbyists. Banking and financial services lobby groups have traditionally had a great deal of influence on state legislatures in the mortgage regulation arena. Moreover, federal banking laws put pressure on state legislatures to accommodate banking interests. Banks are allowed to "export" interest rate and fee regulations from their "home" state. As a result, banks aggressively lobby state legislatures for favorable regulations that they can then use to override regulations in other states.

Economic development has frequently been used as a major argument in such lobbying. Lenders sometimes agree to maintain facilities – or simply the "main office" location – in the home state in exchange for favorable regulations. Some states have gone so far as passing laws aimed at encouraging bank locations and facilities by reducing regulations in exchange for economic development commitments by the institutions. Delaware passed a law in 1981 that eliminated fee and rate restrictions on consumer loans and reduced income taxes in exchange for employing at least one hundred people in the state. Other banks have worked to win regulatory concessions on mortgage regulations, which they can then export around the country. A very large bank lobbied the Illinois legislature unsuccessfully in 2000 and 2001 to gain exemption from essentially any regulations on fees for second mortgages, a freedom that it would then be able to export to other states. The bank holding company argued that economic development would occur as a result of the policy and threatened to locate its new main charter in Ohio or another state if the deregulatory bill did not pass (Hinz 2001).

A key set of actors in the state-level policy debate were the GSEs Fannie Mae and Freddie Mac and the three primary credit rating agencies, Standard & Poor's, Moody's, and Fitch. These firms had significant leverage over state policymakers. The GSEs could refuse to purchase certain types of loans in the state. The rating agencies could refuse to rate mortgage-backed securities containing loans covered by certain state laws, essentially eliminating the regular liquidity and marketability for such loans – or for even greater numbers of loans due to the mixing of loans in securitized pools. Beginning in Georgia in early 2003, the GSEs and the credit rating agencies became actively involved in influencing state legislation by proclaiming that it would not rate securities containing any loans covered by the state's new antipredatory lending law.

In 2001, on the heels of the hearings held around the country on predatory lending by federal agencies, Senator Vincent Fort introduced an antipredatory lending bill in the Georgia legislature. In the next session in 2002, Governor Roy Barnes, an ally of Fort's on the predatory lending issue, introduced what was to become the Georgia Fair Lending Act (GFLA). After undergoing a number of changes, the bill was passed and went into effect in late 2002. The law was immediately considered one of the strongest state antipredatory lending laws in the country. Based on North Carolina's statute, the Georgia law was stronger, especially because it held purchasers of loans accountable for violations of the law, in what is known as assignee liability, something the North Carolina law lacked. Assignee liability was a key issue, because it meant that a regulatory violation followed the loan through the securitization process and affected subsequent parties in the chain of capital. This essentially overrode the problem created by the holder-in-due-course doctrine, which enabled funders of loans to shield themselves from liabilities created by predatory and abusive practices in the origination process.

Immediately after the law went into effect, the lending and mortgage brokerage industry began a concerted campaign to overturn it, especially after Governor Barnes lost his reelection bid in late 2002 (Milligan 2004). They were aided by a prominent local conservative radio host and others in this effort. But they gained their most important ally in early 2003, when Standard & Poor's issued a press release saying that it would not rate securities backed by Georgia mortgages for fear that some of the underlying loans might violate GFLA:

> Loans governed by the GFLA are categorized as "Home Loans," "Covered Home Loans," or "High Cost Home Loans," with each category having its own requirements and, in the case of Covered Home Loans and High Cost Home Loans, fees, points, and annual percentage rate tests. According to Standard & Poor's, violations of the statute will subject non-complying parties to potentially severe liability. Most importantly, however, the GFLA subjects assignees of Home Loans that violate the Act to potential liability. Thus, transaction parties in securitizations, including depositors, issuers and servicers, might all be subject to penalties for violations under the GFLA.
>
> (Mortgage Bankers Association 2003)

This press release, which was later followed by similar actions by Moody's and Fitch, was the critical factor in enabling opponents of GFLA to severely weaken the law by essentially removing the assignee liability provision. In a letter to S&P's chief executive officer, Senator Fort pointed out that S&P misconstrued the original GFLA assignee liability provision, which actually only applied to high-cost loans (Fort 2003). The letter also asked S&P to identify and explain the firm's financial relationships with lenders, issuers, and brokers, suggesting that the firm may have been suffering from conflicts of interest and benefiting from continued securitization of high-risk products. It was not long before lending industry advocates had managed to replace GFLA with a much weaker law that effectively gutted the assignee liability provisions.

Contrary to some of the media discussion that followed the Georgia debate, rating agencies could rate securities with assignee liability provisions, as long as the potential damages from the provisions could be quantified (Engel and McCoy 2007; Reiss 2006). Nonetheless, efforts to create assignee liability provisions in state or federal regulations, even when damages were made quantifiable, were a key flashpoint for industry advocates in mobilizing against regulation.

Federal agencies study abusive lending and regulators warn of subprime risks to banks

In 1999 and 2000, a variety of developments were putting pressure on federal regulators to act on the predatory lending problem. In 1998 lower mortgage rates and higher prepayment rates lowered subprime lender profitability. Moreover, many subprime lenders experienced higher default rates than they had anticipated (U.S. Office of the Comptroller of the Currency 1999). On top of this the Asian and Russian financial crises of 1997 and 1998 made raising capital much more difficult. The result was that a significant number of subprime lenders failed.

On the policy front, states were looking closely at the North Carolina law and a variety of localities were considering local ordinances aimed at slowing abusive lending. In 1999, the U.S. Department of Housing and Urban Development and the U.S. Treasury Department created a task force to develop federal policy recommendations to address "predatory lending," which includes excessive or unnecessary charges, prepayment penalties, repeated refinancings, and other abuses. The HUD-Treasury Task Force held hearings in five large cities in the spring of 2000 and issued a report in June containing a number of federal policy recommendations, including calling on the Federal Reserve Board to use more of its authority under HOEPA to outlaw predatory practices.

In Congress, separate and opposing bills were introduced backed by consumer and industry interest groups. In May 2000, the House Banking Committee held a hearing on predatory lending in which the Federal Reserve Board was chastised by Chairman Jim Leach (R-IA) for not using its authority to act on the issue. The Federal Reserve had not acted on the recommendations made in the 1998 joint Federal Reserve-HUD HOEPA report. Chairman Leach asked "if there is a problem out there, if Congress has given very strong authority to regulators and the Federal Reserve, our regulators, is the Federal Reserve AWOL? That is a question that I think demands a response" (Leach 2000).

Even before the surge of federal policy activity in 1999 and 2000, federal bank regulators had recognized the growth of subprime lending and at least its risks to lenders. In March 1999, the four bank and thrift regulators issued an "Interagency Guidance on Subprime Lending" (U.S. Office of the Comptroller of the Currency 1999). However, this guidance was clearly focused on the need for depository institutions to minimize any institutional risk that they may have in holding high-risk subprime loans on their balance sheets. The eight-page guidance devoted less than half of a page to concerns over consumer protection, and much of this was concerned with how well banks "identify, monitor and control the consumer protection hazards associated with subprime lending." The

guidance did address some of the risks that originators faced in making and securitizing subprime loans, but it did not address the risks that banks and thrifts took on in purchasing subprime mortgage-backed securities to hold on their balance sheets.

State and local policy developments, the HUD-Treasury report, and public and congressional concern led the Federal Reserve Board to hold public hearings in four large cities in the summer and fall of 2000 on potential revisions to HOEPA regulations. At the end of 2000, the Board proposed some significant, albeit modest, changes to the HOEPA rules. The largest changes in the rules involved classifying single-premium credit insurance (SPCI) within the definition of fees under HOEPA and lowering the interest rate threshold at which a loan would be classified as "high-cost." The former meant that almost any loan with single-premium credit insurance would be classified as a high-cost loan under HOEPA (since SPCI typically exceeds the 8 percentage point fee trigger in the law), thereby increasing the disclosures and protections associated with the loan. The latter meant that more high-rate loans would be covered by HOEPA.

The most successful effort by consumer and community advocates was the push to effectively ban single-premium credit insurance. Considered by many to be an egregious predatory practice, SPCI involved selling people insurance that covers loan payments should some calamity (e.g., death or disability) occur. However, SPCI was relatively unique among insurance products in that it was financed completely up-front into the loan. With SPCI, rather than pay the premiums monthly or some other periodic way, the borrower paid the entire 5–10 years of insurance up front via the premium being added onto the mortgage amount. The lump-sum premiums for such policies could easily amount to 15 percent of the principal amount of the loan. This increased the loan amount and reduced borrower equity. Moreover, unlike in the case of insurance that is paid monthly, if the borrower got into trouble, she could not stop paying the insurance portion of her monthly payment without defaulting on the mortgage.

Consumer and community groups began focusing on problems with the product as a key focus of their antipredatory lending campaigns. By the summer of 2000, consumer activism on

SPCI, and the inherent problems with the product, compelled Fannie Mae and Freddie Mac to pledge not to purchase loans containing the product. Following this, the product was condemned in the HUD/Treasury report, and later in 2000 the Federal Reserve recommended including SPCI in the HOEPA definition of points and fees. Then, by the summer of 2001, three large sellers of single-premium credit insurance voluntarily announced that they would no longer offer it. By the end of 2001, the Federal Reserve finalized its proposal to include SPCI in the definition of points and fees, which essentially made any loan with SPCI a high-cost loan under HOEPA and therefore subject to heightened regulation.

The OCC and OTS preempt state regulation of high-risk lending

As more states began to adopt predatory lending regulations in 2001 and 2002, lenders began to turn to Washington to push for lender-friendly federal policies that would override state laws. Lenders argued that state laws would create a "patchwork" of regulation across the country that would reduce the efficiency of the banking system by making it difficult for lenders and secondary-market firms to operate national lending operations. Advocates of state laws, including governors and legislators, countered that states have a right to protect their citizens, especially when it came to something as important as protection of homeowners and borrowers. Moreover, a good deal of real estate law – including foreclosure law – already varied by state, and lending markets had accommodated such differences without causing significant harm to loan availability. In fact, by the early 2000s vendors had begun marketing software that enabled lenders to monitor compliance with various state antipredatory lending laws. One firm, for example, marketed a product called the "Predatory Lending Monitor," which interfaced with major loan origination systems. From September 2002 to March 2003, the company completed nineteen installations of the product (Experity 2003).

To block state antipredatory lending laws in the early 2000s, the lending industry pursued a mixed strategy of seeking a federal statute aimed at preempting state laws and, at the same time, trying to get federal bank regulators to preempt state laws. The first approach would remain difficult as long as Democrats held significant power in the Senate and, perhaps more important, as long as Senator Paul Sarbanes, a supporter of increased mortgage regulation, retained the ranking Democratic seat on the Senate Banking Committee. Therefore, lenders – particularly banks, thrifts, and bank-owned mortgage companies – also adopted the second strategy. Both thrifts and national banks appealed to their federal regulators (the Office of Thrift Supervision and the Office of the Comptroller of the Currency, respectively) to preempt state predatory lending regulations. The OTS regulates federal thrifts and the OCC oversees national banks. Federal law gave both regulators significant ability to preempt state consumer protection regulations. In the late 1990s and early 2000s, they wielded such power aggressively, rebuffing states' attempts to adapt consumer protection laws to a changing financial marketplace – something Congress and federal regulators were not doing.

Unfortunately for those who favor state authority in this arena, some federal regulators have a vested interest in preempting state consumer protection laws. The ability to preempt state law is perhaps the greatest source of value in the federal thrift and national bank charters. Regulators can gain political power based on the number and size of the banks that fall under their regulatory supervision. In some cases, a regulator's operations are funded by levying fees on the institutions they regulate. This can encourage an agency to pursue policies that are friendly to banks – especially larger ones. If a regulator does not use its ability to allow banks under its supervision to preempt state consumer protection regulations, the bank may change its charter so that it is regulated by a more lender-friendly agency. The impacts of charter changes can be significant. Even one very large bank shifting its charter to another regulator can significantly affect an agency's revenues. When Chase Manhattan Bank (now J.P. Morgan Chase) merged with Chemical Bank in 1995 and changed from a national to a state charter, it was estimated that the OCC lost 2 percent of its budget in fees (Rosen 2002). Even if an agency's funding is not directly tied to the banking assets under its supervision, if fewer and fewer institutions fall under its supervisory umbrella, its power and relevance will be called into question. In the long run, this could jeopardize the agency's very existence.

The more power that a regulator has to effectively override state regulations – and the more it exercises such power – the more likely it is that institutions will want to be chartered under that regulator's authority. In the past, competition between regulators was mostly restricted between the national bank (OCC) charter and the state charter (FDIC, Federal Reserve, and state regulators). However, as thrifts were allowed to behave more like commercial banks, and banks became more involved in mortgage markets, the thrift-bank distinction became less meaningful, increasing the competition between regulators.

In 1974, Arthur Burns, chairman of the Federal Reserve Board, expressed concerns over a "competition in laxity" among the regulators (Scott 1977). Since then, there have been repeated concerns that banks "forum shop" to find the most comfortable regulator (Dennis 1978; Matasar and Pavelka 1998). Since at least the late 1990s, this "race for the bottom" includes regulators vying to offer banks as much preemption power as they can. Demonstrating the importance of preemption to the value of a charter type, a banking attorney was quoted in the *American Banker* regarding the OCC's preemption actions as asking, "Why would you want a national charter but for the preemption authority?" (Davenport 2003).

The OTS moved first to override state mortgage regulations by preempting key provisions of Georgia's antipredatory lending law in January 2003, making federal thrifts exempt from the law. A week later, it preempted New York's predatory lending law. State regulators immediately objected to the OTS moves. Community groups saw the OTS's action – under Bush appointee James Gilleran – as particularly antagonistic, given that the preceding director of the OTS, Clinton appointee Ellen Seidman, had voiced some of the strongest concerns over predatory lending among federal regulators (Blackwell 2003).

The OCC was not about to let the thrift charter gain a clear regulatory advantage over the national bank charter. It had issued a letter to national banks in November 2002 asserting its jurisdiction over all state regulators and asked banks to inform it if a state regulator had asserted its authority over a national bank. In comments to the press after the OTS decision, the OCC pointed out that it needed a request from a bank before it could follow the OTS's preemption move (Blackwell 2003).

It was not long before a national bank, National City Bank of Cleveland, requested that the OCC preempt the Georgia law. Community groups, governors, attorneys general, and state legislatures argued that the OCC should not move to preempt state consumer protection laws. In the summer of 2003, the OCC did preempt the Georgia antipredatory lending law, even after industry interests had succeeded in weakening the law at the state level. The agency went on to suggest that it would preempt all similar state laws, and issued proposed regulations to do so. The OCC's move in some ways was a more assertive move in defense of banks to ignore state laws, because its authority under banking statutes to preempt state consumer protection laws was less well established.

Federal regulators went even further and argued that even mortgage lenders that were subsidiaries of national banks or federal thrifts would benefit from federal preemption. The federal courts upheld this position when challenged by state regulators. The financial services regulator for the state of Michigan challenged the ability of a mortgage company subsidiary of a national bank to escape state regulation (U.S. Supreme Court 2007). The state regulator argued that, because the mortgage company, Wachovia Mortgage, was not itself a national bank but only the subsidiary of a national bank, Michigan's laws should not be preempted.

In 2007, the U.S. Supreme Court found in favor of the bank, stating that the preemption powers given by the National Banking Act covered subsidiaries of national banks as well as the banks themselves.

The policy debate between state and federal regulators over preemption became quite heated, with some advocates for state regulation being particularly outspoken. Foremost among these was Elliott Spitzer, attorney general for New York. In 2003, Spitzer threatened to sue the OCC over its preemption activities (*New York Times* 2003). However, after he initiated an investigation into racially discriminatory behavior by national banks in New York, the OCC joined an industry trade group in suing him and effectively prevented his investigation

(Bloomberg News 2005). Although Spitzer had a higher profile than other advocates for the rights of states to regulate lending, he was not alone. Many other state regulators and attorneys general also argued against the federal agency's aggressive preemption practices.

Notwithstanding the aggressive use of preemption powers by some federal regulators, it is not true that most states took aggressive actions to stem the tide of high-risk lending. Mortgage banker and broker lobbies at the state level were generally successful in repelling substantive efforts to improve mortgage regulation in the late 1990s and early 2000s. The laws that did pass were often quite weak. Of course, the actions in the early 2000s most likely blunted any ongoing efforts by states to improve or strengthen regulations after about 2002, knowing that their laws would cover only a portion of the industry and that national banks and federal thrifts could, if necessary, acquire state-regulated lenders to move them out of the state regulatory umbrella.

During the second high-risk boom in the mid-2000s, exotic mortgage products became more widespread in both the prime and subprime markets. As banks and thrifts increasingly became drawn into higher-risk markets, and as the performance of such products began to show some weaknesses, banking regulators issued some warnings about their use. In 2003, the OCC issued another warning about the risks posed by subprime loans to the banks it regulated. The agency was particularly concerned that national banks might suffer "legal, reputation and other" risks in acquiring loans through mortgage brokers or by purchasing loans from originators (U.S. Office of the Comptroller of the Currency 2003a).

Despite their warnings about the risk to lenders involved in subprime lending, with the exception of the modest changes to HOEPA in 2001, federal policymakers made essentially no substantive changes in regulations aimed at curbing lending abuses and the growth of excessively risky lending practices in the subprime market. In fact, federal regulators facilitated the expansion of high-risk lending and paved the way for the second high-risk boom by actively preempting states' attempts to increase lending regulations when federal policymakers would not.

The second high-risk boom saw an increase in the use of "alternative" or exotic loan structures, including interest-only, negative amortization, and payment-option loans. These structures were applied to both the subprime and prime markets. Subprime loans increasingly were structured as hybrid adjustable rate loans in which the interest rate would be fixed for two or three years and then allowed to adjust. Many prime loans were also structured with adjustable rates. As different exotic features were layered on top of each other, many observers became increasingly worried about the underlying risk in the mortgage marketplace.

In the early to mid-2000s, consumer advocates and the U.S. General Accounting Office called on federal regulators to do more to regulate the affiliates and subsidiaries of banks that were increasingly dominating the subprime and high-risk loan markets. In general, the supervision of these lenders was left to state financial service regulators and to the Federal Trade Commission, both of which did not have nearly the level of supervisory resources as the federal banking regulators. In early 2004, the General Accounting Office issued a report calling for stronger regulatory supervision in the subprime market and specifically calling for giving the Federal Reserve more explicit power to conduct regular examinations of lenders affiliated with banks through bank holding company structures (U.S. General Accounting Office 2004). Earlier in 2000, Edward Gramlich, a Federal Reserve Board governor, had urged Federal Reserve chairman Alan Greenspan to direct examiners to examine the lending of bank-affiliated mortgage companies on a pilot basis (Andrews 2007). The suggestion was rebuffed by Greenspan.

More generally, even though federal regulators had issued cautions to banks holding subprime loans directly on their balance sheets, they generally supported the growth of the subprime mortgage market. The most important support came in the form of the preemption of state consumer protection laws. But key federal regulators also issued statements and studies that argued that subprime lending was enabling increased homeownership among minority and lower-income groups, which in turn gave support to similar arguments made by industry lobbyists working against efforts to increase regulation in Congress. The evidence presented for these claims, however, was quite limited, and there was little analysis of the benefits and costs associated with subprime lending or even whether subprime-financed homeownership was economically beneficial to borrowers.

In July 2003, the OCC released a controversial working paper, "Economic Issues in Predatory Lending," during the agency's decision making over its first preemptions of state consumer protection laws (U.S. Office of the Comptroller of the Currency 2003b). The OCC study argued that state antipredatory lending laws reduced levels of subprime lending and suggested that this was a negative outcome because it reduced "credit availability." It now looks quite likely that subprime markets were, in fact, providing socially inefficient amounts and types of credit. The OCC report relied primarily on a study by the industry-funded Credit Research Center at Georgetown University, which found that the number of subprime originations in North Carolina had declined by approximately 14 percent as a result of the state passing the first antipredatory lending law. The OCC paper suggested that this was an undesirable effect of the law. However, many would now likely question whether a decline in subprime lending of 14 percent was an undesirable result. By restricting abusive practices and reducing the number of loans with excessive up-front fees, such laws are likely to discourage the riskiest loans.

The OCC was not alone in its support for the booming subprime industry. Federal Reserve governor Edward Gramlich gave a speech in 2004 that, while acknowledging the problems of higher foreclosure rates in the subprime market, clearly came down on the side of viewing higher levels of subprime lending as a positive trend: "Despite the caveats, the net social evaluation of these trends is probably a strong positive" (Gramlich 2004). Only three years later, Gramlich seemed much less certain on this count (Gramlich 2007). Gramlich had also argued in 2004 that "subprime lending represents a natural evolution of credit markets." Gramlich was clearly not alone in this opinion, especially among economists at the federal regulatory agencies. Subprime lending was often viewed as generally an organic, natural outgrowth of technological and financial innovation that was somehow purely the product of unfettered free markets. Yet the history of deregulation and supportive policies supporting structured mortgage finance tells us otherwise. Housing finance markets are politically and socially constructed. They are the products of

decades of lobbying and policy debates at the state and federal level.

In late 2005, as the market for exotic loans boomed and increasingly involved both prime and subprime loans, the four banking regulators issued a proposed guidance on "nontraditional" mortgage products – what many called exotic loans – and issued a final guidance in October 2006 (U.S. Office of the Comptroller of the Currency et al. 2006). In responding to the late 2005 proposal, consumer groups warned that regulators were not going nearly far enough. In particular, they argued that regulators should direct lenders to underwrite adjustable rate loans using the maximum interest rate to which a loan might adjust. In fact, many subprime and other adjustable rate loans were approved based on initial, low fixed introductory or "teaser" interest rates that later could adjust upward a great deal. Advocates also generally called for the essential prohibition of no-documentation or stated-income loans, while regulators merely discouraged the use of such products. Of course, the guidance was inherently limited in its impact on the mortgage market, because it applied only to depository institutions directly regulated by the four regulators and not to the many affiliate and independent mortgage companies that were, on average, more active in the subprime and high-risk markets.

In 2006 and early 2007, as problems in subprime and higher-risk market segments became much clearer and caused significant disruptions to broader financial markets, regulators responded with additional proposals and hearings. The Federal Reserve Board held hearings related to subprime and predatory lending in both 2006 and 2007. In early 2007, it issued a draft proposal for increased regulation of the subprime market. After the 2007 hearings, the Board issued a more complete set of regulatory proposals with particular attention to using HOEPA to regulate a substantially broader segment of the subprime market, rather than just the very high-cost segment that HOEPA had been used to address previously.

After the fall 2006 election, when Democrats gained control of the House of Representatives and Barney Frank took over as chair of the House Financial Services Committee, there was also some movement in the legislative arena. Frank sponsored a bill that contained many substantive regulations that consumer advocates had been proposing for over a decade. However, the bill that eventually passed the House in 2007 also contained some key language that would preempt some state efforts to impose assignee liability in a stronger way than the federal law would. Despite the fact that the 2007–08 subprime crisis had been caused in large part by breakdowns in the mortgage supply chain – which is precisely what assignee liability is designed to guard against – industry lobbyists had once again successfully weakened the law in this regard.

Of course, by late 2007 a good deal of the damage done by the second boom in high-risk lending had already been put in motion and the subprime market had been substantially shut down. Therefore, proposals to increase regulation would be relevant in the longer term, to prevent a repeat of mortgage market excesses and abuses. Many of the proposals both in the Frank bill and in the proposed HOEPA regulations would constitute significant regulatory improvements and help set the stage for sounder lending markets. These sorts of proposals will be discussed in the last chapter in the broader context of establishing policies for promoting sound and fair lending markets.

FORECLOSURE MITIGATION RESPONSES TO THE 2007–2008 MORTGAGE CRISIS

A good deal of attention by policymakers during the mortgage and foreclosure crisis of 2007 and 2008 concerned what could – or should – be done to assist homeowners who were in danger of, or in the process of, losing homes through foreclosure. As foreclosure rates increased dramatically during 2007 and into 2008, policymakers, lenders, investment firms, and consumer advocates offered numerous policy proposals to stem the tide of foreclosures, assist homebuyers, and, in some cases, slow the fall of the overall housing market. The debates over these proposals were very high profile, especially compared to most issues in the arena of housing policy, which have often been relegated to the pages of specialized media and policy publications. By late 2007 and early 2008, daily newspapers covered national policy debates on a regular basis about voluntary interest-rate freezes, plans to use the FHA to refinance unaffordable loans, foreclosure moratoria, and a variety of more complicated proposals. The

mortgage crisis spawned a number of specialized websites and blogs that tracked the extent of the crisis but also were focused heavily on the debate over various proposals to reduce foreclosures or their impact.

***

Although the precise date of the beginning of the 2007–08 mortgage crisis is difficult to pinpoint, many would point to April 2007, when New Century Financial, one of the largest subprime lenders in the country, filed for bankruptcy. Smaller players in the subprime industry, such as Ownit Mortgage Solutions and People's Choice, had filed for bankruptcy in preceding months, but the failure of a lender the size of New Century revealed the scale of the crisis. In the same month, Senator Charles Schumer, the chair of the Joint Economic Committee, called attention to the impact that foreclosures were having on local neighborhoods and communities by issuing a report, "Sheltering Neighborhoods from the Subprime Foreclosure Storm," and calling for federal intervention to help distressed borrowers (U.S. Senate Joint Economic Committee 2007b).

Initially, in the late spring and early summer of 2007, policymakers such as Fed Chairman Ben Bernanke and HUD Secretary Alonzo Jackson called for federal funding for foreclosure prevention counseling. In June, the investment banking firm Bear Stearns revealed that it was pledging over $3 billion to bail out one of its hedge funds that had lost money on subprime mortgage investments, and in July the rating agencies begin to downgrade some subprime RMBS. Two Bear Stearns hedge funds declared bankruptcy and investors filed suit against the parent company. Things deteriorated even more in August, as more investors, in the United States and Europe, announced large losses in RMBS and CDO investments. By mid-August, credit markets had essentially seized up, as more investment losses were revealed and financial stock prices fell. The Federal Reserve quickly moved to lower interest rates. However, by late 2007 the securitization market for subprime mortgages had essentially shut down.

As delinquencies grew and foreclosure rates increased dramatically in late 2007, with some increases in the prime as well as subprime markets, policymakers introduced a variety of proposals to help delinquent homeowners keep their homes. One of the first legislative proposals introduced separately in the House and Senate in the fall of 2007 was a measure to allow bankruptcy judges to modify the outstanding balance on home loans for borrowers in bankruptcy.

When distressed homeowners do not file for bankruptcy, lenders may voluntarily modify the terms of distressed loans. But lenders often are reluctant to do so, and the complex structured securitization of mortgages created many barriers to loan modifications. Under Chapter 13 bankruptcy, borrowers file debt reorganization plans with the bankruptcy court. Federal bankruptcy law gives the court the ability to modify certain outstanding loans. In the case of most secured loans, bankruptcy judges have the authority to "cram down" the principal balance of the loan without the lender's permission, with the lower limit on such cram-downs typically being the fair market value of the collateral. However, this ability does not extend to loans secured by owner-occupied residences. Bankruptcy judges can modify the loan balance on a vacation home or on an investment property, for example, but not for a borrower's principal residence.

Bills introduced by Senator Richard Durbin (D-IL) in the Senate and Representatives Brad Miller (D-NC) and Linda Sanchez (D-CA) in the House aimed to temporarily remove the exclusion from the cram-down of owner-occupied mortgages, which would have allowed bankruptcy judges to modify loans on owner-occupied homes as a way of reducing foreclosures and keeping people in their homes. Given the challenges of voluntary loan modifications for securitized loans, there was a strong argument for using bankruptcy courts – which, after all, are in the business of restructuring consumer debt – to facilitate the modification of loans to affordable levels.

The key argument in favor of Chapter 13's special protection for lenders making loans on owner-occupied properties is that it enables them to offer lower interest rates and thus encourages home ownership. This presumption, however, was not empirically established prior to the development of the owner-occupancy exception. Only recently have any researchers examined the evidence on the impact of cram-downs on interest rates.

In strongly opposing the bankruptcy cram-down proposals, lending industry representatives argued that the proposal would raise interest rates on owner-occupied loans by 1.5 percentage points (Mortgage Bankers Association 2008). As evidence for this claim, they cited higher interest rates for investment property mortgages (whose interest rates are not generally 1.5 percentage points higher) but also factored in higher down-payment requirements and higher origination fees. Yet, the greater financing costs for such loans are due more to the greater risks involved in investor property mortgages.

Levitin and Goodman (2008) measured the impact of cram-down on interest rates using historical data. From 1979 to 1993, federal judicial districts varied in the degree to which they allowed for mortgage cram-downs on principal residences. These differences allowed Levitin and Goodman to identify the impact that cram-downs have on mortgage rates. They found that mortgage cram-downs resulted in, at most, only a 0.05 to 0.15 percentage point increase in interest rates, a far cry from the 1.5 percentage points asserted by the Mortgage Bankers Association.

Despite the evidence suggesting that permitting bankruptcy cram-downs for owner-occupied loans would not have a significant impact on overall mortgage rates, industry advocates continued to maintain otherwise. Industry lobbyists lobbied aggressively against these proposals, even though they were designed to be temporary. Consumer advocates continued to argue that this proposal would be an important and efficient tool in slowing foreclosures, but by April 2008 congressional proponents of the proposal had largely conceded defeat. The proposal to allow bankruptcy cram-downs continued to be discussed throughout 2008 as foreclosures continued to mount.

Hope now – the bully pulpit runs into structural obstacles

In late November and early December 2007, after the administration had opposed the bankruptcy cram-down proposals, Secretary of the Treasury Henry Paulson introduced the Hope Now initiative, a voluntary initiative developed in cooperation with the securities and loan servicing industry to develop ways to speed up and "streamline" loan modifications of subprime adjustable rate mortgages. Hope Now was coordinated by the Homeownership

Preservation Initiative of Minneapolis, a lender-funded coalition that had been managing a national foreclosure hotline.

The Hope Now proposal was heavily criticized by consumer advocates as being a meager response in part because it was entirely voluntary on the part of servicers and investors. The plan merely laid out a proposed set of methods to identify borrowers for speedier consideration for loan modifications. Although the plan was generally described as one focused on freezing interest rates on adjustable rate loans for five years, the voluntary nature of the plan and the constraints imposed by securitization schemes made such arrangements unlikely in most cases. The proposal was also structured to target a narrow band of homeowners who met specific criteria; even for these borrowers, though, there was no strong incentive for investors to agree to modify loans. The very narrow segment of borrowers eligible to be *considered* for streamlined modifications had to meet the following conditions

1. borrowers had to be living in the residences covered by the mortgage; loans had to be hybrid ARMs with initial fixed interest rate periods of thirty-six months or less;
2. borrowers had to be no more than thirty days past due at the time that the loan modification is being considered and no more than sixty days past due more than once over the past twelve months;
3. loans had to be included in securitized pools; loans had to be originated between January 1, 2005, and July 31, 2007;
4. loans had to have an adjustable interest rate that would reset between January 1, 2008, and July 31, 2010;
5. payments had to be scheduled to increase by more than 10 percent after the reset; the amount of the first-lien loan had to be greater than 97 percent of the home's value;
6. borrowers had to have credit scores below 660 and less than 10 percent higher than their scores at the time of origination.

Estimates of the proportion of subprime ARM borrowers that would fit these requirements fell in the range of 3 to 12 percent.

The focus of Hope Now on borrowers that were current with mortgages prior to an interest rate reset was not well aligned with the scope of the foreclosure problem. A very large number of

delinquent subprime borrowers – on the order of 30 percent or more depending on different estimates – had not even encountered their initial interest rate reset. Rather, the loans were so badly underwritten that they were unsustainable even at the introductory rates. Hope Now was also criticized, including by the Office of the Comptroller of the Currency, for not being able to provide standardized, reliable progress reports on how many borrowers were receiving loan modifications of different sorts or on the success of those modifications (U.S. Office of the Comptroller of the Currency 2008).

[One] of the difficulties in modifying distressed loans that have been securitized is that the cash flows to investors in different tranches are derived differently, so that reducing the interest rate on a loan may hurt one type of investor more than the other. Conversely, lengthening a loan term to reduce payment amounts or reducing the outstanding principal will impose different costs on different investors, again potentially causing a sort of "tranche warfare" (Eggert 2007).

Another obstacle to loan modifications was the heavy use of junior mortgages in the subprime market. As Rosengren (2008) has pointed out, the junior mortgages were often securitized separately from the senior mortgages, even if the same lender originated both loans. This means that modifying a borrower's mortgage debt may involve working with two different servicers and two different securitization structures, greatly compounding the complexity of satisfying securitization agreements and investors. Second-lien mortgages were very prevalent in some markets. The proportion of senior mortgages that had associated junior mortgages increased in Massachusetts from 26 percent in the second quarter of 2003 to 65 percent in the third quarter of 2005 (Rosengren 2008).

The legal agreements and arrangements that undergird structured finance are also obstacles to negotiating large numbers of loan modifications. The pooling and servicing agreements that allow servicers to modify loans often have limits of how many loans can be modified in different ways. Frequently, the agreements stipulate that modifications cannot be made unless the loan is in default or default is reasonably expected, a decision that generally was designed to be made on a case-by-case basis. If mass modifications are made, some servicers may fear litigation by investors. As Rosengren (2008) has argued, the legal structure for securitization "clearly did not foresee the widespread emergence of distressed borrowers, delinquencies, and foreclosures."

In the "old days" of originate-to-hold lending, a distressed borrower would be able to contact the lender that originated the loan. Given the physical costs of the foreclosure process, the interests of the borrower and lender would often align over avoiding a foreclosure and modifying the loan in such a way that the borrower could afford it. Even when GSE securitization began to dominate, the relatively unstructured nature of pass-through securities meant that investor and borrower interests could be rather easily aligned and servicers' decision making and constraints in modifying loans were much less complicated. Although the engineers of structured finance products may have correctly predicted that these products would increase the flow of capital into higher-risk mortgage markets, they clearly did not consider their impacts on the difficulty of modifying mortgages, especially in the event of a need to modify hundreds of thousands of mortgages in a fairly short period of time.

Congressional foreclosure rescue proposals move slowly

While the Bush Administration pushed the voluntary Hope Now investment-industry-led partnership as an alternative to the bankruptcy bill or other legislative proposals, and especially after the bankruptcy bill failed, some members of Congress continued to push for a more active role for the federal government in mitigating foreclosure, arguing that such intervention was necessary in part to slow the flood of vacant housing spilling into an already weak housing market. A variety of proposals were put forward, including various programs to use the FHA to offer refinance loans to finance 80 to 90 percent of the outstanding balance of distressed loans. The FHA had earlier in late 2007 announced its "FHA Secure" program that would make refinance loans to borrowers with subprime adjustable rate loans. However, the program was relatively restrictive, requiring borrowers to be current on their loans prior to any reset in their interest rate – even though many subprime

foreclosures were due to defaults occurring well before the reset period. The FHA Secure Program did not constitute a substantial change to existing FHA refinance products. Nonetheless, the agency did increase the overall number of refinance loans significantly after it announced the program. Thus, although the program may not have served borrowers in proximate danger of losing their home, it likely led to refinancing a substantial number of borrowers into safer, fixed-rate loans.

Notwithstanding FHA's increased re-financing activity, foreclosures continued to rise in late 2007 and 2008. Despite the continuing problem, those arguing for a more muscular federal role in refinancing distressed borrowers met with substantial opposition. Critics of such proposals argued that many borrowers were actually "speculators" and therefore should be held responsible for their fate. Although, depending on the local market, significant portions of foreclosures were non-owner-occupied properties, held either for investment or vacation home purposes (or both), this "speculator" argument was a distraction, because the proposals for refinancing distressed borrowers were all designed only for borrowers who could document owner-occupancy.

There were also suggestions that some large portion of distressed owner-occupants were well-informed, knowledgeable borrowers who had knowingly taken on loans that they knew they could not afford but were betting that their property would appreciate so quickly that they would be able to refinance or sell before their interest rate reset. Again, however, little to no evidence was provided to show that such borrowers were a very sizable portion of distressed homeowners. Although some borrowers might have fit this scenario, many certainly did not, especially in many parts of the country that did not see wild rises in property values but still had experienced large increases in foreclosures.

Some critics argued that assisting distressed borrowers would create a "moral hazard," in that risky behavior would be rewarded rather than punished, suggesting that borrowers receiving such help would go right out again and take out another risky loan because they would now assume that they would be "bailed out" once again. Such arguments were quite effective with the media and the general public, even though there was little evidence of a moral hazard in the case of most owner-occupiers. There may be cases when moral hazards may present themselves in taking out risky loans, but these are much more likely to involve investment properties. Homeowners are less likely to view their home as purely a financial investment and to willingly reengage in activity that put them into high-cost loans and subjected them to the heavy personal costs and humiliation of mortgage default.

Many media reports suggested that owner-occupants whose property values had declined below their outstanding mortgages were walking away from their homes, in what pundits called "jingle mail," implying that homeowners would just send their house keys to the lender and walk away from the house and the mortgage even if they could afford their existing mortgage payments. Again, it is important to distinguish investors from owner-occupants here. Investors are much more likely to walk away from a property whose value has declined significantly. This explains the inherently greater risk of lending to non-owner-occupied properties.

In the case of owner-occupant loans, however, there is substantial evidence that the great majority of borrowers in "negative equity" situations do not abandon their homes. Based on data for Massachusetts, Rosengren (2008) pointed out that the percentage of borrowers who default on loans when the loan amount exceeds home value is only on the order of 6 to 10 percent. This supports the notion that homeowners do not view their home as only a highly liquid investment that they will dump as its value falls. Rather, there are a wide variety of social and economic factors [that] a homeowner will take into consideration. If values drop very far, many owner-occupants may decide to default, especially if their mortgage payments are large relative to their income.

None of this is to say that home values are unimportant factors in determining foreclosure rates. But weak housing markets are typically not sufficient causes for very high foreclosure rates among owner-occupants. An increase in borrower risk – which can be caused by loan features and terms as well as economic conditions and shocks – will increase the number of borrowers in distress. Subprime and high-risk loans are more vulnerable to borrower economic shock such as unemployment, health crises, and divorce. There is less cushion in large part due to the higher debt-to-income ratios in

such loans. But when house prices are rising, distressed borrowers can usually find ways to either refinance their loans or sell their homes. Flat or declining housing prices will leave such borrowers with little alternative but foreclosure, unless lenders or policy-makers step in to somehow help reduce monthly debt burdens.

Finally, by July 2008, with the spillover of the mortgage crisis affecting the economy more broadly and a national election coming up in the fall, there was more pressure to do something about the foreclosure problem. On top of this, there were now concerns that the GSEs might need federal intervention in the form of borrowing or even an equity investment from the federal government. The administration, which had initially opposed any funding in the legislation for local governments struggling with vacant and abandoned properties due to foreclosures, finally dropped its opposition in order to get the bill approved. The result was a complex, multifaceted legislative package – labeled the Housing and Economic Recovery Act (HERA) of 2008 – that contained tax breaks for residential builders, a complicated first-time-homebuyers tax credit, provision for a $300 billion FHA loan program to restructure the loans of distressed homeowners. The bill also contained a provision allowing the Treasury to extend credit to and possibly invest in the GSEs. Finally, it contained almost $4 billion for the Neighborhood Stabilization Program (NSP). The NSP is an eighteen-month program of block grants to state and local governments for reclaiming and redeveloping vacant, foreclosed homes.

The $300 billion "Hope for Homeowners" program, which went into effect in October 2008 and was run by the FHA, required lenders to write down mortgages and refinance borrowers into loans up to 90 percent of the current value of the home. The program also required borrowers to share a portion of their equity gain with the FHA when they sell the property.

The $4 billion in NSP funds was allocated according to a formula based on foreclosure-related activity, although each state was given a minimal level of funding, even if it had experienced few foreclosures. Local governments can use the NSP funds to purchase, reclaim, or demolish vacant homes.

Despite the July 2008 HERA bill and the Hope for Homeowners program, which began operations in October, mounting foreclosures and continued weakening in the housing market continued to press on the larger economy. In early September, Fannie Mae and Freddie Mac were placed into a government "conservatorship," giving their regulator control over the firms. A week later, Merrill Lynch, the investment bank, was sold to Bank of America and Lehmann Brothers filed for bankruptcy after seeking and being rejected for federal aid.

In the third week of September, the Federal Reserve Board rescued the large financial services firm AIG. AIG had been a heavy participant in the credit default swap market, a market that was hit hard by, and amplified the aggregate damage from, the mortgage crisis. The Board made the firm an $85 billion loan and essentially took control of the firm.

As commercial paper markets froze after the collapse of Lehman Brothers, officials in the Treasury Department quickly introduced a $700 billion proposal to allow it to purchase troubled financial assets, including mortgage-backed securities, from financial institutions. After only two weeks of high-profile debate and an initial defeat in the House of Representatives, the Emergency Economic Stabilization Act (EESA) was passed and signed into law on October 3. Together with many earmarked tax breaks and initiatives not clearly related to the financial crisis, EESA contained, as its principal component, the Troubled Assets Recovery Program (TARP). EESA gave the Treasury Department unprecedented authority to purchase distressed financial assets through TARP. It also gave the department the ability to make equity investments in financial institutions. Soon after the bill was approved, various European governments, led by the United Kingdom, began making equity investments in large banks. The U.S. approach of relying more on purchasing mortgage-and asset-backed securities was widely criticized as being an inefficient approach to unfreeze credit markets. By mid-October, the Treasury Department announced that it would use $250 billion in TARP funds to purchase equity in financial institutions and that half of these funds would go to nine very large financial institutions.

***

Although rapid foreclosure processes and lender-friendly foreclosure laws may encourage high-risk lending and make alternatives to foreclosure more difficult, there are also reasons to avoid excessively slow or bureaucratic foreclosure processes. If foreclosure processes cause properties to sit vacant for very long periods of time, they may exacerbate the negative effects of foreclosures on surrounding communities (Mallach 2008). Thus, it is likely that, depending on market conditions and the regulatory climate, a period of well more than a few months but less than a year is the appropriate period of time between the foreclosure notice and the final consummation of the foreclosure sale.

REFERENCES

Andrews, E. 2007. "Fed and Regulators Shrugged as the Subprime Crisis Spread." *New York Times*, December 18.

Blackwell, R. 2003. "Second OTS Preemption: Predator Law in N.Y." *American Banker*, January 31.

Bloomberg News. 2005. "Court Blocks Spitzer Inquiry into Loan Data." *New York Times*, October 13.

Bostic, R., K. Engel, P. McCoy, A. Pennington-Cross, and S. Wachter. 2008. "State and Local Antipredatory Lending Laws: The Effect of Legal Enforcement Mechanisms." *Journal of Economics and Business* 60: 47–66.

Davenport, T. 2003. "Why OCC May Tread Lightly on Georgia Law." *American Banker*, April 9.

Dennis, W. 1978. "The Community Reinvestment Act of 1977: The Legislative History and Its Impact on Applications for Changes in Structure Made by Depository Institutions to the Four Federal Financial Supervisory Agencies." Credit Research Center Working Paper No. 24. Washington, D.C.: Pottinger and Company.

Eggert, K. 2007. "Testimony before the Senate Banking, Housing, and Urban Affairs Committee's Subcommittee on Securities, Insurance, and Investments at a Hearing Regarding Subprime Mortgage Market Turmoil: Examining the Role of Securitization." April 17. http://banking.senate.gov/public/_files/eggert.pdf (accessed May 12, 2008).

Engel, K., and P. McCoy. 2007. "Turning a Blind Eye: Wall Street Finance of Predatory Lending." *Fordham Law Review* 75: 102–62.

Experity. 2003. Press release, www.experity. com/press_releases/PR_3_19_2003.html (accessed June 23, 2003).

Fort, V. 2003. "Letter to Leo C. O'Neill, President, Standard & Poor's." January 28. http://www.federalreserve.gov/secrs/ 2006/august/2 0060808/op-i 253/op-1253_5_1.pdf (accessed May 20, 2008).

Gramlich, E. 2004. "Subprime Mortgage Lending: Benefits, Costs, and Challenges." Speech before the Financial Services Roundtable Annual Housing Policy Meeting, Chicago. May 21. http://www. federalreserve.gov/boarddocs/speeches/ 2004120040521/default.htm (accessed June 22, 2008).

Gramlich, E. 2007. *Subprime Lending: America's Latest Boom and Bust.* Washington, D.C.: Urban Institute Press. http://www.federalreserve.gov/newsevents/ press/bcreg/bcreg20060929al.pdf (accessed June 20, 2008).

Hinz, G. 2001. "Lobbying Bid Falls Short for Bank One. *Crain's Chicago Business*, November 19.

Leach, J. 2000. "Statement of Chairman of the Banking and Financial Services Committee, Hearings on Predatory Lending Practices, U.S. House of Representatives, Committee on Banking and Financial Services." May 24.

Levitin, A., and J. Goodman. 2008. "The Effect of Bankruptcy Strip-Down on Mortgage Markets." Georgetown University Law Center. Research Paper No. 1087816. February 6.

Levitt, A. 2008. "Regulatory Underkill." *Wall Street Journal*, March 21, Al3.

Mallach, A. 2008. "Tackling the Mortgage Crisis: 10 Action Steps for State Government." Washington, D.C.: Metropolitan Policy Program at the Brookings Institute. May. http://www.brookings.edu/papers/2008/ 0529_mortgage_crisis_vey.aspx.

Matasar, A., and D. Pavelka. 1998. "Federal Bank Regulators' Competition in Laxity: Evidence from CRA Audits." *International Advances in Economic Research* 4: 56- 69.

Milligan, J. 2004. "Learning the Hard Way: The History of the Antipredatory Lending Law in Georgia Is a Case Study in How Well-Intentioned Lawmakers Carne Close to Closing Down the Mortgage Market." *Mortgage Banking*, September.

Mortgage Bankers Association. 2003. "Standard & Poor's to Disallow Georgia Fair Lending Act Loans." http://www.mortgage bankers.org/NewsandMedia/PressCenter /32153.htm (accessed June 14, 2008).

Mortgage Bankers Association. 2008. "Stop the Cram-Down Resource Center Puts a Price Tag on Bankruptcy Reform." January 15. http://www.mortgagebankers.org/ NewsandMedia/PressCenter/59343.htm.

National Conference of State Legislatures. 2003. "Banking and Financial Services: Predatory Mortgage Lending."

New York Times. 2003. "Spitzer Threatens to Sue U.S. Regulator over Loan Exemption." *New York Times*, December 13.

Reiss, D. 2006. "Subprime Standardization: How Rating Agencies Allow Predatory Lending to Flourish in the Secondary Mortgage Market." *Florida State Law Review* 33: 985–1065.

Rosen, R. 2002. "Is Three a Crowd? Competition among Regulators in Banking." Paper presented at the 2002 Federal Reserve Bank of Chicago Bank Structure Conference, May 8.

Rosengren, E. 2008. "Current Challenges in Housing and Home Loans: Complicating Factors and the Implications for Policymakers." Speech at the New England Economic Partnership's Spring Economic Outlook Conference on Credit, Housing, and the Consequences for New England. May 30. www.bos.frb.org/news/speeches/ rosengren/2008/053 008.htm.

Scott, K. 1977. "The Dual Banking System: Model of Competition in Regulation." *Stanford Law Review* 30:1-49.

U.S. General Accounting Office. 2004. *Consumer Protection: Federal and State Agencies Face Challenges in Combating Predatory Lending.* GA0-04-280. January. http://www.ncsl.org/programs/banking/ bankmenu.htm (accessed June 24, 2003).

U.S. Office of the Comptroller of the Currency. 1999. "Letter to Chief Executive Officers of National Banks, Department and Division Heads, and All Examining Personnel, OCC 99-10." Cover letter for Interagency Guidance on Subprime Lending. March 3. http://www.ffiec.gov/ ffiecinfobase/resources/retail/occ-bl-99-lO_interag_guid_subprime_lending.pdf (accessed June 20, 2008).

U.S. Office of the Comptroller of the Currency. 2003a. "Avoiding Predatory and Abusive Lending Practices in Brokered and Purchased Loans." Advisory Letter 2003-3. February 21. http://www.occ.treas.gov/ftp/advisory/2003-3.pdf.

U.S. Office of the Comptroller of the Currency. 2003b. *Economic Issues in Predatory Lending.* July 30.

U.S. Office of the Comptroller of the Currency. 2008. *OCC Mortgage Metrics Report: Analysis and Disclosure of National Bank Mortgage Loan Data, October-2007-March 2008.* June. http://www.occ.treas.gov/ftp/release/2008-65b.pdf.

U.S. Office of the Comptroller of the Currency, Board of Governors of the Federal Reserve System, Federal Deposit Insurance Corporation, Office of Thrift Supervision, and National Credit Union Administration. 2006. *Interagency Guidance on Nont1·aditional Mortgage Product Risks.* September 29.

U.S. Senate Joint Economic Committee. 2007b. "Sheltering Neighborhoods from the Subprime Foreclosure Storm." April 11. http://jec.senate.gov/index.cfm?Fuse Action=Reports.Reports&ContentRecord _id=c780213f-7e9c-9af9-761d-fd7e597 b5cfe&Region_id=&Issue_id= (accessed June 23, 2008).

U.S. Supreme Court. 2007. *Watters, Commissioner, Michigan Office of Insurance and Financial Services V. Wachovia Bank, N. A., et al.* No. 05-1342. Argued November 29, 2006 – decided April 17, 2007. http://www.supremecourtus.gov/Opinions/06pdf/05-1342.Pdf (accessed March 22, 2008).

PART FOUR

Shifting emphases in the provision of affordable housing

Plate 4 Harbor Hills Housing Project, 26607 Western Avenue, Lomita, Los Angeles, CA (source: Historic American Buildings Survey).

As the effects of the Great Depression were alleviated first through New Deal policies, and then by the onset of World War II, the imperative for governmental provision of housing for the poor waned. FHA and other federal policies were not geared toward housing production, and the private market failed to produce enough housing to meet demand. In 1949, Congress passed a housing act that called for "a decent home and a suitable living environment for every American family." The real estate lobby continued to oppose any government production programs, believing that "housing projects competed with private businesses but did not pay taxes, were the opening wedge in an eventual takeover of the private housing industry by the government, and undermined the initiative and independence of American citizens." (von Hoffman 2000, 304). As a result, the policy strategies that followed failed to live up to the strong rhetoric of the Housing Act of 1949.

Reacting to the combined failures of public housing and the FHA to build adequate affordable housing, and the lack of bold action in response to the 1949 law, from 1960 to 1972, Congress sought to expand housing programs at all levels. These included rental production programs, rehabilitation programs, and subsidized financing mechanisms. For the first time since the advent of public housing, the federal government became a significant producer of housing for America's poor. However, even new, high-volume production programs failed to build new units fast enough to meet the growing demand (Hartman 1998, 230–231). Furthermore, the new programs were not without their critics. While not as blatantly ideological as in the past, policy opposition was still rooted in arguments regarding the proper role of the federal government, along with critiques of previous programs. Faced with mounting challenges to the growing array of housing programs, and still lacking an overarching housing policy strategy, Richard Nixon instituted a moratorium on the federal production of subsidized housing.

Following the 1972 moratorium, federal housing policy has focused on three broad types of programs: block grants, vouchers, and tax credits. These programs employ vastly different mechanisms to make housing more affordable to low-income households. Each of these programs enables limited and indirect government involvement in the provision and financing of housing for the poor. Block grants provide funding to municipalities for a variety of community development and housing programs; vouchers provide rental assistance to low-income households living in private-sector units; and tax credits provide incentives to private developers to produce housing for low-income Americans.

Until the establishment of the Low Income Housing Tax Credit (LIHTC) by the Reagan administration, the block grant and voucher programs were the primary vehicles for U.S. federal housing policy. The LIHTC represented a significant shift in approach. Under IRS rules, federal Low Income Housing Tax Credits are awarded to affordable housing developers competitively and can then be sold to investors in order to raise funds for development. The LIHTC is run through the IRS, so it does not appear as a budget outlay. Furthermore, the LIHTC enables the production of low-income housing by the private sector, keeping the role of government to a minimum.

The Public Housing program was under particular fire after the highly publicized demolition of the award-winning Pruitt-Igoe projects in 1972. While public housing units built prior to the moratorium remained, production of new public housing essentially ceased at that point. Ending the public housing program did not end the significant needs of existing housing units for upkeep, maintenance, and revitalization. The HOPE VI program was established in 1993 as an attempt to respond to the challenges facing existing public housing. It has done so mainly by allowing the demolition of distressed high-rise buildings and introducing a mixed-income population into newly rehabilitated housing developments. Over time, these newly reconstituted public housing communities are intended to reduce the concentration of poverty in these areas and provide increased opportunities for poor households both within and without public housing.

As the current home foreclosure crisis continues to unfold, affordable housing will become even more important to households across America. Yet the existing stock of affordable units is aging and in need of renewed investment. According to the National Low Income Housing Coalition, "for every new affordable apartment created, two are lost due to deterioration, abandonment or conversion to more expensive housing" (Crowley et al. 2011). Achtenberg (2006) details the history of preservation efforts and describes how they have served to prevent hundreds of thousands of affordable units from being lost. Nonetheless, expiring use contracts, Section 8 opt-outs, and subsidized loan prepayments have caused many units to be lost from the nation's stock of affordable housing. Furthermore, renovation and revitalization of existing subsidized housing can spark private investment, increase tenure security for low income families, and stem gentrification – ensuring that long time and low-income residents can remain in communities that are on the rise, rather than displaced to communities that are in decline. Preserving existing affordable housing can also be cheaper and greener than new construction.

For decades, the federal government was the primary provider of very low-income rental housing via public housing (Wallace 1995). As a result of devolution, consolidation, and retrenchment, nonprofit and private developers are now the principle providers of federally subsidized housing. These fundamental changes have implications for which groups are likely to be served. For-profit producers have greater capacity but are less likely to layer subsidies to reach the poor, while nonprofit housing agencies are mission-driven but have limited financial and organizational capacity (Bratt 2009; Hebert and Wallace 1998; Keyes et al. 1996; Koschinsky 1998). Together these factors limit the production of affordable housing for low and very-low income households, and shape its siting in a way that undermines fair housing goals.

Nonprofit housing agencies target households and neighborhoods with the greatest need for affordable housing, yet they are at a disadvantage when competing for funding and are extremely vulnerable to delays or loss of financing mechanisms that might sink a project. Nonprofit housing agencies currently provide nearly 1.5 million households with affordable housing – nearly 25 percent more than the current stock of public housing (Bratt 2009). Nonprofit developers are also much more likely than for-profit entities to provide housing to low and very-low income households (those earning less than 50 percent of Area Median Income (AMI) and 30 percent of AMI, respectively), and they tend to develop larger units that can be made available to families (Bratt 2008). They are also more apt to redevelop distressed areas (Hebert and Wallace 1998; Keyes et al. 1996; Koebel 1998). The combination of loss of funding and the shift in provision to more profit-driven entities will likely result in less emphasis placed on the needs of the poorest households (Mueller and Schwartz 2008).

The marginalization of nonprofit, especially community-based, producers has other consequences for communities. Community Development Corporations often serve other community needs aside from housing, including job training, education, and health service provision. This diversification can be problematic for organizations already stretched in terms of finances and personnel, but such services provide a necessary connection with the community, ensuring continued support for all of the activities of the organization. CDCs are caught between needing to maintain their ties to the communities they serve, and to provide critical missing services and the need to maintain their reputation as good producers with city administrators (Silverman 2008; Bratt and Rohe 2007).

Decades of federal programs with mixed results, and a return to a pre-Depression outlook on the role of government have resulted in a retrenchment in housing policy. The nature of poverty and government's role in remedying it continue to be at the heart of the debate over housing. As government shifts away from the provision of housing for the poor, however, this debate is likely to shift away from a debate over who to serve to one over *where* they should live.

IN THIS PART:

Chapter 17: Orlebeke, Charles J. (2000). "The evolution of low-income housing policy, 1949 to 1999." *Housing Policy Debate*, 11(2): 489–520.
Chapter 18: O'Regan, Katherine M., and John M. Quigley. (2000). "Federal policy and the rise of nonprofit housing providers." *Journal of Housing Research*, 11(2): 297–317.
Chapter 19: McClure, Kirk. (2000). "The Low-Income Housing Tax Credit as an aid to finance: How well has it worked?" *Housing Policy Debate*, 11(1): 91–114.
Chapter 20: Turner, Margery Austin. (2003). Strengths and weaknesses of the Housing Voucher Program. *Congressional Testimony prepared for the Committee on Financial Services, Subcommittee on Housing and Community Opportunity, United States House of Representatives, June 17, 2003*. Washington, D.C.: The Urban Institute.
Chapter 21: Achtenberg, Emily Paradise (2006). "Federally-assisted housing: Privatization vs. preservation," Chapter 7 in *A Right to Housing: Foundation of a New Social Agenda*, Rachel G. Bratt, Michael E. Stone and Charles Hartman, eds., Philadelphia, PA: Temple University Press.

REFERENCES AND FURTHER READING

Achtenberg, Emily P. (2006). "Federally-assisted housing: Privatization vs. preservation," Chapter 7 in *A Right to Housing: Foundation of a New Social Agenda*, Rachel E. Bratt, Michael E. Stone and C. Hartman, eds., Philadelphia, PA: Temple University Press.
Basolo, Victoria and Mai Nguyen. (2005). "Does mobility matter? Neighborhood conditions of housing voucher holders by race and ethnicity." *Housing Policy Debate*, 16(3/4): 2973–24.
Bockmeyer, Janice. (2003). "Devolution and the transformation of community housing activism." *The Social Science Journal*, 40(2): 175–88.
Bratt, Rachel G. 2008. "Nonprofit and for-profit developers of subsidized rental housing: Comparative attributes and collaborative opportunities." *Housing Policy Debate*, 19(2): 323–65.
Bratt, Rachel G. (2009). "Challenges for nonprofit housing organizations created by the private housing market." *Journal of Urban Affairs*, 31(1):67–96.
Bratt, Rachel G., and W. M. Rohe. (2007). "Challenges and dilemmas facing community development corporations in the United States." *Community Development Journal*, 42(1): 637–8.
Crowley, Sheila, Elina Bravve, Megan DeCrappeo, and Danilo Pelletiere. (2011). *Out of Reach 2011: Renters Await Recovery*. Washington, D.C.: National Low Income Housing Coalition.
Cummings, Jean, and Denise DiPasquale. (1999). "The low-income housing tax credit: An analysis of the first ten years." *Housing Policy Debate*, 10(2): 251–307.
Hartman, Chester. (1998). "The case for a right to housing." *Housing Policy Debate*, 9(2): 223–246.
Hebert, Scott, and James Wallace. (1998). "Nonprofit housing: A study of costs and funding." In *Shelter and Society: Theory, Research, and Policy for Nonprofit Housing*, edited by C. T. Koebel. Albany, NY: State University of New York Press.

Keyes, Langley C., Alex Schwartz, Avis Vidal, and Rachel Bratt. (1996). "Networks and nonprofits: Opportunities and challenges in an era of federal devolution." *Housing Policy Debate*, 7(2): 2012–31.

Koebel, C. Theodore, ed. (1998). *Shelter and Society: Theory, Research, and Policy for Nonprofit Housing.* Edited by J. Bohland and P. Edwards, *SUNY Series in Urban Public Policy.* Albany, NY: State University of New York Press.

Koschinsky, Julia. (1998). "Challenging the third sector housing approach: The impact of federal policies (1980–1996)." *Journal of Urban Affairs*, 20(2): 1171–35.

Listoken, David. (1991). "Federal housing policy and preservation: Historical evolution, patterns, and implications." *Housing Policy Debate*, 2(2): 157–85.

Melendez, Edwin, Alex Schwartz, and Alexandra de Montrichard. (2008). "Year 15 and preservation of tax-credit housing for low-income households: An assessment of risk." *Housing Studies*, 23(1): 67–87.

Mueller, Elizabeth J., and Alex Schwartz. (2008). "Reversing the tide: Will state and local governments house the poor as federal direct subsidies decline?" *Journal of the American Planning Association*, 74(1):1221–35.

Silverman, R. M. (2008). "The influence of nonprofit networks on local affordable housing funding: Findings from a national survey of local public administrators." *Urban Affairs Review*, 44(1): 1261–41.

Turville, Jane (Director). (2011). *The Greenest Building.* USA. Wagging Tails Productions.

von Hoffman, A. (2000). "A study in contradictions: The origins and legacy of the Housing Act of 1949." *Housing Policy Debate*, 11(2): 299–326.

Wallace, J. (1995). "Financing affordable housing in the United States." *Housing Policy Debate*, 6(4): 785–814.

17

"The evolution of low-income housing policy, 1949 to 1999"

From *Housing Policy Debate* (2000)

Charles J. Orlebeke

University of Illinois at Chicago

INTRODUCTION

Shelter is one of the three basic human needs, and a responsible society has an obligation to prevent people from dying out in the cold. In 1949, however, the United States set a goal that would take this minimum obligation several steps further – to "a decent home and a suitable living environment for every American family." This declaration moved the nation beyond the obligation to provide mere shelter and into the realm of "housing," a market commodity produced by a complex and politically influential industry. It also embraced "every American family," not just the obviously needy found huddled under viaducts. This challenge meant confronting the issues of defining who besides the immediately desperate might receive housing assistance, what form such assistance might take and for what types of "decent" housing, and who should be administratively responsible for running the system. Since Congress's famous formulation in 1949, efforts to achieve the goal have turned on such questions.

The 50 years since passage of the Housing Act of 1949 can be divided roughly into two segments: The first ran from 1949 to the 1973 Nixon moratorium on housing production subsidies, which marked the end of the federal government's aspirations to dominate the assault on the national housing goal through federally enacted and administered production programs. The second segment, from 1973 to the present, has seen the evolution of a mixed system of low-income housing policy with a much diminished federal role in program design and outcomes, an ascendant role for state and local governments, and the opportunity for the recipients of housing vouchers to scout the private market for the best deal they can find.

This article traces the rise and demise of the federal leadership model in housing policy up to 1973 and focuses on the development of three important and reasonably effective policy instruments that have come to mark the devolution of housing policy and programs: housing vouchers, housing block grants, and the Low-Income Housing Tax Credit (LIHTC). Given that only rental housing assistance can claim to serve households with the lowest incomes, the emphasis is on rental housing. The article does not explore the many fascinating and complex issues related to the national policy of advancing homeownership across the broadest possible spectrum of incomes.

THE HOUSING GOAL: OVERVIEW OF THE FIRST 50 YEARS

For low-income housing advocates, the Housing Act of 1949 promised that the federal government, given the means and the authority, could solve the nation's housing problems through the exercise of committed political leadership at the top and the implementation muscle of a technically skilled, socially conscious bureaucracy working its will with an eager housing industry and compliant local governments. The years that followed were initially inauspicious: Public housing, the only low-income program available, fell far short of authorized production targets; new programs were started but failed to gain momentum; and executive responsibility for housing was fragmented. The turnaround began in 1965 with the creation of the U.S. Department of Housing and Urban Development (HUD). Then, in 1968, the notion of federal leadership and efficacy in housing triumphed: Reaffirmation of the 1949 goal with quantified production targets and timetable, new housing subsidy programs generously funded, planning requirements aimed at dispersing low-income housing throughout metropolitan regions, and even a new fair housing act outlawing racial discrimination – all the tools were there.

The enchanting possibilities of the Housing Act of 1968 soon began unraveling. For the first few years of the Nixon administration, production targets for subsidized housing were met, but attacks on the production-dominated strategy were mounting from both inside and outside the federal government. In January 1973, President Richard M. Nixon abruptly imposed a moratorium on all new subsidy commitments, and forever after, the soon-to-be-disgraced president would be remembered chiefly for that action rather than for the 1.6 million units of subsidized housing started during his administration. The moratorium forced a reexamination of federally administered production programs and a search for better alternatives.

Since the 1973 moratorium, three policy instruments have arisen from the debris of tried and canceled programs, experimentation, partisan contention, ideological conflict, and – surely not least – scholarly research, analysis, and debate. The first is the emergence of housing voucher-type programs – known variously as housing allowances, rent certificates, housing payments, and currently as housing choice vouchers – as the preferred subsidy vehicle instead of large-scale subsidized housing production programs. The "triumph" (Winnick 1995) of vouchers was ratified as early as 1988, when a panel of housing experts convened by the Urban Institute concluded that the "heated voucher/production debate" had "largely subsided" (Turner and Reed 1990, 7):

Demand-side subsidies make the most sense when affordability is the greatest housing problem to be resolved. And the evidence is convincing that this is indeed the case – in most housing markets and for most types of units.

(Turner and Reed 1990, 7)

The housing voucher has evolved, although much tinkered with, from the modest progenitor created in 1965, called the Section 23 Leased Housing program. Today, it has been widely embraced as the most useful, cost-effective form of subsidy.

The second instrument is the formal transfer of most housing program control from the federal government to state and local governments. In this case, the milestone is the Housing Act of 1990, which created the HOME housing block grant to states and cities as the sibling to the popular, well-established Community Development Block Grant (CDBG) enacted in 1974. Under HOME, federal money would continue to flow to housing production and rehabilitation for both renters and lower-income owners, but local officials, not federal officials or Congress, would determine the mix of applications. This transfer of power is also indicated in the HOPE VI program, created in 1993, which provides lump-sum grants of $50 million to cities for dealing with their distressed public housing inventory. Demolition, new construction, and social services are all permitted uses. As I will argue later, the pre-block grant program models of the 1960s and 1970s involved a presumption of federal control that was at least partly illusory, while at the same time the federal government bore the entire political weight of their evident short-comings. Thus, politically and administratively, the logic of transferring power eventually prevailed.

The third instrument to gain wide acceptance is a relatively new variation on an old theme – namely, the use of the tax system to induce desired housing outcomes. Here I am referring to the LIHTC for the production of low-income rental housing. Enacted in 1986 and only haltingly employed for several years, the LIHTC has survived its many critics and at this writing seems about to be expanded. Part of the reason for its success is that it dovetails with the move toward greater program control by states and cities, which determine the allocation of the credits to specific projects. HUD is largely shut out of LIHTC action; responsibility for monitoring and enforcement is shared by state housing agencies and the U.S. Internal Revenue Service (IRS). Politically, the LIHTC is also helped by being a tax expenditure rather than a spending item; as such, its cost tends to be hidden below the horizon of general public awareness.

These three – vouchers, block grants, and tax credits – form the core of postmoratorium low-income housing strategy. How this came to be will be taken up after a historical sketch of the first quarter century following the original declaration of the housing goal in 1949.

THE 1949 GOAL: NEITHER TIMETABLE NOR MEANS

In 1973, HUD's National Housing Policy Review referred to the 1949 housing goal with some understatement as "a commitment without a timetable and without adequate means of accomplishment" (HUD 1973b, 1–13). Congress, in stating the goal, made no specific reference to helping poor people in their quest for a decent home. In fact, the language leading up to the goal itself cites the need for "housing production," presumably at market prices, "to remedy the serious housing shortage," and for aggressive "clearance of slums and blighted areas" (HUD 1973b, 1–13). If anything, the production of housing that the poor could not afford and the destruction of places where many of them lived worked against such an objective.

In the 1949 act, the only housing subsidy vehicle specifically aimed at low-income families was public housing, first enacted in 1937 as a way to house the temporarily unemployed and, not incidentally, to create jobs for the building trades. Although public housing was built and managed by local housing authorities, the federal government paid the entire capital cost through "annual contribution contracts" to retire bonds issued by the authorities. Rent collections were expected to cover all operating costs without federal help. Despite the sense of urgency inspired by the Depression, public housing had been strongly opposed by private real estate interests that failed to prevent its passage but then succeeded in holding down its implementation to a handful of units in its early years.

After World War II, public housing reemerged, this time as a potential instrument for helping low-income families cope with the postwar housing shortage and for replacing housing in cleared slums. President Harry S. Truman was a vigorous advocate of program expansion, as was "Mr. Conservative," Republican Senator Robert Taft of Ohio. They and their allies finally prevailed in 1949, when Congress authorized the construction of 810,000 units of public housing over the next six years.

It was not much of a victory. "Authorization" means little unless it is followed by appropriations – actual commitment of money – and local implementation. The opponents of public housing were influential in both arenas. In the 1950s, congressional appropriating committees typically provided money for about 25,000 units, while at the local level, battles over public housing sites could be settled only by placing public housing in the least desirable parts of town where poor families were already concentrated. Thus, 10 years after the 6-year, 810,000 unit total had been set, less than a quarter of the units were in place. (The program would gain some momentum and struggle to its 1949 authorization level in another 10 years.)

The 1960s: Alternatives to public housing

Compared with the 1950s, the years leading up to the Housing Act of 1968 were a time of activism and innovation – but low production. Morton Schussheim in his monograph on "the legacy of the sixties" called the housing acts of 1961, 1964, 1965, and 1966 major pieces of legislation, but noted pointedly: "Production of housing for lower-income families, a major aim of the [Kennedy and Johnson] Administrations, never reached a significant level" (Schussheim 1969, 1). The programs of the 1960s did, however, test the political and administrative waters for subsidy alternatives that could augment the always troubled public housing program and engage the interest and energy of the private sector. Characteristically, President John F. Kennedy, like his predecessors, looked to the economic stimulus value of housing production.

The 1961 Housing Act launched the Section 221(d)(3) program, a rental program for moderate-income families considered needy but too well-off to qualify for public housing. This group occupied what was known as the "20 percent gap," referring to the legally mandated gap between the rents public housing authorities could charge and the rents for private standard housing. Apartments could be built by nonprofit sponsors or private developers willing to take a limited profit. The subsidy mechanism was a so-called BMIR (below-market interest rate) loan at 3 percent, which allowed the sponsor to pass along lower development costs in the form of lower rents – 15 to 20 percent below comparable unsubsidized housing. To complete the subsidy two-step, Fannie Mae, a government corporation until it was spun off by the Housing Act of 1968, bought the entire project mortgage from the sponsor's lender at market rate, absorbing the difference between that rate and 3 percent. Production of "(d)(3)s" was constrained by a lack of qualified sponsors ready to come forward, as well as by government-imposed cost constraints and limited availability of sites. It was also unpopular with Treasury and budget officials because the government's purchases of large project mortgages were a direct hit on the federal budget.

In 1965, to address the shortcomings of Section 221(d)(3), President Lyndon B. Johnson presented the Rent Supplement program as the wave of the future. "If it works as well as we expect," he said, "it should be possible to phase out most of our existing programs of low-interest loans" (Schussheim 1969, 15). Instead of using BMIR financing as a subsidy method, rent supplement projects would receive direct rent-reduction payments to make up the difference between 25 percent of tenant income and a fair market rent; therefore, the immediate budget impact would be relatively small and spread over many years. As introduced, rent supplements were aimed at an income group similar to that targeted by Section 221(d)(3). As the proposal emerged from a notably unreceptive Congress, the subsidy method was adopted but broadened to include low-income families eligible for public housing. Congress also choked off any possibility of volume production by refusing to appropriate any money for the program in 1965 and approving only half of Johnson's 1966 request with a rider requiring local government approval of each rent supplement site (Hays 1995). Five years after enactment, only 31,000 units would be in place (Listokin 1991).

On the public housing front, some housing authorities in urban areas that were losing population saw an opportunity in the supply of vacant units in the private housing stock. But public housing was structured solely as a development program with no authority to lease existing, privately owned apartments. The Section 23 Leased Housing program changed that. For the first time, the federal government authorized deep subsidies for renters occupying standard housing in the existing stock, leased on the open market by a public agency. It was a low-profile initiative with a big future.

THE 1968 REAFFIRMATION: BOTH TIMETABLE AND MEANS

In 1968, Congress reaffirmed the 1949 housing goal, again putting it in the context of a housing shortage: "The supply of the Nation's housing is not increasing rapidly enough to meet the national housing goal." But this time there is no reference to clearing "slums and blight," the besmirched code words for the urban renewal program, also launched in 1949, that by 1968 had become known for destroying housing, especially in low-income neighborhoods, and replacing little of it. The most notable feature of the 1968 reaffirmation, however, was the determination by Congress that "this national housing goal ... can be substantially achieved within the next decade by the construction or rehabilitation of twenty-six million housing units, six million of these for low- and moderate-income families." To show that it meant business, Congress instructed the president to prepare a year-by-year schedule for meeting the goal and to report annually on progress. Both the unsubsidized and subsidized components of the goal were stunningly ambitious: The housing industry had only once produced 2 million units in a single year and that was in 1950; in the two years leading up to the declaration, 1966 and 1967 *combined*, there were only about 2.5 million starts.

The 6 million target – an average of 600,000 annually – was even more of a stretch. In the 1950s, subsidized starts under the public housing program hit a peak of 71,000 in 1951, drifted down to about 20,000 in the mid-1950s, and closed the decade at about 34,000 units, a mere 2.2 percent of total housing starts. Even with the addition of two subsidized direct loan programs – the Section 202 program for elderly housing in 1959 and the Section 221(d)(3) program for moderate-income renters in 1961 – total annual production of subsidized housing amounted to only about 72,000 in 1966 and 91,000 in 1967. For the two years combined, subsidized starts made up 6.5 percent of total starts, the first time since the 1949 act that assisted starts had broken 5 percent (Downs 1972). Reacting to such a piddling performance, the 1968 act intended to move beyond rhetoric to a serious run at a quantified goal and a disciplined timetable.

The chief means of accomplishing the subsidized housing goal were two new programs also enacted in 1968: Section 235, which provided eligible home purchasers with mortgages insured by the Federal Housing Administration (FHA) and subsidized to a rate as low as 1 percent, and Section 236, which gave apartment developers FHA-insured 1 percent mortgage financing, thus enabling them to offer below-market rents to low- and moderate-income tenants. The mortgage interest subsidy mechanism had the advantage of causing little budget impact in the initial years of production.

THE NIXON ADMINISTRATION EMBRACES THE 1968 GOALS

At the time the 1968 act was passed, the methodological crudeness of the goal calculation and the implausibility of being able to wipe out all housing problems in 10 years were not seriously raised as issues. Nor did it matter that the Johnson administration, which had championed the goal, was on the way out after the 1968 election, to be replaced by a presumably more conservative Nixon administration. On the contrary, Nixon installed as HUD secretary the production-minded Governor George Romney of Michigan, the former head of American Motors and briefly Nixon's challenger for the Republican presidential nomination. Early in Nixon's first term, Romney told the Subcommittee on Housing of the House of Representatives: "I accept these goals, not as an engineer's measure, but as a reasonable expression of our national need by a knowledgeable and humane Congress which sought to give some definite expression to the ends we seek in housing" (HUD 1969, 20). Reflecting on the 1949 goal, Romney said: "The challenge to us all is that

today, twenty years later, we are so dismally far from having achieved that goal. The problem is how we can best see its realization, not in the remote future, but in the years that lie immediately ahead" (HUD 1969, 20).

In contrast to the authorization/appropriation shell game that followed the 1949 act, Congress provided full funding to the Section 235 and 236 programs, as a galvanized FHA bureaucracy set out to prove that it was capable of managing an unprecedented production mandate. It succeeded. Subsidized production spiked to 197,000 starts in 1969, to 431,000 in 1970, and promised to head even higher in 1971. Henry Schecter, a strong proponent of the 1968 goal from his influential position as senior HUD economist in the 1960s, and coauthor Marion Schlefer noted with satisfaction that the amazing run-up in production "must raise serious doubts about the validity of oft-repeated claims that the complexities and red-tape involved in the present subsidized housing programs are serious impediments to volume production" (Schechter and Schlefer 1971, 5). There was, however, little sense of celebration in the Nixon administration or in Congress.

SECOND-GUESSING THE PRODUCTION STRATEGY: THE 1971 REPORT ON THE NATIONAL HOUSING GOAL

Although the *President's Third Annual Report on National Housing Goals* took bows for exceeding the production timetable laid out in the first goals report, it bristled with cautions and second-guessing. "Production," the report stated, "is not the sole measure of progress, and may not even be the most important" (*President's Third Annual Report* 1971, 21). The production surge, according to the report, had raised a number of troubling issues that needed to be addressed "so that necessary reforms in basic policy can be identified, developed, and implemented as quickly as possible" (*President's Third Annual Report* 1971, 21). But why reform a "basic policy" that seemed to be working? After all, the 1968 goal had called for record production, and record production, surprising skeptics, was clearly happening.

For one thing, by the early 1970s, one of the critical underpinnings of the quantified goal was looking increasingly shaky: the notion of a desperate physical shortage of shelter that could be addressed only by a huge production effort. Housing, including much in reasonably sound condition, was being abandoned in the cities as entire neighborhoods seemed to be emptying out. The middle-class exodus to the suburbs was clearly connected in some way to abandonment, and the report suggested that new subsidized housing might be contributing to this abandonment, which, "if unchecked, could turn our production efforts into a treadmill" (*President's Third Annual Report* 1971, 25). Although a complete explanation of abandonment was elusive – prompting the inevitable round of studies – one thing at least was apparent to the naked eye: A physical shortage of shelter was not the problem.

Cost

The 1971 report grouped its reservations under the headings of "cost," "equity," and "environment." The discussion of cost pointed to rising housing costs and the unprecedented share of subsidized starts – about one of four – in relation to total starts in 1970. This suggested that the federal government was, among other things, feeding "runaway inflation of housing costs" (*President's Third Annual Report* 1971, 22). Translated into federal budget impact, the outlook was ominous: It had been easy to *start* the new subsidy programs because budget outlays in the early years covered only the interest subsidies on the first wave of units; however, as hundreds of thousands of units were piled onto the subsidized stock annually, a huge, scary budget "uncontrollable" loomed. The report cited estimates that subsidized production under way or planned for fiscal year 1970–72 had already obligated the government to "perhaps $30 billion" and that achievement of the 10-year goal might cost "the staggering total of more than $200 billion" over the life of the mortgage contracts (*President's Third Annual Report* 1971, 22). Although the report offered some hope that the problem might eventually yield to HUD's "efforts to advance industrialized methods of housing production, and open up opportunities for large-scale marketing of industrialized housing," it also warned that "the Federal Government could not stand impassively at the cash register and continue to pay out

whatever is necessary to feed runaway inflation of housing costs" (*President's Third Annual Report* 1971, 22).

Equity

The "equity" discussion in the report had familiar echoes of innumerable housing policy debates before and since. First, there was the issue of program coverage – the fact that even the ambitious goals envisioned in the Housing Act of 1968 would still cover only a relatively small fraction of the eligible population, estimated at about 25 million households. The dilemma was that "it will be difficult to continue favoring a select few in the population," but "it is doubtful that the public, and hence the Congress, will be prepared to accept the staggering budgetary cost of a more global coverage" (*President's Third Annual Report* 1971, 23–24). Second, the equity issue was sharpened by the production emphasis on "brand new homes"; this meant not only that the "fortunate few" were getting a housing bargain at taxpayers' expense, but also that their neighbors in similar economic circumstances were "left struggling to meet their monthly payments in older homes purchased without subsidy." Third, "too often the present housing subsidy programs simply cannot help the very poor" (*President's Third Annual Report* 1971, 24). Given statutory limits on the amount of subsidy per unit and the relatively high cost of new construction, "few of the families actually receiving subsidy are at the very low end of the eligible income range" (*President's Third Annual Report* 1971, 24). Programs that had ostensibly been devised to plug the affordability gap for needy families were in fact leaving the most desperate among them to fend for themselves.

Environment

According to the report, issues relating to housing policy and the environment had both physical and social dimensions. Looking back, the report said that the "complex interaction" of federal housing policies and local decision making had "sometimes wrought unfortunate environmental consequences," such as "poorly planned crackerbox developments" in the suburbs after World War II and, in urban areas, "drab, monolithic housing projects, largely segregated, which still stand in our major cities as prisons of the poor – enduring symbols of good intentions run aground on poorly conceived policy, or sometimes simply a lack of policy" (*President's Third Annual Report* 1971, 25). These past failures called for "more explicit attention to the environmental impact of housing programs" and a more active role on the part of state and local governments "in relating community growth, development, and services to the housing needs of citizens of all income levels" (*President's Third Annual Report* 1971, 26).

The report offered its analysis as a "broad framework for evaluating housing programs and policies in the coming year" (*President's Third Annual Report* 1971, 26); it did not spell out specific proposals for change. Yet certain policy themes were clearly signaled – the unsustainability of future housing claims on the federal budget, the top-heavy emphasis on new construction at the expense of "second fiddle" housing preservation programs, the neglect of the poor in housing programs, and the enlistment of state and local governments in comprehensive housing and community development programming. Even as the housing production numbers in the early 1970s indicated a triumphant march toward the 1978 goal, the emerging policy debate foreshadowed a much rockier prospect.

Attacks on the production programs from all sides

Partly in response to the report, the *National Journal* ran a story in June 1971 pointing to "a full-scale and bi-partisan revolt against the nation's 37-year-old builder-oriented policy" (Lilley 1971, 1535). The article quotes numerous members of Congress, mayors, and HUD officials, all of whom found things not to like about the subsidy programs in place: high cost, shoddy construction, poor administration, inapplicability to big-city housing problems, failure to help low-income families, and lack of planning on a metropolitan scale. But pitted against the possibilities for change, according to the story, was "by far the most potent of the housing lobbies" (Lilley 1971, 1535), the National Association of Home Builders (NAHB), joined by the Mortgage Bankers

Association and the National Association of Real Estate Boards. Not that it was all that clear what shape "reform" might take. Some critics wanted more emphasis on housing rehabilitation, some were attracted to housing allowances (then at a very early experimental stage), and some called for a radical restructuring of the subsidy delivery system through block grants to metropolitan housing agencies. In the absence of political consensus of any sort, the production juggernaut rolled on.

In late 1971, an internal HUD report to the White House called "1972 Outlook" reflected a characteristic ambivalence, calling subsidized housing production "unquestionably one of the Administration's great success stories," but also warned that

> it carries the seeds of vulnerability.... Instances of negligent administration, inferior projects, excessive profits, and overbuilding a particular market can be expected to crop up in spite of our best efforts to prevent them, particularly since our manpower is dangerously thin in such key functions as inspections and appraising
> (HUD 1971b, 1)

The seeds of vulnerability had in fact already been amply sown far and wide and would continue to yield an unwelcome bumper crop of criticism in 1972.

THE PROXMIRE ATTACK

On the eve of the 1972 elections, the Joint Economic Committee of Congress released six papers it had commissioned from housing policy experts such as Henry Aaron of the Brookings Institution and Henry Schecter of the Congressional Research Service (U.S. Congress 1972a). Committee chairman Senator William Proxmire, who also served as a member of the Housing Subcommittee of the Senate Banking Committee and chaired the Senate Appropriations Subcommittee on Housing, launched a broadside attack in a press release accompanying the papers:

> Taken together, these studies form a damning indictment of our present housing programs and their administration. One thing is abundantly clear – reform of housing

programs is long overdue. ... I intend to pursue the issue of housing programs and housing reform until we get some order out of the present chaos.... The last Congress found the housing subsidy area such a complicated mess that it could not decide what to do.

(U.S. Congress 1972b, 1)

Indeed. Like many others, Senator Proxmire found it much easier to flail the housing programs than to propose and adopt better alternatives. He noted in his statement, for example, that Aaron advocated a housing allowance entitlement program "arguing that it would be free of many of the inequities and rigidities of existing subsidies"; Schecter, however, "warns against the notion that housing allowances are a panacea for existing housing problems" because of the threat of "strong inflationary pressures in housing markets with limited housing supply" (U.S. Congress 1972b, 6). Proxmire did have a good word for the Section 23 Leased Housing program, a small program reviewed in a paper by Frank deLeeuw and Sam Leaman. Section 23 permitted local public housing authorities to lease rental units in existing private housing for its low-income clients. It was much cheaper than conventional public housing and better accepted by "both tenants and the community" (U.S. Congress 1972b, 7).

THE 1973 MORATORIUM

After Richard Nixon's landslide reelection in 1972, the White House and the Office of Management and Budget (OMB) clearly signaled to HUD that housing subsidy programs were in deep trouble and might be shut down entirely. Word also filtered out to the FHA bureaucracy, which hustled pending applications through the commitment process to beat the anticipated ax. Romney by this time was fed up with the subsidy programs and had, in any case, stated before the election that he would not be around for a second Nixon term. Still, he strenuously opposed the "virtually complete 'moratorium,'" effective January 1, 1973, that OMB wrote into the fiscal year 1974 draft executive budget. In his budget appeal letter to the president, Romney stated that he had

no objection to a substantial cutback in these programs while we pursue the development of an alternative housing strategy. I do object, however, to the abrupt, across-the-board character of the moratorium which will cause widespread disruption in the housing industry, and will prevent the Federal Government from keeping existing specific commitments for subsidized housing.

(HUD 1972, 1)

Romney argued that "the complex network of building and financial institutions that has formed to take advantage of Federal subsidy programs" deserved some "lead-time to adjust to new circumstances rather than suddenly being put out of business" (HUD 1972, 2). He also warned that a complete moratorium will "raise havoc with many existing commitments for subsidized housing, which frequently interlock with related federally-financed efforts," citing as examples urban renewal, new communities financed with federally guaranteed bonds, disaster housing, and "fair-share" subsidized housing distribution plans prepared by metropolitan planning agencies with HUD's encouragement (HUD 1972, 2). Wrote Romney: "[T]urning our back on these commitments would invite a wave of protest and justified cynicism on the part of those with whom we have [been] conducting public business in good faith" (HUD 1972, 2). If the federal budget was too tight to "allow an orderly transition" to a new housing strategy, he recommended a "staged reduction in the mortgage interest and property tax deductions" taken by middle- and upper-income families — a suggestion that was not adopted (HUD 1972, 4).

The bad news on the moratorium was delivered personally by Romney in a speech to the NAHB on January 8, 1973, in Houston. His profound ambivalence about the major subsidy programs was revealed again in this speech, which refers to the apparent success of Sections 235 and 236 in many parts of the country; however, "they have been too frequently abused and made the vehicle of inordinate profits gained through shoddy construction, poor site location, and questionable financing arrangements" (Romney 1973, 8). Sounding much like Senator Proxmire a few months earlier, Romney referred to the housing programs as a "Rube Goldberg structure" (1973, 8) and as a "statutory and administrative monstrosity" (1973, 7). The time had come, he said, "to pause, to re-evaluate, and to seek out better ways" (Romney 1973, 6). He also pointedly refused to use the term "moratorium," instead calling the action a "temporary hold" and noting that the pipeline of approved subsidy applications would keep production going at quite high levels – around 250,000 units – for another 18 months. Beyond that, Romney stated somewhat vaguely that "projects which are necessary to meet statutory or other specific program commitments will be approved in coming months" (1973, 7).

These arguments against a complete moratorium had some effect, with the help of a more flexible domestic affairs staff at the White House countering the hard-liners at OMB. In negotiations after the NAHB speech, it was determined that all Section 235 and 236 projects that had reached the HUD "feasibility approval" stage of processing by January 5, 1973, would escape the moratorium and could go forward to final processing and construction. In addition, OMB agreed to allow 60,000 extra units for the balance of fiscal year 1973 for "specific program commitments" yet to be defined, and "informally" approved 75,000 for fiscal year 1974 (HUD 1973a, 1).

Such palliatives prevented a complete shutdown of subsidized production activity, and advocates from the housing industry and low-income housing supporters would continue to push with limited success for a resumption of large-scale, federally sponsored production programs. But the 1973 moratorium had squashed what was left of the spirit of '68, and the search for better ways in the next quarter century would lead in other directions, specifically to demand-side subsidies and devolution of low-income production decisions to state and local governments.

The history and development of the three program types – vouchers, block grants, and tax credits – that have come to dominate the current phase of the half-century quest for the national housing goal will be considered next.

HOUSING VOUCHERS: RETOOLING AN OLD IDEA

Housing vouchers, then called rent certificates, were first advanced in the 1930s by the National Association of Real Estate Boards as an alternative to government-sponsored new housing for the poor, but in 1937, public housing prevailed as the vehicle of choice. The rent certificate idea stayed alive in the postwar debates leading up to the Housing Act of 1949, again losing out to public housing advocates. In the Eisenhower administration, the President's Committee on Government Housing Policies took up the idea again in 1953 with the same result:

> The committee concluded that rent certificates would be degrading to recipients, that they would not "add to the housing supply," that they would deter participation by private enterprise, that appropriate administration of the program would be organizationally complex, and that there would be no feasible way to limit the scale of such a program.
>
> (Carlson and Heinberg 1978, 49)

The realtors' persistent lobbying for rent certificates also suggested, of course, that their real motive was to take advantage of public funds to jack up rents in their least desirable properties.

Housing vouchers reemerged in the 1960s in the context of softening urban housing markets and public housing authorities that were caught between local opposition to development sites and their bulging waiting lists for low-rent housing. The first significant step came with the Section 23 Leased Housing program authorized by the Housing Act of 1965. Section 23 allowed public housing authorities to lease standard housing units from private landlords and sublease them to their clients. The authority paid the landlord a market rent, the low-income family paid what it could afford as determined by an income-driven formula, and the government made up the difference. Usually, the authority searched the market for appropriate units and then negotiated terms with the landlords, but a few authorities also experimented with a "finders-keepers" method whereby prospective tenants did their own shopping and brought a unit to the authority for approval. Either way, Section 23 cut the tie between a subsidized renter and a physical project built solely for low-income occupancy and in so doing, opened up new opportunities for both geographic mobility and economic – perhaps even racial – integration.

In the late 1960s, vouchers – then known as housing allowances – were considered by another presidential advisory body, the President's Committee on Urban Housing (known as the Kaiser Committee after its chairman, industrialist Edgar Kaiser), which recommended that experimental tests of housing allowances should be initiated. In 1970, Senator Edward Brooke of Massachusetts led the way for such experiments, sponsoring Section 504 of the Housing Act of 1970, which authorized HUD to spend $20 million in fiscal years 1972 and 1973 for the Experimental Housing Allowance Program (EHAP). Meanwhile, two cities that were part of the Model Cities program – Kansas City, MO, and Wilmington, DE – launched small demonstration programs (about 250 families in Kansas City and 80 in Wilmington) to test housing allowances.

The EHAP

Working with the Urban Institute, HUD immediately set about designing the program. Even as the department was in the midst of a huge subsidized housing production effort, the attractions of the housing allowance were compelling. As summed up by HUD Assistant Secretary for Research and Technology, Harold Finger: It "would get the Department out of the business of reviewing particular housing development applications for particular localities, thereby avoiding the problem of local resistance to Federally assisted housing development" (HUD 1971a, 1). It could be less costly and easier to administer than production programs. It could act as an important housing preservation tool by encouraging landlords to meet code standards to qualify for renting to allowance holders, who would then ensure a stable rental income stream. It "could eventually eliminate the development of public housing with its concentration of large families, welfare families, fatherless households" (HUD 1971a, 2). But to make a convincing case for all these benefits, housing allowances had to be tried in settings approximating, as far as possible, actual operating conditions.

As implemented during the 1970s in 12 sites at a cost of about $175 million, the EHAP was indeed, in Louis Winnick's delightfully dismissive phrase, a "rich feeding ground for the policy elite" (Winnick 1995, 96). In the real world of

postmoratorium housing politics, as opposed to the contrived world of the experiments, Congress preempted the EHAP's research findings in 1974 by adopting an allowance-like component of the new subsidy program called Section 8. Yet the EHAP's mountains of data and careful design, and the scrupulous objectivity of the analytical team all played their part in wrapping up the debate on the workability of housing allowances. In particular, the "supply experiments" carried out for five years in Green Bay, WI, and South Bend, IN, and designed to test the market effects of a full-scale allowance entitlement, "resulted in no detectable marketwide rise in rents," thus blunting the traditional chief line of attack by allowance opponents (Winnick 1995, 108).

Vouchers and production: Head-to-head competition

Showing that a program can work is not the same as demonstrating that it is superior, however. The contest between the allowance component (Existing Housing) of Section 8 and the production components (New Construction and Substantial Rehabilitation) played out in the postmoratorium 1970s. Under Romney's successor, James T. Lynn, the Existing Housing component – which replaced the already operating Section 23 leasing program – moved ahead quickly, but the production components lagged. As a result of the delay, Carla Anderson Hills, who took over from Lynn in March 1975, inherited production programs for which no regulations were in place and not a single subsidy commitment was in sight (Foote 1995). Hills, an energetic administrator with a point to prove – her nomination by President Gerald R. Ford had been opposed by housing lobbyists because of her lack of housing experience – took hold of the production programs and succeeded in increasing subsidy commitments from no units at all in fiscal year 1975 to 85,000 units by March 1976 (Hills 1976). Still, congressional critics charged HUD with a bias toward the Existing Housing program, a misdirected attack in Hills's case because she had gotten the Section 8 production programs running smoothly and in addition was reactivating the dormant Section 235 program for subsidized homeownership production. Nevertheless, Congress wrote mandates into the 1977 appropriations act requiring HUD to spend a bigger share of Section 8 on production (Harney 1976). As discussed in the next section, the incessant wrangling with Congress over subsidy types and mix helped persuade Hills that a housing block grant was a better way to organize housing spending.

Jimmy Carter's election in 1977 brought in an administration eager to establish an activist posture in housing and urban policy. As applied to housing, this meant going with the tide of congressional support for stepped-up production and with developers who by that time had mastered Section 8's lucrative profit potential. The Existing Housing component continued as a lower-profile adjunct to the main action.

The "triumph" of vouchers

After Ronald Reagan was elected president in 1980, he appointed the President's Commission on Housing to conduct yet another review of housing programs and make recommendations. Citing gains in both housing supply and quality since the 1950s, as well as the EHAP in the 1970s, the commission concluded that "massive production of new apartments for the poor" was not the answer; rather, a "Housing Payments Program … for lower-income consumers is the most efficient way to help the largest number of poor families in their quest for a decent home" (President's Commission on Housing 1982, xxiii). In making their recommendation, the commission also pointed to the large future budget obligations attached to Section 8 contracts already in force – $121 billion in fiscal year 1982. Armed with the commission's report, Reagan called for repeal of the production components of Section 8 and Congress complied, leaving Section 8 certificates as the only large-scale form of federal housing subsidy. In 1985, the Reagan administration introduced a "voucher" variant of the Section 8 program, which gave the recipient the option of choosing a unit costing more than the HUD-approved fair market rent and paying the difference out of his or her own pocket. The "certificate" and "voucher" programs operated – somewhat confusingly – side by side until merged in 1999 under the name "Housing Choice Vouchers."

"The Triumph of Housing Allowance Programs," as laid out in Winnick's insightful account, "stems from the confluence of discrete trends" (1995, 99), including the fact that the extraordinary utility and versatility of vouchers have progressively widened their base of political support to embrace both urban housing preservationists and metropolitan housing dispersalists. Vouchers also benefit from *not* being production programs, which seem forever burdened with the weighty baggage of blighting projects, excessive cost, social pathologies, bureaucratic bungling, and outright scandal. Staunch defenders of production programs will protest with some reason the unfairness of this judgment, but the images of program failures are too deeply stamped in the collective mind to be dislodged. Vouchers profit in the image game from being largely invisible and from involving financial stakes too small to invite conspicuous fraud. Most important is the recognition across the policy spectrum that "in a better housed America, the core housing problem stemmed, predominantly, not from deficits in supply but from deficits in income" (Winnick 1995, 97).

BLOCK GRANTS AND THE ILLUSION OF FEDERAL CONTROL

For about 40 of the 50 years since the Housing Act of 1949, housing programs for the poor labored under a crippling paradox. Federal money filled the subsidy gap in one way or another: Federal laws and regulations created the program structures for a parade of initiatives, and federal officials – both civil servants and political appointees – acted as gatekeepers, holding in their hands the keys to the federal cashbox. Quite properly, the programs in force at any particular time were labeled "federal." Yet the programs were inescapably "local" as well. Federal housing laws and budget appropriations do not build a single house or apartment anywhere: Actual building requires a local entrepreneur, a site, a complicit local government, and consumers willing to buy or rent. Even with voluminous federal "standards" and regulations in place, this mix of local actors presents a host of vulnerabilities: the home builder who cuts corners and turns out a shoddy product, the apartment developer who fabricates projected expenses and cash flow to "make the numbers work" on a subsidized project, local governments who proffer sites intended to wall off and segregate their poor and minority citizens, and consumers who conceal income to qualify for subsidies. When abuses crop up, as they inevitably do, the federal government is left holding the bag and is deemed responsible. As Secretary Romney, referring to the Section 235 program, testified in April 1971 to the Housing Subcommittee of the House Appropriations Committee:

> As I take a look at this program ... I find no real incentive in there for anybody to see that this program is going to operate on the soundest possible basis other than those of us in the federal government. And everybody is out to take advantage of the situation. It is not structured in a way so that you have any incentives to do other than take advantage of the situation .... The builders like to build them. The real estate people like to sell them. But we are in a position where we have to protect the consumer, we have to protect the government ... under circumstances far more difficult to protect the basic interest than I ever had to contend with before in any field I have ever been in
>
> (Lilley 1971, 1537)

The tension between the federal and local roles in producing subsidized housing was further complicated by the somewhat ambiguous role of the HUD/FHA field offices. The field staff were of course responsible to their masters in Washington for administering the laws and regulations emanating from Congress and the HUD central office. They were also assigned program production targets that they were under pressure to meet. Although they were guardians of the federal interest, however, their very effectiveness as program implementers depended in large part on how "local" they could be – in other words, how accommodating they could be to the profit motives of local builders and the political agendas of local governments and often members of Congress as well, who took considerable interest in how their financial contributors from the housing industry were being treated by HUD field personnel.

The cross-pressures on the field staff from local constituencies and from Washington led to many lapses of judgment and sometimes to outright corruption. As a result, the production programs confronted every HUD secretary with the dilemma of how much centralized control to impose on the field. Should all major project decisions require a Washington review and sign-off, thus slowing down the approval process and hobbling the effectiveness of able field office directors? Or should field staff be trusted with real decision-making authority, subject only to monitoring and spot checks by Washington? Whatever the decisions individual secretaries made on these matters, there were trade-offs and risks that would become all too real on the next trip to Capitol Hill.

Further complicating federal and local roles was federal prescription of the nature and mix of the available programs. When public housing was the only game in town, local governments built public housing. When the 1968 housing goal and new production targets were the emphasis, cities whose priorities were preservation and rehabilitation had very little to work with. After the 1973 moratorium, it was hard to know from year to year what to expect, as Congress engaged in what HUD Secretary Carla Hills referred to as "fits and starts, backing and filling," constantly fiddling with the mix between new construction and leased housing, and between public housing and Section 8, all the while floating numerous proposals for new or redesigned programs (Harney 1976, 1271).

Housing block grants: Competing models in the mid-1970s

By the mid-1970s, the pattern of national housing initiatives had become familiar: the fanfare accompanying enactment, the implementation scramble, the analysis of results, the counting of costs in budget and social terms, the second thoughts and recriminations, and finally the search for a new model. At the heart of this tiresome cycle was the tension between the pretense of federal policy control and the messy realities of local implementation. "I'm damn tired of people in a delivery system objecting to change when everyone knows that the delivery system is clearly failing," said Representative Thomas "Lud" Ashley in 1971 (Lilley 1971, 1537). Ashley, the influential chairman of the Housing Subcommittee of the Banking Committee, was an early, though not consistent, advocate for a housing block grant that would cut the connection between the private developer and the federal bureaucracy by interposing metropolitan planning agencies as recipients of the block grant. As a condition of getting the grant, metropolitan agencies would be required to develop areawide housing plans for distributing subsidized housing throughout the suburbs, thereby mitigating suburban exclusionary zoning and the concentration of housing for poor minorities in central cities. Such a planning requirement had already been inserted into the Housing Act of 1968, but the planning agencies, dominated by local officials, had been slow to respond; a housing block grant would presumably goad them into action. Despite Ashley's advocacy and influence, the idea was too radical; it was introduced but went nowhere.

Not long afterward, however, the block grant concept was taken up again, although in different form and without Ashley's visionary planning and social agenda. This time the leading sponsor was Secretary Hills. Hills was inspired by the model of the CDBG, enacted in 1974, a consolidation of eight separate (mainly non-housing) programs on the "Urban Development" side of HUD. The CDBG predecessor programs, including urban renewal, model cities, open space, and water and sewer grants, had suffered under many of the same tensions as the housing programs: federal funding approval on a competitive, case-by-case basis, detailed federal regulatory control, and the political responsibility for anything that might go wrong as local officials adapted federal policies to local circumstances. CDBG virtually eliminated federal funding discretion by providing automatic, formula-based annual grants to all cities with populations of more than 50,000, to urban counties, and to states for distribution to nonmetropolitan areas. With regard to housing, the CDBG statute permitted funds to be used for housing rehabilitation but not new construction. Hills characterized the difference between CDBG and the old categorical programs as "like night and day" (Harney 1976, 1271). She saw no reason why what worked for community development would not also work for housing.

In one sense, however, CDBG sharpened the conflict between federal and local roles in housing by requiring a local Housing Assistance Plan (HAP) that was supposed to embrace all assisted housing. The difficulty, as laid out in a HUD staff analysis, was that

> responsibility for actual delivery of assisted housing rested primarily with semi-autonomous public housing agencies, private

builders and HUD, leaving local governments with only a peripheral role in implementing their own HAP goals. As a result, HAP preparation often is viewed as a paperwork exercise, with its quality reflecting that attitude.

(HUD 1976, 5)

Despite the indifferent quality of the HAPs, Congress was quick to jump on the fact that in the aggregate, they showed a preference for New Construction and Substantial Rehabilitation over Existing Housing assistance by about a 60 to 40 ratio, while HUD's actual performance in fiscal year 1976 indicated the reverse. The conference committee report on the Housing Act of 1976 chided HUD for

> disregarding the contents of housing assistance plans in allocating housing assistance … failing to use the traditional public housing program to provide needed new units … and administering the Section 8 program in a way to make it a virtual nullity as a useful tool to assist newly constructed and rehabilitated units

(HUD 1976, 6)

On the one hand, Congress directed HUD to pay more attention to the local HAPs, but on the other, the Appropriations Act mandated specific spending earmarks for "a veritable maze of programs," including conventional public housing, with no indication as to how HUD was to mesh these mandates with local plans. As the HUD staff paper put it: "This 'halfwayhouse' approach to housing assistance is rapidly becoming an administrative nightmare for the cities, for HUD, and for the intended recipients of the assistance" (1976, 7–8).

Hills directed her staff to prepare draft legislation for a housing assistance block grant that would have been presented as the centerpiece of a 1977 housing reform initiative. But time ran out on the abbreviated Ford administration; in 1977, President Jimmy Carter's appointees were in charge.

Housing block grants: An idea in eclipse

During the Carter administration, the block grant idea lacked powerful sponsors in either the executive or legislative branches. Carter's

HUD inherited from Hills a Section 8 New Construction program with the early bugs worked out. The old axis between HUD and developers was back, and HUD wanted to show its commitment to low-income housing by running up the highest production numbers since the 1973 moratorium. A block grant would have disrupted that agenda.

After Carter's defeat in 1980, Ronald Reagan, the newly elected president, appointed a study commission to recommend the future course of housing policy. As already noted, the main recommendation of the President's Commission on Housing was for a "housing payments" (voucher) program. However, the block grant idea also reemerged as an important commission recommendation, partly as a concession to supporters of production subsidies. The proposal was to tack on a new "Housing Component" to the CDBG that would permit new construction. The Reagan administration chose to adopt the voucher recommendation and dismissed the block grant proposal.

The housing establishment endorses block grants; Congress eventually agrees

With the Reagan administration locked into an antiproduction, voucher-only housing policy, and with the 1988 election on the horizon, housing advocates in the Senate and the housing industry gathered their forces in 1987 under the banner of the National Housing Task Force, a privately funded group "organized to help set a new national housing agenda" (*A Decent Place to Live* 1988, ii). Led by developer/philanthropist James Rouse, founder of the Enterprise Foundation, and David O. Maxwell, chairman and chief executive officer of Fannie Mae, the 26-member body reviewed 72 position papers from housing interest groups and 20 papers prepared by scholars and practitioners. The report of the task force, issued in March 1988, had as its centerpiece recommendation a $3 billion, freestanding housing block grant to state governments and cities. Christened the Housing Opportunity Program (HOP), the federal block grant was to "be provided with maximum flexibility and minimum regulation" (*A Decent Place to Live* 1988, 13). As for the forms of assistance to be provided for low-income housing, the task

force report recited the menu of subsidy choices that Congress had been scrapping over for 40 years – "grants, loans, interest reduction subsidies, operating support, or any other mechanisms" – and concluded that state and local governments should decide on whatever combinations they "found appropriate and effective" (*A Decent Place to Live* 1988, 21). Twelve years after Secretary Hills had called for a housing block grant, the pillars of the housing establishment came around to the same view. In those intervening years, the task force believed, state and local housing agencies had gathered "both capacity and experience," enabling them to "contribute significantly to meeting the housing goals set by the Task Force" (*A Decent Place to Live* 1988, 26). Congress eventually agreed. The issue of a housing block grant versus a new, HUD-run rental production program was fought out in 1990. On the Senate side, sponsors of the housing bill pushed for the task force's HOP proposal, but on the House side, sponsors adopted a rental production program paired with a small block grant to help community-based, nonprofit housing developers. In the conference committee, the Senate side prevailed: HOP emerged as the HOME Investment Partnerships program, funded at $1.5 billion, with 15 percent set aside for community-based nonprofits.

After Congress acted, some analysts claimed that the 1990 act would deflect assistance from the neediest households (Nelson and Khadduri 1992). But Gordon Cavanaugh, former head of the Philadelphia Housing Authority, commented that such criticisms

> miss the point of [the 1990 act], which was to reestablish local roles. The thrust of the HOME program is to create a housing program free of HUD's constant bureaucratic interference…. HUD does not know best.
> (Cavanaugh 1992, 68, 75)

The legacy of past rental production programs was all around to see: public housing projects in ruins and Section 236 and Section 8 projects built on financial quicksand demanding billions of federal dollars to keep them from going under. Enthusiasts for local control believed that state and local governments could do better; almost everyone agreed that they could do no worse.

THE LIHTC

Tax advantages linked to real estate investment in general and to low-income rental housing in particular have long been tied to stimulating subsidized production. As Case has written: "Virtually all privately financed housing for low- and moderate-income families over the past two decades [1970–1990] has received a substantial subsidy through the tax system" (1991, 343), almost all through the sale of limited partnerships to investors who are able to use tax credits or depreciation allowances to shelter other income from taxation. The process of organizing and marketing such benefits is called syndication. For developers, syndicators, and limited partners, investing in low-income housing is a way of doing well by doing good, especially when the federal government eliminates much of the risk by insuring the mortgage.

The rules of the syndication game are set by Congress in the tax laws, which can change abruptly to enhance or reduce housing-related tax provisions in response to a perceived need for housing stimulus or for cooling an overbuilt market. In the 1980s version of this story, Congress reacted to bottom-scraping housing production – fewer than a million units in 1981 – by shortening depreciation schedules for multifamily construction, which was especially depressed, at only 319,000 units nationwide. The stimulus had the desired effect, and more: Apartment construction more than doubled by 1985, causing a glut of overbuilding in many markets that would shortly contribute to the S&L debacle of the late 1980s. Congress reacted again in 1986 by taking aim at the 1981 incentives in order to slow down speculative building. But low-income housing developers and advocates, who had been hurting since the termination of Section 8 production programs three years earlier, pleaded that their cause constituted a special case. Congress threw them a bone: a new low-income housing tax credit even more lucrative than the incentives it replaced. After a slow start, it "has become the primary production vehicle for low-income housing in the United States" (Wallace 1995, 793).

How the LIHTC works

Individuals and companies who invest in low-income housing can take a tax credit (a dollar-for-dollar offset against other taxes) equal to their investment in 10 annual installments. To qualify for tax credit investment, properties must rent at least 20 percent of their units to households earning 50 percent of the area median income or less, *or* at least 40 percent of their units to households earning less than 60 percent of median income. The rents charged may not exceed 30 percent of a household's income. Units meeting these standards must remain in service for at least 15 years. As implemented, most developments end up being 100 percent occupied by renters meeting the 60 percent of median income standard.

The number of units generated by tax credits is limited by the total allocation permitted under federal law, which established a formula calling for annual allocations to states based on population; each state receives $1.25 per resident. State housing agencies distribute the credits to local housing agencies or directly to sponsors of low-income developments. Program compliance on the development side of the program is the responsibility of state agencies, while the IRS is responsible for enforcing the federal tax code.

LIHTC as a production program

After enactment, the LIHTC got off to a slow start. Congress gave the unfamiliar incentive only a three-year life; the IRS took its time preparing implementing regulations; and developers and investors, not wanting to get caught in yet another congressional change of heart, were cautious. Between 1989 and 1993, the tax credit was kept alive with annual extensions until a persistent lobbying effort persuaded Congress to make it permanent. In 1995, however, supporters had to stave off a determined effort by the House Ways and Means Committee to "sunset" the tax credit in 1997 as part of a broader assault on deficit-swelling "corporate welfare" (Stanfield 1995). Politically, it seems out of danger now: In 1998 and 1999, Congress considered increasing the per resident limit from $1.25 to $1.75, and it seems likely that an upward adjustment along those lines will eventually be adopted.

Estimates of production linked to the LIHTC vary, depending on the source and the method used to count a unit – apartment construction is a multiyear process spanning the time between the initial allocation of credits to a project (which might never be built) and the date it is "placed in service." Using the latter definition, HUD (1996) estimated on the basis of a survey of state housing agencies that 224,446 low-income units had been produced in the 1990–94 period. The U.S. General Accounting Office surveyed the same agencies and got slightly different answers adding up to 172,000 units in the 1992–94 period (White 1997). Cummings and DiPasquale estimate that "roughly 550,000 to 600,000 units were put in place in [LIHTC's] first ten years" (1999, 303). And according to data provided to me by the National Council of State Housing Agencies, tax credits allocated from program inception (1987) through 1998 have provided financing for more than a million low-income apartments.

LIHTC as a block grant

However one sorts out the production numbers, the LIHTC is a very substantial contributor to the low-income housing stock. In addition, from the state and local perspective, a key feature is that it functions administratively "as a form of tax block grant," a flexible source of funds "to provide for local housing needs, including rehabilitated or newly constructed apartment buildings, townhomes or single-family homes, free of federal interference" (Patterson 1996, 7). It has also become a very important production engine for the thousands of nonprofit community development corporations (CDCs) operating in cities across the nation. National nonprofit intermediaries, principally the Local Initiatives Support Corporation and the Enterprise Foundation, act as packagers of corporate tax credit investments, which are then funneled to local CDCs for specific projects (Orlebeke 1997; Walker 1993). Thus, although the LIHTC law required each state to set aside at least 10 percent of its allocation for nonprofit sponsors, the efforts of the intermediaries have resulted in a larger share – more than a quarter – of the credits being committed to nonprofit sponsors (HUD 1996). For CDCs, tax credits typically form one layer of a much more complex financing package combining subsidies from other sources such as low-interest financing from state or local housing agencies, philanthropic grants, donated land, or CDBG or HOME block grants. These financial gymnastics

are necessary because the LIHTC by itself cannot get rents low enough for the lowest-income households.

The LIHTC's friends and critics

The LIHTC has many friends, but also many critics. One line of attack has been that the relative complexity of the program necessarily involves quite high transaction costs. Particularly in the LIHTC's early years, much of the tax credit dollar – perhaps 20 to 30 percent or even more – was never applied to bricks and mortar, but instead was drained off to pay the fees of lawyers and accountants who put together tax credit deals. Also, as just noted, the LIHTC falls short of serving very low income households, forcing sponsors to hunt for other subsidies if the community's neediest families are to be served. These issues lead to an examination of the efficiency of the tax credit in relation to its cost to the federal treasury as a tax expenditure (revenue that is forgone), as well as to the question of whether there is a simpler, more direct way to achieve low-income housing construction that costs less in money and energy.

According to congressional staff estimates, the tax expenditure triggered by the LIHTC was $3.2 billion in fiscal year 1998 and is projected to be $19.6 billion over five years (1998–2002) (Schussheim 1998). It can be argued that the high return on investment that these numbers represent is an unwarranted windfall for corporations lured by tax credits and that the benefits should therefore be reduced or auctioned off. Surely, as some suggest, one could devise a more efficient low-income production program by scrapping the costly and convoluted tax credits and substituting an up-front capital grant similar to the current small-scale Section 202 program for elderly and handicapped housing (Case 1991).

The LIHTC debate is the latest variation on a recurring theme in low-income housing politics. Housing advocates who have the interests of the poor at heart call for government grants and other incentives to stimulate desired production. In the nature of things, such inducements attract, indeed require, the participation of profit-motivated developers, investors, and professional experts such as lawyers and accountants who master the intricacies of a given subsidy technique. (Even "nonprofit" corporations must make money somehow to survive.) When the inducements succeed and production flows, the second-guessing ensues. Project overhead and construction costs, swelled by government regulation, are high; developer and investor profits seem excessive, plundering the federal treasury. Housing advocates motivated by altruism may recoil from these realities, but at the same time, they are reluctant to give up a technique that, however costly and clumsy, works. Economists and policy analysts, meanwhile, scrutinize the incentive and offer more efficient alternatives. The LIHTC has been operating in this challenging terrain.

The difference between the LIHTC and previous tax incentives, as noted above, is that it functions as a form of block grant to states and cities, and in so doing is part of the pattern of devolution marking the postmoratorium period. Devolution has brought with it the highly varied, pragmatic, and often resourceful application of multiple public, nonprofit, and private sources of support that have gathered under the much celebrated banner of "public-private partnerships." Although the community-based arms of these partnerships often lead a harried and precarious existence, complicated by the exertion required to assemble development deals, it seems that their professionalism and productivity are gaining rather than losing strength, and the LIHTC has come to occupy a key place in their worthy efforts to improve housing and neighborhoods.

Moreover, in recent years, as private and nonprofit developers have become more adept in putting together tax credit deals, the LIHTC has also become much less vulnerable to charges of wastefulness and inefficiency. Michael Stegman, an early critic of the LIHTC as a "highly inefficient and relatively inaccessible subsidy mechanism" (1991, 359), now points to "enormous gains in LIHTC efficiency" so that "a growing portion of every tax credit dollar is going into building affordable housing rather than to paying syndication costs or higher investor returns" (1999, 323–24). With the reservation that the LIHTC allocation formula should be adjusted to target more poor households, Stegman asserts – and I agree – that the LIHTC "should continue to be the core of the country's low-income housing production system well into the twenty-first century" (1999, 323).

CONCLUSION

In this article, I have sought both to describe the evolution of important low-income housing policies since 1949 and to suggest that these policies generally make sense: specifically, that they evolved during an extended period of trial and error, that as far as can be determined they are achieving their objectives reasonably well, and that they appear to enjoy a fairly stable political consensus unusual in a chaotic half century of federal housing policies.

In recent years, the most significant turbulence occurred after the 1994 midterm elections when Republicans took control of Congress. Some Republicans, looking for ways to shake up the federal domestic program establishment, focused on HUD as a target for radical reform or elimination, and it was not clear that the Clinton administration would try very hard to stop them. In an attempt to stave off the threat, HUD Secretary Henry Cisneros convened his top staff shortly after the 1994 elections to put together a "Reinvention Blueprint," which included a striking outburst of contrition and a proposed revamping of the department's programs. The tactic succeeded in blunting the movement to get rid of HUD and was a remarkable signal of how much the housing policy landscape had changed since 1949 and 1968.

The Reinvention Blueprint declared as "undeniable truths" HUD's "slavish loyalty to non-performing programs and insufficient trust in the initiatives of local leaders" (HUD 1994, 1) "… [who] know best how to set community and housing priorities and make them work" (HUD 1994, 4). As applied to low-income housing programs, the blueprint called for ending within three years the entire federal system of public and assisted housing tied to project subsidies and replacing it with vouchers issued to tenants who could either stay in place or take them into the private market. State and local governments would be responsible for managing the new voucher system and would also continue receiving housing block grants for new construction and rehabilitation.

Although the main elements of the blueprint have not been adopted and implemented – and are not likely to be anytime soon – the proposal to demolish up to 100,000 units of the "worst public housing developments" is moving forward (HUD 1995, 8). Local governments, usually with the help of the flexible, $50 million HOPE VI grants first authorized in 1993, are now able to tear down derelict public housing as part of a plan to "transform public housing communities from islands of despair and poverty into a vital and integral part of larger neighborhoods" (Epp 1996, 570). In addressing the transformation challenge, cities will be drawing on a wide range of public and private investment sources, including the voucher, block grant, and tax credit programs discussed here.

Unfortunately, as the case of public housing illustrates, the expansion of programs that work is severely limited by the burden of paying for programs that have not. Billions of dollars have been and will be spent to prop up, and now tear down and partially replace, urban public housing. Added to that are the billions that have been and will be committed to preserve the affordability of some 4,000 multifamily properties built under the subsidized production programs of the 1960s and 1970s (Smith 1999). During this period, a fundamental principle had somehow eluded federal policy makers. As David A. Smith has put it: "Identifying and finding the resources to build affordable housing is straightforward; managing it over time is much more difficult" (1999, 147).

HUD's current preservation strategy, known by the shorthand term "mark-to-market," is governed by the Multifamily Assisted Housing Reform and Affordability Act (MAHRA) passed in 1997. MAHRA capped a decade of legislative effort to deal with the many problems of the federally insured multifamily inventory, including troubled projects with chronic maintenance and financial burdens and better-off projects whose owners are eager to terminate expiring subsidy contracts and convert to market-driven rents, thereby pushing current lower-income tenants out the door. Mark-to-market entails a multiyear process of enormous complexity that calls for a project-by-project analysis of the inventory. Project mortgages and rents are to be restructured and put into line with local market values; where necessary, funds for repairs and capital improvements can also be bundled with the refinancing package. Fully implementing mark-to-market will be costly: A 1995 estimate by Smith put the net cost to the FHA insurance fund at about $8.2 billion (1999). Wisely, MAHRA has taken the day-to-day management

of mark-to-market out of HUD's hands by requiring the agency to subcontract with participating administrative entities, usually state housing finance agencies, which will make all the key project-level decisions under HUD's broad oversight – yet another step down the devolution path.

Despite the expensive baggage of past blunders, the three core elements of current low-income housing assistance policy – vouchers, block grants, and tax credits – seem to be securely in place. As always, future Congresses and presidential administrations will still have plenty to fight about in the housing policy arena, but I do not believe we are near another major turning point in housing policy. For low-income housing advocates, this outlook suggests that the most prudent political strategy is to push for a steady expansion of all three program elements as the most promising path to the "realization as soon as feasible" of the nation's housing goals.

Finally, the issue of federal regulatory control versus state and local government discretion continues to be a difficult balancing act. Despite the laudable tendency on the part of Congress and HUD to devolve increasing responsibility to the state and local levels, the impulses to control, prescribe, regulate, and micromanage are powerful. In HUD's 1998 appropriations legislation, for example, the same Congress that authorized the promising idea of up to 100 local "home rule" grant demonstrations combining public housing and Section 8 funds, also enshrined the right of public housing residents to own one or more household pets (Poduska 1998). The federal government must necessarily follow what happens to the money it dispenses. But in recent years, state and local governments have shown commendable initiative in taking on the social and economic challenges posed by their neediest citizens, including the political responsibility for results. A steadily more assertive role in housing is the logical extension of this trend. The federal government would do well to stay on the course of encouraging it.

AUTHOR

Charles J. Orlebeke is a Professor of Urban Planning and Public Affairs at the University of Illinois at Chicago.

REFERENCES

Carlson, David B., and John D. Heinberg. 1978. *How Housing Allowances Work.* Washington, D.C.: Urban Institute.

Case, Karl E. 1991. Investors, Developers, and Supply-Side Subsidies. *Housing Policy Debate* 2(2):341–56.

Cavanaugh, Gordon. 1992. Comment on Kathryn P. Nelson and Jill Khadduri's "To Whom Should Limited Housing Resources Be Directed?" *Housing Policy Debate* 3(1):67–75.

Cummings, Jean L. and Denise DiPasquale. 1999. The Low-Income Housing Tax Credit: An Analysis of the First Ten Years. *Housing Policy Debate* 10(2):251–307.

A Decent Place to Live. 1988. Report of the National Housing Task Force. Washington, D.C.

Downs, Anthony. 1972. *Federal Housing Subsidies: Their Nature and Effectiveness and What We Should Do about Them.* Washington, D.C.: Real Estate Research Corporation.

Epp, Gayle. 1996. Emerging Strategies for Revitalizing Public Housing Communities. *Housing Policy Debate* 7(3):563–88.

Foote, Joseph. 1995. As They Saw It: HUD's Secretaries Reminisce about Carrying Out the Mission. *Cityscape* 1(3):77–79.

Harney, Kenneth R. 1976. Changes May Be in Store for Federal Housing Policy. *National Journal*, September 11, pp. 1270–78.

Hays, R. Allen. 1995. *The Federal Government and Urban Housing.* Albany, NY: State University of New York Press.

Hills, Carla Anderson. 1976. Statement before the Subcommittee on HUD-Independent Agencies, House Committee on Appropriations. March 30, p. 11.

Lilley, William III. 1971. Urban Report/Policy Makers Condemn Housing Programs; Seek Alternative to Builder Subsidy Approach. *National Journal,* July 24, pp. 1535–43.

Listokin, David. 1991. Federal Housing Policy and Preservation: Historical Evolution, Patterns, and Implications. *Housing Policy Debate* 2(2):157–85.

Nelson, Kathryn P., and Jill Khadduri. 1992. To Whom Should Limited Housing Resources Be Directed? *Housing Policy Debate* 3(1):1–55.

Orlebeke, Charles J. 1997. *New Life at Ground Zero: New York, Homeownership, and the Future of American Cities.* Albany, NY: Rockefeller Institute Press.

Patterson, Maurice. 1996. Low-Income Housing Tax Credits Come under Scrutiny. *Nation's Cities Weekly*, March 4, pp. 7, 11.

Poduska, Joseph P. 1998. Congress Approves Public Housing, Section 8 Reform Legislation. *Housing and Development Reporter* 26(24):380.

President's Commission on Housing. 1982. *The Report of the President's Commission on Housing.* Washington, D.C.

President's Third Annual Report on National Housing Goals. 1971. Washington, D.C.: U.S. Government Printing Office.

Romney, George. 1973. Remarks Prepared for Delivery at the 29th Annual Convention of the National Association of Home Builders, Houston, January 8. Press Release, U.S. Department of Housing and Urban Development. Washington, D.C.

Schechter, Henry B., and Marion Schlefer. 1971. Housing Needs and National Goals. In *Papers Submitted to the Committee on Banking and Currency,* pt. 1:5. Washington, D.C.: U.S. Government Printing Office.

Schussheim, Morton J. 1969. *Toward a New Housing Policy: The Legacy of the Sixties.* New York: Committee for Economic Development.

Schussheim, Morton J. 1998. *Housing the Poor: Federal Housing Programs for Low-Income Families.* Washington, D.C.: Congressional Research Service.

Smith, David A. 1999. Mark-to-Market: A Fundamental Shift in Affordable Housing Policy. *Housing Policy Debate* 10(1):143–82.

Stanfield, Rochelle L. 1995. Simple Math. *National Journal*, November 18, pp. 2856–60.

Stegman, Michael A. 1991. The Excessive Costs of Creative Finance: Growing Inefficiencies in the Production of Low-Income Housing. *Housing Policy Debate* 2(2):357–73.

Stegman, Michael A. 1999. Comment on Jean Cummings and Denise DiPasquale's "The Low-Income Housing Tax Credit: An Analysis of the First Ten Years": Lifting the Veil of Ignorance. *Housing Policy Debate* 10(2):321–32.

Turner, Margery Austin, and Veronica Reed. 1990. *Housing America*. Washington, D.C.: Urban Institute.

U.S. Congress, Joint Economic Committee. 1972a. *The Economics of Federal Subsidy Programs: A Compendium of Papers*. Part V – Housing Subsidies. Washington, D.C.: Government Printing Office.

U.S. Congress, Joint Economic Committee. 1972b. Proxmire Releases Studies Evaluating Housing Subsidies. Press release. November 1.

U.S. Department of Housing and Urban Development. 1969. May 12 Statement by George Romney before the Subcommittee on Housing of the U.S. House Committee on Banking and Currency on Housing Goals. Unpublished HUD document.

U.S. Department of Housing and Urban Development. 1971a. January 19 Memorandum from Harold B. Finger to Secretary George Romney and Under Secretary Richard Van Dusen on the Housing Allowance Experiment. Unpublished HUD document.

U.S. Department of Housing and Urban Development. 1971b. *1972 Outlook*. Prepared for the White House by the Office of the Secretary, HUD. Author's files.

U.S. Department of Housing and Urban Development. 1972. December 28 Budget Appeal Letter from Secretary George Romney to President Richard M. Nixon for Fiscal Year 1974. Unpublished HUD document.

U.S. Department of Housing and Urban Development. 1973a. February 5 Memorandum from Harry T. Morley to Secretary James T. Lynn on OMB Actions on HUD Appeal Items. Unpublished HUD document.

U.S. Department of Housing and Urban Development. 1973b. *Housing in the Seventies*. Prepublication transmittal to members of Congress. October 6.

U.S. Department of Housing and Urban Development. 1976. Housing Assistance Block Grants. Unpublished staff paper.

U.S. Department of Housing and Urban Development. 1994. *Reinvention Blueprint*. Washington, D.C.

U.S. Department of Housing and Urban Development. 1995. *HUD Reinvention: From Blueprint to Action*. Washington, D.C.

U.S. Department of Housing and Urban Development. 1996. *U.S. Housing Market Conditions*. Washington, D.C.

Walker, Christopher. 1993. Nonprofit Housing Development: Status, Trends, and Prospects. *Housing Policy Debate* 4(3):369–414.

Wallace, James E. 1995. Financing Affordable Housing in the United States. *Housing Policy Debate* 6(4):785–814.

White, James R. 1997. Tax Credits: Opportunities to Improve Oversight of the Low-Income Housing Program. Testimony before the Subcommittee on Oversight, Committee on Ways and Means, House of Representatives. Washington, D.C.: U.S. General Accounting Office. April 23, pp. 2–4.

Winnick, Louis. 1995. The Triumph of Housing Allowance Programs: How a Fundamental Policy Conflict Was Resolved. *Cityscape* 1(3):95–121.

18

"Federal policy and the rise of nonprofit housing providers"

From *Journal of Housing Research* (2000)

Katherine M. O'Regan and John M. Quigley

INTRODUCTION

Nonprofit housing providers have been explicitly invited to participate in federal housing programs since the 1960s. However, in the past decade – specifically, since the passage of the Tax Reform Act of 1986 (TRA86) – federal housing policy has promoted much more explicitly a distinct role for nonprofit housing providers. Shortly after TRA86 was enacted, Congress began a systematic reevaluation of federal housing policy. The final report of this effort (National Housing Task Force 1988) embraced a multisectored and decentralized housing delivery system in which nonprofit organizations play a critical role. Prescriptions for federal policy included government subsidy but also the notion of government partnerships with private organizations. This theme is reflected in many subsequent federal actions, most notably in the Cranston-Gonzalez National Affordable Housing Act (NAHA) of 1990.

Of particular note, two of the largest federal programs for providing affordable housing include requirements that a specific percentage (a set-aside) of funds be allocated to nonprofit organizations. The Low-Income Housing Tax Credit (LIHTC) program was modified in 1988 (barely two years after it was originally authorized) to require that states allocate at least 10 percent of their annual tax credits to projects sponsored by nonprofit organizations. In 1990, HOME was created as part of NAHA. The HOME program requires that 15 percent of funds be set aside for community-based housing organizations (CBOs), a particular subset of nonprofit providers of housing. While

legislatively separate, these programs not only fund the same organizations but are frequently used to fund *the same housing units*.

This article focuses on these two programs to explore a particular aspect of the new federal role: specifically, federal support of nonprofit provision of affordable housing. Our objective is rather modest. We do not seek to assess programmatic success in providing housing per se but rather to assess the success of these programs in channeling resources to nonprofit housing providers. We first consider reasons why federal support has heightened, based on expressed rationales for nonprofit provision. Some, but not all, objectives in federal housing policy affect the relative importance of nonprofit providers. Recent emphasis on these policy objectives contributes to the increased federal emphasis on nonprofits. We then examine the LIHTC and HOME programs, their design, and their implementation in light of these themes. Finally, we examine issues raised by the design and implementation of these programs for the future course of federal policy toward the nonprofit housing industry.

BACKGROUND

Nonprofit organizations and affordable housing

There is an extensive literature on the role of nonprofit providers of housing – and specifically on the dominant form of such providers, community development corporations (CDCs). For summaries, see Keating, Krumholz, and Star

(1996), Stoutland (1999), Urban Institute (1995), and the U.S. Department of Housing and Urban Development (HUD) (1995). While this literature represents both supporters and detractors, there are common findings that provide the rationale underlying current federal emphasis on nonprofits.

The current model of nonprofit provision by CDCs has its roots in the late 1950s and early 1960s, in the civil rights movement, in urban unrest, and in reactions to the era of top-down urban renewal. Since that time, CDCs have dominated the nonprofit housing industry. CDCs are nonprofits with a distinctly local focus, through resident representation on a governing board and a mission that generally targets a limited geographic area. Thus, CDCs tend to be smaller organizations, producing fewer units of housing, in smaller-scale projects than nonprofit providers that are not community-based, referred to here as regional nonprofits (HUD 1995).

Nonprofits, and CDCs specifically, play a sizable role in providing affordable housing. For example, HUD has estimated that nonprofits produced more than 15 percent of all subsidized units from 1960 to 1990. In 1990, nonprofits produced 36,000 units (17 percent) of federally subsidized housing (HUD 1995). This total does not include units that are subsidized through the LIHTC program or through tax-exempt bonds. Nor does it include federally subsidized housing for the homeless or nonfederal public subsidies. National surveys of CDCs suggest that by 1994, more than 400,000 units of housing had been produced by CDCs (National Congress for Community Economic Development [NCCED] 1995).

Nonprofit production (and capacity to produce) is not uniformly distributed spatially. Nonprofit providers are located dispropor-tionately in larger cities and in the Middle Atlantic, the Pacific, and New England regions (HUD 1995; Urban Institute 1995).

While the importance of nonprofit organizations in the affordable housing industry is clear, the assessment of their performance in producing housing is less clear. Much of the literature on nonprofit housing provision is descriptive, and the case studies reported are not designed to test the relative performance of the organization. Furthermore, assessments of these organizations are complicated by their multiple objectives. Limited information on production costs suggests that nonprofits incur higher costs, perhaps because of inexperience, scale, or the location of production (Bratt, Vidal, and Schwartz 1998; Cummings and DiPasquale 1999; HUD 1995). However, these organizations provide a wider range of services to poorer or more-difficult-to-serve populations (Briggs, Mueller, and Sullivan 1997; HUD 1995). They also seem to have improved over their early experiences, as measured by the costs incurred in construction and by financial management (Cummings and DiPasquale 1998; Stegman 1999a).

Federal support for nonprofit housing providers increased in a sector that had already been found to face particular challenges, most notably maintaining adequate financial support and technical capacity, and overcoming costly patchwork financing (Schwartz et al. 1996; Urban Institute 1995). In audits and surveys of subsidized housing developments, the operating margins of nonprofits were found to be extremely thin (Bratt, Vidal, and Schwartz 1998; Cummings and DiPasquale 1999).

Rationale

The rationale for participation by the nonprofit sector in subsidized housing production is somewhat distinct from the ability of the sector to compete with for-profit developers in minimizing production costs. Three important factors distinguish the rationale from static efficiency comparisons of minimum-cost provision.

First, nonprofits are promoted as a critical component of the affordable housing industry because of their willingness to serve poorer tenants, who live in poorer neighborhoods and in projects with less financial security in economic returns (see, e.g., Urban Institute 1995; Vidal 1992). Arguments are seldom put forward that nonprofits will provide the *same* affordable housing at the *same* cost as for-profit firms, but rather that nonprofits will supply the housing that is the most difficult to induce from for-profit firms. Thus, to the extent that federal housing goals emphasize harder-to-serve populations or those with particularly low incomes, this rationale suggests a greater involvement of nonprofit providers.

Second, local CBOs may possess geograph-ically specific information and knowledge about appropriate solutions to local housing problems. In its pure form, this consideration is similar to the one encountered in deciding upon the provision of public services in a federal system. Decentralization rewards local initiative and knowledge of local needs. Thus, federal devolution of housing programs to state governments and to localities also suggests an increased role for locally based housing providers.

Third, there are clearly articulated goals of housing subsidy policy that are only weakly related to the production of housing units – for example, attention to social and physical externalities, citizen control, and the development of local political organizations. To the extent that federal urban development goals are broader than the physical production of adequate housing, their achievement may be more consistent with production of housing by nonprofit rather than for-profit entities. Note also that attention to these last two goals seems to be more consistent with CDC production than with production by regional nonprofit organizations.

Federal housing policy and the historical role of nonprofits

Large-scale federal support specifically for nonprofit housing arose with passage of the Section 202 Housing Program in 1959, a low-interest loan program providing housing for the elderly. The program was designed exclusively for nonprofit sponsorship. During its first 10 years, more than 45,000 units were produced, all by nonprofits (Rasey 1993). It seems clear that the original motivation for relying on the nonprofits was their presumed comparative advantage in serving the most disadvantaged.

Creation of the U.S. cabinet-level department HUD in 1965 greatly increased the federal presence in housing provision, and the 1968 Housing Act set forth ambitious production goals. The impact of this legislation was seen in the surge of production during the early 1970s (Orlebeke 1993). Because nonprofits were already participating in this industry, they benefited from the increased federal spending on production. While participation by nonprofit institutions was encouraged by the provision of seed money and technical assistance, the motivation was primarily to meet the higher production targets (Rasey 1993).

This federal support for housing production (in which nonprofits actively participated) came to an abrupt halt in 1973 with the Nixon administration's moratorium on new federal housing subsidies. Reevaluation of federal policy resulted in the 1974 Housing and Community Development Act, which shifted federal emphasis in two particularly relevant ways.

First, the 1974 act created the Community Development Block Grant (CDBG) program, a formula grant program that originally consolidated seven separate HUD programs and gave states and localities more control over spending decisions. CDBG is more broadly concerned with development than with the more narrow provision of housing. And it provides funding for a wide range of activities. As suggested above, moving to a decentralized and broadly defined housing program should lead to an increased emphasis on nonprofit provision. This increased emphasis on broader development objectives favors CDCs specifically. In fact, it was reported in the early 1990s that CDBG funding was the single most important source of federal funding for CDC providers of housing (Vidal 1992).

The second major shift in the 1974 act was in reaction to the costs and efficiencies of prior programs. The law mandated a decrease in government housing production. The Section 8 program authorized by the act encouraged private, for-profit, and nonprofit production.

During the 1980s, there was further withdrawal of resources and a reshaping of federal commitments. Federal capital expenditures for housing declined, and support shifted to demand-side housing subsidies, further reducing capital-intensive and production-oriented programs. And finally, the remaining federal resources dedicated to housing were increasingly focused. Several community development programs initiated during the Carter administration were eliminated. Together, these factors led to reduced federal support for nonprofit and community-based housing providers.

The large funding gap arising from changes in federal emphasis was reduced by two particularly important forces. First, more aggressive state and local governments began to take a role in providing affordable housing by creating their own programs, including the creation of independent state housing finance agencies to issue tax-exempt bonds specifically for housing.

Second, private foundations also became more aggressive in their efforts to develop a network of nonprofit housing developers. Two national intermediaries, the Local Initiatives Support Corporation (LISC) and the Enterprise Foundation, were created to operate as foundations, specifically to address the issue of capacity-building in the nonprofit sector. Both organizations provide financial and other assistance in support of neighborhood-based housing. A system of local intermediaries also began flourishing at this time, spurred in some cases by national or local foundations, in others by state and local governmental efforts.

By the late 1980s, CDCs were much less dependent on the federal government for their sources of funding. Diversified funding sources, increased financial security, and experience in housing provision each may have contributed to a more promising performance record during this period than during the 1960s. By 1990, 95 percent of U.S. cities reported CDCs as active developers of housing (Goetz 1992). This increase in the prevalence of nonprofit providers and the changing external perceptions of performance, itself, produced changes in federal policy options. While federal housing policy is not directly credited with these historical developments, current policy builds on the existence of a well-developed system of nonprofit providers whose performance is perceived to have improved substantially.

CURRENT FEDERAL PROGRAMS: LIHTC AND HOME

LIHTC

One notable feature of TRA86 was the removal of a broad array of incentives for real estate development, including removal of accelerated depreciation schedules, the imposition of "at-risk" provisions for depreciation, and the imposition of "line of business" and "passive investor" restrictions on the use of business losses to offset other income.

In anticipation that these changes would reduce incentives for the provision of low-income housing, Congress passed a more narrowly focused tax credit for new production of low-income housing, LIHTC.

LIHTC is administered by the U.S. IRS and state allocating agencies. Each year, the federal government (through the IRS) allocates tax credits of $1.25 per resident to the states. State agencies review applications submitted by developers and allocate the tax credits according to allocation criteria that reflect their own housing policy goals, within general federal guidelines. State plans must give priority to projects that serve the lowest-income tenants and those that ensure affordability for the longest period. Projects may be developed by for-profit or nonprofit organizations, but states must set aside 10 percent of the LIHTC funds they receive for use by nonprofit organizations.

LIHTC projects generally require complicated financial support. Developers typically sell the credits to syndicators, using the proceeds to finance the initial investment. The syndicator acts as the broker between the developer and the ultimate investor in tax credits. The emergence of syndicators, financial intermediaries with housing expertise, has been credited with the increased use of tax credits, and with their increased efficiency (Cummings and DiPasquale 1998; Stegman 1999a). Most LIHTC housing projects receive a variety of additional subsidies.

Several aspects of the LIHTC program suggest an enhanced role for nonprofits. LIHTC is a decentralized, supply-side program and invites the active participation of nonprofits. Allocations are made by state rather than federal agencies, which may benefit nonprofits, at least in those states in which a nonprofit system of housing delivery has been developed. While states may have an interest in using this program in conjunction with other programs to accomplish community development goals, the tax credit program itself does not embrace a broad view of housing services. Thus, it is not surprising that the nonprofit set-asides are not specifically targeted for CBOs.

HOME

HOME is the programmatic cornerstone of NAHA. It is a block grant program with objectives somewhat broader than housing production (including an emphasis on building flexible housing institutions for the provision of locally determined and appropriate housing). Its formal title, Home Investment Partnerships, reveals its emphasis on linkages (partnerships)

– between levels of governments, and between for-profit and nonprofit organizations. The legislation explicitly relies on nonprofit housing developers, noting the importance of increasing the number of capable organizations and the coverage of their networks.

To receive HOME funding, states and localities must submit a five-year comprehensive housing affordability strategy. These housing strategies require the coordination of activities with appropriate housing-related agencies in the private and nonprofit sectors as well as the public sector.

All participating jurisdictions, states as well as localities, must set aside at least 15 percent of HOME funds for Community Housing Development Organizations (CHDOs), community-based housing organizations with at least one year of experience in housing. HOME is thus a very decentralized housing program. States and localities are provided block funding that can be used to meet local needs – supply- or demand-side, ownership or rental. The legislative focus is on local determination of needs, and the broader community development focus suggests a key role for nonprofit CBOs.

NONPROFITS IN CURRENT FEDERAL PROGRAMS

In addition to embracing a larger role for nonprofits, NAHA also charged HUD with the task of assessing their record. HUD's 1995 report includes information on the relative importance of nonprofits in a variety of different federal housing programs (HUD 1995). Table 18.1 reports on the five federal programs producing the largest number of subsidized units during the 1960 to 1990 period. These five programs account for approximately 85 percent of all federally subsidized units created during these three decades. For each of these programs, the table indicates the share of funding that goes to nonprofits.

The variation in the share of funds to nonprofits is quite large. Programs oriented toward a harder-to-serve population (Section 202) and those encompassing broader definitions of housing (CDBG) rely more heavily on nonprofit provision. A comparison of the 1990 percentages to the three-decade averages suggests that the importance of nonprofits in these programs has not changed appreciatively over time. While nonprofits may have increased their presence in housing provision overall during this time period, they did not do so within these federal programs.

Whether nonprofits have increased their federal participation during the decade of the 1990s depends in large part on whether the LIHTC and HOME programs are an ongoing and sizable portion of federal activity and whether nonprofits participate heavily in these programs. Table 18.2 addresses the first question. This table provides time series

| | Percent Nonprofit | |
Program	1960–90	1990
Community development block grants[a]	13.0	13.3
Section 502	3.0	3.0
Section 8 new construction	9.0	–
Section 236 rental[b]	25.1	29.7
Section 515	5.0	5.0
Section 202[c]	100.0	100.0

Table 18.1 Share of funding received by nonprofits in the five largest federal subsidy programs, 1960 to 1990

Source: HUD (1995).

Notes:
[a] Housing portion only.
[b] New commitments for this program are made in Section 221(d)(3).
[c] All funds under Section 202 are reserved by law for nonprofit.

| Year | USDA Section 515 | HUD | | | | | IRS LIHTC* |
		Public Housing	Rent Supplement	Section 236	Section 8	Home	
1987	349,178	1,390,098	23,487	528,174	2,239,503	0	34,491
1988	368,456	1,397,907	23,476	528,174	2,332,462	0	115,899
1989	385,677	1,403,816	20,000	528,000	2,419,866	0	242,099
1990	401,941	1,404,870	20,000	530,625	2,500,462	0	316,128
1991	417,998	1,410,137	20,000	528,115	2,547,995	0	428,098
1992	433,616	1,409,191	20,000	510,422	2,722,477	–	519,398
1993	448,767	1,407,923	19,270	510,105	2,812,008	–	623,154
1994	463,742	1,409,455	18,808	504,966	2,925,959	–	740,253
1995	476,213	1,397,205	20,860	508,358	2,911,692	–	826,596
1996	482,980	1,388,746	20,860	505,305	2,958,162	111,003	903,599
1997	482,980	1,372,260	20,860	494,121	2,943,635	166,086	940,052
1998	482,980	1,295,437	20,860	476,451	3,000,935	209,193	1,041,874
1999	–	1,286,588	20,860	446,658	3,135,850	266,523	1,103,777
2000	–	1,243,100	20,860	420,017	320,583	302,146	–

Table 18.2 Rental dwelling units subsidized by federal programs, 1987 to 1998

Sources: Danter Company (2001), HUD (1992–98b, 1995), National Council of State Housing Agencies (1992), Olsen (2000), Quigley (2000), and Wallace (1998).

Note: *LIHTC numbers represent cumulative allocations. All other figures represent numbers of dwelling units actually subsidized.

information on the number of subsidized units produced by a variety of federally sponsored programs. These numbers are estimates, given data limitations and some double counting (some units receive multiple subsidies).

Since 1987, the number of dwellings subsidized by the Section 515 rural housing program increased by almost 15 percent, while the number of public housing units declined by a similar proportion. Rent supplements and Section 236 subsidies have declined more modestly. In contrast, the number of dwellings subsidized by Section 8 increased by almost half. Dwellings subsidized through the HOME and LIHTC programs have increased rapidly, and the number of LIHTC dwellings allocated is close to the number of dwellings in the public housing inventory. However, these two programs still constitute a small fraction of the entire inventory of federally subsidized rental units. We now analyze the extent to which nonprofits participate in these latter programs.

The early years of LIHTC and HOME

Information on the LIHTC and HOME programs is quite limited. As noted previously, LIHTC is under the oversight of the IRS, which does not report data routinely on this program. There have been several attempts to fill this gap in the past few years; each attempt has surveyed the presence of nonprofits at some point in time. The earliest study, conducted by ICF, Incorporated (1991) found that approximately 9 percent of LIHTC housing projects were sponsored by nonprofit organizations during the first two program years. (This was the period before the mandated 10 percent set-aside for nonprofits.) A subsequent survey by HUD (1996) found nonprofit sponsorship to be increasing, from 18.4 percent of units in 1992 to 26.7 percent in 1994. This is consistent with more recent work by Cummings and DiPasquale (1998, 1999) who estimated that 31 percent of projects were sponsored by nonprofits. The

Cummings and DiPasquale sample covers projects in service through 1996.

The HOME program is overseen by HUD but was slow to start (fiscal year 1992 was the first funding year), and the system for public provision of data is still under development. Two reports have been published that tabulate information on the first few years of the program.

The first report relied on data for HOME commitments made through part of 1994. It found that both state and local jurisdictions committed almost 30 percent of HOME funding to nonprofits, similar to the proportion devoted to nonprofits in the LIHTC housing program (Urban Institute 1995). Slightly less than half of this was for CHDO-sponsored housing, almost equal to the minimum set-aside required by the law. Program administrators reported that meeting the 15 percent CHDO set-aside was a challenge. Subsequent changes in legislation have facilitated the funding of CHDOs by permitting several nonproject uses of HOME funds. Moreover, if jurisdictions have difficulty spending their set-aside on CHDO-sponsored projects, up to 20 percent of the set-aside can be used to fund CHDO "capacity building."

In the more recent report, covering most of fiscal year 1996, jurisdictions reported fewer problems in meeting the CHDO set-aside regulations (Urban Institute 1999). Local jurisdictions reported that CHDOs were expected to receive 20 percent of jurisdictions' cumulative commitments, and nonprofits, as a class, were expected to receive approximately 26 percent.

To analyze more recent trends, we have compiled available data reflecting the cumulative share of funding allocated to nonprofits for each program for 1992 through 1998. Data for the LIHTC program are compiled from a state-level data source. Data for the HOME program are taken from HUD commitment reports. A few points are worth noting before turning to the evidence.

First, these data report the commitment of program allocations, rather than the number of completed units that have entered the inventory. Some fraction of allocations is made to projects that, for a variety of reasons, do not reach completion. Depending on the timing, these commitments may be reallocated (thereby showing up in future commitment data) or they may expire. Thus, to the extent that reallocations

occur frequently, commitment data may not be representative of the actual share of resources going to nonprofits. For the LIHTC program, comparisons of units committed with units in service for the years for which both are available suggest that this is not a problem (O'Regan 2000). For the HOME program data, as commitments have expired or been reallocated, HUD has revised its cumulative data, removing the bulk of double counting. Therefore, these cumulative data more closely reflect the actual level of funding received through HOME.

However, reallocation does mean commitment data will overstate somewhat the aggregate flow of resources. Much of this double counting has been removed from the HUD HOME data. Under the LIHTC program, reallocation appears to have been much more common during the early years of the program.

It is also worth noting that the LIHTC data report the dollar allocation of a tax credit for one year. In fact, these allocations each represent a 10-year stream of benefits. Specifically, each tax-credit dollar allocated provides its owner with 10 dollars of tax credits over a 10-year time period. This should be kept in mind when focusing on the aggregate resources received by nonprofits and when comparing resources across programs.

Table 18.3 presents state-level cumulative data for both programs, by region. As noted previously, the spatial distribution of nonprofit housing providers is not uniform. We thus find large regional differences in commitments of tax credits to nonprofits. Nonprofits received twice as large a share of tax-credit commitments in the Northeast as they did in the South.

Overall, 30 percent of tax credit commitments have been made to nonprofit providers. Compared with other federal housing programs, this is a large fraction. This is also considerably higher than the 10 percent mandated by the law. To the extent that the LIHTC program becomes a more important component of the stock of assisted housing (as suggested in Table 18.2), the presence of nonprofits also will increase.

Table 18.3 presents similar information for CHDO participation in the portions of the HOME program allocated to state and local governments. (Data for a broader definition of nonprofits are generally not available.) Nationally, the proportions of HOME allocations committed to CHDOs are quite similar for the

| Region | Program | Allocations (dollars in thousands) | | |
		Total	Nonprofit or CHDO	Percent to Nonprofits
Northeast	LIHTC*	553,746	256,720	46.40
	HOME (state)	620,310	156,661	25.26
	HOME (local)	1,583,100	329,201	20,80
Midwest	LIHTC*	641,320	187,506	29.20
	HOME (state)	905,812	195,473	21.58
	HOME (local)	1,109,763	295,944	26.70
South	LIHTC*	919,022	186,799	20.30
	HOME (state)	1,426,186	237,277	16.63
	HOME (local)	1,291,857	259,010	20.00
West	LIHTC*	649,643	215,878	33.20
	HOME (state)	601,238	122,644	20.40
	HOME (local)	1,298,602	274,426	21.10
Total U.S.	LIHTC*	2,813,707	862,727	30.70
	HOME (state)	3,601,645	721,741	20.04
	HOME (local)	5,317,101	1,163,729	21.90

Table 18.3 LIHTC and HOME allocations by region (percent of allocations committed to nonprofits or CHDOs, 1992 to 1998)

Source: HUD (1992–98a) and National Council of State Housing Agencies (1992–98).

Note: *Each dollar committed represents a 10-year stream of benefits worth one dollar each year.

portions controlled by states and localities, each near 20 percent. Again, this allocation is somewhat higher than the 15 percent required by legislation. Because CHDOs are only a portion of the nonprofit sector, the presence of nonprofits in the HOME program may be similar in magnitude to that found for LIHTC.

Regional funding patterns for the state portion of HOME funds show a pattern quite similar to that for the LIHTC. Nonprofits (CHDOs) are most prominent in the Northeast and considerably less so in the South. In fact, almost a third of southern states did not meet the required 15 percent CHDO funding set-aside requirement during this time period.

Time series data

While the data maintained by HUD do not permit a time series analysis, some annual data are available for both the LIHTC and state HOME programs through the National Council of State Housing Agencies (NCSHA). These data are limited, but they do permit us to examine trends over time. NCSHA is a nonprofit membership organization for state housing finance agencies (HFAs) that conducts an annual survey of HFA activities, including LIHTC (starting in 1987). Survey results are publicly available beginning with 1992. This source also publishes HOME data, but only for those state HFAs that also administer state HOME funds. Thus, the available data cover only a part of state HOME funds. By 1998, however, 38 of the 52 HOME state jurisdictions were covered by the NCSHA data. In terms of total HOME funding, this accounts for 65 percent of state-level HOME funds.

These data differ not only in coverage of the two programs but also in quality. For the LIHTC program, data reported in different sections of the source books appear to be consistent. They are also internally consistent over time and generally agree with the few external sources that can be used as benchmarks. Our confidence in the LIHTC data is quite high, particularly after the first two years of reporting. The HOME data appear somewhat less consistent.

We speculate that there are two main factors contributing to differences in accuracy of the data. First, double counting is probably more important for HOME funds, since commitments have a longer holding time before expiring. Second, programmatic differences in the commitment processes may be reflected in the quality of data.

To assess the seriousness of these deficiencies, in Table 18.4 we compare data for

	HUD Data	NCSHA Sample		HUD Data	NCSHA Sample
Northeast			*Midwest*		
Connecticut	23.1	–	Illinois	16.2	23.4
Maine	18.1	19.9	Indiana	31.8	37.5
Massachusetts	28.7	32.6	Iowa	14.3	17.2
New Hampshire	30.3	29.8	Kansas	15.8	28.9
New Jersey	18.2	–	Michigan	24.5	47.8
New York	29.6	24.0	Minnesota	22.1	22.3
Pennsylvania	17.0	44.8	Missouri	24.8	16.8
Rhode Island	58.1	51.1	Nebraska	60.2	–
Vermont	23.0	–	North Dakota	15.8	–
Total Northeast	25.3	29.1	Ohio	15.4	–
using NCSHA sample*	27.6		South Dakota	16.8	12.7
			Wisconsin	21.9	–
			Total Midwest	22.6	30.5
			using NCSHA sample*	22.1	
South			*West*		
Alabama	23.1	39.1	Arizona	17.2	27.8
Arkansas	21.9	24.1	California	17.8	–
District of Columbia	14.6	–	Idaho	33.5	30.5
Florida	15.8	16.5	Montana	43.8	43.9
Georgia	12.9	15.2	Nevada	29.5	19.8
Kentucky	15.7	20.9	New Mexico	15.2	14.4
Louisiana	15.2	15.2	Oregon	26.8	44.1
Maryland	22.0	29.8	Utah	15.7	–
Mississippi	18.9	–	Washington	19.6	–
North Carolina	13.8	21.1	Wyoming	17.6	16.4
Oklahoma	30.0	23.1	Total West	20.4	28.8
South Carolina	12.1	30.3	using NCSHA sample*	25.0	
Tennessee	12.8	25.4			
Texas	13.2	18.5			
Virginia	17.3	5.6			
West Virginia	16.7	16.4			
Total South	16.6	21.4	Total U.S.	20.0	25.2
using NCSHA sample*	15.7		using NCSHA sample*	20.1	

Table 18.4 State HOME allocations reserved for CHDOs, 1992 to 1998 (percent)

Sources: HUD (1992–98a) and NCSHA (1992–98).

Note: *Percentage of funds allocated to CHDOs based on HUD data for states that are in the NCSHA data.

our sample of state administrators with the cumulative HUD data presented previously. To control for differences in sample coverage, we also report regional and national percentages using HUD data for the same states that are included in the NCSHA sample.

Nationally, the HUD data indicate a lower share of state HOME funds committed to CHDOs over this seven-year period than do the NCSHA data, 20 compared with 25 percent. Data for some regions and states match quite well; others do not match. The smallest differences are found in the Northeast, with above average CHDO participation reported in both data sources (approximately 28 and 29 percent for both sources using comparable samples).

In the West, the difference in reported regional rates is primarily caused by the difference in sample coverage. In the Midwest and the South, however, the HUD data consistently report lower CHDO commitment rates. As noted, the HUD data have been purged of "unsuccessful" commitments. Thus, the differences in reported rates suggest that states in these two regions have more consistently misjudged the translation of CHDO commitments into final projects, or else that these states have simply had more difficulty completing such projects. Significantly, these are the regions in which networks of nonprofits and CDC housing producers are less well developed.

Table 18.5 is based on the NCSHA data. It presents the share of commitments made to nonprofits generally, for each program in each year, by region. The final two columns provide a summary of allocations for different periods.

As expected, the share of state-level HOME funding committed to nonprofits is higher than for CHDOs. In fact, the share is 50 percent higher. In each region, nonprofits receive a larger portion of HOME funding than of LIHTC funding. In light of the comparisons in Table 18.4, however, some of this difference may simply be attributable to overly optimistic reports of HOME nonprofit commitments. Even if the national rate for HOME is only slightly higher than for LIHTC, however, this would result in more than 30 percent of state HOME resources going to nonprofit housing providers.

Table 18.5 also provides a time series, nationally and by region. Nationally, neither of these programs shows much change in reliance on nonprofits over time. This is consistent with the pattern observed in Table 18.1 for several other federal housing programs. This finding is quite surprising for the HOME program, in light of the extensive discussion among policy makers of capacity-building. As noted earlier, there has been a growth in the participation of nonprofits in the LIHTC program since its formative years. The growth reported during the first years of the program appears to have stopped, however.

While the national figures are remarkably constant, there have been some changes within each of the regions. In the Northeast and the West, the two regions with the largest share of

| Region | Program | Individual Years | | | | | | | Range of Years | |
		1992	1993	1994	1995	1996	1997	1998	1992–93	1994–98
Northeast	LIHTC	57.10	55.20	33.50	44.70	44.80	43.70	49.50	56.10	42.80
	HOME	79.93	53.40	53.24	47.75	68.93	48.78	18.10	55.76	46.99
Midwest	LIHTC	19.80	22.20	25.60	37.30	30.90	33.50	34.30	21.10	31.90
	HOME	36.49	43.88	46.65	32.54	38.15	58.64	35.88	40.60	43.18
South	LIHTC	15.60	12.60	17.30	25.90	23.50	23.50	23.30	13.70	22.50
	HOME	35.92	36.40	38.31	37.55	42.46	51.37	39.52	36.20	41.67
West	LIHTC	49.10	34.90	41.20	35.00	18.50	21.80	24.30	41.50	29.30
	HOME	42.93	90.90	59.64	57.26	35.81	52.90	33.72	66.82	47.34
U.S.	LIHTC	35.20	28.20	28.10	34.90	28.20	30.00	31.00	31.30	30.40
	HOME	38.40	45.48	44.63	39.55	44.94	53.49	35.48	42.87	43.67

Table 18.5 LIHTC and HOME funds allocated by state housing finance agencies to nonprofit organizations, 1992 to 1998 (percent)

Source: NCSHA (1992–98).

commitments to nonprofits for both programs, the share of funds allocated to nonprofits has declined since the early 1990s. In the Midwest and the South, two regions in which nonprofits had the lowest LIHTC participation as of 1992, the share of commitments to nonprofits continued to grow through the mid-1990s. If capacity-building for nonprofits is reflected by the minimum presence of nonprofits, this pattern is consistent with a growth in underlying capacity.

The NCSHA data also indicate the total number of CHDOs by state. Table 18.6 summarizes these data, which may reflect the building of capacity and the growth of nonprofits by region. To control for variations in size among states and regions, we also present the number of CHDOs per million dollars of initial-year HOME allocations.

There was a remarkable growth in the number of CHDOs between 1992 and 1998. The growth has been continuous through 1998 and has occurred in all regions. We note that this growth is in the organizations recognized by

the state government as providing community-based housing. It is possible that much of this growth occurred because an increased number of preexisting providers have undertaken state qualification. This is particularly likely during the first years of the program.

From 1994 onward, CHDO numbers have continued to increase in each region, except the South. In fact, almost all nonsouthern states experienced continual CHDO growth. If some of the increase in the number of CHDOs represents the increased capacity of the local nonprofit housing sector, this pattern suggests only mixed success. The South, which has historically lagged in its CDC provision of housing, continues to lag. But much of the Midwest, which had also lagged in CDC housing provision, has experienced a high rate of CHDO growth.

The increase in number of CHDOs has far outpaced the growth in HOME funding, so it is difficult to attribute the CHDO growth to HOME funding alone. The growth in CHDOs does not appear to be the result of large increases in

	1992	1993	1994	1995	1996	1997	1998
Number of CHDOs							
Northwest	31	103	145	151	221	230	248
Midwest	63	81	139	154	217	259	244
South	108	194	313	365	312	328	383
West	26	31	58	91	106	116	111
U.S.	229	413	660	769	865	942	990
*CHDOs per million dollars**							
Northwest	1.21	2.40	2.73	2.84	4.16	4.33	4.67
Midwest	1.54	1.79	3.06	3.40	3.87	4.62	4.38
South	1.03	1.64	2.63	2.66	2.28	2.64	2.79
West	1.62	2.39	2.51	3.45	4.02	4.40	4.21
U.S.	1.20	1.84	2.70	2.82	3.12	3.56	3.57
Nonproject expenditures (percent)							
Northwest	24.3	0.6	2.2	27.5	1.2	5.5	0.9
Midwest	5.4	2.4	8.8	11.3	6.4	9.2	4.2
South	1.6	3.6	6.6	5.0	5.0	5.4	6.6
West	0.0	2.1	5.3	7.7	11.8	6.8	7.6
U.S.	5.4	2.3	6.1	8.9	5.0	7.1	5.4

Table 18.6 Number of CHDOs and percent of HOME funds spent on nonproject uses, 1992 to 1998

Source: NCSHA (1992–98).

Note: *Number of CHDOs divided by initial year (1992) allocation in millions of dollars.

funding through capacity-building grants or through the funding of operating expenses, either. The share of CHDO funding that goes for nonproject expenses is quite low, and, as noted in Table 18.6, there is no clear trend.

We have compared the simple correlations across states with various measures of the allocations of funds under the HOME and LIHTC programs. Table 18.7 reports a series of simple correlation coefficients, computed separately for each year between 1992 and 1998. In comparing programs, we find small but positive correlations between state shares of funding going to nonprofits in the two programs. This is not surprising, since these state programs operate within the same nonprofit housing networks and local housing conditions. LIHTC funding for nonprofits is much less correlated with the portion of HOME commitments going specifically to CHDOs, however.

The expectation that the availability of nonprofit institutions would affect the share of nonprofit funding is only partially borne out in the data. During the first year or two of the HOME program, states with greater representation of CHDOs spent a significantly larger portion of their funding on both CHDOs specifically and nonprofits generally. But surprisingly, there is essentially no correlation between the level of funding for nonprofits (CHDOs) and the availability of CHDOs after 1993. States with a larger representation of CBOs are not spending a greater share of state HOME funding on nonprofits (CHDOs).

However, after 1993, there is a positive and significant correlation between the presence of CHDOs and LIHTC allocations to nonprofits. States that have a larger number of CHDOs spend a greater share of their LIHTC funding on nonprofits. These results are consistent with the recent evaluation of a national effort to increase CDC funding and capacity that was conducted by the Urban Institute (1998). This evaluation concluded that CDC capacity and LIHTC funding had become much more highly correlated through the 1990s.

Finally, the federal focus on nonprofit providers is based on an assumption that these organizations provide a different product or serve a more disadvantaged clientele than do other providers. Even with the limited data available, it is possible to investigate this assumption. We have assembled state data, from 1992 through 1998, on the share of LIHTC units that serve the lowest income population and the share located in particularly poor census tracts. For the HOME program, we have data only for 1996 to 1998 and only by income category. Simple correlations across states by year are reported in Table 18.8.

There are consistent positive and significant correlations between the characteristics that represent harder-to-serve populations in harder-to-serve neighborhoods and the share of LIHTC allocations committed to nonprofits. These results are consistent with our expectations about the role of nonprofits. However, the limited data for the HOME program provides little positive evidence.

Correlations between	1992	1993	1994	1995	1996	1997	1998
Share of LIHTC allocated to nonprofits and							
Share of HOME to nonprofits	−0.12	0.53	0.39	0.21	0.27	0.08	0.37
Share of HOME to CHDOs	−0.24	0.13	0.31	0.07	0.17	−0.02	0.12
CHDOs per million	−0.02	0.09	0.03	0.34	0.33	0.30	0.21
CHDOs per million dollars and							
HOME share to nonprofits	0.69	−0.04	−0.07	−0.04	−0.20	−0.25	−0.02
HOME share to CHDOs	0.73	0.39	−0.04	0.16	−0.20	−0.19	0.00
Share of CHDOs to nonproject uses	0.20	−0.04	0.25	0.04	0.35	−0.02	0.14

Table 18.7 Simple correlations among state allocations

Source: Authors' calculations based on data reported in NCSHA (1992–98).

Correlation between	1992	1993	1994	1995	1996	1997	1998
Share of LIHTC allocated to nonprofits and							
Share of LIHTC units in poor census tracts	0.35	0.26	0.38	0.39	0.28	0.16	0.13
Share of LIHTC units to lowest-income households	0.01	0.32	0.20	0.48	0.34	0.30	0.29
Share of HOME allocated to lowest-income households and							
Share of HOME to nonprofits	–	–	–	–	0.20	0.15	−0.13
Share of HOME to CHDOs	–	–	–	–	0.27	0.07	−0.04

Table 18.8 Simple correlations between state allocations and uses for hard-to-serve populations

Source: Authors' calculations based on data reported in NCSHA (1992–98).

CONCLUDING COMMENTS

In our examination of the LIHTC and HOME programs, we find that nonprofits do, in fact, receive a larger portion of funding in these programs than they have in other historically important sources of low-income housing production. This suggests that the federal partnering with nonprofits has been more than a rhetorical flourish.

The share of federal funding going to nonprofits under these two programs does not appear to have increased significantly after the first few years of operation. The introduction of the LIHTC and HOME programs seems to have caused a one-time increase in the overall level of federal funding for nonprofits. However, the change in regional patterns indicates that some regions have experienced significant growth in local nonprofit providers, and these are the regions where LIHTC funding has been particularly focused on nonprofits.

This is completely consistent with the existence of a market niche, or a narrow comparative advantage for nonprofit housing providers. Rough evidence from the LIHTC program is consistent with state reliance on nonprofits for exactly these purposes. If this is correct, we should expect to observe a portion, but a stable portion, of funding going to nonprofits.

What is the future of federal policy toward nonprofit housing providers? Support for nonprofit housing providers is likely to depend on the extent to which federal policy emphasizes

the factors for which nonprofit provision has a comparative advantage. Earlier, we suggested three trends in housing policy that converged in the 1990s to increase the participation by nonprofit organizations. Federal efforts to address harder-to-serve populations, to decentralize decision making, and to emphasize broader development objectives are likely to continue. All of these reinforce the position of nonprofit providers. The most likely source of a shift away from federal support for this sector would be an increased emphasis on demand-oriented housing subsidies rather than supply-side funding. Federal housing policy has moved slowly in this direction during the past quarter century.

The future of demand-side subsidies itself raises questions for nonprofit providers. The current LIHTC subsidy level is simply not deep enough to reach particularly low-income households. Yet states have been using LIHTC to serve low-income populations by combining subsidies, including Section 8 certificates. In 1996, for example, 40 percent of LIHTC households also were receiving direct rental subsidies (U.S. General Accounting Office 1997). If this subsidy were curtailed substantially, it would be far more difficult to serve this population using newly constructed LIHTC housing. Moreover, most existing nonprofit housing developments would face serious financial dislocations.

Furthermore, if federal policy generally continues to support activities in which nonprofits specialize, both the HOME and

LIHTC programs will be decentralized, with priorities set by state and local jurisdictions. In the LIHTC program, states have decreased their percentages of funds set aside for nonprofits, suggesting that nonprofits will be competing more directly with other housing providers on the basis of state priorities for project characteristics (Stegman 1999b). Some priorities, such as serving poorer populations or neighborhoods, may suggest continued support of nonprofits. Others, however, may not. For example, several states have explicitly favored preservation of existing stock over production; others have expanded their use of tax credits for public-housing HOPE VI projects. These latter changes in state priorities move resources away from areas in which nonprofit housing activity has been traditionally active.

In summary, it seems clear that the LIHTC and HOME programs have increased federal housing resources for nonprofits. At a time when adequacy of resources was the principal concern for nonprofit performance, this general programmatic characteristic fit the circumstances. However, nonprofit housing finance is complicated by an uncertain system of patchwork financing. This is costly and often requires expertise and capacity that many organizations simply lack. The LIHTC and HOME programs do nothing to address this concern. To the extent that these federal programs continue to support nonprofits, their form could be improved. Improvements in performance are needed beyond those that nonprofits face as housing producers. And those improvements include their performance as managers if they are to have an important role in maintaining the stock of affordable housing. The financial thinness of nonprofit housing projects has been highlighted in recent assessments of nonprofit housing management, suggesting that current forms of programs encouraging nonprofit suppliers are far from ideal.

REFERENCES

Bratt, Rachel, Avis Vidal, and Alex Schwartz. 1998. The Status of Nonprofit-Owned Affordable Housing: Short-Term Successes and Long-Term Challenges. *Journal of the American Planning Association* 64(winter):39–51.

Briggs, Xavier de Souza, Elizabeth Mueller, and Mercer Sullivan. 1997. *From Neighborhood to Community: Evidence on the Social Effects of Community Development*. New York: New School for Social Research, Community Development Research Center.

Cummings, Jean L., and Denise DiPasquale. 1998. *Building Affordable Rental Housing*. Boston: City Research.

Cummings, Jean L., and Denise DiPasquale. 1999. The Low-Income Housing Tax Credit: An Analysis of the First Ten Years. *Housing Policy Debate* 10(2):251–308.

Danter Company. 2001. 1999 Tax Credit Allocation Data. World Wide Web page http://www.danter.com/taxcredit/stats.htm (accessed May 4).

Goetz, Edward. 1992. Local Government Support for Nonprofit Housing: A Survey of U.S. Cities. *Urban Affairs Quarterly* 27(4):420–35.

ICF, Incorporated. 1991. *Evaluation of the Low-Income Housing Tax Credit*. Final Report. Washington, D.C.

Keating, W. Dennis, Norman Krumholz, and Philip Star, eds. 1996. *Revitalizing Urban Neighborhoods*. Lawrence, KS: University of Kansas Press.

National Congress for Community Economic Development. 1995. *Taking Hold*. Washington, D.C.

National Council of State Housing Agencies. 1992–98. *Factbook*. Washington, D.C.

National Housing Task Force. 1988. *A Decent Place to Live*. Washington, D.C.

O'Regan, Katherine. 2000. The Low Income Housing Tax Credit: Adding States to the Analysis. Unpublished paper.

Olsen, Edgar O. 2000. What Do We Know About the Effects of U.S. Housing Programs for the Poor? Paper prepared for the NBER Conference on Means-Tested Transfer Programs in the U.S.

Orlebeke, Charles J. 1993. Federal Housing Policies. In *Affordable Housing and Public Policy: Strategies for Metropolitan Chicago*, ed. Lawrence B. Joseph. Champaign, IL: University of Illinois Press.

Quigley, John M. 2000. A Decent Home: Housing Policy in Perspective. *Brookings Papers on Urban Affairs* 1(1):53–88.

Rasey, Keith P. 1993. The Role of Neighborhood-Based Housing Nonprofits in the Ownership and Control of Housing in U.S. Cities. In *Ownership, Control and the Future of Housing Policy,* ed. R. Allen Hays. Westport, CT: Greenwood Press.

Schwartz, Alex, Rachel Bratt, Avis Vidal, and Langley Keyes. 1996. Nonprofit Housing Organizations and Institutional Support: The Management Challenge. *Journal of Urban Affairs* 18(4):389–407.

Stegman, Michael. 1999a. Comment on Jean L. Cummings and Denise DiPasquale's "The Low Income Housing Tax Credit: An Analysis of the First Ten Years: Lifting the Veil of Ignorance." *Housing Policy Debate* 10(2):251–308.

Stegman, Michael. 1999b. *State and Local Affordable Housing Programs: A Rich Tapestry.* Washington, D.C.: Urban Land Institute.

Stoutland, Sara. 1999. Community Development Corporations: Mission, Strategy, and Accomplishments. In *Urban Problems and Community Development,* ed. Ronald Fergusan and William Dickens. Washington, D.C.: Brookings Institution.

Urban Institute.1995. Implementing Block Grants for Housing: An Evaluation of the First Year of HOME, HC-5898. Washington, D.C.: U.S. Department of Housing and Urban Development.

Urban Institute. 1998. Community Development in the 1990s, ed. Christopher Walker and Mark Weinheimer. Washington, D.C.: U.S. Department of Housing and Urban Development.

Urban Institute. 1999. *Expanding the Nation's Supply of Affordable Housing: An Evaluation of the HOME Investment Partnership Program.* Washington, D.C.: U.S. Department of Housing and Urban Development, Office of Policy Development and Research.

U.S. Department of Housing and Urban Development. 1992–98a. CHDO Reservation Report. Washington, D.C.

U.S. Department of Housing and Urban Development. 1992–98b. HOME Production Report. Washington, D.C.

U.S. Department of Housing and Urban Development. 1995. *Status and Prospects of the Nonprofit Housing Sector.* HUD Report 6758. Washington, D.C.: Office of Policy Development and Research.

U.S. Department of Housing and Urban Development. 1996. *Development and Analysis of the National Low-Income Housing Tax Credit Database.* Washington, D.C.

U.S. General Accounting Office. 1997. *Tax Credits: Opportunities to Improve the Oversight of the Low-Income Housing Program.* Washington, D.C.

Vidal, Avis. 1992. *Rebuilding Communities: A National Study of Urban Community Development Corporations.* New York: New School for Social Research, Graduate School of Management and Urban Policy, Community Development Research Center.

Wallace, James E. 1998. Evaluating the Low Income Housing Tax Credit. In *Evaluating Tax Expenditures: Tools and Techniques for Assessing Outcomes.* San Francisco: Jossey Bass.

19

"The Low-Income Housing Tax Credit as an aid to housing finance: How well has it worked?"

From *Housing Policy Debate* (2000)

Kirk McClure

University of Kansas

INTRODUCTION

The Low-Income Housing Tax Credit (LIHTC) program, which is now over 10 years old, has become the nation's primary mechanism for encouraging the production of housing to be occupied by low- or moderate-income households (Wallace 1995). Efforts are being made to expand and improve on this program to make it more efficient and effective.

The program has been viewed as both a success and a failure. It has been a success in that it has generated many rental housing units that are now occupied by low- and moderate-income households. Although estimates vary, the program has contributed to the rehabilitation or construction of somewhere between 500,000 and 900,000 units (Cummings and DiPasquale 1999; Ernst & Young 1997). This success has been attributed to the program's flexibility. Units have been built across the country, in a variety of markets and serving a broad range of housing needs (Abt Associates, Inc. 1996; Cummings and DiPasquale 1999; Ernst & Young 1997; U.S. General Accounting Office [GAO] 1997). However, those who argue that the program is overly complex and poorly designed to serve the needs of low-income households view it as a failure (Stegman 1991). In addition, it has been criticized for giving excessive subsidies to investors, beyond what is required to induce them to develop the properties (Case 1991).

The research reported here addresses these criticisms. Using a sample of projects developed in Missouri during the first 10 years of the program, it is possible to determine the complexity involved in financing these projects. Specifically, what are the public and private sources of financing? Do the proceeds from the syndication of the tax credits get invested in the property or do they benefit the developer? What are the other sources of equity? Why are additional layers of subsidy needed to make these projects financially feasible?

Review of the program

The intent of the program is to provide enough incentives to ensure that there will be an adequate supply of low-income housing (Guggenheim 1994) by granting tax credits to the owners of selected rental housing developed for occupancy by low- or moderate-income households. Although the subsidy is provided entirely through the federal tax code, it is administered through state government agencies, generally the state housing finance agency. States may allocate these tax credits annually up to a total equaling $1.25 per capita.[1]

The program is discretionary; the subsidy is not given as an entitlement to all housing developments occupied by low- or moderate-income rental households. Rather, proposed developments are selected by the state administrative agency through a competitive process. Winners must develop their project, either through new construction or rehabilitation of an existing property. When the property is occupied, the program begins to grant tax credits against the tax liability of the property owners over a 10-year period, provided that the units maintain restricted-income occupancy for at least 15 years.

Since 1989, occupancy by low- or moderate-income households must be pledged for 30 years, but after 15 years, the owners of the development may notify the state administrative agency of an intention to convert the development to market-rate operation. If within 1 year of receiving this notice, the state agency cannot find a buyer willing to pay a price determined by statutory formula and willing to maintain the property in income-restricted occupancy, then the property may be converted to market-rate operation. If it is converted, however, the tenants at the time of conversion must be held harmless for a period of 3 years. This means that the guarantee of low- or moderate-income occupancy may run for no more than 15 to 18 years, but could run for as long as 30 years.[2]

The development's owners may claim credits only against units occupied by income-eligible households. No credits may be claimed unless either of the following conditions is met:

1. At least 20 percent of the units are occupied by households whose income is less than 50 percent of the metropolitan area's median family income, or
2. At least 40 percent of the units are occupied by households whose income is less than 60 percent of the metropolitan area's median family income

The developer must choose to meet one of these two standards before the housing begins operations.

Annual credits are granted against the costs of the buildings, site improvements, and equipment, which comprise most development expenses other than land cost. Credits are in the amount of about 9 percent of the depreciable costs of the new construction or substantial rehabilitation performed and about 4 percent of the acquisition cost. These amounts are approximate and are adjusted monthly by the government to maintain the present value of the 10 years of credits at 70 percent of the cost of new construction or substantial rehabilitation and 30 percent of the acquisition cost. The present value is calculated using a discount rate determined by the U.S. Department of the Treasury.

Credits of 9 percent are granted only against costs that are not funded through federal subsidies over and above the tax credits. These additional federal subsidies are generally found in the form of publicly assisted financing – for example, funding by the state's housing finance agency. If the development receives tax-exempt financing, then the 9 percent credit rate drops to 4 percent. In addition, if the development benefits from a grant provided through federal sources, such as the HOME program, then the basis against which the credit is applied must be reduced by the amount of the grant.

Rents on the units against which credits are claimed must be determined according to affordability standards set for the metropolitan area. These rents are based on what a family could afford if it paid 30 percent of its income for housing, including contract rent plus tenant-paid utility expenses. These rents vary with the number of bedrooms in the unit. What is important to note is that the allowed rents are based on metropolitan household income and expense criteria, not the income or utility expenses of the actual tenant residing in the unit. As a result, the program does not guarantee that an individual tenant household will not have to pay more than 30 percent of its income for rent, only that the rent will be held down to a level considered affordable by standards within the metropolitan area.

Adherence is enforced by the state administrative agency, which is also called on to periodically inspect the physical condition of the units and to review the process through which property managers certify the tenant household's income eligibility. If the development is failing to comply with any of the program's provisions, then a notice of noncompliance may be issued. If noncompliance becomes sufficiently severe, tax credits may be recaptured and penalties imposed on the property owners.

Program implementation

While the LIHTC program has many intricacies, its implementation tends to follow a relatively standard pattern. Within each state, the administrative agency announces a round of funding. Various developers, both for-profit and nonprofit entities, prepare proposals requesting tax credits for some or all of the units. The state administrative agency selects the most meritorious developments on the basis of published criteria and awards them credits.

If a development receives an award, the developer works to arrange the necessary financing to cover construction costs and to arrange the permanent financing to pay off construction loans when the project is completed. Debt financing is placed with one or more lenders (private sector lenders, public sector lenders, or both). At the same time, the developer seeks equity financing for the project. Usually, this is secured by bringing investors into a limited partnership that will own the property. Investors will make periodic cash contributions through the construction period and, frequently, through the early years of project operation as well. Contributions are given in exchange for the tax credits received over the first 10 years of operation. In addition, the investors may pay for any or all of the other benefits of ownership, including any cash flow that may be experienced, any surplus depreciation generated by the development, and any residual value the property may have when it is sold.

The project is built and goes into operation with periodic inspection by the state administrative agency. Tenants are selected for occupancy just as they are for any other rental property, except that they must also be screened for income eligibility.

Program history

Tax Reform Act of 1986

The LIHTC program was created by the Tax Reform Act of 1986, which significantly reduced the previously generous tax benefits available to all real estate, including low-income housing. During the period leading up to passage of the act, there was a great deal of political pressure for general tax reform. However, a coalition of housing providers and advocacy groups recognized the harm that would be done to low-income housing development if the act contained no special provisions to protect it. Case (1991) describes the response of this

coalition as a "panic" leading them to push for inclusion of the hastily drawn up LIHTC program in the Tax Reform Act. The act was passed, and the program came into existence. However, it began under the cloud of a sunset provision that would kill the program in three years unless Congress extended it.

Omnibus Budget Reconciliation Act of 1989 (Public Law 101–239)

This act extended the life of the LIHTC program, but only for a year. At the time this act was being debated, the problems of expiring subsidy and preserving assisted housing in low-income occupancy were at the center of the debate over assisted housing. Possibly in response to this debate, the act extended the original occupancy period for LIHTC units from 15 to 30 years. The extension was considerably weakened by a provision permitting conversion of the units to market-rate operation if no buyer willing to purchase the development and maintain its restricted-income operation could be found. The act also reduced the annual allocation of tax credits from the original amount of $1.25 per capita to $.9375 per capita.

In the wake of the investigations of U.S. Department of Housing and Urban Development (HUD) scandals and misuse of federal housing contracts, the act prohibited combining subsidy from LIHTC with subsidy from the Section 8 Moderate Rehabilitation program.

The 1989 act also recognized the special problems of developing low- and moderate-income housing in high-cost and low-income areas. Beginning with buildings placed in service in 1990, the act permitted larger tax credits for certain developments. These credits could be 30 percent larger if the development is located in either of two areas:

1. A difficult development area (DDA), a county with high construction, land, and utility costs relative to the income levels of the area, or
2. A qualifying census tract (QT), a tract where at least 50 percent of the households have an income that is less than 60 percent of the area median family income

Finally, the 1989 act began to set minimum standards for the state administrative agencies in terms of how they selected the developments that received tax credits. Housing agencies were required to give highest priority to projects with "the highest percentage of the housing credit dollar amount to be used for project costs" (Section 7108). In other words, emphasis was placed on applying the proceeds of the tax credits to the development rather than having them retained by the developer. In addition, "the housing credit dollar amount … shall not exceed the amount the housing credit agency determines is necessary for the financial feasibility of the project" (Section 7108). This meant that agencies had to check development costs with care, ensuring that, when the credit proceeds were added to available financing, no more credits were awarded than were required to cover development costs. Clearly, Congress had become concerned that credits were not being effectively applied toward the costs of developing housing for low-income households but were being squandered to the benefit of certain very savvy developers.

1990 amendments to the tax code

Only one year after reducing the annual per capita tax credit allocation to each state, Congress restored the allocation to its original $1.25 per capita level. In addition, the LIHTC program was extended for another year.

1993 amendments to the tax code

Up to this point, the LIHTC program was making halting progress, given that the development community could not be sure of its future existence. With the 1993 act, Congress finally made the program permanent. As a result, developers could begin to prepare proposals with the knowledge that the program would survive from year to year.

1994 subsidy layering rule

The federal government continued to be concerned that the LIHTC program was not being used as effectively as possible. Through Administrative Guidelines issued by HUD, administrative agencies were required to follow new, more detailed rules in allocating tax credits.

These guidelines apply only to projects receiving additional subsidies from HUD, but they set an informal standard for the review of all projects. These rules mandated a minimum contribution that each credit recipient must make to the development, ensuring that no more tax credits are awarded to any project than are necessary to fully finance it. These guidelines spelled out, in some detail, how administrative agencies must go about estimating development costs and syndication proceeds.

The guidelines also specified rules with regard to syndication fees charged to offer the tax credits to investors. Total charges may not be more than 15 percent of the total credit amount for public offerings and no more than 5 percent for private offerings. In addition, when setting the amount of credits to be awarded to an individual project, administrative agencies may not estimate syndication proceeds at less than 42 percent of the gross tax credit amount.

PROGRAM PERFORMANCE

The LIHTC program began slowly but gathered speed quickly. During its first year of operation, only 16 percent of the available tax credit authority was used (Herbert and Verdier 1987). This slow start was probably due to the problems associated with the development community's learning how to use it. Now, however, in all states the tax credits are viewed as a scarce resource. Typically, many more developments are proposed in each state than can be funded (Ernst & Young 1997). Currently, the LIHTC program supports about 1,300 projects a year, for approximately 56,000 units annually (Abt Associates, Inc. 1996).

Several studies have examined the portfolio of developments generated by the LIHTC program. These studies have focused on different periods of time in the program's history. Using data obtained from a telephone survey of 50 state program administrators, Herbert and Verdier (1987) examined the first year's production, while ICF, Inc. (1991), using data received from the developers of 104 projects, looked at the first two years of the program's output. Abt Associates, Inc. (1996), employing a national survey that obtained data from 47 of the 54 states and other agencies administering the program, recently examined program production from 1990 through 1994.[3] The GAO (1997) surveyed a nationwide sample of 423 projects placed in service from 1992 through 1994. Cummings and DiPasquale (1999) obtained data from four national tax credit syndicators on 2,554 properties nationwide. These different studies, plus others, found several common patterns in the types of developments produced by the program.

Income mixing

Mixed-income housing is not being produced in great numbers through the LIHTC program. Rather, the vast majority of the developments tend to be fully covered, with tax credits applied to all of the units.

The program probably intended to promote mixed-income housing, since it incorporated minimum requirements that envisioned the mixing of income-restricted units with market-rate units. The program made the minimum requirements less stringent for those developments serving low-income households (below 50 percent of area median family income) than for those serving moderate-income households (below 60 percent of area median family income). No tax credits can be claimed unless at least 20 percent of the units are set aside for low-income occupants or at least 40 percent are set aside for moderate-income occupants. This minimum requirement suggests that the program intended for developers to set aside some, but not all, of the units in a development for income-eligible households, leaving the remainder to be offered at market rates.

Unfortunately, these minimum requirements did not prove to be the decisive factor in developers' calculations. Rather than responding to these minimums, developers looked at operating costs, such as higher management costs with low-income occupancy, and at the rewards offered for any level of program participation. Thus, if tax credits helped the developer create units where the financing would not otherwise be available, the developer would seek tax credits for all of the units, not just some of them. In addition, the program did not provide additional incentives to serve low-income rather than moderate-income households. The benefits derived from the tax credits are identical for low- and moderate-income units. However, allowed rents are higher for units designated for moderate-income households. Thus, designation for moderate-income occupancy brings in more income and the same amount of tax credits, making it very much preferred for low-income occupancy. As a result, units have been designated almost exclusively for moderate-income households.

Construction type and project size

New construction has been favored over rehabilitation. About 60 percent of all LIHTC units have been developed through new construction and the remainder through rehabilitation. Since tax credits are greater for newly constructed units, this is not surprising. While the actual construction costs of either new construction or substantial rehabilitation enjoy the same 9 percent credit rate, the nonland acquisition costs of a development earn only a 4 percent credit rate. Because all rehabilitation projects involve purchasing an existing building, this portion of the total development costs receives a smaller tax credit, making rehabilitation a less favorably treated form of construction.

Independent of construction type, developments tend to be small to medium-sized projects. In the early years, developments averaged about 28 to 30 units each. Now, the average size has grown to 42 units.

Market location

LIHTC units are distributed between metropolitan and nonmetropolitan areas in roughly the proportions found for the population as a whole. About 80 percent of the assisted units are located in metropolitan areas. Among all LIHTC units, 54 percent are located in central cities, 26 percent in suburban areas, and only 20 percent in rural settings. About 37 percent of the projects are located in DDAs or QTs. Given that DDAs and QTs cannot make up more than 20 percent of a jurisdiction's area, the added incentives to build in these high-cost and low-income areas seem to be having some effect, since developments seem to be disproportionately located there.

Developments also tend to be directed toward areas with high concentrations of racial minorities. About one-third of LIHTC units (34 percent) are located in areas with more than 50 percent minority concentrations, and almost one-half (46 percent) are in areas with more than 30 percent minority concentrations.

Typically, LIHTC properties are located in areas with high concentrations of poor households. Among all LIHTC units, 38 percent are located in neighborhoods where the median household income is below 60 percent of the area median family income, while another 26 percent are located in neighborhoods where the median household income is between 60 and 80 percent of the area median family income. While this appears to be targeting units to areas with concentrations of poor households, Nelson (1994) points out that the program is generally producing units with rents that only moderate-income households can afford. Thus, the program may be "creaming" those with the highest incomes in the eligible population and not reaching the households most in need of assistance. However, sample data used by Ernst & Young (1997) suggest that the LIHTC program is in fact serving the poor, with the average tenant's income at 45 percent of the area median family income.[4] The GAO (1997) study finds that three-quarters of the households in LIHTC units have incomes below 50 percent of the area median family income. Unfortunately, little more is known about these households beyond income. For example, their employment status and sources of income are not recorded in any of the studies published to date.

Rents for LIHTC units generally run between $350 and $500 a month. In their sample, Cummings and DiPasquale (1999) found an average rent of $436 in 1996. While this compares favorably with new-to-the-market units in market-rate developments, it is well above the rents found in various forms of subsidized housing. For example, Stegman (1991) found that rents charged for units in public housing run between $100 and $150. Not only are the rents in LIHTC units higher than those found in other subsidized housing, but the LIHTC units that are being produced tend to expand a segment of the rental housing market that may not be in short supply. HUD's own research finds that all regions of the nation have surpluses of units in the rent ranges households with 40 to 80 percent of area median family income can afford. Further, all regions except the Northeast have increasing vacancy rates in this price range (Nelson 1994).

Development by nonprofit sponsors

Increasingly, nonprofit developers have been the sponsors of the housing projects receiving tax credits. In the early years of the program, about 9 percent of the developments had nonprofit sponsors. This has recently risen to about 24 percent (Abt Associates, Inc. 1996). While this is only about one-fourth of the developments that receive tax credits, the program has become a mainstay for nonprofit community development corporations (CDCs). A national survey finds that 94 percent of CDCs use tax credits (Walker 1993). This survey went on to note that, relative to for-profit developers, nonprofit CDCs tend to take on projects in high-cost, low-income areas. Thus, the risk of failure for these projects is high, but CDCs are committed to the location despite the high risk. However, the combination of high-cost locations and very poor tenant populations means that nonprofit developers must often cut corners to achieve financial feasibility. Such projects are often undercapitalized, leading to difficulties after only a few years of operation.

Summary of program performance

The tax credit program appears to have been absorbed into the rental housing development process, but it has not been adopted by market-rate housing developers. Rather, it has been adopted by either nonprofit CDCs or by specialized developers building projects entirely dedicated to low- or moderate-income occupancy. The units are going into largely metropolitan markets containing heavy concentrations of poor, minority households but rents are being charged that make the units affordable to only those poor households with the highest incomes in these areas.

FINANCING

The LIHTC program has been criticized for being excessive in that it grants large subsidies to developers. Case (1991) calculated that the LIHTC program offers the equivalent of a 54 percent grant to developers.[5] This, Case claims, represents an increase in the rewards granted to low-income housing over previous eras of the tax code. The increase has overshot the mark, granting more subsidy than necessary. The

Year	Units	Projects	Federal Credit Amount ($)
1987	1,048	72	1,863,173
1988	2,946	82	5,503,491
1989	3,004	179	5,464,731
1990	1,075	106	3,126,555
1991	2,613	134	4,529,623
1992	884	67	2,337,165
1993	1,909	67	6,321,799
1994	2,488	78	8,182,202
1995	1,800	66	7,209,225
1996	1,996	55	6,732,283

Table 19.1 Projects, units, and tax credits allocated, 1987 through 1996, MHDC

Source: MHDC.

Note: The counts include only projects receiving tax credits from Missouri's annual allocation from the current year or carried over from previous years. No projects that use tax-exempt financing and received tax credits outside of the annual allocation are included.

program has also been criticized as being convoluted and irrational. Stegman (1991) has pointed out that it makes little sense to design a housing program where the poorer the income group served, the more complicated and costly it is to arrange the financing.

The research reported here finds that although the first criticism may have had some validity in the past, the systems put into place to prevent excessive profits from being realized from the LIHTC program seem to be working. Virtually all syndication proceeds are now being applied toward project costs, and excessive profits for developers have been squeezed out of the process. Unfortunately, however, this research suggests that the second criticism is very much on target. The LIHTC program fails to reach deep enough to make projects serving very poor households financially feasible. These developments must pursue the lengthy and expensive process of layering subsidies, one on top of another, until total development costs are covered.

The data for this research come from the Missouri Housing Development Commission (MHDC), which is the state's housing finance agency. In addition to its traditional role in operating multifamily and single-family loan programs, MHDC administers the LIHTC program in the state. The agency has made data available on its portfolio of developments that have received tax credits. The database is an improvement over the national databases mentioned earlier in that more is known about the sources of each project's financing. In addition, this sample covers the full 10 years of program operation, rather than the few years covered in several of the other studies. This span permits a more accurate assessment of the leverage capabilities of the LIHTC program, as well as the many other resources that developers tapped to bring their projects to fruition over the decade that the program has been in operation.

MHDC has participated in the LIHTC program since its inception, so the agency has had a decade of experience in administering it. Through 1996, MHDC allocated tax credits to more than 19,000 units in over 900 projects ranging from single-family dwellings to very large multifamily developments with hundreds of units. The projects are spread statewide but are predominantly found in the metropolitan areas of St. Louis and Kansas City and, to a lesser extent, in the Springfield area in the south-central portion of the state.

MHDC allocates credits to about 2,000 units a year in approximately 70 projects.[6] (See Table 19.1.) These credits are currently worth about $6.7 million a year and are spread across a broad range of markets, ranging from inner-city slum areas to middle-income suburban areas to extremely low-density rural communities.

MHDC is a good source of data in that it is in many ways typical of most administrative agencies. The total portfolio of developments that have received tax credits is very similar to the national database developed from the national survey by Abt Associates, Inc. (1996). Table 19.2 indicates that the projects awarded tax credits by MHDC are comparable to projects nationwide. Although somewhat smaller on average, the MHDC projects are distributed over central cities, suburbs, and rural areas in approximately the same proportions as the national portfolio. Through its Qualified Allocation Plan, MHDC seems to favor rehabilitation over new construction more than is found nationally. However, the distribution of MHDC projects according to market levels of poverty and concentrations of racial minorities are on a par with the national database.

MHDC differs from most agencies administering the LIHTC program in that it administers a state-funded tax credit program as well. Rather than operating independent of the federal programs, the Missouri tax credit program is used to augment it. State tax credits have been awarded to developments since 1992. Initially, they were awarded in the amount of 20 percent of the federal tax credit. This increased to 40 percent in 1994 and may now go as high as 100 percent.

State credits are awarded to all developments that can demonstrate a need for additional financial resources in order to make a project financially feasible. State tax credits operate the same way as federal tax credits. They are syndicated to investors subject to Missouri income tax. As with any other source of financing, the proceeds of this syndication are applied to cover the costs of the development. MHDC staff review all proposals for state tax credits the same way they review proposals for federal tax credits. Not only must each proposal demonstrate a need for the subsidy, but each must also demonstrate that the amount requested is not in excess of the sum necessary to make the project financially feasible.

A sample of 142 developments, including projects granted tax credits beginning in 1987 and running through 1995, was selected from MHDC's entire portfolio. The sample was drawn in a stratified manner to reflect the total portfolio of developments in terms of location in the state, development size, and the year the tax credits were awarded. Cost certification documents were obtained for all developments. These documents disclose the form of ownership (to distinguish nonprofit from for-profit sponsors),

Characteristic of developments	MHDC	National sample
Average project size	14	42
Percentage of developments with tax credits applied to all units in the project	92%	98%
Percentage of developments built through new construction	47%	61%
Percentage of developments in		
Central cities	60%	54%
Suburban areas	27%	26%
Rural areas	13%	20%
Mean percentage of the population below the poverty level in the tract	33%	32%
Mean percentage of the population in a racial minority in the tract	49%	40%
Percentage of developments in DDAs or QTs	41%	41%

Table 19.2 Characteristics of low-income housing tax credit projects: comparing Missouri Projects with the national sample

Source: MHDC data and Abt Associates, Inc., 1996.

the sources of debt financing (conventional loans, public sector loans, and grants), and the amount of the syndication proceeds applied toward the financing (and, in some cases, the amount of syndication fees paid). These data were merged with information on total development costs, location, and unit counts to form the database for this research.

FINDINGS

What do projects receive from syndicating tax credits, and what does this cost?

Because the LIHTC program provides tax benefits to the owners of developments rather than providing a direct capital contribution toward building the development, some mechanism must be put in place to translate the tax benefits received over time into ready cash when construction begins. Syndication is that mechanism, and it is a complex one.

Investors make cash contributions to the development based on the tax benefits they receive. The amount of the contribution made at the time the development is built is less than the value of the tax credits. The amount of the discount is a function of the amount of time that passes between making the investment and receiving the tax credits as a return on that investment as well as the risk inherent in it (McClure 1990). The investment is made at the beginning of the construction period, which may take a year or more, while the tax credits begin to flow only after the project begins operations. There is no certainty that the development will be a success. If it fails to meet LIHTC program requirements or if it is a financial failure, the investor could lose the money or could have some responsibility to provide further resources. As a result of the time and risk involved in investing in low-income housing, the discount rate associated with syndication has been fairly high. Fortunately, very few projects awarded credits through MHDC have ever failed, and these tend to be very small projects (two to four units each) that encountered management problems.

Prior experience

John M. Ols Jr., director, Housing and Community Development Issues, GAO, testified to Congress on the discount rate applied to tax credits as part of the syndication process and stated that, for a sample of developments, developers typically receive investor contributions equal to about 43 percent of the tax credit amount paid out over the 10-year period (Ols 1990). This translates into a discount rate of about 19 percent. However, he found the variation in the discount rate to be fairly wide, ranging from a low of 10 percent to a high of 22 percent. The data did not permit detailed analysis of the variation, but higher risk seemed to be associated with developments built for family occupancy versus elderly occupancy, projects built through rehabilitation rather than new construction, and projects built in urban areas rather than suburban or rural ones. The Cummings and DiPasquale study (1999) found that the tax credit program had improved over time. For their sample of projects, the syndication proceeds were 47 percent of the tax credit allocation in 1987 but had risen to 55 percent in 1994.

The syndication process itself incurs costs as well. The firms that market tax credits to investors must be paid a fee for their services; this fee contributes to the discount between the gross amount of the tax credits and the amount of the net syndication proceeds the development receives. For publicly offered syndications, the fees averaged about 27 percent of the gross syndication proceeds in 1990 (Ols 1990). These fees also ranged widely, from 17 to 34 percent in Ols's sample and from 20 to 30 percent in a later study by Wallace (1995). Ernst & Young (1997) find that these fees have now fallen to less than 10 percent.

MHDC experience

Syndication plays an important role in financing MHDC developments. In the sample of developments, net syndication proceeds as a percentage of the total credit amount averaged about 47 percent over all years. There has been a slow upward trend in this figure over time. (See Table 19.3.) The early years of the program (1987 to 1989) saw average net proceeds of 42 to 45 percent. This figure peaked at 53 percent in 1994 but fell again to 45 percent in 1995. However, MHDC now analyzes proposals for developments, estimating net syndication proceeds to be 52 percent of the gross credit

Year	Average (%)
1987	42
1988	45
1989	43
1990	48
1991	47
1992	46
1993	47
1994	53
1995	45
All years	47

Table 19.3 Net Syndication proceeds as a percentage of total federal credit amount, 1987 through 1995 MHDC LIHTC developments

Source: MHDC.

amount, and routinely sees estimates in excess of 60 percent. A net proceeds amount of 60 percent translates into a discount rate of about 11 percent by the investor.

It is important to note that the 60 cents on the tax-credit dollar received through syndication proceeds often represents more than just the sale of the tax credits. Rather, it is the net amount received after a variety of benefits and costs have been factored into the transaction. On the benefits side, the investor receives the tax credits each year for the first 10 years of operation. In addition, the investor may be purchasing an interest in some share of any cash flow or surplus depreciation deductions the project may generate after paying all other expenses. Finally, the investor may be purchasing some share of the residual value of the property if it is sold and generates a profit.

On the cost side, syndication proceeds will be reduced by the amount of the fees charged by the syndicator for structuring the investment. In addition, the syndicator may make a bridge loan to the development so that all the syndication proceeds are available at construction, well before the syndicator receives any contributions. Investors usually make their capital contributions over a period of years. However, because developers typically need all of the capital before construction begins, they must often take out a bridge loan to be repaid by the investors' capital contributions as they are received. Frequently, the syndicator provides the bridge loan, charging interest and fees for this service (Thorne-Thompson 1994). Such arrangements make it relatively difficult to separate out the exact amount of syndication fees paid, independent of the costs of the bridge loan. Thus, the 60 cents on the dollar represents the end payment after all of these items have been factored in. Few developments reported adequately on all of these factors. As a result, it is not clear how much of the increase in net syndication proceeds is due to decreases in the market's assessment of the risk associated with purchasing tax credits and how much is investment in expected cash flow, depreciation, or residual value.

Only a small portion of the developments in the MHDC sample fully disclosed the amount of syndication fees paid. Because syndication arrangements were very complex, it is doubtful that developments were willfully concealing any information. However, for those that did provide complete reports, the average amount of syndication fees paid was 25 percent of the total credit amount. These fees ranged from a low of 15 percent to a high of 44 percent. However, during 1994 and 1995, fees have consistently averaged 15 percent.

Have syndication proceeds gone to the developer or the development?

The net syndication proceeds from the federal tax credits amounted to about 33 percent of

| | | Non-FmHA Primary Lender | | | |
	Private	MHDC	Other	All Non-FmHA Projects	FmHA Projects
Debt financing					
First mortgage	41.8%	31.0%	58.6%	39.9%	78.6%
Private subordinate	1.9%	5.4%	0.0%	2.7%	0.0%
Public subordinate	17.1%	23.8%	0.0%	18.1%	0.0%
Equity Financing					
Syndication, federal credits	31.2%	36.9%	41.3%	32.9%	17.3
Syndication, state credits	4.6%	1.0%	0.0%	3.6%	1.7%
Cash and other equity	3.4%	1.9%	0.1%	2.9%	2.4%
Total development costs	100.0%	100.0%	100.0%	100.0%	100.0%
Number of developments	81	26	4	111	31

Table 19.4 Percentage of total development costs by type of financing

Source: MHDC.

Note: Columns may not sum to 100 because of rounding.

total development costs for developments not financed through the Farmer's Home Administration (FmHA).[7] (See Table 19.4.) There is no apparent trend in this average figure: It has been relatively constant over time. This 33 percent of total development costs figure may be low, however. A few developments reported net syndication proceeds that appear to be very low. It is possible that these developments received more from syndication than was reported. They may have simply reported the amount pledged to the development. However, all of them were in the early years of the program, before tighter controls on the use of syndication proceeds were in place. If these suspect numbers are omitted, the net syndication proceeds are barely more than one-third of total development costs.

Those projects receiving FmHA financing received 4 percent tax credits, rather than the standard 9 percent, because they are federally financed. As a result, their syndication proceeds are commensurately lower, averaging 17 percent of total development costs.

Net syndication proceeds are generally pledged to the development. They become a form of equity contribution by the ownership toward financing the development. For the vast majority of projects, owners applied all of the syndication proceeds toward the project's financing. In fact, when added to the various loans, additional equity contributions were still required with most projects. As a result, developers were not able to look to tax credits as a form of profit. Rather, they used the proceeds as one of many sources of financing. They had to look to developer's fees or management fees received as repayment for their efforts. In many cases, even developer's fees were waived in order to make the development feasible. This was especially true with nonprofit developers.

Although the proceeds from tax credits directly capitalized rental housing for most projects, some of the developments were over-financed. For a few projects, the sum of various loans leveraged plus the net syndication proceeds exceeded total development costs. Where this is the case, it is possible for a developer to pocket some of the syndication proceeds as a form of excess profit. This was true for 14 of the 142 sample developments, or about 10 percent of the portfolio. This small subset of developments did not appear to consist of any one type of project. Some had only conventional financing; some had subsidized financing. Some were located in rural areas, and some were metropolitan.

Before 1990, there were no guidelines on applying syndication proceeds toward project costs. Safeguards are now in place to prevent excessive allocation of tax credits and to ensure that all proceeds are applied toward the costs of completing the project. If a project is given an initial allocation that proves, on completion, to provide more syndication proceeds than are needed, the allocation of tax credits can be reduced.

What is the role of conventional financing?

Conventional financing was used in 81 of the 142 developments (57 percent). The remaining 43 percent relied entirely on public sector financing. Conventional financing was the only form used for 39 of the 142 developments (27 percent). Thus, almost three-quarters of the developments had to seek some level of financing from public sources.

Why were private lenders and investors unwilling to provide the necessary funds, which, when added to the syndication proceeds, would be enough to develop the project? The answer frequently offered is that the rents for LIHTC projects are too low to support the debt. This simple analysis is not adequate. Comparing the loss of debt leverage from program participation with the gain in syndication proceeds from receiving tax credits shows them to be about the same.

Private sector developments typically have 70 percent debt financing and 30 percent equity financing (Hess and Skinner 1997). The average loan-to-value ratio for the subset of developments that received conventional loans was 42 percent, clearly well below the 70 percent industry average. However, if setting the units aside for low- or moderate-income occupancy brings in syndication proceeds worth about 30 percent of the total development costs, then the reduction in the amount of debt financing from 70 percent to 42 percent would appear to be acceptable. Syndication proceeds would simply offset the reduced loan amount. Unfortunately, the problem is not so simple. Equity investors, who would normally finance about 30 percent of the total development costs in a market-rate development, will turn away from a LIHTC development. While investors are willing to purchase tax credits through syndication, they are no longer willing to invest in the housing itself for the simple reason that the property is unlikely to generate an adequate return on investment.

One of the impacts of the long-term occupancy requirements is that the development cannot be sold, refinanced, and renovated periodically as is common with market-rate developments. Rather, the LIHTC property must remain in low- or moderate-income occupancy for anywhere from 15 to 30 years. This means that investors treat the property as having little or no residual value at the end of this period (Ernst & Young 1997; Thorne-Thompson 1994). As a result, investors see little opportunity for repayment of their investment from the appreciation of the value of the property. Also, the developments generally operate at or close to a breakeven level, generating little or no cash flow. Thus, investors see little opportunity for repayment of their investment from operating the property. Instead, to provide a return on their investment, investors must look to tax credits alone, not the cash flow from or the residual value of the property.

The result is that using LIHTC not only reduces rents below market levels, which reduces the ability to leverage conventional debt financing, but it reduces the developer's ability to raise equity. The developer can expect to receive loans from conventional lenders and the proceeds from syndication of the tax credits. If these two sources do not cover the full cost of developing the project, additional subsidies will be necessary. As Table 19.4 suggests, conventional lenders reduce their loans from 70 percent of total development costs to about 44 percent for LIHTC projects. Equity investors reduce their participation from about 30 percent to only 3 percent. Thus, available financing is reduced by a total of 53 percent, while the proceeds from syndication generate only about 31 percent, leaving 22 percent of project costs to be financed through various layers of subsidy over and above the federal tax credit.

What is the role of additional layers of subsidy?

Only 15 percent of the developments had syndication proceeds from federal tax credits as the only form of subsidy. Put another way, only 15 percent of the developments were able to finance all development costs through conventional loans and the proceeds of syndicating federal tax credits alone. The remaining 85 percent of the developments had at least one additional layer of subsidy over and above the federal tax credit.

Most developments had several layers of subsidy, with two and three layers being the most common. About 35 percent of the projects had two layers, and 33 percent had three. In this layering, federal tax credits were counted as one layer, state tax credits as another, and grants or loans from any public entity were each counted as additional layers. The average number of layers was 2.6, which compares favorably with the North Carolina experience, where the average was five layers (Stegman 1991).

The Missouri state tax credit generated anywhere from 1 to 8 percent of total development costs, depending on the amount of credits awarded. Among only those projects that were privately financed and received Missouri state tax credits, the proceeds from syndication averaged just under 5 percent of total development costs.

If the development is in a high-cost area or an area with extremely low levels of household income, the LIHTC program grants an increased basis against which credits can be claimed. This mechanism was an attempt to avoid the need for excessive layering of subsidies. The goal was to grant more tax credit subsidy where the situation warranted it, thus reducing the need for additional subsidies. The experience in Missouri with the DDAs and QTs did not reduce the need for additional layers. Of the projects located in DDAs or QTs, 92 percent had additional layers over and above the increased tax credits available to them because of their location. This is even higher than the 85 percent found among all developments.

The MHDC experience with nonprofit developers is also instructive. Compared with for-profit developers, nonprofit developers were able to cover more of their project's total development costs through syndication. Nonprofit developers obtained 37.3 percent of project costs through syndication, compared with 30.5 percent among for-profit developers. This higher level of syndication was experienced despite the perceived risk associated with the more difficult projects taken on by nonprofit developers. This risk is found in the lower loan-to-value ratios among conventionally financed developments. The conventional loans of for-profit developers averaged 50.4 percent of total development costs, while nonprofit developers were able to leverage only 22.7 percent. Despite the higher risk, nonprofit developers were able to gain just as many, if not more, housing resources out of the tax credits awarded to them.

CONCLUSION

Efficiency of the tax credit

It has been established that the tax credit is a very inefficient subsidy delivery mechanism (Stegman 1991). If the federal government grants tax credits of $1,000 ($100 a year for 10 years), then the present value of these credits to the government is about $780, discounting at the government's long-term cost of borrowing.[8] When evaluating tax credits as an investment, however, investors employ an even greater discount rate, found here to be about 11 percent. This means that the $780 of housing subsidy from the government will produce only $590 in housing. Clearly this is a significant loss of value (about 24 percent) from the use of tax credits as the vehicle to deliver the housing subsidy. However, it is doubtful that the most efficient mechanism for providing government aid to the development of low-income housing – a capital grant – will be adopted in lieu of tax credits. If the tax credit mechanism is here to stay, its continued implementation needs to find all possible efficiencies.

Efficiency of syndication process

Assuming that the tax credit is to continue, is it becoming more efficient? The net syndication proceeds being realized by developments are going up as a percentage of total tax credits allocated. However, net syndication cannot increase much more. The improvements found in the past 10 years reflect a maturation of the LIHTC program. Investors have come to know and understand it, and syndicators have streamlined the process. This has brought greater efficiency to the tax credit program. A lower risk factor is being applied to investment in tax credits, and a lower percentage of the proceeds is consumed in fees. However, it seems unlikely that the discount being applied to tax credits can be pushed much lower. The current 11 percent discount rate is comparable to the performance of alternative investments with similar risk. If the return falls much lower, it seems doubtful that investors will move much capital into low-income housing tax credits and away from other investments. Syndication fees have been pushed down to less than 10 percent, and, again, it seems unlikely that they can go much lower. As a result, the 50 to 60 percent net proceeds being realized by developers from the tax credits are probably about as high as can be expected. Further efficiencies are being squeezed out of the process by selling surplus depreciation, cash flow, and residual value. This has raised syndication proceeds to 60 percent of the tax credit amount. While this is beneficial to developments, additional syndication proceeds are available only to those developments in markets capable of generating strong cash flows or high residual values. It is doubtful that these higher syndication proceeds will eliminate the need for additional layers of subsidy in most developments.

The increased efficiency is also found in the level of demand for tax credits. Table 19.1 lists the amount of tax credits allocated to projects from 1987 through 1996. What the table shows is that from 1993 on, the state of Missouri has been able to award its entire $6.7 million dollar allocation of tax credits and exceed it by awarding unused tax credits carried over from previous years.

Excessive rewards to developers

In general, proceeds from the syndication of tax credits are applied toward financing the developments, and safeguards are in place to prevent their diversion into developers' hands. The contention that the tax credit program provides excessive grants to developers was true for only a small fraction of projects in the early years of the program.

Fixed credit rate

If the program is not providing windfall profits to developers and has become more efficient over time, why do so many developments have to seek out multiple layers of subsidy? The answer seems to be found in the fixed credit rate

applicable to all projects. The property owner realizes the tax credit over a long period. However, it is not a subsidy to the operation of the property. Few rental housing developments generate any large amount of cash flow from operations that could be sheltered from taxation by a tax credit. This is especially true of developments with rents below market-rate levels. These developments frequently struggle just to break even. As a result, the tax credit is only very rarely a benefit to operations. Rather, it must be translated, through syndication, into a form of financing to cover the initial costs of development, just like any other loan or grant. It is here that the fixed credit rate (9 percent on most developments) becomes a problem.

For developments located in markets where the rents permitted in LIHTC units are close to market rate and where construction and development costs are relatively low, the 9 percent credit rate may be more than enough to make a project financially feasible. The net syndication proceeds combined with conventional financing may cover more than the total development costs. In these cases, so as not to waste scarce federal subsidies, the state administering agency must prevent the developer from pocketing any surplus syndication proceeds. However, where the rents in the LIHTC units are low and where construction and development costs are high (a combination found in most inner-city markets), the 9 percent credit rate is not enough to make a project financially feasible. Even if all the syndication proceeds are applied toward financing, the project is unable to secure all of the needed funds from conventional lenders. Such developments must seek out additional forms of financing, which usually means multiple layers of subsidized financing. This seems to be true for all but a few developments.

Attempts have been made to add more flexibility to the process by increasing the subsidy to developments in DDAs and QTs. While this is a step in the right direction, it has fallen short of providing the flexibility planners and developers need. The proceeds from syndication need to cover the shortfall between total development costs and the conventional loans available to the development. This will vary from project to project and from market to market. What is needed is a mechanism that permits planners to adjust the amount of the tax credits up or down. If planners had the flexibility to award higher credit amounts to more worthy developments, then layers of additional subsidy could be removed. If these credit amounts were enough to cover the shortfall between total development costs and conventional loan and equity amounts, the developers could be freed from the burden of chasing additional layers of subsidy to finance their projects. Given this flexibility, the agencies that administer the LIHTC program could use their ability to award different credit amounts to make developers address a range of housing needs. The agencies could induce developers who would not otherwise include low-income units in their market-rate developments to do so. They could induce developers to target some units to the poorest of the poor instead of those who have more income. Finally, they could help developers finance meritorious developments in markets where, even with several layers of subsidy, projects are simply not feasible.

Notes

1 States may be able to allocate credits in excess of this amount, since they may receive credits from a national pool generated from credits recalled from states unable to use their full allocation.

2 Many states call for developers to make income-restricted occupancy commitments of longer than 30 years, some for as long as 50 years.

3 Each state administers the program, plus there are separate agencies for Chicago, the District of Columbia, Puerto Rico, and the Virgin Islands.

4 This particular sample includes only tenants not receiving additional rental assistance. Tenants with additional rental assistance tend to be much poorer, with an average income at 23 percent of area median family income (Ernst & Young 1997).

5 This amount is the present value of the tax credits granted. Discounted at 10.6 percent, each $10,000 of tax credits offered to developers over the 10-year period is worth about $5,400 to the government during the year the credit was awarded.

6 These figures include only those units given credits from the state's annual allocation of tax credits. Additional units receive tax credits exempt from the annual allocation because they are existing developments using tax-exempt financing.

7 FmHA provided below-market interest rate financing to developments. This program was suspended in 1995 when the FmHA became the Rural Housing Service.

8 In November 1998, U.S. Treasury 10-year notes were trading at 4.86 percent.

REFERENCES

Abt Associates, Inc. 1996. *Development and Analysis of the National Low-Income Housing Tax Credit Database.* Washington, D.C.: U.S. Department of Housing and Urban Development, Office of Policy Development and Research.

Case, Karl E. 1991. Investors, Developers, and Supply-Side Subsidies: How Much Is Enough? *Housing Policy Debate* 2(2):341–56.

Cummings, Jean L., and Denise DiPasquale. 1999. The Low-Income Housing Tax Credit: An Analysis of the First Ten Years. *Housing Policy Debate* 10(2):251–307.

Ernst & Young LLP, Kenneth Leventhal Real Estate Group. 1997. *The Low-Income Housing Tax Credit: The First Decade.* Boston.

Guggenheim, Joseph. 1994. *Tax Credits for Low-Income Housing: Opportunities for Developers, Nonprofits, and Communities under Permanent Tax Act Provisions.* 8th ed. Glen Echo, MD: Simon.

Herbert, Christopher, and James M. Verdier. 1987. *Early Experience with the Low-Income Housing Rental Housing Tax Credit.* Washington, D.C.: National Council of State Housing Agencies.

Hess, Robert C., and Ronald Skinner. 1997. Lenders Wage Battle for Market Share. *Real Estate Capital Markets Report* 6(5):22–24.

ICF, Inc. 1991. *Evaluation of the Low-Income Housing Tax Credit.* Washington, D.C.: U.S. Department of Housing and Urban Development.

McClure, Kirk. 1990. Low and Moderate Income Housing Tax Credits: Calculating Their Value. *Journal of the American Planning Association* 56:363–69.

Nelson, Kathryn P. 1994. Whose Shortage of Affordable Housing? *Housing Policy Debate* 5(4):401–42.

Ols, John M. Jr. 1990. *Low-Income Housing Tax Credit Utilization and Syndication: Testimony before the Subcommittee on HUD/Moderate Rehabilitation Investigations, Committee on Banking, Housing, and Urban Affairs, United States Senate, April 27.* Washington, D.C.: U.S. General Accounting Office.

Stegman, Michael A. 1991. The Excessive Cost of Creative Finance: Growing Inefficiencies in the Production of Low-Income Housing. *Housing Policy Debate* 2(2):357–73.

Thorne-Thompson, Thomas. 1994. Low-Income Housing Tax Credit: Bridge Loan Opportunities. *Real Estate Finance* 11:24–31.

U.S. General Accounting Office. 1997. *Tax Credits: Opportunities to Improve Oversight of the Low-Income Housing Program.* Washington, D.C.

Walker, Christopher. 1993. Nonprofit Housing Development: Status, Trends, and Prospects. *Housing Policy Debate* 4(3):369–414.

Wallace, James E. 1995. Financing Affordable Housing in the United States. *Housing Policy Debate* 6(4):785–814.

20
"Strengths and weaknesses of the Housing Voucher Program"

From *Congressional Testimony of Margery Austin Turner, Director, Metropolitan Housing and Communities Policy Center, The Urban Institute, prepared for the Committee on Financial Services, Subcommittee on Housing and Community Opportunity, United States House of Representatives, June 17, 2003*

Margery Austin Turner

Thank you for the opportunity to testify today on the strengths and weakness of the federal housing voucher program. My testimony reviews the importance of the Housing Choice Voucher Program and the benefits it provides, and describes challenges facing the program. I argue that the administration's proposal to convert the voucher program into a state block grant does nothing to address these challenges and indeed could make them harder to overcome. Finally, I suggest three strategies that could strengthen the basic voucher program design, substantially improving outcomes for families. My remarks are based on research I and my colleagues at the Urban Institute have conducted on federal housing assistance programs and needs as well as on the work of researchers at the Department of Housing and Urban Development and other public and private organizations.

SUMMARY

The federal Housing Choice Voucher Program plays a critical role in helping to address housing needs for extremely low-income households. Its most important advantage is that vouchers give recipients the freedom to choose the kinds of housing and the locations that best meet their needs. As a consequence, many voucher recipients live in healthy neighborhoods that offer social, educational, and economic opportunities for themselves and their children.

The current housing voucher program certainly does not work perfectly. Vouchers have not been as effective in promoting residential mobility and choice among minority recipients as they have been for whites. But even for African Americans and Hispanics, vouchers perform better than public and assisted housing projects in giving families access to low-poverty and racially mixed neighborhoods.

Not all families who receive vouchers are able to find a house or apartment where they can use them. Shortages of moderately priced rental housing, tight market conditions, racial and ethnic discrimination, landlords who are unwilling to accept voucher payments, and ineffective local administration all contribute to this problem. And the program's "portability" feature, which allows recipients to use their vouchers to move from one jurisdiction to another, is a bureaucratic nightmare, not only for families but also for the sending and receiving housing authorities.

The single biggest problem with the current housing voucher program is that federal spending for affordable housing is woefully inadequate. Only about one in every three eligible families gets assistance. Thus, even though vouchers work quite well for those lucky enough to receive them, 6.1 million low-income renters still face severe housing hardship – paying more than half their monthly income for housing, or living in seriously run-down or overcrowded housing.

Converting vouchers to a block grant does not address any of the program's current limitations – and in fact, could well exacerbate existing problems. Some states might use a block grant's flexibility to implement programmatic models that would potentially undermine the success of the voucher approach, creating new problems and worsening the housing hardships that low-income families already face. Moreover, because funding for the voucher program would no longer be tied to a formula that reflects actual program costs and rents, the gap between housing needs and resources would almost certainly widen over time, undermining states' ability to operate the program effectively.

Three promising strategies for making the basic voucher design work better could be implemented within the existing program structure and could potentially improve outcomes for families substantially: 1) *mobility counseling and assistance* can help voucher recipients understand the locational options available, identify housing opportunities, and negotiate effectively with landlords; 2) *aggressive landlord outreach, service, and incentives* can substantially expand the housing options available to voucher recipients; and 3) *regional collaboration and/or regional administration* of the voucher program can help address the administrative barriers to portability across jurisdictions, and make the program more transparent to both landlords and participants. Although it is possible that some states might choose to use a voucher block grant to implement one or more of these promising strategies, this choice seems unlikely absent a programmatic mandate or incentive system.

VALUE OF THE HOUSING CHOICE VOUCHER PROGRAM

The federal housing voucher program supplements rent payments for 1.7 million low-income families and individuals, making it the nation's largest housing assistance program. Recipients choose a house or apartment available in the private market and contribute about 30 percent of their incomes toward rent, while the federal government pays the difference – up to a locally defined "payment standard." Compared to unassisted households at comparable income levels, voucher recipients are far less likely to be paying unaffordable housing cost burdens, and more likely to be living in decent quality housing (HUD 2000). And because the voucher program relies upon the existing housing stock, it is less costly than programs that build new projects for occupancy by the poor (HUD 2000).

The most important advantage of housing vouchers is that they give recipients the freedom to choose the kinds of housing and the locations that best meet their needs. Federal housing construction programs have historically clustered assisted families in low-income, central city neighborhoods, contributing to both concentrated poverty and racial segregation. For example, 37 percent of public housing residents live in neighborhoods where the poverty rate exceeds 40 percent (Newman and Schnare 1997), and most African-American residents of public housing live in neighborhoods that are majority black (Goering, Kamely, and Richardson 1994). Even more recent housing production programs, such as the Low Income Housing Tax Credit and the HOME Program have placed a disproportionate share of assisted units in poor and minority neighborhoods. For example, almost half of LIHTC units are located in neighborhoods that are predominantly black (Buron *et al.* 2000).

In contrast, vouchers have generally allowed assisted families to disperse more widely and to live in lower-poverty, less segregated neighborhoods. In fact, the latest research finds at least some voucher recipients living in eight out of ten neighborhoods in large metropolitan areas. Specifically, Devine *et al.* (2003) analyze the spatial distribution of voucher recipients in the nation's 50 largest metropolitan areas, and conclude that virtually every census tract in these areas contains some housing at rent levels accessible to voucher recipients; voucher recipients are currently living in 83 percent of these census tracts. As a consequence, 58.6 percent of voucher recipients live in neighborhood that are less than 20 percent poor, and only 22.2 percent live in neighborhoods with poverty rates in excess of 30 percent.

Vouchers have not been as effective in promoting residential mobility and choice among minority recipients as they have been for whites. White voucher recipients have gained access to housing in a substantially wider range of metropolitan neighborhoods than have African Americans and Hispanics. African-American and Hispanic voucher holders are over-represented in neighborhoods where vouchers are clustered, and under-represented in neighborhoods where they are more widely dispersed (Devine *et al.* 2003). Moreover, 25.2 percent of African-American recipients and 27.9 percent of Hispanics live in high-poverty neighborhoods (with poverty rates over 30 percent), compared with only 8 percent of whites (Devine *et al.* 2003). Nevertheless, even among African Americans and Hispanics, voucher recipients are more likely than public and assisted housing residents to live in low-poverty and racially mixed neighborhoods (Turner and Wilson 1998).

VOUCHERS DO NOT WORK PERFECTLY

This is not to say that the current housing voucher program works perfectly. Some families who receive vouchers are unable to find a house or apartment where they can use them. The most recent study of success rates among voucher recipients (Finkel and Buron 2001) finds that about 69 percent of households that receive a voucher are successful in using it, down from 81 percent in the late 1980s. In some communities, moderately priced rental housing (affordable with a voucher) is in short supply, particularly in good neighborhoods. Historically, many suburban jurisdictions have used zoning and land use regulations to limit the development of rental housing, especially more affordable rental housing, in order to maintain their property tax base and ensure social homogeneity (Advisory Commission on Regulatory Barriers to Affordable Housing 1991; Malpezzi 1996). Few states require jurisdictions to build or accommodate their "fair share" of affordable housing (Burchell *et al.* 1994). As a consequence, the stock of rental housing tends to be somewhat concentrated in central cities, older suburbs, and less affluent neighborhoods (Orfield 1997).

Moreover, during the late 1990s and early 2000s, rental markets in many metropolitan areas were very tight, vacancy rates were low, and rents were rising rapidly (HUD 1999). These hot market conditions made it difficult for voucher recipients to find vacant units at rent levels they could afford. HUD increased allowable subsidy levels in many metropolitan areas to address this problem, but some local housing agencies continued to face high turn-back rates, as families failed to find units where they could use their vouchers.

Even when suitable rental units are available, landlords may be unwilling to participate in the voucher program. When demand for rental housing is reasonably strong, landlords do not need the voucher program to lease the units they own. Some may have doubts about whether the low-income households who receive vouchers will be good tenants, and whether program regulations will prevent them from rejecting unqualified applicants or evicting problem tenants. And some landlords are simply skeptical about participating in the program for fear of becoming entangled in red tape and bureaucratic hassles.

In some jurisdictions, the fears of rental property owners about participating in the voucher program have been fueled by the poor reputation of the local housing agency. A housing agency known for delays in conducting inspections and approving leases, unreliability in making subsidy payments, and lack of responsiveness to landlord inquiries or complaints is likely to have serious problems convincing local landlords to participate in the voucher program (Turner, Popkin, and Cunningham 2000). Voucher recipients have the greatest difficulty when tight market conditions combine with ineffective program administration, because landlords can easily find tenants for available units, and see real disadvantages to dealing with the local housing agency. Under these circumstances, there may be only a small pool of "Section 8 landlords" who are familiar with the program and readily accept voucher-holders as tenants, sometimes because their properties are located in less desirable areas and might not otherwise be fully leased up (Turner, Popkin and Cunningham 2000).

Another challenge for the voucher program is effectively using the "portability" provisions that allow recipients to use their vouchers in any jurisdiction. Transferring vouchers from one locality to another can be a bureaucratic nightmare, not only for families but also for the sending and receiving housing authorities. When a family receives its voucher from one housing authority but wants to move to the jurisdiction of a different housing authority, the "sending" PHA has a choice; it can either transfer the family to the new PHA (which must agree to "absorb" the transfer by issuing one of its own vouchers) or it can pay the "receiving" PHA for performing administrative functions such as income certifications, housing inspections, and lease renewals. Many urban PHAs have agreements with neighboring jurisdictions that they will automatically "absorb" vouchers from each other rather than administering complex "billing" arrangements. But this arrangement is also undesirable, requiring the receiving PHA to use up a unit of housing assistance that could have served a family on its own waiting list (Feins et al. 1997).

In addition to problems with program administration and regulations, racial discrimination and segregated housing markets exacerbate the challenges that minority recipients face when they try to find housing with their vouchers. Although discrimination against African-American renters has declined over the last decade, minority homeseekers still face high levels of adverse treatment in urban housing markets (Turner et al. 2002). And although increasing numbers of minority households have gained access to suburban neighborhoods, researchers continue to find evidence that minorities face significant barriers to entry into white suburban neighborhoods (South and Crowdar 1998; Stearns and Logan 1986). In addition, some suburban communities have resisted the influx of voucher recipients from other jurisdictions, due to prejudice and fear about racial and economic change, and about the crime and social service needs that these new residents are expected to bring (Churchill et al. 2001).

Families who receive vouchers to relocate from severely distressed public housing as part of HOPE VI initiatives often have particular difficulty finding and retaining housing in the private market. A substantial proportion of these households lack previous experience with the private market and have complex personal problems – substance abuse, depression, domestic violence, gang affiliation – that make it difficult for them to search effectively for housing

and make them less appealing to landlords (Popkin et al. 2002). Landlords may be less willing to rent to public housing families with children, limiting their choices of housing and neighborhoods. Further, long-term public housing residents may not be able to take advantage of any mobility opportunities – their personal situations may make them seem particularly risky to landlords and their own fears of moving to unfamiliar areas may prevent them from even considering these options (Popkin and Cunningham 2000, 2002). Finally, even those former public housing residents who do manage to find housing may encounter problems. Recent research indicates that many are facing hardship due to higher utility costs and the challenges of dealing with individual landlords (Buron et al. 2002). Complex personal situations – such as illegal household members and domestic violence – can place them at risk for losing their assistance altogether (Popkin and Cunningham 2002; Venkatesh 2002).

A BLOCK GRANT COULD MAKE THE SITUATION WORSE

Converting vouchers to a block grant does not address any of the program's current limitations – and in fact, may exacerbate existing problems. The single biggest limitation of the current housing voucher program is that federal spending for affordable housing is woefully inadequate. Only about one in every three eligible families gets assistance. Thus, even though vouchers work well for those lucky enough to receive them, 6.1 million low-income renters still face severe housing hardship – paying more than half their monthly income for housing, or living in seriously run-down or overcrowded housing (Millennial Housing Commission 2002). Under a block grant, funding for the voucher program would no longer be tied to a formula that reflects actual program costs and rents. As a consequence, the gap between needs and resources would almost certainly widen over time (Sard and Fischer 2003).

Moreover, some states might use a block grant's flexibility to implement programmatic models that would potentially undermine the success of the voucher approach, creating new problems and worsening the housing hardships that low-income families already face. For example, they might reduce subsidy payments in order to serve more families, limiting the range of locational options accessible and undermining the program's effectiveness in making decent housing affordable for the poorest households. Or states might impose time limits in hopes of encouraging self-sufficiency, leaving working poor families to face unaffordable market rent levels. Or they might divert voucher funds to build new housing projects ear-marked for the poor, potentially exacerbating the concentration of assisted housing in poor and minority neighborhoods.

All of these so-called "reforms" are untested. We lack the rigorous evaluation results to assess the effectiveness of alternative program models such as time limits. HUD's Moving to Work demonstration, which provides statutory and regulatory waivers to selected housing authorities as an experiment in deregulation, includes several housing authorities that are testing variations in voucher program rules. These include fixed subsidy levels, minimum tenant contributions, and time limits. However, the impacts of these alternative approaches are not being rigorously evaluated, because Moving to Work was not designed for this purpose (Abravanel *et al.* 2000). Thus, if states were offered a housing assistance block grant, they would have little evidence on which to base decisions about alternative voucher program designs.

Further, none of these alternative models eliminates the fundamental dilemma of inadequate funding to meet housing needs, and there is good reason to believe that these types of changes would undermine vouchers' proven effectiveness in making decent housing affordable for low-income families. If block grant funding failed to keep pace with the costs of serving needy households, states would face pressures to use Section 8 administrative fees to cover other costs rather than implementing program improvements, or limit voucher recipients to housing in the least costly neighborhoods.

THE TANF EXPERIENCE IS NOT RELEVANT

Supporters of block grants claim welfare reform as a model for converting the housing voucher program to block grants, but none of the factors that contributed to declining case loads under TANF apply to housing. Unlike the proposal to convert housing vouchers to block grants, welfare reform was preceded by years of experimentation and evaluation of alternative models for promoting work and self-sufficiency. And TANF established clear goals and performance standards for the states, providing incentives to get more people working and off the welfare rolls. The housing block grant proposes no clear goals or performance requirements, and offers no proven models for more effective program design.

When TANF was launched, policymakers had good reason to believe that investing up-front in job training and placement services would reduce families' long-term need for cash assistance, increasing employment and cutting the welfare rolls. The same is not true for housing. A majority of voucher recipients already work. Further, affordable housing is out of reach for many working households – in 2002, there was no city in the United States in which a minimum wage worker working full-time could afford the rent for a standard two-bedroom apartment (NLIHC 2002). Regardless of how states tweaked voucher program rules, the need for housing assistance would stay essentially the same.

THE VOUCHER PROGRAM CAN AND SHOULD BE STRENGTHENED

A growing body of experience from programs around the country point to three promising strategies for making the basic voucher design work better. All of these strategies could be implemented within the existing program structure and could potentially improve outcomes for families substantially.

- *Mobility counseling and assistance* can help voucher recipients understand the locational options available, identify housing opportunities, and negotiate effectively with landlords. A growing body of evidence from assisted housing mobility programs across the country indicates that this kind of supplemental assistance can significantly improve locational outcomes for voucher recipients, resulting in greater mobility to low-poverty and racially mixed neighborhoods for families who might otherwise find it difficult to move out of distressed, inner-city neighborhoods (Goering, Tebbins, and Siewert 1995; HUD 1996, 1999; Turner and Wilson 1998).

- *Aggressive landlord outreach, service, and incentives,* though sometimes viewed as a component of mobility counseling, actually involve very different activities. Housing agencies can significantly expand the options available to voucher recipients and improve recipients' success in finding suitable housing by continuously recruiting new landlords to participate in the program, listening to landlord concerns about how the program operates, addressing red tape and other disincentives to landlord participation, and – in some cases – offering financial incentives to landlords to accept voucher recipients.

- *Regional collaboration and/or regional administration* of the voucher program can potentially help address the administrative barriers to portability across jurisdictions, and make the program more transparent to both landlords and participants. Almost no urban regions in the U.S. are served by a single, regional housing agency, but in a few, the jurisdiction of the central city PHA has expanded to encompass all or much of the metropolitan region (Feins *et al.* 1997). In addition, housing authorities in some metropolitan areas have entered in formal agreements that facilitate the movement of voucher recipients among regions. All of these examples illustrate the potential for greater regional coordination as a mechanism for strengthening voucher program performance (Katz and Turner 2001).

Although it is possible that some states might use a voucher block grant to implement one or more of these promising strategies, this seems unlikely absent a programmatic mandate or incentive system. Instead, the quality of local program administration could well deteriorate, particularly given states' current fiscal distress.

Since 1949, federal housing policy has had as its goal "a decent home in a suitable living environment for every American family." We are still a long way from achieving that goal, and the existing housing voucher program needs to be strengthened to move us in the right direction. But replacing the voucher program with a block grant would take us backward. Instead of resolving the fundamental dilemma of inadequate funding for affordable housing, a block grant would make housing hardship a state problem rather than a federal problem, and open the door to untested program changes that could undermine the proven strengths of the voucher approach.

REFERENCES

Abravanel, Martin, Margery Austin Turner, Robin Ross Smith. 2000. *Housing Agency Responses to Federal Deregulation: A Baseline Report on HUD's Moving to Work Demonstration.* Washington, D.C.: The Urban Institute.

Advisory Commission on Regulatory Barriers to Affordable Housing. 1991. *Not in My Backyard: Removing Barriers to Affordable Housing.* Washington, D.C.: U.S. Department of Housing and Urban Development.

Burchell, Robert W. *et al.* 1994. *Regional Housing Opportunities for Lower Income Households: A Resource Guide to Affordable Housing and Regional Mobility Strategies.* Washington, D.C.: U.S. Department of Housing and Urban Development.

Buron, Larry *et al.* 2000. *Assessment of Economic and Social Characteristics of LIHTC Residents and Neighborhoods.* Cambridge, Mass.: Abt Associates.

Buron, Larry, Susan Popkin, Diane Levy, Laura Harris, and Jill Khadurri. 2002. *The HOPE VI Resident Tracking Study: A Snapshot of the Current Living Situation of Original Residents from Eight Sites.* Report prepared by Abt Associates, Inc. and the Urban Institute for the U.S. Department of Housing and Urban Development. Washington, D.C.: The Urban Institute.

Churchill, Sarah, Mary Joel Holin, Jill Khadduri, and Jennifer Turnham. 2001. *Strategies that Enhance Community Relations in the Tenant-Based Housing Choice Voucher Program, Final Report.* Washington, D.C.: U.S. Department of Housing and Urban Development.

Devine, Deborah J. *et al.* 2003. *Housing Choice Voucher Location Patterns: Implications for Participant and Neighborhood Welfare.* Washington, D.C.: U.S. Department of Housing and Urban Development.

Feins, Judith *et al.* 1997. *State and Metropolitan Administration of Section 8: Current Models and Potential Resources.* Bethesda, MD: Abt Associates.

Finkel, Meryl, and Larry Buron. 2001. *Study on Section 8 Voucher Success Rates.* Washington, D.C.: U.S. Department of Housing and Urban Development.

Goering, John, Ali Kamely, and Todd Richardson. 1994. *The Location and Racial Composition of Public Housing in the United States.* Washington, D.C.: U.S. Department of Housing and Urban Development.

Goering, John, Helene Stebbins, and Michael Siewert. 1995. *Promoting Housing Choice in HUD's Rental Assistance Programs.* Washington, D.C.: U.S. Department of Housing and Urban Development.

HUD. 1996. *Expanding Housing Choices for HUD-Assisted Families: First Biennial Report to Congress.* Washington, D.C.: U.S. Department of Housing and Urban Development.

HUD. 1999. *Waiting in Vain: An Update on America's Housing Crisis.* Washington, D.C.: U.S. Department of Housing and Urban Development.

HUD. 2000. *Section 8 Tenant-Based Housing Assistance: A Look Back After 30 Years.* Washington, D.C.: U.S. Department of Housing and Urban Development.

Katz, Bruce J., and Margery Austin Turner. 2001. "Who Should Run the Housing Voucher Program? A Reform Proposal." *Housing Policy Debate.* 12(2): 239–62.

Malpezzi, Stephen. 1996. "Housing Prices, Externalities, and Regulation in U.S. Metropolitan Areas." *Journal of Housing Research* 7(2): 209–41.

Millennial Housing Commission. 2002. *Meeting Our Nation's Housing Challenges.* Washington, D.C.: Bipartisan Millennial Housing Commission.

National Low Income Housing Coalition (NLIHC). 2002. *Out of Reach 2002.* http://www.hlich.org/oor2002/index.htm.

Newman, Sandra, and Ann B. Schnare. 1997. "]'... And a Suitable Living Environment': The Failure of Housing Programs to Deliver on Neighborhood Quality." *Housing Policy Debate* 8(4): 703–41.

Orfield, Myron. 1997. *Metropolitics: A Regional Agenda for Community and Stability.* Washington, D.C.: Brookings Institution Press.

Popkin, Susan J., and Mary K. Cunningham. 2000. *Searching for Rental Housing With Section 8 in Chicago.* Urban Institute Report. Washington, D.C.: The Urban Institute.

Popkin, Susan J., and Mary K. Cunningham. 2002. *CHA Relocation Counseling Assessment Final Report.* Report prepared for the John D. and Catherine T. MacArthur Foundation. Washington, D.C.: The Urban Institute.

Popkin, Susan J., Diane K. Levy, Laura E. Harris, Jennifer Comey, Mary K. Cunningham, and Larry F. Buron. 2002. *HOPE VI Panel Study: Baseline Report.* Washington, D.C. The Urban Institute.

Sard, Barbara, and Will Fischer. 2003. "Housing Voucher Block Grant Bills Would Jeopardize An Effective Program and Likely Lead to Cuts in Assistance for Low-Income Families." http://www.Cbpp1/data/media/michelle/POSTINGS/5-14-03hous-pdf.doc.

South, Scott J., and Kyle D. Crowdar. 1998. "Leaving the 'Hood: Residential Mobility Between Black, White, and Integrated Neighborhoods." *American Sociological Review* 63(1): 17–26.

Stearns, Linda Brewster, and John R. Logan. 1986. "The Racial Structuring of the Housing Market and Segregation in Suburban Areas." *Social Forces* 65(1): 28–42.

Turner, Margery Austin, Susan J. Popkin, and Mary K. Cunningham. 2000. *Section 8 Mobility and Neighborhood Health.* Washington, D.C.: The Urban Institute.

Turner, Margery Austin, and C. Wilson. 1998. *Affirmatively Furthering Fair Housing: Neighborhood Outcomes for Tenant-Based Assistance in Six Metropolitan Areas.* Washington, D.C.: The Urban Institute.

Turner, Margery Austin, Stephen Ross, George Galster, and John Yinger. 2002. *Discrimination in Metropolitan Housing Markets: Results from Phase I of HDS2000.* Washington, D.C.: U.S. Department of Housing and Urban Development.

Venkatesh, Sudhir. 2002. *The Robert Taylor Homes Relocation Study.* Center for Urban Research and Policy Research Report. New York: Columbia University.

21

"Federally-assisted housing in conflict: Privatization or preservation?"

From *A Right to Housing: Foundation of a New Social Agenda* (2006)

Emily Paradise Achtenberg

Until 1996, the attractive townhouses known as Manassas Park Village in suburban Virginia – 20 minutes by commuter rail from Washington, DC – were home to 167 low- and moderate-income families. Today, the "Glen at White Pines" boasts new dishwashers and dryers and a computer room instead of a laundry, at double the rent (Foong 1996:30).

In 1999, 110 low-income elderly and disabled residents of three Iowa housing complexes learned that their rents would be going up by 67 percent (*Housing and Development Reporter* 1999:661 and HUD 1999a:vii). With few other affordable apartments in the vicinity, tenants faced the grim choice of sacrificing food, medicine and other necessities or leaving their friends, family and communities of 20 years.

Scenarios like these have been repeated all across the country, as private owners of government-assisted projects exercise the right to prepay their subsidized mortgages or opt out of their expiring rent subsidy contracts and convert to market-rate housing. They are the latest manifestations of a protracted struggle that has been waged for decades in the federal policy arena between private property rights and social housing needs in subsidized rental housing.

PREPAYMENT OF SUBSIDIZED MORTGAGES

The problem

The subsidized-mortgage prepayment problem is the legacy of the federal government's first attempt to stimulate private-sector production of low- and moderate-income housing, under Section 221(d)(3) and Section 236 of the National Housing Act. Conceived as an alternative to public housing, these programs produced some 560,000 units during the late 1960s and early 1970s.

In exchange for federally insured loans at subsidized interest rates, tax incentives and virtually no cash investment, developers were required to restrict occupancy to low- and moderate-income families at regulated rents. As an added inducement, most owners were permitted to prepay their 40-year subsidized mortgages after just 20 years, terminate affordability restrictions, and convert the property to its "highest and best" use.[1]

Twenty years later, a typical project built for $20,000 per unit had a market value of $40,000 and an outstanding mortgage debt of just $15,000, leaving a residual equity value of $25,000 per unit. The same project had become a tax liability for its owner, as depleted depreciation and mortgage interest deductions no longer offset taxable income. This created a substantial incentive for owners to prepay, refinance and convert to market housing.

The federal preservation program

In the late 1980s, the first wave of prepayments galvanized tenants and sparked a heated national policy debate over the future of this at-risk housing stock. Owners claimed that prepayment restrictions would constitute a breach of contract and an unconstitutional taking of private property by the federal government. Preservation advocates argued that the original social purpose of the housing should take precedence over paying windfall profits to owners that reflected unanticipated changes in market circumstances.

Faced with the prospect of massive tenant displacement, Congress passed emergency legislation in 1987,[2] followed by a "permanent" statute in 1990,[3] to address the prepayment problem. The new program embraced the view that

> preservation ... is, by far, the most cost effective strategy available to the government and ... can be accomplished in a way that protects the interests of the owners, the tenants and the communities in which the housing is located.
>
> (U.S. Congress 1990:107)

While effectively prohibiting mortgage pre-payment, the preservation program guaranteed owners fair market value incentives to keep the housing affordable to lower-income households for at least another 50 years, at the federal government's expense. The U.S. Department of Housing and Urban Development (HUD) provided additional mortgage insurance, supported by project-based rental subsidies, to finance the owner's "equity takeout" ($25,000 per unit in the previous illustration). Owners could either retain ownership or sell the property on a priority basis to a tenant- or community-based nonprofit purchaser who agreed to the same restrictions.

Privatization and prepayment

By 1991, the political consensus around this "permanent" preservation policy had begun to unravel. Not surprisingly, most owners preferred to secure the incentives for themselves rather than sell their properties to nonprofits, and reports of lucrative equity takeouts with little or no funds reinvested in the property created the appearance of yet another boondoggle for the subsidized housing industry (Grunwald 1994). The HUD Inspector General called the program "an emerging scandal" that could cost taxpayers more than $74 billion over 40 years (HUD 1994:2).

After the 1994 Republican sweep of Congress, bipartisan efforts to discredit preservation began in earnest. Indeed, the Democratic Administration was desperately seeking to abandon the now dysfunctional props (rental subsidies and mortgage guarantees) created earlier to manage the conflict between private profit and social housing needs, which threatened to cause a budgetary and fiscal crisis of massive proportions. A new federal consensus was emerging around the notion of deregulating the assisted housing stock, "vouchering out" existing tenants, and eliminating any ongoing federal involvement with the real estate. The preservation program, with its focus on protecting the existing subsidized housing stock, was completely at odds with this approach.

Accordingly, in November 1994, the White House's Office of Management and Budget (OMB) proposed to repeal the preservation program, restore owners' prepayment rights and provide affected tenants with vouchers (mobile tenant-based subsidies – OMB 1994:30). OMB also sought to rescind funds that were previously appropriated for preservation. These efforts were supported in varying degrees by the U.S. General Accounting Office (GAO), the Congressional Budget Office and HUD (see, for example, HUD 1995).

Preservation and social ownership

During the summer of 1995, tenant organizations, nonprofit groups and housing advocates across the country mounted an unprecedented grassroots campaign to save the preservation program. Using nationally coordinated tactics, such as letter-writing campaigns, press advocacy and lobbying directed at key legislative targets, advocates sought to "put a human face" on the preservation program and demonstrate the economic, social and political costs of prepayment.

Against formidable odds, these efforts achieved remarkable success. While the prepayment right was restored in March 1996, making preservation purely voluntary, the preservation program was extended with an additional $624 million in funding. This represented a 250 percent increase over the prior year appropriation, while the overall HUD budget was slashed by 25 percent (and funding for new housing vouchers was eliminated). Additionally, the revised program effectively targeted preservation funds for sales to resident and community-based nonprofits and replaced HUD mortgage guarantees with direct capital grants – a far more cost-effective approach conducive to long-term preservation.

Between 1996 and 1998, some 25,000 prepayment-eligible units in more than 30 states were converted to virtually debt-free social ownership with permanent affordability guarantees[4] – a transfer unprecedented in the history of U.S. housing. The average cost of preservation sales with capital grants (including both equity takeout and rehabilitation costs) was approximately $36,000 per unit (GAO 1997:60) – less than one-half the cost of building new subsidized housing in most markets at that time.

Nevertheless, the GAO and OMB resumed their attacks with new vigor, charging the capital grant program with excessive rehabilitation costs and inadequate oversight (GAO 1997:60). The subsidized housing industry, which no longer derived significant benefits from preservation, lent tacit support to this critique. HUD, threatened with extinction by the Republican Congress and abandoned by the Democratic Administration, was unwilling and unable to mount an adequate defense. In October 1997, all preservation funding was terminated. Some 50,000 units awaiting capital grants and loans were left in the approved but unfunded HUD preservation "queue" (HUD 1996b).

Post-preservation trends

In total, some 100,000 units were preserved under the various federal programs, including 33,000 units transferred to new owners who were primarily nonprofit purchasers using capital grants (National Housing Trust n.d.). Since the demise of the preservation program, another 110,000 subsidized units have been lost to mortgage prepayment (National Housing Trust 2002a). For prepayments occurring before 1999, the average rent increase was 57 percent (National Housing Trust 2001). While low income tenants who choose to remain after prepayment can receive "enhanced" preservation vouchers (subject to annual appropriations) at the prevailing market rent, these units are permanently lost as housing affordable to lower income households once the original tenants move.

EXPIRING SECTION 8 CONTRACTS

The problem

Starting in 1974, the federal government provided a new incentive to private developers and owners under Section 8 of the National Housing Act, in the form of a direct contract to subsidize the market rents of low- and moderate-income tenants. These contracts were either "project based" (tied to the unit) or "tenant-based" (mobile certificates or vouchers).

The Section 8 project-based housing stock – now larger than the inventory of traditional public housing units – consists of 1.5 million units and encompasses many different programs. Sixty percent (900,000) of the units are also covered by HUD-insured mortgages. Some of the properties originally were developed under Section 236 and Section 221(d)(3), with Section 8 subsidies added later to make a portion of the units more affordable to lower-income households. These projects typically have below market rents due to their subsidized mortgages and HUD rent regulation. Historically, these Section 8 contracts have been short-term (five year renewable).

In other projects originally built or substantially rehabilitated with Section 8, HUD underwrote the initial development by establishing rents high enough to cover market interest rates and construction costs in difficult-to-develop areas. In these projects, HUD also permitted automatic annual rent adjustments, with the result that rents often were above-market. These projects typically have long-term (20+ years) Section 8 contracts.

In the mid-1990s, the combination of long-term and short-term Section 8 contracts expiring simultaneously in the face of new budget constraints catapulted HUD into the spotlight of a looming fiscal crisis. Between FY1996 and FY1998, the cost of renewing all existing Section 8 contracts was projected to grow from about $5 billion to almost $14 billion, with an estimated 1.8 million units expiring – enough to consume the entire HUD budget (Dunlap 1995:12).[5] At the same time, failure to renew contracts with above-market rents could trigger widespread defaults and foreclosures of HUD insured mortgages, resulting in massive claims on the HUD mortgage insurance fund.

Mark to market

Struggling for survival, HUD developed a response to the Section 8 crisis that was to become the cornerstone of its 1995 "reinvention" blueprint. HUD concluded that not only was the long-term cost of continuing to provide Section 8 project-based assistance unsustainable, but the subsidy system itself was "deeply flawed" because it eschewed market principles. While above-market units were over-subsidized, below market units were under-subsidized and under-capitalized, providing perverse incentives for owners. Tenants without market choices were trapped. The federal government, as both subsidy provider and mortgage insurer, was essentially shooting itself in the foot, forced to keep paying for "bad housing" in order to avoid mortgage insurance claims (Retsinas 1995).

Accordingly, HUD proposed that these contracts, upon expiration, would no longer be renewed. Instead, the projects would be "vouchered out" with rents "marked to market" (up or down) and completely deregulated, while residents received tenant-based subsidies. HUD would auction off its mortgages to the highest private bidder (with a partial write down claim against the insurance fund, if necessary), who would restructure project finances, operations,

occupancy and, in some cases, ownership. In this way, HUD hoped to restore market discipline to a substantial portion of the federally assisted housing stock while ending the government's long-standing involvement with, and responsibility for, the real estate (Retsinas 1995).

In response, preservation advocates charged that HUD's proposal would trigger massive tenant displacement and loss of housing that was affordable to lower-income households through mortgage defaults and rent increases. Alternatively, they noted, any savings from "marking down" rents in the above-market stock would be outweighed by the cost of protecting tenants in "below-market" units with new vouchers at the marked-up rents (Bodaken 1995). Joining the groundswell of opposition was a growing alliance of subsidized housing developers and investors concerned about the adverse tax consequences of debt write downs, the potential loss of control over their investments, and the generally increased risk of requiring projects long reliant on HUD guarantees to compete in the open market (Grunwald 1995).

In 1997, Congress finally enacted mark-to-market legislation with a decidedly more preservation-oriented flavor.[6] Under this program, HUD was generally mandated to reduce rents and restructure debt in above-market properties with expiring Section 8 contracts while renewing their project-based subsidies. HUD would retain a deferred second mortgage in the amount of the debt write down – a device not dissimilar to the preservation capital grant, which would minimize adverse tax consequences to owners while facilitating continued public control over the housing. Debt restructuring was required to be carried out by state and local public entities (such as housing finance agencies) on a priority basis.

In exchange for debt restructuring, owners were required to extend low-income affordability restrictions and renew their Section 8 contracts, subject to availability of appropriations, for 30 years. Tenants, nonprofits, and state and local governments were given the right to comment on the restructuring plans.

Once launched, the program encountered substantial owner resistance. And with the general tightening of rental markets during the late 1990s, fewer properties than HUD had originally anticipated appeared to be eligible for or in need of debt restructuring. The majority of owners who did participate elected to absorb voluntary rent decreases without actually restructuring their mortgages, thereby avoiding any long-term affordability or tenant/community participation requirements.

At the same time, the responsibility for administering mark to market shifted increasingly from the public to the private sector. With alternative investment opportunities in the improving economy, many of the original housing finance agency participants balked at HUD's restrictive compensation structure and defected from the program (*Housing and Development Reporter* 2000:549). The new private entities replacing them lent tacit, if not explicit, support to mark to market's drift toward private sector accommodation.

Frustrated by these tendencies, preservation advocates sought to restore some of the program's original social purpose by launching a campaign to facilitate the sale of mark-to-market properties to nonprofit purchasers (National Association for Housing Partnerships and Recapitalization Advisors, Inc. 1999). Many hoped that mark to market – like the earlier federal preservation programs – would provide an "exit strategy" for private owners to transition the housing to nonprofit ownership, supported by federal debt write downs and long-term affordability restrictions.

In September 2000, HUD announced a new package of incentives to make mark to market more profitable for private owners and encourage their participation in the program (HUD 2000). At the same time, HUD agreed to forgive the deferred second mortgage debt for qualified nonprofits that purchased within three years of debt restructuring and to cover a significant portion of their transaction costs.

In recent years, this "owner-friendly" posture, combined with the general softening of the real estate market, has generated an increased volume of mark-to-market activity. Many owners now perceive mark to market as a beneficial opportunity to put their projects on firmer economic footing, with HUD continuing to absorb the risk through mortgage insurance and subsidies. Private lenders as well are now comfortable with mark to market, which enables them to earn fees – and Community Reinvestment Act (CRA) credits – for refinancing and servicing their existing loans (*Housing and Development Reporter* 2003:115).

As of October 2003, 2,030 properties have completed the mark-to-market process, with another 679 in the active pipeline (HUD 2003a). While the inventory is heavily concentrated in the heartland (e.g., Ohio, Pennsylvania, Kentucky), virtually every state has some mark-to-market projects (HUD 2003b). In contrast to early program trends, 63 percent of the completed properties have undergone full debt restructuring, and 95 percent of the pipeline projects have initially elected this option (HUD 2003a).

While some nonprofit groups have succeeded in buying mark-to-market properties using the new purchaser initiatives, the program as currently administered has not been conducive to this outcome. A primary factor is the failure of the private administrative entities to adequately reflect property rehabilitation and operating requirements in the debt restructuring process, resulting in the need for nonprofits to raise additional funds to ensure long-term project viability.

Section 8 opt-outs

While the 1997 statute focused primarily on "above-market" Section 8 properties, it also permitted HUD to renew project-based contracts in "below-market" properties – but only at the owner's option. Additionally, to facilitate budgetary management and Congressional scrutiny, all expiring Section 8 contracts were renewed only on a year-to-year basis.

With rents escalating rapidly in most markets nationwide, an increasing number of owners found themselves with both motive and opportunity to "opt-out" of their subsidy contracts at the point of expiration. Between October 1996 and April 1999, more than 30,000 units in 500 subsidized properties were lost as housing affordable to lower-income households when owners quit the Section 8 program in search of higher market-rate rents (HUD 1999a).[7]

Once again, preservation advocates focused national attention on the problem through targeted media campaigns in key legislative districts. After the notorious and well-publicized Iowa opt-outs in early 1999, HUD acknowledged that the record-level "worst-case" housing needs documented by its own studies were attributable, in part, to federal policies that facilitated the loss of subsidized units (HUD 1999b). HUD noted that while Section 8 opt-outs had occurred in 47 states, regular replacement vouchers at the local housing authority's "payment standard" often did not protect tenants from displacement. Additionally, HUD found that opt-outs were threatening the best housing in the country affordable to lower income households and located in good neighborhoods with good schools and economic opportunities.

In the spring of 1999, HUD developed an emergency initiative, subsequently enacted into law,[8] to stem the tide of Section 8 opt-outs. In most cases, HUD will now renew below-market Section 8 contracts at rents "marked up" to prevailing market levels for at least a five-year term (subject to annual appropriations). Where owners choose to opt out instead, tenants will receive enhanced vouchers at prevailing market rents for the property, similar to the prepayment program. Subject to appropriations, all enhanced vouchers, whether for prepayments or opt-outs, are now required to be renewed at market levels in future years.

Preliminary indications suggest that opt-outs have slowed since the advent of the mark-up-to-market program. As of July 2001, owners had opted out of contracts covering some 47,000 assisted units (National Housing Trust 2002b), reflecting an opt-out rate of 600 units per month since April 1999 (down from 1,000 units per month previously). However, it is too soon to tell whether owners who participate in "mark up to market" view the program as a long-term commitment or as a convenient way to transition to market at the government's expense. Additionally, while some nonprofit purchasers have utilized mark-up-to-market to purchase Section 8 properties, without additional resources to support market-rate acquisition in strong market areas, the utility of this program as a tool for social ownership conversion is limited.

CONCLUSION

In a sense, with mark-up-to-market, federal preservation efforts have come full circle. The current cost of preserving a single subsidized unit with market-determined subsidies (whether project-based or tenant-based) is approximately $6,400 per year (U.S. Department of Housing and Urban Development 2003c: N-4). Over five-and-a-half years, this is roughly the same as the average cost of the upfront capital grants provided to nonprofits under the federal preservation programs ($35,000). Over eleven years, market-based subsidies cost twice as much as preservation capital grants, without considering the additional cost of annual rent escalation. And while preservation capital grants provided permanently affordable housing through social ownership, units marked up to market remain at risk every five years, despite the continued public investment in the housing. In effect, the current market-based strategy retains all of the costs of socially oriented preservation with none of the benefits.

Increasingly, preservation advocates have turned to state and local governments for more permanent, cost-effective preservation solutions with some success (Achtenberg 2002; Galle 1999). For example, many states now earmark a portion of their federal low-income housing tax credits, and, in some cases, tax exempt bond allocations as well, for subsidized housing preservation. Some states and cities have issued preservation bonds backed by special appropriations or other non-federal revenue sources. These resources generally are targeted to nonprofit purchasers in exchange for long term use restrictions, sometimes in conjunction with "rights of first refusal" or purchase options if a federally subsidized property is sold. With these additional funds and tools, federal programs such as mark to market, mark up to market and even enhanced vouchers can be used to facilitate a more permanent preservation solution through social ownership conversion.

To be sure, in the context of state and local resource constraints these preservation initiatives will have limited impact and will succeed only at the expense of much-needed new construction. In recent years, preservation advocates have forged new alliances with city, state and grassroots groups to press for a federal matching grant program that would reward state and local preservation funding with federal dollars. These proposals have gained bi-partisan support and are now merged with an even broader campaign to create a federal housing trust fund for both production and preservation of housing affordable to lower-income families.

Yet, with renewed Republican efforts to diminish even further the federal government's role in subsidized housing, emerging alliances between preservation advocates and state and local governments will surely be put to the test.

In early 2003, the Bush Administration proposed to convert the entire Section 8 voucher program, including enhanced vouchers that protect tenants when owners prepay or opt out, to a state-administered block grant with few federal standards and no guaranteed funding levels. This is widely viewed as a strategy to reduce Section 8 funding while devolving political accountability to the states (Sard and Fischer 2003). Since funding shortfalls will encourage states to reduce existing voucher subsidy levels, market-based enhanced vouchers could be especially vulnerable to attack.

With 30-year hindsight, the failure of federal efforts to provide and preserve housing for low and moderate-income families through the private sector is readily apparent. The conflict between private property rights and social housing needs, inherent in the original structure of the federally-assisted housing programs, has never been resolved but only managed in ways that have ultimately served to exacerbate the conflict. Preservation has been possible only when private interests are served as well; when this is not expedient or becomes too costly, social needs are sacrificed.

At the same time, the history of these federal programs shows how organized grassroots constituencies can sometimes fundamentally alter political processes and program outcomes to create meaningful opportunities for social housing ownership and finance, facilitating long term preservation even under the most adverse of circumstances – an equally important lesson for the future.

Notes

1 Some categories of owners, including nonprofits and for-profit developers who received special benefits such as direct federal rehabilitation loans ("flexible subsidy") were prohibited from prepaying their mortgages without HUD consent.
2 The Emergency Low Income Housing Preservation Act (ELIHPA), Title II of the Housing and Community Development Act of 1987, P.L. 100–242, February 5, 1988, as amended.
3 The Low Income Housing Preservation and Resident Homeownership Act (LIHPRHA), Title II of the Cranston-Gonzalez National Affordable Housing Act, P.L. 101-625, November 28, 1990, as amended.
4 Extrapolated by the author from HUD 1996a, 1997.
5 This estimate includes both project-based and tenant-based Section 8 subsidies.
6 The Multifamily Assisted Housing Reform and Affordability Act of 1997 (MAHRA), Title V of the FY98 VA, HUD, and Independent Agencies Appropriations Act, P.L. 105–65.
7 This estimate does not include Section 8 units lost in conjunction with subsidized housing mortgage prepayments.
8 "The Preserving Affordable Housing for Senior Citizens and Families into the 21st Century Act of 1999," Section 501 of the FY00 Departments of Veterans Affairs, HUD, and Independent Agencies Appropriations Act, P.L. 106–74.

REFERENCES

Achtenberg, Emily P. 2002. *Stemming the Tide: A Handbook on Preserving Subsidized Multifamily Housing*. New York: Local Initiatives Support Corporation.
Bodaken, Michael. 1995. We must preserve the nation's supply of affordable housing. *Shelterforce*, July/August.
Dunlap, Helen M. 1995. Mark to market: A strategy to recapitalize HUD's assisted housing inventory. *Shelterforce*, July/August.
Foong, L. Keat. 1996. Market-rate bandwagon. *Multihousing News*, October/November.
Galle, Brian. 1999. Preserving federally-assisted housing at the state and local level: A legislative tool kit. *Housing Law Bulletin*, 29:183.
Grunwald, Michael. 1994. More HUD money flows to Boston landlords. *Boston Globe*, December 19.
——1995. Investors wary of HUD plan. *Boston Globe*, July 5.
Housing and Development Reporter. 1999. Decision of Iowa owners to terminate contracts raises concern for tenants. *Current Developments*, Vol. 26, No. 42, February 22.
——2000. California, New York City opt out of mark-to-market program. *Current Developments*, Vol. 27, No. 30, January 10.

——2003. Mark-to-market program has made progress, OMHAR director says. *Current Developments*, vol. 31, No. CD-4, February 17.

National Association for Housing Partnerships and Recapitalization Advisors, Inc. 1999. *Mark to Market and Non-Profits: Results from the Demonstration and Implications for the Permanent Program.* Boston: The Association.

National Housing Trust. n.d. Funded Title II and VI projects. Washington, DC: The Trust.

——2001. Prepayment summary as of 12/31/98. May 7. Washington, DC: The Trust.

——2002a. All mortgage prepayments by state as of 12/31/01. June 27. Washington, DC: The Trust.

——2002b. All Section 8 optouts by state as of 7/31/01. June 27. Washington, DC: The Trust.

Office of Management and Budget. 1994. FY1996 Passback: Department of Housing and Urban Development, November 21.

Retsinas, Nicholas, P. 1995. Statement before the Housing, Banking, and Financial Services Subcommittee on Housing and Community Opportunity, June 13.

Sard, Barbara, and Will Fischer. 2003. Housing voucher block grant bills would jeopardize an effective program and likely lead to cuts in assistance for low income families. Washington, DC: Center on Budget and Policy Priorities, May 14.

U.S. Congress. 1990. Managers' Report (Joint Explanatory Statement) – H.REP. No. 922, 101st Cong. 2nd Sess., October 22.

U.S. Department of Housing and Urban Development. 1994. Office of Inspector General, review of multifamily preservation programs. Office of Audit – Region X. Washington, DC, April 20.

——1995. Office of Inspector General, HUD's Multifamily Preservation Program. Office of Audit – New England. Washington, D.C., July 14.

——1996a. Office of Housing, projects funded in FY96. Washington, D.C., July 24.

——1996b. Office of Housing, preservation funding queue. Washington, D.C., November 12.

——1997. 1997 preservation funding queue database. Washington, D.C., December 10.

——1999a. Opting in: Renewing America's commitment to affordable housing. Washington, D.C.

——1999b. Waiting in vain: An update on America's rental housing crisis. Washington, D.C.

——2000. Office of Multifamily Housing Assistance Restructuring. Initiatives for M2M owners and purchasers. Washington, D.C., September 11.

——2003a. Office of Multifamily Housing Assistance Restructuring. Mark-to-market pipeline summary report. Washington, D.C., October 30.

——2003b. Office of Multifamily Housing Assistance Restructuring. PAE and assigned property status report. Washington, D.C., October 31.

——2003c. Fiscal year 2004 budget: Congressional Justifications for estimates. Washington, D.C.

U.S. General Accounting Office (GAO). 1997. Housing preservation: Policies and administrative problems increase costs and hinder program operations. GAO/RCED 97–169, Appendix VIII, July.

Competing goals: Place as community or opportunity?

Plate 5 **Make this neighborhood mixed income** (photography by Craig Morse, Culture: Subculture Photography, www.culturesubculture.com).

INTRODUCTION TO PART FIVE

The "people versus place" debate is ongoing in discussions of urban social policy. For housing policy, this has particular resonance: should we focus on improving conditions in low-income communities or facilitate the de-concentration of poverty? Is our interest in shaping new types of places or in reforming existing ones? Are solutions targeted to existing residents or anyone in need of affordable housing? This section focuses on how evolving views of the relationship between place and housing opportunities have been incorporated into policy.

Funding rules notwithstanding, current housing policy discussions often begin with the assumption that low-income residents should be encouraged to move out of poor communities. The list of problems associated with residence in a neighborhood of "concentrated poverty" is long and well accepted (Ellen and Turner 1997; Wilson 1987). Yet many arguments currently advanced for dispersal of affordable housing and low-income residents – civil rights, opportunity – were also advanced by those who argued for place based strategies forty years ago. Woven throughout the various programs that have focused on people, place or community since the Second World War are differing assumptions about the role of neighborhood setting for residents, the goals of redevelopment projects, and the reasons residents are moving out.

For advocates of urban renewal policies in the 1950s and 1960s, redevelopment was about creating vibrant new places, as part of larger strategies aimed at attracting jobs and residents back to cities from the suburbs. The wholesale destruction of minority and ethnic communities that often came with urban renewal projects, provoked a backlash and – for a brief period – a very different view of place-based policy. The Special Impact Program, funded under Title I-D of the Economic Opportunity Act of 1964 and described by Perry, one of the program's instigators, was explicitly about putting control of neighborhood upgrading in the hands of residents through locally controlled community development corporations (CDCs). It was rooted in the civil rights politics of the era and recognition of the overlap between race, neighborhood and (lack of) political voice.

Fifty years later, the community development movement has largely shifted away from issues of community control. CDCs struggle to develop affordable housing for low-income residents in the context of dwindling resources and local politics (Rubin 2000; Bratt and Rohe 2004). Critics argue that the work of CDCs has become less about empowerment and holistic community uplift and more about inclusion in larger city development agendas (DeFillipis 2008; Stoecker 2008). Newman and Ashton argue that in many struggling cities, neighborhood revitalization strategies are driven primarily by local political actors and community development organizations working in resource-poor environments. But rather than enabling community controlled redevelopment, they contend, this publicly driven process may constitute a new form of gentrification.

While community development advocates were pushing for change in the central city, fair housing advocates were trying to dismantle racial discrimination that limited minority residents' housing choices at the regional scale. As Goetz recounts, policy makers sought to change the location of affordable housing opportunities for minorities through a 1962 executive order ending discrimination in public housing, the Fair Housing Act of 1968, the U.S. Department of Housing and Urban Development's (HUD) short lived regional fair share initiative, and through the advent of scattered site public housing. Yet by 1974, when housing certificates and vouchers were introduced through the new Section 8 program, the rationale had shifted from discrimination to cost cutting. By the 1990s, Goetz argues, the rationale for dispersal rested almost entirely on the need to de-concentrate poverty. Poverty, rather than race, became the focus based on a growing literature documenting the "neighborhood effects" of concentrated poverty (see Ellen and Turner, 1997). This has had the effect of shifting the conversation away from rights and justice. Goetz argues that the rationale for the destruction of communities of color and dispersal of the poor has not been matched by a clear vision of the communities in which displaced residents should be resettled. Lawsuits challenging racial segregation in public housing have resulted in the clearest goals regarding desirable neighborhoods, emphasizing rights and choice (see Julian, Chapter 34 in this volume).

Public housing has long been concentrated in low-income, minority communities. Until the 1960s, local authorities had complete control over the siting of public housing and patterns followed the racially segregated patterns of the era. In Chicago, the city council held veto power over proposed sites, resulting in a near total concentration of units in low-income, black neighborhoods. The series of court cases now known as Gautreaux successfully challenged this situation and laid the groundwork for subsequent lawsuits, Along with the focus on de-concentration of poverty came a focus on the problems of "distressed public housing" – largely in the form of high rise, family buildings. Subsequent policies have attempted to address both concerns by demolishing high rise public housing and replacing it with lower rise, mixed income developments, housing many fewer extremely low-income households. Whether residents end up in less poor neighborhoods is highly dependent on program implementation and local political will. Resistance to scattered site development and the commitment required to make vouchers usable in non-poor areas have limited progress. Efforts to learn more about the benefits of de-concentration have also suffered: resistance to implementation of the Moving to Opportunity demonstration program in non-poor neighborhoods killed it.

All of these tensions are embodied in the HOPE VI program. The program brings together ideas about poverty de-concentration and urban redevelopment. HOPE VI sought to transform not only distressed public housing communities, but also to enable residents to become self-sufficient. Popkin's review of evidence from the HOPE VI Panel Study emphasizes the benefits for public housing families that have relocated to less poor communities. However, her findings also point out the limited understanding we have of how neighborhood context affects residents' lives. The lack of effects on employment, in particular, call into question assumptions about peer effects and access to job networks based on residential setting. As Popkin notes, health challenges may matter more to residents' ability to work – a concern beyond the purview of housing policy. Finally, the diversity of outcomes in terms of neighborhood conditions across cities brings us back to dilemmas of implementation. Can we reduce the share of residents who end up in the worst settings? Can we achieve better outcomes across neighborhood types?

The weak and complex outcomes of mixed income development bring us back to the assumptions upon which such policies were based. Some of the loftiest goals were based on expectations of relationship building between high and low-income residents. Joseph's discussion of the conceptual arguments for the benefits of mixed income development makes clear that there are other ways that benefits might be generated. For example, higher income residents might foster greater informal social control over norms of behavior, resulting in safer neighborhoods. Or they might model more socially acceptable and constructive behavior, leading to a new culture regarding work, respect for property, or other norms. Finally, higher income residents might spur higher demand for higher quality public and private goods and services in neighborhoods. Joseph does find some evidence to support the idea that the addition of higher income residents leads to greater social control and improved community attributes. On the whole, however, he concludes that policy makers should both clarify and lower their expectations regarding the potential effects of mixed-income development. His discussion of the factors that might affect relationship-building among community members –

including the degree of income mixing in the community – might also be applied to gentrifying low-income neighborhoods.

Perhaps the people-versus-place dichotomy is just not that helpful anymore. Davidson argues that this dichotomy obscures more than it reveals. As he says,

> Every individual-level public investment in poverty reduction and mobility is constrained by geography and at the same time directly affects the places those individuals live. Likewise, every public investment in a given place not only has a direct impact on the people in that place but more importantly shapes the incentives that people have to remain, leave, avoid, or move to that place.

Rather, it is the interactions between policies focused on people and on place that we should attend to. If the reality is that low-income people will live in a variety of places, thinking about policy in more integrated terms makes more sense. Neighborhoods are not only sites of concentrated poverty, they may also be simultaneously sites of redevelopment, creating new opportunities. Suburban neighborhoods are likewise complex: areas lacking rental housing that could allow for poverty de-concentration may need to be regarded as sites for affordable housing development in order to broaden opportunities. Finally, the meaning of race and strategies for achieving justice must be placed in the complicated context of local politics.

IN THIS PART:

Chapter 22: Perry, Stewart E. (1973). "Federal support for CDCs: Some of the history and issues of community control." *Review of Black Political Economy*, 3(3): 17–42.

Chapter 23: Newman, Kathe and Ashton, Philip. (2004). "Neoliberal urban policy and new paths of neighborhood change in the American inner city." *Environment and Planning A*, 36: 1151–1172.

Chapter 24: Goetz, Edward G. (2003). "Housing dispersal programs." *Journal of Planning Literature*, 18(1): 3–16.

Chapter 25: Popkin, Susan J., Levy, Diane K., and Buron, Larry. (2009). "Has HOPE VI transformed residents' lives? New evidence from the HOPE VI Panel Study." *Housing Studies*, 24(4): 477–502.

Chapter 26: Joseph, Mark L. (2006). "Is mixed-income development an antidote to urban poverty?" *Housing Policy Debate*, 17(2): 209–234.

Chapter 27: Davidson, Nestor M. (2009). "Reconciling people and place in housing and community development policy." *Georgetown Journal on Poverty Law & Policy*, 16(1), 10pp.

REFERENCES AND FURTHER READING

Bolton, R. (1992). "Place Prosperity" vs. "People Prosperity" Revisited: An Old Issue with a New Angle, *Urban Studies*, 29(2): 185–203.

Bratt, Rachel and William Rohe. (2004)." Organizational Changes Among CDCs: Assessing the Impacts and Navigating the Challenges." *Journal of Urban Affairs*, 26(2): 197–220.

Briggs, Xavier de Sousa, ed. (2005). *The Geography of Opportunity: Race and Housing Choice in Metropolitan America*. Washington, D.C.: The Brookings Institution.

Cisneros, Henry G., Lora Engdahl, and Kurt L. Schmoke. (2009). *From Despair to Hope: Hope VI and the New Promise of Public Housing in America's Cities*. Washington, D.C.: Brookings.

DeFillipis, James. (2008). "Community control and development: the long view," in James DeFillipis, James and Susan Saegert, eds. *The Community Development Reader*. New York: Routledge.

Ellen, Ingrid G., and Margery A. Turner. (1997). "Does neighborhood matter? Assessing the evidence." *Housing Policy Debate*, 8(4): 833–866.

Fainstein, S., and A. Markusen. "1992–1993". "The urban policy challenge: Integrating across social and economic development policy." 71 *North Carolina Law Review*, 1463 (1992–1993).

Fischel, W. (2001). *The Homevoter Hypothesis: How Home Values Influence Local Government Taxation, School Finance, and Land-Use Policies*. Cambridge, MA: Harvard University Press.

Freeman, Lance, and Frank Branconi. (2004). "Gentrification and displacement: New York City in the 1990s." *Journal of the American Planning Association*, 70(1): 39–52.

Galster, G. (2005). "Consequences from the redistribution of urban poverty during the 1990s: A cautionary tale." *Economic Development Quarterly*, 19(2): 119–125.

Glaeser, E. (2005). "Should the government rebuild New Orleans, or just give residents checks?" *The Economists' Voice*, 2(4): article 4.

Imbroscio, David. (2008). "[U]nited and actuated by dome common impulse of passion: Challenging the dispersal consensus in American housing policy research." *Journal of Urban Affairs*, 30(2): 111–130.

Newman, Kathe, and Elvin Wyly. (2006). "The right to stay put revisited: Gentrification and resistance to displacement in New York City." *Urban Studies*, 43(1): 23–57.

Rubin, Herbert. (2000). *Renewing Hope within Neighborhoods of Despair*. Albany, NY: SUNY Press.

Stoecker, Randy. (2008). "The CDC model of urban development: A critique and an alternative," in James DeFillipis and Susan Saegert, eds. *The Community Development Reader*. New York: Routledge.

Williamson, Anne R., Marc T. Smith, and Marta Strambi-Kramer. (2009). "Housing choice vouchers, the Low-Income Housing Tax Credit, and the federal poverty deconcentration goal." *Urban Affairs Review*, 45(1): 119–132.

Wilson, William J. (1987). *The Truly Disadvantaged: The Inner City, the Underclass, and Public Policy*. Chicago: University of Chicago Press.

Winnick, L. (1966). "Place prosperity vs. people prosperity: Welfare considerations in the geographic redistribution of economic activity." Real Estate Research Program, UCLA, *Essays in Urban Land Economics in Honor of the Sixty-Fifth Birthday of Leo Grebler*, pp. 273–283.

Zhang, Yan, and Gretchen Weismann. (2006). "Public Housing's Cinderella," in *Where are Poor People to Live?* Larry Bennet, Janet L. Smith, and Patricia A. Wright (eds). New York: M.E. Sharpe.

22
"Federal support for CDCs: Some of the history and issues of community control"[1]

From *Review of Black Political Economy* (1973)

Stewart E. Perry

I. INTRODUCTION

This paper introduces the history and reasoning that stood behind the program in the Office of Economic Opportunity, for the Community Development Corporations in low-income areas. Of course, the CDC is not just an OEO-funded organization; it was a social invention of low-income neighborhoods long before OEO decided to fund such groups to carry out their own economic development programs.

[…]

The paper initiates with the story of how OEO came to support the CDCs, first in black urban neighborhoods and later in all low-income neighborhoods, urban and rural, black, chicano, Appalachian, white ethnic, and others. I will briefly show how the program developed, how the law changed, and how the projects were evaluated in comparison with other federal economic development efforts. After this background, I will present the definition of community economic development as the main idea behind the CDC program.

[…]

II. HISTORY

The CDC program at OEO was created in 1967–68 from the authority provided originally by the Special Impact Program amendment to the Basic OEO legislation. This crucial amendment had become effective July 1966, as Title I-D of the Economic Opportunity Act of 1964. Sponsored by Senators Robert Kennedy and Jacob Javits, it promoted a particular and different concept of anti-poverty action. Previous OEO programs (aside from the Community Action Programs) were single purpose services – such as Head Start, job counseling, manpower training, youth recreation, VISTA, and so on. And the CAPs were supposed to mobilize resources for these individual services, by bringing the poor and the rest of the society together in joint boards to guide the services for the poor and by organizing the poor to get more of the services they needed. But the Special Impact amendment implies that CAPs and services would not break the cycle of poverty in deteriorated areas. Note the key term "areas." This implies that the problem of poverty is a problem of poor areas (poor communities), *not* a problem of poor *individuals*. That is crucial, for it means that the *total* community area in all its complexity is the target of anti-poverty work, not just the individual poor resident of that area.

Targetting the area, rather than the individual poor people in that area was the outcome of a tour of Bedford-Stuyvesant, the black Brooklyn slum, that Senator Kennedy once took and that convinced him that the problems of poverty were so inter-locked that something had to be done on a different level.[2] The area focus required a re-thinking of what might be done. Three ideas seemed important. First, the problem of the poverty area is too complicated for service programs, even a whole array of service programs, and so a multi-purpose, comprehensive, and coordinated *development* program including services at each community level is necessary. Development means the renewal and rebuilding of physical and institutional resources for the area – such as facilitating the availability of mortgage money for homes or actually building the homes or apartment dwellings.

Second, a very important part of that comprehensive development attack has to include economic and business development. That is, there has to be emphasis upon new businesses and other opportunities for employment and productive service to the community.

Finally, there had to be a new approach to the financing of such a program at the community level. It seemed to the legislators that any one project would have to be very heavily financed to make any dent at all on a large deteriorated neighborhood. So to make a comprehensive "special impact," limited funds ought to be concentrated in a few projects instead of being spread all around to every area that needed attention. This of course poses political problems, since every district wants to get into a program that gives federal grants. The Special Impact Program has, however, generally resisted that kind of political pressure. Probably it has been able to do so, mainly because it has always been a small unpublicized program. Model Cities legislation was also designed for a limited number of projects for concentrated impact, but that program was more heavily funded and more publicized, and it never managed to resist the tug of political demands for spreading the limited funds in a thin layer throughout the country.

The Special Impact Program was, in fact, very close in concept to the later, larger Model Cities program. As a comprehensive development program, it was to deal with housing as well as job counseling, with environmental and physical community development as well as organizing, and so on. The language of the amendment was very broad and really permitted OEO the widest flexibility to do any kind of development work as long as it was comprehensive.

The CAPs really already emphasized the idea of coordinating multi-purpose programs, but only in the matter of services. The Special

Impact program broadened that idea of coordination to include housing and physical development, specifying that two other federal agencies – HUD and EDA – should assist in the revitalization of the Special Impact areas. But probably the most significant new element in the amendment was the idea of local economic or business development with its aim of creating new jobs, especially managerial and entrepreneurial opportunities for residents of low-income areas. Economic development was not originally important in the Model Cities program.

[...]

It so happened that a group of planners[3] in OEO were also dissatisfied with certain aspects of the basic OEO programs; and the Congressional pressure gave them a chance to design a new program, using the Special Impact authority to support ideas being promoted by low-income communities themselves. That was how the OEO model of a CDC got its start. The planners had already taken a look at the Labor Department's model, the Bedford-Stuyvesant project, and had decided that model could be improved upon by making community control much more important.

The Bedford-Stuyvesant project was, as is well known, a creation of Senator Kennedy and his staff. He persuaded important business and financial figures to join the D & S Corporation (which mobilizes the resources in the establishment world on behalf of Bedford-Stuyvesant) and recruited a leading black judge to choose a range of representatives from the Bedford-Stuyvesant district to form the all-black Bedford-Stuyvesant Restoration Corporation. Thus, while a most impressive array of resources in the persons of financial and other leaders was brought to bear on the problems of the area, the project was clearly an outside-initiated affair. It was not then what might be appropriately called a community-controlled organization.[4] And it was just this factor that appeared to be the final necessary piece to an effective Special Impact program.

However, Congressional pressure for more comprehensive development projects like Bedford-Stuyvesant combined with another influence. The forthcoming report of the President's Commission on Civil Disorders also put OEO on the spot to demonstrate its recognition of the dissatisfactions of the young male Blacks who avoided the poverty programs and formed the main force in the series of urban riots in that period. The OEO planning group had also been asked to make a special attempt to survey what was missing in the range of poverty programs and why they were not enlisting some of the people who most needed them in the urban ghetto.

Actually, this task closely fitted the goals of the Special Impact amendment which authorized programs that would combat "dependency, chronic unemployment, and *rising community tension.*"[5] Bedford-Stuyvesant had experienced a serious riot, and it was commonsense long before the Commission report that the tensions in the ghettos were related to the economic discrimination faced by the black city dweller. However, no federal program would be likely to erase that discrimination even over a decade, nor could any federal program be expected to reverse definitively the ghetto poverty cycle in that period of time. It had taken many decades to bring Bedford-Stuyvesant, for example, to the disaster area it had become, and it would take at least as many to rescue it.

Therefore, the realistic policy question for program design was not what solutions could be whipped up to solve the long-standing and recalcitrant problems of a society that produced urban economic and social disaster areas, but what program, if any, could at least promise the chance, to residents of those areas, of concrete advances upon their local problems.[6] Hope was a psychological matter, not an economic one. Economic development had to be based upon what the residents themselves wanted to do and upon *their* definition of their problems. No long-term, abstractly designed economic development program – no matter how technically sophisticated – would work without the support and energies of the residents themselves, who could be expected to respond only if they saw something intrinsically hopeful and self-respecting in it – and that seemed to mean neighborhood community control.

The program design formally proposed by the OEO planning group was based on taking a new look at what the low-income urban black communities were already trying to do for themselves, and what it seemed that these neighborhoods (especially the young men) most wanted – that is, self-determination, programs without strings, community control, and something besides services, something more real somehow, like business development or housing. [...] There were youth projects that focussed on youth business; there was the multipurpose programs in economic and community development in rural areas, such as HELP in New Mexico, SWAFCA, the farmers cooperative in Alabama, and the Crawfordsville project in Georgia, where low-income people had started a sewing plant. Perhaps even more significant were the efforts, like those of the Reverend Leon Sullivan and the Zion Investment Associates or DeForest Brown and Hough Area Development Corporation or Minister Franklin Florence and FIGHT in Rochester, N. Y. – programs initiated by black residents of the inner city to begin comprehensive economic development. In late 1967, there was already a lot going on that the OEO planners could learn from.

B. Program control

The staff proposal originally recommended that local groups, fully controlled by neighborhood residents (not CAPs, which were mainly controlled by nonresidents), receive substantial administrative and investment funds to create their own comprehensive neighborhood economic and community development projects. However, by the specific decision of the OEO director, the proposed no-strings feature for the local use of investment money was compromised: Each neighborhood would have the chance to create its own projects, but after being given a basic investment budget to work with, each specific investment from that budget would have to be approved by OEO. The idea of full community control was not 100 percent accepted then, but at least the local projects would be initially designed locally by local residents themselves. This remains true today, although the program administrators are currently considering a "Venture Autonomy System" which would give the more effective CDCs more freedom to invest without specific OEO approval.

The main idea, then, that the OEO planners initially added to the framework provided by the Special Impact amendment was a real measure of local, low-income neighborhood control over the design and execution of the project. It was true that OEO had previously emphasized "maximum feasible participation," but as everyone now recognizes, participation by the poor was all too often, due to the CAP program history and design, neither maximum, feasible, nor very effective participation.[7] And whenever, in fact, the participation had become too troublesome, the agency had often bowed to political pressure from the establishment to cut it off. Furthermore, just at this particular time (late 1967), the so-called Green amendment was being passed, which gave each local establishment (through local government) the right to take over any CAP program that seemed to be getting out of hand. However, the Green amendment happened to have been written so it applied only to the CAP part of the law. CDCs under the new Special Impact proposal, exempt from Green amendment structures could emphasize the community self-determination that had not been realized under the CAP concept, and now with the Green amendment never would be. The idea of locally controlled community economic development was translated by the OEO planners into a program proposal, but actually the idea came from the inner-city communities themselves, especially places like Hough in Cleveland which had already organized a community development corporation of its own.[8]

The CDC program, then, was an attempt to maintain the idea of poor people's participation and to make that idea more real than it had been. For the planning staff recognized that the black identity movement had a tremendous amount of energy which, given the financial resources to back it up, could do a job that nothing else could in the deteriorated inner-city black neighborhoods. Thus, the CDC program began explicitly with the consideration that the social movement energies of a neighborhood had to be capitalized upon. At that time, it was mainly the black people who had come to a politically conscious and high awareness of their own identity, and the program was especially focussed on them originally. Since then, of course, other minorities (including white ethnics) have been mobilized on the basis of group identity and have begun the same path towards self-determination in their neighborhoods, and OEO's CDC program has responded to their energies as well.[9]

[…]

True resident control meant that the groups that would carry out the program had to be local creations. They could not be organized by or even organized in response to an OEO funding program. The federal agency must reach out to groups already organized, already demonstrating their capacity for constructing and executing a community economic development project. Of course, the availability of funds would inevitably suggest to community groups that they should move in the program direction, suggested by that availability, but since funds would permit only a very small number of possible projects, that influence would probably be minimal; and in fact the agency could select capable groups from those that already showed a capacity to create and run their own programs and who were already looking for economic development funds. That prior track record became a criterion for selecting the initial projects.[10]

C. The experiment

The OEO's version of the CDC program was argued for on the grounds that, although, of course no one could guarantee it, full community control by low-income people would probably produce a better program than any other administrative design. That idea was already mentioned, not fully accepted in the agency, and so the CDC program was adopted only as an experiment to test whether or not community control would work. The first year, a research firm compared the one CDC project that was funded (the Hough Area Development Corporation) with other federal programs using Special Impact funds. […]

The history of the OEO/CDC program is, in fact, a history of a continuous struggle to maintain the integrity of the design, of the program, and of the funds. Part of this struggle may be traced to an incredible turnover rate in many jobs in the higher echelons of OEO. As each new official came in, he looked askance at the CDC program, saw the funds available for it, and thought about using the funds a different way, or thought about saving federal money by cutting back on the program. It was this long history of indecision and outright hostility that resulted in a new substitute amendment to the OEO legislation – an amendment made law in 1972.

Today, OEO's program of support for CDCs takes it authority and funds from the new Title VII of the Economic Opportunity Act. That title or part of the law is labelled "Community Economic Development," instead of "Special Impact." The new title retains much of the language of Title I, Part D, but it specifically requires OEO to provide support for comprehensive community economic development programs by locally controlled groups, "community development corporations." Thus, the concept of the low-income CDC is now in the law. Title VII also requires OEO, if appropriations are large enough, to begin a new kind of support for poor people's cooperatives and CDCs – a revolving loan fund, which will supplement the grant funds for investment purposes in business and other community ventures. This and other language again emphasizes the need to fund a few projects heavily enough and long enough to make a real impact.

Because each neighborhood or rural area has its own individuality and its own history of community organizations, it was virtually impossible for Congress (actually the Senate Subcommittee on Employment, Manpower, and Poverty which initiated the Title VII amendment), to come up with a definition to CDCs that would be both precise and at the same time general enough to cover all possible forms of community control. The legal language apparently could not be made to fit the rich reality of the CDCs, so the final form merely required that the CDC be "responsive to the residents of the area under guidelines established by" the OEO director. [...]

III. COMMUNITY ECONOMIC DEVELOPMENT

The most general basic idea that energizes a CDC is of course "community-based economic development" or, more simply worded, "community economic development." People may differ somewhat on what that exactly means – depending upon their interests and experience. Perhaps because I am a specialist in organizations, I would emphasize that it means building organizations in the economic sector of life. Trying to define it carefully, I would say that community economic development is the creation or strengthening of economic organizations (or, more technically, economic institutions) that are controlled or owned by the residents of the area in which they are located

or in which they will exert primary influence. The organizations that are owned or controlled locally can include such forms as business firms, industrial development parks, housing development corporations, banks, credit unions, and the cooperatives and CDCs themselves as the most broadly generalized, guiding institutions. They might also include organizations (or services) that upgrade the human and social environment in such a way as to increase the economic value and energy of the community.

The process of economic development at the community level means that the community, through its leaders, builds a variety of economic organizations that will (1) attract outside capital into the area on terms that the community approves; (2) improve the physical environment either directly or through, again, outside resources, such as municipal or state or federal investments in streets, schools, housing, and so forth; (3) increase the job and entrepreneurial opportunities for area residents, either indirectly by providing training or directly by the creation of businesses open to and controlled by the residents; (4) provide or encourage others to provide services and goods on a more accessible basis for area residents (e.g., local taxi service or convenience shopping centers); and (5) generally in these and other ways, create the conditions under which the community can participate in the economic advantages and growth of the rest of the society.

From this it should be clear that community economic development is *not* merely starting new local businesses. It is also not merely locating new resources in that community (as in urban displacement through urban renewal) but creating them under the guidance of the local residents. One such instrument for guiding the economic development is the community development corporation.

A. Central goal

Local control by residents enhances the power and the influence of the low-income community to obtain what it needs to end the poverty area cycle. The central and immediate goal of community economic development is to increase that power and influence by providing economic muscle for a representative community organization. That organization would thereby be able to promote the satisfaction of neighborhood needs – for example, for new and improved services (welfare, health, education, garbage collection, police, street lighting, or whatever) as well as for their share of the employment and business opportunities that are ordinarily denied them.

Note that the immediate aim of community economic development is *not* to end poverty. That is, the new firms and banks, and so on, will *not* ensure a job for every able-bodied person in the neighborhood; the new firms *never will, never could.* And they will never produce enough profits to make a meaningful income supplement for all residents. For example, realistically, there will never be enough money in the Special Impact program to start enough new job-creating businesses, locally owned and controlled, where local residents can be employed or receive substantial dividends from profits.

There are several reasons for this. For one, to provide that much money to local groups would upset the established wealth and power relationships in the country. From the Yankee, Indian, or French poverty areas of Northern Maine to the ghettos and barrios of Southern California those relationships are too strong to permit such swift massive change. Yet it is also not economically sensible to plan that the rural or urban slums, can, with their own new businesses, retrieve and support the poor people of this country. Community economic development by low-income people cannot be expected to correct all the problems caused by the economic system of our society.[11] A CDC must have a more limited objective.

It is true that community economic development will and should provide a certain muscle politically for more support for the guaranteed annual income, which would end individual poverty immediately. It is also true that the political muscle of CDCs can increasingly demand and receive for their communities a more and more equitable share of the productivity and wealth of the country. But that share will not come primarily from the businesses, jobs, and profits provided by the CDCs. It will come indirectly through the social, political, and economic strength of the communities and neighborhoods invigorated by CDC projects. That will be the (all too slow) way that the CDCs can contribute most importantly to the ending of poverty in America. If this is true, then the poor people who support their

CDCs as members, as residents, need to be clear about it. The CDCs are not the full answer to their plight.

Someone might ask, "If the main aim of the CDC in community economic development is to establish power and influence for the community, why not simply create a political organization instead of getting all involved in technical problems of business development, housing, and so on?" Indeed, that is a reasonable question. For one thing, a single-purpose political organization can do a lot more politically than an organization that spends time on other problems. The hitch is that politics by itself is not the game. The problems of the low-income area are not just political, any more than they are merely the poor housing, or lack of local businesses, or ethnic discrimination. All of these are involved, and so the CDC must be concerned with all of them.

This is not to say that there is no room for single-purpose organizations in an area that has a successfully functioning CDC. In the best organized community that has a CDC, different organizations have specialized tasks; where there is no CDC, any effective organization is important, even if it is doing only one small part of the job. However, the special task of the CDC is to see all of the problems together, the whole picture of poverty in the neighborhood and how the activities of the entire neighborhood, its organizations, and its individuals can fit together in an over-all comprehensive development approach.[12] The reason the CDC can perform this task is that it is not just a planning agency. It can do things. That is the crucial reason why it must, in fact, be involved in an actual program, and not be merely an important think-tank [...].

Notes

1   This paper was originally prepared at the request of the Ad Hoc Committee of Board Members of CDCs funded under OEO's economic development program.

2   See Jack Newfield, *Robert Kennedy: A Memoir* (New York: Bantam, 1970).

3   They included an economist, James Robinson, a psychologist, T. M. Tomlinson, and two sociologists, Barbara Williams and myself, who headed the working group for the design of the new program proposal. Upon preliminary approval of our

proposal, we were joined by Geoffrey Faux from the Community Action Program, which was to administer the new project.

4 As it has developed, the Bedford-Stuyvesant Restoration Corporation has moved more and more in the direction of seeking ways to be responsive and accountable to the area residents it serves. The D & S Corporation remains an outside group, but its staff collaborates intimately with initiatives taken by Restoration staff; and Restoration itself has been organizationally renewed by more community in-put. Some of these changes took place after the project was transferred for administrative and financial supervision to OEO, which tended to press every CDC to maintain or increase its accountability to its own community.

5 Title 1, Part D, section 150 of the Economic Opportunity Act. (Italics supplied.)

6 Of course, if, as expected, the program was, on the local level, economically, socially, and psychologically successful, its success (and its limitations) would provide the experience and the political demand for more and more emphasis on this type of program and more and more funds for it – with all that that would require in our society. Thus, the long-term and basic solutions to the poverty community problems would grow out of a well-designed, initial program for localities.

7 For example, 100 percent of an objectively chosen sample of CAPs were initially organized without any participation by poor people whatsoever. Moreover, the allocation of resources even in 1966 (before the Green amendment) was only 3 percent for some kind of institutional change activity but 97 percent for service programs, etc. See Stephen Rose, *The Betrayal of the Poor* (Cambridge, Mass.: Schenkman, 1972), pp. 128 and 141–142. For a view that the poor cannot control local programs for their benefit, see Daniel P. Moynihan, *Maximum Feasible Misunderstanding* (New York: Free Press, 1969).

8 The idea was springing up everywhere at that time, independently. That is, different people in different parts of the country were thinking along the same lines, but not realizing that others were too. For example, it was during this time that two Senatorial aides and a black civil rights leader were drafting the proposed Community Self-Determination Act, that was introduced by a large number of Senators and Congressmen in June, 1968. That proposed legislation never went any further, but it expressed in a proposed comprehensive law what the new OEO program was trying to accomplish under the Special Impact Amendment. The authors of the CSDA were Gar Alperovitz (an aide to Senator Gaylord Nelson) and John McClaughry (an aide to Senator Charles Percy), and they worked closely with Roy Innis of CORE. (This evidence of Congressional interest, occurring spontaneously, came as a surprise to OEO.)

9 As the first administrator of the program, Geoffrey Faux was responsible for recognizing very early in 1969 the claims of other minorities, including inner-city white ethnic areas for assistance under the Special Impact Program. This expansion was undoubtedly crucial in increasing the base of support for the CDC concept in OEO at a critical early stage.

10 For a brief discussion of the criteria used, see Stewart E. Perry, "Black Institutions, Black Separatism, and Ghetto Economic Development," *Human Organization* (1972) 31:271–279; esp. p. 273.

11 In the U.S., the ending of individual poverty is actually a much more simple task – actually less disturbing of the wealth and power relationships than community economic development – and therefore more likely. That can be accomplished by some type of guaranteed annual income or negative income tax to insure that the richer areas and populations – via taxes – will share enough for the basics – food, etc. – to go to those in need.

12 I should emphasize most strongly that the CDC does not necessarily get directly involved in all community development activities. For example, generally the Hough Area Development Corporation deliberately stays out of direct development of housing but may assist other organizations doing housing. A CDC will always (or should) find, cooperate with, or develop other local groups and organizations to do a part of the job. No one organization can do it all.

23

"Neoliberal urban policy and new paths of neighborhood change in the American inner city"

From *Environment and Planning A* (2004)

Kathe Newman, Philip Ashton

INTRODUCTION

After decades of disinvestment, population flight, and housing abandonment, a number of very-low-income urban neighborhoods became sites for reinvestment in the late 1990s, suggesting that a new process of neighborhood change was at work. This reinvestment bears much in common with what is traditionally or popularly thought of as gentrification: in-migration of higher income residents, transformation of neighborhood culture, and potential displacement of existing residents. Yet this new reinvestment process differs from conventional gentrification in important respects. In particular, high crime rates, and a lack of locational advantages or an attractive housing stock make this reinvestment all the more surprising and worthy of further investigation. Our goal in this paper is to explore this process of neighborhood change that emerged during the course of the 1990s, using as our illustrative case the West Side Park neighborhood in Newark, New Jersey (Figure 23.1). We undertake a close analysis of this change, examine its context, the agents that initiated it, and the policy and political frameworks that support it, and we suggest possible implications.

We argue that a nexus of forces have come together over the last decade to create this new process of neighborhood change in distressed cities such as Newark. In particular, a neoliberal policy regime, emphasizing poverty deconcentration, mixed-income neighborhoods, home-ownership support, and reliance on the private market rather than the state, has played a key role in spurring new construction and a corresponding influx of eligible moderate-income, minority households. The local state is a key player in this process, seeking to organize the community development sector and neighborhood political constituencies through its control over discretionary funds, access to land, and ability to provide linkages to resources from county, state, and federal governments. Rather than representing an idiosyncratic case, however, we trace the lineage of the patterns we identify in Newark outwards and argue that this form of neighborhood change is increasingly prevalent. We argue that this process deserves critical scrutiny for its reconstitution of community development and its effects on long-term neighborhood residents, especially very-low-income residents. We also analyze the potential limits of such a strategy, suggesting that it may do little to reverse the long-term trends of disinvestment that may ultimately threaten to devalue new developments.

THINKING ABOUT NEIGHBORHOOD CHANGE

In the 1960s, gentrification, as a theory of neighborhood change, challenged the then dominant succession theories of change. By finding a gentry reinvesting in a working-class London neighborhood, Glass (1964) challenged the succession assumptions that urban neighborhoods follow a unidirectional downward

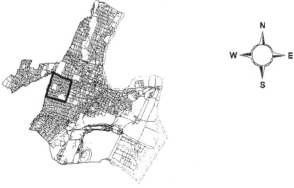

Figure 23.1 West Side Park, Newark, NJ (sources: land use, RCOPC, 2002; parcel map, Department of Engineering, 2000).

trajectory. Her research suggested that neighborhoods could be sites of reinvestment as well as disinvestment. Since her observations, researchers have struggled to explain this form of reinvestment, its sources, processes, and effects. Gentrification is often defined as a class-based process of neighborhood upgrading, with residential displacement generally used as the litmus test to separate it from other types of reinvestment. However, there is a growing consensus that there is no one form or process of gentrification. Beauregard (1986) suggests that it is chaotic, that there are many gentrification processes. Lees (2000) and Ley (1997) suggest that there is a geography of gentrification, so we should expect many forms of gentrification depending on local contexts.

Emerging perspectives on gentrification have also emphasized the temporality of reinvestment and the role of the state in shaping the complexity of gentrification processes and outcomes. Gentrification processes have changed dramatically since the 1960s, when they were a relatively new and somewhat unexpected phenomenon that affected only a few select neighborhoods. By the 1980s and 1990s, the reinvestment that so surprised succession theorists had become commonplace. Since then, the scope of reinvestment has expanded from Berry's (1985) "islands of renewal in seas of decay" to Wyly and Hammel's (1999) "islands of decay in seas of renewal". Hackworth and Smith (2001) have subsequently conceptualized the evolution of gentrification processes in New York City as waves of reinvestment that expand in relation to economic cycles. Economic booms push speculative real-estate markets further away from the downtown core; recessions stop or impede the expansion. The economic recession and demographic shifts of the early 1990s led some to question whether gentrification had run its course without the money or people to fuel the changes (Bourne, 1993). But the late-1990s economic boom fueled a new tsunami-size investment wave that dramatically expanded gentrification processes in global cities such as New York and London and in cities further down the urban hierarchy (Smith, 2002). Cities such as Detroit, Newark, and Cleveland, the very cities that Clay (1980) found had minimal expectations for revitalization in the 1970s, saw reinvestment in the late 1990s. The booming regional labor markets and low interest rates that enabled newly wealthy stock owners – 'financiers' – to hypergentrify neighborhoods such as Brooklyn Heights (Lees, 2000) also augmented the purchasing power of many working-class, middle-class, and upper-middle-class households, suggesting that sites other than the "hottest gentrifying neighborhoods" are important for understanding the most recent wave of gentrification (Smith, 2002, page 8).

Although gentrification is generally understood as a private market activity, the role of the state in creating the conditions for disinvestment-reinvestment cycles has always been acknowledged. More recently, however, policymakers have taken gentrification to heart by adopting it as an expected and desirable revitalization strategy. In the 1970s and to some extent in the 1980s, there was some concern about the effects of gentrification on the poor and in some quarters, but by the 1990s gentrification had become an acceptable path of neighborhood change. This belies a creeping "generalization of gentrification in the urban landscape" and in policy discourse in the USA and the United Kingdom (Smith, 2002, page 2). Although much of this discourse is cloaked in the desirable goals of returning people to cities to achieve 'social balance', Smith argues this is not about creating social balance but rather about drawing the middle class back to urban neighborhoods:

> the appeal to bring people back into the city is always a self-interested appeal that the white middle and upper middle classes retake control of the political and cultural economies as well as the geography of the largest cities.
>
> (Smith, 2002, page 17)

This represents an expansion of neoliberal policy within cities, which offer little resistance.

> The new phase of gentrification therefore dovetails with a larger class conquest not only of national power but of urban policy, and by the end of the twentieth century, gentrification, marking a concerted and systematic partnership of public planning with public and private capital, has moved into the vacuum left by the end of liberal urban policy.
>
> (Smith, 2002, page 11)

The partnership of planning and capital in generalizing gentrification discourse has highlighted the consolidation of a neoliberal urban policy regime emphasizing local competitiveness and revitalizing cities through poverty deconcentration and community reinvestment. For Crump (2002), 'deconcentrating poverty' is the 'blight' of the late 1990s and early 2000s – a favored term used to justify demolishing neighborhoods to make way for capital investment. Over the last two decades, concentrated poverty has come to be seen in policy communities as a source of poverty itself, which has helped legitimate the demolition of high-rise public housing projects and the construction of moderate and market rate housing in very-low-income neighborhoods. For Crump, policymakers adopted the term 'deconcentrating poverty' and let go of the complex factors that produce poverty, thereby reducing poverty to a spatial problem – a spatial problem for which they produced spatial remedy. In many cases, gentrification is a condition that has made poverty deconcentration and mixed-income development a political and economic reality; Wyly and Hammel (2000, page 189) argue

that gentrification has been accepted as the prerequisite for local attempts to redevelop distressed public housing to achieve the goals of privatization and cross-subsidies of market-rate, moderate-income and low-income residents.

We would add that this occurs even in the absence of existing gentrification; the generalization of gentrification has incorporated the desire to use mixed-income development to end concentrated poverty into the imagination of local political leaders and policymakers envisioning alternative futures for their cities. This has been further compounded by financial reregulation and a reemphasis on community reinvestment, which has helped transform the discourse on inner cities from 'redlining' to 'reinvestment' to 'tapping underserved markets' (Listokin and Wyly, 2000). A confluence of policies and regulations have structured this shift, ranging from more aggressive enforcement of the 1977 Community Reinvestment Act under the Clinton administration to the proactive policies of secondary market institutions in providing capital for loans in underserved areas.

Although the impetus for these changes was to overcome historical barriers to credit and assets for low-income and minority households, a crucial outcome has been a surge of liquidity for investments in inner-city neighborhoods (Avery et al., 2000; Wyly et al., 2001).

This changing discourse of gentrification, revitalization, and poverty provides legitimacy for local governments seeking to revitalize their cities and reduce their responsibilities towards the poor. Weber (2002) argues that cities in the USA are increasingly entrepreneurial in the context of globalization and the dismantling of the welfare state. But despite the withdrawal of federal resources through devolution and welfare-state retrenchment the federal government has provided mayors with the flexible dollars and tools they need to transform their skylines and neighborhoods, aiding competitive activities by local governments. Local governments continue to receive a bundle of federal block grants, providing them with resources to influence the process of local development, and the 'new federalist' regime of devolving responsibilities to states and localities has become the established methodology for organizing state involvement in urban re-development. The Community Development Block Grant (CDBG) provides flexible funds for revitalization; the Home Improvement Partnership Program (HOME) provides funds for low-income housing construction, and HOPE VI provides dollars to demolish public housing and facilitate redevelopment. Some cities received multi-million dollar grants through the federal Empowerment Zones and Enterprise Communities programs, which required community participation to identify spending priorities for a flexible array of social services, economic development, and housing but which in many cities became dominated by local government redevelopment preferences (Gittell et al., 1998). Even these programs are now offered on a competitive basis, forcing cities to compete for public redevelopment resources.

Even though these federal programs were ostensibly designed to expand benefits to low-income residents in disinvested environments, local political contexts as well as local needs can remake these federal resources into the anchors of neighborhood change strategies involving the deconcentration of poverty through the demolition of high-rise public housing or increased homeownership for the middle class (Goetz, 2000; Hackworth and Smith, 2001). Davis (1994) elaborates how progressive urban regimes have capitalized transfer payments and other sources of revenue into what he calls an 'affordable city' that expands privileges for the poor. More commonly, however, cities have used these resources to transform their images by physically removing housing for very poor people. The combination of HOPE VI dollars to demolish public housing, increased access to capital for homeownership, and federal policy eliminating the need to replace each demolished public housing unit with a new unit (one-for-one replacement) removes some of the last federal protection for very-low-income residents, further allowing local governments the freedom to pursue their own development agendas (Crump, 2002; Hackworth and Smith, 2001; Wyly and Hammel, 1999). Newark is a case in point; it has used its funds to demolish the high-rise public housing that was a highly visible reminder of a legacy of urban poverty on the fringes of Newark's downtown hub. Before demolition, Newark had 11 868 public housing units. Newark lost 6931 public housing units and its skyline has been forever transformed. Only 2497 of those units will be replaced.

We argue that this neoliberal policy regime, with its emphasis on revitalizing cities through gentrification, deconcentrating poverty, and increasing low-income and moderate-income homeownership, has created a new funding and decision environment for the redevelopment of inner-urban neighborhoods. To that end, we turn to an analysis of recent developments in the West Side Park neighborhood in Newark. As Newark is sometimes held to be the next frontier of New York's resurgent property market, and West Side Park is the site of a major share of the city's recent housing development, we undertake a close analysis of the changes underway, the contexts enabling them, and the agents involved, before examining the possible implications of the changes taking place there. Although the results may not be gentrification in the usual sense of a class-based process of neighborhood upgrading, the exploration of nontraditional cases such as West Side Park is a crucial starting point to understanding how neoliberal urban policy is spurring new forms of neighborhood change (Figures 23.2 and 23.3).

Figure 23.2 Housing under construction.

Figure 23.3 Traditional housing.

WEST SIDE PARK, NEWARK, NEW JERSEY

Newark is an exciting place to explore the effects of this new form of neighborhood change. In the shadow of the New York City skyline, Newark is in the midst of a self-proclaimed urban renaissance. After decades of extreme disinvestment, the rate of construction of residential housing in Newark has soared since the mid-1990s. Building permits for new construction were filed for more than 700 new housing units per year in 1997, 1999, and 2000 (Buildings Department, 1999–2001). Growth has accelerated despite the recent economic downturn, in part because of the demand for space in Newark resulting from the destruction of the World Trade Center; since 2001, commercial property owners report a strong market in downtown Newark, and permits have been filed for an additional 1883 housing units (Martin, 2002). Just west of downtown, the city is planning two major commercial redevelopment projects, including a US$84 million project to revitalize an 11-acre site just west of downtown that will include a supermarket, office space, and 324 units of 'upscale housing'. A new home depot is planned for the area further west in the West Side Park neighborhood.

West Side Park is a 120-square-block, predominantly residential, neighborhood on Newark's western border with the city of Irvington. The neighborhood's story is similar to that of many other urban neighborhoods in declining industrial cities – population flight, racial change, disinvestment, severe property abandonment, arson, loss of housing units, concentrated poverty, crime, and gangs. It is this context that makes a rush of new residential development in the neighborhood in the late 1990s and early 2000s all the more surprising to long-term residents and observers alike. By 2001 West Side Park had become a neighborhood of sharp contrasts. Long-term trends of disinvestment were joined and complemented by reinvestment in the form of new housing construction and commercial revitalization. Construction teams are visible throughout the neighborhood. Cranes, bulldozers, and asbestos-removal experts remove the old, and construction teams pour foundations and build the frames for the new.

The continuing disinvestment and contrasting reinvestment trends were confirmed by the

recent release of the 2000 Census. The broad effects of housing abandonment are clearly evident: the total number of housing units in the neighborhood continued to decrease, from 5330 in 1990, to 4683 in 2000, down from 11 434 in 1970 (figure 23.4). The number of units in structures with three or four units decreased by 21% between 1990 and 2000; the number of units in structures with more than five units decreased by 28%. Changes in housing-market activity attributable to the construction of new housing are also clear. Despite the long-term and dramatic loss of units, the census identified some 880 units added to the neighborhood between 1990 and 2000, mostly taking the form of single-family units. Given these changes, it is perhaps not surprising that a shift in the tenure composition of the neighborhood is also evident. The percentage of homeowners in West Side Park increased from 19% of occupied units in 1990, to 27% in 2000, marking the first time in sixty years that the percentage of renters dropped below 80% (USBC, 1940–2000).

In order to explore the recent dimensions of neighborhood change in West Side Park, we conducted an in-depth analysis that included multiple components. First, we examined demographic and housing changes using US Census data from 1940 to 2000. We included data from tracts 18, 26–29, and 32–38. Although tract 18 extends beyond the northern border of the neighborhood, all the data from that tract are included. Tract 30/31 (the number changes in different census years) is not included as only two blocks are located within West Side Park. Two blocks within tract 29 are included even though they extend beyond the eastern border of the neighborhood. Second, we used the results of a two-month inventory of land-use and building conditions that was conducted on a parcel-by-parcel basis for neighborhood planning (RCOPC, 2002). Third, we gathered building permit data for new construction and rehabilitation from the City of Newark for the period 1999–2001 (Buildings Department, 1999–2001), as well as mortgage data gathered under the Home Mortgage Disclosure Act (HMDA, 1975; FFIEC, 1998–2000), to further pinpoint the sources and patterns of change in the neighborhood. Below we review the findings of this research, and examine alternative interpretations of the changes taking place in the neighborhood before turning to our own interpretation of West Side Park as an example of a new form of neighborhood change.

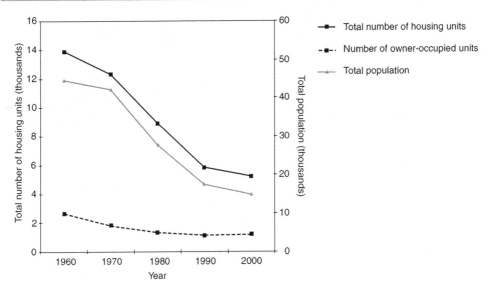

Figure 23.4 Housing unit and population change, West Side Park, Newark, NJ, 1960–2000 (source: USBC, 1940–2000).

WEST SIDE PARK: THE LONG-TERM CONTEXT OF DISINVESTMENT

A predominately white neighborhood in the 1940s and 1950s, West Side Park began to lose residents in the 1950s and was transformed to a majority black neighborhood during the 1960s. As white people left West Side Park for suburban opportunities, the neighborhood became a destination for black people, many of whom were most probably displaced by nearby urban renewal and highway construction projects, including the construction of Interstates 78 and 280 and the construction of the University of Medicine and Dentistry of New Jersey (UMDNJ). Despite 'white flight', the total population of the neighborhood remained stable until 1970, at around 40000 residents. After 1970, however, both the resident population and the number of housing units declined precipitously. Arson and property abandonment devastated the neighborhood and the city as a whole (Sternlieb and Burchell, 1973), both responses to disinvestment and racial change that were in all likelihood accelerated by the civil disturbances in 1967 (Hayden, 1967). Although the disturbances spurred population flight and a collapse of housing demand across the city, the epicenter

of the disturbances just east of West Side Park brought lootings along the neighborhood's two major commercial corridors – Springfield Avenue and South Orange Avenue – as well as fires along Springfield Avenue and in the interstitial residential portions of the neighborhood.

These events accelerated decline and abandonment that continues to this day. West Side Park lost more than 35000 residents between 1940 and 2000, leaving fewer than 15000 by the end of the period. The effects of disinvestment are clearly visible in the built environment. Since the late 1960s the neighborhood has lost a total of 8693 housing units, 87% of which were renter occupied. An aggressive demolition program carried out by the city razed many of the vacant and fire-damaged structures, leaving extensive swathes of vacant land throughout the neighborhood. In 2002, 28% of the neighborhood's parcels were vacant land, and another 10% were used as accessory or parking lots. Furthermore, 9% of existing structures were vacant and/or boarded (figure 23.5).

These conditions provided a rationale for including West Side Park in numerous federal and state urban revitalization programs. The city classified the area east of 10th Street and north of Springfield Avenue as predominantly

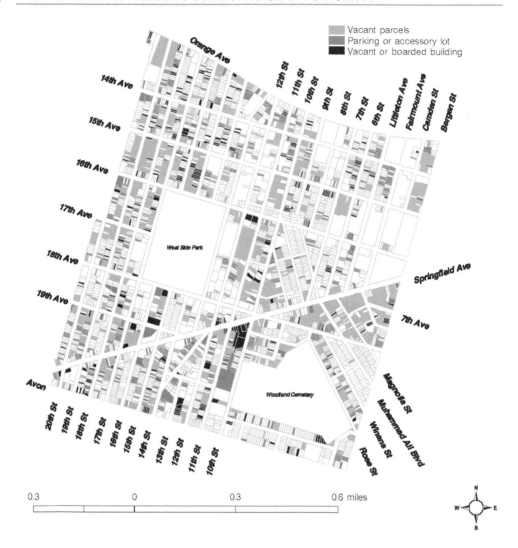

Figure 23.5 Parcel occupancy, West Side Park, Newark, NJ, 2002 (sources: parcel survey, RCOPC, 2002; parcel map, Department of Engineering, 2000).

blighted, qualifying the area for a variety of assistance programs; a new school was built along with new housing in the 1968 urban renewal plan (Housing Authority, 1968). Subsequently, the neighborhood was targeted in the 1960s by the federal Model Cities program (an urban revitalization demonstration program), by the federal Empowerment Zones and Enterprise Communities programs in the 1990s (a broad urban revitalization program), by New Jersey's Urban Coordinating Council (UCC, the state's urban revitalization program), by the state's Urban

Homeownership Recovery Program (UHORP, which encourages homeownership in devastated neighborhoods), and by the state's Enterprise Zone program (which promotes economic development and revitalization). Despite all this attention, only a few small areas of West Side Park were rebuilt before 1990. Some areas in the western portion of the neighborhood were rebuilt but were in such poor condition that the buildings were razed.

After decades of disinvestment, all data clearly point to a process of reinvestment that was well underway by the end of the 1990s. First, our survey of the neighborhood identified many of the markers of more affluent development, including suburban style tract development, new cars, renewed activism to improve the neighborhood's 31-acre Olmsted-designed park, and aggressive organizing to reduce the incidence of crime. Second, as mentioned earlier, the census reported 880 new housing units added between 1990 and 2000; this pattern was confirmed by recent building permit activity, with 171 permits for new construction issued between 1999 and 2001 (Buildings Department, 1999–2001). Census data also point to a shift in tenure composition towards greater homeownership, most likely a result in some part of the in-migration of new homeowners and the continued demolition of apartment buildings, removing rental units.

Home mortgage data for the period 1992–2000 further probe this dynamic by providing a picture of who is buying homes in West Side Park. Under the HMDA, financial institutions are required to report selected applicant and loan data, including race, income, and census tract location for the loan. We pooled HMDA data for the years 1992 through 2000. All loan applications for tracts 18, 26–30, 34, 35, 37, and 38 were included, and yielded 3764 applications. We filtered this database to identify 540 owner-occupant home-purchase originations, which fall into two distinct groups. The first, overwhelmingly made between 1992 and 1994, were loans made to households with incomes less than US$20 000 a year. The location and nature of the loans corresponds to Mount Calvary Commons, a homeownership demonstration project undertaken jointly by Summit Bank and Community Urban Renewal Enterprises Inc., a nonprofit housing developer, with subsidies from the Home Loan Bank of New York. HMDA data identified most of the loans in this first group as originated by Summit Bank. A second group of loans was made predominately between 1998 and 2000 and corresponds more closely to the patterns of change identified through Census data and our neighborhood survey. Two-thirds of these loans were concentrated in the four census tracts identified with the most new construction activity, and HMDA data show the borrowers to be of moderate or middle income. Some 78% of borrowers were black; 12% were white or Hispanic; 10% did not report race. The median

loan was a conventional origination of $104 000, made to a black household with an income of $43 000, well above the 2000 $26 913 median income for Newark, and just below the 2000 $44 944 median income for the predominantly white and affluent Essex County. This confirms an emerging pattern of reinvestment and neighborhood change; the question that remains is how to interpret these changes.

MARKET-DRIVEN DEVELOPMENT

The physical and social characteristics of current redevelopment, along with a perception that Newark is the next frontier for the New York regional housing market, suggest the possibility that a resurgent private market is driving revitalization in West Side Park. Mainstream and political economy theories of inner-city housing markets support the idea of gentrification in West Side Park. Although they differ on the source and implications of change, the two perspectives agree that the long-term processes of abandonment and neighborhood decline have formed valuable assets on which development can capitalize (Smith, 1979; 1996). The loss of population creates an oversupply of housing that drives prices down. For mainstream housing economics this is the end of the filtering process, and the destruction of housing units aids in the stabilization of housing prices. Large tracts of vacant land and a depressed housing market make investment cost effective, especially when proximity to downtown business districts and regional transportation are factored in.

For political economy interpretations, the nexus of federal guarantees for suburban mortgage lending, the decline of employment in the city, and the growing specter of Newark as 'dangerous' and 'forbidden' compound this market dynamic. Redlining and other forms of financial exclusion ensured the collapse of real-estate values and the spatial displacement of demand. Existing owners cannot sell their homes, either because buyers cannot be found or because prospective buyers are unable to secure mortgage financing. With no equity to trade, property owners and businesses are forced either to 'dig in' or to abandon their homes or properties. The situation is particularly tenuous for renters, as tenement landlords opt to disinvest in their properties through deferred maintenance, leading to further declines in housing quality and, ultimately, abandonment. The proliferation of dilapidated structures further stigmatizes the neighborhood in the eyes of investors and consumers. All of these factors aid the formation of a 'rent gap' (Smith, 1979; 1996).

Mixed with the context of Newark as a seeming frontier of regional housing markets, the idea that West Side Park is an emerging market niche makes some sense. It is close to downtown Newark and to major transportation connections between the city and suburban Essex County. The influx of more affluent homebuyers is the basis for the commonsense argument that this is a class-based physical and social transformation of the neighborhood. On the demand side, expanding employment and wages in the 1990s increased effective demand among moderate-income and middle-income minority households looking for affordable homeownership opportunities in the superheated and often racially discriminatory markets of northern New Jersey (Anglin, 2003). Correspondingly, rent-seeking developers have invested in transforming the neighborhood into a new market niche, seeing in West Side Park's low-cost land and good transportation connections an opportunity for excess profits over other, more developed, locations.

Although the above scenario may characterize part of the reinvestment process in West Side Park, our analysis identified two reasons to be skeptical of explaining this as the result of purely private, market-driven development. First, recent housing development has shown little interest in the neighborhood's existing housing stock. The new construction identified by our neighborhood parcel inventory has been almost exclusively tract-style single-family homes and townhouse duplexes. Although there has been a small amount of infill development, both of these development patterns have preferred vacant lots – the former large tracts of half a block or more. Although this in itself is not sufficient to discount private market activity, it is curious that the heightened level of demand has had little spillover effect on the undervalued sites with existing buildings. A possible explanation for the lack of spillover into purchase –'rehab' activity is the neighborhood's housing stock, which is mostly older wood-frame three-floor flats in fair to poor condition. Subsequent analysis of changes in ownership

on the city tax rolls between 1999 and 2001 showed that the small amount of private market activity among existing properties included 'house-flipping' schemes, in which home improvement contractors purchase a property, make minimal repairs, and 'flip' the property for a significant profit. These activities may be connected to predatory lending schemes, which fraudulently raise the appraised value of homes to garner high loans guaranteed by the Federal Housing Administration (FHA) and then use foreclosure to recoup the insurance (Hevesi, 2002). Such activity is not indicative of a rise in market-based arm's-length transactions.

CDC-LED NEIGHBORHOOD REVITALIZATION

A closer analysis of the development process highlights the role played by the new funding and policy environment in spurring partnerships between public and private investors and local nonprofit housing actors and suggests that these partnerships are more successful than are market-based explanations in explaining the timing and scale of revitalization in West Side Park. Building permit data for new construction show that community development corporations (CDCs) sponsored more than half the recent developments. Of the 171 building permits filed with the city for new construction in West Side Park between January 1999 and October 2001, 61% were filed for properties owned by CDCs. The remainder are almost entirely accounted for by the Newark Public Housing Authority (Figure 23.6).

Two aspects of the current funding and policy environment have been particularly important. First, as argued earlier, a consensus has developed within mainstream policy circles over the last decade emphasizing the deconcentration of poverty and asset accumulation by low-income households and neighborhoods, through workforce development, homeownership, and geographically targeted economic development (Retsinas and Belsky, 2002). These ideas have cycled through the public and philanthropic sectors, couched as a new strategy for urban revitalization that provides an opportunity structure spurring wealth creation in concentrated poverty areas (Enterprise Foundation, 1999; Oliver and Shapiro, 1997; Page-Adams and Sherraden,

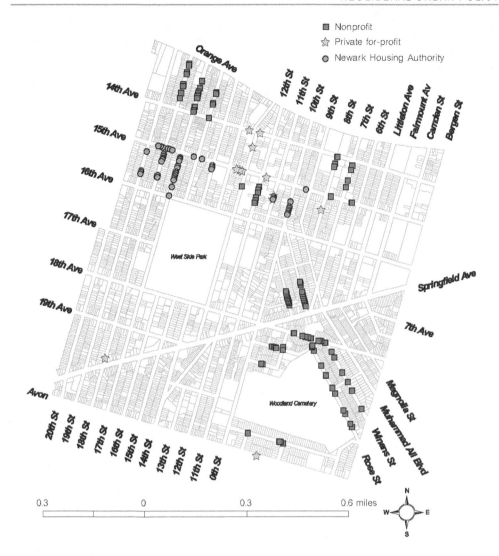

Figure 23.6 Residential construction permits and activity, West Side Park, Newark, NJ, 1999–2001 (sources: permit data, Buildings Department, 2002; parcel map, Department of Engineering, 2000).

1997). Financial intermediaries that provide crucial development funds for CDCs also support the agenda. The director of Newark's Local Initiatives Support Corporation (LISC) said 'We want mixed-income areas, and we are encouraging CDCs, when appropriate, to do more unsubsidized or market-rate units' (quoted in Axel-Lute, 2001). The state of New Jersey has been a major underwriter of this policy regime in West Side Park, supporting mixed-income development with a substantial homeownership component. For example, the

New Jersey Home Mortgage Finance Agency (NJHMFA), a stage agency charged with increasing the availability of affordable housing, has provided construction financing for the development of 144 homes in West Side Park as of June 2000 (NJHMFA, 2000). Even though the new housing units are listed as affordable housing, they are beyond the reach of many current neighborhood residents: estimated sales prices for NJHMFA-assisted homes range from a low of $76 900 to a high of $160 000 (http://www.state.nj.us/dca/hmfa/singfam/100acti.

htm). NJHMFA is joined by a variety of other public and private institutional actors in providing support for these developments. The billboard-like signs announcing future residential developments provide a glimpse into the number and variety of private and public entities investing in the revitalization: federal, state, and local government agencies and elected officials, private lenders, foundations, not-for-profit developers, and the occasional for-profit developer partners are all listed.

Second, financial reregulation and the reemphasis on community reinvestment have helped to create a surge of investment in historically underserved areas (Squires, 2003). Wyly *et al.* (2001) point to a confluence of policies and regulations as structuring this shift, ranging from more aggressive enforcement of the Community Reinvestment Act under the Clinton administration to the proactive policies of secondary-market government-sponsored enterprises (GSEs) in purchasing loans from underserved areas. Nonprofits organizations and other third parties play a key role in managing the risks of inner-city investment, spurring partnerships with lenders and developers (Avery *et al.*, 2000; Listokin and Wyly, 2000).

As an example of the development process spurred by these arrangements, the community development banking arm of First Union Bank helped to package the financing for at least two major developments undertaken by Corinthian Housing Development Corporation in the neighborhood over the last five years. Corinthian recruits prospective homeowners, providing a stream of applicants for First Union mortgages. As a result, First Union Mortgage Company originated one-third of the mortgage loans in West Side Park during the 1998 to 2000 period (FFIEC, 1998; 1999; 2000). This example is typical of the organizational arrangements that have been used to implement most of the new development in the neighborhood. CDCs assume the risks of organizing finance, of gaining regulatory approvals, of marketing units, and of pre-qualifying mortgage applicants. In addition, many of the CDCs rely on for-profit developers to carry out the actual construction on a turnkey basis in return for a small development fee.

These arrangements prove to be a lucrative and relatively low-risk undertaking for private developers and lenders, who have otherwise continued to forsake the neighborhood. These arrangements resonate with the neoliberal policy consensus on neighborhood revitalization, which argues that the successful creation of individual and community assets requires public funds and community energy to leverage private investment, in the process attracting new residents and new commercial activity to provide opportunities or spillovers to existing neighborhood residents. The form of development in West Side Park corresponds to best practices identified in the literature. Not only is large-scale CDC activity seen as necessary for stabilizing distressed neighborhoods, but scale is often associated with the development of a track record and the accumulation of community development capacity (Vidal, 1992).

THE ENTREPRENEURIAL CITY

A second component of the current process of neighborhood change, which further distinguishes it from the model of market-led development, is the central organizing role played by the city of Newark. The city is a major force behind the neighborhood's revitalization and holds considerable power because of the resources under its control. Although private market actors might be beholden to the city for regulatory approvals or important subsidies, CDCs are in an even more tenuous position as they often need local government support not only for those regulatory approvals and minimal subsidies but also for land and grant dollars.

Our analysis identified three dimensions in the role played by the city. First, the city controls the major development resource in the neighborhood – the supply of vacant land accumulated through tax foreclosure and abandonment. In 2002, 65% of vacant parcels in the neighborhood were owned by the city of Newark or other public agencies – more than one quarter of all the lots in West Side Park. Further, 28% of vacant and/or boarded buildings are owned by the city of Newark or other public agencies. The city has used its ownership of tax-foreclosed properties strategically, implementing a disposition process to control access. Interviews with CDC developers in West Side Park indicated that access to city-owned land is a major factor in the timing, scale, and location of their activity. One CDC leader explained 'A few years ago, the city owned 60% of the land. That's starting to be gone …. Supply of land is a big problem …. It used to be if there is land and you have the capacity to develop it, you'll get it' (interview, 2002).

Second, in spite of the city's poor fiscal condition it controls access to valuable development resources in the form of discretionary block grants. The city provides funding for the demolition of abandoned structures, an expensive process that puts new development beyond the reach of many CDCs. The city used 24% of its 2001 CDBG funds ($2 837 680) for demolition (City of Newark, 2002). The city also provides direct subsidies to CDCs and for-profit developers to encourage new housing construction. Three of the CDCs that have developed and/or are currently developing new housing in West Side Park have received HOME dollars. Further, the city uses its direct connections with Trenton, the state capital, or Washington, D.C., to direct resources to projects it champions.

Third, the city has used its leverage to facilitate the suburban style of development typified by recent construction in West Side Park. A motivating factor in this process has been the current administration's desire to remake Newark's image as a resurgent center of the new economy, with key elements in this agenda including downtown corporate-centered development and the demolition of high-rise public housing. Moderate-income housing development, in turn, promises not only to increase the tax base of an underresourced local government but also, and more generally, offers to change the city's complexion from being composed of a series of concentrated poverty neighborhoods. Mayor Sharpe James stated his preference for low-rise mixed-income neighborhoods rooted in homeownership during his first run for mayor in the 1980s, and he recently reiterated his belief that homeownership is necessary for neighborhood stability: 'If you want to drive drug dealers out of a neighborhood, [if] you want to drive undesirables out, put a homeowner there' (quoted in Carter, 2002). More-over, like many other urban mayors, he views housing development as an economic development strategy (James, 2003).

Kennedy and Leonard (2001) suggest that mayors have recognized that creating sport and entertainment districts downtown is not sufficient to revitalize their cities; instead, they have recognized that, for cities to be transformed, they need to lure the middle class back as residents, not just as tourists. In Newark, the city has used the resources at its disposal – block grants, transfer payments, and streams of private capital investment – to support market-rate housing development over other alternatives. In our interviews, CDC developers also identified pressure from city officials to focus on market-rate single-family homeownership, rather than other types of housing such as rental or multifamily housing.

The city's role has contributed to the politicization of the development process in a way that keeps community organizations in a clientist position. The resource allocation process has allowed the city to enforce its preferences for certain styles of development, and this has ensured a level of control over the behavior of local nonprofit actors. For instance, the city's resource allocation process encourages CDCs to work within tightly defined territories, which has further balkanized the already fragmented local community development system that is marked by numerous weak actors (Lake and Newman, 2002). An emphasis on turnkey developments and homeownership means that CDCs do not develop assets of their own, and they are beholden to the circulation of subsidies and project development fees to pay overhead. Although they may be able to develop programmatic capacity in the form of skilled staff, this environment has proven difficult for many CDC directors, staff, and organizers, who have chosen to leave the neighborhood and even the city. Consequently, in spite of the relative scale of CDC-sponsored construction activity in recent years, the human resource base of neighborhood organizations is remarkably thin and unstable. Overall, this translates into a local community development system that cannot implement alternative, resident-centered paths of neighborhood change. A handful of high-capacity CDCs in Newark – those with exceptionally strong staff, neighborhood networks, and access to resources outside of the city – have broken through these constraints.

REVITALIZING VERY-LOW-INCOME NEIGHBORHOODS IN THE 2000S

How do the changes taking place in West Side Park constitute a 'new' form of gentrification that nonetheless remains a class-based process of physical and social spatial transformation? What distinguishes this pattern of neighborhood change are its sources as well as its implications. This type of revitalization has three dimensions that we were able to identify in our research in Newark, each operating at a variety of scales.

First, the context of contemporary (after 1993) gentrification has changed the 'calculus' for development in many neighborhoods, not just for those experiencing market-led redevelopment or those that are easily described by traditional definitions of gentrification. West Side Park continues to experience disinvestment and abandonment, but it now does so in an environment patterned by expanding regional labor and property markets. This has not translated into market-led gentrification, but it has changed the decision environment within which space is evaluated, and it has provided openings for local regimes to pursue development strategies that were previously beyond their capacity. Ironically, it is the level of prior disinvestment in the area that helps to facilitate its revitalization. The severe rent gap helps to make West Side Park a target for revitalization (Smith, 1979; 1996).

Second, and just as important, is a new funding and decision environment for development in inner-city neighborhoods. The new kind of neighborhood change we identify marks the targeting of concentrated poverty neighborhoods by entrepreneurial political regimes seeking to increase their competitiveness. Policy regimes emphasizing inner-city reinvestment, poverty deconcentration, and asset accumulation by households and communities are providing a new resource base to fund this style of development, in many cases legitimizing local decisions to transform neighborhoods by removing housing for very-low-income residents and replacing it with mixed-income housing.

Third, a different context and a new funding environment have in turn reinforced forms of clientist politics that have long characterized resource-poor cities such as Newark. The contemporary expansion of labor and property markets has turned one of the markers of the city's underdevelopment – its stock of vacant, abandoned land – into a new resource that it can use to lever politically motivated growth. This places additional stress on the inherent tensions CDCs face in rebuilding neighborhoods and maintaining relationships with local government. For their part, CDCs, further weakened by decades of clientist politics and with few resources for other types of redevelopment, have little capacity or resources with which to challenge this type of development and offer alternatives.

IMPLICATIONS

The remaining question in this analysis of neighborhood change involves the consequences and effects of the emerging approach to revitalization. How do we evaluate the patterns of physical and social transformation occurring in neighborhoods such as West Side Park? By many accounts, the changes taking place mark a significant turnaround for the neighborhood. The new housing construction is increasing access to homeownership for many who otherwise could not afford it. And the new residents are not the typical gentry; they are neither white nor upper class. Instead, they are mostly working-class and middle-class families of color. In the blocks of West Side Park where there is substantial revitalization, the neighborhood is quiet. The drug dealing that pervades much of the neighborhood is not immediately obvious, and the gang tags are nowhere in sight. Even skeptics of this process have a difficult time pointing to directly adverse consequences of reinvestment in West Side Park. Much of the newly developed land had been vacant and unproductive, and new population increases the viability of commercial activity. Further, development activity helps increase the track record of local community development organizations, contributing to their capacity to sustain neighborhood revitalization activity (Glickman and Servon, 1998). Finally, new development brings income diversity to West Side Park at a time when the value of mixed-income neighborhoods is increasingly vaunted within policy and advocacy circles (Cityscape 1998).

The redevelopment of West Side Park and neighborhoods like it looks like neighborhood-based redevelopment, but is it? Have the rhetoric and aspirations of broad-based community revitalization been hijacked and used to mask a new process of gentrification? Has community development or community revitalization with the goal of eliminating concentrated poverty become a way to legitimize processes of gentrification? In West Side Park, the politicization of development means that the promise of asset accumulation is selective for direct beneficiaries and may not necessarily translate into benefits for inner-city neighborhoods as a whole. Indeed, the vision of mixed-income neighborhoods touted in current policy circles is further stunted as CDCs are systematically prevented from capturing spillovers from development and channeling them into alternative models that can strengthen the position of long-term residents. In addition, the process of change in West Side Park may ultimately prove unsuccessful. The new housing developments are changing both the physical face and the social character of the neighborhood, but they do not address the underlying causes of poverty and the problems associated with poverty that continue to plague the neighborhood such as high unemployment, substance abuse, crime, and poor schools. Our evidence suggests that the larger context of inner-city disinvestment provides a constant threat to the value of new housing investments.

The process we describe marks the targeting of concentrated poverty neighborhoods by political regimes seeking to offer selective benefits to moderate-income and middle-income groups. Moreover, the process may not translate into the 'linear' path of neighborhood change postulated by mainstream community development proponents. This all suggests the need for further inquiry into the long-term effects of horizontal and vertical inequity in neoliberal policies affecting neighborhoods and into policy options that could create real development alternatives in neighborhoods such as West Side Park. Although our research into these areas is still preliminary, we feel there are at least three distinct causes for concern.

First, although our research has highlighted how a publicly organized development process has created a path of physical and social change in West Side Park, a body of mainstream economic theory argues there is a major difference between building houses and reconstructing a neighborhood economy. As Carr (1999) has argued, the promise of market-based approaches to community development is that they will produce self-sustaining economic activity in disadvantaged communities so as to integrate them better into the economic and social mainstream. This argument points to the undervalued assets of inner-city neighborhoods – including cheap, vacant land, available labor pools, and good transportation connections, as resources that can be harnessed by investors, developers, and buyers. Once market actors become 'savvier' about creating, financing, and marketing viable investments in these neighborhoods, they will increase the overall supply of capital flowing into those neighborhoods and spur the process of revitalization. Market reforms spurring investment in 'underserved' markets aid the connections between these 'investment-grade assets' in inner-city neighborhoods and broader financial markets (Carr, 1999, pages 20–21). This is a partial explanation for the surge in development in West Side Park, as neoliberal or market-oriented public policy has helped to channel public and private resources into the hands of local actors working to transform those undervalued assets into marketable products.

But even if this were to happen in West Side Park, there is little to suggest that these benefits would reach long-term residents. Moreover, reinvestment patterns will become self-sustaining only if these investments remain stable or appreciate in value. In fact, our research identified two patterns of neighborhood change at work in West Side Park: the reinvestment trends discussed and the long-term forces of disinvestment and abandonment still clearly at work in the neighborhood. This disinvestment functions to create the resources – in the form of undervalued assets – that make the neighborhood attractive for investment. However, the same disinvestment also constitutes a threat to recent development. The undervalued assets prized by Carr are produced through the social dislocations and poverty brought about by extreme disinvestment. This leads to the risk profiles characteristic of disadvantaged communities, namely in the form of negative externalities or social costs that hamper investment – factors such as dilapidated or abandoned properties, property and personal crime, poor schools and other public services, and low levels of commercial activity. Unless development reaches a sufficient scale, or is coordinated through the intervention of a 'superplayer' that can regulate these costs, developers and consumers will face uncertainty about the future value of their investments, perpetuating barriers to investment or isolating and devaluing existing developments (Dymski, 1997).

Evidence of this tension between disinvestment and reinvestment are evident in West Side Park. Construction workers pour new foundations and frame new single-family homes across the street from rows of empty liquor bottles, bouquets of dead flowers, and sheets bearing scrawled memorials to slain gang members. Down the block from new homes, gang tags offer unavoidable reminders of the neighborhood's continuing tragedies: 'RIP [slain gang member]'. Like other big cities, Newark's crime rate decreased over the course of the 1990s but has risen since. The number of homicides in Newark increased from 59 in 2000, to 97 in 2001 (Kleinknecht, 2002). In West Side Park, drug dealing and car chases are pervasive, and gang violence in adjacent Irvington has mobilized local, state, and federal agencies. The summer of 2003 was particularly violent, with eighteen shootings in eight days (Kleinknecht and Roberts, 2003).

These threats to the sustainability of inner-city development cast the physical changes in West Side Park in a different light. The publicly organized development process we have identified at work in the neighborhood is adept at leveraging resources to create new housing units and to qualify moderate-income borrowers to purchase them, but so far it is unable to address the creation of a viable and self-sustaining niche in the regional housing market. A downturn in the economy or an increase in interest rates will further narrow the range of potential buyers. These failures would be unfortunate for the investors and consumers immediately affected, but they also could further marginalize the neighborhood as a whole. Possible outcomes include widespread defaults and foreclosures and the overall devaluation of new properties, resulting in negative-equity homes worth less than the mortgages outstanding on them (Cassidy, 2002).With the decline of the post-recession expansion in employment that played a role in creating West Side Park as a development niche, optimism about market-based approaches to revitalization may not translate into long-term success.

Second, development focused on the upper end of low-income residents has begun to show itself in new forms of neighborhood politics. Davis (1991) argues that neighborhoods are fractured places, where politics is patterned by the material and symbolic cleavages between groups with different interests in and relationships to property. Our research suggests that the publicly led physical changes in the neighborhood over the last decade have also spurred new, class-based, forms of neighborhood politics. Interviews with neighborhood homeowners show them to be clearly worried about neighborhood conditions that adversely affect their quality of life and the value of their properties. The new development perpetuates polarization between homeowners and renters, where homeowners view renters as a liability in terms of property values and neighborhood stability. As one CDC staff member explained, 'everything is being developed. New people are coming in but we don't have a connection to the new. The current residents aren't associated with new residents' (interview, 2001). Predictably, there is tension between new residents and longer term residents; class, not race, is the source of these divisions. Although many neighborhood issues transcend property interests, such as the recent political mobilization to improve the county park at the center of the neighborhood, others more directly pit new homeowners against low-income renters. An emerging issue is the enforcement of building codes in dilapidated multifamily buildings. New homeowners point to multifamily buildings as eyesores and as centers of drug trafficking and juvenile delinquency. Where these campaigns are successful, they may lead to further displacement of very-low-income residents, as tenement landlords choose tax foreclosure or abandonment rather than investment, ultimately displacing the current residents. This new form of neighborhood change, which is cloaked in the rhetoric of improving the conditions of concentrated poverty, may put further pressure on the tenuous position of long-term neighborhood residents.

Finally, our research problematizes the role and orientation of the community development sector in Newark. This is particularly the case as community development organizations have directly participated in the social and physical transformations in West Side Park. The focus on moderate-income development begs the question of how other strategies might result in a path of neighborhood change that addresses the needs of low-income and very-low-income residents as well as the middle class. For instance, Carr (1999) maintains that market-driven approaches to community development work best if there is a social mortgage on community assets; he argues that community-based institutions need to develop strategies that recapture and recycle value for community building purposes if inner-city residents are to participate equitably in neighborhood change. Further, to the extent that community building involves the identification and mobilization of community assets, it is a local endeavor that is by its nature contextual and customized:

> The most significant seeds for revitalizing new neighborhoods involve nearly invisible small scale entrepreneurial or developmental efforts. Therefore, only a local structure can find and enhance these projects, and connect them with larger development strategies (Kretzmann and McKnight, 1993, page 361)

The inherent tension within CDCs and distance from their neighborhoods, the neoliberal funding environment, and, in Newark, the clientist position of many of the city's smaller CDCs have cut CDCs off from pursuing either community control of neighborhood development or comprehensive community building.

A NEW PROCESS OF NEIGHBORHOOD CHANGE

West Side Park is but one example of how a nexus of forces have come together over the last decade to create this new process of neighborhood change. Like traditionally defined gentrification, it is a class-based process of neighborhood upgrading that transforms the character of a neighborhood and ultimately threatens very-low-income residents. This new process of neighborhood change, however, is distinguished from more conventional forms of gentrification by its sources and its implications. Unlike traditionally defined gentrification, the primary actors shaping and implementing the changes are public and nonprofit rather than for-profit. This process may seem familiar to students and practitioners of community development who have looked over the last four decades to public and community action to remedy concentrated poverty and revitalize disadvantaged neighborhoods. However, the

process we identify bears only a token resemblance to the aspirations of community development advocates; we argue that it marks the targeting of concentrated poverty neighborhoods by political regimes in resource-poor cities, such as Newark, seeking to remake the city.

The neighborhood-level changes take place within a broader context shaped by globalization and a dominant neoliberal policy agenda that together are contributing to a vast restructuring of urban space. West Side Park continues to experience disinvestment and abandonment, but it now does so in an environment patterned by the expanding regional labor and property markets of the New York region. This has not translated into market-led gentrification, but it has changed the decision environment within which space is evaluated and it has provided openings for local regimes to imagine and pursue development strategies that were previously beyond their capacity. They are supported in this by a neoliberal policy regime that emphasizes poverty deconcentration, mixed-income neighborhoods, homeownership, and reliance on the private market. This has provided the local state with the resources – in the form of block grants and discretionary funds, political persuasion, and land taken through decades of tax foreclosure – to enforce a pattern of development.

The new form of neighborhood change has different implications. Although we did not find widespread displacement of very-low-income residents as predicted by conventional accounts of gentrification, the implications we identify are no less insidious or threatening. The politically motivated, publicly organized neighborhood change process we identify has led to the reorganization of the community development sector and neighborhood political constituencies around support for a particular type of redevelopment that eliminates other forms of neighborhood change. Revitalization that focuses on drawing in higher income residents and on increasing homeownership has the effect of targeting benefits away from those with very low incomes; almost no funding goes towards multifamily housing, housing rehabilitation, or permanent affordability, and neighborhood service providers continue to struggle to keep up with demand for health and social services. In addition, it spurs new forms of neighborhood politics that turn low-income housing and youth into 'nuisances' for recently arrived homeowners, making such 'nuisances' open to regulation by building inspectors and police. Moreover, this does little to reverse the long-term trends of disinvestment in the neighborhood; without attention to the needs of long-term residents and the overall quality of life in the neighborhood, new developments face a process of devaluation that may further marginalize the neighborhood. These implications suggest that additional research is needed to unpack the links between larger scale trends and neighborhood changes and to explore the implications of these changes for the most disadvantaged, who are once again triaged out of urban revitalization policy.

REFERENCES

Anglin R, 2003, "Residential segregation in New Jersey", Policy News Brief 1, New Jersey Public Policy Research Institute, New Brunswick, NJ.

Avery R, Bostic R, Canner C, 2000, "CRA special lending programs" *Federal Reserve Bulletin* 86 711–731.

Axel-Lute M, 2001, "Tales of three cities: the trickiest part of dealing with gentrification may be deciding when to start" *Shelterforce Online* (May/June), http://www.nhi.org/online/issues/117/ThreeCities.html.

Beauregard B, 1986, "The chaos and complexity of gentrification", in *Gentrification of the City* Eds N Smith, P Williams (Allen and Unwin, Boston, MA) pp. 35–55.

Berry B, 1985, "Islands of renewal in seas of decay", in *The New Urban Reality* Ed. P Peterson (The Brookings Institute, Washington, D.C.) pp. 69–96.

Bourne L S, 1993, "The demise of gentrification? A commentary and prospective view" *Urban Geography* 14 95–107.

Buildings Department, 1999–2001, "Building permit data", Office of the Construction Official, Buildings Department, City of Newark, 920 Broad Street, Newark, NJ 07102.

Carr J H, 1999, "Community, capital and markets: a new paradigm for community reinvestment" *NeighborWorks Journal* 17(3) 20–23.

Carter B, 2002, "Newark service group adds homes in North Ward" *The Star Ledger* 19 March, http://www.guide2newark.com/.

Cassidy J, 2002, "The next crash" *The New Yorker* 11 November, pp. 123–129.

City of Newark, 2002, "Block Grant Distribution reports", Business Administrator, City of Newark, Newark City Hall, 920 Broad Street, Newark, NJ 07102.

Cityscape 1998, "Racially and ethnically diverse urban neighborhoods", Special issue 4(2), http://www.huduser.org/periodicals/cityscpe/vol4num2/current.html.

Clay P, 1980, "The rediscovery of city neighborhoods: reinvestment by long-time residents and newcomers", in *Back to the City: Issues in Neighborhood Renovation* Eds S B Laska, D Spain (Pergamon Press, New York) pp. 1–26.

Community Reinvestment Act, 1977, 12 USC 2901, implemented by Regulations 12 CFR parts 25, 228, 345, and 563e (U.S. Government Printing Office, Washington, D.C.).

Crump J, 2002, "Deconcentration by demolition: public housing, poverty, and urban policy", *Environment and Planning D: Society and Space* 20 581–596.

Davis J E, 1991, *Contested Ground: Collective Action and the Urban Neighborhood* (Cornell University Press, Ithaca, NY).

Davis J E, 1994, "Beyond the market and the state: the diverse domain of social housing", in *The Affordable City: Toward a Third Sector Housing Policy* Ed. J E Davis (Temple University Press, Philadelphia, PA) pp. 1–38.

Department of Engineering, 2000, "Digital parcel map", Department of Engineering, City of Newark, 920 Broad Street, Newark, NJ 07102.

Dymski GA, 1997, "Business strategy and access to capital in inner-city revitalization", in *The Inner City* Eds T D Boston, C L Ross (Transaction Books, New Brunswick, NJ) pp. 51–64.

Enterprise Foundation, 1999, "Building individual and community assets" http://www.enterprisefoundation.org/resources/ERD/browse.asp?c=25.

FFIEC, 1998–2000 *Home Mortgage Disclosure Act: Raw Data on CD-ROM*

Federal Financial Institutions Examination Council, Washington, D.C., http://www.ffiec.gov/hmda/default.htm.

Gittell M, Newman K, Bockmeyer J, Lindsay R, 1998, "Expanding community participation: the Federal Urban Empowerment Zones" *Urban Affairs Review* 33 530–558.

Glass R, 1964 *London: Aspects of Change* (McGibben and Kee, London).

Glickman N, Servon L, 1998, "More than bricks and sticks: five components of Community Development Corporation capacity" *Housing Policy Debate* 9 497–539.

Goetz E, 2000, "The politics of poverty deconcentration and housing demolition" *Journal of Urban Affairs* 22(2) 157–174.

Hackworth J, Smith N, 2001, "The changing state of gentrification" *Tijdschrift voor Economische en Sociale Geografie* 92 464–477.

Hayden T, 1967 *Rebellion in Newark: Official Violence and Ghetto Response* (Random House, New York).

Hevesi D, 2002, "New curbs on predatory loans" *The New York Times* 10 November.

Home Mortgage Disclosure Act, 1975, Implemented by Federal Reserve Board Regulation C (U.S. Government Printing Office, Washington, D.C.).

Home Mortgage Disclosure (Amendment) Act, 1989, Implemented by Federal Reserve Board Regulation C (U.S. Government Printing Office, Washington, D.C.).

Housing Authority, 1968 *Community Urban Renewal Plan* copy may be consulted at Newark Public Library.

James S, 2003, *State of the City Address*, http://www.ci.newark.nj.us/Speech/Speech.htm.

Kennedy M, Leonard P, 2001, "Dealing with neighborhood change: a primer on gentrification and policy choices", discussion paper prepared for the Brookings Institution on Urban and Metropolitan Policy and PolicyLink, April, http://www.brook.edu/dybdocroot/es/urban/gentrification/gentrification.pdf.

Kleinknecht W, 2002, "Newark sees a surge in crime" *The Star-Ledger* 7 January.

Kleinknecht W, Roberts R, 2003, "Reputed gangster charged in two shootings" *The Star-Ledger* 14 April.

Kretzmann J P, McKnight J L, 1993 *Building Communities from the Inside Out* (ACTA Publications, Chicago, IL).

Lake B, Newman K, 2002, "Differential citizenship in the shadow state" *GeoJournal* 58(2–3) 109–120.

Lees L, 2000, "A re-appraisal of gentrification: towards a 'geography of gentrification'" *Progress in Human Geography* 24 389–408.

Ley D, 1997 *The New Middle Class and the Remaking of the Central City* (Oxford University Press, Oxford).

Listokin D, Wyly E, 2000, "Making new mortgage markets: case studies of institutions, home buyers, and communities" *Housing Policy Debate* 11 575–644.

Martin A, 2002, "Calculating impact of proposed arena" *The New York Times* 10 November, page 4.

NJHMFA, 2000, "Ground breaking at Newark's newest for-sale homes housing construction in UCC neighborhood to begin", press release, 21 June, New Jersey Home Mortgage Finance Agency, http://www.state.nj.us/dca/hmfa/.

Oliver M, Shapiro T, 1997 *BlackWealth: WhiteWealth* (Routledge, London)

Page-Adams D, Sherraden M, 1997, "Asset building as a community revitalization strategy" *Social Work* 42 423–434.

RCOPC, 2002, West Side Park Parcel Inventory, Rutgers Community Outreach Partnership Center, Center for Urban Policy Research, Rutgers University, New Brunswick, NJ.

Retsinas N, Belsky E, 2002 *Low Income Homeownership: Examining the Unexamined Goal* (Brookings Institution Press and Harvard Joint Center for Housing Studies, Washington, D.C.).

Smith N, 1979, "Toward a theory of gentrification: a back to the city movement by capital not people" *Journal of the American Planning Association* 45 538–548.

Smith N, 1996, *The New Urban Frontier: Gentrification and the Revanchist City* (Routledge, London).

Smith N, 2002, "Gentrification generalized, new urbanism: gentrification as a global urban strategy", paper presented at "Upward Neighborhood Trajectories

Conference" Glasgow; copy available from the author, Graduate Center, City University of New York, New York.

Squires G, 2003, *Organizing Access to Capital: Advocacy and the Democratization of Financial Institutions* (Temple University Press, Philadelphia, PA).

Sternlieb G, Burchell R, 1973, "Residential abandonment: the tenement landlord revisited", Center for Urban Policy Research, Rutgers University, New Brunswick, NJ.

USBC, 1940–2000, *Surveys of Population and Housing Long Form and Short Form 1940–2000* U.S. Bureau of the Census, Washington, D.C..

Vidal A, 1992, "Rebuilding communities: a national study of urban community development", Community Development Research Center, New School for Social Research, New York.

Weber R, 2002, "Extracting value from the city: neoliberalism and urban redevelopment" *Antipode* 34 519–541.

Wyly E, Hammel D, 1999, "Islands of decay in seas of renewal: housing policy and the resurgence of gentrification" *Housing Policy Debate* 10 711–771.

Wyly E, Hammel D, 2000, "Capital's metropolis: Chicago and the transformation of American housing policy" *Geografiska Annaler* 82 181–20.

Wyly E, Cooke T J, Hammel D J, Holloway S R, Hudson M, 2001, "Low- to moderate-income lending in context: progress report on the neighborhood impacts of homeownership policy" *Housing Policy Debate* 12 87–127.

24
"Housing dispersal programs"

From *Journal of Planning Literature* (2003)

Edward G. Goetz

Current federal housing policy and the planning approaches of many local governments focus on the dispersal of subsidized families. Dispersal is seen as both an end in itself, helping to reform and improve the nation's stock of subsidized housing, and as a means of deconcentrating poverty in American urban areas. The current efforts constitute, in fact, a second generation of dispersal policy. The first, occurring in the late 1960s through the mid-1970s, was part of the fair housing movement that was aimed at addressing issues of racial discrimination and suburban exclusionism in housing. Both generations of dispersal efforts, regardless of their differing justifications, use roughly the same policy strategies. This article begins by offering a schematic interpretation of dispersal policy during the past thirty-five years. A typology of programs is used as the framework for a discussion of the evolution of dispersal efforts in the United States. The bulk of the article presents the policy history of dispersal.

The first wave of dispersal efforts emerged at the end of the 1960s as a result of the "open housing" movement. Dispersal of subsidized housing was a way of reversing past discrimination and promoting integration. Thus, the first generation of dispersal marked a turnaround for the federal government and its housing policy. After decades of contributing to problems of residential segregation and discrimination, the federal government moved in the 1960s toward acknowledgment of the problems and some initial, hesitant steps to reverse direction. These steps included Executive Order 11063 signed by President Kennedy in 1962 ending discrimination in federally assisted housing programs, the *Fair*

Housing Act of 1968, the creation of scattered-site public housing, the end of high-rise public housing developments, and the first steps toward support of regional housing initiatives to disperse subsidized units.

These first steps toward antidiscrimination and dispersal were halting and, for the most part, ineffective. The *Fair Housing Act of 1968* was limited in important ways and proved very cumbersome in the fight to end racial discrimination in housing (Massey and Denton 1993). Implementation of the act was undermined by successive presidential administrations uninterested in pursuing enforcement and through cuts in enforcement staffing. Dispersal policy and scattered-site efforts have been similarly limited. Scattered-site public housing remained less than 10 percent of subsidized units in most cities (Hogan 1996). The Department of Housing and Urban Development's (HUD) first regionalism initiatives of 1970–72, including support for regional councils of government and regional fair-share housing approaches, quickly evaporated in the face of suburban resistance. Dispersal, as a policy objective, was put on the back burner. HUD did not consciously return to the old practices of concentrating assisted housing, yet visible attempts to significantly disperse subsidized housing disappeared from the agency's agenda.

Ironically, efforts to disperse subsidized housing were waning at just the moment Congress created perhaps the most appropriate means of scattering subsidized households, the Section 8 housing allowance. This program was enacted in 1974 not as part of a larger

Target	Form of housing assistance	
	Tenant-based approaches	Unit-based approaches
Neighborhoods of concentrated poverty		HOPE VI Vacancy consolidation Vouchering out *The Quality Housing and Work Responsibility Act of 1998*
Nontargeted	Section 8 Vacancy consolidation Vouchering out Regional opportunity counseling Portability	Mixed-income developments
Nonconcentrated neighborhoods	Mobility programs (Moving to Opportunity, Gautreaux, etc.)	Scattered site Fair share Other regional production programs

Table 24.1 Housing dispersal programs

desegregation and dispersal effort but more as a means of reducing costs in housing programs and distributing housing resources through the market.

When dispersal reemerged as a sustained and multidimensional approach, it was tied not to the issue of racial discrimination and segregation but to a "new" problem, the concentration of poverty in American cities. Henry Cisneros, onetime mayor of San Antonio, and President Clinton's first secretary of HUD, called "highly concentrated minority poverty urban America's toughest challenge" (HUD 1996, 1). In 1995, Cisneros toured the country and talked at each stop about the mistake in previous HUD policy of "warehousing poor people in high-rise buildings" (Hartung and Henig 1997, 404). The policy response to concentrated poverty has focused on scattering subsidized households across a greater geographic area within regions, providing families with a housing allowance (the Section 8 or Housing Choice Voucher) that allows them to choose their own units on the open market and does not constrain them to units financed by the public sector. Deconcentration has also meant, to a very significant extent, the demolition/ conversion of existing units of subsidized housing and the forced relocation of assisted families to other neighborhoods, achieved through HUD's HOPE VI program and the "vouchering out" of project-based subsidies

(the conversion of housing subsidies from project-based to tenant-based usually associated with the demolition or conversion of the housing to market rate).

Dispersal programs (of both generations) can be distinguished by their characteristics along two dimensions (see Table 24.1). The first is whether the subsidies are unit based or tenant based. This is important because unit-based subsidies have been highly concentrated in the nation's most distressed neighborhoods. Tenant-based subsidies have been more widely distributed and are regarded by many as easier to use when introducing subsidized housing into communities that have previously had little (see Rubinowitz and Rosenbaum 2001).

The second dimension is how (or whether) the subsidies are targeted. Some dispersal programs work by deconcentrating families within neighborhoods of concentrated poverty. For example, HOPE VI takes previously high concentrations of poverty in older distressed public housing developments and transforms them into lower-density, mixed-income developments. Mobility programs, on the other hand, rely on tenant-based assistance and target their assistance in nonconcentrated neighborhoods by requiring families to use them only in low-poverty areas. Some programs, such as the regular Section 8 program and mixed-income development, are untargeted in that they can be used in either high-poverty or low-poverty areas.

"Vouchering out" works in both ways, breaking up concentrations of subsidized households by converting their subsidies to allowances that are then used in a nontargeted manner throughout the local housing market. By highlighting the method of housing assistance and the programmatic target (if any), the typology in Table 24.1 helps to identify the potential impacts of different dispersal approaches. A reliance on measures targeting concentrated neighborhoods, for example, would reflect a redevelopment approach to dispersal in which segregation (income or racial) is addressed by dismantling communities of the poor (or of color). On the other hand, greater relative reliance on programs that work in nonconcentrated areas indicates a greater willingness to open up previously restricted markets.

The typology also serves as a means of identifying the level and source of potential political opposition. Tenant-based forms of assistance are much less visible and thus generate less resistance than project-based programs that typically require a process of public approval. At the same time, the level of opposition to assisted housing in more affluent and whiter neighborhoods (the lower, right-hand cell) is a long-standing characteristic of the American political landscape (and, indeed, what has contributed to the concentration of subsidized units in the first place). The redevelopment approach to dispersal (represented by programs in the upper right cell), if it generates political opposition at all, typically stimulates resistance from lower-income communities with fewer political resources at their disposal. Thus, Table 24.1 also identifies a scale of increasing political vulnerability for dispersal programs that flows from the top left to the bottom right cells.

FIRST-GENERATION DISPERSAL PROGRAMS

Scattered-site programs

For three decades from 1937 to the middle of the 1960s, the dominant model of public housing was the high-density "project." Although efforts to disperse public housing began as early as the 1950s (Hogan and Lengyel 1985; Chandler 1990), the Section 23 program,

enacted in 1965, was the first significant program to facilitate a more scattered approach. Section 23 allowed local public housing authorities (PHAs) to lease private homes on a scattered-site basis to public housing tenants.

The shift to a scattered-site approach was gradual, however. In the 1960s, many of the officials who were running local housing authorities were simply not prepared to use their programs to achieve desegregation. One survey in 1967 found that close to one-half of PHA officials did not think that public housing should promote integration (Hartman and Carr 1969). Fewer than one-fourth of the housing authorities in the survey had initiated scattered-site programs by the end of the 1960s (Hartman and Carr 1969). Because most public housing authorities began their scattered-site programs in the early 1970s, scattered-site units constituted only 9 percent of all assisted housing by the early 1980s (Hogan 1996). After another decade, scattered sites remained less than 10 percent of assisted units in urban areas despite the fact that local officials generally regarded the programs as successful (Hogan 1996).

HUD received further impetus to move toward scattered-site housing from the courts. In the case of *Gautreaux et al. v. Chicago Housing Authority et al.* (1967), the court ruled that the Chicago Housing Authority (CHA) had to end its policy of concentrating public housing in minority and poor neighborhoods. The court mandated that the city disperse future public housing throughout the city and, specifically, build it in low-minority neighborhoods. The CHA responded by refusing to build anymore public housing units for most of the following two decades. In the end, the court appointed a receiver to implement the scattered-site program, and more than 1,800 units were built. Community opposition to the program was persistent, however (Rubinowitz and Rosenbaum 2001).

The growth of the scattered-site program across the county was limited by high land and property costs outside of core neighborhoods, the opposition of residents in the receiving neighborhoods, and the lukewarm commitment of local housing officials to the goal of scattered-site assisted housing.

In addition to embarking on dispersal in a limited way through scattered-site development, HUD moved away from the practice of building public housing in high-rises. In *Shannon et al. v. United States Department of Housing and Urban Development* (1970), the court ruled that HUD and local PHAs could no longer locate subsidized housing only in nonwhite areas (Tein 1992). HUD responded with regulations adopted in 1972 that restricted new construction of subsidized housing in nonwhite areas, except in cases where there were comparable opportunities for nonwhite families in white neighborhoods.

Fair-share housing programs

Concurrent with these efforts to redirect the federal public and assisted housing programs, HUD and Congress began to feel their way into supporting regional initiatives in subsidized-housing dispersal. During this period, several special presidential commissions focused on the exclusionary practices of predominantly white suburban areas and the lack of subsidized, affordable housing outside of central cities. The National Advisory Commission on Civil Disorders, created in 1967 after the Detroit and Newark riots; the National Commission on Urban Problems (the Douglas Commission); the President's Committee on Urban Housing (the Kaiser Committee); and the President's Task Force on Suburban Problems each called for a greater dispersion of federally subsidized housing and specifically for greater development of such housing in suburban areas (Danielson 1976). The Kaiser Committee went so far as to suggest that HUD be given the authority to override local zoning regulations that were exclusionary in intent and effect. Even the Task Force on Urban Renewal, reporting two years into the Nixon administration, recommended withholding federal aid from communities that did not make an effort to expand low-income housing (Danielson 1976).

In the years following the *Fair Housing Act of 1968*, the federal government provided support and funds for the development of area-wide councils of government (COGs) and provided a brief period of support for the metropolitan dispersal of assisted housing (Keating 1994). HUD's Open Communities Program, for example, provided water, sewer, and infrastructure funds based on local governments' compliance with fair-share housing concerns.

Congress authorized COGs to review local applications for federal aid to ensure that proposed projects were consistent with regional development plans. The number of COGs nationwide grew dramatically in response to this new procedural requirement. Some COGs used this authority to downgrade applications from communities that had not made progress in meeting affordable housing goals. This mechanism led to the creation of fair-share housing programs in several metropolitan areas.

Fair-share programs, according to Listokin (1976), are designed to "improve the status quo by allocating units in a rational and equitable fashion. A primary impetus for and emphasis of fair share is expanding housing opportunity usually, but not exclusively, for low-and moderate-income families" (p. 1). Because they require the cooperation of municipalities throughout a metropolitan area, fair-share programs typically are operated by regional governments.

The cities of Dayton, Chicago, San Francisco, Washington, D.C., and others had brief experiments with fair-share housing programs (Keating 1994; Craig 1972; Listokin 1976). As the federal government withdrew support, fair share became strictly a local initiative. It survived where there was sufficient local interest in assuring that subsidized-housing opportunities existed in an equitable fashion throughout the central city and the developing suburban areas. That is to say, it survived almost nowhere. Instead, and as with the dispersal of HUD-subsidized housing, fair share continued only where the courts demanded it.

The country's largest fair-share program in New Jersey is the result of a series of state Supreme Court rulings. The first Mt. Laurel case decided by the New Jersey Supreme Court in 1975 held that communities could not zone to exclude low-income housing. Two subsequent lawsuits were required to fully implement the court's mandate of regional fair-share strategies throughout the state. In 1985, the New Jersey legislature created the Council on Affordable Housing (COAH) to oversee statewide implementation of fair-share requirements. Communities in New Jersey are assigned low-income housing obligations based on existing housing mix, present and projected employment, and amount of open land (Anglin 1994). The COAH was also responsible for setting time limits for compliance and was given the power to enforce its regulations. In the first six years of the program, the COAH had facilitated the development of fourteen thousand affordable housing units in New Jersey suburbs, or 9 percent of new housing construction in the state (Haar 1996).

The program allows communities to fulfill up to half of their low-cost housing obligation by paying other localities to build the housing. In practice, this has meant whiter and more affluent communities have paid poorer communities with greater percentages of people of color to take a portion of their obligation. Among the fifty-four such agreements reached in New Jersey between 1987 and 1996, all but one involved the transfer of affordable housing obligations from wealthier to poorer communities. The average sending community had a population that was 2 percent African American, whereas the average receiving community was 27 percent African American (Field *et al.* 1997). Suburban areas can fulfill the rest of their obligation by providing low-cost housing for the elderly and by imposing residency preferences that allow them to direct the units to families already residing in the community.

Among units that have been built in suburban areas, most are occupied by white families who had previously lived in the suburbs (Wish and Eisdorfer 1997). In fact, the amount of city-to-suburb dispersal of lower-income and minority households through the Mt. Laurel program has been minuscule. Wish and Eisdorfer (1997) traced the movement of more than 2,600 households and found that only 6.8 percent were families that moved from the city to the suburbs. Less than 2 percent of the families were African Americans who moved from city to the suburbs. When the movement of African Americans from the suburbs into the city is taken into account, there has been a net rate of African American dispersal of less than 1 percent.

Regional housing production programs

Some local and state governments have instituted a variety of programs aimed at increasing the amount of low-and moderate-income housing in suburban areas of metropolitan regions. These include inclusionary zoning programs (e.g., Montgomery County, Maryland, and New Jersey) that require a percentage of units in new developments to be set aside for low-and moderate-income occupancy (Brown 2001; Mallach 1984; Boger 1996; Calavita *et al.* 1997), "builders' remedies" (in Connecticut, Massachusetts, and Rhode Island) that provide opportunities for developers to appeal permit and zoning decisions of local governments (Morgan 1995), and state programs (such as those in California, New Hampshire, and Oregon) that require local communities to provide reasonable opportunities for the development of affordable housing (Morgan 1995; Cummins 1996). These objectives typically are achieved through incentives or through direct regulation of the development process. These programs shift the costs of supplying subsidized housing to developers and market-based home buyers and require a strong market to succeed (Polikoff 1997). If market conditions are met, the potential for significant production of affordable units in areas that traditionally, or otherwise, would not have them is considerable. In Montgomery County, Maryland, for example, one of the wealthiest suburban counties in the nation, more than twelve thousand units of low-and moderate-income housing have been built since 1974.

Gautreaux

The most notable lawsuit dealing with desegregation and deconcentration is the *Gautreaux* case. There were, in fact, two *Gautreaux* cases. In 1969, a U.S. district court found that the CHA discriminated in the placement and leasing of public housing and ordered it to provide additional units on a scattered-site basis in predominantly white areas. After an appellate court had ruled in a parallel case that HUD was also culpable, the Supreme Court ruled in 1976 that a metropolitan-wide remedy was possible (Rubinowitz 1992). As a result, the ultimate remedy that was adopted, or what came to be known as the Gautreaux program, encompassed the entire six-county Chicago metropolitan area in which HUD operated programs.

The metropolitan remedy allowed for the use of a then-new policy instrument, the tenant-based Section 8 certificate, by African American public housing residents in areas of the region that were less than 30 percent black. In the twenty years of the program, six thousand participants moved to mostly white areas. The majority moved into the city's predominantly white suburbs (Rubinowitz and Rosenbaum 2001).

The program provided an orientation workshop, an initial credit check, and a home visit for interested families. A mobility counselor was assigned to each family to help locate potential apartments and to provide information the tenants would need after their move, such as referrals to local service agencies. Rubinowitz (1992) argues that many families would not have participated had it not been for the counseling element of the program. To get landlords to participate, the program screened applicants for them. In addition to the credit checks and home visits, the program also required letters of reference for each applicant. Participating landlords were assured of both confidentiality and the fact that the program would avoid reconcentrating participants (Rubinowitz 1992).

Program officials consciously attempted to keep the program low profile. Careful screening of families and limits to the number of families relocated in any given community were established to avoid political backlash in the receiving communities and to retain as much as possible the "invisible" nature of housing allowances.

Despite criticisms of the design of the research that showed positive outcomes for Gautreaux families, the experience of the program convinced many that mobility programs that integrate landlord recruitment, tenant counseling, and placement services could begin to overcome patterns of residential segregation and improve the lives of poor families (Goering et al. 1995).

Section 8 program

In 1968, the President's Commission on Housing, known as the Kaiser Commission, recommended a form of housing allowance for lower-income families. The argument in favor of tenant-based assistance focused on three matters, only one of which was related to its potential to reduce the levels of segregation by race and poverty that characterize unit-based housing assistance programs. The main argument in favor of Section 8 was the growing criticism that unit-based programs were too costly and not serving enough families. In addition, tenant-based assistance was favored

because it allowed families a greater level of choice in units and neighborhoods and represented less interference in the private market (Friedman and Weinberg 1983).

Consideration of tenant-based forms of housing assistance dates to the formation of the public housing program in 1937 (Friedman and Weinberg 1983). Congress considered a program of tenant-based assistance when creating the *Housing Act of 1937* and again in 1944. In both cases, Congress decided that slum clearance and the construction of more and newer housing units to deal with a shortage that had emerged during the Great Depression and grown during the war were the national priority. Furthermore, housing allowances might merely subsidize profits in slum neighborhoods (Friedman and Weinberg 1983; Semer et al. 1976). The idea did not go away, however. Congress considered and rejected the idea again in 1949 and 1953. The riots of the 1960s highlighted the extent of residential segregation and substandard housing conditions for the poor in central cities and brought the dispersal potential of housing allowances to center stage (Hartung and Henig 1997).

Although no immediate action was taken on the Kaiser Commission's recommendation, Congress authorized a national experiment in the use of tenant-based assistance in 1971. Called the Experimental Housing Allowance Program (EHAP), the initiative was meant to run for the better part of a decade, and the results were to be used to determine if a national program would be created. However, Congress and the Nixon administration decided in 1974 to not wait for the results and created the Section 8 program. The program was expanded in the 1980s to include vouchers as well as certificates.

Section 8 of the *Housing and Community Development Act of 1974* consisted of three separate housing assistance programs. The Section 8 New Construction and Section 8 Substantial Rehabilitation programs worked very much like the old project-based programs in which the subsidy was tied to the units built (or rehabilitated). The Section 8 existing program was the truly tenant-based subsidy in which the household could use the certificate in the marketplace. The tenant-based Section 8 program caught on quickly and in just five years became the nation's second largest low-income housing program behind public housing (Rasmussen 1980).

The program worked by allowing certificate holders to rent any unit in the market that met quality standards and rented at or below a HUD-established fair market rent (FMR) for that region. The certificate paid for the difference between the market rent of the unit and 25 percent of the household's income. In 1982, the certificate formula was changed so that households were responsible for paying 30 percent of their incomes. FMRs are adjusted annually by HUD, and the legislation established that FMRs were to be set at the median rent for units of similar size in each regional market. In 1984, FMRs were reduced to the 45th percentile, and in 1995, they were reduced again to the 40th percentile (Turner 1998).

Vouchers

In 1983, Congress, at the urging of the Reagan administration, created a demonstration program of housing vouchers. Vouchers were similar to Section 8 certificates, except that they had fewer geographic restrictions (certificates were limited to the jurisdiction of the local agency that administered them, whereas vouchers were valid throughout the United States) and families could rent units above the FMR if they absorbed the extra cost (and thus paid more than 30 percent of their incomes on housing). In 1999, Congress merged the certificate and voucher programs retaining most of the features of the vouchers.

Over time, the emphasis and expenditures of federal housing policy have shifted from building units to providing housing allowances (Struyk 1991; McClure 1998; Hartung and Henig 1997). The ratio of vouchers and certificates compared to project-based assistance (including public housing) shifted from 0.6 in the 1970s to 4.75 by the 1990s (Hartung and Henig 1997). By 1997, 72 percent of new federal rental assistance funds went to tenant-based subsidies and only 28 percent to project-based programs (McClure 1998), and roughly one-third of all households assisted by the federal government received allowances (Newman and Schnare 1997; McClure 1998).

Section 8 vouchers form the basis of the mobility approach now favored at the federal level. The record of Section 8 shows a much greater dispersion of assisted households compared to project-based programs. This effect was accentuated with the introduction of vouchers, allowing families to venture into neighborhoods where prevailing rents were above FMR limits. Because households receiving tenant-based assistance are more evenly distributed across metropolitan regions than are residents of project-based subsidized housing, the overall geographic dispersion of HUD-assisted households has increased over time (Gray and Tursky 1986).

Portability

During the 1970s, HUD took some preliminary steps to encourage the use of Section 8 certificates across jurisdictional boundaries. HUD's voluntary Areawide Housing Opportunity Plan encouraged municipalities within metropolitan areas to collaborate in planning for low-income housing and to facilitate cross-jurisdictional mobility by certificate holders (Tegeler et al. 1995, 456). The Regional Housing Mobility Program, designed to assist area-wide planning organizations in facilitating the interjurisdictional mobility of low-income and minority households, was abandoned by HUD at the beginning of the Reagan administration (HUD 1994).

In 1987, Congress amended Section 8 to allow certificate holders to use their subsidies throughout the metropolitan area in which the subsidy was issued or in a contiguous metropolitan area. In 1990, Congress expanded the so-called portability provision to allow statewide mobility by certificate holders. Despite these changes, most local housing authorities did not implement portability guidelines quickly (Donovan 1994). A national survey in 1991 found that only 3 percent of Section 8 certificates and vouchers had been ported across jurisdictional boundaries (Polikoff 1997).

Portability was not vigorously adopted by local housing authorities for several reasons (Turner 1998). The first is the policy followed by many local authorities of establishing residency preferences for admission to the Section 8 programs. An internal HUD survey of its fifty-one field offices found that 42 percent of 2,541 local public housing authorities had such residency preferences (Tegeler et al. 1995). Tegeler et al. (1995) argue that "the practice of ranking current local residents above out-of-town applicants may be the single most significant factor excluding eligible minority households from access to Section 8 subsidies once the certificates have been allocated to a region" (p. 21). In addition, the program often resulted in a loss of administrative revenues to local authorities each time a resident "ported out."

In 1992, Congress pulled back on portability, requiring recipients who did not already live in the jurisdiction of an issuing housing authority to remain within that jurisdiction for at least twelve months before moving with it (Schill and Wachter 1995; Tegeler *et al.* 1995). Portability is now a permanent feature of the new Housing Choice Voucher program (the new name for the Section 8 program since 1998).

SECOND-GENERATION DISPERSAL

In the early 1990s, as the concentration-of-poverty argument was reaching ascendancy, the framework for federal housing policy shifted. Congress began not only to recognize the "failures" of public housing but began to associate those failures with an emerging understanding of concentrated poverty as the driving problem in American urban areas. In 1988, along with encouraging portability in Section 8, Congress created the National Commission on Severely Distressed Public Housing. Legislators were looking for a way to change the face of existing public housing by looking at options for the worst such housing in the stock and by increasing the income diversity of public housing residents. The new Clinton appointees brought this same framework with them in 1993, and throughout most of the 1990s, HUD policy moved toward a paradigm that emphasized dispersion. The work demonstrating the connection between federal housing policy and concentrated poverty (see Massey and Kanaiaupuni 1993; Holloway *et al.* 1998; Carter *et al.* 1998) provided the larger rationale for dispersion. HUD was not simply correcting old mistakes; it was addressing what it regarded as the most significant problem facing American cities at the end of the century.

The second generation of dispersal has been a two-pronged approach. On one hand, there is a strong reliance on "mobility programs" that use tenant-based Section 8 subsidies to move families out of neighborhoods of concentrated poverty. These programs are part of a larger shift in federal housing subsidies from project-based to tenant-based assistance that has been taking place for more than twenty years (Nenno 1998). On the other hand, there has been a concerted effort to redefine and redevelop existing public and assisted housing projects by introducing a greater mix of incomes and uses at the project sites and by improving site design to encourage community building within the projects (Popkin, Buron, *et al.* 2000; Epp 1996).

Mobility programs

Programs that combine Section 8 tenant-based assistance with mobility counseling and other special efforts (or special program requirements) to deconcentrate subsidized households are referred to as "mobility programs." Mobility programs go beyond the regular Section 8 program in any of three different ways: (1) participants who volunteer for the programs are *required* to move to nonconcentrated neighborhoods, (2) they incorporate forms of mobility counseling in order to assist households in choosing neighborhoods they would not necessarily have chosen without greater information, and (3) the programs include an active recruitment of landlords in neighborhoods not traditionally receptive to Section 8 families.

As described earlier, the barriers to interjurisdictional mobility using Section 8 are significant. Suburban communities often establish residency preferences for Section 8 and other assisted housing programs that work to reduce opportunities for central city residents to take advantage of subsidized housing in the suburbs. PHAs cannot own or operate facilities outside of their jurisdiction unless they enter into agreements with housing authorities in those areas, which have been rare (Polikoff 1997). Mobility programs are attempts to overcome the limited amount of dispersal typical of the regular Section 8 and public housing programs.

There are five major categories of mobility programs currently in operation in the United States (Turner 1998). The first is the result of recent efforts on the part of the federal government to shift project-based subsidies to tenant-based assistance. In HUD-subsidized buildings that are no longer financially viable, or that have high vacancy rates, or in which the project-based subsidies have expired or are prepaid, families are given Section 8 vouchers in a process called "vouchering out." These families are then assisted in using these vouchers on the open market, relocating to a neighborhood and housing unit of their choice. I include this in the category of a mobility program because of the counseling provided to households and because one of the major policy objectives in vouchering out is to disperse subsidized households.

The second category of mobility program stems from a set of litigation settlements across the country. These lawsuits were typically filed as housing discrimination cases in which it was alleged that the local housing authority and HUD willfully and negligently segregated subsidized housing projects in predominantly minority neighborhoods (Popkin, Galster, *et al.* 2000). The most famous of these suits is the *Gautreaux* case resulting in a mobility program that became a national model for other efforts. More recently, HUD has taken to settling these cases out of court where possible (Hartman 1995). Many of the resulting consent decrees incorporate Gautreaux-like mobility efforts.

The third category of mobility program is the federal government's Moving to Opportunity (MTO) program. This demonstration program, enacted by Congress in 1992, was influenced by the documented outcomes of the Gautreaux program and incorporated many of the features of the Gautreaux effort (Briggs 1997; Stoll 1999). Fourth, HUD has created several Regional Opportunity Counseling programs around the country to promote collaboration in Section 8. These programs combine landlord recruitment and mobility counseling to enhance dispersal (Williams 1998). Finally, there are a variety of local programs around the country, such as the Hartford voluntary program (Donovan 1994), that combine elements of counseling and placement to facilitate the mobility of low-income households. In all, there are more than fifty of all types of programs operating in more than thirty-five metropolitan areas across the country (Briggs 1997; Williams 1998).

Moving to opportunity

The MTO program was authorized by Section 152 of the *Housing and Community Development Act of 1992*. Congress appropriated $20 million in 1992 and another $50 million in 1993 for the program. Authorized as a demonstration program, MTO operates in five cities: New York, Los Angeles, Chicago, Boston, and Baltimore. The program is designed to provide Section 8 tenant-based assistance to families living in public housing or project-based Section 8 in areas with high poverty concentrations (greater than 40 percent of residents below the poverty level) (HUD 1999, 1996). Although modeled after Gautreaux, MTO differs from that litigation-based program in one important way: the receiving neighborhoods are defined by their degree of poverty, not by their degree of racial concentration. Similar to Gautreaux, however, MTO uses nonprofit agencies to recruit landlords to participate and to provide screening of program participants, mobility counseling, and support in the search and resettlement process (HUD 1999, 1996). The program was operational in all five cities by February 1995. Each of the five local housing authorities established a waiting list of those eligible for MTO and then proceeded with recruitment and the random assignment of volunteers to one of three groups – the MTO experimental group, the Section 8 comparison group, and the stay-in-place control group. The experimental group members were referred to the nonprofit counseling agency to begin their counseling and search for housing. They were given Section 8 tenant-based subsidies and were required to relocate into census tracts where less than 10 percent of the population was below the poverty level. The Section 8 comparison group was also given a Section 8 certificate but thereafter treated no differently than any other regular program participant. Thus, their housing search was not restricted to low-poverty areas, and they received no special mobility counseling. Finally, the in-place control group members remained in their public housing or project-based Section 8 units (HUD 1999, 1996). Program participants were randomly assigned to one of the three experimental groups to determine more precisely whether differences in outcome that occur across the groups are attributable to the counseling and assistance received by the treatment. HUD (1999, 1996) plans to monitor the families during a ten-year period to document their educational, employment, and social experiences.

The program implementation was delayed in Baltimore when local political candidates publicized the program and generated strong opposition in some inner suburbs (Moberg 1995). Ironically, these suburbs were not eligible to actually receive MTO families because their poverty rates exceeded 10 percent. The trouble was such that Maryland's two senators succeeded in cutting future funding for the program.

The initial studies of MTO participants indicate significant benefits to families who move to nonconcentrated neighborhoods in terms of greater neighborhood satisfaction and reduced fear of crime (HUD 1999; Johnson *et al.* 2002). Other studies show gains in employment and earnings in some cities but not in others (Hanratty *et al.* 1997; Rosenbaum *et al.* 1998). Similarly, the experience of children in their new schools is mixed, with improvements in some areas and not others (Norris and Bembry 1998; Ludwig *et al.* 2001).

Vouchering out

Vouchering out occurs when HUD project-based assistance is terminated either through a building conversion to market rate rents or through a demolition of an older project, and the displaced households are provided with tenant-based subsidies to use when finding a new apartment. Typically, families that are vouchered out are given some form of mobility or relocation counseling and assistance. As Polikoff (1997) argues, programs that demolish housing units and replace them with Section 8 certificates have the largest impact on "eliminating localized poverty clusters" (p. 20). Vouchering out is significantly different from other mobility programs in that the families are involuntarily displaced from their homes. This can have important implications for the experiences of the families who move.

Varady and Walker (2000) report that long-term residents and older residents were the least happy to move from four sites studied by HUD. Vouchered-out residents also tended to move into nearby neighborhoods rather than disperse widely. This same study reports enhanced satisfaction among residents who were vouchered out, less fear of crime, but no employment impacts (Varady and Walker 2000).

Redefining public and assisted housing

HOPE VI

The National Commission on Severely Distressed Public Housing reported in 1992 that approximately 86,000 units, or 6 percent of public housing, could be considered severely distressed. Congress reacted to the commission's report by authorizing HOPE VI in the same year. The program was aimed at eliminating the worst public housing developments in cities across the country. In order for this to occur, HUD and Congress revised several important policies related to public housing. The first was the one-for-one replacement law, originally a part of the *Housing and Community Development Act of 1987*, requiring housing authorities to produce a new unit of affordable housing for every one they demolished. In addition, HUD eliminated the set of federal preferences that reserved public housing for the lowest-income households (Salama 1999).

The program works primarily to demolish or rehabilitate large and troubled public housing projects, redeveloping the sites into lower-density, mixed-use, mixed-income developments. The redevelopment usually includes some units of public housing on-site but also results in the conversion of many public housing families into Section 8 voucher holders. Thus, the program results in a net loss of public housing units, reduces concentrations of subsidized families, and contributes to the general federal conversion to household-based forms of housing assistance. HOPE VI projects typically result in triple deconcentration: there are fewer public housing units on-site, they are mixed with more nonpublic housing units, and the income mix within public housing is greater than before.

The one-for-one replacement law was the largest obstacle to the implementation of HOPE VI. This rule, combined with the lack of federal funding for the development of new units, made the demolition of dysfunctional public housing developments virtually impossible (Williams-Bridgers 1994). The program could not result in any large-scale activity until the replacement requirement was repealed. HUD Secretary Henry Cisneros was instrumental during the first two years of his administration in trying to convince fellow Democrats to waive the rule for public housing. One Senate Republican aide said the secretary was "doing what no Republican Housing Secretary could have gotten away with" (Weisman 1996, 2517). Cisneros advocated the repeal of the rule even before the 1994 election gave Republicans the majority and threatened the very future of HUD. After the election, however, "every word out of Cisneros' mouth … is about the need for demolition" (Weisman 1996, 2517). One-for-one replacement was eliminated in 1995 and permanently repealed in the 1998 public housing bill.

In the first three years of the program, only PHAs from the forty largest cities or PHAs on HUD's list of troubled housing authorities were eligible for HOPE VI funds (General Accounting Office [GAO] 1997). There was little doubt from the beginning that the biggest impact of HOPE VI would be in the demolition of thousands of units of public housing. Initial HUD targets were to demolish 100,000 units of public housing by the end of the century. Almost 25,000 were demolished by the end of 1996 (Weisman 1996). The first five years of HOPE VI projects were designed to demolish 37,449 units of public housing and replace 27,526 (GAO 1997). The difference was to be made up in vouchers for families who had previously inhabited public housing (GAO 1997). By the end of the 1990s, HUD had planned to replace roughly 60,000 of the 100,000 they wished to demolish. Although replacement housing is a goal of the program, HOPE VI does not provide funding for it. PHAs are required to channel other sources of public housing funds into the replacement housing. In Atlanta, for example, there were plans to build replacement housing off-site using the cash flow from the profitable on-site HOPE VI housing (Salama 1999).

In practice, the scope of HOPE VI has extended beyond the most "severely distressed" projects to include any public housing development in which demolition and replacement costs are similar to rehabilitation costs. In some cities, these guidelines would have virtually remade the face of public housing. In Chicago, which had a high percentage of distressed public housing projects, HUD guidelines called for demolition of 18,000 of the city's 41,000 public housing units (Wright 1998). Many of the city's most notorious public housing projects are to be demolished under HUD plans. The Robert Taylor Homes are to see the demolition of more than 4,000 units

with only 1,276 rebuilt (Rogal 1999). On the city's north side, Cabrini-Green is slated to lose 1,200 units with less than 600 being rebuilt (Bennett and Reed 1999). There is some evidence that HOPE VI is failing to deconcentrate significantly because (1) it is being applied to less-distressed public housing projects, (2) the most common destination for displaced families is other public housing, and (3) those who are given vouchers are simply moving to other neighborhoods of high-minority and poverty status (National Housing Law Project 2002; Rumbler 1998).

Residents who are displaced by the HOPE VI program are, like vouchered-out households, involuntarily dispersed. There are two important implications of this. First, it reduces the enthusiasm that program participants may have for the program. Second, because involuntarily displaced households are not forced to relocate to nonconcentrated neighborhoods, the degree to which families are dispersed is limited, and the experiences that they report in their new communities are less positive compared to participants in voluntary programs (Goetz 2002b). Another group of HOPE VI participants stay in whatever public housing units are rehabilitated and maintained on-site, and so they experience deconcentration in place similar to those in mixed-income developments.

The program's heavy reliance on demolition and forced dispersal have produced significant opposition in some cities, and as some observers have noted, an unsettling resemblance to the old urban renewal program (Keating 2000; National Housing Law Project 2002).

Mixed-income developments

Mixed-income developments (referred to as mixed-income new communities, or MINCS; see Schill 1997) are attempts to create and maintain a greater range of incomes within a single subsidized project. The *Cranston-Gonzalez National Affordable Housing Act of 1990* authorized four public housing authorities to lease up to half of the units in selected developments to families with low, but not very low, incomes (Schill 1997). The public housing reform bill of 1998 (the *Quality Housing and Work Reform Act*) institutionalizes the mixed-income approach. The act directs PHAs to reserve as little as 40 percent of public housing units for the very poor, opening up the rest for families with higher incomes (up to the public housing income ceiling, of course). At the same time, the act tries to facilitate the deconcentration of the poor by setting aside 75 percent of all new Section 8 subsidies for very low-income households (Popkin, Buron, et al. 2000).

What separates the mixed-income model from scattered-site housing is that it reverses the dispersal model. Instead of mixing low-income people into wealthier neighborhoods, it attempts to attract higher-income groups into more disadvantaged communities by offering attractive housing options in previously concentrated project areas. This formula requires several elements to be successful. The developments must offer amenities attractive to market-rate residents, and the projects must be considered safe, thus necessitating strict enforcement of management rules and tenant screening (Schill 1997).

Mixed-income developments and recent reforms in the resident preferences for public housing signal a return to the original premise of public housing (Nyden 1998). Public housing was originally meant as a way station for the working poor. Over time, resident preference policies ensured that the program was targeted to the neediest families, whereas changes in the fiscal structure of the program and in the larger urban political economy ensured that the experience was long term and even multigenerational for some families (Spence 1993).

The rationales for a mixed-income approach to subsidized housing are similar to those for dispersal programs; communities are simply not viable without a cadre of employed residents to sustain businesses, provide role models, and increase social capital. A greater mix of incomes allows the public housing to fit more completely into the surrounding community; that is, it reduces the chances that the public housing will be seen as a pocket of disadvantage within the larger community. Finally, according to the neighborhood effects argument, there is the expectation that very low-income households will benefit from the inclusion of higher-income families in the projects they inhabit (Nyden 1998).

On the other hand, there is reason to expect little integration of groups in mixed-income developments. Studies of mixed-income projects have found that in many cases, mixed income means simply "having two populations living side-by-side with little interaction" (Rosenbaum et al. 1998, 71; see also Brophy and Smith 1997). The literature on mixed-income housing does not provide guidance on the conditions under which middle-income households will reside in mixed-income developments, the specific income mixes that work best, or (and most fundamentally) what the impacts are on poor households (Schwartz and Tajbakhsh 1997).

Desegregation lawsuits

Although the Gautreaux cases are the oldest and perhaps best-known court cases alleging discrimination and segregation in public housing, a number of other lawsuits have been filed in cities across the country. During the Clinton administration, HUD decided to settle with plaintiffs whenever possible. HUD has entered into consent decrees in more than twelve of these cases nationwide. Although the settlements differ in detail, there are several common themes that run through them all. Typically, the settlements call for the demolition of some public housing, construction of scattered-site replacement housing, and the development of mobility programs (with counseling) in which those in the plaintiff class are provided with tenant-based assistance to make desegregative moves (Popkin, Galster, et al. 2000). In addition, several of the settlements call for the merging of Section 8 and public housing waiting lists, and community development in areas surrounding the public housing stock.

The combination of public housing demolition, redevelopment, and mobility programs makes these legal settlements hybrids of the HOPE VI and MTO programs. The settlements deal with older public housing much as the HOPE VI program does – by emphasizing demolition and redevelopment of the sites into lower-density, mixed-use developments. Many of the consent decree sites have, in fact, made use of HOPE VI program funds to accomplish just those objectives. In addition, however, the lawsuits incorporate the MTO model of geographically restricted Section 8 vouchers and mobility counseling to facilitate deconcentration of households.

Typically, the demolition of public housing has proceeded without much delay. Dallas has demolished more than 2,500 units, and in Omaha, more than 700 units were taken down in a two-year period. "In Omaha, tenants were relocated so quickly that some ended up in substandard housing and have to be relocated a second time" (Popkin, Galster, *et al.* 2000, 42). In Minneapolis, more than 350 units went down in less than two years and another 350 after a protracted political struggle (Goetz 2002a).

The development of scattered-site housing, the creation of interjurisdictional mobility programs, and the provision of tenant-based subsidies are typically the most difficult to implement. For example, the development of replacement housing has not occurred on a large scale at any of the sites studied (Popkin, Galster, *et al.* 2000) with the exception of Minneapolis (Goetz 2002a). In some cases, the delays have been due to community resistance to the development of scattered-site housing, in other cases because of a lack of interest from private developers. In Dallas, two lawsuits by homeowners associations have been filed to stop the development of scattered-site units in suburban areas. In one case, the Fifth Circuit Court of Appeals for Texas ruled that the scattered-site development of new public housing in predominantly white areas violated the equal-protection rights of homeowners in those neighborhoods (Popkin, Galster, *et al.* 2000), in effect ending the scattered-site program in Dallas.

The mobility programs launched as part of the decrees have also proven difficult to implement. In some cities, there was reluctance on the part of many people to make desegregative moves. Many participants feared discrimination in the housing search and harassment in the new communities. Others shied away from the mobility programs because of perceived financial barriers to the relocation process, whereas still others were reluctant to move away from areas with which they were familiar and away from support networks on which they relied. In Omaha, for example, where families could use their Section 8 subsidies in any area if after four months they were unable to locate a suitable unit in a nonconcentrated neighborhood, many simply waited and then moved into an impacted neighborhood. In New Haven, members of the plaintiff class did not want to move to the suburbs, away from friends and support networks (Popkin, Galster, *et al.* 2000). These patterns suggest that long-term

support might be necessary to keep families from moving back into impacted areas.

Mobility programs were also hindered by a lack of units at or below the FMRs. Very tight rental housing markets in New York City, Minneapolis, Dallas, and Omaha made the competition for units very intense and made it difficult for the housing authorities to recruit landlords to participate in their programs. Finally, many mobility participants suggested that the lack of transportation in nonimpacted communities was a barrier to mobility. Even where bus routes existed, the distances are so great that getting to and from work and stores was very difficult. Families that did move, however, reported greater (although not uniformly so) satisfaction with their neighborhoods and their children's schools.

AMBIGUOUS OBJECTIVES, EQUIVOCAL POLICY

The typology presented in Table 24.1 provides a framework for understanding dispersal policy and organizing expectations about program outcomes. The lack of tenant-based programs targeted to concentrated neighborhoods, for example, underscores the fact that mobility programs have had little to do with conditions of segregated neighborhoods. Their impact is tied to the outcomes of poor/minority families in receiving neighborhoods. Their limitations are similarly tied to the politics of receiving communities. Project-based dispersal efforts produce a different set of planning dynamics. Those that operate in receiving communities (scattered-site and fair-share programs) have always faced extreme opposition and for that reason have never achieved a significant scale of operation. The redevelopment approach to dispersal (project-based programs in concentrated neighborhoods) either tends toward demolition and displacement (HOPE VI) or the mixed-income approach. The benefits of either of these to low-income households remain unproven.

Dispersal policy is an arena in which the objectives have not always been clear. Emerging first in the late 1960s, after decades of explicitly discriminatory and segregationist practices siting subsidized housing, dispersal policy marked a significant redirection for federal housing policy. Housing officials, long accustomed to the old ways, were sometimes reluctant to embrace dispersal or integration. Even after the federal policy shift, there remained differences on occasion between official Washington policy and the practices undertaken by local housing authorities (see Goering 1986).

The most prevalent confusion in dispersal efforts is whether they are aimed at eliminating discriminatory barriers or whether they go further to attempt to achieve actual integrative outcomes (see Galster 1990). During the first generation of dispersal efforts, there was a clear merging of antidiscrimination efforts on one hand and integrationist objectives on the other. When this became politically insupportable, the Nixon administration separated the two. Stripped of the legitimacy provided by an antidiscrimination justification, dispersal quickly died as political support for integration was insufficient. In an echo of the first wave of dispersal, many of the lawsuits that serve as the foundation for current dispersal programs in cities across the county originated as antidiscrimination suits. The remedies, however, focus on dispersal or integration of low-income families into more affluent neighborhoods. This time there is an uneasy combination of antidiscrimination impulses with the desire to deconcentrate poverty. The elimination of discriminatory subsidized housing siting practices, for which there is significant political consensus, will not, by itself, lead to a significant deconcentration of poverty. More direct steps to facilitate deconcentration through integrating the poor into more affluent communities simply do not enjoy the same level of consensus.

Congressional support for deconcentration and dispersal has been uneven and inconsistent. Congress in the early 1970s would not support a direct effort to integrate suburban areas but in 1974 supported creation of the Section 8 program in an effort to introduce greater choice for subsidized households. Congress approved the MTO program in the 1990s but immediately pulled the plug on its expansion at the first sign of suburban resistance. This has left the courts, in both the first and second generation of dispersal, as the most important initiator of dispersal and integration efforts. Massive and consistent suburban opposition to deconcentration, backed in Congress and in state houses by the growing political clout of America's suburbs, leaves dispersal in a precarious place. What can be agreed upon without much political contention, and therefore what has occurred in greatest quantity, is the demolition of "dysfunctional" or "pathological" central neighborhoods dominated by the poor and by people of color. The path of least resistance seems to be, as it has in the past, the demolition of communities of poverty and the dispersal of the poor and people of color. In practice, this leaves us perilously close to repeating the worst aspects of the Urban Renewal program.

REFERENCES

Anglin, Roland. 1994. Searching for justice: Court-inspired housing policy as a mechanism for social and economic mobility. *Urban Affairs Quarterly* 29, 3: 432–53.

Bennett, Larry, and Adolph Reed Jr. 1999. The new face of urban renewal: The Near North Redevelopment Initiative and the Cabrini-Green neighborhood. In *Without justice for all: The new liberalism and our retreat from racial equity*, Adolph Reed Jr., ed. New York: Westview.

Boger, John C. 1996. Toward ending residential segregation: A fair share proposal for the next reconstruction. In *Race, poverty, and American cities*, John C. Boger and Judith W. Wegner, eds. Chapel Hill: University of North Carolina Press.

Briggs, Xavier de Souza. 1997. Moving up versus moving out: Neighborhood effects in housing mobility programs. *Housing Policy Debate* 8, 1: 195–234.

Brophy, Paul C., and Rhonda N. Smith. 1997. Mixed-income housing: Factors for success. *Cityscape: A Journal of Policy Development and Research* 3, 2: 3–32.

Brown, Karen Destoral. 2001. *Expanding affordable housing through inclusionary zoning: Lessons from the Washington metropolitan area*. Washington, D.C.: The Brookings Institution Center on Urban and Metropolitan Policy.

Calavita, Nico, Kenneth Grimes, and Alan Mallach. 1997. Inclusionary housing in California and New Jersey: A comparative analysis. *Housing Policy Debate* 8, 1: 109–42.

Carter, W. H., Michael Schill, and Susan M. Wachter. 1998. Polarization, public housing and racial minorities. *Urban Studies* 35: 1889–1911.

Chandler, Mittie Olion. 1990. Dispersed public housing: Does it make any difference? Paper presented at the Urban Affairs Association meeting, April, 18–21, Charlotte, North Carolina.

Craig, Lois. 1972. The Dayton area's "fair share" housing plan enters the implementation phase. *City* January/February: 50–56.

Cummins, Justin D. 1996. Recasting fair share: Toward effective housing law and principled social policy. *Law and Inequality* 14, 2: 339–90.

Danielson, Michael N. 1976. *The politics of exclusion*. New York: Columbia University Press.

Donovan, Shaun. 1994. Moving to the suburbs: Section 8 mobility and portability in Hartford. Working paper W94-3. Joint Center for Housing Studies, Cambridge, MA.

Epp, Gayle. 1996. Emerging strategies for revitalizing public housing communities. *Housing Policy Debate* 7, 3: 563–88.

Field, Patrick, Jennifer Gilbert, and Michael Wheeler. 1997. Trading the poor: Intermunicipal housing negotiation in New Jersey. *Harvard Negotiation Law Review* 2, 1: 1–33.

Friedman, Joseph, and Daniel H. Weinberg. 1983. History and overview. In *The great housing experiment*, Vol. 24, Urban Affairs Annual Review, Joseph Friedman and Daniel H. Weinberg, eds. Beverly Hills, CA: Sage.

Galster, George C. 1990. Federal fair housing policy: The great misapprehension. In *Building foundations: Housing and federal policy*, Denise DiPasquale and Langley C. Keyes, eds. Philadelphia: University of Pennsylvania Press.

Gautreaux et al. v. Chicago Housing Authority et al., 265 F. Supp. 582, 583 (N.D. Ill. 1967).

Goering, John M. 1986. Introduction to Section IV. In *Housing desegregation and federal policy*, John M. Goering, ed. Chapel Hill: University of North Carolina Press.

Goering John, H. Stebbins, and M. Siewart. 1995. *Promoting housing choice in HUD's rental assistance programs*. Washington, D.C.: Office of Policy Development and Research, Department of Housing and Urban Development.

Goetz, Edward G. 2002a. *Deconcentrating poverty in Minneapolis: Hollman v. Cisneros*. Minneapolis, MN: Center for Urban and Regional Affairs.

Goetz, Edward G. 2002b. Forced relocation vs. voluntary mobility: The effects of dispersal programmes on households. *Housing Studies* 17, 1: 107–24.

Gray, Robert, and Steven Tursky. 1986. Location and racial/ethnic occupancy patterns for HUD-subsidized family housing in ten metropolitan areas. In *Housing desegregation and federal policy*, John M. Goering, ed. Chapel Hill: University of North Carolina Press.

Haar, Charles M. 1996. *Suburbs under siege: Race, space, and audacious judges*. Princeton, NJ: Princeton University Press.

Hanratty, Maria, Sara McLanahan, and Elizabeth Pettit. 1997. The impact of the Los Angeles Moving to Opportunity program on residential mobility: Neighborhood characteristics and early child and parent outcomes. Presented at the U.S. Department of Housing and Urban Development's Moving to Opportunity Research Conference, November 20–21, Washington, D.C.

Hartman, Chester. 1995. Shelterforce interview: Roberta Achtenberg. *Shelterforce*, no. 79 (January/February): 7.

Hartman, Chester W., and Gregg Carr. 1969. Housing authorities reconsidered. *Journal of the American Institute of Planners* 35, 1: 10–21.

Hartung, John M., and Jeffrey R. Henig. 1997. Housing vouchers and certificates as a vehicle for deconcentrating the poor: Evidence from the Washington, D.C., metropolitan area. *Urban Affairs Review* 32, 3: 403–19.

Hogan, James. 1996. *Scattered-site housing: Characteristics and consequences*. Washington, D.C.: U.S. Department of Housing and Urban Development.

Hogan, James B., and Dorothy L. Lengyel. 1985. Experiences with scattered-site housing. *Urban Resources* 2 (winter): 9–14.

Holloway, Steven R., Deborah Bryan, Robert Chabot, Donna M. Rogers, and James Rulli. 1998. Exploring the effects of public housing on the concentration of poverty in Columbus, Ohio. *Urban Affairs Review* 33, 6: 767–89.

Johnson, Michael P., Helen F. Ladd, and Jens Ludwig. 2002. The benefits and costs of residential mobility programmes for the poor. *Housing Studies* 17, 1: 125–38.

Keating, Larry. 2000. Redeveloping public housing: Relearning urban renewal's immutable lessons. *Journal of the American Planning Association* 66, 4: 384–97.

Keating, W. Dennis. 1994. *The suburban racial dilemma*. Philadelphia: Temple University Press.

Listokin, David. 1976. *Fair share housing allocation*. New Brunswick, NJ: Center for Urban Policy Research.

Ludwig, Jens, Helen F. Ladd, and G. J. Duncan. 2001. The effects of urban poverty on educational outcomes: Evidence from a randomized experiment. In *Brookings-Wharton papers on urban affairs*, Vol. 2, W. G. Gale and J. Pack, eds. Washington, D.C.: Brookings Institution Press.

Mallach, Alan. 1984. *Inclusionary housing programs: Policies and practices*. New Brunswick, NJ: Center for Urban Policy Research.

Massey, Douglas, and Nancy Denton. 1993. *American apartheid: Segregation and the making of the underclass*. Cambridge, MA: Harvard University Press.

Massey, Douglas, and Shawn M. Kanaiaupuni. 1993. Public housing and the concentration of poverty. *Social Science Quarterly* 74, 1: 109–22.

McClure, Kirk. 1998. Housing vouchers versus housing production: Assessing long-term costs. *Housing Policy Debate* 9, 2: 355–71.

Moberg, David. 1995. No vacancy! *Shelterforce* no. 79 (January/February): 11–13.

Morgan, Jennifer M. 1995. Zoning for all: Using inclusionary zoning techniques to promote affordable housing. *Emory Law Journal* 7, 1: 359–97.

National Housing Law Project. 2002. *False HOPE: A critical assessment of the HOPE VI public housing redevelopment program*. Oakland, CA: National Housing Law Project.

Nenno, Mary K. 1998. New directions for federally assisted housing: An agenda for the Department of Housing and Urban Development. In *New directions in urban public housing*, David P. Varady, Wolfgang F. E. Preiser, and Francis P. Russell, eds. New Brunswick, NJ: Rutgers University, Center for Urban Policy Research.

Newman, Sandra J., and Ann B. Schnare. 1997. "And a suitable living environment": The failure of housing programs to deliver on neighborhood quality. *Housing Policy Debate* 8, 4: 703–41.

Norris, Donald F., and James X. Bembry. 1998. Moving to Opportunity in Baltimore: Neighborhood choice and neighborhood satisfaction. Paper presented at the annual meeting of the Urban Affairs Association, April 21–25, Fort Worth, TX.

Nyden, Philip. 1998. Comment on James E. Rosenbaum, Linda K. Stroh, and Cathy A. Flynn's "Lake Parc Place: A study of mixed-income housing." *Housing Policy Debate* 9, 4: 741–48.

Polikoff, Alexander, ed. 1997. *Housing mobility: Promise or illusion?* Washington, D.C.: The Urban Institute.

Popkin, Susan J., Larry F. Buron, Diane K. Levy, and Mary K. Cunningham. 2000. The Gautreaux legacy: What might mixed-income and dispersal strategies mean for the poorest public housing tenants? *Housing Policy Debate* 11, 4: 911–42.

Popkin, Susan J., George Galster, Kenneth Temkin, Carla Herbig, Diane K. Levy, and Elise Richer. 2000. *Baseline assessment of public housing desegregation cases: Cross-site report*. Vol. 1. Washington, D.C.: U.S. Department of Housing and Urban Development.

Rasmussen, David W. 1980. The urban impacts of the Section 8 existing housing assistance program. In *The urban impacts of federal policies*, Norman J. Glickman, ed. Baltimore, MD: Johns Hopkins University Press.

Rogal, Brian J. 1999. Tayloring plans: Section 8 questioned. *The Chicago Reporter*. Retrieved June 21, 1999, from http://www. chicagoreporter.com/1999/06-99/0699cha.htm.

Rosenbaum, James E., Linda K. Stroh, and Cathy A. Flynn. 1998. Lake Parc Place: A study of mixed-income housing. *Housing Policy Debate* 9, 4: 703–40.

Rubinowitz, Leonard S. 1992. Metropolitan public housing desegregation remedies: Chicago's privatization program. *Northern Illinois University Law Review* 12, 3: 590–669.

Rubinowitz, Leonard, and James E. Rosenbaum. 2001. *Crossing the class and color lines: From public housing to white suburbia*. Chicago: University of Chicago Press.

Rumbler, Bill. 1998. Despite Section 8 vouchers, segregation perpetuates. *Chicago Sun Times* (December 6).

Salama, Jerry J. 1999. The redevelopment of distressed public housing: Early results from HOPE VI projects in Atlanta, Chicago, and San Antonio. *Housing Policy Debate* 10, 1: 95–142.

Schill, Michael H. 1997. Chicago's mixed income new communities strategy: The future face of public housing? In *Affordable housing and urban redevelopment in the United States: Urban Affairs Annual Reviews 46*, Willem van Vliet--, ed. Thousand Oaks, CA: Sage.

Schill, Michael H., and Susan M. Wachter. 1995 The spatial bias of federal housing law and policy: Concentrated poverty in urban America. *University of Pennsylvania Law Review* 143: 1284–349.

Schwartz, Alex, and Kian Tajbakhsh. 1997. Mixed-income housing: Unanswered questions. *Cityscape: A Journal of Policy Development and Research* 3, 2: 71–92.

Semer, Milton P., Julian H. Zimmerman, Ashley Foard, and John M. Frantz. 1976. *Housing in the seventies: Working papers*. Vol. 1, *National Housing Policy Review*. Washington, D.C.: Government Printing Office.

Shannon et al. v. United States Department of Housing and Urban Development, 436 F. 2d 809 (3d Cir. 1970).

Spence, L. H. 1993. Rethinking the social role of public housing. *Housing Policy Debate* 4, 3: 355–68.

Stoll, Michael A. 1999. Spatial mismatch, discrimination, and male youth employment in the Washington, D.C. area: Implications for residential mobility policies. *Journal of Policy Analysis and Management* 18, 1: 77–98.

Struyk, Raymond J. 1991. Preservation policies in perspective. *Housing Policy Debate* 2, 2: 383–411.

Tegeler, Philip D., Michael L. Hanley, and Judith Liben. 1995. Transforming Section 8: Using federal housing subsidies to promote individual housing choice and desegregation. *Harvard Civil Rights-Civil Liberties Law Review* 30: 451–86.

Tein, Michael R. 1992. The devaluation of nonwhite community in remedies for public housing discrimination. *University of Pennsylvania Law Review* 140: 1463–1503.

Turner, Margery Austin. 1998. Moving out of poverty: Expanding mobility and choice through tenant-based housing assistance. *Housing Policy Debate* 9, 2: 373–94.

U.S. Department of Housing and Urban Development (HUD). 1994. Residential mobility programs. Urban Policy Brief Number 1. Washington, D.C.: U.S. Department of Housing and Urban Development.

U.S. Department of Housing and Urban Development (HUD), 1996. *Expanding housing choices for HUD-assisted families: First biennial report to Congress: Moving to Opportunity for Fair Housing and urban development*. Washington, D.C.: U.S. Department of Housing and Urban Development.

U.S. Department of Housing and Urban Development (HUD). 1999. *Moving to Opportunity for Fair Housing demonstration program: Current status and initial findings*. Washington, D.C.: U.S. Department of Housing and Urban Development.

U.S. General Accounting Office (GAO). 1997. *HOPE VI demonstration*. Washington, D.C.: U.S. General Accounting Office.

Varady, David P., and Carole C. Walker. 2000. Vouchering out distressed subsidized developments: Does moving lead to improvements in housing and neighborhood conditions? *Housing Policy Debate* 11, 1: 115–62.

Weisman, Jonathan. 1996. True impact of GOP Congress reaches well beyond bills. *Congressional Quarterly* 54, 36: 2515–20.

Williams, Kale. 1998. Fair housing for everybody – Including the poor. *The Fair*

Housing Report, winter: 15–16. Washington, D.C.: Fair Housing Council of Greater Washington, D.C.

Williams-Bridgers, Jacquelyn. 1994. Public housing: Housing agency officials want more flexibility in replacing deteriorated housing. Testimony before the Employment, Housing and Aviation Subcommittee, U.S. House Committee on Banking Finance, Urban Affairs, 103d Congress. 22 March.

Wish, Naomi Bailin, and Stephen Eisdorfer. 1997. The impact of Mount Laurel initiatives: An analysis of the characteristics of applicants and occupants. *Seton Hall Law Review* 27: 1268–1337.

Wright, Pat. 1998. The privatization of public housing leads to affordable housing crisis. *PRAGmatics* 1, 2: 3, 13.

25

"Has HOPE VI Transformed Residents' Lives? New Evidence from the HOPE VI Panel Study"

From *Housing Studies* (2009)

Susan J. Popkin, Diane K. Levy and Larry Buron

INTRODUCTION

Since the early 1990s, the HOPE VI (Housing Opportunities for People Everywhere) program has been the United States' largest, most ambitious community revitalization program. Under the auspices of the US Department of Housing and Urban Development (HUD), HOPE VI targeted the nation's worst public housing – government-subsidized developments suffering from years of neglect and overwhelmed with drug trafficking and violent crime. Exacerbating the problems, many of these developments were extraordinarily segregated – both racially and economically – and often located in isolated, extremely distressed neighborhoods (Popkin, 2007).

The reasons that some public housing developments in the US became such terrible places to live were complex. By the end of the 1980s, public housing was regarded as one of the biggest and most visible failures of American social welfare policy (National Commission, 1992). The vast majority of public housing in the US was built prior to the 1970s, when housing segregation was either the law or implicitly condoned. As a result, most central city public housing was located in high-poverty neighborhoods and occupied primarily by African-Americans. The racial and economic isolation of these developments was exacerbated by tenant selection policies that targeted housing subsidies to those with the most severe housing problems (including homeless families), effectively making many public housing developments housing of last resort. By limiting occupancy to the "poorest of the poor", these policies created even more severe concentrations of distress (Turner *et al.*, 2009).

Administrative failures exacerbated the problems: US public housing was consistently under-funded and many developments were poorly maintained. Ineffective housing authority management and inadequate federal funding left huge backlogs of repairs, creating hazardous conditions that placed residents at risk for injury or disease (Landrigan and Carlson, 1995; Manjarrez *et al.*, 2007; Rosenstreich *et al.*, 1997). Further exacerbating these problems was the lack of effective security or policing; violent criminals and drug dealers dominated many of the developments, and residents lived in constant fear (Popkin *et al.*, 2000a). Finally, the neighborhoods that surrounded the developments generally had deficient public services and few resources – such as stores, financial institutions or hospitals – and even fewer employment opportunities.

The HOPE VI program was a key element of a bold effort to transform US public housing policy. HOPE VI was intended to comprehensively address the challenges of distressed developments – and demonstrate that public housing programs could produce good results for residents and communities. Unlike earlier efforts, HOPE VI sought to not only replace the physical structures, but to improve the life chances of the families who had endured the terrible conditions, offering them opportunities to move into new developments or to use housing vouchers to move to less poor, less distressed neighborhoods (National Commission, 1992). In a departure from earlier efforts to rehabilitate public housing, HOPE VI sought to move beyond "bricks and mortar, and provided funding for supportive services for residents". The program's goals included "improving the living environment for residents of severely distressed public housing" and "providing housing that will avoid or decrease the concentration of very poor families". The hope of the policy makers who created the program was that the combination of the improvements in the quality of their neighborhoods and supportive services would also help residents in other ways, in particular, in becoming self-sufficient and improving their economic circumstances (Popkin et al., 2004a).

With the program now up for reauthorization, it is time to assess how close it has come to achieving these ambitious goals. For much of the history of the program, there has been only limited information about how it has affected residents' lives. Nearly a decade after HOPE VI began, many critics were citing low rates of return to new HOPE VI developments as evidence that relocation and involuntary displacement were leaving residents worse off, sending them to other poor communities that were little better than the distressed developments they left behind (cf. Bennett et al., 2006; Keating, 2001; National Housing Law Project, 2002). To answer questions about what happened to the original residents of HOPE VI developments, the US Congress commissioned two systematic, multi-city studies in 1999: The HOPE VI Panel Study and the HOPE VI Resident Tracking Study. Both were intended to address the question of how the transformation of public housing has affected the lives of the families who lived in developments targeted for HOPE VI redevelopment.[1] The Tracking Study (Buron et al., 2002) was intended to provide a snapshot of living conditions and well-being of former residents of eight HOPE VI sites in early 2001; the HOPE VI Panel Study (Popkin et al., 2002) focused on five sites and tracked living conditions and well-being of residents as they went through the relocation process.

In an earlier paper based on the first phases of this research, the author and colleagues raised critical questions about whether HOPE VI would achieve its potential as a powerful

force for improving the lives of low-income families. Findings from the Tracking Study seemed to suggest that some relocatees had experienced real benefits, but many were living in neighborhoods that were still very poor and racially segregated and others had simply moved to other traditional public housing developments. Baseline findings from the HOPE VI Panel Study suggested that many residents had complex personal problems – with physical and mental health, large family sizes, low labor force attachment – that were likely to make relocation very challenging (Popkin et al., 2004b).

This paper presents new evidence on how HOPE VI families have fared from the follow-up rounds of the HOPE VI Panel Study (Popkin et al., 2002). The long-term findings from the HOPE VI Panel Study paint a more positive picture than our earlier research led us to expect, showing that the program has, in fact, had profound benefits for many public housing families, particularly those who have relocated to less poor communities. However, the long-term results also highlight the limitations of the HOPE VI approach and point to the need for new and creative strategies for addressing some of the worst consequences of concentrated poverty. Finally, these findings raise questions about whether these benefits can be sustained in light of the economic downturn.

TRANSFORMING HOUSING, TRANSFORMING LIVES?

As discussed above, a central premise of HOPE VI is that it is possible to improve the lives of residents of distressed public housing developments either by helping them to relocate to better neighborhoods or by creating a new, healthier community on the same site. Researchers and policy makers have become increasingly concerned about the negative effects of living in concentrated poverty – communities with poverty rates of 40 per cent or more. In the late 1980s, Wilson (1987) argued that the rise of what he called the "urban underclass" was a direct consequence of the isolation of poor families in inner-city communities with limited employment opportunities, inadequate municipal services, and a lack of middle and working-class working residents to serve as role models and to support local institutions such as schools and stores.

Since Wilson, many scholars have examined the evidence on how neighborhood environments affect residents' life chances (cf. Ellen and Turner, 1997; Jencks and Mayer, 1990). In particular, researchers have documented the many ways in which growing up in high poverty neighborhoods harms children and adolescents, including poor physical and mental health, risky sexual behavior and delinquency (Ellen and Turner, 1997; Leventhal and Brooks-Gunn, 2000, 2004; Sampson et al., 2002). Boys growing up in these communities are at great risk of becoming involved in criminal activity; girls face high risks of pressure for early sexual initiation and sexual violence (Popkin et al., 2008). Children of both genders are at risk of dropping out of school and becoming disconnected from the labor market.

High-crime communities like the severely distressed public housing developments targeted by the HOPE VI program are among the worst environments for children – and adults – in the US. In these communities, residents are very likely to suffer some of the most severe consequences of concentrated poverty, including drug addiction, abuse or neglect by drug-addicted parents, being killed or injured in the drug wars, arrested or incarcerated or simply traumatized by the stress of coping with the constant violence and disorder (Popkin et al., 2000a). Profound social disorder and reduced "collective efficacy" is associated with a range of negative outcomes, including high rates of asthma, high homicide rates and low birth weight (Morenoff, 2001; Sampson et al., 1997). Further, exposure to violence can have profound – and lingering – effects on children's mental health and development (Garbarino et al., 1991; Kilpatrick et al., 2000).

In the US, expectations for how HOPE VI might transform public housing residents' lives were very high, based largely on positive research findings from studies of Chicago's Gautreaux Housing Desegregation Program (Popkin et al., 2000b). This program stemmed from a legal settlement in which the courts found that the Chicago Housing Authority (CHA) and HUD had discriminated against African-American tenants by concentrating them in large-scale developments located in poor, black neighborhoods. The decision against the housing authority in 1969 called for the creation of new public housing at "scattered sites" in predominantly white communities. In addition, the court ordered the housing authority to provide Section 8 certificates that African-American public housing residents (and families on the waiting list for public housing) could use to move to racially integrated suburban areas (Polikoff, 2006; Rubinowitz and Rosenbaum, 2000).

Gautreaux program participants received counseling to help them find housing – assistance searching in unfamiliar communities, support during the search process, help in negotiating with landlords and referrals for social services (Feins et al., 1997; Polikoff, 2006). Research on outcomes for families who made these moves suggested that adults were more likely to be employed and children did better in school than their counterparts who remained in the city (Kaufman and Rosenbaum, 1992; Popkin et al., 1993; Rubinowitz and Rosenbaum, 2000). Although the Gautreaux research was limited by small sample sizes, retrospective data collection and lack of a rigorous control group, the findings fueled a policy argument that poverty deconcentration might be a means to dramatically improve the life circumstances of poor minority families (Briggs et al., forthcoming).

Buoyed by the Gautreaux experience, the Clinton Administration promoted innovative strategies such as public housing demolition and replacement with mixed-income housing, and assisted housing mobility initiatives for voucher recipients (Popkin et al., 2004a; Turner et al., 2009). Policy makers had high hopes that mixing residents of different income levels – through a combination of mixed-income redevelopment and mobility strategies – would both expose very low-income public housing residents to working and middle-class role models and provide them access to neighborhoods with better services and greater access to economic opportunities. Proponents argued that aggressively pursuing these strategies could lead to a range of benefits including: improved job and educational opportunities for low-income families; positive role models; more stable communities; better public services; better management; and investments in the larger neighborhood (Goetz, 2003; Joseph et al., 2005; Popkin et al., 2000b; Schwartz and Tajbakhsh, 1997).

[...]

The effects of public housing transformation in the US

In the US, the research evidence to date on the impact of mixed-income and mobility strategies on residents' lives suggests some significant benefits for residents, but not the transformative effects policy makers and scholars had envisioned (Popkin, 2007; Turner et al., 2009). Much of what we know about the US comes from research on HUD's Moving to Opportunity (MTO) Demonstration. Modeled on the Gautreaux program, the MTO experiment targeted very low-income public housing residents located in extremely high-poverty neighborhoods (more than 40 per cent poor) in five cities (Orr et al., 2003). Volunteers were randomly assigned to one of three treatment groups: a "control group" (families retained their public housing unit and received no new assistance); a "Section 8 comparison group" (families received the standard counseling and voucher subsidy, for use in the private housing market); or an "experimental group" that received vouchers usable only in low-poverty neighborhoods (less than 10 per cent poor as of the 1990 Census), and relocation counseling. MTO experimental participants ended up in considerably better housing in safer, if still moderately poor, neighborhoods (Kingsley and Pettit, 2008).

These changes in neighborhood environment seem to have had important benefits for residents' well-being. MTO found that adult women who used vouchers to move to less poor neighborhoods experienced significant and large improvements in mental health. In addition, MTO experimental group movers realized improvements in physical health, such as significant lower rates of obesity relative to the control group. However, the MTO results for adolescents showed puzzling differences by gender, with girls experiencing health benefits and reductions in risky behavior relative to the control group, while boys actually fared worse (Briggs et al., forthcoming; Clampett-Lundquist et al., 2006; Orr et al., 2003; Popkin et al., 2008).

Despite these important gains in quality of life and overall well-being, many have viewed these results as disappointing because they have not fully realized the promise of Gautreaux. For example, MTO findings show no consistent impacts on educational outcomes for youth (Briggs et al., 2008; Orr et al., 2003).Thus far,

MTO results show no statistically significant employment or earnings gains across the full sample of MTO families, although there are some indications of modest effects at two sites (New York and Los Angeles) (Cove et al., 2008).

HOPE VI differs from MTO in several important ways; as a result, it is not clear whether it is reasonable to expect even the same positive benefits for residents' quality of life, let alone any impact on self-sufficiency. MTO was an experiment that compared the impact of providing vouchers that could only be used in low-poverty areas with traditional vouchers and traditional public housing. Because it was a demonstration, participants volunteered to be relocated and received counseling and support in finding suitable housing. Finally, participants' developments were not slated for demolition at the time they volunteered, although some later did become HOPE VI sites. In contrast, HOPE VI involved redeveloping entire public housing communities; because of the redevelopment, residents did not volunteer to move, but rather had to relocate as part of the regeneration initiative. While most sites offered some relocation assistance, there was no requirement that residents move to low poverty communities. Finally, although HOPE VI provided funding for *Community and Supportive Services* for residents, there was no consistent requirement for what types of services housing authorities should offer or whether these services should begin prior to relocation.

Many advocates and researchers argued that the impact of HOPE VI on original residents would almost certainly be negative. While the redevelopment would probably benefit the neighborhood, these critics argued that residents would lose important social ties, and would likely end up in other poor neighborhoods that were just as bad as – or even worse than – those they left.[2] Advocates pointed to the low numbers of returning residents – 11 per cent in an early report – and the fact that plans called for replacing less than half of the original, deeply-subsidized public housing units as evidence that these very poor residents would be left with fewer housing options rather than gaining from new redevelopment (National Housing Law Project, 2002; Wexler, 2000; Zeilenbach, 2002). Other scholars (cf. Fullilove, 2004; Goetz, 2003; Venkatesh et al., 2004) focused on the potential loss of social ties as a critical issue for these very low-income families, arguing that many of these public housing developments were close-knit communities where residents had highly developed social networks on which they relied to cope with the challenges of daily living.

During the first years of the program, accurate information about what was happening to public housing families displaced by HOPE VI redevelopment was sparse. HUD funded a set of case studies of the effects of HOPE VI on individual public housing sites (Holin et al., 2003), but not a long-term study of impact on residents comparable to the research on outcomes of MTO participants. As noted above, much attention was focused on the relatively low rates of return, but that indicator alone cannot tell whether or not residents are worse off, for example, they could have chosen a voucher so they could move to a better neighborhood.[3] Indeed, studies of individual HOPE VI sites suggested that many former residents who had moved to private market housing with vouchers perceived real improvements in their neighborhood conditions, including substantial reductions in crime. Research from Chicago, which had more distressed public housing than any other city and had launched an ambitious, city-wide transformation of its blighted developments, highlighted both the potential benefits and the pitfalls of the HOPE VI approach. In Chicago, residents who succeeded in moving with vouchers were generally doing well and living in better quality housing in dramatically safer communities, but a substantial number of other households, too troubled to qualify for vouchers, had been left behind and were still living in profoundly distressed housing (Popkin and Cunningham, 2002; Popkin et al., 2003). Another study documented residents from the Robert Taylor Homes struggling with relocation, and especially with the loss of important social supports (Venkatesh et al., 2004). Studies in Seattle, Fort Worth, Philadelphia and Minneapolis found similar results; relocated residents were generally satisfied with the lower crime and better amenities in their new communities, but had some anxiety about living in unfamiliar communities (Barrett et al., 2002–2003; Clampett-Lundquist et al., 2006; Goetz, 2003; Kliet and Manzon, 2003).

[...]

In the US, the *HOPE VI Resident Tracking Study* provided the first cross-site, systematic evidence about how former residents were faring. Findings from the study generally showed that as in MTO and the single-site research, most relocated residents were living in better housing in safer neighborhoods and, despite the loss of community, were generally satisfied with their move. But there were important differences across sites; where housing authorities handled relocation poorly, residents did not realize even these modest gains and ended up in other, very poor, racially segregated communities. Further, there were worrying indications that some residents relocated to housing in the private market were struggling to make ends meet because of high utility costs (Buron et al., 2002; Popkin et al., 2004b).

While these early studies seemed to suggest a more positive picture for many original residents than the one many advocates had feared, they raised important questions about how residents were faring, especially those who did not end up in better neighborhoods. In addition, these studies all had significant limitations that made it difficult to know how accurately they depicted the situation for HOPE VI residents overall. Single-site studies allowed in-depth exploration of the experiences of residents in a particular city, but could not capture the variation and complexity of the ways the HOPE VI program might be affecting residents across the US. The *Tracking Study* offered considerably more breadth, but was limited by the fact that it was retrospective, had no information on residents' perceptions of their living conditions or economic struggles before HOPE VI, and, further, necessarily included only those residents who were relatively easy to find several years after being relocated.[4]

[...]

LONG-TERM OUTCOMES FOR HOPE VI FAMILIES

After tracking residents through the relocation process, the *HOPE VI Panel Study* is able to address effectively the question of whether HOPE VI has succeeded in its goal of improving residents' life circumstances or whether the critics' dire predictions have been realized. For the most part, the long-term results show tremendous improvements in quality of life for former residents: most are living in neighborhoods that are dramatically safer and offer far healthier environments for themselves and their children. However, some are struggling with the challenges of living in the private market, and a substantial minority continues to live in traditional public housing developments that are only marginally better than the distressed developments they left. These findings demonstrate the ways in which HOPE VI has improved the life circumstances of many original residents, while underscoring the need to continue to seek solutions for the problems that have kept too many families from being able to take advantage of new opportunities.

Pre-HOPE VI conditions were terrible

At baseline in 2001, survey respondents at all five sites reported intolerable conditions – conditions that put their health and safety at risk and that were substantially worse than those experienced by other poor renters in the US.[5] Approximately one-third said that their unit was so cold during the past winter that it had caused discomfort, 42 per cent reported water leaks, and 25 per cent had broken toilets. About one-third of respondents reported peeling paint or plaster in their units (problems that can cause lead poisoning), about one-quarter reported cockroach infestation and excessive mold in their units, and another 16 per cent reported serious problems with rats and mice. Underscoring the severity of their situations, about one-third reported two or three housing problems, and one in five reported more than three problems (Popkin *et al.*, 2004b).

This substandard housing was located in very high poverty communities; in the census tracts where the Panel Study developments were located, poverty rates exceeded 40 per cent. These neighborhoods were predominantly minority, and had high rates of unemployment, welfare recipiency and other social ills. Crime was rampant; at baseline, virtually all (90 per cent) of the respondents reported serious problems with drug trafficking, drug use and gang activity. Even worse, about 75 per cent viewed violent crime (shooting, assaults and rape) as "big problems". Interview respondents described witnessing shootings and carefully

restricting when and where their children went around their developments. The comments from children were especially poignant, with some recounting harrowing incidents of bullets coming into their rooms or friends who narrowly escaped being shot. In 2001, Jackson and Keiron,[6] two boys who lived in Durham, NC's Few Gardens described the types of incidents that had left them afraid even inside their own homes. Jackson said:

> One time I got shocked 'cause there was a man standing by the fence and they was shooting at him, and then the fence was blocking him 'cause they was in a fight and the man got shot in the leg. So that's why I got scared.

Keiron described a terrifying incident in his apartment:

> They was shooting one night … and they shot into our door and my little brother, he was by the door, but he didn't get shot.

Despite these terrible conditions, at baseline, many respondents were anxious about re-location and most (70 per cent) said that they hoped to return to the new development. By the first follow-up in 2003, about two-thirds of the families had been relocated, most moving to the private market with housing choice vouchers. Most relocatees reported being satisfied with their new housing situation and the proportion who wanted to return had fallen slightly to 64 per cent (Cunningham, 2004).

Most residents have not moved back

At the second follow-up in 2005, 84 per cent of the families in the *HOPE VI Panel Study* had relocated from the five Panel Study sites. The remaining 16 per cent of the respondents still living in their original developments were from either Atlantic City's Shore Park or Chicago's Wells, where the housing authorities were doing staged relocation. The largest number of families – 43 per cent – had received vouchers and moved to housing in the private market and 22 per cent had moved into other traditional public housing developments. Another 10 per cent were renting private market units with no assistance and 4 per cent had become homeowners. Approximately 1 per cent of the *HOPE VI Panel Study* respondents were either homeless or in prison in 2005.

Redevelopment was underway in all of the sites by 2005, although none was completed. Therefore, it is not surprising that only 5 per cent of the Panel Study respondents had moved into a newly remodeled HOPE VI unit by the 2005 follow-up. Atlantic City's Shore Park, where the housing authority was building a revitalized unit for every household that wanted one, had the greatest share of original families (14 per cent) who had moved back into redeveloped HOPE VI units. Other research suggests that return rates to HOPE VI sites overall have varied considerably from less than 10 per cent to 75 per cent, with the largest numbers returning to sites that were rehabilitated rather than demolished and rebuilt – not the case in any of these five sites. Based on this evidence, it seems likely that the final figures for returning for the *HOPE VI Panel Study* sites will increase somewhat over time, but will remain relatively low.[7] Thus, for most original residents, HOPE VI has meant relocation, not living in a new, mixed-income community.

Better housing in safer neighborhoods

Although most residents have not moved back, and probably will not, the majority have experienced meaningful improvement in their quality of life as a result of HOPE VI relocation. Panel Study respondents who moved to the private market or mixed-income developments reported substantial improvements in the quality of their housing. The survey asked families to rate their current housing as "excellent, good, fair, or poor". In 2005, more than two-thirds of private market movers rated their housing as excellent or good; more than three-quarters (85 per cent) of families living in the new HOPE VI units gave their units high ratings. In contrast, a much smaller share of households in public housing rated their housing as excellent or good. Just over one-third (39 per cent) of those in the original public housing (those that had not yet been relocated) gave their units high ratings in 2005. Only about half of those relocated into other public housing (49 per cent) rated their housing as excellent or good.

At baseline in 2001, respondents from all five sites reported intolerable and hazardous housing conditions. In 2005, circumstances had improved substantially for those respondents who had moved to the private market. For example, while slightly more than half of respondents who ultimately moved to the private market reported having two or more housing problems at baseline, just a quarter of voucher holders and unassisted renters reported two or more problems in 2005. In contrast, those who remained in traditional public housing – either their original development or a different one – experienced virtually no improvement in housing quality over time; about 40 per cent of those living in other public housing and about 60 per cent of those in the original public housing units reported having two or more problems at the baseline and at the 2005 follow-up (Comey, 2007).

Beyond basic housing quality, relocation had a profound impact on residents' life circumstances. While most respondents were not living in new, mixed-income developments, those who had left traditional public housing were living in communities that were much less poor than their original public housing developments. After relocation, half of those renting in the private market were living in neighborhoods that had poverty rates below 20 per cent – despite the fact that the HOPE VI program did not provide mobility counseling to encourage and assist residents to move to low-poverty communities. Another indicator of improved neighborhood quality was that private market relocatees were living in communities with lower unemployment rates – about five percentage points lower than rates in their original public housing neighborhoods. However, while relocatees were living in less poor neighborhoods, there has been little change in racial segregation – nearly all *HOPE VI Panel Study* families moved into predominantly African-American neighborhoods. While private market movers were living in less distressed communities, residents who relocated to other public housing developments have not experienced the same benefits – they were living in communities only slightly less poor and no less racially segregated than those in which they lived at the baseline in 2001 (Buron et al., 2007; Comey, 2007).

Fear of crime has profound implications for residents, causing stress and social isolation. In both 2003 and 2005, the survey asked respondents a range of questions about neighborhood conditions, including perceptions of crime and disorder,[8] sense of safety, and neighborhood social cohesion and trust (collective efficacy).[9] The analysis here shows a dramatic improvement in respondents' sense of safety and that the reduction in fear of crime is the biggest and most important effect of HOPE VI relocation overall. For example, the proportion of *Panel Study* respondents reporting "big problems" with drug sales in their community dropped from 78 per cent at baseline to 47 per cent in 2003 and declined even further to 33 per cent in 2005, a drop of 45 percentage points. The trends for virtually every measure of neighborhood safety showed the same dramatic decline (Popkin and Cove, 2007).

The trends for respondents who had moved to mixed-income developments or to the private market (with vouchers or on their own) were even more striking. [...] These respondents report extraordinary improvements in their conditions. For example, while about 80 per cent of voucher holders and HOPE VI movers had reported big problems with drug trafficking in their original neighborhoods at baseline, only 16 per cent reported the same problems in their new neighborhoods in 2005.

The trends for perceptions of violent crime were the same; at baseline, more than two-thirds of the respondents reported big problems with shooting and violence in their developments; in 2005, just 17 per cent of voucher holders reported big problems in their new communities. The trends for the relatively small numbers of HOPE VI movers, unassisted renters and homeowners were identical. Finally, private market movers also consistently reported significant improvements on a wide variety of other neighborhood indicators, including the amount of trash in public areas and quality of schools. Nicole, a voucher holder from Richmond's Easter Hill, described the best things about her new neighborhood in 2005 as:

> There's no gun violence. There's no drugs. There is no alcohol. There's no bottles, broken glass, and everything and everywhere ...

Living in safer neighborhoods has had a profound impact on residents' quality of life. Relocatees' comments reflected a wide range of life changes, including allowing their children to play outside more frequently, less fighting among neighborhood children, sleeping better and generally feeling less worried about drug dealing and shootings in the neighborhood. Comparable to findings from MTO, statistical analysis shows that those who have moved with vouchers report less worry and anxiety and have lower depression scores than those who remain in traditional public housing (Buron *et al.*, 2007).[10]

Respondents' comments reflect the enormous changes in their circumstances. Emma and her granddaughter, Carla were residents of Chicago's Wells development. In 2001, before relocation, they described a community so dangerous that they were afraid to even sit outside on their own porch. Emma said:

> Well about two weeks ago the kids was outside, maybe about 7:00, and good thing that my kids ... are actually usually on the porch. They [the gangs] did a drive by. So it's no different between the day and night. There's no difference.

Carla, who was 14 in 2001, also talked of her fears:

> I don't really like the neighborhood. There's too many shootings and killings going on. A lot of the little kids are starting to come out and play because it's the summer, and it's really not safe enough, because you never know when they're going to shoot or you know drive by. You never know.

In 2005, Emma had a voucher and the family had moved to a neighborhood of single-family homes on the far south side of Chicago. In her new neighborhood, she felt safe and, as she told the interviewer, more "relaxed".

> You don't have to worry about shooting. And ain't nobody going to break in your house. You can leave your stuff laying out there in the yard, and it'll be there when you wake up. It's peace and quiet. You can sleep over here. Over there, it made me feel kind of nervous and scary. But over here, you get to feel more – relaxed.

Carla, now 18, said she no longer had to worry about violence:

> Up here it's quieter. I can get more peace up here than I would have gotten in the Wells. I

can sit out on the porch and just sit there all night, without having to worry about somebody coming up and messing with [me]. You don't have to worry about no shooting – anything like that.

Public housing relocatees got less "safety benefit"

While HOPE VI relocation succeeded in providing a significantly improved environment for respondents who moved to the private market or new mixed-income developments, many respondents remain in public housing and continue to live in dangerous, unhealthy communities. Respondents who moved from their HOPE VI development to another traditional public housing development did not gain the same "safety benefit" as those who moved to the private market or mixed-income housing. While public housing movers do report statistically significant improvements in perceptions of safety over time, they are clearly still living in extremely troubled communities, only slightly better than the distressed developments they left behind. For example, [...], the proportion reporting "big problems" with drug sales declined from 70 per cent at baseline to just under 50 per cent in 2005. This change represents a statistical improvement, but means that residents are still living in communities that are dominated by drug trafficking and violent crime, only slightly less dangerous than their original developments.

Most interview respondents who moved into other public housing said their new developments still had substantial problems with crime and disorder, and described feeling unsafe because of pervasive drug trafficking and gambling in neighborhood streets and sporadic shootings. Youth, in particular, expressed a sense of loss of protection because of moving away from their friends and family, and talked of feeling threatened by other youth and gangs in their new neighborhoods.

Further [...] the 16 per cent of respondents who had not been relocated by 2005 were living in conditions that were just as bad as at baseline in 2001. Most of these residents were from Chicago, where conditions seemed to be getting even worse as vacancy rates increased and physical structures deteriorated. As residents who were easier to relocate, i.e. those who did not have problems that kept them from qualifying for a voucher or new mixed-income housing, moved out, the remaining population became increasingly troubled. The families that remained noted that there was some reduction in drug trafficking as other residents left, but they also noted a decrease in police presence. In addition, families from Chicago's Ida B. Wells development described increasing disorder, including problems with squatters and non-residents sleeping in vacant units and hallways, locks and lights not being repaired, and trash collecting in hallways and stairwells.

Relocation benefits children

Children are particularly vulnerable to the effects of HOPE VI relocation. On the one hand, children are the most likely to benefit in important ways from improved housing quality – and reduced exposure to risks such as lead paint or mold – and from safer, less distressed neighborhoods. On the other hand, moving can disrupt their education and friendships and even put older youth at risk for conflict with local gangs. The *HOPE VI Panel Study* survey included questions on parental reports of children's behavior – an indicator of children's mental health – to see how children were affected by relocation. Overall, the long-term results showed that children whose families received vouchers and moved to the private market fared better after relocation than those who moved to other traditional public housing developments (Gallagher and Bajaj, 2007).[11] Parents of children in families that relocated with vouchers reported lower rates of behavior problems[12] in 2005 than in 2001, prior to relocation. In 2001, 53 per cent of children in voucher households demonstrated two or more behavior problems, but by 2005, this proportion dropped to 41 per cent. Although the pattern was the same for both boys and girls in voucher households, only the decline for girls was statistically significant. Again, because the numbers are small, it is not possible to see statistically accurate trends for households who moved to mixed-income developments, but given the similar trends for housing and neighborhood quality, their outcomes are likely similar to those for voucher holders.

Jamal, an 18-year-old boy from Durham's Few Gardens, described how his attitude toward life had changed since he and his family relocated to a private market apartment:

> The friends I have now, we hang out. We go to the movies, chill out, go to the bowling alley, go play basketball. But if I would have still been hanging with the other friends now, I probably be in a whole mess of trouble ... used to think of life as a joke. I used to say that I didn't really care ... Now, I just look at life like it's something you got to be glad of. You got to be positive.

However, in contrast, while children who moved to the private market were doing better, those whose families moved to other public housing were not faring as well. In 2005, children in voucher households were more likely than children in other public housing to exhibit five out of six positive behaviors (62 versus 43 per cent).[13] They were also marginally less likely to exhibit two or more delinquent behaviors (3 versus 12 per cent).[14] The trends for delinquent behavior for the children still living in traditional public housing were especially disturbing. The incidence of delinquent behaviors increased for youth still living in their original development (by 12 percentage points) and youth in other public housing (by 10 percentage points), while it changed in no significant way for youth in the voucher households. The analysis here shows that the incidence of delinquent behaviors skyrocketed (by 24 percentage points since 2001) for those girls still living in their original development – mostly in Chicago – waiting for relocation. This spike is primarily driven by increasing rates of school suspensions (28 percentage points) and going to juvenile court (24 percentage points). This finding suggests that girls, in particular, are suffering from the ill effects of being left behind in developments that are becoming increasingly dangerous and chaotic as vacancies increase.

Private market challenges

While HOPE VI residents who have moved to private market housing with vouchers are doing well in many ways, as in earlier research (Buron et al., 2002), findings from the Panel Study show that many are having difficulty making ends meet (Buron et al., 2007). Moving out of public housing presents new financial management challenges: private market property managers can be less forgiving of late rent payments than public housing managers, making it imperative that rent is paid on time. In addition, since utilities are generally included in the rent in public housing, many former public housing residents are inexperienced in paying utility bills. They can find coping with seasonal variation in utility costs, particularly heating costs in the winter or spikes in gas costs, very daunting.[15]

At the 2005 follow-up, it was found that voucher holders were significantly more likely than public housing movers to report financial hardships related to paying utilities and providing adequate food for their family. Nearly half (45 per cent) of voucher holders reported trouble paying their utility bills, compared with just 8 per cent of residents in other public housing. Likewise, voucher holders (62 per cent) were more likely than public housing households (47 per cent) to report financial hardships paying for food. However, voucher holders were significantly less likely than public housing residents to be late paying their rent. In essence, these findings suggest that, when faced with the trade-offs, most voucher holders chose to pay their rent on time to avoid risking their housing and instead delayed their utility payments and cut back on food or other items. This problem is one that is likely to also affect residents who move to mixed-income developments where utilities are not included in rents.

Comments from Shenice, a voucher holder from Chicago's Wells, illustrate the financial challenges that private market relocatees face:

> We really had to use our gas, and it was high, and got behind and I was at risk ... I did end up getting on the payment plan. But this is the school season, so what am I going to do about uniforms and everything? ... My kids have school fees, my high school kids, and it's hard on me right now.

HOPE VI did not affect employment

In addition to providing residents with an improved living environment, the HOPE VI program sought to help them attain self-sufficiency. However, while the Panel Study results document dramatic improvements in quality of life for many respondents, there have been no changes in employment or self-sufficiency for either private market movers or those who remain in traditional public housing (Levy and Woolley, 2007). At baseline, 48 per cent of the working-age respondents were not working, even part-time, the same share as at the 2003 and the 2005 follow-up. Findings from the *Panel Study* suggest that HOPE VI relocation and community supportive services are unlikely to affect employment or address the many factors that keep these extremely disadvantaged residents out of the labor force.

A major factor affecting employment status is health, and the findings here show that *HOPE VI Panel Study* respondents are in extremely poor health. In 2005, two out of every five respondents (41 per cent) rated their overall health as either "fair" or "poor" (Manjarrez *et al.*, 2007). At every age level, *HOPE VI Panel Study* respondents are much more likely to describe their health as fair or poor than other adults overall and even than black women, a group with higher-than-average rates of poor health.[16] Further, *HOPE VI Panel Study* respondents report high rates of a range of chronic, debilitating conditions, including arthritis, asthma, obesity, depression, diabetes, hypertension and strokes. Mental health is a very serious problem for these respondents – not only depression, but reported rates of anxiety and other indicators were also very high: overall, 29 per cent of HOPE VI respondents indicated poor mental health.[17]

As in MTO, relocation seems to have had a major impact on mental health, reducing anxiety and depression for private market movers (Buron *et al.*, 2007). However, despite expectations that relocation might improve environmentally-triggered conditions like asthma or stress-related conditions like hypertension, there has been no improvement in physical health conditions overall; in fact, respondents' physical health appears to have deteriorated over time, with more rating their health as "fair" or "poor". A housing-only intervention may not have been sufficient to address the serious, chronic health needs of these vulnerable residents. They may require much more targeted and intensive health services than HOPE VI provided. But even the more holistic intensive NDC intervention in the UK has failed to improve health outcomes for adult residents (CRESR, 2005). It may be that a

more realistic goal for these vulnerable individuals is helping them better manage their chronic health conditions.

Analysis of the panel data shows that for HOPE VI respondents, health problems are by far the biggest barrier to employment, and that moving to the private market or mixed-income housing made no difference for employment outcomes. Among working-age respondents, nearly a third (32 per cent) reported poor health, and most of them (62 per cent) were unemployed. The strongest predictor of not working was having severe challenges with physical mobility. Forty per cent of respondents reported moderate or severe difficulty with mobility; less than half (38 per cent) of these respondents were employed in 2005. [A] typical respondent with no employment barriers had a roughly 82 per cent chance of being employed; severe mobility problems lowered this probability by 40 percentage points.[18] Depression also substantially reduced the probability of being employed, as did having been diagnosed with asthma. Obesity did not have a direct effect on employment but rather was associated with other serious health problems. Relative to non-obese respondents, obese respondents were more likely to report having mobility difficulties, asthma, and an overall health status of "fair" or "poor".

While health was clearly the biggest obstacle to obtaining and keeping a job for *HOPE VI Panel Study* respondents, other factors also affected employment.

Specifically, not having a high school diploma, having children under the age of 6 years and having problems with adequate child care also reduced the probability of employment for working-age respondents.

HOPE VI is not the solution for the "hard-to-house"

Finally, the *Panel Study* results show that "hard-to-house" residents – families coping with multiple complex problems such as mental illness, severe physical illness, substance abuse, large numbers of young children, weak labor-market histories and criminal records, were less likely than other residents to realize significant improvements in their quality of life as a result of HOPE VI revitalization. Findings from the first follow-up of the *Panel Study* showed that these residents made up a substantial proportion of the population at all five sites and more than two-thirds of the households in Chicago's Wells and Washington's East Capitol developments (Popkin et al., 2005). In 2005, analysis showed that, at every site, hard-to-house families were more likely to end up in traditional public housing than in the private market, and so ended up little better off than they were at baseline. Placing them in other traditional developments – or, as in Atlantic City's Shore Park and Chicago's Wells, leaving them in the parts of the development awaiting revitalization – may well have kept them from becoming homeless. However, concentrating multi-problem families in a few traditional developments may well mean that those developments rapidly become as distressed – or even more distressed – than the developments from which these families came. Further, without adequate services and support, there is a risk that these families could become literally homeless. If they fail to meet even the minimal requirements of traditional public housing, they could face eviction, a very real risk as housing authorities in the US begin to more strictly enforce lease requirements (Popkin et al., 2008).

WHERE DO WE GO FROM HERE?

The expectations for US public housing transformation initiatives such as HOPE VI and MTO, which offered the promise of helping very low-income families to move to low poverty and mixed-income communities, were very high. Indeed, because of the findings from research outcomes for participants in the Gautreaux program, scholars and policy makers hoped these initiatives would be truly transformative for residents, not only improving the quality of their lives, but providing them with access to opportunities that could help them improve their economic circumstances. Advocates hoped that by moving to better neighborhoods or living in mixed-income housing, residents would find jobs, earn more, gain access to role models and have better schools for their children. On the other hand, many critics and advocates predicted that HOPE VI was simply another version of urban renewal, one that would simply displace residents of distressed communities to make way for higher-income households.

Results from the *HOPE VI Panel Study* show that, for the most part, the critics' worst fears have not been realized – many former residents now have a considerably better quality of life as a result of HOPE VI relocation. Specifically, for those who have moved to the private market with vouchers, become homeowners, moved off assistance, or moved to new mixed-income developments, the HOPE VI program has more than met its goal of providing an improved living environment. These residents are living in communities that are much less poor and have dramatically lower rates of crime and disorder. There is no question that the enormous improvement in safety and consequent reduction in fear of crime is the biggest benefit for many original residents. With these major improvements in life circumstances, it is possible that living in these safer neighborhoods may have long-term benefits for the mental and physical health of adults and children.

However, even with these very real benefits for residents, the findings raise serious questions about the full extent of the impact of HOPE VI on residents' lives. In many ways, the program has not lived up to its optimistic vision for how public housing transformation could affect residents' lives. First, with low rates of return, relatively few original residents will ever have the experience of living in new, mixed-income housing; for most original residents, the major impact of HOPE VI will be relocation. Only a small number of *Panel Study* respondents have returned to revitalized HOPE VI communities; past experience suggests that the proportion will increase as new units become available, but will never exceed more than about 30 to 40 per cent. The reasons for this low rate of return are both positive and negative. With the shift to mixed-income developments, there are simply fewer public housing units on site. Some sites have imposed relatively stringent screening criteria that have excluded some former residents. On the positive side, as the *Panel Study* results show, many former residents who have received vouchers are satisfied with their new housing and are not interested in returning – this lack of interest in returning suggests that the loss of social ties was not as great a concern for HOPE VI families as some critics feared. Finally, at a few more troubled sites, long histories of mismanagement and neglect mean that residents do not trust the housing authority's promises of better conditions and choose not to return (Buron *et al.*, 2002; Popkin *et al.*, 2004a).

Second, while HOPE VI relocation has helped many residents move to lower poverty communities, it has not reduced racial segregation. The communities these residents have moved to are moderate income, predominantly minority neighborhoods. While offering a better quality of life in many ways, these communities still lack the resources such as good schools, excellent municipal services, and amenities such as stores and restaurants offered by comparable white communities. It is not clear that HOPE VI, and public housing transformation overall, can achieve its full potential to improve the lives of poor, minority families without explicitly acknowledging the ways racial segregation has contributed to the problems in distressed public housing and developing strategies to address the problem directly (Popkin, 2007; Turner *et al.*, 2009).

Third, while relocation has improved the life circumstances for many former residents, a substantial minority of original residents (about one-third) have not gained the same benefit. A relatively small number – about 16 per cent of *Panel Study* respondents – remain in their original developments, living in conditions that are rapidly deteriorating as vacancies increase. This problem is the result of both the housing authorities' choice to stage relocation and redevelop sites in phases and of some families' complex personal situations, which make it very hard-to-house them in either the private market or in new mixed-income developments that have stringent screening criteria. Another group of residents (about 22 per cent of the survey respondents) moved to other traditional public housing developments. Although these residents report statistically significant reductions in perceptions of drug trafficking and violent crime, the reality is that these communities are still extremely dangerous and few would regard them as an improvement from their original distressed developments. Further, the most troubled families are the most likely to end up in these traditional developments and thus are less likely to have truly benefited from the HOPE VI intervention.

Fourth, it is also clear that HOPE VI, like MTO, has not lived up to expectations that it would truly transform residents' lives and help them achieve self-sufficiency. The *HOPE VI*

Panel Study results indicate no impact on employment overall; more than half of working-aged residents continue to be disconnected from the labor force. In part, this finding highlights the limitations of a housing-only strategy; although HOPE VI included community and supportive services, there was no consistent employment strategy. Other research has documented the potential for place-based employment strategies in distressed public housing to improve employment rates and earnings (Turner and Rawlings, 2005). However, HOPE VI had no such employment component. Moreover, residents were being relocated, making a place-based program impractical. Even if HOPE VI had included a more systematic employment strategy, the reality is that these residents face such serious physical and mental health challenges that most of them are unlikely to be able to hold a job that requires even a basic level of fitness (e.g. ability to stand for two hours, climb a flight of stairs or walk four blocks). Again, HOPE VI services did not consistently target health and a housing-focused intervention was probably not enough to help these vulnerable individuals. Given their level of debility, for these residents a strategy focusing on helping them to effectively manage their health challenges may prove more effective in promoting self-sufficiency than a traditional employment program (Levy and Woolley, 2007).

Finally, these results indicate that HOPE VI has not been a solution for the most troubled residents – those "hard-to-house" families with multiple, complex problems that make them ineligible for mixed-income housing or even for vouchers. In many US cities, public housing has served as the housing of last resort for decades, with the poorest and least desirable tenants warehoused in the worst developments. As these developments are demolished, these vulnerable families are simply being moved from one distressed development to another, and with a concentration of extremely troubled families and a lack of adequate supportive services, these new developments have the potential to become even worse environments than those from where these families started.

In the 17 years since its inception, HOPE VI has benefited many former residents of distressed public housing developments, offering them opportunities to live in communities that are considerably less poor and distressed. With the HOPE VI program now up for reauthorization, there is an opportunity to learn from the challenges identified by the *HOPE VI Panel Study* and help the program truly realize its potential for transforming the lives of very low-income families. For example, the next generation of HOPE VI should encourage more families to choose vouchers rather than rely on traditional public housing as a relocation resource. If the goal of HOPE VI is to improve families' living environments, then relocating them to other public housing undermines the program's intent. While emphasizing vouchers, HUD should also require housing authorities to offer meaningful relocation counseling to help residents make informed choices and provide long-term support to help more families succeed in the private market or, ultimately, to return to new, mixed-income housing. A "vouchers-plus" model where relocatees receive ongoing case management and support for a period of at least two years would ensure that families make a successful transition and are able to remain in safer neighborhoods. Housing authorities should track and maintain contact with voucher movers so those families can make effective choices about whether or not to return to the revitalized development. Finally, policy makers should make sure that utility allowances for voucher holders and mixed-income movers keep pace with heating costs so that they are not at risk of hardship and housing instability.

In addition to strengthening relocation assistance and supportive services overall, the next generation of HOPE VI should focus particular attention on the most vulnerable residents. Partially vacated HOPE VI sites are not safe places for children, possibly because of increased gang activity, social disorder and isolation. It is also critical that redevelopment plans consider the needs of families with children by scheduling family moves during the summer and giving priority to families with children so they are not left in partially vacated HOPE VI sites. Relocation services also need to be strengthened to take into account the needs of residents with serious health challenges

If self-sufficiency is to remain a goal of the HOPE VI program, then efforts that address key barriers could prove more effective than job training or placement efforts alone in improving the chances that former and current public housing residents move into employment or retain jobs they already have. From this perspective, efforts to improve the physical mobility of adults and help people manage their asthma more effectively could be considered employment-related initiatives (Levy and Woolley, 2007). Identifying adults with severe mobility limitations and working with them to stabilize or improve their mobility could improve health and possibly even employment rates more effectively than directing them first to employment-related services. Similarly, assessing mental health and encouraging treatment could also be viewed as an employment-related service, as could helping people access safe and affordable child care for both preschool-age and school-age children. Encouraging adults without a high school education to earn a General Equivalency Diploma (GED)[19] might also lead to improvements in employment rates over time. Housing authorities should consider incorporating work-related initiatives into new, mixed-income developments that include supports and incentives for employment. They also need to structure flexibility into their screening criteria to reflect the fact that some otherwise good tenants are not going to be able to meet employment requirements because of health or other barriers.

A new HOPE VI needs to include a real strategy for serving hard-to-house families so they do not remain concentrated in high-poverty, traditional public housing developments. If housing authorities continue to move their most troubled residents to other public housing, those communities will rapidly become as unpleasant and dangerous as the distressed developments that received the HOPE VI grant. To avoid perpetuating the problem, we need new and creative approaches to help this very needy population, including intensive case management and family-supportive housing that offers a rich package of services on site. There are no simple solutions to this problem and none that are low cost, but it is both cost effective and a way to try to help these families find safe and stable housing situations.

Finally, because relocation has been the main impact of HOPE VI on original residents, it is still not known whether or how these very low-income public housing families might benefit from living in a mixed-income community. Other poor families will ultimately move into the new housing developments, but they may not be as distressed as the public housing families who were displaced. Regardless, there is still a need for high quality research that tracks the experiences of both low- and higher-income families who move into mixed-income developments, and answers to critical questions about the sustainability of these communities, especially during economic downturns such as the one we are currently experiencing.

ACKNOWLEDGMENTS

The authors wish to thank their collaborators on the *HOPE VI Panel Study* research: Megan Gallagher, Jennifer Comey, Mark Woolley, Elizabeth Cove and Beata Bajaj.

Notes

1   The studies were conducted by The Urban Institute and its partner, Abt Associates Inc. The HOPE VI Resident Tracking Study was supported entirely by a grant from HUD. The *HOPE VI Panel Study* was supported by a consortium of funders, including HUD; the John D. and Catherine T. MacArthur Foundation; the Annie E. Casey Foundation; the Rockefeller Foundation; the Robert Wood Johnson Foundation; the Fannie Mae Foundation; and the Chicago Community Trust.

2   For critiques of HOPE VI and the potential impact on residents, see Bennett *et al.* (2006); Goetz (2003); Keating (2001); Venkatesh *et al.* (2004).

3   See Popkin *et al.* (2004b) for a discussion of the rate of return issue.

4   Because of the retrospective design, the sample under-represents unassisted tenants and others who were more difficult to locate. In general, those who are difficult to find are those who move frequently, double-up with another family, are homeless, or have moved out of the area. These former residents are likely to have experienced more problems than those we were able to survey.

5   The level of problems reported was substantially higher than that for poor renters nationally in the American Housing Survey. See Popkin *et al.* (2002) for a discussion of these issues.

6   All respondent names are pseudonyms.

7   For other studies that have examined rates of return, see Buron *et al.* (2002); Holin *et al.* (2003); and National Housing Law Project (2002).

8   Perceptions of disorder are highly correlated with crime rates, and are often a better predictor of levels of fear (Perkins and Taylor, 1996).

9   See Sampson *et al.* (1997). The concept of 'collective efficacy' comes from the Project on Human Development in Chicago Neighborhoods and is intended as a measure of neighborhood health. It is highly correlated with crime rates and other indicators such as low birth weight.

10 With such small numbers of respondents living in mixed-income communities, it is not possible to see accurate statistical trends, but given that they experienced the same improvements in housing quality and neighborhood safety, it is likely that they have experienced the same benefits in terms of quality of life as those who received vouchers.

11 Trends for the small numbers of homeowners, unassisted renters, and mixed-income movers were similar, but the sample sizes are too small to permit meaningful analysis.

12 Behavior Problems Measure: Respondents were asked to indicate how often the child exhibited any one of the seven specific negative behaviors, taken from the Behavior Problems Index: trouble getting along with teachers; being disobedient at school; being disobedient at home; spending time with kids who get in trouble; bullying or being cruel or mean; feeling restless or overly active; and being unhappy, sad, or depressed. The answers ranged from 'often' and 'sometimes true' to "not true". The study tracked the proportion of children whose parents reported that they had demonstrated two or more of these behaviors often or sometimes over the previous three months.

13 Positive Behavior Measure: This scale requires respondents to rate how closely each of the following six positive behaviors describes their child: usually in a good mood; admired and well liked by other children; shows concern for other people's feelings; shows pride when doing

something well or learning something new; easily calms down after being angry or upset; and is helpful and cooperative. The list of behaviors was derived from the 10-item Positive Behavior Scale from the Child Development Supplement in the *Panel Study* of Income Dynamics. Each behavior was rated on a scale ranging from 1 ('not at all like this child') to 5 ('completely like this child'). The study tracked the proportion of children with at least five out of six behaviors rated relatively high ('a lot' or 'completely like this child').

14 Delinquent Behavior Measure: Respondents were asked if over the previous year their child had been involved in any of the following five activities: being suspended or expelled from school; going to a juvenile court; having a problem with alcohol or drugs; getting into trouble with the police; and doing something illegal for money. The study tracked the proportion of children involved in two or more of these behaviors.

15 See, for example, Buron *et al.* (2002) and Orr *et al.* (2003).

16 Many health problems vary significantly by gender and race, and because over 88 per cent of the adults in the *HOPE VI Panel Study* are women and 90 per cent are black, a sample of black women nationally is used as the comparison group. The national data cited in this testimony are published by the US Department of Health and Human Services, calculated from the National Health Interview Survey in 2005. National Health Interview Survey data are broken down by sex and race, but not further by poverty status. Nationally, approximately one-third of all black women live in households with incomes below the poverty level. Therefore, the comparison data are biased slightly upward in terms of better health because of the relatively better economic well-being of the national population of black women compared with the HOPE VI sample. However, even limiting the comparisons to similar gender, race and age groups, adults in the HOPE VI study experience health problems more often than other demographically similar groups.

17 Indication of mental health was based on a scale derived from the CIDI-12, or Composite International Diagnostic Interview Instrument. The series includes two types of screener questions that assess the degree of depression and the length of time it has lasted. The index is then created by summing how many of the seven items respondents reported feeling for a large share of the past two weeks. If a respondent scores three or higher on the index, their score indicates a major depressive episode.

18 The study tested the difference in the probability of employment with and without a specific employment barrier for an unmarried, high-school-educated, African-American female respondent using a housing voucher and facing no additional employment barrier. Unless otherwise noted, statistical significance is reported for probability values of 5 per cent or less.

19 A GED is the equivalent of a high school diploma.

REFERENCES

Barrett, E. J., Geisel, P. and Johnston, J. (2002–2003) *The Ramon Utti Report: Impacts of the Ripley Arnold Relocation Program Year 1* (Arlington, TX: University of Texas).

Bennett, L., Smith, J. L. and Wright, P. A. (Eds) (2006) *Where are Poor People to Live? Transforming Public Housing Developments* (Armonk, NY: M.E. Sharpe).

Briggs, X. de Sousa, Popkin, S. J. and Goering, J. (forthcoming) *Moving to Opportunity: The Story of An American Experiment to Fight Ghetto Poverty* (Oxford: Oxford University Press).

Briggs, X. de Souza, Ferryman, K., Popkin, S. J. and Rendon, M. (2008) Why didn't the Moving to Opportunity experiment get children to better schools? *Housing Policy Debate*, 19, pp. 53–91.

Buron, L., Levy, D. and Gallagher, M. (2007) How did people who relocated from HOPE VI with vouchers fare? *HOPE VI: Where Do We Go from Here?* Brief 3 (Washington DC: The Urban Institute). http://www.urban.   org/UploadedPDF/311487_HOPEVI_Vouchers.pdf.

Buron, L., Popkin, S., Levy, D., Harris, L. and Khadduri, J. (2002) *The HOPE VI Resident*

Tracking Study: A Snapshot of the Current Living Situation of Original Residents from Eight Sites (Washington DC: The Urban Institute). Available at http://www.urban.org/publications/410591.html.

CRESR (Centre for Regional Economic and Social Research) (2005) *New Deal for Communities 2001–2005: An Interim Evaluation, Research Report 17* (Sheffield: Sheffield Hallam University).

Clampet-Lundquist, S., Edin, K., Kling, J. R. and Duncan, G. J. (2006) *Moving at-Risk Teenagers Out of High-Risk Neighborhoods: Why Girls Fare Better than Boys* (Princeton University).

Comey, J. (2007) HOPE VI'ed and on the move: mobility, neighborhoods, and housing, *HOPE VI: Where Do We Go from Here? Brief 1* (Washington DC: The Urban Institute). Available at http://www.urban.org/UploadedPDF/311485_HOPEVI_Mobility.pdf.

Cove, E., de Souza Briggs, X., Turner, M. A. and Duarte, C. (2008) Can escaping from poor neighborhoods increase employment and earnings? *Three-City Study of Moving to Opportunity Policy Brief No. 4* (Washington DC: The Urban Institute). Available at http://www.urban.org/uploadedpdf/411640.html.

Cunningham, M. K. (2004) An improved living environment? Relocation outcomes for HOPE VI relocatees, *A Roof Over Their Heads Policy Brief No. 1* (Washington DC: The Urban Institute). Available at http://www.urban.org/url.cfm?ID=311057.

Ellen, I. G. and Turner, M. A. (1997) Does neighborhood matter? Assessing recent evidence, *Housing Policy Debate*, 8, pp. 833–866.

Feins, J., McInnis, D. and Popkin, S. (1997) *Counseling in the Moving to Opportunity Demonstration Program*. Report prepared by Abt Associates Inc. for the US Department of Housing and Urban Development.

Fullilove, M. T. (2004) *Root Shock: How Tearing Up Neighborhoods Hurts Americans and What We Can Do About It* (New York: Ballantine Books).

Gallagher, M. and Bajaj, B. (2007) Moving on: assessing the benefits and challenges of HOPE VI for children. *HOPE VI: Where Do We Go from Here? Brief 4* (Washington

DC: The Urban Institute). Available at http://www.urban.org/UploadedPDF/311488_HOPEVI_Children.pdf.

Garbarino, J., Kostelny, K. and Dubrow, N. (1991) *No Place to be a Child: Growing Up in a War Zone* (Lexington, MA: Lexington Books).

Goetz, E. G. (2003) *Clearing the Way: Deconcentrating the Poor in Urban America* (Washington DC: Urban Institute Press).

Holin, M. J., Buron, L. F. and Baker, M. (2003) *Interim Assessment of the HOPE VI Program: Case Studies* (Bethesda, MD: Abt Associates).

Jencks, C. and Mayer, S. (1990) The social consequences of growing up in a poor neighborhood, in: L. Lynn and M. McGeary (Eds) *Inner-City Poverty in the United States*, pp. 111–186 (Washington DC: National Academy Press).

Joseph, M. L., Chaskin, R. and Weber, H. S. (2005) The theoretical basis for addressing poverty through mixed-income development. Working Paper (Chicago).

Kaufman, J. E. and Rosenbaum, J. E. (1992) The education and employment of low-income black youth in white suburbs, *Educational Evaluation and Policy Analysis*, 14, pp. 229–240.

Keating, L. (2001) *Atlanta: Race, Class, and Urban Expansion* (Philadelphia: Temple University Press).

Kilpatrick, D. G., Acierno, R., Saunders, B., Resnick, H. S., Schnurr, P. P. and Best, C. (2000) Risk factors for adolescent substance abuse and dependence: data from a national sample, *Journal of Consulting and Clinical Psychology*, 36, pp. 19–30.

Kingsley, G. T. and Pettit, K. (2008) Have Moving to Opportunity families lost access to opportunity neighborhoods over time? *Three-City Study of Moving to Opportunity Policy Brief No. 2* (Washington DC: The Urban Institute). Available at http://www.urban.org/publications/411637.html.

Kliet, R. G. and Manzon, L. C. (2003) To move or not to move: determinants of resident relocation choices in HOPE VI. Paper presented at the joint meeting of the Association of the Collegiate Schools of Planning and the Association of European Schools of Planning, Baltimore, July.

Landrigan, P. J. and Carlson, J. E. (1995) Environmental Policy and Children's Health, *The Future of Children*, 5(2), pp. 34–52.

Leventhal, T. and Brooks-Gunn, J. (2000) The neighborhoods they live in: effects of neighborhood residence upon child and adolescent outcomes, *Psychological Bulletin*, 126, pp. 309–337.

Leventhal, T. and Brooks-Gunn, J. (2004) Diversity in developmental trajectories across adolescence: neighborhood influences, in: R. M. Lerner and L. Steinberg (Eds) *Handbook of Adolescent Psychology*, pp. 451–486, 2nd edn (New York: John Wiley and Sons).

Levy, D. K. and Woolley, M. (2007) Employment barriers among HOPE VI families, *HOPE VI: Where Do We Go from Here? Brief 6* (Washington DC: The Urban Institute). Available at http://www.urban.org/UploadedPDF/311491_HOPEVI_Employment.pdf.

Manjarrez, C., Popkin, S. and Guernsey, E. (2007) Poor health: the biggest challenge for HOPE VI families? *HOPE VI: Where Do We Go from Here? Brief 5* (Washington DC: The Urban Institute). Available at http://www.urban.org/UploadedPDF/311489_HOPEVI_Health.pdf.

Morenoff, J. D. (2001) *Place, Race and Health: Neighborhood Sources of Group Disparities in Birthweight*, Report No. 01-482 (University of Michigan, Institute for Social Research, Population Studies Center).

National Commission on Severely Distressed Public Housing (US) (1992) *The Final Report of the National Commission on Severely Distressed Public Housing: A Report to the Congress and the Secretary of Housing and Urban Development* (Washington DC: The Commission). For sale by the US GPO, Supt. of Docs.

National Housing Law Project (2002) *False Hope: A Critical Assessment of the HOPE VI Public Housing Redevelopment Program* (Washington DC: Center for Community Change).

Orr, L., Feins, J., Jacob, R., Beecroft, E., Sanbonmatsu, L., Katz, L. F., Liebman, J. B. and Kling, J. R. (2003) *Moving to Opportunity for Fair Housing Demonstration, Interim Impacts Evaluation* (Washington DC: US Department of Housing and Urban Development).

Perkins, D. D. and Taylor, R. B. (1996) Ecological assessments of community disorder: their relationship to fear of crime and theoretical implications, *American Journal of Community Psychology*, 24, pp. 63–107.

Polikoff, A. (2006) *Waiting for Gautreaux: A Story of Segregation, Housing, and the Black Ghetto* (Evanston, IL: Northwestern University Press).

Popkin, S. J. (2007) Race and public housing transformation in the US, in: B. Harris (Ed.) *Neighborhood Renewal and Housing Markets: Community Engagement in the US and UK*, pp. 138–162 (London: Blackwell).

Popkin, S. J. and Cunningham, M. K. (2002) *CHA Relocation and Mobility Counseling Assessment Final Report*, Report prepared by the Urban Institute for the John D. and Catherine T. MacArthur Foundation (Washington DC: The Urban Institute). Available at http://www.urban.org/publications/410549.html.

Popkin, S. J. and Cove, E. (2007) Safety is the most important thing: how HOPE VI helped families, *HOPE VI: Where Do We Go from Here? Brief 2* (Washington DC: The Urban Institute). http://www.urban.org/UploadedPDF/311486_HOPEVI_Safety.pdf.

Popkin, S. J., Rosenbaum, J. E. and Meaden, P. M. (1993) Labor market experiences of low-income black women in middle-class suburbs: evidence from a survey of Gautreaux Program participants, *Journal of Policy Analysis and Management*, 12, pp. 556–573.

Popkin, S. J., Cunningham, M. K. and Woodley, W. T. (2003) *Residents at Risk: A Profile of Ida B. Wells Homes and Madden Park Residents*, A Report to the Ford Foundation (Washington DC: The Urban Institute). Available at http://www.urban.org/publications/310824.html.

Popkin, S. J., Cunningham, M. K. and Burt, M. (2005) Public housing transformation and the hard to house, *Housing Policy Debate*, 16, pp. 1–24.

Popkin, S. J., Leventhal, T. and Weissman, G. (2008) Girls in the 'hood: the importance of feeling safe, *Three-City Study of Moving* to Opportunity Policy Brief No. 1 (Washington DC: The Urban Institute). Available at http://www.urban.org/publications/411636.html.

Popkin, S. J., Gwiasda, V. E., Olson, L. M. and Rosenbaum, D. P. (2000a) The Hidden War: Crime and the Tragedy of Public Housing in Chicago (New Brunswick, NJ: Rutgers University Press).

Popkin, S. J., Buron, L. F., Levy, D. K. and Cunningham, M. K. (2000b) The Gautreaux legacy: what might mixed-income and dispersal strategies mean for the poorest public housing tenants? Housing Policy Debate, 11, pp. 911–942.

Popkin, S. J., Levy, D. K., Harris, L. E., Comey, J., Cunningham, M. K. and Buron, L. F. (2002) HOPE VI Panel Study: Baseline Report (Washington DC: The Urban Institute). Available at http://www.urban.org/publications/410590.html.

Popkin, S. J., Katz, B., Cunningham, M. K., Brown, K. D., Gustafson, J. and Turner, M. A. (2004a) A Decade of HOPE VI: Research Findings and Policy Challenges (Washington DC: The Urban Institute). Available at http://www.urban.org/publications/411002.html.

Popkin, S. J., Levy, D. K., Harris, L. E., Comey, J., Cunningham, M. K. and Buron, L. F. (2004b) The HOPE VI Program: what about the residents? Housing Policy Debate, 15, pp. 385–414.

Rosenstreich, D. L., Eggleston, P., Kattan, M., Baker, D., Slavin, R. G., Gergen, P., Mitchell, H., McNiff-Mortimer, K., Lynn, H., Ownby, D. and Malveaux, F. (1997) The role of cockroach allergy and exposure to cockroach allergen in causing morbidity among inner-city children with asthma, New England Journal of Medicine, 336, pp. 1356–1363.

Rubinowitz, L. S. and Rosenbaum, J. E. (2000) Crossing the Class and Color Lines: From Public Housing to White Suburbia (Chicago: University of Chicago Press).

Sampson, R. J., Raudenbush, S. W. and Earls, F. (1997) Neighborhoods and violent crime: a multilevel study of collective efficacy, Science, 277, pp. 918–924.

Sampson, R. J., Morenoff, J. D. and Gannon-Rowley, T. (2002) Assessing 'neighborhood effects': social processes and new directions in research, Annual Review of Sociology, 28, pp. 443–478.

Schwartz, A. and Tajbakhsh, K. (1997) Mixed-income housing: unanswered questions, Cityscape: A Journal of Policy Development and Research, 3, pp. 71–92.

Turner, M. A. and Rawlings, L. (2005) Overcoming Concentrated Poverty and Isolation (Washington DC: The Urban Institute). http://www.urban.org/UploadedPDF/311205_Poverty_FR.pdf.

Turner, M. A., Popkin, S. J. and Rawlings, L. (2009) Public Housing and the Legacy of Segregation (Washington DC: The Urban Institute Press).

Venkatesh, S. A., Celimli, I., Miller, D., Murphy, A. and Turner, B. (2004) Chicago public housing transformation: a research report. Center for Urban Research and Policy Working Paper (New York, NY: Columbia University). Available at http://www.columbia.edu/cu/curp/publications2/PH_Transformation_Report.pdf.

Wexler, H. J. (2000) HOPE VI market means/public ends. Working Paper Series PM (Yale University).

Wilson, W. J. (1987) The Truly Disadvantaged: the Innercity, the Underclass, and Public Policy (Chicago: University of Chicago Press).

Zeilenbach, S. (2002) The Economic Impact of HOPE VI on Neighborhoods, Housing Research Foundation Report (Washington DC: US Department of Housing and Urban Development).

26
"Is mixed-income development an antidote to urban poverty?"

From *Housing Policy Debate* (2006)

Mark L. Joseph
Case Western Reserve University

INTRODUCTION

Mixed-income development[1] is becoming increasingly popular in cities across the United States as a means of revitalizing urban areas and transforming public housing (Bohl 2000; Boston 2005; Briggs 1997; Brophy and Smith 1997; Epp 1996; Goetz 2003; Khadduri 2001; Popkin *et al.* 2000, 2004; Rosenbaum, Stroh, and Flynn 1998; Schwartz and Tajbakhsh 1997; Smith 2002; Turbov and Piper 2005a; von Hoffman 1996). A primary rationale for mixed-income development is that it is a way to reverse decades of racial and socioeconomic segregation in urban America. The negative effects of highly concentrated inner-city poverty have been well documented (Jargowsky 1997; Massey and Denton 1993; Wilson 1987, 1996).

In an earlier work (Joseph, Chaskin, and Webber 2006), my coauthors and I examine in detail the theoretical basis for the mixed-income development strategy. This article builds on that work with an eye to providing a much more concise and policy-oriented assessment of the potential for mixed-income development as a means of confronting urban poverty. I am particularly interested in trying to better articulate the possible impact of mixed-income developments on low-income families. Why do we expect mixed-income development to promote a higher quality of life and upward mobility for low-income families? How might specifying our expectations for the benefits of this strategy more clearly inform current policy debates on how best to invest in housing for poor families?

Although thousands of units of mixed-income housing have been built and occupied across the country, it is still not clear exactly what policy makers expect mixed-income development to accomplish and how. Several studies have made important contributions to our understanding of mixed-income development (Briggs 1997; Brophy and Smith 1997; Epp 1996; Khadduri 2001; Khadduri and Martin 1997; Kleit 2005; Mason 1997; Popkin *et al.* 2000; Rosenbaum, Stroh, and Flynn 1998; Schwartz and Tajbakhsh 1997; Smith 2002; Turbov and Piper 2005a). Yet, as Schwartz and Tajbakhsh assert, until we can develop a better understanding of why mixed-income housing should work and how well it actually works, "advocacy of mixed-income housing will be based largely on faith and on dissatisfaction with the previous thrust of low-income housing policy" (1997, 81).

In part, mixed-income development is a policy response to a growing consensus about some of the key factors that have generated unprecedented levels of urban poverty since the mid-1970s. Wilson (1987) described a new urban poverty characterized by the geographic concentration of high rates of joblessness and welfare dependency; high proportions of female-headed households, out-of-wedlock births, and teen pregnancies; and high levels of social disorganization, violence, and crime in certain neighborhoods. Several explanations have been offered for these trends, including a "skills mismatch" created by the restructuring of the U.S. economy from a largely manufacturing one to an information- and service-based one; a "spatial mismatch" created by the exodus of businesses to the suburbs; high levels of geographic racial segregation; and persistent structural racism in employment, education, and the criminal justice system (Bell 1992; Darity and Mason 1998; Hacker 1992; Holzer 1991; Jencks and Mayer 1990a; Kain 1968, 1992; Kasarda 1983, 1990; Kirschenman and Neckerman 1991; Massey and Denton 1993; Pager 2003; Wilson 1987, 1996).

As a strategy to confront urban poverty, mixed-income development responds largely to one critical factor: the social isolation of the urban poor, in particular blacks. While positive in many ways, the loosening of racial discrimination in housing markets in the suburbs and other parts of cities in the 1960s and 1970s led to an exodus of black middle-class and working-class residents from urban neighborhoods. This exodus, it is argued, had very negative effects on the inner city (Jargowsky 1997; Jargowsky and Bane 1990; Ricketts and Sawhill 1986; Wilson 1987, 1996), including a loss of resources from the incomes of those families, a decrease in the presence of families with "mainstream" patterns of norms and behavior, and a loss of families that were more likely to exert pressure within the community for order and safety and to place demands on external actors to provide high-quality goods and services (Wilson 1987).

The most extreme effects of social isolation were experienced in public housing. Originally intended as temporary housing for families facing difficult times, public housing became a permanent home to generations of families with severe economic and social challenges (Bowly 1978; Hirsch 1998; Popkin et al. 2000; Vale 2002; Venkatesh 2000).

The current national attention on mixed-income development is largely due to the high-profile redevelopment of public housing, much of it funded by HOPE VI (Housing Opportunities for People Everywhere), a $5 billion effort launched by the federal government in 1992 to rehabilitate the most severely distressed public housing around the country (Naparstek, Freis, and Kingsley 2000; Popkin et al. 2004; Turbov and Piper 2005a). The redevelopment and design principles that undergird the HOPE VI program draw on the ideas and experience of New Urbanism, a national movement that promotes the planning and design of more diverse and livable communities (Bohl 2000).

The other primary approach being used to deconcentrate poverty and reform public housing consists of dispersal programs, such as the national Moving to Opportunity for Fair Housing Demonstration Program and the Gautreaux Assisted Housing Program in Chicago. These efforts focus on facilitating the relocation of residents to lower-poverty communities in the metropolitan area (for a review of dispersal programs, see Varady and Walker 2003). I will reflect on the comparative promise of both approaches later in this article.

Citing a lack of cost-effectiveness, the Bush administration has sought to end the HOPE VI program, influencing the reduction of HOPE VI funds from $574 million in fiscal year 2002 to $99 million in fiscal year 2006 and seeking in each of the past four years to eliminate the program altogether (Wayne 2006). Thus far, Congress has continued to fund HOPE VI, though at reduced levels, and in 2005, Senator Barbara Mikulski, the original sponsor of the HOPE VI legislation, proposed a reauthorization bill to fund the program at $600 million annually for another five years. The bill was referred to committee and, according to the senator's office, is still pending.

Even the program's strongest supporters acknowledge concern with its implementation. Public housing units that have been demolished far outnumber the replacement units that are planned, there have been extended delays in the delivery of replacement units, and resources and strategies to support the residents during the relocation process have been insufficient (Popkin et al. 2004). The legislation proposed by Senator Mikulski attempts to address some of these concerns. Those who support renewed funding for HOPE VI argue that continued federal investment is key to leveraging local resources to invest in large-scale efforts to provide housing for the poor.

Despite the debate at the federal level about future support for mixed-income development, for the time being there continues to be strong public and private sector investment in this approach in cities across the country (Cisneros and Katz 2004; Smith 2002). Thus, even though the expected and actual benefits of mixed-income development are unclear, local investment in this strategy is increasing at a time when public sector budgets are shrinking and demand for affordable urban housing is growing. (For detailed case studies of private sector investment leveraged through mixed-income development in four U.S. cities, see Turbov and Piper 2005b, 2005c, 2005d, and 2005e.) Within this policy context, I suggest that a much more detailed exploration and assessment of the expected benefits of mixed-income development for low-income families is needed.

In this article, I describe four main propositions drawn from social networks, social control, culture and behavior, and political economy of place theories to describe how mixed-income development might improve the quality of life for low-income families. After presenting the theoretical bases for these propositions, I provide a conceptual framework that delineates the pathways through which these effects might occur. I then review the evidence from existing mixed-income research about the relevance of these propositions. Given the scale of the federal HOPE VI program and the literature on its implementation, I pay particular attention to what we have learned from this effort. I draw on information from other mixed-income efforts where possible and intend for the analysis to be broadly relevant to efforts to develop housing that will attract and retain a socioeconomically diverse population. Finally, I describe the limitations of this approach and consider the policy implications for future mixed-income development.

FOUR PROPOSITIONS REGARDING MIXED-INCOME DEVELOPMENT AND URBAN POVERTY

Social networks as "social capital"

The social networks argument asserts that by attracting higher-income residents back to the inner city, mixed-income development can facilitate the re-establishment of effective social networks and social capital for low-income residents. Granovetter (1973, 1983, 1995) has argued that networks providing people with access to information and opportunities are an important source of upward mobility, particularly for employment. Most important are those relationships – "weak ties" or "bridging social capital" – that provide people with access to resources beyond their networks of close association (see also Briggs 1997; Elliott 1999; Gittell and Vidal 1998; Lin and Dumin 1986; Lin,

Vaughn, and Ensel 1981; Stoloff, Glanville, and Bienenstock 1999).

Research has demonstrated that social networks are indeed valuable in securing employment (Granovetter 1995; Lin and Dumin 1986; Lin, Vaughn, and Ensel 1981; Stoloff, Glanville, and Bienenstock 1999). The social networks of lower-income individuals and blacks tend to be more localized than those of people with higher incomes (Campbell and Lee 1992; Elliott 1999; Fischer 1982; Lee, Campbell, and Miller 1991; Oliver 1988). Weak ties appear particularly advantageous for those with lower socioeconomic status (Granovetter 1995; Lin and Dumin 1986; Lin, Vaughn, and Ensel 1981). If mixed incomes are found in a community, lower-income residents may be able to build weak ties with affluent neighbors and thereby improve access to employment networks and other resources.

Studies of how people build networks have shown that although residents of modern urban neighborhoods generally rely less on neighbors for intimate support than in previous eras (Fischer 1982; Fischer et al. 1997; Wellman 1979; Wellman and Leighton 1979), proximity still influences network formation (Fischer 1982; McPherson, Smith-Lovin, and Cook 2001; Wellman 1979; Wellman and Wortley 1990) and instrumental support (Chaskin 1997). Studies on the impact of the physical environment on communal relations suggest that opportunities for contact, proximity to others, and appropriate space in which to interact are key factors that can promote and shape social interaction (Fleming, Baum, and Singer 1985; Keane 1991; Wilner, Walkley, and Cook 1952, 1955; Yancey 1972). Thus, it is theorized that mixed-income developments, if appropriately designed, may shape relationships among individual residents. Others have criticized this view, suggesting that spatial determinism only holds where there is real or perceived homogeneity among residents (Michelson 1976; see also Briggs 1997 and Gillis 1983).

Social control

The social control argument posits that the presence of higher-income residents – in particular, homeowners – will lead to higher levels of accountability to norms and rules through increased informal social control and thus to increased order and safety for all residents. The loss of stable, working families from the inner city meant the loss of people who were more likely to exert pressure within the community for order and safety. Effective social control requires interdependent relationships in a community and collective supervision to prevent and address local problems (Coleman 1988; Freudenburg 1986; Janowitz 1975; Kasarda and Janowitz 1974; Kornhauser 1978; Sampson and Groves 1989; Shaw and McKay 1969). Another important element of social organization is local participation in formal and voluntary organizations, which builds a community's ability to defend its interests.

Sampson and Groves (1989) have shown that higher levels of socioeconomic status, residential stability, and homeownership lead to increased social organization, which in turn leads to reduced levels of crime and delinquency. Sampson, Raudenbush, and Earls (1997) found that high socioeconomic status and homeownership were associated with elevated levels of collective efficacy – residents' perceptions of social cohesion and trust among neighbors and the extent to which neighbors are willing to take action on behalf of the community – which in turn was found to be strongly negatively associated with self-reported violence. Thus it is proposed that higher-income residents will be more likely to take action to maintain social control in the community, benefiting residents of all income levels.

Culture and behavior

A third proposition is that the presence of higher-income residents in mixed-income developments will lead other families to adapt more socially acceptable and constructive behavior, including seeking regular work, showing respect for property, and abiding by other social norms. In this way, mixed-income development is a policy response to the hotly debated notion of a "culture of poverty" – the theory that a key factor in the persistence of poverty is the destructive, antisocial habits that have been adopted by many low-income inner-city families and are counterproductive to their well-being and upward mobility (Auletta 1982; Jencks and Peterson 1991; Kasarda 1990;

Lemann 1986a, 1986b; Lewis 1969; Mead 1992; Murray 1984; Wilson 1987). Other scholars have criticized the notion of a culture of poverty as offensive and assert that it unfairly attributes to "culture" what is in fact an adaptation to a structural position in society (Katz 1993; Valentine 1968). Further, the notion of role-modeling by one income group for another risks being seen as demeaning and paternalistic (Rosenbaum, Stroh, and Flynn 1998).

There is an extensive literature that examines neighborhood effects, in particular the impact of living in a neighborhood with a greater proportion of affluent residents (see, for example, Briggs 1997; Ellen and Turner 1997; Galster and Killen 1995; Gephart 1997; Jencks and Mayer 1990b). In general, there is increasing evidence that the presence of middle-class, affluent neighbors benefits low-income children and adolescents in such areas as educational outcomes, health, and sexual activity, although direct effects are relatively small compared with the influence of family-level characteristics (Briggs 1997; Brooks-Gunn et al. 1997; Crane 1991; Datcher 1982; Ellen and Turner 1997; Gephart 1997). The strongest research findings have documented the influence of affluent adults on lower-income children and adolescents, rather than adult-to-adult influence, leading some researchers to focus the hypothesized influence of mixed-income developments on the relations between adults and children (Ellen and Turner 1997; Khadduri and Martin 1997).

To the extent that role-modeling does occur, it could take two different forms. In some cases, behavioral change could happen through distal role-modeling, that is, observing the actions of others, such as a neighbor going to work every day or a neighbor's children attending school regularly, over time. In other cases, role-modeling may be more proximal, with residents of different income levels interacting directly and role-modeling occurring in a much more intimate way, through direct advice, feedback, and accountability, for example.

The political economy of place

The fourth proposition suggests that the influence of higher-income residents will generate new market demand and political pressure to which external political and economic actors are more likely to respond, thereby leading to higher-quality goods and services available to a cross-section of residents in the community. An important explanation for the conditions in inner-city neighborhoods is the neglect and marginalization of these areas due to a variety of powerful market and political forces at the city, regional, national, and even global levels. In the context of these forces, the absence of residents who can advocate effectively on behalf of the community, demand high-quality goods and services, and influence public policy is a serious detriment (Crenson 1983; Logan and Molotch 1987; Verba, Scholzman, and Brady 1995).

Homeowners have a greater vested interest in soliciting public and private investment in the community, and higher-income families will demand better performance from neighborhood schools and other local institutions (Khadduri 2001; Sampson, Raudenbush, and Earls 1997). In addition, the greater spending power of higher-income residents should make the community more attractive for retail and commercial development and services such as banking. It can be expected that more affluent residents will bring more personal resources, broader networks of influence, and greater control over their time, thus building the community's capacity to help confront neighborhood challenges and opportunities (Chaskin 2001; Chaskin et al. 2001).

However, while certain improved community amenities may meet the needs of all residents, there may be important instances where the needs and priorities of low-income residents differ from those of other residents. The unequal distribution of influence among residents may lead to community benefits that are not necessarily accessible or valuable to all.

Putting it all together: An ecological framework

The four propositions having been defined, it is useful to examine them in the context of the relationship between the neighborhood and the individual. For this purpose, I adapt an ecological framework developed by Aber et al. (1997).

The framework presented in Figure 26.1 integrates two major areas of theory – Shaw and McKay's social disorganization theory (1969) (see also Sampson and Morenoff 1997) and Bronfenbrenner's (1979) structural-ecological approach to human development – and specifies three levels of context that influence developmental outcomes. Table 26.1 describes the key processes I hypothesize to be at work at each level of context in a mixed-income environment.

In addition to the levels, three pathways of influence can be delineated (see Figure 26.1):

1. From community processes to interpersonal processes to individual processes to individual and family outcomes (Pathway A)
2. From community processes to individual processes to outcomes (Pathway B)
3. From community processes directly to individual outcomes (Pathway C)

Table 26.2 provides examples of how the pathways might work in practice and demonstrates that each proposition can be hypothesized to work through different combinations of the pathways of influence.

Level	Mixed-income processes
Community	Increased social control that promotes greater accountability to social norms
	Individual and collective leveraging of external resources
	The generation of a culture of work and social responsibility
Interpersonal	Interaction across income levels, including information sharing, the building of social networks, and role-modeling
Individual	Behavior modification (self-regulation, use of time, job search methods), change in aspirations, and sense of efficacy

Table 26.1 Level of neighborhood context and mixed-income processes

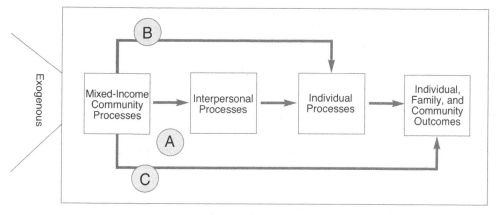

Figure 26.1 Effects of a mixed-income context (source: adapted from Aber *et al.* 1997, 45).

Proposition	Pathway(s)	Description
Social networks	A	Proximity and interpersonal contact at the community level provide opportunities for social interaction between residents of different income levels and backgrounds. Social interaction leads to the building of familiarity and trust and eventually to the exchange of information and resources that support individual processes such as employment search. Enhanced individual processes leads to improved individual, family and community outcomes such as higher employment and greater self-sufficiency.
Social control	A	New and strengthened interpersonal relationships among particular individuals lead to greater accountability to each other and to others whom they both know, such as their children. People who commit a delinquent act while in these new networks are more likely to be recognized and held accountable by others. Less delinquent behavior leads to improved outcomes, such as fewer arrests and lower rates of incarceration for people in these networks.
	B	Increased social control at the community level as a whole and an increased collective sense of vigilance on behalf of the community promote individual behavior modification among those previously inclined to delinquency and crime. As noted, abstaining from these activities reduces contact with the criminal justice system.
	C	Greater social control at the community level promotes greater neighborhood safety and reduced crime, which directly improve the quality of life for the individuals and families.
Culture and behavior	A	Proximity and interpersonal contact at the community level provide opportunities for social interaction, which may include proximal role-modeling * Individuals modify their behaviors based on the direct influence and mentoring of others, and these modified behaviors lead to improved outcomes, such as school achievement and better employment.

Proposition	Pathway(s)	Description
	B	The socioeconomic diversity in the community creates a dominant culture of work and social responsibility. This leads to distal role-modeling whereby the actions and routines of more affluent families are observed at a distance and emulated by others. As in other pathways, individual behavior modification in turn leads to improved individual outcomes, as well as greater self-sufficiency among families and reduced illicit activity at the community level.
Political economy of place	C	Individual and collective leveraging of external resources leads to higher-quality local services and infrastructure, thus directly promoting an improved quality of life for local residents

Table 26.2 Mixed-income propositions and pathways of influence

* By the definition used here, proximal role-modeling requires direct interaction, as distinct from distal role-modeling, which involves observing and emulating the actions of others from a distance.

An important point to note is that only Pathway A requires direct interpersonal interaction across income levels. Thus, even *without* social interaction, a theoretical case can be made for the benefit of mixed-income housing for low-income residents. This is significant since, as we shall see, the assumption that such interaction can be easily facilitated through mixed-income housing is open to serious question. It is also important to note that just as there may be benefits to living in a mixed-income development, such a move also has potentially significant costs. Challenges for low-income families could include a loss of existing support networks, an increased sense of stigma and isolation, and the negative effects of a sense of relative deprivation.

THE RELEVANCE OF THESE PROPOSITIONS IN MIXED-INCOME DEVELOPMENTS

Research on the past decade of mixed-income development in the United States is quite limited. Drawing on case studies of HOPE VI developments, comparative studies of mixed-income developments, and other available research, I will now assess the four propositions in light of the nation's experience thus far.

Social networks

Current evidence about the formation of social networks across income levels is limited and inconclusive. Most studies have found little interaction across income levels at mixed-income developments (Brophy and Smith 1997; Buron et al. 2002; Hogan 1996; Mason 1997; Ryan et al. 1974). However, the two most comprehensive studies of social interaction in mixed-income developments to date – Rosenbaum, Stroh, and Flynn's (1998) study of Lake Parc Place in Chicago and Kleit's (2005) study of the New Holly HOPE VI development in Seattle – did find evidence of neighboring relationships across income levels. However, both developments have important characteristics that prevent generalization.

At Lake Parc Place, units were reserved for low-income and moderate-income residents, and there were no market-rate units. Sixty percent of the moderate-income residents had lived in public housing before and therefore had a shared life experience with the residents of the public housing units. At New Holly, Kleit (2005) found that proximity within the development and shared attributes (ethnicity, language, education, marital status, owner/renter status) were associated with higher levels of social ties. She also found that children in the household can act as bridges to other families with children. Community facilities and activities were relatively well attended by the full range of residents of the mixed-income development. However, New Holly has a unique level of diversity; the development is home to whites, blacks, and new immigrants from Southeast Asia and East Africa. Families living in the development speak 12 different languages.

Only limited empirical evidence so far supports the proposition that mixed-income development will lead to changes in residents' social networks. Most studies have found little interaction across income levels, and those that have found such interaction have not been able to demonstrate that it has led to information about jobs or other resources (Brophy and Smith 1997; Smith 2002).

Social control

The available evidence is inconclusive about whether increased levels of social control have been observed in existing mixed-income developments and, if so, what the source of that increased control is. On the basis of their surveys of residents, Rosenbaum, Stroh, and Flynn (1998) found that the higher-income residents at Lake Parc Place provided strong support for rules and enforcement. Only 5.4 percent of the moderate-income residents felt that there were too many rules, but 26.8 percent of the low-income residents felt that way. And while only 3.6 percent of the moderate-income residents felt that management was too strict, 12.5 percent of the low-income residents felt that way. However, in their study of eight HOPE VI sites, Buron et al. (2002) found no difference in the levels of social control reported by public housing residents of HOPE VI sites, Housing Choice Voucher Program apartments, unsubsidized apartments, and public housing developments. The one exception was that control of graffiti was perceived to be significantly lower in public housing sites. Smith (2002) reports that according to his conversations with property managers and developers, strong property management seemed relatively more important for social control than residents' actions. It may be that the combination of strong management and more active informal control by residents is the most effective means of maintaining social

order. Although empirical evidence for increased social organization in mixed-income communities is very limited, the strong empirical evidence for the impact of socioeconomic status, homeownership, and residential stability on informal social control in more general neighborhood studies makes this proposition compelling (Sampson and Groves 1989; Sampson, Raudenbush, and Earls 1997).

Culture and behavior

In addition to the controversial nature of the proposition about role-modeling and behavior, it is a very difficult phenomenon to measure empirically. There is no evidence in the limited research on mixed-income developments as to whether role-modeling is taking place and, if so, what effect it has. Residents with whom Mason (1997) spoke, for example, downplayed the importance of modeling (see also Rosenbaum, Stroh, and Flynn 1998). When they surveyed residents of mixed-income developments about social opinions and lifestyle values, Ryan et al. found that "contrary to conventional wisdom, people at different income levels display pretty much the same distribution of values, social attitudes, and lifestyles" (1974, 22). While there is certainly a difference between holding a value and acting on it, there may well be less to be gained from income mixing in terms of changing values than is assumed. Lower-income residents answered only one question on Ryan et al.'s (1974) survey differently from higher-income residents. The question asked whether the respondent agreed with the statement that the only significant difference between poor people and the rest of society is that the poor do not have as much money. Ryan et al. (1974) report that while low-income residents tended to agree with this statement, higher-income residents did not, thus suggesting that low-income residents would not subscribe to the proposition that they would benefit from using higher-income residents as role models. This raises the question referenced earlier by Valentine (1968) as to whether inner-city residents are isolated from mainstream values or simply from mainstream opportunities. Further, if there is a benefit to role-modeling, perhaps it lies in modeling life skills rather than in modeling values.

Although the presence of middle-class role models has become a fundamental and commonly accepted rationale for mixed-income development, my review raises serious questions about the relative importance of this proposition. It is possible that distal role-modeling is more prevalent than proximal, one-on-one interactions across income levels. Certainly it seems more likely that role-modeling from adults to children will be more readily observed than role-modeling between adults.

The political economy of place

No research on mixed-income developments examines the role of higher-income residents in leveraging external resources. In his interviews with developers and property managers, Smith (2002) found some evidence that market pressure ensures that development properties are well maintained. On the basis of his review of other literature on urban development, Smith asserts: "Much research has shown that attracting non-poor households to a community is critically important to creating a market for services ... and exerting political power to improve municipal services" (2002, 26). With regard to private services, the argument is not that higher-income residents directly leverage private investments and services, although some may work through local community organizations and government officials to lobby for particular investments. It is more likely that market actors will respond to the presence of higher-income residents and increase investments in neighborhoods and their services. Despite a lack of empirical evidence, this proposition remains a compelling argument for mixed-income development based on expectations that homeowners will have greater residential stability, participation in community organizations, likelihood of voting, and spending power.

Assessment of propositions based on available evidence

In my review, I do not finding compelling evidence for the propositions about network formation and role-modeling through social interaction across income levels. In the short term at least, these pathways are unlikely to hold much promise as a way to improve individual and family outcomes for low-income residents. Over time, depending on the level of residential stability in mixed-income developments and the level of investment in activities that promote social interaction, we may see higher levels of relationship building that lead to benefits for low-income residents. Eventually, role-modeling of a more distal nature among adults, as well as more proximal role-modeling between adults and children, may take place.

However, given the evidence cited earlier, I find the propositions that the presence of higher-income residents will lead to greater informal social control and improved community attributes much more compelling. Higher-income residents, particularly homeowners, will likely be more stringent about upholding rules and regulations and promoting informal social control. We can certainly expect that, with a mixed-income constituency, the market and external institutions will respond differently to demands for higher-quality goods and services. The limited available empirical evidence thus indicates that propositions relating to social control and political economy of place hold more promise at this time.

POLICY IMPLICATIONS

The need to clarify expectations

Policy makers and developers should be urged to be clearer about their expectations and priorities for any mixed-income development they undertake. Is the motivation for the development to revitalize the local area and provide additional housing options for urban dwellers, to provide low-income residents with higher-quality housing, to help lift low-income families out of poverty, or some combination of the three? Unless the motivation for mixed-income development is clearer, the ability to evaluate the success of this approach, compare various design and development strategies, and advise policy makers and implementers on relative values and the most effective means of promotion is somewhat limited.

The need to lower expectations

There is a tremendous amount of hyperbole about and hope for mixed-income development. My analysis suggests that we should lower our expectations about its impact on low-income residents. Short- to medium-term effects in terms of social order and increased quality of goods and services seem to be reasonable. The new developments seem certain to improve the overall living environment for the low-income families that move in and thus will have an indirect effect on their well-being. However, it is also possible that low-income families may experience significant personal and familial challenges in the new environment, including social isolation, stigma, a sense of relative deprivation, increased scrutiny, and competition with more affluent residents for scarce local resources (Briggs 1997; Jencks and Mayer 1990b).

Further, mixed-income development alone cannot reasonably be expected to promote more direct effects such as behavioral change and substantial gains in employment and self-sufficiency. Promoting sustainable changes in the lives of low-income residents who move from neighborhoods with concentrated poverty to mixed-income developments will generally require combining housing with investments in social services, education, job readiness, training and placement, and transportation. Moreover, it will require, above all, attention to more fundamental structural barriers that constrain access to opportunity by race and class.

Housing design

For those mixed-income developments where social interaction is an explicit priority, there seems to be great potential to think creatively about design in order to facilitate more interaction among residents. Drawing on New Urbanist ideas, developers can prioritize the physical integration of various unit types; the avoidance of characteristics that would make the units of residents with different income levels distinguishable from the outside; the incorporation of comfortable and accessible shared space such as hallways, walkways, courtyards, and other common areas; and the creation of common civic space such as parks, community centers, and libraries (Barnett 2003; Katz 1994; Leccese and McCormick 1999).

Community building

Existing research suggests that simply sharing the same space will not build the level of interaction needed to promote the meaningful exchange of information and support. Property managers and others responsible for the ongoing oversight of developments must decide how much to invest in actively facilitating interpersonal connections to help residents identify areas of common interest. Events – such as cookouts, potlucks, community meetings, and celebrations – may be important venues for bringing residents into the same space and providing an opportunity for repeated interaction and relationship building. The formation of resident organizations such as block clubs and civic associations is another important means of building meaningful bonds. Also important is the role of local institutions such as schools, day care centers, and recreational facilities to the extent they can be expressly designed, financed, and managed to serve families with a range of income levels.

Income mix

We have much to learn about the implications of various proportions of residents of different income levels within a development, but we can be certain that the mix affects outcomes. The higher the proportion of low-income and subsidized residents, the greater the contribution to the city's stock of quality affordable housing. The higher the proportion of homeowners and market-rate renters, the more revenue there is to finance the development, the greater the residential and social stability, and the greater the expected subsequent investment in services. To the extent that promoting social interaction is an important goal, it appears that interaction is more easily generated among residents of proximal income levels – low-income and moderate-income for example. This suggests that including a moderate-income tier may help facilitate social interaction across income levels.

Mixed-income versus dispersal strategies

Despite the need to lower short-term expectations for mixed-income development, this strategy appears no less promising than dispersal programs, such as the national Moving to Opportunity for Fair Housing Demonstration Program (Goering and Feins 2003; Orr *et al.* 2003) and the Gautreaux Assisted Housing Program in Chicago (Rosenbaum 1995; Rosenbaum *et al.* 1991), the other current policy alternatives for deconcentrating poverty and reforming public housing. (For a review of dispersal programs, see Varady and Walker 2003.) Available research indicates that the clearest benefit of dispersal programs for low-income families is increased community safety and order – the same benefit we expect from mixed-income developments. But a key difference is that dispersal programs benefit only those households that move out of high-poverty areas. Mixed-income developments may benefit all residents of the neighborhood receiving the development, although it is possible that the greatest benefits may accrue to the lower-income residents of the development itself. While we do not expect a significant impact on earnings for residents of mixed-income developments, dispersal strategies have so far failed to demonstrate any impact on earnings either. Both strategies require families to adapt to new environments and establish new social networks, but families in mixed-income developments have the advantage of remaining in the inner city and living in close proximity to other low-income families.

Criticisms of the mixed-income approach, particularly the HOPE VI program, include the reduction of units available for low-income families, the substantial costs of redevelopment, and extensive delays in construction and unit delivery. However, dispersal programs face significant administrative and political challenges of their own, including resistance from suburban communities, that make it difficult to take that approach to scale. In this light, mixed-income development seems an important component of a response to urban poverty and should continue to be explored.

Toward a comprehensive strategy for housing the urban poor

As a strategy for meeting the needs of the urban poor, mixed-income development has some important limitations. While it holds promise as a way to provide housing quality and residential stability, it cannot, in and of itself, address the

major barriers to self-sufficiency – unstable employment, limited education and work skills, problematic credit history, and health challenges – experienced by many low-income families (Bohl 2000). As Popkin and her colleagues conclude from their review of the HOPE VI program:

> [W]hile it is clearly feasible to create a healthy mixed-income development that will attract higher-income tenants and provide a pleasant and safe community for all residents, it remains less clear what conditions are required to ensure that living in these communities will have substantial payoffs for the social and economic status of low-income families over the long term.
> (2004, 23–24)

In particular, as Cunningham, Popkin, and Burt (2005) note, the urban poor include a substantial proportion of families that could be termed "hard-to-house," meaning that their personal circumstances present major challenges to retaining their housing. These challenges include employability, substance abuse, mental health, or criminal background issues, as well as family demands related to a physical disability, elderly status, or grandparents caring for grandchildren in the absence of the parents.

Only a very small proportion of low-income residents will be able to move into mixed-income developments. Not only is there a substantial net loss of public housing units across the country due to the federal government's elimination of the one-for-one replacement requirement in 1995, but in many cases stringent screening criteria for residence in the new developments excludes most of the local public housing population (Venkatesh *et al.* 2004). Popkin *et al.* (2000) make the vital observation that mixed-income developments will be unavailable to many of the most challenged families among the urban poor.

CONCLUSION

We must continue efforts to end the decades of social isolation for the poor and the resulting concentration of poverty effects that have limited the life chances of generations of inner-city residents of color. Through the mechanisms outlined here – increased informal social control, more effective demand for local services and amenities, and perhaps exposure to a broader range of possibilities for youth – mixed-income development appears to be a strategy that can improve the quality of life for many low-income families. There is still much to be learned about the challenges of living in mixed-income developments and the extent to which benefits beyond improved environmental conditions are experienced.

However, while promising in some significant ways, mixed-income development can be only one component of a more comprehensive strategy for housing poor families. To fully address the increasing shortage of affordable housing for the urban poor, complementary efforts are needed to improve housing conditions in high-poverty neighborhoods and to facilitate moves to low-poverty areas of the city (Briggs 2005). These might include the increased availability of well-maintained public and subsidized housing with access to strong supportive services and strategies to connect the residents to resources in the surrounding neighborhoods. Deconcentration efforts, through the Housing Choice Voucher Program, for example, can be strengthened through stronger support and oversight of landlords and more resources to support families' search for housing and ongoing housing stability.

Producing thousands of units of mixed-income housing nationwide has required a great deal of vision, creativity, and persistence on the part of the public and private sectors. This same level of ambition and commitment will be needed not only to stay the course, but also to determine how to enhance and complement current approaches for maximal impact on low-income households across the country.

ACKNOWLEDGEMENTS

I would like to acknowledge Robert J. Chaskin and Henry S. Webber, who were my coauthors on an earlier version of this work, as well as two anonymous reviewers for helpful comments on an earlier draft. The research assistance of Meegan Bassett, Michelle Freeman, Ranada Harrison, and Kayla Hogan was invaluable. This research was partly funded by the Rockefeller Foundation and supported by a postdoctoral scholarship at the School of Social Service Administration at the University of Chicago.

Note

1 Mixed-income development ranges from private-sector, market-rate developments that include a small percentage of affordable housing to developments built exclusively for moderate- and low-income families. Like Brophy and Smith, my interest in this article is any development or community initiative where the mixing of income groups is a "fundamental part of [the] financial and operating plans" (1997, 5). My focus here is on mixed-income developments built in inner-city locations as a means of attracting middle-income residents and revitalizing surrounding areas.

REFERENCES

Aber, J. Lawrence, Martha A. Gephart, Jeanne Brooks-Gunn, and James P. Connell. 1997. Development in Context: Implications for Studying Neighborhood Effects. In *Neighborhood Poverty. Volume I. Contexts and Consequences for Children*, ed. Jeanne Brooks-Gunn, Greg J. Duncan, and J. Lawrence Aber, 44–61. Newark, NJ: Russell Sage Foundation.

Auletta, Ken. 1982. *The Underclass*. New York: Random House.

Barnett, Jonathan. 2003. *Redesigning Cities: Principles, Practice, Implementation*. Chicago: Planners.

Bell, Derrick. 1992. *Faces at the Bottom of the Well: The Permanence of Racism*. New York: Basic.

Bohl, Charles C. 2000. New Urbanism and the City: Potential Applications and Implications for Distressed Inner-City Neighborhoods. *Housing Policy Debate* 11(4):761–801.

Boston, Thomas D. 2005. Environment Matters: The Effect of Mixed-Income Revitalization on the Socioeconomic Status of Public Housing Residents: A Case Study of Atlanta. Working Paper No. 1. Georgia Institute of Technology.

Bowly, Devereaux. 1978. *The Poorhouse: Subsidized Housing in Chicago, 1895–1976*. Carbondale, IL: Southern Illinois University Press.

Briggs, Xavier de Souza. 1997. Moving Up versus Moving Out: Neighborhood Effects in Housing Mobility Programs. *Housing Policy Debate* 8(1):195–234.

Briggs, Xavier de Souza, ed. 2005. *The Geography of Opportunity: Race and Housing Choice in Metropolitan America.* Washington, D.C.: Brookings Institution Press.

Bronfenbrenner, Urie. 1979. *The Ecology of Human Development: Experiments by Nature and Design.* Cambridge, MA: Harvard University Press.

Brooks-Gunn, Jeanne, Greg J. Duncan, Tama Leventhal, and J. Lawrence Aber. 1997. Lessons Learned and Future Directions for Research on the Neighborhoods in Which Children Live. In *Neighborhood Poverty. Volume I. Context and Consequences for Children*, ed. Jeanne Brooks-Gunn, Greg J. Duncan, and J. Lawrence Aber, 279–97. Newark, NJ: Russell Sage Foundation.

Brophy, Paul C., and Rhonda N. Smith. 1997. Mixed-Income Housing: Factors for Success. *Cityscape: A Journal of Policy Development and Research* 3(2):3–31.

Buron, Larry E., Susan J. Popkin, Diane K. Levy, Laura E. Harris, and Jill Khadduri. 2002.
The HOPE VI Resident Tracking Study: A Snapshot of the Current Living Situation of Original Residents from Eight Sites. Report prepared by Abt Associates, Inc., and the Urban Institute for the U.S. Department of Housing and Urban Development. Washington, D.C.: Urban Institute.

Campbell, Karen E., and Robert A. Lee. 1992. Sources of Personal Neighbor Networks: Social Integration, Need, or Time? *Social Forces* 70(4):1077–1100.

Chaskin, Robert J. 1997. Perspectives on Neighborhood and Community: A Review of the Literature. *Social Service Review* 7(4):521–47.

Chaskin, Robert J. 2001. Community Capacity: A Definitional Framework and Implications from a Comprehensive Community Initiative. *Urban Affairs Review* 36(3):291–323.

Chaskin, Robert J., Prudence Brown, Sudhir Venkatesh, and Avis Vidal. 2001. *Building Community Capacity.* New York: Aldine de Gruyter.

Cisneros, Henry, and Bruce Katz. 2004. Keep HOPE (VI) Alive. *Atlanta Journal-Constitution,* May 17. World Wide Web page http://www.brookings.edu/urban/20040517_metroview.htm (accessed April 28, 2006).

Coleman, James S. 1988. Social Capital in the Creation of Human Capital. *American Journal of Sociology* 94:95–121.

Crane, Jonathan. 1991. The Epidemic Theory of Ghettos and Neighborhood Effects on Dropping Out and Teenage Childbearing. *American Journal of Sociology* 96(5):1226–59.

Crenson, Matthew A. 1983. *Neighborhood Politics.* Cambridge, MA: Harvard University Press.

Cunningham, Mary K., Susan J. Popkin, and Martha Burt. 2005. *Public Housing Transformation and the "Hard to House."* A Roof over Their Heads Policy Brief No. 9. Washington, D.C.: Urban Institute.

Darity, William A. Jr., and Patrick L. Mason. 1998. Evidence on Discrimination in Employment: Codes of Color, Codes of Gender. *Journal of Economic Perspectives* 12(2):63–90.

Datcher, Linda. 1982. Effects of Community and Family Backgrounds on Achievement. *Review of Economics and Statistics* 64(1):32–41.

Ellen, Ingrid Gould, and Margery Austin Turner. 1997. Does Neighborhood Matter? Assessing Recent Evidence. *Housing Policy Debate* 8(4):833–66.

Elliott, James R. 1999. Social Isolation and Labor Market Insulation: Network and Neighborhood Effects on Less-Educated Urban Workers. *Sociological Quarterly* 40(2):199–216.

Epp, Gayle. 1996. Emerging Strategies for Revitalizing Public Housing Communities. *Housing Policy Debate* 7(3):563–88.

Fischer, Claude S. 1982. *To Dwell among Friends: Personal Networks in Town and City.* Chicago: University of Chicago Press.

Fischer, Claude S., Robert M. Jackson, Ann C. Stueve, Kathleen Gerson, Lynne McAllister-Jones, and Mark Baldassare. 1997. *Networks and Places: Social Relations in the Urban Setting.* New York: Free.

Fleming, Raymond, Jerome Baum, and Jerome E. Singer. 1985. Social Support and the

Physical Environment. In *Social Support and Health*, ed. Sheldon Cohen and S. Leonard Syme, 327–45. Orlando, FL: Academic.

Freudenburg, William R. 1986. The Density of Acquaintanceship: An Overlooked Variable in Community Research? *American Journal of Sociology* 92(1):27–63.

Galster, George C., and Sean P. Killen. 1995. The Geography of Metropolitan Opportunity: A Reconnaissance and Conceptual Framework. *Housing Policy Debate* 6(1):7–43.

Gephart, Martha A. 1997. Neighborhoods and Communities as Contexts for Development. In *Neighborhood Poverty*. Volume I. *Contexts and Consequences for Children*, ed. Jeanne Brooks-Gunn, Greg J. Duncan, and J. Lawrence Aber, 1–43. Newark, NJ: Russell Sage Foundation.

Gillis, A. R. 1983. Strangers Next Door: An Analysis of Density, Delinquency, and Scale in Public Housing Projects. *Canadian Journal of Sociology* 8:1–20.

Gittell, Ross, and Avis Vidal. 1998. *Community Organizing: Building Social Capital as a Development Strategy*. Thousand Oaks, CA: Sage.

Goering, John, and Judith Feins, eds. 2003. *Choosing a Better Life: Evaluating the Moving to Opportunity Social Experiment*. Washington, D.C.: Urban Institute Press.

Goetz, Edward. 2003. Housing Dispersal Programs. *Journal of Planning Literature.* 18(1):3–16.

Granovetter, Mark. 1973. The Strength of Weak Ties. *American Journal of Sociology.* 78(6):1360–80.

Granovetter, Mark. 1983. The Strength of Weak Ties: A Network Theory Revisited. *Sociological Theory* 1:201–33.

Granovetter, Mark. 1995. *Getting a Job: A Study of Contacts and Careers*. Chicago: University of Chicago Press.

Hacker, Andrew. 1992. *Two Nations: Black and White, Separate and Unequal*. New York: Scribner's.

Hirsch, Arnold R. 1998. *Making the Second Ghetto: Race and Housing in Chicago 1940–1960*. Chicago: University of Chicago Press.

Hogan, James. 1996. *Scattered-Site Housing: Characteristics and Consequences*. Washington, D.C.: U.S. Department of Housing and Urban Development, Office of Policy Development and Research.

Holzer, Harry J. 1991. The Spatial Mismatch Hypothesis: What Has the Evidence Shown? *Urban Studies* 28(1):105–22.

Janowitz, Morris. 1975. Sociological Theory and Social Control. *American Journal of Sociology* 81(1):82–108.

Jargowsky, Paul A. 1997. *Poverty and Place: Ghettos, Barrios, and the American City*. New York: Russell Sage Foundation.

Jargowsky, Paul A., and Mary J. Bane. 1990. Ghetto Poverty: Basic Questions. In *Inner-City Poverty in the United States*, ed. Laurence E. Lynn and Michael G. H. McGeary, 16–67. Washington, D.C.: National Academy Press.

Jencks, Christopher, and Susan E. Mayer. 1990a. Residential Segregation, Job Proximity, and Black Job Opportunities. In *Inner-City Poverty in the United States*, ed. Laurence E. Lynn and Michael G. H. McGeary, 187–222. Washington, D.C.: National Academy Press.

Jencks, Christopher, and Susan E. Mayer. 1990b. The Social Consequences of Growing Up in a Poor Neighborhood. In *Inner-City Poverty in the United States*, ed. Laurence E. Lynn and Michael G. H. McGeary, 111–86. Washington, D.C.: National Academy Press.

Jencks, Christopher, and Paul E. Peterson, eds. 1991. *The Urban Underclass*. Washington, D.C.: Brookings Institution.

Joseph, Mark L., Robert J. Chaskin, and Henry S. Webber. 2006. The Theoretical Basis for Addressing Poverty through Mixed-Income Development. Unpublished paper. University of Chicago, School of Social Service Administration.

Kain, John F. 1968. Housing Segregation, Negro Employment, and Metropolitan Decentralization. *Quarterly Journal of Economics* 82(2):175–97.

Kain, John F. 1992. The Spatial Mismatch Hypothesis: Three Decades Later. *Housing Policy Debate* 3(2):371–460.

Kasarda, John D. 1983. Entry-Level Jobs, Mobility, and Urban Minority Unemployment. *Urban Affairs Quarterly* 19(1):21–40.

Kasarda, John D. 1990. City Jobs and Residents on a Collision Course: The

Urban Under-class Dilemma. *Economic Development Quarterly* 4(4):313–19.

Kasarda, John D., and Morris Janowitz. 1974. Community Attachment in Mass Society. *American Sociological Review* 39(3):328–39.

Katz, Michael B. 1993. *The Underclass Debate.* Princeton, NJ: Princeton University Press.

Katz, Peter. 1994. *The New Urbanism: Toward an Architecture of Community.* New York: McGraw-Hill.

Keane, Carl. 1991. Socioenvironmental Determinants of Community Formation. *Environment and Behavior* 23(1):27–96.

Khadduri, Jill. 2001. Deconcentration: What Do We Mean? What Do We Want? *Cityscape: A Journal of Policy Development and Research* 5(2):69–84.

Khadduri, Jill, and Marge Martin. 1997. Mixed-Income Housing in the HUD Multifamily Stock. *Cityscape: A Journal of Policy Development and Research* 3(2):33–69.

Kirschenman, Joleen, and Kathryn M. Neckerman. 1991. "We'd Love to Have Them, but…": The Meaning of Race for Employers. In *The Urban Underclass*, ed. Christopher Jencks and Paul E. Peterson, 203–32. Washington, D.C.: Brookings Institution.

Kleit, Rachel Garshick. 2005. HOPE VI New Communities: Neighborhood Relationships in Mixed-Income Housing. *Environment and Planning A* 37(8):1413–41.

Kornhauser, Ruth R. 1978. *Social Sources of Delinquency.* Chicago: University of Chicago Press.

Leccese, Michael, and Kathleen McCormick, eds. 1999. *Charter of the New Urbanism.* New York: McGraw-Hill.

Lee, Barrett A., Karen E. Campbell, and Oscar Miller. 1991. Racial Differences in Urban Neighboring. *Sociological Forum* 6(3):525–50.

Lemann, Nicholas. 1986a. The Origins of the Underclass, Part I. *Atlantic Monthly*, June, pp. 31–55.

Lemann, Nicholas. 1986b. The Origins of the Underclass, Part II. *Atlantic Monthly*, July, pp. 54–68.

Lewis, Oscar. 1969. The Culture of Poverty. In *Perspectives on Understanding Poverty: Perspectives from the Social Sciences,* ed. Daniel P. Moynihan, 187–200. New York: Basic.

Lin, Nan, and Mary Dumin. 1986. Access to Occupations through Social Ties. *Social Networks* 8:365–85.

Lin, Nan, John C. Vaughn, and Walter M. Ensel. 1981. Social Resources and Occupational Attainment. *Social Forces* 59(4):1164–81.

Logan, John R., and Harvey L. Molotch. 1987. *Urban Fortunes: The Political Economy of Place.* Berkeley, CA: University of California Press.

Mason, Maryann. 1997. Mixed-Income Public Housing: Outcomes for Tenants and Their Community. A Case Study of the Lake Parc Place Development in Chicago, Illinois. Ph.D. diss. Loyola University of Chicago.

Massey, Douglas S., and Nancy A. Denton. 1993. *American Apartheid: Segregation and the Making of the Underclass.* Cambridge MA: Harvard University Press.

McPherson, Miller, Lynn Smith-Lovin, and James M. Cook. 2001. Birds of a Feather: Homophily in Social Networks. *Annual Review of Sociology* 27:415–44.

Mead, Lawrence. 1992. *The New Politics of Poverty.* New York: Basic.

Michelson, William. 1976. *Man and His Urban Environment: A Sociological Approach* (with revisions). Reading, MA: Addison-Wesley.

Murray, Charles. 1984. *Losing Ground: American Social Policy 1950–1980.* New York: Basic.

Naparstek, Arthur J., Susan R. Freis, and G. Thomas Kingsley (with Dennis Dooley and Howard E. Lewis). 2000. *HOPE VI: Community Building Makes a Difference.* Washington, D.C.: U.S. Department of Housing and Urban Development.

Oliver, Melvin L. 1988. The Urban Black Community as Network: Toward a Social Network Perspective. *Sociological Quarterly* 29(4):623–45.

Orr, Larry, Judith D. Feins, Robin Jacob, Erik Beecroft, Lisa Sanbonmatsu, Lawrence B. Katz, Jeffrey B. Liebman, and Jeffrey R. Kling. 2003. *Moving to Opportunity for Fair Housing Demonstration Program: Interim Impacts Evaluation.* Report prepared by Abt Associates, Inc., and the National Bureau of Economic Research. Washington, D.C.: U.S. Department of

Housing and Urban Development, Office of Policy Development and Research.

Pager, Devah. 2003. The Mark of a Criminal Record. *American Journal of Sociology* 108(5):937–75.

Popkin, Susan J., Larry F. Buron, Diane K. Levy, and Mary K. Cunningham. 2000. The Gautreaux Legacy: What Might Mixed-Income and Dispersal Strategies Mean for the Poorest Public Housing Tenants? *Housing Policy Debate* 11(4):911–42.

Popkin, Susan J., Bruce Katz, Mary K. Cunningham, Karen D. Brown, Jeremy Gustafson, and Margery Austin Turner. 2004. *A Decade of Hope VI: Research Findings and Policy Challenges.* Washington, D.C.: Urban Institute.

Ricketts, Erol Roy, and Isabel V. Sawhill. 1986. *Defining and Measuring the Underclass.* Washington, D.C.: Urban Institute.

Rosenbaum, James. 1995. Changing the Geography of Opportunity by Expanding Residential Choice: Lessons from the Gautreaux Program. *Housing Policy Debate* 6(1):231–69.

Rosenbaum, James, Susan J. Popkin, Julie E. Kaufmann, and Jennifer Rusin. 1991. Social Integration of Low-Income Black Adults in Middle-Class White Suburbs. *Social Problems* 38(4):448–61.

Rosenbaum, James E., Linda K. Stroh, and Cathy A. Flynn. 1998. Lake Parc Place: A Study of Mixed-Income Housing. *Housing Policy Debate* 9(4):703–40.

Ryan, William, Allan Sloan, Mania Seferi, and Elaine Werby. 1974. *All in Together: An Evaluation of Mixed-Income Multi-Family Housing.* Boston: Housing Finance Authority.

Sampson, Robert J., and Byron W. Groves. 1989. Community Structure and Crime: Testing Social Disorganization Theory. *American Journal of Sociology* 94(4):774–802.

Sampson, Robert J., and Jeffery D. Morenoff. 1997. Ecological Perspectives on the Neighborhood Context of Urban Poverty: Past and Present. In *Neighborhood Poverty.* Volume II. *Policy Implications in Studying Neighborhoods*, ed. Jeanne Brooks-Gunn, Greg J. Duncan, and J. Lawrence Aber, 1–22. Newark, NJ: Russell Sage Foundation.

Sampson, Robert J., Stephen Raudenbush, and Felton Earls. 1997. Neighborhoods and Violent Crime: A Multilevel Study of Collective Efficacy. *Science* 277:918–24.

Schwartz, Alex, and Kian Tajbakhsh. 1997. Mixed-Income Housing: Unanswered Questions. *Cityscape: A Journal of Policy Development and Research* 3(2):71–92.

Shaw, Clifford R., and Henry D. McKay. 1969. *Juvenile Delinquency and Urban Areas: A Study of Rates of Delinquency in Relation to Differential Characteristics of Local Communities in American Cities.* Chicago: University of Chicago Press.

Smith, Alistair. 2002. *Mixed-Income Housing Developments: Promise and Reality.* Cambridge, MA: Harvard University, Joint Center for Housing Studies.

Stoloff, Jennifer A., Jennifer L. Glanville, and Elisa Jayne Bienenstock. 1999. Women's Participation in the Labor Force: The Role of Social Networks. *Social Networks* 21:91–108.

Turbov, Mindy, and Valerie Piper. 2005a. *HOPE VI and Mixed-Finance Redevelopments: A Catalyst for Neighborhood Renewal.* Washington, D.C.: Brookings Institution.

Turbov, Mindy, and Valerie Piper. 2005b. *HOPE VI and Mixed-Finance Redevelopments: A Catalyst for Neighborhood Renewal. Atlanta Case Study.* Washington, D.C.: Brookings Institution.

Turbov, Mindy, and Valerie Piper. 2005c. *HOPE VI and Mixed-Finance Redevelopments: A Catalyst for Neighborhood Renewal. Louisville Case Study: Park DuValle.* Washington, D.C.: Brookings Institution.

Turbov, Mindy, and Valerie Piper. 2005d. *HOPE VI and Mixed-Finance Redevelopments: A Catalyst for Neighborhood Renewal. Pittsburgh Case Study: Manchester.* Washington, D.C.: Brookings Institution.

Turbov, Mindy, and Valerie Piper. 2005e. *HOPE VI and Mixed-Finance Redevelopments: A Catalyst for Neighborhood Renewal. St. Louis Case Study: Murphy Park.* Washington, D.C.: Brookings Institution.

Vale, Lawrence J. 2002. *Reclaiming Public Housing: A Half Century of Struggle in Three Public Neighborhoods.* Cambridge, MA: Harvard University Press.

Valentine, Charles A. 1968. *Culture and Poverty: Critique and Counter Proposals.* Chicago: University of Chicago Press.

Varady, David, and Carole Walker. 2003. Housing Vouchers and Residential Mobility. *Journal of Planning Literature* 18(1):17–30.

Venkatesh, Sudhir A. 2000. *American Project: The Rise and Fall of a Modern Ghetto.* Cambridge, MA: Harvard University Press.

Venkatesh, Sudhir A., Isil Celimli, Douglas Miller, Alexandra Murphy, and Beauty Turner. 2004. *Chicago Public Housing Transformation: A Research Report.* New York: Columbia University, Center for Urban Research and Policy.

Verba, Sidney, Kaye Scholzman, and Henry E. Brady. 1995. *Voice and Equality: Civic Voluntarism in American Politics.* Cambridge, MA: Harvard University Press.

von Hoffman, Alexander. 1996. High Ambitions: The Past and Future of American Low-Income Housing Policy. *Housing Policy Debate* 7(3):423–46.

Wayne, Alex. 2006. Bush Making Progress in Efforts to End Public Housing Renewal Program. *Congressional Quarterly Today,* February 9. World Wide Web page http://www.knowledgeplex.org/news/148152.html?p=1 (accessed February 26).

Wellman, Barry. 1979. The Community Question: The Intimate Networks of East Yorkers. *American Journal of Sociology* 84(5):1201–27.

Wellman, Barry, and Barry Leighton. 1979. Networks, Neighborhoods, and Communities: Approaches to the Study of the Community Question. *Urban Affairs Quarterly* 14(3):363–90.

Wellman, Barry, and Scot Wortley. 1990. Different Strokes from Different Folks: Community Ties and Social Support. *American Journal of Sociology* (96)3:558–88.

Wilner, Daniel, Rosabelle P. Walkley, and Stuart W. Cook. 1952. Residential Proximity and Intergroup Relations in Public Housing Projects. *Journal of Social Issues* 8(1):45–69.

Wilner, Daniel, Rosabelle P. Walkley, and Stuart W. Cook. 1955. *Human Relations in Interracial Housing.* Minneapolis: University of Minnesota Press.

Wilson, William Julius. 1987. *The Truly Disadvantaged: The Inner City, the Underclass, and Public Policy.* Chicago: University of Chicago Press.

Wilson, William Julius. 1996. *When Work Disappears: The World of the New Urban Poor.* New York: Knopf.

Yancey, William L. 1972. Architecture, Interaction, and Social Control. In *Environment and the Social Sciences: Perspectives and Applications,* ed. Joachim F. Wohlwill and Daniel H. Carson, 126–36. Washington, D.C.: American Psychological Association.

27
"Reconciling people and place in housing and community development policy"

From *Georgetown Journal on Poverty Law and Policy* (2009)

Nestor M. Davidson

INTRODUCTION

A central debate in housing and community development policy has long revolved around the dichotomy between people-based and place-based policies.[1] As this divide is conventionally framed, people-based strategies invest in individuals, often with the explicit goal of allowing those individuals to move to a better life, while place-based strategies target specific communities or locations, often with the explicit goal of revitalizing entrenched pockets of poverty.[2] Thus, for example, tenant-based rental housing vouchers and "moving-to-opportunity" programs seek to empower low-income residents to escape failing communities, in a subsidized version of the perennial American penchant for new horizons. Conversely, some forms of project-based rental housing subsidies and many urban renewal policies seek to reinvigorate distressed neighborhoods.[3] Arguments about the proper focus of policymaking in this arena continue unabated.[4]

This Essay argues that this dichotomy is much more illusory than the traditional debate assumes, or, at the very least, it is more complicated. Every individual-level public investment in poverty reduction and mobility is constrained by geography and at the same time directly affects the places those individuals live. Likewise, every public investment in a

given place not only has a direct impact on the people in that place but more importantly shapes the incentives that people have to remain, leave, avoid, or move to that place. In short, to an extent the conventional discourse significantly obscures, people are place, and place is people, and it is important to focus on the interaction between these foci of policy-making.

This is not only an academic question. Insisting on framing policy choices in terms of a dichotomy between people and place – or between mobility and community – distorts the real tradeoffs at issue. Those tradeoffs have much more to do with persistently inadequate levels of public investment and seemingly mundane ground-level details of programmatic design that are, in practice, critical. Bringing to the fore the interaction between people and place, mobility and community, is a more fruitful way to approach policy design than using proxies that inadequately capture the real consequences of housing and community development strategies.

To explore this interactionist perspective, this Essay first reviews the conventional debate between people-based and place-based responses to poverty, then unpacks several fallacies underlying this perceived dichotomy, and, finally, outlines other conceptual models that might address more appropriately the concerns that have been channeled into this debate.

I. PEOPLE OR PLACE –
AN INTRACTABLE DILEMMA?

The debate about place-based versus people-based approaches has been etched in the evolution of housing and community development policy since at least the post-War era of urban renewal and the controversies over the significant displacement that those policies engendered. The "slum clearance" program launched by the federal Housing Act of 1949 and the later Model Cities programs were perhaps the classic place-based policies. These programs sought to eradicate poverty by radically changing the places where poverty (or, at least, urban poverty) most strongly persisted. Urban renewal – the infamous "federal bulldozer"[5] – leveled communities wholesale, guided by a top-down planning vision that not only ignored existing urban fabric, but also paid far too little heed to those living in the communities targeted by that renewal.[6]

The fact that the urban renewal policies of the 1950s and 1960s are generally, although not universally, understood to have failed spectacularly has fueled interest in policies that focus more on individuals in poverty and on preserving existing communities. Thus, in the 1960s, housing policy began to move from public housing to public-private partnerships that provided incentives for private owners to build and operate subsidized housing,[7] a model that was reinvented in the late 1980s through the Low-Income Housing Tax Credit (LIHTC) program.[8] In the 1970s, the pendulum in housing policy swung even more forcefully toward subsidies that were not tied to specific projects, notably with Section 8 of the Housing and Community Development Act of 1974, which opened the door to tenant-based rental vouchers as a predominant form of housing subsidy.[9]

Two recent innovations in housing policy illustrate the on-going tension in practice between mobility and place. In the 1990s, the HOPE VI program and the Moving to Opportunity for Fair Housing (MTO) demonstration program represented divergent progressions in the evolution of housing policy. HOPE VI provides funds to demolish and revitalize the most severely distressed public housing, seeking to replace pockets of extreme poverty with mixed-income communities designed in a new-urbanist spirit. HOPE VI has been controversial among some housing advocates, particularly on the ground that it does not sufficiently account for the displacement that comes from failing to replace public housing on a unit-for-unit basis. Nonetheless, it has become a contemporary symbol of the promise of place-making policies.

By contrast, the MTO program, modeled largely on the Chicago program that grew out of the famous *Gautreaux* litigation,[10] provided subsidies for families to move out of high-poverty neighborhoods. The premise of such mobility strategies is that individuals will fare better if they are in better neighborhoods, with less threat of crime, different peer groups, and better access to jobs and public services. The evidence supporting this premise is mixed,[11] but is sufficiently promising that mobility policies have become entrenched in the spectrum of approaches, offering – like place does in HOPE VI – the most recent model of individual intervention.

The people/place dichotomy is a staple of urban development and economic development writ large, as local governments vie for subsidies and favorable sources of tax revenue, but likewise work through individual citizens. This plays out, however, in particular ways in housing policy. The basic divide in the housing arena involves demand-side subsidies, particularly what are now called Housing Choice Vouchers, versus supply-side subsidies, which can include a variety of up-front capital or long-term operating subsidies. Vouchers are thought to promote individual preferences and mobility, have less impact on housing markets, and reduce the government's risk. Project-based subsidies, by contrast, are said to represent stable investments in quality housing, are less subject to the vicissitudes of local housing markets, and are an efficient locus for other social services.

Any number of other programs – from the 1977 Community Reinvestment Act, which sought to eliminate redlining in lending,[12] to an array of individual-level interventions such as job training, Temporary Assistance to Needy Families, the Earned-Income Tax Credit, and others – can be added to this mosaic. Although varying on many levels, all of these programs can be catalogued based on whether they seek in the first instance to revitalize specific places or emphasize poverty reduction by subsidizing and empowering individuals.

The pendulum that these competing approaches represent has generated sustained academic discourse.[13] One of the first commentators to frame the terms of the debate was Louis Winnick in his 1966 essay, *Place Prosperity versus People Prosperity*.[14] Winnick argued against place-based policies, which he colorfully derided as "planned intervention in favor of economically deficient areas."[15] Winnick asserted that place-based policies merely redistributed, rather than increased in the aggregate, employment, retail opportunities, and housing (with cities seeking to poach from suburbs, in his view). He described this cycle as "at best ... clumsy, expensive, and often inequitable."[16]

Winnick's skepticism about place-based strategies continues to engender critique.[17] Some commentators have argued that these policies address the external symptoms of poverty without attacking underlying causes, ironically adding to the concentration of poverty.[18] Others have argued that place-based policies incentivize individuals to remain in economically distressed communities, are cost-ineffective ways to solve localized externalities, and are not well designed to target appropriate recipients.[19]

On the other hand, place-based strategies have their defenders. Even skeptics of such policies acknowledge what economists describe as "spatial externalities."[20] Concentrated poverty brings a kind of localized multiplier effect, where the geographic nature of the lack of economic opportunity, often coupled with failing public services and a lack of public safety undermine individual attempts to break out of poverty.[21] Thus, many policymakers recognize that the only way to create real opportunity for many communities is to intervene to overcome the negative feedback loops that play out in some locations. Moreover, even severely distressed communities contain largely unappreciated economic and social capital, and can have a valuable "sense of place" that is potentially put at risk by policies that foster "escape."[22] The resulting reality is that in housing, community development, and in urban policy more generally, the current landscape represents an uneasy amalgam of place-based and people-based policies. Each new policy proposal – or event, like the devastation of New Orleans wrought by Hurricane Katrina – becomes an opportunity to rehash the debate.[23]

II. RECONCILING PEOPLE AND PLACE

Despite the length and strength of the debate on people-based versus place-based strategies, it is an unnecessary distraction. Thoughtful commentators have sought to transcend the dichotomy in several ways. Some have argued, for example, that "people" and "place" represent proxies for different problems that are in turn amenable to different solutions.[24] Others have argued that policy must pay attention to people and place at the same time, recognizing the conceptual pull of the dichotomy, but emphasizing the need for policies to respond to both sides of the divide.[25]

These are valuable perspectives with much force, but this Essay takes a different approach. Rather than isolate two seemingly oppositional targets of housing and community development policy, this Essay argues that it is important to explore the *interaction* between them. Every policy that seeks to alleviate individual poverty is constrained by location and, if successful, alters communities. Every policy that seeks to respond to the spatial concentration of poverty works through individuals.

A. How place constrains and is shaped by people-based strategies

Every investment in individual poverty reduction must confront the reality that individuals are constrained by their geography.[26] Income support of any kind, job training, housing vouchers, and other individual interventions flow to people who then must confront existing labor and housing markets and specific communities where the daily struggles of life play out. Markets that have, by definition, failed and in turn produced persistent poverty in the United States are largely geographically linked at the local level, even as they are increasingly shaped by global trade and capital markets. Thus the very housing, labor, retail, and related markets that generate the need for individual investments in turn constrain the impact of those investments.

For example, people receiving housing vouchers can only use those vouchers in pre-existing local housing markets, and there are significant psychic and material costs to leaving communities. It is hardly surprising, then, that without mobility counseling, individual voucher holders tend to utilize their vouchers in many of the same high poverty neighborhoods they were living in without subsidies.[27] Likewise, job training can only prepare people for those labor opportunities that are available. A similar recognition of the impact of context can apply to most individual-level interventions.

To some extent, describing policies as "people-based" is often used as a shorthand for mobility, with individual investments designed not just to lift people out of poverty but more specifically to subsidize their move to different communities. This emphasis on individual mobility, however, somewhat ironically elevates the centrality of place.[28] Indeed, one way to think about mobility policies is as place-based strategies disguised as people-based strategies. An underlying premise of programs like Gautreaux and MTO is that by moving to a new social context, individuals in poverty will experience better individual outcomes. There are many theories as to why place might make this difference – peer group effects, for example, or the added material and psychic benefits of lower-crime environments, among many others – but the premise remains that a new place means better outcomes.

If people are able to move out of pockets of poverty, however, they must still make their new lives work in a specific place. Indeed, some recipients of mobility subsidies are pushed to move back to higher poverty communities because of changes in the communities to which they moved (such as rising rents).[29] In this way, mobility as an anti-poverty strategy can be understood as being about capturing the benefits of place.

Mobility, moreover, can have a controversial impact on the places to which people move. Some critics of mobility programs argue that such programs merely export social dysfunction,[30] a proposition that is hotly contested by many experts.[31] This kind of exchange highlights the proposition that it is at least possible that places can be altered by individual mobility.

Conversely, if investments in individuals are successful, the mobility such investments generate can have significant effects on the communities left behind. As people move, the social fabric of a community can be damaged by the loss of certain members and a strategy that incentivizes that movement can have direct consequences on the communities from which people are escaping. If a job training or mobility voucher or other support leads people to find a better community, the place they leave behind is changed by that movement. To the extent that the success of mobility programs is predicated in part on the nature of the communities in which people live, creating incentives to break up distressed communities can further isolate those not able or willing to leave. Recognizing this fact is by no means meant to advocate relegating anyone to pockets of poverty, and mobility has always been a core aspect of the American identity. Rather, this is simply to highlight the reality that when some members of a community exit, that exit affects both those who leave and those who remain.[32]

B. How people shape and react to place-based strategies

Just as every investment in a given individual is constrained by place and changes the places where people live, every investment in a given place impacts specific people and, more importantly, changes the underlying incentive structure for individual mobility. On the most basic level, it is impossible to invest in a place without that investment at the same time being in the people in that place. It is true that a tax incentive or rezoning for a business to locate in a community benefits that business in the first instance, and geographically targeted incentives are not mobile. But someone has to fill the jobs that that new business creates and even if the fit between those for whom those opportunities are intended and the people who actually take advantage of them is imperfect (people shaping place-based policies), it is not entirely tangential.

Beyond the direct impact of place-based policies on individuals in those places, such policies shape incentives that influence where individuals live and work. Critics of place-based policies, like Glaeser, tend to underplay the reality that the individuals who are the focus of mobility policies are embedded in specific communities.[33] This is particularly odd given recognition by economists in particular of the interaction between place-based policies and individual mobility incentives in other contexts. Indeed, a significant vein in the literature on local governments and public finance depends largely on a vision of individuals as mobile consumers of place. This theory is generally associated with the economist Charles Tiebout, who famously argued that local governments can be understood to compete for mobile residents, offering different mixes of tax burdens and service levels in a never-ending process of "market" adjustments.[34] This so-called "Tiebout sorting" is predicated on the proposition that location is not fungible and that public investments in changing places will have relatively predictable effects on the individual incentive structure for mobility.[35]

Put another way, people move or stay where they are based in no small measure on opportunities, so changing places changes the structure of choice.[36] People move or stay based on the resources they have as well as the opportunities they can access, and mobility programs directly target resource questions.[37] But changing a place not only changes whether or not people want to stay in or leave that place. Such policies also ripple to how others around that place choose to interact with it. For example, public investments in distressed communities often spark gentrification. Although the predicates for gentrification are classically place-based – infrastructure, public safety, incentives for developers, and the like – the consequences are decidedly personal. As communities become more desirable, more affluent residents are drawn in. At the same time, low-income residents are too often required to move to other high-poverty communities because that is all that they can afford. Place-based interventions thus become unintentional "mobility" programs in an unfortunate mirror to programs like MTO and Gautreaux.

Places are dynamic communities of individuals who are subject to incentives to move. It is only a question of time horizon for a successful place-based intervention to change the community it targets as well as those connected to it in any way. Today's "economically deficient areas"[38] can be tomorrow's boom towns – as locations across the country have experienced in the past fifteen years – and every intervention creates a new set of incentives for people to move.[39]

To the extent, then, that a significant critique of place-based policies turns on targeting,[40] it is certainly true that any effort to create new economic and social conditions will inevitably change the individuals who live in the targeted communities, and those individuals will not have any entitlement to remain. That, however, is less a critique of place-based policymaking than a recognition of a certain shortsightedness in implementation.

III. REFRAMING THE DEBATE

Reconciling people-based and place-based policies in housing and community development requires a renewed focus on the interaction between people and place, recognizing that while geography is destiny, all places are interconnected and places are largely significant because of the people in those places. This insight brings to the fore more pressing questions, such as whether relevant markets – for housing, for labor, for other opportunities – are failing and whether the response to those market failures is sufficiently robust and appropriately sensitive to long-term consequences. What matters most is how any given investment in poverty reduction is structured, how it operates, and whether it is sufficiently funded. Individual housing vouchers can be a tool for community revitalization if they carry the right level of subsidy and are structured to account for neighborhood effects. Likewise, project-based subsidies can alleviate rather than contribute to concentrated poverty and segregation if new construction and subsidies for the preservation of existing housing focus on a diverse set of communities. And public housing can be – and in some communities, increasingly has become – an engine of economic and racial integration rather than segregation.

On the other hand, each of these programs can have negative consequences in the place/people nexus – creating the wrong kinds of incentives, concentrating poverty, and undermining the very goals to which affordable housing and community development policy are dedicated. Any argument that public interventions on one side or the other of that nexus (or on both people and place with insufficient attention to how each affects the other) is sufficient in and of itself ignores a vital interactive reality.

Debates about the relative merits of supply-side and demand-side subsidies should thus become debates about whether rent levels and operating subsidies are set appropriately, whether public investments are being managed wisely, and whether the communities these policies are helping to form are sustainable, diverse, and vibrant. These all raise knotty empirical questions beyond the scope of this brief Essay, but the important point is that it is necessary to see the interaction between people and place in every program.

Ultimately, then, understanding the nexus between these two foci of policy can give renewed impetus to arguments for additional support and can serve as a reminder that the micro-level details of policy design are critical. Every policy has unintended consequences, but poverty programs are destined to repeat past failures if they are not designed carefully to address holistically individual incentives, market forces, the nature of community, and the importance of context. People are place and places are people, and understanding this is vital to any effort to alleviate poverty.

Notes

1 See Randall Crane and Michael Manville, People or Place? Revisiting the Who Versus Where of Urban Development, *20 Land Lines* 2 (July 2008); William Wheaton, Commentary, *Brookings-Wharton Papers on Urban Affairs 2000*, at 93–96 (discussing place-based versus people-based policies); Roger Bolton, Place Prosperity vs. People Prosperity Revisited: An Old Issue with a New Angle, *29 Urban Stud.* 185 (1992); see also John M. Quigley, A Decent Home: Housing Policy in Perspective, *Brookings-Wharton Papers on Urban Affairs 2000*, at 84–85 (discussing project-based versus tenant-based housing subsidies); cf. Matthew Edel, 'People' versus 'Places' in Urban Impact Analysis, in *The Urban Impacts of Federal Policies* 175 (Norman J. Glickman ed., 1980).

2 See Crane and Manville, supra note 1, at 3–4.

3 Although this conceptual distinction is a staple of housing and community development policy, it is by no means unique to that policy arena. A similar debate, for example, plays out in education policy, pitting advocates of neighborhood schools against proponents of school vouchers, framed around similar arguments about community versus choice.

4 This debate even featured, albeit briefly, in the recent presidential campaign – a rare moment in which poverty policies have garnered national attention. See David Brooks, Edwards, Obama and the Poor, *New York Times*, July 30, 2007, at A19 (comparing the anti-poverty policies of Senator Barack Obama and former Senator John Edwards based on their relative emphasis on place-based and person-based approaches); Edward Glaeser, Where Edwards is Right, *New York Sun*, Aug. 7, 2007 (arguing that Edwards' person-based policies are preferable to Obama's place-based policies because they focus more on "helping poor people than poor places").

5 See generally *Martin Anderson, The Federal Bulldozer: A Critical Analysis of Urban Renewal 1942–1962* (1964).

6 See Wendell Pritchett, The Public Menace of Blight: Urban Renewal and the Private Uses of Eminent Domain, 21 *Yale L. and Pol'y Rev.* 1 (2003).

7 See Quigley, supra note 1, at 61–62.

8 Production subsidies at the federal level declined significantly for decades outside the context of the LIHTC, which was passed as part of the Tax Reform Act of 1986. See generally Charles J. Orlebeke, The Evolution of Low-Income Housing Policy, 1949 to 1999, 11 *Housing Pol'y Debate* 489 (2000). Recently, Congress created a National Housing Trust Fund as part of the Housing and Economic Recovery Act of 2008 (H.R. 3221), signed into law on July 30, 2008. The Trust Fund has the potential to represent a significant new source of federal housing funding, although because the Fund was to have been capitalized through Fannie Mae and Freddie Mac, the current economic crisis has significantly complicated this promise.

9 See Quigley, supra note 1, at 64.

10 See Nestor Davidson, Cooperative Localism: Federal-Local Collaboration in an Era of State Sovereignty,93 VA. L. REV. 959, 1029–31 (2007) (discussing the Gautreaux litigation and its aftermath). In the Gautreaux Program, African-American families received Section 8 subsidies to move to white or racially-mixed

communities. See generally *Alexander Polikoff, Waiting for Gautreaux: A story of segregation, housing, and the black ghetto* (2006).

11 See, e.g., Margery Austin Turner and Xavier Briggs, Assisted Housing Mobility and the Success of Low-Income Minority Families: Lessons for Policy, Practice, and Future Research, *Urban Institute Metropolitan Housing and Communities Center Brief* (March 2008); John Goering, Place-Based Poverty, Social Experimentation, and Child Outcomes: A Report of Mixed Effects, 13 *Children, Youth and ENV.* 1 (2003).

12 See Michael S. Barr, Credit Where It Counts: The Community Reinvestment Act and Its Critics, 80 N.Y.U. L. REV. 513 (2005).

13 See sources cited, supra note 1.

14 Louis Winnick, Place Prosperity versus People Prosperity: Welfare Considerations in Geographic Redistribution of Economic Activity, in *Essays in Urban Land Economics* 273 (1966); see Crane and Manville, supra note 1, at 4 (discussing Winnick's role in this debate).

15 Winnick, supra note 14, at 274.

16 Id. at 280.

17 See Crane and Manville, supra note 1, at 3.

18 See Wheaton, supra note 1, at 95; see also Michael H. Schill and Susan M. Wachter, The Spatial Bias of Federal Housing Law and Policy: Concentrated Poverty in Urban America, 143 U. PA. L. REV. 1285 (1995) (arguing that "federal housing law and policy have exhibited a locational bias that has promoted the growth of large concentrations of poor people in the inner city" for most of the twentieth century).

19 See Edward L. Glaeser and Joshua D. Gottlieb, The Economics of Place-Making Policies, *Brookings Papers on Economic Activity* (Douglas W. Elmendorf, N. Gregory Mankiw, and Lawrence H. Summers, eds., 2008).

20 See Crane and Manville, supra note 1, at 3.

21 Cf. *William Julius Wilson, The Truly Disadvantaged: The Inner City, The Underclass, and Public Policy* (1987).

22 See Bolton, supra note 1, at 193.

23 See, e.g., Edward L. Glaeser, Should the Government Rebuild New Orleans, Or Just Give Residents Checks?, 2 (4) *The Economists' Voice*, Art. 4, available at http://www.bepress.com/ev/vol2/iss4/art4Edward Glaeser; Crane and Manville, supra note 1.

24 See Crane and Manville, supra note 1, at 3–4 (arguing that the debate should be viewed not as a dichotomy, but as "two distinct, although not wholly separate problems": individual poverty, on the one hand, and the provision of "community-based shared goods" on the other); id. at 6.

25 See Turner and Briggs, supra note 11, at 1 (arguing that "initiatives that promote housing mobility should not substitute for investing in the revitalization of distressed communities; both place-based and people-based strategies should be vigorously pursued.").

26 There is a burgeoning critical literature on law and geography that usefully identifies the spatial aspects of legal questions and the interaction between place, space and power. See David Delaney, Richard T. Ford, and Nicholas Bromley, Preface: Where is Law?, in *The Legal Geographies Reader: Law, Power, and Space* (Nicholas Bromley *et al.* eds., 2001). A central insight from this literature that is relevant to debates about people-based versus place-based policies is the social construction of space. Id. Hence, the notion of "place" itself deserves interrogation and much of the criticism of place-based strategies may be chafing at the contested nature of how localities are constituted.

27 See Turner and Briggs, supra note 11, at 3.

28 It is also important to recognize that discrimination remains a formidable barrier that shadows the entire people-based and place-based debate. Thus, the Gautreaux and the MTO programs were as much about racial integration as they were or are about economic opportunity.

29 See Turner and Briggs, supra note 11, at 3.

30 See Hannah Rosin, American Murder Mystery, *Atlantic Monthly* (July/Aug. 2008).

31 See Xavier de Souza Briggs and Peter Dreier, Memphis Murder Mystery? No, Just Mistaken Identity, *Shelterforce* (July 22, 2008), available at http://www.shelterforce.org/article/special/1043/.

32 Of course, if individual interventions were ever sufficiently robust to lift individuals out of poverty on a wholesale basis, that would clearly make significant place-based changes.

33 See supra text accompanying notes 13–19.

34 See Charles M. Tiebout, A Pure Theory of Local Expenditures, 64 *J. POL. ECON.* 416 (1956).

35 See id.

36 Cf. *Albert O. Hirschman, Exit, Voice, and Loyalty: Responses to Decline in Firms, Organizations, and States* (1970).

37 And, as noted, forces such as discrimination can constrain individuals. Fair housing and similar legislation can be understood as an attempt to overcome such constraints.

38 Winnick, supra note 14, at 274.

39 It bears noting that the critique of place-based policies that they create incentives for individuals to remain in economically distressed locations assumes that such policies can have no actual effect in transforming those places. Surely, many place-based policies fail (just as many individual-based policies do), but it would be impossible to look at the work of community development corporations and local governments across the country and declare such work a universal failure. The list of communities that have been turned around is significant – even in some of the most challenging circumstances. This is not to endorse place-based policies, but merely to note that equating investments in place with a singular outcome (the concentration of poverty) is to misunderstand the nature of such investments.

40 See Crane and Manville, supra note 1, at 3.

The relationship between land use regulations and housing choices

Plate 6 "Suburbia" – Highlands Ranch, a Denver suburb, Adams County, Colorado, July 15, 1997 (photograph: Airphoto – Jim Wark).

INTRODUCTION TO PART SIX

The regulation of land use and building form – through land use planning, zoning ordinances and building codes – has been a central function of planning since the early twentieth century. Early regulations were justified by the public health threats posed by overcrowded tenements and by the impediments to investment that the lack of certainty about neighboring properties produced. In response to these concerns, local zoning ordinances enabled the separation of land uses thought incompatible and regulated height and building mass to ensure that sunlight and fresh air reached the streets. Over time, health and safety became the rationale for suburban single family home settlements, and the assumed threats to property values posed by proximity to other types of housing and non-residential land uses became enshrined in local planning practice. Selections included in this section highlight the disagreement among researchers and policy makers regarding the purposes of regulation and thus, on how to best judge costs and benefits.

The rising cost of housing and increase in environmental regulation since the late 1970s has prompted increasing debate over the impact of various forms of regulation on housing costs and prices. Since the first Bush administration in the early 1990s, HUD has placed increased emphasis on identifying and removing regulatory barriers to the development of affordable housing. Over time, this discussion has broadened to encompass the barriers posed to residential development more generally. Indeed, economists Quigley and Raphael (2004) have attributed at least part of the increase in housing prices during the 1990s to regulations limiting the supply of housing. In his article "Regulations and Housing Development: What We Know," Michael H. Schill presents a daunting list of regulations with the potential to reduce the supply of housing and thus increase market prices. To his list he adds the costs imposed by lengthy government review processes. Despite agreement on the connection between reduced housing supply, rising quality standards and rising housing prices, Schill reminds us that such costs may be justified by the public purposes behind regulations. Absent agreement on these purposes, it is not possible to understand or place a meaningful value on costs generated by regulations or to balance them against benefits, and judge how both costs and benefits are distributed.

Historically, the argument against zoning has centered on its use a tool for racial exclusion. The groundwork for the postwar segregation of U.S. cities and suburbs was set through Depression-era FHA mortgage insurance guidelines, which favored new construction, single-family detached housing and racial exclusion, and by the Housing Acts of 1949 and 1954, which gave local jurisdictions control over production and siting of public housing.

Before 1950, zoning regulations and deed-restrictions could legally block minority households from moving into white neighborhoods. However, after Brown v. Board of Education and passage of the Civil Rights and Fair Housing Acts, explicitly racial zoning was no longer tolerated by the courts. Instead, exclusion of minorities was accomplished through the creation of independent suburban jurisdictions that were able to set their own zoning rules and effectively price out lower income, minority households.

Of course, regulations do not have to explicitly target racial groups to be discriminatory – they can accomplish much the same thing by excluding particular types of housing where minority groups are more likely to reside. Many postwar white suburban communities became adept at setting lot sizes and other zoning rules to exclude apartments and modest homes for sale, ostensibly to protect single family home values. In "Local Land Use and the Chain of Exclusion," Rolf Pendall examines the relationship between four types of land use regulations and racial exclusion, and finds the strongest evidence of a relationship for large lot zoning. Through the "chain of exclusion," low-density development reduces overall housing growth, and limits development of multi-unit housing, targeted mostly to renters. Both have the effect of reducing options for minority households. The net effect was to keep rental housing out of the suburbs and concentrate it in cities.

Disagreements over the public purposes of regulations are often obscured by ideological debates. The debate over inclusionary zoning provides a stark example. On the whole, the literature on inclusionary housing policies and programs largely divides into two camps: one largely focused on documenting the effects on the housing market of regulation, where costs are presented largely absent discussion of countervailing benefits, and another focused on describing the rather diverse array of existing programs, the strategies used to achieve them, and their performance in terms of affordable units produced – with less explicit discussion of who bears the costs.

Bento, et al.'s article, "Housing Market Effects of Inclusionary Zoning," presents an economic analysis of the impact of inclusionary zoning on housing prices, housing starts, and single-family home size under California's policies between 1988 and 2005. They carefully note the impacts on both single family and multifamily housing, but refrain from assessing the impact of the program on "social welfare." Their finding that the California program has increased production of multifamily units could arguably be presented as a very positive result, consistent with the public purpose of increasing housing choices for low-income and minority households.

Arguably, environmental concerns are driving the most sweeping changes in land use, zoning and building codes since the 1920s. Public awareness and concern regarding the impact of unchecked population growth on the environment has motivated a succession of strategies for controlling, managing or re-shaping urban growth, dating back to the 1970s (Fischel 2004). In the context of jurisdictional fragmentation, efforts to limit growth are often imposed unevenly and have the potential to reinforce or create new exclusionary patterns. By adopting "smart growth" techniques and mechanisms, local governments can effectively, whether intentionally or not, price out many residents.

As with inclusionary zoning, growth management or sustainable growth policies differ from place to place. Existing research largely chronicles the experience of leaders in the field, with debate focused on determining the costs and benefits of Portland's metropolitan growth boundary, in particular. Portland places severe restrictions on subdivision of farmland, preserves open space, and discourages all growth outside the boundary. At the same time, the law allows for dramatically higher densities inside the growth boundary. Nelson and Wachter argue, in "Growth Management and Affordable Housing Policy," that while many existing policies have provoked a rise in housing prices, by increasing housing densities, mandating a mix of housing types and promoting fair share or inclusionary housing requirements, such policies can successfully balance environmental and social goals.

The focus on increased density is also found in current proposals to use density to foster greater use of public transportation, particularly rail-based transit. Rather than acting to moderate housing prices, recent research suggests that redevelopment in "transit rich neighborhoods" – particular those adding light rail lines – may have the unintended consequence of pricing out low income renters (Pollack, et al. 2011). Whether current efforts can avoid creating a new "chain of exclusion" for low income renters, and justify the inclusionary mandates or public spending necessary to do so, remains to be seen.

In the end, discussion of regulation must return us to the public purposes of regulation and link these to the distribution of costs and benefits. Land use and building regulations, reflecting local planning priorities, will continue to shape where low income residents can live and the types and prices of housing available to them. Emerging rationales return us to the health and safety of the public – this time through arguments about how development patterns affect the environment. We must continue to examine the connection between these new approaches to planning for sustainability and the location and accessibility of housing to low income and minority residents.

IN THIS PART:

REFERENCES AND ADDITIONAL READINGS

Calavita, Nico, Kenneth Grimes and Allan Mallach. (1997). "Inclusionary housing in California and New Jersey: A comparative analysis." *Housing Policy Debate*, 8(1): 109–42.
Fischel, William A. (2004). "An economic history of zoning and a cure for its exclusionary effects." *Urban Studies*, 41(2): 317–40.
Ihlanfeldt, Keith. (2007). "The effect of land use regulation on housing and land prices." *Journal of Urban Economics*, 61(3): 420–35.
Jackson, Kenneth. (1985). *Crabgrass Frontier: The Suburbanization of the United States*. New York: Oxford University Press. Chapter 11: "Federal subsidy and the suburban dream: How Washington changed the American housing market," pp. 190–218
McClure, Kirk. (2010). "The prospects for guiding housing choice voucher households to high opportunity neighborhoods." *Cityscape: A Journal of Policy Development and Research*, 12(3): 101–22.
Quigley, John M. and Steven Raphael. (2004). "Is housing unaffordable? Why isn't it more affordable?" *Journal of Economic Perspectives*, 18(1): 191–214.
Schuetz, Jenny, Rachel Meltzer, and Vicki Been. (2009). "31 flavors of inclusionary zoning: Comparing policies from San Francisco, Washington, D.C., and suburban Boston." *Journal of the American Planning Association*, 75(4): 441–56.

28
"Regulations and housing development: What we know"

From *Cityscape* (2005)

Michael H. Schill

University of California, Los Angeles

INTRODUCTION

In recent years, policymakers and academics have paid increasing attention to the costs of federal, state, and local regulations. Perhaps nowhere is this research more important than in the area of housing. From 1990 to 2002, the median sales price of new homes rose by 52 percent, outpacing the change in the Consumer Price Index by a substantial margin (National Association of Home Builders, 2004). At least part of this increase in price is attributable to increased land costs caused by government regulation (Quigley and Raphael, 2004). Inflated land and construction costs, in turn, reduce total housing supply and, in many jurisdictions, contribute to affordability problems.[1] In some municipalities, the high cost of housing may even retard economic growth.

This article will assess the current state of knowledge about the impacts of federal, state, and local regulations on the supply and cost of housing. [...] [W]e know very little about the effect of many forms of government intervention, such as building codes and environmental regulations, on housing prices in general, let alone the impact on affordable housing. Even where the literature is most abundant (that is, zoning and land use regulation), we have wide gaps in our knowledge.

Part 1 of this article briefly explores the concept of regulatory barriers to development. In common parlance, regulatory barrier is used to refer to something negative, a rule that rational lawmakers should seek to repeal or eliminate. Defining a regulatory barrier precisely, however, is difficult and often value laden.

Studies that seek to estimate the costs and benefits of regulations, while perhaps not the final word on whether a given regulation should be rejected or modified, do have an important role to play in helping policymakers analyze the tradeoffs involved. Part 2 summarizes the existing state of knowledge about the effects building codes, land use regulations, impact fees, environmental regulations, and administrative delays have on the cost and supply of housing, in general, and affordable housing, in particular.

The ambiguity of the concept of regulatory barriers and the gaps of knowledge concerning the impacts of regulations are two reasons why proposals to eliminate expensive government red tape and regulatory requirements have had only limited success in the United States. Part 3 describes these efforts and presents reasons for why the problem is so impervious to solution.

PART 1. WHAT ARE REGULATORY BARRIERS?

Many regulations that increase the cost of housing or reduce its supply typically are not characterized as regulatory barriers. For example, many municipalities enact building codes that mandate the use of fire-retardant materials or zoning laws that prohibit housing in close proximity to chemical plants. These laws make housing less affordable, but we think of this effect as an unfortunate byproduct of rules necessary to promote health and safety, not as a barrier to be removed. In his 1990 request to former U.S. Department of Housing and Urban Development (HUD) Secretary Jack Kemp to create what came to be known as the Advisory Commission on Regulatory Barriers to Affordable Housing, President George H.W. Bush characterized the problem as "excessive rules, regulations, and red tape that add unnecessarily to the cost of housing ..." (Advisory Commission on Regulatory Barriers to Affordable Housing, 1991: 1).

Distinguishing between unnecessary regulatory barriers that should be removed and necessary or useful regulation that should be preserved is an extraordinarily difficult task. Governments frequently enact regulations for a variety of reasons that directly and indirectly affect the supply and cost of housing. In many instances, the regulations are deemed necessary to promote the health and well-being of either the residents of buildings or the community as a whole. For example, housing codes were promulgated in the late 19th century to prevent disease and unhealthful conditions by setting minimum requirements for sanitary facilities, light, and air (Lubove, 1962). Building codes were enacted to prevent fire and ensure the safety of adjacent buildings and their residents, as well as firefighters (Wermiel, 2000).

Many other regulations are justified on the grounds of externalities that might be less immediately threatening. For example, in 1926, when the U.S. Supreme Court ruled in Euclid v. Ambler Realty (272 U.S. 365 [1926]) that zoning was a constitutional exercise of the police power, it did so expressly on the ground that zoning would prevent nuisances. The prohibited activity need not be something illegal but might be "merely a right thing in the wrong place – like a pig in the parlor instead of the barnyard." Large lot zoning, minimum setbacks, and required architectural standards all fit within this set of purposes.

A wide variety of environmental regulations also fits, ranging from federal and state laws to preserve wetland habitats to those that limit development that would endanger certain species of animals. More recently, efforts to limit suburban sprawl also may be thought of as efforts to internalize externalities such as automobile pollution and traffic congestion.

Governments also enact regulations to fund needed or desired facilities and public services. Subdivision regulations typically require developers to set aside land for roadways, schools, and parks. Impact fees, at least in theory, are imposed to charge developers the marginal costs of services that arise from new housing and its occupants.

Each of these regulations serves an important public purpose. Their potentially negative impact on the supply and cost of housing is a secondary byproduct of the government action. Of course, these same regulations can be adopted by governments for the primary purpose of inhibiting the supply of housing built in a jurisdiction and/or increasing its price. Such regulations could promote scarcity, thereby increasing the values of existing homes and the wealth of residents (Thorson, 1996).

More commonly, local governments will seek to limit housing development for fiscal reasons. Because local governments must raise taxes to fund schools and other needed public services, they typically are under pressure to promote certain types of development over others. Commercial uses and large homes that generate substantial tax collections (known as "fiscal zoning") are favored; dense housing developments and low-cost housing that increase demand for schools and social services beyond the tax revenues they generate are disfavored. Large lot zoning, expensive subdivision regulations, excessive building codes, and prohibitions on multifamily housing can effectively ensure that the price of housing is so expensive as to prevent cross-subsidization (Hamilton, 1978).

While sometimes difficult to distinguish from fiscal zoning, many of these same regulations can be used by municipalities to promote social or racial homogeneity. In some instances, residents of a town will be concerned with the disamenities that could arguably arise from close proximity with people who are different from themselves. In other instances, residents may be motivated by racist or classist impulses.

Indeed, the difficulty of distinguishing an economically valid use of government regulation from a less acceptable use is exemplified by the Euclid case itself. Much of the court's opinion in Euclid was devoted to a defense of efforts to separate apartment buildings from single-family homes, even though that issue was not implicated by the facts of the case. This defense has led many to believe that the decision is less a case about externality prevention than a case about the use of government regulation to preserve income homogeneity.[2] In seeking to separate "bad" regulations (that is, regulatory barriers) from "good" ones, it is extremely perilous to look solely at the effects of these regulations on the price of housing. Many regulations may increase the price of housing by affecting the desirability of the neighborhood where it is located or the quality of the structure. Increased demand induced by the greater amenities required by the laws may generate price increases (Fischel, 1990).

Thus, one is immediately drawn to the concept of economic efficiency. To the extent that the social costs of a regulation exceed its social benefits, it would seem that the rule or ordinance would meet President Bush's criteria of excessive and unnecessary. A more difficult question surrounds those regulations that are efficient but generate unsatisfactory distributional results. For example, some regulations may generate a surplus of benefits over costs, but the benefits will primarily inure to higher income families and the costs to low- and moderate-income families. This problem is highlighted in Vicki Been's article on impact fees (2005). Theoretically, impact fees could be imposed in such a way as to promote an economically efficient level of development activity in a jurisdiction if they were set at an amount that reflected the marginal cost of development to that community. At the same time, to the extent that the impact fees were to be passed forward to future owners of housing or were to cause an owner of land to substitute other, more expensive housing types for dense, moderate-income housing, this gain in economic efficiency might be achieved at the cost of affordability.[3] Is the impact fee a barrier to affordable housing, or is affordable housing an inefficient use of land in this community?

To some degree, the answer to both of these questions is "yes." The question of whether a regulation constitutes a barrier that needs to be removed may sometimes depend on how much housing is valued compared to other social objectives. Research may not provide a clear answer to a question that is inexorably intermixed with politics and difficult moral and social questions. Social science, however, can

still be helpful. Cost/benefit analyses of regulations can be useful in identifying which laws do little except drive up the cost of housing. Presumably, those regulations in which economic costs exceed their benefits, and which reduce affordable housing, would be prime candidates for removal. Even in instances when economic efficiency and equity concerns point in different directions, careful theoretical and empirical research can help us understand the relevant tradeoffs and identify which regulations are least beneficial and/or most problematic. Such research also may provide us with information to modify existing regulations to reduce their negative effects on affordable housing.

PART 2. REGULATIONS AND HOUSING: AN ASSESSMENT OF THE LITERATURE

The articles prepared for this volume extensively review the theoretical and empirical literature on the effects of regulation on the supply and cost of housing. One of the most consistent findings [in existing theoretical and empirical literature on the effects of regulation on the supply and cost of housing] is how little we know about the subject. For some regulations, such as building codes and environmental regulations, the literature barely exists. For others, such as land use regulations and impact fees, many studies exist, but the results are often contradictory and difficult to interpret.

Building codes

Building codes set forth the minimum standards that developers are required to meet when they construct housing. There is consensus that building codes are both a legitimate and necessary exercise of government's police powers. The fact that codes may raise the price of housing is unsurprising because, in many instances, the housing built under the codes is of a higher quality than would be constructed otherwise.

Building codes, however, also can become regulatory barriers under certain circumstances (Downs, 1991). For example, some codes require the use of materials or production processes that go well beyond minimum health and safety requirements. Sometimes, the reason for this is benign, such as legislative delays in revising a code to keep current with new technology. States and municipalities also might mandate redundant, or "belt and suspenders," regulations out of an overabundance of caution. In other instances, however, expense-generating code provisions might result from lobbying by building materials manufacturers or labor unions. Alternatively, building codes may be a covert way to exclude housing that is affordable to low- and moderate-income families.

In recent years, we have made tremendous progress in promoting the adoption of model building codes throughout the nation. Most recently, three regional codes have been supplanted by two national/international codes. Yet, a few jurisdictions have not adopted either of the model codes. Many more have made significant changes to the model code provisions. The ability of states and municipalities to customize codes can serve important public purposes, especially when the type of construction in a jurisdiction or the jurisdiction's soil or seismic conditions are sufficiently different from those in the rest of the country. As building codes become less uniform because of these jurisdictional changes, however, more complexity is introduced, and the likelihood increases that they could serve as barriers to entry for national developers. Each of these factors could lead to higher production costs. Complexity also can create delay because of the greater need for discretionary approvals or explanations from government officials.

The literature on the impact of building codes on the price of housing is extremely thin. Much of it is so old as to be useful only for historic interest. Among the handful of studies completed after 1980, almost all are based on anecdotal accounts or poorly specified models. According to Listokin and Hattis (2005), the more quantitative studies suggest that the impact of building codes on price is no more than 5 percent.

Depreciation reduces the quantity of housing services a given housing unit provides over time. Building codes, therefore, also can affect housing supply by hindering the rehabilitation of buildings. In many jurisdictions, rehabilitation is subject to the same minimum standards as new construction. Therefore, to meet the requirements imposed by newer technologies, entire systems will have to be replaced at great expense. In an effort to overcome those costs, some states have enacted "smart codes" specifically geared toward rehabilitation. For example, according to Listokin and Hattis (2005), the adoption of a rehabilitation code by the state of New Jersey may have reduced rehabilitation costs by between 10 and 40 percent and increased the amount of building renovation activity substantially.

Environmental regulations

Over the past 25 years, the scope and quantity of environmental protection regulations have grown tremendously. Many of these laws have a direct or indirect impact on housing development. Among the two most important laws are the federal Clean Water Act, which limits development in wetlands, and the Endangered Species Act, which restricts development in areas where more than 600 species live. Many states also have enacted environmental protection laws limiting where and how development can take place. In addition, governments at all levels often require developers who need discretionary government approvals or who build on government land to undertake extensive environmental impact analyses, sometimes culminating in the preparation of voluminous environmental impact statements.

More recently, states and municipalities have enacted additional regulations under the banner of "smart growth." Smart growth is a catchall phrase that typically encompasses a variety of policies to limit growth at the periphery of metropolitan areas and, in some formulations, incentives to increase density in more central areas. Municipalities, most often those located in the outer suburban rings, have reduced permitted densities or begun to ration building permits. A few jurisdictions, most notably in the state of Oregon, have adopted urban growth boundaries – severe restrictions on residential construction at the periphery. The stated purpose of these regulations is to preserve greenfields, reduce traffic congestion, and, occasionally, promote reinvestment and development in more dense, urbanized areas.

Economic theory unambiguously predicts that environmental regulations will increase the price of housing. For example, regulations could affect the price of developable land.

Assuming constant demand, as the supply of land available for development decreases, the price of land should increase. In addition, at least some environmental protection statutes should generate amenities that may increase demand, thereby further intensifying the price effect.

Government rules requiring developers and/or public entities to undertake environmental impact analyses also are likely to generate higher costs and lead to a diminished supply of housing for two reasons. First, the review itself and the possible resulting environmental impact statement could be very costly. Second, potential lawsuits from neighbors or environmental activists challenging the review could be even more problematic. In addition to assuming the costs of defending the case, the developer would have to factor into the project the costs of delay and settlement. In some instances, this uncertainty actually may deter builders from undertaking projects, thereby reducing the overall supply of housing and increasing price.

Surprisingly, very few academic studies have investigated the relationship between environmental protection statutes and housing supply and prices. As Kiel (2005) indicates, the few studies that have been completed tend to show that, as expected, the value of land that is restricted falls and demand for land nearby tends to increase. The most relevant study by Frech and Lafferty (1984) of land preservation regulations implemented by the California Coastal Commission found that the prices of homes close to restricted areas increased by between $2,882 and $5,040 in 1975 dollars, and that those further inland went up by $989 to $1,700. The difference between these two sets of numbers captures the amenity effect, whereas the increases further away capture the supply effects of the regulations.

Portland, Oregon's urban growth boundary, while not technically an environmental regulation, has been the subject of much debate and recent analysis. Some studies have suggested that the restrictions on development imposed by the greenbelt increased housing prices (Staley and Mildner, 1999). Other studies have argued that any increase in housing prices in Portland was more attributable to increased demand for living in the city and other demographic factors (Downs, 2002; Phillips and Goodstein, 2000).

Zoning and land use

Zoning and land use regulations are ubiquitous in the United States. Traditionally, zoning sought to separate uses that might be incompatible – industrial uses were to be located in certain portions of a municipality and residential uses in another. Over time, ordinances made finer distinctions within each type of use (for example, single-family versus multifamily) and imposed an array of requirements on the permitted size and bulk of the buildings allowed (for example, height restrictions and minimum floor area requirements). In addition to promulgating traditional zoning requirements, municipalities enacted requirements for developers who sought to subdivide their properties. Oftentimes, developers would need to provide roads, schools, and other public facilities to the municipality in return for the privilege of being able to develop and sell the housing. Over time, the variety of land use regulations has mushroomed. Today, many jurisdictions have implemented growth control ordinances that ration the number of building permits that will be granted in any particular year. In addition, many municipalities prescribe and enforce architectural standards through their land use and subdivision regulations.

As described in Part I, municipalities have a variety of motives for imposing limitations on the use and density of new housing, including the desire to reduce negative externalities, keep tax rates low, achieve monopoly profits, and promote racial and economic homogeneity. Just as with environmental regulations, typical zoning and land use regulations, if enforced, are likely to increase the price of housing. Limitations on density or requirements that developers provide costly amenities to a community, if not capitalized into the price of land, will be passed forward to the ultimate purchasers or renters of housing. Even if the cost of the regulations is passed back to the owners of vacant land, density restrictions (and growth controls) of the type imposed by most towns and cities will lead to lower levels of production, and, therefore, higher prices for existing housing. At the same time, to the extent that land use regulations successfully protect against negative externalities, housing prices will go up because of increased demand.

In contrast to building codes and environmental regulations, many studies examine the impact of land use regulations on the price and quantity of housing. According to Quigley and Rosenthal (2005: 69), "[c]aps on development, restrictive zoning limits on allowable densities, urban growth boundaries, and long permit-processing delays have all been associated with increased housing prices." With the exception of a few studies suggesting that some municipalities use zoning as a way to achieve monopoly pricing, however, the research largely fails to sort out whether the supply effect or the amenity effect predominates.

Impact fees

In addition to, or in lieu of, subdivision exactions, many jurisdictions levy impact fees on the developers of new housing. The purpose of these fees, at least in theory, is to promote efficient development by requiring developers or consumers of new housing to absorb the marginal cost of the development to the municipality. A second related purpose is to shift the financial burden of new development away from existing residents. Of course, as with zoning, land use regulations, and subdivision controls, impact fees also can intentionally be used to discourage new development by raising its cost.

As Been (2005) demonstrates, economic theory does not provide us with a clear answer to the question of whether impact fees lead to more or less expensive housing in a given jurisdiction. In the end, much will depend upon who bears the fee. If the impact fee is passed back to the owner of vacant land, then it should not affect either the quantity of housing produced or its price, unless the owner is permitted under applicable zoning to substitute different and less costly (from the perspective of the impact fee) forms of housing or other uses. For example, if a municipality imposes a flat fee based upon the number of apartments or homes built, a developer might choose to build larger homes, thereby leading to less overall supply and higher prices. A similar result could occur if the landowner could choose to build a commercial development in place of the housing. If the fee is not passed back to the owner of the land or is borne by the developer, then it will fall upon the ultimate consumer of the housing. This will cause the housing to be more expensive and likely lead to less overall supply.

Been (2005) adds two additional complications to the difficult issue of how impact fees affect the price and quantity of housing. The adoption of an impact fee by a municipality is endogenous to its other land use regulatory decisions. In other words, a municipality's decision to adopt an impact fee will be affected by its other land use regulations. For example, if the municipality were not to adopt an impact fee, it might instead choose to restrict housing construction with large lot zoning or growth controls because it wishes to avoid having to raise taxes to pay for the incremental costs of the development. Thus, it is possible that the ability to impose an impact fee might make a municipality more – not less – willing to permit housing to locate within its borders. Second, some impact fees will selectively exempt affordable housing from the fee, and, thus, actually may be neutral or positive regarding this type of accommodation.

Several studies have examined the effect of impact fees. These studies generally show that impact fees are associated with higher housing prices for newly constructed housing, as well as existing housing. In many instances, researchers have found that the increase in price is significantly higher than the fee itself. Once again, as was the case with each of the regulations discussed so far, increased prices for housing do not necessarily mean that an impact fee is a barrier that should be removed. To the extent that the impact fee is calculated in such a way that housing consumers value the amenities it pays for, the price increase may reflect only increased demand. Nevertheless, while the impact fee might be efficient under this scenario, it effectively may make housing in the jurisdiction unaffordable to low- and moderate-income families. Furthermore, the empirical result showing that impact fees seem to have a positive impact on existing housing, as well as newly constructed housing, may be attributable to the fact that fees are structured in such a way as to exceed the marginal cost of the new development, thereby providing a cross-subsidy to existing homeowners.

Administrative processes

According to the academic literature, each of the regulations discussed so far (building codes, environmental regulations, zoning and land use regulations, and impact fees) is likely to increase housing prices. These price increases are ambiguous in terms of social welfare because increased housing prices might reflect the benefits (not just the burdens) the regulations generate. The final regulatory barrier to be covered in this part of the article, however, is unambiguous. In many municipalities throughout the nation, the costs of regulation are multiplied as a result of inefficient and duplicative government administrative processes.

As government regulations become more complex, housing developers and government officials must interact more frequently. These contacts might take place at the approval stage for a project when the developer must negotiate a zoning change or variance, satisfy an environmental review, or obtain a building permit. Long, costly delays frequently occur and may be attributable to insufficient staffing of governmental agencies, long backlogs in processing, and antiquated procedures. The problems are multiplied when, as often happens, the developer must deal with multiple agencies, and even multiple governments, to obtain permits and approvals.

In addition, the more times a developer must come into contact with government, the greater the opportunity for politics to intervene. Much development will require discretionary government approvals, which frequently will be influenced by public pressure, sometimes from community residents or other developers threatened with increased competition. In addition, each government approval provides citizens with the opportunity to raise concerns, voice opposition, and bring lawsuits against a project. In many instances, the uncertainty generated can be more detrimental to a project than any of the substantive regulations described in this article.

Research on administrative processes affecting the development process is truly embryonic. Most estimates of the impact of administrative inefficiency and delay on development come from anecdotal accounts or surveys of developers, which may be biased. Most of these studies, as described by May (2005), suggest that administrative roadblocks add significantly to the cost of housing and truly constitute barriers to development. This finding is further supported by the findings from a recent analysis by Glaeser and Gyourko (2003)

in which the relationship among several measures of housing and land cost and an index based on the average length of time between an application for rezoning and the issuance of a building permit was studied. The authors found that the increase in time to obtain a permit is strongly associated with rising land and housing prices.[4]

OVERALL IMPACTS

[…]Importantly, though, a housing developer is likely to encounter many of these regulations (and others) simultaneously. For example, to successfully complete one development in the suburbs, a typical builder will need to apply for subdivision approval, pay an impact fee, obtain a building permit and a certificate of occupancy and, if he is unlucky enough, apply for a rezoning or a variance. Thus, the costs generated by government regulations and their impacts on housing are cumulative.

Several studies have sought to examine the cumulative impact of different types of local development regulations on the cost of housing, and each found it to be quite substantial. For example, the National Association of Home Builders (NAHB) (1998) surveyed builders in 42 metropolitan areas in 1998 and asked them to provide a detailed breakdown of the cost of constructing a 2,150-square-foot house on a 7,500- to 10,000-square-foot lot. The average sales price of such a home was estimated to be $226,668. Of this total, the builders estimated that approximately 10 percent could be shaved off "if unnecessary government regulations, delays, and fees were eliminated."

Luger and Temkin (2000) also used survey data from developers, engineers, and planners to estimate the impact of "discretionary" or "excessive" costs imposed by regulation in New Jersey municipalities. They found these costs to be sizable, albeit somewhat more modest than those reported in the NAHB study, ranging from $10,000 to $20,000 per unit on a home with a median sales price of $236,000. The authors further concluded that the impact of those regulations is more likely to be felt at the lower end of the market.

Two recent studies used indices of regulatory restrictiveness to estimate the impact of varying levels of land development regulation across metropolitan areas. According to estimates by

Green and Malpezzi (2003), moving from a lightly regulated environment to a heavily regulated environment would raise rents by 17 percent, increase house values by 51 percent, and lower homeownership rates by 10 percentage points. According to Mayer and Somerville (2000), a metropolitan area with a 4.5-month delay in approval and two different types of growth-control restrictions would have an estimated 45 percent less construction than a metropolitan area with a 1.5-month delay and no growth management policy.

PART 3. REMOVING REGULATORY BARRIERS TO HOUSING: A SHORT HISTORY

Concerns about the impact of regulatory barriers on the housing market have existed for decades. For example, in 1968, the National Commission on Urban Problems described how different building code standards impeded the development of housing in the United States. The proposition that regulation stood in the way of affordable housing was echoed by the President's Commission on Housing in 1982 and found its fullest exposition in the report of the 1991 Advisory Commission on Regulatory Barriers to Affordable Housing. In its report entitled "Not in My Back Yard: Removing Barriers to Affordable Housing," the Commission set forth a comprehensive program for deregulation with state governments playing pivotal roles. The approach of using states as a fulcrum was justified because local governments derive their regulatory powers from the states. In addition, states were thought to be in a better position than the federal government to take into account interregional variations, while at the same time being sufficiently centralized to take into account the extra-municipal effects of local actions.

The 1991 Commission report proposed that the federal government "inspire" state and local governments to reform their regulations using a "carrot and stick" approach. All states and localities that received federal assistance would be required to include in annual reports to the government a description of what they were doing to reduce regulatory barriers. HUD would have the power to condition assistance on satisfactory barrier removal strategies. A state that failed to adequately remove regulatory barriers to housing development would lose its ability to issue tax-exempt bonds for housing and its authority to allocate tax credits to developers of low- and moderate-income housing.

Congress never adopted the Commission's proposals, despite praise from some quarters (Schill, 1992). Instead, Congress required that jurisdictions that receive federal housing submit a comprehensive housing affordability strategy that would include an explanation of whether the cost of housing in the jurisdiction was affected by policies such as land use controls, zoning ordinances, building codes, and growth limits.[5] The existence of these regulations, however, would not justify HUD disapproval of assistance.[6] In 1992, Congress passed a minor piece of legislation authorizing HUD to make grants to states and localities to develop removal strategies for regulatory barriers, including drafting model legislation and simplifying and consolidating administrative procedures. In addition, HUD created the Regulatory Barriers Clearinghouse to facilitate the dissemination of best practices about barrier removal strategies. Several years later, an even more modest effort to require the federal government to publish a cost impact statement when it imposes regulations that would drive up the cost of housing was not passed by Congress despite being proposed several times.

At the federal level, the issue of regulatory barriers to development was dormant throughout the Clinton administration but has been revitalized by the George W. Bush administration. HUD has established a new departmentwide initiative, America's Affordable Communities Initiative, to tackle the problem. Thus far, HUD has set aside funds for research on regulatory barriers and sought to build coalitions to address the problem. More tangibly, in 2004, the Department published a Federal Notice announcing its intent to include in most of its competitive fiscal year 2004 funding opportunities (Notice of Funding Availability) a series of questions on the local regulatory environment (U.S. Department of Housing and Urban Development, 2004). Applicants for HUD funds have an opportunity, if they desire, to respond to these questions; those applicants who meet the requisite minimum criteria for regulatory reform can receive additional "points," which can assist them in the competitive selection process.

In addition, a number of states and cities have shown renewed interest in the issue of regulatory barriers. For example, several jurisdictions have sponsored studies that outline strategies for barrier removal (Colorado Department of Local Affairs, 1999; Commonwealth of Massachusetts, 2000; Salama, Schill, and Stark, 1999). A few have even implemented the proposals. For example, California, Florida, and New Jersey require municipalities to plan for affordable housing[7] Other states have taken steps to expedite permitting procedures for affordable housing[8] or to exempt some affordable housing projects from environmental impact requirements.[9] New York City, long known for chronic housing shortages exacerbated by cumbersome development rules, also has seemingly changed its approach. In 2002, Mayor Michael Bloomberg announced an ambitious agenda to rezone manufacturing land for housing development and adopt a model building code (New York City Department of Housing Preservation and Development, 2002).

Nevertheless, most states and municipalities do business as usual. With the exception of a handful of states that either have passed statutes or had activist courts require fair share housing plans (Schill, 2002), regulatory barriers abound and may even be intensifying. The persistence of regulatory barriers in the United States, despite the prevalence of rising housing prices and extraordinary rent-to-income burdens among many renters, can be explained by many factors. The simplest and most important of these factors is that in our federal system, states have traditionally vested the police power in municipalities. Because each city or town pursues its own parochial interest, it is not forced to consider the cumulative impact of regulation on housing in the metropolitan area or region. Indeed, each municipality has strong fiscal incentives to erect regulatory barriers to avoid tax increases to pay for needed services. In addition, direct participation by citizens tends to be most intense and effective with respect to local governments. Many existing residents would prefer to avoid development because they want to preserve the status quo, are concerned about congestion, or want to maintain racial or economic homogeneity. Although some states have shown interest in statewide planning, many more are interested in responding to the desires of their suburban constituents. Thus, instead of reducing regulatory barriers, many states have clamped down on development, sometimes under the banner of smart growth.

Smart growth presents both an opportunity and a hazard for those who wish to remove regulatory barriers to development. In many ways, smart growth is more of a political slogan than a coherent set of proposals. To suburban residents, it represents an opportunity to erect barriers to development, slow demographic change, and reduce congestion on the roads. To environmentalists, it means the preservation of greenfields and the reduction of air pollution. To urban advocates, it holds out the promise for renewed interest in dense development as options in the suburbs are restricted.

Smart growth, however, is a risky strategy for those who would like to see increased production of affordable housing. Because cities and suburbs are politically independent, there is no guarantee that restrictions at the periphery would be matched by increased development in the city. City dwellers may wonder why they should have to shoulder the burden of increased development, both in terms of increased service costs and congestion. In the absence of some form of regional or state authority, smart growth could merely exacerbate current inequities and make affordable housing even scarcer for low- and moderate-income Americans.[10]

At the federal level, Congress has never strongly supported the removal of regulatory barriers, partly because members of Congress, like state legislators, are ultimately responsive to their increasingly suburban constituencies. In addition, advocates for reducing regulatory barriers have repeatedly failed to form effective coalitions among natural allies. Unfortunately, the only vocal groups consistently advocating for barrier removal are the home-building and real estate industries. Traditional low-income housing advocates, with the exception of some groups dedicated to the fight against exclusionary zoning, are – at best – generally silent, or – at worst – hostile when the debate turns to deregulation. One explanation for this reaction may be sympathy with the purposes underlying many of the regulations that so negatively affect housing production, such as environmental protection.

An additional impediment to effective mobilization on the issue of regulatory barriers is the simple fact, described in detail above, that we know too little about the subject. […].

Notes

1. Many households pay extremely high proportions of their incomes for housing, leaving little at the end of the month for other necessities. For example, according to the American Housing Survey (U.S. Department of Commerce, 2002), in 2001, 23.2 percent of all renter and 9.8 percent of all homeowner households in the United States paid more than half their incomes for housing.

2. This interpretation of the function of the village's zoning ordinance was offered by the lower court judge in a decision that would have invalidated the ordinance: "The purpose to be accomplished is to classify the population and segregate them according to their income or situation in life." 297 F. 307, 316 (N.D. Ohio 1924).

3. One possible way to resolve the conflict between efficient regulations and affordability concerns might be to increase levels of housing subsidies. In today's fiscal environment, however, it is doubtful that the amount of public resources devoted to housing will be substantially augmented.

4. Glaeser and Gyourko regress two dependent variables over the index values, the log of median family income and percentage population growth. The first dependent variable is the fraction of units in a metropolitan area that are valued at or above 140 percent of construction costs. The second is an "implied zoning tax" that is derived by subtracting the cost of land estimated by a nonlinear hedonic equation from the cost of land obtained by subtracting the structure cost from total home value.

5. See 42 U.S.C. sec. 12705(b)(4).

6. "[T]he adoption of a public policy identified pursuant to subsection (b)(4) of this section shall not be a basis for the Secretary's disapproval of a housing strategy." 42 U.S.C. sec. 12705(c)(1).

7. See Cal. Gov. Code sec. 65580 et seq.; Fla. Stat. Ann. Sec. 163.3191; N.J. Stat. sec. 52:27D-301-334.

8. See Fla. Stat. Ann. Sec. 373.4141 (requiring expedited permitting procedures for affordable housing developments).

9. See, for example, Cal. Pub. Res. Code sec. 21080.14 (exempting from CEQA affordable housing of up to 100 units).

10. Smart growth also can be criticized for restricting opportunities for minority households to live in suburban locations and for infringing on property rights. See Schill (2003).

REFERENCES

Advisory Commission on Regulatory Barriers to Affordable Housing. 1991. *"Not In My Back Yard": Removing Barriers to Affordable Housing.* Final report. Washington, D.C.: U.S. Department of Housing and Urban Development.

Been, Vicki. 2005. "Impact Fees and Housing Affordability," *Cityscape* 8 (1): 139–186.

Colorado Department of Local Affairs, Division of Housing. 1999. *Reducing Housing Costs Through Regulatory Reform: A Handbook for Colorado Communities.* Denver.

Commonwealth of Massachusetts, Executive Office for Administration and Finance. 2000. *Bringing Down the Barriers: Changing Housing Supply Dynamics in Massachusetts.* Boston.

Downs, Anthony. 2002. "Have Housing Prices Risen Faster in Portland than Elsewhere?" *Housing Policy Debate* 13 (1): 7–31.

——1991. "The Advisory Commission on Regulatory Barriers to Affordable Housing: Its Behavior and Accomplishments," *Housing Policy Debate* 2 (4): 1095–1137.

Fischel, William A. 1990. *Do Growth Controls Matter?: A Review of Empirical Evidence on the Effectiveness and Efficiency of Local Government Land Use Regulation.* Cambridge, MA: Lincoln Institute of Land Policy.

Frech, H.E., III, and Ronald N. Lafferty. 1984. "The Effect of the California Coastal Commission on Housing Prices," *Journal of Urban Economics* 16: 105–123.

Glaeser, Edward L., and Joseph Gyourko. 2003. "The Impact of Building Restrictions on Housing Affordability," *Federal Reserve Bank of New York Economic Policy Review* 9 (2): 21–39.

Green, Richard K., and Stephen Malpezzi. 2003. *A Primer on U.S. Housing Markets and Housing Policy*. Washington, D.C.: The Urban Institute.

Hamilton, Bruce W. 1978. "Zoning and the Exercise of Monopoly Power," *Journal of Urban Economics* 5: 116–128.

Kiel, Katherine A. 2005. "Environmental Regulations and the Housing Market: A Review of the Literature," *Cityscape* 8 (1): 187–208.

Listokin, David, and David B. Hattis. 2005. "Building Codes and Housing," *Cityscape* 8 (1): 21–68.

Lubove, Roy. 1962. *The Progressives and the Slums: Tenement House Reform in New York City, 1890–1917*. Westport, CT: Greenwood Press.

Luger, Michael I., and Kenneth Temkin. 2000. *Red Tape and Housing Costs*. New Brunswick: Center for Urban Policy Research, Rutgers, The State University of New Jersey.

May, Peter J. 2005. "Regulatory Implementation: Examining Barriers From Regulatory Processes," *Cityscape* 8 (1): 209–232.

Mayer, Christopher J., and C. Tsuriel Somerville. 2000. "Land Use Regulation and New Construction," *Regional Science and Urban Economics* 30 (6): 639–662.

National Association of Home Builders. 2004. *Annual New Home Sales (1963–2003)*. Washington, D.C.: National Association of Home Builders.

——1998. *The Truth About Regulatory Barriers to Housing Affordability*. Washington, D.C.: National Association of Home Builders.

New York City Department of Housing Preservation and Development. 2002. *The New Housing Marketplace*. New York: New York City Department of Housing Preservation and Development.

Phillips, Justin and Eban Goodstein. 2000. "Growth Management and Housing Prices: The Case of Portland, Oregon," *Contemporary Economic Policy* 18 (3): 334–344.

Quigley, John M., and Steven Raphael. 2004. "Is Housing Unaffordable? Why Isn't It More Affordable?" *Journal of Economic Perspectives* 18 (1): 191–214.

Quigley, John M., and Larry A. Rosenthal. 2005. "The Effects of Land Use Regulation on the Price of Housing: What Do We Know? What Can We Learn?" *Cityscape* 8 (1): 69–138.

Salama, Jerry J., Michael H. Schill, and Martha E. Stark. 1999. *Reducing the Cost of New Housing Construction in New York City*. A Report to The New York City Partnership and Chamber of Commerce, The New York City Housing Partnership and The New York City Department of Housing Preservation and Development. New York: New York University School of Law, Center for Real Estate and Urban Policy. http://www.law.nyu.edu/realestatecenter/CREUP_Papers/Cost_Study_1999/NYCHousingCost.pdf.

Schill, Michael H. 2003. Comments on Smart Growth and Affordable Housing. Paper presented at the Brookings Symposium on the Relationships Between Affordable Housing and Growth Management, Brookings Institution, May 29, 2003.

——2002. "Regulatory Barriers to Housing Development in the United States, in Land Law. In *Comparative Perspective 101* edited by A. Gambaro and M. Jordan. The Hague: Kluwer Law International.

——1992. "The Federal Role in Reducing Regulatory Barriers to Affordable Housing in the Suburbs," *Journal of Law and Politics* 8: 703.

Staley, Samuel R., and Gerard Mildner. 1999. *Urban Growth Boundaries and Housing Affordability*. Los Angeles: Reason Public Policy Institute.

Thorson, James A. 1996. "An Examination of the Monopoly Zoning Hypothesis," *Land Economics* 72 (1): 43–55.

U.S. Department of Commerce, Bureau of the Census. 2002. *American Housing Survey for the United States: 2001*. Washington, D.C.: U.S. Department of Commerce.

U.S. Department of Housing and Urban Development (HUD). 2004. "America's Affordable Communities Initiative. HUD's Initiative on Removal of Regulatory Barriers: Announcement of Incentives Criteria on Barrier Removal in HUD's FY 2004 Competitive Funding Allocations," *Federal Register* 69 (55): 13449–13454.

Wermiel, Sara E. 2000. The Fireproof Building: Technology and Public Safety in the *Nineteenth-Century American City*. Baltimore: Johns Hopkins University Press.

ADDITIONAL READING

U.S. Department of Commerce, Bureau of the Census. 1991. *American Housing Survey for the United States: 1989.* Washington, D.C.: U.S. Department of Commerce.

29
"Local land use regulation and the chain of exclusion"

From *Journal of the American Planning Association* (2000)

Rolf Pendall

American metropolitan areas are indisputably segregated by race (Farley and Frey, 1994). For decades, racial segregation has characterized city blocks (Farley, 1993), neighborhoods (Massey and Denton, 1993), and even entire jurisdictions (Keating, 1994). Such jurisdiction-level segregation, referred to in this article as *exclusion,* persists despite substantial movement of African Americans to the suburbs since 1970 (Schneider and Phelan, 1993). Some observers (Galster, 1991) contend that racial segregation has grown even worse in many metropolitan areas as White non-Hispanics have moved to ever more distant suburban locations.

Many forces interact to produce racial segregation in neighborhoods, including household preferences and discrimination or institutionalized racism within the private and public sectors (Clark, 1986; Galster, 1988). This article concerns land use controls, the most prominent example of how local institutions may have exclusionary effects. Zoning, for example, was invented in part to keep minorities away from non-Hispanic Whites (Weiss, 1987). Even after racial zoning was found to be unconstitutional by the U.S. Supreme Court, large-lot zoning and other land use controls with the potential to exclude racial minorities remained available to municipalities throughout the United States, often as a very thin cover for racial bias (Danielson, 1976). Not until the 1970s did state legislatures and courts in Massachusetts, New Jersey, and California begin to restrain these exclusionary practices (Anglin, 1994; Calavita and Grimes, 1998; Stockman, 1992). In the same decade, the first of more than a dozen state legislatures began to enact new measures to coordinate and require local planning for growth management (Bollens, 1992). Growth management, recently rechristened "Growing Smart" by a coalition of governmental and nongovernmental organizations, seeks primarily to contain scattered, low-density development ("sprawl"") and to create more certainty in local development approval processes (American Planning Association, 1998). The racial consequences of these evolving state land use policies remain uncertain, however. Under certain circumstances, growth management can make development more "compact," but this higher density will not always benefit low-income or minority residents. It may instead promote gentrification. Under other circumstances, growth management may not induce compact development at all, because land use controls do not always work as intended or advertised (Landis, 1992).

The new enthusiasm for "smart growth" thus revives old questions about land use controls and racial segregation. How are they connected? Do Blacks and Hispanics respond differently to different land use controls and to different housing supply conditions? The study reported here used data from over 1,000 jurisdictions in the 25 largest U.S. metropolitan areas to conclude that exclusive low-density zoning reduces rental housing in the municipalities and counties that use it. The resulting shortage of rental housing, in turn, limits the number of Black and Hispanic residents who can move into these municipalities and counties. Building permit caps are also associated with lowered proportions of Hispanic residents. Other land use controls have either very limited or no average effects on either housing types or racial distributions.

EXCLUSIONARY LAND USE CONTROLS IN CONTEXT

No single factor can explain exclusion; individual preferences, household choices, and moving decisions play an important role in racial segregation (Clark, 1986). White non-Hispanics have historically had low tolerance for African American neighbors, while African Americans tend to prefer racially mixed neighborhoods (Farley et al., 1997). This gap between Whites' tolerances and Blacks' preferences can segregate neighborhoods even in the absence of discriminatory actions or policies by the private sector or government (Schelling, 1971). Real estate agents have exacerbated these underlying preference-related tendencies toward segregation by steering people to neighborhoods where others of their race dominate. Banks and insurance companies have discriminated against minorities seeking mortgages and insurance and erected obstacles to housing transactions in minority neighborhoods. Landlords also discriminate against racial minorities (Massey and Denton, 1993). Congress has responded with such measures as the Fair Housing Act and the Home Mortgage Disclosure Act to exact penalties for discrimination (Kushner, 1995). Even so, private-sector discrimination continues (Cloud and Galster, 1993).

Municipal governments have also fostered racial discrimination and exclusion. Many jurisdictions adopted and implemented racial zoning even after the U.S. Supreme Court ruled it unconstitutional in 1917 (Buchanan v. Warley; cited in Kushner, 1995). A large body of evidence from legal cases shows that jurisdictions still use land use controls both to segregate – that is, to ensure that low-income and minority residents may live only in certain neighborhoods – and to exclude low-income and minority households entirely from the municipality (see, for example, Kirp et al., 1995; Keating, 1997).

The courts have not consistently told planners and local decision makers that land use controls with racially exclusionary effects are impermissible. Federal Constitutional case law suggests that even if a land use control system has racially exclusionary effects, it will survive challenges unless plaintiffs can prove that the local government in question explicitly intended to exclude suspect classes when it adopted the regulations (Arlington Heights v.

Metropolitan Housing Development Corp. 1977). Title VIII of the 1968 Fair Housing Act, however, provides a statutory basis for challenges to land use controls with exclusionary effects, regardless of any findings of intent (Kushner, 1995). In U.S. v. City of Black Jack (1978), for example, the Eighth Circuit Court invalidated a suburban incorporation because its proposed zoning ordinance would have eliminated apartments, thereby excluding many African Americans. The Seventh Circuit Court, on the other hand, included intent among its criteria for finding a violation of Title VIII in the Arlington Heights (1977) case. The Supreme Court has yet to decide which of these interpretations of Title VIII should be the law of the land.

State-level challenges to exclusionary zoning have been more successful, but these cases have concentrated on exclusion of lower-income households, not racial minorities. Case law in Pennsylvania (Fernley v. Board of Supervisors, 1985), New Jersey (Southern Burlington NAACP v. Township of Mount Laurel, 1975, 1983), and New Hampshire (Britton v. Town of Chester; 1991), for example, has resulted in more receptive local environments for construction of multifamily housing. Whether this environment will also foster racial inclusion is an open question that is partially answered by the research reported here.

Planners' ethical codes contrast starkly with the lack of clarity from the federal and state courts about racially exclusionary zoning. The American Institute of Certified Planners (AICP) Code of Ethics and Professional Conduct and the American Planning Association (APA) Ethical Principles in Planning both include the following language regarding planners' obligations:

> A planner must strive to expand choice and opportunity for all persons, recognizing a special responsibility to plan for the needs of disadvantaged groups and persons, and must urge the alteration of policies, institutions, and decisions which oppose such needs.
>
> (AICP, 1991 [1978])

This language suggests that planners have a responsibility to dismantle land use controls that exclude on the basis of class or income, not to mention those that have exclusionary effects on racial or ethnic minorities. However, no systematic national study has yet statistically linked land use controls to racial exclusion. As a result, planners do not necessarily know what to expect from any particular land use control. Can planners use permit caps, very-low-density zoning, or urban growth boundaries, for example, and still expect to "expand choice and opportunity for all persons"? How, indeed, might land use controls lead to exclusion? This chain of events requires specification and systematic testing.

HOUSING MARKETS AND INCLUSION: HYPOTHESES

Four important housing market conditions promote inclusion of African Americans and Hispanics: new housing supply, multifamily housing supply, rental housing supply, and affordable rental housing. New neighborhoods, especially neighborhoods of new, moderately priced houses, will presumably be more racially mixed than established ones, because younger Whites tend both to move more often and to have higher tolerance for minorities generally (Schuman et al., 1985) and for minority neighbors (Farley et al., 1997).

A healthy supply of multifamily housing is particularly important to minority residents because it tends to be rented, and when owner-occupied it tends to cost less than detached houses. Rental housing allows more Black and Hispanic households to move into communities for two reasons. First, fewer than 45% of Blacks and Hispanics nationally own their dwellings, compared to nearly 70% of White non-Hispanics (U.S. Census Bureau, 1998a). Without built-up equity or good credit ratings, Blacks and Hispanics face high financial burdens when they try to buy houses; consequently, places with less rental housing will attract fewer Blacks and Hispanics. Second, Black and Hispanic households have lower incomes than non-Hispanic White households; the median income for African American or Hispanic households in 1997 was under $30,000, compared to $40,577 for White non-Hispanic households (U.S. Census Bureau, 1998b). Lower incomes hinder saving for down payments. Third, Black home buyers may prefer to locate in places with higher proportions of rentals because more Blacks

already live there. Survey data indicate that most African Americans prefer integrated neighborhoods but would choose mostly Black over mostly White neighborhoods (Farley et al., 1997). Finally, where rental housing is scarce, some landlords may select White tenants because of racial prejudice. Where rental housing is plentiful, landlords are less likely to profit from discriminatory behavior, and if one landlord discriminates, other rental options may be available in the same neighborhood.

Their lower incomes also make African Americans and Hispanics more dependent on affordable rental housing than non-Hispanic Whites. Therefore, one would expect to find higher concentrations of Blacks and Hispanics in places with higher proportions of multifamily, rental, and affordable rental units. One would also expect the concentrations of both groups to increase over time in places where these housing types become more common.

There are also hypothetical indirect links among these four important market factors. Most observers agree that an adequate housing supply can stabilize prices and enhance affordability (Dowall, 1984). The relationship between housing supply and the proportion of multifamily and rented dwellings is harder to predict. A constrained supply of housing may encourage owners of rented single-family homes to sell their units to occupants, thereby reducing the proportion of rental housing. On the other hand, constrained supply can also lead owners of single-family houses to convert them to dwellings for more than one household if local zoning and building laws permit such conversions. An adequate supply of attached dwellings can indirectly support inclusion. Attached housing units tend to be rented and to be more affordable when sold. Adequate supplies of rental housing, in turn, should also foster rental housing affordability.

When the housing supply is tight and rentals scarce, a landlord or a real estate agent can turn away African Americans and Hispanics because the landlord or agent may be confident that a White non-Hispanic household will eventually rent or buy the unit. Robust and open housing market conditions can reduce competition among households for dwellings, creating a renter's or buyer's market, and theoretically undercutting discrimination.

Control	Definition	Direct effect on housing			
		Supply	Multifamily	Rentals	Affordability
Low-density-only zoning	Gross residential density (units/total land area) limited to fewer than eight dwelling units per acre	−	−	−	−
Building permit cap	Annual limit on new residential building permits; in effect at least 2 years	−	−	?	−
Building permit moratorium	Total stoppage of residential building permit issuance in effect at least 2 years	−	−	?	−
Adequate public facilities ordinance (APFO)	"Levels of service" set for more than two urban infrastructure or public service systems	?	?	?	?
Urban growth boundary	Permanent or temporary limits on expansion of the urban edge	?	+	?	?
Boxed-in status	Urban expansion precluded by political boundaries or water bodies	?	+	?	?

Table 29.1 Land use controls and their effect on housing outcomes

+ Hypothesized to have a positive effect
− Hypothesized to have a negative effect
? No hypothesized direction for effect

LAND USE CONTROLS AND HOUSING MARKETS: HYPOTHESES

How, then, might municipal land use controls contribute to an exclusionary housing market? This study examined the ways in which five major land use controls and one land use condition (inability to annex) may contribute to exclusion. These controls, shown with their definitions and their effects on housing conditions in Table 29.1, were selected based on a review of literature on common land use controls in the U.S. (Pendall, 1995) and further specified through interviews with American Planning Association chapter presidents in

1994. Figure 29.1 summarizes the hypothesized pathway that leads from exclusionary land use controls through the housing market to racial exclusion.

Exclusive large-lot zoning, or low-density-only zoning, often precludes any residential development throughout a jurisdiction except as detached, single-family houses.[1] Low-density-only zoning can restrict the housing supply in a community by reducing construction even in areas well suited to development. Low-density-only zoning may even reduce rental affordability because rentals may be in greater demand. Communities composed entirely of single-family homes may have better

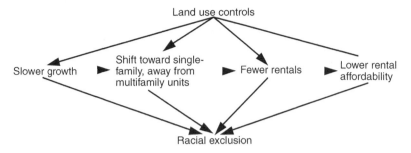

Figure 29.1 The chain of exclusion: hypothesized relationships.

services and less traffic than mixed-density communities. Thus low-density-only zoning can impose constraints on supply, attached dwellings, rental dwellings, and housing affordability, all four of the conditions that hypothetically promote racial inclusion.

Building permit caps and *building permit moratoria* both reduce the annual supply of housing units. Permit caps allow some construction and tend to be adopted for long periods of time; moratoria (as defined here) allow no construction, but are usually temporary responses to infrastructure shortages. Permit caps and moratoria may also give builders incentives to build a smaller number of larger, more expensive houses (Zorn et al., 1986). Permit caps may reduce the affordability of rental housing because the programs used to implement them often allocate scarce permits to higher-quality housing units (Schwartz et al., 1984). Long-lasting moratoria may disrupt housing production and reorient units built after the moratorium is lifted.

Adequate public facilities ordinances (APFOs) condition approval of development upon availability of public facilities according to locally adopted standards or levels of service (Nelson and Duncan, 1995). There are no clear reasons to expect that APFOs will have consistent effects on housing supply, type, tenure, or affordability. On one hand, APFOs may hinder development because they add costs. On the other, they may facilitate development by making new facilities available (Altshuler and Gómez-Ibáñez, 1993). APFOs can theoretically lead to either lower or higher proportions of detached houses; builders may respond to infrastructure fees by building

more densely (Landis, 1995) or by building larger houses that more easily recapture the cost of additional infrastructure (Bay Area Council, 1988).

Urban growth boundaries, urban limit lines, or *greenbelts* attempt to contain the extent of urbanization, but may permit or promote higher-density development in urbanized areas (Nelson and Duncan, 1995). A final condition, *"boxed-in"* city, applies to jurisdictions surrounded by other incorporated areas or bodies of water. Boxed-in status differs from the others because local governments "inherit" rather than adopt it, but, like greenbelts, it may limit urban expansion. Urban growth boundaries and boxed-in status may encourage high-density (multifamily) development by raising land prices (Knaap, 1985). However, the direct effects of growth boundaries and boxed-in status on housing supply, rentals, and rental affordability are more difficult to predict.

PREVIOUS STUDIES LINKING LAND USE CONTROLS AND EXCLUSION

Many of the historic studies and lawsuits discussed earlier have revealed particular cases in which land use controls have had exclusionary outcomes. Some have even provided evidence of intent to use land use controls in a racially discriminatory manner. These cases have not, however, constituted enough evidence to convince judges or planners that certain land use controls almost inevitably exclude racial minorities or that communities using those land use controls should prove that their versions of the controls do not exclude Blacks and Hispanics.

An extensive review of the literature reveals no broad quantitative studies that have tested the entire "chain of exclusion" from land use controls, through housing markets, to discriminatory outcomes. Studies do, however, show that restrictive land use controls are more common in communities with high proportions of wealthy, non-Hispanic Whites than in communities with many minorities (Burnell and Burnell, 1989; Bates and Santerre, 1994). Places where single-family detached dwellings dominate have also been shown to have a larger proportion of White non-Hispanic residents than places with multifamily dwellings (Pogodzinski and Sass, 1994). A study of southern California showed that places with restrictive growth policies have lower proportions of Blacks but found no significant relationship between such controls and the proportion of Hispanics (Donovan and Neiman, 1995). An early national survey that characterized 228 population-growth-managing communities found only one subset of 15 communities with comparatively high proportions of ethnic minority residents (Dowall, 1980).

None of these studies necessarily shows that the land use controls in question led to exclusion; rather, they may simply show that wealthy and White places are more likely to adopt restrictive land use controls. In fact, recent research has raised questions about whether zoning and land use controls "work" at all (Landis, 1992) that is, whether they produce a different landscape than would be produced in their absence. Sometimes local governments adopt and amend their zoning ordinances in the anticipation that builders would like to satisfy market demand in the very places "permitted" by the zoning map (Wallace, 1988). Building permit limitations, another much studied "growth control," may have loopholes that allow business as usual in local housing construction (Warner and Molotch, 1995). If these land use controls do not, in fact, affect the housing market, then they cannot logically be classified as exclusionary.

TESTING THE LINKS: NEW RESEARCH ON EXCLUSION BY LAND USE CONTROLS

In the remainder of this article, I build the case that low-density-only zoning is a potent exclusionary land use control and that building permit caps warrant caution. I find little evidence that other land use controls exacerbate exclusion.

The model

The following questions were addressed in this study: Do land use controls result in exclusionary housing conditions, and do these conditions lead in turn to racial exclusion? Based on the literature discussed above, I present a formal model for attempting to answer these questions. Let Y be the dependent variable, X be a set of local-level explanatory variables, L be a set of land use control variables, M be a set of metropolitan-level explanatory variables, and y be unobserved characteristics. Let the subscript t stand for time, i for community, and a for metropolitan area. This model takes the form:

$$Y_{i,t} = a + bX_{i,t-1} + c(X_{i,t-1}) + dL_{i,t-1} + eM_{a,t-1} + f(M_{a,t} - M_{a,t-1}) + gY_{i,t-1} + h(y_i) + e_{i,t}$$

In the vernacular, and as it applies to this study, the formal model translates as follows. Housing characteristics or racial composition in 1990 is a function of a set of local explanatory variables in 1980; the change between 1980 and 1990 in the value of these variables; a set of land use controls known to be extant in the community between 1980 and 1990; a set of metropolitan characteristics extant in 1980; the change between 1980 and 1990 in the value of these metropolitan characteristics; unobserved fixed local characteristics; and random error.

In practice, I have no way to estimate the unobserved fixed effects (y_i), which may result in biased estimates of the effects of land use controls and other local characteristics. This might have been resolved with a difference approach that estimated the changes in the dependent variable as a function of changes in community characteristics, metropolitan characteristics, and land use controls. However, my database (described in the next section) does not contain a detailed history of land use control adoption from 1980 to 1990. Thus I cannot rule out the possibility that the changes observed in housing conditions and racial composition result from unobserved variables.

Hence the results reported here must be considered provisional and exploratory.

Data and analysis

In 1994, I surveyed 1,510 cities, towns, counties, and townships in the largest 25 metropolitan areas in the United States[2] using the mail-survey method advocated by Dillman (1978). A jurisdiction was included if it had at least 10,000 residents in 1990 and had sole zoning authority;[3] such jurisdictions had a combined 1990 population of just over 97 million residents, nearly 40% of the U.S. total. In most cases, the survey was mailed to the planning director; for communities without a planning director, the survey was addressed to the municipal executive, engineer, planning board/commission chair, or retained planning consultant. In all, 1,168 jurisdictions (77%) responded, representing 83% of the population of the surveyed communities and 32% of the nation's residents in 1990. Over three fourths of the respondent jurisdictions had fewer than 50,000 residents in 1990, but the majority of the population lived in jurisdictions with over 100,000 residents. The surveys were short and simple, resulting in a high completion rate for the questions relating to the presence or absence of land use controls.[4]

The surveys asked whether each community employed the land use controls discussed earlier. Over 90% of the respondents had zoning ordinances, but only 15% had low-density-only zoning (see Table 29.2). Seventeen percent of respondents responded "yes" when asked, "Does your community have an 'urban limit line' or other growth boundary, imposed by such policies as decisions to limit extension of urban services or designation of a 'greenbelt' of open space around it?" Thirty percent of respondents had

APFOs, but an APFO applying to only one subject – schools, transportation, public safety facilities, water and wastewater infrastructure, or parks – may not constitute a strict control. Thus the research tests the effects of only those APFOs that apply to more than two of these infrastructure systems (16% of respondents). Only 4% of respondents had used building permit caps for at least 2 years in the 1980s, and 4% had imposed moratoria on residential permits for 2 years or more. Over half of the jurisdictions could not annex (were boxed in).

To analyze links with racial concentration, I extracted data from the 1980 and 1990 Censuses of Population and Housing at the city, township, county, and metropolitan levels.[5] The data included population by major racial category and Hispanic ethnicity; dwelling units by structure type, occupancy status, tenure, age, and for rental units the number of bedrooms; and the occupational status, educational attainment, and average commute time of the adult population. The affordability of the rental housing stock was calculated consistent with U.S. Department of Housing and Urban Development (HUD) standards: the proportion of local rental units whose monthly gross rent did not exceed 30% of 80% of the monthly median income in the Consolidated Metropolitan Statistical Area (CMSA) or Metropolitan Statistical Area (MSA) in 1989.

The analysis tested the chain of exclusion in three steps. In the first step, I used independent sample t-tests to identify significant differences between the racial composition in 1980 of places with and without each land use control. Here, racial composition is measured compared to a metropolitan average; the local percent Blacks[6] is divided by the regional percent Blacks, so that places with higher concentrations of Blacks than the regional average have an index

Land Use Control	Respondents with control	
	Number	Percent
Low-density-only zoning	171	15.1
Permit cap	43	3.8
Long-lasting moratorium	49	4.3
Adequate public facilities ordinance (APFO)	191	16.6
Urban growth boundary	198	17.3
Boxed-in status	596	52.6

Table 29.2 Restrictive residential land use controls in place, metropolitan survey, 1994

over 1. In the second and third steps, I used ordinary least squares (OLS) regression to test the model outlined above. The second step identified the independent association between each land use control and race-related outcomes, and the third in turn showed the effects of land use controls on housing and the effects of housing on racial groups. The regressions considered all the jurisdictions together as well as only jurisdictions that began the decade with relatively low concentrations of Blacks and Hispanics (defined by having fewer than 10% Black or Hispanic residents).

FINDINGS

Did fewer minorities live in controlled communities in 1980?

Several land use controls were associated with lower concentrations of minorities in 1980 (see Table 29.3), a finding consistent with earlier studies. The concentration of Blacks (that is, the index between the local and regional percent Black population) in places with low-density-only zoning (0.20) was less than half that of places allowing higher-density residential

Land Use Control	With control	Without control	Difference
Low-density-only zoning	170	959	
Black index	0.20	0.45	−0.24
Hispanic index	0.45	0.73	−0.28
Building permit cap	43	1,088	
Black index	0.29	0.42	−0.13
Hispanic index	0.82	0.68	n.s.
Long-lasting moratorium	48	1,082	
Black index	0.38	0.42	n.s.
Hispanic index	0.59	0.69	n.s.
APFO, more than 2 subjects	189	958	
Black index	0.45	0.41	n.s.
Hispanic index	0.68	0.69	n.s.
Urban growth boundary	198	939	
Black index	0.35	0.43	−0.08
Hispanic index	0.77	0.66	0.11
Boxed-in cities	594	534	
Black index	0.40	0.43	n.s.
Hispanic index	0.63	0.76	−0.13

Table 29.3 Independent samples t-tests, land use controls and race, 1980

Notes:
1 First line in each group refers to the number of respondents with or without the control.
2 Indices are equivalent to location quotients. They divide the percent of Blacks or Hispanics in a local area (city, town, or unincorporated county area) into the percent of Blacks or Hispanics in the local area's metropolitan region. For example, if a local area's population were 10% Hispanic and its metropolitan region's population 20% Hispanic, then the local area would have a Hispanic index of 0.50.
3 Numbers with controls do not equal Table 29.2 because of missing data for some communities.
4 All differences are significant at p <0.1 unless labeled as n.s. (not significant).

development (0.45); these places also had much lower concentrations of Hispanics (0.45 with and 0.73 without low-density-only zoning). Places with permit caps and urban growth boundaries (UGBs) had lower concentrations of African Americans but not significantly lower concentrations of Hispanics. In fact, places with UGBs had higher concentrations of Hispanics relative to their metropolitan areas than those without UGBs.

Do communities with land use controls lose minorities?

The next step tested for differences in percent Blacks and Hispanics in 1990 after controlling for the proportion of Black and Hispanic residents in 1980. Differences among the 1990 values will therefore equate to net change in local racial composition during the 1980s. The analysis also held constant metropolitan characteristics of Blacks and Hispanics (percent of total in 1980, percent change 1980–1990); logically, we would expect jurisdictions to add more minority residents if their metropolitan areas had higher concentrations or faster-growing populations of minorities.

Low-density-only zoning, moratoria, urban growth boundaries, and permit caps were all associated with lower proportions of Blacks and Hispanics in 1990 after controlling for Black and Hispanic concentrations in 1980 at the local and metropolitan levels (see Table 29.4). In other words, minority representation fell in these jurisdictions while suburbs nationally were gaining minority population (Schneider and Phelan, 1993). The Black and Hispanic percentages of the total population fell by 0.8 and 0.5 percentage points respectively in communities with low-density-only zoning in the 1980s. Since the average responding jurisdiction was about 6.5% Black and 7.2% Hispanic in 1990, even such a small effect may be interpreted as an indicator of racial exclusion. This result pertained not only to the entire tested set of 1,168 jurisdictions but also to 986 jurisdictions with fewer than 10% Black residents?[7]

Building permit caps also had exclusionary effects in the 1980s, but only on Hispanics. The Hispanic share of population in communities with permit caps fell by 1.8 percentage points across all jurisdictions and by 0.6 percentage points in the 975 communities with fewer than 10% Hispanic residents. Permit caps are most common where Hispanics are the dominant minority: San Francisco, Los Angeles, and San Diego. Moratoria reduced the share of Blacks (full set only), and UGBs reduced the share of Hispanics in low-Hispanic jurisdictions. As expected, regional minority shares in 1980 and growth in the 1980s were associated with higher local proportions of the same minorities in 1990. (The high R-square statistics in these equations result from the inclusion of the 1980 minority proportion and thus are not especially remarkable.)

Do land use controls influence housing outcomes? Does housing influence racial composition?

This third step identified housing outcomes in jurisdictions with and without land use controls and the effect of these housing outcomes on racial composition, while holding constant a series of other important factors. This step was addressed with two questions. First, how did each land use control affect housing growth, the proportion of single-family and multifamily units, the proportion of units rented, and the proportion of affordable rentals, and how did each of these supply conditions affect the others? Second, how did housing and land use controls influence racial outcomes? (The hypotheses corresponding to these questions and a diagram of the expected relationships appear in Table 29.1 and Figure 29.1 and their accompanying text.)

Many additional local housing and population characteristics need to be held constant to test for these independent effects; Table 29.5 summarizes these variables and their hypothesized effects on housing and race-related outcomes. In addition, regional characteristics must be controlled; for example, regional housing growth rates in the 1980s will logically influence local growth rates. Hence each regression included a metropolitan-scale analog in 1990 as a control variable.

	% Black, 1990		% Hispanic, 1990	
	All	Low-Black	All	Low-Hispanic
Land use controls in place in the 1980s				
Low-density-only zoning	−0.008*	−0.005*	0.005†	0.002
Permit cap	−0.001	−0.002	−0.018**	−0.006†
Long-lasting moratorium	−0.011†	−0.005	−0.001	0.002
AFPO, > 2 subjects	0.004	0.002	0.000	0.002
Urban growth boundary	−0.004	−0.004	−0.004	−0.004*
Boxed-in status	0.001	−0.001	0.001	0.003*
Race, 1980				
% Black non-Hispanic	1.037**	1.197**		
% Hispanic			1.139**	1.512**
Metro area, 1980 and shifts 1980–1990				
Metro % Black non-Hispanic	0.150**	0.094**		
Metro % growth, Black non-Hispanic	0.025**	0.024**		
Metro % Hispanic			0.148**	0.038**
Metro % growth, Hispanic			0.012**	0.007**
Constant	−0.010*	−0.006†	−0.002	−0.005**
R2	0.8751	0.4906	0.9369	0.8332
N	1,168	986	1,168	975

Table 29.4 Parameter estimates, land use controls and racial change, 1980–1990

Notes
1 Low-Black and low-Hispanic communities had less than 10% Black or Hispanic residents, respectively, in 1980.
2 APFO: Adequate public facilities ordinance.
†p<.10, *p<.05, **p<.01

	Housing growth	Percent Multi-family	Percent Rental units	Percent Rentals affordable	Percent Black or Hispanic	Rationale
Housing stock, 1980						
# housing units	−	+	+	?	+	Larger jurisdictions grow more slowly than small ones, accommodate more high density housing, minorities.
% units rented			+		+	Higher proportions of rentals lead to affordability, higher proportions of minorities.
% of rentals affordable					+	Jurisdictions with high rental affordability will attract more minority residents.

	Housing growth	Percent Multi-family	Percent Rental units	Percent Rentals affordable	Percent Black or Hispanic	Rationale
>75% on septic systems	?	−	−	?		High reliance on septic systems reduces multifamily and rental housing opportunities.
Vacancy rate	?	?	?	+	+	High vacancy rates may either dampen new production or signify large amounts of recent construction; should increase affordability, create opportunities for minorities.
% rentals built before 1960						Old rentals should be less expensive, according to filtering theory (Weicher and Thibodeau, 1988)
% rentals in structures of >5 units				−		Larger complexes should become less affordable over time because their managers tend to be professionals who know when they can raise rents (Applebaum and Gilderbloom, 1986).
% rentals less than 2 bedrooms (1990)				+	−	
Race, 1980						
% minority (Black non-Hisp./Hispanic)	?/+	+	+	+	+/?*	Increased immigration in 1980s; high percentages of Blacks and Hispanics in 1980 should lead to more inclusive housing outcomes. Black neighborhoods may attract more Hispanics.
Socioeconomic status (SES) and community location, 1980						
% college graduates	−	−	−	−	−	Places with high SES in 1980 should become more exclusive in the 1980s as incomes bifurcate (Karoly, 1992)

	Housing growth	Percent Multi-family	Percent Rental units	Percent Rentals affordable	Percent Black or Hispanic	Rationale
% sales admin support	+	+	+	+	+	Places with high proportions of residents in sales and administrative support occupations should have become less exclusive in the 1980s; they provide low-cost labor to expanding suburban employment centers (U.S. Congress Office of Technology Assessment, 1995).
Local/ metro commute	+	−	−	−	−	Places with long commutes should attract more rapid – but also more exclusive – growth, in part because while Blacks have moved into the suburbs Whites have moved even farther (Galster, 1991).
Old housing, dense population	−					Congested central cities with old housing should grow more slowly.

Table 29.5 Hypothesize effects of control variables on housing and race-related outcomes

+ Hypothesized to have a positive effect.
− Hypothesized to have a negative effect.
? No hypothesized direction for effect.
*hypothesized effect on growth in the other minority group.

The analysis found that low-density-only zoning contributed significantly to four exclusive housing market outcomes, after holding all these other conditions constant (see Table 29.6). First, communities with low-density-only zoning grew about 5% more slowly in the 1980s than other communities surveyed;[8] Second, the share of multifamily housing dropped by 0.6 percentage points in low-density-only communities, while third, their share of single-family housing increased by 1.1 percentage points. That is, a community with low-density-only zoning that had been 20% multifamily in 1980 would have dropped to 19.4% multifamily in 1990, all else being equal. Fourth, the rental share dropped by 0.7 percentage points in the 1980s. Contrary to expectations, however, the small and shrinking stock of rentals in low-density-only communities became more, not less, affordable in the 1980s. I will return to this result after discussing the intermediate effects of housing supply, unit type, and tenure on rental affordability.

	Housing growth 1980–90 (LN)	% multi-family 1990	% single-family 1990	% rental 1990	% of rentals affordable 1990
Land use controls in place of 1980s					
Low-density-only zoning	−0.47**	−0.006†	0.011**	−0.007†	0.023*
Permit cap	0.003	0.000	0.008	0.003	−0.008
Long-lasting moratorium	0.023	0.000	0.002	−0.005	−0.037**
APFO, >2 subjects	0.018	0.005†	−0.003	−0.004	−0.011
Urban growth boundary	0.002	−0.037	0.002	0.000	−0.002
Boxed-in status	0.022†	0.006	−0.009**	0.004	−0.025**
Housing stock, 1980					
#housing units (LN)	−0.052**	0.006**	−0.006**	−0.003**	0.001
% multifamily units		0.922**			
% single-family units			0.951**		
% units rented				0.808**	0.173**
% of rental units affordable				0.039**	0.740**
>75% on septic systems	−0.018	−0.007†	0.000	−0.015**	0.011
Vacancy rate (LN)	0.035**	−0.003	0.004	0.011**	0.013**
% rentals built < 1960					−0.069**
% rentals in structures of >4 units					−0.060**
% rentals <2BR (1990)					0.178**
Change in housing, 1980–1990					
Change in housing units (LN)		0.005**	−0.082**	0.017**	−0.032**
Change in % single-family units (LN)				−0.171**	0.049
Change in multifamily units (LN)				0.047**	−0.012
Change in % rental units (LN)					0.072**
Race, 1980					
% non-Hispanic Black (LN)	−0.028	0.006	0.015	0.069**	0.032
% Hispanic (LN)	0.281**	−0.032*	−0.005	0.092**	0.222**
Socioeconomic status and community location, 1980					
% college graduates	0.011	−0.002	0.002	−0.002	0.056**
% sales/admin. support	0.717**	0.094*	−0.028	0.223**	0.169*
Local/metro commute	−0.121**	−0.028**	0.025**	−0.033**	0.003
Old housing, dense pop.	−0.140**				
Metro area, 1980 and shifts 1980–1990					
Metro housing growth, 1980s (LN)	0.049**				
Metro % multifamily		0.008			
Metro multifamily shift, 1980s (LN)		0.162**			
Metro % single-family			0.018		
Metro single-family shift, 1980s (LN)			0.111**		
Metro % rentals				0.047*	

	Housing growth 1980–90 (LN)	% multi-family 1990	% single-family 1990	% rental 1990	% of rentals affordable 1990
Metro rental shift, 1980s (LN)				0.224**	
Metro % affordable rentals					0.205**
Metro affordable rental shift, 1980s (LN)					0.534**
Constant	0.726**	−0.212**	−0.038	0.245**	−0.568**
R²	0.577	0.928	0.941	0.933	0.838
F	94.86**	793.13**	986.72**	729.33**	229.43**
N	1102	1102	1102	1102	1102

Table 29.6 Parameter estimates, land use controls and housing, 1980–1990

APFO: Adequate public facilities ordinance
LN: Natural logarithm
†p<.10, *<.05,**p<.01

Of the *25* remaining housing outcomes tested – five housing outcomes for each of the five land use controls – only two were significant and exclusionary: Moratoria and boxed-in status reduced the 1990 share of affordable rentals by 3.7 and 2.5 percentage points, respectively. Boxed-in status was also associated with two inclusionary outcomes: faster population growth and a falling proportion of single-family housing. APFOs encouraged a shift toward multifamily housing, although this association was slight and only marginally significant. In all, therefore, these data lend support to recent findings that growth controls do not always work (Landis, 1992); in fact, the most effective growth control is low-density-only zoning, which has often been left out of recent growth-control studies.

How did housing supply, unit type, tenure, and affordability affect one another? Housing growth had inclusionary effects on unit type and tenure (see Table 29.6). It correlated with significant but small shifts from single-family to multifamily units; the average community added 0.01 percentage point to its multifamily housing share for every 1 percentage point increase in housing units and lost 0.2 percentage point of its single-family housing share.[9] A 1 percentage point increase in housing growth was also associated with a 0.04 percentage point decrease in the share of units rented; even

though the proportion of rented dwellings fell, however, the number of rented dwellings in such growing communities would have risen, an inclusive outcome. As expected; shifts toward single-family housing slightly reduced the rental share, and shifts toward multifamily housing slightly increased it. Rental housing supply, in turn, improved rental affordability. For example, if two cities, "Smith" and "Jones," both had 30% affordable rentals in 1980, but Smith had 10% more rental housing than Jones, then by 1990, 31.7% of Smith's rental housing stock would be affordable while Jones' share of affordable rentals would be stuck at 30%. Rental affordability also grew in communities that shifted toward rentals in the 1980s.

Communities with low-density-only zoning therefore became more exclusive in the 1980s in three ways. They grew more slowly; they shifted further from multifamily to single-family units; and they shifted further away from renter occupancy. Since shifts toward multifamily and rental housing were also associated with shifts toward rental affordability, low-density-only zoning indirectly contributed to lower rental affordability, although its direct effect on rental affordability seemed positive when all other housing factors were held constant.

How do housing outcomes influence racial composition? This next set of regressions suggests that Blacks and Hispanics respond differently to exclusionary housing outcomes (see Table 29.7). Rental housing made a significant but small difference in local shares of Black residents. For example, in 1980 Smith and Jones cities were (hypothetically) both 7% Black, and 10% of Smith's and 60% of Jones's dwellings were rented. During the 1980s, Smith's rental share remained at 10% while that of Jones grew to 72%. By 1990, Jones's Black share would have grown by about 1.2 percentage points because it began with 50% more rental housing, and by another 0.3 percentage points because of the shift toward even more rentals.

	% Black, 1990		% Hispanic, 1990	
	All	Low-Black	All	Low-Hispanic
Land use controls in place in the 1980s				
Low-density-only zoning	−0.001	−0.001	0.002	0.000
Permit cap	0.000	−0.002	−0.015**	−0.005
Long-lasting moratorium	−0.009	−0.004	−0.003	0.001
APFO, > 2 subjects	0.003	0.002	−0.001	0.001
Urban growth boundary	−0.001	−0.002	0.000	−0.002
Boxed-in status	0.002	−0.001	0.002	0.003*
Housing stock, 1980				
% of units rented	0.035**	0.024*	0.020*	0.006
% of rentals affordable	0.007	0.006	0.015†	0.004
Vacancy rate	−0.001	−0.069	0.200**	0.090**
% rentals <2BR, 1990	−0.047**	−0.023*	0.023*	0.011*
<10,000 dwellings	0.020*	0.012	0.003	−0.002
10,000-25,000 dwellings	0.018*	0.010	0.003	−0.001
25,000-50,000 dwellings	0.015†	0.012	0.011†	0.003
50,000-150,000 dwellings	0.019†	0.007	0.007	−0.003
1990:1980 Housing ratios (change in housing)				
Change in number of dwellings	−0.003	0.000	−0.009**	0.001
Change in % singe family	−0.003	−0.002	0.000	0.000
Change in % multifamily	0.015	−0.001	−0.021	0.004
Change in % of units rented	0.028**	0.017**	0.006	0.001
Change in % of rentals affordable	0.000	0.000	0.003	0.001
Race, 1980				
% Black non-Hispanic	1.050**	1.219**	0.017†	−0.013*
% Hispanic	−0.006	0.007	1.091**	1.432**
Socioeconomic status and community location, 1980				
% college graduates	−0.025†	−0.024*	−0.032**	−0.023**
% sales/administrative support	0.264**	0.176**	−0.001	0.030*
Local/metro commute	0.007	0.005	0.000	−0.010**
Metro area, 1980 and shifts 1980–1990				
% Black non-Hispanic	0.109**	0.070**		
% growth, Black non-Hispanic	0.016†	0.016*		
% Hispanic			0.189**	0.057**
% growth, Hispanic			0.012**	0.008**

	% Black, 1990		% Hispanic, 1990	
	All	Low-Black	All	Low-Hispanic
Constant	−0.138**	−0.084**	−0.011	−0.015
R²	0.884	0.523	0.944	0.845
N	1,168	986	1,168	975

Table 29.7 Parameter estimates, land use controls, housing characteristics, and racial change, 1980–1990

Notes:
Low-Black and low-Hispanic communities have less than 10% Black or Hispanic residents.
APFO: Adequate public facilities ordinance
†p<. 10, *p<.05, **p<.01

The share of Hispanics grew in the 1980s primarily in response to housing vacancies and affordability. For example, if Smith and Jones cities both had 25% Hispanic residents in 1980, but Smith had a 12% housing vacancy rate and Jones a 4% rate, then Smith would have 26.6% Hispanics in 1990 while Jones would remain at 25%. Even though vacancies strengthened Hispanic representation, housing growth slightly but significantly reduced the Hispanic share in the analysis of all jurisdictions. (The low-Hispanic subset showed no significant effect.) It may be that in fast-growing jurisdictions, new non-Hispanic residents so outnumber new Hispanic residents that the overall share of Hispanics declines. Rental housing affordability also slightly but significantly boosted the share of Hispanics in the 1980s.

Land use controls became almost entirely insignificant once the housing and other variables were held constant. The sole exception was that building permit caps were associated with significant reductions in the share of Hispanic residents. (This result is not significant for the low-Hispanic subset). It is unlikely that Hispanics moved out or failed to move in because of building permit caps. Local vacancy rates had significant and strong effects on the share of Hispanic residents, but additional analysis (results not reported here) revealed that permit caps had no significant effects on the vacancy rate. Hispanics may therefore have responded to yet another set of untested housing conditions, or to other conditions (e.g., discrimination or steering) that happened to be at work more intensely in places with permit caps in the 1980s. In such case, permit caps would correlate, but have no causal relationship, with the reduction in Hispanics.

CHAINS OF EXCLUSION: LAND USE CONTROLS, RACE, AND HOUSING

This research confirms the long-known connection between low-density-only zoning and racial exclusion. In 1980, jurisdictions with low-density-only zoning housed about half as many Blacks, and two thirds as many Hispanics, as other jurisdictions within their regions. Jurisdictions with low-density-only zoning also failed to gain as many Black and Hispanic residents between 1980 and 1990 as did similar communities that permitted higher-density residential development. In 1990, these 171 jurisdictions had 153,316 Black and 156,943 Hispanic residents. Had the dynamics of racial transition in these places been similar to those in places without exclusionary zoning, they would have housed approximately 31,300 more Blacks and 21,600 more Hispanics: 20% and 14%, respectively, of the Black and Hispanic residents who actually lived there.

The study also found connections between building permit caps and racial exclusion. The Hispanic share in places with building permit caps fell by an average of 1.8 percentage points in the 1980s. Together, the 43 jurisdictions with permit caps had 564,118 Hispanic residents in 1990; that number would have been approximately 60,150 higher if caps had no statistically significant association with exclusion. Permit caps did not have significant effects on the Black population.

It may be no coincidence that the land use control with the most exclusionary effects on Blacks predominates in the northeastern and midwestern U.S., while the control with the most exclusionary effects on Hispanics is most common in California. Jurisdictions with low-density-only-zoning are disproportionately located in a few areas: Boston, New York, Philadelphia, Pittsburgh, and Cleveland, whose Black-White dissimilarity indices ranged from 0.73 to 0.88 in 1980, among the highest in the nation (Massey and Denton, 1988).[10] In Boston, low-density-only zoning applied to over half the land area in responding jurisdictions. Almost half of the responding jurisdictions in Boston and more than a quarter of those in New York restricted residential densities to fewer than eight units per acre. In both metropolitan areas, jurisdictions with populations between 10,000 and 25,000 were more likely than others to have low-density-only zoning. Therefore, even more low-density-only zoning would have been reported if small jurisdictions had responded at the same rate as large ones and if jurisdictions with fewer than 10,000 residents had been surveyed.

Permit caps, by contrast, are rare outside California. Only 42 of the 1,168 responding jurisdictions had permit caps, and 35 of these were in metropolitan San Francisco, Los Angeles, and San Diego. The Hispanic population in these regions grew nearly 70% between 1980 and 1990, from 3.6 million to 6.1 million residents. California's courts have been very permissive about permit caps, and some cities using permit caps – such as Livermore, California – have been held up as growth management models for the rest of the country (Landis, 1992; Nelson and Duncan, 1995). This qualified support by planning researchers for permit caps contrasts with the links reported here between caps and exclusion of Hispanics, and suggests a need for additional research and action, especially considering Census Bureau projections that the U.S. Hispanic population will grow from 30.5 million in July 1999 to 96.5 million in 2050 (U.S. Census Bureau, 1996).

Although land use controls have evident connections with the exclusion of Blacks and Hispanics, the mechanisms through which these effects occur are not straightforward. Land use controls are not signs that advertise "Whites only." If land use controls exclude Blacks and Hispanics, they do so over time by building residential environments that attract or accommodate large numbers of non-Hispanic White residents while failing to accommodate Blacks and Hispanics. I refer to this indirect connection between land use controls and racial exclusion as the "chain of exclusion." Figure 29.2 depicts this chain of exclusion.

In the first link of the chain, low-density-only zoning reduced housing growth in the 1980s. Second, low-density-only zoning combined with slower growth to reduce the share of multifamily units and boost the single-family share. Third, low-density-only zoning, slow growth, and reductions in multifamily housing correlated with a falling proportion of rental units. Fourth, slow growth, reductions in multifamily housing, and falling rentals all correlated with reductions in the affordability of the rental stock. Among the other land use controls, only boxed-in status and permit moratoria were associated with exclusionary effects, and in these cases, the effect was limited to one characteristic only: reduced rental housing affordability. In the fifth link of the chain, a restricted multifamily and rental housing stock dampened growth in the minority population.

These findings on land use controls and housing are consistent with other recent research. According to this study, permit caps and growth boundaries, often modeled as supply constraints that will inexorably elevate house prices (Elliott, 1981; Frech and Lafferty, 1984; Schwartz and Zorn, 1988), did not consistently reduce housing growth in the 1980s. Neither did they have any consistent average effect on housing unit types, tenure, or affordability (or on vacancy rates, which were tested in an unreported analysis). Since local governments or voters often impose permit caps after growth spurts, the "limits" often exceed a normal year's construction (Landis, 1992). Many jurisdictions also allow "borrowing" from later years' allocations and make exceptions for small developments, so that even a high cap can be exceeded (City of Livermore, 1992). Growth boundaries often encircle areas that are much larger than needed to accommodate future housing construction. Growth boundaries can also be moved, and large numbers of houses are sometimes permitted outside a permanent boundary (Nelson and Moore, 1996). In short, permit caps and growth boundaries sometimes have exclusionary effects, but often they are little more than symbols of concern about the pace and shape of new growth.

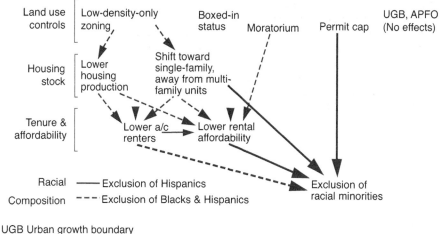

Figure 29.2 The chain of exclusion: significant relationships.

Low-density-only zoning imposes a strong, long-lasting, and uniform ceiling on housing density. This study classified as "low density only" any jurisdiction that prohibits housing construction at a gross density of higher than eight dwelling units per acre. This limit leaves ample room for variation; it would apply to both a jurisdiction permitting a 60-unit apartment complex on a minimum 10-acre lot and a jurisdiction whose most permissive residential zoning allows single-family homes on 6,000-square-foot lots. Even so, such a density ceiling would reduce housing growth and the share of multifamily and rental housing.

Housing conditions affected Blacks and Hispanics differently. Rental housing promoted growth in the share of Blacks consistently and strongly, while rental housing affordability and vacancy rates had no appreciable effect. Rising rental affordability and ample housing vacancies, by contrast, were consistently significant and important for Hispanics; rental housing also had a positive influence on the Hispanic share, but not in the subset of low-Hispanic communities.

The precise effects of exclusionary low-density-only zoning must still, however, be considered exploratory for at least two reasons. First, because of data limitations I was unable to control statistically for any unobserved fixed community characteristics that may have been hidden causes for housing or racial change. Second, land use controls are themselves sometimes an outcome of patterns of community change, including housing and racial change. Further research and analysis would be helpful to gain greater certainty about dynamics of the relationship between community change and land use controls.

Despite these caveats, this research is entirely consistent with previous case-study findings and research about both zoning and other land use controls. In this context, the study should be sufficient to suggest that planners should, in the terms of the AICP code of ethics, urge the alteration of low-density-only zoning as an institution that "opposes the needs of disadvantaged groups and persons" (AICP, 1991). Planners can consider at least two existing policies to alter exclusionary zoning. The "fair share" model, most actively applied in California and New Jersey, requires local governments to zone land and develop programs to help meet housing needs for all income levels. The "anti-snob zoning" approach, used in southern New England, permits subsidized housing developers to appeal local governments' decisions to deny their projects when fewer than 10% of the town's or city's dwellings are subsidized.[11] The results of this study suggest that variants of the fair share approach will more likely promote economic and racial integration than anti-snob zoning, which is reactive and places the burden on developers to appeal local decisions, thereby subjecting them to possible retribution on subsequent projects. Anti-snob zoning laws also fail to remove obstacles to market-rate multifamily rental housing in communities that have already provided their share of subsidized units. Since the share of rental housing is consistently more important for Blacks than the share of affordable rental housing, the anti-snob zoning approach constitutes only a partial solution to the problem of racial exclusion.

In summary, this research shows that low-density-only zoning has historic and current connections with racial exclusion. When local governments adopt zoning ordinances or building permit caps, they directly influence the use of land and the pace of development. They also indirectly control who may live within their boundaries. Because land use controls have only an indirect effect on a place's eventual residents, however, legal challenges to exclusionary land use controls seldom succeed. Even the most successful lawsuits usually result in court orders to allow construction of particular affordable housing projects, not in comprehensive programs to rewrite communities' zoning ordinances.

Although local legal challenges offer little hope for comprehensive solutions to exclusionary zoning, other approaches may gain legitimacy in the future. Myron Orfield's (1997) *Metropolitics* relates that in Minneapolis, inner cities and inner suburbs have begun to forge a consensus for a state fair-housing policy. Similar coalitions may be possible in other metropolitan areas. Beyond ethnic and economic exclusion, low-density-only zoning exacerbates "sprawl" (Pendall, 1999), which in turn can require huge investments in new infrastructure, produce more nonpoint source air and water pollution, and further fragment wildlife habitat. All these effects present opportunities for coalition building to promote inclusive housing.

ACKNOWLEDGMENTS

Thanks to Elizabeth Deakin, Matthew Drennan, Ann-Margaret Esnard, Marshall Feldman, William Goldsmith, John Landis, Dowell Myers, Sidney Saltzman, and the anonymous reviewers for substantive comments on various drafts. Joanne Pendall and Trudie Calvert provided editorial assistance; Leda Black created Figure 29.2. Any errors or misinterpretation remain my responsibility. This research was funded in part by the University of California at Berkeley's Center for Real Estate and Urban Economics.

Notes

1 The study uses eight units per gross acre as a measure of single-family densities. Some low-density-only jurisdictions allow apartment construction but constrain development by mandating large lots and substantial parking and landscaping.

2 The metropolitan areas were the Atlanta MSA, Baltimore MSA, Boston-Lawrence-Salem-Lowell-Brockton NECMA, Chicago-Gary-Lake County CMSA, Cincinnati-Hamilton CMSA, Cleveland-Akron-Loraine CMSA, Dallas-Ft. Worth CMSA, Denver-Boulder CMSA, Detroit-Ann Arbor CMSA, Houston-Galveston-Brazoria CMSA, Kansas City MSA, Los Angeles-Anaheim-Riverside CMSA, Miami-Fort Lauderdale CMSA, Milwaukee-Racine CMSA, Minneapolis-St. Paul MSA, New York-Northern New Jersey-Long Island CMSA, Philadelphia-Wilmington-Trenton CMSA, Phoenix MSA, Pittsburgh-Beaver County CMSA, San Diego MSA, San Francisco-Oakland-San Jose CMSA, Seattle-Tacoma CMSA, St. Louis MSA, Tampa-St. Petersburg-Clearwater MSA, and Washington MSA, all as defined in June 1990 by the U.S. Office of Management and Budget.

3 That is, if the jurisdiction had authority to adopt a zoning ordinance and exercised primary control over local zoning within its territory. This excluded Texas counties, which do not zone, and counties in most northeastern and midwestern states, which play at most an advisory role in town- or township-controlled zoning decisions.

4 The survey also included questions about the availability of vacant land for multifamily housing and about affordable housing policies. The completion rate on these questions was lower. Blank survey forms are available from the author on request.

5 Data for 1990 came from CD-ROMs containing summary results from the 100% census (STF1A) and the long-form 16% census sample (STF3A); 1980 data were extracted from the tape version of STF3. The 1980 and 1990 data sometimes apply to different geographic areas; between 1980 and 1990, 31 places incorporated as cities. Twenty-five of these were listed as census-designated places (CDPs) in 1980; the data from these CDPs were used alongside the incorporated-area data in the analysis. Of the 756 places that were incorporated in 1980, 118 (16%) increased in land area by more than one third between 1980 and 1990, presumably as a result of annexation. No methods were used to hold the land area of cities and villages constant at their 1980 or 1990 limits. As a result, some changes between 1980 and 1990 resulted from annexation of housing in previously unincorporated areas. A complete listing of the precise tables and variables used is available from the author on request.

6 The term Black is used throughout this analysis instead of African American to provide consistency with terminology in the 1980 and 1990 U.S. Census of Population; Blacks as measured in this research may be African American, Caribbean, Afro-European, or African.

7 Data were missing for about 65 jurisdictions in this test. Descriptive statistics are available from the author on request.

8 This regression measures housing growth as the natural logarithm of the ratio of 1990 housing units to 1980 housing units; the natural log was used to correct for positive skew and outliers.

9 These numbers are obtainable by taking the antilog of the parameters in Table 29.6.

10 The dissimilarity index (D) ranges from 0 to 1 and is conventionally interpreted to represent the proportion of Blacks or Whites who would have to move to achieve racial evenness across a region.

11 Connecticut General Statutes § 8-30g; Massachusetts General Laws Chapter 40B §§20-23; R.I. Gen.

REFERENCES

Altshuler, A. A, and Gómez-Ibáñez, J. A (1993). *Regulation for revenue: The political economy of land use exactions.* Washington, D.C., and Cambridge, MA: Brookings Institution Press/Lincoln Institute of Land Policy.

American Institute of Certified Planners. (1991). *AICP code of ethics and professional conduct* [On-line]. Available: http://www.planning.org/abtaicp/conduct.html (Adopted 1978, amended 1991).

American Planning Association. (1998). *Growing Smart^SM* [Online]. Available: http://www.planning.org/plnginfo/GROWSMAR/gsindex.html.

Anglin, R. (1994). Searching for justice: Court-inspired housing policy as a mechanism for social and economic mobility. *Urban Affairs Quarterly, 29,* 432–453.

Appelbaum, R. P., and Gilderbloom, J. I. (1986). Supply-side economics and rents: Are rental housing markets truly competitive? In R. G. Bratt, C. Hartman, and A. Meyerson (Eds.), *Critical perspectives on housing* (pp. 165–179). Philadelphia: Temple University Press.

Arlington Heights v. Metropolitan Housing Development Corp., 429 U.S. 252 (1977).

Bates, L. J., and Santerre, R. E. (1994). The determinants of restrictive residential zoning: Some empirical findings. *Journal of Regional Science, 34,* 253–263.

Bay Area Council. (1988). *Taxing the American dream: Development fees and housing affordability.* San Francisco: Author.

Bollens, S. A (1992). State growth management: Intergovernmental frameworks and policy objectives. *Journal of the American Planning Association, 58,* 454–466.

Britton v. Town of Chester, 595 A2d 492 (NH 1991). Buchanan v. Warley, 245 U.S. 60 (1917).

Burnell, B. S., and Burnell, J. D. (1989). Community interaction and suburban zoning policies. *Urban Affairs Quarterly,* 24, 470–482.

Calavita, N., and Grimes, K. (1998). Inclusionary housing in California: The experience of two decades. *Journal of the American Planning Association,* 64, 150–169.

City of Livermore Planning Department. (1992). *1992–1993 Housing implementation program* [Brochure]. Livermore, CA: Author.

Clark, W. A. V. (1986). Residential segregation in American cities: A review and interpretation. *Population Research and Policy Review,* 5, 95–127.

Cloud, C., and Galster, G. (1993). What do we know about racial discrimination in mortgage markets? *The Review of Black Political Economy,* 22, 101–120.

Danielson, M. N. (1976). *The politics of exclusion.* New York: Columbia University Press.

Dillman, D. A (1978). *Mail and telephone surveys: The total design method.* New York: Wiley.

Donovan, T., and Neiman, M. (1995). Local growth control policy and changes in community characteristics. *Social Science Quarterly,* 76, 780–793.

Dowall, D. E. (1980). An examination of population-growth-managing communities. *Policy Studies journal,* 9, 414–427.

Dowall, D. E. (1984). *The suburban squeeze.* Berkeley: University of California Press.

Elliott, M. (1981). The impact of growth control regulations on housing prices in California. *AREUEA Journal,* 9, 115–133.

Fair Housing Act of 1968, 42 U.S. C. §§2000d-1, -2.

Farley, J. E. (1993). Racial housing segregation in St. Louis, 1980–1990: Comparing block and census tract levels. *Journal of Urban Affairs,* 15, 515–527.

Farley, R., and Frey, W. H. (1994). Changes in the segregation of Whites from Blacks during the 1980s: Small steps toward a more integrated society. *American Sociological Review,* 59, 23–45.

Farley, R., Fielding, E. L., and Krysan, M. (1997). The residential preferences of Blacks and Whites: A four-metropolis analysis. *Housing Policy Debate,* 8, 763–800.

Fernley v. Board of Supervisors, 502 A2d 585 (Pa 1985).

Frech, H. E., III, and Lafferty, R.N. (1984). The effect of the California Coastal Commission on housing prices. *Journal of Urban Economics,* 16, 105–123.

Galster, G. (1988). Residential segregation in American cities: A contrary review. *Population Research and Policy Review,* 7, 93–112.

Galster, G. (1991). Black suburbanization: Has it changed the relative location of races? *Urban Affairs Quarterly* 26, 621–628.

Karoly, L. A (1992). *The trend in inequality among families, individuals, and workers in the United States: A twenty-five year perspective.* Santa Monica, CA: RAND.

Keating, W. D. (1994). *The suburban racial dilemma.* Philadelphia: Temple University Press.

Keating, W. D. (1997). The Parma housing racial discrimination remedy revisited. *Cleveland State University Law Review,* 45, 235–250.

Kirp, D. L., Dwyer, J. P., and Rosenthal, L. A. (1995). *Our town: Race, housing, and the soul of suburbia.* New Brunswick, NJ: Rutgers University Press.

Knaap, G. (1985). The price effects of urban growth boundaries in metropolitan Portland, Oregon. *Land Economics,* 61, 26–35.

Kushner, J. A (1995). *Fair housing: Discrimination in real estate, community development, and 1'evitalization* (2nd ed.). Deerfield, IL: Clark Boardman Callaghan.

Landis, J. D. (1992). Do growth controls work? A new assessment. *Journal of the American Planning Association,* 58, 489–508.

Landis, J. D. (1995). Imagining land use futures: Applying the California Urban Futures model. *Journal of the American Planning Association,* 61, 438–457.

Massey, D. S., and Denton, N. A (1988). Suburbanization and segregation in U.S. metropolitan areas. *American Journal of Sociology,* 94, 592–626.

Massey, D. S., and Denton, N. A (1993). *American apartheid: Segregation and the making of the underclass.* Cambridge, MA: Harvard University Press.

Nelson, A. C,. and Duncan, J. B. (1995). *Growth management principles and practices.* Chicago: Planners Press.

Nelson, A. C., and Moore, T. (1996). Assessing growth management policy implementation. *Land Use Policy, 13,* 241–259.

Orfield, M. (1997). *Metropolitics: A regional agenda for community and stability.* Washington, D.C., and Cambridge, MA: Brookings Institution Press/Lincoln Institute of Land Policy.

Pendall, R. (1995). *Residential growth controls and racial and ethnic diversity: Making and breaking the chain of exclusion.* Unpublished doctoral dissertation, University of California, Berkeley.

Pendall, R. (1999). Do land use controls cause sprawl? *Environment and Planning B: Planning and Design, 26,* 555–571.

Pogodzinski, J. M., and Sass, T. R. (1994). The theory and estimation of endogenous zoning. *Regional Science and Urban Economics, 24,* 601–630.

Schelling, T. (1971). Dynamic models of segregation. *Journal of Mathematical Sociology, 1,* 143–86.

Schneider, M., and Phelan, T. (1993). Black suburbanization in the 1980s. *Demography, 30,* 269–279.

Schuman, H., Steeh, C., and Bobo, L. (1985). *Racial attitudes in America: Trends and interpretation.* Cambridge, MA: Harvard University Press.

Schwartz, S. I., and Zorn, P.M. (1988). A critique of quasiexperimental and statistical controls for measuring program effects: Application to urban growth control. *Journal of Policy Analysis and Management, 7,* 491–505.

Schwartz, S. I., Hansen, D. E., and Green, R. (1984). The effect of growth control on the production of moderate priced housing. *Land Economics, 60,* 110–14.

Southern Burlington NAACP v. Township of Mount Laurel (Mount Laurel I), 336 A2d 713 (NJ 1975).

Southern Burlington NAACP v. Township of Mount Laurel (Mount Laurel II), 456 A2d 390 (NJ 1983).

Stockman, P. K. (1992). Anti-snob zoning in Massachusetts: Assessing one attempt at opening the suburbs to affordable housing. *Virginia Law Review, 78,* 535–580.

U.S. Census Bureau. (1996). *Resident population of the United States: Middle series projections, 2035–2050, by sex, race, and Hispanic origin, with median age* [On-line]. Available: http://www.census.gov/population/projections/nation/nsrh/nprh3550.txt.

U.S. Census Bureau. (1998a). *Moving to America: Moving to homeownership* [On-line]. Available: http://www.census.gov/hhesjwww/homeown.html.

U.S. Census Bureau. (1998b). *Historical income tables: Households* [On-line]. Available: http://www.census.gov/hhes/income/histinc/hOS.html.

U.S. Congress Office of Technology Assessment. (1995). *The technological reshaping of metropolitan America* (OTA-ETI-643). Washington, D.C.: U.S. Government Printing Office.

U.S. v. City of Black Jack, 508 F2d 1179 (8th Cir 1974), cert denied, 434 U.S. 1025 (1978).

Wallace, N. E. (1988). The market effects of zoning undeveloped land: Does zoning follow the market? *Journal of Urban Economics, 23,* 307–326.

Warner, K., and Molotch, H. (1995). Power to build: How development persists despite local controls. *Urban Affairs Review, 30,* 378–406.

Weicher, J. C., and Thibodeau, T. G. (1988). Filtering and housing markets: An empirical analysis. *Journal of Urban Economics, 23,* 21–40.

Weiss, M.A. (1987). *The rise of the community builders.* New York: Columbia University Press.

Zorn, P.M., Hansen, D. E., and Schwartz, S. (1986). Mitigating the price effects of growth control: A case study of Davis, California. *Land Economics, 62,* 47–57.

30
"Housing market effects of inclusionary zoning"

From *Cityscape* (2009)

Antonio Bento
Cornell University

Scott Lowe
Boise State University

Gerrit-Jan Knaap
University of Maryland, College Park

Arnab Chakraborty
University of Illinois, Urbana-Champaign

INTRODUCTION

As concerns about affordable housing have grown across the country, local governments have responded by adopting a variety of affordable housing programs. An increasing number of local governments are considering an inclusionary zoning approach, which requires developers to sell a certain percentage of newly developed housing units at below-market rates to lower income households. Although specific details of these programs vary widely, they are politically attractive because they are viewed as a way to promote housing affordability without raising taxes or using public funds.

No program, of course, is cost free. According to standard economic theory, inclusionary zoning acts like a tax on housing construction. And just as with other taxes, the burdens of inclusionary zoning are passed on to housing consumers, housing producers, and landowners. More specifically, economic theory suggests that inclusionary zoning requirements act to decrease the supply of housing at every price, raise housing prices, and slow housing construction. As a result, inclusionary zoning policies could exacerbate the affordable housing problem that they are designed to address.

Although debate over the merits of inclusionary zoning has continued for nearly three decades, no rigorous studies have been done on their effects on housing prices and starts. This article offers such an analysis. Specifically, this article presents an analysis of the effects of inclusionary zoning policies on single-family housing prices, single-family and multifamily housing starts, and the size of single-family housing units in California during the period from 1988 through 2005.

The analysis found that inclusionary zoning policies have measurable effects on housing markets. Specifically, it found that, in jurisdictions that adopt inclusionary zoning, the share of multifamily housing increases, the price of single-family houses increases, and the size of single-family houses decreases. The analysis did not examine the purported benefits of inclusionary zoning, such as whether these policies increase the supply of affordable housing or serve to integrate low- and high-income residents. Therefore, the analysis cannot ascertain whether inclusionary zoning increases social welfare. It demonstrates, however, that such benefits do not come without measurable costs.

BACKGROUND

The first inclusionary zoning program was adopted in 1974 by Montgomery County, Maryland. The original Montgomery County ordinance required that 15 percent of new developments with more than 50 housing units be sold at a price affordable to low-income households. In return, the county provided developers with a density bonus that allowed them to build at a density up to 20 percent higher than the maximum density allowed by zoning. Since then, inclusionary zoning policies have grown in number and variety across the country. For example, between 1990 and 2003, the number of California communities with inclusionary zoning grew from 29 to 107 (Powell and Stringham, 2004). As of 2004, an estimated 350 to 400 local jurisdictions had inclusionary zoning programs, with the vast majority of these programs enacted in California, Massachusetts, and New Jersey (Porter, 2004).

The economic effects of inclusionary zoning are similar to those of a tax on housing construction, as show in Exhibit 1. As more

units are sold at a discount, the cost of development increases. Developers must raise the price on market-rate units to compensate for the cost of discounted units. As a result, the price of market-rate housing rises and the production of such housing declines. This decline in housing production can manifest as both a reduction in housing starts and as a reduction in housing size.

The features of inclusionary zoning programs vary widely, as shown in Exhibit 2. The economic impacts of inclusionary zoning vary based on the different program features. A voluntary program that relies on incentives might not have any economic impacts, while a mandatory program that requires many, deep, and long-term discounts could have significant adverse economic effects.

Previous research on inclusionary zoning has produced mixed results. Although most research has been theoretical and dominated by case studies, some studies have sought to quantify the benefits and potential costs.

An early study by Clapp (1981) described the potential reaction of developers to inclusionary zoning programs. Tombari (2005) similarly described the potential adverse effects on housing prices and starts. Powell and Stringham (2004), in their study for the Reason Public Policy Institute, provided quantitative support for the concerns raised by Clapp and Tombari. Specifically, using data from the San Francisco Bay area, they provided evidence to suggest that inclusionary zoning makes market-priced homes more expensive, restricts the supply of new homes, and produces few affordable units.

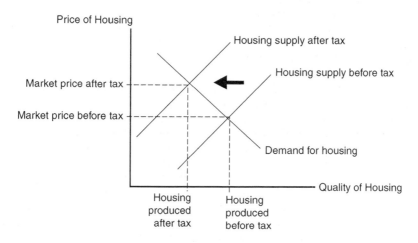

Exhibit 1 The economic effects of inclusionary zoning.

Feature	IZ Programs
Size and types of developments subject to inclusionary requirements	Some programs are voluntary; others impose inclusionary requirements only on large, single-family projects; and ther impose inclusionary requirements on all types of projects of all sizes
Percent of units that must be affordable	Some programs require only 5 percent of new units to be sold at a discount; others require percentages as high as 30 percent
Depth and duration of price discounts	The depth of price discounts often varies by the target population. For example, many programs require that units be made affordable to those at 80 percent of median household incomes, while others set different standards. The period of affordability often varies from 10 to 99 years
Incentives or allowances offered in compensation	Most programs offer some form of incentives or compensation for providing affordable units. Incentives and compensation often include density bonuses waivers of subdivision requirements, or fee reductions. Some programs permit payments in lieu of inclusionary units

Exhibit 2 Distinguishing features of inclusionary zoning programs.

IZ = inclusionary zoning

A considerable volume of case study research, however, comes to quite opposite conclusions. Using data from Los Angeles, Rosen (2002) found no correlation between the adoption of an inclusionary housing policy and housing starts in 28 California cities. Multiple case studies by Calavita (Calavita, 2004; Calavita and Grimes, 1998; Calavita, Grimes, and Mallach, 1997) and his colleagues in California and New Jersey concluded that inclusionary zoning is a viable strategy for increasing the supply of affordable housing and mixing low- and high-income residents. The National Housing Conference (2002) drew similar conclusions in case studies conducted in Massachusetts.

In a study of the inclusionary zoning programs in the Greater Washington metropolitan area, Brown (2001) concluded that inclusionary zoning programs work best in jurisdictions with large amounts of undeveloped land and less effectively in dense, more mature metropolitan areas. The Non-Profit Housing Association of Northern California (NPH) and the California Coalition for Rural Housing (2003) published the results of a survey on the prevalence and components of inclusionary housing programs in California. The study found significant variation in both the prevalence and the components of the programs

in California and concluded that the effects of such programs depend in part on such programmatic details. The study presented in the following section tests this proposition using data from the NPH survey.

SCOPE AND CONTEXT OF THE STUDY

This article examines housing markets in local jurisdictions in California during the period from 1988 through 2005. During this period, for a number of reasons, California offers a good setting for examining the effects of inclusionary zoning. First, the state is large and includes many municipalities with distinct regulatory environments. Second, California is an often-studied state with very good data available for housing market analysis. Third, and most importantly, inclusionary zoning programs became increasingly common in California during the study period. Time-series analyses of housing markets in California from 1988 through 2005 included observations of many cities with existing inclusionary zoning policies, cities without inclusionary zoning policies, and cities that adopted inclusionary zoning policies within the study period. For each individual city in this sample we controlled for unobserved, time-invariant characteristics that might affect housing starts or the types of houses that are built. By doing so, we were able to isolate the effects of the inclusionary zoning programs, relative to other factors that might be influencing new housing developments. It is the variation in the use of inclusionary zoning across the state and over time that helps to isolate the effects of this policy from other factors.

Although the study setting is well suited for this analysis, any such analysis must be interpreted in the context of prevailing market conditions. As shown in Exhibits 3 and 4, housing

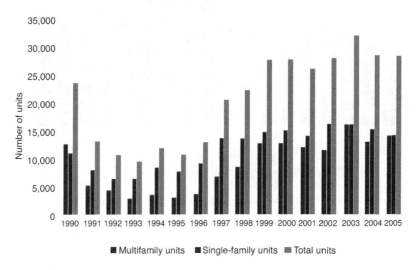

■ Multifamily units ■ Single-family units ■ Total units

Exhibit 3 New housing construction for all cities in California.

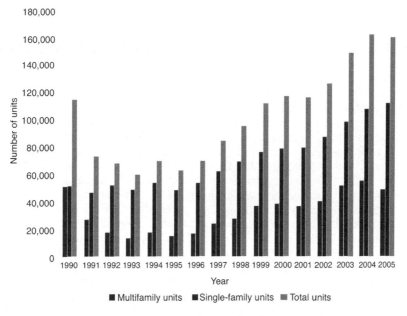

Year

■ Multifamily units ■ Single-family units ■ Total units

Exhibit 4 New housing construction for cities in California with inclusionary zoning.

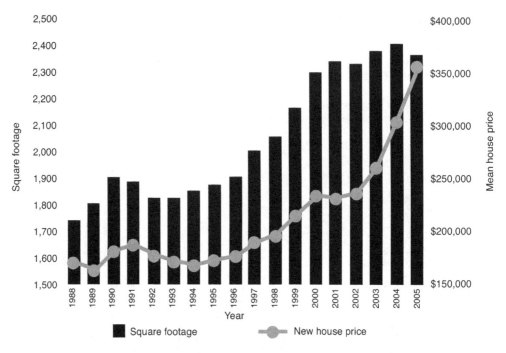

Exhibit 5 Square footage and new house prices in the San Francisco and Sacramento metropolitan areas.

starts in California were strongly influenced by national business cycles during the study period. Housing starts bottomed in the early 1990s as the national economy fell into recession but increased fairly consistently as the economy recovered. New housing prices were similarly affected by national business cycles, as shown in Exhibit 5 for the San Francisco and Sacramento metropolitan areas, but did not rise until 1996. The average size of a new, single-family house, however, rose slowly but consistently during the study period, as shown in Exhibit 5.

Although these trends primarily reflect national business cycles, housing markets in California have several location-specific characteristics of note. According to Landis *et al.* (2000), since the 1980s, housing markets in California have not produced housing units commensurate with the rapid growth in demand. The specific reasons for this are numerous, although limitations in the supply of land, capital, and infrastructure are all likely factors. Regulatory constraints probably also played a role. According to Pendall, Puente, and Martin (2006), local governments in California have adopted more growth management instruments

than their counterparts in other parts of the country. Thus, it is important to note that this study was conducted in markets characterized by strong demand-side pressures and significant and varied supply-side constraints.

DATA AND DESCRIPTIVE STATISTICS

The data for this analysis, derived from a variety of sources, are used to compile two distinct data sets. The primary sources of these data include the California Construction Industry Research Board (CIRB), the Census Bureau, and DataQuick News Service Custom Reports. [...] The first data set uses municipalities as the unit of analysis and includes information about the physical, demographic, and economic characteristics of cities throughout California, including information on location, regulatory environment, and natural setting. In addition, the data set includes information about whether the municipality had an inclusionary zoning program and, if so, when the program was first adopted. Data were obtained for the period 1988 through 2005. This first data set is used to

| Variable | Inclusionary Zoning Cities | | | |
	Mean	Sd	Min.	Max.
Offsite allowances	57%	50%		
In-lieu fees	76%	43%		
Land dedications	25%	43%		
Developer credit transfers	13%	34%		
Target population very low income	41%	49%		
Target population low income	77%	42%		
Target population moderate income	61%	49%		
Period of affordability[a]	34	12	10	55
Minimum project size to qualify[b]	12	50	0	400
Percent of units as part of IZ	12%	6%	0%	30%
Cities (N)	65			
Observations[c]	1,011			

Exhibit 6 Descriptive statistics.

IZ = inclusionary zoning, N = number, Sd = standard deviation
[a] In years
[b] Number of units
[c] Years of data * N
Note: The study included 65 municipalities.

study the effects of inclusionary zoning on the number and composition (single family vs. multifamily) of housing units built, controlling for other factors.

As shown in Exhibit 6, 65 municipalities included in this study had adopted an inclusionary zoning program after 1989 but before the end of the study period. On average, the minimum project size at which a development became subject to inclusionary requirements was 12 housing units and the percentage of units that had to be made available to low-income households was 12 percent. Of the 65 municipalities with inclusionary policies, 57 percent allowed offsite allowances, 76 percent allowed in-lieu fees, 25 percent offered land dedication allowances, and 13 percent allowed developer credit transfers. The average length of time affordable units must remain affordable is 34 years, although many municipalities have stipulated that the units remain affordable in perpetuity.

As illustrated in Exhibit 7, cities that adopted inclusionary programs are located throughout the state but are most common in the coastal areas, especially in the San Francisco and Sacramento metropolitan areas and the Los Angeles metropolitan area. In general, municipalities that

had inclusionary zoning programs, relative to those that did not, had higher incomes, higher housing prices, higher growth rates, and more neighbors with similar policies. In addition, these municipalities were closer to the coast.

The second data set uses new single-family home sales as the unit of analysis. This data set includes information about newly constructed housing units in the San Francisco and Sacramento metropolitan areas, and it includes the physical features of the house, the neighborhood in which the house is located, and the policies of the pertinent governmental jurisdiction – including the features of any applicable inclusionary zoning programs. The second data set was used to estimate the impacts of inclusionary zoning on the price and size of new homes sold.

Descriptive statistics of the new homes sold from 1988 through 2005 in the San Francisco and Sacramento metropolitan areas are presented in Exhibit 8. The costs and size changes, mirrored in Exhibit 5, indicate the recession of the early 1990s and the upward trend toward larger homes. The mean price of new home sales, even after correcting for inflation, increased steadily after 1995.

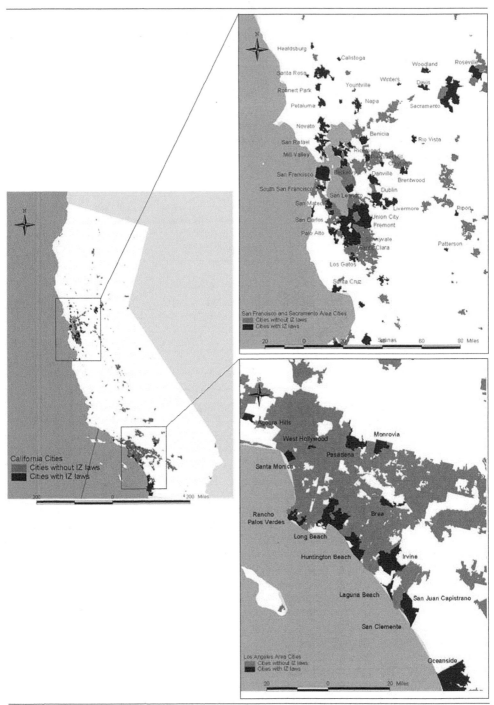

IZ = inclusionary zoning.

Exhibit 7 Inclusionary zoning programs in California.

Year	Number	Mean Cost[a] ($)	Mean Number of Bathrooms	Mean Number of Bedrooms	Mean Floor Space[b]
1988	14,580	167.68	2.31	3.07	1.74
1989	21,165	161.31	2.36	3.22	1.81
1990	18,694	180.66	2.42	3.35	1.90
1991	12,526	185.27	2.41	3.28	1.89
1992	11,158	176.67	2.36	3.24	1.83
1993	8,022	170.02	2.38	3.30	1.83
1994	13,189	167.12	2.39	3.35	1.85
1995	11,718	170.87	2.42	3.39	1.88
1996	13,813	175.26	2.43	3.37	1.91
1997	15,482	188.78	2.48	3.47	2.00
1998	15,768	195.86	2.49	3.49	2.06
1999	17,834	213.63	2.55	3.57	2.17
2000	17,977	233.04	2.61	3.62	2.30
2001	18,967	230.40	2.64	3.67	2.35
2002	21,954	235.82	2.60	3.58	2.34
2003	20,773	259.16	2.63	3.58	2.39
2004	21,827	304.15	2.68	3.61	2.41
2005	23,268	354.67	2.67	3.50	2.37
Avg.	16,595	209.46	2.49	3.43	2.06

Exhibit 8 Descriptive statistics – San Francisco and Sacramento metropolitan areas new home sales.

[a] Thousands of dollars in 1988 dollars
[b] Thousands of square feet

METHODS

To explore the effects of inclusionary zoning, we conducted a multivariate statistical analysis of housing starts, prices, and size. The results are presented in Exhibits 9 through 12. Exhibits 9 and 10 present the stock and composition effects of inclusionary zoning on housing starts. Exhibit 11 presents the effects of inclusionary zoning on housing prices. Exhibit 12 presents the results of the analysis on housing size. Each analysis includes city-level "fixed" effects to capture market-specific differences between jurisdictions that are assumed constant over time.

Model Dependent Variable: $([HU_{1+1} - HU_1] / HU_1)(*100)$	(1) Total Housing Units	(2) Single-Family Housing Units	(3) Multifamily Housing Units
Inclusionary zoning program	0.1536	−0.1885	0.3601
	(0.1478)	(0.1918)	(0.2605)
$[HU_1 - HU_{1-1}]$	1.03e-05	4.32e-05	3.93e-06
	(2.22e-06)***	(4.00e-06)***	(1.71e-06)**
Observations	5,509	5,509	5,509
City fixed effects	Yes	Yes	Yes
Year controls	Yes	Yes	Yes
R-squared	0.07	0.14	0.01

Exhibit 9 New housing stock change models.

HU = housing units
* Significant at 10%
** Significant at 5%
*** Significant at 1%
Note: Robust standard errors are in parentheses

Dependent Variable: % Single-Family Units1 +1 (*100)	(1)	(2)	(3)
Inclusionary zoning program	−6.8868		
	(1.9365)***		
Inclusionary zoning program requiring 10% or less of the units for low-income households		−2.9150	
		(2.5151)	
Inclusionary zoning program requiring more than 10% of the units for low-income households		−12.1033	
		(2.8076)***	
Inclusionary zoning program and a threshold of less than 10 units			−9.6961
			(2.1297)***
Inclusionary zoning program and a threshold of 10 or more units			−0.9995
			(3.7497)
Percent of single-family units$_1$	0.0671	0.0664	0.0663
	(0.0173)***	(0.01734)***	(0.01734)***
Observations	5,880	5,880	5,880
City fixed effects	Yes	Yes	Yes
Year controls	Yes	Yes	Yes
R-squared	0.03	0.03	0.03

Exhibit 10 New housing composition change models.

* Significant at 10%
** Significant at 5%
*** Significant at 1%
Note: Robust standard errors are in parentheses

Dependent Variable: Cost in 1988 Dollars	(1)	(2)	(3)
House price sample[a]	All	< $187,000	> $187,000
Inclusionary zoning program	0.022	−0.008	0.050
	(0.003)***	(0.004)***	(0.003)***
Observations	298,715	149,253	149,462
Beds, baths, and floor space included	Yes	Yes	Yes
Census block group boundary fixed effects	Yes	Yes	Yes
Year of sale controls	Yes	Yes	Yes
Quarter of sale controls	Yes	Yes	Yes
School district boundary controls	Yes	Yes	Yes
Lot size controls	Yes	Yes	Yes
Dummies for missing data	Yes	Yes	Yes
Clustered errors at the block group level	No	No	No
R-squared (within)	0.60	0.31	0.58

Exhibit 11 The effect of inclusionary zoning on new housing values.

[a] In 1988 dollars
* Significant at 10%
** Significant at 5%
*** Significant at 1%
Note: Robust standard errors are in parentheses. Samples includes all Bay Area and Sacramento new house sales of homes with fewer than 12 bedrooms or bathrooms, less than 30,000 square feet of living space, and more than 250 sqare feet of living space and that cost more than $20,000.

Dependent Variable: New House Interior Square Footage (Floor Space)/1,000	(1)	(2)	(3)
House price sample[a]	All	< $187,000	> $187,000
Inclusionary zoning program	−0.048	−0.033	0.001
	(0.006)***	(0.007)***	(0.008)
Observations	298,715	149,253	149,462
Beds and baths included	Yes	Yes	Yes
Census block group boundary fixed effects	Yes	Yes	Yes
Year of sale controls	Yes	Yes	Yes
Quarter of sale controls	Yes	Yes	Yes
School district boundary controls	Yes	Yes	Yes
Lot size controls	Yes	Yes	Yes
Dummies for missing data	Yes	Yes	Yes
Clustered errors at the block group level	No	No	No
R-squared (within)	0.53	0.52	0.46

Exhibit 12 The effect of inclusionary zoning on square footage of new houses.

[a] In 1988 dollars
* Significant at 10%
** Significant at 5%
*** Significant at 1%
Note: Robust standard errors are in parentheses. Samples includes all Bay Area and Sacramento new house sales of homes with fewer than 12 bedrooms or bathrooms, less than 30,000 square feet of living space, and more than 250 sqare feet of living space and that cost more than $20,000.

This analysis of housing starts specified the dependent variable as the percentage change in housing units so that the coefficients could be interpreted as elasticities – that is, the percentage change in starts resulting from a percentage (or unit) change in the dependent variable. Controls included city and year fixed effects that allowed us to account for any unobserved city-level characteristics (such as proximity to the coast, elevation, or desirable amenities) and for characteristics that are uniform across cities but vary across time (such as changing market conditions or statewide recessionary periods).

The analysis of housing prices specified the dependent variable as the logarithm of the sales price, and the analysis of house size specified the dependent variable in 1,000 square feet of living space. As with the housing starts models, we controlled for unobserved spatial and temporal characteristics of the houses that might affect their prices. Specifically, we controlled for the year and quarter the home was sold and for the neighborhood and school district within which the house is located. These controls allowed us to carefully account for any outside factors that may have influenced housing prices, thus isolating the effects of the inclusionary zoning programs.

RESULTS

In this section, we present the key results of this study. We focus on effects on housing starts, composition of housing starts, prices of new homes sold, and the size of new homes sold.

Effects on housing starts

As column 1 of Exhibit 9 shows, our findings indicate that inclusionary zoning programs had a small and insignificant effect on total housing starts during the study period. The analysis suggests that housing starts in municipalities were 0.15 percent greater in municipalities with an inclusionary zoning program compared to those without. This estimate, however, is not statistically significant at the 90-percent confidence level.

As column 2 of Exhibit 9 shows, our findings indicate that inclusionary zoning programs had a small and statistically insignificant effect on single-family housing starts. The analysis

suggests that single-family housing starts were 0.19 percent lower in municipalities that had an inclusionary zoning program compared with those that did not. This estimate, however, also is not statistically significant at the 90-percent confidence level.

As column 3 of Exhibit 9 shows, our findings indicate that inclusionary zoning programs had a small and statistically insignificant positive effect on multifamily housing starts. The estimate indicates that multifamily housing starts were 0.36 percent higher in municipalities that had an inclusionary zoning program compared with those that did not. Once again, however, this estimate is not statistically significant at the 90-percent confidence level.

Effects on composition of housing starts

As column 1 of Exhibit 10 shows, our estimates indicate that the adoption of inclusionary zoning had a significant effect on the share of single-family housing starts. Holding all other variables constant, the share of single-family housing starts in municipalities that implemented inclusionary zoning programs was nearly 7 percentage points lower than the share in those municipalities that did not implement such a program. This result is very significant: the chances are less than 0.01 percent that there was no effect of inclusionary zoning on this ratio of housing mix.

As columns 2 and 3 of Exhibit 10, respectively, show, the effect of inclusionary zoning on housing mix varied significantly with the percentage of housing units required to be sold to low-income households and with the minimum project size subject to inclusionary zoning requirements. Compared with jurisdictions without inclusionary zoning programs, municipalities with an inclusionary zoning program in which the percentage of new homes to be sold at a discount requirement was more severe (greater than 10 percent of a project's units) experienced a 12-percent shift from single-family to multifamily housing starts. Similarly, the inclusionary zoning regulation resulted in a 10-percent shift from single-family to multifamily housing starts in jurisdictions with an inclusionary zoning program in which the threshold that required participation in the inclusionary zoning program was more severe (for example, inclusionary zoning regulations that apply only to projects with fewer than 10 units).

Effects on prices of new homes sold

Estimates of the effects of inclusionary zoning programs on housing prices are presented in Exhibit 11. As column 1 shows, our estimates indicate that inclusionary zoning programs raise housing prices by approximately 2.2 percent. Also, as columns 2 and 3 show, our estimates indicate that the effects on inclusionary zoning are greater in higher priced housing markets. Specifically, our estimates indicate that inclusionary zoning programs lowered the price of housing that sold for less than $187,000 (in 1988 dollars) by about 0.8 percent and increased the price of housing that sold for more than $187,000 by about 5.0 percent.

Effects on the size of new homes sold

Estimates of the effects of inclusionary zoning on the size of single-family housing are presented in Exhibit 12. As column 1 shows, our estimates indicate that the implementation of an inclusionary zoning program lowers the mean housing size by approximately 48 square feet. Further, as columns 2 and 3 show, the effects of inclusionary zoning on housing size are greater on lower priced homes. Specifically, our estimates indicate that houses that sold for less than $187,000 are approximately 33 square feet smaller in inclusionary zoning jurisdictions, while houses that sold for more than $187,000 are larger in inclusionary zoning jurisdictions by a statistically insignificant amount.

CONCLUSIONS

Although inclusionary zoning programs have been around for some time, they remain controversial. Proponents argue that such programs are effective tools for increasing the supply of affordable housing and for helping to integrate low- and high-income residents. Opponents argue that such programs impose cost burdens on developers, increase the price of market-rate units, and lower the supply of market-rate housing. This study provides no new information about the validity of the

arguments of the proponents; however, it does offer new information about the arguments of the opponents.

Overall, our findings show that inclusionary zoning programs had significant effects on housing markets in California from 1988 through 2005. Although cities with existing or new programs during the study period did not experience a significant reduction in the rate of single-family housing starts, they did experience a statistically insignificant increase (at a 90-percent confidence level) in multifamily housing starts. As a consequence, our findings show that cities with inclusionary housing programs experienced a significant and relatively large increase in the ratio of multifamily to single-family housing production. That is, having an inclusionary housing program increased a city's multifamily housing starts share by 7 percent. The reasons for this shift are relatively clear. Housing markets in California cities, persistently constrained by regulatory barriers, expanded rapidly during the 1990s as the national and California economies recovered from the 1991 recession. Inclusionary zoning programs in cities where they were adopted placed a small additional burden on single-family development and less of a burden on multifamily development. Under the pressure of growing demand, single-family starts declined slightly and multifamily starts increased significantly. The economic recovery, paired with a more rigid regulatory environment, caused a significant shift toward multifamily housing development during the 1990s. This shift was greater in cities that required a larger percentage of the new units to be sold at below-market rates and in cities that required inclusionary units in developments with smaller numbers of units. No net effect, however, was evident on total housing starts.

Findings also indicate that housing prices in cities that adopted inclusionary zoning increased approximately 2 to 3 percent faster than in cities that did not adopt such policies. In addition, our findings show that housing price effects were greater in higher priced housing markets than in lower priced markets. That is, housing that sold for less than $187,000 (in 1988 dollars) decreased by only 0.8 percent, but housing that sold for more than $187,000 increased by 5.0 percent. These findings suggest that housing producers, in general, did not respond to inclusionary requirements by slowing the rate of construction of single-family housing but did pass the increase in production costs on to housing consumers. Further, housing producers were better able to pass on the increase in costs in higher priced housing markets than in lower priced housing markets.

Finally, our findings indicate that the size of market-rate houses in cities that adopted inclusionary zoning increased more slowly than in cities without such programs. Specifically, our findings show that housing size in cities with inclusionary zoning programs was approximately 48 square feet smaller than in cities without inclusionary programs. Further, most of the reductions in housing size occurred in houses that sold for less than $187,000. These findings suggest that inclusionary zoning programs caused housing producers to increase the price of more expensive homes in markets in which residents were less sensitive to price and to decrease the size of less expensive homes in markets in which residents were more sensitive to price.

Once again, these results must be understood in context. The California housing market expanded rapidly over the 1990s as pent-up demand exploded following the 1991 recession. The imposition of inclusionary zoning requirements was not strong enough to slow the overall rate of housing production but did cause a measurable shift from single-family to multifamily housing production. The magnitude of this shift varied with the stringency of the inclusionary requirements. The imposition of inclusionary requirements was strong enough, however, to cause a rise in housing prices and a reduction in housing size. Price effects were larger in high-priced markets, and size effects were larger in low-priced markets.

These results are fully consistent with economic theory and demonstrate that inclusionary zoning policies do not come without cost. In robust housing markets, such as those of California during the 1990s, inclusionary zoning requirements were not strong enough to slow the rate of housing production, although they did cause housing prices to rise and housing size to fall. In less robust markets, it is more likely that inclusionary requirements have stronger effects on housing starts than on housing prices and size. Confirmation of such speculation, however, is beyond the scope of this study.

[...]

ACKNOWLEDGMENTS

The work reported in this article was accomplished at the National Center for Smart Growth Research and Education with funding from the National Association of Home Builders.

REFERENCES

Brown, Karen Desterol. 2001. *Expanding Affordable Housing Through Inclusionary Zoning: Lessons From the Washington Metropolitan Area.* Washington, D.C.: The Brookings Institution Center on Urban and Metropolitan Policy.

Calavita, Nico. 2004 (February). "Origins and Evolution of Inclusionary Housing in California," *NHC Affordable Housing Policy Review* 3 (1): 3–8.

Calavita, Nico, and Kenneth Grimes. 1998. "Inclusionary Housing in California: The Experience of Two Decades," *Journal of the American Planning Association* 64 (2): 150–169.

Calavita, Nico, Kenneth Grimes, and Alan Mallach. 1997. "Inclusionary Housing in California and New Jersey: A Comparative Analysis," *Housing Policy Debate* 8 (1): 109–142.

California Coalition for Rural Housing and the Non-Profit Housing Association of Northern California. 2003. *Inclusionary Housing in California: 30 Years of Innovation.* San Francisco, CA: California Coalition for Rural Housing and the Non-Profit Housing Association of Northern California.

Clapp, John M. 1981. "The Impact of Inclusionary Zoning on the Location and Type of Construction Activity," *Journal of the American Real Estate & Urban Economics Association* 9: 436–456.

Landis, John D., Michael Smith-Heimer, Michael Larice, Michael Reilly, Mary Corley, and Oliver Jerchow. 2000. *Raising the Roof: California Housing Development Projections and Constraints, 1997–2020.* Berkeley, CA: Institute of Urban and Regional Development at the University of California, Berkeley.

National Housing Conference. 2002 (January), "Inclusionary Housing: Lessons

Learned in Massachusetts," *NHC Affordable Housing Policy Review* 2 (1): 1–28.

Pendall, Rolf, Robert Puentes, and Jonathan Martin. 2006 (August). *From Traditional to Reformed: A Review of the Land Use Regulations in the Nation's 50 Largest Metropolitan Areas.* Washington, D.C.: The Brookings Institution, Metropolitan Policy Program.

Porter, Douglas R. 2004. *Inclusionary Zoning for Affordable Housing.* Washington, D.C.: Urban Land Institute.

Powell, Benjamin, and Edwards Stringham. 2004 (April). "Housing Supply and Affordability: Do Affordable Housing Mandates Work?" *Policy Study No. 318.* Los Angeles, CA: Reason Foundation.

Rosen, David Paul. 2002 (September 25). *City of Los Angeles Inclusionary Housing Study.* Report prepared for the Los Angeles Housing Department. Irvine, CA: David Paul Rosen & Associates. Available at http://www.cityofla.org/LAHD/DRAexsum.pdf.

Tombari, Edward A. 2005 (November). *Smart Growth, Smart Choices Series: The Builder's Perspective on Inclusionary Zoning.* Washington, D.C.: National Association of Home Builders.

31
"Growth management and affordable housing policy"

From *The Journal of Affordable Housing and Community Development Law* (2003)

Arthur C. Nelson and Susan M. Wachter

I. INTRODUCTION

Let us begin by transporting ourselves to a Sunbelt metropolitan area in 2033. Look around and you will see that half to two-thirds of the built environment will have been constructed between 2003 and 2033. In some fast-growing metropolitan areas, such as Las Vegas, three-quarters of everything that you see will have been built since 2003. Nationally, half or more of the built environment in 2033 will have been built between now and then.[1] How will that future look? Where will people live?

Now look back in time and imagine two metropolitan areas that grew in population and jobs at about the same rate between 1990 and 2000. Their household incomes also grew by about the same rate. But the similarities end there. The two regions represent two extremes in their planning approaches: metropolitan Portland, Oregon, and metropolitan Atlanta, Georgia. Since the late 1970s, Portland has been considered the quintessentially contained metropolitan area by means of policy.[2] In contrast, Atlanta is the quintessentially sprawled metropolitan area because it has pursued a "business as usual" approach to growth.[3] In Portland, the metropolitan landscape is required to accommodate regional development needs within an urban growth boundary and to connect land uses in a variety of ways.[4] During the 1990s, both cities experienced similar growth rates. Yet, across many objective measures, Atlanta's quality of life deteriorated while Portland's improved.[5]

The differences do not end with land use. Consider an additional measure: the change in the index of dissimilarity between whites and African Americans.[6] Between 1990 and 2000, the index of dissimilarity for all metropolitan areas fell from 58.8 to 51.4 (12.6 percent).[7] In Atlanta, the index fell from 68.8 to just 65.6, or just 4.7 percent, considerably less than the average while that for Portland fell from 62.4 to 48.1, or 22.9 percent, more than twice the national average.[8]

Land-use patterns that result from managed growth initiatives such as Portland's are associated with an increase in housing costs. Over a similar period of time (1986–95 in Portland compared with 1987–96 in Atlanta), housing prices rose by 25 percent in Atlanta but nearly doubled in Portland.[9] Growth management policies can have the effect of raising housing costs but, when implemented with full attention to housing affordability issues, they do not necessarily preclude affordable housing. Growth management policies can impact housing affordability through several paths.[10] The word "affordability" itself is used to mean the price of housing in relationship to income. That is, affordability is defined as the capacity of households to consume housing services. Land use regulations directly and indirectly impact affordability. A community may lack affordable housing because zoning laws preclude the building of homes on small lots, thereby raising the minimum cost of a home. Housing affordability also takes into consideration the quality of housing. An index of housing affordability may be constructed for a typical home in a community, the median-priced house, or a minimally adequate house as determined by compliance with local building codes. Housing affordability is increased if the supply of minimally adequate homes at a given price relative to income is also increased. In this article, we consider the theory and evidence of the impact of growth management initiatives on housing prices and on housing affordability.[11]

This article advances the proposition that affordable housing policy can be a key component of growth management and, when properly construed, need not be in conflict with the goal of housing affordability. Part II defines the goals and principles of growth management, "smart growth," and examines growth management land use's specific policies that impact housing affordability. Part III reviews the evidence on the economic implications of growth management initiatives for housing prices. Part IV analyzes the state role and Part V the existing and potential federal role in affordable housing policy within the context of growth management and Part VI concludes.

II. WHAT IS GROWTH MANAGEMENT?

Smart growth aims to balance the costs and benefits of development, particularly by internalizing public costs and benefits that are not priced by private markets. One of the authors (Nelson) has previously suggested that smart growth is composed of five goals:[12]

1. *Preserve public goods.* Air; water; open space for air cleansing and flood control; historically, culturally, and scientifically significant places; scenic views and vistas; sensitive landscapes; and wildlife habitat all may be "public" goods, that is, goods with benefits that go beyond this private consumption value.
2. *Minimize adverse and maximize positive interactions of land uses.* For example, industrial plants with air pollution and odors may have an adverse impact on residential land uses. Conversely, the co-location of apartments and shopping centers can have positive impacts on the value of the apartment and retail sites.
3. *Minimize public fiscal costs.* This goal is close to the pocketbook of taxpayers with its aim

of creating infrastructure systems and government services that impose the least burden on taxpayers for benefits generated.
4. *Maximize accessibility of jobs and housing.* Suburban sprawl, with its low-density, single-use, development pattern may pose barriers to the employment of low-income workers. The social costs of unemployment may justify planning efforts to link transportation to jobs.
5. *Maximize quality of life.* What this means can be elusive. Nelson suggests that quality of life means creating family-friendly, safe neighborhoods where social assets and networks can increase life chances.

To implement these goals, Porter outlines general operational smart growth practices as follows:[13]

1. *Use infrastructure efficiently.* In doing so, infill and redevelopment become more economically feasible and transportation options may improve.
2. *Stimulate inner-area revitalization.* The decline of many central cities has led to industrialized infrastructure capacity leading to redevelopment opportunities to accommodate a large share of a region's growth.
3. *Use design to create attractive places.* Integrating land uses with infrastructure and transportation networks and creating visually attractive places can support the development of higher-density sense of communities and help revitalize the declining urban core.
4. *Preserve natural resources.* Negative externalities of the overuse of water, air, and land can reduce quality of life. Preservation of environmental resources, especially those in urban areas, can contribute to the rebuilding of desirable urban neighborhoods.
5. *Reorient transportation.* The need for transportation options has become more apparent. In particular, cost-efficient, public-transit-oriented development can provide options for additional modes of travel, including walking, and can decrease road congestion and provide increased access to jobs.

Growth management principles and operational practice impact land use outcomes and have direct bearing on housing markets: Growth controls can decrease the supply of developable land sites and, potentially, the availability of affordable housing. Growth management policies that are sensitive to housing affordability, however, also can result in increased housing options. They can do so by (1) expanding the availability of housing beyond the single-family detached mode, through integration of housing with commercial uses accessible to transportation; (2) using design to increase the density of housing; and (3) revitalizing declining housing markets. We focus here on these operational principles that expand the availability of housing. The role of the state in what has been termed inclusionary zoning, as a response to exclusionary zoning, is the focus of Part IV.[14]

1. *Integrate land uses with housing and providing for diverse housing options.* Ever since *Euclid, Ohio v. Ambler Realty Co.*,[15] planning in the United States has been preoccupied with separating land uses. Residential subdivisions not only ban commercial uses, such as the corner grocery, but typically separate housing several miles from shopping. A vision of smart growth is to integrate land uses to recreate urban and urbane land uses. By doing so, the options for both housing types and housing supply can be increased.[16] A way to accomplish integrated land use is to concentrate transit-oriented development (TOD)-intensifying activity around mass-transit stops. By increasing density and combining housing, retail, and office space in close proximity around subway or light rail stations, cities can provide residents with a wider range of housing options.[17]

2. *Elevate the role of design.* Good design includes developing infrastructure, recreation, and transportation systems, and more broadly land use systems to create a sense of place.[18] In addition, design can play a role in mitigating NIMBYism. The general public has negative perceptions about what affordable housing and "higher-density" development both look like. Good design may help alleviate negative perceptions about the aesthetics of affordable housing built at higher densities.[19] The American Planning Association (APA) has proposed model statutes for smart growth housing options that both are attractive and increase the supply of housing through increased density. Several states have adopted the proposed APA language that enables localities to implement these denser design plans.[20]

3. *Revitalize the center.* Smart growth, broadly construed, can be seen to have two parts:

policies that address problems associated with poorly structured growth outcomes in suburbs and policies that address the decline of central cities. Both need to be addressed concurrently. Rising housing costs due to restrictive land use practices that may or may not be associated with smart growth can be mitigated by policies that increase the supply of sites where redevelopment at higher levels of density is economically feasible, which is likely to be at the urban core. Moreover, the decline of livable neighborhoods in inner cities and increased abandonment directly decrease the stock and also set in motion a cycle of further destabilization and neighborhood and housing abandonment. Considerable vacant land and abandoned property exist in older manufacturing cities, especially in the Midwest and Northeast. These sites can be brought back on line, increasing housing supply and accessible family-friendly neighborhoods. The revitalization of inner city neighborhoods to reverse the cycle of decline can provide opportunity for residential redevelopment at higher levels of density, where density is most desired at central locations.

Whether smart growth initiatives on balance increase or decrease the supply of housing sites depends on the implementation of these development principles and on the interaction of growth management initiatives with traditional suburban restrictive zoning policies.[21]

III. THE ECONOMICS OF HOUSING PRICES AND GROWTH MANAGEMENT

The net effect of growth management on the availability of sites for new or redeveloped housing determines the impact of smart growth on housing prices. Is there a question as to whether smart growth initiatives cause housing price increases? When urban growth boundaries limit land supply, they drive up developable land prices and, thus, apparently, housing prices as well. The data, as seen by the comparisons of Atlanta house price increases to those of Portland, support this link. However, there are several potentially offsetting economic effects of smart growth initiatives on housing prices,

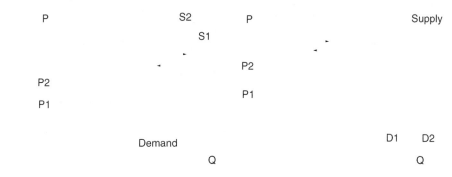

Figure 31.1

both on current restrictive policies and on the supply of housing in the urban core, and the determination and measurement of the net effect are not straightforward.

To illustrate these effects in a simplified model, Figure 31.1 displays supply and demand curves for a typical community's housing market. The demand curve slopes downward, indicating that at lower prices more housing is demanded (either by existing residents or new movers). The supply curve slopes upward, indicating that the costs of supply increase at higher levels of housing activity, primarily because land costs rise due to scarcity of development sites at higher levels of housing construction, although building costs also may increase.

The typically understood positive impact of smart growth on housing prices derives from an assumed net inward shift of the supply curve, as Figure 31.1 illustrates. On the left-hand side, we observe that a supply curve shift of *S1* to *S2* raises the price of housing from *P1* to *P2*. The implementation of a smart growth initiative may cause developable land to become scarcer, resulting in this supply curve shift. For example, development sites may be withdrawn from available land with the imposition of a growth boundary beyond which land will not be serviced with necessary infrastructure. However, it is also possible that developable land sites and housing supply will increase because of anti-exclusionary policies and higher allowable densities, especially in urban infill housing, shifting supply outward and decreasing prices from *P1* to *P2*. The impact of a smart growth

policy on the price of housing must be determined empirically. The finding of whether in fact housing prices increase is complicated by measurement issues: Figure 31.1 illustrates this problem. On the left-hand side, we observed that a land supply restriction of *S1* to *S2* will raise the price of housing from *P1* to *P2*. On the right-hand side, the effect of making the community more attractive and thus stimulating demand from *D1* to *D2* has a similar effect. Thus, in a comprehensive review of these issues, Fischel concludes that "confronted simply with evidence that prices of housing rose as a result of a public growth management program, we cannot say which scenario is the dominant cause."[22]

Besides the empirical issue of whether developable sites increase or not and the measurement difficulty of empirically identifying that change, there is a conceptual issue that affects whether a significant restriction of supply raises housing prices in a smart growth community. In a region where some communities employ smart growth restrictions and many do not, smart growth initiatives need not raise areawide housing prices, except to the extent that they increase quality. As illustrated in Figure 31.2, if the demand curve for housing in a specific community is elastic, as the supply curve shifts to the left, the only impact is a decrease in quantity; there is no increase in prices. Indeed, this open-city model, where supply is essentially expandable elsewhere so that each community is a "price taker," is exactly what many economists believe to be true for U.S. housing markets.

P   S2   S1

P2   Demand

                               Q

Figure 32.2

Thus, the question of whether prices increase or not is an empirical issue. Much of the empirical literature that summarizes economists' views of what the effects of smart growth policies have been centered on the housing market of Portland, which became the poster child for smart growth with the designation of an urban growth boundary (UGB) as early as 1979, long before smart growth was in vogue nationally. In perhaps the most extensive study of the impact of growth management on housing prices in Portland, Downs performs regression analysis of eighty-five large U.S. metropolitan areas from 1980 to 2000 and shows that a dummy variable measuring the effect of Portland's UGB has statistically significant effects on home prices only in the first half of the 1990s, but the impact is slight.[23] Downs finds from this that the adoption of UGBs does not in itself cause home prices to rise. Rather what matters is whether the UGB is stringently drawn or tightly enforced. If so, the UGB might drive up house prices in the short term if there is also strong demand. He concludes that the lack of impact in Portland stems from the fact that the area inside the UGB is too large for the land market to be affected.

In a response to Downs, two views have been expressed that interpret his findings somewhat differently. Nelson attributes the lack of importance of the Portland dummy variable in Downs's regression analysis as being due to an unmeasured increase in supply that occurred in Portland over this period,[24] due to the difficulty of tracking the increase in supply caused by adding accessory units to existing dwellings. Fischel interprets the lack of significance as being due to the comparison regions that Downs uses, which according to Fischel are themselves subject to exclusionary or restrictive zoning land use constraints.[25]

Exclusionary zoning, as Fischel points out, is a popular policy throughout the West during the study period, and the West is heavily represented in Down's data comparisons.

In sum, the finding that Portland home prices do not increase relative to those in other metropolitan areas is interpreted variously as being due to (1) the nonconstraining nature of the urban growth boundary; (2) an increase in the supply of housing units that accompanies the urban growth boundary in Portland; and (3) the comparison with other metro areas that adopted land use restrictions, but not smart growth policies, in this period. Thus, the significant housing price increase in Portland in recent decades is not definitive evidence that smart growth policies were responsible for driving up housing prices more than other policies being adopted at the same time in similarly situated MSAs. Moreover, the implementation of smart growth policies and, specifically, whether policies are adopted to increase aggregate housing supply, is key to whether this result holds.[26]

IV. THE STATE'S ROLE

The supply of affordable housing in a region may be constrained, not by smart growth policies, but by restrictive zoning practices.

In the United States, under principles of federalism, land use law is the domain of the states, and, to a large extent, states have devolved this responsibility to localities that, acting as state agents, are incentivized to adopt restrictive land use policies.[27] The adoption of statewide growth management plans has resurrected the states' local oversight role in several areas: statewide infrastructure planning; model enabling statutes; and, most importantly, explicit affordable housing components of growth management that counter localities' incentives to adopt exclusionary zoning practices. Some observers have hypothesized that although other state-initiated approaches have failed or have had only limited success, statewide growth management may be effective in countering these practices.[28]

A newly engaged state role in land use planning is most obvious in the direction of state infrastructure investment to areas with greater density. Maryland's recently imple-mented smart growth plan is illustrative. The state established "priority funding areas" consisting of Maryland's center cities and other designated areas that meet density, sewer, and water system requirements. Under the Act, the state is prohibited from funding any growth-related projects that are located outside the priority funding areas. With this measure, Maryland hopes to revitalize older, developed areas while simultaneously curbing sprawl.

A second role of the states is the adoption of model enabling statutes, in particular, those intended to increase the diversity of housing options. In 2002, the American Planning Association (APA) published a legislative guidebook incorporating local enabling model statutes.[29] The APA identified land use tools that localities could choose to implement to provide for affordable housing options, including expanding or rehabilitating public infrastructure, designating sites to be zoned at densities conducive to low- or moderate-income housing, and establishing controls to preserve lower-income housing.[30]

A third and more controversial role is for states to target directly the incentives for localities to provide for affordable housing. As noted above, state legislatures delegate zoning powers to the individual municipalities, and thus legislatures clearly retain the power to restrict the ability of municipalities to enact exclusionary ordinances for the overall public good. Thus, growth management statutes allow for implementation of statewide land use policies to oversee whether municipalities can exercise zoning power in the interest of the state as a whole rather than in the local interest.

Localities have strong fiscal incentives to engage in restrictive zoning, whether or not local zoning power is exercised in the service of the interest of the states. Urban economists have examined the fiscal reasons many local governments are incentivized to create communities of homogenous income groups by enacting restrictive land use ordinances. As demonstrated by Tiebout, people can avoid cross-subsidizing others by forming homogeneous communities.[31] To prevent cross-subsidization, each household in a jurisdiction must pay the same amount in taxes (head taxes) for public goods provided by the jurisdiction. Because a major purpose of zoning is to prevent free riders, local land use ordinances, regardless of their source, are likely to restrict affordable housing in many communities.[32]

A number of states have enacted measures to review access to affordable housing through oversight of local land use regulations. However, it is only recently that land use planning has addressed housing needs explicitly. To be sure, housing districts were part of ancient city plans, but they were designed principally to separate classes of people and, except for needs of ruling classes, the number and configuration of housing for lower classes appears to be conspicuous by its absence.[33] In the early history of the United States, housing concerns were directed principally to public safety and health concerns. For example, the early plan for Philadelphia restricted construction of wood-frame buildings, including homes, to reduce the risk of fire.[34] Throughout the nineteenth century, high residential density was seen as compromising public health and safety.[35] Even into the twentieth century, housing needs seemed secondary to creating a "City Beautiful."[36]

The issue of housing needs was first placed on the national agenda with the advent of the 1949 Housing Act. It still took nearly a generation before the idea was broached that local communities consider adaptation of inclusionary housing policies to provide housing options to households at different income levels.[37] The watershed housing case emanating from Mount Laurel, New Jersey, in the late 1970s and early 1980s advanced the idea that providing for housing needs in every community was required by the state's constitution.[38]

The late 1970s and 1980s saw other state efforts to require local governments to address local housing needs through inclusionary policies.[39] Not that many states ventured into this arena nor were the states that did so – notably California, Connecticut, Florida, Georgia, Idaho, Oregon, Rhode Island, Vermont, and Washington – very successful.[40] Moreover, most states still do not actually monitor performance of local governments in providing affordable housing.[41]

Thus, despite a half century of federal interest in housing and a few leading court cases, exclusionary zoning remains the rule. Many communities use "adequate public facility" ordinances and "concurrency" to deny housing developments other than high-value, single-family homes by contending that local public facilities are inadequate to accommodate the impact of such developments.[42] To provide facilities needed to accommodate the needs of new development, many communities impose "impact fees" structured to target lower-value housing more than higher-value housing with exclusionary effect.[43] Fiscal impact studies often used to measure the extent to which new development pays its own way[44] can be designed to assure that only high-value housing pays its own way.[45] But these are complex ways to perpetuate exclusion. More direct ways remain: large lot zoning and large minimum house sizes[46] or simply conditions imposed on higher-density housing proposals.[47]

There have been attempts to soften the impact of exclusionary zoning on low-income homebuyers through legislative and judicial action: The prime example of an attempted judicial invalidation of exclusionary zoning is the *Mt. Laurel* decisions in New Jersey. However, *Mt. Laurel* demonstrates the difficulty of formulating judicial remedies. A recent *Harvard Law Review* article critiques these measures for being developer-led and maintains that inclusionary zoning is likely to work better if implemented as part of a statewide growth management initiative.[48] The argument rests on the ability of proactive statewide planning to overcome the incentives of local communities to shift the fiscal burdens of affordable housing elsewhere. Portland is put forth as an exemplar of this approach. While there have been too few examples to support the thesis that inclusionary zoning is more likely to succeed in a statewide growth management context, there are economic reasons to support this view. Localities have less of an incentive to zone out lower-income affordable housing if they are not threatened by the disposable community syndrome associated with neighborhood decline.

V. TOWARD A ROLE FOR THE FEDERAL GOVERNMENT

The U.S. General Accounting Office (GAO) has produced three reports on sprawl and smart growth-related issues. In its first two reports, the GAO found little measurable impact of or rationale for federal actions on urban sprawl.[49] In a more recent GAO report, environmental concerns are cited as a federal interest. The GAO concludes that the direct impact of federal policy on sprawl was difficult to detect.[50]

The federal government has a much longer history with policies intended to revitalize central cities, arguably also an important component of smart growth. A number of federal programs are directed at rejuvenating urban areas. For example, the 1974 Community Development Block Grants (CDBG) program aids projects in cities that benefit low- and moderate-income residents; the 1993 legislated empowerment zones (EZ) and enterprise communities (EC) and the recently adopted New Markets Tax Credits stimulate development in distressed communities. HUD is also directly responsible for affordable housing policy, for example, through housing vouchers.

A possible additional role for the federal government that could enhance the federal interest in affordable housing is to provide incentives for states to promote affordable housing outcomes. Federalism could be exploited to incentivize experimentation in the development of state programs to respond to the federal interests.

The design of a reward program would include incentives to go to the states that, in turn, would pass a share of the reward to local governments. Measurement of positive outcomes would need to be developed for such policy to be efficient. The index could be simple, such as the number of "affordable" housing units per capita, or an index of housing segregation between housing types and prices among communities. Whatever measurement system is used, the index must be developed to appropriately align state incentives to the federal interest.

VI. CONCLUDING OBSERVATIONS

Growth management and smart growth have emerged as somewhat contentious land management principles and practices that lead to denser and more compact regions as an alternative to sprawl. Affordable housing policies can be a component of smart growth. Such policies, however, depend on local implementation that runs counter to both local home rule principles and local fiscal incentives.

During the next thirty years, up to half of the built environment existing will have been constructed. The opportunity to build with attention to the affordability of housing outcomes as well as to the shape of the built environment has not been equaled since perhaps the end of World War II. Now is the time to shape a vision to assure that the future built environment will generate more benefits for more people.

The authors wish to thank their research assistants Rebecca Sohmer and Joseph Lucas.

Notes

1 Unpublished estimates by one of the authors (Nelson) for the Brookings Institution. The figure includes new development to accommodate growth as well as replacement of existing structures because of age, destruction, or other factors. This estimate assumes a 25 percent increase in structures to support population and employment growth, and demolition of just 1 percent of the present building stock annually.

2 Arthur C. Nelson, *Oregon's Urban Growth Boundary as a Landmark Planning Tool, in Planning the Oregon Way* (Abbott, Howe and Adler eds. 1993).

3 R.D. Bullard, G.S. Johnson, and A.O. Torres, *Atlanta Megasprawl,*14 *Forum for Applied Research & Pub. Pol'y* 3, at pp. 17–23 (Fall 1999).

4 *See* Arthur C. Nelson and James B. Duncan, *Growth Management Principles and Practices* (Am. Planning Ass'n 1995).

5 For details, see A.C. Nelson, *Smart Growth or Business as Usual: Which Is Better at Improving Quality of Life and Central City Vitality, in Bridging The Divide (Proceedings)* (Susan M. Wachter, R. Leo Penne, and Arthur C. Nelson eds. HUD 2000). In general, Portland's air pollution (ozone) problem was nearly eliminated, and the city saw its dependency on single-occupant vehicles fall, neighborhood quality rise, energy consumption fall, density rise, overcrowding fall, preservation of open spaces rise, and incompatible land uses fall.

6 The index of dissimilarity measures the change needed to make all units of observation identical. In the context of racial segregation, a score of 100 means that all members of a race live in just one area while a score of 0 means that each area has the same proportion of that race.

7 Calculated from 1990 and 2000 indices of dissimilarity provided by the Lewis Mumford Center at the State University of New York at Albany. A score of 60.0 is considered indicative of systematic racism in settlement patterns, based on work by Denton and Massey. *See Douglas S. Massey and Nancy A. Denton, American Apartheid: Segregation and the Making of the Underclass (1994).*

8 *Id.*

9 *See* Nelson, *supra* note 5, at 100.

10 The joint achievement of these two goals, curbing urban sprawl while improving housing affordability, has been described as fair growth. Fair growth is the connection between social equity issues, such as fair housing and antidisplacement policies, and smart growth issues, such as growth management and urban revitalization. The term refers to land use practices that attempt to curb urban sprawl without endangering housing affordability and access to jobs for minorities and low-income residents.

11 *Arthur C. Nelson, Rolf Pendall, Casey J. Dawkins, and Gerrit J. Knaap, The Link Between Growth Management and Housing Affordability: The Academic Evidence* (Brookings Inst. 2002), *available at* www.brook.edu/dybdocroot/es/urban/publications/growthmang.pdf.

12 *Id.;* see also Robert W. Burchell and Catherine C. Galley, *Inclusionary Zoning: Pros and Cons, in Inclusionary Zoning: A Viable Solution to the Affordable Housing Crisis?* (Cent. for Hous. Pol'y 2000), *available at* www.inhousing.org/NHC-Report/NHC-0.htm.

13 Douglas R. Porter, *Whither Eastward Ho! Strategies for Strengthening Regional Stewardship in Southeastern Florida: A Report to the Region from Two Strategy Forums* (1999), *available at* www.jc.fau.edu/3publications/whithereastward-ho.pdf. Mills and Hamilton define "exclusionary zoning" as local land-use requirements that effectively exclude from a community those whose homes would not pay the residents' shares of the cost of local government services. They provide examples of exclusionary land-use policies such as minimum lot sizes and square feet of floor space, and prohibition of multifamily

housing. *Edwin S. Mills and Bruce Hamilton, Urban Economics* 339 (5th ed. 1993).

14 Inclusionary zoning refers to local government programs and regulations that force developers to build dwellings for low-income households. *See Paul Davidoff and I. Davidoff, Opening the Suburbs: Toward Inclusionary Controls, in Management and Control of Growth: Techniques in Application 54050* (1975); *Herbert M. Franklin, David Faulk, and Arthur J. Levin, In-zoning: A Guide for Policy Makers on Inclusionary Land Use Programs* (Potomac Inst. 1974); Seymour I. Schwartz & Robert A. Johnston, *Inclusionary Housing Programs,* 49 APA J. 1, at pp. 3–21 (Winter 1983) (publication of the Am. Planning Ass'n, Chicago).

15 97 F. 307 (D. Ohio 1924), *rev'd,* 272 U.S. 365 (1926).

16 Demographic trends suggest that there is a growing market for housing options provided by mixed-use, mixed-income, infill development. By far, the dominant mode of housing in the United States is the single-family residential unit (composed of detached, attached, and manufactured home types). But demographics are changing – the household of the 1960s was very different from the average family of 2000. In 1974, 42.1 percent of all households had children, but this figure had fallen to 38.1 percent by 1995. The percentage of single-person households is on the rise, having increased from 19.5 percent of all households in 1974 to 24.6 percent in 1995. Elderly households (in which the householder is more than sixty-five years of age) also have increased, rising from 19.5 percent of all households in 1974 to 23.3 percent in 1995. Because of our changing demographic trends, there is a growing demand for more diverse housing types. One promise of smart growth is to provide just that. *See* S. Burlington Cty. NAACP v. Mt. Laurel Twp., 336 A.2d 713 (N.J. 1975), *rev'd,* 456 A.2d 390 (N.J. 1983).

17 Dena Belzer and Gerald Autler, *Transit-Oriented Development: Moving from Rhetoric to Reality* (discussion paper prepared for the Brookings Inst. June 2002), *available at* www.brook.edu/dybdocroot/es/urban/publications/belzertodexsum.htm.

18 Recent publications demonstrate the value of design and the housing market's receptiveness to it. *See Mark J. Eppli and Charles C. Tu, Valuing the New Urbanism: The Impact of the New Urbanism on Prices of Single Family Homes* (Urban Land Inst. 1999); *see also Steven Fader, Density by Design* (Urban Land Inst. 1999). For more information on the role of design in achieving higher densities, see the website of the Congress for New Urbanism, *at* www.cnu.org. A leading designer of innovative affordable housing is Michael Pyatok, whose website may be found *at* www.pyatok.com.

19 William Fulton, *Density: Reality, Perception, and Policy Issues, in Bridging the Divide (Proceedings)* (Susan M. Wachter, R. Leo Penne and Arthur C. Nelson eds. HUD 2000).

20 *Growing Smart Legislative Guidebook: Model Statutes for Planning and the Management of Change* (Stuart Meck ed. 2002).

21 Edwin S. Mills, *Truly Smart "Smart Growth," Illinois Real Estate Letter* 6–7 (summer 1999), *available at* www.cba.uiuc.edu/orer/V13-3-1.pdf (published by the Office of Real Estate Research at the University of Illinois at Urbana-Champaign).

22 William A. Fischel, Comment on Anthony Downs's *Have Housing Prices Risen Faster in Portland Than Elsewhere?,* 13 Hous. *Pol'y Debate* (2002), *available at* www.fanniemaefoundation.org/programs/hpd/pdf/hpd-1301-fischel.pdf.

23 Anthony Downs, *Have Housing Prices Risen Faster in Portland Than Elsewhere,* 13 Hous. *Pol'y Debate* (2002), *available at* www.fanniemaefoundation.org/programs/hpd/pdf/hpdl301_downs.pdf.

24 Arthur C. Nelson, Comment on Anthony Downs's *Have Housing Prices Risen Faster in Portland Than Elsewhere?,* 13 Hous. *Pol'y Debate* (2002), *available at* www.fanniemaefoundation.org/programs/hpd/pdf/hpd.1301nelson.pdf.

25 Fischel, *supra* note 22.

26 Robert Lang and Steven Hornburg, *Planning Portland Style: Pitfalls and Possibilities,* 8 Hous. *Pol'y Debate* (1997),

available at www.mi.vt.edu/Research/PDFs/PortlandLang.pdf.

27 Municipalities are "creations of the states alone." Jett v. Dallas Indep. Sch. Dist., 491 U.S. 701, 728 (1989). The quotation is attributed to one Rep. Blair during the congressional debates on the Civil Rights Act of 1871, *id.* at 728 (quoting *Cong. Globe*, 42d Cong., 1st Sess., 795 (1871)). *See also* Monell v. Dep't of Social Serv., 436 U.S. 658 (1978).

28 Note, *State-Sponsored Growth Management as a Remedy for Exclusionary Zoning*, 108 HARV. L. REV. 1127 (1995). Exclusionary zoning can be defined as zoning that, whether by purpose or as an unintended consequence, has the effect of raising housing prices within a community and excluding low-income purchasers from the housing market.

29 *AM. Planning Ass'n, Planning for Smart Growth: 2002 State of the States* (2002), *available at* www.planning.org/growingsmart/pdf/states2002.pdf.

30 *See AM. Planning Ass'n, Growing Smart Legislative Guidebook* 492 through 4-115 (2002), *available at* www.planning.org/guidebook/pdf/guidebook/chapter4.pdf.

31 Charles Tiebout, *A Pure Theory of Local Public Expenditure*, 64 J. POL. ECON. 416-24 (1956).

32 Local governments frequently enact land use regulations – such as zoning ordinances, impact fees, and growth controls – that have the effect of limiting the supply of low-cost housing. These ordinances may be motivated by the desire to preserve environmental amenities and avoid overcrowding of public facilities. In addition, middle- and upper-income residents may prefer to live in communities composed of households of similar socioeconomic composition. *See Wlliam A. Fischel, Regulatory Takings: Law, Economics, and Politics* (1990). Further, homeowners may want to preserve or enhance the value of their investments in their homes by preventing the construction of lower-valued housing nearby, which they believe will reduce market prices. Michael H. Schill and Susan M. Wachter, *Housing Market Constraints and Spatial Stratification by Income and Race*, 6 Hous. POL'Y DEBATE (1995), *available at* www.fanniemaefoundation.org/programs/hpd/pdf/hpd 0601_schill.pdf.

33 *See A.E.J. Morris, History of Urban Form: Before the Industrial Revolution* (3d ed. 1996).

34 *Charles M. Haar, Land-use Planning: A Casebook on the Use, Misuse, and Re-use of Urban Land* (1989).

35 *See Lewis Mumford, The City in History (1972); Mel Scott, American City Planning since 1890* (1969).

36 *William I. Goodman & Rric C. Freund, principles and practice of urban planning* (1968). *See Jerry Weitz, Sprawl Busting (1999); R.H. Freilich, From Sprawl to Smart Growth (1999); Julian Conrad Juergensmeyer & Thomas H. Roberts, Land Use Planning and Control Law* (Hornbook series) (1998). Indeed, the planning profession's principal textbook from the late 1960s through the 1970s did not include a single chapter on housing, despite having 584 text pages organized into twenty chapters. It is only in relatively recent times that conventional planning has addressed housing issues and then only in a few states.

37 *Anthony Downs, Opening Up the Suburbs, an Urban Strategy for America* (1975).

38 *See* S. Burlington Cty. NAACP v. Mt. Laurel Twp., 336 A.2d 713 (N.J. 1975), *rev'd*, 456 A.2d 390 (N.J. 1983).

39 *See State-Sponsored Growth Management, supra* note 28.

40 *See American Planning Association, supra* note 30.

41 *See Freilich, supra* note 36; *Weitz, supra* note 36.

42 *See Nelson and Duncan, supra* note 4 (review of these techniques).

43 *See James C. Nicholas, The Calculation of Proportionate-Share Impact Fees* (Am. Planning Ass'n, Planning Advisory Service No. 408, 1988); James C. Nicholas, *On the Progression of Impact Fees*, 58 J.AM. *Planning Ass'n* 4, at 517 (Autumn 1992).

44 *See R.H. Burchell and David LIstokin, Fiscal Impact Handbook* (Cent. for Urban Pol'y Res. 1978).

45 The Cost of Community Services studies of the American Farmland Trust load all school, public safety, and other costs onto only residential development, thereby

showing that such development per se fails to pay its way but commercial, industrial, and even open space activities more than pay their way. The logical outcome is local antithesis to new residential development generally and a predisposition to favor only high-value residential development. *See* www. farmlandinfo.org/fic/tas/tafs-cocs.html.

46 *See Juergensmeyer and Roberts, supra* note 36.

47 In Henry County v. Tim Jones Properties, 539 S.E.2d 167 (Ga. 2000), the county approved rezoning for residential development only if the developer of 300 proposed houses install an eight-acre park, construct a half-mile-long, four-lane divided "parkway" connecting the development to a two-lane road, build an Olympic-sized swimming pool for the sole use of the residents, and other requirements. One of us (Nelson) also learned that a proposed apartment building in a suburb of Atlanta was approved, based on the conditions of reducing density from twelve to eight units per acre, construction of a razor-wire fence around the perimeter, and installation of a gate with a guard posted twenty-four by seven to monitor entry with complete video monitoring.

48 Case Note, 115 HAR v. L. REV. 2058 (2002) (analysis of Home Builders Ass'n of Northern California v. City of Napa, 108 Cal. Rptr. 2d 60 (Ct. App. 2001)).

49 *U.S. Gen. Acct. Office*, Report No. GAO/ RCED-99-87, *Extent of Federal Influence on Urban Dprawl is Unclear* (1999); *see also Gen. Acct. Office*, Report No. GAO/ RCED-00-178, *Local Growth Issues-Federal Opportunities and Challenges* (2000).

50 In 2001, GAO released the results of a survey on how the federal government could incentivize states to create land use policies that protect the environment. GAO found that most states and localities do not "comprehensively assess the impacts of land use on air and water quality and develop ways to mitigate any adverse effects." The respondents recommended three ways in which the federal government could help localities implement better land use practices: (1) financial incentives for transportation, environmental, and land use officials to collaborate; (2) technical assistance in land use assessment; and (3) public education on environmental impacts. GAO, Report No. GAO/RCED-00-178, *supra* note 49.

32
"Neighborhood change and transit: What we learned"

From *Maintaining Diversity in America's Transit-Rich Neighborhoods* (2011)

Stephanie Pollack, Barry Bluestone and Chase Billingham

Dukakis Center for Urban and Regional Policy at Northeastern University

To better understand patterns of neighborhood change in newly transit-rich neighborhoods, this chapter presents the results of new research analyzing socioeconomic change in 42 neighborhoods in 12 metropolitan areas first served by rail transit between 1990 and 2000. Because prior research on gentrification and TRNs has looked at only a limited number of neighborhood characteristics, we decided to explore a much broader range of factors related to population, housing and transportation across a variety of different transit systems. After explaining how the research was accomplished and what was learned, we present our conclusions about the likely mechanisms underlying the observed patterns of change in transit-rich neighborhoods.

METHODS AND DATA

We began this research by identifying 12 metropolitan areas in which one or more new heavy, light or commuter rail stations had opened between the 1990 Census and the 2000 Census. We chose to focus on those that opened by 1997 to allow time for demographic changes to emerge before the 2000 Census. Having divided U.S. transit systems into four categories based on their age and number of stations served [...], we made certain to include new stations added to the oldest and most extensive legacy transit systems (Chicago and San Francisco) as well as stations added to smaller and slower growing modest transit systems (Cleveland and St. Louis). Not surprisingly, the largest number of new stations was found in evolving transit systems, the growing transit systems in growing metropolitan areas. We identified new stations built between 1990 and 1997 in the three largest evolving transit systems in Los Angeles, Portland, and Washington, D.C.; in the medium-sized evolving systems in Atlanta, Baltimore, Dallas and San Diego; and in the small but fast-growing transit system in Denver. (The fourth category of transit systems, which we call emerging transit systems, are those which first opened rail transit stations after 2000 and so could not be included in our analysis of neighborhood change that occurred between 1990 and 2000.) We selected a subset of stations that avoided data limitations and complications, where the census information for 1990 and 2000 could be compared to geographies that covered roughly the same half-mile radius around each station as explained below. We also made certain to include station areas with different kinds of rail, stations with and without parking and stations in various types of neighborhoods. The resulting set of 42 stations in 12 different metropolitan areas [...] is sufficiently robust and heterogeneous to provide important insights into the difficult question of whether and how neighborhoods in different metropolitan areas change due to the presence of transit.

For each of the new stations identified for consideration, we examined census block group maps to construct approximations of the station's surrounding neighborhood. A census block group contains a number of census tracts including between 600 and 3,000 individuals with an ideal number of about 1,500 residents. A block group was included in the defined transit-rich neighborhood if the majority of its land area was within a one-half mile radius of the station. With the proper block groups identified, we collected data from Summary Files 1 and 3 of the 1990 and 2000 U.S. Census for each selected block group and aggregated the block-group level data into TRN-level data.

Since prior research had frequently looked at only a few variables – such as housing values but not rents, or proportion of college-educated residents but not household income – and often could not explain why some neighborhoods gentrified while others did not, we decided to explore a broad range of potential factors. For each of the 42 transit station areas to be analyzed, we decided to examine changes between 1990 and 2000 in population growth, housing units (both total number and tenure), racial and ethnic composition, household income (both median income and households with incomes above $100,000), housing costs (both gross rents and home values), in-migration, public transit use for commuting and motor vehicle ownership. We collected data on the same variables at the level of the metropolitan statistical area (MSA) for each of the 12 MSAs where the new transit stations were located.

We analyzed the data in three stages. First, we calculated percentage changes on each variable for each station and its corresponding MSA. For comparison, we measured the 1990–2000 demographic change in each TRN against the corresponding change in the surrounding MSA. Researchers frequently use the MSA in which a neighborhood is embedded as a reference area when studying neighborhood change (Freeman, 2005). This comparison is designed to control for any systemic fixed effects, which are changes that occurred throughout the metropolitan area for reasons presumably unrelated to the siting of a new transit station. The numerical difference between the percentage change on each variable in each TRN and the percentage change on each variable in the MSA is used to determine whether there has been a significant change in a demographic factor that might be due to the siting of a transit stop.

Second, after examining the raw differences in the rate of change between each station area and the surrounding MSA in our first analysis, we re-analyzed all of the data using a more conservative approach because small differences in the results between TRNs and their metro areas may not truly reflect real differences due to the small size of the samples. This "large differences" approach considered a transit station difference from its MSA to be meaningful where the value for the 1990–2000 percentage change in a station neighborhood is 20 percentage points higher or lower than the 1990–2000 percentage change in the MSA variable.

Third, to determine whether patterns of neighborhood change vary depending on the type of transit built (light rail, heavy rail or commuter rail), we divided the 42 stations into three groups based on transit types and all of the data were re-analyzed for these three categories of TRNs. [...]

INITIAL ANALYSIS AND CONCLUSIONS

Our first analysis involved determining how much and in what direction a particular demographic change in each of the 42 transit-rich neighborhoods differs from that of each TRN's metropolitan area. The numerical difference between the percentage change on each variable in each TRN and the percentage change on each variable in the MSA is used to determine whether there has been a change that might be due to the siting of a transit station.

Population growth

For nearly two-thirds (64 percent) of the 42 transit stations in this study, the population grew more quickly between 1990 and 2000 in the TRN than in its metropolitan area as a whole. This disproportionate increase in population was seen in 27 out of the 42 TRNs.

Housing units

Not surprisingly, an increase in population requires a boost in housing production. In 55 percent of the TRNs, housing production increased more dramatically in the neighborhood than in the metropolitan area as a whole. Similarly, in the neighborhoods around 62 percent of the stations the proportion of owner-occupied units increased more than in the surrounding metropolitan area.

Racial and ethnic composition

One measure of gentrification is a change in the racial composition of a TRN. If an area becomes more attractive because of a new station and the amenities it brings, the population in the TRN might become more non-Hispanic white with a decline in the ranks of black and Hispanic households. But this does not always seem to be the case in the 42 TRNs in our study. Roughly half of the TRNs experienced an increase in the proportion of non-Hispanic white households relative to the change for the TRN's metro area. The other half, however, saw their non-Hispanic white population either decline between 1990 and 2000 or increase but more slowly than the rate of increase in their metro areas.

Household income

While the racial and ethnic composition does not seem to have changed in any consistent way within the new TRNs, the economic composition of those neighborhoods did. Median household income increased more than in the surrounding metro area in more than three-fifths (62 percent) of the TRNs. The proportion of households with incomes exceeding $100,000 a year also rose more sharply than their metro areas in 60 percent of the TRNs.

Housing costs

The increase in incomes in these neighborhoods is reflected in the cost of housing. Median gross rent increased faster than in their metro areas in nearly three-quarters (74 percent) of the TRNs. The impact on home prices was even more dramatic, with nearly nine out of ten (88 percent) TRNs experiencing an increase in median housing values greater than the increase in home prices in the metro area.

In-migration

That new transit stations attract new residents is shown by both the increase in population in these neighborhoods and by in-migration trends (the rate of people reporting that they did not live in their current home five years earlier). In more than seven out of ten (71 percent of) TRNs, the percentage of neighborhood residents who had lived in a different house five years earlier exceeded the in-migration rate increase for the associated metro area. For most TRNs, this would seem to reflect both absolute growth in population and, potentially, the substitution of new households for ones that had previously lived in these neighborhoods.

Public transit use for commuting

One would expect that with a new transit station, the proportion of nearby residents using public transit for their commutes would increase. In fact, this is not always the case. In 17 of the 42 TRNs (40 percent), public transit use for commuting actually declined relative to the change in transit use in the metro area once the new station opened. [...] [T]o the extent that increased housing costs drive out lower income families who are more likely to use public transit, a new transit station can reduce the percentage of the neighborhood population using public transit. Total transit boardings may still increase, however, if the neighborhood population rises fast enough or if neighborhood residents use transit for trips other than commuting trips.

Motor vehicle ownership

The relative reduction in the proportion of the TRN households using public transit in 40 percent of the neighborhoods studied is consistent with the finding that automobile ownership increased faster in nearly three-quarters (71 percent) of these neighborhoods, with ownership of two or more autos increasing in nearly three in five (57 percent). When upper income households move into an area, they are more likely to own motor vehicles and to use them for their commute.

A number of important conclusions can be drawn from this first round of analysis. The first is that a new transit station frequently catalyzes neighborhood growth and in-migration of new neighborhood residents. In two-thirds of the station areas, the population grew faster in the TRN than in the metro as a whole. In more than 70 percent of the TRNs, the number of people reporting that they did not live in their current home five years earlier is higher in the TRN than in the corresponding metro.

Newly transit-served neighborhoods not only grow – they change. The most predominant pattern of change is that after a transit station goes into operation, the typical neighborhood resident is wealthier and the housing stock more expensive, two indicators of gentrification. In more than 60 percent of the TRNs, median household income rose faster than in the surrounding metros; in nearly two-thirds of the TRNs, the proportion of households with annual incomes exceeding $100,000 rose more sharply than in their metro areas. We also found a stunningly high incidence of disproportionately rising rents and housing values. Rents increased faster than in their metro areas in nearly three-quarters of the TRNs. The impact on home prices was even more dramatic, with nearly nine out of ten TRNs experiencing an increase in median housing values greater than the increase in home prices in their metropolitan area. Hence, gentrification occurred in an overwhelming majority of the newly transit-served neighborhoods that we studied, if gentrification is defined […] as a neighborhood change process characterized by increasing property values and incomes.

Given these findings, we wanted to explore whether neighborhoods that began with a larger number of renters were more susceptible to gentrification, as other studies have found (Chapple, 2009). To discern whether gentrification occurs more often in neighborhoods with initially high proportions of renters rather than homeowners, we looked for a correlation between the rate of homeownership in 1990 (before the transit station opened) on the one hand and both the percentage change in the non-Hispanic white population between 1990 and 2000 and the percentage change in median household income between 1990 and 2000 on the other. In both cases we found that a higher initial proportion of renters was correlated with a larger change in racial and ethnic composition and larger increases in median household income.[1] This provides plausible evidence that neighborhoods with a large number of renters are more susceptible to gentrification.

While we can confidently say that our analysis found evidence of gentrification in the majority of newly transit-served neighborhoods, it is more difficult to determine whether this gentrification was accompanied by involuntary displacement of former neighborhood residents. Displacement can be difficult to detect and document, even with far more sophisticated data than were available for our analysis (Freeman, 2005; McKinnish, Walsh and White, 2008). In this initial round of analysis, the data indicate that a new transit station does not automatically lead to a fundamental change in the racial or ethnic composition of the TRN. On the other hand, the higher in-migration rate and rapid increase in incomes in a majority of TRNs suggest that lower income residents may be leaving the area.

Displacement is not, however, the only problem associated with gentrification. Another negative consequence of gentrification involves not those neighborhood residents who leave but those who remain behind. We found larger increases in both rents and home values in the newly transit-served neighborhoods than in the corresponding metropolitan areas in roughly three-quarters of the TRNs studied. For existing homeowners in these TRNs, this was a boon. For existing renters, however, this likely caused many to pay a higher proportion of their income for shelter and could eventually force them to seek housing elsewhere. Our findings therefore raise the concern that new transit is associated with higher housing cost burdens for renters who remain in the neighborhood.

Another troubling finding from the first round of analysis was that the placement of a new transit station did not consistently increase the number of neighborhood residents reporting that they used public transit for their commute. Indeed, in over half of the TRNs we studied, public transit use for commuting by neighborhood residents actually declined relative to the change in transit use in the metro area after the new station opened. This was perhaps not surprising since automobile ownership increased more than in the corresponding metro area in nearly three-quarters of these newly transit-served neighborhoods, with ownership of two or more autos increasing in nearly three in five. Another adverse consequence of the gentrification observed in newly transit-served neighborhoods is that the higher income households living in the TRN bring and use more vehicles and may therefore undermine efforts to shift commuting trips to the newly-built transit.

Gentrification [...] can be a positive or destructive form of neighborhood change. This initial round of analysis found evidence of gentrification and of at least two negative consequences of such gentrification in TRNs: higher housing cost burdens for renters and an influx of automobile owning households less likely to use transit for commuting.

LARGE DIFFERENCES ANALYSIS

The preceding analysis was based on simple point estimate differences in each of the factors under investigation. However, the demographic data used in this analysis come from a 5 percent sample of the U.S. Census of population for 1990 and 2000. Because of the sample size, small differences in the results between TRNs and their metro areas may not truly reflect real differences. To provide more confidence in our results, we re-analyzed all of the data under the condition that a large difference between demographic changes in the TRN and those experienced in the metro area as a whole would be said to exist only where there was at least a 20 percentage point difference between the TRN and its surrounding metro area. If we were to discover only a few such cases, we would have to conclude that – while there were theoretical reasons that new transit has an impact on the surrounding neighborhood's demographics – there was not sufficient evidence that a new transit station in fact contributes to such neighborhood change. If, however, we were to discover many cases in which such large differences existed between the changes seen in TRNs and those in the corresponding metros, such a finding would reinforce the results of our initial analysis.

Population growth

Using this criterion, in about half of the TRNs the growth in population in the TRN was within 20 percentage points of that in the surrounding metro area during the decade in which the transit station opened. However, in nearly a third of the TRNs, the population grew at least 20

percentage points more than in the metro area as a whole, while in only one eighth of the cases did it grow substantially less.

Housing units

Unsurprisingly, given the population growth, in nearly three quarters of all cases (74 percent), the change in the number of housing units in the TRN was within 20 percentage points of that of its MSA. However, in nearly one-fourth (10 TRNs, or 24 percent) of the new TRNs, the percentage increase in new housing units constructed between 1990 and 2000 exceeded the percentage increase in the MSA by at least 20 percentage points. By contrast, in only one TRN was the increase in housing units at least 20 percentage points lower than in the surrounding MSA.

Changes were also seen in the tenure of neighborhood housing stock. A full third of the TRNs experienced an increase in homeownership that was at least 20 percentage points greater than the surrounding metro area. In only one case did a TRN experience a rise in home-ownership rate at least 20 percent lower than its MSA.

Racial and ethnic composition

In about half (52 percent) of the TRNs we did not find a difference of 20 percentage points or more between the TRN and its metro area in the relative rate of change in the non-Hispanic white population. Indeed, where the relative change was substantial, the non-Hispanic white population in the new TRNs was nearly twice as likely (31 percent versus 17 percent) to experience a much larger decrease in its representation in these new transit-rich neighborhoods (or a much lower increase) than the surrounding MSA. The results for non-Hispanic blacks appear to confirm this finding. Relative to their MSAs, the non-Hispanic black populations in the new TRNs were actually a bit more likely to experience an increase (29 percent) in their ranks than a decrease (19 percent). Three-fourths (75 percent) of the TRNs experienced a substantial percentage change in their Hispanic representation, but the number experiencing a substantial growth relative to their MSAs was about the same as the number experiencing a relatively lower growth rate (38 percent versus 36 percent). These results are consistent with the findings of the initial analysis that, whatever else a new transit station may portend for its neighborhood, neighborhood racial and ethnic composition does not change substantially.

Household income

As was true in the initial round of analysis, greater change was seen in neighborhood economic composition than in racial and ethnic composition. Over half (57 percent) of the 42 TRNs experienced change in their median household income that was within 20 percentage points of the change in their respective MSAs. But of the remaining 18 TRNs, 13 (31 percent) saw incomes rise much faster than their surrounding metro areas, while only five (12 percent) experienced incomes that increased much slower. Further, 55 percent of the TRNs experienced a substantial increase in the proportion of families earning at least $100,000 per year; in only about a quarter (26 percent) of the TRNs did median household income rise by substantially less than the surrounding metro area.

Housing costs

Nowhere did we find a more pronounced difference between TRNs and their metro areas than in the data on increasing median housing value. In more than two-thirds (29) of the 42 TRNs, home values increased at least 20 percentage points faster between 1990 and 2000 than in their surrounding metro areas. In only four did home values increase at a much slower rate than their surrounding MSAs. Although the evidence for rising rents is not quite so strong as for rising home values, more than a third of the TRNs in the study experienced median gross rent increases in excess of 20 percentage points more than their surrounding MSAs while only one TRN out of the 42 experienced a substantially lower increase than its metro area.

In-migration

In the initial analysis a substantial majority of TRNs were more likely to experience more

rapid in-migration (the rate of people reporting that they did not live in their current home five years earlier) than their surrounding metro areas, but the large differences analysis found that in four-fifths of the cases the in-migration rate in the TRN was within 20 percentage points of the rate in the corresponding MSA. In seven of the remaining TRNs (17 percent), the TRN in-migration rate exceeded the MSA in-migration rate by at least 20 percentage points, and in only one case out of 42 was the TRN in-migration rate at least 20 percentage points lower than the overall MSA rate.

Public transit use for commuting

The results of this more strenuous +20/−20 percent test for public transit use by commuters found that transit utilization rates in the TRNs were not substantially different from those for the entire metro about half of the time. In about one-third (31 percent) of the TRNs, reported use of transit for commuting rose substantially faster than in the surrounding metro area, with the new transit station apparently succeeding in attracting residents who were also transit commuters. However, in one-fifth (19 percent) of the TRNs the use of public transit rose substantially less than in the MSA or fell by more.

Motor vehicle ownership

In 70 percent of the cases, the increase in household car ownership is within 20 percentage points of that in the corresponding MSA. However, motor vehicle ownership rates rose substantially faster in the TRN than in the corresponding MSA in more than one-quarter of TRNs (26 percent) and rose by substantially less than their surrounding metro areas in only one case.

As expected, the +20/−20 percent test produces a smaller number of TRNs in which substantial demographic shifts are observed. For almost all of the factors studied, at least half of the time the change in a given variable is within 20 percentage points of the same changes seen throughout the metro area. But focusing on those cases in which the TRN experiences substantially greater change than its metropolitan area, the direction of change is consistent with the findings from our initial round of analysis, with most of the TRNs experiencing the same type of change seen in the initial analysis and only a handful of TRNs experiencing a different pattern of change. So even this very conservative method of analysis, in which change in the newly-transit served area must exceed that in the metro area by 20 or more percentage points to be considered meaningful, provides further support for many of our initial conclusions.

While cause and effect are always difficult to prove conclusively, the large-differences analysis strongly suggests that gentrification concerns are well-founded. New transit stations are associated with a pattern of neighborhood change marked by sizeable increases in population and household income, particularly at the high end of the income spectrum, and by rising homeownership rates, housing values and residential rents. In more than two-thirds of the TRNs, home values increased at least 20 percentage points faster between 1990 and 2000 than in their surrounding metro areas. More than a third of the TRNs experienced median gross rent increases in excess of 20 percentage points more than their surrounding MSAs. Three out of every five TRNs saw the proportion of families earning at least $100,000 per year grow more than 20 percentage points faster than in the metro as a whole. In line with rising income, a full third of the TRNs experienced an increase in homeownership which was at least 20 percentage points greater than the surrounding metro area.

The large-differences analysis also reinforces the concern that neighborhood gentrification in too many newly transit-served neighborhoods is associated with undesirable changes in travel behavior. In more than one-quarter of the TRNs, automobile ownership rose at a rate more than 20 percentage points greater than that in the surrounding metro. Similarly, in roughly one-fifth of the TRNs the use of public transit rose substantially less than in the MSA or fell by more. The good news is that reported use of transit for commuting rose substantially faster than in the surrounding metro area in nearly one-third of the TRNs, with the new transit station apparently succeeding in attracting residents who were also transit commuters. However, given the recent investment in new transit, the finding that use of public transit for commuting in one-fifth of TRNs was substantially less than that in the corresponding metro area is troubling.

The large-differences analysis, like the initial analysis, did not find clear evidence of involuntary displacement. In-migration rates in most of the TRNs were within 20 percentage points of those for the corresponding metros. And while household income rose faster in many of the TRNs, this did not seem to correlate with a displacement of non-Hispanic black families or Hispanic households. We cannot conclude that rising household incomes or rising property values are due to wealthy households moving into TRNs and directly displacing lower income families. Instead, as other recent studies of gentrification have found (McKinnish, Walsh and White, 2008), the mechanism may be one of succession or replacement rather than displacement. Rents rise in the existing rental stock and are higher in the new housing stock, more for-sale housing is built, and higher income residents join their lower-income predecessors in the newly transit-served neighborhood. The result, however, is similar: on average, the changed neighborhood post-transit is wealthier, rents are higher and residents are more likely to own cars.

TRANSIT TYPE ANALYSIS

The first two rounds of analysis were designed to evaluate whether the construction of new transit stations of any type could cause changes in neighborhood demographics including gentrification and displacement. But it is possible that certain types of transit lead to a much higher potential for both gentrification and displacement. By separately studying heavy rail, commuter rail, and light rail transit stations, we were able to dig deeper into the gentrification and displacement phenomenon. Hence, a third and final round of analysis, in which we sorted the 42 TRNs by their types of stations, helps explain where gentrification is most likely to occur. The results of this transit type analysis demonstrate that neighborhoods surrounding new light rail stations experience considerably more substantial demographic shifts than those surrounding new heavy rail and commuter rail stations.

Population growth

Light rail neighborhoods saw their populations increase at a rate that exceeded their metro areas by 21 percentage points, on average.

Meanwhile, heavy rail neighborhoods outpaced their MSAs by an average of only five percentage points and commuter rail neighborhoods actually lagged their MSAs in population growth.

Housing units

A similar finding emerged from an analysis of added housing units. On average, the growth in housing around light rail transit stations exceeded housing construction in surrounding metro areas by 82 percentage points; the corresponding figures for heavy rail and commuter rail neighborhoods were 11 and four percentage points, respectively.

Moreover, owner-occupied units became much more prevalent in light rail TRNs. Owner occupancy increased at a rate that exceeded the surrounding metro areas by 146 percentage points, on average, where light rail was developed. In heavy rail and commuter rail neighborhoods, the differential was negligible.

Racial and ethnic composition

In both commuter rail and heavy rail neighborhoods, the growth in the white population trailed that of the metro area as a whole. By contrast, light rail neighborhoods became slightly whiter, on average, than their metro areas. The growth in the black population in heavy rail neighborhoods substantially exceeded that of their surrounding metro areas (although the increase is only 74 percent when 2 stations are eliminated as outliers). For commuter rail neighborhoods, the differential was 18 percentage points. By comparison, light rail neighborhoods became less black, on average, than their metro areas between 1990 and 2000.

Median household income

On average, light rail neighborhoods saw their median income rise by 77 more percentage points than their metro areas; for heavy rail neighborhoods, the difference was 18 percentage points, and for commuter rail neighborhoods it was just two percentage points.

Housing costs

While the median value of owner-occupied homes rose by 24 more percentage points in commuter rail neighborhoods than in their metro areas, the differential was 217 percentage points for heavy rail neighborhoods, and a staggering 500 percentage points for light rail neighborhoods.

Median rent rose by 50 percentage points more in light rail neighborhoods than in their metro areas. By comparison, rents in the new heavy rail TRNs exceeded the increase in rents in their MSAs by just 30 percentage points, and in commuter rail neighborhoods by just 10 percentage points.

In-migration

Neighborhoods served by different types of transit experienced different patterns of in-migration (the rate of people reporting that they did not live in their current home five years earlier). Both light rail and commuter rail neighborhoods saw increases in in-migration that exceeded rates in their MSAs, by 4 percentage points for light rail and more than 15 percentage points for heavy rail. Commuter rail neighborhoods, by contrast, experienced slightly less in-migration than their corresponding metro areas.

Public transit use for commuting

Where heavy rail and commuter rail stations were placed, the increase in public transit use exceeded that in their MSAs. But use of public transportation for commuting in light rail neighborhoods actually declined in 12 of the 16 light rail TRNs after the transit station went into operation.

Motor vehicle ownership

The percentage of households owning no car fell dramatically in the light rail TRNs, while the growth in the percentage of households owning two or more cars outpaced the metro areas by 52 percentage points, on average. In the heavy rail and commuter rail neighborhoods, however, the percentage of households owning no car increased. The percentage of households owning two or more cars increased more modestly in the heavy rail than in the light rail neighborhoods and declined slightly in the commuter rail neighborhoods. These changes in the commuter rail and light rail neighborhoods may reflect a process of self-selection in which some new residents choose to live near transit and reduce their car ownership and/or use (Cervero, 2007). In the light rail neighborhoods, car ownership patterns – fewer households without a vehicle and more households with two or more – may instead reflect the neighborhood's higher income levels.

This final round of analysis revealed significant differences in neighborhood change patterns associated with different types of transit. A new light rail station (as opposed to heavy rail or commuter rail) magnifies almost every aspect of neighborhood change. To confirm this finding, we conducted additional statistical analyses. We conducted a series of two-tailed t-tests on all of these variables, comparing the neighborhood-metro area differentials of light rail TRNs to those of TRNs surrounding all other types of transit stations. The results are displayed in Table 32.1. Light rail neighborhoods experienced statistically significant changes in many of the variables compared to neighborhoods with new commuter rail or subway stations. The most striking differences included greater increases in median income and in the proportion of owner-occupied homes, as well as increases in the percentage of households with two or more cars.[2]

	Total Population		Total Housing Units		Percent White		Percent Black		Percent Hispanic	
	Mean	S.E.	Mean	S.E.	Mean	S.E.	Mean	S.E.	Mean	S.E.
All Others	0.022	0.056	0.089	0.08	−0.086	0.051	1.91	1.071	0.278	0.211
Light Rail	0.0206	0.066	0.822	0.491	0.083	0.094	−0.156	0.071	0.114	0.249
t-statistic	−2.06	*	−1.94	+	−1.71	+	1.46		0.48	

	Median Household Income		Median Gross Rent		Median Housing Value		Percent Owner-Occupied	
	Mean	S.E.	Mean	S.E.	Mean	S.E.	Mean	S.E.
All Others	0.125	0.076	0.237	0.088	1.523	1.066	0.057	0.052
Light Rail	0.769	0.293	0.503	0.213	4.996	2.147	1.461	0.658
t-statistic	−2.69	*	−1.35		−1.62		−2.86	**

	Percent of Residents Living in a Different House 5 Years Ago		Percent of Workers Taking Public Transit to Work		Percent of Households with 0 Cars		Percent of Households with 2+ Cars	
	Mean	S.E.	Mean	S.E.	Mean	S.E.	Mean	S.E.
All Others	0.093	0.039	0.341	0.121	0.319	0.229	0.076	0.059
Light Rail	0.042	0.031	−0.047	0.099	−0.177	0.066	0.524	0.524
t-statistic	0.89		2.19	*	1.58		−3.39	**

Table 32.1 Comparison of means (light rail TRNs vs. heavy rail and commuter rail TRNs)

+ p<.10, * p<.05, ** p<.01

These differences in neighborhood change patterns between 1990 and 2000 likely reflect differences in where light rail, heavy rail and commuter rail stations are located. In the light rail neighborhoods, nearly three-fourths (74 percent) of the households were renters and they had an average median household income of only $14,028, less than 40 percent of the commuter rail station average. Median household income in the nine commuter rail station neighborhoods averaged $36,825 in 1990 and only 53 percent of the housing units in these neighborhoods were renter-occupied. Rental occupancy and median household income in the heavy rail station neighborhoods fell in between that in light rail and commuter rail neighborhoods, but closer to the latter. Nearly 58 percent of the households in heavy rail neighborhoods were renters and they averaged $29,791 in median income. As the light rail neighborhoods were initially dominated by lower income renters, the addition of higher income families to these neighborhoods apparently magnified patterns of neighborhood change and accelerated gentrification and some of its adverse consequences.

CONCLUSIONS

As in prior studies, we found that patterns of neighborhood change varied across the transit-rich neighborhoods we studied. Many of the TRNs changed in ways that were roughly similar to the underlying pattern of change in their larger metro areas. Taking into account all of the information provided in the three sets of analyses, however, we conclude that there are substantial shifts in demographic and economic characteristics associated with the siting of a new public transit station. Focusing particularly on TRNs where changes were more pronounced than those in the surrounding metropolitan area, a predominant pattern of neighborhood change could be discerned: with the addition of transit, housing became more expensive, neighborhood residents wealthier and vehicle ownership more common. Many TRNs therefore experience gentrification, a pattern of neighborhood change marked by rising housing costs and incomes.

Our research also supports the conclusion that neighborhoods with a large number of renters are more susceptible to gentrification.

Indeed, when we specifically looked at the neighborhoods where the new stations were light rail – neighborhoods which, in our study, were more likely to be dominated pre-transit by low-income, renter households than those in the heavy rail and commuter rail neighborhoods – almost every aspect of neighborhood change was magnified: rents rose faster and owner-occupied units became more prevalent, for example. In these TRNs, with their high population of low-income renters before the light rail station opened, in-migration by higher-income families appears to have disproportionately changed the demographic structure and substantially increased the risk and pace of gentrification.

While we can confidently say we found some evidence of gentrification in the majority of newly transit-served neighborhoods, it is more difficult to determine whether this gentrification was accompanied by involuntary displacement of former neighborhood residents. Our research did not find strong evidence of disproportionate changes in the racial/ethnic composition of the newly transit-served neighborhoods. Despite evidence of gentrification based on housing values, rents and incomes, we did not find that new transit stations led to a reduction in the proportion of blacks and Hispanics or a substantial increase in the proportion of non-Hispanic white households in most TRNs. Perhaps the relatively higher retention of higher-income black and Hispanic households and/or the in-migration of racially mixed, higher-income residents results in a wealthier neighborhood, but one with a racial composition similar to that of the pre-transit neighborhood.

Displacement is not, however, the only problem associated with gentrification. Gentrification can be a positive form of neighborhood change, one associated with neighborhood revitalization, better amenities for all neighborhood residents and rising home values that benefit existing homeowners. But gentrification can also have adverse consequences and our analysis found evidence of at least two negative consequences of gentrification in transit-rich neighborhoods: higher housing cost burdens for renters and an influx of automobile-owning households less likely to use transit for commuting.

New transit brings with it rising rents and home values, particularly when light rail is located in previously lower-income neighborhoods

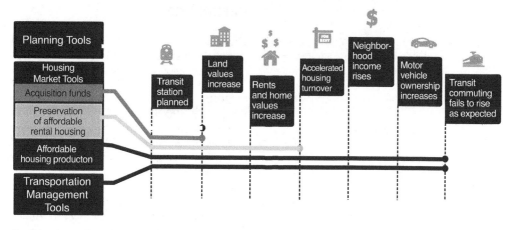

Breaking the cycle of unintended consequences in transit-rich neighborhoods.

dominated by rental housing. While neighborhood incomes also increase, the income of individual households will not necessarily change. As landlords raise rents, households that choose to remain and take advantage of the new transit may suffer from higher housing cost burdens.

A new transit station may also set in motion a cycle of unintended consequences that reduces neighborhood residency by those groups most likely to use transit in favor of groups more likely to drive. In some newly transit-served neighborhoods, rising rents and home values attract not only higher-income residents but also car-owning residents. Use of public transit for commuting in this problematic subset of newly transit-served neighborhoods actually rose slower (or, in some cases, declined faster) than in the metropolitan area as a whole. Whether by displacement or replacement, or a combination of the two, in some transit-rich neighborhoods the pattern of change is working against the goal of attracting transit-oriented neighbors: the most likely potential transit riders are being crowded out by car owners less likely to be regular users of transit. This cycle raises concerns both about equity, because core transit riders are predominantly people of color and/ or low income, and about the success of new transit investments in attracting desired levels of ridership. But, as illustrated [in the figure] policy tools can be deployed to produce more equitable patterns of neighborhood change.

ACKNOWLEDGMENTS

We gratefully acknowledge the funding support of the Rockefeller Foundation's Promoting Equitable, Sustainable Transportation initiative and, in particular, the insights and patience of Managing Director Nick Turner.

We also acknowledge the invaluable research support of Jessica Herrmann and Marc Horne for their work constructing the transit station geographies used in this study and the equally invaluable efforts of Ishwar Khatiwada and Mykhaylo Trubskyy of Northeastern University's Center for Labor Market Studies in constructing the database of 1990 and 2000 Census data. Additional thanks go to research associate Anna Gartsman and interns Gabriella Paiella and Dan Drazen for their research assistance.

Finally, we wish to thank Diana Williams at the Funders' Network for Smart Growth and Livable Communities and Mary Skelton Roberts at the Barr Foundation for organizing two roundtable convenings at which we were able to present our initial research findings and conclusions; we similarly thank the many researchers, funders and advocates who participated in the two sessions and provided valuable feedback and insights.

While the authors are grateful to all of the aforementioned individuals and organizations, the report's research and conclusions are solely the responsibility of the authors.

Notes

1 We ran simple zero-order correlations between the rate of homeownership in 1990 in the TRNs in each city with the percentage change in the non-Hispanic white population between 1990 and 2000 and separately with the 1990–2000 percentage change in median household income. Across all 42 TRNs in the 12 MSAs in the study, there was a negative correlation ($-.596$) between the initial homeownership rate and racial/ethnic change and a nearly identical negative correlation ($-.580$) with the change in median household income.

2 For the differences between light rail neighborhoods and all others on the change in median income, $t=-2.69$. For the change in percent owner occupied housing, $t=-2.86$. For the change in the percentage of households with two or more cars, $t=-3.39$. The differences are large enough in many cases that, despite the relatively small sample size, they are statistically significant at $<.05$.

REFERENCES

Cervero, R. (2007). Transit-Oriented development's ridership bonus: A product of self-selection and public policies. *Environment and Planning*, 39, 2068–2085.

Chapple, K. (2009). *Mapping susceptibility to gentrification: The early warning toolkit*. Berkeley, CA: University of California Berkeley Center for Community Innovation.

Freeman, L. (2005). Displacement or succession? Residential mobility in gentrifying neighborhoods. *Urban Affairs Review* 40 (4), 463–491.

McKinnish, T, Walsh, R. and White, K. (2008). *Who gentrifies low-income neighborhoods?* Cambridge, MA: National Bureau of Economic Research (Working Paper 14026).

Housing and race: Enduring challenges, debated strategies

Plate 7 Detroit, Michigan. Riot at the Sojourner Truth homes, a new U.S. federal housing project, caused by white neighbors' attempt to prevent Negro tenants from moving in. Sign with American flag "We want white tenants in our white community" directly opposite the housing project (photographer: Arthur S. Siegel).

INTRODUCTION TO PART SEVEN

It is widely perceived that racial discrimination and segregation in housing is a thing of the past – a remnant of a divisive and confrontational history. The terms themselves conjure up images of government policies that forced separation between the races in schools and neighborhoods; of urban violence in response to injustice and inequality; of hard and fast rules about what groups constituted racial and ethnic minorities, where they could go, and what they could do. Until the Civil Rights and Fair Housing Acts of the 1960s, most government housing policies and practices contained unconcealed racial inequities. While great strides have been made toward racial equality, discrimination and racism persist in our social, educational, and political structures, as well as in the minds of many Americans. These issues are collectively embodied in the places we live, making addressing discrimination and segregation especially divisive and problematic in housing policy. Although racial equality in housing is now the law, minorities have continued to experience severe discrimination when seeking housing, as well as unequal access to financing (Galster and Godfrey 2005).

Large-scale governmental involvement in the housing market began during the Great Depression. The largest effect of New Deal era housing policies was to dramatically reduce the risk of lending. This system enabled an entirely new class – the middle class – to become homeowners. However, it did little to address the needs of the most disadvantaged populations. Discriminatory practices codified in FHA regulations allowed only White residents to utilize the new system of mortgage finance, thereby excluding minority groups entirely from this vast expansion of the egalitarian ideal.

Not only were many minority borrowers excluded from obtaining home loans, but entire neighborhoods were off-limits to potential investors. These regulations, commonly known as "redlining," utilized a hierarchical rating system to measure neighborhood suitability for mortgage investment. This system used four color-coded ratings to determine the health of a neighborhood, and therefore the risk in providing a mortgage in that neighborhood. Most Black neighborhoods received the least desirable "red" rating, preventing prospective buyers from obtaining financing to purchase or upgrade properties in those neighborhoods. Together, lending discrimination and redlining excluded minority households from the opportunities afforded whites. Instead, Black families, trapped in increasingly poor and crowded neighborhoods, lacked access to capital for improving their homes or establishing businesses. Such trends became starker as huge numbers of African-Americans migrated north during the 1940s and 1950s. As government policies enabled working class whites to leave the increasingly crowded city centers, the residents of publicly supported housing located in cities became increasingly poor and increasingly minority. Public housing was one of the few options left for those who could not qualify for homeownership.

Redlining and FHA rules so constrained the supply of housing and housing finance in Black neighborhoods, that upwardly mobile Blacks began to look to White neighborhoods, where prices were lower (Mehlhorn 1998). Such moves were facilitated through "blockbusting" – a process through which unscrupulous real estate agents reaped large profits by scaring white residents into selling their homes to agents rather than risk watch their home values fall once Blacks moved in. The agents would then re-sell the homes at much higher prices to Black households (Massey and Denton 1993).

In response to the deterioration of urban neighborhoods and job centers, national urban policy shifted its focus to economic development. These new priorities manifested in the Housing Act of 1949, which included measures intended to improve the public perception of American cities and to improve housing conditions for those in the greatest need. The majority of the funding stemming from the 1949 Housing Act went into the slum clearance portion of the program (generally known as "Urban Renewal"). To replace the slums, the Housing Act authorized the construction of thousands of brand new housing units. However, fewer units were built than were demolished. Those constructed were generally reserved for middle and upper class households, while public housing for low income families followed previously established siting patterns – namely, placement in isolated areas far from established communities and job centers.

Poor siting, mismanagement, and underfunding reduced support for the public housing program, and "The Projects" became identified with urban poverty, blight, and crime. As it became clear that the public housing program could not meet the needs of those who lacked adequate housing, the federal government embarked on numerous experimental housing programs under the umbrella of the War on Poverty. These programs included voucher programs, demonstration mobility programs, and production programs for both rental and owner-occupied low-income housing. However, even these new high-volume production programs failed to supply units fast enough for the growing demand.

Compounding the variety issues in public housing were ongoing challenges in implementing racial equality. Racial desegregation ordered by *Brown v. the Board of Education* and the 1964 Civil Rights Act, along with the widespread violence in U.S. cities following the assassinations of Robert Kennedy and Martin Luther King, Jr., eventually led to the enactment of the 1968 Fair Housing Act. This act took the strides made by the Civil Rights Act and applied them specifically to housing. As such, the Fair Housing Act represents the legal foundation for residential racial desegregation. However, this elimination of de jure segregation did not mean that de facto racial discrimination disappeared from real estate practices, housing development, and lending, as both Galster and Godfrey, and Charles discuss in their contributions to this section. Furthermore, as pointed out in the report of the National Commission on Fair Housing, the Fair Housing Act did not provide strong enough policy tools to implement its goals, and requires considerable political will to successfully implement and enforce its requirements. As a result, discriminatory practices, though now illegal, continue to pose a threat to true racial equality in the housing market.

In addition to ongoing problems in the private market, it became clear that federal housing programs were not countering entrenched patterns of racial segregation in metropolitan areas. In fact, housing programs arguably compounded, rather than rectified, racial segregation. Elizabeth Julian, a former HUD Assistant Secretary for Fair Housing during the Clinton Administration, presents a critique of housing policy, arguing that the federal government has failed to integrate housing and community development policy strategies, thus undermining progress toward meaningful fair housing outcomes.

The intersection of housing policy and racial discrimination in the United States has placed heavy burdens upon poor and minority groups. While a number of very popular government actions – from the Homestead Act to FHA insurance – provided opportunities for individuals to enter the middle classes through property ownership, African Americans and other racial minorities were excluded from these benefits. Conversely, policies designed to provide housing opportunities to the poor or minorities – including public housing, the Community Reinvestment Act, and Section 8 vouchers – continue to carry a stigma and face significant political opposition to implementation. Furthermore, racial and class segregation and concentration of poverty continue to present a major problem for U.S. communities. Policymakers must directly address both the inequality and discrimination that pervades the housing market and the role government action has in shaping or enabling these problems.

IN THIS PART:

REFERENCES AND FURTHER READING

Bratt, Rachel G., ed. (1989). *Rebuilding a Low-Income Housing Policy*. Philadelphia: Temple University Press.

Cashin, Sheryll. (2004). *The Failures of Integration: How Race and Class are Undermining the American Dream*. 1st ed. New York: Public Affairs.

Eaddy, Randy, Carolyn Sawyer, Ahimizu Kazuhiro, Ray McIlwain, W. Swain Wood, and Debbie Segal. (2003). *Residential Segregation, Poverty, and Racism: Obstacles to America's Great Society*. Washington, D.C.: Lawyers' Committee for Civil Rights Under the Law.

Farley, Reynolds. (1996)."Racial differences in the search for housing: Do whites and blacks use the same techniques to find housing?" *Housing Policy Debate*, 7(2): 367–85.

Freund, David. (2007). *Colored Property: State Policy and White Racial Politics in Suburban America*. Chicago: University of Chicago Press.

Galster, George C. (1990). "Racial steering by real estate agents: Mechanisms and motives." *Review of Black Political Economy*, 19(1): 39–63.

Galster, George C. (1991). "Housing discrimination and urban poverty of African-Americans." *Journal of Housing Research*, 2(2): 87–122.

Galster, George and Erin Godfrey. (2005). "By words and deeds: Racial steering by real estate agents in the U.S. in 2000." *Journal of the American Planning Association*, 71(3): 251–268.

Goering, John, and Ron Wienk, eds. (1996). *Mortgage Lending, Racial Discrimination, and Federal Policy*. Washington, D.C.: Urban Institute Press.

Haurin, Donald R., Christopher Herbert, and Stuart Rosenthal. (2007). "Homeownership gaps among low-income and minority households." *Cityscape*, 9(2): 5–52.

HUD. (2008). *Historical Census of Housing Tables - Homeownership*. US Department of Housing and Urban Development 2004. Online, available from: www.census.gov/hhes/www/housing/census/historic/owner.html [accessed November 29, 2008].

Immergluck, Dan. (2002). "Redlining redux: Black neighborhoods, black-owned firms, and the regulatory cold shoulder." *Urban Affairs Review*, 38(22): 22–41.

Lukas, J. Anthony. (1985). *Common Ground*. Boston: Knopf.

Massey, Douglas S., and Nancy A. Denton. (1993). *American Apartheid: Segregation and the Making of the Underclass*: Cambridge, MA: Harvard University Press.

Mehlhorn, Dmitri. (1998). "A requiem for blockbusting law, economics, and race-based real estate speculation." *Fordham Law Review*, 67(3): 1145–92.

Orfield, Gary. (2004). "Why segregation is inherently unequal: The abandonment of Brown and the continuing failure of Plessy." *New York Law School Law Review*, 49: 1041–52.

Orfield, Gary, and Susan E. Eaton. (1996). *Dismantling Desegregation*. New York: New Press.

Patterson, Orlando. (1997). *The Ordeal of Integration: Progress and Resentment in America's "Racial" Crisis*. New York: Civitas/Counterpoint.

Schill, Michael H., and Susan M. Wachter. (1995). "Housing market constraints and spatial stratification by income and race." *Housing Policy Debate*, 6(1): 141–67.

Squires, Gregory, and Charis Kubrin. (2005). "Privileged places: Race, uneven development and the geography of opportunity in urban America." *Urban Studies*, 42(1): 47–68

Thernstrom, Stephan, and Abigail Thernstrom. (1997). *America in Black and White: One Nation, Indivisible*. New York: Simon and Schuster.

Turner, Margery A. (1992). "Discrimination in urban housing markets: Lessons from fair housing audits." *Housing Policy Debate*, 3(2): 185–215.

Wilson, William Julius. (1980). *The Declining Significance of Race: Blacks and Changing American Institutions*. 2nd ed. Chicago: University of Chicago Press.

Yinger, John. (1998). "Housing discrimination is still worth worrying about." *Housing Policy Debate*, 9(4): 893–927.

Yinger, John. (1999). "Sustaining the Fair Housing Act." *Cityscape*, 4(3): 99–106.

33

"By words and deeds: Racial steering by real estate agents in the U.S. in 2000"

From *Annual Review of Sociology* (2005)

George Galster and Erin Godfrey

Residential segregation on the basis of race or ethnicity is a long-established characteristic of metropolitan America (Farley and Frey, 1994; Iceland *et al.*, 2002; Massey and Denton, 1993; McEntire, 1960; Taeuber *et al.*, 1985). Three distinct, not mutually exclusive causes of residential segregation have been proposed: *class, self-segregation,* and *discrimination* (Charles, 2003; Dawkins, 2004; Freeman, 2000; Galster, 1987b). The class theory attempts to explain residential segregation in terms of average interracial differences in ability to pay for housing. The self-segregation theory holds that Whites (and perhaps other groups) prefer to live in areas predominantly occupied by members of their own group because they perceive either something undesirable about other groups and/or something positive about their own. The discrimination theory posits that minorities are prevented from moving into areas that their incomes and preferences might otherwise allow because of discriminatory barriers in the housing market. Although some (Clark, 1986; Orlebeke, 1997; Thernstrom and Thernstrom, 1997) have argued that discrimination plays a negligible role in residential segregation, Galster (1986,1987b; Galster and Keeney, 1988) has provided econometric evidence that cross-metropolitan variations in housing discrimination are significantly correlated with differences in residential segregation, and recent reviews concur regarding the continued importance of discrimination (Charles, 2003; Dawkins, 2004; Freeman, 2000).

One form of discrimination in the housing market is *steering,* which may be defined as behaviors by real estate agents that differentially direct clients toward particular neighborhoods and away from others on the basis of race or ethnicity. Steering distorts the spatial patterns of housing demands by White and minority homebuyers in such a fashion that segregation is perpetuated and stable integration is discouraged. It is not surprising, then, that steering has been prohibited by federal law since passage of the Fair Housing Act of 1968, and subsequently by numerous substantially equivalent state and local ordinances (Schwemm, 1992). Specifically prohibited practices include directing people to a particular community or neighborhood because of their race or ethnicity, discouraging people from occupying any dwelling because of the race or ethnicity of the persons in the neighborhood, failing to inform people of desirable features of a dwelling or neighborhood in order to perpetuate such discouragement, and communicating to prospective purchasers that they would not be comfortable or compatible with existing residents of a neighborhood (U.S. Department of Housing and Urban Development [HUD], 1989). Even given these clear and longstanding legal prohibitions against steering and the evidence linking it to segregation, does steering persist in American metropolitan housing markets?

Historically there is no doubt that steering was widely practiced (Helper, 1969; McEntire,

1960; Palmer, 1955). The first systematic studies of the phenomenon were conducted for their communities by local fair housing organizations in the early 1970s, and employed *paired testers* (Fix and Struyk, 1993): closely matched White and minority investigators who independently visited real estate offices posing as home-buyers and recorded treatment afforded them (e.g., Bish *et al.*, 1973; Greater Dallas Housing Opportunity Center, 1974). These were soon followed by scholars applying more sophisticated statistical analyses of testing results in case study sites (Feins and Bratt, 1983; Galster 1990b; Hall *et al.*, 1983; James *et al.*, 1984; Pearce, 1979; Roychoudhury and Goodman, 1992, 1996). By the end of the 1980s, at least three dozen testing-based steering studies of a wide variety of communities had been completed (see the summaries in Galster, 1990a).

The totality of this evidence indicated that steering, though widespread during the period, typically did not limit the number of different areas available to minority homebuyers nor preclude all options to see predominantly White neighborhoods. Rather, steering most often constituted a failure to show White homebuyers options in neighborhoods and school districts with nontrivial proportions of minorities, and a propensity to show minority home-buyers disproportionately in areas currently possessing or soon expected to possess significant proportions of minorities. Differential commentary that encouraged or discouraged the choice of particular areas occurred more frequently than differential showings of homes. No valid national estimate of the incidence of steering can be deduced from these studies, unfortunately, due primarily to nonrandom samples and incomparable methods and measures (Galster, 1990a).

HUD sponsored two paired testing-based studies of housing discrimination during this period that afforded the first opportunity to estimate reliably how often steering occurred nationwide. In 1979 the Housing Market Practices Survey (HMPS) of White and Black home seekers was conducted in 40 metropolitan areas (Wienk *et al.*, 1979). The weighted average incidence of steering across the sample was estimated at 20–30% of the tests, depending on the measure of steering used (Newburger, 1981, 1989). In 1989 the Housing Discrimination Study (HDS) was conducted in 24 metropolitan areas to ascertain treatment of White, Black,

and Hispanic home seekers (Turner, Struyk, *et al.*, 1991). The steering revealed by HDS was analyzed by Turner, Edwards, and Mikelsons (1991); Turner and Mikelsons (1992); and Yinger (1995). They reported for both Black/White and Hispanic/White tests an average incidence of 12% of steering that promoted racial/ethnic segregation, a slightly lower estimate of steering that promoted income class segregation, and an overall steering index incidence of 20% (Turner and Wienk, 1993). Under certain circumstances, the incidence of steering appeared even higher. If the advertised unit that anchored the paired test was located in a predominantly minority neighborhood and the real estate agent had access to homes in predominantly White neighborhoods through a Multiple Listing Service (MLS), there was an 80% chance that the White tester would gain more access to the latter homes (Yinger, 1995).

Just before HDS went into the field, Congress passed the Fair Housing Amendments Act of 1988. In a variety of ways, it was designed to strengthen Federal strictures against steering and other forms of housing discrimination. It extended the number of protected classes, provided for a more speedy adjudication process through administrative law judges, gave HUD the power to initiate suits, and toughened penalties for violators, among other features (Schwemm, 1992; U.S. Commission on Civil Rights, 1994).

Unfortunately, during the ensuing decade there was little evidence to assess whether steering and other discriminatory acts were persisting in this new statutory environment. Only one paired-testing report (prepared by a fair housing group) focusing on discrimination in the housing sales market came to light during the 1990s, and this did not deal with steering (Yinger, 1998). As a result, some scholars have argued that steering and other forms of housing discrimination have largely ceased (Orlebeke, 1997; Thernstrom and Thernstrom, 1997).

The topic of this article is therefore of great relevance. We analyze steering data produced by the Housing Discrimination Study conducted during 2000, which largely replicated and extended the paired-testing and analysis strategies of the 1989 HDS. Steering of non-Hispanic White (*White* hereafter) compared to non-Hispanic Black *(Black* hereafter) or Hispanic testers is investigated, depending on the site. We comprehensively examined nine potential avenues of steering in our nationally represen-tative sample of 20 metropolitan study sites:

- three *types of steering*, information, segregation, and class;
- three *mechanisms of steering*, home inspecting, recommending, and editorializing;
- and *three levels:* census tracts, municipalities, and school districts.

Our goal was to ascertain how often steering of various types occurs at various geographic scales, what mechanisms are used to perpetrate it, and whether its incidence has declined during the last decade.

The article begins with a discussion of the concept of steering wherein all the foregoing terms are explained. The second describes the HDS 2000 and our methodological approach. The third section presents findings on the incidence of steering of Whites, Blacks, and Hispanics for the nation as a whole. Both quantitative and qualitative evidence related to steering via editorial commentary by agents is presented. Finally, we consider whether the incidence of steering has fallen appreciably since 1989. We conclude with a summary of key findings, the linkage of steering and interracial wealth differentials in a vicious circle, and implications for reforming fair housing enforcement strategies to better combat steering.

STEERING AS A FORM OF HOUSING DISCRIMINATION: CONCEPTUAL ISSUES

Definition of steering

For the purposes or our investigations, steering is defined as follows:

A behavior by home sales agents in which minority and White homebuyers are provided information about respective sets of homes having systematically different spatial patterns in terms of numbers of neighborhoods represented, neighborhood racial/ethnic composition, and/or neighborhood socio-economic class composition.

Three *types* of steering (defined by the nature of the difference in spatial pattern) and three

mechanisms through which steering can occur (what home sales agents show or recommend, and what areas they comment upon) are implicit in this definition. Both the types and mechanisms are explained below.

Types of steering

All of the steering we investigated in HDS 2000 may be considered in some sense *racial/ethnic steering*, inasmuch as the tester teammates differed on this dimension, three distinct types of steering can be identified within this overall context, however. We label these: *information*, *segregation*, and *class* steering.

- *Information steering* is spatial patterns of home showings that differ between minority and White homebuyers in the number of areas represented.
- *Segregation steering* is spatial patterns of home showings in which areas shown minority homebuyers have larger (or growing, or more proximity to concentrations of, etc.) specified minority populations than areas shown Whites, on average.
- *Class steering* is spatial patterns of home showings in which areas shown minority homebuyers have lower socioeconomic status (lower incomes, homeownership rates, property values, etc.) than areas shown Whites, on average.

All three types have intrinsic interest. Although not often analyzed (Galster, 1990a, b), information steering is important because unless both White and minority homebuyers are shown or recommended homes in the same areas, they are potentially receiving vastly different amounts and/or types of information about alternative neighborhood opportunities. It is easy to see that the homebuyers shown fewer neighborhoods will be offered an inferior amount of spatial information. It is more problematic conceptually if numerically equivalent but different (perhaps partially intersecting) sets of neighborhoods are shown. Such a difference necessarily provides different information, but it is difficult to ascertain *a priori* which homebuyer is being treated unfavorably.

Segregation steering is the most conventional form considered by previous researchers and fair housing enforcement groups. This form of steering holds the potential to limit the housing choices of both minority and White homebuyers in such ways that it undermines stable, racially diverse neighborhoods and perpetuates segregation.

Class steering, though less frequently considered (Galster, 1990a; Pearce, 1979), is also of potential concern insofar as minorities prove to be systematically directed into lower-class neighborhoods. Such lower-status areas are likely to constitute inferior environments in which to raise children, to have opportunities for high-quality public services and education, and to garner capital gains on one's home.

We investigated all three types of steering. In particular, we compared measures of different types of steering within each of three geographic scales to probe the extent to which the patterns are consistent across types.

Mechanisms of steering

Agents can engage in steering in three (non-mutually exclusive) ways: through inspecting, recommending, and editorializing. They can *inspect* homes in person with clients, *recommend homes* to clients from the Multiple Listing Service (MLS) or other listings, and they can *editorialize* (provide gratuitous positive or negative evaluations) about certain areas the client should or should not consider.

Steering accomplished by inspecting or recommending homes can manifest information, segregation, or class types. In other words, the homes inspected or recommended can be distributed among a different number of areas (i.e., information-type steering) and/or the areas can differ systematically in their racial/ethnic composition (i.e., segregation-type steering) or socioeconomic class composition (i.e., class-type steering).

Analogously, steering accomplished by editorializing can produce information, segregation, or class types. That is, the comments about areas may differ in their frequency, and/or serve to direct certain testers to certain types of areas differing systematically in their racial/ethnic or class composition.

We conducted parallel analyses of all three potential mechanisms of steering at alternative geographic scales to probe the extent to which the patterns of how steering is promulgated are consistent across differing definitions of area.

For any given area, we also explored how the three mechanisms of steering may work in a mutually reinforcing fashion.

Geographic scale of steering

Although all types of steering involve differential patterns of geographic areas shown minority and White clients, there is no *a priori* best formulation of *area*. Obviously, one must define areas sufficiently small such that meaningful differences in the racial/ethnic, class, and other dimensions of local quality of life can be observed. On the other hand, specifying inappropriately small areas may preclude obtaining important or accurate data on many characteristics.

We responded to this challenge by estimating measures of steering at three spatial scales. We operationalized area alternatively by using administrative boundaries for census tracts, census-defined municipalities, and school districts.

A multilevel analysis of steering is required if we are to gain an unbiased portrait of how it operates. It is conventional to measure steering only at the neighborhood (census tract) level, but doing so may overlook other important dimensions. For example, agents may show White and minority homebuyers different sets of neighborhoods that are identical in their racial or class composition, but if the sets are located in school districts or municipalities with distinctly different racial/class profiles and fiscal capacities, the two sets may not offer equal opportunities (Pearce, 1980). As another illustration, it has been shown that agents may practice segregation and class steering at the neighborhood level not by differential patterns of neighborhood showings, but rather by racially selective editorial commentary about the school districts or municipalities in which neighborhoods are located (Galster, 1990b; Pearce, 1980).

THE HOUSING DISCRIMINATION STUDY (HDS) OF 2000

Sponsored by the U.S. Department of Housing and Urban Development, the 2000 HDS studied 20 of the 25 metropolitan areas used in the 1989 HDS and was weighted to make the results

Test sites	# Black/White paired tests	# Hispanic/White paired tests
Black/White		
Atlanta, GA	89	n/a
Birmingham, AL	66	n/a
Dayton-Springfield, OH	70	n/a
Detroit, MI	72	n/a
Macon/Warner Robins, GA	74	n/a
New Orleans, LA	76	n/a
Orlando, FL	76	n/a
Philadelphia, PA	27	n/a
Pittsburgh, PA	50	n/a
Washington, DC	71	n/a
Hispanic/White		
Pueblo, CO	n/a	76
San Antonio, TX	n/a	85
San Diego, CA	n/a	75
Tucson, AZ	n/a	75
Black/White and Hispanic/White		
Austin, TX	75	72
Chicago, IL	70	74
Denver, CO	71	78
Houston, TX	78	76
Los Angeles, CA	69	69
New York, NY	78	79

Table 33.1 Summary of metropolitan areas and paired tests in HDS 2000

nationally representative. Metropolitan areas with populations over 100,000 were included in the 1989 sampling frame if the proportion of Blacks or Hispanics in their central cities were greater than their national average analogues. In 10 2000 HDS sites, we conducted only Black/White tests, in 4 we conducted only Hispanic/White tests, and in 6 we conducted both. In all, 1,112 Black/White and 759 Hispanic/White paired tests of real estate sales offices were completed. Table 33.1 presents the 20 metropolitan areas in which testing occurred, along with the number of paired tests conducted. Table 33.2 presents total and minority population figures and estimates of the level of segregation (dissimilarity indices) for each metropolitan area.

Random samples of homes advertised in the major newspaper(s) of each metropolitan area were selected on a weekly basis, and paired testers posing as homebuyers independently visited the real estate offices representing the sampled homes as soon as possible after sampling. It should be recognized that homes advertised in the metropolitan newspaper are not a random sample of all homes available on the market (Galster et al., 1987; Turner and Mikelsons, 1992; Turner and Wienk, 1993), so the steering measured here is only applicable to this one portal of accessing housing (National Research Council, 2002).

Testers requested to be shown the advertised home and "any similar properties," giving no other geographic preferences. Multiple visits with agents, typically involving home inspections, often occurred. Testers recorded their experiences and information they were provided, including addresses of homes that were recommended and shown by the agent and any sorts of comments made by agents about geographic areas or people living there. Tester teammates independently filed their reports with the local test coordinator, who verified and recorded the information.

Tester partners were assigned financial characteristics that rendered them equally qualified to buy the sampled home. They also were assigned closely matched characteristics related to gender, employment, education, family circumstances, and housing preferences. Testers were thoroughly trained and supervised by a local fair housing agency with testing experience.

NATIONAL FINDINGS ON STEERING

Black/White tests

Our analysis of steering relies upon a net measure of differential treatment: the difference between the percentage of cases where the White tester was favored over the minority teammate and the percentage of cases where the opposite was true. The details of how we measured differences in treatment and the statistical tests we performed are presented in the Appendix.

There were few statistically significant net measures of steering discrimination promulgated either through agent's recommendations

Test sites	Total	Population Black (%)		Hispanic (%)		Dissimilarity White/ Black	White/ Hispanic
Black/White							
Atlanta, GA	4,112,198	1,216,230	30%	268,851	7%	0.645	0.511
Birmingham, AL	921,106	279,452	30%	16,598	2%	0.701	0.460
Dayton-Springfield, OH	950,558	142,143	15%	11,329	1%	0.698	0.255
Detroit, MI	4,441,551	1,045,652	24%	128,075	3%	0.846	0.456
Macon/ Warner Robins, GA	322,549	122,481	38%	6,665	2%	0.514	0.303
New Orleans, LA	1,337,726	508,464	38%	58,545	4%	0.684	0.358
Orlando, FL	1,644,561	245,054	15%	271,627	17%	0.541	0.387
Philadelphia, PA	5,100,931	1,065,713	21%	258,606	5%	0.720	0.601
Pittsburgh, PA	2,358,695	202,160	9%	17,100	1%	0.671	0.290
Washington, DC	4,923,153	1,335,065	27%	432,003	9%	0.625	0.480
Hispanic/White							
Pueblo, CO	141,472	2,685	2%	53,710	38%	0.384	0.318
San Antonio, TX	1,592,383	105,618	7%	816,037	51%	0.492	0.507
San Diego, CA	2,813,833	161,480	6%	750,965	27%	0.535	0.506
Tucson, AZ	843,746	25,594	3%	247,578	29%	0.379	0.488
Black/White and Hispanic/White							
Austin, TX	1,249,763	105,909	8%	327,760	26%	0.508	0.456
Chicago, IL	8,272,768	1,602,248	19%	1,416,584	17%	0.797	0.611
Denver, CO	2,109,282	131,312	6%	397,236	19%	0.605	0.500
Houston, TX	4,177,646	749,864	18%	1,248,586	30%	0.663	0.551
Los Angeles, CA	9,519,338	999,747	11%	4,242,213	45%	0.664	0.631
New York, NY	9,314,235	2,451,277	26%	2,339,836	25%	0.810	0.667

Table 33.2 Total and minority populations and segregation in HDS 2000 metropolitan areas (census 2000 data)

Source: U.S. Census Bureau (2000).

Note: Population figures based on census tracts using definitions as of June 30, 1999.

or inspections of homes. The most robust finding was Black/White segregation steering driven by inspections and recommendations at the census tract level. Editorial comments made by real estate agents were a much more pervasive mechanism, however, evincing higher incidences of information, segregation, and class steering at all spatial levels.

Information steering

We found no statistically significant differences in the percentage of cases where either Black or White testers received a greater number of inspections or recommendations about different tracts, municipalities, or school districts (see Table 33.3). Percentages of gross White-favored and Black-favored tests were highest at the neighborhood level and lowest at the school district level. Information steering was consistently observed, however, when we examined editorializing by real estate agents. As shown in the bottom panel of Table 33.3, in 12–15% of the tests there was systematic discrimination in the number of different census tracts, municipalities, and school districts about which commentary was provided. Moreover, White testers consistently received more comments than their Black teammates about

tracts, municipalities, and school districts – more positive comments, more negative comments, and more comments of any sort, regardless of whether recommended or inspected homes were considered (results not shown in Table 33.3). The net discrimination measures associated with the above differences were all highly statistically significant (p <.01) and ranged from 11 to 17 percentage points.

Thus, it does not appear that there is a systematic, nationwide pattern of real estate agents showing Black and White testers different numbers of tracts, municipalities, or school districts via recommending and inspecting homes. On the other hand, agents give Whites more information about residential options than they give Blacks through their commentary, especially when it comes to neighborhoods defined by census tracts.

Segregation steering

Table 33.4 summarizes our findings related to the incidence of tests where the behavioral patterns worked to further segregation *(pro-segregation* outcome) or to further integration *(pro-integration* outcome). We found a statistically significant net measure of Black/White segregation steering at the census tract level of

	Differential treatment in 2000		
	White favored	Black favored	Net measure
Recommended homes			
# Different census tracts	14.1%	13.5%	0.6%
# Different municipalities	6.0%	5.3%	0.7%
# Different school districts	3.7%	4.5%	−0.8%
Inspected homes			
# Different census tracts	10.0%	7.8%	2.2%
# Different municipalities	3.3%	2.6%	0.7%
# Different school districts	1.6%	2.0%	−0.4%
Editorial comments			
# Different census tracts	38.5%	23.5%	15.0%***
# Different municipalities	28.8%	16.9%	11.9%***
# Different school districts	30.2%	17.7%	12.5%***
# Total comments (positive and negative)	48.6%	35.0%	13.6%***

Table 33.3 National incidence of information steering: Black/White tests

* *p*<.10   ** *p*<.05   ***p*<.01 (two-tailed tests)

geography using both recommendations and inspections. As shown in the top two panels of Table 33.4, the net differences in treatment in both mechanisms were nearly 4 percentage points.

Editorializing again proved to be a commonly u.sed mechanism for promulgating segregation steering of Blacks and Whites, at all geographic levels (see the bottom panel of Table 33.4). There were highly statistically significant (p<.01) differences, ranging from 12 to 14 percentage points, between the percentages of tests where comments promoted racial segregation and where they promoted integration, regardless of whether comments were associated with homes recommended or inspected.

Class steering

Only one of the nine indicators of class steering for both recommended and inspected homes proved even modestly statistically significant in the Black/White tests (see the top two panels of Table 33.5). There was a 2-percentage-point net measure of class steering via recommended homes at the municipal level when class was defined as the percentage of nonpoor residents estimated for 1999. As in the case of segregation steering, the dominant mechanism of class steering was editorializing. Comments that encouraged White testers more than Black testers to choose low-poverty tracts, municipalities,

| | Differential treatment in 2000 | | |
	Pro-segregation	Pro-integration	Net measure
Recommended homes			
% White in census tract	16.5%	12.7%	3.8%*
% White in municipality	6.9%	5.3%	1.6%
% White in school district	6.5%	5.3%	1.2%
Inspected homes			
% White in census tract	12.1%	8.3%	3.8%*
% White in municipality	4.8%	3.2%	1.6%
% White in school district	4.1%	3.3%	0.8%
Editorial comments			
% White in census tract	37.1%	23.4%	13.7%***
% White in municipality	29.7%	17.8%	11.9%***
% White in school district	31.2%	17.9%	13.3%***

Table 33.4 National incidence of segregation steering: Black/White tests

* p<.10   ** p<.05   ***p<.01 (two-tailed tests)

| | Differential treatment in 2000 | | |
	White favored	Black favored	Net measure
Recommended homes			
% Owner occupied in census tract	17.8%	18.5%	−0.7%
% Owner occupied in municipality	7.5%	6.0%	1.5%
Median home price in census tract	24.1%	22.2%	1.9%
Median home price in municipality	9.8%	8.3%	1.5%
Per capita income in census tract	20.1%	19.4%	0.7%
Per capita income in municipality	7.4%	5.2%	2.2%
% Nonpoor in census tract	6.9%	5.1%	1.8%
% Nonpoor in municipality	4.3%	2.5%	1.8%*
% Nonpoor in school district	3.7%	4.5%	0.0%

	Differential treatment in 2000		
	White favored	Black favored	Net measure
Inspected homes			
% Owner occupied in census tract	12.6%	12.4%	0.2%
% Owner occupied in municipality	5.1%	3.1%	2.0%
Median home price in census tract	16.6%	15.9%	0.7%
Median home price in municipality	5.5%	5.0%	0.5%
Per capita income in census tract	13.5%	13.3%	0.2%
Per capita income in municipality	4.2%	3.2%	1.0%
% Nonpoor in census tract	5.2%	3.3%	1.9%
% Nonpoor in municipality	2.9%	1.7%	1.2%
% Nonpoor in school district	2.8%	3.5%	−0.7%
Editorial comments			
% Nonpoor in census tract	34.9%	23.4%	11.5%***
% Nonpoor in municipality	29.7%	17.8%	11.9%***
% Nonpoor in school district	32.4%	18.0%	14.4%***

Table 33.5 National incidence of class steering: Black/White tests

* $p<.10$ ** $p<.05$ *** $p<.01$ (two-tailed tests).

and school districts occurred 12–14 percentage points more frequently ($p<.01$) than the reverse (see the bottom panel in Table 33.5).

Steering in Black/White tests of the same agent

To assess the robustness of the results, we conducted a parallel analysis with the subset of the Black/White tests where both tester teammates saw the same real estate agent. One might expect there to be fewer nonsystematic differences in treatment observed when the same agent is involved with both testers. Steering results for Black/White tests involving the same agent were consistent with results for the full sample, with two exceptions. These exceptions suggest that some of the interracial differences observed in editorializing may have been attributable to different agents, though it remained an important mechanism for steering.

Hispanic/White tests

Echoing the results for the Black/White tests, we found few net measures of Hispanic/White steering promulgated by homes recommended or inspected that were statistically significant. The most robust finding was, again, segregation steering promulgated by inspections and recommendations at the census tract level. Unlike Black/White tests, however, editorializing was not a frequently applied mechanism, appearing in Hispanic/White tests only as a means of promulgating segregation steering at the tract level and information steering by the overall number of comments offered.

Information steering

We found no statistically significant differences in the percentages of cases where either White or Hispanic testers received a greater number of inspections or recommendations about

	Differential treatment in 2000		
	White favored	Hispanic favored	Net measure
Recommended homes			
# Different census tracts	15.4%	13.5%	1.9%
# Different municipalities	6.3%	5.6%	0.7%
# Different school districts	5.0%	4.5%	0.5%
Inspected homes			
# Different census tracts	9.9%	8.4%	1.5%
# Different municipalities	3.6%	3.6%	0.0%
# Different school districts	3.4%	2.5%	0.9%
Editorial comments			
# Different census tracts	35.0%	32.2%	2.8%
# Different municipalities	26.1%	24.6%	1.5%
# Different school districts	24.8%	21.4%	3.4%
# Total comments (positive and negative)	46.8%	40.2%	6.6%*

Table 33.6 National incidence of information steering: Hispanic/White tests

* $p<.10$ ** $p<.05$ *** $p<.01$ (two-tailed tests)

different tracts, municipalities, or school districts (see the top two panels of Table 33.6). Moreover, there was no evidence that editorial comments about different geographic areas were provided differentially by ethnicity of tester (see the bottom panel of Table 33.6). However, there was some evidence of information steering via editorializing when overall intensity of commentary is considered. White testers were offered more comments in total ($p<.10$) and more negative comments ($p<.01$) than their Hispanic teammates when they inspected homes or had homes recommended. The net measure of information steering associated with total comment differentials was 7 percentage points, and the net measure for negative comments was 8 percentage points.

Segregation steering

We found a statistically significant incidence of Hispanic/White segregation steering at the census tract level of geography using inspections (but not recommendations). As shown in the middle panel of Table 33.7, the net difference in treatment was 5 percentage points. This pattern was consistent with segregation steering at the tract level promulgated via editorializing. Tests in which racial segregation was encouraged by comments exceeded those in which integration was encouraged by 6 percentage points ($p<.05$; see the bottom panel of Table 33.7).

Class steering

Out of the numerous indicators of class steering we analyzed, none proved statistically significant in the Hispanic/White tests (see Table 33.8).

	Differential treatment in 2000		
	Pro-segregation	Pro-integration	Net measure
Recommended homes			
% White in census tract	17.1%	15.7%	1.4%
% White in municipality	7.0%	6.5%	0.5%
% White in school district	8.6%	7.4%	1.2%
Inspected homes			
% White in census tract	15.0%	10.0%	5.0%**
% White in municipality	4.8%	4.1%	0.7%
% White in school district	6.6%	5.1%	1.5%
Editorial comments			
% White in census tract	35.1%	28.9%	6.2%*
% White in municipality	28.3%	24.7%	3.6%
% White in school district	27.2%	24.3%	2.9%

Table 33.7 National incidence of segregation steering: Hispanic/White tests

* *p*<.10   ** *p*<.05   ***p*<.01 (two-tailed tests)

	Differential treatment in 2000		
	White higher	Hispanic higher	Net measure
Recommended homes			
% Owner occupied in census tract	19.9%	18.3%	1.6%
% Owner occupied in municipality	7.0%	5.0%	2.0%
Median home price in census tract	24.3%	26.7%	−2.4%
Median home price in municipality	10.4%	9.4%	1.0%
Per capita income in census tract	18.1%	20.5%	−2.4%
Per capita income in municipality	6.1%	6.6%	−0.5%
% Nonpoor in census tract	7.0%	6.0%	1.0%
% Nonpoor in municipality	2.6%	2.3%	0.3%
% Nonpoor in school district	8.5%	6.9%	1.6%
Inspected homes			
% Owner occupied in census tract	14.7%	14.7%	0.0%
% Owner occupied in municipality	5.2%	3.7%	1.5%
Median home price in census tract	19.4%	21.5%	−2.1%
Median home price in municipality	6.7%	7.5%	−0.8%
Per capita income in census tract	15.6%	14.9%	0.7%
Per capita income in municipality	4.6%	5.5%	−0.9%
% Nonpoor in census tract	5.1%	4.1%	1.0%
% Nonpoor in municipality	1.9%	1.4%	0.5%
% Nonpoor in school district	5.9%	4.5%	1.4%

| | Differential treatment in 2000 | | |
	White higher	Hispanic higher	Net measure
Editorial comments			
% Nonpoor in census tract	30.7%	29.9%	0.8%
% Nonpoor in municipality	26.9%	25.2%	1.7%
% Nonpoor in school district	26.8%	24.4%	2.4%

Table 33.8 National incidence of class steering: Hispanic/White tests

* *p*<.10   ** *p*<.05   ***p<.01 (two-tailed tests)

Steering in Hispanic/White tests of the same agent

Our analyses of Hispanic/White tests involving the same agent reinforced most conclusions above, although there were some differences. As in the case of Black/White tests, confining the Hispanic/White analysis to tests when the same agent saw both teammates generally preserved and sometimes increased the net measures of all types of steering promulgated by recommendations or inspections, but reduced the net measures of steering associated with editorializing. Again, our results appear robust.

Steering by words: A portrait of neighborhood editorializing

Agents gratuitously offering neighborhood commentary on a selective basis to White and minority homebuyers appears to be the most frequently employed mechanism of steering. In this section, we explore in more depth the sorts of comments that agents offered in their attempts to influence residential choices.

We coded agent comments transcribed by testers into several close-ended categories depending on the topic and whether the commentary was positive or negative [...].

The dominant topic mentioned by agents was the racial/ethnic composition of neighborhoods; fully 70% of all comments offered information about racial mix. Almost two thirds of these comments (45% of all comments) were neutral in nature, merely mentioning the *fact* without apparent approbation or denigration.

Over 90% of these neutral comments indicated to the homebuyer in question that the neighborhood had some degree of racial/ethnic diversity; less than 10% noted that the area was exclusively White occupied. In fairness, it must be noted that many of the comments we labeled *neutral* carried an implicit message that Whites who might consider living amid minority neighbors were unusual, as revealed in the following agent quotes:

> "There are a lot of Blacks there, but that's up to you." (Birmingham, AL)

> "If it's a mixed neighborhood, that's all right. But you want to make sure it's mixed; you don't want to be the only White person there." (Los Angeles, CA)

Other *neutral* comments about mixed areas provided revealing subtexts, such as the case of the Chicago, IL, agent who said, "That neighborhood is very diverse; all races are accepted there, except n____s – I mean, Blacks."

The remaining comments related to neighborhood composition all indicated that there was some degree of racial/ethnic diversity, and were almost evenly split between ones that lauded this attribute (12% of all comments) and ones that deplored it (13% of all comments). Some of the *positive* comments might be viewed as faint praise, indeed, inasmuch as the speakers tended to qualify their statements. For example, a Macon, GA, agent said, "Black people do live around here, but it has not gotten bad yet." On the other hand, the negative comments lacked any subtlety in their message:

"I would not recommend [area A], it's totally Black, And I don't like [area B], it's pretty mixed." (Los Angeles, CA)

"It is not the neighborhood in which to buy a home; too many Hispanics living there." (New York, NY)

"That area is full of Hispanics and Blacks that don't know how to keep clean." (Los Angeles, CA)

"[Area] is very mixed. You probably wouldn't like it because of the income you and your husband make. But I don't want to sound prejudiced." (San Diego, CA)

The remaining comments that did not relate explicitly to racial/ethnic composition tended to provide overarching evaluations applied to entire neighborhoods (e.g., "good place to live," "you wouldn't like it," "safe"). Such editorializing typically was negative in tone (19% of all comments), serving to discourage prospective homebuyers from considering an area. Given the findings of Pearce (1980) and Galster (1990b), we were surprised that so few comments were offered about local schools (5% of all comments), though what was offered tended to be critical. In only one comment was school quality and race explicitly linked. A Detroit, MI, agent said, "[Area] schools are not so good, and you would know by looking if we were in [area] now."

Has steering lessened since 1989?

Estimating changes over time in the incidence of steering across U.S. metropolitan areas must be done carefully to ensure comparability in samples, methods, and operational definitions of steering. Thus, though tempting, it would be inappropriate to take at face value the estimates reported (Newburger, 1981, 1989; Turner, Edwards, et al., 1991) by the earlier nationwide studies of steering – HMPS (1977) and HDS (1989) – and contrast them to those reported above for the current study. Across all three studies there were important differences in the samples of metropolitan areas analyzed, methods for sampling addresses for paired testing, and techniques for identifying and measuring acts of steering.

It is possible, however, to construct a few valid intertemporal comparisons for the 1989–2000 period. We examined the 20 metropolitan areas where paired tests were conducted in both the 1989 and the 2000 HDS investigations employing the same methodology, and reconstructed steering indicators that could be generated identically from data available in both years. In this fashion we were able to construct for both Black/White and Hispanic/White tests one comparable net measure tor the incidence of segregation steering and two for class (per capita income and median house value) steering at the census tract level, promulgated via inspections.

We could identify no statistically significant changes in these six measures to support the hypothesis that steering involving Black/White or Hispanic/White homebuyers had decreased from 1989 to 2000. On the contrary, we a found statistically significant *increase* in the net measure of segregation steering in Black/White tests. This stands in marked contrast to the diminution in many other forms of discrimination in sales and rental markets observed during this period (Turner *et al.*, 2002).

CONCLUSIONS AND POLICY IMPLICATIONS

We have conducted a comprehensive analysis of steering by real estate sales agents, based on extensive Black/White and Hispanic/White paired testing conducted in a nationally representative sample of metropolitan areas in 2000. Our work extends the portrait of this form of discrimination beyond the conventional dimension of differential home inspections or recommendations across neighborhoods according to their racial composition. We examined three types of steering (information, segregation, and class) potentially perpetrated by three mechanisms (inspecting, recommending, and editorializing) at three spatial levels (census tract, municipality, and school district). We find that steering of various types continues, perpetrated by words and deeds, unabated over the last decade. Core findings are summarized in Table 33.9.

The lower-bound, net measures of incidence indicate that steering of all three types is occurring, especially consistently at the tract level, when Black and White homebuyers are

Steering type	Black/White tests			Hispanic/White tests		
	Recommend	Inspect	Comment	Recommend	Inspect	Comment
Information	0.6%	2.2%	15.0%***	1.9%	1.5%	2.8%
Segregation	3.8%*	3.8%*	13.7%***	1.4%	5.0%**	6.2%*
Class	1.8%	1.9%	11.5%***	1.0%	1.0%	0.8%

Table 33.9 Summary of core findings: Net measures of incidence of discrimination

1. $* p<.10$ $** p<.05$ $*** p<.01$ (two-tailed tests)
2. Results shown are net measures of steering incidence at census tract scale of geography.
3. Class steering is measured here by percent of non-poor population in tract.

involved. Editorializing appears by far the most prevalent sort of Black/White steering mechanism; it is observed across all types of steering and at all spatial levels. The net measures suggest that in at least 12 to 15% of the cases, agents systematically provide gratuitous geographic commentary that provides more information to White homebuyers and encourages them to choose areas with more White and fewer poor households.

The multidimensional occurrences of steering observed in the Black/White tests are not observed in Hispanic/White tests. The only statistically significant net measures of discrimination (5–6%) occur in the case of segregation steering at the census tract level, perpetrated either by home inspections or editorializing.

Perhaps the most sobering finding is that steering does not appear to have decreased since tougher fair housing laws were introduced in 1988. On the contrary, the incidence of Black/White segregation steering appears to have increased during this period. Indeed, the totality of findings reported here from the 2000 HDS bear an uncanny similarity to those produced by paired testing conducted by fair housing groups during the 1980s (Galster, 1990a, b). The unambiguous consequence of these practices is encouraging the segregation of homebuyers on the basis of race/ethnicity and economic class, as has been recently documented by Immergluck (1998). While involuntary segregation in turn may pose many obstacles to minorities (Galster, 1987b; Galster and Keeney, 1988; Massey and Denton, 1993). one is especially pernicious and is therefore discussed below.

Perpetuating interracial wealth differentials through a vicious circle of steering

Persistent and massive disparities in the wealth accumulated by White, Black, and Hispanic households have been well documented (e.g., Oliver and Shapiro, 1995). A sizeable fraction of this differential can be explained, in turn, by interracial differences in homeownership rates (see the recent review by Charles and Hurst, 2002). Still more may be explained by observed differences in the rates at which homes owned by different groups appreciate (Kim, 2003). These latter differences interrelate with steering in a mutually reinforcing fashion.

As this article has demonstrated, through words and deeds some real estate agents continue to steer minority homebuyers (especially Blacks) into neighborhoods where minorities are overrepresented and White homebuyers into neighborhoods that are overwhelmingly White occupied. Given that White homebuyers typically dominate most

U.S. metropolitan housing markets, both numerically and in terms of purchasing power, such steering helps to skew the pattern of demands such that different rates of home appreciation are evinced in minority and White neighborhoods (Kim, 2003). Directly, this perpetuates interracial wealth differentials among homeowners by affecting accumulation of home equity. Indirectly, lower appreciation in minority neighborhoods perpetuates interracial wealth differentials by discouraging in two ways minorities from purchasing homes in the first place. First, minorities will have less access to transfers of wealth accumulated by relatives that might serve as a down payment on a home purchase. Second, lower prospects for appreciation raise the effective cost of home owning (Charles and Hurst, 2002). As the wealth of individual minorities and appreciation of their neighborhoods lags further. White real estate agents may have their stereotypes reinforced in turn. Their motives to steer therefore may be intensified, as they perceive minorities to be less desirable prospective entrants into White neighborhoods and minority neighborhoods to offer less desirable investment prospects for their White customers. Thus, steering forms a key link in what might be termed a *vicious circle* of mutual reinforcing relationships that abets interracial differentials in homeownership and wealth accumulation.

Fair housing policy: Enhanced education or enforcement?

Our findings suggest that geographic steering warrants considerably more attention as the object of fair housing activities. Unfortunately, most fair housing enforcement initiatives in the past have focused on the rental housing sector, probably because such testing demands considerably less effort, expense, and expertise on the part of testers, their project coordinators, and the sponsoring agency. Although there have been considerable efforts to train real estate agents about the requirements of fair housing laws and to educate the public about their rights, it is clear that such efforts have not eradicated steering. Indeed, we would argue that even prospectively enhanced education and outreach initiatives are likely to show only modest payoffs.

In the case of real estate agents, knowledge of fair housing law and practice may simply be unpersuasive in comparison to the compelling economic motives for steering. At least three, non-mutually exclusive steering motives have been theoretically identified and have received some empirical support (Galster, 1987a, 1990b; Ondrich, Ross, *et al.*, 2001a, b; Ondrich, Strieker, *et al.*, 1998; Yinger, 1995). First, agents may hold racial/ethnic stereotypes about their customers' ability to pay and/or their preferences for neighborhood racial composition. They therefore steer to avoid *wasting time* by showing houses that their customers would be unwilling or unable to buy, thereby potentially losing sales commissions or at least needlessly prolonging the transaction. Second, agents who have

established reputations in exclusively White neighborhoods and/or those in danger of racial *tipping* may steer out of fear that White homeowners will cease listing their homes with agents who show minorities homes there. Finally, agents who have not established reputations in particular neighborhoods may steer in ways to promote the racial/ethnic or class transition of these areas, fomenting fear-based home sales and maximizing their commissions thereby. Steering's economic motivations could potentially be countered by a credible threat of legal sanctions, but, as explained below, the current enforcement system provides little deterrence.

Analysis of agent comments made during HDS 2000 strongly supports our claim that fair housing training for agents will be insufficient to change their behavior in light of the aforementioned economic motives. In 4% of the comments made, the agent revealed knowledge of fair housing requirements but blatantly violated them nevertheless. Consider the following illustrations:

> "[Area] has a questionable ethnic mix that you might not like. I could probably lose my license for saying this!" (Chicago, IL)

> "[Area] is different from here; it's multicultural … I'm not allowed to steer you, but there are some areas that you wouldn't want to live in." (Detroit, MI)

> "There are a lot of Latinos living there … I'm not supposed to be telling you that, but you have a daughter and I like you." (Los Angeles, CA)

> "I''s against the law for me to be saying so, but I could steer you toward some neighborhoods and away from some others." (New Orleans, LA)

> "I would not send you to this area. I'm not supposed to say this but I'm probably old enough to be your father. [When tester asked why, agent said tentatively] Because it's primarily an ethnic neighborhood and I wouldn't send you there." (San Antonio, TX)

Then there were agents who tried mightily to obey the letter of the law while steering nevertheless:

"You notice the people in yards and walking along the street? [When tester asked what she meant, agent responded] You see mostly Caucasians, not any African-Americans." (Los Angeles, CA)

"You would not like homes around [area] because it is 'densely populated.' How do I put this nicely? [After thinking for a moment, the agent sighed and said] There are some things in real estate that I just can't say." (Philadelphia, PA)

Whether enhanced fair housing education and outreach efforts to homebuyers could prove sufficient to stop steering similarly seems doubtful to us. Typically, agents' most egregious failures to show a prospective homebuyer areas where their race/ethnicity is underrepresented and to offer negative commentary about minority-occupied areas occur when dealing with White clients. We would argue that White homebuyers are less likely to file a civil rights suit, even when they suspect that they have been steered illegally. On the other hand, because minority homebuyers typically are shown *some* homes in predominantly White areas and offered *some* commentary, they are unlikely to suspect that they are being steered. Merely making the public more aware that steering may occur, it is illegal, and individuals may seek redress and compensatory damages is not, therefore, likely to generate many additional victim-initiated suits, in our opinion.

Tougher fair housing laws only provide a heightened deterrent when they are accompanied by a credible chance that illegal acts will be challenged successfully in court (Galster, 1990c). Unfortunately, in the case of steering as practiced in contemporary American housing markets, this necessary condition appears far from being fulfilled. The current approach of victim-initiated complaints is flawed because, as we have seen, few victims of steering are likely to suspect it *and* file suit were they to become suspicious.

What is needed is a new enforcement strategy that builds the capacity of local, state, and federal civil rights agencies to conduct widespread, ongoing paired testing investigations of real estate sales offices, structured in many ways analogously to HDS. Both tests of agencies suspected of steering and tests of randomly selected agencies should be conducted. Agencies that consistently evince equal treatment of testers could receive commendations or other forms of valuable public relations benefits. On the other hand, evidence suggesting steering or other illegal practices would form the basis of suits initiated by the enforcement agency, yielding the prospect of substantial legal costs as well as punitive damages. In this fashion, the relative benefits and costs to steering as perceived by agents will be tilted decidedly toward the latter, thereby creating a credible deterrent. In the absence of such a new strategy, we fear that real estate agents will continue to have compelling economic reasons to engage in steering, by words and deeds.

REFERENCES

Bish, M., Bullock, J., and Milgram, J. (1973). *Racial steering: The dual housing market and multiracial neighborhoods.* Washington, D.C.: National Neighbors, Inc.

Charles, C. (2003). The dynamics of racial residential segregation. *Annual Review of Sociology, 29,* 167–207.

Charles, K., and Hurst, E. (2002). The transition to home ownership and the Black-White wealth gap. *Review of Economics and Statistics, 84,* 281–297.

Clark, W. (1986). Residential segregation in American cities: A review and interpretation. *Population Research and Policy Review, 5,* 95–127.

Dawkins, C. (2004). Recent evidence on the continuing causes of Black-White residential segregation. *Journal of Urban Affairs, 26,* 379–400.

Farley, R., and Frey, W. (1994). Changes in the segregation of Whites from Blacks during the 1980s: Small steps toward a more integrated society. *American Sociological Review, 59,* 23–45.

Feins, J., and Bratt, R. (1983). Barred in Boston: Racial discrimination in housing. *Journal of American Planning Association, 49,* 344–355.

Fix, M., and Struyk, R. (Eds.). (1993). *Clear and convincing evidence: Measurement of discrimination in America.* Washington, D.C.: Urban Institute Press.

Freeman, L. (2000). Minority housing segregation: A test of three perspectives. *Journal of Urban Affairs, 22,* 15–35.

Galster, G. (1986). More than skin deep: The effect of discrimination on the extent and pattern of racial residential segregation. In J. Goering (Ed.), *Housing desegregation and federal policy* (pp. 119–138). Chapel Hill: University of North Carolina Press.

Galster, G. (1987a). The ecology of racial discrimination in housing: An exploratory model. *Urban Affairs Quarterly, 23,* 84–107.

Galster, G. (1987b). Residential segregation and interracial economic disparities. *Journal of Urban Economics, 21,* 22–44.

Galster, G. (1990a). Racial steering in urban housing markets: A review of the audit evidence. *The Review of Black Political Economy, 18,* 105–129.

Galster, G. (1990b). Racial steering by real estate agents: Mechanisms and motives. *The Review of Black Political Economy, 19,* 39–63.

Galster, G. (1990c). Federal fair housing policy: The great misapprehension. In D. DiPasquale and L. C. Keyes (Eds.), *Building foundations: Housing and federal policy* (pp. 137–156). Philadelphia: University of Pennsylvania Press.

Galster, G., Freiberg, F., and Houk, D. (1987). Racial differences in real estate advertising practices: An exploratory case study. *Journal of Urban Affairs, 9,* 199–215.

Galster, G., and Keeney, M. (1988). Race, residence, discrimination, and economic opportunity. *Urban Affairs Quarterly, 24,* 87–117.

Greater Dallas Housing Opportunity Center. (1974). *A study of discrimination and steering practices by real estate agents.* Dallas, TX: Author.

Hall, D., Peterman, W., and Dwyer, J. (1983). *Measuring discrimination and steering in Chicago's southern suburbs* (Technical Report no. 1–83). Chicago: Nathalie P. Voorhees Center for Neighborhood and Community Improvement at the University of Illinois–Chicago.

Helper, R. (1969). *Racial policies and practices of real estate brokers.* Minneapolis: University of Minnesota Press.

Iceland, J., Weinberg, D., and Steinmetz, E. (2002). *Racial and ethnic segregation in the United States: 1980–2000.* Washington, D.C.: U.S. Government Printing Office, Bureau of the Census Series CENSR-3.

Immergluck, D. (1998). Progress confined: Increases in Black home buying and the persistence of residential segregation. *Journal of Urban Affairs, 20,* 443–457.

James, F., McCummings, B., and Tynan, E. (1984). *Minorities in the sunbelt.* New Brunswick, NJ: Rutgers University Press.

Kenney, G., and Wissoker, D. (1994). An analysis of the correlates of discrimination facing young Hispanic job-seekers. *American Economic Review, 84,* 674–683.

Kim, S. (2003). Long-term appreciation of owner-occupied single-family house prices in Milwaukee neighborhoods. *Urban Geography, 24,* 212–231.

Massey, D., and Denton, N. (1993). *American apartheid: Segregation and the making of the underclass.* Cambridge, MA: Harvard University Press.

McEntire, D. (1960). *Residence and race.* Berkeley: University of California Press.

National Research Council, Committee on National Statistics. (2002). *Measuring housing discrimination in a national study.* Washington, D.C.: National Academy Press.

Newburger, H. (1981, December). *The nature and extent of racial steering practices in U.S. housing markets* (Working Paper). Washington, D.C.: U.S. Department of Housing and Urban Development.

Newburger, H. (1989). Discrimination by a profit-maximizing real estate broker in response to White prejudice. *Journal of Urban Economics, 26,* 1–19.

Oliver, M., and Shapiro, T. (1995). *Black wealth/White wealth.* New York: Routledge.

Ondrich, J., Ross, S. L., and Yinger, J. (2001a, June). *Now you see it, now you don't: Why do real estate agents withhold houses from Black customers?* (Working Paper No. 24). Syracuse, NY: Syracuse University, Center for Policy Research.

Ondrich, J., Ross, S. L., and Yinger, J. (2001b). Geography of housing discrimination. *Journal of Housing Research, 12,* 217–238.

Ondrich, J., Stricker, A., and Yinger, J. (1998). Do real estate brokers choose to discriminate? Evidence from the 1989 Housing Discrimination Study. *Southern Economic Journal, 64,* 880–901.

Orlebeke, C. (1997). [Review of the book *Closed doors, opportunities lost: The continuing costs of housing discrimination*]. *Journal of Policy Analysis and Management, 16,* 180–185.

Palmer, S. (1955). *The role of real estate agents in the structuring of residential areas: A study of social control.* Unpublished doctoral dissertation, Yale University, New haven, CT.

Pearce, D. (1979). Gatekeepers and home-seekers: Institutional patterns in racial steering. *Social Problems, 26,* 325–342.

Pearce, D. (1980). *Breaking down barriers: New evidence on the impact of metropolitan school desegregation on housing patterns* (Final Report to the National Institute of Education). Washington, D.C.: Center for National Policy Review, School of Law, Catholic University.

Roychoudhury, C., and Goodman, A. (1992). An ordered probit model for estimating racial discrimination through fair housing audits. *Journal of Housing Economics, 2,* 358–373.

Roychoudhury, C., and Goodman, A. (1996). Evidence of racial discrimination in different dimensions of housing search. *Real Estate Economics, 24,* 161–178.

Schwemm, R. (1992). *Housing discrimination law and litigation.* Deerfield, IL: Clark, Boardman, Callaghan.

Taeuber, K., Monfort, F., and Massey, P. (1985). *The trend for metropolitan racial residential segregation.* Madison: Center for Demography and Ecology, University of Wisconsin.

Thernstrom, S., and Thernstrom, A. (1997). *America in black and white: One nation, indivisible.* New York: Simon and Schuster.

Turner, M., Edwards, J., and Mikelsons, M. (1991). *Housing Discrimination Study: Analyzing racial and ethnic steering.* Washington, D.C.: U.S. Department of Housing and Urban Development.

Turner, M., and Mikelsons, M. (1992). Patterns of racial steering in four metropolitan areas. *Journal of Housing Economics, 2,* 199–234.

Turner, M., Ross, S., Galster, G., Yinger, J., Godfrey, E., Bednarz, B., Herbig, C., and Lee, S. (2002). *Discrimination in metropolitan housing markets: National results from Phase I HDS 2000.* Washington, D.C.: Urban Institute.

Turner, M., Struyk, R., and Yinger, J. (1991). *Housing Discrimination Study: Synthesis.* Washington, D.C.: U.S. Department of Housing and Urban Development.

Turner, M., and Wienk, R. (1993). The persistence of segregation in urban areas: Contributing causes. In G. Kingsley and M. Turner (Eds.), *Housing markets and residential mobility* (pp. 193–216). Washington, D.C.: Urban Institute Press.

U.S. Census Bureau. (2000). *Housing patterns – metropolitan areas* [Data File]. Retrieved October 26, 2004, from http://www.census.gov/hhes/www/resseg.html

U.S. Commission on Civil Rights. (1994). *The Fair Housing Amendments Act of 1988: The enforcement report.* Washington, D.C.: Author.

U.S. Department of Housing and Urban Development. (1989, January23). *Implementation of the Fair Housing Amendments Act of 1988.* Available at: http://www.efn.org/~fairhous/eng/legalres/federal/fhactreg.html

Wienk, R., Reid, C., Simonson, J., and Eggers, F. (1979). *Measuring racial discrimination in American housing markets: The Housing Market Practices Survey.* Washington, D.C.: U.S. Department of Housing and Urban Development, Policy Development and Research.

Yinger, J. (1995). *Closed doors, opportunities lost: The continuing cost of housing discrimination.* New York: Russell Sage Foundation.

Yinger, J. (1998). Housing discrimination is still worth worrying about. *Housing Policy Debate, 9,* 893–927.

34
"The dynamics of racial residential segregation"

From *Annual Review of Sociology* (2003)

Camille Zubrinsky Charles

INTRODUCTION

Sociologists and policymakers have long viewed racial residential segregation as a key aspect of racial inequality, implicated in both intergroup relations and in larger processes of individual and group social mobility. At the dawn of the twentieth century, Du Bois (1903) recognized the importance of neighborhoods – the "physical proximity of home and dwelling-places, the way in which neighborhoods group themselves, and [their] contiguity" – as primary locations for social interaction, lamenting that the "color line" separating black and white neighborhoods caused each to see the worst in the other (1990, pp. 120–21). Indeed, students of racial inequality, from Myrdal (1944) to Taeuber and Taeuber (1965), believed that segregation was a major barrier to equality, asserting that segregation "inhibits the development of informal, neighborly relations," "ensures the segregation of a variety of public and private facilities" (Taeuber and Taeuber 1965, p. 1), and permits prejudice "to be freely vented on Negroes without hurting whites" (Myrdal 1944, p. 618). Moreover, residential segregation "undermines the social and economic well-being" irrespective of personal characteristics (Massey and Denton 1993, pp. 2–3). Whether voluntary or involuntary, living in racially segregated neighborhoods has serious implications for the present and future mobility opportunities of those who are excluded from desirable areas. Where we live affects our proximity to good job opportunities, educational quality, and safety from crime (both as victim and as perpetrator), as well as the quality of our social networks (Jargowsky 1996; Wilson 1987).

By the late 1960s, unrest in urban ghettos across the country brought residential segregation – and its implication in racial inequality – to the public's attention, leading to the now famous conclusion of the Kerner Commission that America was "moving toward two societies, one black, one white – separate and unequal" (U.S. National Advisory Commission on Civil Disorders 1988) and the passage of the Fair Housing Act in 1968. In addition to ending legal housing market discrimination, passage of the Fair Housing Act marked the end of public discussion of residential segregation, as many believed that antidiscrimination legislation was the beginning of the end of residential segregation. With legal barriers to educational, occupational, and residential opportunities removed, blacks could finally achieve full-fledged integration, and social scientists, politicians, and the general public ignored this dimension of the color line for the next two decades (Massey and Denton 1993; Meyer 2000). By the late 1970s, conditions in the nation's urban areas – where the majority of blacks were still concentrated – had declined precipitously. Social scientists scrambled to explain the emergence of a disproportionately black urban underclass, paying little or no attention to persisting residential segregation by race.

In *The Truly Disadvantaged* (1987), Wilson outlined the most widely accepted theory of urban poverty: Geographically concentrated poverty and the subsequent development of a ghetto underclass resulted from structural changes in the economy combined with the exodus of middle- and working-class black families from many inner-city ghetto neighborhoods. The shift from a goods- to a service-producing economy saw huge declines in the availability of low-skilled manufacturing jobs that paid enough to support a family; owing to past discrimination, blacks were disproportionately concentrated in these jobs and therefore suffered massive unemployment. Having benefited more substantially from civil rights gains that included affirmative action policies as well as antidiscrimination legislation, Wilson argued, middle- and working-class blacks were able to take advantage of residential opportunities outside of the ghetto. The impact of these events was an "exponential increase" in the now well-known social dislocations associated with sudden and/or long-term increases in joblessness – under- and unemployment, welfare dependence, out-of-wedlock births, and a blatant disregard for the law. The emigration of nonpoor blacks, Wilson argued, removed an important "social buffer," leaving poor blacks in socially isolated communities that lacked material resources, access to jobs and job networks, exposure to conventional role models, and therefore "generate[d] behavior not conducive to good work histories" (Wilson 1987, pp. 56–60).

Massey and Denton (1993) show, however, that without residential segregation, these

> structural changes would not have produced the disastrous social and economic outcomes observed in inner cities … Although rates of black poverty were driven up by the economic dislocations Wilson identifies, it was segregation that confined the increased deprivation to a small number of densely settled, tightly packed, and geographically isolated areas.

Retooling existing theories of urban poverty, they argue, resolves unanswered questions regarding the disproportionate representation of blacks and Puerto Ricans in the ranks of the underclass, as well as the concentration of underclass communities in older, larger cities of the Northeast and Midwest. In the largest urban areas, blacks and Puerto Ricans were the only groups to experience extreme residential segregation and steep rises in poverty at the same time, the latter stemming from the fact that areas of black concentration were also hit especially hard by the economic reversals of the 1970s (Massey and Denton 1993, pp. 146–47). Emphasizing the interaction of segregation and rising poverty also furthers our understanding of the inability of nonpoor blacks to escape segregation and its consequences, despite increasing class segregation within black communities (Jargowsky 1996; Massey and Denton 1993, pp. 146–47). Focusing on a black middle-class exodus, they argue, detracts attention from the devastating consequences of residential segregation for all blacks, irrespective of socioeconomic status.

The publication of *American Apartheid* (Massey and Denton 1993) was singularly influential in shifting public discourse "back to issues of race and racial segregation" as "fundamental to … the status of black Americans and the origins of the urban underclass." The book argued persuasively that "the missing link" in each of the underclass theories prevalent at the time was "their systematic failure to consider the important role that segregation has played in mediating, exacerbating, and ultimately amplifying the harmful social and economic processes they treat" (Massey and Denton 1993, p. 7). As a result, social scientists have rediscovered racial residential segregation as a constituent factor in persistent racial inequality in the United States. Recent research addresses several key issues, including the following: (a) trends in the residential segregation of racial/ethnic groups, (b) factors that influence the spatial distribution of groups, and (c) the social and economic consequences of segregation.

This review addresses each of these issues. I begin with a summary of trends in the residential segregation of blacks, Hispanics, and Asians from whites since 1980. Despite declines in black-white segregation, blacks remain severely segregated in the majority of U.S. cities. As a result of massive immigration, Hispanic and Asian segregation from whites is on the rise; but except for a small number of cases among Hispanics, both groups still remain only moderately segregated from whites. Following the discussion of trends in segregation, I review recent literature dedicated to understanding the causes of residential segregation. Two broad theoretical perspectives shape this discussion and are indicative of ongoing sociological – indeed, societal – debates regarding the relative importance of race and class in determining social outcomes. The spatial assimilation model posits that objective differences in socioeconomic status and acculturation across racial/ethnic groups are primarily responsible for residential segregation, squarely addressing the issue of social mobility in its suggestion that increased education, occupational prestige, and income will lead to greater racial residential integration. This explanation adequately describes the residential mobility of both phenotypically white Hispanics and of Asians. Alternatively, the place stratification model emphasizes the persistence of prejudice and discrimination – key aspects of intergroup relations – that act to constrain the residential mobility options of disadvantaged groups, including supra-individual, institutional-level forces. Available evidence suggests that this model better characterizes the inability of those who are phenotypically black (both African Americans and black Hispanics) to escape segregation. At first glance, these perspectives may appear oppositional. Upon closer inspection, however, these seemingly oppositional explanations complement one another. Race still matters; however, its relative importance – and that of socioeconomic status – depends on group membership. Finally, I end with a discussion of the consequences of residential segregation, followed by a discussion of the current state of knowledge regarding the dynamics of racial residential segregation, including suggestions and/or efforts to alleviate segregation and its consequences.

TRENDS IN RESIDENTIAL SEGREGATION, 1980–2000

Blacks in 16 metropolitan areas were hyper-segregated from whites in 1980, exhibiting extreme isolation on at least four of five standard measures of residential distribution (Massey and Denton 1989). By 1990, that number had nearly doubled: In 29 U.S. metropolitan areas – containing 40% of the total black population – blacks experienced "extreme, multidimensional, and cumulative residential segregation" (Denton 1994, p. 49). Blacks are unique in this experience, which contrasts sharply with the limited and temporary segregation experienced by other groups (Denton 1994; Massey and Denton 1993). Hispanics and Asians are only moderately

segregated from whites, although their levels of segregation and isolation are increasing as a result of continuous, high-volume immigration since 1970. Preliminary data from the 2000 Census (Logan 2001a) documents nationwide increases in the relative size of the Hispanic and Asian populations since 1980 and declines in the relative size of the white population; the relative size of the black population changed little (an average of 1.5%). With no end to immigration in sight, non-Hispanic whites are projected to become a numerical minority in the United States some time during this century (Edmonston and Passel 1992; Massey 1995), and the trend is well underway: 8 of the 50 largest metro areas are already majority-minority (whites are less than half the total population) and two others will be majority-minority by the 2010 Census.

These compositional shifts influence residential segregation in meaningful ways. Isolation is generally low for small groups but is expected to rise with increasing group size even if the group's level of segregation remains constant. Moreover, the larger the relative size of an out-group's population, the greater exposure to that group is likely to be. Both exposure and isolation are influenced by group settlement patterns. Specifically, chain migration patterns common among both Hispanic and Asian immigrants concentrate rapidly growing groups in a small number of metropolitan areas – and within a small number of neighborhoods within an area – increasing their isolation and decreasing exposure to out-groups (Logan 2001a; Massey and Denton 1987).

Table 34.1 reports black, Hispanic, and Asian segregation from whites (dissimilarity), isolation, and exposure to whites for the 50 largest metropolitan regions in 2000 (and parenthetically, the change between 1980 and 2000). Both Hispanics and Asians show increasing segregation and isolation, along with declining exposure to whites. These patterns are consistent with their rapid population growth, settlement patterns, and declining white population share. Over the same period, blacks show declines in both segregation and isolation; trends in exposure to whites are mixed, but overall reflect a slight increase. These patterns are consistent with the shifts in population composition outlined above and their anticipated effects on spatial distribution. These changes also contributed to declining black isolation: In many instances, Hispanic settlement patterns concentrate them in areas of traditional black settlement, increasing black-Hispanic contact (Alba *et al.* 1995).

Nearly half of the metro regions experienced declines in black-white segregation of at least 10 percentage points over the 20-year period. Still, the degree of black-white segregation remains extreme (over 60) in 28 regions. More than half of these are Eastern and Midwestern regions, where black-white segregation has been most resistant to change (Farley and Frey 1994; Massey and Denton 1993), and many of the most segregated regions saw little or no change in black-white segregation over the two decades. At the same time, segregation declined enough in some mid-sized regions with sizable black populations to be characterized as moderate (under 50). Areas with the largest declines (15% or more) tend to be multiethnic (an above-average presence of at least one other nonwhite group) and/or have relatively small black populations (between 5% and 10%); these metro areas are located in the newer cities of the West and Southwest (Farley and Frey 1994; Frey and Farley 1993; Logan 2001a). Finally, approximately half of the areas show double-digit declines in isolation, although in many cases, exposure to whites either declined or remained constant. Thus, for the 50 regions, black isolation declined by an average of 12%, but exposure to whites increased by only 1%, on average. As indicated previously, the majority of the decline in black isolation is due mainly to their increasing exposure to Hispanics (Alba *et al.* 1995; Frey and Farley 1993; Logan 2001a).

Trends in Hispanic and Asian segregation are the opposite of those observed for blacks. In most areas, Hispanic-white segregation remains moderate, isolation low, and exposure to whites meaningful, despite explosive population growth. Overall, increases in segregation range from small to moderate. Hispanic-white dissimilarity never exceeds 68 (and only five areas exceed 60, compared to 28 for blacks) and averages a low of 43 in the South and a high of 57 in the East. Isolation increased more substantially, yet the average Hispanic resides in a neighborhood that is between 16% and 42% same-race (compared to the average black person, whose neighborhood is between 18% and 59% same-race). Exposure to whites declined more substantially. Finally, Asians remain the least-segregated nonwhite group. Increases in dissimilarity and isolation

(except for the West, where Asians are most concentrated) are generally less than 10% (the average increase for the 50 regions was 3%), and declines in exposure to whites are comparable to those experienced by Hispanics, once again reflecting the rapid population growth of these largely immigrant groups, concentrated settlement patterns, and declining white population share. In contrast to the residential patterns of blacks, Hispanics, and Asians, whites' exposure to minorities increased steadily over the past two decades: In 2000, the minority percentage in the average white person's census tract was a nontrivial 20%, and research by Alba and colleagues (1995) documents sharp declines in the number of all-white neighborhoods since 1970. In short, although segregation persists or increases for minority group members, the average white person experiences modest integration.

Finally, a brief mention of trends in suburban segregation is warranted. In 2000, nearly 60% of Asians, 50% of Hispanics, and 40% of blacks lived in the suburbs, compared to 71% of whites. These percentages represent substantial increases in minority representation; however, they have not been accompanied by meaningful declines in suburban residential segregation. Patterns of suburban segregation mirror those of the larger metropolitan area of which they are a part, indicating that new minority residents are moving to suburbs where coethnics were already present in 1990. Where groups are smallest in number, they are least segregated and least likely to establish suburban enclaves; however, in the regions where the majority of blacks, Hispanics, and Asians live and are, therefore, a larger share of the suburban population, "segregation is higher, more unyielding over time, and minority population growth is more likely to be associated with the creation or intensification of ethnic enclaves" (Logan 2001b). Increasing minority suburbanization within the context of persisting segregation helps to explain the rising economic segregation among both blacks and Hispanics documented by Jargowsky (1996). Minority suburbs – although better off than poor minority neighborhoods – tend to be less affluent, have poorer quality public services and schools, and experience more crime and social disorganization compared to the suburbs that comparable whites reside in (Alba *et al.* 1994; Logan *et al.* 2002; Pattillo-McCoy 1999).

Metro area	Blacks Dissimilarity (80-00Δ)	Blacks Isolation (80-00Δ)	Blacks Exposure (80-00Δ)	Hispanics Dissimilarity (80-00Δ)	Hispanics Isolation (80-00Δ)	Hispanics Exposure (80-00Δ)	Asians Dissimilarity (80-00Δ)	Asians Isolation (80-00Δ)	Asians Exposure (80-00Δ)
Western areas									
Los Angeles/Long beach	63 (−14)	34 (−26)	16 (0)	63 (+6)	63 (+13)	17 (−17)	48 (+1)	29 (+14)	31 (−17)
Riverside/San Bernardino	46 (−9)	15 (−5)	38 (−17)	43 (+4)	50 (+17)	36 (−23)	38 (+7)	11 (+8)	46 (−27)
Orange County	37 (−9)	3 (−2)	48 (−17)	56 (+13)	54 (+21)	31 (−28)	40 (+12)	26 (+19)	46 (−29)
San Diego	54 (−10)	15 (−12)	38 (−6)	51 (+9)	44 (+16)	38 (−20)	47 (+1)	22 (+11)	45 (−17)
Seattle/Bellevue/Everett	50 (−18)	14 (−15)	59 (+4)	31 (+11)	8 (+6)	70 (−16)	35 (−5)	19 (+7)	65 (−8)
Oakland	63 (−11)	35 (−21)	26 (−2)	47 (+11)	30 (+12)	36 (−25)	42 (+4)	29 (+17)	41 (−22)
Portland/Vancouver	48 (−21)	16 (−16)	67 (+7)	35 (+14)	15 (+12)	74 (−17)	32 (+3)	9 (+6)	78 (−12)
San Francisco	61 (−7)	23 (−18)	31 (−3)	54 (+8)	34 (+12)	36 (−17)	49 (−2)	40 (+10)	38 (−12)
San Jose	41 (−8)	4 (−3)	38 (−18)	52 (+6)	41 (+9)	30 (−23)	42 (+9)	38 (+27)	37 (−28)
Sacramento	56 (−3)	18 (−4)	44 (−13)	40 (+5)	21 (+7)	52 (−17)	49 (+1)	20 (+7)	48 (−19)
Western area average	52 (−11)	18 (−12)	41 (−7)	47 (+9)	36 (+13)	42 (−20)	42 (+3)	24 (+13)	48 (−19)
Southwestern areas									
Houston	68 (−9)	47 (−19)	22 (−1)	56 (+5)	49 (+13)	31 (−19)	49 (+6)	15 (+9)	45 (−26)
Dallas	59 (−19)	42 (−26)	33 (+9)	54 (+5)	45 (+21)	37 (−23)	45 (+6)	11 (+9)	60 (−22)
Phoenix/Mesa	44 (−18)	9 (−14)	51 (+4)	53 (0)	46 (+12)	44 (−13)	28 (+1)	4 (+3)	70 (−13)
Denver	62 (−7)	24 (−19)	47 (+4)	50 (+1)	38 (+9)	50 (−13)	30 (+4)	5 (+3)	70 (−9)
Fort Worth/Arlington	60 (−18)	35 (−28)	40 (+10)	48 (0)	37 (+11)	46 (−17)	42 (+5)	8 (+6)	61 (−25)
San Antonio	50 (−12)	20 (−15)	34 (+1)	51 (−7)	66 (−1)	27 (−2)	32 (+2)	4 (+2)	49 (−13)
Las Vegas	43 (−20)	19 (−31)	48 (+7)	43 (+20)	34 (+23)	49 (−30)	30 (+9)	9 (+6)	62 (−20)
Salt Lake City/Ogden	37 (−20)	3 (−6)	74 (−1)	43 (+8)	22 (+12)	70 (−15)	30 (+5)	6 (+4)	76 (−13)
Austin/San Marcos	52 (−13)	21 (−22)	40 (+5)	47 (0)	40 (+4)	45 (−7)	41 (+6)	9 (+7)	63 (−13)
Southwestern area average	53 (−15)	24 (−20)	43 (+4)	49 (+4)	42 (+12)	44 (−15)	36 (+5)	8 (+5)	62 (−17)

	Blacks			Hispanics			Asians		
	Dissimilarity	Isolation	Exposure	Dissimilarity	Isolation	Exposure	Dissimilarity	Isolation	Exposure
Midwestern areas									
Chicago	81 (–8)	73 (–10)	16 (+5)	62 (–2)	48 (+10)	38 (–13)	44 (–3)	15 (+6)	63 (–12)
Detroit	85 (–3)	79 (0)	17 (–2)	46 (+4)	19 (+12)	62 (–13)	46 (+5)	8 (+6)	76 (–8)
Minneapolis/St. Paul	58 (–10)	23 (–6)	58 (–4)	47 (+10)	10 (+6)	67 (–20)	43 (+13)	12 (+10)	68 (–25)
St. Louis	74 (–9)	65 (–9)	32 (+8)	29 (0)	4 (+2)	77 (–4)	43 (+1)	5 (+3)	80 (–8)
Cleveland/Lorain/Elyria	77 (–8)	71 (–7)	25 (+5)	58 (0)	17 (+4)	65 (–9)	38 (+3)	5 (+3)	80 (–7)
Kansas City	69 (–9)	53 (–14)	38 (+9)	46 (+5)	17 (+7)	64 (–13)	35 (+1)	4 (+2)	77 (–7)
Cincinnati	75 (–4)	58 (–6)	39 (+4)	30 (–1)	2 (+1)	81 (+1)	42 (+2)	4 (+3)	82 (–5)
Indianapolis	71 (–9)	53 (–12)	41 (+7)	44 (+15)	7 (+6)	70 (–14)	39 (0)	3 (+2)	79 (–8)
Columbus	63 (–10)	48 (–9)	47 (+6)	38 (+9)	6 (+5)	71 (–12)	42 (–3)	7 (+5)	78 (–10)
Milwaukee/Waukesha	82 (–2)	67 (–2)	25 (–2)	60 (+4)	33 (+17)	51 (–20)	41 (+10)	5 (+4)	65 (–25)
Midwestern area average	74 (–7)	59 (–8)	34 (+4)	46 (+4)	16 (+7)	65 (–12)	41 (+3)	7 (+4)	75 (–12)
Southern areas									
Washington, DC	63 (–7)	59 (–8)	28 (–1)	48 (+16)	20 (+15)	45 (–25)	39 (+7)	14 (+9)	57 (–18)
Atlanta	66 (–11)	63 (–10)	28 (+2)	53 (+21)	20 (+18)	49 (–27)	45 (+9)	8 (+7)	59 (–27)
Baltimore	68 (–7)	66 (–7)	29 (+4)	36 (+3)	4 (+2)	66 (–7)	39 (+1)	7 (+5)	71 (–10)
Tampa/St. Petersburg/Clearwater	65 (–14)	43 (–16)	42 (+7)	45 (–5)	23 (+4)	61 (–9)	34 (0)	4 (+3)	75 (–12)
Miami	74 (–7)	63 (–5)	11 (–7)	44 (–9)	71 (+13)	18 (–16)	31 (+3)	3 (+2)	29 (–29)
Orlando	57 (–17)	41 (–21)	41 (+5)	41 (+10)	27 (+21)	55 (–30)	36 (+4)	5 (+4)	62 (–26)
Ft. Lauderdale	62 (–22)	53 (–18)	31 (+6)	32 (+4)	23 (+17)	55 (–29)	28 (+1)	4 (+3)	59 (–30)
Norfolk/Virginia Beach/Newport News	46 (–13)	52 (–9)	42 (+5)	32 (+1)	5 (+2)	60 (–11)	34 (–4)	6 (+2)	63 (–14)
Charlotte/Gastonia/Rock Hill	55 (–8)	45 (–10)	44 (+2)	50 (+18)	13 (+12)	55 (–18)	43 (–4)	4 (+3)	65 (–19)
New Orleans	69 (–2)	71 (0)	24 (–2)	36 (+9)	8 (+2)	61 (–10)	48 (–3)	11 (0)	51 (–7)
Greensboro/Winston-Salem/High Point	59 (–8)	49 (–11)	41 (+3)	51 (+19)	11 (+10)	58 (–16)	46 (+3)	4 (+3)	67 (–19)

	Blacks			Hispanics			Asians		
	Dissimilarity	Isolation	Exposure	Dissimilarity	Isolation	Exposure	Dissimilarity	Isolation	Exposure
Nashville	57 (−9)	46 (−10)	48 (+5)	46 (+23)	9 (+8)	68 (−12)	42 (−1)	4 (+3)	75 (−12)
Raleigh/Durham/Chapel Hill	46 (−6)	43 (−11)	46 (+1)	43 (+19)	12 (+11)	55 (−19)	41 (0)	7 (+5)	70 (−14)
Southern area average	61 (−10)	53 (−10)	35 (+2)	43 (+10)	19 (+10)	54 (−18)	39 (+1)	6 (+4)	62 (−18)
Eastern areas									
New York	82 (0)	60 (−3)	11 (−4)	67 (+2)	46 (+6)	21 (−10)	51 (+1)	27 (+11)	40 (−15)
Philadelphia	72 (−6)	62 (−7)	28 (+2)	60 (−3)	27 (+5)	43 (−7)	44 (+3)	10 (+7)	66 (−12)
Boston	66 (−11)	39 (−14)	40 (+4)	59 (+3)	21 (+9)	54 (−13)	45 (−3)	13 (+1)	71 (−7)
Nassau/Suffolk	74 (−3)	41 (−8)	34 (−8)	47 (+10)	23 (+13)	56 (−22)	36 (+5)	8 (+6)	75 (−14)
Pittsburgh	67 (−6)	47 (−7)	50 (+6)	30 (−1)	1 (0)	84 (−3)	49 (+3)	5 (+4)	85 (−7)
Newark	80 (−3)	67 (−3)	17 (−4)	65 (−2)	36 (+9)	36 (−11)	35 (+4)	9 (+7)	69 (−11)
Bergen/Passaic	73 (−7)	36 (−10)	27 (−6)	58 (−3)	39 (+11)	38 (−13)	36 (+2)	16 (+13)	65 (−20)
Providence/Fall River/Warwick	59 (−13)	13 (−10)	56 (−5)	68 (+18)	32 (+24)	48 (−31)	43 (+10)	6 (+5)	69 (−20)
Eastern area average	72 (−6)	46 (−8)	33 (−2)	57 (+3)	28 (+10)	48 (−14)	42 (+3)	12 (+7)	68 (−13)
Overall average	62 (−10)	41 (−12)	37 (+1)	48 (+6)	27 (+10)	51 (−16)	40 (+3)	11 (+6)	62 (−16)

Table 34.1 Black, Hispanic and Asian segregation from white in the 50 largest metropolitan regions, 1980–2000

Source: U.S. Bureau of the Census and The Lewis Mumford Center for Comparative Urban and Regional Research.
Notes: Due to space limitations, indices and changes are rounded to the nearest whole number.

THEORETICAL PERSPECTIVES ON RESIDENTIAL SEGREGATION

A large body of research attempts to explain the persistence of residential segregation – particularly among blacks – despite the passage of antidiscrimination legislation, more favorable racial attitudes among whites, and the dramatic expansion of the black middle class. This section summarizes three competing explanations for persisting racial residential segregation that garner the most research attention – objective differences in socioeconomic status, prejudice, and housing-market discrimination – and reviews major research findings circa 1980. Explanations emphasizing group differences in social class status are consistent with the spatial assimilation model, whereas the place stratification model includes explanations placing primacy on persisting prejudice and/or discrimination. Where appropriate, I consider alternative explanations that do not fit neatly into either theoretical perspective.

Spatial assimilation

Racial group differences in socioeconomic status characteristics are well documented. On average, blacks and Hispanics complete fewer years of school and are concentrated in lower-status occupations, earn less income, and accumulate less wealth compared to whites (Farley 1996a; Oliver and Shapiro 1995). The persistence and severity of these differences lead easily to the conclusion that residential segregation by race is simply the logical outcome of these differences in status and the associated differences in lifestyle (Clark 1986, 1988; Galster 1988; see also Jackman and Jackman 1983 on class identities as involving lifestyle considerations). This assumption is the basis of the spatial assimilation model, which asserts that individuals convert socioeconomic gains into higher-quality housing, often by leaving ethnic neighborhoods for areas with more whites; for immigrants, it also involves acculturation – the accumulation of time in the United States and English language fluency. It should also be noted that spatial assimilation is influenced by the metropolitan-area characteristics discussed in the previous section (i.e., group size, rates of group population

change, and suburbanization) (Alba and Logan 1993; Farley and Frey 1994; Massey and Denton 1985).

Socioeconomic status differences

Tests of this hypothesis dominate segregation research over the past two decades, and findings consistently show that Asians and Hispanics are always substantially less segregated from whites than blacks are. As Asian and Hispanic socioeconomic status improves and generations shift from immigrant- to native-born, segregation from whites declines substantially. Conversely, objective differences in socioeconomic status explain only part of blacks' residential outcomes (Alba and Logan 1993; Denton and Massey 1988; Logan and Alba 1993, 1995; Logan et al. 1996; Massey and Denton 1987, 1993; Massey and Fischer 1999). Moreover, studies distinguishing among white, black, and mixed-race Hispanics find that black and mixed-race Hispanics' residential patterns mirror those of African Americans. The exceptional experience of groups with black skin leads Massey and Denton (1989, Denton and Massey 1989) to conclude that blacks pay a "higher constant penalty" for their race that is not explained by socioeconomic status disadvantage.

Until recently, the bases for these conclusions were aggregate-level analyses, primarily from the Massey-Denton segregation research project that culminated in the publication of *American Apartheid*. Modeling aggregate-level studies suffer from several potentially important limitations, however. In particular, modeling individual-level processes at the aggregate level (either tract- or metropolitan-area level) risks problems of ecological inference and introduces multicollinearity that limits the number of explanatory measures (Alba and Logan 1993; Massey et al. 1987; see also Massey and Denton 1987). Particularly problematic, homeownership is never included in aggregate-level studies, despite its obvious implications for residential outcomes (Alba and Logan 1993; Charles 2001; Oliver and Shapiro 1995; Yinger 1995). Finally, these studies measure and/or predict segregation or, less frequently, central-city versus suburban location across metropolitan areas. At least as important, however, is to understand variations in the characteristics of the neighborhoods – both central-city and suburban – where various racial/ethnic groups actually live. For example, suburban blacks tend to live in older, inner suburbs that are less affluent, less white, and experience more crime and social disorganization compared to the suburbs where comparable whites live (Alba et al. 1994; Logan and Schneider 1984; Pattillo-McCoy 1999); thus, not all suburbs are equal, and aggregate analyses cannot detail these important experiential differences.

Individual-level analyses address these limitations and substantially enhance our knowledge of residential outcomes by race; locational attainment models (Alba and Logan 1991, 1992) have been particularly influential in this regard. An innovative method introduced by Alba and Logan (1991, 1992) transforms aggregate level Census data (mainly STF3 and STF4 files) into the functional equivalent of individual-level Public Use Microdata Sample data with characteristics of each person's community of residence appended, eliminating issues of ecological inference and multicollinearity [Logan et al. 1996, p. 858; for a detailed explanation of the method, see Alba and Logan (1991, 1992)]. Models employ a broad range of social class indicators, most notably homeownership and family status to predict neighborhood-level outcomes (e.g., median income and exposure to crime, as well as percent non-Hispanic white and suburban versus central-city residence). Analyses compare the characteristics of suburbs inhabited by whites, blacks, Hispanics, and Asians rather than aggregate-level segregation.

These improvements have yielded interesting and important information. Most interesting, perhaps, is that at the individual-level, blacks exhibit a positive association between socioeconomic status and residential outcomes, although their returns to education and income are significantly lower than for other groups. Especially troubling is the negative effect of homeownership on blacks' residential outcomes. Counter to the benefits typically associated with owning a home (rather than renting), black homeowners reside in neighborhoods that are more segregated and less affluent than their renting counterparts – they are the only group that is consistently penalized for owning a home (Alba et al. 2000a; Logan et al. 1996). Together, these differences keep blacks from reaching parity with whites at any level of affluence – blacks live in neighborhoods that are, on

average, 15% to 20% less affluent than other groups with comparable status. Additionally, contrary to the assertion that black residential segregation is unchanged by increasing socioeconomic status, Alba et al. (2000a) find that middle-class and affluent blacks in the most segregated U.S. cities live in areas with substantially more whites than their poor, inner-city counterparts do. This is counterbalanced, however, by the generally lower status of their white neighbors. Thus, the suburban areas where middle-class and affluent blacks live are significantly less white and less affluent than those of comparable whites.

Patterns for Asians and Hispanics, on the other hand, are more similar to those observed in the aggregate. Both show substantial residential gains with improved socioeconomic status, and effects for homeownership are mixed (often nonsignificant and occasionally negative, although less so than for blacks); effects of education and income are large enough, however, that average and affluent native-born Hispanics and Asians live in communities that are roughly equivalent to those of comparable whites (Logan et al. 1996; Alba et al. 1999). A comparison of 1980 and 1990 data suggests a weakening of the traditional spatial assimilation model regarding the importance of acculturation. Being native-born and speaking only English still improves Hispanics' locational attainment, but the latter is less important in 1990 compared to 1980; by 1990, neither characteristic disadvantaged Asians. The emergence of ethnic suburban enclaves may account for this apparent weakening of the traditional spatial assimilation process by making residence in high-status, suburban communities an option for recently arrived non-English speakers with at- or above-average social class characteristics (Alba et al. 1999, 2000b; Logan et al. 2002). Furthermore, "perceptible African ancestry" costs black Hispanics between $3500 and $6000 in locational returns, placing them in neighborhoods that are comparable to those of black Americans (Alba et al. 2000a, p. 613).

Much of the research discussed to this point focuses heavily on the use of statistically convenient, but homogenizing, racial categories. Considering characteristics specific to immigration may account for some intragroup diversity, and it is certainly a step in the right direction; however, an important body of research documents meaningful differences among national-origin groups within the same broad racial category, suggesting the importance of analyses that are sensitive to these differences (see, for example, Portes and Rumbaut 1996; Waldinger and Bozorgmehr 1996; Waters 1990, 1999). At the aggregate level, Massey and Bitterman's (1985) comparison of Mexicans in Los Angeles and Puerto Ricans in New York – demonstrating that differences in segregation are attributable to the latter group's generally lower socioeconomic status and "blackness" – represents both an important exception to this general tendency and evidence of potentially important intragroup variation.

A final advantage of the individual-level analyses detailed above is the serious attention several studies have paid to national-origin differences within each of the four major racial categories. Consistent with assimilation hypotheses, for example, Logan and Alba (1993) find that the more recently settled Irish-, Italian-, and Polish-origin whites tend to reside in lower-income neighborhoods than the earlier-arriving (e.g., British, French, and German) and other white ethnic groups, net of individual-level characteristics. For "blacks," results are consistent with those detailed above: Afro-Caribbean blacks experience more favorable outcomes and see better returns to their human capital than African Americans do (Alba et al. 1999; Crowder 1999; Logan and Alba 1993, 1995).

National-origin differences are most pronounced among Asians and Hispanics, the two most heterogeneous and rapidly growing groups. Logan and Alba (1993) find that Asian Indians, Filipinos, and Vietnamese tend to reside in less affluent neighborhoods than Chinese, Japanese, Koreans, and other Asian groups do, suggesting that this effect may be tied to the extreme poverty circumstances of their home countries compared to those of other Asian groups. Alternatively, Asian Indians and Filipinos are not at all disadvantaged by poor English skills; in this case, the researchers suggest that this is because English is widely used in both India and the Philippines. As a result, these groups arrive with more exposure to English; therefore, the "census self-assessment of English ability has a different meaning for them" (Alba et al., 1999 p. 457; see also Jasso and Rosenzweig 1990). The disadvantage associated with poor English

skills, moreover, declined considerably between 1980 and 1990 for the Chinese and Koreans, but increased among the Vietnamese. None of the Asian groups is meaningfully disadvantaged by recent arrival (Alba et al. 1999).

Both national-origin and racial classification matter for Hispanics. Puerto Ricans, Cubans, and all black Hispanics reside, on average, in lower socioeconomic status neighborhoods relative to other Hispanics, net of other individual characteristics (Alba and Logan 1993, pp. 260–64). Poor English skills negatively impact the likelihood of suburban (versus central-city) residence for Mexicans and Cubans, but not for Dominicans and Salvadorans. Also, in sharp contrast to the Asian groups, recent immigration to the United States is detrimental to the likelihood of suburban residence for all Hispanic groups (Alba et al. 1999). Although limited in number, these analyses highlight important variation in residential outcomes and in the factors that influence those outcomes that are hidden by the use of broad, analytically convenient racial categories; future research should continue to expose the complicated social realities hidden by this social science convention.

On the whole, conclusions of aggregate-level studies remain intact. The experiences of Hispanics and (for the most part) Asians are largely consistent with the spatial assimilation model; blacks (African Americans and black Hispanics) on the other hand, do not see the same payoff for improved social class status. This is best illustrated by the negative effect of homeownership. Alba and colleagues suggest that this represents the operation of a dual housing market that restricts black homeowners – but not black renters – to black neighborhoods, making it difficult for them to enter some neighborhoods and adding to the cost they pay for housing. Mixed effects of homeownership among Asians and Hispanics suggest that a dual housing market may operate to a lesser extent for them as well (Alba and Logan 1993; Alba et al. 1999; Logan et al. 1996; Massey and Denton 1993). Finally, non-Hispanic whites live in largely white and generally more affluent neighborhoods irrespective of their social class characteristics. The oppositional experiences of blacks and whites contradict the tenets of spatial assimilation and suggest the persistence of an enduring system of racial stratification.

Place stratification

The emergence of racially separate neighbor-hoods resulted from a combination of individual- and institutional-level actions. Scholars generally agree that all levels of government, as well as the real estate, lending, and construction industries, played critical roles in creating and maintaining a dual housing market that constrained the mobility options of blacks (for detailed discussions, see Massey and Denton 1993; Meyer 2000; Yinger 1995). It was assumed by many, however, that passage of the 1968 Fair Housing Act marked the beginning of the end of segregation. This, however, has not been the case: residential segregation persists, and substantial evidence points to continued resistance to more than token numbers of black (and, to a lesser extent, Hispanic) neighbors (Bobo and Zubrinsky 1996; Charles 2000, 2001; Farley et al. 1993, 1994; Meyer 2000; Zubrinsky and Bobo 1996) and discriminatory practices in the real estate and lending markets (Massey and Lundy 2001; Galster 1990;Yinger 1995). The place stratification model punctuates the centrality of these issues, arguing that "[r]acial/ ethnic minorities are sorted by place according to their group's relative standing in society, [limiting] the ability of even the socially mobile members to reside in the same communities as comparable whites" (Alba and Logan 1993, p. 1391). Whites use segregation to maintain social distance, and therefore, present-day residential segregation – particularly blacks' segregation from whites – is best understood as emanating from structural forces tied to racial prejudice and discrimination that preserve the relative status advantages of whites (Bobo and Zubrinsky 1996; Logan et al. 1996; Massey and Denton 1993; Meyer 2000).

Despite general agreement regarding the role of prejudice and discrimination (both individual and institutional) in the emergence of racially segregated neighborhoods, the extent to which these factors are implicated in the persistence of segregation remains contested. Alternative explanations downplay the continuing salience of prejudice and/or discrimination in favor of other race-related attitudes and perceptions. The in-group preference hypothesis argues that all groups have "strong desires" for neighborhoods with substantial numbers of coethnics (Clark 1992, p. 451) that reflect a simple, natural ethnocentrism rather than outgroup hostility or an effort to preserve relative status advantages. A stronger version contends blacks' own preference for self-segregation explains current levels of black-white segregation (see, for example, Patterson 1997; Thernstrom and Thernstrom 1997). According to the racial proxy (Clark 1986, 1988; Harris 1999, 2001) and the race-based neighborhood stereotyping hypotheses (Ellen 2000), it is the collection of undesirable social class characteristics associated with blacks or the neighborhoods where they are concentrated – joblessness, welfare dependence, proclivity to criminal behavior – not race per se, that motivates aversion to black neighbors, not only among out-groups, but among blacks themselves. Still, race is central to each of these alternatives, and direct assessments of the role of prejudice often include one or more of these alternative explanations. As such, I address these alternative explanations within the context of stratification-based explanations.

Neighborhood racial composition preferences

A well-established literature details black-white differences in preferences for integration. In their classic article, "Chocolate City, Vanilla Suburbs," Farley and colleagues (1978) introduced an innovative and highly regarded method for measuring views on residential segregation. In the experiment, white respondents are asked about their comfort with and willingness to enter neighborhoods with varying degrees of integration with blacks; black respondents receive a similar experiment: rating neighborhoods of various racial compositions from most to least attractive and indicating their willingness to enter each of the areas. In both cases, scenarios represent realistic assumptions regarding the residential experiences and options of both groups; neighborhood cards similar to those used by Farley and colleagues are presented in Figure 34.1 (for details, see Farley et al. 1978, 1993).

Results revealed substantial resistance by Detroit-area whites to even minimal levels of integration: 25% said the presence of a single black neighbor would make them uncomfortable, 40% said they would try to leave an area that was one-third black, and nearly twice as many would leave the majority black neighborhood

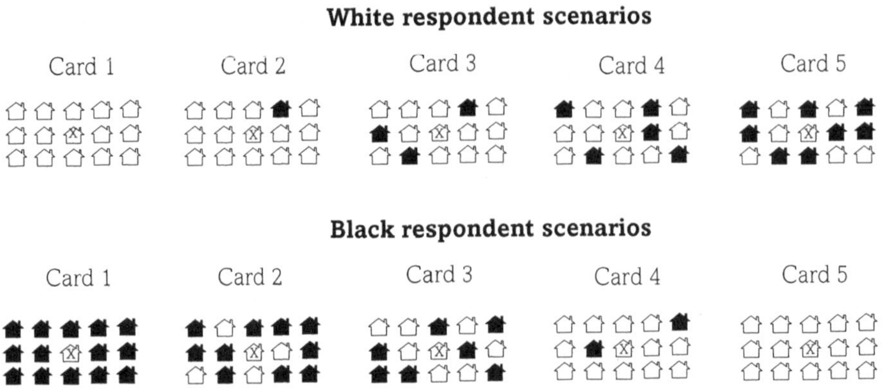

White respondent scenarios

Card 1   Card 2   Card 3   Card 4   Card 5

Black respondent scenarios

Card 1   Card 2   Card 3   Card 4   Card 5

Figure 34.1 Farley-Schuman neighborhood cards for black and white respondents from the 1992–1994 Multi-City Study of Urban Inequality.

(Farley et al. 1978). Blacks, on the other hand, showed a clear preference for integration. Eighty-five percent chose the 50-50 neighborhood as their first or second choice; when asked to explain their selection, two thirds stressed the importance of racial harmony (Farley et al. 1978, p. 328). Virtually all blacks were willing to enter all three integrated neighborhoods, and 38% of Detroit-area blacks said they would move into an otherwise all-white neighborhood.

As part of the 1992–1994 Multi-City Study of Urban Inequality (MCSUI), the Farley-Schuman showcard methodology was replicated in Atlanta, Boston, Detroit, and Los Angeles; to enhance our understanding of preferences in multiethnic contexts, the experiment was modified to include Hispanics and Asians. Analyses of neighborhood racial composition preferences based on the MCSUI data highlight the influence of both respondent- and target-group race on attitudes toward residential integration (Charles 2001; Clark 2002; Farley et al. 1993, 1997; Zubrinsky and Bobo 1996). Relative to the 1970s, whites express greater comfort with higher levels of integration and fewer said they would be unwilling to enter racially mixed areas. Although a sizeable majority of whites express comfort with a one-third out-group neighborhood, a rank ordering of out-groups is evident: whites feel most comfortable with Asians and least so with blacks (Hispanics fall in between), and comfort declines as the number of out-group members increases. The

pattern of responses regarding whites' willingness to enter racially mixed neighborhoods is similar, except that the decline in willingness to enter begins earlier and is never as high as comfort with neighborhood transition; thus, 60% of whites are comfortable with a neighborhood that is one-third black, but only 45% of whites are willing to move into that same neighborhood (Charles 2001). Although reflecting meaningful improvements in whites' attitudes, Detroit-area whites stand out as more resistant to integration compared to whites in the other cities (Farley et al. 1997).

Blacks, Hispanics, and Asians all appear to want both meaningful integration and a substantial coethnic presence. The relative importance of these competing desires, however, depends on both the respondent- and target-group race. The overwhelming majority of blacks selected one of the two most integrated alternatives irrespective of out-group race, although the one with 10 black and 5 out-group households is slightly more attractive than the one that best approximates a 50-50 neighborhood. For Hispanics and Asians, on the other hand, target-group race is especially important: when potential neighbors are white, their most attractive neighborhoods are the same as those of blacks (Cards 2 and 3), although the order is reversed. When potential neighbors are black, however, between 60% and 80% of both Hispanics and Asians find one of the two least-integrated alternatives most attractive (Cards 1 and 2). Across respondent racial categories, the all-the-same-race alternative is least attractive when potential neighbors are white; however, Hispanics and Asians generally find this neighborhood more attractive than blacks do. Both groups are also twice as likely as blacks to select the all-white neighborhood as their first or second choice (approximately 10% for Hispanics and Asians, compared to 5% of blacks), although for all three groups, the all-out-group alternative is the least attractive. Patterns of willingness to enter neighborhoods mirror those for attractiveness. For blacks, these patterns suggest a slight shift away from a preference for 50-50 neighborhoods and a significant decline in willingness to be the only black family in an otherwise all-white area since 1976 (Charles 2001; Farley et al. 1993, 1997).

Other multiethnic studies of preferences yield similar results. Bobo and Zubrinsky (1996) analyze multiracial data but measure attitudes toward one group at a time using a single forced-choice item. Consideration of a single target group is a limitation of the Farley-Schuman methodology in multiethnic contexts as well, as are differences between white and nonwhite experiments that make direct comparisons difficult. Charles (2000) presents a major innovation on the Farley-Schuman experiment that allows the simultaneous consideration of whites, blacks, Hispanics, and Asians as potential neighbors, using a single item in which all respondents are asked to draw their ideal multiethnic neighborhood. Regardless of the measure, the pattern of results is the same. All groups exhibit preferences for both meaningful integration and a substantial presence of same-race neighbors, although preferences for same-race neighbors are not uniform across groups: whites exhibit the strongest preference for same-race neighbors and blacks the weakest. Moreover, preferences vary by the race of the target group and demonstrate a racial rank ordering of out-groups in which whites are always the most desirable out-group and blacks are always the least desirable. Finally, preferences for integration decline as the number of out-group members increases. These bivariate patterns make it clear that race is influential in the residential decision-making process (Bobo and Zubrinsky 1996; Charles 2001; Farley et al. 1993, 1997; Zubrinsky and

Bobo 1996). Therefore, the next logical question is how does race matter?

Prejudice versus the alternatives

Although suggestive, the patterns detailed above are not conclusive evidence of the primacy of racial prejudice; however, several multivariate analyses detail whether and how race matters at the individual level. Using the MCSUI data for Detroit, Farley and colleagues (1994) showed that anti-black stereotypes are strongly associated with whites' discomfort with black neighbors, their likelihood of fleeing an integrating area, and their willingness to enter mixed neighborhoods. Similarly, Timberlake (2000) concludes that negative racial stereotypes and perceptions of group threat from blacks are the strongest predictors of whites' resistance to integration, based on analysis of MCSUI data for Atlanta. For Atlanta blacks, negative racial stereotypes and (to a lesser extent) the perception of whites as tending to discriminate against other groups contribute to their integration attitudes. Bobo and Zubrinsky (1996) and Charles (2000) analyzed multiracial data from Los Angeles, concluding that negative out-group stereotypes reduce openness to integration across racial categories and influence preferences for both out-group (Bobo and Zubrinsky 1996; Charles 2000) and same-race neighbors (Charles 2000).

Each of these analyses includes a measure of respondents' perceptions of the social class positions of out-groups relative to their own group as a test of the racial-proxy argument; Bobo and Zubrinsky (1996), Charles (2000), and Timberlake (2000) also include measures of in-group attachment to assess the relative importance of ethnocentrism. In all instances, racial stereotypes are the most powerful predictors of preferences. Effects for both perceived social class disadvantage and in-group attachment are always smaller and often nonsignificant; indeed, this pattern persists across respondent racial categories for both out-group and same-race neighbors (Charles 2000). Nationally representative data from the 2000 General Social Survey both confirm and strengthen the results of these single-city analyses.

Target group race	Respondent race		
	Whites	Blacks	Hispanics
Whites			
Mean %	57.11%	30.40%	31.50%
No whites	0	9.21	1.28
All whites	20.28	0	0
Blacks			
Mean %	16.80%	42.01%	18.77%
No blacks	24.71	0.66	17.95
All blacks	0	6.58	0
Hispanics			
Mean %	12.82%	14.47%	33.61%
No Hispanics	32.17	27.63	2.56
All Hispanics	0	0	1.28
Asians			
Mean %	13.27%	13.11%	16.11%
No Asians	32.75	32.24	19.23
All Asians	0	0	0
Number of cases	858	152	78

Table 34.2 Summary statistics, multiethnic neighborhood showcard experiment, 2000 General Social Survey

Notes: The percentage of each racial group in a respondent's ideal neighborhood is the sum of each group included in the experiment, divided by the total number of houses (14), excluding the respondent's.
$p < .001$ except: all Hispanics ($p < .01$), no Asians ($p < .05$), and mean percent Asian ($p < .10$).

Table 34.2 summarizes preferences for white, black, and Hispanic respondents and reveals a pattern of preferences similar to those found by both Bobo and Zubrinsky (1996) and Charles (2000). Compared to the data from Los Angeles, however, both whites and blacks prefer more same-race neighbors (8% and 5%, respectively), but the opposite is true for Hispanics. Nationally, whites are much more likely to exclude an out-group entirely: 25% of whites want no blacks in their ideal neighborhood (compared to one fifth in Los Angeles) and as many as one third exclude Hispanics and Asians (compared to 16%–17% in Los Angeles). Blacks are also substantially more exclusionary at the national level, exhibiting rates of Hispanic and Asian exclusion between three and five times higher than for Los Angeles.

Finally, Table 34.3 presents correlations between neighborhood racial composition preferences and each of the race-related attitudes outlined above – perceived social class difference, racial stereotyping, and in-group attachment. In addition to preferences for various out-group neighbors, the bottom panel of Table 34.3 reports correlations between the selected racial attitudes and preferences for same-race neighbors. The perceived social class difference and racial stereotyping measures are scaled from -6 to $+6$. High (positive) scores indicate unfavorable ratings of out-groups relative to one's own group, low (negative) scores indicate favorable ratings of out-groups, and a score of zero indicates no perceived difference. In-group attachment captures the extent to which respondents "feel close" to members of their racial group; scores range from 0 (not at all close) to 8 (very close). This item was only asked of white and black respondents.

Target group race	Respondent race			
	Whites	Blacks	Hispanics	Total
Percentage of white neighbors				
Perceived social class difference	–	–.108	–.077	–.095
Racial stereotyping	–	–.148[+]	–.192[+]	–.167*
In-group attachment[a]	–	.119	–	.109**
Percentage of black neighbors				
Perceived social class difference	–.056	–	–.302**	–.082*
Racial stereotyping	–.390***	–	–.454***	–.390***
In-group attachment[a]	–.091*	–	–	–.037
Percentage of Hispanic neighbors				
Perceived social class difference	–.034	–.019	–	–.065*
Racial stereotyping	–.319***	–.104	–	–.305***
In-group attachment[a]	–.150*	–.095	–	–.141***
Percentage of Asian neighbors				
Perceived social class difference	–.051	–.003	.048	–.051
Racial stereotyping	–.285***	–.204*	–.202[+]	–.269***
In-group attachment[a]	–.105*	.040	–	–.082*
Percentage of same-race neighbors				
Perceived social class difference[b]	.041	–.074	.285*	.208***
Racial stereotyping[b]	.429***	–.162[+]	.500***	.421***
In-group attachment[a]	.142**	–.064	–	.104**

Table 34.3 Correlations of race-related attitudes and perceptions and neighborhood racial composition preferences, 2000 General Social Survey

Notes: Figures are Pearson correlations with preferences for the corresponding group as neighbors. The perceived social class difference and racial stereotyping measures are scaled from –6 to +6. High (positive) scores indicate unfavorable ratings of out-groups relative to one's own group; low (negative) scores indicate favorable ratings of out-groups; 0 indicates no perceived difference. Internal consistency (Cronbach's alpha) among the traits included in the stereotype difference score (intelligence, laziness, violent, committed to strong families, committed to fairness and equality for all) vary by target group as follows: for whites, $\alpha = .6217$; for blacks, $\alpha = .6736$; for Hispanics, $\alpha = .5719$; and for Asians, $\alpha = .6384$.
[a]In-group attachment questions ask about feelings of closeness to whites and blacks only.
[b]In the panel of correlations between racial attitudes and preferences for same-race neighbors, measures of perceived social class difference and racial stereotypes are combined for all out-groups (e.g., for Hispanic respondents these measures reflect perceptions of/attitudes about whites, blacks, and Asians).
[+]$p < .10$; * $p < .05$; ** $p < .01$; *** $p < .001$.

Consistent with Bobo and Zubrinsky (1996), racial stereotyping is the race-related attitude or perception most correlated with preferences, irrespective of respondent or target-group race. As stereotypes of out-groups become increasingly unfavorable, preferences for those groups as neighbors decline and preferences for same-race neighbors increase. This is especially true among whites, where correlations between racial stereotyping and preferences are between two and four times larger than for in-group attachment and those for perceived social class difference are both weak and nonsignificant. Correlations among these variables are weakest for blacks. Of 12 figures, 3 barely meet the most-liberal limits of statistical significance acknowledged in the social sciences. Hispanics are in between these extremes, exhibiting the highest correlation between both perceived social class difference and racial stereotyping, and preferences for black neighbors; stereotyping is only marginally correlated (p<.10) with preferences for white and Asian neighbors. Despite some differences, preliminary evidence from the 2000 General Social Survey substantiates prior findings from single-city analyses and highlights the primary importance of racial prejudice relative to both concerns about social class disadvantage and/or ethnocentrism in understanding neighborhood racial composition preferences.

More recently, Krysan and Farley (2002) supplement quantitative analyses with an examination of black MCSUI respondents' open-ended explanations of their integration attitudes. Contrary to proponents of both the ethnocentrism and racial proxy hypotheses, they find that belief in the principle of integration and/or a desire to improve race relations drives blacks' preferences for integration: This was the most common explanation for the attractiveness of the two most popular (and most integrated) neighborhoods (see Figure 34.1, Cards 2 and 3). Moreover, strong desires for a substantial coethnic presence are "inextricably linked" to fears of discrimination and white hostility (Krysan and Farley 2002, pp. 968–69); the latter is consistent with other descriptive analyses detailing an inverse association between perceived white hostility and overall neighborhood desirability (Charles 2001; Farley et al. 1993; Zubrinsky and Bobo 1996). They find virtually no support for either the ethnocentrism or the racial-proxy hypothesis. Few blacks invoke ethnocentric attitudes, even when favoring the all-black over the 50-50 neighborhood; contrary to the assertion that blacks (and whites) use race as a proxy for negative neighborhood characteristics, only 10% of black respondents cite negative neighborhood characteristics as the primary reason to avoid all-black areas.

A similar analysis examines open-ended elaborations from "whites who say they'd flee" (Krysan 2002). Once again, evidence of ethnocentrism is spare when considering integration with blacks. Concerns about cultural differences were more salient for whites in Los Angeles contemplating integration with Asians and Hispanics, and are expressed mainly in terms of language differences. Consistent with the racial-proxy and race-based neighborhood stereotyping hypotheses, whites offer race-associated reasons most often (e.g., concerns about crime and/or property values); however, meticulous analysis of the characteristics of whites offering clearly racial versus race-associated responses finds that education makes the difference. More educated whites are both less willing to negatively stereotype out-groups and more likely to offer race-associated explanations for their decision to flee an integrated area. Krysan (1998) suggests that because better-educated respondents are both more susceptible to social desirability pressures and more adept at articulating their racial group's interest in more subtle ways (Jackman and Muha 1984), the difference between explicitly racial and so-called race-associated explanations is semantic: "[I]n the end, each of the reasons is an articulation of a racial stereotype" (Krysan 2002).

The analyses discussed to this point represent important methodological, empirical, and substantive contributions to our understanding of integration attitudes. Especially insightful are those analyses that elaborate preferences in multiethnic contexts and those that employ multiple methods to gain leverage on the complexities of racial attitudes. Nonetheless, critics aptly point to important limitations associated with studies that rely on measures of expressed preferences. In particular, because it is clear to respondents that their racial attitudes are at issue, responses are susceptible to social desirability pressures and the difficulty of distinguishing between the direct effect of the racial composition of the neighborhood and the indirect effect of the neighborhood characteristics that respondents may associate with the racial composition of the neighborhood. Although preference studies include a measure of perceived social class difference, other unmeasured aspects of the proxy argument (e.g., crime, school quality) are left uncontrolled. Each of these limitations can bias results (Ellen 2000; Emerson et al. 2001; Harris 1999). Alternatively, tests of the racial-proxy hypothesis that use respondents' actual residential location and the value of their homes as indicators of neighborhood desirability are confounded by the fact that "[e]ven if people prefer to live in racially mixed neighborhoods, they may not end up in such neighborhoods" because of discrimination or a shortage of housing (Emerson *et al.* 2001, p. 924).

A recent analysis by Emerson *et al.* (2001) stands out for creatively and effectively addressing these limitations using a factorial experiment to assess whites' attitudes toward integration with blacks, Hispanics, and Asians. Respondents are asked to imagine that they have two school-aged children and are looking for a house; they have found a house they like better than any other (it has everything the respondent is looking for) that is both close to work and within their price range. Before asking whites if they would buy the home, they are offered a set of randomly generated neighborhood characteristics – public school quality, crime level, direction of property value change, home value compared to others in the neighborhood, and racial composition (between 5% and 100% Asian, black, or Hispanic). They find that the presence of Hispanics and Asians does not matter to whites, but black neighborhood composition matters significantly even after controlling for proxy variables. Whites are neutral about buying a home in a neighborhood between 10% and 15% black and are unlikely to buy the home in a neighborhood over 15% black. This pattern is especially pronounced among families with children.

The overall conclusion to be drawn is that active racial prejudice is a critical component of preferences for integration, and therefore, the persistence of racially segregated communities. Whites' racial prejudice is a double whammy: influential not only for its effect on their own integration attitudes, but also for its implications for minority group preferences and residential search behavior. Areas perceived as hostile toward particular minority groups are also perceived as less attractive, even when other aspects of the communities should be desirable (Charles 2001). Indeed, blacks openly admit that fears of white hostility motivate desires for more than a handful of coethnic neighbors (Krysan and Farley 2002). Although the influence of racial stereotyping is the same for all groups, all three nonwhite groups want substantially more integration than whites do. Contrary to the popular adage that "birds of a feather flock together," ethnocentrism plays a minimal role at best; moreover, with respect to blacks, the most thorough and detailed analyses to date suggest that whites move out because blacks move in – black density matters because the presence of too many blacks (and, to a lesser extent, Hispanics and Asians) suggests a change in "traditional status relations of relative dominance and privilege" (Bobo and Zubrinsky 1996, p. 904; see also Charles 2000; Krysan 2002). In sum, the attitudes, preferences, and (potential) behaviors of whites alone cannot fully account for actual residential patterns; all groups express some desire for coethnic neighbors, and these preferences play a role in shaping actual outcomes (Clark 2002). A much more sizable share of available evidence, however, points to the influential role of racial prejudice, both as a motivating factor in the avoidance of particular out-groups and as a motivator of minority group preferences for same-race neighbors.

Housing market discrimination

The institutional practices that created and maintained residential segregation represent the translation of white prejudice into "systematic, institutionalized racial discrimination" in the housing market (Massey and Denton 1993, p. 51; Meyer 2000; Yinger 1995). A growing body of empirical evidence points to the persistence of discrimination in the housing market, although the form that present-day discrimination takes is markedly different than in previous eras (Bobo 1989; Cutler *et al.* 1999). Although formal barriers to integration have been eliminated, discriminatory white tastes remain; segregation persists, it is argued, through a process of decentralized racism, in which "whites pay more" to live in predominantly white areas (Cutler *et al.* 1999, pp. 445). As such, discriminatory behavior has become more subtle and therefore more difficult to detect even by its victims (Galster 1990, 1992; Yinger 1995). Since the mid-1950s, audit studies have proven useful in detecting these subtle forms of discrimination. In an audit study, pairs of trained testers – one white and the other either black or Hispanic – with similar economic and family characteristics successively inquired about housing, carefully detailing their experiences with the real estate agent or landlord. After a visit, each auditor completes a detailed report of her experiences; discrimination is defined as systematically less favorable treatment of the black or Hispanic tester and is documented by direct observation during the interaction (Ondrich *et al.* 1998). Housing units are sampled randomly from metropolitan-area newspapers; examples of experiences detailed by auditors range from seemingly race-neutral aspects of interaction such as the promptness of returning phone calls or volunteering to show an audit pair additional units, to the obviously racial act of steering minority auditors toward mixed or segregated areas.

Despite its advantages, the audit methodology is not without critics, most notably Heckman and Siegelman (1993) (see also Heckman 1998). By sampling housing units only from major newspapers, for example, audit studies likely underestimate the incidence of discrimination. Other aspects of the method run the risk of overstating the frequency of discrimination. As part of the training process, auditors are fully informed of the purpose of the study and as a result may be unintentionally motivated to find it; similarly, it has been suggested that other characteristics of the individual auditors may influence agent behavior (i.e., the presence or absence of facial hair and/or an accent). There is also concern about the use of gross measures of discrimination that count "all errors made" by agents/landlords as unfavorable or discriminatory treatment, arguing that this inaccurately assumes that firms never make race-neutral errors, and confounds random and systematic effects. Heckman and Siegelman (1993, p. 272) suggest beginning with a net measure of discrimination experienced by minority testers relative to their white teammates because (a) it takes race-neutral errors into account, and (b) if the net measure reveals evidence of discrimination, the gross measure will as well.

In response, Yinger (1993, 1995, 1998) agrees that audit studies measure discrimination in a major segment of the housing market – units advertised in major newspapers – that is accessible to all homeseekers, irrespective of race or ethnicity; although results cannot be generalized to all housing transactions, they do account for a large share of the action. Conceding the potential benefits of blind audits for avoiding experimenter effects, proponents of full disclosure argue for deliberately informing auditors of the nature and purpose of the study while at the same time emphasizing the importance of accurate, complete reporting avoids other kinds of "experimenter effects."

Specifically, some minority auditors may be upset by blatant mistreatment and unable to accurately complete their evaluations, invalidating the audit. Moreover, both members of an audit team must receive identical training to minimize behavioral differences. Bringing teammates together without full disclosure opens the door for (inaccurate) speculation among the auditors about the purpose of the study and/or appropriate behavior. With respect to aspects of auditors' appearances or behavior – aside from race – that could influence agents' behavior, more recent audit studies are more careful in the selection of testers, particularly with respect to the presence or absence of an accent (Yinger 1995).

Finally, although simple gross measures of discrimination almost certainly overestimate the frequency of systematic discrimination and should be interpreted as upper-bound estimates of discrimination, net measures subtract both random and systematic differences in treatment and probably underestimate the frequency of discrimination. As a consequence, net measures underestimate the gross incidence of discrimination (Yinger 1995, pp. 45–46). Analyses of audit studies generally present net measures followed by gross measures. Yinger points out that the "story told by the simple net measure is bleak enough … in some ways the story may be even worse" (1995, p. 46). In light of such intense scrutiny, research on housing market discrimination based on audit studies is highly regarded in both the research and legal communities and is now widely accepted for use both as enforcement tools and as evidence of discrimination in U.S. courts (Metcalf 1988; Yinger 1998).

Both national- and local-level studies find evidence of substantial discrimination that has not changed meaningfully over time (Yinger 1995, 1998). In a review of 50 local audit studies completed throughout the United States during the 1980s, Galster (1990) concluded that racial discrimination is a dominant feature of the housing market, conservatively estimating that (a) housing discrimination against black and Hispanic home and apartment seekers occurs in roughly half of their interactions with agents or landlords, (b) the discrimination is subtle and difficult for the individual to detect, and (c) the frequency of discrimination had not changed over time (Galster 1992, p. 647). These figures are confirmed by evidence from the 1989

Housing Discrimination Study (HDS), the most recent national audit study. In *Closed Doors, Opportunities Lost,* Yinger (1995) delivers a comprehensive and influential discussion of housing market discrimination, using HDS data to detail the incidence and severity of discrimination. At the beginning of a transaction, an individual inquires about an advertised unit and then asks about the availability of other, similar units, at which time an agent may withhold information or limit the number of units shown to the client. In the second stage, the actions taken by agents to facilitate the transaction are considered. These would include the discussion of terms and conditions, the agent's sales effort, and/or assistance in securing financing; at this point, an agent may offer less assistance to minority clients. The third aspect of the interaction involves the geographic location of units other than the advertised unit that opened the interaction. Access to housing is constrained if a client is only shown housing in neighborhoods with particular racial/ethnic make-ups (Yinger 1995, pp. 31–33).

During the first stage of the interaction, Yinger found that blacks and Hispanics are denied access to housing between 5% and 10% of the time – information is completely withheld. More often, minority access to housing was constrained: Black and Hispanic testers learned about 25% fewer units than comparable whites. Whites were also significantly more likely to receive other forms of favorable treatment, including follow-up calls, positive comments about an available unit, and special rental incentives (e.g., one month's free rent or a reduced security deposit). Minority auditors suffered many minor inconveniences, including waiting longer to be served, inattention to their housing needs but overemphasis on their incomes, and less assistance with obtaining financing. Racial/ethnic steering is also common. Yinger estimates that black and Hispanic homeseekers visiting four real estate agents will encounter steering 40% and 28% of the time, respectively, whereas whites are more likely to hear negative comments about integrated areas. Racial/ethnic steering of this sort is prohibited by fair housing legislation; however, steering through marketing practices is completely legal, and evidence suggests that real estate agencies do much of their steering through their marketing practices. Units in black

neighborhoods are not advertised as often, have fewer open houses, and are more likely to be represented by firms that are not part of a Multiple Listing Service. This may also be an issue for units in predominantly Hispanic areas. These practices are the exact opposite of those employed for units in white neighborhoods (Yinger 1995, pp. 55–59).

A growing body of evidence documents racial discrimination in lending as well (Dedman 1988, 1989; Jackson 1994). The Boston Fed Study compares conventional loan denial rates for whites, blacks, and Hispanics in Boston using 1990 data from the Home Mortgage Disclosure Act supplemented with other variables known to influence credit decisions. Together, these data offer "the most comprehensive set of credit characteristics ever assembled" (Yinger 1995, p. 71; for details, see Munnell *et al.* 1996). Results from the Boston Fed Study indicate that controlling for "the risk and cost of default and for loan and personal characteristics," blacks and Hispanics are 56% more likely than whites to be denied a conventional mortgage loan, which amounts to a minority denial rate of 17%, compared to a white rate of 11%. Analysis of the Boston Fed data by Carr and Megbolugbe (1993) found that minorities receive systematically lower credit ratings. This means that a "slow paying" white applicant, for example, would be considered creditworthy, but a similar black applicant would not. There is evidence of racial bias in nearly every other aspect of the lending process, including private mortgage insurance, redlining by home insurance companies, methods of advertising and outreach (Yinger 1995, p. 83–85), and bank branch locations and closing patterns (Caskey 1992), in addition to evidence of an association between the likelihood of blacks' loan approval and the racial composition of the financial institution workforce (Squires and Kim 1995). The latter confirms evidence that prejudice and economic interests motivate biased behavior (Yinger 1995, Ondrich *et al.* 1998).

More than a decade has passed since the collection of the 1989 HDS. To remedy this, researchers at the Urban Institute are back in the field for HDS 2000. This updated study promises to be the most ambitious and thorough analysis to date. In addition to black/white and Hispanic/white tests replicated from the 1989 HDS for comparative purposes, HDS 2000 will ultimately include tests of housing market discrimination against both Asians and Native Americans (Turner *et al.* 2002). Newly released Phase I results offer mixed messages about changes in the incidence of housing market discrimination against blacks and Hispanics since the 1989 study, revealing both improvement and persistent discrimination. Improvements in the sales market are encouraging; in 2000, both blacks and Hispanics were significantly less likely than they were in 1989 to receive consistently unfavorable treatment relative to whites. For blacks, the overall incidence of white-favored treatment dropped to 17% in 2000, down 12 percentage points over the 10-year period. Despite this overall improvement, blacks are now more likely to be steered away from predominantly white neighborhoods than they were 10 years ago. The overall incidence of discrimination against Hispanics declined by 7.1 percentage points over the decade (to 19.7%) and saw no significant change in the likelihood of geographic steering (Turner *et al.* 2002). The experience of black and Hispanic renters, however, offers little optimism. Blacks are significantly less likely to receive unfavorable treatment than in the previous decade; however, the decline is much smaller (9%) than in the sales market. More troubling is that Hispanic renters show no significant change in their likelihood of receiving unfavorable treatment relative to whites, and they now experience a higher incidence of discrimination (26%) than their black counterparts (Turner *et al.* 2002).

In preparation for the Asian and Native American audits, Phase I of the 2000 HDS includes pilot studies for both groups – Chinese and Koreans in Los Angeles, Southeast Asians in Minneapolis, and Native Americans in Phoenix. In Los Angeles, results suggest that Chinese and Korean renters "may face different patterns of adverse treatment" than their black and Hispanic counterparts do (Turner *et al.* 2002, p. 4.18). Results indicate that both groups are told about and shown more units than their non-Asian minority counterparts; on the other hand, black and Hispanic testers received better service from agents than either Asian group. Discrimination against Chinese and Koreans in the sales market, however, is similar to that of blacks and Hispanics – indeed, Korean homebuyers have the highest overall net estimate of discrimination (22.2%) for any of the minority groups studied in Los Angeles (Turner *et al.* 2002).

Turner and colleagues (2002) reported that local organizations had difficulty recruiting and retaining Southeast Asian and Native American testers because (a) little testing has been conducted with these groups in the past and (b) few of these testers had any experience with homeownership and found it especially difficult to complete sales audits. These challenges help to inform subsequent tests. As a result, pilot-test results are only available for the rental market, where both groups appear to experience significant discrimination (Turner *et al.* 2002, p. 2.6). Southeast Asian renters in Minneapolis face more adverse treatment than either of the Asian groups in Los Angeles, and their experiences more closely mirror national results for black and Hispanic renters, particularly in the areas of housing availability and inspections. Native American renters experience adverse treatment at levels slightly above those found at the national level for blacks and Hispanics (Turner *et al.* 2002). These exploratory results illustrate the value of full-fledged multiethnic/multiracial analyses of residential processes; we look forward to the completion and dissemination of results from Phases II and III of the 2000 HDS.

The important information provided by national audit studies comparable to both the 1989 and the 2000 HDSs is juxtaposed by significant challenges involved in utilizing the method (e.g., training, recruiting, and maintaining minority testers); chief among these challenges is, no doubt, the substantial expense of these studies. Recent research by Massey and Lundy (2001) offers a lower-cost alternative to the in-person audit method used in the 1989 and 2000 HDSs: conducting a telephone-based audit study of racial discrimination in the Philadelphia rental housing market. Citing evidence that individuals "are capable of making fairly accurate racial attributions on the basis of linguistic cues," the authors argue that a good deal of discrimination is likely to occur before a personal encounter can take place (Massey and Lundy 2001, p. 454). They find that this is, in fact, the case: Compared to whites, blacks were significantly less likely to speak to the rental agent and, if they spoke to a landlord, significantly less likely to be told of a unit's availability. Alternatively, blacks were more likely than whites to have their credit worthiness mentioned as a potential obstacle in qualifying for a lease (Massey and Lundy 2001, p. 466).

Thus, in one way or another, and to a greater or lesser degree, discrimination in the housing market constrains the ability of nonwhites to rent and/or purchase housing. Access to housing is constrained, the search process is more unpleasant (i.e., more visits, more waiting, etc.), homeseekers receive far less assistance from lenders in the mortgage application process and are more likely to have their applications denied, and their moving costs are higher. Yinger estimates that every time that black and Hispanic households search for housing – whether they encounter discrimination or not – they pay a "discrimination tax" of approximately $3,000. Cumulatively, he estimates that blacks and Hispanics pay $4.1 billion per year in higher search costs and lost housing opportunities. Included in this estimate is the decision of 10% of blacks and 15% of Hispanics not to look for housing because they anticipate discrimination (Yinger 1995, pp. 95–103; for more on the impact of anticipated discrimination on search behavior, see Farley 1996b). By making it more difficult for minorities to purchase housing, discrimination contributes to racial disparities in homeownership and wealth accumulation, which in turn foster persisting suburban residential segregation.

THE CONSEQUENCES OF RESIDENTIAL SEGREGATION

A voluminous body of research documents the powerful influence of place on individual life chances. Concentrated poverty neighborhoods exhibit high rates of long-term joblessness, out-of-wedlock births, school drop-out, crime and social disorder, and lower average wages for those who work (Cutler and Glaeser 1997; Jargowsky 1996; Krivo and Peterson 1996; Massey and Denton 1993; Wilson 1987). Without sufficient resources, public services – particularly public schools – deteriorate as well. Residential segregation is, as detailed at the outset, deeply implicated in the concentration of poverty in black communities. Yet, even after accounting for the social and economic disadvantages associated with residential segregation, Cutler and Glaeser (1997, p. 865) found that "a one-standard-deviation reduction in segregation (13 percent) would eliminate one-third" of white-black differences in rates of high school completion, single parenthood, and employment as well as earnings.

The neighborhoods where poor blacks are concentrated are characterized by extreme levels of disadvantage, and middle-class and affluent blacks are exposed to higher levels of neighborhood disadvantage than their status would imply (Alba et al. 1994; Massey and Fischer 1999; Pattillo-McCoy 1999; Wilson 1987). Suburban blacks are as segregated as their central-city counterparts; their suburbs are part of a contiguous set of black neighborhoods that are, collectively, the ghetto, differentiated only by their status as the "best, mixed, and worst areas" (Galster 1991; Jargowsky and Bane 1991; Logan 2001a; Morenoff and Sampson 1997; Pattillo-McCoy 1999). Indeed, the well-known perils associated with ghetto life documented by quantitative researchers (Jargowsky 1996; Cutler and Glaeser 1997; Wilson 1987) and ethnographers like Anderson (1990, 1999) and Venkatesh (2000) are found, albeit to a lesser degree, in the neighborhoods of middle-class blacks (see, for example, Alba et al. 1994; Pattillo-McCoy 1999; Timberlake 2002). In a study of Philadelphia, Massey and colleagues (1987) documented rates of welfare dependence, out-of-wedlock births, and below-average educational outcomes several times higher than those of comparable whites, and the experience of middle-class blacks is only marginally improved over that of poor blacks.

The clustering of blacks within an expansive ghetto undermines black homeownership, either because housing in these areas is unattractive to residents or because of difficulties associated with securing lending; segregation also undermines Hispanic home ownership (Flippen 2001, pp. 354–5). The dwellings occupied by blacks (and black Hispanics) are older, of poorer quality, and depreciated in value relative to similar whites (Massey and Denton 1993; Rosenbaum 1994, 1996), and differences in home values and rates of ownership are implicated in persisting black and Hispanic wealth disparities – $414 billion and $186 billion, respectively, relative to whites (Oliver and Shapiro 1995; Yinger 1995). Exposure to crime is also a persistent concern because "even the most affluent blacks are not able to escape from crime, for they reside in communities as crime-prone as those housing the poorest whites (Alba et al. 1994, p. 427). Thus, whites' worst urban contexts are better than "the average context of black communities" (Sampson and Wilson 1995, p. 42).

Thus, as a consequence of residential segregation, the vast majority of blacks experience residential circumstances that are – to a greater or lesser degree – detrimental to their future social mobility because "any process that concentrates poverty within racially isolated neighborhoods will simultaneously increase the odds of socioeconomic failure within the segregated group" (Massey and Denton 1993, p. 179). Indeed, in-depth interviews with employers reveal that space is used as a mechanism for discriminating against minority job applicants (Kirschenman and Neckerman 1991; Wilson 1996). A recent study of participants in the Gautreaux program – one of the first scattered-site, low-income housing programs – details substantial improvements in the educational and employment outcomes of those who moved with their families from segregated urban housing projects to predominantly white suburban communities. Compared to their city-dwelling counterparts, Gautreaux participants were significantly more likely to be in high school, in a college-prep track, enrolled in a four-year college, employed with benefits, and not outside either the educational or employment systems. Many of the suburban participants said that safety contributed a great deal to their success (Rubinowitz and Rosenbaum 2000).

Ongoing research by Massey, Charles, and colleagues (Massey and Fischer 2002; Charles 2002) finds a similar relationship between neighborhood violence and the educational outcomes of middle-class and affluent students at selective colleges and universities. For both blacks and Hispanics, growing up under segregated circumstances significantly lowers later academic performance. The negative effect holds after controlling for socioeconomic status and is not attributable to differences in school quality or variations in intellectual, social, or psychological preparation among students from integrated and segregated neighborhoods. Apparently, segregation matters because it results in exposure to unusually high levels of violence while growing up. These students are also more likely to experience stressful life events that lead to greater family stress, poorer health, and greater family involvement while in college – all of which negatively impact academic performance (Charles 2002).

Although substantially better off than their poor counterparts, residential segregation limits black and Hispanic students' ability to reach their full potential.

CONCLUSION

The past decade has seen a remarkable increase in our understanding of the processes that maintain racially segregated neighborhoods in the United States. Increasing attention to the multiethnic character of many metropolitan areas – and of our nation – has improved our understanding of group differences in locational returns to human capital and how the racial attitudes of the four major racial groups contribute to residential patterns. Indeed, with so little information regarding the racial attitudes of nonwhites or of whites toward Hispanics and Asians, this alone is a boon to the study of race relations. The use of audit methodology has forever altered the landscape of discussion regarding discrimination in the housing and lending markets, detailing widespread, current discrimination against blacks, Hispanics, and preliminarily Asians and Native Americans that occurs at virtually every point in the search process. The expansion of much of this work to include the four major racial categories is an advance that cannot be underscored enough. As our nation becomes increasingly "prismatic," understanding the dynamics of race relations and processes of social mobility becomes both more complicated and more important.

Logan and colleagues (2002, p. 320) recently lamented that "we are near the limit of what can be accomplished through the analysis of publicly available census data." Their research is particularly illustrative of the benefits of highlighting the nation's increasing multi-ethnicity; still, locational attainment models that rely solely on census data cannot adequately assess the effect of massive disparities in accumulated wealth, nor can they account for the manner in which respondents' attitudes influence their residential outcomes. The major limitation to research of this sort, then, is its inability to capture the dynamic nature of residential segregation. This is a monumental task at the national level, but seems possible in selected metropolitan areas.

Future research should continue to actively engage this complexity. To date, much of what we know regarding the racial attitudes of Hispanics and Asians is limited to analyses of Los Angeles (and, to a lesser extent, Boston). Regional differences in settlement patterns and the vast heterogeneity within these broad racial categories make it imperative that we continue to pursue information on these groups and push past the convenience of broad racial classification schemes. In the area of individual-level racial attitudes, the factorial experimental design introduced recently by Emerson and colleagues (2001) presents a substantial improvement on prior methods and should be pursued. Future research should vary factors that they did not (e.g., the presence of children), consider the importance of the characteristics of surrounding neighborhoods, move beyond biracial neighborhoods and offer the full, multiethnic complement of neighbors, and incorporate nonwhite respondents (Emerson 2001, p. 932).

Qualitative analyses – whether from elaborations to closed-ended questions or in-depth interviews – represent another direction for future research. The next logical step in this case is to explore the attitudes, perceptions, and justifications of Hispanics and Asians for their neighborhood racial composition preferences; this is particularly important for capturing the importance of immigration-related characteristics. Ongoing research by Charles (unpublished observations), for example, details important differences in the motivations behind preferences for same-race neighbors based on immigrant status and English language ability. Results from Phases II and III of the 2000 HDS, moreover, will provide new and much-needed information on the housing market experiences of Asians and Native Americans, and for the first time, the ability to make comparisons among nonwhite groups. What we have already learned from the Phase I results provides valuable information about changes in the experiences of blacks and Hispanics since the 1989 study. Periodic follow-ups of nationwide housing market audit studies similar to the 2000 HDS would continue to keep us abreast of the extent to which discrimination in the housing market persists. Similarly, updated analysis of nationally representative, multiracial lending market data, preferably at regular intervals, would provide crucial and complementary

information on this aspect of the residential sorting process.

Finally, as is characteristic of social science research, the tendency has been to focus on the problem – segregation. Without doubt, this has been justified, given the deleterious effects of segregation on intergroup relations, social mobility, personal safety, and ultimately, efforts to reduce racial inequality in America. Relative to the body of research on segregation, however, far too little attention is paid to understanding the processes that produce and maintain the small but meaningful number of stably integrated neighborhoods. Although not discussed at length in this review, efforts to understand racial residential patterns that focus on the comparatively small but critically important number of success stories rather than our well-known failures are a much-needed breath of fresh air, reminding us that, although fragile and few and far between, "racially integrated neighborhoods are not, as once thought, inevitably doomed to rapid resegregation" (Ellen 2000, p. 152).

To wit, a study of 14 stably integrated urban communities estimates that as many as 10 million Americans reside in racially/ethnically diverse communities, areas defined as having racial/ethnic compositions closest to city racial/ethnic averages in both 1980 and 1990, although most have been integrated for longer (Nyden et al. 1998, p. 6). More recently, Ellen (2000) examines the characteristics of stably integrated neighborhoods and their residents, analyzing data for 34 U.S. metropolitan areas. She estimates that nearly 20% of all U.S. neighborhoods were racially mixed in 1990; these neighborhoods were home to 15% of whites and roughly one third of blacks. Moreover, more than 75% of neighborhoods that were integrated (between 10% and 50% black) in 1980 remained so a decade later (Ellen 2000, p. 1).

Both studies find that stably integrated communities tend to be economically diverse, including middle-class, college-educated homeowners with professional occupations, as well as low-income families in entry-level, service-sector jobs. This economic diversity tends to reflect the presence of varied housing opportunities, including rental housing constituting at least 25% of housing units. Integrated communities also tend to have attractive physical characteristics (e.g., good location, architecturally interesting homes, and a secure set of neighborhood amenities), places where cross-racial interaction takes place as part of day-to-day life (e.g., grocery stores, schools, parks, or neighborhood festivals), and strong community-based organizations and social institutions committed to maintaining diversity – either directly or indirectly by addressing communitywide, nonracial service issues (largely schools and safety, but also neighborhood preservation) and/or promoting cross-group dialogue (Ellen 2000; Nyden et al. 1998). Stable integration is also more likely in communities that are more distant from an area's central minority concentration and in areas with smaller overall black populations without an intense racial competition for housing and widespread neighborhood change (Ellen 2000, pp. 153–54). Whether by design or by circumstance, residents of these communities are both aware of and value the diversity of their communities and work to promote and maintain it (Nyden et al. 1998), and they are likely to have more tolerant racial attitudes. Clearly then, future research should increase and expand analyses of the "substantial and increasing minority of neighborhoods that are currently integrated and likely to stay that way for many years" (Ellen 2000, p. 176). The central consideration of Hispanics will be crucial here. Given both the size and heterogeneity of this group, their residential trajectory will have a large effect on overall residential patterns. Their ability to integrate – particularly those who are phenotypically black – may introduce new options for increasing the residential integration of non-Hispanic blacks.

In the dawn of the new millennium, a color line more complex than the one Du Bois described continues to separate our neighborhoods, maintaining our tendency "to see commonly the worst of each other" (Du Bois 1990, p. 121) and thwarting the upward social mobility of a substantial portion of our population. Recent efforts to understand the causes of persisting residential segregation highlight the complexity of our emerging multiethnic world at the same time that they remind us, matter-of-factly, that race still matters. As the dominant group, whites have the luxury of living in relatively affluent, safe neighborhoods with high-quality schools and services, even when their own financial resources are limited. Although recent immigrants may be initially

disadvantaged by low socioeconomic status and limited English proficiency, they can be assured of gradually making their way into neighborhoods comparable to those of whites. As has been the case for much of our history, however, groups racially defined as black continue to face profound barriers to their quest for the American dream.

The agenda for both social science and public policy should also include the articulation of policy responses that are both economically feasible and likely to have wide public appeal. Yinger (1995) offers a set of responses of this type that involve attacking racial disparities through policies that address social and economic outcomes "for which the minority-white disparities are greatest" but are available to all qualified applicants regardless of race. Programs that support and encourage low-income homeownership and/or assist public schools in poor communities are good examples of this. Moreover, given the large number of minorities and the increasing number of whites who are willing to enter integrated communities, programs that support stable integration at all levels of social class should also be pursued. This could include (a) the expansion of Gautreaux-type programs as an alternative to traditional public housing programs, (b) aggressive public relations campaigns and community betterment projects that promote the general attractiveness of integrated neighborhoods, and (c) affirmative marketing and pro-integrative mortgage incentives that encourage blacks to enter predominantly white areas and whites to enter racially mixed neighborhoods (Ellen 2000; Yinger 1995).

The past three decades have witnessed meaningful improvement in whites' racial attitudes and unparalleled expansion of the black middle class. Nonetheless, black-white segregation remains so extreme and its consequences so severe that Denton (1994, p. 74) forcefully concluded "[w]hatever we are now doing to combat residential segregation is not nearly enough and in many cases is not working at all" (see also Glazer 1980; Massey and Denton 1993; Yinger 1995). In places where Hispanics are heavily concentrated, they may soon confront similar circumstances. We have learned a great deal about the dynamics of racial residential segregation during this period and documented significant declines in the degree of residential separation. Continued improvement is crucial if we are to realize our full national potential, and future research should advance the achievement of this most important goal.

REFERENCES

Alba RD, Denton NA, Leung SJ, Logan JR.1995. Neighborhood change under the conditions of mass immigration: the New York City region, 1970–1990. *Int. Migr. Rev.*31(3):625–56.

Alba RD, Logan JR. 1991. Variations on two themes: racial and ethnic patterns in the attainment of suburban residence. *Demography* 28:431–53.

Alba RD, Logan JR. 1992. Analyzing locational attainments: constructing individual-level regression models using aggregate data. *Sociol. Methods Res.* 20:367–97.

Alba RD, Logan JR. 1993. Minority proximity to whites in suburbs: an individual level analysis of segregation. *Am. J. Sociol.* 98(6):1388–427.

Alba RD, Logan JR, Bellair PE. 1994. Living with crime: the implications of racial/ethnic differences in suburban location. *Soc. Forces* 73(2):395–434.

Alba RD, Logan JR, Stults BJ. 2000a. The changing neighborhood contexts of the immigrant metropolis. *Soc. Forces* 79(2):587–621.

Alba RD, Logan JR, Stults BJ. 2000b.How segregated are middle-class African Americans? *Soc. Probl.* 47(4):543–58.

Alba RD, Logan JR, Stults BJ, Marzan G, ZhangW. 1999. Immigrant groups in the suburbs: a reexamination of suburbanization and spatial assimilation. *Am. Sociol. Rev.* 64:446–60.

Anderson E. 1990. *Streetwise: Race, Class, and Change in an Urban Community.* Chicago: Univ. Chicago Press.

Anderson E. 1999. *Code of the Street: Decency, Violence, and the Moral Life of the Inner City.* New York: Norton.

Blumer H. 1958. Race prejudice as a sense of group position. *Pacific Soc. Rev.* 1(1):1–7.

Bobo L. 1989. Keeping the linchpin in place: testing the multiple sources of opposition to residential integration. *Int. Rev. Soc. Psychol.* 2(3):305–23.

Bobo L, Zubrinsky C. 1996. Attitudes toward residential integration: perceived status differences, mere in-group preference, or racial prejudice? *Soc. Forces* 74(3):883–909.

Carr JH, Megbolugbe IF. 1993. The Federal Reserve Bank of Boston study on mortgage lending revisited. *J. Housing Res.* 4(2):277–313.

Caskey J. 1992. Bank representation in low income and minority urban communities. Work. Pap., Res. Div. Fed. Reserve Bank Kansas City.

Charles CZ. 2000. Neighborhood racial composition preferences: evidence from a multiethnic metropolis. *Soc. Probl.* 47(3):379–407.

Charles CZ. 2001. Processes of residential segregation. In *Urban Inequality: Evidence From Four Cities*, ed. A O'Connor, C Tilly, L Bobo, pp. 217–71. New York: Russell Sage.

Charles CZ. 2002. *Comfort zones: immigration, assimilation, and the neighborhood racial-composition preferences of Latinos and Asians.* Paper presented at Annu. Meet. Amer. Soc. Assoc., Chicago.

Clark WAV. 1986. Residential segregation in American cities: a review and interpretation. *Popul. Res. Policy Rev.* 5:95–127.

Clark WAV. 1988. Understanding residential segregation in American cities: interpreting the evidence, a reply to Galster. *Popul. Res. Policy Rev.* 8:193–97.

Clark WAV. 1992. Residential preferences and residential choices in a multiethnic context. *Demography* 29(3):451–66.

Clark WAV. 2002. Ethnic preferences and ethnic perceptions in multi-ethnic settings. *Urban Geogr.* 23(3):237–56.

Crowder KD. 1999. Residential segregation of West Indians in the New York/New Jersey metropolitan areas: the roles of race and ethnicity. *Int. Migr. Rev.* 33:79–113.

Cutler DM, Glaeser EL. 1997. Are ghettos good or bad? *Q. J. Econ.* 112(3):827–72

Cutler DM, Glaeser EL, Vigdor JL. 1999. The rise and decline of the American ghetto. *J. Polit. Econ.* 107(3):455–506.

Dedman B. 1988. The color of money. *Journal, Atlanta Journal Constitution*, May 1–4.

Dedman B. 1989. Blacks turned down for home loans from SandLs twice as often as whites. *Atlanta Journal, Atlanta Journal Constitution,* Jan. 22.

Denton NA. 1994. Are African Americans still hypersegregated? In *Residential Apartheid: The American Legacy,* ed. R Bullard, C Lee, JE Grigsby, pp. 49–79. Los Angeles: UCLA Cent. Afr. Am. Stud.

Denton NA, Massey DS. 1988. Residential segregation of blacks, Hispanics, and Asians by socioeconomic status and generation. *Soc. Sci. Q.* 69:797–817.

Denton NA, Massey DS. 1989. Racial identity among Caribbean Hispanics: the effect of double minority status on residential segregation. *Am. Sociol. Rev.* 54:790–808.

Du Bois WEB. 1990 (1903). *The Souls of Black Folk: Essays and Sketches.* New York: Vintage Books.

Edmonston B, Passel JS. 1992. Immigration and immigrant generations in population projections. *Int. J. Forecast.* 8(3):459–76.

Ellen IG. 2000. *Sharing America's Neighborhoods: The Prospects for Stable Racial Integration.* Cambridge, MA: Harvard Univ. Press.

Emerson MO, Yancey G, Chai KJ. 2001. Does race matter in residential segregation? Exploring the preferences of white Americans. *Am. Sociol. Rev.* 66(6):922–35.

Farley R. 1996a. *The New American Reality: How We Are, How We Got There, Where We Are Going.* New York: Russell Sage.

Farley R. 1996b. Racial differences in the search for housing: Do whites and blacks use the same techniques to find housing? *Hous. Policy Debate* 7:367–86.

Farley R, Fielding EL, Krysan M. 1997. The residential preferences of whites and blacks: a four-metropolis analysis. *Hous. Policy Debate* 8(4):763–800.

Farley R, Frey WH. 1994. Changes in the segregation of whites from blacks during the 1980s: small steps toward a more integrated society. *Am. Sociol. Rev.* 59:23–45.

Farley R, Schuman H, Bianchi S, Colasanto D, Hatchett S. 1978. Chocolate city, vanilla suburbs: Will the trend toward racially separate communities continue? *Soc. Sci. Res.* 7:319–44.

Farley R, Steeh C, Jackson T, Krysan M, Reeves K. 1993. Continued racial segregation in Detroit: chocolate city, vanilla suburbs. *J. Hous. Res.* 4(1):1–38

Farley R, Steeh C, Krysan M, Jackson T, Reeves K. 1994. Stereotypes and segregation: neighborhoods in the Detroit area. *Am. J. Sociol.* 100(3):750–80.

Flippen CA. 2001. Residential segregation and minority home ownership. *Soc. Sci. Res.* 30(3):337–62.

Frey WH, Farley R. 1993. Latino, Asian, and black segregation in multi-ethnic metro areas: findings from the 1990 Census. Res. Rep. Popul. Stud. Cent., Univ. Mich.

Galster GC. 1988. Residential segregation in American cities: a contrary review. *Popul. Res. Policy Rev.* 7:93–112.

Galster GC. 1990. Racial steering in housing markets during the 1980s: a review of the audit evidence. *J. Plan. Educ. Res.* 9:165–75.

Galster GC. 1991. Black suburbanization: Has it changed the relative location of races? *Urban Aff. Q.* 26:621–28.

Galster GC. 1992. Research on discrimination in housing and mortgage markets: assessment and future directions. *Hous. Policy Debate* 3(2):639–83.

Glazer N. 1980. Race and the suburbs. In *The Work of Charles Abrams,* ed. OH Koenigsberger, S Groak, B Bernstein, pp. 175–80. Oxford: Pergamon Press.

Harris DR. 1999. "Property values drop when blacks move in, because …": Racial and socioeconomic determinants of neighborhood desirability. *Am. Sociol. Rev.* 64:461–79.

Harris DR. 2001. Why are whites and blacks averse to black neighbors? *Soc. Sci. Res.* 30(1):100–16.

Heckman JJ. 1998. Detecting discrimination. *J. Econ. Perspect.* 12(2):101–16.

Heckman JJ, Siegelman P. 1993. The Urban Institute Audit Studies: their methods and findings. In *Clear and Convincing Evidence: Measurement of Discrimination in America,* ed. M Fix, RJ Struyk, pp. 187–258, 271–76. Washington, D.C.: Urban Inst. Press.

Jackman MR, Jackman RW. 1983. *Class Awareness in the United States.* Berkeley, CA: Univ. Calif. Press.

Jackman MR, Muha MJ. 1984. Prejudice, tolerance, and attitudes toward ethnic groups. *Soc. Sci. Res.* 6:145–69.

Jackson WE III. 1994. Discrimination in mortgage lending markets as rational economic behavior: theory, evidence, and public policy. In *African Americans and the New Policy Consensus: Retreat of the Liberal State*, ed. ME Lashley, MN Jackson, pp. 157–78. Westport, CT: Greenwood Press.

Jargowsky PA. 1996. *Poverty and Place: Ghettos, Barrios, and the American City.* New York: Russell Sage.

Jargowsky PA, Bane MJ. 1991. Ghetto poverty in the United States, 1970–1980. In *The Urban Underclass*, ed. C Jencks, PE Peterson, pp. 235–73. Washington, D.C.: Brookings Inst.

Jasso G, Rosenzweig M. 1990. *The New Chosen People: Immigrants in the United States.* New York: Russell Sage.

Kirschenman J, Neckerman KM. 1991. "We'd love to hire them, but …": the meaning of race for employers. In *The Urban Underclass*, ed. C Jencks, PE Peterson, pp. 203–32. Washington, D.C.: Brookings Inst.

Krivo LJ, Peterson RD. 1996. Extremely disadvantaged neighborhoods and urban crime. *Soc. Forces* 75:619–48.

Krysan M. 1998. Privacy and the expression of white racial attitudes: a comparison across three contexts. *Public Opin. Q.* 62:506–44.

Krysan M. 2002. Whites who say they'd flee: Who are they, and why would they leave? *Demography* 39(4):675–96.

Krysan M, Farley R. 2002. The residential preferences of blacks: Do they explain persistent segregation? *Soc. Forces* 80:937–80.

Logan JR. 2001a. Ethnic diversity grows, neighborhood integration lags behind. Rep. Lewis Mumford Cent. Comp. Urban Reg. Res.

Logan JR. 2001b. The new ethnic enclaves in America's suburbs. Rep. Lewis Mumford Cent. Comp. Urban Reg. Res.

Logan JR, Alba RD. 1993. Locational returns to human capital: minority access to suburban community resources. *Demography* 30(2):243–68.

Logan JR, Alba RD. 1995. Who lives in affluent suburbs? Racial differences in eleven metropolitan regions. *Sociol. Focus* 28(4):353–64.

Logan JR, Alba RD, Leung S-Y. 1996. Minority access to white suburbs: a multiregional comparison. *Soc. Forces* 74(3):851–81.

Logan JR, Alba RD, Zhang W. 2002. Immigrant enclaves and ethnic communities in New York and Los Angeles. *Am. Sociol. Rev.* 67:299–322.

Logan JR, Schneider M. 1984. Racial segregation and racial change in American suburbs, 1970–1980. *Am. J. Sociol.* 89(4):874–88.

Massey DS. 1995. The new immigration and ethnicity in the United States. *Popul. Dev. Rev.* 21(3):631–52.

Massey DS, Bitterman B. 1985. Explaining the paradox of Puerto Rican segregation. *Soc. Forces* 64(2):306–31.

Massey DS, Condran GA, Denton NA. 1987. The effect of residential segregation on black social and economic well-being. *Soc. Forces* 66:29–57.

Massey DS, Denton NA. 1985. Spatial assimilation as a socioeconomic outcome. *Am. Sociol. Rev.* 50:94–106.

Massey DS, Denton NA. 1987. Trends in the residential segregation of blacks, Hispanics, and Asians: 1970–1980. *Am. Sociol. Rev.* 52(6):802–25.

Massey DS, Denton NA. 1989. Hypersegregation in U.S. metropolitan areas: black and Hispanic segregation along five dimensions. *Demography* 26(3):373–91.

Massey DS, Denton NA. 1993. *American Apartheid: Segregation and the Making of the Underclass.* Cambridge, MA: Harvard Univ. Press.

Massey DS, Fischer MJ. 1999. Does rising income bring integration? New results for blacks, Hispanics, and Asians in 1990. *Soc. Sci. Res.* 28:316–26.

Massey DS, Fischer MJ. 2002. *The Long Term Consequences of Segregation.* Paper presented at Ann. Meet. Popul. Assoc. Am., Atlanta.

Massey DS, Lundy G. 2001. Use of black English and racial discrimination in urban housing markets: new methods and findings. *Urban Aff. Rev.* 36(4):452–69.

Metcalf GR. 1988. *Fair Housing Comes of Age.* New York: Greenwood.

Meyer SG. 2000. *As Long as They Don't Live Next Door: Segregation and Racial*

Conflict in American Neighborhoods. New York: Rowman and Littlefield.

Morenoff JD, Sampson RJ 1997. Violent crime and the spatial dynamics of neighborhood transition: Chicago, 1970–1990. *Soc. Forces* 76:31–64.

Munnell AH, Tootell GMB, Browne LE, McEneaney J. 1996. Mortgage lending in Boston: interpreting HMDA data. *Am. Econ. Rev.* 86(1):25–53.

Myrdal G. 1972 (1944). *An American Dilemma: The Negro Problem and Modern Democracy.* New York: Random House.

Nyden P, Lukehart J, Maly MT, Peterman W, eds. 1998. Racially and ethnically diverse urban neighborhoods. In *Cityscape* 4(2):1–28, 261–69.Washington, D.C.: US Dep. Hous. Urban Dev.

Oliver ML, Shapiro TM. 1995. *Black Wealth/White Wealth: A New Perspective on Racial Inequality.* New York: Routledge.

Ondrich J, Stricker A, Yinger J. 1998. Do real estate brokers choose to discriminate? Evidence from the 1989 housing discrimination study. *South. Econ. J.* 64(4):880–902.

Patterson O. 1997. *The Ordeal of Integration: Progress and Resentment in America's Racial Crisis.* Washington, D.C.: Civitas.

Pattillo-McCoy M. 1999. *Black Picket Fences: Privilege and Peril Among the Black Middle Class.* Chicago: Univ. Chicago Press.

Portes A, Rumbaut RG. 1996. *Immigrant America:A Portrait.* Berkeley, CA: Univ. Calif. Press.

Purnell T, Idsardi W, Baugh J. 1999. Perceptual and phonetic experiments on American English dialect identification. *J. Lang. Soc. Psychol.* 18(1):10–30.

Rosenbaum E. 1994. The constraints on minority housing choices, New York City 1978–1987. *Soc. Forces* 72(3):725–47.

Rosenbaum E. 1996. The influence of race on Hispanic housing choices, New York City, 1978–1987. *Urban Aff. Rev.* 32(2):217–43.

Rubinowitz LS, Rosenbaum JE. 2000. *Crossing the Class and Color Lines: From Public Housing to White Suburbia.* Chicago: Univ. Chicago Press.

Sampson RJ, Wilson WJ. 1995. *Toward a Theory of Race, Crime and Urban Inequality.* In *Crime and Inequality,* ed. J Hagen, RD Peterson, pp. 37–54. Stanford, CA: Stanford Univ. Press.

Squires GD, Kim S. 1995. Does anybody who works here look like me?: mortgage lending, race, and lender employment. *Soc. Sci. Q.* 76(4):823–38.

Taeuber KE, Taeuber AF. 1965. *Negroes in Cities: Residential Segregation and Neighborhood Change.* West Hanover, MA: Atheneum.

Thernstrom S, Thernstrom A. 1997. *America in Black and White: One Nation, Indivisible.* New York: Simon and Schuster.

Timberlake JM. 2000. Still life in black and white: effects of racial and class attitudes on prospects for residential integration in Atlanta. *Sociol. Inq.* 70(4):420–45.

Timberlake JM. 2002. Separate, but how unequal? Ethnic residential stratification, 1980 to 1990. *City Community* 1(3):251–66.

Turner MA, Ross SL, Galster GC, Yinger J. 2002. Discrimination in metropolitan housing markets: national results from Phase I HDS 2000. US Dep. Hous. Urban Dev., Washington, D.C.

US Natl. Advis. Comm. Civil Disord. 1988. *The Kerner Report.* New York: Pantheon Books.

Venkatesh SA. 2000. *American Project: The Rise and Fall of a Modern Ghetto.* Cambridge, MA: Harvard Univ. Press.

Waldinger R, Bozorgmehr M. 1996. The making of a multicultural metropolis. In *Ethnic Los Angeles,* ed. R Waldinger, M Bozorgmehr, pp. 3–37. New York: Russell Sage Found.

Waters MC. 1990. *Ethnic Options: Choosing Identities in America.* Berkeley, CA: Univ. Calif. Press.

Waters MC. 1999. *Black Identities: West Indian Immigrant Dreams and American Realities.* New York: Russell Sage Found.

Wilson WJ. 1987. *The Truly Disadvantaged: The Inner City, the Underclass, and Public Policy.* Chicago: Univ. Chicago Press.

Wilson WJ. 1996. *When Work Disappears: The World of the New Urban Poor.* New York: Knopf.

Yinger J. 1993. Audit methodology: comments. In *Clear and Convincing Evidence: Measurement of Discrimination in America*, ed. M Fix, RJ Struyk, pp. 259–70. Washington, D.C.: Urban Inst. Press.

Yinger J. 1995. *Closed Doors, Opportunities Lost: The Continuing Costs of Housing Discrimination.* New York: Russell Sage Found.

Yinger J. 1998. Evidence on discrimination in consumer markets. *J. Econ. Perspect.* 12(2):23–40.

Zubrinsky CL, Bobo L. 1996. Prismatic metropolis: race and residential segregation in the city of the angels. *Soc. Sci. Res.* 25:335–74.

35

"Fair housing and community development: Time to come together"

From *Indiana Law Review* (2008)

Elizabeth K. Julian

INTRODUCTION

Forty years ago, shortly before the passage of the Fair Housing Act, the National Advisory Commission on Civil Disorders, more generally known as the Kerner Commission, famously declared that the country was "moving toward two societies, one black, one white – separate and unequal." The Commission urged, among other things, the enactment of a "comprehensive and enforceable federal open housing law" (Kerner 1968). It recognized, however, that many poor people of color were locked in the ghettos of the inner city by a poverty that had its roots deep in the soil of segregation and that discrimination and prejudice in the public and private housing markets would not abate overnight. The report concluded that "no matter how ambitious or energetic the program, few Negroes now living in central cities can be quickly integrated" and called for large scale "enrichment" of the Black ghetto as an adjunct strategy to address the findings regarding race, housing, and community conditions in America (Kerner 1968).

Two months after the Kerner Commission issued its report and call for action, Congress passed the Fair Housing Act. While the bill was not the "comprehensive and enforceable federal open housing law" urged by the report, the sponsors hoped that its passage would usher in a society in which residential segregation would no longer define American housing patterns and community landscape (Lamb 2005). It was

the last major piece of civil rights legislation of the 1960s and struck at the heart of our attitudes about race: who could live next door (Fair Housing Act 1986) It was long overdue.

However, passage of the Fair Housing Act, which came in the wake of the assassination of Dr. King on April 4, 1968, did not abate white resistance to residential integration (Goering 1986; Bell 2008; Rubinowitz and Shelton 2008; Rubinowitz and Perry 2002; Meyer 2000). Progressives quickly turned to the second recommendation of the Kerner Commission, "enrichment" of the black ghetto, to address the problems that existed in minority communities as a result of Jim Crow (Kerner 1968). During the 1968 presidential campaign, when Robert Kennedy, vying for the Democratic Party nomination, proposed "community development" as a counter to Eugene McCarthy's support for letting minorities move to white areas, it was seen by some as a crass political move (Schlesinger 1978). But it was also a practical and realistic effort to respond to the frustration felt by many blacks who saw their communities struggling with the legacy of segregation: extreme poverty, dilapidated and deteriorating housing stock, inadequate public services, and little or no investment – much less re-investment – by the public or private sectors. Place-based community development initiatives appeared to offer a more empowering way for people of color to deal with the harms of segregation, one that did not require the receptiveness of white people. While it would entail public expenditure, it meant that blacks would be staying where they belonged, and not demanding to come where they did not, i.e., white neighborhoods. For white liberals, it provided a respectable alternative to taking on a fight that was both socially uncomfortable and politically difficult. The modern community development movement was born.

The fundamental rights that the Fair Housing Act explicated were already imbedded in our Constitution and legal rulings before they were recognized by the people's representatives (42 U.S.C. § 1982 (2000); Jones v. Alfred H. Mayer Co., 392 U.S. 409, 1968; Shelley v. Kraemer, 334 U.S. 1 (1948); Lamb 2005). The Fair Housing Act was nevertheless an important statement of national purpose. However, forty years after the passage of the Fair Housing Act, the dream of its sponsors has not been realized. In many ways segregation seems more entrenched than ever, particularly, but not exclusively, for lower income people of color (Goering 1986; Massey and Denton 1993; Briggs 2005). Moreover, discrimination continues to limit housing choice for people of color at every income level (Turner *et al.* 2002).The reasons for that can be debated, but the reality of it cannot. Neither can the relationship between geography and opportunity. Today it is truer than ever that where you live determines what sort of life chances you and, perhaps more importantly, your children will have, and where you live depends a great deal on your race and income (Briggs 2005).

It is at the intersection of race and poverty where the fair housing and community development movements have had their greatest challenges (Massey and Denton 1993; Briggs 2005). Both are progressive movements seeking to address either explicitly or implicitly the negative impact that racial segregation and discrimination had on minority individuals and communities. However, over the past forty years, neither movement has been individually successful in either creating open and inclusive communities of opportunity or making separate equal. At best the movements have seemed to operate in parallel universes and, at worst, have reflected tension and even conflict that belie their common commitment to social and racial justice. That tension is clearly related in part to the perceived inconsistency between the goal of "integration" and the goal of strengthening existing minority communities. But is it also

related to the reality of scarce resources? The fundamental principles of housing choice and equal opportunity appear to collide with the perceived need to focus those scarce resources, particularly federal housing dollars, on community revitalization work. However, this is a false dichotomy. Fair housing and community development are two sides of the same coin. They grew out of the need to address the twin evils of Jim Crow: separate and unequal. It is the thesis of this Article that the two goals are best advanced together.

[…]

I. THE FAIR HOUSING MOVEMENT

> We're going to make this an open city, because it's right. We're going to make it an open city, because it's practical. We're going to make it an open city, because it's sound economics. We're going to make it an open city, because we're tired of being humiliated.
> Rev. Dr. Martin Luther King, Jr. Chicago 1966
> (Breymaier 2007).

The modern fair housing movement, theoretically empowered by passage of the Fair Housing Act, has not made significant strides toward creating a nation of open and inclusive communities of opportunity (Massey and Denton 1993; Schwemm 2007, 2008; Turner 2008). There are, no doubt, many reasons for that, including ambivalence about the goal of racial integration. Certainly, the political environments in which the movement has operated over the past forty plus years and the shortcomings of the Act itself, particularly related to enforcement, contributed as well (Lamb 2005; Massey and Denton 1993). The Act reflected the difficult compromises involved in securing its adoption, and it was never as effective of a tool to promote real residential integration or to deal with the complicated legacy of segregation at the community level as proponents had hoped (Lamb 2005). This has been due, in part, to the relatively singular focus of the fair housing movement on individual acts of discrimination in real estate-related transactions and its failure to effectively collaborate with other community-based social justice efforts in the face of governmental policies that reinforce segregation at every turn (Schwemm 2007; Sidney 2005).

However, the overarching failure has been that of political will. The alchemy of race and housing has seldom produced a politician's finest moments, nor our people's. The failures have been, and continue to be, bi-partisan failures. Segregation by race and income presents the progressive community with one of its greatest challenges, and our response in the coming decades will determine the country we become.

II. THE COMMUNITY DEVELOPMENT MOVEMENT

Despite forty years of work, the investment of considerable public and private resources, and greater political support than the fair housing movement, the community development movement working in low-income minority communities has failed to make separate equal (Lemann 1994). Critics have faulted the community development movement for over-looking the role of race in creating unacceptable living conditions and limited opportunities in many low-income communities (O'Connor 2008). While a plethora of public and private programs and associated resources have "targeted" struggling low-income communities for "revitalization," the conditions in underserved minority neighborhoods were rarely dressed *as legacies of segregation* (Tegeler 2005; Julian 2007). The reluctance to do so and to employ strategies, including litigation, which seek remedies for racial discrimination and the structural conditions that it begat have resulted in the movement's limited effectiveness (Julian 2007). In criticizing the community "revitalization" movement for not taking "structural racism and social class inequality" into account in either defining the problem or formulating solutions, Henry Louis Taylor, Jr. (2001) suggests a new way of thinking about community development. This perspective acknowledges that the adverse conditions in low income communities have often resulted from decades of illegal racial and class-based segregation (Taylor and Cole 2001). Remedies must therefore be structural and comprehensive in nature, and the demand for them must derive its legitimacy from civil rights law, not just moral or political authority (Taylor and Cole 2001).

III. AMIABLE APARTHEID

During the past forty years, the importance of eradicating segregation and the value of living in diverse communities have been challenged and debated. In addition to white attitudes, ambivalent at best and hostile at worst, minority attitudes, which have always rightly found offensive any notion that they must live among whites to be able to access equal opportunity, have increasingly grown tired of the effort – an attitude that Sheryll Cashin describes clearly in her book, *The Failures of Integration* (Cashin 2004). It may be argued that we have not sufficiently/meaningfully attempted integration, but in any event the appetite for dealing with the issue of segregation in the early part of the twenty-first century is not hearty. Despite sometimes sympathetic rhetoric and token efforts, significant segments of the progressive community – including anti-poverty, affordable housing, and environmental advocates, following in the footsteps of their community development counterparts – have not embraced the principle of fair housing and an open society as an essential component of their work (Bullard 1990). Moreover, conservative whites, hardly enthusiastic supporters of the goals of the Fair Housing Act in the first place, have been happy to watch "those people" struggle to deal with the effect of segregation and the structural racism that it begat in "their" communities from across the tracks, the river, the levee, or whatever "natural" divide separates those who have from those who have not, secure in their belief that no political will exists to bridge or breech it (Bullard 1990).

Along with the demographic data that shows our continuing segregated condition (U.S. Census 2002; Briggs 2005), recent academic studies and legal developments have reinvigorated those who would argue that the goal of an integrated society is utopian at best and undesirable or even illegal at worst. The Supreme Court's recent decisions in the Seattle and Kentucky public education cases have, in an almost complete rejection of the heart and soul of *Brown v. Board of Education* (347 U.S. 483 (1954)), limited the most reasonable voluntary tools to address racial segregation in public education. Arguments in the briefs filed by amici curiae on behalf of fair housing and civil rights groups regarding the effects of housing segregation on the ability to desegregate public schools were generally ignored by the Court (*Parents Involved*, 127 S. Ct. 2738 (2007)). The silver lining may be, however, that by erecting barriers to voluntary local efforts to provide desegregated educational opportunities, the Court's decision has put the issue of housing segregation back on the national agenda (Julian 2007).

The recent research of Robert Putnam, based upon an extensive survey taken at the time of the 2000 Census of people living in a range of diverse and homogenous environments, has likewise given succor to those who would declare the goal of an integrated society unworthy (Putnam 2007). Putnam concludes, he says reluctantly, that at least in the "short run" living in a racially and ethnically diverse environment is stressful and difficult (Putnam 2007, 149–151). He finds that such environments result in loss of a sense of community and cause us to withdraw from desirable social interaction to stay at home and watch T.V. (Putnam 2007; Kushner 2008). Not surprisingly, these rather grim research findings have resulted in widespread discussion in the popular media and communication venues suggesting that the national belief in the value of diversity is misplaced. As one major newspaper characterized the Putnam findings: "diversity hurts civic life" (Jonas 2007). Another commentator opined: "Greater Diversity Equals More Misery" (Mercer 2007). While Putnam's research will likely be used in connection with the debate on immigration, it also poses serious issues given our already diverse population and projections that we will become increasingly so regardless of immigration policies (U.S. Minority Business Development Agency 1999). A critique of the conclusions and methodology of the research is beyond the scope of this Article, but a discussion of its implications for fair housing and open communities is not. If we are not currently comfortable living in racially and ethnically diverse environments, does the research suggest that we can never be so? Does it suggest that we would be happy, socially and civically engaged citizens if we were just allowed to retreat to our racial or ethnic enclaves? And, if so, can society choose policies that foster that condition if they only serve to undercut our ideal of a free, open society where people can choose where to live, regardless of race? The

implications of the Putnam research are not so much about the validity of its conclusions about our *present*, which after all capture attitudes toward race less than fifty years after we outlawed official segregation. They are about what sort of *future* we believe is possible. Can we continue to honor the principles of our Constitution and laws, and acknowledge the mistakes of our past, if we embrace segregation as a goal for our future?

Another instance of research being used to argue against policies that support racial and economic integration is found in the recent work on HUD's Moving To Opportunity (MTO) Demonstration (Goering 2005; DeLuca 2007) that concluded that "[a]t least for the children in the Moving to Opportunity experiment, the promise that better neighborhoods would bring greater academic achievement has thus far gone unfulfilled" (Sanbonmatsu *et al.* 2007). These findings again have prompted calls for an end to initiatives that create opportunities for those who are poor to live among those who are not poor (and, implicitly, racial minorities to live among whites) (Hoover Institute 2007). MTO was designed in response to research regarding the effect of the *Gautreaux* housing mobility program in Chicago, part of the remedy in a public housing desegregation lawsuit, Gautreaux v. Chicago Housing Authority (Rosenbaum *et al.* 2005; Institute for Policy Research 2008; Rosenbaum and DeLuca 2008). The Gautreaux program, because it was a remedy in a civil rights lawsuit, was explicitly designed to remedy racial discrimination (Gautreaux, 690 F.2d at 619). Families choosing a housing mobility remedy moved to both lower poverty and non-minority suburban neighborhoods and communities. Unlike Gautreaux, MTO did not include a racial component to the movers' opportunities. Many MTO participants who moved to lower poverty areas continued to live in overwhelmingly minority communities, a point particularly worth noting given the relation of racial geography to opportunity so compellingly set out in The Geography of Opportunity (Briggs 2005). The Gautreaux research gives a more positive picture of the impact on the families, particularly the children, who made a mobility move (Rosenbaum *et al.* 2005). That research, by James Rosenbaum and others, followed families over a much longer period than the MTO experiment and focused on a number of quality of life conditions that improved for movers, including education (Rosenbaum *et al.* 2005).

The rush to declare housing mobility a "failed social policy" based on the limited results from the MTO program, particularly as it relates to providing a remedy to racial segregation, reflects less a policy concern that housing mobility will not succeed than a political concern that it will. There are already indications that such policies might find support in the next (2008) national administration. [...] Indeed, Alex Polikoff, the indefatigable father of *Gautreaux*, has already developed a policy proposal for the next administration to consider that would create a *Gautreaux*-style housing mobility program on a national scale (Polikoff 2005). No doubt the naysayers will continue their efforts to dismiss and discredit efforts to give low income minority families an escape route out of the ghetto; however, conductors on the modern day "Underground Railroad" like Polikoff can be expected to press for such policies as one of the most effective ways to provide relief to individual families who want access to the greater opportunities that exist beyond the borders of the ghetto.

It remains to be seen how best to respond to the challenges these developments present. Advocates and others in the progressive community who find abandoning the goal of an open inclusive society unacceptable and unsupportable need to be more engaged and aggressive in stating that position. Advocates who recognize that conditions in low-income communities are often vestiges of segregation should insist that the nation not move on until it effectively addresses that legacy. It is especially important that advocates from the fair housing and community development movements overcome their longstanding divide in order to ensure that a new strain of an old disease does not take hold in our body politic.

IV. THE BATTLEGROUND: LOW-INCOME HOUSING

The tensions between fair housing/civil rights and community development often play themselves out in the realm of low-income housing policy. Despite barriers that have been removed to housing choice and opportunity for more affluent people of color over the past forty years, low-income families of color continue to be dependent upon public policy decisions about where they can live. In recent years these tensions and conflicts have surfaced in the policy discussions and advocacy work surrounding public housing and the low-income housing tax credit program, as well as in the context of zoning and other local land use policies.

The public housing program, which began in 1937, was expanded and institutionalized in 1949 (HUD 2007). The program continues to provide affordable housing to very low-income people in communities throughout the country. Public housing's current incarnation is most visible in the HOPE VI program that provides funds for the transformation of public housing using a mixed income housing model (HOPE VI 2008). The Low Income Housing Tax Credit program (LIHTC) was first authorized by Congress in 1987 and has financed approximately 1.5 million units of affordable housing nationwide using a tax incentive-based, private development and management approach (HUD 2008). Both are housing programs, but have increasingly come to be viewed as instruments of community development. Both have also perpetuated, rather than ameliorated, existing housing and community segregation, despite the mandates of the Fair Housing Act that federal housing and community development programs "affirmatively further fair housing" (Exec. Order No. 12892 1994; 42 U.S.C. § 3608 2000).

A. Public housing/HOPE VI

The role of federal housing policy in creating a public housing system that is both separate and unequal has been the subject of extensive litigation and academic and political commentary (Roisman 2005). However, effective remedies for those conditions continue to evade both advocates and public policy makers.

During the Clinton Administration, efforts were made to affirmatively further fair housing when resolving civil rights litigation against federal and local housing agencies, albeit with limited success (Julian 2004). These initiatives sought to transform the ghetto conditions in public housing communities, expand housing opportunities by deconcentrating the location of public housing, and create more choices through the administration of the voucher program (Julian 2004). Civil rights advocates successfully litigated and argued that continuation of the status quo with regard to low-income housing policy perpetuated prior official segregation and was not only bad policy, but also unconstitutional (Roisman 2007). Remedies negotiated by the plaintiffs and HUD focused on increasing housing choices and addressing the large public housing projects that were built to segregate and had deteriorated to the point that they blighted communities and destroyed lives (Roisman 2007).

The litigation settlements evolved alongside the policy imperative of expansion of the voucher program and public housing transformation, most visibly in the implementation of the HOPE VI Program (Julian 2007). The story of HOPE VI is a story of improved housing opportunities and revitalized communities, but it is also a story of broken promises, missed opportunities, outright failures, and bad faith. Rather than using the HOPE VI program to remedy the harmful legacy of segregation that public housing represented, the program became the vehicle by which many local communities and developers sought to implement a revitalization strategy without sufficient regard to what happened to the people who were displaced. In other communities, the HOPE VI process was used to continue the containment of low-income minority families in segregated conditions by rebuilding as much housing as possible on sites in blighted communities. Despite an undisputed need for such housing, policymakers refused to insure that all housing units being demolished for "revitalization" purposes were replaced, opting instead for a strategy that both reduced the low-income housing inventory and perpetuated segregation (Popkin and Cunningham 2005).

[...]

While an in-depth discussion of New Orleans public housing debate following the Katrina disaster is beyond the scope of this Article, that situation highlights the need to realize a more equitable, expansive vision for the future of low-income housing. Stacy Seicshnaydre, founder of the Greater New Orleans Fair Housing Center and professor at the Tulane University School of Law, has written a compelling piece, entitled "The More Things Change, the More They Stay the Same: In Search of a Just Public Housing

Policy Post-Katrina" (Seicshnaydre 2007). In the article, Seicshnaydre pleads with those who are truly concerned about the future of New Orleans public housing and its residents, past and future, to embrace a more just and more demanding vision for low-income housing in the New Orleans region. The fundamental issue in New Orleans today, and in the public housing debate in general, is whether segregation is a problem that must or even should be addressed at the national level. Before the passage of the 1949 Housing Act, the argument made against addressing segregation was one of postponement – get the housing now, and we can integrate it later (Julian and Daniel 1989). Today, that argument is being supplanted by the contention that concerns about segregation are out of date and that the value of integration and diversity in contemporary American culture is open to serious question. This is an opportunity for civil rights/fair housing advocates and community development/low-income housing advocates to find common ground and support policies that do not repeat the mistakes of the past, but rather address them with a new vision and vigor.

B. LOW INCOME HOUSING TAX CREDIT PROGRAM

The Low Income Housing Tax Credit Program ("LIHTC program") is the leading source of new housing units for low-income families (Roisman 1998; Freeman 2004). It is also the most recent example of the federal government's failure to incorporate fair housing principles in the administration of a low-income housing program (Roisman 1998). The LIHTC program was initiated long after the passage of the Fair Housing Act and in full light of the growing awareness of the role that federal housing policy played in creating and exacerbating housing segregation for low-income families. Despite that knowledge, there has been virtually no effort to ensure that the LIHTC program does not continue to perpetuate segregation, and criticism of the program on those grounds has been growing over the past fifteen years (Roisman 1998). While the tax credit agencies are not required to maintain civil rights related data regarding the developments, available information suggests that in many places the LIHTC program is continuing the pattern of concentrating developments in high poverty, predominately minority areas or failing to ensure that units built in non-minority areas are available to low-income minority families (Roisman 1998). For those familiar with the history of public housing, it is a new version of an old story.

As finally happened with public housing, litigation has begun to challenge the administration of the LIHTC program for perpetuation of segregation and failure to affirmatively further fair housing as required by the Fair Housing Act. In New Jersey, fair housing advocates challenged the State's Qualified Allocation Plan (U.S.C.A. § 42(m)(1)(B) 2007) for failing to affirmatively further fair housing by concentrating housing finance agencies that set out tax credit units in the predominantly minority urban areas, thereby perpetuating the historic residential segregation (N.J. Super. Ct. App. Div. 2004). Community based organizations and others active on low-income housing issues (such as the Local Initiatives Support Corporation, known as LISC) came to the State's defense. They argued that tax credits should be used as tools of community development and given to inner city non-profits rather than to developers who would produce units for occupancy in the whiter, more affluent, and higher opportunity suburbs (N.J. Super. Ct. App. Div. 2004). The New Jersey Superior Court struck down the challenge, deferring to the state housing finance agency's determination about how to allocate credits in a way that "affirmatively further[s]" fair housing. To date, a federal court has not spoken on the issue of the LIHTC program's obligations under the Fair Housing Act, but there is every indication that further litigation is planned, which will remedy that lack of perspective. Recognizing that it is now the primary vehicle for the production of affordable housing units, national and local civil rights advocates have turned their attention to the LIHTC program, after years of urging by a few visionary scholar/advocates who understand the implications of this important program for addressing the difficult problem of segregation.

The debate continues about the responsibilities of the public housing and LIHTC programs under the Fair Housing Act and other civil rights laws. This debate provides an important opportunity for fair housing, civil rights, low-income housing, and community development advocates to develop a unified agenda to provide housing in higher opportunity areas as well as in areas where the provision of such resources will further the revitalization of a community and prevent unwelcome displacement. This sort of balance was urged upon the court by the Institute for Social Justice in New Jersey in its very persuasive amicus brief before the New Jersey Supreme Court (848 A.2d 1 (No.A-10–02T2)). Such an approach would build upon the work of those who, in many ways, should be natural allies in pursuing racial justice and equal opportunity in low-income housing. The policies must acknowledge the role that race has played in the challenges faced by low-income people of color and the communities in which they live. They must not assume that the people affected are monolithic in the choices they will make or the paths that they wish to take, today or for the next generation. Those who consider themselves part of the fair housing, low-income housing, and community development movements should come together on this pivotal issue to stand up for the rights of low-income people of color in hope of providing them real and effective choices about where they live, who they live with, and the opportunities that those choices bring.

V. COMING TOGETHER

Why, one might ask, should we? In a world of limited resources, every dollar spent to open an exclusive white suburb is one less dollar spent to improve or protect an existing minority neighborhood or community and vice versa. It is true that resources dedicated to addressing the evils of racism and poverty are, of course, particularly scarce. However, during the past forty years the divided fair housing and community development movements have not succeeded in either dismantling the vestiges of segregation in communities of color or in creating an open and inclusive society. These movements have just causes that are best advanced together (Marcantonio. 1956). If the deal is implicitly made that addressing the vestiges of segregation in minority neighborhoods will keep people of color out of white neighborhoods, it is a deal that should fail. If the deal is implicitly made that making resources available for housing mobility and choice can excuse the neglect of minority communities, or permit gentrification and "disperse" people regardless of their wishes, it is a deal that should fail. Finally, if the deal is that "we'll take the east side and you can take the west side," such racial partitioning of our nation's people and geography is inconsistent with our highest ideals and most concrete promises, and it should fail.

As the above discussion suggests, one of the most effective replacements for old de jure segregationist strictures has been local land use policy in the form of zoning ordinances and similar municipal laws (Kushner 2008; Roisman 2001; Troutt 2008). While neutral on their face, they are as effective, and perhaps even more effective than their predecessor laws, in effectuating racial exclusion, racial containment, and racial oppression (Huntington Branch NAACP v. Town of Huntington 488 U.S. 15 1988; Metro Housing Corp. v. Arlington Heights 558 F.2d 1283 (7th Cir. 1977); Miller. v. City of Dallas, WL 230834 2002). Some communities may forbid multifamily development altogether, or use density standards or design requirements to price affordable development out of the municipality. Other communities use zoning and land use policies to continue the placement of undesirable uses, such as landfills and other environmental hazards, in low-income minority communities, while protecting predominately white communities from such impacts, or to ensure that the housing stock in minority communities is kept modest, while allowing growing white communities to use lot size and other policies to ensure that their tax base grows, and their population is affluent. Place-based community development corporations generally do not challenge these local laws because the policies either exist in places where community development corporations do not operate and will not go, or the cost of legal challenges, both financial and political, is beyond their capacity. Fair housing organizations also leave these conditions unchallenged because the policies involve systemic structures of racial exclusion and are not about individual acts of discrimination. As a consequence, neither movement is currently positioned to make real change. That can be overcome, but it will require that the community development and fair housing movements, along with their more muscled affordable housing and civil rights advocates at the national level, come together to forge a common agenda to address these challenges (Blackwell and Bell 2005).

Such an agenda must be based upon the belief that people who live in this country have the right to live where they choose and to access opportunity wherever it can be found, unlimited by de jure or de facto assumptions about race. We must invest in the difficult task of creating inclusive communities of opportunity, and truly take seriously the Fair Housing Act mandate to "affirmatively further fair housing" in every aspect of our housing and community development work. Many might suggest that the urgency surrounding the continued devastating impact of poverty, environmental degradation, and the very real affordable housing crisis may have made the issue of segregation seem too controversial to take on and that "fair housing" is a baggage that those issues cannot afford to carry; however, these conceptions are wrong. Housing is more than shelter and there is a racial dimension at work in all those areas. Housing can be an instrument of social containment and oppression or a means to access opportunity, security, and wealth. While poverty afflicts people of all races, the debilitating effects of concentrated poverty are not visited upon poor whites to the same degree as upon low income people of color, and the communities in which poor whites live are not marred by the same sort of indicators of "distress" as those in which poor people of color reside (Houk *et al.* 2007).

However, even if one believes that "separate" can be "equal" and is a more desirable social organizing principle, opportunities in our nation still depend greatly on where one lives, and where one lives depends greatly on one's race. Fair housers should join community development practitioners in making the unequal conditions and mistreatment of minority communities a civil rights issue, and demanding a remedy in the statehouse and the courthouse. People of color, particularly those who find themselves at the intersection of race and poverty, should be able to access the opportunities that already exist in more racially diverse or white communities and should be supported in that choice. Failure to help low-income people of color in asserting that right does not strengthen the community development movement and indeed will only perpetuate the injustice it seeks to overcome.

CONCLUSION

America is growing more diverse by the day. Individuals cannot be forced to stay in or return to their respective racial enclaves in order to capture the range of social and financial capital that such an arrangement might provide, however attractive that might seem from a community development perspective. In spite of all odds, and for many reasons, people will continue to choose to live outside their racial and economic comfort zone if provided the opportunity. Those choices must be supported, and we must build a theory of community that values those choices.

The legal and moral imperative of fair housing is real and can be put to effective use as part of a combined fair and affordable housing and equitable community development agenda. Fair housing, affordable housing, and community development activists can continue to fight over the small pie that is currently available to feed our hunger for racial and social justice, or they can come together to demand a bigger pie that can be distributed more equitably. The current political environment should be receptive to the agenda of social justice advocates able to find common ground on the issues of fair housing and community development that will finally erase the vestiges of segregation. For that reason, fair housing/civil rights and community development/affordable housing advocates should come together and begin to build their respective movements anew on a foundation that respects and supports the other's core values. They must understand their dual histories, including where goals have diverged and why, and how they can become stronger by coming together around an agenda that deals honestly but optimistically with the issue of race.

As advocates seek to preserve old communities or build new ones, they should commit themselves to the principle that those communities must be inclusive, and find ways to make such a proposition less threatening. These ultimately are not legal challenges, though legal tools will continue to be useful. They are personal and group challenges to our own identities and call upon our individual and collective sense of responsibility and possibility. A community development movement that embraces fair housing as a meaningful component of its mission will be a more powerful and effective movement going forward. A fair housing movement that recovers its birthright, and moves from the fringes to the forefront of the battle for a truly open society of equal opportunity, will be more powerful and relevant going forward. These social justice movements can unite around a commitment to equal opportunity for all, created through access to safe neighborhoods, affordable housing, good schools, jobs, and a healthy environment in open, equitably developed, and inclusive communities. It is a vision and a goal worthy of our future.

REFERENCES

Bell, Jeannine. 2008. The Fair Housing Act and Extralegal Terror, 41 *Indiana Law Review* 537, 545–46.

Blackwell, Angela Glover and Judith Bell. 2005. Equitable Development for a Stronger Nation: Lessons from the Field, in *The Geography Of Opportunity: Race and Housing Choice in Metropolitan America*, Xavier de Souza Briggs, ed., Washington, D.C. Brookings Institution, at 289, 289.

Breymaier, Rob. 2007. Affirmative Furthering of Fair Housing: The 21st Century Challenge, *Poverty & Race*, May–June, at 10, 10.

Briggs, Xavier de Souza, ed. 2005. *The Geography Of Opportunity: Race and Housing Choice in Metropolitan America*, Washington, D.C. Brookings Institution.

Bullard, Robert D. 1990. *Dumping In Dixie: Race, Class, And Environmental Quality*. Westview Press. Chapter 1, Environmentalism and Social Justice, available at http://www.ciesin.org/docs/010-278/010-278chpt1.html.

Cashin, Sheryll. 2004. *The Failures Of Integration*. New York: Public Affairs, at 17–28.

DeLuca, Stefanie. 2007. All Over the Map: Explaining Educational Outcomes of the Moving to Opportunity Program, *Education Next*, 7, 4, at 28–36, available at http://media.org/documents/edunext_200 74_28.pdf.

Executive Order No. 12892, 59 Fed. Reg. 2939 (January 17, 1994).

Freeman, Lance. 2004. *Siting Affordable Housing: Location and Neighborhood*

Trends of Low Income Housing Tax Credit Developments in the 1990s, at 2, available at http://www.brookings.edu/~/media/Files/rc/reports/2004/04metropolitanpolicy_freeman/20040405_Freeman.pdf.

Goering, John M. 1986.Introduction to *Housing Desegregation and Federal Policy* 9, 9 (John M. Goering ed.) University of North Carolina Press.

Goering, John M. 2005. Expanding Housing Choice and Integrating Neighborhoods: The MTO Experiment, in *The Geography Of Opportunity: Race and Housing Choice in Metropolitan America*, Xavier de Souza Briggs, ed., Washington, D.C. Brookings Institution.

HOPE VI (2008) Homeownership and Opportunity for People Everywhere Program (HOPE VI Program), 42 U.S.C.A. § 1437v (West 2003 and Supp. 2007).

Hoover Institute. 2007. Relocating Poor Families to More-Affluent Neighborhoods Doesn't Necessarily Lead to Improved Student Achievement. August 14, http://www.hoover.org/publications/ednext/9126936.html.

Houk, Diane L., Erica Blake, and Fred Freiberg. 2007. Increasing access to low-poverty areas by creating mixed-income housing, 82–85, available at: http://www.helpusa.org/fhjc_files/Entire_Report.pdf.

HUD (U.S. Department of Housing and Urban Development). 2007. HUD Historical Background, http://www.hud.gov/offices/adm/about/admguide/history.cfm (last visited April 9, 2008).

Institute for Policy Research, Northwestern University. 2008. *IPR Research on Gautreaux and Other Housing Mobility Programs*, http://www.northwestern.edu/ipr/publications/Gautreaux.html (last visited Apr. 9, 2008);

Jonas, Michael, 2007. The Downside of Diversity, *Boston Globe*, August 5, at D1.

Julian, Elizabeth K. 2004. "Deconcentration" as Policy: HUD and Housing Policy in the 1990s, in *The NIMBY Report, Deconstructing "Deconcentration"* 5, 6–8 (March).

Julian, Elizabeth. 2007. An Unfinished Agenda: Why It's Time for Fair Housing and Community Development to Reunite to Fight the Vestiges of Segregation, *Shelterforce*, issue 152.

Julian, Elizabeth K. and Michael M. Daniel. 1989. Separate and Unequal: The Root and Branch of Public Housing Segregation, *Clearinghouse Review*, 23: 666, 668–71.

Kerner Commission. 1968. *Report Of The National Advisory Commission On Civil Disorders*. Washington, D.C.: U.S. Government Printing Office.

Kushner, James A. 2008. Urban Neighborhood Regeneration and the Phases of Community Evolution After World War II in the United States, 41 *Indiana Law Review* 575, 599–600.

Lamb, Charles M. 2005. *Housing Segregation In Suburban America Since 1960*, New York: Cambridge University Press, at 47–50.

Lemann, Nicholas. 1994. The Myth of Community Development, *New York Times*, January 9, at § 6, 27.

Marcantonio, Vito, Annette T. Rubinstein, ed. 1956. *I Vote My Conscience: Debates, Speeches and Writings of Vito Marcantonio 1935–1950*, New York: Vito Marcantonio Memorial, at 307–08.

Massey, Douglas S., and Nancy A. Denton. 1993. *American Apartheid: Segregation and The Making Of The Underclass*, Cambridge: Harvard University Press.

Mercer, Ilana. 2007. Greater Diversity Equals More Misery; Harvard Political Scientist Robert Putnam Has Found That Diversity Is Not a Strength, but a Weakness, *Orange County Register*, July 22, http://www.ocregister.com/opinion/putnam-diversity-social-1781099-racial-greater.

Meyer, Stephen Grant. 2000. *As Long As They Don't Move Next Door: Segregation And Racial Conflict In American Neighborhoods*. Lanham: Rowman and Littlefield.

O'Connor, Alice. 2008. *Historical Perspectives on Race and Community Revitalization*, Aspen Institute, http://www.aspeninstitute.org/atf/cf/%7BDEB6F227-659B-4EC88F84-8DF23CA704F5%7D/9OConnor.pdf.

Polikoff, Alex. 2005. A Vision for the Future: Bringing *Gautreaux* to Scale, in *Keeping the Promise: Preserving and Enhancing Housing Mobility in the Section 8 Housing Choice Voucher Program* 137, 141–50, Phillip Tegeler, Mary Cunningham, and Margery Austin Turner, eds., available at http://www.prac.org/pdf/KeepingPromise. pdf.

Popkin, Susan J. and Mary K. Cunningham. 2005. Beyond the Projects: Lessons from Public Housing Transformation in Chicago, in *The Geography Of Opportunity: Race and Housing Choice in Metropolitan America*, Xavier de Souza Briggs, ed., Washington, D.C. Brookings Institution.

Putnam, Robert D. 2007. E Pluribus Unum: Diversity and Community in the Twenty-first Century, 30 *Scandinavian Political Studies* 137.

Roisman, Florence Wagman. 1998. Mandates Unsatisfied: The Low Income Housing Tax Credit Program and the Civil Rights Laws, 52 *University of Miami Law Review* 1011, 1012 n.1 (1998) (citing U.S. Gen. Accounting Office, Tax Credits: Opportunities to Improve Oversight of the Low Income Housing Program Sec. 2 (Mar. 1997)).

Roisman, Florence Wagman. 2001. Opening the Suburbs to Racial Integration: Lessons for the 21st Century, 23 *Western New England Law Review* 65, 92–95.

Roisman, Florence Wagman. 2005. Keeping the Promise: Ending Racial Discrimination and Segregation in Federally Financed Housing, 48 *Howard Law Journal 913*, 913–16.

Roisman, Florence Wagman. 2007. Affirmatively Furthering Fair Housing in Regional Housing Markets: The Baltimore Public Housing Desegregation Litigation, 42 *Wake Forest Law Review* 333, 336–46.

Rosenbaum, James E., and Stefanie DeLuca. 2008. What Kinds of Neighborhoods Change Lives? The Chicago Gautreaux Housing Program and Recent Mobility Programs, 41 *Indiana Law Review* 653, 659–62.

Rosenbaum, James, Stefanie DeLuca, and Tammy Tuck. 2005. New Capabilities in New Places: Low-Income Black Families in Suburbia, in *The Geography Of Opportunity: Race and Housing Choice in Metropolitan America*, Xavier de Souza Briggs, ed., Washington, D.C. Brookings Institution, at 150, 156.

Rubinowitz, Leonard S., and Imani Perry. 2002. Crimes Without Punishment: White Neighbors' Resistance to Black Entry. 92 *Journal of Criminal Law and Criminology* 335.

Rubinowitz, Leonard S., and Kathryn Shelton. 2008. Non-Violent Direct Action and the Legislative Process: The Chicago Freedom Movement and the Federal Fair Housing Act, 41 *Indiana Law Review* 663.

Sanbonmatsu, Lisa. Jeffrey R. Kling, Greg J. Duncan, and Jeanne Brooks-Gunn. 2007. New Kids on the Block: Results from the Moving to Opportunity Experiment, *Education Next*, Fall, at G1, G2 available at http://media.hoover.org/documents/ednext_20074_60.pdf.

Schlesinger, Arthur M., Jr. 1978. *Robert Kennedy and his Times*, Boston: Houghton Mifflin, at 910–11.

Schwemm, Robert G. 2007. Why Do Landlords Still Discriminate (And What Can Be Done About It)?, 40 *John Marshall Law Review* 455, 456–57, 471.

Schwemm, Robert G. 2008. Cox, Halprin and Discriminatory Municipal Services Under the Fair Housing Act, 41 *Indiana Law Review* 717, 718 n.4, 718–19.

Seicshnaydre, Stacy E. 2007. The More Things Change, the More They Stay the Same: In Search of a Just Public Housing Policy Post-Katrina, *Poverty & Race*, September–October at 3.

Sidney, Mara S. 2005. Fair Housing and Affordable Housing Advocacy: Reconciling the Dual Agenda, in *The Geography Of Opportunity: Race and Housing Choice in Metropolitan America*, Xavier de Souza Briggs, ed., Washington, D.C. Brookings Institution, at 266–67.

Taylor, Henry Louis Jr., and Sam Cole. 2001. *Structural Racism and Efforts To Racially Reconstruct The Inner-City Built Environment*, University of Buffalo Center for Urban Studies, http://www.thecyberhood.net/documents/papers/taylor01.pdf.

Tegeler, Philip D. 2005. The Persistence of Segregation in Housing Programs, in *The Geography Of Opportunity: Race and Housing Choice in Metropolitan America*, Xavier de Souza Briggs, ed., Washington, D.C. Brookings Institution, at 203–05.

Troutt, David D. 2008. Katrina's Window: Localism, Resegregation, and Equitable Regionalism, 55 *Buffalo Law Review* 1109, 1141–71.

Turner, Margery Austin. 2008. Limits on Housing and Neighborhood Choice: Discrimination and Segregation in U.S. Housing Markets, 41 *Indiana Law Review* 797, 797–800.

Turner, Margery Austin, Stephen L. Ross, George Galster, and John Yinger. 2002. *Discrimination In Metropolitan Housing Markets: National Results From Phase 1 Housing Discrimination Study 2000*, Urban Institute, at 8–1 to –12, available at http://www.huduser.org/publications/hsgfin/phase1.html.

U.S. Census Bureau. *2002. Racial and Ethnic Residential Segregation in the United States: 1980–2000*, at 15, http://www.censusbureau.biz/hhes/www/housing/housing_patterns/pdf/paa_paper.pdf.

U.S. Minority Business Development Agency. 1999. *Dynamic Diversity: Projected Changes in U.S. Race and Ethnic Composition 1995 to 2050*, at 1–3, Washington, D.C.: U.S. Department of Commerce, available at http://www.mbda.gov/documents/unpubtext.pdf.

36
The Future of Fair Housing (2008)

National Commission on Fair Housing and Equal Opportunity

EXECUTIVE SUMMARY

> Injustice anywhere is a threat to justice everywhere. We are caught in an inescapable network of mutuality, tied in a single garment of destiny. Whatever affects one directly, affects all indirectly.
>
> Dr. Martin Luther King, Jr.

That "inescapable network of mutuality" described by Martin Luther King, Jr. begins in our communities. Where we live shapes our lives, our interactions with others, our work life, our health, and our education. Each of us has a role to play in creating communities that are welcoming, safe, and open to all.

Today, this goal is more important than ever because the nation is becoming increasingly diverse. Currently, African Americans, Latinos, Asian Americans and Native Americans make up more than 30 percent of our population. In a few decades, those groups are projected to represent a majority of U.S. residents. These groups represent our future workers, the people whose skills and talents must be harnessed to ensure the nation's economic viability.

Forty years ago, congress passed Title VIII of the Civil Rights Act Of 1968 (the "Fair Housing Act"), which prohibits discrimination in public and private housing markets that is based on race, color, national origin, religion, sex, disability, or familial status. The act requires communities and the federal government to proactively further fair housing, residential integration, and equal opportunity goals; however, equal opportunity in housing remains a major challenge, with collateral impact far beyond four walls and a roof.

That is why the Leadership Conference on Civil Rights/Education Fund, the National Fair Housing Alliance, the NAACP Legal Defense and Educational Fund, and the Lawyers' Committee for Civil Rights Under Law came together to form the National Commission on Fair Housing and Equal Opportunity to investigate the state of fair housing in this 40th anniversary year.

Our seven-member commission was co-chaired by two former U.S. Housing and Urban Development (HUD) Secretaries, The Honorable Jack Kemp, a Republican, and the Honorable Henry Cisneros, a Democrat, confirming that fair housing is not a partisan issue. Over the past six months, we held hearings in five major U.S. cities – Chicago, Houston, Los Angeles, Boston, and Atlanta – to assess our progress in achieving fair housing for all.

The hearings exposed the fact that despite strong legislation, past and ongoing discriminatory practices in the nation's housing and lending markets continue to produce levels of residential segregation that result in significant disparities between minority and non-minority households, in access to good jobs, quality education, homeownership attainment and asset accumulation. This fact has led many to question whether the federal government is doing all it can to combat housing discrimination. Worse, some fear that rather than combating segregation, HUD and other federal agencies are promoting it through the administration of their housing, lending, and tax programs.

We heard testimony from hundreds of witnesses that there are still far too many segregated neighborhoods where skin color determines school quality and economic opportunity; and where municipal services track race and income, rather than need.

The hearings showed us that discrimination continues to be endemic, intertwined into the very fabric of our lives. Ironically, even though more Americans than ever are living in diverse communities, residential segregation remains high. Sustaining the racial and ethnic stability in diverse communities remains a challenge because of perceptions and prejudices that devitalize them. And while nationally the incidence of discrimination is down, there are at least 4 million fair housing violations in our country every year. That is far too many.

Demographics tell the tale.

Today, two-thirds of new households being formed are either racial or ethnic minorities or immigrants. This population is now looking for housing for the first time. In addition, now more than ever, individuals with disabilities are rightfully seeking greater access to opportunities in every sector. Equal opportunity in housing offers the chance to live, work, and interact in richly diverse settings and opens doors to other opportunities – in education, health care and employment.

For all of these reasons, our communities and neighborhoods must reflect a richer, more robust heterogeneity, one that draws on the strengths of all Americans. Everyone recognizes that our nation's ability to achieve any measure of economic, educational, or social justice is tied to our ability to promote fairness in our housing system.

While what we learned about the state of fair housing was sobering, this report is by no means gloomy. We have made progress. The combined efforts of leaders within our communities, fair housing advocates, committed members of the housing industry and government action has ensured that housing opportunities are fairer than they were four decades ago. Most states and many localities have fair housing laws, some of which provide greater protection than the federal Fair Housing Act. The ethical codes of most housing industry groups include a commitment to fair housing, and state real estate licensing laws require fair housing training and continuing education. HUD's 2000 housing discrimination study showed a reduction in the overall discrimination rate in residential sales and information on housing availability, though an increase in racial steering.

And our witnesses did not just testify about problems. People came forward with solutions. All over America, thoughtful advocates, housing experts, and families are working to find ways to build equal opportunity in housing.

Over time, Americans have become more interested in living in communities that are racially and ethnically diverse. Many fair housing organizations are well established and provide a broad range of fair housing services to our communities, including work to build alliances with housing industry groups and local governments to produce quality training and effective outreach, working to build public support for fair housing.

Yet much more is needed.

Equal housing opportunity must be our collective goal. But as recent history has demonstrated, we cannot get there working in silos. Only together, with a mix of education, enforcement, and policy tools, working across partisan lines, with government and private partnerships coordinated at the local, state, regional and federal level, can we begin to make our dreams real.

SUMMARY OF RECOMMENDATIONS

The following is a summary of the recommendations in our report. These recommendations attempt to capture the innovation, ideas, and spirit of change from people from all over the country who are working to make equal opportunity happen for all of us. We believe that the following actions are critical to move us forward toward our vision of creating and sustaining stable, diverse, inclusive neighborhoods across America.

Create an independent fair housing enforcement agency

In order to address the longstanding and systemic problems with fair housing enforcement, we recommend the creation of an independent fair housing enforcement agency to replace the existing fair housing enforcement structure at HUD. Support for an independent fair housing enforcement agency was the most consistent theme of the hearings.

A reformed independent fair housing enforcement agency would have three key components: (1) career staff with fair housing experience and competence as the key criteria for employment; (2) an advisory commission appointed by the president with the advice and consent of the senate that is broadly representative of industry, advocates, and enforcers; and (3) adequate staff and resources to make fair housing a reality. Such an agency would be empowered at the public policy level to work with the HUD secretary to advance proactively all of the fair housing issues that are critical to building stronger communities.

The Government Accountability Office should immediately conduct a study of the options for establishing an independent fair housing agency or commission that would provide national leadership for change on fair housing related issues. The agency would focus solely on fair housing enforcement, required by Section 810 of the Fair Housing Act, 42 U.S.C. §3610, and fair housing and fair lending education. Although this type of structural change is not without costs and challenges, making the agency independent should help restore credibility to the effort in light of the many problems experienced with placement of fair housing enforcement at HUD.

As an interim step to seeking legislation for an independent agency, HUD should act immediately to strengthen its fair housing work by dividing the current office of fair housing and equal opportunity into two offices, separating fair housing enforcement from fair housing program compliance.

The Office of Fair Housing, headed by a Deputy Secretary, would retain sole authority for all aspects of fair housing enforcement and education, including the Fair Housing Initiatives Program, which funds private fair housing groups and fair housing education, and the Fair Housing Assistance Program, which funds state and local enforcement agencies. It would include investigative staff and lawyers to work jointly on strengthened enforcement (including investigations), rapid response to cases requiring immediate attention, and improved training and quality assurance in investigations. The Office of Civil Rights, headed by an Assistant Secretary, would retain internal programmatic and compliance responsibilities for fair housing – including HUD'S responsibility for affirmatively furthering fair housing in its own programs and among HUD grantees and its obligation to enforce other civil rights laws, such as Section

504 of the 1973 Rehabilitation Act and Title VIof the 1964 Civil Rights Act. A third office, the President's Fair Housing Council, would work with both of the new offices in promoting compliance with fair housing.

Revive the President's Fair Housing Council

In order to build, sustain, and grow strong, stable, diverse communities, we need strong federal leadership that coordinates fair housing policy and practice across agencies. In order to accomplish this, we strongly recommend that the President's Fair Housing Council be revived and given a stronger mandate in the new administration. It must be staffed and reconvened as soon as possible – either within HUD or as part of the proposed White House Office of Urban Policy.

All of the federal agencies with responsibility over housing and urban development activities are obligated not only to promote fair housing, but to "*cooperate with the Secretary* [of HUD] to further such purposes" (42 U.S.C. § 3608). This requirement has generally been honored in the breach.

Executive Order 12892 (1994) took this requirement of cooperation one step further, by establishing the President's Fair Housing Council, which is required to "review the design and delivery of federal programs and activities to ensure that they support a coordinated strategy to affirmatively further fair housing." The Fair Housing Council has been severely underutilized, and to our knowledge has only met once. Yet the Council has the potential to go beyond the housing-related agencies delineated in the Fair Housing Act to bring in virtually every other cabinet agency whose work may directly or indirectly affect housing.

The Commission also recommends that the federal agencies participating in the council expressly require collaboration between their grantees at the metropolitan and regional level to support fair housing goals. The collaborative cross-agency work of the Council should be mirrored in every metropolitan area.

The Fair Housing Council, working through federal agencies such as the Department of the Treasury, Department of Education, and financial institution regulators, would play a critical role in coordinating the work of the various federal government agencies that influence housing and lending policy and practice. As a key element of a proposed White House strategy on metropolitan policy, the Fair Housing Council could ensure that fair housing is an integral part of the strategy to rebuild our urban infrastructure and create diverse and thriving regions.

Ensure compliance with the "affirmatively furthering fair housing" obligation

One of the basic principles in the Fair Housing Act and the Housing and Community Development Act of 1974 is that the federal government, and all of its programs and activities, must take proactive steps to advance fair housing, not just to avoid discriminating. Unfortunately, the government and its grantees have not taken this mandate seriously. In order to make this statutory obligation a reality, we must make changes in federal programs and activities to avoid further segregation and promote wider housing choices for families.

Since 1968, the Fair Housing Act has contained a requirement that HUD and other federal agencies engaged in housing and urban development and grantees that they fund, act in an affirmative way to further fair housing. The courts have consistently recognized that this affirmatively furthering duty requires HUD to "do more than simply not discriminate itself; it reflects the desire to have HUD use its grant programs to assist in ending discrimination and segregation, to the point where the supply of genuinely open housing increases."[1]

However, despite the strong statutory underpinning for the affirmatively furthering obligation, the testimony unanimously reported that the process was not functioning as intended. HUD has not been successful in bringing the affirmatively furthering obligation to life.

The federal government's three largest federal housing programs (Section 8, public housing, and the Low Income Housing Tax Credit) serve more than 4.5 million families and yet do very little to further fair housing and, in some cases, work to create and/or maintain segregated housing patterns. These programs must be reoriented to focus, in part, on helping families move to less racially and economically segregated communities.

For example, the Section 8 housing choice voucher program, which creates a portable housing benefit that can be used by an eligible family to rent private apartments in multiple locations, could be reformed to increase access of eligible families to high opportunity communities,[2] by including higher rents where necessary, improving administrative portability of vouchers across jurisdictional lines, re-establishing housing mobility programs to assist voucher-holders seeking to move to higher opportunity areas, creating strong incentives and performance goals for administering agencies, and providing incentives to recruit new landlords into the program. We should mandate that families be provided information and counseling about their range of housing choices, including choices in more integrated areas.

The Low Income Housing Tax Credit (LIHTC) program, administered by the Internal Revenue Service and state housing finance agencies, is the nation's largest low-income housing production program and yet has operated with little or no civil rights oversight since its inception in 1986. This program must be reformed to include fair housing requirements for site selection, affirmative marketing, and reporting of racial/ethnic data to ensure that this program works to further fair housing goals.

Other federal housing initiatives, including HOPE VI, the Community Development Block Grant, the HOME Program, USDA housing programs, and emerging programs such as the National Housing Trust Fund, must also be held to high fair housing standards.

And HUD must do more to stop segregation of people with disabilities within its own housing programs.

With federal leadership that includes a more powerful structure for this affirmatively furthering fair housing concept, communities will be empowered to develop and implement their own coordinated strategies for moving fair housing forward in a way that advances diversity and inclusion in neighborhoods and throughout metropolitan areas.

Strengthen compliance with the affirmatively furthering fair housing obligation by federal grantees

The current federal system for ensuring fair housing compliance by state and local recipients of housing assistance has failed. HUD must reform its current structure by strengthening its leadership in enforcement of the affirmatively furthering obligation.

Currently, HUD only requires that communities that receive federal funds "certify" to their funding agency that a jurisdiction is affirmatively furthering fair housing. HUD requires no evidence that anything is actually being done as a condition of funding, and it does not take adverse action if jurisdictions are directly involved in discriminatory actions or fail to affirmatively further fair housing.

Instead, a regulatory structure must provide guidance and direction to ensure that programs receiving federal funds advance fair housing. A reformed structure should be based on existing guidance in HUD's Fair Housing Planning Guide but expanded to contain specific activities that are required to be undertaken consistent with this report.

HUD must also provide training and technical assistance to support the reformed affirmatively furthering initiative, including training and technical assistance to support groups that will work locally and regionally in communities to advance fair housing principles.

Through regulations, HUD should confirm its authority to undertake reviews of grantees for their compliance with the affirmatively furthering fair housing obligation, and specific sanctions should be spelled out for grantees found to be in non-compliance.

Strengthen the fair housing initiatives program (FHIP)

Funding for the Fair Housing Initiatives Program must be significantly increased. The Fair Housing Initiatives Program was created in the late 1980s to support and fund fair housing enforcement and education across the country. While the program has been an effective change agent in communities, severe funding constraints and an erratic funding stream have limited its usefulness.

Current appropriation levels are grossly inadequate to fund existing private fair housing groups to perform enforcement activities. A full service private fair housing group that successfully competes in FHIP can be awarded no more than $275,000 per year, whether it is located in New York City or Savannah, Georgia.

Although about 140 agencies have received enforcement grants over the past ten years, current funding levels permit many fewer groups to be funded every year to conduct enforcement activities. Only 28 groups in the country received consistent funding over the five year period from FY 2003–2007 and 26 private fair housing groups, including some of the oldest and most respected groups, have closed or are at risk.

Additional funds will allow a significant increase in the presence and effectiveness of the program, increasing the public's awareness about fair housing rights, developing partnerships with industry leaders in communities, supporting increased fair housing enforcement and helping build, or rebuild, diverse communities.

Also, the FHIP program should have eligibility and performance standards established in joint consultation between federal program personnel and private fair housing groups, to ensure that organizations receiving FHIP funds use them effectively.

Adopt a regional approach to fair housing

To make real progress toward equal housing opportunity, all of the jurisdictions within a metropolitan area must be coordinated in their efforts.

The starting point for a comprehensive regional fair housing process begins with fair housing performance goals for each federal housing program and each state and local grantee in a region. Funding of state and local entities through the popular HOME and Community Development Block Grant (CDBG) programs should be conditioned on meeting these goals. Each federal housing program in the region – including Section 8, LIHTC, and public housing – should also be redirected to support a share of specific regional opportunity goals.

A key aspect of this enhanced regional coordination should be to revive a regional planning coordination system such as the federal government's prior "A-95 review process," which required regional planning organizations to develop fair housing plans with specific target performance goals for each major metropolitan area. This process empowered regional planning agencies to review and sign off on federal grants to municipalities for their conformance with the regional plan. Just as the President's Fair Housing Council seeks to coordinate federal activities across agencies to support fair housing, all the agencies operating in a metropolitan area should coordinate their activities, with fair housing as a central component. Implementation of major investments in transportation, employment, education, commercial development, and other infrastructure enhancements should be aligned with fair housing goals, to support and develop diverse, sustainable communities with access to opportunity for all residents of the region.

Ensure that fair housing principles are emphasized in programs addressing the mortgage and financial crisis

The current mortgage crisis has its roots in decades of discriminatory housing and lending practices. Exploitative predatory lending has had its most devastating effects in communities that are predominantly Black and Latino, causing an unprecedented loss of wealth to those communities given this, it is critical that the solutions that have been proposed to address our current mortgage crisis comply with the mandate that all government housing and lending programs affirmatively promote fair housing. In the foreclosure context, this means assessing the racial impacts of alternative plans and seeking approaches that are racially fair – approaches that do not further segregate and isolate low-income communities of color, but rather promote diverse neighborhoods.

In addition, fair lending enforcement by the federal government must be improved by: (1) fostering better coordination between HUD's administrative enforcement of the Fair Housing Act, the Department of Justice, the bank regulatory agencies, and private fair housing groups; (2) prioritizing fair housing and fair lending litigation to identify and eliminate discriminatory predatory lending practices and policies; and (3) ensuring the legal standard for violation of the Fair Housing Act and the Equal Credit Opportunity Act includes the well-established disparate impact standard.

HUD should also implement a special fair lending initiative to fund the investigation and redress of discriminatory practices in the lending sector. This initiative must include an evaluation of programs like the Neighborhood Stabilization Program to ensure that they promote fair housing goals.

Create a strong, consistent, fair housing education campaign

Despite all of the evidence that deeply entrenched discrimination and segregation continue, and the evidence that large parts of our communities are at risk, there has been no national government leadership, and no national message, about the importance of these issues.

HUD should use its direct budget authority to fund basic education and outreach materials, written in easy-to-understand language, in multiple languages, and in accessible formats. These materials should be available in many formats, such as Power Points, videos, fact sheets, public service announcements, and brochures targeted to the different types of consumers of fair housing services.

In particular, the FHIP program should fund a five-year coordinated national multimedia campaign with two components: one that will educate consumers to recognize and report all types of discrimination for all protected classes and to recognize the value of challenging discrimination; and one that will recognize and advance the idea that diverse communities are stronger communities. A five-year program is necessary to achieve real inroads into the reported lack of public knowledge about fair housing and the high numbers of people who are unwilling to challenge housing discrimination. Both campaigns will chip away at stereotypes, an essential element in the plan to promote neighborhood diversity.

Many industry groups have already moved into the area of education. Successful programs can be identified by a reformed fair housing office, replicated, and made available through the internet. The materials must include basic and advanced content. Many housing providers have developed relative sophistication in this area, but many others have not. A variety of different approaches will be needed to reach housing industry representatives of all types, including HUD-funded and tax credit properties.

A revitalized approach to fair housing research will be an important component of a strengthened fair housing presence by developing data and analyzing the effectiveness of strategies to power new approaches to advancing fair housing.

Create a new collaborative approach to fair housing issues

No single agency or approach can change the face of our communities. We must develop and support a new collaborative spirit to bring muscle to the strategies we envision. We can replicate strategic partnerships developed between some real estate associations and private fair housing centers to educate and monitor rental and sales practices and develop partnerships with corporations who support workplace diversity to help create neighborhood diversity. This new approach will search out best practices and the most effective strategies from the housing industry, corporations, state and local governments, and fair housing practitioners and advocates to strengthen our communities. It will seek to involve constituencies at the local level that can bring new ideas and new energy to revitalize and empower our communities to promote residential integration.

Passage of the Fair Housing Act 40 years ago was the beginning, not the end, of our struggle to achieve equality in pursuit of the American dream. We know that our dream cannot be fulfilled without calling on the best and brightest leadership from communities across our country to work with federal, state and local officials from many different offices and perspectives. But we also know that our country cannot reach its fullest potential – one nation, indivisible, with liberty and justice for all – without a national commitment to address injustice and recognize that the success or failure of our communities depends on us all.

Notes

1   *N.A.A.C.P. V. Sec"y Of Housing & Urban Development*, 817 F.2d 149, 155 (1st Cir. 1987) (Breyer, J.)

2   See testimony of john powell (Los Angeles); Kirwan Institute For The Study Of Race And Ethnicity, *The Geography Of Opportunity: Review Of Opportunity Mapping Initiatives* (July 2008) (Los Angeles Exhibit).

Copyright acknowledgements

von Hoffman, Alexander, 'The lost history of urban renewal.' Reprinted with permission from Joint Center of Housing Studies, Harvard University.

Marcuse, Peter, 'Housing policy and the myth of the benevolent state'. Reprinted with permission from *Social Policy*.

Krumholz, Norman, 'The Reluctant Hand'. Reprinted with permission from the author.

Bratt, Rachel, Stone, Michael and Hartman, Chester, 'Why a right to housing is needed and makes sense' and Achtenberg, Emily, 'Federally-assisted housing'. Reprinted with permission from Temple University Press.

Glaeser, Edward and Gyuorko, Joseph, 'How do we know when housing is "affordable"?'. Reprinted with permission from American Enterprise Institute for Public Policy Research.

Tegeler, Philip and Bernstein, Scott, 'Counterpoint'. Reprinted with permission from Shelterforce.

Powell, John, 'Remedial Phase Report of john powell in Thompson v. HUD'. Reprinted with permission from the Kirwin Institute for the Study of Race and Ethnicity, Ohio State University.

Shlay, Anne, 'Low income homeownerships' and Goetz, Edward, 'Housing dispersal programs'. Reprinted with permission from Sage.

Davis, John, 'More than money'. Reprinted with permission from *Journal of Affordable Housing and Community Development Law*.

Rohe, William, van Zandt, Shannon and McCarthy, George, 'The social benefits and costs of homeownership'. Reprinted with permission from the Brookings Institution.

Immergluck, Dan, 'High risk lending and public policy'. Reprinted with permission from Cornell University Press.

O'Regan, Katherine and Quigley, John, 'Federal policy and the rise of nonprofit housing providers'. Reprinted with permission from *Journal of Housing Research*.

Turner, Mary, 'Strengths and weaknesses of the Housing Voucher Program'. Reprinted with permission from The Urban Institute.

Perry, Stuart, 'Federal support for CDCs'. Reprinted with permission from Springer.

Newman, Kathe and Ashton, Philip, 'Neoliberal urban policy and new paths of neighbourhood change in the American inner city'. Reprinted with permission from Pion Ltd.

Davidson, Nestor, 'Reconciling People and Place in Housing and Community Development Policy'. Reprinted with permission from *Georgetown Journal on Poverty Law and Policy*.

Pendall, Rolf, 'Local land use regulation and the chain of exclusion' and Galster, George and Godfrey, Erin, 'By words and deeds'. Reprinted with permission from *Journal of the American Planning Association*.

Nelson, Arthur and Wachter, Susan, 'Growth management and affordable housing policy'. Reprinted with permission from the National Association of Housing and Redevelopment Officials.

Pollack, Stephanie, Bluestone, Barry and Billingham, Chase, 'Neighbourhood change and transit'. Reprinted with permission from Dukakis Center for Urban and Regional Policy, Northeastern University.

Charles, Camille, 'The dynamics of racial residential segregation'. Reprinted with permission from *Annual Review of Sociology*.

National Commission of Fair Housing and Equal Opportunities for 'The Future of Fair Housing'. Reprinted with their permission.

Every effort has been made to contact and acknowledge copyright owners. If any material has been included without permission, the publishers offer their apologies. The publishers would be pleased to have any errors or omissions brought to their attention so that corrections may be published at later printing.

Index

Please note that page references to non-textual content such as illustrations will be in *italics*, while the letter 'n' will follow references to Notes.

Johnson, L.B., 26, 240, 241; Committee on Urban Housing, 31–5; "Crisis of the Cities" message, 32
Joint Center for Housing Studies, 59, 67n, 98
Joseph, M.L., 374–90
Julian, E.K., 528–36

Kaiser, E. F., 33–5, 246
Kaiser Commission on Medicaid and the Uninsured, 117
Kaiser Committee on Urban Housing, 246, 340, 342
Katz, B., 125
Kemeny, J., 155
Kengott, G.F., 82
Kennedy, J.F., 239, 337
Kennedy, M., 329
Kiel, K.A., 408
Killen, S., 137, 148n
King, M.L., 540
Kingsley, G.T., 146n
Kingston, P.W., 172, 205, 206
Kleit, R.G., 380
Knaap, G.-J., 438–51
Knickerbockers (early Manhattan aristocracy), 6
Kozol, J., 56
Kramer, F., 21
Krueckeberg, D.A., 151, 155–65
Krumholz, N., 4, 44–52
Krysan, M., 514
Kutty, N.K., 103, 105, 107n

Lafferty, R.N., 408
Lake Parc Place, Chicago, 380, 381
Lam, J., 198
Lamb, M., 8
land sales and homesteads, 158–9
land use regulations (local), and exclusion, 416–37; adequate public facilities ordinances, 420; Blacks and Hispanics, 433; building permit caps and moratoria, 420, 432; chains of exclusion, 420, 431–4; whether communities with land use controls lose minorities, 424; data and analysis, 422–3; ethical codes, 417; exclusionary land use controls, context, 417–18; whether fewer minorities live in controlled communities in 1980, 423–4; whether housing influences racial composition, 424; housing markets and inclusion, hypotheses, 418; land use controls and housing markets, hypotheses, 419–20; whether land use controls influence housing outcomes, 424;

large-lot zoning, exclusive, 419; low-density-only zoning, 421, 432; previous studies linking, 420–1; research findings, 423–31, 425–6, 428–9, 430–1; research model, 421–31; urban growth boundaries, urban limit lines or greenbelts, 420
Lane, T.S., 80–1, 90, 98, 101
large differences analysis, 467–9
Lawrence, D., 15
Le Play, F., 81
Lea, M., 169
Leach, J., 218
lead poisoning, 55, 66n
Leadership Council for Metropolitan Open Communities, 123, 132
Leased Housing program, 1965, 245
Lees, L., 318
Lehmann Brothers, bankruptcy of, 228
lending: below-market interest rate, 240; exotic loans, 222; high-risk see high-risk lending; originate-to-hold, 226; "predatory," 152, 177, 218; subprime, 152, 177, 214, 215, 217–19
Leonard, P., 329
Lerman, D.L., 97
Levitin, A., 224
Levy, D.K., 355–73
Ley, D., 318
Libby, J., 191
Limited Equity Cooperatives (LECs), 187, 189, 190
limited equity housing, 187, 188
Lincoln, A., 158, 159
Linneman, P., 85
Lipman, B.J., 163
Listokin, D., 171, 340, 407
Local Initiatives Support Corporation (LISC), 26, 252, 260; Newark, New Jersey, 327
Local Law Enforcement and Blueprint for Neighborhood Conservation, 19
location of housing: low-income homeownership, 176–7; true costs, 116–17
Lochearn, Baltimore County suburb, 131
Lockwood, R., 20, 22
Logan, J., 143n, 144n, 145n, 508
London, 7, 12
low income housing, and urban redevelopment, 17–18
Lowe, S., 438–51
Lower East Side, New York, 16
low-income families, housing policy alternatives for, 177–9; access improvement, 178; alternative tenure forms, support for, 179; rental housing, increasing support for, 178–9